Antitrust Law and Intellectual Property Rights

Antitrust Law and Intellectual Property Rights

CASES AND MATERIALS

CHRISTOPHER R. LESLIE

OXFORD
UNIVERSITY PRESS

OXFORD
UNIVERSITY PRESS

Oxford University Press, Inc., publishes works that further Oxford University's objective
of excellence in research, scholarship, and education.

Oxford   New York
Auckland   Cape Town   Dar es Salaam   Hong Kong   Karachi   Kuala Lumpur   Madrid   Melbourne
Mexico City   Nairobi   New Delhi   Shanghai   Taipei   Toronto

With offices in
Argentina   Austria   Brazil   Chile   Czech Republic   France   Greece   Guatemala   Hungary   Italy
Japan   Poland   Portugal   Singapore   South Korea   Switzerland   Thailand   Turkey   Ukraine
Vietnam

Copyright © 2011 by Oxford University Press, Inc.

Published by Oxford University Press, Inc.
198 Madison Avenue, New York, New York 10016

Oxford is a registered trademark of Oxford University Press
Oxford University Press is a registered trademark of Oxford University Press, Inc.

All rights reserved. No part of this publication may be reproduced, stored in a retrieval system, or transmitted, in any
form or by any means, electronic, mechanical, photocopying, recording, or otherwise, without the prior permission
of Oxford University Press, Inc.

___

Library of Congress Cataloging-in-Publication Data

Leslie, Christopher R.
  Antitrust law and intellectual property rights : cases and materials / Christopher R. Leslie.
     p. cm.
  Includes bibliographical references and index.
  ISBN 978-0-19-533719-8 ((hardback) : alk. paper)
  1. Intellectual property—United States. 2. Antitrust law—United States. I. Title.
  KF3116.L47 2010
  346.7304'8—dc22   2010020812

___

Note to Readers
This publication is designed to provide accurate and authoritative information in regard to the subject matter covered. It is
based upon sources believed to be accurate and reliable and is intended to be current as of the time it was written. It is sold
with the understanding that the publisher is not engaged in rendering legal, accounting, or other professional services. If legal
advice or other expert assistance is required, the services of a competent professional person should be sought. Also, to confirm
that the information has not been affected or changed by recent developments, traditional legal research techniques should be
used, including checking primary sources where appropriate.

*(Based on the Declaration of Principles jointly adopted by a Committee of the
American Bar Association and a Committee of Publishers and Associations.)*

> You may order this or any other Oxford University Press publication by
> visiting the Oxford University Press website at www.oup.com

For Tony

CONTENTS

Preface and Acknowledgments — xix

PART ONE:
THE FOUNDATIONS OF THE INTERSECTION BETWEEN ANTITRUST LAW AND INTELLECTUAL PROPERTY RIGHTS — 1

1. A Primer on Intellectual Property Law — 3
A. Patents — 5
B. Copyrights — 11
C. Trademarks — 14
D. Trade Secrets — 18
E. Other Forms of Intellectual Property — 19
Comments and Questions — 19
Bibliography of Additional Resources — 21

2. A Primer on Antitrust Law — 23
A. Sherman Act (1890) — 25
   Section One of the Sherman Act — 25
   Section Two of the Sherman Act — 27
      Monopolization — 28

Attempted Monopolization	31
Conspiracies to Monopolize	32
B. Clayton Act (1914)	33
Tying Arrangements	33
Mergers	34
Other Aspects of the Clayton Act	35
C. Federal Trade Commission Act (1914)	35
Remedies	35
Comments and Questions	36
Bibliography of Additional Resources	37

3 The Tension Between Antitrust and Intellectual Property — 39

A. A Brief History on the Relationship Between Antitrust Law and Intellectual Property Rights	39
Atari Games Corp. v. Nintendo of America, Inc.	44
Comments and Questions	46
B. The Relationship Between Intellectual Property and Market Power	46
DOJ-FTC Antitrust Guidelines for the Licensing of Intellectual Property, Sec. 2.2	47
Illinois Tool Works v. Independent Ink, Inc.	47
Comments and Questions	54
Bibliography of Additional Resources	56
C. Antitrust Law and the Misuse of Intellectual Property	56
1. Patent Misuse	57
County Materials Corp. v. Allan Block Corp.	57
Comments and Questions	60
2. Copyright Misuse	61
Lasercomb America, Inc. v. Reynolds	61
Comments and Questions	64
3. Trademark Misuse	66
Bibliography of Additional Resources	67

D. Economic Concepts	68
1. Price Discrimination	68
Note on the Robinson-Patman Act	70
Comments and Questions	71
2. Efficiency	72
Thomas O. Barnett, Interoperability Between Antitrust and Intellectual Property	72
Comments and Questions	73
3. Networks Effects	73
U.S. v. Microsoft Corp.	73
Comments and Questions	83
Bibliography of Additional Resources	84

PART TWO:
THE ANTITRUST IMPLICATIONS OF UNILATERAL CONDUCT BY INTELLECTUAL PROPERTY OWNERS — 87

4. Enforcement of Intellectual Property Rights — 89

A. Enforcement of a Fraudulently Procured Patent	89
Walker Process Equipment v. Food Machinery & Chemical Corp.	89
Comments and Questions	92
Dippin' Dots, Inc. v. Mosey	94
Comments and Questions	99
Brunswick Corp. v. Riegel Textile Corp.	100
Comments and Questions	103
Bibliography of Additional Resources	104
B. Sham Litigation	104
CVD, Inc. v. Raytheon Co.	104
Comments and Questions	110
Note on the Noerr-Pennington Doctrine	111
Professional Real Estate Investors v. Columbia Pictures	113
Comments and Questions	118
Note on *Filmtec Corp. v. Hydranautics*	120

x Contents

Primetime 24 Joint Venture v. National Broadcasting Co.		123
Comments and Questions		128
Bibliography of Additional Resources		129

5 Tying Arrangements and Intellectual Property — 131

U.S. Dep't of Justice & Federal Trade Commission, Antitrust Enforcement and Intellectual Property Rights: Promoting Innovation and Competition (2007) — 131

DOJ-FTC Antitrust Guidelines for the Licensing of Intellectual Property, Sec. 5.3 — 131

A. Tying Arrangements and Patented Products — 132
International Salt Co. v. United States — 132
Comments and Questions — 135

B. Antitrust Implications of Block-Booking of Copyrighted Works — 139
United States v. Paramount Pictures, Inc. — 139
Comments and Questions — 140
United States v. Loew's, Inc. — 141
Comments and Questions — 145
Outlet Communications, Inc. v. King World Productions, Inc. — 147
Comments and Questions — 149

C. Copyrighted Software and Tying — 149
Digidyne Corp. v. Data General Corp. — 149
Comments and Questions — 153

D. Trademarks and Tying — 154
Siegel v. Chicken Delight, Inc. — 154
Comments and Questions — 157
Krehl v. Baskin-Robbins Ice Cream Co. — 158
Comments and Questions — 162
Tominaga v. Shepherd — 162
Comments and Questions — 165
Bibliography of Additional Resources — 165

6 Unilateral Refusals to License or Deal — 167

DOJ-FTC Antitrust Guidelines for the Licensing of Intellectual Property, Sec. 2.2 — 167

Data General Corp. v. Grumman Systems Support Corp.	167
Comments and Questions	176
Image Technical Serv. v. Eastman Kodak	178
Comments and Questions	189
In re Independent Service Organizations Antitrust Litigation (Xerox)	190
Comments and Questions	195
Note on Market Power in Aftermarkets	199
Note on the Digital Millennium Copyright Act	200
Intergraph Corp. v. Intel Corp.	203
Comments and Questions	212
Bibliography of Additional Resources	213

7 Design Changes and Predatory Innovation — 215

Berkey Photo, Inc. v. Eastman Kodak Co.	215
Comments and Questions	227
Foremost Pro Color, Inc. v. Eastman Kodak Co.	231
Comments and Questions	235
C.R. Bard, Inc. v. M3 Systems, Inc.	236
Comments and Questions	240
Automatic Radio Manufacturing Co. v. Ford Motor Co.	243
Comments and Questions	245
Abbott Laboratories v. Teva Pharmaceuticals USA, Inc.	245
Comments and Questions	253
Bibliography of Additional Resources	255

8 Deceptive Conduct before Standard-Setting Organizations — 257

In the Matter of Dell Computer Corp.	257
Comments and Questions	261
Broadcom Corp. v. Qualcomm Inc.	262
Comments and Questions	273
Rambus, Inc. v. FTC	274
Comments and Questions	282

xii Contents

Note on Section 5 of the Federal Trade Commission Act	284
Bibliography of Additional Resources	287

PART THREE:
THE ANTITRUST IMPLICATIONS OF HORIZONTAL
AGREEMENTS INVOLVING INTELLECTUAL PROPERTY — 289

9 Price Fixing and Intellectual Property — 291

A. Patents and Cartels	291
United States v. United States Gypsum Co.	291
Comments and Questions	298
Addamax Corp. v. Open Software Foundation, Inc.	300
Comments and Questions	305
B. Patent Pooling and Price Fixing	305
DOJ-FTC Antitrust Guidelines for the Licensing of Intellectual Property, § 5.5 Cross-licensing and pooling arrangements	305
Standard Oil Co. v. United States	307
Comments and Questions	311
Matsushita Electrical Industrial Co. v. Cinram	316
Comments and Questions	321
Federal Trade Commission In the Matter of Summit Technology	323
Comments and Questions	327
C. Blanket Licensing of Copyrighted Works	327
Broadcast Music, Inc. v. CBS	327
Comments and Questions	336
Note on Agreements to Fix a Maximum Price	338
D. Standard-setting Organizations	339
U.S. Dep't of Justice & Federal Trade Commission, Antitrust Enforcement and Intellectual Property Rights: Promoting Innovation and Competition (2007)	340
Sony Electronics, Inc. v. Soundview Technologies, Inc.	340
Comments and Questions	345
Bibliography of Additional Resources	349

Contents xiii

10 Market Allocation and Intellectual Property Rights — 351

A. Patents and Market Allocation — 351
    Hartford-Empire Co. v. United States — 351
        Comments and Questions — 355

B. Trademarks and Market Allocation — 355
    Timken Roller Bearing Co. v. United States — 355
        Comments and Questions — 356
    United States v. Sealy — 357
        Comments and Questions — 362
    United States v. Topco Associates, Inc. — 362
        Comments and Questions — 369
    Palmer v. BRG of Georgia, Inc. — 369
        Comments and Questions — 371
    Clorox Co. v. Sterling Winthrop, Inc. — 371
        Comments and Questions — 377

C. Copyrights and Market Allocation — 378
    Auwood v. Harry Brandt Booking Office, Inc. — 378
        Comments and Questions — 380

D. International Intellectual Property Regimes and Market Allocation — 381
    Metro Industries, Inc. v. Sammi Corp. — 381
        Comments and Questions — 385

E. DOJ-FTC Antitrust Guidelines for the Licensing of Intellectual Property, Sec. 5.1 — 385

11 Pharmaceutical Settlements and Reverse Payments — 387

In re Cardizem CD Antitrust Litigation — 387
    Comments and Questions — 393
Schering-Plough Corp. v. F.T.C. — 394
    Comments and Questions — 410
C. Scott Hemphill, *An Aggregate Approach to Antitrust: Using New Data and Rulemaking to Preserve Drug Competition*, 109 Columbia Law Review 629 (2009) — 412

xiv Contents

In re Tamoxifen Citrate Antitrust Litigation	413
Comments and Questions	427
Bibliography of Additional Resources	431

12 Agreements to Buy and Sell Intellectual Property as an Antitrust Violation — 433

A. Acquisition of IP as a Conspiracy to Restrain Trade	433
United States v. Singer Manufacturing, Co.	433
Comments and Questions	442
B. Agreements to Acquire Intellectual Property and Merger Law	444
DOJ-FTC Antitrust Guidelines for the Licensing of Intellectual Property § 5.7	444
Antitrust Modernization Commission: Report and Recommendations (2007)	444
A Note on Technology and Innovation Markets	449
DOJ-FTC Antitrust Guidelines for the Licensing of Intellectual Property §3.2	449
Federal Trade Commission In the Matter of Ciba-Geigy Ltd.	450
Comments and Questions	458

13 Group Boycotts and Concerted Refusals to Deal or License — 459

A. Antitrust Treatment of Concerted Refusals to Deal	459
Fashion Originators Guild of America v. Federal Trade Commission	459
Comments and Questions	462
B. Concerted Refusals to Deal with a Patentee	462
Jones Knitting Corp. v. Morgan	462
Comments and Questions	465
C. Group Boycotts and Copyrights	465
Primetime 24 Joint Venture v. National Broadcasting Co.	465
Comments and Questions	467
The Movie 1 & 2 v. United Artists Communications, Inc.	468
Comments and Questions	472

Contents xv

PART FOUR:

THE ANTITRUST IMPLICATIONS OF VERTICAL AGREEMENTS INVOLVING INTELLECTUAL PROPERTY 473

14. Vertical Price Restraints and Intellectual Property ... 475

A. The Foundation of Antitrust's Treatment of Vertical Price Restraints ... 475

    Dr. Miles Medical Co. v. John D. Park & Sons Co. ... 475

        Comments and Questions ... 479

B. *General Electric* and the Ability of Patent Owners to Set Resale Prices ... 480

    United States v. Line Materials Co. ... 480

        Comments and Questions ... 486

C. Vertical Price Fixing and Copyrighted Works ... 489

    United States v. Paramount Pictures, Inc. ... 489

        Comments and Questions ... 491

    LucasArts Entertainment Co. v. Humongous Entertainment Co. ... 492

        Comments and Questions ... 495

    A Note on the First Sale Doctrine ... 495

D. Resale Price Maintenance and Trademarked Goods ... 496

    U.S. v. Frankfort Distilleries ... 496

    Hudson Distributors, Inc. v. Eli Lilly & Co. ... 497

        Comments and Questions ... 500

E. The Demise of *Dr. Miles* ... 500

    Leegin Creative Leather Products, Inc. v. PSKS, Inc. ... 500

        Comments and Questions ... 509

15. Non-price Licensing Restrictions ... 511

DOJ-FTC Antitrust Guidelines for the Licensing of Intellectual Property, § 2.3 ... 511

B. Braun Med., Inc. v. Abbott Labs ... 512

    Comments and Questions ... 515

A Note on Exhaustion Doctrine ... 515

United States v. Studiengesellschaft Kohle ... 517
    Comments and Questions ... 527
DOJ-FTC Antitrust Guidelines for the Licensing of Intellectual Property, Examples of Licensing ... 527
Transparent-Wrap Machine Corp. v. Stokes & Smith Co. ... 528
    Comments and Questions ... 531
Bibliography of Additional Resources ... 534

16 The Antitrust Implications of Structuring Royalties ... 535

Automatic Radio Manufacturing v. Hazeltine Research ... 535
    Comments and Questions ... 538
Brulotte v. Thys Co. ... 539
    Comments and Questions ... 541
Zenith Radio Corp. v. Hazeltine Research, Inc. ... 543
    Comments and Questions ... 548
Scheiber v. Dolby Laboratories, Inc. ... 549
    Comments and Questions ... 552
Bibliography of Additional Resources ... 553

PART FIVE: INJURY, REMEDIES, JURISDICTION AND PROCEDURAL ISSUES ... 555

17 Standing and Antitrust Injury ... 557

A. Competitor Standing ... 557
    Handgards, Inc. v. Ethicon, Inc. ... 557
        Comments and Questions ... 559
    Bourns, Inc. v. Raychem Corp. ... 560
        Comments and Questions ... 564
B. Consumer Standing ... 564
    In re Ciprofloxacin Hydrochloride Antitrust Litigation ... 564

Molecular Diagnostics Laboratories v. Hoffmann-La
Roche Inc. ... 565
    Comments and Questions ... 567
Bibliography of Additional Resources ... 567

18. Remedies ... 569

U. S. v. Glaxo Group Ltd. ... 569
    Comments and Questions ... 573
Bibliography of Additional Resources ... 576

19. Jurisdiction and Procedural Issues ... 577

Christianson v. Colt Industries Operating Corp. ... 578
Holmes Group, Inc. v. Vornado Air Circulation Systems, Inc. ... 583
    Comments and Questions ... 585
Hydranautics v. FilmTec Corp. ... 586
    Comments and Questions ... 587
Bibliography of Additional Resources ... 588

APPENDICES ... 589

Appendix A: Statutory Supplement ... 591
Appendix B: Antitrust Guidelines for the Licensing of Intellectual Property ... 617
Appendix C: Microeconomic Analysis and Graphs ... 647

Table of Cases ... 659
Index ... 669

PREFACE AND ACKNOWLEDGMENTS

Typically, courses in intellectual property law focus primarily on the philosophy behind protecting intellectual property rights, how to secure and enforce the rights, and the scope of such intellectual property rights. Patents, copyrights, and trademarks are characterized by the range of exclusionary rights associated with each body of law. Intellectual property rights can, in some circumstances, confer considerable market power upon their owners. Such firms sometimes exercise this power in ways that exceed the legitimate bounds of their intellectual property rights. While substantive IP law defines the scope of the exclusionary rights, it is antitrust law that often provides the most important consequences when IP owners inappropriately exercise their rights in a way that harms consumers or illegitimately excludes competitors. Antitrust law defines the limits of what intellectual property owners can do with their IP rights.

This book's primary focus is doctrinal antitrust law, as applied to issues involving intellectual property rights. Aside from the introductory primer on intellectual property rights in the first chapter, the book does not concentrate on substantive intellectual property law. Instead it focuses on what conduct firms can and cannot engage in while acquiring and exploiting their intellectual property rights. This casebook explores those aspects of antitrust law that are necessary for both antitrust practitioners and intellectual property attorneys, involved in either litigation or transactions, to understand.

This book is the culmination of a decade of work and the input of many talented colleagues and students. I have taught my course on Antitrust Law and Intellectual Property Rights at New York University School of Law, University of Texas School of Law, the University of Illinois College of Law, and my former home institution, the Chicago-Kent College of Law. My interactions with the students helped considerably in developing this casebook. Several students—Inya Baiye,

Karin Hessler, Ben Kleinman, and Kate Stutt—provided line edits and other useful suggestions.

I owe special thanks to three of my former students from New York University School of Law—Jason Adler, Cedric Logan, and Jonathan Salzberger. I had the pleasure of teaching them in my seminar Antitrust Law and Intellectual Property Rights, after which each of them helped research and write some of the Comments and Questions following the case excerpts.

Several law professors provided invaluable feedback and suggestions after either teaching from a draft version of the book or reviewing a draft manuscript. These included Tom Cotter, Dan Crane, Carol Handler, Mark Lemley, Barak Orbach, and Tony Reese. The book is much improved because of their input.

My faculty assistant, Lisa Payne, provided excellent assistance in making the graphs in the Economics Appendix.

Finally, this casebook would not exist but for the hard work of Lori Wood who shepherded the proposal through Oxford University Press and provided both guidance and encouragement.

Christopher R. Leslie
Irvine, California

PART ONE

THE FOUNDATIONS OF THE INTERSECTION BETWEEN ANTITRUST LAW AND INTELLECTUAL PROPERTY RIGHTS

CHAPTER 1

A Primer on Intellectual Property Law

In many ways, property rights provide one of the critical foundations of modern capitalist society. Free market economies assume the ownership of real estate and moveable objects that can be voluntarily traded for the mutual gain of both buyers and sellers. Capitalism could not exist without property rights.

Intellectual property (IP) refers to "[a] category of intangible rights protecting commercially valuable products of the human intellect. The category comprises primarily trademark, copyright, and patent rights, but also includes trade-secret rights, publicity rights, moral rights, and rights against unfair competition."[1] The fact that intellectual property is intangible distinguishes it from physical property. The consumption of physical goods is generally rivalrous. One person's consumption of a physical good depletes the supply for others. For example, two people cannot each eat the entirety of the same apple. In addition, physical property is generally appropriable. The owner of physical property can exclude others from using the property by securing it (in the case of goods or chattels) or by preventing trespass (in the case of land or other real estate) by, for example, building walls.

In contrast, the consumption of the subjects of intellectual property is generally nonrivalrous because one person's use of an invention does not diminish another person's ability to exploit that invention by making a copy. The nonrivalrous aspect of intellectual property has both positive and negative attributes. On the positive side, sharing and distribution often entails a relatively low cost. Once a disease-curing drug has been invented, it can be manufactured at a low cost and made affordable to low-income individuals afflicted with the particular disease. One person's enjoyment of a work of authorship, such as a song, does not prevent

---

[1] BLACK'S LAW DICTIONARY (8th ed. 2004).

other people from also enjoying that same song. In addition, it is usually difficult for inventors and authors to exclude other people from the benefits of their creations, at least if the creators want to exploit their economic value, which generally requires disclosing the creations to the public. Once an invention or work of authorship is disclosed, it can be difficult to keep others from copying it.

The difficulty of excluding others from the economic benefits of intellectual creations has a negative side. Invention generally requires a significant investment of time and labor. New products and ideas often result from an arduous process of trial and error—combined with both ingenuity and luck. In contrast, conversion is substantially quicker than creation. Reverse engineering—the process of taking a product apart to see how it is built in order to reconstruct one's own version of the product—is often cheaper than invention from scratch. Similarly, writing a novel often takes years; copying it may take minutes. The copier can generally undersell the innovator because the copier does not have to recoup the costs of creating and developing the work and instead bears only the cost of producing the copies (costs that the original creator also faces in producing her own copies for sale). In many instances, products that are protected by intellectual property have relatively high fixed costs (the cost of creation) but have relatively low marginal costs (the cost of manufacturing each additional unit of output of a patented invention or a printed volume of copyrighted work). This makes copying an attractive competitive strategy because the copier incurs none of the high fixed costs of creation and, thus, can sell the product at a relatively low price.

However, if one's ideas or inventions can be readily misappropriated by others, then a creator has less incentive to invest in creating new products or authoring new works. Firms and individuals would be less willing to invest their resources into research and development if they feared the result of their efforts could be appropriated by their competitors, who could undersell them since the copier has fewer costs to recoup. If competitors in a particular market all wait for their rivals to do the heavy lifting of creation, no firm would engage in meaningful research and development. All firms and consumers would be worse off. Similarly, many artists—be they writers, painters, choreographers, or moviemakers—would be less likely to invest their time and energy creating works of authorship—and many commercial entities would be less likely to invest in the dissemination of such works—if they suspected their efforts could be readily copied.

Intellectual property law attempts to solve this problem by granting exclusionary rights to inventors and authors. Protecting physical property is relatively straightforward. Moveable objects can be put under lock and key, while real estate (and large immovable objects) can be fenced off. (Of course, some forms of physical property may be difficult to protect against trespass, such as vast tracts of land in remote locations.) If physical barriers fail, property owners can sue for trespass or conversion.

Physical exclusion is trickier with intellectual creations. Once an idea or artistic work becomes public, it can be hard for an inventor to exclude others from using or copying it. Intellectual property law addresses this problem by affording IP owners the right to sue infringers. In doing so, IP law seeks to create proper incentives for investment in innovation by granting inventors exclusionary rights to prevent others from copying (or otherwise using) their ideas or works in particular ways. In addition to the economic arguments, moral arguments based on the principle that inventors deserve rewards for the successful work also inform some intellectual property regimes, particularly in Europe.

Expansive statutory regimes define the scope of protection afforded to owners of patents, copyrights, trademarks, and trade secrets. Because this book explores the intersection of antitrust law and intellectual property rights, it is useful to understand the basics of each area of law.

The goal of this chapter is not to provide a comprehensive treatise on intellectual property law generally. It is to provide a sufficient overview of those intellectual property law concepts that are discussed in the antitrust cases throughout the rest of the book. More in-depth treatment can be found in the respected treatises listed at the end of this chapter.

A. Patents

Evolution of the American Patent System

Both patent law and copyright law have their foundations in the U.S. Constitution. Article I, section 8, clause 8 of the Constitution grants Congress the authority "To promote the Progress of Science and useful Arts, by securing for limited Times to Authors and Inventors the exclusive Right to their respective Writings and Discoveries." Congress exercised its constitutional authority by enacting the first Patent Act in 1790. Congress has modified patent law many times in the ensuing years. The Patent Act of 1952 represented the most recent fundamental overhaul of federal patent law and remains the basis of the current statute (codified in Title 35 of the U.S. Code), though the statute has been amended numerous times in the last 50 years.

Acquisition of Patent Rights

The formal patenting process begins when an inventor files a patent application with the Patent and Trademark Office (PTO). The patent application describes the invention and often includes diagrams that explain how the invention is constructed. The most important part of the application is the claims. The claims define the metes and bounds of the invention for which the applicant is seeking exclusive rights. The claims are the starting point for determining whether the applicant is entitled to a patent and, if a patent issues, the claims will be the basis for determining whether other parties' conduct infringe the patent. Within a patent application, some claims may be valid even while others are not.

The PTO assigns each patent application to an individual patent examiner. A patent issues only if the examiner affirmatively approves the patent application. The examination process, usually called prosecution, is ex parte; the application is filed confidentially and the PTO examiner interacts only with the patent applicant (though typically through her counsel), not with the other market participants and potential infringers. Though patent applications are kept confidential for the first 18 months after the patent application is filed, most patent applications are published after that period, even though the examination process is still ongoing.

The patent examiner must determine whether the invention claimed in the patent application is valid and falls within the scope of patentable subject matter. This subject matter is limited to processes, machines, articles of manufacture, and compositions of matter. 35 U.S.C. § 101. Patent law requires that the invention be useful, novel, and nonobvious, and that the patent application properly disclose and claim the invention.

Utility. In order to qualify for patent protection, the patent applicant must show that its invention is useful. 35 U.S.C. § 101. This is a very low standard. The patent applicant need only demonstrate that the invention does *something*. She need not show that its invention is equal to or better than competing products on the market.

Novelty. The described invention must also be novel. 35 U.S.C. § 102. The applicant's precise invention must not have been known or used or described in any patent or printed publications, before the date on which the applicant invented it. Even if the applicant did not know of the prior existence of the invention and independently created it, this prior existence will anticipate the invention, which will thus fail to meet the novelty requirement.

Nonobviousness. Even if the applicant's invention has not been anticipated by an identical previous invention, the invention will still not be patentable unless it is also nonobvious. 35 U.S.C. § 103. This standard requires that, at the time the invention was made, it would not have been obvious to a person having ordinary skill in the art to which the invention pertains. This requirement ensures that an applicant is not granted the exclusive rights for an invention that is a trivial or inevitable advancement. Obviousness is often nuanced and reasonable people may disagree whether the patent applicant's invention would have been obvious to one with ordinary skill based on the information available at the time.

Both the novelty and nonobviousness determinations clearly require comparing the claimed invention to what was already in existence at the time the invention was made. The body of existing inventions and knowledge that is the basis for the comparison is called "prior art." Prior art includes, among other things, printed publications, prior patents, and prior patent applications, as well as information that was known to people other than the applicant. Prior art may render a patent claim either obvious or anticipated; in either case, the claim is invalid.

Even if the patent applicant can satisfy the three requirements of patentability—usefulness, novelty, and nonobviousness—attorneys prosecuting patent applications must also pay attention to additional concerns. These include how the patent applicant discloses her invention, whether any statutory bars could preclude the patent from issuing, and whether any other inventors may lay claim to the invention.

Disclosure. The patent application must adequately disclose the invention and enable a person of ordinary skill in the art to make and use the described invention. Further, section 112 requires disclosure of the so-called "best mode" of practicing the invention. 35 U.S.C. § 112.

Statutory Bars. Even if the applicant's invention is novel, nonobvious, and useful, and her application meets the disclosure requirements, the patent statute will bar her from obtaining a patent under certain circumstances. Most importantly, the inventor will lose her right to a patent if the invention was in public use or on sale in the United States more than one year before she files her patent application. 35 U.S.C. § 102(b). In essence, the law gives an inventor a one-year grace period, from the time she (or someone else) puts the invention on sale or in public use, in which she can file her patent application. Much patent case law focuses on the question of what constitutes a sale, an offer for sale, or a public use.

Priority. If two different patent applicants file separate applications for similar inventions, U.S. law (unlike that of most nations) provides that the first to invent, rather than the first to file a patent application, is entitled to the patent. The PTO procedure for determining which inventor has priority, according to fairly complex rules, is known as an *interference*.

If the patent examiner determines that a claimed invention meets all of the statutory requirements and approves the patent application, the patent will issue. If the patent examiner rejects the patent application, she must explain her reasons for rejection. The patent applicant is given an opportunity to amend the claims or to argue against the rejection. If the examiner finally rejects the application, the inventor can appeal within the PTO and, ultimately, in federal court. After a patent issues, it may still be challenged through re-examination. However, such reexaminations are rare.

Scope of Protection

The patent does not give the patent holder the affirmative right to manufacture the patented product. Patent rights are exclusionary rights. The patent grants the patent holder "the right to exclude others from making, using, offering for sale, or selling the invention throughout the United States or importing the invention into the United States" so long as the patent remains in force. 35 U.S.C. § 154(a)(1)–(2).

A person or firm may hold a patent and yet remain unable to actually manufacture or sell any products covered by that patent. One example is in the context of *blocking patents*. Two firms may each hold a patent on a characteristic of a larger product. Neither firm can make the product without infringing the other's patent. In such a case, the patents are said to block each other. Fortunately, patents are alienable; they can be bought, sold, traded, or licensed. Solutions to the problem of blocking patents include one firm purchasing the other firm's patent, or both firm agreeing to cross-license their patents. Cross-licensing of patents is discussed in Chapter 9.

An improvement patent is a patent on an improvement to an existing product. If the existing product is patented by someone other than the holder of the improvement patent, then neither firm can practice the improvement. "The holder of the basic patent can block the improver's sale of improved devices, but similarly, the improver can use its patent to block the holder of the basic patent from selling the improved device."[2]

Duration of Protection

Patents expire twenty years after the effective filing date of the application that led to the patent (though patent protection does not start until the patent is actually issued). Because the patent application process can take two or three years, and sometimes longer, the actual life of a patent is less than twenty years.

Infringement

Patent infringement is essentially any act that encroaches on the exclusive rights of the patent holder. "Patent infringement occurs when a party 'without authority makes, uses, offers to sell or sells any patented invention.'"[3] A party may make an otherwise infringing product if she has a license from the patentholder, in which case she has authority to engage in the conduct. Even if a third party has independently created her own invention without knowing of the patent, her invention can infringe the patentee's invention.

A competing product infringes the patent if the product infringes any claim of the patent. A product need not infringe all of the claims of the patent in order to infringe. "Determining patent infringement is a two-step process: (1) the court must interpret the [patent] claim, and then (2) it must compare the allegedly infringing device against the properly construed claim."[4] The process of claim construction, which requires interpreting the words of the patent claim to determine exactly what constitutes the patented invention, is often a contested process. Once the claim is construed, if the allegedly infringing device is identical in all elements to the patented invention, then the device literally infringes the patent.

Even if the product does not literally infringe the claims of a patent, a product can be found to infringe a claim under the doctrine of equivalents. If a product differs only inconsequentially from the patented product but "performs substantially the same function, in substantially the same way, to achieve substantially the same result as the claimed invention"[5] then the new product will be found to be an infringing equivalent. The consequences of a finding of infringement by equivalent are the same as a finding of literal infringement.

---

[2] Herbert Hovenkamp, Mark D. Janis, Mark A. Lemley & Christopher R. Leslie, Antitrust Law and Intellectual Property §2.2c2 at 2–24 (2d edition).
[3] HollyAnne Corp. v. TFT, Inc., 199 F.3d 1304, 1308 (Fed. Cir. 1999) (quoting 35 U.S.C. 271(a) (1994)).
[4] Research Plastics, Inc. v. Fed. Packaging Corp., 421 F.3d 1290, 1295 (Fed.Cir.2005).
[5] Anchor Wall Systems, Inc. v. Rockwood Retaining Walls, Inc., 340 F.3d 1298, 1313 (Fed. Cir. 2003).

In addition to condemning direct infringement (through actually making, using, selling, offering to sell, or importing the potential invention), patent law also condemns inducement to infringement and contributory infringement. 35 U.S.C. § 271 (b) & (c).

Patent owners can sue infringers in any appropriate federal district court. However, the appeal of a patent infringement suit will be heard by the Court of Appeals for the Federal Circuit, not the regional court of appeal in which the district judge sits. Congress created the Federal Circuit in 1982 in response to a perceived lack of uniformity and high error rate among the regional circuit courts of appeal in patent cases. The losing party before the Federal Circuit may petition for certiorari to the Supreme Court. As Chapter 19 discusses, regional courts of appeal may still hear patent cases in some circumstances, such as when patent infringement is asserted as a counter-claim in antitrust litigation.

Remedies for Infringement

The successful patentee in an infringement suit is entitled to compensatory damages that can not be "less than a reasonable royalty for the use made of the invention by the infringer, together with interest and costs as fixed by the court." 35 U.S.C. § 284. Whether the compensatory damages are calculated by the jury or the judge, the judge retains the discretion to increase the damages up to three times the assessed damages. Id.

Patent holders may also obtain preliminary and/or permanent injunctive relief when appropriate. 35 U.S.C. § 283. Injunctive relief may include an order preventing a competitor from selling an infringing product.

Defenses

Accused of patent infringement, a defendant has several possible defenses to avoid liability for infringement. This section highlights the four most common defenses: non-infringement, patent invalidity, inequitable conduct, and patent misuse. While other defenses are available, these are the defenses that typically are mentioned in patent litigation that has an antitrust component, such as a patent infringement lawsuit in which an antitrust counterclaim is filed.

Non-infringement. Firms accused of patent infringement generally argue that their products do not infringe the patent at issue. This requires the court to construe the patent claims and determine whether or not the defendant's product falls within any of the claims. Unlike the other defenses discussed in this section, non-infringement is not an affirmative defense; in other words, the defendant does not have the burden of proof. Rather, the patentee must prove infringement. When a defendant argues that it has not infringed, it is arguing that the plaintiff has not proven its prima facie case.

Patent invalidity. A firm cannot be held liable for patent infringement if the patent being sued upon is invalid. Thus, infringement defendants often argue that the plaintiffs' patent is invalid. Although the PTO makes an initial determination of validity in issuing a patent, that determination is not conclusive and a patent's validity can be challenged in court. However, because patents are presumed to be valid, an infringement defendant must prove patent invalidity with clear and convincing evidence.[6] Nevertheless, the defense often succeeds. One recent study found that forty-six percent of litigated patents were held invalid.[7] A court can find a patent invalid on any ground that could have barred the patent from issuing in the first place (such as lack of novelty, obviousness, inadequate disclosure, a barring sale or public use, etc.).

Inequitable conduct. A patent applicant engages in inequitable conduct when it makes material misrepresentations or omissions to the PTO in its patent application and during its patent prosecution with the intent to deceive to the PTO. If a patent applicant has engaged in inequitable conduct, the entire patent is rendered unenforceable. Inequitable conduct generally takes the form of concealing relevant information from the PTO. The Federal Circuit has defined the elements of inequitable conduct as follows:

> Inequitable conduct due to failure to disclose material information must be proven by clear and convincing evidence of: (1) prior art that was material; (2) knowledge chargeable to an applicant of that prior art and of its materiality; and (3) failure of the applicant to disclose the art resulting from an intent to mislead the PTO. Such proof of inequitable conduct may be rebutted by a showing that: (a) the prior art was not material; (b) if the prior art was material, a showing that the applicant did not know of that art; (c) if the applicant did know of that art, a showing that the applicant did not know of its materiality; or (d) a showing that the applicant's failure to disclose the art did not result from an intent to mislead the PTO.[8]

Inequitable conduct is not synonymous with fraud (though infringement defendants will often argue patent fraud as well). Fraud is more difficult to prove and "requires higher threshold showings of both intent and materiality than does a finding of inequitable conduct."[9] Properly distinguishing between fraud and inequitable conduct is important because a patent applicant's commission of fraud against the PTO can give rise to antitrust liability, as discussed in Chapter 4.

Patent Misuse. An infringement defendant may also argue that the patentee has engaged in patent misuse. The patent misuse defense is essentially an "extension of the equitable doctrine of unclean hands."[10] Patent misuse is a broad concept that generally means the patentee has engaged in conduct to improperly expand either of the scope or duration of its patent in some manner. The Federal Circuit

---

[6] Eli Lilly and Co. v. Barr Labs, 222 F.3d 973, 980 (Fed. Cir. 2000).Furthermore, because patents are often made up of many claims, some claims may be held to be invalid while others survive and provide the basis for a successful infringement suit.

[7] *See* John R. Allison & Mark A. Lemley, *Empirical Evidence on the Validity of Litigated Patents*, 26 AIPLA Q.J. 185, 205 (1998); *see also* Mark A. Lemley, *An Empirical Study of the Twenty-Year Patent Term*, 22 AIPLA Q.J. 369, 420 (1994).

[8] Elk Corp. v. GAF Building Materials Corp., 168 F.3d 28, 30 (Fed. Cir. 1999) (citations omitted).

[9] Nobelpharma AB v. Implant Innovations, 141 F.3d 1059, 1070–71 (Fed. Cir. 1998).

[10] B. Braun Med., Inc. v. Abbott Labs., 124 F.3d 1419, 1427 (Fed. Cir. 1997).

has noted that an infringement defendant may employ this defense when the patentee misuses "the patent to obtain market benefit beyond that which inheres in the statutory patent grant."[11] Some forms of patent misuse may also constitute antitrust violations.

In general, patent misuse takes place after a patent has issued, while inequitable conduct occurs during the application process. Unlike inequitable conduct, patent misuse technically can be "cured." Patent misuse does not mean that the patent is invalid; rather, it means that it is unenforceable until the misuse has been purged.[12]

B. Copyrights

Copyrights protect works of authorship fixed in a tangible medium, such as books, film, diagrams, and sound recordings. Copyright does not protect ideas or facts. The federal copyright statute explicitly states that copyright protection does not extend to "any idea, procedure, process, system, method of operation, concept, principle, or discovery, regardless of the form in which it is described, explained, illustrated, or embodied in such work." 17 U.S.C. § 102(b). Rather, copyright protection extends to how an idea is expressed. This is often referred to as the idea/expression distinction in copyright. The dividing line between idea and expression is often hard to define, particularly in cutting edge areas of copyright protection such as software.

Acquisition of Copyright Protection

Unlike inventors, authors need not affirmatively apply for government approval in order to secure intellectual property rights. Copyright protection for eligible works attaches as soon as the work is fixed "in any tangible medium of expression, now known or later developed, from which they can be perceived, reproduced, or otherwise communicated, either directly or with the aid of a machine or device." 17 U.S.C. §102 (a). For example, the papers that students write for their classes are protected by federal copyright law once the original expressions are written on paper or typed into a word processor and saved. While copyright owners can register their works with the Copyright Office, registration does not actually bestow copyright protection on submitted works, but instead confers important procedural and remedial benefits.

Before 1989, copyright law imposed a number of formalities on the acquisition of federal copyright. For most of U.S. history, the placement of a proper copyright notice (e.g., © 1972 Jane Doe) on every published copy of a work was a condition to obtaining or maintaining copyright protection, and failure to comply with that requirement generally meant that a work did not obtain a copyright,

---

[11] Mallinckrodt, Inc. v. Mediport, Inc., 976 F.2d 700, 704 (Fed. Cir. 1992).
[12] See Minebea Co., Ltd. v. Papst, 444 F.Supp.2d 68, 209 (D.D.C.2006) ("Patent misuse is an equitable defense against patent infringement; it renders the patent unenforceable until the misuse is cured and thus provides a temporary defense.").

or lost that protection, and entered the public domain. No such formalities are required any longer; copyright protection begins as soon as the work is fixed in a tangible medium.

To be eligible for copyright protection, a work must be original. Originality, however, entails a low threshold and requires only that the work be independently created and reflects a minimal level of creativity. The originality requirement does not require that a work be completely original. Copyright protection extends to derivative works as well. A derivative work is a new work that builds upon an existing work in some way. For example, the musical *Wicked* is a derivative work of L. Frank Baum's book *The Wizard of Oz*. Copyrights in a derivative work extend only to the newly contributed material that is independently created and minimally creative, not aspects of the pre-existing work. If the underlying work is itself protected by copyright, then the derivative work could potentially be infringing if it used the underlying work without the consent of its copyright owner. (Baum's original book, though not the MGM movie based on it, is in the public domain and thus no longer protected by copyright and free for anyone to copy or to use as the basis for a derivative work.)

Also, a new compilation of existing works can be entitled to copyright protection. The originality in a compilation is seen in the decisions of what materials to include in the compilation and how to order them. Protection even extends to compilations of uncopyrightable material, such as facts, if the selection and arrangement of these facts is independently created and minimally creative, but the copyright in such a fact compilation will protect only the author's selection and arrangement, and not the underlying facts themselves.

Scope of Protection

Copyright law provides the owners of copyrights a series of exclusive rights. These include the rights to exclude others from reproducing, distributing, publicly performing, or publicly displaying the protected work, and from preparing a derivative work based upon it. The rights of reproduction, distribution, and adaptation apply to all copyrighted works, while the public performance and display rights attach only to specifically enumerated categories of work. Each right is independent, and a single course of conduct could simultaneously infringe several rights.

All of these rights are subject to a long catalog of exceptions and limitations, which specify activities that are not infringing, even though they come with the scope of the copyright owner's rights. See 17 U.S.C. §§ 107-122. Fair use, discussed below, is the broadest of these exceptions; many other limitations are much more narrowly focused on publication rights, particular kinds of works, or particular uses.

Duration of Protection

Due to amendments to copyright law, there is no one set duration of copyright protection equivalent to the relatively straightforward twenty-year term of a patent.

The duration of copyright protection is a function of who created the work, and when the work was created. Works published before 1923 are in the public domain. For works published between 1923 and 1977 inclusive, if all of the necessary formalities were complied with, then copyright protection generally began when the work was published and lasted for an initial term of 28 years. The copyright could be renewed (this generally required the copyright owner to register for renewal), and the length of the renewal copyright, originally 28 years, was extended in 1978 to 47 years and again in 1998 to 67 years. Thus, a work first published in this period could possibly be protected for 95 years from publication.

For works created after 1977, the basic term of copyright is the life of the author plus seventy years. (In the case of works by multiple collaborators, the term runs from the life of the last surviving author). If the work was created by an employee but owned by the employer (under the copyright doctrine known as "works for hire"), then the term is not measured by an author's life, but instead runs 95 years from publication, or 120 years from creation, whichever is shorter.

Infringement

While a patent can be infringed even if the infringing party was unaware of the patent, copyright infringement requires that the defendant somehow copy the protected work. The elements of a copyright infringement claim require the owner of a valid copyright to prove both that the defendant actually copied from the copyrighted work (which is usually proven circumstantially by showing that the defendant had access to the work and that the defendant's work has "probative similarities" to the plaintiff's work) and that the defendant's copying amounted to improper appropriation. Making that second showing generally requires demonstrating that the defendant copied protected expression and that audiences will perceive substantial similarities between the works.

While the Copyright Act does not explicitly provide for contributory infringement or vicarious liability, courts have created causes of action under these theories of liability.[13]

Remedies for Infringement

The successful plaintiff in a copyright infringement suit may collect either (1) actual damages and the infringer's profits or (2) statutory damages. Pursuing the statutory damages measure, the court may award the copyright owner "a sum of not less than $750 or more than $30,000 as the court considers just." 17 U.S.C. § 504(c)(1). However, in cases of willful infringement, the court may award up to $150,000. In its discretion, the court may also award costs and attorney's fees to the prevailing party under certain conditions. Injunctive relief is also available, and courts routinely grant permanent injunctions to prevailing copyright plaintiffs. Finally, willful copyright infringement is, under some circumstances, a criminal offense.

---

[13] *See* Gershwin Pub. Corp. v. Columbia Artists Mgmt., Inc., 443 F.2d 1159 (2nd Cir. 1971).

Defenses

Fair use represents perhaps the most common and complicated defense to charges of copyright infringement. Although the defense was initially developed by the courts, Congress later codified it in the federal copyright statute. Section 107 of the copyright statute provides that copying a protected work does not constitute infringement so long as the copying represents "fair use":

> In determining whether the use made of a work in any particular case is a fair use the factors to be considered shall include—(1) the purpose and character of the use, including whether such use is of a commercial nature or is for nonprofit educational purposes; (2) the nature of the copyrighted work; (3) the amount and substantiality of the portion used in relation to the copyrighted work as a whole; and (4) the effect of the use upon the potential market for or value of the copyrighted work. 17 U.S.C. §107.

While fair use discussions are highly contextual, courts often focus on whether or not the challenged copying was commercial in nature and whether or not the challenged copying potentially undermined the market for the copyrighted work. Because software is protected by copyright, recent cases have debated whether or not reverse engineering of copyrighted software constitutes copyright infringement or fair use.[14]

Courts and commentators are currently debating whether or not copyright law should recognize a defense of copyright misuse—analogous to the defense of patent misuse—and, if so, what its relationship should be to antitrust law.

C. Trademarks

Trademarks "include[] any word, name, symbol, or device, or any combination thereof used by a person. . . to identify and distinguish his or her goods [or services]. . . from those [of]. . . others and to indicate the source of the goods [or services], even if that source is unknown." 15 U.S.C. §1127. Trademark protection is important for both quality control and to prevent consumer confusion about the source of goods and services.[15] Firms employ trademarks to differentiate their products from competing ones. Absent trademark protection, businesses may have insufficient incentive to invest in building the goodwill of their product, service, or franchise system. If any burger restaurant could call itself McDonald's and employ the familiar Golden Arches motif in its signage, consumer confusion would reign.

Trademarks can include the name of a business (such as McDonald's), as well as the names of individual products (Chicken McNuggets, for example). Trademark protection can extend to logos or designs used by a manufacturer, such as the Nike Swoosh, as well as the shape of a product or its container, such as the distinctive

---

[14] *See Sega Enter. Ltd. v. Accolade Inc.*, 977 F.2d 1510 (9th Cir. 1993).
[15] A service mark is essentially the equivalent of a trademark used by businesses that provide a service.

shape of a Coca-Cola bottle. Trademark protection may extend to sounds (e.g., the three chimes associated with television network NBC), colors (e.g., Tiffany's blue boxes), and even scents.[16] Of course, not all names, logos, and shapes are eligible for trademark protection. Much trademark law focuses on which terms and designs are properly trademarked.

The 1946 Lanham Act, 15 U.S.C. §§ 1051 et seq., provides the foundation for federal trademark law. But unlike patent and copyright, trademarks are also a function of state law.[17] State and federal trademark doctrine are generally very similar.

Acquiring Trademark Protection

As the name implies, the Patent and Trademark Office examines trademark applications as well as patent applications. Businesses can register their trademarks with the PTO. Trademark examination is generally less arduous than the patent application process. If the examiner approves the initial trademark application, the PTO publishes the application and third parties are given the opportunity to oppose the registration. For trademark applicants denied registration, an administrative appeals system exists, which may eventually lead to litigation in the federal courts.

However, unlike patents, businesses need not follow the registration procedures of the Lanham Act in order to receive trademark protection. Unregistered names and symbols that qualify as trademarks can be protected from infringement under both state and federal law. But those firms that do register trademarks are entitled to several significant advantages. For example, trademark "registration constitutes prima facie evidence of ownership, validity, and the exclusive right to use the registered mark" and provides "nationwide constructive notice as of the registration date. . ."[18]

Trademark Requirements

To be enforceable under federal law, a trademark must satisfy three criteria: distinctiveness, non-functionality, and use in commerce.

Distinctiveness. A trademark must be sufficiently distinctive of the goods or services with which it is used—that is, the mark must distinguish the trademark owner's product from products of other suppliers. Purported trademarks are often evaluated along a spectrum: generic; descriptive; suggestive; arbitrary or fanciful.

Generic terms are not capable of serving as trademarks. A purported trademark is deemed generic if it merely names the category that the product belongs in, such as granny smith apples that are sold under the brand name Apples. Generic terms cannot be distinctive and are not protected by trademark.

---

[16] *See, e.g.,* In re Clarke, 17 U.S.P.Q.2d 1238 (Trademark Tr. & App. Bd. of the PTO 1990) (permitting trademark for plumeria scent on sewing thread).

[17] While state common law copyright still can cover some unfixed works, copyright is essentially a function of federal law. Federal patent law has no meaningful state counterpart.

[18] HOVENKAMP, JANIS, LEMLEY & LESLIE, *supra* note 2, at 2–63.

Descriptive marks describe some quality or attribute of the product, such as granny smith apples that are sold under the name Crunchy Green Apples. Descriptive terms cannot receive trademark protection unless the mark has sufficiently permeated the consumer consciousness so as to acquire "secondary meaning." If that happens, consumers understand the term not merely as a description of the product, but as an indicator of a single source of the product. The term has thus acquired distinctiveness, and is capable of protection as a mark. For example, the artificial sweetener "Sweet'N Low" is both sweet and low in calories, but the name is protected by trademark because the phrase has acquired secondary meaning among consumers.

Suggestive, arbitrary, and fanciful marks receive trademark protection more easily because they are regarded as "inherently distinctive." A suggestive mark suggests but does not directly describe the underlying good or some characteristic of it. "Suggestive marks are eligible for protection without any proof of secondary meaning, since the connection between the mark and the source is presumed."[19] An arbitrary mark takes a real word and applies to a completely unrelated product (such as Apple Computers or Apple Records). Finally, a fanciful mark often creates a new word entirely, such as Kodak or Rolls-Royce.

Non-functionality. When the trademark relates to a feature of the product—such as design, color, or scent—that feature can only be trademarked if it is non-functional. The Supreme Court has defined a product feature as functional "if it essential to the use or purpose of the article or if it affects the cost or quality of the article."[20] For example, Coca-Cola could not have trademarked the distinctive shape of its Coke bottles if that shape served the functional purpose of making the bottle easier to grip and drink from. If a product feature is functional, then it may be protected by patent, if the applicant can satisfy the requirements of patentability, but it may not be protected by trademark.

Use in Commerce. In order to secure and maintain federal trademark protection, the trademark owner must use the mark "in the ordinary course of trade." The use must be bona fide and "not made merely to reserve a right in a mark." 15 U.S.C. § 1127. Under federal trademark law, a trademark owner who fails to use its mark in commerce may be deemed to have abandoned the mark. This is in distinct contrast to patent and copyright protection. A patentee need not practice her invention and the copyright owner need not market his works; neither will lose their intellectual property rights due to non-use.

Duration of Trademark Protection

A trademark may last in perpetuity so long as the trademark owner continues to use the trademark in business and the mark retains its distinctiveness. This differs dramatically from patents, which expire twenty years after application, and

---
[19] Two Pesos, Inc. v. Taco Cabana, Inc., 505 U.S. 763, 773 (1992) (quoting Thompson Medical Co. v. Pfizer Inc., 753 F.2d 208, 216 (2d Cir. 1985)).
[20] Inwood Labs v. Ives Labs., 456 U.S. 844, 850 n.10 (1982).

copyrights, which by Constitutional command cannot be perpetual. Federal registrations, however, must be periodically renewed to remain in force.

Scope of Protection

Trademark owners can bring suit under two distinct theories: infringement or dilution.

Infringement. In order to establish infringement, a trademark owner must show that the alleged infringer has engaged in unauthorized use of the mark that is "likely to cause confusion" among consumers as to source of the goods being offered for sale or as to sponsorship or affiliation. Much trademark law focuses on the factors and application of this "likelihood of confusion" test.

Dilution. While many states have long recognized a cause of action for dilution, federal law did not until Congress enacted the Federal Trademark Dilution Act, which became effective in 1996.[21] Under federal law, only owners of so-called "famous" marks can also sue for dilution. Most trademarks are not famous marks. To determine whether or not a mark is famous requires a balancing of several factors, a non-exhaustive list of which is codified in the Lanham Act. 15 U.S.C. § 1125(c)(2)(B)(i)-(vi). Dilution can take different forms, including dilution by tarnishment and dilution by blurring. The complexities of dilution doctrine do not generally affect the antitrust-trademark intersection and thus will not be discussed here.

Remedies for infringement

The Lanham Act provides for injunctive relief and damages (including treble damages and attorneys' fees in exceptional cases). 15 U.S.C. § 1117. In the case of infringing goods, the Lanham Act authorizes destruction of the offending products. 15 U.S.C. § 1118. Finally, the Lanham Act creates criminal liability for trafficking in counterfeit goods. 18 U.S.C. § 2320.

Defenses

Defendants in trademark infringement suits have several defenses at their disposal, including that they have engaged in fair use,[22] though it should be noted that the fair use defense in trademark differs from fair use in copyright law. A defendant will often challenge the validity of a mark or its registration. The defendant in a trademark case can also argue that the plaintiff's trademark registration was fraudulently procured if the trademark applicant made misrepresentations to the PTO with the intent to deceive. However, the defense is disfavored.[23] Finally, although some courts have recognized trademark misuse as a defense, the theory is not widely accepted as of yet.

---

[21] For background on dilution theory, see Ringling Brothers Barnum & Bailey Combined Shows v. Utah Division of Travel Dev., 170 F.3d 449, 453–462 (4th Cir. 1999).
[22] *See* KP Permanent Make-Up, Inc. v. Lasting Impression I, Inc., 543 U.S. 111 (2004).
[23] Aveda Corp. v. Evita Marketing, 706 F.Supp. 1419, 1425 (D. Minn. 1989).

D. Trade Secrets

The final form of intellectual property relevant to the intersection of antitrust and IP is the law of trade secrets. A trade secret is information from which a firm derives value because the information is not generally known. This can include recipes and formulas (like the recipe for Coca-Cola), a process for making products, customer lists, and software code, among others. The intersection of antitrust law and trade secret law is relatively slight compared to patent, copyrights, and trademarks. Trade secrets are far less likely to be involved in litigation alleging antitrust violations. Still, to the extent that some antitrust cases discuss trade secrets, it is worthwhile to understand the basics of trade secret law.

While patents, copyrights, and trademarks are products of federal law, trade secrets are primarily governed by state law. Most states have adopted the Uniform Trade Secrets Acts, albeit often with modifications that somewhat reduce national uniformity. Many courts also rely heavily on the Restatement of the Law of Unfair Competition in resolving cases.

Acquisition of Trade Secret Protection

To qualify for trade secret protection, a firm must undertake reasonable efforts to protect the secrecy of its proprietary information. And while absolute secrecy is not required, if information is either generally known or readily ascertainable from public sources, then it is not subject to trade secret protection in most jurisdictions.

In contrast to patents and trademarks, trade secret protection requires no public disclosure—indeed, it essentially forbids it. However, if a competitor were to independently and legally ascertain the secret, the competitor could practice the discovery, license it, or even publicly disclose it (thereby destroying its secrecy). In contrast, a patent protects against independent discovery such that even a competitor who invents a product on her own cannot make or sell it if another firm has already patented it.

Scope of Protection

Trade secret law protects the trade secret owner against misappropriation. Misappropriation includes stealing a trade secret, paying an insider to disclose the secret, and other forms of industrial espionage. Trade secret law prohibits those with a duty to protect the secret from using or disclosing the information in breach of their duty. Thus, former employees cannot use their ex-employers' trade secrets in another business venture. Misappropriation can include using a trade secret known to have been accidentally disclosed. However, reverse engineering—the process of taking a product apart in order to determine how it is made—does not generally constitute misappropriation.

The owner of a trade secret can license that secret to other firms. Such licensing does not expose the secret in a manner that eliminates trade secret protection, so long as the licensee has a duty to maintain the secret in confidence.

Duration

Trade secret protection can potentially last in perpetuity. This advantage forces inventors to make a decision: upon discovery of an innovation, firms often have to choose between filing a patent application or relying on trade secret protection. Patent protection lasts twenty years from the date of application and requires the applicant to publicly disclose its invention, so that competitors could practice the invention after the patent expires. Trade secret protection is potentially perpetual but could perish abruptly without warning should another firm make a similar discovery on its own or the information otherwise becomes publicly available.

Remedies for Misappropriation

A finding of misappropriation generally entitles the plaintiff in a trade secret case to injunctive relief, compensatory damages, and in exceptional cases, punitive damages and attorneys' fees.

Defenses

Traditional defenses to accusations of trade secret misappropriation include arguments that the purported information was not legally a trade secret and that it was not misappropriated. Most commonly, a defendant will argue that it came up with the idea on its own. Because independent development is a complete defense—and the plaintiff bears the burden of proof on misappropriation—trade secrets can represent a more precarious form of protection.

Antitrust Issues

Most trade secret cases raise no antitrust issues. However, in some instances, trade secret licenses may include provisions that implicate antitrust law. For example, trade secret licenses sometimes include noncompetition clauses.[24]

E. Other Forms of Intellectual Property

Intellectual property rights exist beyond patents, copyrights, trademarks, and trade secrets. They include the right to publicity, plant variety protection, protection for boat hull designs, and privacy torts that sometimes get included in broader discussions of intellectual property (such as public disclosure of private facts). These intellectual property rights rarely raise any antitrust issues and thus are not included in this brief overview of intellectual property law.

Comments and Questions

1. One long-standing question in intellectual property policy remains the proper duration for intellectual property rights. What would be the consequences

---

[24] Firemen's Ins. Servs. v. CIGNA Property & Cas. Ins. Agency, 693 A.2d 1330 (Pa. 1997) (holding for antitrust defendant).

if the duration of protection were too short? What would be the consequences if the duration of protection were too long? Should the law err on the side a granting intellectual property protection that is too short or too long? How should policymakers decide the appropriate duration for intellectual property rights?

2. The optimal duration of a patent may be a function of the type of industry that the patent owner competes in. For example, a patent owner in a pharmaceutical market recoups its investment at a different rate than an inventor in a software market. Would it be feasible to have varying patent lengths for different industries?

3. Different forms of intellectual property have different durations of protection. Why is this appropriate? Does it make sense that patent protection expires after twenty years while trademark and trade secret protection can be perpetual?

4. Each form of intellectual property has its own system for acquiring legal protection. As a result, it is significantly more burdensome to acquire patent protection than copyright protection. Why does that make sense?

5. Trademark rights can be lost if the owner abandons the mark. In contrast, patent and copyright protection persists regardless of the owner's lack of use. (Patent owners must pay scheduled maintenance fees in order to maintain their patent rights, but they do not have to actually market or license their patented invention.) Why does that make sense? Does the application of trademark law change depending on whether one views trademarks as a property right or as a means of preventing consumer confusion about the source a product?

6. One of the primary justifications for affording exclusionary rights to the owners of intellectual property is that IP is relatively easy to "steal" through copying without permission. However, in some high-tech markets, owners of IP are able to prevent widespread copying, such as when software and digital media are protected through digital rights management (DRM) and related technologies. Does this undermine the rationale for IP protection? Should owners of IP that is difficult to copy be entitled to the same exclusionary rights as owners of easy-to-copy information? Why or why not?

7. As noted, consumption of intellectual property is generally described as nonrivalrous: "[i]ntellectual creations are susceptible to 'nonrivalrous consumption,' in the sense that their possession or use by one person does not preclude others from possessing or using them as well." Michael Madow, *Private Ownership of Public Image: Popular Culture and Publicity Rights*, 81 CAL. L. REV. 127, 222 n.445 (1993). *See also* Thomas F. Cotter, *Do Federal Uses of Intellectual Property Implicate the Fifth Amendment?*, 50 FLA. L. REV. 529, 562-63 (1998) ("to refer to something as 'nonrivalrous' means that another person can use it without simultaneously depriving anyone else of its use.").

But simply because concurrent consumption is physically possible does not mean that the value of that consumption is unaffected. For example, a trade secret is information that "derives independent economic value, actual or potential, from not being generally known or readily ascertainable by others who can obtain economic value from its disclosure or use." BLACK'S LAW DICTIONARY (8th ed. 2004). The exposure of the trade secret necessarily hurts the inventor by reducing her competitive advantage even though she can continue to use the particular process or device in her business.

Also, some may consider the consumption of some luxury goods to be rivalrous. Many consumers may derive value from certain high-status items precisely because the goods are not readily available to others. If the goods could be readily copied and sold, they would lose their cachet. However, that does not mean that originators necessarily suffer. For example, fashion design generally falls outside of IP protection and copying is common, as new red-carpet designs are replicated and sold in lower-end stores. Under traditional IP theory, this should reduce the flow of original designs into the marketplace. However, Professors Raustiala and Sprigman have argued that "copying fails to deter innovation in the fashion industry because, counter-intuitively, copying is not very harmful to originators. Indeed, copying may actually promote innovation and benefit originators. . . .[C]opying functions as an important element of—and perhaps even a necessary predicate to—the apparel industry's swift cycle of innovation." Kal Raustiala & Christopher Sprigman, *The Piracy Paradox: Innovation and Intellectual Property in Fashion Design*, 92 VA. L. REV. 1687 (2006). Professors Raustiala and Sprigman explain that copying in high-end clothing markets creates the need for yet more cutting-edge fashion, generating more work for innovators.

Bibliography of Additional Resources

DONALD S. CHISUM, CHISUM ON PATENTS (1978; updated)

PAUL GOLDSTEIN, GOLDSTEIN ON COPYRIGHT (3RD ED. 2005; updated annually)

J. THOMAS MCCARTHY, MCCARTHY ON TRADEMARKS AND UNFAIR COMPETITION (4TH ED. 1996)

MELVILLE B. NIMMER & DAVID NIMMER, NIMMER ON COPYRIGHT (1978; updated quarterly)

CHAPTER 2

A Primer on Antitrust Law

Antitrust laws in general . . . are the Magna Carta of free enterprise. They are as important to the preservation of economic freedom and our free enterprise system as the Bill of Rights is to the protection of our fundamental personal freedoms. And the freedom guaranteed each and every business, no matter how small, is the freedom to compete. . . .

United States v. Topco Assocs., 405 U.S. 596, 610 (1972)

It is axiomatic that the antitrust laws were passed for 'the protection of competition, not competitors.'

Brooke Group Ltd. v. Brown & Williamson Tobacco Corp., 509 U.S. 209 (1993) (quoting Brown Shoe Co. v. United States, 370 U.S. 294, 320 (1962)).

Antitrust law is essentially the law of competition. Indeed, other legal systems—such as the European Union and Canada—refer to their analogous legal regimes as "competition law." American antitrust law seeks to encourage multiple sellers to compete against each other to attract business. Competition in the marketplace serves many related goals. Competition benefits consumers because, in order to attract customers, rival firms will often lower prices, improve quality and service, and generally be responsive to consumer needs. In contrast, a monopolist—a firm without significant rivals—does not face such competitive pressure. In particular, if a firm is not price disciplined by other firms, it can charge the so-called monopoly profit-maximizing price.

Various forms of competition can be characterized as static or dynamic. Static competition focuses primarily on price, such as when two firms sell similar products and attempt to earn sales by offering consumers a lower price. The addition of new features to an existing product is also sometimes viewed as a variant of static competition. In contrast, dynamic competition represents the process of product evolution in which firms develop entirely new systems for performing tasks. For example, record players competed against each other (in something approximating static competition) until CD players came along and replaced record players in large measure. The manufacturers of CD players engaged in static competition in this new product market by offering new features and competitive prices. All the while, dynamic competition still continued out of view of the music-consuming public until the release of digital music players, such as the iPod. Both forms of competition are important—dynamic competition ensures that new products enter the economy while static competition facilitates lower prices for existing products.

Competition serves the goal of efficiency. In order to increase price, a monopolist will generally reduce output. (Another way to think about this is that when the price increases, some consumers will no longer be willing or able to pay the higher price and, thus, fewer sales will necessarily occur.) While some customers may be priced out of the market, the fact that the remaining customers are paying a higher price more than compensates the monopolist for any lost sales. As competitors enter the market, they will try to lure sales away from the dominant firm by reducing price (and sometimes by improving quality or service). This in turn leads to both the optimal output and lower prices for consumers. This is referred to static efficiency. Static efficiency can be achieved relatively quickly when firms promptly lower prices in response to their rivals' price reductions. Dynamic competition is a longer term process and dynamic efficiency is achieved over time if firms make appropriate investments in technological innovation.[1]

Monopoly pricing does not achieve static efficiency and hurts consumers in two distinct ways. First, some consumers will be priced out of the market and be denied the product altogether even though they are willing and able to pay the competitive price at which the product could be supplied. It would be more efficient for these sales to occur because the consumers value the product more than it costs to make that product. Society is made worse off as beneficial sales fail to transpire. Economists refer to this reduction in social wealth as "deadweight loss." It is illustrated graphically in Appendix C of this casebook.

Second, those consumers who continue to purchase the product will pay a higher price than they would in a competitive market. This represents a wealth transfer from consumers to producers. Whether unable to purchase the product or compelled to pay a higher price, all consumers suffer when faced with monopoly pricing.

There are two main threats to competitive markets: monopolies and cartels. First, a single firm may employ predatory tactics to destroy its competitors and thus secure a monopoly. With its competitors vanquished, the firm will raise its price. Second, firms in a marketplace may form a cartel by ceasing to compete against each other and instead collude by agreeing to reduce output and charge the monopoly price. Antitrust law attempts to address these threats in order to create and restore competitive markets.

---

[1] Howard A. Shelanski & J. Gregory Sidak, *Antitrust Divestiture in Network Industries*, 68 U. CHI. L. REV. 1, 18 (2001).

American antitrust law has its roots in the English common law against restraints of trade. In the 1800s, several states followed English tradition and recognized that agreements among competitors in restraint of trade were unenforceable. However, the common law as recognized in the American states did not affirmatively condemn price-fixing agreements with civil or criminal sanctions. Rather, the agreements were merely unenforceable such that if a member of a cartel violated the understanding by not raising price, it would have a defense to any subsequent breach of contract suit: the underlying contract was unenforceable because it was in restraint of trade. In an effort to circumvent state law, rival firms formed trusts, which were essentially cartels that effectively evaded legal prohibitions on price-fixing agreements. In many industries, the trusts increased dramatically the prices of consumer goods.

Congress laid the foundation of federal antitrust law in 1890 with the Sherman Act. In response to perceived deficiencies of the Sherman Act, the 1914 Congress enacted two additional statutes: the Clayton Act and the Federal Trade Commission Act. All three statutes are contained in the Statutory Supplement found in Appendix A of this casebook. The most relevant sections of each of these laws are presented here.

A. Sherman Act (1890)

The Sherman Act contains two main provisions. Section One of the Sherman Act condemns agreements that unreasonably restrain trade. Section Two of the Sherman Act focuses on unilateral conduct by firms seeking to acquire or maintain monopoly power in a particular market. Each section will be discussed in turn.

Section One of the Sherman Act

Section One of the Sherman Act provides, in relevant part: "Every contract, combination in the form of trust or otherwise, or conspiracy, in restraint of trade or commerce among the several States, or with foreign nations, is declared to be illegal." 15 U.S.C. § 1. By condemning "every contract . . . in restraint of trade," Section One appears to be extraordinarily sweeping, because every contract restrains trade in some way.[2] After all, if I agree to sell my car to you, then I am also agreeing not to sell it to someone else. Unfortunately, the 1890 Congress provided virtually no guidance on what precise contracts it intended to outlaw.

To prevent the Sherman Act from overreaching and condemning beneficial contracts, the Supreme Court in its famous *Standard Oil* opinion held that Section One prohibits only *unreasonable* restraints of trade.[3] Modern courts have developed a multi-element test for determining Section One violations. Although judicial opinions may articulate the elements differently, most include the following elements: (1) Agreement or concerted action; (2) which constitutes an

---

[2] State Oil Co. v. Khan, 522 U.S. 3, 10 (1997).
[3] Standard Oil Co. of N.J. v. United States, 221 U.S. 1 (1911).

unreasonable restraint of trade; and (3) that has an effect on interstate commerce. The third element is rarely an issue in antitrust cases involving intellectual property. The first two elements will be discussed in turn.

Agreement. The agreement element can be established by direct evidence of an agreement, such as a written contract, audio or video tape, or the testimony of someone who observed the agreement being made. In the absence of such direct evidence, a plaintiff can show an agreement through circumstantial evidence. This process of proving agreement among competitors is often called "conscious parallelism." It requires the plaintiff to show both that the defendants consciously engaged in parallel conduct and the presence of so-called "plus factors"—such as communications among the defendants, radical and simultaneous changes in business practices, and evidence that each individual firm's action would not have made sense in the absence of an agreement. Conscious parallelism alone does not establish an agreement; relatively simultaneous conduct (including price increases) happens in competitive markets, as well as cartelized ones. The analysis of plus factors is intended to distinguish between parallel conduct resulting from similar competitive pressures and parallel conduct that is a consequence of collusion.

Unreasonable restraints of trade. The heart of most Section One jurisprudence and scholarship is the second element, determining whether an agreement has an unreasonably anticompetitive effect. Courts can employ one of three different legal tests to hold that an agreement unreasonably restrains trade: the per se rule, the rule of reason, and quick look analysis.

Per Se Rule. Some types of agreements are condemned as per se illegal. The per se rule is categorical; if an agreement falls in a per se category, then the agreement violates Section One, without any analysis of the agreement's actual effect on competitive conditions. The anticompetitive effect is presumed as a matter of law. Per se condemnation is reserved for concerted action "that would always or almost always tend to restrict competition and decrease output."[4] The Supreme Court recently noted that "[p]er se liability is reserved for only those agreements that are 'so plainly anticompetitive that no elaborate study of the industry is needed to establish their illegality.'"[5] Examples of per se categories of restraints include agreements among competitors to fix prices or to allocate customers among each other. Some group boycotts are also considered per se illegal.

Rule of Reason Analysis. When a court evaluates a restraint under the rule of reason, the plaintiff must establish that the agreement has or will likely injure competition, for example, by decreasing output or increasing price through collusion. The Rule of Reason takes "into account a variety of factors, including specific information about the relevant business, its condition before and after the restraint

---

[4] Northwest Wholesale Stationers, Inc. v. Pacific Stationery & Printing Co., 472 U.S. 284, 289–90 (1985) (quoting Broadcast Music, Inc. v. Columbia Broadcasting System, Inc., 441 U.S. 1, 19–20 (1979)).

[5] Texaco, Inc. v. Dagher, 547 U.S. 1 (2006) (quoting National Society of Professional Engineers v. United States, 435 U.S. 679, 692 (1978)).

was imposed, and the restraint's history, nature, and effect."[6] If the rule of reason applies to the agreement, the defendants are able to argue that they had a legitimate procompetitive justification for their agreement that outweighs the anticompetitive effects presented by the plaintiff.

Quick Look. Beginning in the 1980s, federal courts began to develop a middle tier of analysis that falls somewhere between the immediate condemnation of the per se rule and drawn-out inquiry associated with full-blown rule of reason analysis. This mid-level test goes by several names: quick look, abbreviated rule of reason, and truncated rule of reason. These are different labels for the same legal concept. An agreement can be held to violate Section One under quick look analysis if "observer with even a rudimentary understanding of economics could conclude that the arrangements in question would have an anticompetitive effect on customers and markets."[7] The precise contours of quick look analysis, including when a particular agreement falls within its ambit, are unclear. The Court seems to prefer a quick look approach instead of the per se rule when the defendant is a non-profit organization.[8]

Much antitrust litigation focuses on whether a challenged agreement falls in a per se category or should be evaluated under the rule of reason. Courts are significantly more likely to treat an agreement as per se illegal if they characterize the restraint as horizontal, i.e., between competitors.[9] Vertical restraints—for example, agreements between a manufacturer and its distributors or between a wholesaler and a retailer—are evaluated under the Rule of Reason.[10] Agreements on price are much more likely to be condemned under the per se rule than concerted action without price agreements.[11] This means that plaintiffs will try to characterize a challenged restraint as horizontal and related to price, whereas defendants (in addition to denying any agreement, if possible) will argue that their relationship is vertical in nature and that any agreement does not set price.

Section Two of the Sherman Act

Section 2 of the Sherman Act provides, in relevant part: "Every person who shall monopolize, or attempt to monopolize, or combine or conspire with any other person or persons, to monopolize any part of the trade or commerce among the several States, or with foreign nations, shall be deemed guilty of a felony. . . ." 15 U.S.C. § 2. Thus, there are three separate causes of action: monopolization, attempted

---

[6] State Oil Co. v. Khan, 522 U.S. 3, 10 (1997).
[7] California Dental Ass'n v. FTC, 526 U.S. 756 (1999).
[8] *See, e.g.*, National Collegiate Athletic Ass'n v. Board of Regents of University of Oklahoma, 468 U.S. 85 (1984).
[9] U.S. v. Topco Associates, Inc., 405 U.S. 596 (1972).
[10] Leegin Creative Leather Prods., Inc. v. PSKS, Inc., 127 S. Ct. 2705 (2007); Continental T. V., Inc. v. GTE Sylvania Inc., 433 U.S. 36 (1977).
[11] *See, e.g.*, F.T.C. v. Superior Court Trial Lawyers Ass'n, 493 U.S. 411 (1990).

monopolization, and conspiracies to monopolize. Each of these causes of action has its own elements that a plaintiff must prove in order to establish liability.

Monopolization

In the early decades of the Sherman Act, a debate ensued over whether Section 2 condemned monopoly structures (i.e., the mere possession of a monopoly) or monopoly conduct (i.e., a firm's acquisition or maintenance of monopoly power through the commission of predatory acts). The latter approach prevailed: "The offense of monopoly under § 2 of the Sherman Act has two elements: (1) the possession of monopoly power in the relevant market and (2) the willful acquisition or maintenance of that power as distinguished from growth or development as a consequence of a superior product, business acumen, or historic accident."[12] The second element is often referred to as the monopoly conduct requirement.

A firm may acquire a monopoly legally in a variety of ways, including marketing a superior product protected by intellectual property rights, such as a copyright or patent. But that does not mean that every monopolist that owns intellectual property rights is necessarily safe from antitrust liability. Much Section 2 jurisprudence is devoted to defining the boundary between illegal anticompetitive conduct and legitimate competitive activity. Because monopolists sometimes possess intellectual property rights that they exercise to exclude competitors, properly defining this boundary is particularly important for intellectual property right owners.

The following provides an overview of the two elements of illegal monopolization:

(1) Possession of Monopoly Power in a Relevant Market

Before a plaintiff can ask a federal judge to scrutinize the defendant's allegedly anticompetitive conduct, it must prove that the defendant possesses monopoly power in a relevant market. The relevant market has two components—what the relevant product is and where that product is sold. As a result, the first element of a monopolization claim requires the plaintiff to perform three separate tasks: define the relevant product market, define the relevant geographic market, and prove that the defendant has monopoly power in that properly defined antitrust market.

Courts determine the relevant product market by asking what products are reasonably interchangeable with the defendant's product. This often requires examining the cross-elasticity of demand and cross-elasticity of supply. Cross-elasticity of demand asks what products consumers would buy instead of the defendant's product if the defendant raised its price above the price that would be charged in a competitive market. Those products compete against the defendant's product and should be included in the relevant market. If the defendant's customers would not shift to another product in response to a significant price hike, that suggests that consumers do not view other products as reasonably interchangeable with the

---
[12] United States v. Grinnell Corp., 384 U.S., 563, 570–571 (1966).

defendant's product. For example, if the defendant is the only seller of butter, she is not necessarily a monopolist. It depends if other products compete against butter. If the defendant attempted to raise the price of butter from a competitive price to a monopoly price and this caused a significant number of consumers to switch to margarine, then the relevant market includes both butter and margarine. Cross-elasticity of supply asks if suppliers—who are not currently making a reasonably interchangeable product—would start making such a product that competes with the defendant's product if the defendant began charging a supra-competitive price. If other suppliers would start making a competing product, their productive capacity should be included in the relevant market because it could enter the market in response to a price hike by the defendant and, thus, their presence price disciplines the defendant, e.g., deters the defendant from raising price.

The relevant geographic market includes those areas in which consumers can obtain substitute products or from which alternative suppliers of the relevant product can bring their products to local consumers. The Fifth Circuit has noted "that the geographic market is a measure of capacity of competing firms to sell beyond their immediate location, and 'determines whether a particular product market is national, regional or even narrower.'"[13] This may require the court to consider "such factors as transport costs, price relationships and actual sales patterns in the area, and buyer convenience and preferences."[14] To define the breadth of the geographic market, courts consider both where the defendant's current customers would go to buy from an alternative supply source and where new suppliers would come from to enter the defendant's market in response to a price increase by the defendant.

After defining the relevant product and geographic markets—which combine to delineate the relevant market—the plaintiff must prove that the defendant has monopoly power in that properly defined market. Monopoly power is the power to control prices or exclude competition in a relevant market.[15] In general, monopoly power is difficult to measure directly so courts look at the defendant's market share, whether there are barriers to entry, and other indicators of monopoly power.

Market Share. The first, and most important, indicator of monopoly power is the defendant's market share in the relevant market. The higher the defendant's market share, the more likely a court is to conclude that the defendant has monopoly power in that market. While there are no hard and fast rules, some courts are willing to find monopoly power if a defendant has a market share of about 75 percent or higher. Conversely, in most cases if the defendant has a market share of 50 percent or lower, this is generally insufficient to establish monopoly power. But it is important to remember that courts have not articulated a uniform market share that marks the threshold between monopoly power and a lack thereof.

---

[13] Hornsby Oil Co. v. Champion Spark Plug Co., 714 F.2d 1384, 1393 (5th Cir. 1983) (quoting Areeda and Turner, Antitrust Law II, at 355).
[14] Jayco Sys., Inc. v. Savin Bus. Mach. Corp., 777 F.2d 306, 319–20 (5th Cir. 1985) (citing 2 P. Areeda & D. Turner, Antitrust Law §§ 522–525 (1978)).
[15] United States v. E. I. du Pont de Nemours & Co., 351 U.S. 377, 391 (1956).

Barriers to Entry. Although some courts rely heavily on the market share indicator, market share alone may paint a deceptive picture of whether the defendant has monopoly power. In general, evidence highlighting the presence or absence of barriers to entry provides the context in which the market share data should be analyzed. For example, if the defendant has very high market share in a relevant market and the barriers to entry are low, then the defendant may not have monopoly power because if she were to attempt to raise price, competitors could easily enter the market and bid the price down (since the barriers to entry are so low). Thus, even though the defendant has high market share, she does not automatically have monopoly power. Conversely, depending on market structure, if the defendant has a low market share (say, 40 percent) and barriers to entry are significant, then that defendant may be able to raise price profitably. Examples of barriers to entry include patents, government regulations, and a lack of access to capital, qualified labor, raw materials, or other necessary inputs.

Other Indicators of Monopoly Power. In addition to market share and barriers to entry, which sophisticated courts almost always consider, other factors may also point to a defendant's market power. These include monopoly pricing by the defendant, persistent price discrimination, and ever-increasing market concentration as competitors exit the market. These are neither dispositive nor necessary but can be persuasive, especially when the defendant has high market share and barriers to entry appear present.

Beware the Cellophane Trap. Because monopoly power is the ability to raise price, the argument goes, if one cannot profitably raise price this indicates an absence of market power. Using this same argument, DuPont convinced the Supreme Court that it did not have monopoly power over cellophane despite its apparently high market share.[16] The Supreme Court's opinion on this point is universally regarded as wrong, so much so that this form of mistake is called "the Cellophane Trap" or "the Cellophane Fallacy." The flaw is that the defendant may already be charging the monopoly price. Thus, while it may be true that the defendant cannot increase its price even more without losing many sales, that is not necessarily evidence that the defendant does not have a monopoly. It may be evidence that the defendant is already exercising its monopoly power and charging the monopoly profit-maximizing price.

If an antitrust plaintiff cannot prove that the defendant possesses monopoly power in a relevant market, then the defendant will prevail on a Section 2 monopolization claims. If the plaintiff does establish the defendant's monopoly power, the court will proceed to consider the next element, whether the defendant engaged in monopoly conduct to either acquire or maintain its monopoly power.

(2) Monopoly Conduct

The Sherman Act does not condemn a business for simply having a monopoly. Mere possession of a monopoly is not illegal. The Sherman Act condemns the use

---

[16] United States vs. E. I. du Pont de Nemours & Co., 351 U.S. 377 (1956).

of anti-competitive conduct in order to acquire or maintain a monopoly. In the absence of anti-competitive conduct, there is no violation. Courts use the phrases monopoly conduct, anti-competitive conduct, predatory conduct, and exclusionary conduct interchangeably in Section Two jurisprudence.

There is no accepted single test for what constitutes monopoly conduct sufficient to satisfy the second element of the *Grinnell* test. However, the Supreme Court has stated that "'exclusionary' comprehends at the most behavior that not only (1) tends to impair the opportunities of rivals, but also (2) either does not further competition on the merits or does so in an unnecessarily restrictive way."[17] This is more of a principle than a legal test that lower courts can apply to various fact patterns. Antitrust law is essentially common law; monopoly conduct is defined by the case law. To determine whether a monopolist's conduct is illegal, lawyers and judges must compare that behavior to other acts by monopolists that courts have either condemned or permitted. Parts 2 and 3 of this book present a wide range of cases in which courts have held that an IP owner either has or has not engaged in impermissible exclusionary conduct. These cases provide the foundation from which antitrust attorneys give advice to their clients as to what IP owners can and cannot do with their intellectual property.

Attempted Monopolization

Section 2 of the Sherman Act also condemns attempted monopolization. Attempted monopolization is a separate cause of action that has its own elements. The Supreme Court in *Spectrum Sports* held that "to demonstrate attempted monopolization a plaintiff must prove (1) that the defendant has engaged in predatory or anti-competitive conduct with (2) a specific intent to monopolize and (3) a dangerous probability of achieving monopoly power."[18]

The third prong of the attempted monopolization test, dangerous probability of success, is similar to the first prong of *Grinnell* test (monopoly power in a relevant market). The dangerous probability element requires the plaintiff to define the relevant product and geographic markets and to show that, as a result of the defendant's anti-competitive conduct, there is a dangerous probability that the defendant will monopolize this market. The primary difference between the third prong of attempted monopolization and the first prong of *Grinnell* is that the former is easier to satisfy. While monopolization requires the plaintiff to show that the defendant actually has monopoly power, attempted monopolization only requires the plaintiff to establish that there is a "dangerous probability" of the defendant acquiring such power. The *Spectrum Sports* opinion explained: "In order to determine whether there is a dangerous probability of monopolization, courts

---

[17] Aspen Skiing Co. v. Aspen Highlands Skiing Corp., 472 U.S. 585, 605 n.32 (1985) (quoting 3 P. Areeda & D. Turner, Antitrust Law 78 (1978)).
[18] Spectrum Sports, Inc. v. McQuillan, 506 U.S. 447, 456 (1993) (citing 3 Areeda & Turner, Antitrust Law, ¶ 820, at 312).

have found it necessary to consider the relevant market and the defendant's ability to lessen or destroy competition in that market."[19]

This basically requires the analysis that would be performed under the first prong of the *Grinnell* monopolization test, but the market share requirements will be lower in an attempted monopolization claim. "An attempted monopolization claim necessarily involves conduct which has not yet succeeded; otherwise, the plaintiff would bring an actual monopolization claim."[20] Thus, whereas the first prong of *Grinnell* generally requires the defendant to have a market share around 75 percent or higher, plaintiffs can satisfy the dangerous probability element for attempted monopolization by showing that the defendant has a market share of around 35 percent or higher, depending on the presence of barriers to entry. Again, these numbers are rough estimates.

Because the market share requirement for attempted monopolization is lower, the cause of action requires that plaintiffs show the additional element of specific intent to monopolize the market. The specific intent required for attempted monopolization must be "something more than an attempt to compete vigorously."[21] The plaintiff must show that the defendant had a "specific intent to destroy competition or build monopoly."[22] Specific intent to monopolize is a fairly nuanced concept and the line that separates the intent to compete vigorously from the intent to monopolize a market is difficult to draw.

The first prong of the attempted monopolization test essentially parallels the second element of the *Grinnell* test for illegal monopolization. Monopoly conduct under *Grinnell* is the same as "predatory or anticompetitive conduct" under *Spectrum Sports*, and vice-versa.

Conspiracies to Monopolize

Finally, Section 2 of the Sherman Act condemns conspiracies to monopolize. This, too, is a separate cause of action with its own elements. In order to prevail on a conspiracy to monopolize claim, the plaintiff must prove: "(1) an agreement to restrain trade, (2) deliberately entered into with the specific intent of achieving a monopoly rather than a legitimate business purpose, (3) which could have had an anticompetitive effect, and (4) the commission of at least one overt act in furtherance of the conspiracy."[23]

Much less case law addresses this cause of action. This is not surprising because a conspiracy to monopolize is more difficult to prove than a conspiracy in restraint of trade under Section One, yet it is hard to imagine a factual scenario that would constitute a conspiracy to monopolize, but not a Section One violation. Because both causes of action should provide the same remedy, savvy plaintiffs will pursue

---

[19] Spectrum Sports, Inc. v. McQuillan, 506 U.S. 447, 456 (1993).
[20] Taylor Publishing Co. v. Jostens, Inc., 216 F.3d 465, 474 (5th Cir. 2000).
[21] Spectrum Sports, 506 U.S. at 459.
[22] Times Picayune Publishing Co. v. United States, 345 U.S. 594, 626 (1953).
[23] U.S. Anchor Mfg., Inc. v. Rule Indus., Inc., 7 F.3d 986, 998 (11th Cir. 1993); *see also* Multistate Legal Studies, Inc. v. Harcourt Brace Jovanovich Legal and Prof'l Publ., Inc., 63 F.3d 1540, 1556 (10th Cir. 1995); North Mississippi Communications, Inc. v. Jones, 792 F.2d 1330 (5th Cir.1986).

a Section One claim instead. (Of course, the plaintiff could bring both conspiracy to restrain trade and conspiracy to monopolize claims, but the plaintiff gains little by pleading the latter claim.)

B. Clayton Act (1914)

Tying Arrangements

Although Congress in 1890 decided to leave interpretation of the Sherman Act's vague edicts to the federal judiciary, Congress in later years was not always enamored with the Supreme Court's construction of antitrust law. In particular, Congress took umbrage with the Court's decision in *Henry v. A.B. Dick*,[24] which held that a patentholder could compel its customers to agree to purchase unpatented supplies for use with their patented product. Today we call this type of contractual requirement a tying arrangement. A tying arrangement exists when a seller will provide or sell one product (the "tying product") only on the condition that the buyer agrees to also purchase another separate product (the "tied product").[25] Section 3 of the Clayton Act condemned tying arrangements where the effect "may be to substantially lessen competition or tend to create a monopoly in any line of commerce."[26]

Tying case law has grown significantly since 1914 and soon after Congress enacted the Clayton Act, the Supreme Court held that tying arrangements can violate Section One of the Sherman Act as well. Although the Court initially announced different legal tests, today the legal tests for condemning tie-ins under Sherman and Clayton Acts are essentially identical. The major difference is that the Clayton Act is limited to products, while the Sherman Act applies to services as well.

Under either Section One of the Sherman Act or Section Three of the Clayton Act, a tying arrangement is illegal if the plaintiff can prove: "1) that there are two separate products, a 'tying' product and a 'tied' product; 2) that those products are in fact 'tied' together—that is, the buyer was forced to buy the tied product to get the tying product; 3) that the seller possesses sufficient economic power in the tying product market to coerce buyer acceptance of the tied product; and 4) involvement of a 'not insubstantial' amount of interstate commerce in the market of the tied product."[27] Some courts interpret the fourth element as requiring the *foreclosure* of a substantial volume of commerce in the tied product market, and not mere involvement.[28] In addition, in at least two circuits—the Second and the

---

[24] 224 U.S. 1 (1912).

[25] Northern Pac. Ry. Co. v. United States, 356 U.S. 1, 5–6 (1958); Jefferson Parish Hosp. Dist. No. 2 v. Hyde, 466 U.S. 2, 12 (1984); Eastman Kodak Co. v. Image Technical Services, Inc., 504 U.S. 451, 461 (1992) ("A tying arrangement is 'an agreement by a party to sell one product but only on the condition that the buyer also purchases a different (or tied) product, or at least agrees that he will not purchase that product from any other supplier.'").

[26] 15 U.S.C. § 14.

[27] Technical Resource Serv. v. Dornier Med. Sys., 134 F.3d 1458, 1464–65 (11th Cir. 1998) (citing Tic-X-Press, Inc. v. Omni Promotions Co., 815 F.2d 1407, 1414 (11th Cir.1987)). *See also* Eastman Kodak Co. v. Image Technical Servs., Inc., 504 U.S. 451, 462 (1992).

[28] *See, e.g.,* Town Sound & Custom Tops, Inc. v. Chrysler Motors Corp., 959 F.2d 468, 493 (3d Cir.1992).

Fifth—the plaintiff must also show that the "tie has an anticompetitive effect on the tied market."[29] If the plaintiff can establish the prima facie case, the defendant is allowed to argue that it had a legitimate business justification for imposing the tying requirement.

Courts refer to tying arrangements as per se illegal, making tie-ins one of the categories of per se violations. But scholars uniformly recognize that this label is a misnomer. If tying arrangements were truly per se illegal, the plaintiff would not have to establish the defendant's market power or any effect on commerce; nor would the defendant be allowed to argue a legitimate business justification defense. These are all hallmarks of the rule of reason, not the per se rule. While some Supreme Court justices have indicated their desire to stop referring to tying arrangements as per se illegal, the majority have declared that "[i]t is far too late in the history of our antitrust jurisprudence to question the proposition that certain tying arrangements pose an unacceptable risk of stifling competition and therefore are unreasonable 'per se.'"[30]

Section Three of the Clayton Act also condemns exclusive dealing arrangements that unreasonably restrain competition. An exclusive dealing arrangement can take one of several different forms. A supplier may agree to sell all of its output to one particular buyer. Alternatively, a buyer (often a distributor or a retailer) may agree to handle the goods of only one particular seller. For example, a retail store may agree to carry only one brand of tape or ice cream. To determine whether an exclusive dealing arrangement unreasonably restrains trade, courts examine, among other things, what percentage of the relevant market is foreclosed by the arrangement, how long the period of exclusivity lasts, and whether the excluded competitors have alternative distribution channels. Exclusive dealing arrangements may also be in violation of Section One or Section Two of the Sherman Act, provided the plaintiff can prove the necessary elements of those antitrust causes of action.

Mergers

Section 7 of the Clayton Act (as amended in 1950) condemns mergers and acquisitions where "the effect of such acquisition may be substantially to lessen competition or to tend to create monopoly" in "any line of commerce." Although private plaintiffs can challenge mergers (provided that they can establish that they have standing), the federal government takes primary responsibility for merger enforcement. Both the Antitrust Division of the Department of Justice and the Federal Trade Commission have authority to challenge proposed mergers. After congressional enactment of the Hart-Scott-Rodino Act in 1976, merging parties above a certain size must submit a Hart-Scott-Rodino filing to the federal antitrust agencies in advance of their proposed merger. This provides the Antitrust Division and the FTC an opportunity to challenge and enjoin the merger before it is consummated.

---

[29] *See, e.g.*, Hack v. Yale College, 237 F.3d 81, 86 (2d Cir. 2000); United Farmers Agents Assn. v. Farmers Insurance Exchange, 89 F.3d 233, 235 n.2 (5th Cir. 1996) (citation omitted).
[30] Jefferson Parish, 466 U.S. 2, 9 (1984).

Relatively little case law exists on mergers—and no Supreme Court cases have been decided in the last thirty years—because when the government challenges a merger, the parties often abandon the deal.

Other Aspects of the Clayton Act

The Clayton Act also addresses interlocking directorates and other issues that are not particularly relevant to the overlap of antitrust and intellectual property laws and, thus, are not discussed here.

C. Federal Trade Commission Act (1914)

The 1914 Congress debated whether to take a narrow or broad approach to dealing with the perceived deficiencies of judicial interpretation of the Sherman Act. The narrow approach would prohibit those specific practices that Congress had identified as warranting antitrust condemnation, like tying arrangements. The broad approach would create a structure to address unforeseen forms of anticompetitive conduct.

Ultimately, Congress pursued both paths. While the Clayton Act proscribes some specific conduct, Congress in 1914 also passed the Federal Trade Commission Act (FTCA), which created the Federal Trade Commission and authorized it to enforce the FTCA provisions, most notably Section 5. Section 5 of the FTCA declares unlawful any "unfair methods of competition in or affecting commerce and unfair or deceptive acts or practices in or affecting commerce."[31] The call of the provision is broad. Much conduct that violates the Sherman or Clayton Acts will necessarily violate Section 5 of the FTCA as well. But Section 5 goes further, prohibiting deceptive trade practices even if they do not restrain competition as defined by the antitrust laws.

Unlike the Sherman and Clayton Acts, the FTCA provides for no private right of action. Only government enforcers may bring actions pursuant to the FTCA. The FTCA authorizes the FTC to "hit at every trade practice... which restrain[s] competition or might lead to such restraint if not stopped in its incipient stages."[32]

Remedies

Antitrust laws may be enforced by federal and state officials, as well as by private plaintiffs. Private plaintiffs can seek damages or injunctive relief. With limited exceptions, any damage award received by a successful antitrust plaintiff is automatically trebled. The trebling is not a matter of judicial discretion. In light of treble damages, antitrust does not provide for punitive damages. In order to recover damages, private plaintiffs must show that they have suffered antitrust injury, which "injury of the type the antitrust laws were intended to prevent and

---

[31] 15 U.S.C. § 45(a)(1).
[32] FTC v. Cement Institute, 333 U.S. 683, 693 (1948).

that flows from that which makes defendants' acts unlawful."[33] In other words, the plaintiff's alleged injury must flow from a decrease in competition. Generally, consumers who pay an inflated price to a cartel member or an illegal monopolist have suffered antitrust injury in the form of the overcharge.

Injunctive relief includes both structural remedies and conduct remedies. Structural remedies seek to change the market in which the defendant operates, such as by dissolving a dominant firm into smaller independent companies that compete against each other, as happened with Standard Oil in the 1910s. Conduct remedies require the defendant to change its individual policies. Examples of conduct remedies include the mandate that Microsoft share certain technical information with software developers.

Both the Federal Trade Commission and Department of Justice's Antitrust Division are entrusted to enforce federal antitrust laws. When successful, federal antitrust authorities are entitled to injunctive relief and single damages.[34] In addition, state attorneys general bring civil antitrust suits as parens patriae actions. This means that they are suing in the name of their states' consumers, who have been injured by the alleged antitrust violation.

Most importantly, prosecutors within the DOJ's Antitrust Division can bring criminal antitrust cases. Individuals convicted of criminal antitrust violations can be sentenced up to ten years in federal prison. Although the Sherman Act does not clearly delineate what conduct is criminal and what conduct creates only civil liability, in reality, criminal prosecutions are brought solely against hard-core antitrust violators, such as bid-riggers and price-fixers in a cartel.

Comments and Questions

1. Section Two does not prohibit all monopolies. Instead courts focus on the process by which a firm acquires or maintains its monopoly power. Should antitrust law condemn all monopolies? In other words, should monopolies be illegal per se? Why or why not?

2. What standard should courts use to distinguish between legitimate zealous competition and illegal anticompetitive conduct?

3. The Sherman Act creates a separate cause of action for attempted monopolization. Why should antitrust law condemn attempted monopolization in addition to actual monopolization? Antitrust law does not condemn attempted violations of Section One. Should it?

4. Courts and commentators have routinely observed that antitrust is concerned with consumer welfare. Should the purpose of antitrust law be to maximize consumer welfare or total social welfare, as measured by the wealth of both consumers and producers combined? Is it always easy to determine who is a consumer

---

[33] Atlantic Richfield Co. v. USA Petroleum Co., 495 U.S. 328, 334 (1990).
[34] Pfizer, Inc. v. Government of India, 434 U.S. 308, 317 (1978) (Congress "affirmatively intended to exclude the United States from the treble-damages remedy.")

and who is a producer? How does defining the goals of antitrust law affect how the law may be applied?

If antitrust is primarily concerned with consumer welfare, should consumers be able to combine and form a buyers' cartel in order to compel sellers to charge lower prices?

If antitrust law is designed to protect consumer welfare, should competitors have standing to bring antitrust litigation? Should antitrust laws protect small businesses from being driven out of business by larger firms if those larger firms are more efficient?

Bibliography of Additional Resources

Phillip E. Areeda & Herbert Hovenkamp, Antitrust Law (2008 and supplements)

Robert Bork, The Antitrust Paradox (1978)

Lawrence Sullivan & Warren Grimes, The Law of Antitrust: An Integrated Handbook (2001)

Herbert Hovenkamp, Federal Antitrust Policy: The Law of Competition and Its Practice (2005)

Herbert Hovenkamp, The Antitrust Enterprise: Principle and Execution (2008)

Keith N. Hylton, Antitrust Law: Economic Theory and Common Law Evolution (2003)

Earl W. Kintner and Joseph P. Bauer, Federal Antitrust Law (1998)

William Letwin, Law and Economic Policy in America: The Evolution of the Sherman Antitrust Act (1965)

Richard A. Posner, Antitrust Law (2d ed. 2001)

E. Thomas Sullivan, The Political Economy of the Sherman Act: The First One Hundred Years (1991)

CHAPTER 3

The Tension Between Antitrust and Intellectual Property

A. A Brief History on the Relationship Between Antitrust Law and Intellectual Property Rights

Federal patent law predates federal antitrust law by a century. During that century, courts were largely deferential to patent owners and "treated a patentee's exclusive rights to make, sell, and use the patented invention as virtually sacrosanct."[1] The 1790 Congress also enacted the first copyright statute and began a long process of expanding the reach and scope of copyright protections.[2]

In the early days after the passage of the Sherman Act, antitrust law did little to affect the supremacy of intellectual property rights. Antitrust law evolved separately from the various intellectual property regimes. Courts afforded little weight to the idea that the anticompetitive effects of intellectual property rights could implicate antitrust concerns. For example, early decisions upheld the ability of patentholders to impose tying arrangements, most notably the Sixth Circuit opinion in *Heaton-Peninsular Button-Fastener Co. v. Eureka Specialty Co.*[3] The case is referred to as the Button-Fastener Case because the owner of a patented button-fastening machine required customers to purchase unpatented fasteners.

At the beginning of the twentieth century, the Supreme Court considered the relationship between antitrust law and patent rights in *E. Bement & Sons v. National Harrow*.[4] The *Bement* Court examined a patent pool that set the price that pool members could charge for their final products. This is the type of conduct

---

[1] Alan J. Weinschel, *Intellectual Property and the Antitrust Laws, in* ANTITRUST ADVISOR 5–6 (Irving Scher ed., 2006).
[2] *See* R. Anthony Reese, *Innocent Infringement in U.S. Copyright Law: A History,* 30 COLUM. J.L. & ARTS 133 (2007).
[3] 77 F. 288 (6th Cir. 1896).
[4] 186 U.S. 70 (1902).

that would seem to represent a clear antitrust violation today.[5] However, when one licensee challenged the license agreements used by the patent pool, the Court interpreted patent rights very broadly:

> [T]he general rule is absolute freedom in the use or sale of rights under the patent laws of the United States. The very object of these laws is monopoly, and the rule is, with few exceptions, that any conditions which are not in their very nature illegal with regard to this kind of property, imposed by the patentee and agreed to by the licensee for the right to manufacture or use or sell the article, will be upheld by the courts. The fact that the conditions in the contracts keep up the monopoly or fix prices does not render them illegal.[6]

As with the Button-Fastener case, the opinion endorsed extreme deference to patentholders.

The conflict between antitrust and IP commenced in earnest in the early 1910s, when both courts and Congress began to more closely scrutinize the conduct of intellectual property owners. Following the lead of the Button-Fastener Case, the Supreme Court endorsed a patent owner's ability to impose a tying arrangement between patented and unpatented products in *Henry v. A.B. Dick*.[7] Perhaps not surprisingly, Horace Lurton, who as a Sixth Circuit judge authored the Button-Fastener Case, wrote the majority opinion in *A.B. Dick*. However, this time the Court's opinion provoked a congressional response.

In 1914, largely in response to the Supreme Court's decision in *A.B. Dick*,[8] Congress enacted the Clayton Act, Section 3 of which condemned tying arrangements that substantially lessened competition. Because Section 3 specifically condemned anticompetitive tying arrangements even if the tying product was patented, the passage of the Clayton Act signaled a change in legal treatment of patentholders accused of violating antitrust laws. Three years after passage of the Clayton Act, the Supreme Court in *Motion Picture Patents Co. v. Universal Film Manufacturing Co.*,[9] reversed its decision in *A.B. Dick*. The patentee in *Motion Picture Patents* attempted to limit whose films could be played using its patented projector. The Court analyzed the claims of the patent and determined that the patent covered only the projector and not the films shown with it. The Court noted that the "scope of every patent is limited to the invention described in the claims..."[10] The Court concluded that the patentee had sought to expand its market power beyond the legitimate scope of its patent. The decision brought tying arrangements within the ambit of the Sherman Act, as well as the Clayton Act. More importantly, the decision in *Motion Picture Patents* signaled patentholders that possession of a valid patent would no longer serve to essentially immunize them from antitrust liability.

---

[5] *See* Chapter 9.
[6] 186 U.S. at 91.
[7] 224 U.S. 1 (1912).
[8] *See* IBM v. United States, 298 U.S. 131, 137 (1936).
[9] 243 U.S. 502 (1917).
[10] *Id.* at 510.

A patentee's action that restrained competition beyond the scope of its patent could rightfully be a concern for antitrust law.

For the next several decades, the federal courts wrestled with defining the appropriate boundaries between the legitimate exercise of exclusionary IP rights and the congressional call to prevent unreasonable restraints of trade. This judicial dialogue on the intersection of antitrust and intellectual property took place in the context of a larger expansion of antitrust law's reach. While the 1914 Acts revived antitrust laws, enforcement again become relatively dormant with the onset of the Great Depression, during which time the federal government facilitated pricing coordination through the National Recovery Administration and the Supreme Court permitted price fixing among competitors in depressed industries, such as coal.[11] However, when Thurman Arnold took over the helm of the DOJ's Antitrust Division, he reinvigorated antitrust enforcement and convinced the federal courts to take a harder line against a wider range of business arrangements.[12] Beginning with horizontal price fixing, the Supreme Court began to develop and expand the list of activities declared per se illegal under the antitrust laws.[13] By the early 1970s, the list of per se illegal agreements eventually included tying arrangements,[14] resale price maintenance,[15] vertical nonprice restraints,[16] and horizontal agreements to divide markets or allocate customers.[17] In the area of mergers, the Supreme Court consistently condemned mergers in which the merging firms had very small market shares.[18] This led Justice Stewart to observe in the mid-1960s that the "sole consistency that I can find is that in [merger cases], the Government always wins."[19] In sum, in almost all areas of antitrust, the scales were heavily weighted in favor of the plaintiff.

This steady expansion of antitrust law generally also influenced how courts interpreted the rights of intellectual property owners. Courts tried to balance the competing interests. On the one hand, the Supreme Court opined that a patent "is an exception to the general rule against monopolies and to the right to access to a free and open market."[20] But the Court also showed a willingness to condemn some anticompetitive conduct by patentholders. For example, the Supreme Court in this period held that tying arrangements, including where the tying product was patented, were per se illegal.[21] The relationship between antitrust and intellectual property became more entrenched with the evolution of the doctrine of patent misuse, whereby patents could be rendered unenforceable if a patentholder exploited its

---

[11] Appalachian Coals v. U.S., 288 U.S. 344 (1933).
[12] *See* SPENCER WEBER WALLER, THURMAN ARNOLD: A BIOGRAPHY (2005).
[13] United States v. Socony-Vacuum Oil Co., 310 U.S. 150 (1940).
[14] Northern Pacific Ry. Co. v. United States, 356 U.S. 1 (1958).
[15] Dr. Miles Medical Co. v. John D. Park & Sons Co., 220 U.S. 373 (1911).
[16] United States v. Arnold, Schwinn & Co., 388 U.S. 365 (1967).
[17] United States v. Topco Associates, Inc., 405 U.S. 596 (1972).
[18] United States v. Von's Grocery Co., 384 U.S. 270, 272 (1966); Brown Shoe Co. v. United States, 370 U.S. 294, 315, 343–44 (1962).
[19] United States v. Von's Grocery Co., 384 U.S. 270, 301 (1966) (Stewart, J., dissenting).
[20] Precision Instrument Mfg. Co. v. Auto. Maintenance Mach. Co., 324 U.S. 806, 816 (1945).
[21] International Salt Co. v. U.S., 332 U.S. 392 (1947).

exclusionary rights in a manner that illegitimately expanded the patent's scope. Patent misuse was primarily a defense employed by defendants in patent infringement cases. However, patent misuse melded with antitrust jurisprudence as courts began to hold that much conduct that represented patent misuse also violated the antitrust laws.[22] Many courts found antitrust and patent laws to be inherently in conflict. Invoking cases from the early era, some courts observed that "there is an obvious tension between the patent laws and the antitrust laws" since "[o]ne body of law protects monopoly power while the other seeks to proscribe it."[23] As courts attempted to balance IP rights and antitrust concerns, antitrust interests often prevailed. This mid-century judicial balancing act is reflected in many of the cases excerpted in Parts 2 through 4 of this book.

By the early 1970s, the ascension of antitrust over IP interests became evident when the Deputy Assistant Attorney General in the Department of Justice's Antitrust Division announced the "Nine No-No's." These reflected government views about the actions that patent owners could not take without drawing the attention of, and perhaps a lawsuit from, the Antitrust Division. The list included:

(1) tying arrangements;
(2) grantback provisions, which forced a licensee to assign future patents back to the patentee;
(3) restrictions on the resale of patented products;
(4) restrictions on a licensee's ability to sell unpatented products;
(5) provisions precluding a licensee from entering into future licenses with other patentees;
(6) mandatory package licensing;
(7) royalty provisions to collect royalties on the sale of unpatented items;
(8) restrictions on a licensee's use of a product made pursuant to a patented process; and
(9) resale price restrictions.

Some of these were common practices and the Nine No-No's put patent owners on notice that it would not be business as usual, although many of these practices did, in fact, continue. While not announced publicly until the early 1970s, the philosophy behind the Nine No-No's began in the late 1960s. Government attorneys crafted the list of Nine No-No's at a time when most antitrust violations were evaluated under the per se rule, including vertical price restraints and vertical non-price restraints. The Nine No-No's were part and parcel of a larger antitrust regime that treated almost all business relationships with suspicion.

Beginning in the mid-1970s, the Supreme Court began to retreat from its heavy reliance on antitrust's per se rule. Most significantly, with its decision in *Continental T. V., Inc. v. GTE Sylvania Inc.*,[24] the Court removed vertical non-price restraints

---

[22] This is explored more fully in Chapter 3.
[23] United States v. Westinghouse Electric Corp., 648 F.2d 642, 646 (9th Cir.1981) (citing E. Bement & Sons v. Nat'l Harrow Co., 186 U.S. 70, 91 (1902)).
[24] 433 U.S. 36 (1977).

from the per se illegal category. Many of the items on the Nine No-No's hit list are properly characterized as vertical non-price restraints. Thus, as vertical non-price restraints shifted from being condemned per se to being subjected to rule of reason analysis, the Nine No-No's became inconsistent with antitrust law as interpreted by the courts.

The election of Ronald Reagan signaled the official demise of the Nine No-No's,[25] as the Antitrust Division under President Reagan took a decidedly less dim view of these once-suspect licensing practices. In 1983, the head of the Antitrust Division, Assistant Attorney General William F. Baxter, urged greater deference to IP owners:

> The antitrust laws should be clarified to prohibit the courts from condemning intellectual property licensing as per se unlawful. To enable intellectual property owners to obtain the maximum legitimate rewards possible for their efforts, it is crucial that the courts carefully consider procompetitive benefits when evaluating the lawfulness of intellectual property licensing under the antitrust laws. While many courts appreciate the competitive benefits of intellectual property, the occasional judicial hostility shown toward intellectual property in the context of antitrust suits must be proscribed. A law clearly stating that intellectual property licensing cannot be deemed per se illegal would inform the courts that intellectual property licensing arrangements generally enhance rather than impede innovation and productivity and that the antitrust laws must be sensitive to this fact. . . .It is also necessary to clarify the patent and copyright doctrines of misuse to mitigate the danger that the courts will use those doctrines as a vehicle for venting judicial hostility toward intellectual property. The misuse doctrine, which the courts use to justify a refusal to enforce patent and copyrights, can provide a devastating disincentive to innovate. If the doctrine is to continue to exist, the courts must be required to apply it in a manner that is consistent with the procompetitive exploitation of intellectual property. The law should clearly provide that before the courts can find that the exploitation of a patent or copyright constitutes misuse, they must determine, pursuant to an analysis grounded in economic theory, that the conduct is anticompetitive and a violation of the antitrust laws.[26]

Lest there be any doubt about the ramifications of this new thinking on the Nine No-No's policy of the past, Roger B. Andewelt, then Deputy Director of Operations for the Antitrust Division removed it in a speech in July 1985 when he declared:

> the Nine No-No's never were consistent with the case law and more importantly always represented unsound and counter-productive competition policy. Each of the nine provisions potentially could be an integral part of a procompetitive license. Therefore, instead of reverting to per se treatment, patent licenses should

---

[25] Willard K. Tom & Joshua A. Newberg, *Antitrust and Intellectual Property: From Separate Spheres to Unified Field,* 66 ANTITRUST L.J. 167, n.67 (1997).
[26] WEINSCHEL, *supra* note 59 at 5-9–5-10 (quoting W. Baxter, *Antitrust Law and the Stimulation of Technological Invention and Innovation,* discussion paper for Preparatory Conf. on Govt. Organization & Operation & the Role of Govt. in the Economy, Univ. San Diego (July 19–21, 1983)).

be judged under the antitrust rule of reason so that licensors have an opportunity to demonstrate any such procompetitive effects."[27]

The shift away from the Nine No-No's may have been influenced in part by the growing influence of IP owners and the perception that IP was playing an increasingly important role in the American economy.

During the same time frame, Congress also made life easier for owners of intellectual property by enacting the National Cooperative Research Act of 1984—amended by the National Cooperative Research and Production Act and the Standards Development Organization Advancement Act of 2004—which facilitated technical collaboration by eliminating per se treatment and treble damages for certain agreements.[28] In addition to these amendments to the antitrust statutes, Congress also revised patent law to reflect a greater deference to patent owners. The Patent Misuse Reform Act of 1988 provided that a patentholder does not commit patent misuse by imposing a tying requirement—i.e., conditioning the licensing (or sale) of the patented product on the licensee (or buyer) also licensing (or buying) another separate product—unless the patentholder possesses market power in the relevant market in which the patented product competes.[29] In other words, market power would not be presumed from the mere presence of the patent. This alteration in patent law ultimately changed antitrust common law, as we will explore later in this chapter.

As economic thinking evolved and scholars embarked on writing more about how to properly balance the concerns of the antitrust and intellectual property legal regimes, many courts began issuing more nuanced opinions on the intersection of these two areas of law. The following excerpt from the Federal Circuit is an example:

Atari Games Corp. v. Nintendo of America, Inc.
897 F.2d 1572 (Fed. Cir. 1990).

When the patented product is merely one of many products that actively compete on the market, few problems arise between the property rights of a patent owner and the antitrust laws. [citation omitted] However, when the patented product is so successful that it creates its own economic market or consumes a large section of an existing market, the aims and objectives of patent and antitrust laws may seem, at first glance, wholly at odds. However, the two bodies of law are actually complementary, as both are aimed at encouraging innovation, industry and competition. [citation omitted]

There may on occasion exist, therefore, a fine line between actions protecting the legitimate interests of a patent owner and antitrust law violations. On the one

---

[27] WEINSCHEL, *supra* note 59 at 5-10–5-11 (quoting R.B. Andewelt, *The Antitrust Division's Perspective on Intellectual Property Protection and Licensing In the Past, the Present and the Future*, Remarks before ABA Patent, Trademark and Copyright Section (July 16, 1985)).

[28] These are discussed more fully in Chapter 9 and the statutes are located in Appendix A of this casebook.

[29] 35 U.S.C.A. § 271 (d)(5).

hand, the patent owner must be allowed to protect the property right given to him under the patent laws.

On the other hand, a patent owner may not take the property right granted by a patent and use it to extend his power in the marketplace improperly, i.e. beyond the limits of what Congress intended to give in the patent laws. The fact that a patent is obtained does not wholly insulate the patent owner from the antitrust laws. [citation omitted] When a patent owner uses his patent rights not only as a shield to protect his invention, but as a sword to eviscerate competition unfairly, that owner may be found to have abused the grant and may become liable for antitrust violations when sufficient power in the relevant market is present. Therefore, patent owners may incur antitrust liability for enforcement of a patent known to be obtained through fraud or known to be invalid, where license of a patent compels the purchase of unpatented goods, or where there is an overall scheme to use the patent to violate antitrust laws.

After the rejection of the overreaching of the Nine No-No's era, the next major Federal Government announcement on the relationship between antitrust law and intellectual property rights came in 1995, when the Federal Trade Commission and the DOJ's Antitrust Division jointly issued *Antitrust Guidelines for the Licensing of Intellectual Property*. The 1995 Licensing Guidelines were decidedly more balanced and nuanced than prior government policies. The Guidelines began from the premise that: "The intellectual property laws and the antitrust laws share the common purpose of promoting innovation and enhancing consumer welfare." The 1995 Guidelines advanced three brought principles: (1) for purposes of antitrust analysis, intellectual property is treated as comparable to any other form of property; (2) the antitrust enforcement agencies do not presume that intellectual property creates market power; and (3) Agencies recognize that intellectual property licensing is generally procompetitive because it allows firms to combine complementary factors of production. The Guidelines present the federal agencies' views on a wide range of licensing practices that implicate antitrust concerns.

The 1995 Guidelines do not constitute substantive antitrust law and are not binding on federal judges deciding antitrust cases. The Guidelines officially only reflect the antitrust agencies' philosophy on these antitrust issues. However, litigants routinely cite the Guidelines and courts have treated the Guidelines as persuasive authority and, thus, they have been relatively influential. Because the Guidelines provide a concise explanation on the relationship between antitrust and IP rights—and because they reflect the federal government's enforcement priorities—many scholars and attorneys use the Guidelines as the starting point for discussions on this hybrid area of law. Given their importance, it would be a good idea to familiarize yourself with the Guidelines. They may be found in their entirety in Appendix B of this casebook, and sections of the Guidelines are excerpted throughout this casebook where relevant to the case discussion.

The thrust of the 1995 Guidelines' theme that antitrust law and intellectual property law are complementary continues to reflect the federal antitrust enforcement agencies' thinking. In 2007, the Department of Justice's Antitrust Division and the Federal Trade Commission jointly issued a report that both detailed the prior conflicts between antitrust and IP law and also reiterated that the two areas of law are more complementary than irreconcilable. The report noted:

> Over the past several decades, antitrust enforcers and the courts have come to recognize that intellectual property laws and antitrust laws share the same fundamental goals of enhancing consumer welfare and promoting innovation. This recognition signaled a significant shift from the view that prevailed earlier in the twentieth century, when the goals of antitrust and intellectual property law were viewed as incompatible: intellectual property law's grant of exclusivity was seen as creating monopolies that were in tension with antitrust law's attack on monopoly power. Such generalizations are relegated to the past. Modern understanding of these two disciplines is that intellectual property and antitrust laws work in tandem to bring new and better technologies, products, and services to consumers at lower prices.[30]

Despite the passage's rosy tone, tensions remain. Owners of intellectual property often engage in conduct that licensees, competitors, consumers, and/or government actors believe constitutes a violation of federal antitrust laws. The IP owners often win, but antitrust plaintiffs have also achieved some major litigation victories. In some instances, federal courts have reached opposing legal conclusions on virtually identical facts. In sum, the intersection of antitrust and IP rights remains a confusing area of jurisprudence in which reasonable people can disagree on how antitrust law should or should constrain IP owners.

Comments and Questions

1. Was there any virtue in the government announcing a list of Nine No-No's?

2. Should any of the Nine No-No's be *per se legal*? If so, which ones and why?

B. The Relationship Between Intellectual Property and Market Power

Chapter 2 noted the importance of market power in antitrust analysis. In particular, Section 2 monopolization requires the plaintiff to prove that the defendant possesses monopoly power in a relevant market. Attempted monopolization requires proof that there is a dangerous probability of the defendant acquiring monopoly power. In Section One cases evaluated under the rule of reason, courts consider the market power of the parties to the challenged agreement.[31] Finally, the third element of a tying claim requires the plaintiff to prove that the

---

[30] U.S. Dep't of Justice & Federal Trade Commission, Antitrust Enforcement and Intellectual Property Rights: Promoting Innovation and Competition 1 (2007).
[31] *See, e.g.*, Total Ben. Serv., Inc. v. Group Ins. Admin., Inc., 875 F.Supp. 1228, 1233 (E.D.La. 1995) ("[I]f the defendants lack market power, that is, the power to raise prices above competitive levels, their conduct is not likely to have the required impact on competition.") (citations omitted).

defendant has sufficient economic power over the tying product that it can force consumer to purchase the tied product.

This raises the question of the relationship between intellectual property rights and market power. The 1995 Guidelines addressed the issue as follows:

> **DOJ-FTC Antitrust Guidelines for the Licensing of Intellectual Property, Sec. 2.2**
>
> Market power is the ability profitably to maintain prices above, or output below, competitive levels for a significant period of time. The Agencies will not presume that a patent, copyright, or trade secret necessarily confers market power upon its owner. Although the intellectual property right confers the power to exclude with respect to the specific product, process, or work in question, there will often be sufficient actual or potential close substitutes for such product, process, or work to prevent the exercise of market power. ***

When they were issued, the Guidelines were at odds with well-established Supreme Court precedent. However, while the Supreme Court in its tying case law had long presumed that patents, as well as copyrights, conferred market power over the tying product, the Court revisited that presumption in *Illinois Tool Works v. Independent Ink, Inc.* The Court's reasoning relied in part on the 1995 Guidelines.

Illinois Tool Works v. Independent Ink, Inc.
547 U.S. 28 (2006)

Justice Stevens delivered the opinion of the Court.

In *Jefferson Parish Hospital Dist. No. 2 v. Hyde*, 466 U.S. 2 (1984), we repeated the well-settled proposition that "if the Government has granted the seller a patent or similar monopoly over a product, it is fair to presume that the inability to buy the product elsewhere gives the seller market power." [citation omitted] This presumption of market power, applicable in the antitrust context when a seller conditions its sale of a patented product (the "tying" product) on the purchase of a second product (the "tied" product), has its foundation in the judicially created patent misuse doctrine. [citation omitted] In 1988, Congress substantially undermined that foundation, amending the Patent Act to eliminate the market power presumption in patent misuse cases. See 102 Stat. 4674, codified at 35 U.S.C. § 271(d). The question presented to us today is whether the presumption of market power in a patented product should survive as a matter of antitrust law despite its demise in patent law. We conclude that the mere fact that a tying product is patented does not support such a presumption.

I.

Petitioners, Trident, Inc., and its parent, Illinois Tool Works Inc., manufacture and market printing systems that include three relevant components: (1) a patented piezoelectric impulse ink jet printhead; (2) a patented ink container, consisting of a bottle and valved cap, which attaches to the printhead; and (3) specially designed, but unpatented, ink. Petitioners sell their systems to original equipment manufacturers (OEMs) who are licensed to incorporate the printheads and containers into printers that are in turn sold to companies for use in printing barcodes on cartons and packaging materials. The OEMs agree that they will purchase their ink exclusively from petitioners, and that neither they nor their customers will refill the patented containers with ink of any kind.

Respondent, Independent Ink, Inc., has developed an ink with the same chemical composition as the ink sold by petitioners. After an infringement action brought by Trident against Independent was dismissed for lack of personal jurisdiction, Independent filed suit against Trident seeking a judgment of noninfringement and invalidity of Trident's patents. In an amended complaint, it alleged that petitioners are engaged in illegal tying and monopolization in violation of §§ 1 and 2 of the Sherman Act. [citation omitted]

After discovery, the District Court granted petitioners' motion for summary judgment on the Sherman Act claims. [citation omitted] It rejected respondent's submission that petitioners "necessarily have market power in the market for the tying product as a matter of law solely by virtue of the patent on their printhead system, thereby rendering [the] tying arrangements per se violations of the antitrust laws." [citation omitted] Finding that respondent had submitted no affirmative evidence defining the relevant market or establishing petitioners' power within it, the court concluded that respondent could not prevail on either antitrust claim. [citation omitted] The parties settled their other claims, and respondent appealed.

After a careful review of the "long history of Supreme Court consideration of the legality of tying arrangements," [citation omitted] the Court of Appeals for the Federal Circuit reversed the District Court's decision as to respondent's § 1 claim [citation omitted]. Placing special reliance on our decisions in *International Salt Co. v. United States*, 332 U.S. 392 (1947), and *Loew's*, 371 U.S. 38, as well as our *Jefferson Parish* dictum, and after taking note of the academic criticism of those cases, it concluded that the "fundamental error" in petitioners' submission was its disregard of "the duty of a court of appeals to follow the precedents of the Supreme Court until the Court itself chooses to expressly overrule them." [citation omitted] We granted certiorari to undertake a fresh examination of the history of both the judicial and legislative appraisals of tying arrangements. [citation omitted] Our review is informed by extensive scholarly comment and a change in position by the administrative agencies charged with enforcement of the antitrust laws.

II.

American courts first encountered tying arrangements in the course of patent infringement litigation. [citation omitted] Such a case came before this Court in *Henry v. A.B. Dick* Co., 224 U.S. 1 (1912), in which, as in the case we decide today, unpatented ink was the product that was "tied" to the use of a patented product through the use of a licensing agreement. Without commenting on the tying arrangement, the Court held that use of a competitor's ink in violation of a condition of the agreement—that the rotary mimeograph "'may be used only with the stencil, paper, ink and other supplies made by A.B. Dick Co.'"—constituted infringement of the patent on the machine. [citation omitted] Chief Justice White dissented, explaining his disagreement with the Court's approval of a practice that he regarded as an "attempt to increase the scope of the monopoly granted by a patent... which tend[s] to increase monopoly and to burden the public in the exercise of their common rights." [citation omitted] Two years later, Congress endorsed Chief Justice White's disapproval of tying arrangements, enacting § 3 of the Clayton Act. *See* 38 Stat. 731 (applying to "patented or unpatented" products); see also *Motion Picture Patents Co. v. Universal Film Mfg. Co.*, 243 U.S. 502, 517–518, 37 S.Ct. 416, 61 L.Ed. 871 (1917) (explaining that, in light of § 3 of the Clayton Act, *A.B. Dick* "must be regarded as overruled"). And in this Court's subsequent cases reviewing the legality of tying arrangements we, too, embraced Chief Justice White's disapproval of those arrangements. [citation omitted]

In the years since *A.B. Dick*, four different rules of law have supported challenges to tying arrangements. They have been condemned as improper extensions of the patent monopoly under the patent misuse doctrine, as unfair methods of competition under § 5 of the Federal Trade Commission Act, [citation omitted] as contracts tending to create a monopoly under § 3 of the Clayton Act, [citation omitted] and as contracts in restraint of trade under § 1 of the Sherman Act. In all of those instances, the justification for the challenge rested on either an assumption or a showing that the defendant's position of power in the market for the tying product was being used to restrain competition in the market for the tied product. As we explained in Jefferson Parish, [citation omitted] "[o]ur cases have concluded that the essential characteristic of an invalid tying arrangement lies in the seller's exploitation of its control over the tying product to force the buyer into the purchase of a tied product that the buyer either did not want at all, or might have preferred to purchase elsewhere on different terms."

Over the years, however, this Court's strong disapproval of tying arrangements has substantially diminished. Rather than relying on assumptions, in its more recent opinions the Court has required a showing of market power in the tying product. ***

In rejecting [in *Jefferson Parish*] the application of a per se rule that all tying arrangements constitute antitrust violations, we explained:

> "[W]e have condemned tying arrangements when the seller has some special ability—usually called 'market power'—to force a purchaser to do something that he would not do in a competitive market. . . .
>
> . . . . .
>
> "Per se condemnation—condemnation without inquiry into actual market conditions—is only appropriate if the existence of forcing is probable. Thus, application of the per se rule focuses on the probability of anticompetitive consequences. . . .

> "For example, if the Government has granted the seller a patent or similar monopoly over a product, it is fair to presume that the inability to buy the product elsewhere gives the seller market power. United States v. Loew's Inc., 371 U.S., at 45–47. Any effort to enlarge the scope of the patent monopoly by using the market power it confers to restrain competition in the market for a second product will undermine competition on the merits in that second market. Thus, the sale or lease of a patented item on condition that the buyer make all his purchases of a separate tied product from the patentee is unlawful." Id., at 13–16.

Notably, nothing in our opinion suggested a rebuttable presumption of market power applicable to tying arrangements involving a patent on the tying good. [citation omitted] Instead, it described the rule that a contract to sell a patented product on condition that the purchaser buy unpatented goods exclusively from the patentee is a per se violation of § 1 of the Sherman Act.

Justice O'Connor wrote separately in *Jefferson Parish,* concurring in the judgment *** In her opinion, she questioned not only the propriety of treating any tying arrangement as a per se violation of the Sherman Act, [citation omitted] but also the validity of the presumption that a patent always gives the patentee significant market power, observing that the presumption was actually a product of our patent misuse cases rather than our antitrust jurisprudence. [citation omitted] It is that presumption, a vestige of the Court's historical distrust of tying arrangements, that we address squarely today.

III.

Justice O'Connor was, of course, correct in her assertion that the presumption that a patent confers market power arose outside the antitrust context as part of the patent misuse doctrine. That doctrine had its origins in *Motion Picture Patents Co. v. Universal Film Mfg. Co.,* 243 U.S. 502 (1917), which found no support in the patent laws for the proposition that a patentee may "prescribe by notice attached to a patented machine the conditions of its use and the supplies which must be used in the operation of it, under pain of infringement of the patent," [citation omitted]. Although Motion Picture Patents Co. simply narrowed the scope of possible patent infringement claims, it formed the basis for the Court's subsequent decisions creating a patent misuse defense to infringement claims when a patentee uses its patent "as the effective means of restraining competition with its sale of an unpatented article." [citation omitted]

Without any analysis of actual market conditions, these patent misuse decisions assumed that, by tying the purchase of unpatented goods to the sale of the patented good, the patentee was "restraining competition," [citation omitted] or "secur[ing] a limited monopoly of an unpatented material," [citation omitted] In other words, these decisions presumed "[t]he requisite economic power" over the tying product such that the patentee could "extend [its] economic control to unpatented products." Loew's, 371 U.S., at 45–46.

The presumption that a patent confers market power migrated from patent law to antitrust law in *International Salt Co. v. United States,* 332 U.S. 392 (1947). In that case, we affirmed a District Court decision holding that leases of patented machines requiring the lessees to use the defendant's unpatented salt products violated § 1 of the Sherman Act and § 3 of the Clayton Act as a matter of law. [citation omitted] Although the Court's opinion does not discuss market power or the patent misuse doctrine, it assumes that "[t]he volume of business affected by these contracts cannot be said to be insignificant or insubstantial and the tendency of the arrangement to accomplishment of monopoly seems obvious." [citation omitted]

The assumption that tying contracts "ten[d]... to accomplishment of monopoly" can be traced to the Government's brief in *International Salt,* which relied heavily on our earlier patent misuse decision in *Morton Salt.* The Government described *Morton Salt* as "present[ing] a factual situation almost identical with the instant case," and it asserted that "although the Court in that case did not find it necessary to decide whether the antitrust laws were violated, its language, its reasoning, and its citations indicate that the policy underlying the decision was the same as that of the Sherman Act." [citation omitted] Building on its assertion that *International Salt* was logically indistinguishable from *Morton Salt,* the Government argued that this Court should place tying arrangements involving patented products in the category of per se violations of the Sherman Act. [citation omitted]

Our opinion in *International Salt* clearly shows that we accepted the Government's invitation to import the presumption of market power in a patented product into our antitrust jurisprudence. While we cited *Morton Salt* only for the narrower proposition that the defendant's patents did not confer any right to restrain competition in unpatented salt or afford the defendant any immunity from the antitrust laws, [citation omitted] given the fact that the defendant was selling its unpatented salt at competitive prices, [citation omitted] the rule adopted in International Salt necessarily accepted the Government's submission that the earlier patent misuse cases supported the broader proposition "that this type of restraint is unlawful on its face under the Sherman Act." [citation omitted]

Indeed, later in the same Term we cited *International Salt* for the proposition that the license of "a patented device on condition that unpatented materials be employed in conjunction with the patented device" is an example of a restraint that is "illegal per se." *United States v. Columbia Steel Co.,* 334 U.S. 495, 522–523, and n. 22 (1948). And in subsequent cases we have repeatedly grounded the presumption of market power over a patented device in *International Salt.* [citation omitted]

IV.

Although the patent misuse doctrine and our antitrust jurisprudence became intertwined in *International Salt,* subsequent events initiated their untwining. This process has ultimately led to today's reexamination of the presumption of per se illegality of a tying arrangement involving a patented product, the first case since 1947 in which we have granted review to consider the presumption's continuing validity.

Three years before we decided *International Salt*, this Court had expanded the scope of the patent misuse doctrine to include not only supplies or materials used by a patented device, but also tying arrangements involving a combination patent and "unpatented material or [a] device [that] is itself an integral part of the structure embodying the patent." Mercoid, 320 U.S., at 665. [citation omitted] In reaching this conclusion, the Court explained that it could see "no difference in principle" between cases involving elements essential to the inventive character of the patent and elements peripheral to it; both, in the Court's view, were attempts to "expan[d] the patent beyond the legitimate scope of its monopoly." Mercoid, 320 U.S., at 665.

Shortly thereafter, Congress codified the patent laws for the first time. [citation omitted] At least partly in response to our *Mercoid* decision, Congress included a provision in its codification that excluded some conduct, such as a tying arrangement involving the sale of a patented product tied to an "essential" or "nonstaple" product that has no use except as part of the patented product or method, from the scope of the patent misuse doctrine. § 271(d) [citation omitted]. Thus, at the same time that our antitrust jurisprudence continued to rely on the assumption that "tying arrangements generally serve no legitimate business purpose," [citation omitted] Congress began chipping away at the assumption in the patent misuse context from whence it came.

It is Congress' most recent narrowing of the patent misuse defense, however, that is directly relevant to this case. Four years after our decision in *Jefferson Parish* repeated the patent-equals-market-power presumption, 466 U.S., at 16, Congress amended the Patent Code to eliminate that presumption in the patent misuse context. [citation omitted] The relevant provision reads:

> (d) No patent owner otherwise entitled to relief for infringement or contributory infringement of a patent shall be denied relief or deemed guilty of misuse or illegal extension of the patent right by reason of his having done one or more of the following:... (5) conditioned the license of any rights to the patent or the sale of the patented product on the acquisition of a license to rights in another patent or purchase of a separate product, *unless, in view of the circumstances, the patent owner has market power in the relevant market for the patent or patented product on which the license or sale is conditioned.* 35 U.S.C. § 271(d)(5) (emphasis added).

The italicized clause makes it clear that Congress did not intend the mere existence of a patent to constitute the requisite "market power." Indeed, fairly read, it provides that without proof that Trident had market power in the relevant market, its conduct at issue in this case was neither "misuse" nor an "illegal extension of the patent right."

While the 1988 amendment does not expressly refer to the antitrust laws, it certainly invites a reappraisal of the per se rule announced in *International Salt*. A rule denying a patentee the right to enjoin an infringer is significantly less severe than a rule that makes the conduct at issue a federal crime punishable by up to 10 years in prison. *See* 15 U.S.C. § 1. It would be absurd to assume that Congress intended to provide that the use of a patent that merited punishment as a felony would not constitute "misuse." Moreover, given the fact that the patent misuse doctrine provided the basis for the market power presumption, it would be anomalous to preserve the presumption in antitrust after Congress has eliminated its foundation. [citation omitted]

*** While some [tying] arrangements are still unlawful, such as those that are the product of a true monopoly or a marketwide conspiracy, [citation omitted] that conclusion must be supported by proof of power in the relevant market rather than by a mere presumption thereof.

V.

Rather than arguing that we should retain the rule of per se illegality, respondent contends that we should endorse a rebuttable presumption that patentees possess market power when they condition the purchase of the patented product on an agreement to buy unpatented goods exclusively from the patentee. [citation omitted] Respondent recognizes that a large number of valid patents have little, if any, commercial significance, but submits that those that are used to impose tying arrangements on unwilling purchasers likely do exert significant market power. Hence, in respondent's view, the presumption would have no impact on patents of only slight value and would be justified, subject to being rebutted by evidence offered by the patentee, in cases in which the patent has sufficient value to enable the patentee to insist on acceptance of the tie.

Respondent also offers a narrower alternative, suggesting that we differentiate between tying arrangements involving the simultaneous purchase of two products that are arguably two components of a single product—such as the provision of surgical services and anesthesiology in the same operation, [citation omitted] or the licensing of one copyrighted film on condition that the licensee take a package of several films in the same transaction, [citation omitted]—and a tying arrangement involving the purchase of unpatented goods over a period of time, a so-called "requirements tie." [citation omitted] According to respondent, we should recognize a presumption of market power when faced with the latter type of arrangements because they provide a means for charging large volume purchasers a higher royalty for use of the patent than small purchasers must pay, a form of discrimination that "is strong evidence of market power." [citation omitted]

The opinion that imported the "patent equals market power" presumption into our antitrust jurisprudence, however, provides no support for respondent's proposed alternative. In International Salt, it was the existence of the patent on the tying product, rather than the use of a requirements tie, that led the Court to presume market power. [citation omitted] Moreover, the requirements tie in that case did not involve any price discrimination between large volume and small volume purchasers or evidence of noncompetitive pricing. Instead, the leases at issue provided that if any competitor offered salt, the tied product, at a lower price, "the lessee should be free to buy in the open market, unless appellant would furnish the salt at an equal price." [citation omitted]

*** [T]he vast majority of academic literature recognizes that a patent does not necessarily confer market power. Similarly, while price discrimination may provide evidence of market power, particularly if buttressed by evidence that the patentee has charged an above-market price for the tied package, see, e.g., 10 Areeda ¶ 1769c, it is generally recognized that it also occurs in fully competitive markets. [citation omitted] We are not persuaded that the combination of these two factors should give rise to a presumption of market power when neither is sufficient to do so standing alone. Rather, the lesson to be learned from *International Salt* and the academic commentary is the same: Many tying arrangements, even those involving patents and requirements ties, are fully consistent with a free, competitive market. For this reason, we reject both respondent's proposed rebuttable presumption and their narrower alternative.

It is no doubt the virtual consensus among economists that has persuaded the enforcement agencies to reject the position that the Government took when it supported the per se rule that the Court adopted in the 1940's. In antitrust guidelines issued jointly by the Department of Justice and the Federal Trade Commission in 1995, the enforcement agencies stated that in the exercise of their prosecutorial discretion they "will not presume that a patent, copyright, or trade secret necessarily confers market power upon its owner." [citation omitted] While that choice is not binding on the Court, it would be unusual for the Judiciary to replace the normal rule of lenity that is applied in criminal cases with a rule of severity for a special category of antitrust cases.

Congress, the antitrust enforcement agencies, and most economists have all reached the conclusion that a patent does not necessarily confer market power upon the patentee. Today, we reach the same conclusion, and therefore hold that, in all cases involving a tying arrangement, the plaintiff must prove that the defendant has market power in the tying product. . . .

Reversed

Comments and Questions

1. The word "monopoly" means different things in different disciplines. In antitrust law, monopoly power is the ability to raise prices in a properly defined market. But other areas of law use the word more casually. As Judge Richard Posner explained, a "patent confers a monopoly in the sense of a right to exclude others from selling the patented product. But if there are close substitutes for the patented product, the patent 'monopoly' is not a monopoly in a sense relevant to antitrust law." *Asahi Glass Co. v. Pentech Pharm., Inc.*, 289 F.Supp.2d 986, 995 (N.D. Ill. 2003) (Posner., J.). Thus, when judges or commentators use the word "monopoly," it is important for the reader to determine in what sense the author is using the word.

2. Long before the decision in *Illinois Tool Works*, the Supreme Court had recognized that a so-called "patent monopoly" is not necessarily an economic monopoly as that term is used in antitrust jurisprudence. For example, in 1958 the Court opined that "[i]t is common knowledge that a patent does not always confer a monopoly over a particular commodity. Often the patent is limited to a unique form or improvement of the product and economic power resulting from the patent privileges is slight. As a matter of fact the defendant and *International Salt* offered to prove that competitive salt machines were readily available which were satisfactory substitutes for its machines (a fact the Government did not controvert), but the Court regarded such proof as irrelevant." *Northern Pacific Railway Co. v. United States*, 356 U.S. 1, 9 (1958). Despite this early acknowledgement, for over half a century that the Court nonetheless retained its presumption that if the tying product is patented, then the tying seller must possess market power.

3. The *Illinois Tool Works* Court relied on the fact that Congress had amended the patent laws such that infringement defendants arguing a patent misuse defense would have to prove that the patentee had market power—such power could not be presumed from the mere existence of the patent. Congress debated amending the antitrust laws in addition to changing patent laws and left the antitrust laws untouched. Should that affect the judicial analysis of whether the congressional amendment of the patent laws warrants a reversal of antitrust precedent?

4. The *Illinois Tool Works* Court stated: "Many tying arrangements, even those involving patents and requirements ties, are fully consistent with a free, competitive market." Can you think of examples?

5. The *Illinois Tool Works* opinion did not hold that patents never confer market power, only that such power should not be presumed. Intellectual property rights often bestow market power on their owners. Of patents, copyrights, and trademarks, which form of intellectual property is most likely to confer market power on its owner? Why? Of patents, copyrights, and trademarks, which form of intellectual property is least likely to confer market power on its owner? Why? Should there ever be a rebuttable presumption of market power? If so, how should the presumption be rebutted?

6. Whether or not a patent confers market power on its owner may be a function of the relevant industry. For example, in pharmaceutical markets, one patent is more likely to confer meaningful market power and perhaps monopolize a relevant product market, than in software or semi-conductor markets where more than one patent is generally necessary to make products. *See* Dan L. Burk & Mark A. Lemley, *Policy Levers in Patent Law*, 89 VIRGINIA LAW REVIEW 1575 (2003).

7. Some markets in which IP rights are important have corresponding black markets. For example, some businesses knowingly sell products that infringe patents, or are illegal copies of copyrighted works, or are counterfeit versions of branded luxury goods, such as purses. Black market sales generally occur at a price less than that charged by the seller of the legitimate goods. Because many goods protected by IP rights cost little to manufacture or copy—for example, pharmaceuticals and

CDs—black market sellers can charge a very low price but still earn considerable profits. Indeed, digital copies of music, movies, and software have a marginal cost that approaches zero. Should the presence of black market sales affect the court's determination of whether the owner of intellectual property possesses market power? In particular, should black market sales be included in the relevant product market? For an argument that black market sales should not expand the definition of the relevant product market, see James M. Sellers, *Comment: The Black Market and Intellectual Property: A Potential Sherman Act Section Two Antitrust Defense?*, 14 ALB. L.J. SCI. & TECH. 583 (2004). Should the fact that black market sales are illegal affect the antitrust analysis? Which litigants would want to include black market sales in the analysis, and why?

8. One of the core questions of this book—and the entire field of Antitrust Law and IP Rights—is how should courts resolve the tension between intellectual property and antitrust laws. If a monopolist has monopoly power as a result of its ownership of intellectual property—whether patent, copyright, or trademark—should there be any constraints on what the monopolist can do with its intellectual property? If so, what? If not, why not?

9. Antitrust laws act as a constraint on property rights. For example, antitrust laws would preclude a dominant firm from acquiring the factories of its sole competitor. Should antitrust law treat intellectual property rights differently than other property rights? If so, why? If not, why not? Given that intellectual property rights are specifically found in the Constitution, does that mean that intellectual property laws should necessarily trump antitrust laws?

Bibliography of Additional Resources

Regina A. DeMeo, *Losing the Presumption of Market Power for Antitrust Purposes, and its Affect on the Software Industry*, 14 SANTA CLARA COMPUTER & HIGH TECH. L.J. 491 (1998)

Paul S. Grunzweig, *Prohibiting the Presumption of Market Power for Intellectual Property Rights: The Intellectual Property Antitrust Protection Act of 1989*, 16 J. CORP. L. 103 (1990)

James M. Sellers, *The Black Market and Intellectual Property: A Potential Sherman Act Section Two Antitrust Defense?*, 14 ALB. L.J. SCI. & TECH. 538 (2004)

C. Antitrust Law and the Misuse of Intellectual Property

The Supreme Court gave rise to the patent misuse defense in its 1917 opinion in *Motion Picture Patents Co. v. Universal Film Manufacturing Co.* The patent owner had a patent on film projectors and imposed a requirement that its licensees (and their lessees) could only use the patented projectors to show films from patentee-approved sources. The Court held that the patentee could not use its patent on projectors to compel exhibitors to show only its films. The Court reasoned: "Whatever the right of the owner may be to control by restriction the materials to be used in operating the machine, it must be a right derived through the general law from the ownership of the property in the machine, and it cannot be derived from or protected by the patent law, which allows a grant only of the right to an exclusive use of the new and useful discovery which has been made—this and nothing more." *Motion Picture Patents Co. v. Universal Film Mfg. Co.*, 243 U.S. 502, 513 (1917). Interpreting this holding, lower courts held that when a patentee attempts to control the sale and usage of unpatented complementary products. The doctrine generally provides that if an owner of an IP right has engaged in misuse, the court will refuse to enforce the owner's IP right until the misuse ends.

Many of the cases excerpted in this casebook make references to the misuse of intellectual property. For example, in *Illinois Tool Works* the Supreme Court explained how its 1944 *Mercoid* opinion expanded the patent misuse doctrine to reach patentees that imposed tying arrangements between a patented tying product and an unpatented tied product. Congress responded to the *Mercoid* opinion by codifying the patent misuse defense and by specifying circumstances that do not constitute misuse. Notably, the new patent law provided that a patentee does not misuse its patent by imposing a tying requirement when the tied product has no use except in conjunction with the patented tying product.

The focus of this casebook is when the conduct of IP owners violates antitrust law. Misuse is a concept in IP law, not antitrust law. Nevertheless, courts have sometimes defined misuse in relation to antitrust law and vice versa, as the following cases illustrate.

1. Patent Misuse

County Materials Corp. v. Allan Block Corp.
502 F.3d 730 (7th Cir. 2007)

WOOD, Circuit Judge.

*** Two companies, County Materials Corporation and Allan Block Corporation, entered into a production agreement ("the Agreement") giving exclusive rights to County Materials to manufacture Allan Block's patented concrete block; the issue is whether County Line was free to sell an allegedly non-infringing product, despite the presence of a covenant not to compete in the Agreement in which County Line promised not to sell competing products for 18 months if it stopped making Allan Block's product. Following the termination of the Agreement, County Line decided not to wait for the full 18 months before jumping back into the market with a competing product. Allan Block threatened to sue, but County Line beat it to the courthouse with this suit for a declaratory judgment. County Line wanted the district court to declare that the covenant not to compete was unenforceable because it violated federal patent policy, essentially raising an anticipatory patent misuse defense to its planned breach of the Agreement. The district court granted summary judgment to Allan Block, finding no violation of federal patent policy or Minnesota law. We agree with the district court's conclusions and affirm.

County Materials is in the business of manufacturing concrete blocks. Allan Block develops, markets, and licenses technology for the manufacturing of concrete blocks;

it does not manufacture blocks itself. In April 1993, County Materials's predecessor in interest, County Concrete Corporation, entered into a production agreement with Allan Block. The Agreement granted to County Materials the exclusive right to manufacture Allan Block's patented block products in northwest Wisconsin. County also was granted the right to sell these products under the Allan Block trademark. Finally, Allan Block agreed to provide County Materials with significant technical, marketing, and strategic support while the Agreement was in effect.

The Agreement included a limited covenant not to compete, which allowed County Materials to make and sell two specific competing block products, without any time restrictions. The non-compete provision also required that for the 18 months following the termination of the Agreement, County Materials could not "directly or indirectly engage in the manufacture and/or sale of any other [competing]... block."

In 2005, Allan Block notified County Materials that it would be terminating the Agreement. Shortly thereafter, County Materials completed its own design for a new concrete block that would compete directly with the Allan Block products that it had been manufacturing and selling in northwest Wisconsin. As County Materials took steps to begin producing this new block, Allan Block threatened that it would sue to enforce the non-compete provision from the terminated Agreement. County Materials decided to move first, and so it filed this suit alleging that the inclusion of the non-compete provision in the Agreement constituted patent misuse, which made the Agreement void. ***

This court reviews a district court's decision to grant summary judgment de novo. [citation omitted] The parties appear to agree that the production agreement is a patent license, which is the way that we too would characterize it. County Materials essentially claims that the inclusion of the covenant not to compete in the patent license here was per se unlawful patent misuse and the improper result of patent leverage. While at one time this argument might have had traction, in certain circumstances, it is at least disfavored today, if not entirely rejected. Today, the concept of patent misuse is cabined first by statute, 35 U.S.C. § 271(d), which essentially eliminates from the field of "patent misuse" claims based on tying and refusals to deal, unless the patent owner has market power, and second by case law. As the Federal Circuit explained in *Virginia Panel Corp. v. MAC Panel Co.*, 133 F.3d 860 (Fed.Cir.1997), there are certain practices that court identified as "constituting per se patent misuse," including "arrangements in which a patentee effectively extends the term of its patent by requiring post-expiration royalties." Id. at 869 [citation omitted]. The practices identified in § 271(d), in contrast, may not be branded "misuse." *Va. Panel Corp.*, 133 F.3d at 869.

If a practice is not per se unlawful nor specifically excluded from a misuse analysis by § 271(d)

> a court must determine if that practice is reasonably within the patent grant, i.e., that it relates to subject matter within the scope of the patent claims. If so, the practice does not have the effect of broadening the scope of the patent claims and thus cannot constitute patent misuse. If, on the other hand, the practice has the effect of

extending the patentee's statutory rights and does so with an anti-competitive effect, that practice must then be analyzed in accordance with the rule of reason. Under the rule of reason, the finder of fact must decide whether the questioned practice imposes an unreasonable restraint on competition, taking into account a variety of factors, including specific information about the relevant business, its condition before and after the restraint was imposed, and the restraint's history, nature, and effect.

Id. (internal citations and quotation marks omitted).

County Materials is not claiming that Allan Block was trying to extend the term of its patent by requiring post-expiration royalties. It is wrong, therefore, to argue that some form of per se analysis applies here. *** The covenant not to compete in the agreement before us must therefore be assessed under a rule of reason. County Materials argues that this clause is unreasonable because it allows Allan Block to use its patent to exclude competition in the market from unpatented products. ***

The Federal Circuit's decision in *Windsurfing Int'l, Inc. v. AMF, Inc.*, 782 F.2d 995 (Fed.Cir.1986), provides helpful guidance in deciding whether a particular use of a patent might amount to "misuse" and thus furnish the defense to a licensing agreement that County Materials is looking for. In *Windsurfing*, the Federal Circuit said that patent misuse does not exist unless the party asserting it can "show that the patentee has impermissibly broadened the 'physical or temporal scope' of the patent grant with anti-competitive effect." 782 F.2d at 1001 (emphasis added). This standard is satisfied by showing some overall harm to competition, and so, contrary to County Materials's contentions, it fully takes into account the fact that patents exist to "spur progress and innovation." The *Windsurfing* standard for patent misuse necessarily considers whether progress and innovation have been stymied and allows courts concretely to answer the vague question whether progress has been slowed. ***

Anticompetitive effects, in short, are a critical element of any patent misuse case that is evaluated under a rule of reason approach. *Windsurfing* was one of the first cases to recognize this; it required "a factual determination [that]... reveal[s] that the overall effect of the license *tends* to restrain competition unlawfully in an appropriately defined relevant market." 782 F.2d at 1001–02 (emphasis added). A plaintiff is not required to show a defendant's subjective intent to obtain some kind of leverage over its patent. We assume, for the sake of argument, that it is also not necessary for a plaintiff to plead a case that would suffice to show that the antitrust laws have been violated. But, at the summary judgment stage, some evidence tending to show an adverse effect in an economically sound relevant market is essential for any claim governed by the rule of reason.

With these principles in mind, we are ready to assess County Materials's case. To begin with, the Agreement between County Materials and Allan Block shows no sign of one-sidedness or abuse of power on Allan Block's part. County Materials received significant benefits, starting with the right to use the patented technology for the manufacture of the concrete blocks, and continuing with the right to use Allan Block's trademark and the right to receive supporting technical, marketing, and strategic services from Allan Block. In return, County Materials had to promise to pay royalties to Allan Block and to devote significant efforts to the exploitation of Allan Block's patent. If County Materials had been free to pick and choose among all potentially competing products on the market, Allan Block may have signed over the rights to use its patent and know-how for little or nothing in return. Allan Block's services alone have considerable value for any company undertaking the manufacture and sale of these products (or so the parties could have concluded), whether or not they are tied to a patented product. Nothing in these facts suggests that Allan Block needed or used any kind of leverage made possible by the patent to secure County Materials's promise to refrain from working with all but the designated two competing products, or its promise to refrain from using other products for 18 months after the expiration of the Agreement.

In fact, this was not a particularly onerous covenant not to compete. It allowed County Materials to continue to manufacture and sell not one but two competing products, which the district court reasoned would "guarantee plaintiff could always compete with defendant in the landscape block market." In addition, the clause had both temporal and geographical limits. It lasted for only 18 months after the Agreement's termination (a period which no one contends goes beyond the duration of Allan Block's patent) and applied only to County Materials's exclusive production territory, which was a section of Wisconsin. Although the non-compete clause may have hurt County Materials's ability to compete as aggressively as it would have liked in the concrete block market in northwest Wisconsin, there does not appear to be any evidence in the record showing that these limited requirements have hurt competition for cement blocks in County Materials's former exclusive territory. In the related field of antitrust, the Supreme Court has said that "[i]t is axiomatic that the antitrust laws were passed for the protection of competition, not competitors." *Brooke Group Ltd. v. Brown & Williamson Tobacco Corp.*, 509 U.S. 209, 224 (1993) (internal quotation marks omitted). *Independent Ink, supra,* held that the principles underlying the patent misuse doctrine are closely aligned to those underlying antitrust law. Without a showing that this clause had any effect on the broader market for concrete block (as opposed to an effect only on County Materials), its purported patent misuse defense cannot succeed. ***

The judgment of the district court is Affirmed.

Comments and Questions

1. The relationship between patent misuse and antitrust law is complicated. The Federal Circuit has explained that "[t]he concept of patent misuse arose to restrain practices that did not in themselves violate any law, but that drew anticompetitive strength from the patent right, and thus were deemed to be contrary to public policy. The policy purpose was to prevent a patentee from using the patent to obtain market benefit beyond that which inheres in the statutory patent right." *Mallinckrodt, Inc. v. Medipart, Inc.*, 976 F.2d 700 (Fed. Cir. 1992). Thus, patent misuse was distinct from antitrust violations.

Over time, the patent misuse defense has come to resemble an antitrust inquiry. The Federal Circuit has noted: "Patent misuse is an affirmative defense to an accusation of patent infringement, the successful assertion of which 'requires that the alleged infringer show that the patentee has impermissibly broadened the "physical or temporal scope" of the patent grant with anticompetitive effect.'" *Virginia Panel Corp. v. MAC Panel Co.*, 133 F.3d 860 (Fed. Cir. 1997). The court went on to describe some types of patentee conduct constituting "per se misuse" and others being misuse under a rule of reason approach. The "per se" and "rule of reason" dichotomy is lifted directly from antitrust jurisprudence. For the past three decades, most instances of patent misuse have involved conduct that violates antitrust laws as well. HERBERT HOVENKAMP, ANTITRUST ENTERPRISE 273 (2005).

Still, however, patent misuse is theoretically broader than antitrust because an antitrust plaintiff must show that it has suffered antitrust injury as well as showing all of the elements of the substantive antitrust claim, such as monopoly power in the case of a Section 2 monopolization claim. The Federal Circuit has noted that proving an antitrust violation "requires more exacting proof than suffices to demonstrate patent misuse." *Virginia Panel Corp. v. MAC Panel Co.*, 133 F.3d 860 (Fed. Cir. 1997). Can you think of examples of conduct that would constitute patent misuse but not an antitrust violation?

What should be the proper relationship between the patent misuse defense and substantive antitrust law? Should they be coextensive? Why or why not?

2. Professor Thomas Cotter has argued that misuse doctrine is but one of the intellectual property doctrines that emphasizes the importance of competition. Thomas F. Cotter, *The Procompetitive Interest in Intellectual Property Law*, 48 WM. & MARY L. REV. 483 (2006). Such doctrines suggest that the antitrust law and intellectual property law are not inherently in tension.

3. In addition to its patent misuse defense, County Materials also argued that the covenant not to compete violated Minnesota law. Covenants not to compete are governed by state law. The Seventh Circuit opined that, under Minnesota state law, to be enforceable the covenant "must (1) protect a legitimate interest of the party in whose favor it is imposed, (2) be reasonable as between the parties, and (3) not be injurious to the public." (citing *Haynes v. Monson*, 224 N.W.2d 482, 484 (1974)). The Seventh Circuit upheld the covenant not to compete.

What is the danger posed by covenants not to compete?

Should they be per se illegal? Why or why not?

Given that the covenant not to compete in *County Materials* allowed the licensee to make and sell two specific competing block products, without any time restrictions, was the Seventh Circuit correct to uphold the agreement?

2. Copyright Misuse

Lasercomb America, Inc. v. Reynolds,
911 F.2d 970 (4th Cir. 1990)

SPROUSE, Circuit Judge:

*** Holiday Steel and Lasercomb were competitors in the manufacture of steel rule dies that are used to cut and score paper and cardboard for folding into boxes and cartons. Lasercomb developed a software program, Interact, which is the object of the dispute between the parties. Using this program, a designer creates a template of a cardboard cutout on a computer screen and the software directs the mechanized creation of the conforming steel rule die.[2]

In 1983, before Lasercomb was ready to market its Interact program generally, it licensed four prerelease copies to Holiday Steel which paid $35,000 for the first copy, $17,500 each for the next two copies, and $2,000 for the fourth copy. Lasercomb informed Holiday Steel that it would charge $2,000 for each additional copy Holiday Steel cared to purchase. Apparently ambitious to create for itself an even better deal, Holiday Steel circumvented the protective devices Lasercomb had provided with the software and made three unauthorized copies of Interact which it used on its computer systems. Perhaps buoyed by its success in copying, Holiday Steel then created a software program called "PDS-1000," which was almost entirely a direct copy of Interact, and marketed it as its own CAD/CAM die-making software. ***

There is no question that defendants engaged in unauthorized copying, and the purposefulness of their unlawful action is manifest from their deceptive practices. ***

On March 24, 1986, the district court entered a preliminary injunction, enjoining defendants from marketing the PDS-1000 software. ***

Misuse of Copyright Defense

A successful defense of misuse of copyright bars a culpable plaintiff from prevailing on an action for infringement of the misused copyright. Here, appellants claim Lasercomb has misused its copyright by including in its standard licensing agreement clauses which prevent the licensee from participating in any manner in the creation of computer-assisted die-making software. ***

The district court rejected the copyright misuse defense for three reasons. First, it noted that defendants had not explicitly agreed to the contract clauses alleged to constitute copyright misuse. Second, it found "such a clause is reasonable in light of the delicate and sensitive area of computer software." And, third, it questioned whether such a defense exists. We consider the district court's reasoning in reverse order.

A. Does a "Misuse of Copyright" Defense Exist?

We agree with the district court that much uncertainty engulfs the "misuse of copyright" defense. We are persuaded, however, that a misuse of copyright defense is inherent in the law of copyright just as a misuse of patent defense is inherent in patent law.

---

[2] This genre of software is called CAD/CAM, which stands for "computer assisted design and computer assisted manufacture."

The misuse of a patent is a potential defense to suit for its infringement, and both the existence and parameters of that body of law are well established. [citation omitted] ***

2. The Misuse of Patent Defense

Although a patent misuse defense was recognized by the courts as early as 1917, most commentators point to *Morton Salt Co. v. G.S. Suppiger*, 314 U.S. 488 (1942), as the foundational patent misuse case. In that case, the plaintiff Morton Salt brought suit on the basis that the defendant had infringed Morton's patent in a salt-depositing machine. The salt tablets were not themselves a patented item, but Morton's patent license required that licensees use only salt tablets produced by Morton. Morton was thereby using its patent to restrain competition in the sale of an item which was not within the scope of the patent's privilege. The Supreme Court held that, as a court of equity, it would not aid Morton in protecting its patent when Morton was using that patent in a manner contrary to public policy. [citation omitted] *** [T]he Supreme Court endorsed "misuse of patent" as an equitable defense to a suit for infringement of that patent.

Since *Morton Salt*, the courts have recognized patent misuse as a valid defense and have applied it in a number of cases in which patent owners have attempted to use their patents for price fixing, tie-ins, territorial restrictions, and so forth. [citation omitted] The patent misuse defense also has been acknowledged by Congress in the 1988 Patent Misuse Reform Act, Pub.L. No. 100–703, 102 Stat. 4676 (1988) (codified at 35 U.S.C. § 271(d)(4) & (5)), which limited but did not eliminate the defense.[15]

3. The "Misuse of Copyright" Defense

Although the patent misuse defense has been generally recognized since Morton Salt, it has been much less certain whether an analogous copyright misuse defense exists. [citation omitted] This uncertainty persists because no United States Supreme Court decision has firmly established a copyright misuse defense in a manner analogous to the establishment of the patent misuse defense by Morton Salt. The few courts considering the issue have split on whether the defense should be recognized ***.

We are of the view, however, that since copyright and patent law serve parallel public interests, a "misuse" defense should apply to infringement actions brought to vindicate either right. ***

Thus, we are persuaded that the rationale of *Morton Salt* in establishing the misuse defense applies to copyrights. ***

Having determined that "misuse of copyright" is a valid defense, analogous to the misuse of patent defense, our next task is to determine whether the defense should have been applied by the district court to bar Lasercomb's infringement action against the defendants in this case.

---

[15] The primary effect of the Patent Misuse Reform Act is to eliminate the presumption that use of a patent license to create a tie-in is per se misuse. *See* Calkins, Patent Law, at 196–97.

B. The District Court's Finding that the Anticompetitive Clauses Are Reasonable

*** Both the presentation by appellants and the literature tend to intermingle antitrust and misuse defenses. [citation omitted] A patent or copyright is often regarded as a limited monopoly—an exception to the general public policy against restraints of trade. Since antitrust law is the statutory embodiment of that public policy, there is an understandable association of antitrust law with the misuse defense. Certainly, an entity which uses its patent as the means of violating antitrust law is subject to a misuse of patent defense. However, *Morton Salt* held that it is not necessary to prove an antitrust violation in order to successfully assert patent misuse ***.

So while it is true that the attempted use of a copyright to violate antitrust law probably would give rise to a misuse of copyright defense, the converse is not necessarily true—a misuse need not be a violation of antitrust law in order to comprise an equitable defense to an infringement action. The question is not whether the copyright is being used in a manner violative of antitrust law (such as whether the licensing agreement is "reasonable"), but whether the copyright is being used in a manner violative of the public policy embodied in the grant of a copyright.

Lasercomb undoubtedly has the right to protect against copying of the Interact code. Its standard licensing agreement, however, goes much further and essentially attempts to suppress any attempt by the licensee to independently implement the idea which Interact expresses. The agreement forbids the licensee to develop or assist in developing any kind of computer-assisted die-making software. If the licensee is a business, it is to prevent all its directors, officers and employees from assisting in any manner to develop computer-assisted die-making software. ***

The language employed in the Lasercomb agreement is extremely broad. Each time Lasercomb sells its Interact program to a company and obtains that company's agreement to the noncompete language, the company is required to forego utilization of the creative abilities of all its officers, directors and employees in the area of CAD/CAM die-making software. Of yet greater concern, these creative abilities are withdrawn from the public. The period for which this anticompetitive restraint exists is ninety-nine years, which could be longer than the life of the copyright itself. ***

We think the anticompetitive language in Lasercomb's licensing agreement *** amounts to misuse of its copyright. Again, the analysis necessary to a finding of misuse is similar to but separate from the analysis necessary to a finding of antitrust violation. The misuse arises from Lasercomb's attempt to use its copyright in a particular expression, the Interact software, to control competition in an area outside the copyright, i.e., the idea of computer-assisted die manufacture, regardless of whether such conduct amounts to an antitrust violation.

Comments and Questions

1. The Fourth Circuit approach in *Lasercomb* has proved influential. See, e.g., *DSC Communications Corp. v. Pulse Communications, Inc.*, 170 F.3d 1354

(Fed. Cir. 1999) ("Copyright misuse is a defense to a claim of copyright infringement."); *Alcatel USA, Inc. v. DGI Technologies, Inc.*, 166 F.3d 772 (5th Cir. 1999) *Practice Mgmt. Info. Corp. v. American Med. Ass'n*, 121 F.3d 516, 521 (9th Cir.1997) ("We agree with the Fourth Circuit that a defendant in a copyright infringement suit need not prove an antitrust violation to prevail on a copyright misuse defense.").

However, the copyright misuse defense is not as widely accepted as the patent misuse defense. In particular, Congress has not codified the copyright misuse defense as it has the patent misuse defense.

2. Applying a rule developed for the patent misuse defense, the *Lasercomb* court went on to note that "the defense of copyright misuse is available even if the [infringement] defendants themselves have not been injured by the misuse." Does this make sense? Why or why not?

3. The court clarified that its "holding, of course, is not an invalidation of Lasercomb's copyright. Lasercomb is free to bring a suit for infringement once it has purged itself of the misuse." Do you agree with this rule? If an IP owner engages in misuse, should it lose its IP rights forever? Why or why not?

4. In a case that predated *Lasercomb*, Judge Posner of the Seventh Circuit suggested that copyright misuse could not exist absent a violation of antitrust law:

> Noting the convergence of patent-misuse principles with antitrust principles, we said in *USM Corp. v. SPS Technologies, Inc.*, 694 F.2d 505, 512 (7th Cir.1982): "If misuse claims are not tested by conventional antitrust principles, by what principles shall they be tested? Our law is not rich in alternative concepts of monopolistic abuse; and it is rather late in the date to try to develop one without in the process subjecting the rights of patent holders to debilitating uncertainty." This point applies with even greater force to copyright misuse, where the danger of monopoly is less. We hold that a no-contest clause in a copyright licensing agreement is valid unless shown to violate antitrust law.

Saturday Evening Post Co. v. Rumbleseat Press, Inc., 816 F.2d 1191 (7th Cir. 1987).

In a later case, Judge Posner opined that it was an "open [] question whether copyright misuse, unless it rises to the level of an antitrust violation, is a defense to infringement" and he explained the rationale for decoupling the two legal concepts:

> The argument for applying copyright misuse beyond the bounds of antitrust, besides the fact that confined to antitrust the doctrine would be redundant, is that for a copyright owner to use an infringement suit to obtain property protection, here in data, that copyright law clearly does not confer, hoping to force a settlement or even achieve an outright victory over an opponent that may lack the resources or the legal sophistication to resist effectively, is an abuse of process.

Assessment Technologies of WI, LLC v. WIREdata, Inc., 350 F.3d 640, 647 (7th Cir. 2003).

What is the proper relationship between antitrust law and the copyright misuse defense? Why?

3. Trademark Misuse

Whereas all jurisdictions recognize the patent misuse defense and many, if not most, recognize the copyright misuse defense, the development of a meaningful trademark misuse defense has failed to gain traction. Just as the *Lasercomb* court developed the copyright misuse defense as a logical extension of the patent misuse defense, courts have noted the salient differences between patents and trademarks in questioning the existence of a trademark misuse defense:

> We recognize that the forces favoring exercise of [a court's equity] power in a trademark suit are much weaker than those calling for its exercise in patent litigation, and that decisions upholding an antitrust misuse defense in the latter are not necessarily authoritative in the trademark field. See, for example, *Morton Salt Co. v. G. S. Suppiger Co.*, 314 U.S. 488 (1942). The distinction arises from the fact that a patent represents a grant of a limited monopoly that in most instances would, absent its legalization by Congress, constitute an unlawful restraint of trade. The limited monopoly is granted in exchange for disclosure of the patented invention to the public so that it may be utilized in free competition upon expiration of the patent. A valid trademark, on the other hand, merely enables the owner to bar others from use of the mark, as distinguished from competitive manufacture and sale of identical goods bearing another mark, or even no mark at all, since the purpose of trademark enforcement is to avoid public confusion that might result from imitation or similar unfair competitive practices rather than to authorize restraints upon trade.
>
> Thus, although misuse of a patent almost inevitably is accompanied by unlawful restraints, the opportunity for effective antitrust misuse of a trademark, as distinguished from collateral anti-competitive activities on the part of the manufacturer or seller of the goods bearing the mark, is so limited that it poses a far less serious threat to the economic health of the nation. As a result, it has been recognized that a sharp distinction must be drawn between the antitrust misuse defense in patent infringement suits, on the one hand, and its use in trademark suits, on the other.

Carl Zeiss Stiftung v. V. E. B. Carl Zeiss, Jena, 298 F. Supp. 1309 (S.D.N.Y. 1969)

The skepticism of the *Carl Zeiss* court remains today. One district court went so far as to describe the trademark misuse defense as a "phantom" and a "non-existent legal theory." *Northwestern Corp. v. Gabriel Mfg. Co., Inc.*, 48 U.S.P.Q.2d 1902, 1998 WL 525431 (N.D. Ill. 1998).

Other courts have acknowledged the possibility—but improbability—of the defense succeeding:

> There is general agreement that "[a]n essential element of the antitrust misuse defense in a trademark case is proof that the mark itself has been the basic and fundamental vehicle required and used to accomplish the violation. Although the burden of establishing such a direct misuse is a heavy one, it is not insuperable."

[citation omitted] As the cases cited above make clear, an antitrust-related trademark misuse case is not impossible to maintain as a matter of law. Nevertheless, the defense is extremely narrow. "[I]n almost every reported instance where the antitrust misuse of a trademark has been raised as a defense, it has been rejected[, because the defendant did not demonstrate] that the trademark, as distinguished from collateral activities with respect to goods bearing the trademark, was itself being used as the prime and effective instrument to effectuate the antitrust activity."

Estée Lauder Inc. v. Fragrance Counter Inc., 189 F.R.D. 269 (S.D.N.Y. 1999) (quoting *Carl Zeiss*).

Should courts recognize a trademark misuse defense? If so, what should be the relationship between that defense and substantive antitrust law? Should it make a difference what kind of mark is being used (e.g., a word mark or a product configuration mark)?

Bibliography of Additional Resources

Phillip Abromats, *Copyright Misuse and Anticompetitive Software Licensing Restrictions: Lasercomb America, Inc. v. Reynolds*, 52 U. Pitt. L. Rev. 629 (1991)

Roger Arar, *Redefining Copyright Misuse*, 81 Colum. L. Rev. 1291 (1981)

Kevin J. Arquit, *Patent Abuse and the Antitrust Laws*, 59 Antitrust L. J. 739 (1990–91)

Joel R. Bennett, *Patent Misuse: Must an Alleged Infringer Prove an Antitrust Violation?*, 17 AIPLA Q.J. 1 (1989)

Byron A. Bilicki, *Standard Antitrust Analysis and the Doctrine of Patent Misuse: A Unification Under the Rule of Reason*, 46 U. Pitt L. Rev. 209 (1984)

Kenneth J. Burchfield, Patent Misuse and Antitrust Reform: *"Blessed Be the Tie?"*, 4 Harv. J.L. & Tech. 1 (1991)

Ilan Charnelle, *The Justification and Scope of the Copyright Misuse Doctrine and its Independence of the Antitrust Laws*, 9 UCLA Ent. L. Rev. 167 (2002)

John T. Cross & Peter K. Yu, *Competition Law and Copyright Misuse*, 56 Drake L. Rev. 427 (2008).

Stephen J. Davidson & Nicole A. Engisch, *Copyright Misuse and Fraud on the Copyright Office: An Escape for Infringers?*, 13 No. 1 Computer Law. 14 (1996)

Robin C. Feldman, *The Insufficiency of Antitrust Analysis for Patent Misuse*, 55 Hastings L.J. 399 (2003)

Brett Frischmann & Dan Moylan, *The Evolving Common Law Doctrine of Copyright Misuse: A Unified Theory and its Application to Software*, 15 Berkeley Tech. L.J. 865 (2000)

Ramsey Hanna, *Misusing Antitrust: The Search for Functional Copyright Misuse Standards*, 46 Stanford L. Rev. 401 (1994)

Robert J. Hoerner, *The Decline (and Fall?) of the Patent Misuse Doctrine in the Federal Circuit*, 69 Antitrust L.J. 669 (2002)

Kathryn Judge, *Rethinking Copyright Misuse*, 57 Stan. L. Rev. 901 (2004)

Dennis S. Karjala, *Copyright Protection of Operating Software,* Copyright *Misuse, and Antitrust*, 9 Cornell J.L. & Pub. Pol'y 161 (1999)

68 *Antitrust Law and Intellectual Property Rights*

Marshall Leaffer, *Engineering Competitive Policy and Copyright Misuse*, 19 U. Dayton L. Rev. 1087 (1994)

Mark A. Lemley, *The Economic Irrationality of the Patent Misuse Doctrine*, 78 Cal. L. Rev. 1599 (1990)

Scott A. Miskimon, *Divorcing Public Policy from Economic Reality: The Fourth Circuit's Copyright Misuse Doctrine in* Lasercomb America, Inc. v. Reynolds, 69 N.C. L. Rev. 1672 (1991)

William E. Ridgway, *Revitalizing the Doctrine of Trademark Misuse*, 21 Berkeley Tech. L.J. 1547 (2006)

Douglas L. Rogers, *Give the Smaller Players a Chance: Shaping the Digital Economy through Antitrust and Copyright Law*, 5 Marquette Intell. Prop. L. Rev. 13 (2001)

D. Economic Concepts

1. Price Discrimination

The Court in *Illinois Tool Works* discusses price discrimination in the context of market power. Price discrimination exists when a seller charges different prices to different consumers. To understand the economics of price discrimination, one must first understand the nature of consumer demand. In most markets, different consumers are willing to pay different prices. For example, one consumer may be willing to pay $500 for a particular bicycle while another is willing to pay no more than $300 for the same bike. (Either sale would be profitable.) We say that the second consumer has a lower reservation price than the first—a reservation price being the highest price that a consumer is willing to pay for a particular product.

Suppose that the monopolist must set one price to charge all customers. If the monopolist charges $500, it loses a profitable sale. If it charges $300, however, the monopolist foregoes extracting an additional $200 from the high-reservation price consumer. The firm maximizes its profits by charging different prices to different consumers, namely higher prices to consumers with higher reservation prices and lower prices to consumers with lower reservation prices. Price discrimination can mitigate some of the inefficiency associated with monopolies. Most firms would prefer to effectively price discriminate, instead of charging a single price.

Two problems may prevent firms from pursuing this strategy. First, firms may not be able to discern consumers' reservation prices. If a firm misidentifies a low-value consumer as a high-value consumer and consequently insists on charging the higher price, the firm will lose a profitable sale. Conversely, if a firm misidentifies a high-value consumer as a low-value consumer and consequently charges the lower price, the firm will earn less on that sale than it would if it had simply charged the higher price of $500. Exacerbating the problem is the fact that consumers have an incentive to represent themselves as low-value consumers, regardless of their actual reservation price. Because of this, price discrimination is difficult to implement.

Second, even if a firm could accurately distinguish between high- and low-value consumers, it would still have to contend with the problem of arbitrage. The firm could identify and sell to a low-value consumer at a low price, who in turn resells the product at a higher price to a high-value consumer. The low-value consumer earns a profit by reselling instead of using the product. Arbitrage, however, reduces the profitability of price discrimination if a firm faces too much competition from its own customers.

Despite these problems, price discrimination sometimes succeeds. In particular, copyright owners have found ways to price discriminate. Professor Michael Meurer has explained:

> A seller price discriminates by charging different prices to buyers when the price difference cannot be explained by a cost difference in supplying the copyrighted work. Given identical versions of a work that have identical production and distribution costs, any price difference amounts to price discrimination. A familiar example is a movie ticket price discount for senior citizens. Moreover, given two versions of works that are not identical, price discrimination occurs if the price difference between the versions exceeds the cost difference in making the versions. An example is the relatively high price of hardcover books. Publishers normally set a price difference between hardcover and paperback books that exceeds the cost difference in publishing the two formats.

Michael J. Meurer, *Copyright Law and Price Discrimination,* 23 CARDOZO L. REV. 55 (2001).

The imposition of a tying arrangement is another strategy that can allow a firm to engage in price discrimination. One advantage of using tying to effect price discrimination is that it can minimize the risk of arbitrage:

> For example, suppose the Xymox Corporation manufactures and sells both copiers and copy paper. It sells copiers to two consumer profiles, a large paper-intensive business (such as a law firm) and a small business that has fewer copying needs (such as a real estate office). The law firm cannot operate without the ability to do large amounts of copying, and therefore it values the copier more than does the real estate firm, which does less copying. Suppose the law firm were willing to pay $50,000 for a decent copier, whereas the real estate firm is willing to pay $5,000. Ideally, Xymox would like to charge the law firm $50,000 and the real estate firm $5,000. However, it cannot. *** [T]here is a significant risk of arbitrage because the real estate firm could buy the copier for $5,000 and then sell it to the law firm for $30,000, a beneficial arrangement for everybody but Xymox. Xymox's dilemma is to find a way to price its copiers so that it does not lose sales to low-volume users, such as the real estate firm, but still extracts a significant amount of the consumer surplus from high-volume users, such as the law firm. Tying may do the trick. Xymox can impose a tying arrangement between its copiers and its copy paper, whereby purchasers of Xymox copiers must exclusively use Xymox paper. Xymox can then price its copiers at $4,000 and its paper at a supra-competitive price, say 10¢ per sheet. The low-volume user, who does not use much paper, will end up spending $5,000 over the life of the copier. Conversely, the high-volume user, who uses substantial quantities of copy paper, will end up paying closer to $50,000 for the copier and paper supplies over the life of the copier. Both low- and high-volume

users will find the arrangement cost-beneficial and Xymox will extract maximum consumer surplus from different consumer groups. However, because both sets of consumers see the same shelf-price for their copiers, there is no blatant price discrimination. Additionally, there is no risk of arbitrage because the low-volume user cannot sell her copier to a high-volume user in a mutually beneficial trade; thus, the tying-implemented price discrimination is not easily circumvented.

Christopher R. Leslie, *Unilaterally Imposed Tying Arrangements and Antitrust's Concerted Action Requirement*, 60 Ohio St. L. J. 1773 (1999).

Arguably, Illinois Tool Works was attempting to pursue this strategy: instead of charging a single monopoly price for its printheads, it charged a lower price for printheads and imposed a tying requirement while charging a supracompetitive price for the tied ink. As a result, high-volume customers who consumed more ink would end up paying an effectively higher price for their printheads than low-volume users. If this were Illinois Tool Works' goal, should antitrust law care? Why or why not?

Note on the Robinson-Patman Act

There is a specific antitrust statute, called the Robinson-Patman Act, 15 U.S.C. §13 et seq., that condemns some forms of price discrimination. In 2002, Congress authorized the creation of the Antitrust Modernization Commission (AMC), a bipartisan panel designed to review the state of American antitrust law and to make appropriate recommendations to Congress. As part of its mission, the AMC explained the origins of and evaluated the wisdom of the Robinson-Patman Act:

> Congress passed the Robinson-Patman Act in 1936 to respond to the concern of small businesses— such as "mom and pop" grocery stores—that they were losing share to larger supermarkets and chain stores and in some cases were being forced to leave the market. Small businesses complained that they could not obtain from suppliers the same price discounts that larger businesses demanded and received. To address this concern, Congress passed the Robinson-Patman Act (RP Act or Act), which prohibits sellers from offering different prices to different purchasers of "commodities of like grade and quality" where the difference injures competition. Different discount levels, or lower prices, can be offered only where: (1) the same discount is practically available to all purchasers; (2) a lower price is justified by a lower per-unit cost of selling to the "favored" buyer; (3) a lower price is offered in good faith to meet (but not beat) the price of a competitor; or (4) a lower price is justified by changing conditions affecting the market or marketability of the goods, such as where goods are perishable or seasonal or the business is closing or in bankruptcy. Other provisions of the Robinson-Patman Act ensure the goal of equal pricing by restricting the use of commissions and promotional expenses, for example. ***
>
> In its operation, however, the Act has had the unintended effect of limiting the extent of discounting generally and therefore has likely caused consumers to pay

higher prices than they otherwise would. *** Moreover, the Act ironically appears increasingly to be ineffective even in protecting small businesses. Over time, many businesses have found ways to comply with the Act by, for example, differentiating products, so they can sell somewhat different products to different purchasers at different prices. Such methods are likely to increase the seller's costs—and thus increase costs to consumers—but do nothing to protect small businesses. The Act generally appears to have failed in achieving its main objective. ***

Robinson-Patman Act claims generally can be characterized as either primary-line or secondary-line claims. Primary-line claims allege that price discrimination by a manufacturer injures competition at the manufacturer level by harming one or more of the manufacturer's competitors. The theory behind primary-line claims is that a manufacturer might sell its product below cost to certain stores, so that a competing manufacturer would not be able to meet the lower prices and would go out of business; this theory depends on high entry barriers that would prevent entry to replace the lost competitor. In such a case, the competing manufacturer would complain of a primary-line injury. ***

A broad range of cases may raise claims of secondary-line injury, however. Secondary-line claims involve injury alleged at the level of the distributor or retailer, one step removed from the manufacturer that offered the discount. For example, a small retailer that did not receive the same discount as a larger retailer from the same manufacturer might allege secondary-line injury. ***

By broadly discouraging price discounts, the Robinson-Patman Act potentially harms competition and consumers. The goal of the antitrust laws is to protect *competition* that benefits consumers. The Robinson-Patman Act does not promote competition, however. Instead, the Act protects *competitors*, often at the expense of competition that otherwise would benefit consumers, thereby producing anticompetitive outcomes. The Act prevents or discourages discounting that could enable retailers to lower prices to consumers.

Not surprisingly, the AMC urged the repeal of the Robinson-Patman Act in its entirety. Other government reports have similarly supported repeal. To date, such attempts to prod Congress have proven unsuccessful. There is very little litigation under the Robinson-Patman Act, however. The government has not brought a case in nearly twenty years. Very few private lawsuits are brought either. Nevertheless, while the antitrust statute designed to address one form of price discrimination remains relatively inactive, the economic concept of price discrimination animates some of the strategies pursued by IP owners, as you may see when reading some of the cases in this book.

Comments and Questions

1. The Supreme Court in *Illinois Tool Works* concluded that businesses can engage in price discrimination even if they do not possess market power. Do you agree? Can you think of examples where a firm price discriminates even though it competes in a relatively competitive market?

2. Should antitrust law limit a firm's ability to charge different prices to different customers for the same product or service? Does your answer depend on whether the firm possesses monopoly power?

2. Efficiency

Efficiency is a critical concept in antitrust jurisprudence. Many scholars, particularly those associated with the Chicago School, argue that maximizing efficiency is the sole purpose of antitrust law.[32] This view of antitrust has been roundly criticized by other scholars,[33] but nonetheless remains persuasive. Regardless of one's position in this debate, it is important to note that efficiency comes in different forms, as the following excerpt explains:

Thomas O. Barnett,
Interoperability Between Antitrust and Intellectual Property,
September 13, 2006[*]

This concept of efficiency is crucial to understanding how IP law interacts with the world of antitrust. To some, "efficiency" can mean static efficiency, which occurs when firms compete within an existing technology to streamline their methods, cut costs, and drive the price of a product embodying that technology down to something close to the cost of unit production. Static efficiency is a powerful force for increasing consumer welfare, but economists tell us that an even greater driver of consumer welfare is dynamic efficiency. Dynamic efficiency refers to gains that result from entirely new ways of doing business. The Austrian economist Joseph Schumpeter explained dynamic efficiency as:

> ... competition from the new commodity, the new technology, the new source of supply, the new organization... competition which commands a decisive cost or quality advantage and which strikes not at the margins of the profits and the outputs of the existing firms but at their foundations and their very lives.[3]

A more colloquial term for dynamic efficiency, but a helpful one, is leapfrog competition — competition that does not merely improve upon old methods, but leaps ahead into something new.

It follows from the Schumpeterian view that antitrust law, with its focus on improving consumer welfare, has a keen interest in protecting innovation. Fostering innovation requires recognition of the benefits of dynamic efficiency and the dangers of focusing myopically on static efficiency. The same forces that yield the benefits of static efficiency—conditions that encourage rivals quickly to adopt a new business method and drive their production toward marginal cost—can discourage innovation (and thus dynamic efficiency) if the drive toward marginal

---

[32] ROBERT BORK, THE ANTITRUST PARADOX: A POLICY AT WAR WITH ITSELF 427 (2d ed. 1993).
[33] Robert H. Lande, *Wealth Transfers As The Original And Primary Concern Of Antitrust: The Efficiency Interpretation Challenged*, 34 HASTINGS L.J. 65 (1982).
[*] *Available at* http://www.usdoj.gov/atr/public/speeches/218316.htm#N_3_.
[3] Joseph Schumpeter, Capitalism, Socialism and Democracy 84 (Harper Perennial 1976) (1942).

costs occurs at such an early stage that it makes innovation uneconomical. Where innovation requires substantial up-front research and development (R&D) costs, a rational firm will elect not to innovate if it anticipates a selling environment that too quickly resolves to marginal cost of production. This problem is sometimes described as the need to recoup R&D costs and an expected profit sufficient to induce firms to direct their capital to risky R&D ventures.

Seen in this light, strong intellectual property protection is not separate from competition principles, but rather, is an integral part of antitrust policy as a whole. Intellectual property rights should not be viewed as protecting their owners *from* competition; rather, IP rights should be seen as encouraging firms to engage *in* competition, particularly competition that involves risk and long-term investment.

Comments and Questions

1. The cases excerpted in Parts 2 through 5 of this book often discuss efficiency, either explicitly or implicitly. It is important to ask yourself whether the challenged conduct is efficient and, if so, what type of efficiency is at issue?

If the conduct excludes competitors and/or raises price, but is still arguably efficient, should antitrust law condemn it?

2. How might these two forms of efficiency trade off against each other? Which form of efficiency is most important?

3. To the extent that antitrust law is about efficiency and intellectual property is about innovation, this raises the question: What is the relationship between innovation and the various forms of efficiency?

3. Networks Effects

U S. v. Microsoft Corp.
253 F.3d 34 (D.C. Cir. 2001)

PER CURIAM:

Microsoft Corporation appeals from judgments of the District Court finding the company in violation of §§ 1 and 2 of the Sherman Act and ordering various remedies.

The action against Microsoft arose pursuant to a complaint filed by the United States and separate complaints filed by individual States. The District Court determined that Microsoft had maintained a monopoly in the market for Intel-compatible PC operating systems in violation of § 2 ***

We decide this case against a backdrop of significant debate amongst academics and practitioners over the extent to which "old economy" § 2 monopolization doctrines should apply to firms competing in dynamic technological markets characterized by network effects. In markets characterized by network effects, one product or standard tends towards dominance, because "the utility that a user derives from consumption of the good increases with the number of other agents consuming the good." Michael L. Katz & Carl Shapiro, Network Externalities, Competition, and Compatibility, 75 am. Econ. Rev. 424, 424 (1985). For example, "[a]n individual consumer's demand to use (and hence her benefit from) the telephone network . . . increases with the number of other users on the network whom she can call or from whom she can receive calls." Howard A. Shelanski & J. Gregory Sidak, Antitrust Divestiture in Network Industries, 68 U. Chi. L. Rev. 1, 8 (2001). Once a product or standard achieves wide acceptance, it becomes more or less entrenched. Competition in such industries is "for the field" rather than "within the field." See Harold Demsetz, Why Regulate Utilities?, 11 J.L. & Econ. 55, 57 & n.7 (1968) (emphasis omitted).

In technologically dynamic markets, however, such entrenchment may be temporary, because innovation may alter the field altogether. See Joseph A. Schumpeter, Capitalism, Socialism and Democracy 81-90 (Harper Perennial 1976) (1942). Rapid technological change leads to markets in which "firms compete through innovation for temporary market dominance, from which they may be displaced by the next wave of product advancements." Shelanski & Sidak, at 11–12 (discussing Schumpeterian competition, which proceeds "sequentially over time rather than simultaneously across a market"). Microsoft argues that the operating system market is just such a market.

Whether or not Microsoft's characterization of the operating system market is correct does not appreciably alter our mission in assessing the alleged antitrust violations in the present case. As an initial matter, we note that there is no consensus among commentators on the question of whether, and to what extent, current monopolization doctrine should be amended to account for competition in technologically dynamic markets characterized by network effects. [citation omitted] Indeed, there is some suggestion that the economic consequences of network effects and technological dynamism act to offset one another, thereby making it difficult to formulate categorical antitrust rules absent a particularized analysis of a given market. See Shelanski & Sidak, at 6–7 ("High profit margins might appear to be the benign and necessary recovery of legitimate investment returns in a Schumpeterian framework, but they might represent exploitation of customer lock-in and monopoly power when viewed through the lens of network economics. . . . The issue is particularly complex because, in network industries characterized by rapid innovation, both forces may be operating and can be difficult to isolate."). ***

II. Monopolization

Section 2 of the Sherman Act makes it unlawful for a firm to "monopolize." 15 U.S.C. § 2. The offense of monopolization has two elements: "(1) the possession of monopoly power in the relevant market and (2) the willful acquisition or maintenance of that power as distinguished from growth or development as a consequence of a superior product, business acumen, or historic accident." *United States v. Grinnell Corp.*, 384 U.S. 563, 570–71(1966). The District Court applied this test and found that Microsoft possesses monopoly power in the market for Intel-compatible PC operating systems. Focusing primarily on Microsoft's efforts to suppress Netscape Navigator's threat to its operating system monopoly, the court also found that Microsoft maintained its power not through competition on the merits, but through unlawful means. Microsoft challenges both conclusions. We defer to the District Court's findings of fact, setting them aside only if clearly erroneous. Fed R. Civ. P. 52(a). We review legal questions de novo. [citation omitted] ***

A. Monopoly Power

While merely possessing monopoly power is not itself an antitrust violation, [citation omitted] it is a necessary element of a monopolization charge [citation omitted]. The Supreme Court defines monopoly power as "the power to control prices or exclude competition." *United States v. E.I. du Pont de Nemours & Co.*, 351 U.S. 377, 391 (1956). More precisely, a firm is a monopolist if it can profitably raise prices substantially above the competitive level. [citation omitted] Where evidence indicates that a firm has in fact profitably done so, the existence of monopoly power is clear. [citation omitted] Because such direct proof is only rarely available, courts more typically examine market structure in search of circumstantial evidence of monopoly power. [citation omitted] Under this structural approach, monopoly power may be inferred from a firm's possession of a dominant share of a relevant market that is protected by entry barriers. [citation omitted] "Entry barriers" are factors (such as certain regulatory requirements) that prevent new rivals from timely responding to an increase in price above the competitive level. [citation omitted]

The District Court considered these structural factors and concluded that Microsoft possesses monopoly power in a relevant market. Defining the market as Intel-compatible PC operating systems, the District Court found that Microsoft has a greater than 95% share. It also found the company's market position protected by a substantial entry barrier. [citation omitted]

Microsoft argues that the District Court incorrectly defined the relevant market. It also claims that there is no barrier to entry in that market. Alternatively, Microsoft argues that because the software industry is uniquely dynamic, direct proof, rather than circumstantial evidence, more appropriately indicates whether it possesses monopoly power. Rejecting each argument, we uphold the District Court's finding of monopoly power in its entirety.

1. Market Structure

a. Market definition

"Because the ability of consumers to turn to other suppliers restrains a firm from raising prices above the competitive level," *Rothery Storage & Van Co. v. Atlas Van Lines, Inc.*, 792 F.2d 210, 218 (D.C.Cir.1986), the relevant market must include all products "reasonably interchangeable by consumers for the same purposes." *du Pont*, 351 U.S. at 395. In this case, the District Court defined the market as "the licensing of all Intel-compatible PC operating systems worldwide," finding that there are "currently no products—and . . . there are not likely to be any in the near future-that a significant percentage of computer users worldwide could substitute for [these operating systems] without incurring substantial costs." [citation omitted] Calling this market definition "far too narrow," [citation omitted]

Microsoft argues that the District Court improperly excluded three types of products: non-Intel compatible operating systems (primarily Apple's Macintosh operating system, Mac OS), operating systems for non-PC devices (such as handheld computers and portal websites), and "middleware" products, which are not operating systems at all.

We begin with Mac OS. Microsoft's argument that Mac OS should have been included in the relevant market suffers from a flaw that infects many of the company's monopoly power claims: the company fails to challenge the District Court's factual findings, or to argue that these findings do not support the court's conclusions. The District Court found that consumers would not switch from Windows to Mac OS in response to a substantial price increase because of the costs of acquiring the new hardware needed to run Mac OS (an Apple computer and peripherals) and compatible software applications, as well as because of the effort involved in learning the new system and transferring files to its format. [citation omitted] The court also found the Apple system less appealing to consumers because it costs considerably more and supports fewer applications. [citation omitted] *** Microsoft neither points to evidence contradicting the District Court's findings nor alleges that supporting record evidence is insufficient. ***

Microsoft's challenge to the District Court's exclusion of non-PC based competitors, such as information appliances (handheld devices, etc.) and portal websites that host server-based software applications, suffers from the same defect: the company fails to challenge the District Court's key factual findings. In particular, the District Court found that because information appliances fall far short of performing all of the functions of a PC, most consumers will buy them only as a supplement to their PCs. [citation omitted] The District Court also found that portal websites do not presently host enough applications to induce consumers to switch, nor are they likely to do so in the near future. [citation omitted] Again, because Microsoft does not argue that the District Court's findings do not support its conclusion that information appliances and portal websites are outside the relevant market, we adhere to that conclusion.

This brings us to Microsoft's main challenge to the District Court's market definition: the exclusion of middleware. Because of the importance of middleware to this case, we pause to explain what it is and how it relates to the issue before us.

Operating systems perform many functions, including allocating computer memory and controlling peripherals such as printers and keyboards. [citation omitted] Operating systems also function as platforms for software applications. They do this by "exposing"- i.e., making available to software developers-routines or protocols that perform certain widely-used functions. These are known as Application Programming Interfaces, or "APIs." [citation omitted] For example, Windows contains an API that enables users to draw a box on the screen. [citation omitted] Software developers wishing to include that function in an application need not duplicate it in their own code. Instead, they can "call"- i.e., use-the Windows API. [citation omitted] Windows contains thousands of APIs, controlling everything from data storage to font display. [citation omitted]

Every operating system has different APIs. Accordingly, a developer who writes an application for one operating system and wishes to sell the application to users of another must modify, or "port," the application to the second operating system. [citation omitted] This process is both timeconsuming and expensive. [citation omitted]

"Middleware" refers to software products that expose their own APIs. [citation omitted] Because of this, a middleware product written for Windows could take over some or all of Windows's valuable platform functions-that is, developers might begin to rely upon APIs exposed by the middleware for basic routines rather than relying upon the API set included in Windows. If middleware were written for multiple operating systems, its impact could be even greater. The more developers could rely upon APIs exposed by such middleware, the less expensive porting to different operating systems would be. Ultimately, if developers could write applications relying exclusively on APIs exposed by middleware, their applications would run on any operating system on which the middleware was also present. [citation omitted] Netscape Navigator and Java-both at issue in this case-are middleware products written for multiple operating systems. [citation omitted]

Microsoft argues that, because middleware could usurp the operating system's platform function and might eventually take over other operating system functions (for instance, by controlling peripherals), the District Court erred in excluding Navigator and Java from the relevant market. The District Court found, however, that neither Navigator, Java, nor any other middleware product could now, or would soon, expose enough APIs to serve as a platform for popular applications, much less take over all operating system functions. [citation omitted] Again, Microsoft fails to challenge these findings, instead simply asserting middleware's "potential" as a competitor. [citation omitted] The test of reasonable interchangeability, however, required the District Court to consider only substitutes that constrain pricing in the reasonably foreseeable future, and only products that can enter the market in a relatively short time can perform this function. [citation omitted] Whatever middleware's ultimate potential, the District Court found that consumers could not now abandon their operating systems and switch to middleware in response to a sustained price for Windows above the competitive level. [citation omitted] Nor is middleware likely to overtake the operating system as the primary platform for software development any time in the near future. [citation omitted]

***Because market definition is meant to identify products "reasonably interchangeable by consumers," *du Pont*, 351 U.S. at 395, and because middleware is not now interchangeable with Windows, the District Court had good reason for excluding middleware from the relevant market.

b. Market power

Having thus properly defined the relevant market, the District Court found that Windows accounts for a greater than 95% share. The court also found that even if Mac OS were included, Microsoft's share would exceed 80%. Id. Microsoft challenges neither finding, nor does it argue that such a market share is not predominant. *Cf. Grinnell,* 384 U.S. at 571 (87% is predominant); *Eastman Kodak Co. v. Image Technical Servs., Inc.,* 504 U.S. 451, 481 (1992) (80%); *du Pont,* 351 U.S. at 379, 391 (75%).

Instead, Microsoft claims that even a predominant market share does not by itself indicate monopoly power. Although the "existence of [monopoly] power ordinarily may be inferred from the predominant share of the market," *Grinnell,* 384 U.S. at 571, we agree with Microsoft that because of the possibility of competition from new entrants, see *Ball Mem'l Hosp., Inc.,* 784 F.2d at 1336, looking to current market share alone can be "misleading." [citation omitted] In this case, however, the District Court was not misled. Considering the possibility of new rivals, the court focused not only on Microsoft's present market share, but also on the structural barrier that protects the company's future position. [citation omitted] That barrier-the "applications barrier to entry"-stems from two characteristics of the software market: (1) most consumers prefer operating systems for which a large number of applications have already been written; and (2) most developers prefer to write for operating systems that already have a substantial consumer base. [citation omitted] This "chicken-and-egg" situation ensures that applications will continue to be written for the already dominant Windows, which in turn ensures that consumers will continue to prefer it over other operating systems. [citation omitted] ***

2. Direct Proof

*** Even if we were to require direct proof, moreover, Microsoft's behavior may well be sufficient to show the existence of monopoly power. *** Microsoft never claims that it did not charge the long-term monopoly price. Microsoft does argue that the price of Windows is a fraction of the price of an Intel-compatible PC system and lower than that of rival operating systems, but these facts are not inconsistent with the District Court's finding that Microsoft has monopoly power. [citation omitted]

More telling, the District Court found that some aspects of Microsoft's behavior are difficult to explain unless Windows is a monopoly product. For instance, according to the District Court, the company set the price of Windows without considering rivals' prices, [citation omitted] something a firm without a monopoly would have been unable to do. The District Court also found that Microsoft's pattern of exclusionary conduct could only be rational "if the firm knew that it possessed monopoly power." [citation omitted] It is to that conduct that we now turn.

B. Anticompetitive Conduct

As discussed above, having a monopoly does not by itself violate § 2. A firm violates § 2 only when it acquires or maintains, or attempts to acquire or maintain, a monopoly by engaging in exclusionary conduct "as distinguished from growth or development as a consequence of a superior product, business acumen, or historic accident." *Grinnell,* 384 U.S. at 571 [citation omitted].

In this case, after concluding that Microsoft had monopoly power, the District Court held that Microsoft had violated § 2 by engaging in a variety of exclusionary acts (not including predatory pricing), to maintain its monopoly by preventing the effective distribution and use of products that might threaten that monopoly. Specifically, the District Court held Microsoft liable for: (1) the way in which it integrated IE into Windows; (2) its various dealings with Original Equipment Manufacturers ("OEMs"), Internet Access Providers ("IAPs"), Internet Content Providers ("ICPs"), Independent Software Vendors ("ISVs"), and Apple Computer; (3) its efforts to contain and to subvert Java technologies; and (4) its course of conduct as a whole. Upon appeal, Microsoft argues that it did not engage in any exclusionary conduct.

Whether any particular act of a monopolist is exclusionary, rather than merely a form of vigorous competition, can be difficult to discern: the means of illicit exclusion, like the means of legitimate competition, are myriad. The challenge for an antitrust court lies in stating a general rule for distinguishing between exclusionary acts, which reduce social welfare, and competitive acts, which increase it.

From a century of case law on monopolization under § 2, however, several principles do emerge. First, to be condemned as exclusionary, a monopolist's act must have an "anticompetitive effect." That is, it must harm the competitive process and thereby harm consumers. In contrast, harm to one or more competitors will not suffice. ***

Second, the plaintiff, on whom the burden of proof of course rests, [citation omitted] must demonstrate that the monopolist's conduct indeed has the requisite anticompetitive effect. [citation omitted] In a case brought by a private plaintiff, the plaintiff must show that its injury is "of 'the type that the statute was intended to forestall,'" "[citation omitted] no less in a case brought by the Government, it must demonstrate that the monopolist's conduct harmed competition, not just a competitor.

Third, if a plaintiff successfully establishes a prima facie case under § 2 by demonstrating anticompetitive effect, then the monopolist may proffer a "procompetitive justification" for its conduct. [citation omitted] If the monopolist asserts a procompetitive justification-a nonpretextual claim that its conduct is indeed a form of competition on the merits because it involves, for example, greater efficiency or enhanced consumer appeal-then the burden shifts back to the plaintiff to rebut that claim. [citation omitted]

Fourth, if the monopolist's procompetitive justification stands unrebutted, then the plaintiff must demonstrate that the anticompetitive harm of the conduct outweighs the procompetitive benefit. ***

Finally, in considering whether the monopolist's conduct on balance harms competition and is therefore condemned as exclusionary for purposes of § 2, our focus is upon the effect of that conduct, not upon the intent behind it. Evidence of the intent behind the conduct of a monopolist is relevant only to the extent it helps us understand the likely effect of the monopolist's conduct. [citation omitted]

With these principles in mind, we now consider Microsoft's objections to the District Court's holding that Microsoft violated § 2 of the Sherman Act in a variety of ways.

[*Editor*: The D.C. Circuit affirmed the district court's holdings that Microsoft violated Section Two in myriad ways by engaging in monopoly conduct designed to keep Netscape's market share in the browser market depressed and, thus, to prevent browser technology from evolving in a manner that would undermine the network effects in the operating system market. Microsoft's illegal conduct included:

(1) imposing license restrictions on original equipment manufacturers (OEMs) that effectively prevented them from removing any desktop icons, folders, or "Start" menu entries or otherwise altering the appearance of the Windows desktop, which effectively prevented the OEMs from promoting rival browsers or removing visible means of user access to IE;

(2) integrating Internet Explorer and Windows by "excluding IE from the 'Add/Remove Programs' utility" and "commingling code related to browsing and other code in the same files, so that any attempt to delete the files containing IE would, at the same time, cripple the operating system," which had the effect of "both prevent[ing] OEMs from pre-installing other browsers and deterr[ing] consumers from using them";

(3) entering agreements with internet access providers, such as America Online, "to promote IE exclusively and to keep shipments of internet access software using Navigator under a specific percentage, typically 25%"; and

(4) concluding deals with independent software vendors and Apple Computer designed to reduce the distribution and usage of rival browsers.

The D.C. Circuit did reverse some of the district court's findings (e.g., the lower court's finding that Microsoft's dealings with internet content providers were anticompetitive). However, as to most of the conduct for which the D.C. Circuit affirmed the conclusion of illegality, Microsoft offered no procompetitive justification for the conduct listed above.]

5. Java

Java, a set of technologies developed by Sun Microsystems, is another type of middleware posing a potential threat to Windows' position as the ubiquitous platform for software development. [citation omitted] The Java technologies include: (1) a programming language; (2) a set of programs written in that language, called the "Java class libraries," which expose APIs; (3) a compiler, which translates code written by a developer into "bytecode"; and (4) a Java Virtual Machine ("JVM"), which translates bytecode into instructions to the operating system. [citation omitted] Programs calling upon the Java APIs will run on any machine with a "Java runtime environment," that is, Java class libraries and a JVM. [citation omitted]

In May 1995 Netscape agreed with Sun to distribute a copy of the Java runtime environment with every copy of Navigator, and "Navigator quickly became the principal vehicle by which Sun placed copies of its Java runtime environment on the PC systems of Windows users." [citation omitted] Microsoft, too, agreed to promote the Java technologies-or so it seemed. For at the same time, Microsoft took steps "to maximize the difficulty with which applications written in Java could be ported from Windows to other platforms, and vice versa." [citation omitted] Specifically, the District Court found that Microsoft took four steps to exclude Java from developing as a viable cross-platform threat: (a) designing a JVM incompatible with the one developed by Sun; (b) entering into contracts, the so-called "First Wave Agreements," requiring major ISVs to promote Microsoft's JVM exclusively; (c) deceiving Java developers about the Windows-specific nature of the tools it distributed to them; and (d) coercing Intel to stop aiding Sun in improving the Java technologies.

a. The incompatible JVM

The District Court held that Microsoft engaged in exclusionary conduct by developing and promoting its own JVM. [citation omitted] Sun had already developed a JVM for the Windows operating system when Microsoft began work on its version. The JVM developed by Microsoft allows Java applications to run faster on Windows than does Sun's JVM, [citation omitted] but a Java application designed to work with Microsoft's JVM does not work with Sun's JVM and vice versa. [citation omitted] The District Court found that Microsoft "made a large investment of engineering resources to develop a high-performance Windows JVM," [citation omitted] and, "[b]y bundling its... JVM with every copy of [IE]... Microsoft endowed its Java runtime environment with the unique attribute of guaranteed, enduring ubiquity across the enormous Windows installed base," [citation omitted]. As explained above, however, a monopolist does not violate the antitrust laws simply by developing a product that is incompatible with those of its rivals. [citation omitted] In order to violate the antitrust laws, the incompatible product must have an anticompetitive effect that outweighs any procompetitive justification for the design. Microsoft's JVM is not only incompatible with Sun's, it allows Java applications to run faster on Windows than does Sun's JVM. Microsoft's faster JVM lured Java developers into using Microsoft's developer tools, and Microsoft offered those tools deceptively, as we discuss below. The JVM, however, does allow applications to run more swiftly and does not itself have any anticompetitive effect. Therefore, we reverse the District Court's imposition of liability for Microsoft's development and promotion of its JVM.

b. The First Wave Agreements

The District Court also found that Microsoft entered into First Wave Agreements with dozens of ISVs to use Microsoft's JVM. ***

To the extent Microsoft's First Wave Agreements with the ISVs conditioned receipt of Windows technical information upon the ISVs' agreement to promote Microsoft's JVM exclusively, they raise a different competitive concern. The District Court found that, although not literally exclusive, the deals were exclusive in practice because they required developers to make Microsoft's JVM the default in the software they developed. *** Because Microsoft's agreements foreclosed a substantial portion of the field for JVM distribution and because, in so doing, they protected Microsoft's monopoly from a middleware threat, they are anticompetitive.

Microsoft offered no procompetitive justification for the default clause that made the First Wave Agreements exclusive as a practical matter. [citation omitted] Because the cumulative effect of the deals is anticompetitive and because Microsoft has no procompetitive justification for them, we hold that the provisions in the First Wave Agreements requiring use of Microsoft's JVM as the default are exclusionary, in violation of the Sherman Act.

c. Deception of Java developers

Microsoft's "Java implementation" included, in addition to a JVM, a set of software development tools it created to assist ISVs in designing Java applications. The District Court found that, not only were these tools incompatible with Sun's cross-platform aspirations for Java-no violation, to be sure-but Microsoft deceived Java developers regarding the Windows-specific nature of the tools. Microsoft's tools included "certain 'keywords' and 'compiler directives' that could only be executed properly by Microsoft's version of the Java runtime environment for Windows." [citation omitted] As a result, even Java "developers who were opting for portability over performance... unwittingly [wrote] Java applications that [ran] only on Windows." Conclusions of Law, at 43. That is, developers who relied upon Microsoft's public commitment to cooperate with Sun and who used Microsoft's tools to develop what Microsoft led them to believe were cross-platform applications ended up producing applications that would run only on the Windows operating system.

*** Microsoft documents confirm that Microsoft intended to deceive Java developers, and predicted that the effect of its actions would be to generate Windows-dependent Java applications that their developers believed would be cross-platform; these documents also indicate that Microsoft's ultimate objective was to thwart Java's threat to Microsoft's monopoly in the market for operating systems. One Microsoft document, for example, states as a strategic goal: "Kill cross-platform Java by grow[ing] the polluted Java market." GX 259, reprinted in 22 J.A. at 14514; see also id. ("Cross-platform capability is by far the number one reason for choosing/using Java.") (emphasis in original).

Microsoft's conduct related to its Java developer tools served to protect its monopoly of the operating system in a manner not attributable either to the superiority of the operating system or to the acumen of its makers, and therefore was anticompetitive. Unsurprisingly, Microsoft offers no procompetitive explanation for its campaign to deceive developers. Accordingly, we conclude this conduct is exclusionary, in violation of § 2 of the Sherman Act.

d. The threat to Intel

The District Court held that Microsoft also acted unlawfully with respect to Java by using its "monopoly power to prevent firms such as Intel from aiding in the creation of cross-platform interfaces." [citation omitted] In 1995 Intel was in the process of developing a highperformance, Windows-compatible JVM.

Microsoft wanted Intel to abandon that effort because a fast, cross-platform JVM would threaten Microsoft's monopoly in the operating system market.

*** By 1996 "Intel had developed a JVM designed to run well... while complying with Sun's cross-platform standards." [citation omitted] In April of that year, Microsoft again urged Intel not to help Sun by distributing Intel's fast, Suncompliant JVM. Id. And Microsoft threatened Intel that if it did not stop aiding Sun on the multimedia front, then Microsoft would refuse to distribute Intel technologies bundled with Windows. [citation omitted]

Intel finally capitulated in 1997, after Microsoft delivered the coup de grace.

> [O]ne of Intel's competitors, called AMD, solicited support from Microsoft for its "3DX" technology.... Microsoft's Allchin asked Gates whether Microsoft should support 3DX, despite the fact that Intel would oppose it. Gates responded: "If Intel has a real problem with us supporting this then they will have to stop supporting Java Multimedia the way they are. I would gladly give up supporting this if they would back off from their work on JAVA."

[Findings of Fact] Id. ¶ 406.

Microsoft's internal documents and deposition testimony confirm both the anticompetitive effect and intent of its actions. See, e.g., GX 235, reprinted in 22 J.A. at 14502 (Microsoft executive, Eric Engstrom, included among Microsoft's goals for Intel: "Intel to stop helping Sun create Java Multimedia APIs, especially ones that run well... on Windows."); Deposition of Eric Engstrom at 179 ("We were successful [in convincing Intel to stop aiding Sun] for some period of time.").

Microsoft does not deny the facts found by the District Court, nor does it offer any procompetitive justification for pressuring Intel not to support cross-platform Java. Microsoft lamely characterizes its threat to Intel as "advice." The District Court, however, found that Microsoft's "advice" to Intel to stop aiding cross-platform Java was backed by the threat of retaliation, and this conclusion is supported by the evidence cited above. Therefore we affirm the conclusion that Microsoft's threats to Intel were exclusionary, in violation of § 2 of the Sherman Act. ***

Comments and Questions

1. The Eleventh Circuit has explained why network effects can create a barrier to entry that protects incumbent firms against competition from new rivals:

> Network effects often enhance the monopoly position of firms that operate in industries where a large number of common customers is especially advantageous. See Stuart M. Benjamin, Douglas G. Lichtman, and Howard A. Shelanski, Telecommunications Law and Policy 616 (2002) ("All else equal, wouldn't you have a strong incentive to select the phone company that had the largest number of customers with whom you might want to converse? Once you join, can you see how this same phenomenon would increase the pressure on, say, your friends and family-which in turn would put pressure on their friends and family-to join the same phone network, thus increasing any monopoly tendency already at play

in the market?"). The cost of competing with an incumbent firm in a network industry may well be insurmountable. As the Supreme Court recently explained: "A newcomer could not compete with the incumbent carrier to provide local service without coming close to replicating the incumbent's entire existing network, the most costly and difficult part of which would be laying down the 'last mile' of feeder wire, the local loop, to thousands (or millions) of terminal points in individual houses and businesses." Verizon Communications Inc. v. FCC, 535 U.S. 467 (2001).

Ala. Power Co. v. FCC, 311 F.3d 1357 (11th Cir.2002).

If you were the president of a firm that wanted to enter a market characterized by network effects, what would you do to try to overcome the network effects that protected the incumbent firms?

2. How does the presence of network effects help Microsoft maintain its monopoly power in the market for operating systems?
How would Netscape and Java potentially undermine these network effects?
Do network effects benefit or harm consumers?

3. Intellectual property rights are not necessary to create network effects, but they may increase the exclusionary potential of networks. Why?

4. Microsoft sought to characterize its licensing restrictions on OEMs as the company "exercising its rights as the holder of valid copyrights." The D.C. Circuit rejected this defense:

> Microsoft's primary copyright argument borders upon the frivolous. The company claims an absolute and unfettered right to use its intellectual property as it wishes: "[I]f intellectual property rights have been lawfully acquired," it says, then "their subsequent exercise cannot give rise to antitrust liability." [citation omitted] That is no more correct than the proposition that use of one's personal property, such as a baseball bat, cannot give rise to tort liability.

The D.C. Circuit's analogy seems sound. If it were not, there would be little nuance to the intersection between antitrust law and intellectual property rights because the presence of valid IP rights would provide a defense to any antitrust claims.

5. To read more about network effects, see David McGowan, *Networks and Intention in Antitrust and Intellectual Property*, 24 J. CORP. L. 485 (1999).

Bibliography of Additional Resources

WARD S. BOWMAN, JR., PATENT AND ANTITRUST LAW (1973)

Michael A. Carrier, *Resolving the Patent-Antitrust Paradox through Tripartite Innovation*, 565 VAND. L. REV. 1047 (2003)

Michael A. Carrier, *Unraveling the Patent-Antitrust Paradox*, 150 U. PA. L. REV. 761 (2002)

Ronald A. Cass & Keith N. Hylton, *Preserving Competition: Economic Analysis, Legal Standards and Microsoft*, 8 Geo. Mason L. Rev. 1 (1999)

Andrew Chin, *Antitrust Analysis In Software Product Markets: A First Principles Approach*, 18 Harv. J.L. & Tech. 1 (2004)

Alan Devlin, *The Stochastic Relationship between Patents and Antitrust*, 5 J. Competition L. & Econ. 75 (2009)

Robin Feldman, *Patent and Antitrust Differing Shades of Meaning*, 13 Va. J.L. & Tech. 5 (Spring 2008)

Harry First, *Microsoft and the Evolution of the Intellectual Property Concept*, 2006 Wisc. L. Rev. 1369 (2006)

Daniel J. Gifford, *Antitrust's Troubled Relations with Intellectual Property*, 87 Minn. L. Rev. 1695 (2003)

Daniel J. Gifford, *The Antitrust/Intellectual Property Interface: an Emerging Solution to an Intractable Problem*, 31 Hofstra L. Rev. 363 (2002)

Richard J. Gilbert & Willard K. Tom, *Is Innovation King at the Antitrust Agencies? The Intellectual Property Guidelines Five Years Later*, 69 Antitrust L.J. 43 (2001)

Wendy J. Gordon, *Intellectual Property as Price Discrimination: Implications for Contract*, 73 Chi-Kent L. Rev. 1367 (1998)

Herbert Hovenkamp, Mark D. Janis, Mark A. Lemley & Christopher R. Leslie, Antitrust and IP: An Analysis of Antitrust Principles Applied to Intellectual Property Law (2nd Edition 2009)

Herbert Hovenkamp, *Patents, Property, and Competition Policy*, 34 J. Corp. L. 1243 (2009)

Herbert Hovenkamp, *Restraints on Innovation*, 29 Cardozo L. Rev. 247 (2007)

Louis Kaplow, *The Patent-Antitrust Intersection: A Reappraisal*, 97 Harv. L. Rev. 1813 (1984)

Ariel Katz, *Making Sense of Nonsense: Intellectual Property, Antitrust, and Market Power*, 49 Ariz. L. Rev. 837 (2007)

James Langenfeld, *Intellectual Property and Antitrust: Steps Toward Striking a Balance*, 52 Case W. Res. L. Rev. 91 (2001)

Mark A. Lemley, *A New Balance Between IP and Antitrust*, 13 Sw. J. L. & Trade Am. 237 (2007)

Mark A. Lemley & David McGowan, *Legal Implications of Network Economic Effects*, 86 Cal. L. Rev. 479 (1998)

Michael J. Meurer, *Copyright Law and Price Discrimination*, 23 Cardozo L. Rev. 55, 55 (2001)

Michael J. Meurer, *Price Discrimination, Personal Use and Piracy: Copyright Protection of Digital Works*, 45 Buff. L. Rev. 845, 869–75 (2001)

Joseph Scott Miller, *This Bitter Has Some Sweet: Potential Antitrust Enforcement Benefits from Patent Law's Procedural Rules*, 70 Antitrust L. J. 875 (2003)

Robert Pitofsky, *Antitrust and Intellectual Property: Unresolved Issues at the Heart of the New Economy*, 16 Berkeley Tech. L.J. 535 (2001)

Steven C. Salop & R. Craig Romaine, *Preserving Monopoly: Economic Analysis, Legal Standards, and Microsoft*, 7 Geo. Mason L. Rev. 617 (1999)

Gerald Sobel, *The Antitrust Interface with Patents and Innovation: Acquisition of Patents, Improvement Patents and Grant-Backs, Non-Use, Fraud on the Patent Office, Development of New Products and Joint Research*, 53 ANTITRUST L.J. 681 (1985)

John T. Soma & Kevin B. Davis, *Network Effects in Technology Markets: Applying the Lessons of Intel and Microsoft to Future Clashes Between Antitrust and Intellectual Property*, 8 J. INTELL. PROP. L. 1 (2000)

E. Thomas Sullivan, *The Confluence of Antitrust and Intellectual Property at the New Century*, 1 MINN. INTELL. PROP. REV. 1 (2000)

Willard K. Tom & Joshua A. Newberg, *Antitrust and Intellectual Property: From Separate Spheres to Unified Field*, 66 ANTITRUST L.J. 167 (1997)

PART TWO

THE ANTITRUST IMPLICATIONS OF UNILATERAL CONDUCT BY INTELLECTUAL PROPERTY OWNERS

CHAPTER 4

Enforcement of Intellectual Property Rights

A. Enforcement of a Fraudulently Procured Patent

Walker Process Equipment v. Food Machinery & Chemical Corp.
382 U.S. 172 (1965)

Mr. Justice CLARK delivered the opinion of the Court.

The question before us is whether the maintenance and enforcement of a patent obtained by fraud on the Patent Office may be the basis of an action under § 2 of the Sherman Act, and therefore subject to a treble damage claim by an injured party under § 4 of the Clayton Act. The respondent, Food Machinery, & Chemical Corp. (hereafter Food Machinery), filed this suit for infringement of its patent No. 2,328,655 covering knee-action swing diffusers used in aeration equipment for sewage treatment systems. Petitioner, Walker Process Equipment, Inc. (hereafter Walker), denied the infringement and counterclaimed for a declaratory judgment that the patent was invalid. After discovery, Food Machinery moved to dismiss its complaint with prejudice because the patent had expired. Walker then amended its counterclaim to charge that Food Machinery had 'illegally monopolized interstate and foreign commerce by fraudulently and in bad faith obtaining and maintaining * * * its patent * * well knowing that it had no basis for * * * a patent.' It alleged fraud on the basis that Food Machinery had sworn before the Patent Office that it neither knew nor believed that its invention had been in public use in the United States for more than one year prior to filing its patent application when, in fact, Food Machinery was a party to prior use within such time. The counterclaim further asserted that the existence of the patent had deprived Walker of business that it would have otherwise enjoyed. Walker prayed that Food Machinery's conduct be declared a violation of the antitrust laws and sought recovery of treble damages.

*** We have concluded that the enforcement of a patent procured by fraud on the Patent Office may be violative of § 2 of the Sherman Act provided the other elements necessary to a § 2 case are present. In such event the treble damage provisions of § 4 of the Clayton Act would be available to an injured party.

I.

As the case reaches us, the allegations of the counterclaim, as to the fraud practiced upon the Government by Food Machinery as well as the resulting damage suffered by Walker are taken as true. We, therefore, move immediately to a consideration of the legal issues presented.

Both Walker and the United States, which appears as amicus curiae, argue that if Food Machinery obtained its patent by fraud and thereafter used the patent to exclude Walker from the market through 'threats of suit' and prosecution of this infringement suit, such proof would establish a prima facie violation of § 2 of the Sherman Act. On the other hand, Food Machinery says that a patent monopoly and a Sherman Act monopolization cannot be equated; the removal of the protection of a patent grant because of fraudulent procurement does not automatically result in a § 2 offense. Both lower courts seem to have concluded that proof of fraudulent procurement may be used to bar recovery for infringement, [citation omitted] As the Court of Appeals expressed the proposition, 'only the government may 'annul or set aside' a patent.' [citation omitted] ***

II.

We have concluded, first, that Walker's action is not barred by the rule that only the United States may sue to cancel or annul a patent. It is true that there is no statutory authority for a private annulment suit and the invocation of the equitable powers of the court might often subject a patentee 'to innumerable vexatious suits to set aside his patent.' Mowry, supra, 81 U.S. at 441. But neither reason applies here. Walker counterclaimed under the Clayton Act, not the patent laws. While one of its elements is the fraudulent procurement of a patent, the action does not directly seek the patent's annulment. The gist of Walker's claim is that since Food Machinery obtained its patent by fraud it cannot enjoy the limited exception to the prohibitions of § 2 of the Sherman Act, but must answer under that section and § 4 of the Clayton Act in treble damages to those injured by any monopolistic action taken under the fraudulent patent claim. Nor can the interest in protecting patentees from 'innumerable vexatious suits' be used to frustrate the assertion of rights conferred by the antitrust laws. It must be remembered that we deal only with a special class of patents, i.e., those procured by intentional fraud.

Under the decisions of this Court a person sued for infringement may challenge the validity of the patent on various grounds, including fraudulent procurement. [citation omitted] In fact, one need not await the filing of a threatened suit by the patentee; the validity of the patent may be tested under the Declaratory Judgment Act. [citation omitted] At the same time, we have recognized that an injured party may attack the misuse of patent rights. [citation omitted] To permit recovery of treble damages for the fraudulent procurement of the patent coupled with violations of § 2 accords with these long-recognized procedures. It would also promote the purposes so well expressed in Precision Instrument, 324 U.S. at 816:

> 'A patent by its very nature is affected with a public interest. * * * (It) is an exception to the general rule against monopolies and to the right to access to a free and open market. The far-reaching social and economic consequences of a patent, therefore, give the public a paramount interest in seeing that patent monopolies spring from backgrounds free from fraud or other inequitable conduct and that such monopolies are kept within their legitimate scope.'

III.

Walker's counterclaim alleged that Food Machinery obtained the patent by knowingly and willfully misrepresenting facts to the Patent Office. Proof of this assertion would be sufficient to strip Food Machinery of its exemption from the antitrust laws.[5] By the same token, Food Machinery's good faith would furnish a complete defense. This includes an honest mistake as to the effect of prior installation upon patentability—so-called 'technical fraud.'

To establish monopolization or attempt to monopolize a part of trade or commerce under § 2 of the Sherman Act, it would then be necessary to appraise the exclusionary power of the illegal patent claim in terms of the relevant market for the product involved. Without a definition of that market there is no way to measure Food Machinery's ability to lessen or destroy competition. It may be that the device—knee-action swing diffusers—used in sewage treatment systems does not comprise a relevant market. There may be effective substitutes for the device which do not infringe the patent. This is a matter of proof, as is the amount of damages suffered by Walker.

*** [W]e believe that the case should be remanded for Walker to clarify the asserted violations of § 2 and to offer proof thereon. The trial court dismissed its suit not because Walker failed to allege the relevant market, the dominance of the patented device therein, and the injurious consequences to Walker of the patent's enforcement, but rather on the ground that the United States alone may 'annul or set aside' a patent for fraud in procurement. *** Fairness requires that on remand Walker have the opportunity to make its § 2 claims more specific, to prove the alleged fraud, and to establish the necessary elements of the asserted § 2 violation.

Reversed and remanded.

---

[5] This conclusion applies with equal force to an assignee who maintains and enforces the patent with knowledge of the patent's infirmity.

92 Antitrust Law and Intellectual Property Rights

Mr. Justice HARLAN (concurring)

I join the Court's opinion. I deem it appropriate, however, to add a few comments to what my Brother CLARK has written because the issue decided is one of first impression and to allay possible misapprehension as to the possible reach of this decision.

We hold today that a treble-damage action for monopolization which, but for the existence of a patent, would be violative of § 2 of the Sherman Act may be maintained under s 4 of the Clayton Act if two conditions are satisfied: (1) the relevant patent is shown to have been procured by knowing and willful fraud practiced by the defendant on the Patent Office or, if the defendant was not the original patent applicant, he had been enforcing the patent with knowledge of the fraudulent manner in which it was obtained; and (2) all the elements otherwise necessary to establish a § 2 monopolization charge are proved. Conversely, such a private cause of action would not be made out if the plaintiff: (1) showed no more than invalidity of the patent arising, for example, from a judicial finding of 'obviousness,' or from other factors sometimes compendiously referred to as 'technical fraud'; or (2) showed fraudulent procurement, but no knowledge thereof by the defendant; or (3) failed to prove the elements of a § 2 charge even though he has established actual fraud in the procurement of the patent and the defendant's knowledge of that fraud.

It is well also to recognize the rationale underlying this decision, aimed of course at achieving a suitable accommodation in this area between the differing policies of the patent and antitrust laws. To hold, as we do, that private suits may be instituted under § 4 of the Clayton Act to recover damages for Sherman Act monopolization knowingly practiced under the guise of a patent procured by deliberate fraud, cannot well be thought to impinge upon the policy of the patent laws to encourage inventions and their disclosure. Hence, as to this class of improper patent monopolies, antitrust remedies should be allowed room for full play. On the other hand, to hold, as we do not, that private antitrust suits might also reach monopolies practiced under patents that for one reason or another may turn out to be voidable under one or more of the numerous technicalities attending the issuance of a patent, might well chill the disclosure of inventions through the obtaining of a patent because of fear of the vexations or punitive consequences of treble-damage suits. Hence, this private antitrust remedy should not be deemed available to reach § 2 monopolies carried on under a nonfraudulently procured patent.

These contrasting factors at once serve to justify our present holding and to mark the limits of its application.

Comments and Questions

1. *Walker Process* issues do not generally arise in the context of copyright and trade secrets—and only rarely in the context of trademarks, which do not have to be registered—because these forms of intellectual property do not require government action in order to create IP rights. The Ninth Circuit expanded the reasoning of *Walker Process* in *Handgards, Inc. v. Ethicon, Inc.*, 601 F.2d 986 (9th Cir. 1979). In *Handgards*, the patent owner did not itself commit fraud but

instead legally acquired a patent from another firm that had withheld prior art from the PTO. *Handgards* operationalizes the *Walker Process* dicta in which the majority stated that its opinion "applies with equal force to an assignee who maintains and enforces the patent with knowledge of the patent's infirmity." Walker Process, 382 U.S. at 177 n. 5. An IP owner's attempted enforcement of an IP right that the owner knows is invalid is often called a *Handgards* claim. While Walker Process claims are limited to patents (and perhaps registered trademarks), *Handgards* claims apply to all forms of IP rights. The knowing enforcement of invalid IP rights is discussed more fully later in this chapter.

2. The *Walker Process* Court "concluded that the enforcement of a patent procured by fraud on the Patent Office may be violative of § 2 of the Sherman Act provided the other elements necessary to a § 2 case are present." 382 U.S. at 172. Why doesn't enforcement of a fraudulently procured patent automatically create antitrust liability?

The Court's rule refers to enforcement and not merely procurement of fraudulent patents. Subsequent courts have held that "[w]ithout some effort at enforcement, the patent cannot serve as the foundation of a monopolization case." *California E. Lab., Inc. v. Gould*, 896 F.2d 400, 403 (9th Cir. 1990). The Supreme Court and subsequent courts implicitly argue that absent enforcement, an invalid patent cannot adversely affect competition. For example, the Federal Circuit has held that "[m]ere procurement of a patent, whatever the conduct of the applicant in the procurement, cannot without more affect the welfare of the consumer and cannot in itself violate the antitrust laws." *FMC Corp. v. Manitowoc Co.*, 835 F.2d 1411 (Fed. Cir. 1987). Is that necessarily true?

3. Given that courts require enforcement of the suspect patent in order to create a *Walker Process* claim for excluded competitors, this raises the question of what does it mean to enforce a patent? For decades, most courts defined patent enforcement narrowly to mean only the actual filing of an infringement lawsuit or explicit threats to initiate such litigation imminently. Recently, the Federal Circuit held that a patentee's threats to sue a competitor's customers constituted sufficient enforcement to give that competitor standing to pursue a *Walker Process* claim. *Hydril Co. v. Grant Prideco LP.*, 474 F.3d 1344 (Fed. Cir. 2007). What other conduct should satisfy the enforcement requirement?

Courts have held that the following examples do not constitute patent enforcement: a patentee's publicly flaunting its patent, stating its intent to enforce against infringers, accusing its competitors of infringing, telling a competitor's business partners that the competitor is infringing, collecting royalties for the patent, and refusing to license the patent. *See* Christopher R. Leslie, *Patents of Damocles*, 83 IND. L.J. 133 (2008). Can these activities have an exclusionary effect on the patentee's competitors? If so, should these forms of conduct represent patent enforcement for *Walker Process* claims?

4. It remains unclear how much patent fraud exists. Evidence suggests that many patents are invalid. John R. Allison & Mark A. Lemley, *Empirical Evidence on the Validity of Litigated Patents*, 26 AIPLA Q.J. 185, 205 (1998) (finding that

46 percent of litigated patents were held invalid). This is hardly surprising given the constraints imposed on the Patent & Trademark Office. The PTO reviews over one thousand patent applications every business day. FEDERAL TRADE COMMISSION, TO PROMOTE INNOVATION: THE PROPER BALANCE OF COMPETITION AND PATENT LAW AND POLICY, Executive Summary, 9–10 (Oct. 2003). In recent Federal Trade Commission hearings on competition and patent law, witnesses "estimated that patent examiners have from 8 to 25 hours to read and understand each application, search for prior art, evaluate patentability, communicate with the applicant, work out necessary revisions, and reach and write up conclusions." *Id*. Furthermore, the patent applicant has no affirmative obligation to research for relevant prior art.

The institutional constraints may lead to the issuance of invalid patents. But invalidity is distinct from fraud. All fraudulently procured patents are invalid. *DuPont v. Berkley & Co.*, 620 F.2d 1247, 1274 (8th Cir. 1980) ("A patent procured by fraud by definition would not have issued but for the misrepresentation or non-disclosure. The patent is invalid as improperly issued..."). But not all invalid patents are tainted by fraud.

Patent fraud requires intentional misconduct by the patent applicant to deceive the patent examiner. Most instances of patent invalidity involve situations where prior art invalidates the patent and neither the PTO nor the applicant were aware of the relevant prior art. Furthermore, not all misconduct by a patent applicant rises to the level of fraud, as the Federal Circuit explained in the following case:

Dippin' Dots, Inc. v. Mosey,

476 F.3d 1337 (Fed. Cir. 2007)

Gajarsa, Circuit Judge.

This is a patent infringement and antitrust case dealing with a unique ice cream product. Plaintiffs Dippin' Dots, Inc. and Curt D. Jones (collectively "DDI") appeal from the district court's claim construction and summary judgment of non-infringement of U.S. Patent No. 5,126,156 ("the '156 patent") and from the judgment following jury trial that all claims of that patent are obvious, that the patent is unenforceable due to inequitable conduct during prosecution, and that DDI violated the antitrust laws by asserting a patent that had been procured through fraud on the Patent Office. ***

I. Background

A. The Technology and Patent

The '156 patent, covering subject matter invented by plaintiff Jones and exclusively licensed to plaintiff Dippin' Dots, is directed to a process for making a form of cryogenically prepared novelty ice cream product. *** DDI has commercialized this process. The ice cream it produces, sold under the Dippin' Dots brand, is known to patrons of amusement parks, stadiums, shopping malls, and the like.

B. The Festival Market Sales

Much of the debate in this case centers on the import of sales made at the Festival Market mall in Lexington, Kentucky, more than a year before DDI filed its patent application. Sales made more than one year before the patent's priority date implicate the on-sale bar of 35 U.S.C. § 102(b). For the '156 patent, this critical date is March 6, 1988. Starting on July 24, 1987, Jones sold cryogenically-prepared, largely beaded ice cream at the Festival Market. During Jones's time at Festival Market, which lasted at least until July 29th, over 800 customers purchased his beaded ice cream and others received free samples. The customers were permitted to leave with the product and were not restricted by any kind of confidentiality agreement. Jones later testified that his main goal at the Festival Market was to "get . . . test-marketing information" and not to further develop technical aspects of his product such as particular temperature ranges for storage and service.

It is undisputed that the Festival Market sales were never disclosed to the Patent and Trademark Office ("PTO") during prosecution of the '156 patent. The declaration of commercial success which ultimately persuaded the examiner to grant the patent contained a sworn statement by Jones that "[t]he initial sales were in March of 1988," which was on or after the critical date.

Jones testified that at Festival Market he only practiced the first three steps of the claimed method, not the storing, bringing, or serving steps. He testified that he considered the evidence of what had happened at Festival Market to be irrelevant to patentability. The attorney who prosecuted the '156 patent, Warren Schickli, testified that he considered the sales to have been experimental since the process as practiced at Festival Market could not be feasibly commercially exploited. ***

C. Prior Litigation

The controversy in this case began when several of DDI's distributors severed their relationship, found alternative manufacturing sources, and entered into competition against DDI. DDI initiated a series of patent infringement lawsuits against its new competitors in various judicial districts. *** The defendants counterclaimed for violation of § 2 of the Sherman Act due to DDI's allegation of patent infringement based on a fraudulently acquired patent. This type of antitrust claim has become known as a "*Walker Process*" claim, named for the Supreme Court's decision in *Walker Process Equipment, Inc. v. Food Machinery & Chemical Corp.*, 382 U.S. 172, 177 (1965). ***

By special verdict, the jury found that the sales by Jones prior to March 1988 could be asserted against the patent as prior art and that all claims of the '156 patent were invalid as obvious. The jury also found that both Jones and Schickli had, with intent to deceive, made material misrepresentations or omissions in violation of the duty of candor to the PTO. It also determined that defendants Mini Melts, Inc. and Frosty Bites Distribution had proven all required elements of their antitrust counterclaim, including the requisite fraud on the PTO. ***

II. Discussion

***

C. Inequitable Conduct

We have stated that "[a] patent may be rendered unenforceable for inequitable conduct if an applicant, with intent to mislead or deceive the examiner, fails to disclose material information or submits materially false information to the PTO during prosecution." *Digital Control Inc. v. The Charles Mach. Works*, 437 F.3d 1309, 1313 (Fed.Cir.2006). The party urging unenforceability must show by clear and convincing evidence that the applicant met "thresholds of both materiality and intent." *Molins PLC v. Textron*, 48 F.3d 1172, 1178 (Fed.Cir.1995). Where, as here, those factual findings were made by the district court, we review them for clear error. Id. The ultimate determination of inequitable conduct is committed to the sound discretion of the trial court. We review for abuse of that discretion. *Union Pac. Res. Co. v. Chesapeake Energy Corp.*, 236 F.3d 684, 693-94 (Fed. Cir.2001).

The first prong of the inequitable conduct test, materiality, is clearly met here. As discussed supra, the Festival Market sales render the '156 patent invalid for obviousness. Had those sales been disclosed to the PTO, the patent may or may not have issued. At the very least, the existence of such sales prior to the critical date is a matter that "a reasonable examiner would have considered . . . important in deciding whether to allow the . . . application." *Dayco Prods., Inc. v. Total Containment, Inc.*, 329 F.3d 1358, 1363 (Fed.Cir.2003) [citation omitted].

The question of deceptive intent is a more difficult one, but we find no clear error in the district court's determination on this point. "'Smoking gun' evidence is not required in order to establish an intent to deceive. . . . Rather, this element of inequitable conduct[] must generally be inferred from the facts and circumstances surrounding the applicant's overall conduct." *Paragon Podiatry Lab., Inc. v. KLM Labs. Inc.*, 984 F.2d 1182, 1189 (Fed.Cir.1993). We have noted that omission of sales made before the critical date is especially problematic:

> Absent explanation, the evidence of a knowing failure to disclose sales that bear all the earmarks of commercialization reasonably supports an inference that the inventor's attorney intended to mislead the PTO. The concealment of sales information can be particularly egregious because, unlike the applicant's failure to disclose, for example, a material patent reference, the examiner has no way of securing the information on his own.

Id. at 1193. While DDI wholly neglected to disclose the Festival Market sales to the PTO, it enthusiastically touted sales made after the critical date as evidence of the commercial appeal of its process. That combination of action and omission permits an inference of the minimum, threshold level of intent required for inequitable conduct. The evidence to support a finding of intent may not be particularly strong here (a point we discuss further in Part II.D, infra.) However, the district court was permitted to balance the relatively weak evidence of intent together with the strong evidence that DDI's omission was highly material to the issuance of the '156 patent and to find that on balance, inequitable conduct had occurred. Such a finding, as an exercise of the district court's equitable powers, is within its discretion. [citation omitted] We perceive no abuse of discretion here. The district court's inequitable conduct finding is correct.

D. *Walker Process* Antitrust Claim

The defendants in this case counterclaimed against DDI for violation of § 2 of the Sherman Act, and the same jury that found the patent obvious found DDI liable on that counterclaim. Proof that a patentee has "obtained the patent by knowingly and willfully misrepresenting facts to the Patent Office . . . [is] sufficient to strip [the patentee] of its exemption from the antitrust laws." *Walker Process Equip., Inc. v. Food Mach. & Chem. Corp.*, 382 U.S. 172, 177 (1965). A party who asserts such a fraudulently obtained patent may be subject to an antitrust claim. If a patentee asserts a patent claim and the defendant can demonstrate the required fraud on the PTO, as well as show that "the other elements necessary to a § 2 case are present," the defendant-counterclaimant is entitled to treble damages under the antitrust laws. *Id.* at 175.

The first barrier for a *Walker Process* claimant to clear is the requirement that the patent be obtained through actual fraud upon the PTO. This question is governed by Federal Circuit law. *Nobelpharma AB v. Implant Innovations, Inc.*, 141 F.3d 1059, 1068 (Fed.Cir.1998) (en banc in relevant part). A finding of inequitable conduct does not by itself suffice to support a finding of Walker Process fraud, because "inequitable conduct is a broader, more inclusive concept than the common law fraud needed to support a *Walker Process* counterclaim." *Nobelpharma*, 141 F.3d at 1069. To demonstrate *Walker Process* fraud, a claimant must make higher threshold showings of both materiality and intent than are required to show inequitable conduct. Id. at 1070-71; *C.R. Bard, Inc. v. M3 Sys., Inc.*, 157 F.3d 1340, 1364 (Fed.Cir.1998) (*Walker Process* claimant "must make a greater showing of scienter and materiality than when seeking unenforceability based on conduct before the Patent Office"). Furthermore, a finding of *Walker Process* fraud cannot result from an equitable balancing between the two factors; a strong showing of one cannot make up for a deficiency in the other. *Nobelpharma*, 141 F.3d at 1071. The difference in breadth between inequitable conduct and *Walker Process* fraud admits the possibility of a close case whose facts reach the level of inequitable conduct, but not of fraud before the PTO. This is such a case.

The heightened standard of materiality in a *Walker Process* case requires that the patent would not have issued but for the patent examiner's justifiable reliance on the patentee's misrepresentation or omission. *C.R. Bard*, 157 F.3d at 1364. The defendants have established materiality even under this strict threshold, since the evidence supports a finding that the patent would not have issued if DDI had disclosed the Festival Market sales to the PTO. The difficulty comes in establishing that the omission of those sales was done with fraudulent intent. DDI did make certain statements to the PTO that would have been more completely accurate had it included information about the Festival Market sales. ***

Ultimately, the defendants' fraud case here is built only upon DDI's omission of the Festival Market sales from the prosecution record. While *Walker Process* intent may be inferred from the facts and circumstances of a case, "[a] mere failure to cite a reference to the PTO will not suffice." *Nobelpharma*, 141 F.3d at 1071. This is not to say that an omission always reduces to "mere failure to cite." We acknowledged in *Nobelpharma* "that omissions, as well as misrepresentations, may in limited circumstances support a finding of *Walker Process* fraud . . . because a fraudulent omission can be just as reprehensible as a fraudulent misrepresentation." 141 F.3d at 1070. We believe, though, that to find a prosecution omission fraudulent there must be evidence of intent separable from the simple fact of the omission. A false or clearly misleading prosecution statement may permit an inference that the statement was made with deceptive intent. For instance, evidence may establish that a patent applicant knew one fact and presented another, thus allowing the factfinder to conclude that the applicant intended by the misrepresentation to deceive the examiner. That is not the case with an omission, which could happen for any number of nonfraudulent reasons-the applicant could have had a good-faith belief that disclosure was not necessary, or simply have forgotten to make the required disclosure. In this case, DDI argues that it did not disclose the Festival Market sales to the PTO because it believed that the product there was made without practicing the "storing," "bringing," or "serving" steps of the claim within the specified temperature ranges, and that therefore the Festival Market sales were merely cumulative to other prior art references which also lacked those three steps. The jury was of course allowed to disbelieve or discount evidence tending to support this claim. However, the defendants submitted no evidence of their own-aside from the absence of the Festival Market sales from the prosecution record-which affirmatively shows DDI's fraudulent intent. That intent cannot be shown merely from the absence of evidence which would come about from the jury's discounting DDI's explanation.

Nobelpharma serves as a good example of the sort of facts that do prove *Walker Process* fraud by omission. In that case, the inventors had transmitted to their Swedish patent agent a draft patent application which included a citation to a book written by the patentee in 1977. 141 F.3d at 1062. That book was eventually held to anticipate the patent. *Id.* at 1072. The agent "deleted all reference to the 1977 Book from the patent application that was ultimately filed in Sweden" and then also failed to mention the book in the U.S. application that led to the patent at issue. *Id.* at 1062. When pressed on the issue at trial, the agent "could not explain, even in retrospect, why he deleted all reference to the 1977 Book." *Id.* at 1072. We found that the evidence of actual deletion by the patent agent gave the jury reasonable ground to find intent to defraud by the patentees. Id.

There is no similarly strong evidence that the omission in this case was fraudulent. It might be argued that because the omitted reference was so important to patentability, DDI must have known of its importance and must have made a conscious decision not to disclose it. That argument has some force, but to take it too far would be to allow the high materiality of the omission to be balanced against a lesser showing of deceptive intent by the patentee. Weighing intent and materiality together is appropriate when assessing whether the patentee's prosecution conduct was inequitable. *Molins*, 48 F.3d at 1178. However, when *Walker Process* claimants wield that conduct as a "sword" to obtain antitrust damages rather than as a mere "shield" against enforcement of the patent, *Nobelpharma*, 141 F.3d at 1070, they must prove deceptive intent independently. The defendants have not done so here to the extent necessary for a reasonable jury to find *Walker Process* fraud. The finding of fraud on the PTO is therefore reversed. ***

Comments and Questions

1. The *Dippin' Dots* court makes a critical distinction between fraud and inequitable conduct. Is that distinction persuasive? If a patent applicant engages in inequitable conduct, should that be sufficient to form the basis of an illegal monopolization cause of action (assuming, as the *Walker Process* opinion provides, that the other elements of a Section Two claim are present)? Why or why not?

2. While they are conceptually similar, inequitable conduct and *Walker Process* fraud vary significantly in their legal significance. Inequitable conduct is a defense to a charge of patent infringement while *Walker Process* creates a private cause of action for antitrust plaintiffs. If the defendant can prove inequitable conduct, this should serve as a successful defense in a patent infringement lawsuit, but provides no remedy to the patentee's competitors. However, if the defendant in a patent infringement can prove that the patentee acquired his patent through fraud (and not merely inequitable conduct), this could provide the basis for a *Walker Process* claim, which, if successful, would entitle her to any antitrust damages that she can establish. As the Federal Circuit often says, inequitable conduct is a shield and a *Walker Process* claim is a sword. In short, although one is a defense and one is a counterclaim, they are related and the defendant in a patent infringement would be wise to consider whether one or both of these is an appropriate response.

3. If the patentee in *Dippin' Dots* had a draft of its patent application that included a reference to sales at the state fair and the patentee subsequently removed that reference, would that omission constitute proof of fraud?

4. Because inequitable conduct is a defense in a patent infringement suit, it does not create a private cause of action. The remedy for inequitable conduct is that the patent is unenforceable. Is that a sufficient deterrent for deceptive conduct before the PTO? Why might it not be?

5. Why doesn't the patent applicant's conduct in *Dippin' Dots* rise to the level of fraud? The court tells us that the jury "found that both Jones and Schickli had, with intent to deceive, made material misrepresentations or omissions in violation of the duty of candor to the PTO." Why isn't that fraud sufficient to prove a *Walker Process* claim? Should it be?

Brunswick Corp. v. Riegel Textile Corp.
752 F.2d 261 (7th Cir. 1984)

POSNER, Circuit Judge.

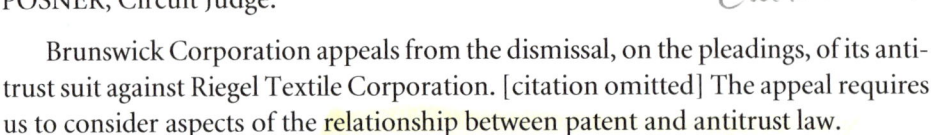

Brunswick Corporation appeals from the dismissal, on the pleadings, of its antitrust suit against Riegel Textile Corporation. [citation omitted] The appeal requires us to consider aspects of the relationship between patent and antitrust law.

The complaint alleges that in 1967 Brunswick invented a new process for making "antistatic yarn," which is used to make garments worn in hospital operating rooms and other areas where there are volatile gases that could be ignited by static electricity. Brunswick, which is not itself a textile manufacturer, disclosed its invention to Riegel, which is. Riegel promised to keep the invention secret. In April 1970 Brunswick applied for a patent on the new process and in August Riegel did likewise—in breach of its agreement with Brunswick. (Riegel denies that this was a breach, but as Brunswick has been given no chance to substantiate the allegations of its complaint we must treat them as true for purposes of this appeal.) Without considering Brunswick's application the Patent Office issued a patent to Riegel in 1972. The Patent Office discovered the Brunswick application in 1973, and in 1975 instituted a patent-interference proceeding to determine priority of invention between Riegel and Brunswick. [citation omitted] That proceeding was still pending before the Patent Office when Brunswick brought this lawsuit in 1982, but since then the Patent Office has held that although Brunswick indeed invented the process first, its patent application was invalid. ***

Brunswick's complaint in this case is that by procuring a patent by fraud and then defending the patent's validity groundlessly in the patent-interference proceeding, Riegel monopolized the production of antistatic yarn in violation of section 2 of the Sherman Act. ***

Getting a patent by means of a fraud on the Patent Office can, but does not always, violate section 2 of the Sherman Act. [citation omitted] A patent entitles the patentee to prevent others from making or selling the patented product or, as here, using the patented production process, and he may be able to use this legal right to restrict competition. If antistatic yarn cannot be produced efficiently other than by using Riegel's patented process, Riegel may be able to exclude competition in the sale of such yarn, in which event it may have "monopoly power"—the "power to control prices or exclude competition." [citation omitted] And to create (or attempt to create, or conspire to create) monopoly power by improper means is to monopolize (or attempt to monopolize, or conspire to monopolize) within the meaning of section 2 of the Sherman Act. [citation omitted]

But "may" is not "does"; and for a patent fraud actually to create or threaten to create monopoly power, and hence violate section 2, three conditions must be satisfied besides proof that the defendant obtained a patent by fraud:

1. The patent must dominate a real market. *See Walker Process Equipment, Inc. v. Food Machinery & Chem. Corp.*, 382 U.S. at 177–78; *American Hoist & Derrick Co. v. Sowa & Sons, Inc.*, 725 F.2d 1350, 1366–67 (Fed.Cir.1984); *Handgards, Inc. v.*

Ethicon, Inc., 601 F.2d 986, 993 n. 13 (9th Cir.1979). Although the Patent Office will not issue a patent on an invention that has no apparent utility, the invention need not have any commercial value at all (other products or processes may be superior substitutes), and it certainly need not have enough value to enable the patentee to drive all or most substitutes from the market. If a patent has no significant impact in the marketplace, the circumstances of its issuance cannot have any antitrust significance.

2. The invention sought to be patented must not be patentable. If the invention is patentable, it does not matter from an antitrust standpoint what skullduggery the defendant may have used to get the patent issued or transferred to him. The power over price that patent rights confer is lawful, and is no greater than it otherwise would be just because the person exercising the rights is not the one entitled by law to do so. The distinction between a fraud that leads the Patent Office to issue a patent on an unpatentable invention (as in a case where the patent applicant concealed from the Patent Office the fact that the invention already was in the public domain) and one that merely operates to take the patent opportunity away from the real inventor (who but for the fraud would have gotten a valid patent that would have yielded him a royalty measured by the monopoly power that the patent conferred) is supported by analogy to cases holding that fraud on the Patent Office, to be actionable as patent fraud, must be material in the sense that the patent would not have been issued but for the misconduct. [citation omitted] Equally, for a fraud to be material in an antitrust sense the plaintiff must show that but for the fraud no patent would have been issued to anyone. If a patent would have been issued to someone, the fraud could but have diverted market power from the one who had the right to possess and exploit it to someone else.

3. The patent must have some colorable validity, conferred for example by the patentee's efforts to enforce it by bringing patent-infringement suits. Indeed, some formulations of the antitrust offense of patent fraud make it seem that the offense is not the fraudulent procuring of a patent in circumstances that create monopoly power but the bringing of groundless suits for patent infringement. [citation omitted] This metamorphosis is natural because most patent-antitrust claims are asserted as counterclaims to patent-infringement suits and because the abusive prosecution of such suits could violate the antitrust laws even if the patent had not been obtained by fraud. [citation omitted] But enforcement actions are not a sine qua non of monopolizing by patent fraud. Since a patent known to the trade to be invalid will not discourage competitors from making the patented product or using the patented process, and so will not confer monopoly power, suing an infringer is some evidence that the patent has (or at least the patentee is seeking to clothe it with) some colorable validity that might deter competitors. But it is not indispensable evidence; the concern of section 2 is with exclusion of competition, not with the particular means of exclusion. Indeed, one might argue that just by virtue of being issued, a patent would have some apparent validity and that no more should be necessary. But this would go too far the other way. Since patents are issued in ex parte proceedings, and since by hypothesis the patent applicant had

to use fraud to persuade the Patent Office to issue the patent, the patent might not fool anybody in the defendant's market.

Let us see whether these three conditions are satisfied by the complaint in this case. Right off the bat there is a problem with condition (1), as Brunswick's complaint does not allege that the business of making and selling antistatic yarn is an economically meaningful market. However, facts are pleaded that allow an inference that antistatic yarn probably does not have good substitutes, in which event its sole producer could maintain its price significantly above the cost of production and sale.

There is a serious problem, however, with condition (2). Far from alleging that the process for making antistatic yarn that Riegel patented is not patentable, the complaint alleges that it is. Brunswick's only objection is to the patentee's identity; it thinks that it rather than Riegel should be the patentee. But as we have already suggested, to say that a patent should have been issued because the invention covered by it is patentable, but should have been issued to a different person and would have been but for fraud (the breach of the promise to Brunswick not to disclose its invention), is to say in effect that the patentee stole the patent from its rightful owner; and stealing a valid patent is not at all the same thing, from an antitrust standpoint, as obtaining an invalid patent. Until unmasked in an infringement or cancellation or other proceeding, a patent on an unpatentable invention may create a monopoly by discouraging (through litigation or other means) others from making the patented product, just as a valid patent may, but the monopoly that such a patent creates is illegal, and hence actionable under antitrust law. The theft of a perfectly valid patent, in contrast, creates no monopoly power; it merely shifts a lawful monopoly into different hands. This has no antitrust significance, although it hurts the lawful owner of the monopoly power.

The purpose of the antitrust laws as it is understood in the modern cases is to preserve the health of the competitive process—which means, so far as a case such as this is concerned, to discourage practices that make it hard for consumers to buy at competitive prices—rather than to promote the welfare of particular competitors. This point was implicit in the famous dictum of *Brown Shoe Co. v. United States*, 370 U.S. 294, 320 (1962), that antitrust law (the Court was speaking of section 7 of the Clayton Act, but the point has been understood to be general) is concerned "with the protection of competition, not competitors "(emphasis in original), and has been repeated with growing emphasis in recent years by this and other courts. [citation omitted] True, competitors as well as consumers still have standing to complain about antitrust violations, but that is because competitors are thought to be effective (maybe indispensable) surrogates for the many consumers who do not realize they are the victims of monopolistic practices, or if they do may lack incentives to bring suit because the harm to an individual consumer may be tiny even though the aggregate harm is immense. [citation omitted] If no consumer interest can be discerned even remotely in a suit brought by a competitor—if, as here, a victory for the competitor can confer no benefit, certain or probable, present or future, on consumers—a court is entitled to question whether a violation of antitrust law is being charged. [citation omitted] ***

We cannot find the consumer interest in this case. Brunswick is complaining not because Riegel is gouging the consumer by charging a monopoly price for antistatic yarn, but because Riegel took away a monopoly that rightfully belonged to Brunswick as the real inventor. ***

It is not a purpose of antitrust law to confer patents or to resolve disputes between rival applicants for a patent. From the standpoint of antitrust law, concerned as it is with consumer welfare, it is a matter of indifference whether Riegel or Brunswick exploits a monopoly of antistatic yarn. [citation omitted] Indeed, if anything, competitive pricing is more likely if Brunswick loses this suit than if it wins it. If Brunswick is confident that Riegel's patent is invalid, it can go into the antistatic-yarn business itself, with little fear of being held liable for patent infringement; and by entering, it will inject some competition into that market for the first time. Brunswick argues that it could not induce textile manufacturers to produce antistatic yarn under license from it since they would fear that Riegel would sue them, however baselessly, for patent infringement. But when a patentee (or, as in this case, a patent applicant) licenses his patent to other firms, he typically agrees to indemnify them for any costs incurred in patent-infringement suits brought against them. Brunswick, a large corporation, can afford to indemnify its licensees and would promise to do so if it really believed that it and not Riegel was the lawful owner of the patent. ***

[I]f a form of wrongdoing (stealing a patentable process) cannot cause antitrust injury to anyone, because it has no tendency to raise prices or reduce output or do anything else that hurts consumer or other interests protected by the antitrust laws, it does not violate those laws at all. It is then not a matter of the case having been brought by the wrong plaintiff, as in Brunswick, but of there being no possible plaintiff because the defendant's conduct has no tendency to injure anyone intended to be benefited by the antitrust laws. ***

The third condition for a patent fraud to violate section 2 of the Sherman Act — that the defendant has made efforts to give the color of validity to his patent on an unpatentable invention — cannot be met in a case where the plaintiff himself asserts that the underlying invention is patentable. This reinforces our conclusion that the complaint states no antitrust cause of action. ***

Comments and Questions

1. In *Brunswick*, Judge Posner writes, "If the invention is patentable, it does not matter from an antitrust standpoint what skullduggery the defendant may have used to get the patent issued or transferred to him." Is that necessarily true? So long as the patent should issue to *someone*, why should antitrust care about who gets it and how they got? (Remember, we're asking why *antitrust law* cares, not fraud or tort or any other area of law.)

Similarly, Judge Posner asserts that "[t]he theft of a perfectly valid patent . . . creates no monopoly power; it merely shifts a lawful monopoly into different hands. This has no antitrust significance, although it hurts the lawful owner of the monopoly power." Can you find "antitrust significance" in Riegel's conduct?

2. Judge Posner's reasoning suggests that no one has an antitrust claim against Riegel, not even the federal government. Do you think that is the correct result? Why or why not?

Bibliography of Additional Resources

Suzanne K. Brown, *Omission Possible: Nobelpharma v. Implant Innovations Makes Material Omissions in Patent Applications a Possible Source of Liability for Antitrust Counterclaims,* 25 J. Corp. L. 179 (1999)

Arun Chandra, *Antitrust Liability for Attempting to Enforce a Fraudulent Patent,* 81 J. Pat. & Trademark Off. Soc'y 201 (1999)

James B. Kobak, Jr., *Professional Real Estate Investors and the Future of Patent-Antitrust Litigation:* Walker Process *and* Handgards *Meet* Noerr-Pennington, 63 Antitrust, L.J. 185 (1994)

B. Sham Litigation

CVD, Inc. v. Raytheon Co.
769 F.2d 842 (1st Cir. 1985)

RE, Chief Judge:

In this action, brought under the antitrust laws of the United States, defendant Raytheon Company (Raytheon) appeals from a judgment, entered pursuant to a special jury verdict, in the District Court for the District of Massachusetts. The judgment awarded plaintiff CVD, Inc. ("CVD") treble damages of $3,180, plus attorneys' fees and costs, granted plaintiffs declaratory relief, and dismissed the defendant's counterclaims.

The dispute between plaintiffs, CVD, Inc., Robert Donadio and Joseph Connolly, both former Raytheon employees, and defendant Raytheon pertains to the manufacture of zinc selenide (ZnSe) and zinc sulfide (ZnS) by a process known as chemical vapor deposition (cvd). On August 28, 1981, plaintiffs Donadio, Connolly, and CVD initiated this action, contending that defendant Raytheon attempted to monopolize the market for ZnSe and ZnS made by the cvd process, in violation of 15 U.S.C. § 2 (1982), and that a licensing agreement between the plaintiffs and Raytheon was an unreasonable restraint of interstate commerce and trade in violation of 15 U.S.C. § 1 (1982). The complaint sought damages and a declaratory judgment that the agreement between Raytheon and CVD, purporting to license the cvd process, was void and unenforceable. The defendant counterclaimed for breach of contract, misappropriation of trade secrets, breach of fiduciary duty, and violation of the Massachusetts consumer protection statute.

After a 27 day trial, in response to special interrogatories formulated by the court, the jury returned a verdict for the plaintiffs. *** Since we find that the jury verdict was supported by sufficient evidence *** the judgment of the district court is affirmed.

Facts

Raytheon, a Delaware corporation with executive offices in Massachusetts, is a diversified company specializing in commercial and military electronics, materials and weapons. In 1959, plaintiff-appellee Donadio was hired as an engineer in the Advanced Materials Department at Raytheon. He was employed there until he resigned in the fall of 1979 in order to form CVD. Plaintiff-appellee Connolly was hired by Raytheon in 1972, and was employed there continuously until he also left to form CVD. Donadio and Connally had signed employment agreements promising to protect Raytheon's proprietary information. Both were involved in the manufacture of zinc selenide and zinc sulfide by chemical vapor deposition (ZnSe/cvd or ZnS/cvd). This process combines vaporized zinc solids with hydrogen sulfide or hydrogen selenide in specially modified, high-temperature (approximately 900° centigrade) vacuum furnaces. The resulting solid materials are further processed into high precision optical materials which are used to make, among other things, infrared windows for lasers, high-speed aircraft, and missiles. These materials are the only suitable materials for certain demanding optical uses. Most of Raytheon's work on these materials had been done under contracts with the federal government. As part of its obligation under these contracts, Raytheon was required to provide periodic reports that detailed the technology and processes used in the production operation.

In the fall of 1979, Donadio informed his supervisor, Dr. James Pappis, the manager of the Advanced Materials Department, that he intended to leave Raytheon to start a new company to manufacture ZnS and ZnSe by the cvd process. Pappis replied that this would present legal difficulties in light of Donadio's employment agreement and Raytheon's trade secrets. The next day Pappis consulted with Leo Reynolds, a patent attorney with Raytheon, who spoke with Pappis briefly, and examined some drawings and the government reports for the purpose of determining whether the cvd process contained trade secrets.

The following day Donadio and Connolly met with Pappis, Reynolds, Joseph Pannone, the Patent Counsel for Raytheon, and another Raytheon executive. Reynolds told Donadio and Connolly that they could not manufacture ZnS and ZnSe by the cvd process without using Raytheon trade secrets. Although Donadio disputed Reynolds' assertion that trade secrets were involved, Reynolds threatened to sue if they began to manufacture ZnS/cvd or ZnSe/cvd without a license from Raytheon. Soon thereafter, Donadio and Connolly were asked to leave Raytheon.

After this meeting, Donadio retained an attorney, Jerry Cohen, who specialized in intellectual property. In discussions with Raytheon, Cohen took the position that there were no trade secrets in Raytheon's chemical vapor deposition process since the technology had been published in government reports, and, therefore, was in the public domain. Raytheon asserted, and later attempted to prove at trial, that important details were not included in the reports, and that, consequently, the reports were too vague to permit anyone to reproduce the cvd system. Cohen asked Reynolds for a list of what Raytheon claimed to be trade secrets. Reynolds refused to comply with the request on the ground he could not provide an "all-inclusive" list.

At a later meeting, Reynolds read orally a list of claimed secrets but Cohen disputed all the items on the list.

In attempting to settle the dispute, Cohen proposed an agreement in which CVD would not be obligated to pay royalties if CVD could prove that no Raytheon trade secrets were used in its operations. This proposal was refused. Several other formulas for resolving the dispute were also discussed. Raytheon, however, held firm to its position that the plaintiffs could not manufacture ZnS/cvd or ZnSe/cvd without using Raytheon trade secrets, and insisted on a royalty rate based upon a flat percentage of revenue or volume for a ten-year period. Eventually, on February 15, 1980, an agreement was signed, providing for a 15% royalty on earnings for ZnSe and 8% for ZnS. No payments were ever made by CVD under the contract, however, and in 1981 plaintiffs filed the present action. ***

Sherman Act

This case presents a difficult question pertaining to the interaction of the federal antitrust laws and state trade secrets law. Guidance in resolving these questions can be found in analogous, but not identical, issues presented in cases in which patent infringement suits have been brought in bad faith with an intent to restrain competition or monopolize. See, e.g., *Walker Process Equipment, Inc. v. Food Machinery & Chemical Corp.*, 382 U.S. 172 (1965) [citation omitted].

In examining "bad faith" patent infringement claims, courts have balanced the public interest in free competition, as manifested in the antitrust laws, with the federal interest in the enforcement of the patent laws, and the first amendment interest in the free access to courts. See, e.g., *Walker Process*, supra, 382 U.S. at 177–78 ***

There are, of course, significant differences between patent and trade secret protection. The scope of protectible trade secrets is far broader than the scope of patentable technology. [citation omitted] Under Massachusetts law, a trade secret may consist of:

> any formula, pattern, device or compilation of information which is used in one's business, and which gives him an opportunity to obtain an advantage over competitors who do not know or use it. It may be ... a process of manufacturing. ... A trade secret is a process or device for continuous use in the operation of the business. Generally it relates to the production of goods, as, for example, a machine or formula for the production of an article.

[citation omitted]

The basis for the federal patent system is found expressly in the Constitution. *See* U.S. Const. art. I, § 8, cl. 8. A patent confers a legal monopoly for a limited period of time. In return for the patent, the patentee must fully disclose the patented invention or process. After the expiration of the statutory period, the patentee loses all exclusive rights to the patent. [citation omitted]

The cornerstone of a trade secret, however, is secrecy. Once a trade secret enters the public domain, the possessor's exclusive rights to the secret are lost.

Enforcement of Intellectual Property Rights

Moreover, unlike a patent, a trade secret affords no rights against the independent development of the same technology or knowledge by others. [citation omitted]

As with patent law, the rationale behind state trade secret law is to encourage invention, and to provide innovators with protection for the fruits of their labors. [citation omitted] In addition, trade secret law is intended to maintain and promote standards of commercial ethics and fair dealing. [citation omitted]

In this case, the court must resolve a dispute which brings into focus the tension between the antitrust laws and the public interest in the licensing of trade secrets. Generally, there is a significant public interest in the licensing of trade secrets. By licensing a trade secret, the licensor partially releases his monopoly position and effectively disseminates information. [citation omitted] The result, it is hoped, is greater competition that will enure to the benefit of the public.

Like the holders of other intellectual property rights, possessors of trade secrets are entitled to assert their rights against would-be infringers and to defend their rights in court. [citation omitted] Nevertheless, the assertion in bad faith of trade secret claims, that is, with the knowledge that no trade secrets exist, for the purpose of restraining competition does not further the policies of either the antitrust or the trade secrets laws. [citation omitted] Thus, it seems clear that the assertion of a trade secret claim in bad faith, in an attempt to monopolize, can be a violation of the antitrust laws. [citation omitted] Similarly, it is well established that an agreement which purports to license trade secrets, but in reality, is no more than a sham, or device designed to restrict competition, may violate the antitrust laws. [citation omitted]

We believe that the proper balance between the antitrust laws and trade secrets law is achieved by requiring an antitrust plaintiff to prove, in addition to the other elements of an antitrust violation, by clear and convincing evidence, that the defendant asserted trade secrets with the knowledge that no trade secrets existed. [citation omitted] To succeed in an attempted monopolization claim under section 2 of the Sherman Act, the plaintiff must prove that the defendant had the specific intent to monopolize the relevant market, and a dangerous probability of success. As other courts have noted, a specific intent to monopolize or restrain competition can often be inferred from a finding of bad faith. [citation omitted]

This case differs from the Walker Process line of cases in that Raytheon did not actually initiate litigation against the plaintiffs. Instead, the evidence indicates that it used the threat of litigation to exact a licensing agreement from the plaintiffs. In this case, litigation with Raytheon would have proved ruinous to the newly formed corporation, and effectively foreclosed competition in the relevant market. Under these circumstances, we hold that the threat of unfounded trade secrets litigation in bad faith is sufficient to constitute a cause of action under the antitrust laws, provided that the other essential elements of a violation are proven.

Relevant Market

It is undisputed that, until CVD's formation, Raytheon was the only company in the world to produce for commercial sale zinc selenide or zinc sulfide by chemical vapor deposition. *** In answer to a special interrogatory, the jury found that the defendant Raytheon had market power as to both zinc sulfide and zinc selenide. This conclusion is amply supported by the evidence.

Trade Secrets and Bad Faith

The proof as to the existence of trade secrets and the defendant's bad faith in asserting them, if they did not exist, is necessarily intertwined. As noted, in order to be protected by law, a trade secret must be kept in secret. [citations omitted] Heroic measures to ensure secrecy are not essential, but reasonable precautions must be taken to protect the information. ***

It is also "well settled that an employee upon terminating his employment may carry away and use the general skill or knowledge acquired during the course of the employment." [citation omitted] This principle effectuates the public interest in labor mobility, promotes the employee's freedom to practice a profession, and freedom of competition. [citation omitted]

The existence of trade secrets in Raytheon's ZnS/cvd and ZnSe/cvd manufacturing process depends upon the degree of public disclosure of the relevant information. It is the determination of this Court that the jury could have found sufficient evidence that the essential information contained in the cvd technology had entered the public domain, and, therefore, Raytheon possessed no trade secrets in this technology. Furthermore, there was sufficient evidence for the jury to find that Raytheon knew that no trade secrets existed. Hence, it was proper for the jury to conclude that Raytheon's assertion of trade secrets and exaction of the licensing agreement were in bad faith.

Specifically, upon the evidence presented, the jury could have found the following facts to support its conclusions. The process of chemical vapor deposition generally was well known in the scientific community. Raytheon regularly published schematics, diagrams, run conditions, and other detailed information related to the production of ZnS/cvd and ZnSe/cvd in periodic reports supplied to the government as part of Raytheon's contractual obligations. Although some of the reports were temporarily classified by the government for security purposes, all of these reports were available to the public by 1979. At trial, the plaintiffs demonstrated that nearly all the details originally claimed as trade secrets were published in the reports. There was also evidence that the details not specifically mentioned in the reports were either obvious or insignificant, or both.

In addition, Raytheon employees had published papers relating to cvd technology in scientific journals. Raytheon had also produced a film about this technology which was shown to a convention of engineers (and later to the jury). Photographs of the interior of the cvd furnace were published in various publications. Raytheon employees gave lectures and speeches on the technology to various groups, often accompanied by viewgraphs or slides of the equipment. Although access to the facility was limited, visitors were permitted to view the furnaces. Donadio testified that, based on the information disclosed to the public, a competent engineer could construct and operate a viable system for the production of zinc selenide or zinc sulfide through chemical vapor deposition. *** [O]n cross-examination, the defendant's experts admitted that many of the details claimed to be trade secrets would occur as logical, if not obvious, choices to a competent engineer designing a system. Under these circumstances, it is not for this Court to judge the credibility of witnesses. The jury, therefore, was entitled to, and apparently did, rely upon and give credence to the plaintiffs' evidence over that of the defendant.

Also significant, as to both the existence of trade secrets and the issue of bad faith, was Raytheon's failure to follow its own established procedures for the protection of trade secrets. For example, despite a written policy that all confidential drawings and documents were to be stamped with a restrictive legend warning of the document's confidential nature, none of the engineering drawings for the cvd furnaces was stamped or marked with any restrictive legend. Furthermore, there was no evidence that Donadio or Connolly took any engineering drawings with them when they left Raytheon. Indeed, there was evidence, albeit inconclusive, tending to suggest that Raytheon had altered drawings after the commencement of this litigation to conform to CVD drawings.

There was also sufficient evidence for the jury to conclude that Raytheon had made a policy decision not to protect at least certain aspects of the cvd process. For example, Raytheon's patent department instructed Raytheon's engineering personnel that an "invention disclosure should be submitted on every new or improved device, system, method or composition of matter . . . which is more than routine engineering." These forms were reviewed by a committee and a determination was made as to how they should be protected. The disclosures were then assigned a status code reflecting the committee's determination. Code 3 meant that the item should be protected as a trade secret. Code 2 indicated that a patent application would not be filed, and that the item was not to be protected as a trade secret. Items that were designated for protection as trade secrets were filed in a file section referred to as the "trade secrets drawer."

Evidence introduced at trial indicated that no invention disclosures relating to the manufacture of zinc selenide or zinc sulfide by the cvd process were ever designated for protection as a trade secret. Moreover, nothing related to ZnS/cvd or ZnSe/cvd was found in the "trade secrets drawer." ***

Other evidence that would tend to prove bad faith includes the fact that Reynolds asserted trade secrets, and threatened litigation, after only a cursory investigation without thoroughly examining the majority of the government reports or the extent of public disclosure. Reynolds also refused to give Cohen a list of claimed secrets. From this, the jury could have inferred that Reynolds could not make such a list because he knew that there were no secrets. There was also testimony that Cohen pointed out to Reynolds that all the items Reynolds claimed were trade secrets at their January 22, 1980 meeting were in fact published in the government reports.

In short, the record reveals the extensive public disclosure, Raytheon's failure to follow its own procedures for trade secret protection, its refusal to specify trade secrets in asserting its claims or in the agreement, and its insistence on a flat ten-year term at 15% and 8% royalty rates. In light of these facts, the jury could have concluded that Raytheon knew it had no trade secrets, yet nevertheless asserted them in bad faith in order to restrain competition and monopolize the ZnS/cvd and ZnSe/cvd markets. ***

The practice at issue in this case, the assertion of claims in bad faith, is a predatory practice under the antitrust laws. As a cause of action, it descends directly from the Walker Process case and its progeny. ***

Conclusion

Our review of the record leads us to conclude that there was sufficient evidence to support the jury's findings of fact. The exaction of a licensing agreement through the bad faith assertion of trade secrets by a party in a far superior bargaining position with the intention of restraining competition and monopolizing the market is a violation of the antitrust laws. ***

Comments and Questions

1. The court states that a "patent confers a legal monopoly for a limited period of time." What does the court mean by "legal monopoly"?

2. The court states: "By licensing a trade secret, the licensor partially releases his monopoly position and effectively disseminates information." Do owners of trade secrets necessarily have a "monopoly position"? Assuming that they do, does the licensing of a trade secret actually undermine the original inventor's monopoly power?

3. The court noted the presence of evidence that Raytheon may have altered its drawings to appear more like CVD's drawings. Assuming that the jury believes this evidence, what is the legal significance of such alterations in an antitrust case?

4. In its appeal, Raytheon argued that CVD did not suffer antitrust injury, "which is to say injury of the type the antitrust laws were intended to prevent …" Courts generally treat antitrust injury as injury caused by an unreasonable restraint of competition. In this case, the First Circuit reasoned that:

> the evidence indicates that Raytheon gave Donadio and Connolly three choices: (1) defend a trade secrets infringement suit against Raytheon; (2) refrain from competing with Raytheon in the manufacture of ZnS/cvd and ZnSe/cvd; or (3) take a license from Raytheon for the use of alleged trade secrets. All of the choices would have had an adverse economic impact on the plaintiffs, as well as an anticompetitive effect. Indeed, the first two alternatives would have been fatal to CVD's existence as a viable concern. Since Raytheon asserted its claim in bad faith, with the intent to restrain competition, it is the type of offense the antitrust laws are designed to prevent. The injury to CVD, legal expenses incurred in attempting to resolve Raytheon's bad faith claims, reflects the anticompetitive effect of acts with an anticompetitive intent.

Should legal expenses constitute antitrust injury?

Enforcement of Intellectual Property Rights 111

5. With this as the measure of antitrust injury, the damages alleged in the case were very low. CVD litigated the case all the way up to the First Circuit and received the damages that it had requested: the federal appeals court upheld the jury's award of $1,060 for legal expenses. Why pursue such a low amount of money?

One objective of CVD was apparently to nullify the licensing agreement that it had entered into with Raytheon. If that is the true goal of the lawsuit, why not just bring a declaratory judgment action to have the contract invalidated? Why did the plaintiff bring suit under the antitrust laws?

6. If Raytheon was merely posturing or puffing up their trade secrets claim in their negotiations with CVD, should that be sufficient to give rise to antitrust liability? Should CDV have signed the licensing agreement, or should they have waited for Raytheon to initiate litigation for violating the state trade secrets law? What advice would you have given CVD if you were its attorney during the licensing negotiations?

Note on the Noerr-Pennington Doctrine

The Supreme Court famously discussed the possibility of antitrust liability predicated on government lobbying efforts in *Eastern Railroad Presidents Conference v. Noerr Motor Freight, Inc.*, 365 U.S. 127 (1961). *Noerr* concerned a publicity campaign by members of the railroad industry to influence the public and the government on the desirability of railroad transportation vis-à-vis trucking. This publicity campaign entailed the use of shell organizations that made exaggerated claims about the dangers and costs of trucking. Members of the trucking industry sued members of the railroad industry for violations of the Sherman Act. The railroad companies

> "admitted that they had conducted a publicity campaign designed to influence the passage of state laws" regulating the trucking industry, but argued that it was within their rights to "to inform the public and the legislatures of the several states of the truth with regard to the enormous damage done to the roads by the operators of heavy and especially of overweight trucks, with regard to their repeated and deliberate violations of the law limiting the weight and speed of big trucks, with regard to their failure to pay their fair share of the cost of constructing, maintaining and repairing the roads, and with regard to the driving hazards they create."

Id. at 131.

The district court agreed with the railroads that simply lobbying for government action was not sufficient to incur antitrust liability. Nevertheless, the court held for the plaintiffs, finding that the railroads' campaign contained "additional factors" that brought it out of First Amendment protection and subjected it to antitrust liability; specifically, the campaign "was malicious and fraudulent-malicious in that its only purpose was to destroy the truckers as competitors . . . and that the railroads' campaign also had as an important, if not overriding, purpose the destruction of the truckers' goodwill, among both the general public and the truckers' existing customers, and thus injured the truckers in ways unrelated to the passage or enforcement of law." *Id.* at 133. The court awarded damages to the truckers' trade association and issued a broad injunction preventing the railroad companies from publicly criticizing the truckers. The court of appeals affirmed.

The Supreme Court reversed and issued a series of opinions that are generally referred to as the *Noerr-Pennington* Doctrine or sometimes simply *Noerr* immunity. District Judge Lowell Jensen of the Northern District of California summarized this evolution as follows:

The Noerr-Pennington Doctrine

In *Eastern Railroad Presidents Conference, et al. v. Noerr Motor Freight, Inc., et al.*, 365 U.S. 127 (1961), the Supreme Court held that the Sherman Act did not bar an association of railroad companies from banding together to influence legislation destructive of the trucking industry. The unanimous opinion of the Court purported only to interpret the antitrust laws. In doing so, the Court considered several factors. First, the Court reasoned that representative democracy depends on "the ability of the people to make their wishes known to their representatives." *Id.* at 137. The Sherman Act was not intended to regulate this type of political activity, but only business activity. Second, interpreting the Sherman Act to bar the railroads' lobbying activities would "raise important constitutional questions." *Id.* at 138. The Court concluded that the railroads' activities were not prohibited under the Sherman Act.

In *United Mine Workers v. Pennington,* 381 U.S. 657 (1965), the Court broadened the Noerr holding to encompass the petitioning of other public officials besides legislators. Pennington also emphasized the irrelevance of the petitioner's underlying purpose. "*Noerr* shields from the Sherman Act a concerted effort to influence public officials regardless of intent or purpose." *Id.* at 670.

Despite this language, *Noerr-Pennington* does not shield all petitioning activity from antitrust liability. The *Noerr* Court recognized a "sham" exception: if petitioning activity, "ostensibly directed toward influencing governmental action, is a mere sham to cover what is actually nothing more than an attempt to interfere directly with the business relationships of a competitor," Sherman Act liability is justified. *Noerr* 365 U.S. at 144. However, it is not a sham if the activity is "a genuine effort to influence legislation and law enforcement practices." *Id.*

The concept of the sham exception was further refined in *California Motor Transport Co. v. Trucking Unlimited,* 404 U.S. 508 (1972). In that case, defendants allegedly conspired to monopolize trade and commerce in the transportation of goods by instituting administrative and judicial proceedings "to resist and defeat [plaintiffs'] applications . . . to acquire operating rights or to transfer or register those rights." The Court, recognizing the applicability of Noerr to petitioning in the courts, distinguished administrative and adjudicatory fora from the legislative lobbying at issue in *Noerr*. Noting that certain types of unethical conduct, "condoned in the political arena," were sanctionable in the adjudicatory context, the Court implied that the scope of protected petitioning activity was narrower in adjudicatory fora than for legislative lobbying. *Trucking Unlimited* at 513. The Court held that institution of baseless, repetitive claims, in order to effectively bar competitors from meaningful access to administrative agencies and the courts, was not "political expression" entitled to First Amendment protection. Such activity fell within *Noerr*'s sham exception, "as adapted to the adjudicatory process."

Trucking Unlimited at 516. USS-POSCO Industries v. Contra Costa County Bldg. & Const. Trades Council, 692 F.Supp. 1166, 1168–69 (N.D.Cal. 1988).

The fact that bringing anticompetitive litigation can provide the basis for antitrust liability is critically important for the owners of intellectual property. IP owners defend their legitimate rights by instituting (or threatening) infringement litigation. Infringement lawsuits can often be characterized as anticompetitive. Consequently, defendants in infringement cases often bring antitrust counterclaims, asserting that the infringement suit is designed to exclude them from the market. The *Noerr-Pennington* doctrine provides an antitrust defense for the IP owners unless their lawsuit is a sham, in which case the IP owner's conduct falls outside of the *Noerr-Pennington* doctrine. (The antitrust plaintiff will still have to prove all of the elements of an antitrust violation, discussed in Chapter 2. Proving that the IP owner's infringement suit is a sham simply eliminates the IP's owner's *Noerr-Pennington* defense to an antitrust claim.) The Supreme Court laid out the current legal test for determining whether litigation is a sham in the following case:

Professional Real Estate Investors v. Columbia Pictures,
508 U.S. 49 (1993)

Justice THOMAS delivered the opinion of the Court.

This case requires us to define the "sham" exception to the doctrine of antitrust immunity first identified in *Eastern Railroad Presidents Conference v. Noerr Motor Freight, Inc.*, 365 U.S. 127 (1961), as that doctrine applies in the litigation context. Under the sham exception, activity "ostensibly directed toward influencing governmental action" does not qualify for *Noerr* immunity if it "is a mere sham to cover . . . an attempt to interfere directly with the business relationships of a competitor." [citation omitted] We hold that litigation cannot be deprived of immunity as a sham unless the litigation is objectively baseless. The Court of Appeals for the Ninth Circuit refused to characterize as sham a lawsuit that the antitrust defendant admittedly had probable cause to institute. We affirm.

I

Petitioners Professional Real Estate Investors, Inc., and Kenneth F. Irwin (collectively, PRE) operated La Mancha Private Club and Villas, a resort hotel in Palm Springs, California. Having installed videodisc players in the resort's hotel

114 *Antitrust Law and Intellectual Property Rights*

rooms and assembled a library of more than 200 motion picture titles, PRE rented videodiscs to guests for in-room viewing. PRE also sought to develop a market for the sale of videodisc players to other hotels wishing to offer in-room viewing of prerecorded material. Respondents, Columbia Pictures Industries, Inc., and seven other major motion picture studios (collectively, Columbia), held copyrights to the motion pictures recorded on the videodiscs that PRE purchased. Columbia also licensed the transmission of copyrighted motion pictures to hotel rooms through a wired cable system called Spectradyne. PRE therefore competed with Columbia not only for the viewing market at La Mancha but also for the broader market for in-room entertainment services in hotels.

In 1983, Columbia sued PRE for alleged copyright infringement through the rental of videodiscs for viewing in hotel rooms. PRE counterclaimed, charging Columbia with violations of §§ 1 and 2 of the Sherman Act, and various state-law infractions. In particular, PRE alleged that Columbia's copyright action was a mere sham that cloaked underlying acts of monopolization and conspiracy to restrain trade.

The parties filed cross-motions for summary judgment on Columbia's copyright claim and postponed further discovery on PRE's antitrust counterclaims. Columbia did not dispute that PRE could freely sell or lease lawfully purchased videodiscs under the Copyright Act's "first sale" doctrine, [citation omitted] and PRE conceded that the playing of videodiscs constituted "performance" of motion pictures, [citation omitted] As a result, summary judgment depended solely on whether rental of videodiscs for in-room viewing infringed Columbia's exclusive right to "perform the copyrighted work[s] publicly." § 106(4). Ruling that such rental did not constitute public performance, the District Court entered summary judgment for PRE. [citation omitted] The Court of Appeals affirmed on the grounds that a hotel room was not a "public place" and that PRE did not "transmit or otherwise communicate" Columbia's motion pictures. [citation omitted]

On remand, Columbia sought summary judgment on PRE's antitrust claims, arguing that the original copyright infringement action was no sham and was therefore entitled to immunity under *Eastern Railroad Presidents Conference v. Noerr Motor Freight, Inc., supra.* Reasoning that the infringement action "was clearly a legitimate effort and therefore not a sham," [citation omitted] the District Court granted the motion ***. The Court of Appeals affirmed. ***

II

*** Those who petition government for redress are generally immune from antitrust liability. We first recognized in *Eastern Railroad Presidents Conference v. Noerr Motor Freight, Inc.*, 365 U.S. 127 (1961), that "the Sherman Act does not prohibit ... persons from associating together in an attempt to persuade the legislature or the executive to take particular action with respect to a law that would produce a restraint or a monopoly." *Id.*, at 136. Accord, *Mine Workers v. Pennington*, 381 U.S. 657, 669 (1965). In light of the government's "power to act in [its] representative capacity" and "to take actions . . . that operate to restrain trade," we reasoned that the Sherman Act does not punish "political activity" through which "the people . . . freely inform the government of their wishes." *Noerr*, 365 U.S., at 137. Nor did we "impute to Congress an intent to invade" the First Amendment right to petition. *Id.*, at 138.

Noerr, however, withheld immunity from "sham" activities because "application of the Sherman Act would be justified" when petitioning activity, "ostensibly directed toward influencing governmental action, is a mere sham to cover . . . an attempt to interfere directly with the business relationships of a competitor." *Id.*, at 144. ***

In *California Motor Transport Co. v. Trucking Unlimited*, 404 U.S. 508 (1972), we elaborated on *Noerr* in two relevant respects. First, we extended *Noerr* to "the approach of citizens . . . to administrative agencies . . . and to courts." 404 U.S., at 510. Second, we held that the complaint showed a sham not entitled to immunity when it contained allegations that one group of highway carriers "sought to bar . . . competitors from meaningful access to adjudicatory tribunals and so to usurp that decisionmaking process" by "institut[ing] . . . proceedings and actions . . . with or without probable cause, and regardless of the merits of the cases." *Id.*, at 512. We left unresolved the question presented by this case— whether litigation may be sham merely because a subjective expectation of success does not motivate the litigant. We now answer this question in the negative and hold that an objectively reasonable effort to litigate cannot be sham regardless of subjective intent.

Our original formulation of antitrust petitioning immunity required that unprotected activity lack objective reasonableness. *Noerr* rejected the contention that an attempt "to influence the passage and enforcement of laws" might lose immunity merely because the lobbyists' "sole purpose . . . was to destroy [their] competitors." 365 U.S., at 138. *** Whether applying *Noerr* as an antitrust doctrine or invoking it in other contexts, we have repeatedly reaffirmed that evidence of anticompetitive intent or purpose alone cannot transform otherwise legitimate activity into a sham. [citation omitted] ***

III

We now outline a two-part definition of "sham" litigation. First, the lawsuit must be objectively baseless in the sense that no reasonable litigant could realistically expect success on the merits. If an objective litigant could conclude that the suit is reasonably calculated to elicit a favorable outcome, the suit is immunized under *Noerr*, and an antitrust claim premised on the sham exception must fail.[5] Only if challenged litigation is objectively meritless may a court examine the litigant's

---

[5] A winning lawsuit is by definition a reasonable effort at petitioning for redress and therefore not a sham. On the other hand, when the antitrust defendant has lost the underlying litigation, a court must "resist the understandable temptation to engage in post hoc reasoning by concluding" that an ultimately unsuccessful "action must have been unreasonable or without foundation." Christiansburg Garment Co. v. EEOC, 434 U.S. 412, 421-422 (1978). [citation omitted] The court must remember that "[e]ven when the law or the facts appear questionable or unfavorable at the outset, a party may have an entirely reasonable ground for bringing suit." Christiansburg, *supra*, 434 U.S., at 422.

subjective motivation. Under this second part of our definition of sham, the court should focus on whether the baseless lawsuit conceals "an attempt to interfere directly with the business relationships of a competitor," *Noerr,* supra, 365 U.S., at 144 (emphasis added), through the "use [of] the governmental process—as opposed to the outcome of that process—as an anticompetitive weapon," *Omni,* 499 U.S., at 380 (emphasis in original). This two-tiered process requires the plaintiff to disprove the challenged lawsuit's legal viability before the court will entertain evidence of the suit's economic viability. Of course, even a plaintiff who defeats the defendant's claim to Noerr immunity by demonstrating both the objective and the subjective components of a sham must still prove a substantive antitrust violation. Proof of a sham merely deprives the defendant of immunity; it does not relieve the plaintiff of the obligation to establish all other elements of his claim.

Some of the apparent confusion over the meaning of "sham" may stem from our use of the word "genuine" to denote the opposite of "sham." [citation omitted] The word "genuine" has both objective and subjective connotations. On one hand, "genuine" means "actually having the reputed or apparent qualities or character." Webster's Third New International Dictionary 948 (1986). "Genuine" in this sense governs Federal Rule of Civil Procedure 56, under which a "genuine issue" is one "that properly can be resolved only by a finder of fact because [it] may reasonably be resolved in favor of either party." [citation omitted] On the other hand, "genuine" also means "sincerely and honestly felt or experienced." Webster's Dictionary, at 948. To be sham, therefore, litigation must fail to be "genuine" in both senses of the word.[6]

IV

We conclude that the Court of Appeals properly affirmed summary judgment for Columbia on PRE's antitrust counterclaim. Under the objective prong of the sham exception, the Court of Appeals correctly held that sham litigation must constitute the pursuit of claims so baseless that no reasonable litigant could realistically expect to secure favorable relief. [citation omitted]

The existence of probable cause to institute legal proceedings precludes a finding that an antitrust defendant has engaged in sham litigation. The notion of probable cause, as understood and applied in the common law tort of wrongful civil proceedings, requires the plaintiff to prove that the defendant lacked probable cause to institute an unsuccessful civil lawsuit and that the defendant pressed the

---

[6] In surveying the "forms of illegal and reprehensible practice which may corrupt the administrative or judicial processes and which may result in antitrust violations," we have noted that "unethical conduct in the setting of the adjudicatory process often results in sanctions" and that "[m]isrepresentations, condoned in the political arena, are not immunized when used in the adjudicatory process." California Motor Transport, 404 U.S., at 512-513. We need not decide here whether and, if so, to what extent Noerr permits the imposition of antitrust liability for a litigant's fraud or other misrepresentations. Cf. Fed.Rule Civ.Proc. 60(b)(3) (allowing a federal court to "relieve a party . . . from a final judgment" for "fraud . . ., misrepresentation, or other misconduct of an adverse party"); Walker Process Equipment, Inc. v. Food Machinery & Chemical Corp., 382 U.S. 172, 176-177 (1965); id., at 179-180 (Harlan, J., concurring).

action for an improper, malicious purpose. [citation omitted] Probable cause to institute civil proceedings requires no more than a "reasonabl[e] belie[f] that there is a chance that [a] claim may be held valid upon adjudication" [citation omitted] Because the absence of probable cause is an essential element of the tort, the existence of probable cause is an absolute defense. [citation omitted] Just as evidence of anticompetitive intent cannot affect the objective prong of *Noerr*'s sham exception, a showing of malice alone will neither entitle the wrongful civil proceedings plaintiff to prevail nor permit the factfinder to infer the absence of probable cause. [citation omitted] When a court has found that an antitrust defendant claiming Noerr immunity had probable cause to sue, that finding compels the conclusion that a reasonable litigant in the defendant's position could realistically expect success on the merits of the challenged lawsuit. Under our decision today, therefore, a proper probable cause determination irrefutably demonstrates that an antitrust plaintiff has not proved the objective prong of the sham exception and that the defendant is accordingly entitled to Noerr immunity.

The District Court and the Court of Appeals correctly found that Columbia had probable cause to sue PRE for copyright infringement. Where, as here, there is no dispute over the predicate facts of the underlying legal proceeding, a court may decide probable cause as a matter of law. [citation omitted] Columbia enjoyed the "exclusive righ[t] . . . to perform [its] copyrighted" motion pictures "publicly." 17 U.S.C. § 106(4). Regardless of whether it intended any monopolistic or predatory use, Columbia acquired this statutory right for motion pictures as "original" audiovisual "works of authorship fixed" in a "tangible medium of expression." § 102(a)(6). Indeed, to condition a copyright upon a demonstrated lack of anticompetitive intent would upset the notion of copyright as a "limited grant" of "monopoly privileges" intended simultaneously "to motivate the creative activity of authors" and "to give the public appropriate access to their work product." [citation omitted]

When the District Court entered summary judgment for PRE on Columbia's copyright claim in 1986, it was by no means clear whether PRE's videodisc rental activities intruded on Columbia's copyrights. At that time, the Third Circuit and a District Court within the Third Circuit had held that the rental of video cassettes for viewing in on-site, private screening rooms infringed on the copyright owner's right of public performance. [citation omitted] Although the District Court and the Ninth Circuit distinguished these decisions by reasoning that hotel rooms offered a degree of privacy more akin to the home than to a video rental store, [citation omitted] copyright scholars criticized both the reasoning and the outcome of the Ninth Circuit's decision. [citation omitted] The Seventh Circuit expressly "decline[d] to follow" the Ninth Circuit and adopted instead the Third Circuit's definition of a "public place." [citation omitted] In light of the unsettled condition of the law, Columbia plainly had probable cause to sue.

Any reasonable copyright owner in Columbia's position could have believed that it had some chance of winning an infringement suit against PRE. Even though it did not survive PRE's motion for summary judgment, Columbia's copyright action was arguably "warranted by existing law" or at the very least was based on an objectively "good faith argument for the extension, modification, or reversal of existing law." Fed. Rule Civ. Proc. 11. By the time the Ninth Circuit had reviewed all claims in this litigation, it became apparent that Columbia might have won its copyright suit in either the Third or the Seventh Circuit. Even in the absence of supporting authority, Columbia would have been entitled to press a novel copyright claim as long as a similarly situated reasonable litigant could have perceived some likelihood of success. A court could reasonably conclude that Columbia's infringement action was an objectively plausible effort to enforce rights. Accordingly, we conclude that PRE failed to establish the objective prong of *Noerr*'s sham exception. ***

We affirm the judgment of the Court of Appeals.

Comments and Questions

1. What does it mean for a lawsuit to be objectively baseless? Did Justice Thomas define the concept in different ways? Some commentators argue that establishing antitrust liability for sham litigation is exceedingly difficult:

> The 'objective baselessness' prong of the *PRE* test, as interpreted by some courts, as transformed the 'sham' exception into an almost insurmountable hurdle. It is no longer accurate to describe the 'sham' exception as an analogue to Rule 11 or other standards governing the misuse of process. Rule 11 petitions occasionally succeed. The 'sham' exception, in contrast, is an endangered species, and rumors of its extinction abound.

John T. Delacourt, *Protecting Competition by Narrowing Noerr: A Reply*, 18-FALL ANTITRUST 77 (2003).

The Supreme Court asserts in footnote 5 that: "A winning lawsuit is by definition a reasonable effort at petitioning for redress and therefore not a sham." Is that necessarily always true?

Antitrust lawsuits based on claims that the defendant has threatened or pursued sham litigation rarely succeed. Why do parties even bother asserting it?

2. Why does the Court frame the objective component as a threshold issue before inquiry may begin into a party's subjective motivation?

One effect of making the objective element a threshold requirement is to limit the discovery on the subjective element of intent. In *PRE*, the lower court had denied the antitrust plaintiff's request for discovery on Columbia's intent in bringing the copyright action. The Supreme Court held that this refusal to permit discovery was proper because "Columbia's economic motivations in bringing suit … were rendered irrelevant by the objective legal reasonableness of the litigation." Do you agree that courts should limit discovery on that IP owner's intent until the antitrust plaintiff can prove the IP owner's legal claims are objectively baseless?

3. What is the role of the subjective element in Justice Thomas's two-part test? Why is the subjective element necessary? Why should the antitrust plaintiff have to prove the subjective element if she can prove the infringement lawsuit was objectively baseless? (Remember, she will still have to prove all of the elements of an antitrust violation in order to prevail on her claim.)

4. Does the subjective element permit a litigant to attempt to enforce a patent it knows to be invalid? Consider this:

> [*Professional Real Estate Investors*] extended *Noerr* immunity to infringement suits even where the patentee fully knows that his patent is invalid or not infringed, provided that he brought the suit with the subjective hope of persuading the court (or, to put it more bluntly, fooling the court) to the contrary position, rather than solely for its harassment value.

James R. Atwood, *Securing and Enforcing Patents: The Role of Noerr/Pennington*, 83 J. PAT. & TRADEMARK OFF. SOC'Y 651, 658 (2001).
Do you agree?

5. The *PRE* decision states: "We need not decide here whether and, if so, to what extent *Noerr* permits the imposition of antitrust liability for a litigant's fraud or other misrepresentations." What is the relationship between *Walker Process* and *Noerr* immunity? Is *Walker Process* a separate and distinct basis of antitrust liability, or is it simply an exception to *Noerr* immunity? *Walker Process* did not discuss the *Noerr* and *Pennington* decisions. Was that an oversight? *See* Atwood at 657 ("[T]he Court in *Walker Process* did not address the *Noerr/Pennington* doctrine, but its holding has been treated as effectively creating an exception to *Noerr*."). Note that the First Circuit in CVD discussed *Walker Process* but did not mention the *Noerr-Pennington* doctrine.

Walker Process and its progeny make a distinction between fraud and inequitable conduct. After *PRE*, should enforcement of a patent obtained through inequitable conduct be considered sham litigation?

6. The Federal Circuit has applied *Noerr* immunity in the context of state tort law unfair competition claims. In Globetrotter Software, Inc. v. Elan Computer Group, Inc., 362 F.3d 1367, 1377 (Fed. Cir. 2004), the court explained:

> Our decision to permit state-law tort liability for only objectively baseless allegations of infringement rests on both federal preemption and the First Amendment. The federal patent laws preempt state laws that impose tort liability for a patentholder's good faith conduct in communications asserting infringement of its patent and warning about potential litigation. In addition, the same First Amendment policy reasons that justify the extension of *Noerr* immunity to pre-litigation conduct in the context of federal antitrust law apply equally in the context of state-law tort claims.

Even if a party is immune from antitrust liability under *Noerr*, could the same party incur liability under other legal theories for the same exact conduct? *See Cardtoons, L.C. v. Major League Baseball Players Ass'n*, 208 F.3d 885 (10th Cir.) (en banc) (holding threats of litigation from copyright owner are not immune from state unfair competition laws).

7. What is the market that the defendants allegedly sought to monopolize? Do you find this to be a credible market?

8. Does the Court's holding in PRE affect the result or the reasoning of the First Circuit's opinion in *CVD, Inc. v. Raytheon Co.?* Why or why not?

Note on *Filmtec Corp. v. Hydranautics*

Courts can disagree about when a patent infringement defendant can rightly become an antitrust plaintiff. In one case, two different courts reached opposing conclusions on exactly the same facts involving the same litigants. In *Filmtec Corp. v. Hydranautics*, 67 F.3d 931 (Fed. Cir. 1995), the Federal Circuit addressed an antitrust counterclaim in a patent infringement suit involving an inventor, John Cadotte, who worked for a not-for-profit research corporation on a government-funded water desalinization project that used reverse osmosis membranes. The inventor left the project, helped found a for-profit corporation (FilmTec) to commercially manufacture such membranes, and filed for a patent on his membrane (the '344 patent), assigning the patent rights to FilmTec.

When FilmTec sued its competitor Hydranautics for infringement, Hydranautics argued that FilmTec's title to the patent was defective. The district court held that FilmTec had good title and enjoined Hydranautics from any commercial activity that would infringe the patent. Hydranautics appealed to the Federal Circuit, which reversed because the inventor had conceived of his invention while working on a government project and the invention rightly belonged to the United States, not FilmTec.

Hydranautics then sued FilmTec in district court for violating Section Two of the Sherman Act, arguing that FilmTec monopolized the relevant market for reverse osmosis membranes by bring sham litigation to enforce an invalid patent. Yet, Hydranautics also sought to raise the same antitrust issues as a counterclaim in the original infringement litigation by way of amending its response to that sought to include an antitrust counterclaim. The district court dismissed the antitrust suit—reasoning the antitrust claims were a compulsory counterclaim to FilmTec's infringement suit—and denied Hydranautics' attempt to amend its response in the infringement suit as untimely.

Hydranautics appealed the dismissal of the antitrust suit to the Ninth Circuit and the denial of its motion to amend to the Federal Circuit. Thus, Hydranautics in effect pursued the same antitrust claims in two separate courts.

The Federal Circuit ruled first. It upheld that district court refusal to allow Hydranautics to amend its response. The Federal Circuit reasoned that such amendment would be futile because FilmTec had a clear defense under *Noerr-Pennington*:

> [T]he *Noerr-Pennington* doctrine does not protect litigation from suit under the antitrust laws if the litigation is a "sham." *** So the question is whether or not FilmTec's infringement litigation could be characterized as a sham. The Supreme Court has recently provided a two-tiered definition of sham litigation.
>
>> First, the lawsuit must be objectively baseless in the sense that no reasonable litigant could realistically expect success on the merits. If an objective litigant could conclude that the suit is reasonably calculated to elicit a favorable outcome, the suit is immunized under *Noerr,* and an antitrust claim premised on the sham exception must fail.

PRE, 508 U.S. at——, 113 S.Ct. at 1928. The second tier, to be reached "only if challenged litigation is objectively meritless," *id.*, is "whether the baseless lawsuit conceals an attempt to interfere *directly* with the business relationships of a competitor through the use of the governmental *process*-as opposed to the *outcome* of that process-as an anticompetitive weapon." *Id.*, 508 U.S. at——,113 S.Ct. at 1928, 26 USPQ2d at 1646 (emphasis in original) (citations omitted).

The first question is thus whether FilmTec's patent infringement suit was objectively baseless. The actual outcome of that suit, although instructive, is not determinative: "The court hearing the antitrust claim must make its own assessment of the objective merits of the predicate suit. . . ." *Boulware v. Nevada Dep't of Human Resources*, 960 F.2d 793, 799 (9th Cir.1992). Had FilmTec ultimately prevailed in its infringement suit, Hydranautics would have a difficult time establishing that FilmTec's suit was a sham. FilmTec would therefore enjoy *Noerr-Pennington* immunity, even if its sole purpose in bringing suit was monopolization of the market. *See PRE*, 508 U.S. at—— n. 5. But FilmTec lost, which complicates the analysis.

On the one hand, the Supreme Court has cautioned that "when the antitrust defendant has lost the underlying litigation, a court must resist the understandable temptation to engage in post hoc reasoning by concluding that an ultimately unsuccessful action must have been unreasonable or without foundation." *Id.* (citations omitted). On the other hand, a preliminary success on the merits does not necessarily preclude a court from concluding that litigation was baseless. *See Boulware*, 960 F.2d at 798–99. ***

Although the question is not without some doubt, we conclude that, taking all of the facts and circumstances into account, it cannot be said that FilmTec's suit against Hydranautics was objectively baseless. The issues on which this litigation hinged, precisely what Cadotte invented, and when, were genuine. On the basis of its understanding of those issues, FilmTec, not without reason, staked a claim to owning the '344 patent as Cadotte's assignee. The trial judge, after full consideration, ruled for FilmTec on this issue. Although that is not controlling, and indeed we found it to be erroneous, it does support the conclusion that FilmTec's theory was more than a sham. In this light, and in view of all that has transpired in the case, allowing Hydranautics to amend its answer by adding an antitrust counterclaim would be a futile act; the decision of the trial court in denying the motion to amend is affirmed.

The Ninth Circuit took a different tack. In reviewing Hydranautics' appeal of the dismissal of its antitrust claim, the Ninth Circuit in *Hydranautics v. FilmTec Corp.*, 70 F.3d 533 (9th Cir. 1995), first held that an antitrust claim based on sham patent infringement litigation is not a compulsory counterclaim to that prior patent infringement suit. The Court then addressed whether *Noerr-Pennington* immunity protected FilmTec from antitrust liability:

> FilmTec claims that it is immunized from an antitrust lawsuit by the Noerr-Pennington doctrine. Hydranautics disagrees. *** We conclude that this

disagreement could not properly be resolved against Hydranautics on the basis of the pleadings. The outcome will depend on evidence. We therefore cannot affirm on this ground.

Application of the Noerr-Pennington doctrine to antitrust claims has recently been clarified by *Professional Real Estate Investors, Inc. v. Columbia Pictures Industries, Inc.*, 508 U.S. 49 (1993) ***. *Columbia Pictures* holds that litigation cannot be deprived of its antitrust immunity as a sham unless it is objectively baseless, regardless of whether the subjective intent of the litigation is to interfere with competition. ***

FilmTec's theory is that its patent infringement lawsuit could not have been "objectively baseless," because FilmTec won in district court. FilmTec argues that its initial victory requires dismissal of antitrust claims based upon FilmTec's ultimately unsuccessful patent infringement lawsuits, regardless of whether it obtained the patents fraudulently. The holdings in Columbia Pictures and Liberty Lake leave open the question of whether an infringement action based on a fraudulently obtained patent is "objectively baseless." Footnote six in Columbia Pictures says the court does "not decide here whether, and, if so, to what extent *Noerr* permits the imposition of antitrust liability for a litigant's fraud or other misrepresentations." Id. at ——, n. 6, 113 S.Ct. at 1929, n. 6.

Columbia Pictures cites *Walker Process Equip., Inc. v. Food Machinery and Chem. Corp.*, 382 U.S. 172 (1965) in footnote 6. In *Walker Process*, the Court held that proof of the claim that the patent holder obtained its patent by knowingly and willfully misrepresenting facts to the Patent Office "would be sufficient to strip [the patent holder] of its exemption from the antitrust laws." *Walker Process*, 382 U.S. at 177. It further held that "enforcement of a patent procured by fraud on the Patent Office may be violative" of the Sherman Act and subject the defendant to treble damages under the Clayton Act. Id. at 174. ***

Columbia Pictures explains that "probable cause" to institute legal proceedings, in the sense in which the phrase is used in tort suits for malicious prosecution of civil claims, establishes that the litigation is not "objectively baseless." At common law, a reversed judgment for the plaintiff in the first action usually is not conclusive as to probable cause in the malicious prosecution action, where the judgment was obtained by fraud. [citation omitted] If the patent was obtained by "intentional fraud," and not merely "technical fraud," see *Walker Process*, 382 U.S. at 176, 179, then a reversed judgment based upon that fraud, where the plaintiff obtained the patent by intentional fraud or was an assignee who knew of the patent's infirmity, would not demonstrate probable cause for a patent infringement suit. See *Walker Process*, 382 U.S. at 177.[1]

---

[1] While we were considering this opinion, we learned that the Federal Circuit decided a parallel case, Filmtec Corp. v. Hydranautics, 67 F.3d 931 (Fed.Cir.1995) *** The Federal Circuit held that as a matter of law, FilmTec's case was not objectively baseless, but said "there is no dispute over the facts." In the procedural posture of the case before us, it would not be correct to say that there is no dispute as to the facts. Hydranautics alleges fraud, and FilmTec denies it. We must assume for the purposes of Rule 12(b)(6) that Hydranautics could prove that FilmTec obtained the patent fraudulently.

Hydranautics asserts facts in its complaint that, if true, would prove that FilmTec obtained its patent by fraud. Its complaint therefore cannot be dismissed short of summary judgment or trial.

Applying the law to the same fact pattern, the Federal Circuit held that *Noerr-Pennington* protected FilmTec from antitrust liability, rendering Hydranautics' antitrust claims futile. In contrast, the Ninth Circuit held that Hydranautics' antitrust case could proceed. Which court's approach do you think is correct? Why? What mistake did the other court make?

Primetime 24 Joint Venture v. National Broadcasting Co.

219 F.3d 92 (2nd Cir. 2000).

WINTER, Chief Judge:

This appeal arises out of an antitrust action brought by PrimeTime 24 Joint Venture ("PrimeTime") against the major television networks, their affiliates' trade associations, independent television stations, and the National Association of Broadcasters. The complaint alleged that appellees violated Section 1 of the Sherman Act, 15 U.S.C. § 1, through concerted, baseless, signal-strength challenges brought under the Satellite Home Viewer Act, 17 U.S.C. § 119 (1995) ***. Judge McKenna granted appellees' motion to dismiss under Fed.R.Civ.P. 12(b)(6) on the ground that their conduct was protected under the Noerr-Pennington doctrine. We reverse.

Background

The complaint alleged the following. PrimeTime retransmits network broadcast signals either directly to satellite dish owners or to direct-to-home satellite distributors who include the network broadcasts in packages of hundreds of channels sold to consumers. When the complaint was filed, PrimeTime was the leading American provider of network television broadcasts to satellite dish owners. It had over two million subscribers and was the "only satellite carrier of network programming . . . neither owned nor controlled by network or cable television interests."

Appellees are the major television networks, ABC, Inc. ("ABC"), CBS, Inc. ("CBS"), the National Broadcasting Company ("NBC"), and the Fox Broadcasting Company ("Fox"); their affiliates' trade associations; the National Association of Broadcasters ("NAB"); and businesses owning and/or operating stations affiliated with the networks. The network companies both supply the affiliates with programming and distribute it directly to consumers through broadcasts from their owned and operated stations. The NAB is a trade association comprising both the networks and the affiliates.

Until recently, consumers received television programming principally through over-the-air broadcasts from stations owned and operated by, or affiliated with,

---

Nor do we decide whether the issue of objective baselessness is res judicata, on account of the Federal Circuit case. These questions should, if raised on remand, be decided in the first instance by the district court.

the network companies. This technology, however, limited adequate reception to signals transmitted by relatively nearby stations. New technology has both provided improved reception and multiplied the programming options available to consumers through the introduction of cable and satellite television.

Unlike conventional broadcasters that transmit free signals and rely on advertising revenues, satellite operators such as PrimeTime charge users a fee. Users can improve reception or access the satellite system's provision of geographically distant station broadcasts. Access to distant stations allows consumers to avoid local preemptions of network programming; to watch sports, news, or other broadcasts from distant stations; or to take advantage of variations in programming timing caused, for instance, by time-zone differences.

Due to its continuing appeal, network programming is essential to the competitive position of satellite operators. However, satellite providers cannot offer copyrighted network television programming without permission or a license. In an effort to balance the networks' copyright interests with consumers' interests in receiving programming through satellites, Congress passed the Satellite Home Viewers Act of 1988 ("SHVA"), [citation omitted] The SHVA, inter alia, requires networks to license their signals to satellite broadcasters at a statutorily fixed royalty fee, for distribution to viewers who cannot receive a sufficiently strong over-the-air broadcast signal. [citation omitted]

Specifically, the SHVA mandatory license extends only to households that "cannot receive, through the use of a conventional, stationary outdoor rooftop receiving antenna, an over-the-air signal of . . . Grade B intensity as defined by the Federal Communications Commission," [citation omitted] and have not received cable service in the preceding 90 days [citation omitted]. Thus, the SHVA establishes a relatively objective signal-strength rule rather than a subjective rule of reception quality. [citation omitted] The signal-strength rule at issue works by station, so that in a local area where the network affiliates' signals originate from different points, the satellite operator might have statutory rights to licenses for the programming of some but not all networks, e.g., ABC and CBS but not NBC. [citation omitted]

Satellite providers initially designate those households for which they claim a statutory right to serve under the mandatory licensing. Local broadcasters have the right under the SHVA to challenge the satellite operators' estimate of the signal-strength received by the designated households. [citation omitted] If the subscriber is "within the predicted Grade B Contour of the station," the satellite operator must either cease providing the disputing broadcaster's channel to the challenged viewers or perform a signal-strength test for that household. [citation omitted] If the test shows that the challenged household is adequately served by the challenging stations, the satellite provider must cease providing the programming from that station; if the test shows that the challenged household is not adequately served, the challenging station must reimburse the satellite provider for the cost of conducting the test. ***

The statute limits the rights of stations to force a satellite provider to conduct signal-strength tests. In any calendar year, a station may challenge no more than five percent of a satellite provider's subscriber base that existed at the SHVA's effective date. [citation omitted] Above the five-percent threshold, a station may challenge service to a household only by conducting its own test, as in the case of households outside the predicted Grade B Contour. [citation omitted]

PrimeTime's complaint alleged that appellees, in concert with themselves and with coordination by the NAB, intentionally abused the SHVA's signal-strength challenge provision by filing baseless challenges for the purpose of raising PrimeTime's cost structure and thereby reducing competition from it. PrimeTime alleged in particular that appellees based their challenges on a common NBC subscriber list, despite the fact that PrimeTime had provided different lists to each network. Because network affiliates broadcast from different points, the predicted Grade B Contours as described in the lists differ for each network. The purpose of using an NBC subscriber list, PrimeTime alleges, was intentionally to over-challenge subscribers, i.e., to challenge subscribers outside particular stations' Grade B Contours. ***

Finally, the complaint alleged that PrimeTime was injured by appellees because it was forced to drop subscribers due to the number of challenges and the cost of conducting signal-strength tests. The complaint also alleged an adverse effect on competition.

In granting a motion to dismiss, Judge McKenna ruled that appellees' actions were protected by the Noerr-Pennington doctrine. *** This appeal followed.

Discussion

*** PrimeTime [argues] that appellees engaged in coordinated efforts to make baseless SHVA challenges to impose costs upon PrimeTime as a way of stifling competition from it ***

Abuse of SHVA Challenge Provision

It is beyond question that a good-faith SHVA challenge by a station to a PrimeTime subscriber within that station's Grade B Contour cannot violate the Sherman Act. That is what the SHVA specifically permits. Nor do we think that it violates the Sherman Act for stations to act in coordination, whether orchestrated by the networks, NAB, or trade associations, in making good-faith SHVA challenges.

We reach that conclusion for two overlapping reasons. First, we believe that Congress intended to allow coordinated efforts among parties such as appellees in making good-faith SHVA challenges, and it would therefore be anomalous to read the Sherman Act to forbid such efforts. Second, even if we were in doubt as to Congress's precise intent, we believe that good-faith SHVA challenges are protected by the Noerr-Pennington doctrine. However, we also conclude that Congress did not intend to permit coordinated SHVA challenges to be made without regard to the merits and for the purpose of imposing upon a satellite carrier unnecessary costs as a means of limiting that carrier's ability to operate and compete. Such bad faith conduct also falls within the "sham" exception to *Noerr-Pennington*.

Turning first to Congress's intent with regard to the SHVA, we note that SHVA challenges are a form of copyright enforcement. The SHVA was designed to "balance[] the rights of copyright owners by ensuring payment for the use of their property rights, with the rights of satellite dish owners, by assuring availability at reasonable rates of retransmitted television signals." H.R.Rep. No. 100-887(I), at 14 (1988), reprinted in 1988 U.S.C.C.A.N. 5611, 5617. Signal-strength challenges are an integral part of the SHVA's design to protect networks' copyright interests and to "respect [] the network/affiliate relationship and promote[] localism." Id.; see generally 17 U.S.C. § 119(a). In its discussion of Section 119(a), the Report of the House Judiciary Committee specifically contemplated cooperation among stations:

> The [SHVA] contemplates that network stations will cooperate with one another (and with the network with which they are affiliated) in monitoring the compliance of satellite carriers with the requirements of [the SHVA]. [citation omitted]

*** Of course, the principle that enforcement of legal rights through coordinated efforts among competitors cannot lead to antitrust liability does not extend to the concerted assertion of baseless claims with the intent of imposing costs on a competing firm to prevent or impair competition from that firm. *See California Motor Transp. Co. v. Trucking Unlimited*, 404 U.S. 508, 516 (1972); Robert H. Bork, The Antitrust Paradox 347-64 (1978). Such conduct is predatory, without any redeeming efficiency benefitting consumers. ***

We turn now to the pertinent analysis under the *Noerr-Pennington* doctrine, a body of caselaw constituting a limitation upon the scope of the Sherman Act. *** Courts have extended *Noerr-Pennington* to encompass concerted efforts incident to litigation, such as prelitigation "threat letters," [citation omitted] and settlement offers [citation omitted]. Litigation, including good faith litigation to protect a valid copyright, therefore falls within the protection of the *Noerr-Pennington* doctrine. [citation omitted]

PrimeTime is of course correct in arguing that SHVA challenges are not literally petitions to the government. Moreover, SHVA signal-strength challenges differ significantly from prelitigation threat letters because SHVA challenges require the satellite carrier either to pay for a signal-strength test or to terminate service. SHVA challenges are, therefore, more immediately harmful to a competitor than are prelitigation threat letters. Nevertheless, SHVA challenges are a form of action authorized by statute and a preliminary step to resort to litigation if necessary. Moreover, the immediate harm has been counterbalanced by a statutory right of reimbursement if the challenge is unsuccessful-a litigation skirmish in miniature. Accordingly, we see no reason to exclude SHVA challenges from the protection afforded by Noerr-Pennington generally to administrative and court proceedings or to steps preliminary to such proceedings.

However, that is not the end of the matter. The *Noerr-Pennington* doctrine does not extend to "every concerted effort that is genuinely intended to influence governmental action," because "[i]f all such conduct were immunized then, for example, competitors would be free to enter into horizontal price agreements as long as they wished to propose that price as an appropriate level for governmental ratemaking or price supports." *Allied Tube & Conduit Corp. v. Indian Head, Inc.,* 486 U.S. 492, 503 (1988) [citation omitted].

In particular, as noted in *Noerr* itself, "[t]here may be situations in which [petitioning activity], ostensibly directed toward influencing governmental action, is a mere sham to cover what is actually nothing more than an attempt to interfere directly with the business relationships of a competitor and the application of the Sherman Act would be justified." 365 U.S. at 144. Elaboration of the "sham exception" occurred in *California Motor Transport,* where the Court noted that "a pattern of baseless, repetitive claims may . . . lead[] the factfinder to conclude that the administrative and judicial processes have been abused." 404 U.S. at 513.

To establish "sham" administrative or judicial proceedings, a plaintiff must show that the litigation in question is: (i) "objectively baseless," and (ii) "an attempt to interfere directly with the business relationships of a competitor through the use of the governmental process-as opposed to the outcome of that process-as an anticompetitive weapon." *Professional Real Estate Investors, Inc. v. Columbia Pictures Indus.,* 508 U.S. 49, 60, 113 S.Ct. 1920, 123 L.Ed.2d 611 (1993) (citations, internal quotation marks, and alterations omitted).

This two-step inquiry, however, applies to determining "whether a single action constitutes sham petitioning." *USS-POSCO Indus. v. Contra Costa County Bldg. & Constr. Trades Council, AFL-CIO,* 31 F.3d 800, 811 (9th Cir.1994) (interpreting *Professional Real Estate*). In cases in which "the defendant is accused of bringing a whole series of legal proceedings," the test is not "retrospective" but "prospective": "Were the legal filings made, not out of a genuine interest in redressing grievances, but as part of a pattern or practice of successive filings undertaken essentially for purposes of harassment?" *Id.* As the Ninth Circuit has noted, it is immaterial that some of the claims might, "as a matter of chance," have merit. The relevant issue is whether the legal challenges "are brought pursuant to a policy of starting legal proceedings without regard to the merits and for the purpose of injuring a market rival." *Id.*

Under this standard, PrimeTime's complaint stated a valid sham claim. PrimeTime alleged that appellees submitted "simultaneous and voluminous challenges . . . without regard to whether the challenges had merit," [citation omitted] PrimeTime alleged in particular that appellees submitted violations based solely on NBC station lists. [citation omitted] Because network affiliates in a particular area generally transmit from different locations, PrimeTime plausibly alleged that "ABC, CBS, and Fox affiliates challenged thousands of subscribers who did not even receive ABC, CBS, or Fox programming." [citation omitted] Furthermore, PrimeTime alleged that appellees submitted numerous challenges to subscribers outside the predicted Grade B Contour. [citation omitted] Although the challenging stations, not PrimeTime, would have the statutory obligation to pay for a signal-strength test outside the Grade B Contour, [citation omitted] PrimeTime alleged that appellees coordinated their efforts to submit huge volumes of challenges simultaneously, [citation omitted] and failed to give PrimeTime "information sufficient to determine which of the challenged subscribers resided within the station's predicted Grade B Contour," [citation omitted] Moreover, PrimeTime alleges that the appellees' coordinated scheme "was done in order to overwhelm PrimeTime 24 and make it difficult and expensive for PrimeTime 24 to comply with [the] SHVA." [citation omitted]

PrimeTime's complaint therefore adequately alleges that the SHVA challenges were "brought pursuant to a policy of starting legal proceedings without regard to the merits and for the purpose of injuring a market rival." *USS-POSCO*, 31 F.3d at 811. PrimeTime essentially alleges "the filing of frivolous objections . . . simply in order to impose expense and delay," the "classic example" of a sham. *City of Columbia v. Omni*, 499 U.S. 365, 380 (1991); *see also California Motor Transp.*, 404 U.S. at 512 ("It is alleged that petitioners instituted the proceedings and actions with or without probable cause, and regardless of the merits of the cases." (internal punctuation marks omitted)). ***

We therefore reverse.

Comments and Questions

1. If the *PrimeTime 24* court had applied the two-part test from *PRE*, would it have reached the same result? Why did the court not apply the *PRE* two-part test?

2. In other litigation against PrimeTime, courts had found that the company had "engaged in a pattern or practice of infringing [network] copyrights." *ABC, Inc. v. PrimeTime 24*, 184 F.3d 348, 350 (4th Cir. 1999); *accord* CBS v. Prime Time 24 Joint Venture, 48 F.Supp.2d 1342, 1357 (S.D. Fla. 1998). In one action, the court imposed a nationwide injunction against PrimeTime. *See id.* at 1360–63. Should that affect the result in this litigation? Why or why not?

3. How many lawsuits does an antitrust defendant need to file in order for the antitrust plaintiff to be able to take advantage of the sham test for repetitious litigation? When a plaintiff alleges that an entity engaged in "repetitive petitioning," what percentage of the lawsuits needs to be frivolous in order for the overall conduct to be considered a sham? Some of them are bound to have some merit. *See* John T. Delacourt, *Protecting Competition by Narrowing Noerr: A Reply*, 18-FALL Antitrust 77, 78 (2003) ("If filed in sufficient numbers—even if the petitioner was indifferent to the merits, and filing solely the purpose of harassing and burdening competitors—odds are that at least some of the petitions would prevail"). Should the antitrust plaintiff have to prove that a majority of the filed (or threatened) lawsuits were objectively baseless?

4. Why is repetitive petitioning an effective strategy to deter competition? Consider this:

> A . . . form of relatively cheap predation involves filing (or threatening) lawsuits for the sake of exclusion, rather than on the merits. These actions can be more costly

for the victim than the predator, and can cause costly delay that harms the rival. For example, there are substantial cost asymmetries in repetitive sham litigation; the incremental cost of filing an additional sham complaint is negligible, but the cost of defending against the complaint is high in comparison.... In nonrepetitive sham litigation cases, costs borne by the two parties may be roughly comparable, but they will nevertheless usually be proportionally larger for the victim in relation to its share of market or expected profits from entry.

Susan A. Creighton, D. Bruce Hoffman, Thomas G. Krattenmaker, Ernest A. Nagata, *Cheap Exclusion*, 72 ANTITRUST L.J. 975, 992–93 (2005) (citations omitted).

Bibliography of Additional Resources

Richard P. Beem, *Recovering Attorney Fees & Damages When Defending Against Bad Faith Patent Litigation*, 80 J. PAT. & TRADEMARK OFF. SOC'Y 81 (1998)

Michael Paul Chu, *An Antitrust Solution to the New Wave of Predatory Patent Infringement Litigation*, 33 WM. & MARY L. REV. 1341 (1992)

Danielle S. Fitzpatrick & David R. Steinman, *Antitrust Counterclaims in Patent Infringement Cases: A Guide to Walker Process and Sham-Litigation Claims*, 10 TEX. INTELL. PROP. L.J. 95 (2001)

James B. Kobak, Jr., *Professional Real Estate Investors and the Future of Patent-Antitrust Litigation: Walker Process and Handgards Meet Noerr-Pennington*, 63 ANTITRUST L.J. 185 (1994)

Gary Myers, *Antitrust and First Amendment Implications of Professional Real Estate Investors*, 51 WASH. & LEE L. REV. 1199 (1994)

CHAPTER 5

Tying Arrangements and Intellectual Property

Chapter 2 provided a brief overview on how antitrust law treats tying arrangements generally. This chapter focuses on specific types of tying arrangements that involve various forms of intellectual property. It is advisable to reread the tying discussion in Chapter 2 before reading the cases in this chapter.

U.S. Dep't of Justice & Federal Trade Commission,
Antitrust Enforcement and Intellectual Property Rights:
Promoting Innovation and Competition 107 (2007)

"Classic "contractual" patent tying occurs when the tying product (such as a mimeograph machine) is patented, the tied product is an unpatented commodity used as an input for the tying product (such as ink or paper), and the sale of the patented product is conditioned on the purchase of the unpatented product. A "technological tie" may be defined as one in which "the tying and tied products are bundled together physically or produced in such a way that they are compatible only with each other.""

DOJ-FTC Antitrust Guidelines for the Licensing
of Intellectual Property, Sec. 5.3

A "tying" or "tie-in" or "tied sale" arrangement has been defined as "an agreement by a party to sell one product . . . on the condition that the buyer also purchases a different (or tied) product, or at least agrees that he will not purchase that [tied] product from any other supplier." *Eastman Kodak Co. v. Image Technical Services, Inc.*, 112 S. Ct. 2072, 2079 (1992). Conditioning the ability of a licensee to license one or more items of intellectual property on the licensee's purchase of another item of intellectual property or a good or a service has been held in some cases to constitute illegal tying. Although tying arrangements may result in anticompetitive effects, such arrangements can also result in significant efficiencies and procompetitive benefits. In the exercise of their prosecutorial discretion, the Agencies will consider both the anticompetitive effects and the efficiencies attributable to a tie-in. The Agencies would be likely to challenge a tying arrangement if: (1) the seller has market power in the tying product, (2) the arrangement has an adverse effect on competition in the relevant market for the tied product, and (3) efficiency justifications for the arrangement do not outweigh the anticompetitive effects. The Agencies will not presume that a patent, copyright, or trade secret necessarily confers market power upon its owner.

Package licensing—the licensing of multiple items of intellectual property in a single license or in a group of related licenses—may be a form of tying arrangement if the licensing of one product is conditioned upon the acceptance of a license of another, separate product. Package licensing can be efficiency enhancing under some circumstances. When multiple licenses are needed to use any single item of intellectual property, for example, a package license may promote such efficiencies. If a package license constitutes a tying arrangement, the Agencies will evaluate its competitive effects under the same principles they apply to other tying arrangements.

A. Tying Arrangements and Patented Products

International Salt Co. v. United States,
332 U.S. 392 (1947)

Mr. Justice JACKSON delivered the opinion of the Court.

The Government brought this civil action to enjoin the International Salt Company, appellant here, from carrying out provisions of the leases of its patented machines to the effect that lessees would use therein only International's salt products. The restriction is alleged to violate § 1 of the Sherman Act, and § 3 of the Clayton Act. ***

It was established by pleadings or admissions that the International Salt Company is engaged in interstate commerce in salt, of which it is the country's largest producer for industrial uses. It also owns patents on two machines for utilization of salt products. One, the 'Lixator,' dissolves rock salt into a brine used in various industrial processes. The other, the 'Saltomat,' injects salt, in tablet form, into canned products during the canning process. The principal distribution of each of these machines is under leases which, among other things, require the lessees to purchase from appellant all unpatented salt and salt tablets consumed in the leased machines.

Appellant had outstanding 790 leases of an equal number of 'Lixators,' all of which leases were on appellant's standard form containing the tying clause[5] and

---

[5] 'It is further mutually agreed that the said Lixate Process Dissolver shall be installed by and at the expense of said Lessee and shall be maintained and kept in repair during the term of this lease by and at the expense of said Lessee; that the said Lixate Process Dissolver shall be used for dissolving and

other standard provisions; of 50 other leases which somewhat varied the terms, all but 4 contained the tying clause. It also had in effect 73 leases of 96 'Saltomats,' all containing the restrictive clause.[6] In 1944, appellant sold approximately 119,000 tons of salt, for about $500,000, for use in these machines.

The appellant's patents confer a limited monopoly of the invention they reward. From them appellant derives a right to restrain others from making, vending or using the patented machines. But the patents confer no right to restrain use of, or trade in, unpatented salt. By contracting to close this market for salt against competition, International has engaged in a restraint of trade for which its patents afford no immunity from the anti-trust laws. [citation omitted]

Appellant contends, however, that summary judgment was unauthorized because it precluded trial of alleged issues of fact as to whether the restraint was unreasonable within the Sherman Act or substantially lessened competition or tended to create a monopoly in salt within the Clayton Act. We think the admitted facts left no genuine issue. Not only is price-fixing unreasonable, per se, [citation omitted] but also it is unreasonable, per se, to foreclose competitors from any substantial market. [citation omitted] The volume of business affected by these contracts cannot be said to be insignificant or insubstantial and the tendency of the arrangement to accomplishment of monopoly seems obvious. Under the law, agreements are forbidden which 'tend to create a monopoly,' and it is immaterial

---

converting into brine only those grades of rock salt purchased by the Lessee from the Lessor at prices and upon terms and conditions hereafter agreed upon, provided:

'If at any time during the term of this lease a general reduction in price of grade of salt suitable for use in the said Lixate Process Dissolver shall be made, said Lessee shall give said Lessor an opportunity to provide a competitive grade of salt at any such competitive price quoted, and in case said Lessor shall fail or be unable to do so, said Lessee, upon continued payments of the rental herein agreed upon, shall have the privilege of continued use of the said equipment with salt purchased in the open market, until such time as said Lessor shall furnish a suitable grade of salt at the said competitive price.'

It further provides as follows:

'Should said Lessee fail to pay promptly the aforesaid rental, or shall at any time discontinue purchasing its requirement of salt from said Lessor, or otherwise breach any of the terms and conditions of this lease, said Lessor shall have the right, upon 30 days' written notice of intention to do so, to remove the said Lixate Process Dissolver from the possession of said Lessee.'

[6] 'It is further mutually agreed that the said Salt Tablet Depositor(s) shall be installed and maintained in good condition during the term of this lease; that the said Salt Tablet Depositor(s) shall be used only in conjunction with Salt Tablets sold or manufactured by the Lessor, and that the Lessee shall purchase from the Lessor or its agent, Salt Tablets for use in the Salt Tablet Depositor(s) at prices and upon terms and conditions hereinafter agreed upon, Provided: If at any time during the term of this lease, a general reduction in Lessor's price of Salt Tablets suitable for use in the Depositor(s) shall be made, said Lessor shall provide said Lessee with Salt Tablets at a like price.'

The lease further provides: '* * * should Lessee fail to pay promptly the aforesaid rental, or at any time discontinue purchasing its requirements of Salt Tablets for said Salt Tablet Depositor(s) from said Lessor, or its agent, or otherwise breach any of the terms and conditions of this lease, said Lessor shall have the right, upon 10 days' written notice of intention to do so, to remove the said Salt Tablet Depositor(s) from the premises and/or possession of said Lessee.'

134 *Antitrust Law and Intellectual Property Rights*

that the tendency is a creeping one rather than one that proceeds at full gallop; nor does the law await arrival at the goal before condemning the direction of the movement.

Appellant contends, however, that the 'Lixator' contracts are saved from unreasonableness and from the tendency to monopoly because they provided that if any competitor offered salt of equal grade at a lower price, the lessee should be free to buy in the open market, unless appellant would furnish the salt at an equal price; and the 'Saltomat' agreements provided that the lessee was entitled to the benefit of any general price reduction in lessor's salt tablets. The 'Lixator' provision does, of course, afford a measure of protection to the lessee, but it does not avoid the stifling effect of the agreement on competition. The appellant had at all times priority on the business at equal prices. A competitor would have to undercut appellant's price to have any hope of capturing the market, while appellant could hold that market by merely meeting competition. We do not think this concession relieves the contract of being a restraint of trade, albeit a less harsh one than would result in the absence of such a provision. The 'Saltomat' provision obviously has no effect of legal significance since it gives the lessee nothing more than a right to buy appellant's salt tablets at appellant's going price. All purchases must in any event be of appellant's product.

Appellant also urges that since under the leases it remained under an obligation to repair and maintain the machines, it was reasonable to confine their use to its own salt because its high quality assured satisfactory functioning and low maintenance cost. The appellant's rock salt is alleged to have an average sodium chloride content of 98.2%. Rock salt of other producers, it is said, 'does not run consistent in sodium chloride content and in many instances runs as low as 95% of sodium chloride.' This greater percentage of insoluble impurities allegedly disturbs the functioning of the 'Lixator' machine. A somewhat similar claim is pleaded as to the 'Saltomat.'

Of course, a lessor may impose on a lessee reasonable restrictions designed in good faith to minimize maintenance burdens and to assure satisfactory operation. We may assume, as matter of argument, that if the 'Lixator' functions best on rock salt of average sodium chloride content of 98.2%, the lessee might be required to use only salt meeting such a specification of quality. But it is not pleaded, nor is it argued, that the machine is allergic to salt of equal quality produced by any one except International. If others cannot produce salt equal to reasonable specifications for machine use, it is one thing; but it is admitted that, at times, at least, competitors do offer such a product. They are, however, shut out of the market by a provision that limits it, not in terms of quality, but in terms of a particular vendor. Rules for use of leased machinery must not be disguised restraints of free competition, though they may set reasonable standards which all suppliers must meet. [citation omitted]

Appellant urges other objections to the summary judgment. The tying clause has not been insisted upon in all leases, nor has it always been enforced when it was included. But these facts do not justify the general use of the restriction which has been admitted here. ***

Judgment affirmed.

Comments and Questions

1. Scholars have advanced many competing theories to explain why firms impose tying arrangements on their customers. Two major schools—and a constellation of individual theories—disagree about the competitive consequences of tie-ins. One argues that tying requirements necessarily reduce competition and the other concludes that tie-ins are either competitively benign or actually procompetitive.

The traditional arguments against tying arrangements are advanced by the Leverage School, which argues that a firm imposes a tying requirement in an effort to extend its monopoly power over the tying product into the market for the tied product. Not long after its opinion in *International Salt*, the Supreme Court opined that "[b]y conditioning his sale of one commodity on the purchase of another, a seller coerces the abdication of buyers' independent judgment as to the 'tied' product's merits and insulates it from the competitive stresses of the open market." Times-Picayune Pub. Co. v. U.S., 345 U.S. 594, 605 (1953). Competition suppressed, the tying seller could convert her monopoly in the tying product market into a second monopoly in the tied product market. Tying doctrine has largely focused on this risk of a dominant firm converting one monopoly into two. Louis Kaplow, *Extension of Monopoly Power Through Leverage*, 85 COLUMBIA L. REV. 515 (1985). Many adherents of the Leverage School argue that antitrust law should condemn tying arrangements because tie-ins eliminate competition on the merits in the tied product market, reduce consumer surplus, force consumers to make unwanted purchases, and erect barriers to entry. Since its advent in the early twentieth century, leverage theory has become more sophisticated as economists have examined how a dominant seller in one market can expand its market power into an adjacent market under certain conditions. *See* Michael D. Whinston, *Tying, Foreclosure, and Exclusion*, 80 AM. ECON. REV. 837 (1990).

In contrast, adherents of the Chicago School argue that tying arrangements cannot be used to extend monopoly power. Some scholars associated with the Chicago School, as such Robert Bork, have argued that leveraging monopoly power across markets is "impossible" and that "there is no viable theory of a means by which tying arrangements injure competition." ROBERT BORK, ANTITRUST PARADOX 367, 372 (1978). They argue that a tying seller must reduce the price of the tying product in order to convince consumers to accept the tying requirement, which often entails a supra-competitive price for the tied product. In this interpretation of tying, the seller opts to receive some of her monopoly profits—profits that she normally would be earning in the tying product market—in the tied product market. The net level of monopoly profits stays the same; it is simply spread across two different markets when there is a tying arrangement. Instead of viewing tying as a means of injuring competition in the tied product market, many Chicagoans believe that sellers employ tying arrangements to effect price discrimination. *See* WARD S. BOWMAN, PATENT AND ANTITRUST 117–18 (1973). Price discrimination occurs when a seller charges a higher price to those consumers willing to pay more and a lower price to those consumers who value the product less. The price discrimination explanation for tying assumes that the tying seller reduces the price of the tying product—below what would be charge absent the tying requirement—and charges a supra-competitive price for the tied product, which is a product used in conjunction with the tying product. The price discrimination explanation is most persuasive when there is a requirements tying contract. "A 'requirements tie-in' sale occurs when a seller requires customers who purchase one product from the seller (e.g., a printer) also to make all their purchases of another product from the seller (e.g., ink cartridges). Such tying allows the seller to, for example, charge customers different amounts depending on their product usage." U.S. DEP'T OF JUSTICE & FEDERAL TRADE COMMISSION, ANTITRUST ENFORCEMENT AND INTELLECTUAL PROPERTY RIGHTS: PROMOTING INNOVATION AND COMPETITION 10 (2007). The tying arrangement acts as a meter; those consumers who use the tying product more will purchase more of the tied product at an inflated price. This explanation assumes that high-intensity users also place a higher value on the tying product and supplies for it (i.e., the tied product). Chicagoans argue that price discrimination reduces neither output nor efficiency, and thus antitrust law should not condemn tie-ins used to effectuate price discrimination. Consequently, scholars who support this theory of tying advocated per se legality for tie-ins.

Which theory about tying arrangements do you find more persuasive? Why?

Does the Court's opinion in *International Salt* reflect the thinking of the Leverage School or the Chicago School?

2. Can either of the major theories explain the tie-in that International Salt imposed? How do the facts of International Salt undermine both the Leverage School and the Chicago School explanations of tying arrangements?

The *International Salt* Court simply asserted that "the tendency of the arrangement to accomplishment of monopoly seems obvious." But scholars estimate that International Salt enjoyed a market share between 2 and 4 percent of the salt market. *See* Victor P. Goldberg, *The International Salt Puzzle*, 14 RESEARCH IN L. & ECON. 31, 36 (1991) ("…the leases involved less than 2% of annual domestic salt production…"); John L. Peterman, *The International Salt Case*, 22 J.L. & ECON. 351, 351 (1979) (4%). How can a tying seller with less than 5 percent of the market for the tied product monopolize that market through a tying arrangement?

Was International Salt engaging in price discrimination? Could International Salt charge a supra-competitive price for salt?

3. International Salt had two separate tying products—the Lixator and the Saltomat—and it imposed a different form of tying requirement depending on which machine the customer was leasing. (These are the contract clauses found in footnotes 5 and 6 of the case.) Lessees of the Lixator agreed to purchase all of the salt used in the machine from International Salt unless they could find a better

deal elsewhere. This is a price-protection clause that prevented International Salt from charging more than its competitors.

In contrast, lessees of the Saltomat agreed to purchase all of their salt used in those machines from International Salt, but "the lessee was entitled to the benefit of any general price reduction in lessor's salt tablets." This is an example of a most-favored nations (MFN) clause, which insures the customer that the seller will not charge less to any one of *its* customers.

If you were a consumer, would you rather have the price-protection clause or the MFN clause in your contract with International Salt? Why?

How does the presence of these clauses affect the ability of the Leverage School and the Chicago School to explain the purpose and likely competitive effects of the tying arrangement in *International Salt*?

4. Alternative Explanations of Tying.

In addition to the two major theories on tying arrangements, other explanations abound. Some argue that tying arrangements represent a way for tying sellers to protect the quality of their tying product. *See* Benjamin Klein & Lester F. Saft, *The Law and Economics of Franchise Tying Contracts*, 28 J. L. & ECON. 345 (1985); *see also* Marius Schwartz & Gregory J. Werden, *A Quality-Signaling Rationale for Aftermarket Tying*, 64 ANTITRUST L. J. 387, 395 (1996). If the tying product uses inputs and lower-quality inputs cause the tying product to malfunction, a seller may require consumers to purchase inputs from it in order to insure that only high-quality inputs are used. The inputs become tied products. The seller imposes the tying requirement out of concern that lower quality inputs can damage the functioning of the tying product and consumers may hold the seller of the tying product responsible, which could damage the seller's goodwill.

International Salt made this argument, asserting that the use of lower quality salt would reduce the functionality of the two salt machines. The Court rejected this argument. 332 U.S. 392, 397-98 (1947). However, at least some courts have found this goodwill explanation persuasive. See, e.g., *Mozart Co. v. Mercedes Benz of N. Am., Inc.*, 833 F.2d 1342 (9th Cir. 1987). In many instances, courts reason that the tying seller can require the consumer to use a particular quality of input, but cannot necessarily require that the input be purchased from the tying seller.

Others suggest that sellers may use tying arrangements to evade price regulation. For example, if government officials set a maximum price for a particular product, a seller might refuse to sell that product unless the consumer agrees to buy an additional (unregulated) product at an inflated price. The seller charges the regulated price for the tying product but a supracompetitive price for the tied product—as a result, the consumer pays the same price for the bundle of goods that he would have paid if there had not been a price cap on the tying product. Is that explanation persuasive in the *International Salt* case?

Some scholars have hypothesized that a tying requirement with a price-protection clause—as was the case in *International Salt*—could be used to stabilize a price-fixing conspiracy. John L. Peterman, *The International Salt Case*, 22 J.L. & Econ. 351, 361 (1979). Cartels are inherently unstable because members of the conspiracy may cheat by charging a lower price. Detecting such cheating can be very difficult. However, if all the members of a cartel impose a tying requirement with a price-protection clause—in which the price of the tied product is fixed—then consumers would expose cheaters by report the lower price offered by a competitor in order to evade the tying requirement. Consumers unwittingly become the cartel's monitoring system.

Finally, Volume Tying Theory argues that some tying arrangements represent an attempt by a firm that is a monopolist in one market to simply increase its sales in the tied product market, which is a competitive market. The tying seller is not trying to monopolize the second market, but merely to increase its sales volume and consequently its profits. Volume Tying Theory argues that even products sold in a so-called competitive market generate profit for the seller, so the seller has an incentive to maximize its sales volume. Christopher R. Leslie, *Cutting Through Tying Theory with Occam's Razor: A Simple Explanation of Tying Arrangements*, 78 Tul. L. Rev. 727 (2004).

5. Following the Court's holding in *International Salt*, federal courts have long categorized tying arrangements as per se illegal. This is a misnomer because tie-ins are only nominally per se illegal. The per se rule against tie-ins is nominal because: 1) it requires the plaintiff to prove that the defendant has market power over the tying product; 2) it requires the plaintiff to demonstrate that a not insubstantial dollar volume of commerce in the tied product market is affected; and 3) it permits the defendant to argue that she has a legitimate business justification for imposing a tie-in. Some circuits even require that the plaintiff prove the actual anti-competitive effects of the tie-in under a per se test. *See, e.g., United Farmers Agents Assn. v. Farmers Insurance Exchange*, 89 F.3d 233, 235 n.2 (5th Cir. 1996). These elements and defenses negate the per se label because when an antitrust violation is truly per se illegal, the plaintiff does not have to demonstrate the defendants' market power or to prove an anticompetitive effect; both are presumed as a matter of law. Nor is the defendant allowed to proffer a business justification for its conduct when per se rules are strictly applied. Despite the fact that antitrust practitioners realize the deceptive nature of the court's per se language in tying cases, the Supreme Court has refused to repudiate its misuse of the per se tag, opining in 1984 that "[i]t is far too late in the history of our antitrust jurisprudence to question the proposition that certain tying arrangements pose an unacceptable risk of stifling competition and therefore are unreasonable 'per se.'" *Jefferson Parish Hosp. Dist. No. 2 v. Hyde*, 466 U.S. 2, 9 (1984).

6. The Court rejected International Salt's defense that its "tying clause ha[d] not been insisted upon in all leases, nor ha[d] it always been enforced when it was included." Why would a firm include tying requirement and then not enforce it?

7. International Salt leased its machines to its customers. Should a patentee have the right to control a machine to which, by leasing out, it still holds title?

B. Antitrust Implications of Block-Booking of Copyrighted Works

United States v. Paramount Pictures, Inc.
334 U.S. 131 (1948)

Block-booking is the practice of licensing, or offering for license, one feature or group of features on condition that the exhibitor will also license another feature or group of features released by the distributors during a given period. The films are licensed in blocks before they are actually produced. All the defendants, except United Artists, have engaged in the practice. Block-booking prevents competitors from bidding for single features on their individual merits. The District Court held it illegal for that reason and for the reason that it 'adds to the monopoly of a single copyrighted picture that of another copyrighted picture which must be taken and exhibited in order to secure the first.' That enlargement of the monopoly of the copyright was condemned below in reliance on the principle which forbids the owner of a patent to condition its use on the purchase or use of patented or unpatented materials. [citation omitted] The court enjoined defendants from performing or entering into any license in which the right to exhibit one feature is conditioned upon the licensee's taking one or more other features.

We approve that restriction. The copyright law, like the patent statutes, makes reward to the owner a secondary consideration. In *Fox Film Corp. v. Doyal*, 286 U.S. 123, 127, Chief Justice Hughes spoke as follows respecting the copyright monopoly granted by Congress 'The sole interest of the United States and the primary object in conferring the monopoly lie in the general benefits derived by the public from the labors of authors.' It is said that reward to the author or artist serves to induce release to the public of the products of his creative genius. But the reward does not serve its public purpose if it is not related to the quality of the copyright. Where a high quality film greatly desired is licensed only if an inferior one is taken, the latter borrows quality from the former and strengthens its monopoly by drawing on the other. The practice tends to equalize rather than differentiate the reward for the individual copyrights. Even where all the films included in the package are of equal quality, the requirements that all be taken if one is desired increases the market for some. Each stands not on its own footing but in whole or in part on the appeal which another film may have. As the District Court said, the result is to add to the monopoly of the copyright in violation of the principle of the patent cases involving tying clauses. ***

Columbia Pictures makes an earnest argument that enforcement of the restriction as to block-booking will be very disadvantageous to it and will greatly impair its ability to operate profitably. But the policy of the anti-trust laws is not qualified or conditioned by the convenience of those whose conduct is regulated. Nor can a vested interest, in a practice which contravenes the policy of the anti-trust laws, receive judicial sanction.

We do not suggest that films may not be sold in blocks or groups, when there is no requirement, express or implied, for the purchase of more than one film. All we hold to be illegal is a refusal to license one or more copyrights unless another copyright is accepted.

Comments and Questions

1. Courts generally treat block-booking as a form of tying arrangement. Most tying arrangements involve complementary products, such as the salt-processing machines and salt at issue in *International Salt*. How is block-booking different from more traditional tying arrangements? What is the tying product and what is the tied product?

2. Coercion is a necessary element for a tying claim. How is coercion present in block-booking? *See* Six West Retail Acquisition, Inc. v. Sony Theatre Mgmt. Corp., 2000-1 Trade Cas. (CCH) ¶ 72,823 (S.D.N.Y. 2000) ("Because block-booking involves a distributor compelling a theatre to accept movies that it does not want, actual coercion 'is an indispensable element' of a block-booking violation.")

3. Who suffers the anticompetitive effects of block-booking?

4. Several possible explanations exist for why studios engaged in block-booking. While courts held that block-booking represented anticompetitive conduct, scholars have suggested more benign, efficient explanations. For example, Professor Herbert Hovenkamp writes: "A likely explanation for block booking is also transaction cost savings. At the time theaters lease films they do not know how strong the demand for a particular film will be. By leasing in blocks suppliers can give theaters a steady supply of films so that another one will always be available on short notice if the audiences for the current film become too small." HERBERT HOVENKAMP, THE ANTITRUST ENTERPRISE: PRINCIPLE AND EXECUTION 265–266 (2005); F. Andrew Hanssen, *The Block Booking of Films Re-examined*, 43 J. L. & ECON. 395 (2000) (supporting transaction costs explanation for block-booking). Others argue that block-booking is efficient because it reduces the search costs for movie theater owners and managers who no longer have to research individual films. *See* Roy Kenney & Benjamin Klein, *The Economics of Block Booking*, 26 J. LAW & ECON. 497 (1983).

In an influential article, economist George Stigler explained how block-booking may operate as a form of price discrimination. George J. Stigler, United States v. Loew's Inc.: *A Note On Block-Booking*, 1963 SUP. CT. REV. 152 (1963). As explained above, scholars associated with the Chicago School argue that tying may reflect price discrimination. The price discrimination explanation works best with requirements tie-ins. However, the theory also works when the tying seller has market power in both the tying and tied products markets so long as consumers desire both products but assign them different relative values. Michael D. Whinston, *Tying, Foreclosure, and Exclusion*, 80 AM. ECON. REV. 837 (1990).

Stigler explained how block-booking can maximize a studio's profits by hypothesizing two theaters that each value two films differently. Theater A is willing to pay $8,000 to lease Film X and $2,500 to lease Film Y. Theater B is willing to pay $7,000 to lease Film X and $3,000 to lease Film Y. Both theaters value Film X more than Film Y, but the strength of the relative preferences is different. Assume that the studio charges the same price to all theaters.

If the studio leased the films separately, it could not charge more than $7,000 for Film X (the most that Theater B is willing to pay) or more than $2,500 for Film Y (the most that Theater A is willing to pay). The studio earns licensing fees totaling $19,000 ($2,500 times 2, plus $7,000 times 2). However, if the studio engaged in block-booking, it could tell the theaters that Films X and Y can only be leased together and the price for the block of movies is $10,000. Theater A would accept the terms because it values the bundle of movies at $10,500 ($8,000 + $2,500) and Theater A would accept the terms because it values the bundle of movies at $10,000 ($7,000 + $3,000). Under this scheme, the studio would receive $20,000, $1,000 more than if it charged the profit-maximizing price absent block-booking.

Which of the explanations for block-booking do you find most persuasive and why?

Given which explanation you find most persuasive, what implications does that have for the legality of block-booking under antitrust laws?

5. Whatever nomenclature courts apply, the federal antitrust agencies have announced that they will rule of reason analysis in determining which tying claims involving IP they will prosecute. *See* U.S. Dep't of Justice & Federal Trade Commission, Antitrust Enforcement and Intellectual Property Rights: Promoting Innovation and Competition 114 (2007) ("Thus, as a matter of their prosecutorial discretion, the Agencies will apply the rule of reason when evaluating intellectual property tying and bundling agreements.").

If block-booking arrangements were analyzed under the Rule of Reason, what factors should the court consider? Under what circumstances would block-booking violate the Rule of Reason?

United States v. Loew's, Inc.

371 U.S. 38 (1962)

Mr. Justice GOLDBERG delivered the opinion of the Court.

These consolidated appeals present as a key question the validity under § 1 of the Sherman Act of block booking of copyrighted feature motion pictures for television exhibition. We hold that the tying agreements here are illegal and in violation of the Act.

The United States brought separate civil antitrust actions in the Southern District of New York in 1957 against six major distributors of pre- 1948 copyrighted motion picture feature films for television exhibition, alleging that each defendant had engaged in block booking in violation of § 1 of the Sherman Act. The complaints asserted that the defendants had, in selling to television stations, conditioned the license or sale of one or more feature films upon the acceptance by the station of a package or block containing one or more unwanted or inferior films. No combination or conspiracy among the distributors was alleged; nor was any

142 *Antitrust Law and Intellectual Property Rights*

monopolization or attempt to monopolize under § 2 of the Sherman Act averred. The sole claim of illegality rested on the manner in which each defendant had marketed its product. The successful pressure applied to television station customers to accept inferior films along with desirable pictures was the gravamen of the complaint.

After a lengthy consolidated trial, the district judge filed exhaustive findings of fact, conclusions of law, and a carefully reasoned opinion, [citation omitted]in which he found that the actions of the defendants constituted violations of § 1 of the Sherman Act. The conclusional finding of fact and law was that

> '* * * the several defendants have each, from time to time *** licensed or offered to license one or more feature films to television stations on condition that the licensee also license one or more other such feature films, and have, from time to time *** refused, expressly or impliedly, to license feature films to television stations unless one or more other such feature films were accepted by the licensee.' [citation omitted]

The judge recognized that there was keen competition between the defendant distributors, and therefore rested his conclusion solely on the individual behavior of each in engaging in block booking. In reaching his decision he carefully considered the evidence relating to each of the 68 licensing agreements that the Government had contended involved block booking. He concluded that only 25 of the contracts were illegally entered into. Nine of these belonged to defendant C & C Super Corp., which had an admitted policy of insisting on block booking that it sought to justify on special grounds.

Of the others, defendant Loew's, Incorporated, had in two negotiations that resulted in licensing agreements declined to furnish stations KWTV of Oklahoma City and WBRE of Wilkes-Barre with individual film prices and had refused their requests for permission to select among the films in the groups. Loew's exacted from KWTV a contract for the entire Loew's library of 723 films, involving payments of $314,725.20. The WBRE agreement was for a block of 100 films, payments to total $15,000.

Defendant Screen Gems, Inc., was also found to have block booked two contracts, both with WTOP of Washington, D.C., one calling for a package of 26 films and payments of $20,800 and the other for 52 films and payments of $40,000. The judge accepted the testimony of station officials that they had requested the right to select films and that their requests were refused.

Associated Artists Productions, Inc., negotiated four contracts that were found to be block booked. Station WTOP was to pay $118,800 for the license of 99 pictures, which were divided into three groups of 33 films, based on differences in quality. To get 'Treasure of the Sierra Madre,' 'Casablanca,' 'Johnny Belinda,' 'Sergeant York,' and 'The Man Who Came to Dinner,' among others, WTOP also had to take such films as 'Nancy Drew Troubleshooter,' 'Tugboat Annie Sails Again,' 'Kid Nightingale,' 'Gorilla Man,' and 'Tear Gas Squad.' A similar contract for 100 pictures, involving a license fee of $140,000, was entered into by WMAR of Baltimore.

Triangle Publications, owner and operator of five stations, was refused the right to select among Associated's packages, and ultimately purchased the entire library of 754 films for a price of $2,262,000 plus 10% of gross receipts. Station WJAR of Providence, which licensed a package of 58 features for a fee of $25,230, had asked first if certain films it considered undesirable could be dropped from the offered packages and was told that the packages could not be split. *** [The Court gave other examples of block booking.]

We shall consider *** the fundamental question whether their activities were in violation of the antitrust laws. ***

I.

This case raises the recurring question of whether specific tying arrangements violate § 1 of the Sherman Act. This Court has recognized that '(t)ying agreements serve hardly any purpose beyond the suppression of competition,' *Standard Oil Co. of California v. United States*, 337 U.S. 293, 305—306. They are an object of antitrust concern for two reasons—they may force buyers into giving up the purchase of substitutes for the tied product, [citation omitted] and they may destroy the free access of competing suppliers of the tied product to the consuming market, see *International Salt Co. v. United States*, 332 U.S. 392, 396. A tie-in contract may have one or both of these undesirable effects when the seller, by virtue of his position in the market for the tying product, has economic leverage sufficient to induce his customers to take the tied product along with the tying item. The standard of illegality is that the seller must have 'sufficient economic power with respect to the tying product to appreciably restrain free competition in the market for the tied product * * *.' [citation omitted] Market dominance—some power to control price and to exclude competition—is by no means the only test of whether the seller has the requisite economic power. Even absent a showing of market dominance, the crucial economic power may be inferred from the tying product's desirability to consumers or from uniqueness in its attributes.[4]

The requisite economic power is presumed when the tying product is patented or copyrighted, *International Salt Co. v. United States*, 332 U.S. 392; *United States v. Paramount Pictures, Inc.*, 334 U.S. 131. This principle grew out of a long line of patent cases which had eventuated in the doctrine that a patentee who utilized tying arrangements would be denied all relief against infringements of his patent. [citation omitted] These cases reflect a hostility to use of the statutorily granted patent monopoly to extend the patentee's economic control to unpatented products.

---

[4] Since the requisite economic power may be found on the basis of either uniqueness or consumer appeal, and since market dominance in the present context does not necessitate a demonstration of market power in the sense of § 2 of the Sherman Act, it should seldom be necessary in a tie-in sale case to embark upon a full-scale factual inquiry into the scope of the relevant market for the tying product and into the corollary problem of the seller's percentage share in that market. This is even more obviously true when the tying product is patented or copyrighted, in which case, *** sufficiency of economic power is presumed. ***

144 *Antitrust Law and Intellectual Property Rights*

The patentee is protected as to his invention, but may not use his patent rights to exact tribute for other articles.

Since one of the objectives of the patent laws is to reward uniqueness, the principle of these cases was carried over into antitrust law on the theory that the existence of a valid patent on the tying product, without more, establishes a distinctiveness sufficient to conclude that any tying arrangement involving the patented product would have anticompetitive consequences. [citation omitted] In *United States v. Paramount Pictures, Inc.*, 334 U.S. 131, 156—159, the principle of the patent cases was applied to copyrighted feature films which had been block booked into movie theaters. ***

Appellants attempt to distinguish the Paramount decision in its relation to the present facts: the block booked sale of copyrighted feature films to exhibitors in a new medium—television. Not challenging the District Court's finding that they did engage in block booking, they contend that the uniqueness attributable to a copyrighted feature film, though relevant in the movie-theater context, is lost when the film is being sold for television use. Feature films, they point out, constitute less than 8% of television programming, and they assert that films are 'reasonably interchangeable' with other types of programming material and with other feature films as well. Thus they argue that their behavior is not to be judged by the principle of the patent cases, as applied to copyrighted materials in Paramount Pictures, but by the general principles which govern the validity of tying arrangements of nonpatented products. [citation omitted] They say that the Government's proof did not establish their 'sufficient economic power' in the sense contemplated for nonpatented products.

Appellants cannot escape the applicability of *Paramount Pictures*. A copyrighted feature film does not lose its legal or economic uniqueness because it is shown on a television rather than a movie screen.

The district judge found that each copyrighted film block booked by appellants for television use 'was in itself a unique product'; that feature films 'varied in theme, in artistic performance, in stars, in audience appeal, etc.,' and were not fungible; and that since each defendant by reason of its copyright had a 'monopolistic' position as to each tying product, 'sufficient economic power' to impose an appreciable restraint on free competition in the tied product was present, as demanded by the Northern Pacific decision. [citation omitted][6] We agree. These findings of the district judge, supported by the record, confirm the presumption of uniqueness resulting from the existence of the copyright itself.

Moreover, there can be no question in this case of the adverse effects on free competition resulting from appellants' illegal block booking contracts. Television stations forced by appellants to take unwanted films were denied access to films marketed by other distributors who, in turn, were foreclosed from selling to the stations.

---

[6] To use the trial court's apt example, forcing a television station which wants 'Gone With The Wind' to take 'Getting Gertie's Garter' as well [is] taking undue advantage of the fact that to television as well as motion picture viewers there is but one 'Gone With The Wind.'

Nor can there be any question as to the substantiality of the commerce involved. The 25 contracts found to have been illegally block booked involved payments to appellants ranging from $60,800 in the case of Screen Gems to over $2,500,000 in the case of Associated Artists. A substantial portion of the licensing fees represented the cost of the inferior films which the stations were required to accept. These anticompetitive consequences are an apt illustration of the reasons underlying out recognition that the mere presence of competing substitutes for the tying product, here taking the form of other programming material as well as other feature films, is insufficient to destroy the legal, and indeed the economic, distinctiveness of the copyrighted product. [citation omitted] By the same token, the distinctiveness of the copyrighted tied product is not inconsistent with the fact of competition, in the form of other programming material and other films, which is suppressed by the tying arrangements.

It is therefore clear that the tying arrangements here both by their 'inherent nature' and by their 'effect' injuriously restrained trade. [citation omitted] Accommodation between the statutorily dispensed monopoly in the combination of contents in the patented or copyrighted product and the statutory principles of free competition demands that extension of the patent or copyright monopoly by the use of tying agreements be strictly confined. There may be rare circumstances in which the doctrine we have enunciated under § 1 of the Sherman Act prohibiting tying arrangements involving patented or copyrighted tying products is inapplicable. However, we find it difficult to conceive of such a case, and the present case is clearly not one.

The principles underlying our *Paramount Pictures* decision have general application to tying arrangements involving copyrighted products, and govern here. *** Enforced block booking of films is a vice in both the motion picture and television industries, and that the sin is more serious (in dollar amount) in one than the other does not expiate the guilt for either. Appellants' block booked contracts are covered by the flat holding in Paramount Pictures [citation omitted] that 'a refusal to license one or more copyrights unless another copyright is accepted' is 'illegal.' ***

Comments and Questions

1. Why is block-booking to television stations exclusionary such that antitrust law should care about it? If the value of those movies in the package that the television station actually wants exceeds the price of the total package, why can't the television station buy the package and then simply not show the inferior movies? After all, some of the packages included over seven hundred films and, in some cases, certain "films were unplayable since they had a foreign language sound track." Does the presence of unplayable films make the block-booking exclusionary?

Is there a difference between licensing a movie for $10,000 and paying the same amount to license a block of movies that includes that movie as well as two others that the station has no interest in showing?

The Court asserted: "A substantial portion of the licensing fees represented the cost of the inferior films which the stations were required to accept." Is that necessarily true?

2. Section One of the Sherman Act is supposed to condemn agreements that unreasonably restrain trade. Where is the anticompetitive effect in this case? The Court argues: "Television stations forced by appellants to take unwanted films were denied access to films marketed by other distributors who, in turn, were foreclosed from selling to the stations." Is that necessarily true?

3. The Supreme Court opinions in *Paramount* and *Loew's* relied on the per se rule established in *International Salt*, which was also the case that served as the basis for the rule that if a tying seller has a patent on the tying product, then the seller can be presumed to possess market power in the tying product market. Does the Supreme Court's opinion in *Illinois Tool Works* (excerpted in Chapter 3), in which the Court invalidated that presumption as applied to patents, affect the per se rule against block booking? *See* Leonard J. Feldman, Rima J. Alaily & Chad D. Farrell, *Independent Ink at the Crossroads of Antitrust and Intellectual Property Law: The Court's Holding Regarding Market Power in Cases Involving Patents and Implications in Cases Involving Copyrights*, 30 SEATTLE U. L. REV. 407 (2007).

4. The Court quotes *Standard Oil* for the proposition that "tying agreements serve hardly any purpose beyond the suppression of competition." Is that true? Why does the Court say this?

5. Is reducing search costs a persuasive explanation of block-booking imposed on TV stations? Do TV stations have different search costs than movie theaters?

6. Tying arrangements can violate Section One or Two of the Sherman Act, Section Three of the Clayton Act, or Section Five of the FTC Act, but most tying claims are brought under Section One. The facts of *Loew's* show the peculiarity of this situation, as the Supreme Court noted: "No combination or conspiracy among the distributors was alleged" and that "there was keen competition between the defendant distributors." Yet the Court still found a violation of Section 1 of the Sherman Act, which prohibits concerted action that unreasonably restrains trade. The *Loew's* decision highlights a quirk of antitrust law in which non-conspiratorial tying arrangements are condemned under the Sherman Act provision that addresses conspiracies. Most courts never mention this anomaly, but a couple of courts have justified condemning tie-ins under Section One because they are contracts between the seller who imposes the tying requirement and the consumer who acquiesces. *See, e.g.,* Systemcare, Inc. v. Wang Labs. Corp., 117 F.3d 1137, 1145 (10th Cir. 1997) (en banc). *See* Christopher R. Leslie, *Unilaterally Imposed Tying Arrangements and Antitrust's Concerted Action Requirement*, 60 OHIO ST. L. J. 1773 (1999) (criticizing *Systemcare* and discussing the origin and consequences of the antitrust anomaly whereby unilateral tying is condemned under Section One). Because tying is, at its heart, unilateral conduct, we discussed it here in Part 2: Unilateral Conduct.

Tying Arrangements and Intellectual Property 147

Outlet Communications, Inc. v. King World Productions, Inc.
685 F.Supp. 1570 (M.D.Fla. 1988)

GEORGE KENDALL SHARP, District Judge.

[The plaintiff—WCPX, a television station in Orlando, Florida—sued King World—the exclusive distributor of the television game show, Wheel of Fortune, which was the highest rated syndicated TV show at the time of the case. WCPX had licensed the program for two years. Then King World allegedly refused to license Wheel of Fortune unless the TV station also purchased licenses for two other TV game shows, Jeopardy and Headline Chasers. When WCPX refused to accept the condition, King World licensed the three programs to WCPX's competitor—WFTV. WCPX alleged that King World violated Section One by coercing WFTV (not WCPX, which declined the tying requirement) into an illegal tying arrangement. The defendant moved for judgment on the pleadings.] ***

Plaintiff claims that defendant possesses an unfair economic advantage over its competitors in the market because of its position as sole distributor of Wheel of Fortune and the success of that game show, and that it coerced the tie-in license agreement that resulted in Wheel of Fortune being obtained by a competitor ***. As a result of defendant's actions, plaintiff alleges that it will lose audience and advertising revenues in excess of $1,000,000.00 for commercial time during the telecast of WHEEL OF FORTUNE as well as for prior and subsequent programming. Plaintiff also claims treble damages, interest, attorneys' fees and costs, pursuant to section 4 of the Clayton Act, 15 U.S.C. § 15. ***

Plaintiff has alleged a tying arrangement by defendant whereby plaintiff economically could not license Wheel of Fortune (the tying product) for 1985–1986 without also licensing Jeopardy! and Headline Chasers (the tied products) from defendant. ***

Plaintiff's complaint has alleged facts that could meet the definitional requirements of a tying arrangement, the analysis that the court must make in deciding a motion for judgment on the pleadings. Plaintiff has represented that, economically, it could not license Wheel of Fortune for 1985–1986 without also licensing the less desirable game shows, Jeopardy! and Headline Chasers. ***

Simply marketing two products together in a package is not an unlawful tying arrangement. ***

In order to prove that a tying arrangement is illegal per se, a plaintiff must establish four elements:

(1) that there are two separate products, a "tying" product and a "tied" product;
(2) that those products are in fact "tied" together-that is, the buyer was forced to buy the tied product to get the tying product;
(3) that the seller possesses sufficient economic power in the tying product market to coerce buyer acceptance of the tied product; and
(4) involvement of a "not insubstantial" amount of interstate commerce in the market of the tied product.

Tic-X-Press, 815 F.2d at 1414 [citation omitted]

148 *Antitrust Law and Intellectual Property Rights*

The court has reservations concerning plaintiff's ability to establish the first element. *** Since Jeopardy! and Headline Chasers, like Wheel of Fortune, also are game shows, plaintiff's complaint is unclear as to whether there are two product markets as opposed to two products within the same market. From the facts stated in plaintiff's complaint, it is questionable to the court that there is any market for the tied product Headline Chasers, and restraint of competition in the tied product market is a crucial component for analysis of a per se illegal tying arrangement. Because plaintiff may be able to prove some set of facts to overcome this potential barrier to its per se illegal tying arrangement claim and because there are possible legal and factual bases for the remaining elements, the court is unwilling to foreclose plaintiff's antitrust allegation on this first element in a motion for judgment on the pleadings.

The second element that a plaintiff must allege is "that the seller forced or coerced the buyer into purchasing the tied product." [citation omitted] The court is cognizant that plaintiff did not purchase or license the alleged tied products for the 1985-1986 broadcast year. *** "It is clear that although competitors do not have to show that they themselves were forced or coerced to do anything, they do have to show that the buyer of the tied package was forced or coerced to buy the tied product." *Tic-X-Press*, 815 F.2d at 1415 n. 15.

Direct evidence of coercive behavior is not required, rather "coercion may be established by showing that the facts and circumstances surrounding the transaction as a practical matter forced the buyer into purchasing the tied product." *Id.* at 1418 [citation omitted] ***

The third element that a plaintiff must plead to prove a per se illegal tying arrangement is that defendant had sufficient "[e]conomic or market power" to force the purchaser into a tying arrangement, which the purchaser would not accept in a competitive market. [citation omitted] *** Plaintiff has alleged that defendant controls or holds the copyright to Wheel of Fortune. There is no dispute that defendant has the exclusive right to distribute Wheel of Fortune, which has the highest audience ratings of any syndicated television show. It appears to the court that plaintiff has demonstrated the uniqueness and desirability of Wheel of Fortune, the tying product, and that defendant has the requisite or sufficient market power. See *Tic-X-Press*, 815 F.2d at 1420.

The fourth element that a plaintiff must allege to prove a per se illegal tying arrangement is involvement of a "not insubstantial" amount of interstate commerce in the market of the tied product. *Id.* at 1414, 1419 [citation omitted]. The Supreme Court has held that the "controlling consideration" in determining whether the volume of commerce in the tied market is "not insubstantial" is "whether a total amount of business, substantial enough in terms of dollar-volume of business so as not to be merely de minimis, is foreclosed to competitors by the tie. . . ." *Fortner*, 394 U.S. at 501 [citation omitted] ***

The facts alleged in plaintiff's complaint are deficient for the court's analysis of the fourth element for establishing an unlawful per se tying arrangement. Not only has plaintiff failed to delineate the tied market, but also it has not provided a dollar amount with respect to the tied market to enable the court to make the de minimis determination. [citation omitted] Although plaintiff has failed to allege adequately two of the four elements of a per se illegal tying arrangement, the court deems it advisable not to preclude plaintiff's antitrust claim on the merits because of pleading deficiencies. Accordingly, defendant's motion for judgment on the pleadings as to *** the antitrust claim *** is DENIED.

Comments and Questions

1. Are there two separate product markets? Why or why not?

2. The court cited the pre-*Illinois Tool Works* rule that when the tying product is copyrighted, economic power is presumed. Did the court need the presumption in this case? Why or why not?

Does the fact that the tying product is copyrighted inform the antitrust analysis?

3. Is competition in the tied product market injured in this case?

4. Does the alleged tying arrangement inflict antitrust injury?

C. Copyrighted Software and Tying

Digidyne Corp. v. Data General Corp.
734 F.2d 1336 (9th Cir. 1984)

BROWNING, Chief Judge:

The issue presented for review is whether Data General's refusal to license its NOVA operating system software except to purchasers of its NOVA central processing units (CPUs) is an unlawful tying arrangement under section 1 of the Sherman Act and section 3 of the Clayton Act [citation omitted]. We conclude that it is.

I.

Defendant Data General manufactures a computer system known as NOVA. The system consists of a NOVA CPU designed to perform a particular "instruction set" or group of tasks, and a copyrighted NOVA operating system called RDOS containing the basic commands for operation of the system. Not all operating systems work with all CPUs. Plaintiffs produce emulator NOVA CPUs designed to perform the NOVA instruction set and thus to make use of defendant's RDOS.

Data General refuses to license its RDOS to anyone who does not also purchase its NOVA CPU. Plaintiffs allege that this constitutes an unlawful tying arrangement; the defendant's RDOS being the tying product, the NOVA instruction set CPU being the tied product.

Plaintiffs filed a number of actions alleging violations of section 1 of the Sherman Act and section 3 of the Clayton Act. The actions were consolidated. The issues of liability and damages were segregated for trial. This appeal is from a judgment on liability.

*** Trial, limited to the issue of defendant's economic power, resulted in a jury verdict for plaintiffs. Defendant's motion for judgment n.o.v. or for a new trial was granted. Plaintiffs appealed.

II.

A tying arrangement is illegal if it is shown to restrain competition unreasonably or is illegal per se, without such a showing, if certain prerequisites are met. [citation omitted] The prerequisites of per se illegality are: (1) separate products, the purchase of one (tying product) being conditioned on purchase of the other (tied product); (2) sufficient economic power with respect to the tying product to restrain competition appreciably in the tied product; and (3) an effect upon a substantial amount of commerce in the tied product. [citation omitted] These prerequisites were satisfied in this case. We therefore do not consider whether competition was in fact unreasonably restrained.

The district court properly granted summary judgment on the first and third of the required elements of a per se violation, holding that on the undisputed facts the NOVA instruction set CPU and defendant's RDOS are separate products and the volume of commerce in NOVA instruction set CPUs tied to the purchase of defendant's RDOS is substantial. [citation omitted]

We adopt the district court's reasoning on these issues, adding that the court's analysis of defendant's "single product" claim is supported by the Supreme Court's recent discussion in *Jefferson Parish Hospital District No. 2 v. Hyde*, 466 U.S. 2 (1984). The undisputed facts summarized in the district court's opinion establish that a demand existed for NOVA instruction set CPUs separate from defendant's RDOS, and that each element of the NOVA computer system could have been provided separately and selected separately by customers if defendant had not compelled purchasers to take both. [citation omitted]

The remaining element necessary to establish a per se violation-defendant's possession of sufficient economic power with respect to the tying product, defendant's RDOS-was tried to a jury and resolved in plaintiffs' favor. The district court erred in setting aside this verdict or, alternatively, ordering a new trial.

III.

*** As the Supreme Court said in *United States v. Loew's, Inc.*, 371 U.S. 38, 45 (1962):

> Market dominance-some power to control price and to exclude competition-is by no means the only test of whether the seller has the requisite economic power. Even absent a showing of market dominance, the crucial economic power may be inferred from the tying product's desirability to consumers or from uniqueness in its attributes.

This position was re-affirmed in the *Fortner* cases. In *Fortner I*:

> The standard of "sufficient economic power" does not, as the District Court held, require that the defendant have a monopoly or even a dominant position throughout the market for the tying product. Our tie-in cases have made unmistakably clear that the economic power over the tying product can be sufficient even though the power falls far short of dominance and *even though the power exists only with respect to some of the buyers in the market*. . . .
>
> . . . [T]he presence of any appreciable restraint on competition provides a sufficient reason for invalidating the tie. Such appreciable restraint results *whenever the seller can exert some power over some of the buyers in the market, even if his power is not complete over them and over all other buyers in the market* . . . . [D]espite the freedom of some or many buyers from the seller's power, other buyers-whether few or many, whether scattered throughout the market or part of some group within the market-can be forced to accept the higher price because of their stronger preferences for the product, and the seller could therefore choose instead to force them to accept a tying arrangement that would prevent free competition for their patronage in the market for the tied product. Accordingly, the proper focus of concern is whether the seller has the power to raise prices, or impose other burdensome terms such as a tie-in, *with respect to any appreciable number of buyers within the market*.

394 U.S. at 502-04 (emphasis added). ***

In accordance with these holdings, we review the record not for what it may reveal as to defendant's position in a defined market in which defendant's RDOS was sold, but only to determine whether the jury reasonably could have concluded defendant's RDOS was sufficiently unique and desirable to an appreciable number of buyers to enable defendant to force those buyers also to buy a substantial volume of defendant's NOVA instruction set CPUs they would have preferred not to buy.

IV.

There was abundant evidence that defendant's RDOS was distinctive and particularly desirable to a substantial number of buyers, and could not be readily produced by other sellers. There was also substantial evidence that defendant's insistence upon licensing its RDOS only to purchasers of defendant's NOVA instruction set CPU, led buyers to purchase defendant's NOVA CPUs who would not have bought them or would have bought them elsewhere absent the tying requirement.

Although expressing some doubt as to the sufficiency of the evidence, the district court assumed defendant's RDOS was superior to competing operating systems and was viewed as uniquely desirable by buyers. [citation omitted] We do not share the court's hesitancy about the adequacy of the proof of the strong preference of many customers for RDOS. It was a most popular product. Experts, customers, and even competitors testified to its many advantages over competitive products. Defendant's own officials expressed the same opinion in pre-litigation documents.

Defendant's RDOS has copyright protection. Defendant also claimed the production of RDOS required use of defendant's trade secrets. The RDOS copyright established both the distinctiveness of RDOS and a legal bar to its reproduction by competitors. "The requisite economic power is presumed when the tying product is patented or copyrighted." *United States v. Loew's, Inc.*, 371 U.S. at 45. The copyright confers upon defendant "some advantages not shared by his competitors in the market for the tying product." *Fortner II*, 429 U.S. at 620 . ***

There is abundant evidence, including testimony of defendant's own executives, customers, and plaintiffs' expert witnesses, that defendant's RDOS could not be reproduced without infringing defendant's copyright and utilizing defendant's trade secrets.[3] Defendant vigorously pursued those who assertedly violated defendant's proprietary rights. Additionally, there was evidence that creating and testing a compatible system would require millions of dollars and years of effort. One of defendant's officers testified that the passage of the time required to reproduce RDOS would render the completed software obsolete.

The power to coerce that RDOS gave the defendant was enhanced by the fact that many of defendant's customers were "locked in" to the use of RDOS. Briefly, defendant sells RDOS and NOVA CPUs primarily to original equipment manufacturers (OEMs) who combine them with application software (a set of instructions that allows the system to accomplish a particular task) to create a complete computer system for resale. Application system software for particular uses is developed by OEMs at substantial expense. Once developed, application software for a particular use may be used by an OEM in producing any number of computer systems for that use for resale to different customers. However, application software is designed to function only with a particular operating system. OEMs who construct their application software to function with defendant's RDOS therefore must purchase an RDOS for each computer system they assemble using that application software. Because of the tying condition, they also must purchase one of defendant's NOVA instruction set CPUS for each such computer system they sell.

An OEM can free itself from this "lock in" only by abandoning its application software compatible with defendant's RDOS, in which it has a substantial investment, or converting the software so that it may be used with another operating system. There was abundant testimony that conversion was not economically feasible.

The defendant argues that "lock-in" is irrelevant in determining its market power because OEMs are aware of the tie when they select an operating system for the computer system they are assembling. At that point, defendant argues, the OEM has made no investment in application software and, as a result, chooses freely among competing systems. [citation omitted] This characterization of the market is not accurate. As the evidence in this case establishes, the initial choice is

---

[3] One of defendant's officers admitted it would be impossible to develop operating system software performing all the functions of defendant's RDOS without violating defendant's copyright and utilizing its trade secrets.

not free of forcing. Defendant's operating system has been shown to be unique as a matter of law and distinctively attractive as a matter of fact. Defendant's initial leverage is magnified by the lock-in. By 1979, 93 percent of defendant's NOVA CPU sales were made to locked-in customers. These buyers were not only forced to buy defendant's CPUs initially to acquire the operating system they found most attractive, they were thereafter forced to buy defendant's CPUs for their subsequent needs in order to acquire the only operating system they could economically use. Not even a decision by CPU manufacturers to broaden their base and compete in the operating system market would have alleviated the problem, for the locked-in customers were not free to choose among competing operating systems. RDOS was the only operating system that would allow them to realize the benefit of their investment in application software, an investment that in some cases totalled millions of dollars.

OEM testimony confirmed defendant's potential power to coerce arising from the lock-in. For example, one OEM witness testified "[w]ithout [the RDOS operating system] I can't operate"; and another: "economically I was in a position where I had to use RDOS. I had no choice at that point." ***

Evidence regarding the potential sources of power with respect to RDOS (copyright, trade secret, and "lock-in"), was submitted to the jury under appropriate instructions. The jury found as a fact that defendant possessed and used the power by means of the tying arrangement to appreciably restrain competition in the market for NOVA instruction set CPUs. The evidence outlined above fully supported the jury's verdict. ***

Comments and Questions

1. Why does the court conclude that it does "not consider whether competition was in fact unreasonably restrained." Is that appropriate? Why or why not?

2. A tying arrangement requires two separate products. Why are the CPU and the software considered two separate products in this case?

3. One element of illegal tying is the tying defendant has sufficient economic power in the market for the tying product. The *Digidyne* court quotes the Fortner I for the proposition that this element can be satisfied if "the seller has the power to raise prices, or impose other burdensome terms such as a tie-in, *with respect to any appreciable number of buyers within the market*." What should constitute an "appreciable number of buyers"?

4. The *Digidyne* court notes when the defendant owns IP rights over the tying product, market power is presumed. As discussed in Chapter 3, *Illinois Tool Works* reversed this presumption for patented tying products—and necessarily undermined as applied to copyrighted tying products. The *Digidyne* court invoked the presumption, but did the court need the presumption in order to find that this defendant had economic power over tying product?

Does the combination of copyright and trade secrets make a stronger case for the defendant possessing market power over the tying product?

D. Trademarks and Tying

Siegel v. Chicken Delight, Inc.
448 F.2d 43 (9th Cir. 1971)

MERRILL, Circuit Judge:

This antitrust suit is a class action in which certain franchisees of Chicken Delight seek treble damages for injuries allegedly resulting from illegal restraints imposed by Chicken Delight's standard form franchise agreements. The restraints in question are Chicken Delight's contractual requirements that franchisees purchase certain essential cooking equipment, dry-mix food items, and trade-mark bearing packaging exclusively from Chicken Delight as a condition of obtaining a Chicken Delight trade-mark license. These requirements are asserted to constitute a tying arrangement, unlawful per se under § 1 of the Sherman Act.

After five weeks of trial to a jury in the District Court, plaintiffs moved for a directed verdict, requesting the court to rule upon four propositions of law: (1) That the contractual requirements constituted a tying arrangement as a matter of law; (2) that the alleged tying products-the Chicken Delight name, symbols, and system of operation -possessed sufficient economic power to condemn the tying arrangement as a matter of law; (3) that the tying arrangement had not, as a matter of law, been justified; and (4) that, as a matter of law, plaintiffs as a class had been injured by the arrangement. The court ruled in favor of plaintiffs on all issues except part of the justification defense, which it submitted to the jury. On the questions submitted to it, the jury rendered special verdicts in favor of plaintiffs. ***

I. Factual Background

Over its eighteen years existence, Chicken Delight has licensed several hundred franchisees to operate home delivery and pick-up food stores. It charged its franchisees no franchise fees or royalties. Instead, in exchange for the license granting the franchisees the right to assume its identity and adopt its business methods and to prepare and market certain food products under its trade-mark, Chicken Delight required its franchisees to purchase a specified number of cookers and fryers and to purchase certain packaging supplies and mixes exclusively from Chicken Delight.

The prices fixed for these purchases were higher than, and included a percentage markup which exceeded that of, comparable products sold by competing suppliers.

II. The Existence of an Unlawful Tying Arrangement

In order to establish that there exists an unlawful tying arrangement plaintiffs must demonstrate: First, that the scheme in question involves two distinct items and provides that one (the tying product) may not be obtained unless the other (the tied product) is also purchased. Times-Picayune Publishing Co. v. United States,

345 U.S. 594, 613-614 (1953). Second, that the tying product possesses sufficient economic power appreciably to restrain competition in the tied product market. *Northern Pacific R. Co. v. United States,* 356 U.S. 1, 6 (1958). Third, that a "not insubstantial" amount of commerce is affected by the arrangement. *International Salt Co. v. United States,* 332 U.S. 392 (1947). Chicken Delight concedes that the third requirement has been satisfied. It disputes the existence of the first two. Further it asserts that, even if plaintiffs should prevail with respect to the first two requirements, there is a fourth issue: whether there exists a special justification for the particular tying arrangement in question. *United States v. Jerrold Electronics Corp.,* 187 F.Supp. 545 (E.D.Pa.1960), aff'd per curiam, 365 U.S. 567 (1961).

A. Two Products

The District Court ruled that the license to use the Chicken Delight name, trademark, and method of operations was "a tying item in the traditional sense," 311 F.Supp. at 849, the tied items being the cookers and fryers, packaging products, and mixes.

The court's decision to regard the trade-mark or franchise license as a distinct tying item is not without precedent. In *Susser v. Carvel Corp.,* 332 F.2d 505 (2d Cir. 1964), all three judges regarded as a tying product the trade-mark license to ice cream outlet franchisees, who were required to purchase ice cream, toppings and other supplies from the franchisor. [citation omitted] Nevertheless, Chicken Delight argues that the District Court's conclusion conflicts with the purposes behind the strict rules governing the use of tying arrangements.

The hallmark of a tie-in is that it denies competitors free access to the tied product market, not because the party imposing the arrangement has a superior product in that market, but because of the power or leverage exerted by the tying product. [citation omitted] Rules governing tying arrangements are designed to strike, not at the mere coupling of physically separable objects, but rather at the use of a dominant desired product to compel the purchase of a second, distinct commodity. [citation omitted] In effect, the forced purchase of the second, tied product is a price exacted for the purchase of the dominant, tying product. By shutting competitors out of the tied product market, tying arrangements serve hardly any purpose other than the suppression of competition. [citation omitted]

Chicken Delight urges us to hold that its trade-mark and franchise licenses are not items separate and distinct from the packaging, mixes, and equipment, which it says are essential components of the franchise system. To treat the combined sale of all these items as a tie-in for antitrust purposes, Chicken Delight maintains, would be like applying the antitrust rules to the sale of a car with its tires or a left shoe with the right. Therefore, concludes Chicken Delight, the lawfulness of the arrangement should not be measured by the rules governing tie-ins. We disagree.

In determining whether an aggregation of separable items should be regarded as one or more items for tie-in purposes in the normal cases of sales of products the courts must look to the function of the aggregation. Consideration is given to such questions as whether the amalgamation of products resulted in cost savings apart from those reductions in sales expenses and the like normally attendant upon any tie-in, and whether the items are normally sold or used as a unit with fixed proportions.◆

Where one of the products sold as part of an aggregation is a trade-mark or franchise license, new questions are injected. In determining whether the license and the remaining ("tied") items in the aggregation are to be regarded as distinct items which can be traded in distinct markets consideration must be given to the function of trade-marks. The historical conception of a trade-mark as a strict emblem of source of the product to which it attaches has largely been abandoned. The burgeoning business of franchising has made trade-mark licensing a widespread commercial practice and has resulted in the development of a new rationale for trade-marks as representations of product quality. This is particularly true in the case of a franchise system set up not to distribute the trade-marked goods of the franchisor, but, as here, to conduct a certain business under a common trade-mark or trade name. Under such a type of franchise, the trade-mark simply reflects the goodwill and quality standards of the enterprise which it identifies. As long as the system of operation of the franchisees lives up to those quality standards and remains as represented by the mark so that the public is not misled, neither the protection afforded the trade-mark by law nor the value of the trade-mark to the licensee depends upon the source of the components.

This being so, it is apparent that the goodwill of the Chicken Delight trade-mark does not attach to the multitude of separate articles used in the operation of the licensed system or in the production of its end product. It is not what is used, but how it is used and what results that have given the system and its end product their entitlement to trade-mark protection. It is to the system and the end product that the public looks with the confidence that established goodwill has created.

Thus, sale of a franchise license, with the attendant rights to operate a business in the prescribed manner and to benefit from the goodwill of the trade name, in no way requires the forced sale by the franchisor of some or all of the component articles. Just as the quality of a copyrighted creation cannot by a tie-in be appropriated by a creation to which the copyright does not relate, United States v. Paramount Pictures, Inc., 334 U.S. 131, 158 (1948), so here attempts by tie- in to extend the trade-mark protection to common articles (which the public does not and has no reason to connect with the trade-mark) simply because they are said to be essential to production of that which is the subject of the trade-mark, cannot escape antitrust scrutiny.

◆ [Note: This is not the current legal test. In *Jefferson Parish*, the Supreme Court held "that the answer to the question whether one or two products are involved turns not on the functional relation between them, but rather on the character of the demand for the two items. ... [N]o tying arrangement can exist unless there is a sufficient demand for the purchase of [the tied product] separate from [the tying product] to identify a distinct product market in which it is efficient to offer [the tied product] separately from [the tying product]." Jefferson Parish Hosp. Dist. No. 2 v. Hyde, 466 U.S. 2 (1984). Editor.]

Chicken Delight's assertions that only a few essential items were involved in the arrangement does not give us cause to reach a different conclusion. The relevant question is not whether the items are essential to the franchise, but whether it is essential to the franchise that the items be purchased from Chicken Delight. This raises not the issue of whether there is a tie-in but rather the issue of whether the tie-in is justifiable, a subject to be discussed below.

We conclude that the District Court was not in error in ruling as matter of law that the arrangement involved distinct tying and tied products.

B. Economic Power

Under the per se theory of illegality, plaintiffs are required to establish not only the existence of a tying arrangement but also that the tying product possesses sufficient economic power to appreciably restrain free competition in the tied product markets. [citation omitted]

Chicken Delight points out that while it was an early pioneer in the fast food franchising field, the record establishes that there has recently been a dramatic expansion in this area, with the advent of numerous firms, including many chicken franchising systems, all competing vigorously with each other. Under the circumstances, it contends that the existence of the requisite market dominance remained a jury question.

The District Court ruled, however, that Chicken Delight's unique registered trade-mark, in combination with its demonstrated power to impose a tie-in, established as matter of law the existence of sufficient market power to bring the case within the Sherman Act. We agree. ***

It can hardly be denied that the Chicken Delight trade-mark is distinctive; that it possesses goodwill and public acceptance unique to it and not enjoyed by other fast food chains.

It is now clear that sufficient economic power is to be presumed where the tying product is patented or copyrighted. ***

Just as the patent or copyright forecloses competitors from offering the distinctive product on the market, so the registered trade-mark presents a legal barrier against competition. It is not the nature of the public interest that has caused the legal barrier to be erected that is the basis for the presumption, but the fact that such a barrier does exist. Accordingly we see no reason why the presumption that exists in the case of the patent and copyright does not equally apply to the trade-mark.

Thus we conclude that the District Court did not err in ruling as matter of law that the tying product—the license to use the Chicken Delight trade-mark—possessed sufficient market power to bring the case within the Sherman Act. ***

Comments and Questions

1. The court noted that Chicken Delight "charged its franchisees no franchise fees or royalties." How does that affect the antitrust analysis?

2. What is the tying product and what is the tied product?

Other state and federal courts have followed Chicken Delight and held that a "trademark or franchise license may be a 'tying product'." Rental Car of New Hampshire v. Westinghouse Elec. Corp., 496 F.Supp. 373, 378 (D. Mass. 1980); Warriner Hermetics, Inc. v. Copeland Refrigeration Corp., 463 F.2d 1002, 1015–16 (5th Cir. 1972). What do you think—should a trademark be considered a tying product?

In *Jefferson Parish*, the Supreme Court held "that the answer to the question whether one or two products are involved turns not on the functional relation between them, but rather on the character of the demand for the two items.... [N]o tying arrangement can exist unless there is a sufficient demand for the purchase of [the tied product] separate from [the tying product] to identify a distinct product market in which it is efficient to offer [the tied product] separately from [the tying product]." Jefferson Parish Hosp. Dist. No. 2 v. Hyde, 466 U.S. 2 (1984). Under this test, are the trademark and the supplies two separate products for tying products?

3. Chicken Delight's policy might more accurately be evaluated as an exclusive dealing agreement instead of as a tying arrangement. Its franchisees did not have to merely purchase additional products from Chicken Delight; they had to use them exclusively. HERBERT HOVENKAMP, ANTITRUST ENTERPRISE at 200. Professor Hovenkamp argues that antitrust plaintiffs characterize the franchisor policies as tying, as opposed to exclusive dealing, in order "to take advantage of tying's irrational 'per se' rule." Id.

4. To some extent, are franchisors selling uniformity? If so, is that a desirable objective? Absent some contractual constraint—such as a tying requirement—what is that the franchisor is concerned its franchisees might do?

5. Chicken Delight argued that it needed to impose the tying requirement in order to protect the quality of its product. The court rejected that argument, asserting that the "sale of a franchise license, with the attendant rights to operate a business in the prescribed manner and to benefit from the goodwill of the trade name, in no way requires the forced sale by the franchisor of some or all of the component articles." Is that true? How does the franchisor maintain quality if franchisees can use any inputs? How can the franchisor insure product quality without using a tying requirement?

6. *See generally* Note, *Trademark Franchising and Antitrust Law: The Two-Product Rule for Tying Arrangements*, 27 SYRACUSE L. REV. 953 (1976); McCarthy, *Trademark Franchising and Antitrust: The Trouble with Tie-ins*, 58 CAL. L. REV. 1085 (1970).

Krehl v. Baskin-Robbins Ice Cream Co.
664 F.2d 1348 (9th Cir. 1982)

*** I. Factual Background

BRICO [Baskin-Robbins Ice Cream Co.] the nation's largest chain of ice cream specialty stores, operates the quintessential franchise system. [citation omitted] Originally a small Southern California ice cream manufacturer, BRICO initially engaged in the direct franchising of retail outlets in California. In 1959, BRICO began a program of expansion through licensing independent manufacturers to produce Baskin-Robbins ice cream and establish Baskin-Robbins franchised stores. This mode of expansion was chosen because shortages of capital and personnel rendered any other method impracticable.

The distribution system employed by BRICO has essentially three tiers. At the top is BRICO itself. It manages the chain of franchised stores, selects the area franchisors, and, through a wholly owned subsidiary, acts as the prime lessor of all Baskin-Robbins store properties.

At the second level of the system are the eight independent manufacturers licensed by BRICO to operate as area franchisors. BRICO, again through a wholly owned subsidiary, also operates at this level, acting as an area franchisor in six exclusive territories. The independent area franchisors are contractually bound to BRICO by Area Franchise Agreements. These agreements provide each area franchisor with an exclusive territory in which to manufacture Baskin-Robbins ice cream products. They also authorize the area franchisors, in conjunction with BRICO, to establish and service Baskin-Robbins franchised stores within their respective territories. Under these agreements, the area franchisors are forbidden to disclose the secret formulae and processes by which Baskin-Robbins ice cream products are manufactured.

The third level of the Baskin-Robbins system is composed of the franchised store owners. These independent businessmen are bound to both BRICO and the area franchisor by the standard form Store Franchise Agreement. Under these agreements, the franchised store may sell only Baskin-Robbins ice cream products purchased from the area franchisor in whose territory the store is located. ***

Certain franchisees of Baskin-Robbins bring this treble damage antitrust suit, ***. First, they contend that Baskin-Robbins ice cream products are unlawfully tied to the sale of the Baskin-Robbins trademark. ***

At the close of franchisees' case in chief, Baskin-Robbins moved to dismiss the action, pursuant to Rule 41(b) of the Federal Rules of Civil Procedure. The District Court, sitting without a jury, granted the motion, holding, inter alia, that: 1) The tie-in claim failed because franchisees did not establish that the Baskin-Robbins trademark was a separate product from Baskin-Robbins ice cream ***.

II. Analysis ***

The Tie-in Claim

It is well settled that there can be no unlawful tying arrangement absent proof that there are, in fact, two separate products, the sale of one (i.e., the tying product) being conditioned upon the purchase of the other (i. e., the tied product). [citation omitted] Franchisees argue that Baskin-Robbins' policy of conditioning the grant of a franchise upon the purchase of ice cream exclusively from Baskin-Robbins constitutes an unlawful tying arrangement. According to franchisees, the tying product is the Baskin-Robbins trademark and the tied product is the ice cream they are compelled to purchase.

The critical issue here is whether the Baskin-Robbins trademark may be properly treated as an item separate from the ice cream it purportedly represents. We conclude, as did the District Court, that it may not.

In support of their tie-in claim, franchisees rely heavily on *Siegel v. Chicken Delight*, Inc., 448 F.2d 43 (9th Cir. 1971). They contend that *Chicken Delight* established, as a matter of law, that a trademark is invariably a separate item whenever the product it represents is distributed through a franchise system. A careful reading of *Chicken Delight*, however, precludes such an interpretation and discloses that it stands only for the unremarkable proposition that, under certain circumstances, a trademark may be sufficiently unrelated to the alleged tied product to warrant treatment as a separate item.

In *Chicken Delight*, we were confronted with a situation where the franchisor conditioned the grant of a franchise on the purchase of a catalogue of miscellaneous items used in the franchised business. These products were neither manufactured by the franchisor nor were they of a special design uniquely suited to the franchised business. Rather, they were commonplace paper products and packaging goods, readily available in the competitive market place. In evaluating this arrangement, we stated that, "in determining whether the (trademark) . . . and the remaining . . . items . . . are to be regarded as distinct items . . . consideration must be given to the function of trademarks." *Chicken Delight*, 448 F.2d at 48. Because the function of the trademark in *Chicken Delight* was merely to identify a distinctive business format, we found the nexus between the trademark and the tied products to be sufficiently remote to warrant treating them as separate products. [citation omitted]

A determination of whether a trademark may appropriately be regarded as a separate product requires an inquiry into the relationship between the trademark and the products allegedly tied to its sale. [citation omitted] In evaluating this relationship, consideration must be given to the type of franchising system involved. In *Chicken Delight*, we distinguished between two kinds of franchising systems: 1) the business format system; and 2) the distribution system. [citation omitted][11] A business format franchise system is usually created merely to conduct business under a common trade name. The franchise outlet itself is generally responsible for the production and preparation of the system's end product. The franchisor merely provides the trademark and, in some cases, supplies used in operating the franchised outlet and producing the system's products. Under such a system, there is generally only a remote connection between the trademark and the products the franchisees are compelled to purchase. This is true because consumers have no reason to associate with the trademark, those component goods used either in the operation of the franchised store or in the manufacture of the end product.

---

[11] Of course, a franchise system may be of the "distribution" type in relation to the end product of the system and of the "format" type in relation to the kinds of incidental supplies tied to the sale of the trademark in Chicken Delight. The crucial inquiry is into the relationship between the trademark and the product allegedly tied to its sale.

> NOT TRUE. IF I go to Baskin Robbins, I want Baskin Robbins ice cream.

"Under such a type of franchise, the trade-mark simply reflects the goodwill and quality standards of the enterprise it identifies. As long as ... franchisees (live) up to those quality standards ... neither the protection afforded the trade-mark by law nor the value of the trade-mark ... depends upon the source of the components." *Id.* at 48–49.

Where, as in *Chicken Delight*, the tied products are commonplace articles, the franchisor can easily maintain its quality standards through other means less intrusive upon competition.[12] Accordingly, the coerced purchase of these items amounts to little more than an effort to impede competition on the merits in the market for the tied products. [citation omitted]

Where a distribution type system, such as that employed by Baskin-Robbins, is involved, significantly different considerations are presented. [citation omitted] Under the distribution type system, the franchised outlets serve merely as conduits through which the trademarked goods of the franchisor flow to the ultimate consumer. These goods are generally manufactured by the franchisor or, as in the present case, by its licensees according to detailed specifications. In this context, the trademark serves a different function. Instead of identifying a business format, the trademark in a distribution franchise system serves merely as a representation of the end product marketed by the system. "It is to the system and the end product that the public looks with the confidence that the established goodwill has created." *Chicken Delight*, 448 F.2d at 49 (emphasis added). Consequently, sale of substandard products under the mark would dissipate this goodwill and reduce the value of the trademark. The desirability of the trademark is therefore utterly dependent upon the perceived quality of the product it represents. Because the prohibition of tying arrangements is designed to strike solely at the use of a dominant desired product to compel the purchase of a second undesired commodity, *id.* at 47, the tie-in doctrine can have no application where the trademark serves only to identify the alleged tied product. The desirability of the trademark and the quality of the product it represents are so inextricably interrelated in the mind of the consumer as to preclude any finding that the trademark is a separate item for tie-in purposes. *exactly as I said above*

In the case at bar, the District Court found that the Baskin-Robbins trademark merely served to identify the ice cream products distributed by the franchise system. Based on our review of the record, we cannot say that this finding is clearly erroneous. Accordingly, we conclude that the District Court did not err in ruling that the Baskin-Robbins trademark lacked sufficient independent existence apart from the ice cream products allegedly tied to its sale, to justify a finding of an unlawful tying arrangement. ***

Affirmed.

---

[12] Provision of specifications for the manufacture of these products is one means often available to insure that franchisees maintain quality standards. See Chicken Delight, 448 F.2d at 51. Where, as here, the alleged tied product is manufactured pursuant to secret formulae, the specification alternative is not available. [citation omitted]

Comments and Questions

1. The court attempts to distinguish *Chicken Delight* by claiming that the tied products in that case "were commonplace paper products and packaging goods, readily available in the competitive market place." The court assigns legal significance to this by asserting that because "the tied products are commonplace articles, the franchisor can easily maintain its quality standards through other means less intrusive upon competition."

    Is the court's characterization of the tied products in *Chicken Delight* accurate? If not, how does that affect the antitrust analysis?

2. The court states that the "desirability of the trademark and the quality of the product it represents are so inextricably interrelated in the mind of the consumer as to preclude any finding that the trademark is a separate item for tie-in purposes." Is that persuasive?

Tominaga v. Shepherd,
682 F.Supp. 1489 (C.D. Cal. 1988)

RAFEEDIE, District Judge.

*** Factual Background

Defendant El Centro is a California corporation and is the franchisor of "Pizza Man-He Delivers" and "Chicken Delight" franchises in Los Angeles and Orange Counties. There are currently forty-five Pizza Man, six combination Pizza Man and Chicken Delight, and one Chicken Delight franchisees in the Southern California area. Defendant Vance Shepherd is the president of El Centro. El Centro has registered its Pizza Man and Chicken Delight service marks with the United States Patent and Trademark Office.

Plaintiff Milton Tominaga does business as P.M. Distributors in the Los Angeles area, and is a wholesale distributor of ingredients for prepared foods and restaurant supplies. He is an authorized distributor of food and packaging products to El Centro's franchisees. Tominaga owned a franchised store from 1975 until 1985. From 1982 to the present, he supplied various Pizza Man franchises with ingredients and supplies. In 1985, Tominaga sold his Pizza Man store, according to his affidavit, because defendant Shepherd told him he would become the exclusive distributor for Pizza Man ingredients and supplies.

El Centro franchisees entered into a franchise agreement with El Centro in order to obtain licenses to operate Pizza Man stores (all facts pertaining to Pizza Man should be assumed to apply to Chicken Delight unless otherwise noted) and to utilize the service mark. Under the franchise agreement, a franchisee is not limited to purchasing its food products and supplies from any one distributor:

> a franchisee may purchase any and all authorized food products and packaging from suppliers of his choice, provided that such food and packaging are uniform

and high quality and comply with the standards and specifications set forth in the Operations Manual.

Also, under the standard form franchise agreements, each El Centro franchisee is obligated to package all goods sold to the public in approved Pizza Man packaging unless such packaging is unavailable, in which case written permission must be obtained from El Centro. Each franchisee is further required to prepare its menu and use ingredients in accordance with the methods and specifications set forth in the Pizza Man Operations Manual.

Tominaga was an authorized distributor of packaging materials and refrigerated food products ***

[When El Centro took action against Tominaga, he sued, claiming that El Centro had imposed an illegal tying arrangement. El Centro moved for summary judgment]

A. Illegal Tying Arrangement Claim

*** In order to prevail under a per se theory, plaintiff must establish the following three elements; "(1) a tie-in between two distinct products or services; (2) sufficient economic power in the tying product market to impose significant restrictions in the tied product market; and (3) an effect on a non-insubstantial volume of commerce in the tied product market." [citation omitted] Plaintiff has failed to present competent evidence that El Centro had market power in the tying market. ***

A distinctive trademark is "unique" in the sense that it constitutes an identifiable property right, but it should not be confused in the franchising context with the existence of market power. [citation omitted] ***

In *Siegel v. Chicken Delight*, 448 F.2d 43 (9th Cir.1971), the court reasoned that Chicken Delight had sufficient market power because "[i]t can hardly be denied that the Chicken Delight trademark is distinctive; that it possesses goodwill and public acceptance unique to it and not enjoyed by other fast food chains." [citation omitted] This analysis, however, has been subjected to a crippling attack by Klein & Saft [Klein & Saft, *The Law and Economics of Franchise Tying Contracts*, 28 J.LAW & ECON. 345 (1985)]:

> It makes no economic sense to attribute significant market power to the Chicken Delight trademark. The important economic distinction that must be made is between pre- and postcontract economic power. Precontract, competition among franchisors (such as McDonald's or Kentucky Fried Chicken) to sign up franchisees prevents Chicken Delight from exercising any economic power in setting contract terms with potential franchisees. Chicken Delight, although it possesses a trademark, does not possess any economic power in the relevant market in which it operates-the fast food franchising (or perhaps, more generally, the franchising) market.

Klein & Saft, *supra*, at 356; Mozart, 833 F.2d at 1346 ("Market power, if any, is derived from the product, not from the name or symbol as such").

In this case, plaintiff argues that it need not rely upon a "presumption" of market power, because El Centro's activity is evidence of market power. Nevertheless, the

164 *Antitrust Law and Intellectual Property Rights*

above referenced analysis is useful in determining the merits of plaintiff's argument. Plaintiff charges that (1) El Centro demonstrated its market power by increasing prices of the service marked supplies, and foreclosing plaintiff from distributing such supplies; and (2) by "locking in" franchisees to the tying product by virtue of their investment in the franchise.

Plaintiff's argument, however, fails to define the relevant market. In *Mozart*, the court emphasized the necessity of defining the relevant market.

> The critical issue is whether MBNE [the Mercedes franchisor] possesses the "market power" to force dealers to purchase the tied product rather than acquire the franchise to sell a different automobile.

Mozart, 833 F.2d 1346. Thus, as recognized in *Mozart*, the relevant market would include other franchises for similar products. Possible relevant markets include take out pizza franchises, fast food franchises or restaurant franchises in general. Klein & Saft, supra, at 356 (the relevant market in Chicken Delight was the fast food franchising market, or perhaps more generally, the franchising market).

Plaintiff's implicit argument is that the relevant market is the "Pizza Man franchising" market. This market definition is erroneous as a matter of law. No reasonable argument can be made that Pizza Man possesses the power to coerce potential franchisees to purchase the tied product rather than sell a different brand of fast food (the tying product). The analysis must take place at the "pre-contract" stage. Klein & Saft, *supra*, at 356. Plaintiff, however, engages in "post-contract" analysis concerning defendant's power over already existing franchisees by virtue of their "sunk costs." This argument was explicitly rejected in *Mozart*.

> Obviously there are costs in surrendering one franchise and acquiring another, but these costs are unrelated to the "market power" of a unique automobile. These costs will enable the car maker to extract concessions from the dealer, but this power is related to the franchise method of doing business, not to the possible uniqueness of the car.

Mozart, 833 F.2d at 1346-47. The court concluded that the district court's jury instruction was "improperly focused" on the particular franchise [Mercedes dealerships], and failed to recognize that the "market" at issue "is the market for dealership franchises." *Id.*[4]

Therefore, plaintiff's argument that the evidence submitted shows there is a material issue of fact as to defendant's market power is based on an improper market definition. El Centro's ability to "coerce" its franchisees to purchase a

---

[4] Klein & Saft come to the same conclusion; "Postcontract ... a franchisor can use the threat of termination to "hold up" a franchisee that has made a specific investment in the marketing arrangement. However, this potential economic power has nothing to do with market power, ultimate consumers' welfare, or antitrust." Klien & Saft, supra, at 356 (emphasis added). The "hold up" of franchisees is a "contract problem," but not an antitrust problem. As the axiom provides, the antitrust laws were designed to protect competition, not competitors; injury to the plaintiff alone (or to the franchisees) is not sufficient to prove injury to competition. Brunswick Corp. v. Pueblo Bowl-O-Mat, Inc., 429 U.S. 477, 488, (1977).

product it may not wish to purchase (postcontract), and its claimed ability to raise prices because of the franchisees sunk investment, does not show market power in the fast food franchising market. The "power" exercised is merely the power of a franchisor over its franchisees. Nothing in the record shows that El Centro had the power (precontract) to "force" potential franchisees to purchase the tied goods. Such power could only be exercised by El Centro if the relevant market for the tying product were Pizza Man franchises. No such showing has been made, nor could such a showing be made.

Plaintiff relies upon *Digidyne Corp. v. Data General Corp.*, 734 F.2d 1336, 1341 (9th Cir.1984), cert denied, 473 U.S. 908 (1985). In *Digidyne*, the court held that market power will be found were [sic] defendant is able to "lock in" the tied product when a customer has made a substantial investment in the tying product. The court in *Mozart* distinguished *Digidyne* on the grounds that it concerned a unique, copyrighted tying product, whereas *Mozart*, as our case, concerns a trademark tying product [Mercedes dealerships and Pizza Man stores]. Moreover, the court in *Mozart* suggested that the *Digidyne* panel erred in failing to engage in market analysis. *Mozart*, 833 F.2d at 1346 n. 4. In any event, the case before this court is on all fours with that before the *Mozart* panel.

Therefore, plaintiff has failed to produce evidence creating a material issue of fact concerning El Centro's market power in the tying product, and summary judgment is appropriate.

***

Comments and Questions

1. Other courts have held that a franchisor may require franchisees to purchase supplies from a list of approved suppliers without violating antitrust laws. *See* Kentucky Fried Chicken Corp. v. Diversified Packaging Corp., 549 F.2d 368, 375–377 (5th Cir. 1977). One key factor is whether the franchisor has a direct economic interest in the seller of the tied product; if not the tying arrangement is not illegal.

The facts of *Tominaga* show how the franchisor tried to operate within the bounds of antitrust law when the court noted that "a franchisee may purchase any and all authorized food products and packaging from suppliers of his choice, provided that such food and packaging are uniform and high quality and comply with the standards and specifications set forth in the Operations Manual." Would that have solved the antitrust problem in *Chicken Delight*?

Bibliography of Additional Resources

David Evans & Michael Salinger, *Why Do Firms Bundle and Tie? Evidence from Competitive Markets and Implications for Tying Law*, 22 YALE J. ON REG. 37 (2005)

Michael H. Kauffman, Image Technical Services, Inc. v. Eastman Kodak Co.: *Taking One Step Forward and Two Steps Back in Reconciling Intellectual Property Rights and Antitrust Liability*, 34 WAKE FOREST L. REV. 471 (1999)

CHAPTER 6

Unilateral Refusals to License or Deal

DOJ-FTC Antitrust Guidelines for the Licensing of Intellectual Property, Sec. 2.2

2.2 Intellectual property and market power

Market power is the ability profitably to maintain prices above, or output below, competitive levels for a significant period of time. The Agencies will not presume that a patent, copyright, or trade secret necessarily confers market power upon its owner. Although the intellectual property right confers the power to exclude with respect to the specific product, process, or work in question, there will often be sufficient actual or potential close substitutes for such product, process, or work to prevent the exercise of market power. If a patent or other form of intellectual property does confer market power, that market power does not by itself offend the antitrust laws. As with any other tangible or intangible asset that enables its owner to obtain significant supracompetitive profits, market power (or even a monopoly) that is solely 'a consequence of a superior product, business acumen, or historic accident' does not violate the antitrust laws. Nor does such market power impose on the intellectual property owner an obligation to license the use of that property to others. As in other antitrust contexts, however, market power could be illegally acquired or maintained, or, even if lawfully acquired and maintained, would be relevant to the ability of an intellectual property owner to harm competition through unreasonable conduct in connection with such property.

Data General Corp. v. Grumman Systems Support Corp.

36 F.3d 1147 (1st Cir. 1994)

STAHL, Circuit Judge.

Grumman Systems Support Corporation ("Grumman") assigns error to the district court's handling of litigation arising from Grumman's acquisition, duplication, and use of MV/Advanced Diagnostic Executive System ("ADEX"), a sophisticated computer program developed by Data General Corporation ("DG") to diagnose problems in DG's MV computers. DG claimed that Grumman had infringed DG's ADEX copyrights and misappropriated trade secrets embodied in ADEX. A jury agreed, awarding DG $27,417,000 in damages (excluding prejudgment interest and attorney's fees). Grumman contends that the district court prematurely dismissed its affirmative defenses and counterclaims and committed several errors during and after the trial.

While this case raises numerous issues touching on copyright law, Grumman's most intriguing argument—presented below as both a defense and a counterclaim—is that DG illegally maintained its monopoly in the market for service of DG computers by unilaterally refusing to license ADEX to Grumman and other competitors. The antitrust claims are intriguing because they present a curious conflict, namely, whether (and to what extent) the antitrust laws, in the absence of any statutory exemption, must tolerate short-term harm to the competitive process when such harm is caused by the otherwise lawful exercise of an economically potent "monopoly" in a copyrighted work.

After a careful analysis, we affirm on all but one relatively minor issue concerning the calculation of damages.

I. Background

DG and Grumman are competitors in the market for service of computers manufactured by DG, and the present litigation stems from the evolving nature of their competitive relationship. DG not only designs and manufactures computers, but also offers a line of products and services for the maintenance and repair of DG computers. Although DG has no more than a 5% share of the highly competitive "primary market" for mini-computers, DG occupies approximately 90% of the "aftermarket" for service of DG computers. As a group, various "third party maintainers" ("TPMs") earn roughly 7% of the service revenues; Grumman is the leading TPM with approximately 3% of the available service business. The remaining equipment owners (typically large companies in the high technology industry) generally maintain their own computers and peripherals, although they occasionally need outside service on a "time and materials" basis.

A. Computer Service: Outputs and Inputs

*** In order to identify the existence and location of a malfunctioning part, a service technician may use diagnostics (now increasingly sophisticated software), schematics (maps of the location and function of hardware elements), and various types of documentation, together with the technician's own experience acquired by diagnosing equipment problems. In order to actually mend a malfunctioning part, a technician might fix the part on the spot with routine tools or sophisticated software (e.g., a software diagnostic that can reformat a disk drive), or send the part to a repair depot run either by the technician's employer or another service organization. *** At the core of this litigation is a dispute about Grumman's access to software diagnostics and other service "tools" produced by DG for use in the repair, upgrading, and maintenance of DG equipment.

B. TPM Access to Service Inputs ***

From 1976 until some point in the mid-1980s, DG affirmatively encouraged the growth of TPMs with relatively liberal policies concerning TPM access to service tools. DG sold or licensed diagnostics directly to TPMs, and allowed TPMs to use diagnostics sold or licensed to DG equipment owners. DG did not restrict access by TPMs to spare parts manufactured by DG or other manufacturers. DG allowed (or at least tolerated) requests by TPMs for DG's repair depot to fix malfunctioning circuit boards, the heart of a computer's central processing unit ("CPU"). DG sold at least some schematics and other documentation to TPMs. DG also sold TPMs engineering change order kits. And finally, DG training classes were open to TPM field engineers. Grumman suggests that DG's liberal policies were beneficial to DG because increased capacity (and perhaps competition) in the service aftermarket would be a selling point for DG equipment. ***

In the mid-1980s, DG altered its strategy. With the goal of maximizing revenues from its service business, DG began to refuse to provide many service tools directly to TPMs. DG would not allow TPMs to use the DG repair depot, nor would it permit TPMs to purchase schematics, documentation, "change order" kits, or certain spare parts. DG no longer allowed TPM technicians to attend DG training classes. Finally, DG developed and severely restricted the licensing of ADEX, a new software diagnostic for its MV computers. The MV series was at once DG's most advanced computer hardware and an increasingly important source of sales and service revenue for DG. ***

DG would also license ADEX for the exclusive use of the in-house technicians of equipment owners who perform most of their own service. However, DG would not license ADEX to its own service customers or to the customers of TPMs. Nor was ADEX available to TPMs from sources other than DG. ***

Grumman found various ways to skirt DG's ADEX restrictions. Some former DG employees, in violation of their employment agreements, brought copies of ADEX when they joined Grumman. In addition, DG field engineers often stored copies of ADEX at the work sites of their service customers, who were bound to preserve the confidentiality of any DG proprietary information in their possession. Although DG service customers had an obligation to return copies of ADEX to DG should they cancel their service agreement and switch to a TPM, few customers did so. It is essentially undisputed that Grumman technicians used and duplicated copies of ADEX left behind by DG field engineers. There is also uncontroverted evidence that Grumman actually acquired copies of ADEX in this manner in order to maintain libraries of diagnostics so that Grumman technicians could freely duplicate and use any copy of ADEX to service any of Grumman's customers with DG's MV computers.

C. The Present Litigation

In 1988, DG filed suit against Grumman in the United States District Court for the District of Massachusetts. *** DG alleged that Grumman's use and duplication of ADEX infringed DG's ADEX copyrights, and requested injunctive relief, [citation omitted] as well as actual damages and profits [citation omitted]. In another count, DG alleged that Grumman had violated Massachusetts trade secrets law by misappropriating copies of ADEX in violation of confidentiality agreements binding on former DG employees and DG service customers. On December 29, 1988, the district court issued a preliminary injunction prohibiting Grumman from using ADEX. [citation omitted] ***

Grumman *** claimed that DG could not maintain its infringement action because DG had used its ADEX copyrights to violate Sections 1 and 2 of the Sherman Antitrust Act [citation omitted][12] Specifically, Grumman charged that DG misused its copyrights by (1) tying the availability of ADEX to a consumer's agreement either to purchase DG support services (a "positive tie") or not to purchase support services from TPMs (a "negative tie"), and (2) willfully maintaining its monopoly in the support services aftermarket by imposing the alleged tie-in and refusing to deal with TPMs. [Editor: The district court rejected Grumman's antitrust arguments and Grumman appealed.] ***

B. Grumman's Antitrust Counterclaims

The district court granted DG's motions for summary judgment with respect to Grumman's *** monopolization claim under Section 2. We affirm ***

2. Monopolization

*** Grumman accused DG of willfully maintaining its monopoly in the aftermarket for service of DG computers in violation of Section 2 of the Sherman Act, 15 U.S.C. § 2, which prohibits the monopolization of "any part of the trade or commerce among the several States." To survive summary judgment on its willful maintenance claim, Grumman must demonstrate a genuine dispute about the existence of two elements: (1) DG's possession of monopoly power in the market for support services of DG computers; and (2) DG's maintenance of that power through "exclusionary conduct." [citation omitted] The district court assumed the existence of monopoly power but granted summary judgment on the grounds that Grumman had not demonstrated the need for a trial on the element of exclusionary conduct. We follow suit.[60]

---

[12] Grumman presented the antitrust claims as independent counterclaims as well.

[60] We note, however, that the record does contain evidence of DG's monopoly power in the assumed service aftermarket for DG computers. In addition to DG's monopoly share (over 90%) of the service aftermarket, the record contains evidence of barriers to entry (e.g., costs to TPMs of obtaining diagnostics and other service "tools"), market imperfections (e.g., high information costs for computer purchasers and high switching costs for DG equipment owners), and more importantly, supracompetitive service prices and price discrimination among DG service customers.

"Exclusionary conduct" is defined as "'conduct, other than competition on the merits or restraints reasonably "necessary" to competition on the merits, that reasonably appears capable of making a significant contribution to creating or maintaining monopoly power.'" [citation omitted] We label as improper that conduct which harms the competitive process and not conduct which simply harms competitors. [citation omitted] That process is harmed when conduct "obstructs the achievement of competition's basic goals—lower prices, better products, and more efficient production methods." [citation omitted] In contrast, exclusionary conduct does not include behavior which poses no unreasonable threat to consumer welfare but is merely a manifestation of healthy competition, an absence of competition, or a natural monopoly. [citation omitted]

Grumman's primary contention is that DG's unilateral refusal to license ADEX to anyone other than qualified self-maintainers constitutes exclusionary conduct. Grumman also attacks as exclusionary DG's refusal to provide other service tools directly to TPMs. We first review the principles governing the analysis of a monopolist's unilateral refusal to deal, and then discuss whether a unilateral refusal to license a copyrighted work might ever deserve to be condemned as exclusionary. We hold below that the desire of an author to be the exclusive user of its original work is a presumptively legitimate business justification for the author's refusal to license to competitors. We hold further that Grumman has not presented sufficient proof to rebut this presumption and thereby avert summary judgment. In particular, we find no merit in Grumman's contention that DG acted in an exclusionary fashion in discontinuing its liberal policies allowing TPM access to diagnostic software. Finally, we conclude that no reasonable jury could find that DG's restrictions on TPM access to other service tools amount to exclusionary conduct.

a. Unilateral Refusals to Deal

Because a monopolization claim does not require proof of concerted activity, even the unilateral actions of a monopolist can constitute exclusionary conduct. [citation omitted] Thus, a monopolist's unilateral refusal to deal with its competitors (as long as the refusal harms the competitive process) may constitute prima facie evidence of exclusionary conduct in the context of a Section 2 claim. See Kodak, 504 U.S. at —— n. 32 (citing *Aspen Skiing Co. v. Aspen Highlands Skiing Corp.,* 472 U.S. 585, 602–05 (1985)). A monopolist may nevertheless rebut such evidence by establishing a valid business justification for its conduct. See Kodak, 504 U.S. at —— n. 32 (suggesting that monopolist may rebut an inference of exclusionary conduct by establishing "legitimate competitive reasons for the refusal"); *Aspen Skiing,* 472 U.S. at 608, 105 S.Ct. at 2860 (suggesting that sufficient evidence of harm to consumers and competitors triggers further inquiry as to whether the monopolist has "persuade[d] the jury that its [harmful] conduct was justified by [a] normal business purpose"). In general, a business justification is valid if it relates directly or indirectly to the enhancement of consumer welfare. Thus, pursuit of efficiency and quality control might be legitimate competitive reasons for an otherwise exclusionary refusal to deal, while the desire to maintain a monopoly market share or thwart the entry of competitors would not. [citation omitted] In essence, a unilateral refusal to deal is prima facie exclusionary if there is evidence of harm to the competitive process; a valid business justification requires proof of countervailing benefits to the competitive process.

Despite the theoretical possibility, there have been relatively few cases in which a unilateral refusal to deal has formed the basis of a successful Section 2 claim. Several of the cases commonly cited for a supposed duty to deal were actually cases of joint conduct in which some competitors joined to frustrate others. [citation omitted] Prior to *Aspen Skiing*, the case that probably came closest to condemning a true unilateral refusal to deal was *Otter Tail Power Co. v. United States*, 410 U.S. 366 (1973), which condemned the refusal of a wholesale power supplier either to sell wholesale power to municipal systems or to "wheel power" when Otter Tail's retail franchises expired and local municipalities sought to supplant Otter Tail's local distributors. The case not only involved a capital-intensive public utility facility—which could not effectively be duplicated and occupied a distinct separate market—but the Supreme Court laid considerable emphasis on "supported" findings in the district court "that Otter Tail's refusals to sell at wholesale or to wheel were solely to prevent municipal power systems from eroding its monopolistic position." 410 U.S. at 378.

In *Aspen Skiing*, the Court criticized a monopolist's unilateral refusal to deal in a very different situation, casting serious doubt on the proposition that the Court has adopted any single rule or formula for determining when a unilateral refusal to deal is unlawful. In that case, an "all-Aspen" ski ticket—valid at any mountain in Aspen—had been developed and jointly marketed when the three (later four) ski areas in Aspen were owned by independent entities. 472 U.S. at 589. Some time after Aspen Skiing Company ("Ski Co.") came into control of three of the four ski areas, Ski Co. refused to continue a joint agreement with *Aspen Highlands Skiing Corp.* ("Highlands"), the owner of the fourth area. *Id.* at 592–93. Although there was no "essential facility" involved, the Court found that it was exclusionary for Ski Co., as a monopolist, to refuse to continue a presumably efficient "pattern of distribution that had originated in a competitive market and had persisted for several years." *Id.* at 603.

It is not entirely clear whether the Court in Aspen Skiing merely intended to create a category of refusal-to-deal cases different from the essential facilities category or whether the Court was inviting the application of more general principles of antitrust analysis to unilateral refusals to deal. We follow the parties' lead in assuming that Grumman need not tailor its argument to a preexisting "category" of unilateral refusals to deal.

b. Unilateral Refusals to License

DG attempts to undermine Grumman's monopolization claim by proposing a powerful irrebuttable presumption: a unilateral refusal to license a copyright can never constitute exclusionary conduct. We agree that some type of presumption is in order, but reach that conclusion only after an exhaustive inquiry touching on the general character of presumptions, the role of market analysis in the copyright

(1) The Propriety of a Presumption

We begin our analysis with two observations. First, DG's rule of law could be characterized as either an empirical assumption or a policy preference. For example, if we were convinced that refusals to license a copyright always have a net positive effect on the competitive process, we might adopt a presumption to this effect in order to preclude wasteful litigation about a known fact. On the other hand, if we were convinced that the rights enumerated in the Copyright Act should take precedence over the responsibilities set forth in the Sherman Act, regardless of the realities of the market, we might adopt a blanket rule of preference. DG's argument contains elements of both archetypal categories of presumptions. ***

We now consider what appears to be an empirical proclamation from DG: "[T]he refusal to make one's innovation available to rivals . . . is pro-competitive conduct." As support, DG cites *Grinnell*, 384 U.S. at 570–71, in which the Court held that willful maintenance of monopoly does not include "growth or development as a consequence of a superior product." It is not the superiority of a work that allows the author to exclude others, however, but rather the limited monopoly granted by copyright law. Moreover, one reason why the Copyright Act fosters investment and innovation is that it may allow the author to earn monopoly profits by licensing the copyright to others or reserving the copyright for the author's exclusive use. [citation omitted] Thus, at least in a particular market and for a particular period of time, the Copyright Act tolerates behavior that may harm both consumers and competitors. [citation omitted]

DG does not in fact argue that consumers are better off in the short term because of the inability of TPMs to license ADEX. Instead, DG suggests that allowing copyright owners to exclude others from the use of their works creates incentives which ultimately work to the benefit of consumers in the DG service aftermarket as well as to the benefit of consumers generally. In other words, DG seeks to justify any immediate harm to consumers by pointing to countervailing long-term benefits. Certainly, a monopolist's refusal to license others to use a commercially successful patented idea is likely to have more profound anti-competitive consequences than a refusal to allow others to duplicate the copyrighted expression of an unpatented idea (although such differences may become less pronounced if copyright law becomes increasingly protective of intellectual property such as computer software). But by no means is a monopolist's refusal to license a copyright entirely "pro-competitive" within the ordinary economic framework of the Sherman Act. Accordingly, it may be inappropriate to adopt an empirical assumption that simply ignores harm to the competitive process caused by a monopolist's unilateral refusal to license a copyright. Even if it is clear that exclusive use of a copyright can have anticompetitive consequences, some type of presumption may nevertheless be appropriate as a matter of either antitrust law or copyright law.

(2) Antitrust Law and the Accommodation of Patent Rights

*** Should an antitrust plaintiff be allowed to demonstrate the anti-competitive effects of a monopolist's unilateral refusal to grant a copyright license? Would the monopolist then have to justify its refusal to license by introducing evidence that the protection of the copyright laws enabled the author to create a work which advances consumer welfare?

The courts appear to have partly settled an analogous conflict between the patent laws and the antitrust laws, treating the former as creating an implied limited exception to the latter. *** The "patent exception" is largely a means of resolving conflicting rights and responsibilities, i.e., a policy presumption. [citation omitted] At the same time, the exception is grounded in an empirical assumption that exposing patent activity to wider antitrust scrutiny would weaken the incentives underlying the patent system, thereby depriving consumers of beneficial products. [citation omitted]

(3) Copyright Law

Copyright law provides further guidance. The Copyright Act expressly grants to a copyright owner the exclusive right to distribute the protected work by "transfer of ownership, or by rental, lease, or lending." 17 U.S.C. § 106. Consequently, "[t]he owner of the copyright, if [it] pleases, may refrain from vending or licensing and content [itself] with simply exercising the right to exclude others from using [its] property." *Fox Film Corp. v. Doyal*, 286 U.S. 123, 127 (1932). *See also Stewart v. Abend*, 495 U.S. 207, 229 (1990). We may also venture to infer that, in passing the Copyright Act, Congress itself made an empirical assumption that allowing copyright holders to collect license fees and exclude others from using their works creates a system of incentives that promotes consumer welfare in the long term by encouraging investment in the creation of desirable artistic and functional works of expression. [citation omitted] We cannot require antitrust defendants to prove and reprove the merits of this legislative assumption in every case where a refusal to license a copyrighted work comes under attack. Nevertheless, *** the Copyright Act does not explicitly purport to limit the scope of the Sherman Act. And, if the Copyright Act is silent on the subject generally, the silence is particularly acute in cases where a monopolist harms consumers in the monopolized market by refusing to license a copyrighted work to competitors. ***

(4) Harmonizing the Sherman Act and the Copyright Act

Since neither the Sherman Act nor the Copyright Act works a partial repeal of the other, and since implied repeals are disfavored, [citation omitted] we must harmonize the two as best we can, id., mindful of the legislative and judicial approaches to similar conflicts created by the patent laws. We must not lose sight of the need to preserve the economic incentives fueled by the Copyright Act, but neither may we ignore the tension between the two very different policies embodied in the Copyright Act and the Sherman Act, both designed ultimately to improve the welfare of consumers in our free market system. Drawing on our discussion above, we hold that while exclusionary conduct can include a monopolist's unilateral refusal to license a copyright, an author's desire to exclude others from use of its copyrighted work is a presumptively valid business justification for any immediate harm to consumers.[64]

c. DG's Refusal to License ADEX to non-CMOs

Having arrived at the applicable legal standards, we may resolve Grumman's principal allegation of exclusionary conduct. Although there may be a genuine factual dispute about the effect on DG equipment owners of DG's refusal to license ADEX to TPMs, DG's desire to exercise its rights under the Copyright Act is a presumptively valid business justification.

Apparently sensing the uphill nature of its allegation of an exclusionary refusal to license, Grumman seeks to overcome any obstacles primarily by characterizing DG's licensing policies as a monopolist's exclusionary withdrawal of assistance within the framework of *Aspen Skiing*. Citing *Aspen Skiing*, Grumman contends that DG's refusal to license ADEX to TPMs, in light of the fact that DG previously allowed TPMs to use DG diagnostics, is exclusionary conduct because "[a] monopolist that has helped a market develop may not withdraw its support without legitimate business justifications." Assuming that such a claim can overcome the presumption that a refusal to license is not exclusionary, we nevertheless hold that *Aspen Skiing* cannot apply to the facts of this case. The reasoning of *Aspen Skiing* has little to do with the fact that defendant Ski Co. withdrew assistance upon which competitors may have relied when entering the market. Rather, the decision turns on a comparison of the behavior of firms in a competitive market (the Aspen ski market) with a monopolist's behavior once competition has been curtailed. The Court noted that the rich soil of competition had produced the all-mountain ticket in Aspen and other multimountain areas, justifying an "infer[ence] that such tickets satisfy consumer demand in free competitive markets." 472 U.S. at 603. *See also* Olympia Equip., 797 F.2d at 377 (suggesting that the facts in Aspen Skiing indicate that "competition required some cooperation among competitors" in the Aspen ski market). Ski Co.'s decision to eliminate the ticket in later years was a sign that the weeds of monopoly had begun to take hold, to the possible detriment of consumer welfare. Aspen Skiing, 472 U.S. at 604. Finally, after canvassing evidence of consumer preferences concerning skiing options at Aspen, the Court concluded that Ski Co.'s new policies did in fact harm consumers. Id. at 605–607. In short, instead of prescribing a categorical approach, Aspen Skiing ultimately calls for an inquiry that is relatively routine in antitrust analysis: namely, whether the monopolist's actions unjustifiably harm the competitive process by frustrating consumer preferences and erecting barriers to competition. Cf. Olympia Equip., 797 F.2d at 379 ("If [Aspen Skiing]

---

[64] Wary of undermining the Sherman Act, however, we do not hold that an antitrust plaintiff can never rebut this presumption, for there may be rare cases in which imposing antitrust liability is unlikely to frustrate the objectives of the Copyright Act.

stands for any principle that goes beyond its unusual facts, it is that a monopolist may be guilty of monopolization if it refuses to cooperate with a competitor in circumstances where some cooperation is indispensable to effective competition.").

Grumman attempts to analogize this case to Aspen Skiing by focusing on the fact that DG once encouraged firms to enter the DG service aftermarket by allowing liberal access to service tools, but no longer does so. The analytical framework of Aspen Skiing cannot function in these circumstances, however, because we are unable to view DG's market practices in both competitive and noncompetitive conditions. While TPMs have made inroads in the market for service of DG computers, DG has always been a monopolist in that market, and competitive conditions have never prevailed. Therefore, it would not be "appropriate to infer" from DG's change of heart that its former policies "satisfy consumer demand in free competitive markets." Aspen Skiing, 472 U.S. at 603.

Nor does it appear that Grumman would be able at trial to overcome the presumption on any other theory. There is no evidence that DG acquired its ADEX copyrights in any unlawful manner ***. And, while there is evidence that DG knew that developing a "proprietary position" in the area of diagnostic software would help to maintain its monopoly in the aftermarket for service of DG computers, there is also evidence that DG set out to create a state-of-the-art diagnostic that would help to improve the quality of DG service. [citation omitted] In fact, there is clearly some evidence that ADEX is a significant benefit to owners of DG's MV computers. ADEX is a better product than any other diagnostic for MV computers. The use of ADEX appears to have increased the efficiency and reduced the cost of service because technicians can locate problems more quickly and, through the use of the software's "remote assistance" capability, can arrive at customer sites having determined ahead of time what replacement parts are necessary. In addition to the possibility of lower prices occasioned by such gains in efficiency, ADEX also promises to lower prices through gains in effectiveness. For example, customers may save the cost of replacing expensive hardware components because the use of advanced diagnostics increases the possibility that technicians can locate a problem and repair the component. ***

In conclusion, Grumman has not produced evidence from which a jury could find that DG engaged in exclusionary conduct by unilaterally refusing to license ADEX***. Therefore, there was no error in the district court's entry of summary judgment on Grumman's monopolization claim.
***

Comments and Questions

1. The first step in any monopolization claim is to define the relevant market. What is the relevant market in this case? Why?

2. Initially, the First Circuit stated its holding as following: "We hold below that the desire of an author to be the exclusive user of its original work is a presumptively legitimate business justification for the author's refusal to license to competitors."

But what exactly is the legitimate business justification?

In defining what constitutes a legitimate business justification, the First Circuit noted: "In general, a business justification is valid if it relates directly or indirectly to the enhancement of consumer welfare." How does the unilateral refusal to deal in this case enhance consumer welfare?

Does this mean that the IP owner does not need to present a legitimate business justification to refuse to sell or license?

Was DG the "exclusive user" of the copyrighted software given that they licensed it to some customers? If not, how does that affect application of the court's holding?

Later, the court articulated its holding as follows: "an author's desire to exclude others from use of its copyrighted work is a presumptively valid business justification for any immediate harm to consumers."

How is this different than the court's first articulation of its holding?

If an IP owner's desire to exclude is "presumptively valid," how can an antitrust plaintiff rebut the presumption?

3. In a footnote supported with cites to several Supreme Court and lower court opinions, the court notes: "It is in any event well settled that concerted and contractual behavior that threatens competition is not immune from antitrust inquiry simply because it involves the exercise of copyright privileges." How do you reconcile this with the court's holding?

The court also states that there may be "rare cases" in which antitrust liability will not frustrate the objectives of the Copyright Act. What are those "rare cases"?

4. The First Circuit relies heavily on the Supreme Court opinion in *Aspen Skiing*, which condemned a monopolist for terminating a profitable joint-lift ticket program with its only competitor in the market for downhill skiing in Aspen, Colorado. Did the Court in *Aspen Skiing* define the relevant market correctly? What would you have argued if you had represented the antitrust defendants in that case?

In discussing *Aspen Skiing*, the First Circuit quotes *Olympia Equipment* for the proposition that "a monopolist may be guilty of monopolization if it refuses to cooperate with a competitor in circumstances where some cooperation is indispensable to effective competition."

Why isn't that the situation here—without cooperation from Data General, there is no effective competition in the relevant market?

The *Data General* court also distinguishes *Aspen Skiing* because "the decision turns on a comparison of the behavior of firms in a competitive market (the Aspen ski market)."

Was there a competitive market in *Aspen Skiing*? Why or why not?

How does your answer affect the First Circuit's antitrust analysis in *Data General*?

Finally, the *Data General* court stated that "Aspen Skiing ultimately calls for an inquiry that is relatively routine in antitrust analysis: namely, whether the monopolist's actions unjustifiably harm the competitive process by frustrating consumer preferences and erecting barriers to competition."

Are consumer preferences being frustrated by Data General's conduct?

After all, consumers who would like to use Grumman or another firm cannot because of Data General's refusal to license.

Image Technical Serv. v. Eastman Kodak,
125 F.3d 1195 (9th Cir. 1997)

BEEZER, Circuit Judge:

Plaintiffs-Appellees Image Technical Services, and ten other independent service organizations ("ISOs") that service Kodak photocopiers and micrographic equipment sued the Eastman Kodak Co. ("Kodak") for violations of the Sherman Act. The ISOs alleged that Kodak used its monopoly in the market for Kodak photocopier and micrographic parts to create a second monopoly in the equipment service markets. A jury verdict awarded treble damages totaling $71.8 million. The district court denied Kodak's post trial motions and entered a ten year permanent injunction requiring Kodak to sell "all parts" to ISOs. Kodak filed a timely appeal, challenging the jury's verdict, the ISOs' evidence, the jury instructions, the damage awards and the permanent injunction. Kodak also seeks reversal on the basis of an alleged biased juror.

This appeal raises questions relating to the application of antitrust principles upon a finding that a monopolist unilaterally refused to deal with competitors. We also address overlapping patent and copyright issues and their significance in the antitrust context. ***

I

Kodak manufactures, sells and services high volume photocopiers and micrographic (or microfilm) equipment. Competition in these markets is strong. In the photocopier market Kodak's competitors include Xerox, IBM and Canon. Kodak's competitors in the micrographics market include Minolta, Bell & Howell and 3M. Despite comparable products in these markets, Kodak's equipment is distinctive. Although Kodak equipment may perform similar functions to that of its competitors, Kodak's parts are not interchangeable with parts used in other manufacturers' equipment.

Kodak sells and installs replacement parts for its equipment. Kodak competes with ISOs in these markets. Kodak has ready access to all parts necessary for repair services because it manufactures many of the parts used in its equipment and purchases the remaining necessary parts from independent original-equipment manufacturers. In the service market, Kodak repairs at least 80% of the machines it manufactures. ISOs began servicing Kodak equipment in the early 1980's, and have provided cheaper and better service at times, according to some customers. ISOs obtain parts for repair service from a variety of sources, including, at one time, Kodak.

As ISOs grew more competitive, Kodak began restricting access to its photocopier and micrographic parts. In 1985, Kodak stopped selling copier parts to ISOs, and in 1986, Kodak halted sales of micrographic parts to ISOs. Additionally, Kodak secured agreements from their contracted original-equipment manufacturers not to sell parts to ISOs. These parts restrictions limited the ISOs' ability to compete in the service market for Kodak machines. Competition in the service market requires that service providers have ready access to all parts.

Kodak offers annual or multi-year service contracts to its customers. Service providers generally contract with equipment owners through multi-year service contracts. ISOs claim that they were unable to provide similar contracts because they lack a reliable supply of parts. Some ISOs contend that the parts shortage forced them out of business.

In 1987, the ISOs filed this action against Kodak, seeking damages and injunctive relief for violations of the Sherman Act. The ISOs claimed that Kodak both: (1) unlawfully tied the sale of service for Kodak machines with the sale of parts in violation of § 1 of the Sherman Act, and (2) monopolized or attempted to monopolize the sale of service for Kodak machines in violation of § 2 of the Sherman Act.

Kodak moved for summary judgment prior to discovery. The district court allowed brief discovery and then granted summary judgment in Kodak's favor. [citation omitted] We reversed. [citation omitted]

Kodak appealed to the Supreme Court, which affirmed the denial of summary judgment. The Court held that the record disclosed sufficient factual disputes to survive summary judgment on both the § 1 and § 2 claims. *Eastman Kodak Co. v. Image Technical Serv., Inc.*, 504 U.S. 451 (1992). The Supreme Court also held that Kodak's lack of market power in the market for high volume photocopiers and micrographic equipment did not preclude, as a matter of law, the possibility of market power in the derivative aftermarkets for parts and service. Id. at 477. ***

After remand, the case proceeded to trial in the district court. Before closing arguments, the ISOs withdrew their § 1 tying and conspiracy claims. The remaining § 2 attempted monopolization and monopolization claims were submitted to the jury. A unanimous verdict awarded damages to the ISO's totaling $71.8 million after trebling. Ten ISOs were awarded damages covering lost service profits in the amount of $12,172,900 (before trebling) and six ISOs were awarded damages covering lost profits for used equipment sales totaling $11,775,400 (before trebling).

After accepting the verdict, the district court crafted a ten year injunction requiring Kodak to sell all parts to ISOs on "reasonable and nondiscriminatory terms and prices." The injunction required Kodak to sell: (1) all parts for Kodak equipment; (2) all parts described in Kodak's Parts Lists; (3) all parts of supply items that are field replaceable by Kodak technicians; (4) all service manuals and price lists; and (5) all tools or devices "essential to servicing Kodak equipment."

II

Section 2 of the Sherman Act prohibits monopolies, attempts to form monopolies, as well as combinations and conspiracies to do so. 15 U.S.C. § 2. The ISOs presented evidence in support of two § 2 theories: attempted monopolization and monopolization. They alleged, and the jury concluded, that Kodak used its monopoly over

Kodak photocopier and micrographic parts to attempt to create and actually create a second monopoly over the service markets.

To prevail on a § 2 attempt claim, the ISOs were required to establish: "(1) a specific intent to control prices or destroy competition; (2) predatory or anticompetitive conduct directed at accomplishing that purpose; (3) a dangerous probability of achieving 'monopoly power,' and (4) causal antitrust injury." [citation omitted] The requirements of a § 2 monopolization claim are similar, differing primarily in the requisite intent and the necessary level of monopoly power. [citation omitted] To prevail on a § 2 monopoly claim the ISOs were required to prove that Kodak: (1) possessed monopoly power in the relevant market and (2) willfully acquired or maintained that power. *Kodak*, 504 U.S. at 481 (citing *United States v. Grinnell Corp.*, 384 U.S. 563, 570–71 (1966)). Section 2 plaintiffs must also establish antitrust injury. [citation omitted] ***

A. Market Power

Kodak first attacks the ISOs' monopoly power theory and its supporting evidence. Monopoly power is "the power to control prices or exclude competition." *Grinnell*, 384 U.S. at 571 (quoting *United States v. E.I. du Pont de Nemours & Co.*, 351 U.S. 377, 391 (1956)). As noted, § 2 monopoly claims require a showing of monopoly power, commonly referred to as market power. [citation omitted] Market power can be proven by either direct or circumstantial evidence. [citation omitted] The ISOs offered proof of market power by both means. We hold that there is sufficient proof of market power by circumstantial evidence. We need not consider the ISOs' direct evidence.

To demonstrate market power by circumstantial evidence, a plaintiff must: "(1) define the relevant market, (2) show that the defendant owns a dominant share of that market, and (3) show that there are significant barriers to entry and show that existing competitors lack the capacity to increase their output in the short run." *Id.* at 1434 (citations omitted). We review these requirements in turn.

1.

We begin with the relevant market determination. The relevant market is the field in which meaningful competition is said to exist. ***

In *Kodak*, the Supreme Court noted two guiding principles pertinent to the relevant market definition here. First, the Court held that service and parts could constitute separate markets. *Kodak*, 504 U.S. at 462–63, 481–82. Second, the Supreme Court held that a single brand could constitute a separate market. *Id.* at 482. Thus, as to the market for Kodak parts, the ISOs proceeded on the theory that Kodak held monopolies over two relevant parts markets: the Kodak photocopier parts market and the Kodak micrographic parts market. Both markets, the ISOs argued, consisted of the entirety of necessary Kodak parts for that field of equipment.

  *** Kodak proposes a segmented parts market. It argues that because no two parts are interchangeable, the relevant markets for parts consist of the market for each individual part for Kodak photocopiers and each single part for Kodak micrographics equipment. Under Kodak's theory there are not two relevant parts markets, but thousands of individual "part" markets. Kodak contends that the ISOs should have been required to demonstrate that they could not obtain particular nonpatented parts and that the failure to obtain that particular part resulted in a Kodak monopoly over service. We reject Kodak's market definition.

Kodak's market definition focuses exclusively on the interchangeability of the parts although ignoring the "commercial realities" faced by ISOs and end users. *** Consideration of the "commercial realities" in the markets for Kodak parts compels the use of an "all parts" market theory. The "commercial reality" faced by service providers and equipment owners is that a service provider must have ready access to all parts to compete in the service market. As the relevant market for service "from the Kodak equipment owner's perspective is composed of only those companies that service Kodak machines," *id.* *** The ISOs argue that through its anticompetitive conduct Kodak has ensured that it will possess the only inventory of all parts for Kodak high volume photocopiers and micrographic equipment. ***

Aggregating the individual parts into a single "all parts" market for photocopiers and a single "all parts" market for micrographics equipment is also necessary for administrative convenience. Kodak photocopiers and micrographic equipment require thousands of individual parts and a supply of all parts is necessary in order to fulfill service contracts. To require the ISOs to prove that Kodak has monopoly power in thousands of markets would be both unduly burdensome and pointless. [citation omitted] Moreover, aggregation does not prejudice Kodak because service providers need all parts to compete in the service market, and Kodak's 100% monopoly power over the 30% of parts it manufactures suggests the same potential for control of the service market under an individual part market theory that the jury found using the "all parts" market. Kodak "can point to no advantage it would enjoy were finer divisions . . . employed." [citation omitted] ***

Kodak has both undisputed 100% monopoly shares for certain parts and an alleged monopoly share in the entire parts market.

2. Market share

Next we turn to the second monopoly power element: market share. A plaintiff relying on circumstantial evidence to establish a § 2 monopolization claim must show that the defendant owned a "dominant share" of the market. *Rebel Oil*, 51 F.3d at 1434. Calculation of the market share allows for a proper understanding of the defendant's influence and relative power in the relevant market. A dominant share of the market often carries with it the power to control output across the market, and thereby control prices. Id. at 1437. Courts generally require a 65% market share to establish a prima facie case of market power. *See American Tobacco Co. v. United States*, 328 U.S. 781, 797 (1946).

In *Kodak*, the Supreme Court stated that Kodak's possession of monopoly power was "easily resolved." 504 U.S. at 481. The Court relied on its earlier discussion of the § 1 claim, where it held that the ISOs had "presented a triable claim that *Kodak* ha[d] the 'power to control prices or exclude competition' in service and parts." *Id.*

Noting that "monopoly power" under § 2 requires "something greater than market power under § 1," the Court held that the "evidence that Kodak controls nearly 100% of the parts market and 80% to 95% of the service market, with no readily available substitutes . . . sufficient to survive summary judgment. . . ." *Id.*

3.

The third and final monopoly power factor concerns barriers to market entry and barriers to expansion. [citation omitted] A § 2 plaintiff, establishing monopoly power by circumstantial evidence, must establish more than just market share. Even a 100% monopolist may not exploit its monopoly power in a market without entry barriers. [citation omitted] A § 2 plaintiff must show that new competitors face high market barriers to entry and that current competitors lack the ability to expand their output to challenge a monopolist's high prices. [citation omitted] Barriers to entry "must be capable of constraining the normal operation of the market to the extent that the problem is unlikely to be self-correcting." [citation omitted] Common entry barriers include: patents or other legal licenses, control of essential or superior resources, entrenched buyer preferences, high capital entry costs and economies of scale. *Id.*

*** Kodak has 220 patents and controls its designs and tools, brand name power and manufacturing capability. Kodak controls original-equipment manufacturers through various contract arrangements. Kodak has consistently maintained a high share of the service market. These factors together with the economies of scale, support a finding of high barriers to entry by new manufacturers and to increased output by established suppliers. [citation omitted] ***

B. Use of Monopoly Power

The second element of a § 2 monopoly claim, the "conduct" element, is the use of monopoly power "to foreclose competition, to gain a competitive advantage, or to destroy a competitor." *Kodak*, 504 U.S. at 482–83 (quoting *United States v. Griffith*, 334 U.S. 100, 107 (1948)). The ISOs proceeded under a "monopoly leveraging" theory, alleging that Kodak used its monopoly over Kodak parts to gain or attempt to gain a monopoly over the service of Kodak equipment. The Supreme Court endorsed this theory in *Kodak* noting: "If Kodak adopted its parts and service policies as part of a scheme of willful acquisition or maintenance of monopoly power, it will have violated § 2." *Id.* (citations omitted). "Willful acquisition" or "maintenance of monopoly power" involves "exclusionary conduct," not power gained "from growth or development as a consequence of a superior product, business acumen, or historic accident." *Grinnell*, 384 U.S. at 570–71. ***

Section 2 of the Sherman Act prohibits a monopolist's unilateral action, like Kodak's refusal to deal, if that conduct harms the competitive process in the absence of a legitimate business justification. *See Kodak*, 504 U.S. at 483 n. 32 (citing *Aspen Skiing*, 472 U.S. at 602). ***

The Supreme Court considered a refusal to deal claim in *Aspen Skiing* without referencing the essential facilities doctrine. Aspen Skiing involved a § 2 challenge by one Aspen ski resort against the owner of the remaining three ski resorts in Aspen, a monopolist in the recreational ski market. *** The Supreme Court began its analysis in *Aspen Skiing* with a discussion of the "right to refuse to deal," a right the Court characterized as highly valued but not "unqualified." *Id.* at 601. The Court, quoting extensively from *Lorain Journal Co. v. United States,* 342 U.S. 143, 155 (1951), held that the right to refuse to deal was "neither absolute nor exempt from regulation" and when used "as a purposeful means of monopolizing interstate commerce" the exercise of that right violates the Sherman Act. *Aspen Skiing,* 472 U.S. at 602. Thus "the long recognized right . . . [to] freely [ ] exercise [one's] own independent discretion as to parties with whom he will deal" does not violate the Sherman Act "[i]n the absence of any purpose to create or maintain a monopoly." *Id.* (quoting *Lorain Journal* 342 U.S. at 155 (emphasis in the original) (citations omitted). In Aspen Skiing the Court noted that a defendant's refusal to deal was evidence of its' intent "relevant to the question whether the challenged conduct is fairly characterized as 'exclusionary' or 'anticompetitive'—to use the words in the trial court's instructions—or 'predatory,' to use a word that scholars seem to favor." *Id.*

Next, the Court reasoned that a monopolist's refusal to deal was not limited to the specific facts of *Lorain Journal,* but also covered the *Aspen Skiing* defendant-monopolist's election "to make an important change in a pattern of distribution that had originated in a competitive market and had persisted for several years." *Id.* at 603. The Court noted that competitors in other markets continued to use interchangeable lift tickets and thus inferred that "such tickets satisfy consumer demand in free competitive markets." *Id.* The Court concluded that although such conduct was not "necessarily anticompetitive," the posture of the case and the strength of the evidence presented compelled the Court to uphold the jury's finding of liability. The Court noted that the challenged instructions correctly required the jury to distinguish "between practices which tend to exclude or restrict competition on the one hand, and the success of a business which reflects only a superior product, a well-run business, or luck, on the other." *Id.* Other instructions properly informed the jury that the defendant's refusal to deal "does not violate Section 2 if valid business reasons exist for that refusal." *Id.* at 605, 105 S.Ct. at 2858. ***

Jury Instructions Nos. 28 and 29 here covered the requirements set forth in Aspen Skiing.[6] Like the Supreme Court in Aspen Skiing, we are faced with a situation in which a monopolist made a conscious choice to change an established pattern of distribution to the detriment of competitors. *Id.* at 603, 105 S.Ct. at 2858. Although the service market prior to Kodak's parts policy had not "originated in a competitive market and persisted for several years," *id.,* the ISO service

---

[6] Jury Instruction No. 28 states in relevant part:

Exclusionary conduct refers to practices that unreasonably or unnecessarily impede fair competition; that is, conduct that impairs the efforts of others to compete for customers in an unnecessarily restrictive way. Such conduct does not refer to ordinary means of competition, like offering better products or services, exercising superior skill or business judgment, utilizing more efficient technology, or exercising natural competitive advantages.

market had existed for three years and was growing rapidly before Kodak implemented its parts policy. Our case is factually distinguishable from Aspen Skiing in several respects: here there are no readily comparable competitive markets; ISO profits were not halved after the imposition of the anticompetitive policies; and there are two markets at issue, rather than only one. Further, *** Aspen Skiing did not involve the effects of a supplier's refusal to deal with its customers in order to control a downstream market. Notwithstanding these distinctions, both the analysis in Aspen Skiing and Kodak footnote 32 suggest that Aspen Skiing applies here. Like the First Circuit in *Data General v. Grumman Systems Support,* 36 F.3d 1147 (1st Cir.1994), we believe the Supreme Court, in Aspen Skiing, endorsed a more general application of § 2 principles to refusal to deal cases. *See Data General,* 36 F.3d at 1183–84 (plaintiff alleging § 2 refusal to deal claim "need not tailor its argument to a preexisting 'category' of unilateral refusals to deal."). The district court's Jury Instruction No. 29 was proper. ***

III

Our conclusion that the ISOs have shown that Kodak has both attained monopoly power and exercised exclusionary conduct does not end our inquiry. Kodak's conduct may not be actionable if supported by a legitimate business justification. When a legitimate business justification supports a monopolist's exclusionary conduct, that conduct does not violate § 2 of the Sherman Act. *See Kodak,* 504 U.S. at 483; *Oahu Gas,* 838 F.2d at 368. A plaintiff may rebut an asserted business justification by demonstrating either that the justification does not legitimately promote competition or that the justification is pretextual. *See Kodak,* 504 U.S. at 483–84 (citing *Kodak,* 903 F.2d at 618). Kodak asserts that the protection of its patented and copyrighted parts is a valid business justification for its anticompetitive conduct and argues that the district court's erroneous jury instructions made it impossible for the jury to properly consider this justification. Kodak attacks the district court's failure both to provide a "less restrictive alternatives" instruction, and to instruct as to Kodak's intellectual property rights. ***

A. Least Restrictive Alternatives

Kodak argues that the district court erred by failing to instruct the jury that it was not to consider whether Kodak could have accomplished its business objectives through less restrictive alternatives. Kodak also questions the sufficiency of the ISOs' pretext evidence. ***

Kodak argues that monopolization, unlike tying, does not require consideration of whether the defendant could have achieved its aims through less restrictive alternatives. Kodak, however, cites no authority mandating an instruction requiring that the jury not consider "less restrictive alternatives." *** As discussed above, the "unnecessarily excluded or handicaps" language was permissible under *Aspen Skiing.* Moreover, the district court's instruction here, Instruction No. 28, was very similar to both the language proposed by Kodak and the language endorsed by the Supreme Court in *Aspen Skiing*, 472 U.S. at 597. Jury Instruction No. 28 defines "exclusionary conduct" as impairing "the efforts of others to compete for customers in an unnecessarily restrictive way." ***

Kodak next argues that the ISOs' primary arguments refuting Kodak's business justifications were "less restrictive alternative" arguments. Kodak focuses on the ISOs' attack on Kodak's quality control justification as one such "less restrictive alternative" argument. Kodak argues that because "the legitimacy of quality control is beyond reproach," the ISOs were forced to establish this justification, and others, were pretextual. The ISOs did establish pretext: they attacked Kodak's quality control justification on the grounds that it was pretextual, not because it was the least restrictive alternative. Counsel for the ISOs argued that Kodak's quality control justification was "a joke" because ISOs do not interfere with the quality of Kodak's service. We hold that the district court did not err in its instructions.

*** The ISOs' evidence suffices to support the jury's rejection of Kodak's business justifications, as the record reflects evidence of pretext. The ISOs presented evidence that: (1) Kodak adopted its parts policy only after an ISO won a contract with the State of California; (2) Kodak allowed its own customers to service their machines; (3) Kodak customers could distinguish breakdowns due to poor service from breakdowns due to parts; and (4) many customers preferred ISO service.

B. Intellectual Property Rights

Kodak also attacks the district court's business justifications instructions for their failure to properly detail Kodak's intellectual property rights. Kodak argues that the court failed to instruct the jury that Kodak's numerous patents and copyrights provide a legitimate business justification for Kodak's alleged exclusionary conduct. Kodak holds 220 valid United States patents covering 65 parts for its high volume photocopiers and micrographics equipment, and all Kodak diagnostic software and service software are copyrighted. The jury instructions do not afford Kodak any "rights" or "privileges" based on its patents and copyrights: all parts are treated the same. In Jury Instruction No. 37, the court told the jury:

> [i]f you find that Kodak engaged in monopolization or attempted monopolization by misuse of its alleged parts monopoly . . . then the fact that some of the replacement parts are patented or copyrighted does not provide Kodak with a defense against any of those antitrust claims.
>
>> In Jury Instruction No. 28, the court stated, over Kodak's objection, that:
>> [s]uch [exclusionary] conduct does not refer to ordinary means of competition, like offering better products or services, exercising superior skill or business judgment, utilizing more efficient technology, or exercising natural competitive advantages.

Kodak proposed to include "exercising lawful patents and copyrights" amongst the list of non-exclusionary conduct in Instruction No. 28, but the district court rejected that language.

Kodak's challenge raises unresolved questions concerning the relationship between federal antitrust, copyright and patent laws. In particular we must determine the significance of a monopolist's unilateral refusal to sell or license a patented or copyrighted product in the context of a § 2 monopolization claim based upon monopoly leveraging. This is a question of first impression.

1.

We first identify the general principles of antitrust, copyright and patent law as we must ultimately harmonize these statutory schemes in responding to Kodak's challenge. Antitrust law seeks to promote and protect a competitive marketplace for the benefit of the public. See *Standard Oil Co. v. United States*, 221 U.S. 1, 58 (1911); *SCM Corp. v. Xerox Corp.*, 645 F.2d 1195, 1203 (2d Cir.1981). The Sherman Act, the relevant antitrust law here, prohibits efforts both to restrain trade by combination or conspiracy and the acquisition or maintenance of a monopoly by exclusionary conduct. 15 U.S.C. §§ 1, 2.

Patent law seeks to protect inventions, while inducing their introduction into the market for public benefit. *SCM Corp.*, 645 F.2d at 1203. Patent laws "reward the inventor with the power to exclude others from making, using or selling [a patented] invention throughout the United States." Id. Meanwhile, the public benefits both from the faster introduction of inventions, and the resulting increase in market competition. Legally, a patent amounts to a permissible monopoly over the protected work. See *Zenith Radio Corp. v. Hazeltine Research, Inc.*, 395 U.S. 100, 135 (1969). Patent laws "are in pari materia with the antitrust laws and modify them pro tanto (as far as the patent laws go)." *Simpson v. Union Oil Co.*, 377 U.S. 13, 24 (1964).

Federal copyright law "secure[s] a fair return for an author's creative labor" in the short run, while ultimately seeking "to stimulate artistic creativity for the general public good." *Twentieth Century Music Corp. v. Aiken*, 422 U.S. 151, 156, 95 S.Ct. 2040, 2044, 45 L.Ed.2d 84 (1975) (internal quotations omitted). The Copyright Act grants to the copyright owner the exclusive right to distribute the protected work. [citation omitted]

Clearly the antitrust, copyright and patent laws both overlap and, in certain situations, seem to conflict. This is not a new revelation. We have previously noted the "obvious tension" between the patent and antitrust laws: "[o]ne body of law creates and protects monopoly power while the other seeks to proscribe it." *United States v. Westinghouse Electric Corp.*, 648 F.2d 642, 646 (9th Cir.1981) (citations omitted). Similarly, tension exists between the antitrust and copyright laws. See *Data General*, 36 F.3d at 1187.

Two principles have emerged regarding the interplay between these laws: (1) neither patent nor copyright holders are immune from antitrust liability, and (2) patent and copyright holders may refuse to sell or license protected work. First, as to antitrust liability, case law supports the proposition that a holder of a patent or copyright violates the antitrust laws by "concerted and contractual behavior that threatens competition." *Id.* at 1185 n. 63 (citation omitted). In *Kodak*, the Supreme Court noted:

> [we have] held many times that power gained through some natural advantage such as a patent, copyright, or business acumen can give rise to liability if 'a seller exploits his dominant position in one market to expand his empire into the next.'

504 U.S. at 479 n. 29 (quoting *Times-Picayune Publishing Co. v. United States*, 345 U.S. 594, 611 (1953) and citing *Northern Pacific R. Co. v. United States*, 356 U.S. 1 (1958); *United States v. Paramount Pictures, Inc.*, 334 U.S. 131 (1948); Leitch Mfg. Co. v. Barber Co., 302 U.S. 458, 463 (1938)).

Case law also supports the right of a patent or copyright holder to refuse to sell or license protected work. See *Westinghouse*, 648 F.2d at 647. In *United States v. Westinghouse Electric Corp.*, we held that "[t]he right to license [a] patent, exclusively or otherwise, or to refuse to license at all, is the 'untrammeled right' of the patentee." *Id.* [citation omitted]

2. *(next section answers this problem)*

Next we lay out the problem presented here. The Supreme Court touched on this question in *Kodak*, i.e., the effect to be given a monopolist's unilateral refusal to sell or license a patented or copyrighted product in the context of a § 2 monopoly leveraging claim. In footnote 29, previously discussed, the Supreme Court in *Kodak* refutes the argument that the possession by a manufacturer of "inherent power" in the market for its parts "should immunize [that manufacturer] from the antitrust laws in another market." 504 U.S. at 479 n. 29, 112 S.Ct. at 2089 n. 29. The Court stated that a monopolist who acquires a dominant position in one market through patents and copyrights may violate § 2 if the monopolist exploits that dominant position to enhance a monopoly in another market. Although footnote 29 appears in the Court's discussion of the § 1 tying claim, the § 2 discussion frequently refers back to the § 1 discussion, and the Court's statement that "exploit[ing] [a] dominant position in one market to expand [the] empire into the next" is broad enough to cover monopoly leveraging under § 2. *Id.* By responding in this fashion, the Court in *Kodak* supposed that intellectual property rights do not confer an absolute immunity from antitrust claims.

The *Kodak* Court, however, did not specifically address the question of antitrust liability based upon a unilateral refusal to deal in a patented or copyrighted product. Kodak and its amicus correctly indicate that the right of exclusive dealing is reserved from antitrust liability. We find no reported case in which a court has imposed antitrust liability for a unilateral refusal to sell or license a patent or copyright. Courts do not generally view a monopolist's unilateral refusal to license a patent as "exclusionary conduct." See *Data General*, 36 F.3d at 1186 [citation omitted].

This basic right of exclusion does have limits. For example, a patent offers no protection if it was unlawfully acquired. [citation omitted] Nor does the right of exclusion protect an attempt to extend a lawful monopoly beyond the grant of a patent.

188 *Antitrust Law and Intellectual Property Rights*

See Mercoid, 320 U.S. at 665. Section 2 of the Sherman Act condemns exclusionary conduct that extends natural monopolies into separate markets. Much depends, therefore, on the definition of the patent grant and the relevant market.

The relevant market for determining the patent or copyright grant is determined under patent or copyright law. ***

Parts and service here have been proven separate markets in the antitrust context, but this does not resolve the question whether the service market falls "reasonably within the patent [or copyright] grant" for the purpose of determining the extent of the exclusive rights conveyed. [citation omitted]

3.

We now resolve the question detailed above. Under the fact-based approaches of *Aspen Skiing* and *Kodak*, some measure must guarantee that the jury account for the procompetitive effects and statutory rights extended by the intellectual property laws. To assure such consideration, we adopt a modified version of the rebuttable presumption created by the First Circuit in *Data General*, and hold that "while exclusionary conduct can include a monopolist's unilateral refusal to license a [patent or] copyright," or to sell its patented or copyrighted work, a monopolist's "desire to exclude others from its [protected] work is a presumptively valid business justification for any immediate harm to consumers." *Data General*, 36 F.3d at 1187.

This presumption does not "rest on formalistic distinctions" which "are generally disfavored in antitrust laws;" rather it is based on "actual market realities." *Kodak*, 504 U.S. at 466–67, 112 S.Ct. at 2082. This presumption harmonizes the goals of the relevant statutes and takes into account the long term effects of regulation on these purposes. The presumption should act to focus the factfinder on the primary interest of both intellectual property and antitrust laws: public interest. [citation omitted]

Given this presumption, the district court's failure to give any weight to Kodak's intellectual property rights in the jury instructions constitutes an abuse of discretion. This error was, however, harmless. The ISOs maintain that Kodak argued protection of intellectual property as a business justification to the jury, which rejected this justification as pretextual. An error in instructing the jury in a civil case does not require reversal if it is more probable than not harmless. [citation omitted] ***

Kodak may assert that its desire to profit from its intellectual property rights justifies its conduct, and the jury should presume that this justification is legitimately procompetitive.

Nonetheless, this presumption is rebuttable. [citation omitted] ***

The *Data General* court noted that the presumption of legitimacy can be rebutted by evidence that the monopolist acquired the protection of the intellectual property laws in an unlawful manner. *See* 36 F.3d at 1188 (citation omitted). The presumption may also be rebutted by evidence of pretext. Neither the aims of intellectual property law, nor the antitrust laws justify allowing a monopolist to rely upon a pretextual business justification to mask anticompetitive conduct.

See Kodak, 504 U.S. at 484 (Because "Kodak's willingness to allow self-service casts doubt on its quality claim . . . . a reasonable trier of fact could conclude that [this justification] is pretextual.") [citation omitted]

Kodak defends its intellectual property rights "justification" against claims of pretext. Kodak argues that its subjective motivation is irrelevant. Kodak also contends, citing *Olympia Equipment Leasing Co. v. Western Union Telegraph Co.*, 797 F.2d 370, 379 (7th Cir.), reh'g denied, (7th Cir.1986), that a desire to best the competition does not prove pretext, nor does hostility to competitors. Kodak's argument and its accompanying authority stands for nothing more than the proposition that a desire to compete does not demonstrate pretext.

Evidence regarding the state of mind of Kodak employees may show pretext, when such evidence suggests that the proffered business justification played no part in the decision to act. Kodak's parts manager testified that patents "did not cross [his] mind" at the time Kodak began the parts policy. Further, no distinction was made by Kodak between "proprietary" parts covered by tooling or engineering clauses and patented or copyrighted products. In denying Kodak's motion for a new trial, the district court commented that Kodak was not actually motivated by protecting its intellectual property rights. Kodak argues that the district court should have allowed the jury to reach this conclusion.

Kodak photocopy and micrographics equipment requires thousands of parts, of which only 65 were patented. Unlike the other cases involving refusals to license patents, this case concerns a blanket refusal that included protected and unprotected products. [citation omitted] From this evidence, it is more probable than not that the jury would have found Kodak's presumptively valid business justification rebutted on the grounds of pretext.

Kodak argues that the existence of some patented and copyrighted products undermines ISOs "all parts" theory. To the contrary, as discussed above, the "all parts" market reflects the "commercial realities" of the marketplace and the lack of identifiable separate markets for individual parts. The fact that Kodak did not differentiate between patented and nonpatented parts lends further support to the existence of these commercial realities. The jury accepted the "all parts" theory and found a scheme to monopolize the service market through Kodak's conduct. We hold that the district court's failure to instruct on Kodak's intellectual property rights was harmless.

***

Comments and Questions

1. The Ninth Circuit defined the relevant product market as "all parts" necessary to maintain and repair Kodak copiers. What was the court's reasoning? Do you find it persuasive? Professor Hovenkamp has argued that the court confused complements and substitutes. Substitutes compete against each other in the same market; in contrast, "[n]ot only do complements not compete with each other; they frequently are made with entirely different technologies and under totally different competitive conditions." HOVENKAMP, ANTITRUST ENTERPRISE at 158.

190 *Antitrust Law and Intellectual Property Rights*

Did the Ninth Circuit improperly define a market comprised on complements? If so, how did it affect the analysis in the case?

2. Could the Kodak decision be regarded as correct because the liability is based on Kodak's refusal to sell unpatented parts, which made up the majority of parts that Kodak refused to sell? Should Kodak have a duty to sell unpatented products or inputs to its competitors? Is your answer affected by whether or not you think that Kodak has a monopoly over these parts?

3. Assuming that Kodak should be found liable, what is the proper remedy?

4. Court noted: "ISOs began servicing Kodak equipment in the early 1980's, and have provided cheaper and better service at times, according to some customers." How is this relevant to the antitrust analysis?

5. Should a single brand ever constitute a relevant market for antitrust purposes? Why?

In re Independent Service Organizations Antitrust Litigation (Xerox),
203 F.3d 1322 (Fed. Cir. 2000)

MAYER, Chief Judge.

CSU, L.L.C. appeals the judgment of the United States District Court for the District of Kansas, dismissing on summary judgment CSU's claims that Xerox's refusal to sell patented parts and copyrighted manuals and to license copyrighted software violate the antitrust laws. [citation omitted] *** [W]e affirm.

Background

Xerox manufactures, sells, and services high-volume copiers. Beginning in 1984, it established a policy of not selling parts unique to its series 10 copiers to independent service organizations ("ISOs"), including CSU, unless they were also end-users of the copiers. In 1987, the policy was expanded to include all new products as well as existing series 9 copiers. Enforcement of this policy was tightened in 1989, and Xerox cut off CSU's direct purchase of restricted parts. Xerox also implemented an "on-site end-user verification" procedure to confirm that the parts ordered by certain ISOs or their customers were actually for their end-user use. Initially this procedure applied to only the six most successful ISOs, which included CSU.

To maintain its existing business of servicing Xerox equipment, CSU used parts cannibalized from used Xerox equipment, parts obtained from other ISOs, and parts purchased through a limited number of its customers. For approximately one year, CSU also obtained parts from Rank Xerox, a majority-owned European affiliate of Xerox, until Xerox forced Rank Xerox to stop selling parts to CSU and other ISOs. In 1994, Xerox settled an antitrust lawsuit with a class of ISOs by which it agreed to suspend its restrictive parts policy for six and one-half years and to license its diagnostic software for four and one-half years. CSU opted out of that settlement and filed this suit alleging that Xerox violated the Sherman Act by setting the prices on its patented parts much higher for ISOs than for end-users to force ISOs to raise their prices. This would eliminate ISOs in general and CSU in particular as competitors in the relevant service markets for high speed copiers and printers.

Xerox counterclaimed for patent and copyright infringement and contested CSU's antitrust claims as relying on injury solely caused by Xerox's lawful refusal to sell or license patented parts and copyrighted software. Xerox also claimed that CSU could not assert a patent or copyright misuse defense to Xerox's infringement counterclaims based on Xerox's refusal to deal.

The district court granted summary judgment to Xerox dismissing CSU's antitrust claims and holding that if a patent or copyright is lawfully acquired, the patent or copyright holder's unilateral refusal to sell or license its patented invention or copyrighted expression is not unlawful exclusionary conduct under the antitrust laws, even if the refusal to deal impacts competition in more than one market. The court also held, in both the patent and copyright contexts, that the right holder's intent in refusing to deal and any other alleged exclusionary acts committed by the right holder are irrelevant to antitrust law. This appeal followed.

Discussion

The issue is whether the district court erred in granting Xerox's motion for summary judgment on CSU's antitrust claims. ***

A.

Intellectual property rights do not confer a privilege to violate the antitrust laws. *See Intergraph Corp. v. Intel Corp.*, 195 F.3d 1346, 1362, 52 USPQ2d 1641, 1652 (Fed.Cir.1999). "But it is also correct that the antitrust laws do not negate the patentee's right to exclude others from patent property." *Id.* (citation omitted). "The commercial advantage gained by new technology and its statutory protection by patent do not convert the possessor thereof into a prohibited monopolist." *Abbott Lab. v. Brennan*, 952 F.2d 1346, 1354, 21 USPQ2d 1192, 1199 (Fed.Cir.1991). "The patent right must be 'coupled with violations of § 2', and the elements of violation of 15 U.S.C. § 2 must be met." *Id.* (citations omitted). "Determination of whether the patentee meets the Sherman Act elements of monopolization or attempt to monopolize is governed by the rules of application of the antitrust laws to market participants, with due consideration to the exclusivity that inheres in the patent grant." *Id.* at 1354–55, 952 F.2d 1346, 21 USPQ2d at 1199 (citations omitted).

A patent alone does not demonstrate market power. *See id.* at 1355, 952 F.2d 1346. The United States Department of Justice and Federal Trade Commission have issued guidance that, even where it exists, such "market power does not 'impose on the intellectual property owner an obligation to license the use of that property to others.'" *Intergraph*, 195 F.3d at 1362 (citing United States Department of Justice and Federal Trade Comm'n Antitrust Guidelines for the Licensing of Intellectual Property 4 (1995)). There is "no reported case in which a court ha[s] imposed antitrust liability for a unilateral refusal to sell or license a patent...." *Id.*

(citing *Image Technical Servs. v. Eastman Kodak Co.*, 125 F.3d 1195, 1216, 44 USPQ2d 1065, 1079 (9th Cir.1997)). The patentee's right to exclude is further supported by section 271(d) of the Patent Act which states, in pertinent part, that "[n]o patent owner otherwise entitled to relief . . . shall be denied relief or deemed guilty of misuse or illegal extension of the patent right by reason of his having . . . (4) refused to license or use any rights to the patent . . . " 35 U.S.C. § 271(d) (1999) (emphasis added).

The patentee's right to exclude, however, is not without limit. *** [A] patent owner who brings suit to enforce the statutory right to exclude others from making, using, or selling the claimed invention is exempt from the antitrust laws, even though such a suit may have an anticompetitive effect, unless the infringement defendant proves one of two conditions. [citation omitted] First, he may prove that the asserted patent was obtained through knowing and willful fraud within the meaning of *Walker Process Equipment, Inc. v. Food Machinery & Chemical Corp.*, 382 U.S. 172, 177 (1965). [citation omitted] Or he may demonstrate that the infringement suit was a mere sham to cover what is actually no more than an attempt to interfere directly with the business relationships of a competitor. [citation omitted] Here, CSU makes no claim that Xerox obtained its patents through fraud in the Patent and Trademark Office; the *Walker Process* analysis is not implicated.

"[I]rrespective of the patent applicant's conduct before the [Patent and Trademark Office], an antitrust claim can also be based on [an] allegation that a suit is baseless; in order to prove that a suit was within *Noerr*'s 'sham' exception to immunity, [*see Noerr*, 365 U.S. at 144], an antitrust plaintiff must prove that the suit was both objectively baseless and subjectively motivated by a desire to impose collateral, anti-competitive injury rather than to obtain a justifiable legal remedy." *Nobelpharma*, 141 F.3d at 1071 (citing *Professional Real Estate Investors, Inc. v. Columbia Pictures Indus., Inc.*, 508 U.S. 49, 60–61 (1993)). "Accordingly, if a suit is not objectively baseless, an antitrust defendant's subjective motivation is immaterial." *Id.* at 1072. CSU has alleged that Xerox misused its patents but has not claimed that Xerox's patent infringement counterclaims were shams.

To support its argument that Xerox illegally sought to leverage its presumably legitimate dominance in the equipment and parts market into dominance in the service market, CSU relies on a footnote in *Eastman Kodak Co. v. Image Technical Services, Inc.*, 504 U.S. 451, 480 n. 29, 112 S.Ct. 2072, 2089 n. 29, 119 L.Ed.2d 265 (1992), that "[t]he Court has held many times that power gained through some natural and legal advantage such as a patent, . . . can give rise to liability if 'a seller exploits his dominant position in one market to expand his empire into the next.' "Notably, Kodak was a tying case when it came before the Supreme Court, and no patents had been asserted in defense of the antitrust claims against Kodak. Conversely, there are no claims in this case of illegally tying the sale of Xerox's patented parts to unpatented products. Therefore, the issue was not resolved by the Kodak language cited by CSU. Properly viewed within the framework of a tying case, the footnote can be interpreted as restating the undisputed premise that the patent holder cannot use his statutory right to refuse to sell patented parts to gain a monopoly in a market beyond the scope of the patent. [citation omitted] ***

CSU further relies on the Ninth Circuit's holding on remand in Image Technical Services that "'while exclusionary conduct can include a monopolist's unilateral refusal to license a [patent] or to sell its patented ... work, a monopolist's 'desire to exclude others from its [protected] work is a presumptively valid business justification for any immediate harm to consumers.'" 125 F.3d at 1218 (citing *Data General Corp. v. Grumman Sys. Support Corp.*, 36 F.3d 1147, 1187 (1st Cir.1994)). By that case, the Ninth Circuit adopted a rebuttable presumption that the exercise of the statutory right to exclude provides a valid business justification for consumer harm, but then excused as harmless the district court's error in failing to give any instruction on the effect of intellectual property rights on the application of the antitrust laws. *See id.* at 1219–20. It concluded that the jury must have rejected the presumptively valid business justification as pretextual. *See id.* This logic requires an evaluation of the patentee's subjective motivation for refusing to sell or license its patented products for pretext. We decline to follow *Image Technical Services.*

We have held that "if a [patent infringement] suit is not objectively baseless, an antitrust defendant's subjective motivation is immaterial." *Nobelpharma*, 141 F.3d at 1072. We see no more reason to inquire into the subjective motivation of Xerox in refusing to sell or license its patented works than we found in evaluating the subjective motivation of a patentee in bringing suit to enforce that same right. In the absence of any indication of illegal tying, fraud in the Patent and Trademark Office, or sham litigation, the patent holder may enforce the statutory right to exclude others from making, using, or selling the claimed invention free from liability under the antitrust laws. We therefore will not inquire into his subjective motivation for exerting his statutory rights, even though his refusal to sell or license his patented invention may have an anticompetitive effect, so long as that anticompetitive effect is not illegally extended beyond the statutory patent grant. [citation omitted] It is the infringement defendant and not the patentee that bears the burden to show that one of these exceptional situations exists and, in the absence of such proof, we will not inquire into the patentee's motivations for asserting his statutory right to exclude. Even in cases where the infringement defendant has met this burden, which CSU has not, he must then also prove the elements of the Sherman Act violation.

We answer the threshold question of whether Xerox's refusal to sell its patented parts exceeds the scope of the patent grant in the negative. Therefore, our inquiry is at an end. Xerox was under no obligation to sell or license its patented parts and did not violate the antitrust laws by refusing to do so.

B.

The Copyright Act expressly grants a copyright owner the exclusive right to distribute the protected work by "transfer of ownership, or by rental, lease, or lending." 17 U.S.C. § 106(3) (1996). "[T]he owner of the copyright, if [it] pleases, may refrain from vending or licensing and content [itself] with simply exercising the right to exclude others from using [its] property." *Data General*, 36 F.3d at 1186[citation omitted].

The Supreme Court has made clear that the property right granted by copyright law cannot be used with impunity to extend power in the marketplace beyond what Congress intended. *See United States v. Loew's, Inc.*, 371 U.S. 38, 47–48 (1962) (block booking of copyrighted motion pictures is illegal tying in violation of Sherman Act). The Court has not, however, directly addressed the antitrust implications of a unilateral refusal to sell or license copyrighted expression. ***

Perhaps the most extensive analysis of the effect of a unilateral refusal to license copyrighted expression was conducted by the First Circuit in *Data General Corp. v. Grumman Systems Support Corp.*, 36 F.3d 1147. There, the court noted that the limited copyright monopoly is based on Congress' empirical assumption that the right to "exclude others from using their works creates a system of incentives that promotes consumer welfare in the long term by encouraging investment in the creation of desirable artistic and functional works of expression. . . . We cannot require antitrust defendants to prove and reprove the merits of this legislative assumption in every case where a refusal to license a copyrighted work comes under attack." *Id.* at 1186–87. The court went on to establish as a legal standard that "while exclusionary conduct can include a monopolist's unilateral refusal to license a copyright, an author's desire to exclude others from use of its copyrighted work is a presumptively valid business justification for any immediate harm to consumers." *See id.* at 1187. The burden to overcome this presumption was firmly placed on the antitrust plaintiff. The court gave no weight to evidence showing knowledge that developing a proprietary position would help to maintain a monopoly in the service market in the face of contrary evidence of the defendant's desire to develop state-of-the-art diagnostic software to enhance its service and consumer benefit. *See id.* at 1188–89.

As discussed above, the Ninth Circuit adopted a modified version of this *Data General* standard. Both courts agreed that the presumption could be rebutted by evidence that "the monopolist acquired the protection of the intellectual property laws in an unlawful manner." *Image Technical Servs.*, 125 F.3d at 1219 (citing *Data General*, 36 F.3d at 1188). The Ninth Circuit, however, extended the possible means of rebutting the presumption to include evidence that the defense and exploitation of the copyright grant was merely a pretextual business justification to mask anticompetitive conduct. *See id.* The hazards of this approach are evident in both the path taken and the outcome reached. The jury in that case was instructed to examine each proffered business justification for pretext, and no weight was given to the intellectual property rights in the instructions. *See id.* at 1218, 1220 n. 12. This permitted the jury to second guess the subjective motivation of the copyright holder in asserting its statutory rights to exclude under the copyright laws without properly weighing the presumption of legitimacy in asserting its rights under the copyright laws. While concluding that the failure to weigh the intellectual property rights was an abuse of discretion, the Ninth Circuit nevertheless held the error harmless because it thought the jury must have rejected the presumptive validity of asserting the copyrights as pretextual. *See id*. at 1219–20. This is in reality a significant departure from the First Circuit's central premise that rebutting the presumption would be an uphill battle and would only be appropriate in those rare cases in which imposing antitrust liability is unlikely to frustrate the objectives of the Copyright Act. *See Data General*, 36 F.3d at 1187 n. 64, 1188, 32 USPQ2d at 1417 n. 64.

We believe the First Circuit's approach is more consistent with both the antitrust and the copyright laws ***. We therefore reject CSU's invitation to examine Xerox's subjective motivation in asserting its right to exclude under the copyright laws for pretext, in the absence of any evidence that the copyrights were obtained by unlawful means or were used to gain monopoly power beyond the statutory copyright granted by Congress. In the absence of such definitive rebuttal evidence, Xerox's refusal to sell or license its copyrighted works was squarely within the rights granted by Congress to the copyright holder and did not constitute a violation of the antitrust laws.

Conclusion

Accordingly, the judgment of the United States District Court for the District of Kansas is affirmed.

Comments and Questions

1. The Ninth and Federal Circuit disagree about the role of intent in antitrust liability. In contrast to *Kodak*, the Federal Circuit refused to look into Xerox's subjective motivation behind the refusal. The Federal Circuit asserted "the right holder's intent in refusing to deal and any other alleged exclusionary acts committed by the right holder are irrelevant to antitrust law." *Xerox*, 203 F.3d at 1324.

Is that always true? Is intent relevant to sham litigation?

Review the Federal Circuit's rationale for refusing to look at intent. What are the costs and benefits of reviewing subjective intent?

If liability turns on intent, how is it possible to distinguish between a legitimate intent to exercise exclusionary IP rights and an illegitimate intent to engage in impermissible exclusionary conduct? A corporation is comprised of people. Whose intent should courts investigate in finding that a corporation had the intent to injure competition instead of intent to protect its intellectual property rights? Remember that in *Data General*, the court found intent to further monopolization *and* intent to create a more efficient product.

2. Both the Ninth and Federal Circuits' approaches have been criticized. At the DOJ's Antitrust Division and Federal Trade Commission hearings to discuss the relationship between antitrust and intellectual property,

> [p]anelists agreed that neither *Kodak* nor *CSU* provide sufficient guidance on potential antitrust liability for a refusal to license. Most panelists rejected the approach of the U.S. Court of Appeals for the Ninth Circuit in *Kodak*, which

impracticably focused on the subjective intent of the patent holder that had refused to license its patent. As one panelist noted, *Kodak* presents a standard that is out of step with the modern focus of antitrust analysis, which is on objective economic evidence. Panelists also criticized the decision of the U.S. Court of Appeals for the Federal Circuit in *CSU*, which, in dictum, narrowly construed the circumstances in which antitrust liability can arise for a refusal to license. These circumstances—illegal tying, fraud on the U.S. Patent and Trademark Office, and sham litigation—provided little guidance, according to panelists, because they are independent bases for antitrust liability.

U.S. DEP'T OF JUSTICE & FEDERAL TRADE COMMISSION, ANTITRUST ENFORCEMENT AND INTELLECTUAL PROPERTY RIGHTS: PROMOTING INNOVATION AND COMPETITION 5 (2007).

3. The Ninth and Federal Circuits agreed that the critical issue is the scope of the patent. For example, the Ninth Circuit stated that the patentee's "right of exclusion" does not "protect an attempt to extend a lawful monopoly beyond the grant of a patent" and "[m]uch depends, therefore, on the definition of the patent grant and the relevant market." Similarly, the Federal Circuit noted that a "patent holder cannot use his statutory right to refuse to sell patented parts to gain a monopoly in a market beyond the scope of the patent." Despite their agreement on this fundamental principle, neither court actually defined the scope of the patent.

Could the antitrust plaintiff argue that Xerox was engaging in exclusionary conduct to achieve monopoly power "*beyond the scope of the patent*"?

4. Professors Hovenkamp, Janis, and Lemley try to reconcile *Data General*, *Xerox*, and *Image Technical* further by investigating when and how the intellectual property justification came into play in the litigation. In *Image Technical*, Kodak did not present intellectual property as a justification until a few years into litigation. This *post hoc* justification had to be denied by the Ninth Circuit because it was obvious that Kodak was simply offering a litigation strategy and their decision making had nothing to do with intellectual property. Therefore, *Image Technical* should be read as precluding evidence of intent to injure competition, probably because all participants want to injure competition. To Hovenkamp, Janis, and Lemley, all *Image Technical* would allow the plaintiff to demonstrate is that there was no legitimate refusal to license intellectual property rights at stake and that the invocation of intellectual property as a justification was simply post hoc. Thus, evidence of the defendant's intent will only be raised in "very specialized circumstances." Herbert Hovenkamp, Mark D. Janis, & Mark A. Lemley, *Unilateral Refusals to License*, 2 J. COMPETITION L. & ECON. 1, 26 (2006).

5. Professors Hovenkamp, Janis, and Lemley also find that the tying arrangements inherent in *Xerox* and *Image Technical* may account for the differences between the two decisions. At issue were tying claims where the defendant offered their machines only when the customer agreed to purchase their services in the aftermarket as well. While *Xerox* acknowledged that tying involving patents could bring antitrust liability, it did not address the tying facts at issue because these

issues were not raised. *Image Technical* expressed greater concern that Kodak may have been tying its products and been using intellectual property as a pretext for it. Thus, the Ninth Circuit may have condemned tying and not the refusal to license per se. The Federal Circuit skirted the tying issue altogether. Herbert Hovenkamp, Mark D. Janis, & Mark A. Lemley, *Unilateral Refusals to License*, 2 J. COMPETITION L. & ECON. 1, 26–27 (2006). Perhaps then, as a plaintiff, it makes sense to frame the suit as a tying claim and not a refusal to deal case.

The Federal Circuit recognized an exception for tying arrangement. How could the plaintiff in Xerox characterize the defendant's conduct as a form of tying?

6. The relationship between patent misuse and antitrust liability remains unclear, but antitrust courts sometimes invoke the case law on patent misuse when adjudicating antitrust claims. Thus, it is important for antitrust practitioners to have a sense of what conduct constitutes patent misuse. The Patent Misuse Reform Act of 1988 specifically provides that "[n]o patent owner otherwise entitled to relief for infringement or contributory infringement of a patent shall be denied relief or deemed guilty of misuse or illegal extension of the patent right by reason of his having . . . refused to license or use any rights to the patent . . . ." 35 U.S.C. 271(d)(4).

The federal antitrust agencies have noted that "courts have held that section 271(d)(4)'s companion provision, section 271(d)(5), does not immunize patentees from antitrust liability for the conduct it governs—conditioning a license, or sale of a patented product, on the purchase of some other product or the taking of some other license—and it would seem anomalous to read the phrase "illegal extension of the patent right" to immunize patentees from antitrust liability for their refusals to license, but not for such conditioning of licenses." U.S. DEP'T OF JUSTICE & FEDERAL TRADE COMMISSION, ANTITRUST ENFORCEMENT AND INTELLECTUAL PROPERTY RIGHTS: PROMOTING INNOVATION AND COMPETITION 26 (2007).

7. One of the first unilateral refusal to deal cases in the intellectual property context was *SCM Corp. v. Xerox Corp.*, 645 F.2d 1195 (2d Cir. 1981). In that case, Xerox had a patent on a plain paper copier and refused to license its patent to a competitor, SCM, that wished to manufacture its own copier. SCM sued, claiming that the refusal to deal constituted monopolization. The court held that "where a patent has been lawfully acquired, subsequent conduct permissible under the patent laws cannot trigger any liability under the antitrust laws." Xerox had lawfully acquired its patent and therefore could not be found liable for its refusal to deal. Many commentators have termed this the creation of per se legality. *See* Michael A. Carrier, *Refusals to License Intellectual Property After* Trinko, 55 DEPAUL L. REV. 1191 (2006). *See also Miller Insituform, Inc. v. Insituform of North America, Inc.*, 830 F.2d 606 (6th Cir. 1987) (holding that "[a] patent holder who lawfully acquires a patent cannot be held liable under Section Two of the Sherman Act for maintaining the monopoly power he lawfully acquired by refusing to license the patent to others.").

Is Federal Circuit's *Xerox* opinion distinguishable from *SCM*?

Courts hold that a patentholder cannot use IP "to extend his power in the marketplace improperly." Atari Games Corp. v. Nintendo of America Inc.,

897 F.2d 1570, 1576 (Fed. Cir. 1990). But when is an extension of market power "improper"?

Could you explain to your client who wants to obey the law what is a legitimate use and what is a pretextual assertion of IP rights?

8. Federal antitrust enforcement agencies have indicated that they will not pursue antitrust claims based on a patentee's unconditional refusal to license:

> Antitrust liability for mere unilateral, unconditional refusals to license patents will not play a meaningful part in the interface between patent rights and antitrust protections. Antitrust liability for refusals to license competitors would compel firms to reach out and affirmatively assist their rivals, a result that is "in some tension with the underlying purpose of antitrust law." Moreover, liability would restrict the patent holder's ability to exercise a core part of the patent—the right to exclude.

U.S. DEP'T OF JUSTICE & FEDERAL TRADE COMMISSION, ANTITRUST ENFORCEMENT AND INTELLECTUAL PROPERTY RIGHTS: PROMOTING INNOVATION AND COMPETITION 5 (2007). (quoting Trinko, 540 U.S. at 407–08)

9. Note that the above quote referred to "*unconditional* refusals to license patents." Does that mean that conditional refusals are treated differently? Consider this: In one case, the district court asserted that "[b]ecause a patent owner has the legal right to refuse to license his or her patent on any terms, the existence of a predicate condition to a license agreement cannot state an antitrust violation." Townshend v. Rockwell International Corporation, 2000 WL 433505 (N.D. Cal. Mar. 28, 2000). Is that correct?

In their report on the intersection of antitrust law and IP rights, the federal antitrust enforcement agencies recently noted:

> In *Motion Picture Patents Co. v. Universal Film Manufacturing Co.*, the Supreme Court rejected the theory that "since the patentee may withhold his patent altogether from public use he must logically and necessarily be permitted to impose any conditions which he chooses upon any use which he may allow of it." The Court explained that the "defect in this thinking springs from the substituting of inference and argument for the language of the statute and from failure to distinguish between the rights which are given to the inventor by the patent law and which he may assert against all the world through an infringement proceeding, and rights which he may create for himself by private contract which, however, are subject to the rules of general [law] as distinguished from those of the patent law." Conduct going beyond a mere refusal thus may merit scrutiny under the antitrust laws.

U.S. DEP'T OF JUSTICE & FEDERAL TRADE COMMISSION, ANTITRUST ENFORCEMENT AND INTELLECTUAL PROPERTY RIGHTS: PROMOTING INNOVATION AND COMPETITION 30–31 (2007) (quoting Motion Picture Patents, 243 U.S. 502, 514 (1917)).

Can you think of conditions that an IP owner might impose on its licensees that should rise to the level of an antitrust violation?

10. If a unilateral refusal to license can create antitrust liability, that leads to the question of remedy. Is the proper remedy money damages or should it require the defendant to license its IP? If so, should the compulsory licensing be royalty free? Compulsory licensing as an antitrust remedy is discussed in Chapter 18.

Note on Market Power in Aftermarkets

One controversy in antitrust law concerns when a firm possesses market power in so-called aftermarkets. An aftermarket is a relevant market for goods or services used in conjunction with an earlier-purchased product, sometimes called the primary equipment market. For example, after purchasing a car in a primary equipment market, the consumer will have to eventually make purchases in aftermarkets for a replacement battery, oil changes, etc. Some theorists have argued that if a firm does not have market power in the primary equipment market, then it cannot have market power in aftermarkets, also called downstream markets. In *Eastman Kodak Co. v. Image Technical Services, Inc.*, 504 U.S. 451 (1992), the Supreme Court addressed the question of "whether a defendant's lack of market power in the primary equipment market precludes—as a matter of law—the possibility of market power in derivative aftermarkets." (This is the same *Kodak* case that later went to trial and led to the 1997 Ninth Circuit opinion excerpted earlier in this chapter.)

In *Kodak*, the Supreme Court considered a claim that Kodak had illegally monopolized the market for servicing Kodak brand copiers by imposing a tying requirement whereby Kodak would not sell Kodak parts (the tying product) to consumers that did not agree to also purchase Kodak service (the tied product).* Independent services organizations (ISOs) that repaired Kodak copiers claimed that Kodak was using its market power over Kodak parts as leverage to monopolize the aftermarket for repairs. Kodak argued that it did not have market power over Kodak parts because it lacked market power in the primary equipment market for copiers. Kodak contended that when consumers purchase durable equipment they calculate and compare each products' lifecycle cost, which is the cost of the equipment over its useful life, including the initial purchase price and maintenance costs. Kodak could not charge a supracompetitive price for its parts, according to Kodak, because if it did then consumers would not buy Kodak copiers. Absent market power in the parts market, Kodak's argument continued, the ISOs' theory of monopoly leveraging was invalid as a matter of law.

The Supreme Court rejected Kodak's theory on aftermarkets. The majority reasoned, in part, that Kodak's argument assumed that consumers could appreciate the lifecycle costs of equipment. The Court, however, believed that most consumers could not accurately engage in lifecycle pricing because it required too much hard-to-obtain data—"includ[ing] data on price, quality, and availability of products needed to operate, upgrade, or enhance the initial equipment, as well

---

* Kodak customers could buy parts from Kodak in order to service the equipment they owned, but were contractually precluded from purchasing service from a non-Kodak provider.

as service and repair costs, including estimates of breakdown frequency, nature of repairs, price of service and parts, length of 'downtime,' and losses incurred from downtime"—and an ability to "undertake sophisticated analysis." The Court also reasoned that some customers may be locked-in to using Kodak copiers because the switching costs—the expense associated with replacing Kodak copiers with another brand that had lower maintenance costs—would be prohibitively high. For these reasons, the Court concluded that a manufacturer could enjoy economic power in a downstream parts market even if that manufacturer did not dominate the upstream equipment market.

The *Kodak* opinion has not been without controversy and lower courts have tried to determine when a firm that apparently lacks market power in a primary equipment market may nonetheless possess market power in an aftermarket. Many judges and scholars have taken issue with the Court's analysis in *Kodak*. In discussing the *Kodak* opinion, Judge Easterbrook viewed Kodak's change in policy as the crux of the market power issue:

> Kodak sold plain paper copiers in a market with three substantial rivals. At the time of the sale, *** Kodak sold replacement parts, enabling users to repair their copiers or hire independent service organizations (ISOs) to do so. Later Kodak changed its policy and refused to sell parts to ISOs, who alleged that this enabled Kodak to claim the repair business for itself, at supra-competitive prices. The Court held that evidence in the record that prices had increased prevented a grant of summary judgment. It conceded that customers who had anticipated the change of policy could not be exploited; they would have shopped around and purchased copiers based on full-life-cycle costs (purchase price, plus costs of repair, plus costs of consumables). Competition among manufacturers fully protects buyers who accurately calculate life-cycle costs. But not all customers do this, if only because they do not anticipate all changes of policy. Thus Kodak had some ability to extract additional money by raising prices. It could not so do again; once the new policy was known, consumers could shop with full information. *** [I]f spare parts had been bundled with Kodak's copiers from the outset, or Kodak had informed customers about its policies before they bought its machines, purchasers could have shopped around for competitive life-cycle prices.

Digital Equipment Corp. v. Uniq Digital Technologies, Inc., 73 F.3d 756 (7th Cir. 1996).

Do you agree with Judge Easterbrook's analysis? Would customers have been able to calculate and compare life-cycle costs if Kodak's policy had been longstanding? Why or why not?

Do you think that a firm with several rivals in the market for primary equipment can possess market power in downstream markets? Why or why not?

Note on the Digital Millennium Copyright Act

A copyright owner's ability to dominate an aftermarket may also be affected by the anti-circumvention provisions of the Digital Millennium Copyright Act (DMCA),

17 U.S.C. § 1201 et seq. The DMCA creates liability for circumventing copyright protection systems, as well as trafficking in devices to circumvent such technological measures. The Second Circuit explained the history and structure of the DMCA:

> The DMCA was enacted in 1998 to implement the World Intellectual Property Organization Copyright Treaty (WIPO Treaty), which requires contracting parties to provide adequate legal protection and effective legal remedies against the circumvention of effective technological measures that are used by authors in connection with the exercise of their rights under this Treaty or the Berne Convention and that restrict acts, in respect of their works, which are not authorized by the authors concerned or permitted by law. ... The Act contains three provisions targeted at the circumvention of technological protections. The first is subsection 1201(a)(1)(A), the anticircumvention provision. This provision prohibits a person from circumvent[ing] a technological measure that effectively controls access to a work protected under [Title 17, governing copyright]. . . . The second and third provisions are subsections 1201(a)(2) and 1201(b)(1), the anti-trafficking provisions. . . . Subsection 1201(a)(1) differs from both of these anti-trafficking subsections in that it targets the use of a circumvention technology, not the trafficking in such a technology.

Universal City Studios v. Corley, 273 F.3d 429 (2d Cir.2001) (brackets in original). *See also Corley,* 273 F.3d at 440–41 ("[T]he focus of subsection 1201(a)(2) is circumvention of technologies designed to *prevent access* to a work, and the focus of subsection 1201(b)(1) is circumvention of technologies designed to *permit access* to a work but *prevent copying* of the work or some other act that infringes a copyright.") (emphasis in original).

For example, if a copyright owner encrypts its software or DVDs in order to restrict access and thereby prevent copying, a party might violate the DMCA if it disables the encryption technology. Circumvention, however, is not infringement. Copyright infringement must be proven independently of any violation of the DMCA and a violation of the DMCA's anti-circumvention provisions can be proven without a showing of copyright infringement. The Federal Circuit has explained: "Prior to the DMCA, a copyright owner would have had no cause of action against anyone who circumvented any sort of technological control, but did not infringe. The DMCA rebalanced these interests to favor the copyright owner; the DMCA created circumvention liability for 'digital trespass' under § 1201(a)(1). It also created trafficking liability under § 1201(a)(2) for facilitating such circumvention and under § 1201(b) for facilitating infringement (both subject to the numerous limitations and exceptions outlined throughout the DMCA)." *Chamberlain Group, Inc. v. Skylink Technology, Inc.,* 381 F.3d 1178 (Fed. Cir. 2004).

The DMCA creates the risk that firms will attempt to create technical incompatibility that is protected with a layer of encryption technology in order to prevent rivals in downstream markets from competing on the merits. This raises antitrust issues. Courts are beginning to address and define the relationship between the

DMCA and antitrust law, if any. In *Chamberlain Group, Inc. v. Skylink Technology, Inc.*, 381 F.3d 1178 (Fed. Cir. 2004), for example, Chamberlain manufactured automatic garage door opening systems, which included a remote that "incorporate[d] a copyrighted 'rolling code' computer program that constantly changes the transmitter signal needed to open the garage door." Skylink Technology manufactured a so-called universal remote that allows owners to open a Chamberlain garage door. Chamberlain sued Skylink, asserting that its rival was trafficking in a device that circumvented Chamberlain copyrighted code. The Federal Circuit rejected the IP owner's claim, reasoning that

> Chamberlain's proposed construction would allow any manufacturer of any product to add a single copyrighted sentence or software fragment to its product, wrap the copyrighted material in a trivial "encryption" scheme, and thereby gain the right to restrict consumers' rights to use its products in conjunction with competing products. In other words, Chamberlain's construction of the DMCA would allow virtually any company to attempt to leverage its sales into aftermarket monopolies—a practice that both the antitrust laws, *See* Eastman Kodak Co. v. Image Tech. Servs., 504 U.S. 451, 455 (1992), and the doctrine of copyright misuse, Assessment Techs. of WI, LLC v. WIREdata, Inc., 350 F.3d 640, 647 (7th Cir.2003), normally prohibit.
>
> Even were we to assume arguendo that the DMCA's anticircumvention provisions created a new property right, Chamberlain's attempt to infer such an exemption from copyright misuse and antitrust liability would still be wrong. We have noted numerous times that as a matter of Federal Circuit law, "[i]ntellectual property rights do not confer a privilege to violate the antitrust laws. But it is also correct that the antitrust laws do not negate [a] patentee's right to exclude others from patent property." CSU, L.L.C. v. Xerox Corp., 203 F.3d 1322, 1325 (Fed. Cir.2000) (citations omitted). In what we previously termed "the most extensive analysis of the effect of a unilateral refusal to license copyrighted expression," id., among our sister Circuits, the First Circuit explained that: "[T]he Copyright Act does not explicitly purport to limit the scope of the Sherman Act. . . . [W]e must harmonize the two [Acts] as best we can." Data Gen. Corp. v. Grumman Sys. Support Corp., 36 F.3d 1147, 1186–87 (1st Cir.1994). ***
>
> The DMCA, as part of the Copyright Act, does not limit the scope of the antitrust laws, either explicitly or implicitly.

Chamberlain Group, Inc. v. Skylink Technology, Inc., 381 F.3d 1178 (Fed. Cir. 2004).

Should the use of anti-circumvention technology ever help establish antitrust liability? Why or why not? If so, under what circumstances?

For further reading on the DMCA and interoperability, see Jacqueline Lipton, *The Law of Unintended Consequences: The Digital Millennium Copyright Act and Interoperability*, 62 WASH. & LEE L. REV. 478 (2005); Aaron K. Perzanowski, Rethinking Anticircumvention's Interoperability Policy, 42 U.C. DAVIS. L. REV. 1549 (2009).

Intergraph Corp. v. Intel Corp.,
195 F.3d 1346 (Fed. Cir. 1999)

PAULINE NEWMAN, Circuit Judge.

Intel Corporation appeals the grant of a preliminary injunction by the United States District Court for the Northern District of Alabama. We vacate the injunction.

Intel is a manufacturer of high performance computer microprocessors. The microprocessors are sold to producers of various computer-based devices, who adapt and integrate the microprocessors into products that are designed and sold for particular uses. These producers are called original equipment manufacturers, or OEMs. Intergraph Corporation is an OEM, and develops, makes, and sells computer workstations that are used in producing computer-aided graphics. From 1987 to 1993 Intergraph's workstations were based on a high performance microprocessor developed by the Fairchild division of National Semiconductor, embodying what is called the "Clipper" technology. Intergraph owns the Clipper technology and patents thereon. In 1993 Intergraph discontinued use of Clipper microprocessors in its workstations and switched to Intel microprocessors. In 1994 Intel designated Intergraph a "strategic customer" and provided Intergraph with various special benefits, including proprietary information and products, under non-disclosure agreements.

Starting in late 1996 Intergraph charged several Intel OEM customers with infringement of the Clipper patents based on their use of Intel microprocessors. The accused companies sought defense and indemnification from Intel. Negotiations ensued between Intel and Intergraph. Intel inquired about a license to the Clipper patents, but the proposed terms were rejected by Intergraph as inadequate. Intel then proposed certain patent cross-licenses, also rejected by Intergraph. Intel also proposed that the non-disclosure agreement relating to a new joint development project include a license to the Clipper patents; this too was rejected by Intergraph. As negotiations failed and threats continued the relationship deteriorated, and so did the technical assistance and other special benefits that Intel had been providing to Intergraph.

In November 1997 Intergraph sued Intel for infringement of the Clipper patents. Intergraph also charged Intel with other violations of law, including fraud, misappropriation of trade secrets, negligence, wantonness and willfulness, breach of contract, intentional interference with business relations, breach of express and implied warranties, and violation of the Alabama Trade Secrets Act. Intergraph demanded that Intel be enjoined from infringement of the Clipper patents, and the award of compensatory and punitive damages and trebled damages.

Intergraph moved to enjoin Intel pendente lite from cutting off or delaying provision of the special benefits that Intel had previously provided to Intergraph. Following Intel's opposition to this motion Intergraph amended its complaint to charge Intel with violation of the antitrust laws. After a hearing, the district court held that Intel was a monopolist and had violated sections 1 and 2 of the Sherman

204 *Antitrust Law and Intellectual Property Rights*

Act or was likely to be so shown, and issued a preliminary injunction that included the following provisions:

> a. Intel shall supply Intergraph with all Intel product information, including but not limited to technical, design, development, defect, specification, support, supply, future product, product release or sample data, whether existing in product data books, "yellow backs," Confidential Information Transmittal Records, email or other mediums . . . , whether it is on an advance basis for the development of motherboards, graphics subsystems or workstations utilizing Intel's existing, or future generation products (hereinafter "Product Development"), or current products as needed for support of such products. . . .
>
> * * * * * *
>
> c. Intel shall supply Intergraph with an allocation, and set aside a supply of microprocessors, semiconductors, chips, and buses (hereinafter "Chips") on an advance basis for product development ("Chips Samples"), in such quantities as forecasted by Intergraph in the same manner and the same terms as is done by Intergraph's similarly situated Competitors, ...
>
> d. Within eleven (11) days of the date on which Intergraph posts the bond, as required by subsection (h) of this order, Intel shall supply Intergraph with 25 sets of Deschutes Chips Samples, together with all technical data needed to permit Intergraph to develop, design, and manufacture its products. . . .
>
> e. Intel shall supply Intergraph with an allocation, and set aside a supply, of Chips which have been manufactured by or on behalf of Intel for distribution (hereinafter "Production Chips"), as well *1351 as all future chips proposed by, or available from Intel, including but not limited to 333mhz Pentium II, BX, Deschutes and Merced Chips, in accordance with a forecast supplied by Intergraph. . . .
>
> * * * * * *
>
> (ii) Intel shall supply Intergraph with Production Chips not yet available from Intel's authorized distributors ("Early Production Chips") in such quantities as forecasted by Intergraph, or in proportional quantities as supplied to Intergraph's similarly situated Competitors, . . .
>
> * * * * * *
>
> i. Intergraph shall maintain the confidentiality of all Information, Third Party Information, Chip Samples and Early Production Chips, in accordance with the terms, conditions and procedures of the applicable non-disclosure agreements as previously agreed to by the parties. . . .

Intel appeals, arguing that no law requires it to give such special benefits, including its trade secrets, proprietary information, intellectual property, pre-release products, allocation of new products, and other preferences, to an entity that is suing it on charges of multiple wrongdoing and is demanding damages and the shutdown of its core business. Intel states that its commercial response to Intergraph's suit is not an antitrust violation, and that this "garden-variety patent dispute" does not warrant the antitrust remedy here imposed. Intel also states that the scope of the injunction far exceeds the special benefits that had previously been accorded to Intergraph, and that it is unworkable, as well as unfair to Intel's overall business relationships, for the court to promote Intergraph to a disproportionately favored position.

Intergraph's response is that it can not survive in its highly competitive graphics workstation business without these services and benefits from Intel, and that the district court simply acted to preserve Intergraph's prior commercial position while the parties litigate unrelated patent issues. Intergraph states that the national interest requires that patentees be free to enforce their patents without risk of retaliatory commercial response from the accused infringer. Intel disputes these premises, and also points out the incongruity of Intergraph's statement that it is essential to Intergraph's business that it have the products for which it is demanding the shutdown of Intel's production.

Standard of Review

*** In *Lucero v. Operation Rescue*, 954 F.2d 624, 627 (11th Cir.1992) the Eleventh Circuit summarized the criteria for grant of a preliminary injunction as (1) the party seeking the injunction has shown a substantial likelihood of success on the merits, (2) there is a substantial threat of irreparable injury in absence of the injunction, (3) the balance of harms favors the party seeking the injunction, and (4) entry of the injunction does not disserve the public interest. ***

Intel as "Monopolist"

The district court ruled that Intergraph is likely to succeed in showing that Intel is a "monopolist," whereby Intel's withdrawal of the benefits it had previously accorded to Intergraph and other actions were deemed to violate sections 1 and 2 of the Sherman Act. 15 U.S.C. §§ 1, 2. The court relied on several legal theories, viz.: (1) the essential facility theory and the corollary theory of refusal to deal, (2) leveraging and tying, (3) coercive reciprocity, (4) conspiracy and other acts in restraint of trade, (5) improper use of intellectual property ***

Intel states that unlawful monopolization was not shown, as a matter of law, because Intergraph and Intel are not competitors. Unlawful monopolization requires both the existence of monopoly power and anticompetitive conduct. *See* 3 Phillip E. Areeda & Herbert Hovenkamp, Antitrust Law, & 650a, at 66 (1996) ("Unlawful monopolization under § 2 of the Sherman Act requires both power and 'exclusionary' or anticompetitive conduct before any kind of relief is appropriate.") Monopoly power is generally defined as the power to control prices or exclude competition in a relevant market; anticompetitive conduct is generally defined as conduct whose purpose is to acquire or preserve the power to control prices or exclude competition. [c.o] The prohibited conduct must be directed toward competitors and must be intended to injure competition. *See Spectrum Sports, Inc. v. McQuillan*, 506 U.S. 447, 458, 113 S.Ct. 884, 122 L.Ed.2d 247 (1993) ("The law directs itself not against conduct which is competitive, even severely so, but against conduct which unfairly tends to destroy competition itself.") Such conduct must affect the relevant product market, that is, the "area of effective competition" between the defendant and plaintiff. [c.o] ***

The antitrust law has consistently recognized that a producer's advantageous or dominant market position based on superiority of a commercial product and ensuing market demand is not the illegal use of monopoly power prohibited by the Sherman Act. *** Product superiority and the ensuing market position, flowing from a company's research, talents, commercial efforts, and financial commitments, do not convert the successful enterprise into an illegal monopolist under the Sherman Act.

Intel does not dispute the high market share achieved by its high performance microprocessors. However, that is not a violation of law. Intel stresses that it is not in competition with Intergraph in any relevant market; that its relationship with Intergraph is that of supplier and customer, not competitor. Although the district court found that Intel and Intergraph compete or will compete in the future in the "graphics subsystems" market, as we discuss post, Intel points out, and Intergraph does not dispute, that neither firm possesses monopoly power in this market. Intel stresses that violation of the Sherman Act requires the use of monopoly power to exclude competition or maintain prices, [c.o] none of which is here alleged. ***

Intel's market power in the microprocessor market is irrelevant to the issues of this case, all of which relate to the effect of Intel's actions on Intergraph's position in its own markets. ***

The conduct complained of is Intel's withdrawal or reduction of technical assistance and special benefits, particularly pre-release access to Intel's new products, in reaction to Intergraph's suit for patent infringement. However, the Sherman Act does not convert all harsh commercial actions into antitrust violations. Unilateral conduct that may adversely affect another's business situation, but is not intended to monopolize that business, does not violate the Sherman Act. [c.o] Although Intergraph stresses the adverse effect on its business of Intel's proposed withdrawal of these special benefits, the record contains no analysis of the effect of such action on competition among manufacturers of graphics subsystems or high-end workstations. "The antitrust laws were enacted for 'the protection of competition, not competitors,'" *Brunswick Corp. v. Pueblo Bowl-O-Mat, Inc.*, 429 U.S. 477, 488, 97 S.Ct. 690, 50 L.Ed.2d 701 (1977) (emphasis in original) [c.o].

Defining the relevant market is an indispensable element of any monopolization or attempt case, [c.o] for it is the market in which competition is affected by the asserted predatory or anticompetitive acts. It is the market in which sellers compete, based on products that are in competition with each other. [c.o]

The district court found that Intel possessed monopoly power in two "relevant markets": (1) the market for high-end microprocessors, and (2) the submarket of Intel microprocessors. Neither one is a market in which Intergraph and Intel are in competition with each other. Intergraph states that it competes in the microprocessor market by virtue of its Clipper patents. However, the patent grant is a legal right to exclude, not a commercial product in a competitive market. Intergraph abandoned the production of Clipper microprocessors in 1993, and states no intention to return to it. Firms do not compete in the same market unless, because of the reasonable interchangeability of their products, they have the actual or potential ability to take significant business away from each other. [c.o]

The district court also mentioned the graphics subsystems market as a relevant market, describing Intergraph and Intel as competitors in that market, and finding that Intel has plans to enter the workstation market. There was neither evidence nor suggestion of monopoly power by Intel in these markets, or the willful acquisition or maintenance of monopoly power in Intergraph's market. ***

Intel's conduct with respect to Intergraph does not constitute the offense of monopolization or the threat thereof in any market relevant to competition with Intergraph. The Sherman Act is a law in the public, not private, interest. ***

We turn to consideration of the specific grounds on which the district court applied the Sherman Act to the relationship between these entities and, finding a likelihood of violation of the antitrust laws, awarded antitrust-type relief to Intergraph.

The "Essential Facility" Theory

The "essential facility" theory of Sherman Act violation stems from *United States v. Terminal RR Ass'n*, 224 U.S. 383 (1912), wherein a group of railroads formed an association that controlled the railroad terminals, bridges, and switching yards serving the City of St. Louis. The Court held that this association was formed for an anticompetitive purpose, that the railroad terminals, bridges, and yards were facilities essential to competing railroads, and that section 1 of the Sherman Act was violated. [c.o]

The district court found that "the Advance Chips Samples and advance design and technical information are essential products and information necessary for Intergraph to compete in its markets." Reasoning that "[t]he antitrust laws impose on firms controlling an essential facility the obligation to make the facility available on non-discriminatory terms," the court held that Intel's action in withdrawing these benefits violated the Sherman Act. As authority the district court cited *Otter Tail Power Co. v. United States*, 410 U.S. 366 (1973); *Aspen Skiing*, 472 U.S. 585; and *MCI Communications Corp. v. American Telephone & Telegraph Co.*, 708 F.2d 1081, 1132 (7th Cir.1983).

Intergraph argues that the essential facility theory provides it with the entitlement, in view of its dependence on Intel microprocessors, to Intel's technical assistance and other special customer benefits, because Intergraph needs those benefits in order to compete in its workstation market. However, precedent is quite clear that the essential facility theory does not depart from the need for a competitive relationship in order to incur Sherman Act liability and remedy. [c.o] In *Otter Tail Power*, *Aspen Skiing*, and *MCI Communications* the "essential facilities" denied to the plaintiffs were all controlled by competitors.

In *Otter Tail Power* an electric utility withheld access to its power transmission lines from municipalities that wanted to establish their own municipal power distribution systems. Otter Tail Power's use of its monopoly power as a regulated utility, to refuse to "wheel" competitive electricity over its lines, along with its refusal to sell wholesale power to the municipal systems, was held to violate section 2 of the Sherman Act. The Court also noted that Otter Tail Power had entered into a series of territorial allocation schemes with other electric utilities, which were held to be per se antitrust violations.

208 *Antitrust Law and Intellectual Property Rights*

In *Aspen Skiing* the owner of three of the four major ski areas in Aspen raised its revenue demands for continuing a joint lift ticket arrangement with the fourth ski area, such that it was tantamount to refusal to continue the joint ticket program. The Court upheld the jury instruction to determine whether Aspen Skiing "willfully acquired, maintained, or used [monopoly] power by anti-competitive or exclusionary means or for anti-competitive or exclusionary purposes," as well as the instruction that "a firm possessing monopoly power has no duty to cooperate with its business rivals" unless the purpose is predatory or anticompetitive. Having approved these premises and statements of law, the Court stated that it was "unnecessary to consider the possible relevance of the 'essential facilities' doctrine." 472 U.S. at 611 n. 44.

In *MCI Communications*, 708 F.2d at 1132–33, the court enumerated the elements of liability under the "essential facilities" theory as "(1) control of the essential facility by a monopolist; (2) a competitor's inability practically or reasonably to duplicate the essential facility; (3) the denial of the use of the facility to a competitor; and (4) the feasibility of providing the facility." The courts have well understood that the essential facility theory is not an invitation to demand access to the property or privileges of another, on pain of antitrust penalties and compulsion; thus the courts have required anticompetitive action by a monopolist that is intended to "eliminate competition in the downstream market." *Alaska Airlines*, 948 F.2d at 544–45. See *MCI Communications, supra*. This understanding is seriously strained by the district court's holding that "reasonable and timely access to critical business information that is necessary to compete is an essential facility," although the asserted competition is in a different market. A non-competitor's asserted need for a manufacturer's business information does not convert the withholding of that information into an antitrust violation.

Although the viability and scope of the essential facility theory has occasioned much scholarly commentary, no court has taken it beyond the situation of competition with the controller of the facility, whether the competition is in the field of the facility itself or in a vertically related market that is controlled by the facility. That is, there must be a market in which plaintiff and defendant compete, such that a monopolist extends its monopoly to the downstream market by refusing access to the facility it controls. [c.o] Absent such a relevant market and competitive relationship, the essential facility theory does not support a Sherman Act violation. ***

The notion that withholding of technical information and samples of pre-release chips violates the Sherman Act, based on essential facility jurisprudence, is an unwarranted extension of precedent and can not be supported on the premises presented. The district court erred in holding that Intel's superior microprocessor product and Intergraph's dependency thereon converted Intel's special customer benefits into an "essential facility" under the Sherman Act. The court's ruling of antitrust violation can not be sustained on this ground.

Intergraph also phrases Intel's action in withholding access to its proprietary information, pre-release chip samples, and technical services as a "refusal to deal," and thus illegal whether or not the criteria are met of an "essential facility." However, it is well established that "[i]n the absence of any purpose to create or maintain a monopoly, the [Sherman] act does not restrict the long recognized right of a trader or manufacturer engaged in an entirely private business, freely to exercise his own independent discretion as to parties with whom he will deal." *United States v. Colgate & Co.*, 250 U.S. 300, 307, (1919). [c.o] Intel states that it continued to sell its products to Intergraph, that it did not refuse to deal with Intergraph as with any regular customer, and that the antitrust laws do not require it to give preferred treatment to a customer that is suing it.

Courts have recognized that "[t]he relationship between a manufacturer and its customer should be reasonably harmonious; and the bringing of a lawsuit by the customer may provide a sound business reason for the manufacturer to terminate their relations." *House of Materials, Inc. v. Simplicity Pattern Co.*, 298 F.2d 867, 871 (2d Cir.1962) [c.o] Although we have observed a few rulings wherein a court has, for example, barred the termination of a distributor during litigation, no case has held that the divulgation of proprietary information and the provision of special or privileged treatment to a legal adversary can be compelled on a "refusal to deal" antitrust premise.

A "refusal to deal" may raise antitrust concerns when the refusal is directed against competition and the purpose is to create, maintain, or enlarge a monopoly. For example, in *Lorain Journal Co. v. United States*, 342 U.S. 143 (1951) the only newspaper in town refused to sell newspaper advertising to persons who also advertised on a competing radio station; this was held to be an attempt to monopolize the mass dissemination of all news and advertising, and to violate the Sherman Act. [c.o]

Intergraph provided no support for its charge that Intel's action in withholding "strategic customer" benefits from Intergraph was for the purpose of enhancing Intel's competitive position. Although the district court found that there was a lack of business justification for Intel's actions, there was no showing of harm to competition with Intel; thus the need did not arise to establish the defense of business justification. As stated in *California Computer Products, Inc. v. International Bus. Mach. Corp.*, 613 F.2d 727, 744 (9th Cir.1979), a manufacturer is "under no duty to help [plaintiff] or other peripheral equipment manufacturers survive or expand." Absent a duty, justification is unnecessary.

To the extent that Intergraph has presented on this appeal, or the district court relied on, a theory of refusal to deal based on Intel's withdrawal of the special customer benefits (Intel continued to sell to Intergraph as a regular customer), a basis for violation of the antitrust laws has not been established. ***

Coercive Reciprocity and Tying

The district court found that Intel engaged in unlawful "coercive reciprocity," defined by the court as "the practice of using economic leverage in one market coercively to secure competitive advantage in another," by its proposals to settle the patent dispute. The court referred to Intel's "overall course of conduct, including its tying of a continued supply to Intergraph of CPUs and technical information with its demand for Intergraph's relinquishment of its Clipper technology patents without costs to Intel." The court depicted Intel's proposals as a per se antitrust violation "because of its pernicious effect and economic similarity to illegal tying cases," in violation of both sections 1 and 2 of the Sherman Act.

The district court cited cases wherein economic leverage in one product was used to coerce dealing in another product. In *Betaseed, Inc. v. U & I Inc.*, 681 F.2d 1203, 1216 (9th Cir.1982) the court defined coercive reciprocity as a coerced reciprocal dealing "in which two parties face each other as both buyer and seller and one party agrees to buy the other party's goods on condition that the second party buys other goods from it." Illegal tying is similarly defined: "The essential characteristic of a invalid tying arrangement lies in the seller's exploitation of its control over the tying product to force the buyer into the purchase of a tied product that the buyer either did not want at all, or might have preferred to purchase elsewhere on different terms." *Jefferson Parish Hosp.*, 466 U.S. at 12.

To violate the Sherman Act the entity that coerces reciprocal dealing must be a monopolist in one product and thus be positioned to require dealing in the coerced product, which but for the monopolist's coercion could be acquired elsewhere. Thus Betaseed, the only processor of sugar beets geographically accessible to the U & I company, conditioned the processing of U & I's beets on the purchase by U & I of Betaseed's beet seeds, thereby excluding competition in the market for beet seed. Similarly in *Spartan Grain & Mill Co. v. Ayers*, 581 F.2d 419, 424 (5th Cir.1978), also relied on by the district court, Spartan demanded that the producers of breeding chickens purchase Spartan chicken feed and chicks in order for Spartan to buy their eggs (the market in which it had power). These are classical examples of illegal coerced reciprocal dealing.

In contrast, Intel's various licensing proposals furthered no illegal relationship. It is Intergraph, not Intel, that owns the Clipper patents. To the extent that the record mentions these negotiations, it appears that Intergraph is interested in selling or licensing the Clipper patents, but has deemed Intel's various offers to be inadequate. Intel did not demand that Intergraph buy its products, and the record describes no market in which Intel's licensing proposals were shown to have distorted competition. [citation omitted]

***

No threat or actual monopolization is asserted to flow from the various rejected patent license proposals. Commercial negotiations to trade patent property rights for other consideration in order to settle a patent dispute is neither tying nor coercive reciprocity in violation of the Sherman Act. ***

Use of Intellectual Property To Restrain Trade

In response to Intel's argument that its proprietary information and pre-release products are subject to copyright and patents, the district court observed that Intel's intellectual property "does not confer upon it a privilege or immunity to violate the antitrust laws." That is of course correct. But it is also correct that the antitrust laws do not negate the patentee's right to exclude others from patent property. See *Cygnus Therapeutics Sys. v. ALZA Corp.*, 92 F.3d 1153, 1160, 39 USPQ2d 1666, 1671 (Fed.Cir.1996) ("The patent statute grants a patentee the right to exclude others from making, using, or selling the patented invention.") The patent and antitrust laws are complementary, the patent system serving to encourage invention and the bringing of new products to market by adjusting investment-based risk, and the antitrust laws serving to foster industrial competition. See *Loctite Corp. v. Ultraseal Ltd.*, 781 F.2d 861, 866–67, 228 USPQ 90, 100–01 (Fed.Cir.1985) (the purpose of the patent system is to "encourage innovation and its fruits"; the purpose of the antitrust laws is "to promote competition"). The patent and antitrust laws serve the public in different ways, both of importance to the nation.

The district court stated that "[u]nlawful 'exclusionary conduct can include a monopolist's unilateral refusal to license a [patent or] copyright or to sell a patented or copyrighted work,'" quoting from *Image Technical Services*. This quotation, however, is part of a longer passage which imparts a quite different meaning:

> Under the fact-based approaches of Aspen Skiing and Kodak, some measure must guarantee that the jury account for the procompetitive effects and statutory rights extended by the intellectual property laws. To assure such consideration, we adopt a modified version of the rebuttable presumption created by the First Circuit in Data General, and hold that "while exclusionary conduct can include a monopolist's unilateral refusal to license a [patent or] copyright," or to sell its patented or copyrighted work, a monopolist's "desire to exclude others from its [protected] work is a presumptively valid business justification for any immediate harm to consumers."

Image Technical Servs., 125 F.3d at 1218 (alterations in original). In *Image Technical Services* the Ninth Circuit reported that it had found "no reported case in which a court had imposed antitrust liability for a unilateral refusal to sell or license a patent or copyright." 125 F.3d at 1216. Nor have we. In accord is the joint statement of the United States Department of Justice and Federal Trade Comm'n, Antitrust Guidelines for the Licensing of Intellectual Property 4 (1995) that market power does not "impose on the intellectual property owner an obligation to license the use of that property to others." *Id.* at 4. *See* 35 U.S.C. § 271(d)(4) ("No patent owner otherwise entitled to relief for infringement or contributory infringement of a patent shall be denied relief or deemed guilty of misuse or illegal extension of the patent right by reason of his having done one or more of the following: . . . (4) refused to license or use any rights to the patent"). [citation omitted]

Further, Intergraph is not seeking a license under Intel's patents and copyrights, but a preferred position as to the products that embody this intellectual property before they are commercially available, as well as access to trade secrets. In *Bonito Boats, Inc. v. Thunder Craft Boats, Inc.*, 489 U.S. 141, 161, 109 S.Ct. 971, 103 L.Ed.2d 118 (1989) the Court recognized that trade secrets are of value only before the products embodying them are commercially available. Intergraph seeks technical information that is not generally known, samples of new products before they are available to the public, and individualized technical assistance. However, as we have stated, the owner of proprietary information has no obligation to provide it, whether to a competitor, customer, or supplier. Precedent makes clear that a customer who is dependent on a manufacturer's supply of a component can not on that ground force the producer to provide it; there must also be an anticompetitive aspect invoking the Sherman Act. In *Eastman Kodak*, for example, Kodak and the independent service organizations were in direct competition in the market for servicing Kodak's photocopiers and micrographic equipment; the Court assumed, for the purpose of reviewing a grant of summary judgment, that Kodak had the intent to limit competition in the service market and that it succeeded in doing so. 504 U.S. at 455, 458, 112 S.Ct. 2072. The district court herein recognized that there must be an anticompetitive intent, but ignored the absence of competition between Intel and Intergraph.

The district court's conclusory statement that Intel was using its intellectual property to restrain trade was devoid of evidence or elaboration or authority. A Sherman Act violation can not be so imprecisely invoked. ***

The preliminary injunction is vacated.

Comments and Questions

1. The Federal Circuit in Intergraph asserted that "[o]ther than as a remedy for illegal acts, the antitrust laws do not compel a company to do business with anyone-customer, supplier, or competitor." Given your understanding of *Aspen Skiing*, is that correct?

2. The Federal Circuit notes that the Supreme Court condemned the Lorain Journal for violating Section Two. Did the Lorain Journal engage in a conditional or unconditional refusal to deal? Why does the distinction matter?

3. Under the essential facilities doctrine, a monopolist may violate Section Two of the Sherman Act if it controls an input or distribution bottleneck that its rivals must have access to in order to compete, and the monopolist refuses to share in order to monopolize a second, downstream market. In general, the essential facilities doctrine is concerned with a firm extending its monopoly power from one market to another. For example, a firm that controls the only oil pipeline may refuse to lease unused capacity to its competitors because the firm is trying to use its monopoly over the pipeline to create (or maintain) a monopoly over oil. See *United States v. Terminal Railroad Association*, 224 U.S. 383 (1912) (condemning railroad association's denial access to only rail yard in St. Louis to competing railroads).

The essential facilities doctrine is controversial. *See, e.g.,* Phillip E. Areeda, *Essential Facilities: An Epithet in Need of Limiting Principles*, 58 ANTITRUST L.J. 841 (1989). Courts rarely a facility to be "essential." *See, e.g., Alaska Airlines v. United Airlines*, 948 F.2d 536 (9th Cir. 1991) (access to airline computer reservation system deemed not essential). Despite its origins in the Supreme Court cases of *Terminal Railroad* and *Otter Tail Power Co. v. U.S.*, 410 U.S. 366 (1973), the Court recently stated that the justices "have never recognized such a doctrine." *Verizon Communications Inc. v. Law Offices of Curtis V. Trinko, LLP*, 540 U.S. 398 (2004)

Still, the lower federal courts continue to recognize and apply the doctrine. This raises the issue: Should intellectual property be considered an "essential facility" such that IP owners could be forced to license their IP or risk antitrust liability under the essential facilities doctrine?

Before the Federal Circuit heard *Intergraph Corp. v. Intel Corp.*, the Northern District of Alabama had granted Intergraph a preliminary injunction forcing Intel to deal based on an essential facilities claim. *Intergraph Corp. v. Intel Corp.*, 3 F. Supp. 2d 1255 (N.D. Ala. 1998). Intergraph argued that access to Intel's chips was essential for it to compete and that Intel should be forced to deal on reasonable terms. The Federal Circuit reversed the essential facilities claim because Intel and Intergraph were not competitors and thus Intel was not trying to gain a monopoly in a downstream market. *See* also *Aldridge v. Microsoft Corp.*, 995 F. Supp. 728 (S.D. Tex. 1998).

Professors Hovenkamp, Janis, and Lemley note that neither *Intergraph* nor *Aldridge* held that intellectual property could never be an essential facility. The Federal Circuit did not deal with the intellectual property aspects of the case even though they were presented. Herbert Hovenkamp, Mark D. Janis, & Mark A. Lemley, *Unilateral Refusals to License*, 2 J. Competition L. & Econ. 1, 14 (2006). The essential facilities doctrine is still presumably viable. *But see* Verizon Communications Inc. v. Law Offices of Curtis V. Trinko LLP, 540 U.S. 398, 411 (2004) (stating that the Supreme Court "has never recognized such a doctrine.").

For an interesting note on intellectual property as an essential facility, see Note, *Patented Embryonic Stem Cells: The Quintessential Essential Facility?*, 94 Geo. L.J. 205 (2005).

Bibliography of Additional Resources

Charles Allen Black, *The Cure for Deadly Patent Practices: Preventing Technology Suppression and Patent Shelving in the Life Sciences*, 14 Alb. L.J. Sci. & Tech. 397 (2004)

James C. Burling, et. al., *The Antitrust Duty to Deal and Intellectual Property Rights*, 24 J. Corp. L. 527 (1999)

Yee Wah Chin, *Unilateral Technology Suppression: Appropriate Antitrust and Patent Law Remedies*, 66 Antitrust L.J. 441 (1998)

Teague I. Donahey, *At the Intersection of Antitrust and Intellectual Property: Lessons from Intergraph v. Intel and CSU v. Xerox*, 10 Fed. Circuit B.J. 129 (2000)

James B. Gambrell, *The Evolving Interplay of Patent Rights and Antitrust Restraints in the Federal Circuit*, 9 Tex. Intell. Prop. L.J. 137 (2001)

Simon Genevaz, *Against Immunity for Unilateral Refusals to Deal in Intellectual Property: Why Antitrust Law Should Not Distinguish Between IP and Other Property Rights*, 19 Berkeley Tech. L.J. 741 (2004)

Herbert Hovenkamp, *Market Power in Aftermarkets: Antitrust Policy and the Kodak Case*, 40 U.C.L.A. L. Rev. 1447 (1993)

Herbert Hovenkamp, Mark D. Janis & Mark A. Lemley, *Unilateral Refusals to License*, 2 J. Competition L. & Econ. 1 (2006)

Benjamin Klein & Josh Shepard Wiley, *Competitive Price Discrimination as an Antitrust Justification for Intellectual Property Refusals to Deal*, 70 Antitrust L.J. 599 (2003)

Salil Kumar, *Parts and Service Included: An Information-Centered Approach to Kodak and the Problem of Aftermarket Monopolies*, 62 U. Chi. L. Rev. 1521 (1995)

Marina Lao, *Unilateral Refusals to Sell or License Intellectual Property and the Antitrust Duty to Deal*, 9 Cornell J.L. & Pub. Pol'y 193 (1999)

A. Douglas Melamed & Ali M. Stoeppelwerth, *The CSU Case: Facts, Formalism and the Intersection of Antitrust and Intellectual Property Law*, 10 Geo. Mason L. Rev. 407 (2002)

Patrick H. Moran, *The Federal and Ninth Circuits Square Off: Refusals to Deal and the Precarious Intersection Between Antitrust and Patent Law*, 87 Marq. L. Rev. 387 (2003)

R. Hewitt Pate, *Refusals to Deal and Intellectual Property Rights*, 10 Geo. Mason L. Rev. 429 (2002)

Aaron B. Rabinowitz, *When Does a Patent Right Become an Antitrust Wrong? Antitrust Liability for Refusals to Deal in Patented Goods*, 11 Rich J.L. & Tech. 7 (2005)

Kurt M. Saunders, *Patent Nonuse and the Role of Public Interest as a Deterrent to Technology Suppression*, 15 Harv. J. Law & Tech. 389 (Spring 2002)

W. Michael Schuster, *Subjective Intent in the Determination of Antitrust Violations by Patent Holders*, 49 S. Tex. L. Rev. 507 (2007)

CHAPTER 7

Design Changes and Predatory Innovation

Berkey Photo, Inc. v. Eastman Kodak Co.
603 F.2d 263 (2nd Cir. 1979)

IRVING R. KAUFMAN, Chief Judge:

*** This action, one of the largest and most significant private antitrust suits in history, was brought by Berkey Photo, Inc., a far smaller but still prominent participant in the industry. Berkey competes with Kodak in providing photofinishing services the conversion of exposed film into finished prints, slides, or movies. Until 1978, Berkey sold cameras as well. It does not manufacture film, but it does purchase Kodak film for resale to its customers, and it also buys photofinishing equipment and supplies, including color print paper, from Kodak.

The two firms thus stand in a complex, multifaceted relationship, for Kodak has been Berkey's competitor in some markets and its supplier in others. In this action, Berkey claims that every aspect of the association has been infected by Kodak's monopoly power in the film, color print paper, and camera markets, willfully acquired, maintained, and exercised in violation of § 2 of the Sherman Act, 15 U.S.C. § 2. *** Berkey alleges that these violations caused it to lose sales in the camera and photofinishing markets and to pay excessive prices to Kodak for film, color print paper, and photofinishing equipment. A number of the charges arise from Kodak's 1972 introduction of the 110 photographic system, featuring a "Pocket Instamatic" camera and a new color print film, Kodacolor II, but the case is not limited to that episode. It embraces many of Kodak's activities for the last decade and, indeed, from preceding years as well. ***

After deliberating for eight days on liability and five on damages, the jury found for Berkey on virtually every point, awarding damages totalling $37,620,130. Judge Frankel upheld verdicts aggregating $27,154,700 for lost camera and photofinishing sales and for excessive prices on film and photofinishing equipment, but he

216 *Antitrust Law and Intellectual Property Rights*

entered judgment n. o. v. for Kodak on the remainder. Trebled and supplemented by attorneys' fees and costs pursuant to § 4 of the Clayton Act, 15 U.S.C. § 15, Berkey's judgment reached a grand total of $87,091,309.47, with interest, of course, continuing to accrue. ***

I. The Amateur Photographic Industry

*** The principal markets relevant here, each nationwide in scope, are amateur conventional still cameras, conventional photographic film, photofinishing services, photofinishing equipment, and color print paper. The numerous technological interactions among the products and services constituting these markets are manifest. To take an obvious example, not only are both camera and film required to produce a snapshot, but the two must be in compatible "formats." This means that the film must be cut to the right size and spooled in a roll or cartridge that will fit the camera mechanism. Berkey charges that Kodak refused to supply on economical terms film usable with camera formats designed by other manufacturers, thereby exploiting its film monopoly to obstruct its rivals in the camera market. ***

A. The Camera Market

The "amateur conventional still camera" market now consists almost entirely of the so-called 110 and 126 instant-loading cameras. These are the direct descendants of the popular "box" cameras, the best-known of which was Kodak's so-called "Brownie." Small, simple, and relatively inexpensive, cameras of this type are designed for the mass market rather than for the serious photographer.[2]

Kodak has long been the dominant firm in the market thus defined. Between 1954 and 1973 it never enjoyed less than 61% of the annual unit sales, nor less than 64% of the dollar volume, and in the peak year of 1964, Kodak cameras accounted for 90% of market revenues. Much of this success is no doubt due to the firm's history of innovation. In 1963 Kodak first marketed the 126 "Instamatic" instant-loading camera, and in 1972 it came out with the much smaller 110 "Pocket Instamatic." Not only are these cameras small and light, but they employ film packaged in cartridges that can simply be dropped in the back of the camera, thus obviating the need to load and position a roll manually. Their introduction triggered successive revolutions in the industry. Annual amateur still camera sales in the United States averaged 3.9 million units between 1954 and 1963, with little annual variation. In the first full year after Kodak's introduction of the 126, industry sales leaped 22%, and they took an even larger quantum jump when the 110 came to market. Other camera manufacturers, including Berkey, copied both these inventions but for several months after each introduction anyone desiring to purchase a camera in the new format was perforce remitted to Kodak.

---

[2] More complicated cameras, such as those in the 135 format ("35-millimeter") commonly used by professionals and photographic hobbyists, were found not to be part of this market. The jury also rejected Kodak's request to include in the definition "instant" cameras, pioneered by the Polaroid Corporation, which produce a finished print within minutes, or even seconds, after the shutter is snapped.

Design Changes and Predatory Innovation 217

*** In 1968 Berkey began to sell amateur still cameras made by other firms, and the following year the Keystone Division commenced manufacturing such cameras itself. From 1970 to 1977, Berkey accounted for 8.2% of the sales in the camera market in the United States, reaching a peak of 10.2% in 1976. In 1978, Berkey sold its camera division and thus abandoned this market.

B. The Film Market

(Kodak has even more market power in Film, than cameras!)

The relevant market for photographic film comprises color print, color slide, color movie, and black-and-white film. Kodak's grip on this market is even stronger than its hold on cameras. Since 1952, its annual sales have always exceeded 82% of the nationwide volume on a unit basis, and 88% in revenues. Foreign competition has recently made some inroads into Kodak's monopoly, but the Rochester firm concedes that it dominated film sales throughout the period relevant to this case. Indeed, in his summation, Kodak's trial counsel told the jury that "the film market . . . has been a market where there has not been price competition and where Kodak has been able to price its products pretty much without regard to the products of competitors."

Kodak's monopoly in the film market is particularly important to this case, because the jury accepted Berkey's contention, noted above, that it had been used to disadvantage rivals in cameras, photofinishing, photofinishing equipment, and other markets. Of special relevance to this finding is the color print film segment of the industry, which Kodak has dominated since it introduced "Kodacolor," the first amateur color print film, in 1942. In 1963, when Kodak announced the 126 Instamatic camera, it also brought out a new, faster color print film Kodacolor X which was initially available to amateur photographers only in the 126 format. Nine years later, Kodak repeated this pattern with the simultaneous introduction of the 110 Pocket Instamatic and Kodacolor II film. For more than a year, Kodacolor II was made only for 110 cameras, and Kodak has never made any other color print film in the 110 size.

C. Photofinishing Services and Photofinishing Equipment [omitted]

D. The Color Paper Market [omitted]

II. § 2 of the Sherman Act

(§2 is the important section)

The Sherman Antitrust Act of 1890 has been characterized as "a charter of freedom," [citation omitted] For nearly ninety years it has engraved in law a firm national policy that the norm for commercial activity must be robust competition. The most frequently invoked section of the Act is the first, which forbids contracts, combinations, or conspiracies in restraint of trade. But the prohibition of § 1 is incomplete, Standard Oil Co. of New Jersey v. United States, 221 U.S. 1, 60–61 (1911), for it only applies to conduct by two or more actors. If sufficiently powerful, however, a single economic entity may also stifle competition. [citation omitted] Accordingly, in § 2 of the Sherman Act, Congress made it unlawful to "monopolize, or attempt to monopolize, or combine or conspire . . . to monopolize" any part of interstate or foreign commerce. It is § 2 to which we give our principal attention in analyzing this case.

In passing the Sherman Act, Congress recognized that it could not enumerate all the activities that would constitute monopolization. Section 2, therefore, in effect conferred upon the federal courts "a new jurisdiction to apply a 'common law' against monopolizing." 3 P. Areeda & D. Turner, Antitrust Law 40 (1978). In performing that task, the courts have enunciated certain principles that by now seem almost elementary to any student of antitrust law. But, because § 2 must reconcile divergent and sometimes conflicting policies, it has been difficult to synthesize the parts into a coherent and consistent whole. To provide a framework for deciding the issues presented by this case, therefore, we begin by stating what we conceive to be the fundamental doctrines of § 2.

A. Monopoly Power as the Essence of the § 2 Violation

*** It is not a defense to liability under § 2 that monopoly power has not been used to charge more than a competitive price or extract greater than a reasonable profit. Learned Hand stated the rationale in the *Alcoa* case, *United States v. Aluminum Co. of America*, 148 F.2d 416, 427 (2d Cir. 1945). He said in his incisive manner that the Sherman Act is based on the belief:

> that possession of unchallenged economic power deadens initiative, discourages thrift and depresses energy; that immunity from competition is a narcotic, and rivalry is a stimulant, to industrial progress; that the spur of constant stress is necessary to counteract an inevitable disposition to let well enough alone.

Judge Hand explained, in addition, that Congress was not "actuated by economic motives alone" in enacting § 2. *Id.* Considerations of political and social policy form a major part of our aversion to monopolies, for concentration of power in the hands of a few obstructs opportunities for the rest.

Because, like all power, it is laden with the possibility of abuse; because it encourages sloth rather than the active quest for excellence; and because it tends to damage the very fabric of our economy and our society, monopoly power is "inherently evil." [citation omitted] If a finding of monopoly power were all that were necessary to complete a violation of § 2, our task in this case would be considerably lightened. Kodak's control of the film and color paper markets clearly reached the level of a monopoly. And, while the issue is a much closer one, it appears that the evidence was sufficient for the jury to find that Kodak possessed such power in the camera market as well. But our inquiry into Kodak's liability cannot end there.

B. The Requirement of Anticompetitive Conduct

Despite the generally recognized evils of monopoly power, it is "well settled," [citation omitted] that § 2 does not prohibit monopoly Simpliciter or, as the Supreme Court phrased it in the early landmark case of *Standard Oil Co. of New Jersey*, 221 U.S. at 62, "monopoly in the concrete."

Thus, while proclaiming vigorously that monopoly power is the evil at which § 2 is aimed, courts have declined to take what would have appeared to be the next logical step declaring monopolies unlawful per se unless specifically authorized by law. To understand the reason for this, one must comprehend the fundamental tension one might almost say the paradox that is near the heart of § 2. This tension creates much of the confusion surrounding § 2. It makes the cryptic Alcoa opinion a litigant's wishing well, into which, it sometimes seems, one may peer and find nearly anything he wishes.

The conundrum was indicated in characteristically striking prose by Judge Hand, who was not able to resolve it. Having stated that Congress "did not condone 'good trusts' and condemn 'bad' ones; it forbad all," *Alcoa, supra,* 148 F.2d at 427, he declared with equal force, "The successful competitor, having been urged to compete, must not be turned upon when he wins," *Id.* at 430. Hand, therefore, told us that it would be inherently unfair to condemn success when the Sherman Act itself mandates competition. Such a wooden rule, it was feared, might also deprive the leading firm in an industry of the incentive to exert its best efforts. ***

Grinnell instructs that after possession of monopoly power is found, the second element of the § 2 offense is "the willful acquisition or maintenance of that power as distinguished from growth or development as a consequence of a superior product, business acumen, or historic accident." 384 U.S. at 570–71.

This formulation appears to square with the understanding of the draftsmen of the Sherman Act that § 2 does not condemn one "who merely by superior skill and intelligence . . . got the whole business because nobody could do it as well." *United Shoe Machinery Corp.*, 110 F.Supp. at 341 (quoting legislative history). Thus the statement in Alcoa that even well-behaved monopolies are forbidden by § 2 must be read carefully in context. Its rightful meaning is that, if monopoly power has been acquired or maintained through improper means, the fact that the power has not been used to extract improper benefits provides no succor to the monopolist.

But the law's hostility to monopoly power extends beyond the means of its acquisition. Even if that power has been legitimately acquired, the monopolist may not wield it to prevent or impede competition. Once a firm gains a measure of monopoly power, whether by its own superior competitive skill or because of such actions as restrictive combinations with others, it may discover that the power is capable of being maintained and augmented merely by using it. *E. g., Lorain Journal Co. v. United States,* 342 U.S. 143 (1951). That is, a firm that has achieved dominance of a market might find its control sufficient to preserve and even extend its market share by excluding or preventing competition. A variety of techniques may be employed to achieve this end—predatory pricing, lease-only policies, and exclusive buying arrangements, to list a few.

Even if the origin of the monopoly power was innocent, therefore, the Grinnell rule recognizes that maintaining or extending market control by the exercise of that power is sufficient to complete a violation of § 2. As we have explained, only considerations of fairness and the need to preserve proper economic incentives prevent the condemnation of § 2 from extending even to one who has gained his power by purely competitive means. The district court judge correctly indicated that such a monopolist is tolerated but not cherished. Thus, the rule of *Grinnell* must be read together with the teaching of Griffith, that the mere existence of monopoly power "whether lawfully or unlawfully acquired," is in itself violative of § 2, "provided it is coupled with the purpose or intent to exercise that power." 334 U.S. at 107. ***

In sum, although the principles announced by the § 2 cases often appear to conflict, this much is clear. The mere possession of monopoly power does not *ipso facto* condemn a market participant. But, to avoid the proscriptions of § 2, the firm must refrain at all times from conduct directed at smothering competition. This doctrine has two branches. Unlawfully acquired power remains anathema even when kept dormant. And it is no less true that a firm with a legitimately achieved monopoly may not wield the resulting power to tighten its hold on the market. ***

III. The 110 System

We turn now to the events surrounding Kodak's introduction of the 110 photographic system in 1972. *** [By 1966, Kodak] began actively to consider the possibility of developing a new type of Kodacolor film ***, now called Kodacolor II, at the time of introduction. ***

In accord with Kodak's 1967 plan, Kodacolor II was sold only in the 110 format for eighteen months after introduction. It remains the only 110-size color print film Kodak has ever sold.

As Kodak had hoped, the 110 system proved to be a dramatic success. In 1972 the system's first year the company sold 2,984,000 Pocket Instamatics, more than 50% of its sales in the amateur conventional still camera market. The new camera thus accounted in large part for a sharp increase in total market sales, from 6.2 million units in 1971 to 8.2 million in 1972. Rival manufacturers hastened to market their own 110 cameras, but Kodak stood alone until Argus made its first shipment of the "Carefree 110" around Christmas 1972. The next year, although Kodak's competitors sold over 800,000 110 cameras, Kodak retained a firm lead with 5.1 million. Its share of 110 sales did not fall below 50% until 1976. Meanwhile, by 1973 the 110 had taken over most of the amateur market from the 126, and three years later it accounted for nearly four-fifths of all sales.

Berkey's Keystone division was a late entrant in the 110 sweepstakes, joining the competition only in late 1973. Moreover, because of hasty design, the original models suffered from latent defects, and sales that year were a paltry 42,000. With interest in the 126 dwindling, Keystone thus suffered a net decline of 118,000 unit sales in 1973. The following year, however, it recovered strongly, in large part because improvements in its pocket cameras helped it sell 406,000 units, 7% of all 110s sold that year.

Berkey contends that the introduction of the 110 system was both an attempt to monopolize and actual monopolization of the camera market. ***

A. Attempt to Monopolize and Monopolization of the Camera Market

There is little doubt that the evidence supports the jury's implicit finding that Kodak had monopoly power in cameras. The principal issues presented to us regarding the effect of the 110 introduction in the camera market are whether Kodak engaged in anticompetitive conduct and, if so, whether that conduct caused injury to Berkey. It will be useful at the outset to present the arguments on which Berkey asks us to uphold its verdict:

> (1) Kodak, a film and camera monopolist, was in a position to set industry standards. Rivals could not compete effectively without offering products similar to Kodak's. Moreover, Kodak persistently refused to make film available for most formats other than those in which it made cameras. Since cameras are worthless without film, this policy effectively prevented other manufacturers from introducing cameras in new formats. Because of its dominant position astride two markets, and by use of its film monopoly to distort the camera market, Kodak forfeited its own right to reap profits from such innovations without providing its rivals with sufficient advance information to enable them to enter the market with copies of the new product on the day of Kodak's introduction. This is one of several "predisclosure" arguments Berkey has advanced in the course of this litigation.
>
> (2) The simultaneous introduction of the 110 camera and Kodacolor II film, together with a campaign advertising the two jointly, enabled Kodak to garner more camera sales than if it had merely scaled down Kodacolor X to fit the new camera. The jury could conclude that Kodacolor II was an inferior product and not technologically necessary for the success of the 110. In any event, Kodak's film monopoly prevented any other camera manufacturer from marketing such a film-camera "system" and the joint introduction was therefore anticompetitive.
>
> (3) For eighteen months after its introduction, Kodacolor II was available only in the 110 format. Thus it followed that any consumer wishing to use Kodak's "remarkable new film" had to buy a 110 camera. Since Kodak was the leading and at first the only manufacturer of such devices, its camera sales were boosted at the expense of its competitors.

For the reasons explained below, we do not believe any of these contentions is sufficient on the facts of this case to justify an award of damages to Berkey. We therefore reverse this portion of the judgment.

1. Predisclosure

Through the 1960s, Kodak followed a checkered pattern of predisclosing innovations to various segments of the industry. Its purpose on these occasions evidently was to ensure that the industry would be able to meet consumers' demand for the complementary goods and services they would need to enjoy the new Kodak products. But predisclosure would quite obviously also diminish Kodak's share of the auxiliary markets. It was therefore, in the words of Walter Fallon, Kodak's chief executive officer, "a matter of judgment on each and every occasion" whether predisclosure would be for or against Kodak's self-interest.

*** Kodak did not have a duty to predisclose information about the 110 system to competing camera manufacturers.

As *** Berkey concedes, a firm may normally keep its innovations secret from its rivals as long as it wishes, forcing them to catch up on the strength of their own efforts after the new product is introduced. [c.o.] It is the possibility of success in the marketplace, attributable to superior performance, that provides the incentives on which the proper functioning of our competitive economy rests. If a firm that has engaged in the risks and expenses of research and development were required in all circumstances to share with its rivals the benefits of those endeavors, this incentive would very likely be vitiated.

Withholding from others advance knowledge of one's new products, therefore, ordinarily constitutes valid competitive conduct. Because, as we have already indicated, a monopolist is permitted, and indeed encouraged, by § 2 to compete aggressively on the merits, any success that it may achieve through "the process of invention and innovation" is clearly tolerated by the antitrust laws. [citation omitted] ***

[E]nforced predisclosure would cause undesirable consequences beyond merely encouraging the sluggishness the Sherman Act was designed to prevent. A significant vice of the theory propounded by Berkey lies in the uncertainty of its application. Berkey does not contend, in the colorful phrase of Judge Frankel, that "Kodak has to live in a goldfish bowl," disclosing every innovation to the world at large. However predictable in its application, such an extreme rule would be insupportable. Rather, Berkey postulates that Kodak had a duty to disclose limited types of information to certain competitors under specific circumstances. But it is difficult to comprehend how a major corporation, accustomed though it is to making business decisions with antitrust considerations in mind, could possess the omniscience to anticipate all the instances in which a jury might one day in the future retrospectively conclude that predisclosure was warranted. And it is equally difficult to discern workable guidelines that a court might set forth to aid the firm's decision. For example, how detailed must the information conveyed be? And how far must research have progressed before it is "ripe" for disclosure? These inherent uncertainties would have an inevitable chilling effect on innovation. They go far, we believe, towards explaining why no court has ever imposed the duty Berkey seeks to create here. ***

The first firm, even a monopolist, to design a new camera format has a right to the lead time that follows from its success. The mere fact that Kodak manufactured film in the new format as well, so that its customers would not be offered worthless cameras, could not deprive it of that reward. Nor is this conclusion altered because Kodak not only participated in but dominated the film market. ***

Indeed, such authority as exists supports this conclusion. *ILC Peripherals Leasing Corp. v. International Business Machines Corp.*, 458 F.Supp. 423 (N.D.Cal.1978) (Memorex), was a case similar in some respects to this one. IBM was the leading manufacturer of central data processing units (CPUs) and competed with Memorex and others to supply peripheral equipment for use in conjunction with IBM CPUs. When IBM made changes in the intricate interface the "computer 'plug' "by which peripherals are attached to the central system, it did not provide advance information to Memorex, thereby forcing its rival to learn what it could after the new CPUs were shipped to customers. Memorex contended that to compete effectively in the peripherals market it needed to know, under some form of licensing arrangement, about interface changes as soon as IBM announced its products. *Id.* at 436–37. Noting the total absence of authority in support of this position, the district court indicated that plaintiff could properly be left to rely on "reverse engineering" to develop IBM-compatible equipment. IBM would thus be unchallenged for a time in the market for certain peripherals, but "(d)epriving IBM of its lead time would remove its incentive to invent." *Id.* at 437.

The predisclosure demanded here is much more radical than that sought and rejected in Memorex. Berkey claims that it should have been given the information about Kodak's new film format long before product announcement and without any licensing fee. Moreover, the possibility lurking in Memorex that IBM, by creating technological incompatibilities, was tying peripherals sales to its CPUs is not present here. *Cf. Response of Carolina, Inc. v. Leasco Response, Inc.*, 537 F.2d 1307, 1330 (5th Cir. 1976). Kodak's new format was primarily a camera development, and the use of Kodacolor II did not in itself create any incompatibilities with an existing camera. ***

Conclusion. We have held that Kodak did not have an obligation, merely because it introduced film and camera in a new format, to make any predisclosure to its camera-making competitors. Nor did the earlier use of its film monopoly to foreclose format innovation by those competitors create of its own force such a duty where none had existed before. In awarding Berkey $15,250,000, just $828,000 short of the maximum amount demanded, the jury clearly based its calculation of lost camera profits on Berkey's central argument that it had a right to be "at the starting line when the whistle blew" for the new system. The verdict, therefore, cannot stand.

2. Systems Selling

Berkey's claims regarding the introduction of the 110 camera are not limited to its asserted right to predisclosure. The Pocket Instamatic not only initiated a new camera format, it was also promoted together with a new film. As we noted earlier, the view was expressed at Kodak that "(w)ithout a new film, the (camera) program is not a new advertisable system." Responding in large measure to this perception, Kodak hastened research and development of Kodacolor II so that it could be brought to market at the same time as the 110 system. Based on such evidence, and the earlier joint introduction of Kodacolor X and the 126 camera, the jury could readily have found that the simultaneous release of Kodacolor II and the Pocket Instamatic was part of a plan by which Kodak sought to use its combined film and camera capabilities to bolster faltering camera sales. Berkey contends that this program of selling was anticompetitive and therefore violated § 2. We disagree.

It is important to identify the precise harm Berkey claims to have suffered from this conduct. It cannot complain of a product introduction Simpliciter for the same reason it could not demand predisclosure of the new format: any firm, even a monopolist, may generally bring its products to market whenever and however it chooses. Rather, Berkey's argument is more subtle. It claims that by marketing the Pocket Instamatics in a system with a widely advertised new film, Kodak gained camera sales at Berkey's expense. And, because Kodacolor II was not necessary to produce satisfactory 110 photographs and in fact suffered from several deficiencies, these gains were unlawful.

It may be conceded that, by advertising Kodacolor II as a "remarkable new film" capable of yielding "big, sharp pictures from a very small negative," Kodak sold more 110 cameras than it would have done had it merely marketed Kodacolor X in 110-size cartridges. The quality of the end product a developed snapshot is at least as dependent upon the characteristics of the film as upon those of the camera. It is perfectly plausible that some customers bought the Kodak 110 camera who would have purchased a competitor's camera in another format had Kodacolor II not been available and widely advertised as capable of producing "big, sharp pictures" from the tiny Pocket Instamatic. Moreover, there was also sufficient evidence for the jury to conclude that a new film was not necessary to bring the new cameras to market. ***

But necessity is a slippery concept. *** Even if the 110 camera would produce adequate snapshots with Kodacolor X, it would be difficult to fault Kodak for attempting to design a film that could provide better results. The attempt to develop superior products is, as we have explained, an essential element of lawful competition. Kodak could not have violated § 2 merely by introducing the 110 camera with an improved film.

Accordingly, much of the evidence at trial concerned the dispute over the relative merits of Kodacolor II and Kodacolor X. There was ample evidence that for some months following the 110 introduction, Kodacolor II was inferior to its predecessor in several respects. Most notably, it degenerated more quickly than Kodacolor X, so that its shelf life was shorter. It is undisputed, however, that the grain of Kodacolor II, though not as fine as Kodak had hoped, was better than that of the older film.

In this context, therefore, the question of product quality has little meaning. A product that commends itself to many users because superior in certain respects may be rendered unsatisfactory to others by flaws they considered fatal. Millions of consumers, for example, evidently found the 110 camera highly attractive because of its "pocketability." Others, perhaps more concerned over the quality of their flash pictures, found the original models unsatisfactory because of the high incidence of "red-eye." Similarly, some individuals would, if given the option and aware of the relevant factors, select Kodacolor II over Kodacolor X because of its superior grain, which was especially useful for a small camera; others might choose Kodacolor X because the original variety of Kodacolor II had to be used more quickly to produce attractive pictures.

It is evident, then, that in such circumstances no one can determine with any reasonable assurance whether one product is "superior" to another. Preference is a matter of individual taste. The only question that can be answered is whether there is sufficient demand for a particular product to make its production worthwhile, and the response, so long as the free choice of consumers is preserved, can only be inferred from the reaction of the market.

When a market is dominated by a monopolist, of course, the ordinary competitive forces of supply may not be fully effective. Even a monopolist, however, must generally be responsive to the demands of customers, for if it persistently markets unappealing goods it will invite a loss of sales and an increase of competition. If a monopolist's products gain acceptance in the market, therefore, it is of no importance that a judge or jury may later regard them as inferior, so long as that success was not based on any form of coercion. Certainly the mere introduction of Kodacolor II along with the Pocket Instamatics did not coerce camera purchasers. Unless consumers desired to use the 110 camera for its own attractive qualities, they were not compelled to purchase Kodacolor II especially since Kodak did not remove any other films from the market when it introduced the new one. If the availability of Kodacolor II spurred sales of the 110 camera, it did so because some consumers regarded it as superior, at least for the smaller format.

Of course, Kodak's advertising encouraged the public to take a favorable view of both Kodacolor II and the 110 camera, but that was not improper. A monopolist is not forbidden to publicize its product unless the extent of this activity is so unwarranted by competitive exigencies as to constitute an entry barrier. See *American Tobacco Co. v. United States*, 328 U.S. 781, 797 (1946); *Borden, Inc.*, 3 Trade Reg. Rep. (CCH) P 21,490 (FTC 1978). And in its advertising, a producer is ordinarily permitted, much like an advocate at law, to bathe his cause in the best light possible. Advertising that emphasizes a product's strengths and minimizes its weaknesses does not, at least unless it amounts to deception, constitute anticompetitive conduct violative of § 2.

We conclude, therefore, that Kodak did not contravene the Sherman Act merely by introducing Kodacolor II simultaneously with the Pocket Instamatic and advertising the advantages of the new film for taking pictures with a small camera.

3. Restriction of Kodacolor II to the 110 Format

There is another aspect to Berkey's claim that introduction of Kodacolor II simultaneously with the Pocket Instamatic camera was anticompetitive. For eighteen months after the 110 system introduction, Kodacolor II was available only in the 110 format. Since Kodak was the first to have the 110s on the market, Berkey asserts it lost camera sales because consumers who wished to use the "remarkable new film" would be compelled to buy a Kodak camera. This facet of the claim, of course, is not dependent on a showing that Kodacolor II was inferior in any respect to Kodacolor X. Quite the opposite is true. The argument is that, since consumers were led to believe that Kodacolor II was superior to Kodacolor X, they were more likely to buy a Kodak 110, rather than a Berkey camera, so that the new film could be used.

Where a course of action is ambiguous, "consideration of intent may play an important role in divining the actual nature and effect of the alleged anticompetitive conduct," *United States v. United States Gypsum Co.*, 438 U.S. 422, 436 n.13 (1978) [citation omitted]. We shall assume Arguendo that Kodak violated § 2 of the Sherman Act if its decision to restrict Kodacolor II to the 110 format was not justified by the nature of the film but was motivated by a desire to impede competition in the manufacture of cameras capable of using the new film. This might well supply the element of coercion we found lacking in the previous section. We shall assume also that there was sufficient evidence for the jury to conclude that the initial decision to market Kodacolor II exclusively in the 110 format during its introductory period was indeed taken for anticompetitive purposes.

But to prevail, Berkey must prove more, for injury is an element of a private treble damages action. Berkey must, therefore, demonstrate that some consumers who would have bought a Berkey camera were dissuaded from doing so because Kodacolor II was available only in the 110 format. This it has failed to establish. The record is totally devoid of evidence that Kodak or its retailers actually attempted to persuade customers to purchase the Pocket Instamatic because it was the only camera that could use Kodacolor II, or that, in fact, any consumers did choose the 110 in order to utilize the finer-grained film.

To be sure, some of Kodak's advertisements emphasized the superior qualities of Kodacolor II, but the gist of these messages was merely that Kodacolor II, unlike previous films, would yield, "big, sharp pictures" from a small camera. In short, Kodak simply claimed to have achieved its goal of truly developing a Pocket Instamatic system whose color prints would be "as close as possible to the prints currently obtained from 126-size Kodacolor X." Stressing the "pocketability" of the 110 format, Kodak did not emphasize Kodacolor II as an independent reason to choose a photography system. Little of the advertising mentioned Kodacolor II by name. Of even greater weight is the fact that none in any way implied that the new film was available only in the 110 size. Accordingly, the content of Kodak's publicity, standing alone, would not permit a jury rationally to infer that Berkey was injured by the restriction of Kodacolor II to the 110 format.

The abstract possibility nevertheless remains that there might have been some customers who would have purchased a Berkey camera in one of the pre-existing formats but decided to select a Kodak 110 instead because they were aware that there was no alternative means of using Kodacolor II, even in the absence of advertising to that effect. Yet, although millions of amateur photographers bought Pocket Instamatics, Berkey did not produce anyone at the trial to testify that he was so motivated. Nor did Berkey present the testimony of camera dealers, or evidence of any kind, to establish that such customers existed. Indeed, Berkey declined to challenge the testimony of a camera dealer that he never promoted the fact that Kodacolor II was available only in the 110 size. We expressed our concern over the absence of such evidence at oral argument, but Berkey's post-argument brief did not point to any relevant items in the record that we had overlooked. We conclude, therefore, that the jury could not find that Berkey suffered more than de minimis injury, if any, because Kodacolor II was limited to the 110 format. Although the antitrust laws afford latitude in permitting the factfinder to estimate "the extent of the damages" where precise calculation is impossible, they do not allow recovery where there has been no showing that plaintiff suffered cognizable injury. [citation omitted]

Voluminous discovery and a prolonged trial have already given Berkey more than ample opportunity to adduce evidence, which it failed to do, in support of its consistently maintained claim that it lost camera sales because of restriction of Kodacolor II to the 110 format. It would make a mockery of the adversary system in a case of this character, where great expenditures of time and money have been made and where the plaintiff was represented by counsel of extraordinary ability and experience, to afford a new trial so that missing elements of proof could be produced, if, indeed, they exist.

To summarize our conclusions on the 110 camera claims, we hold:

1. Kodak was under no obligation to predisclose information of its new film and format to its camera-making competitors.
2. It is no basis for antitrust liability that Kodacolor II, despite certain deficiencies compared to Kodacolor X, may have encouraged sales of the 110 camera.
3. Finally, although the restriction of Kodacolor II to the 110 format may have been unjustified, there was no evidence that Berkey was injured by this course of action.

We, therefore, reverse so much of the judgment as awarded Berkey damages based on the introduction of the 110 camera.

Comments and Questions

1. At one point in its *Berkey Photo* opinion, the Second Circuit claimed that "the use of monopoly power attained in one market to gain a competitive advantage in another is a violation of § 2 [of the Sherman Act], even if there has not been an attempt to monopolize the second market." That was incorrect. Unilateral conduct short of an actual monopolization or an attempt to monopolize cannot serve as the basis for a Section Two violation. Consider *Spectrum Sports, Inc. v. McQuillan*, 506 U.S. 447, 459 (1993), where the Supreme Court noted that "§ 2 makes the conduct of a single firm unlawful only when it actually monopolizes or dangerously threatens to do so." Several courts declined to adopt *Berkey*'s construction of Section Two as creating a violation for leveraging monopoly power merely to gain a competitive advantage. E.g., *Alaska Airlines, Inc. v. United Airlines, Inc.*, 948 F.2d 536, 547 (9th Cir. 1991) ("We now reject *Berkey*'s monopoly leveraging doctrine as an independent theory of liability under Section 2."); *Fineman v. Armstrong World Industries, Inc.*, 980 F.2d 171 (3d Cir.1992).

2. The Second Circuit rejects Berkey's argument that Kodak had a duty to predisclose its new film. Is there any justification under antitrust law for imposing such a duty? The court found none, and indicated that imposing a duty to disclose would strip firms of a significant incentive to innovate:

> It is the possibility of success in the marketplace, attributable to superior performance, that provides the incentives on which the proper functioning of our competitive economy rests. If a firm that has engaged in the risks and expenses

of research and development were required in all circumstances to share with its rivals the benefits of those endeavors, this incentive would very likely be vitiated.

If a duty to disclose were implemented, how would it be framed? Berkey described it as "a duty to disclose limited types of information to certain competitors under specific circumstances." What sorts of "limited types of information"? Which competitors? What specific circumstances? The court expressed concern that inadministrability of a duty to disclose in this context would chill innovation.

3. The Second Circuit rejects Berkey's argument that Kodak violated Section Two by releasing Kodacolor II and the Pocket Instamatic camera simultaneously. Berkey alleged that the simultaneous introduction of the film and camera meant that customers were forced to purchase Kodak's cameras in order to obtain the benefits of the new film. Several courts have held that decisions as to how or when a product will be released should not be subject to antitrust liability. *See generally Oahu Gas Serv., Inc. v. Pacific Res., Inc.*, 838 F.2d 360, 369 (9th Cir. 1988) ("A line of 'product innovation' cases has consistently rejected antitrust liability for a monopolist's decision about when or whether to market new products."). Are there circumstances under which the innovation of a new product could constitute an antitrust violation?

Professors Janusz Ordover and Robert Willig offer a two-stage approach to "predatory systems rivalry." Professors Ordover and Willig define predatory systems rivalry as the introduction of system components redesigned so as to make them incompatible with formerly compatible components sold by a competitor. Janusz A. Ordover & Willig, Robert D., *An Economic Definition of Predation: Pricing and Product Innovation*, 91 YALE L.J. 8, 30 (1981). In this way, a firm like Kodak, with significant power in the film market, could redesign its film in order to work only with its cameras, thus driving producers of previously compatible cameras out of that market. The first stage of the Ordover-Willig approach is to assess the conditions of the market in order to determine whether the defendant possessed a predatory motive. The second stage entails an examination of whether the defendant made a predatory sacrifice of profits.

Professors Ordover and Willig focus on two decisions which could entail a profit sacrifice: the ex ante decision to invest in research and development for a non-predatory product, and the ex post decision to stop providing preexisting compatible system components. *Id.* at 13. Both types of actions rely on the notion of "compensatory pricing," defined as making preexisting compatible system components available at prices no higher than what is needed to cover any loss in sales of the new components due to the decision to continue providing old components. *Id.* at 31. The first analysis, regarding investment in research and development, is assessed by comparing the cost of the investment to the anticipated net revenues assuming that compatible components will be provided at compensatory prices. The second analysis, regarding the decision as to whether to provide compatible components at compensatory prices, imposes a duty of sorts on innovators to continue providing old versions of system components.

What are the merits of such an approach? Does it sufficiently identify conduct that would inflict the sort of harms with which antitrust is concerned? Is it too broad, punishing conduct that might constitute beneficial innovation? For a rebuttal of the Ordover-Willig approach, see Joseph Gregory Sidak, *Debunking Predatory Innovation*, 83 COLUM. L. REV. 1121 (1983).

4. How else might courts approach claims of predatory innovation? Professor Richard Gilbert evaluates several possible standards in *Holding Innovation to an Antitrust Standard*, Competition Policy International, Spring 2007, including the Ordover-Willig approach. Gilbert argues that while a profit sacrifice test such as the Ordover-Willig approach is theoretically sound, its inquiry into costs and benefits at various stages in the innovation process is too complex for courts to reliably make. *Id.* at 58–59. Do you think Professor Gilbert is correct? How does the complexity of the Ordover-Willig approach compare to other areas of antitrust law requiring an inquiry into the economics of particular business conduct, such as tying or refusals to deal? Might the problem be one of focus rather than degree; that is, would the complexity of the Ordover-Willig approach be as worrisome if it did not focus on the research and development stage? Consider the possibility that in the research and development stage, where incentives for firms to innovate are already fragile, the prospect of having inherently risky business strategies retroactively examined by courts might dissuade firms from engaging in innovation at all.

Gilbert considers four other approaches to predatory innovation. The first approach, a total economic welfare standard, would seek to maximize total welfare by considering the effect of a particular innovation on producer profits and consumer benefits. *Id.* at 53. Is such an approach feasible? Gilbert argues that the complexity of an approach that analyzes such a vast range of effects, both in the present and in the future, would frequently lead to courts punishing conduct that lacks anticompetitive effect or intent and failing to punish conduct that is in fact anticompetitive. *Id.* How does the complexity of this approach compare with the Ordover-Willig approach, which restricts the scope of the analysis to some extent?

The second approach, a consumer welfare standard, would eliminate some of this complexity by focusing solely on consumer surplus. However, the downfalls of a standard that focuses only on consumer welfare are evident. Even where new products provide indirect benefits to consumers (e.g., by providing benefits or incentives to other economic agents that encourage innovation), a consumer welfare standard might punish innovation if there is no easily observable consumer benefit. For instance, Professor Gilbert notes that cost-saving innovations that result in a slight price increase and incremental innovations that do not provide immediate consumer benefits but enable and encourage further innovation that does benefit the consumer would both be impermissible. *Id.* at 56–7. Even if this were not the case, is it possible to formulate a workable consumer welfare standard for courts, taking into account the fact that a particular innovation might benefit some consumers while harming others?

The third approach that Professor Gilbert discusses is the profit sacrifice test proposed by Professors Ordover and Willig, which Professor Gilbert criticizes in part because "innovation is about sacrificing short-term profits for long-term rewards. Does that make the test unworkable?

The fourth approach, a no economic sense test, would only punish conduct that would not make economic sense "but for the tendency to eliminate or lessen competition." *Id.* at 60. How is this different from a profit sacrifice standard? Gilbert contends that the answer to this question depends on how "no economic sense" is defined. If conduct makes economic sense only if it looks to be profitable ex ante, then the no economic sense test and the profit sacrifice standard are equivalent. *Id.* at 77. If, on the other hand, economic sense is defined so as to include a wide range of "sensible" benefits, then all innovation will make economic sense and the test will be the equivalent of the highly deferential test for sham litigation. *Id.* at 61—62. Gilbert contends that given the pitfalls of the other standards and the risk that overzealous application of such standards would chill innovation, the latter definition is preferable. *Id.* at 77.

5. The broadly defined no economic sense test might appeal to some courts, given their conventionally deferential stance toward product innovation. *See, e.g., Expert Masonry, Inc. v. Boone County, Ky.*, 440 F.3d 336, 348 (6th Cir. 2006) (quoting *Crane & Shovel Sales Corp. v. Bucyrus-Erie Co.*, 854 F.2d 802, 809 (6th Cir. 1988)) ("Courts have no experience to make such [business] judgments, and certainly antitrust liability cannot be premised on improvident business decisions."); *United States v. Microsoft Corp.*, 253 F.3d 34, 64 (D.C. Cir. 2001) ("[C]ourts are properly very skeptical about claims that competition has been harmed by a dominant firm's product design changes."); *United States v. Microsoft Corp.*, 147 F.3d 935, 948 (D.C. Cir. 1998) ("Antitrust scholars have long recognized the undesirability of having courts oversee product design.").

However, some courts have been willing to engage in an analysis of product innovation decisions despite these express declarations of deference. The California District Court in *In re IBM Peripheral EDP Devices Antitrust Litig.* noted that if particular product design changes "had no purpose and effect other than the preclusion of [competitors], this Court would not hesitate to find that such conduct was predatory." 481 F.Supp. 965, 1003 (D. Cal. 1979). But the court did not choose to focus only on whether there was "no purpose and effect other than the preclusion of" competition, instead deciding to assess the following factors:

> the effects of the design on competitors; the effects of the design on consumers; the degree to which the design was the product of desirable technological creativity; and the monopolist's intent, since a contemporaneous evaluation by the actor should be helpful to the factfinder in determining the effects of a technological change.

Id. Given what you know about the flaws of the predatory innovation approaches listed above, do you think it was wise for the court to establish such a standard?

6. Some approaches to predatory innovation might demand that courts make quality assessments in order to determine whether the purported improvement has merit. Are courts qualified to make this sort of assessment? The Second Circuit in

Berkey seemed reluctant in this regard: "[N]o one can determine with any reasonable assurance whether one product is 'superior' to another." *Cf. ILC Peripherals v. Int'l Bus. Machines,* 458 F. Supp. 423, 439 (N.D.Cal. 1978) ("[W]here there is a valid engineering dispute over a product's superiority the inquiry should end; the product is innovative and the design is legal.").

Even if courts were capable of reliably identifying quality improvements, should they do so? What are the risks? Is it necessary for them to do so in order to identify which innovations are anticompetitive and which are not?

7. Regarding this question of quality assessments, the Second Circuit notes that the superiority of one product over another "so long as the free choice of consumers is preserved, can only be inferred from the reaction of the market." In the predatory innovation context, how reliable are such inferences likely to be? The court notes that where the innovator has monopoly power, there may be some distortion, but as long as there is no "coercion" the reaction of the market should be conclusive. Can the introduction of an incompatible product coerce consumers to purchase the product? Or is some attendant conduct necessary to create a coercive effect? The *Berkey* court thought so, finding that consumers were not coerced to purchase the Kodacolor II film because other varieties of Kodak film were still available.

8. How would the approaches to predatory innovation listed in this section resolve Berkey's final claim, that the restriction of Kodacolor II to the Kodak 110 camera format was a violation of Section Two?

9. In *Berkey Photo,* 35-millimeter cameras were excluded from the relevant product market. Why is that appropriate, or is it not?

10. What is the significance of Kodak earning 88 percent of the revenues, while selling only 82 percent of the volume of cameras?

Foremost Pro Color, Inc. v. Eastman Kodak Co.

703 F.2d 534 (9th Cir. 1983)

WALLACE, Circuit Judge:

Foremost Pro Color, Inc. (Foremost) appeals from the district court's judgment for Eastman Kodak Co. (Kodak). The district court dismissed Foremost's antitrust claims for failure to state a claim upon which relief could be granted. ***

I.

Kodak is the preeminent firm in the amateur photographic industry in this country, enjoying a dominant position in the markets for photographic film and conventional amateur still cameras. For example, over eighty percent of all photofinishing—the development of negatives and the printing of photographs—is conducted with Kodak-manufactured photofinishing equipment, photographic paper and chemicals.

Foremost is an authorized Kodak dealer and an independent photofinisher. As a dealer, Foremost has purchased photographic film, paper and chemicals

232 *Antitrust Law and Intellectual Property Rights*

from Kodak for resale to consumers. As a photofinisher, Foremost has purchased photographic equipment, paper and chemicals from Kodak and used them in the photofinishing process on orders placed by its consumer customers. Because Kodak is also a photofinisher, although at a significantly smaller level than in the past as a result of a 1954 consent decree negotiated with the United States Department of Justice, Foremost is both a photofinisher customer and competitor of Kodak.

Kodak's dominance of the photographic film and amateur still camera markets "is no doubt due to the firm's history of innovation." *Berkey Photo, Inc. v. Eastman Kodak Co.*, 603 F.2d 263, 269 (2d Cir.1979) [citation omitted]. It is one of those innovations which ignited the present controversy. Similar to *Berkey*, this case arises out of Kodak's undisclosed development and 1972 introduction of its then-newest line of cameras, the 110 "pocket instamatic," and its supporting photographic system. That system included a new generation of film (Kodacolor II), photographic paper, and photographic film processing and printing chemicals. The relevant history of the development and introduction of this system is well-outlined in Berkey. [citation omitted]

Foremost argues that this introduction of a new, integrated photographic system violated several provisions of the antitrust laws. *** Foremost claims that because the 110 cameras could only use new Kodacolor II film and because this film could only be processed with the new papers and chemicals, Kodak implicitly and unlawfully tied the sale of cameras to film, film to chemicals, and chemicals to paper and film in violation of section 1 of the Sherman Act, 15 U.S.C. § 1, and section 3 of the Clayton Act, 15 U.S.C. § 14. ***

Foremost's third amended complaint alleged that because "the new Kodacolor II film . . . was not compatible with any of the then existing film processing procedures or chemical solutions," and because the new "chemistry was not compatible with the then existing . . . paper, [Foremost] was required to discard its complete inventory of the old paper and chemistry and purchase the new . . . papers and . . . chemistry." Foremost alleged that this amounted to the sale of commodities "on an implied contract, condition, agreement or understanding that [Foremost] would purchase other photographic commodities manufactured and sold by [Kodak]." As Foremost has phrased it on appeal, this implied condition, agreement or understanding arose because "whenever Foremost purchased one Kodak product, it necessarily had to purchase additional Kodak commodities "(emphasis in original).

Tying arrangements have long been considered per se unlawful under section 1 of the Sherman Act. *Northern Pacific Railway Co. v. United States*, 356 U.S. 1, 5 (1958). A tying arrangement is an agreement by a party to sell one product only on the condition that the buyer also purchase a different or "tied" product. Id.; [citation omitted] In order to establish an unlawful tying arrangement, a plaintiff must demonstrate the existence of two distinct products or services, that the sale of the "tying" product or service is conditioned on the purchase of the "tied" product or service, that the defendant has "sufficient economic power" in the market for the tying product to appreciably restrain competition in the market for the tied product, and that the amount of commerce involved in the market for the tied

Design Changes and Predatory Innovation 233

product is "not insubstantial." [citation omitted] A significant element of an illegal tying arrangement is coercion by the seller, i.e., the seller must condition the sale of the tying product on the buyer's purchase of the tied product. [citation omitted] If the buyer is free to take either product by itself, "there is no tying problem." [citation omitted] "Some modicum" of involuntariness or coercion is thus essential to the existence of a per se illegal tie-in. [citation omitted]

When these prerequisites are met, tying arrangements are illegal in and of themselves, without any requirement that the plaintiff make a showing of unreasonable competitive effect. *Fortner Enterprises, Inc. v. United States Steel Corp.*, 394 U.S. 495, 498, 89 S.Ct. 1252, 1256, 22 L.Ed.2d 495 (1969). The principal evil of the tying arrangement, that which has traditionally justified its inclusion in the per se category, is that it denies competitors access to the market for the tied product not because the party imposing the arrangement necessarily has a superior product in that market, but rather because of the leverage exerted as a result of its economic power in the market for the tying product and the demand for the tying product. See *Kentucky Fried Chicken Corp. v. Diversified Packaging Corp.*, 549 F.2d 368, 375 (5th Cir.1977); *Siegel v. Chicken Delight, Inc.*, 448 F.2d 43, 47 (9th Cir.1971) [citation omitted]. Thus, competition in the market for the tied product is severely restrained because competitors "cannot offer their products on an equal basis" with the party imposing the tying arrangement. *Moore v. Jas. H. Matthews & Co.*, 550 F.2d at 1212.

Of course, conduct which does not meet the requirements of the per se prohibition against tying arrangements may still constitute a violation of section 1 of the Sherman Act under the "rule of reason" test. *Fortner Enterprises, Inc. v. United States Steel Corp.*, supra, 394 U.S. at 499–500 [citation omitted]. But Foremost has not challenged the alleged tying arrangement under the rule of reason. Thus, the dispositive question before us is whether, under the per se rule, Foremost adequately pleaded the requisite coercion in its complaint.

Although the complaint boldly asserts that the purchase of the tied products was "required," that single word is insufficient to support even an inference of the necessary coercion. [citation omitted] Foremost did not allege that there existed an express requirement to purchase the 110 components as a package, that Kodak threatened to terminate film sales if Foremost did not also purchase paper and chemicals, or that a condition of being an authorized dealer of 110 cameras was the purchase of 110 film, paper and chemicals. Rather, as the complaint itself explains, the reason Foremost insists that it was required to purchase new film, chemicals and paper was that the newly introduced 110 film could not be processed with the then existing technology and these new products were necessary to satisfy consumer demand for 110 products and to process 110 photofinishing orders placed by its customers. Thus, Foremost's complaint pointedly refrains from alleging that Kodak itself required the purchase of film as a condition of the sale of cameras, or required the purchase of chemicals and paper as a condition of the sale of film. Coercion for purposes of the per se rule means "a product sold on the condition that the buyer also purchase a different or tied product or at least that the buyer agrees not to purchase the product from any other supplier." *Betaseed, Inc. v. U and I Inc.*, 681 F.2d at 1222 n. 35. In the absence of an allegation that the purchase of the alleged tied products was required as a condition of sale of the alleged tying products, rather than as a prerequisite to practical and effective use of the tying products, Foremost's complaint failed to plead the coercion essential to a per se unlawful tying arrangement.[4]

Although liberally sprinkled with the word "required," Foremost's tying allegation basically involves the so-called technological tie. In other words, because the new film could not be processed with the old chemicals, and because the needed new photographic paper similarly could not be processed with the old chemicals, it was necessary to purchase an entire package of film, chemicals and paper. We do not believe that, standing alone, such technological interrelationship among complementary products is sufficient to establish the coercion essential to a per se unlawful tying arrangement. Indeed, such a rule could become a roadblock to the competition vital for an ever expanding and improving economy. Product innovation, particularly in such technologically advancing industries as the photographic industry, is in many cases the essence of competitive conduct. Therefore, we decline to place such technological ties in the category of economic restrictions deemed per se unlawful by Northern Pacific and its progeny. [citation omitted]

Nor are the allegations that the new 110 film, chemicals and paper were incompatible with the products offered by Kodak's competitors sufficient to support a per se unlawful tie-in. Quite obviously, a firm that pioneers new technology will often introduce the first of a new product type along with related, ancillary products that can only be utilized effectively with the newly developed technology. Until other, less technologically advanced competitors procure licenses or otherwise develop ancillary products that are compatible with the new product, the technological leader will be faced with no present competition in the newly developed product market. The essence of a per se unlawful tying arrangement, however, is that it forecloses competition in the market for the tied product or products. The creation of technological incompatibilities, without more, does not foreclose competition; rather, it increases competition by providing consumers with a choice among differing technologies, advanced and standard, and by providing competing manufacturers the incentive to enter the new product market by developing similar products of advanced technology. Any short-run absence of competition in the market for the technologically tied product could just as likely be due to the unwillingness or inability of competitors to devote sufficient economic resources to match the pace of technological development set by the industry's leader, as to the abuse of market power by that dominant firm. Thus, the per se rule does not

---

[4] Under the facts alleged in the complaint, there could not as a matter of law be the sort of implicit coercion discussed in *Moore v. Jas. H. Matthews & Co., supra*, 550 F.2d at 1217, because Foremost was not forced to "accept the tied item and forego possibly desirable substitutes." Since the complaint alleges that, when the 110 system was introduced, no competing manufacturers produced chemicals and papers compatible with Kodacolor II film, there could have been no substitutes that Foremost or other photofinishing customers were foreclosed from purchasing.

logically fit and should not be applied. It is clear that a mere technological tie does not present the competitive evils which the per se prohibition of tying arrangements is designed to prevent. See *Kentucky Fried Chicken Corp. v. Diversified Packaging Corp.*, 549 F.2d at 378–79.

As a general rule, therefore, we hold that the development and introduction of a system of technologically interrelated products is not sufficient alone to establish a per se unlawful tying arrangement even if the new products are incompatible with the products then offered by the competition and effective use of any one of the new products necessitates purchase of some or all of the others. Any other conclusion would unjustifiably deter the development and introduction of those new technologies so essential to the continued progress of our economy.

Foremost's tying claim alleged only the introduction of technologically related components incompatible with existing products offered by the competition. It did not allege that the dominant purpose motivating Kodak's design and introduction of the 110 system was to compel purchase of the entire system as a package, rather than to achieve the legitimate goal of marketing new, technologically superior products designed to satisfy consumer demand for smaller, pocket-sized cameras. Therefore, the complaint failed to state a claim for relief predicated on unlawful tying.

Comments and Questions

1. Foremost's claim fails because the Ninth Circuit finds that the development of technological incompatibilities does not alone constitute the coercion sufficient to demonstrate a per se unlawful tying arrangement under Section One of the Sherman Act. How does this compare with the *Berkey* court's formulation of coercion?

2. Not only does the Ninth Circuit find that Kodak's conduct did not constitute coercion, but it also makes the following observation:

> The creation of technological incompatibilities, without more, does not foreclose competition; rather, it increases competition by providing consumers with a choice among differing technologies, advanced and standard, and by providing competing manufacturers the incentive to enter the new product market by developing similar products of advanced technology.

Is this necessarily true? By labeling the technologically incompatible product as "advanced" and the older, compatible version as "standard," the court seems to assume that the distinction is clear. But when it is not obvious that a newer, technologically incompatible product is more "advanced" than the older, compatible version, is it necessarily true that competition will increase? Consider a situation where a product is made technologically incompatible and is no "better," in the eyes of consumers, than the previous version. Under such circumstances, is it true that consumers will benefit? If it is not, is the Ninth Circuit's analysis incorrect in this case? Is the Ninth Circuit's analysis generally applicable to future cases?

3. The *Foremost* court "decline[d] to place such technological ties in the category of economic restrictions deemed per se unlawful" by previous cases. What is the difference between technological tie-ins and contractual tie-ins? Should antitrust law treat them differently?

4. Professor Joseph Gregory Sidak argues that technological ties should be deemed per se legal. Joseph Gregory Sidak, *Debunking Predatory Innovation*, 83 COLUM. L. REV. 1121, 1143 (1983). Sidak contends that technological tie-ins provide benefits to consumers by allowing monopolists to price discriminate, encouraging them to increase output to the socially optimal level. *Id.* at 1126. According to Sidak, price discrimination is often more efficient to accomplish through technological ties than contractual ties due to the ongoing monitoring and enforcement costs necessary to sustain the latter. *Id.* at 1137–38. Sidak argues that even where a technological tie-in cannot be used to price discriminate, other welfare-enhancing effects such as the use of tie-ins as a means for quality control weigh against the justifications for proscribing such conduct. *Id.* at 1136–40. Do you agree?

C.R. Bard, Inc. v. M3 Systems, Inc.

157 F.3d 1340 (Fed. Cir. 1998)

[*The facts are written by Judge Newman, who wrote the majority opinion for every issue except for attempted monopolization and one patent law issue. The majority opinion on those issues was written by Judge Bryson. Judge Newman's opinion on the attempted monopolization issue is in dissent.*]

Before MAYER, Chief Judge, NEWMAN and BRYSON, Circuit Judges.

PAULINE NEWMAN, Circuit Judge.

In suit are United States Patent No. 4,944,308 issued July 31, 1990 (the '308 patent) and United States Reissue Patent No. RE 34,056 issued September 8, 1992 (the '056 patent), both entitled "Tissue Sampling Device." These patents originated with the work of Dr. Per Gunner Lindgren, a physician in Sweden, and are now owned by appellant C.R. Bard, Inc.

The patented inventions are devices for taking samples of body tissue for biopsy purposes, wherein a biopsy needle firing device or "gun" mechanically injects a biopsy needle assembly into the core body tissue. These devices are described as improving the speed, accuracy, ease, and patient comfort of tissue sampling, compared with manually inserted biopsy needles. They are said to be particularly advantageous for sampling small or movable lesions and fibrous or firm tissues, because the rapidly and firmly fired needles can penetrate even fibrotic lesions before the lesions can slip aside. The patented guns and needles have achieved commercial success.

Bard sued M3 Systems in August 1993 in the United States District Court for the Northern District of Illinois, asserting that M3's ProMag biopsy gun and ACN/SACN biopsy needle assemblies infringed the '308 and '056 patents, respectively. M3 raised the defenses that the patents are invalid on several grounds and are not infringed, and also charged Bard with fraud, antitrust law violation, and patent misuse. The jury rendered special verdicts in favor of M3 on every issue ***. The jury also found that Bard perpetrated fraud in the Patent and Trademark Office (PTO) in obtaining both patents, that Bard misused both patents, and that Bard violated antitrust law, awarding $1.5 million in antitrust damages, trebled by the district court. ***

The Patented Inventions

The First Generation Device-The PCT Patent Application

In 1981 Dr. Lindgren, working in Sweden with Jan Allard, an engineer, designed and constructed the first of several successively improved mechanical biopsy guns. This "first generation" gun was designed to fire a commercially available biopsy needle assembly made by the Baxter Travenol Company, having the brand name "Tru-Cut." The Tru-Cut is a double needle consisting of a hollow outer needle called the cannula and an inner needle called the stylet. The stylet is solid except for a recess near its point. In the manual procedure for which the Tru-Cut was designed, the physician would first extend the stylet and insert the assembly into the body tissue, whereupon the tissue to be sampled would flow into the recess in the stylet; the physician would then push the cannula into the body tissue to surround the stylet and cut and trap the tissue sample in the recess.

This procedure required the physician to use both hands to manipulate the needles, while a second physician would hold and manipulate the ultrasound equipment that is usually required to view the interior of the body and direct insertion of the needles. Dr. Lindgren sought to mechanize this procedure in order to improve the speed and accuracy of insertion, to reduce human error, and to permit a physician to perform the biopsy without assistance by providing a sampling device that can be operated with one hand while the other hand holds the ultrasound apparatus.

The first generation gun is a box-like structure fitted with two spring-loaded drivers associated with slots that are configured to hold the cannula and stylet of the Tru-Cut needle assembly. To use this gun the physician must first "cock" each of the spring-loaded drivers. This cocking action, as it was often called at trial, is referred to as pre-tensioning or energizing in the patent documents. Cocking is performed by hand or with a specially designed tool described as a miniature crowbar. After the drivers are cocked, the stylet and cannula are placed in the appropriate slots and the gun housing is closed. The gun is then aimed at the target tissue and a trigger mechanism releases the stylet and cannula in rapid sequence. The needles are then manually retrieved. ***

The Second Generation-The '056 Reissue Patent

Starting in 1984, Dr. Lindgren undertook to improve the gun so that it would not be necessary for the physician to cock the two drivers manually before installing the biopsy needles, a step described as awkward and inefficient. In 1985 Dr. Lindgren, working with Dan Åkerfeldt, an engineer, designed a mechanism whereby the drivers are cocked by external action after the needles are placed in the gun and the housing is closed. In this mechanism rods are attached to each of the spring-loaded drivers, extend out the back of the gun, and culminate in a ring or handle. By pulling the ring or handle the operator simultaneously cocks both drivers, moving the needles rearward. A trigger mechanism then fires the stylet and cannula, in rapid sequence, into the tissue to be sampled.

The Tru-Cut needles were not usable with the second generation gun, for their structure was such that they could not be moved rearward as well as propelled forward. New needles were designed with a modified hub and flange structure and a slit in the stylet flange to facilitate placement in the gun. Corresponding structural changes were made to the gun to accommodate the changes in the needles. ***

The Third Generation Gun-The '308 Patent

Dan Åkerfeldt continued to work on improving these devices. He sought to make the gun easier to use, especially by inexperienced physicians. Because pulling the cocking ring required significant manual force to overcome the simultaneous resistance of both driver springs, he designed an external integrated cocking mechanism that energized the two springs sequentially, thereby requiring less force than did the simultaneous cocking mechanism of the second generation gun. The third generation gun also provided for separate rearward movement of the needles after the biopsy sample was taken, thereby facilitating removal of the tissue from the stylet. Radiplast applied for a United States patent on the third generation gun on November 14, 1988, naming Dan Åkerfeldt as inventor. The patent issued in 1990 and is the '308 patent in suit. ***

Antitrust Issues

Antitrust violation was found on special verdicts that Bard by anticompetitive conduct had monopolized or attempted to monopolize the relevant markets for each of fully automated biopsy guns and needles, guns alone, and replacement needles. The jury instructions on the antitrust count identified three separate claims; first, that the patents were procured by fraud followed by attempts to enforce the fraudulently procured patents; second, that Bard threatened and then brought suit knowing that its patents were invalid, unenforceable, or not infringed; and third, that Bard unlawfully leveraged its monopoly power in the guns to obtain a competitive advantage in replacement needles by modifying its gun to accept only Bard needles. The jury found in favor of M3 Systems and against Bard on every question, and assessed compensatory damages, measured primarily as litigation costs, of $1.5 million, which were trebled as required by section 4 of the Clayton Act. Bard argues that the findings are not supported by substantial evidence, and that judgment as a matter of law should have been granted. ***

Judge Bryson, writing for the majority on the issue of attempted monopolization:

The jury considered evidence that Bard modified its Biopty gun to prevent its competitors' non-infringing, flangeless needles from being used in Bard's guns.

By special verdicts, the jury found that there was a relevant product market for replacement needles for fully automated reusable biopsy guns, that Bard had monopoly power in that market, and that it had acquired or maintained its monopoly power in that market through restrictive or exclusionary conduct.

In order to prevail on its claim of an antitrust violation based on Bard's modification of its Biopty gun to prevent the use of competing replacement needles, M3 was required to prove that Bard made a change in its Biopty gun for predatory reasons, i.e., for the purpose of injuring competitors in the replacement needle market, rather than for improving the operation of the gun. [citation omitted] Bard argues that the evidence showed that absent patent protection for Bard's devices, M3 could still compete in the relevant market. While the evidence of Bard's market power was in dispute, the jury specifically found that Bard enjoyed monopoly power in the market for replacement needles. The evidence was sufficient to support the jury's verdict on that point and also to support the jury's conclusion that Bard maintained its monopoly position by exclusionary conduct, to wit, modifying its patented gun in order to exclude competing replacement needles.

The dissent on this issue starts from the premise that the modification to Bard's Biopty gun was an "improvement" and argues from that premise that to hold Bard liable for the modification would have the "pernicious" effect of penalizing innovators for making improvements to their products. The dissent's premise, however, is contrary to the jury's verdict, which was supported by the evidence. Although Bard contended at trial that it modified its Biopty gun to make it easier to load and unload, there was substantial evidence that Bard's real reasons for modifying the gun were to raise the cost of entry to potential makers of replacement needles, to make doctors apprehensive about using non-Bard needles, and to preclude the use of "copycat" needles. One internal Bard document showed that the gun modifications had no effect on gun or needle performance; another internal document showed that the use of non-Bard needles in the gun "could not possibly result in injury to either the patient or the physician." In view of that evidence, the jury could reasonably conclude that Bard's modifications to its guns constituted "restrictive or exclusionary conduct" in a market over which it had monopoly power. ***

Judge Newman's dissent on the attempted monopolization issue:

M3 Systems proposed that Bard had modified its biopsy gun and needles for the purpose of preventing use of Tru-Cut needles and then to exclude M3's copies so that they did not fit the gun without an adapter. M3 contends that Bard's motives were anti-competitive, pointing to Bard documents showing internal discussions of competitive products and concern for patent scope and market share. ***

Bard was under no duty to facilitate M3's competition by refraining from changing its products. The jury instructions did not distinguish patent-supported products and markets based thereon from actions described to the jury as being in restraint of trade. *** No mention was made of the patentee's statutory right to exclude, and there was no instruction to consider that right.

*** I must, respectfully, dissent from the court's ruling that Bard incurred liability under the Sherman and Clayton Acts by its actions in modifying and improving its patented products, thereby requiring M3 to provide an adapter with its replacement needles for the Bard gun. ***

Both the needle assembly alone and the integrated biopsy gun/needle device were patented. They were subject to Bard's patent-based rights to exclude others from making, using, or selling them. It was not Bard's changes to its biopsy gun or needles that affected M3's sale of replacement needles; it was the patents on these products. To hold that Bard could violate the Sherman Act by changing these products, if M3's business was adversely affected, is a novel and pernicious theory of antitrust law that is contrary to the principles of competition, and fraught with litigation-generating mischief. ***

The proceedings at trial, and the jury instructions, made no mention of the patent rights here present. It is without precedent to find antitrust liability premised on a theory that development of new products is illegally anticompetitive when the new product requires competing suppliers to adjust their product accordingly. Commentators who have considered the question of "whether product innovation can ever be unlawfully 'predatory'" have concluded that "no administrable rule could be fashioned that would not exact an unreasonably heavy toll." 3 Phillip E. Areeda & Herbert Hovenkamp, Antitrust Law § 705b (rev. ed.1996). If this court deems it appropriate to add this burden to patent-based innovation, there should at least be some overriding public benefit. However, antitrust jurisprudence has well understood that the enforcement of the antitrust laws is self-defeating if it chills or stifles innovation. ***

Comments and Questions

1. The case was remanded to determine the proper amount of damages because the jury found for the antitrust plaintiff on three separate antitrust grounds, two of which (a *Walker Process* claim and a sham litigation claim) were reversed by the Federal Circuit. Because the damage award was aggregated and did not attribute specific awards for the predatory redesign cause of action, the Federal Circuit could not affirm the jury award.

2. The Federal Circuit focuses on the role of anticompetitive intent in this case, with Judge Bryson determining that Bard modified its biopsy gun so as to injure competitors in the replacement needle market. Should anticompetitive intent alone constitute an antitrust violation in a predatory innovation case? The California District Court held that with respect to the design change in *In re IBM Peripheral EDP Devices Antitrust Litig.*, it would not, finding that although the "predominant intent in adopting the ... design was undoubtedly to preclude or delay ... competition and gain a competitive advantage," the modification was an improvement, and there was little actual impact on competition. 481 F.Supp. 965, 1005 (D.C. Cal. 1979).

If a dominant firm changes its product solely to make it incompatible with a competitor's complementary product, what role should intent play in the antitrust analysis?

Scholars have vigorously debated the role of intent in antitrust liability. Compare Ronald A. Cass & Keith N. Hylton, *Antitrust Intent*, 74 S. CAL. L. REV. 657 (2001) (cautioning against an intent inquiry in antitrust) with Marina Lao, *Reclaiming a Role for Intent Evidence in Monopolization Analysis*, 54 AM. U. L. REV. 151 (2004) (advocating an intent inquiry in Section Two cases).

Some courts decline to rely on intent evidence, reasoning that it is too difficult to divine so-called "corporate intent." *See In re IBM*, 481 F.Supp 965, 1003 (N.D. Cal. 1979) ("Discerning corporate intent is seldom easy, and, in any event, the law against monopolization is much more concerned with the effect of conduct rather than with its purpose.").

Given that all firms want to take sales away from their rivals, what should count as evidence of anticompetitive intent sufficient to satisfy an intent requirement?

If intent matters for this species of antitrust violation, then how should courts treat a monopolist's good faith attempt to improve the product but still introduces incompatability that drives all competitors from the market?

Should good (i.e., non-anticompetitive) intent save a firm from antitrust liability when the actions have the same anticompetitive effect as an illegal monopolist's premeditated plan to use predatory design changes to force its competitors from the market?

In general, anticompetitive intent alone is not enough to violate § 2—there must also be some overt anticompetitive act. *Rural Telephone Services Co., Inc. v. Feist Publications, Inc.*, 957 F.2d 765, 769 (10th Cir. 1992); *Olympia Equip. Leasing Co. v. Western Union Tel. Co.*, 797 F.2d 370, 379 (7th Cir. 1986). To what extent did the *Bard* court explore whether or not there was anticompetitive conduct? Judge Bryson found that the evidence supported the jury verdict that no "improvement" was made in altering the biopsy gun as Bard did. But even if there was no evident improvement, is this enough to demonstrate that Bard's conduct was objectively anticompetitive?

In determining whether conduct is anticompetitive or not, it is necessary to examine whether the conduct had an anticompetitive *effect*. *Aspen Skiing Co. v. Aspen Highlands Skiing Corp.*, 472 U.S. 585, 605 (1985). How did the *Bard* court examine the effect of the purportedly anticompetitive conduct in this case? How does the decision in this regard comport with the Ninth Circuit's opinion in *Foremost* that technological incompatibilities alone actually increase competition?

3. Judge Newman, in dissent, argues against employing any sort of predatory innovation standard, quoting Areeda & Hovenkamp to find that "no administrable rule could be fashioned that would not exact and unreasonably heavy toll" in terms of chilling innovation. Do you agree?

Even if a rule were flawless in theory, some have argued that the sheer complexity of the rule alone could chill innovation. *E.g.*, Joseph Gregory Sidak, *Debunking Predatory Innovation*, 83 COLUM. L. REV. 1121, 1142 (1983). At what point, if at all, should courts be willing to risk chilling innovation in order to ensure that clearly anticompetitive conduct does not go unpunished?

4. The court noted that the "jury considered evidence that Bard modified its Biopty gun to prevent its competitors' non-infringing, flangeless needles from being used in Bard's guns." Why is it critical that the competitors' needles were non-infringing?

5. Predatory design change claims exist primarily in situations where there are two complementary product markets—the primary and secondary markets. A dominant firm exercises market power in the primary market and competes in the secondary market. In an effort to increase its sales in the secondary market, the dominant changes the design of its product in the primary market and modifies its product in the secondary market so that its version of the product is the one that is compatible. What are the primary and secondary markets in *Berkey Photo*, *Foremost*, and *C.R. Bard*? What effect did the defendant's design decisions have on competition in the secondary market?

6. Should antitrust be less concerned about protecting competitors whose business model depends on the success of another's product?

Is this free-riding? Should the monopolist have a legal right to prevent this form of free riding?

What if the incompatibility makes the defendant's product worse—e.g., slower, less durable, less reliable, more expensive, etc?

Are you concerned that if design changes can form the basis of antitrust liability, then monopolists will be deterred from improving their products?

7. After losing in a split decision before the three-judge panel, M3 Systems requested that the Federal Circuit hear the case en banc. The Federal Circuit declined. Writing a concurrence to the court's decision, Judge Gajarsa explained:

> If fundamental issues at the intersection of patent law and antitrust law were being decided, I would dissent from the court's decision to deny an in banc rehearing. However, those issues are not before us. In this case, the patentee is accused of improperly redesigning a patented product, albeit within the proper scope of the claims, in order to prevent its competition from entering the market for the now unpatented product used in association with the patented device. The patentee, Bard, was charged with redesigning its patented "Biopty" gun to prevent its competitors' needles from being used in that device. The majority opinion on the antitrust issue ultimately determined that substantial evidence supported the jury's verdict that this behavior was "predatory" in violation of antitrust laws. [citation omitted]
>
> Given these facts, the patent bar may, at first glance, be alarmed that the majority opinion opens the floodgates with respect to a new antitrust cause of action. However, it is important for the bar to note that the only argument Bard made on appeal regarding the antitrust violation was directed to the sufficiency of the evidence on this issue. Bard did not argue to this court that modification of a patented product within the scope of the claims by a patentee cannot, as a matter of law, constitute an antitrust violation. *** In light of our limited review of jury findings, the majority affirmed the jury verdict based on its determination that there was substantial evidence to support the verdict. [citation omitted]
>
> Consequently, this case does not establish or endorse a new antitrust theory.

C.R. Bard, Inc. v. M3 Systems, Inc., 161 F.3d 1380 (Fed. Cir. 1998) (Gajarsa, J., concurring in rejection to hear case en banc).

Do you agree with Judge Gajarsa interpretation of the panel's opinion? Why or why not?

Automatic Radio Manufacturing Co. v. Ford Motor Co.

390 F.2d 113 (1st Cir. 1968)

COFFIN, Circuit Judge.

This is an appeal from a denial of a preliminary injunction sought by a manufacturer of automobile radios, Automatic Radio Mfg. Co., Inc. (Automatic), against Ford Motor Company (Ford), to restore its competitive position in the automobile radio market pending the outcome of a private antitrust suit seeking treble damages and injunctive relief ***

Automatic is a substantial manufacturer of custom car radios adapted to fit into the dashboards of particular models and makes of automobiles. Its radios are designed for use in most of the models of the major United States automobile manufacturers. Its immediate customers are distributors who resell the radios to new car dealers. In the instant case, its ultimate customers are Ford car dealers. For years its radios and installation kits have been sold to many of these dealers, particularly in the eastern part of the United States, for approximately $10 less than the cost of a Ford radio installed at the factory.

Until 1964, each Ford model had the same basic instrument panel whether the car was equipped with a radio or not. If an automobile was ordered without a factory installed radio, the opening for the radio was covered by a 'knockout plate'. The dealer could easily remove the plate and, using the accessories contained in kits, install either a Ford radio or one manufactured by appellant or other producers. In the fall of 1964 Ford changed its dashboard styling in two of its models. In cars equipped with factory installed radios a 27 inch wide plastic dashboard cover, with openings for various dashboard gauges and radio knobs, buttons and dial, was used. In cars ordered without radios, the same plastic dashboard cover was used except that it was partly imperforate; it had no openings masked with a 'knockout plate' where a radio would otherwise be located. If a dealer wished to install a Ford radio, the perforated cover, with holes for a radio, would be furnished with the installation kit without extra charge. If a dealer wished to buy a perforated cover separate from a kit, the price ranged from $5 to $7.67. With the introduction of the 1967 Mercury and Deluxe Comet, Ford extended its styling changes and used a different kind of imperforate cover, apparently more difficult to duplicate.

While the inclusion of a perforated cover free of extra charge in the Ford installation kit reduced or in some cases eliminated the price advantage previously enjoyed by Automatic, appellant complains that it is further prejudiced by the time and expense necessary to tool up for and produce its own replicas of Ford's perforated covers. This delay allegedly causes it to miss out on the lucrative first sales months of the automobile year or, in the case of the Mercury and the Comet, to lose

244 *Antitrust Law and Intellectual Property Rights*

sales for the entire year. Automatic complains not only that its sales of radios for Ford cars have been cut in half, and its profits on these sales converted into losses, but also that it has lost its good will as a reliable full line custom radio supplier. It further alleges damage to the consuming public in the erosion of the competition it has hitherto contributed.

The injunction sought by Automatic would require Ford, upon request of its dealers, to deliver automobiles without radios but with perforated dashboard covers and to issue order forms to provide for the ordering of automobiles so equipped. The district court found (1) that Automatic did not establish a causal relationship between Ford's dashboard changes and its own declining sales; (2) that it did not demonstrate that adequate monetary compensation would be impossible or extraordinarily difficult; (3) that the relief requested might prove 'nugatory' or ineffective in achieving any relief; and (4) that supervision of Ford's 7,200 dealers might render enforcement of a decree too difficult. It concluded that the circumstances did not justify the mandatory form of decree requested and that the existence of an illegal tying arrangement had not been established. It said nothing as to alleged Sherman Act violations. ***

We dispose of this appeal on the narrow ground that Automatic has made no compelling case of immediate irreparable injury. *** By so saying, we do not mean to imply that Automatic's claims are insubstantial and frivolous.

We take Automatic's claims of injury warranting injunctive relief in reverse order. As for the public, two arguments are made. The first is that Automatic's continued access to Ford dealers without the barrier of the recent marketing practices is a prerequisite to 'meaningful price competition'. The second, and related, argument is that treble damages are a cheap price to pay for the elimination, pendente lite, of this competition and obtaining a monopoly in the supply of car radios. As to the first contention, the affidavits of the Ford dealers almost uniformly avow that, whatever the source of radios installed in Ford cars, the price of the radio to the consumer is the same. Even if, however, we take note of the likelihood that dealers who realize a greater margin of profit by using an Automatic radio have more to 'play with' in offering a better price, particularly on trade-ins, the second argument is unrealistic in failing to take into account the fact that Automatic, if successful on the merits, would be entitled to permanent injunctive relief which would permit competition to revive.

Automatic next asserts that its good will as a reliable full line supplier of custom radios to Ford dealers is in jeopardy. It phrases the question as 'whether money damages can adequately compensate appellants for lost competitive position and terminated business relationships.' Were Automatic a consumer-oriented enterprise in the sense that its sales depended upon consumer consciousness of its product's availability or non-availability, we might be sympathetic to this claim. But Automatic's immediate customers are distributors who sell to dealers, who, in turn, seek Automatic's product because it is a lower cost product, yielding them a greater profit. *** [T]he basic pricing situations strongly suggest that, should Automatic ultimately prevail on the merits, the status quo ante would be quickly restored to the extent that price advantage remained a critical consideration. In short, we see 'good will' in this situation the result of a very mercurial market- a market geared to the competing advantages of price and demand for service space and personnel rather than the attractiveness to the ultimate consumer of a trade name which he seldom sees. ***

In the meantime, we note that there is no danger of Automatic's demise. Its overall sales, profits, and number of distributors have increased. While such a posture does not negate the possibility that Ford has deprived appellant of lost profits or has caused losses in its business with Ford dealers, it is relevant to the question whether ultimate monetary compensation is likely to be an adequate remedy.

In conclusion, while we do not mean to forejudge the substantial and novel question involving disputed evidence of motivation and causation of Ford's increase and Automatic's decline in sales, we do not feel so compelled by the case made on the affidavits and exhibits as to require, pending trial, cessation of the styling and marketing practice which Ford has pursued for the past three and one half years.

Affirmed.

Comments and Questions

1. The case illustrates that a product redesign can arguably have anticompetitive effects even in the absence of a patented product. Is predatory innovation more likely to take place in markets with patented products? Why or why not?

2. When should antitrust plaintiffs be entitled to injunctive relief? What form should such relief take?

Abbott Laboratories v. Teva Pharmaceuticals USA, Inc.

432 F.Supp.2d 408 (D. Del. 2006)

JORDAN, District Judge

These antitrust actions have been brought by various plaintiffs (collectively "Plaintiffs") against Abbott Laboratories ("Abbott"), and Fournier Industrie et Santé and Laboratoires Fournier S.A. (collectively "Fournier"). Before me is the Defendants' Consolidated Motion to Dismiss Plaintiffs' Complaints. ***

According to Plaintiffs, Abbott and Fournier have manipulated the statutory framework that regulates the market for pharmaceutical drugs in order to prevent generic substitutes for the branded drug TriCor® from having a meaningful opportunity to enter the market. As context for those allegations, a description of the approval process for generic pharmaceutical drugs may be helpful.

A. Generic Drugs and the Operation of the Hatch-Waxman Act

Before a pharmaceutical drug is released into the market, it must be approved by the Food and Drug Administration ("FDA"), pursuant to the Food, Drug, and Cosmetic Act, 21 U.S.C. §§ 301 et seq. [citation omitted] The manufacturer of a new branded drug must submit detailed safety and efficacy data for the drug to the FDA in a New Drug Application ("NDA"). 21 U.S.C. § 355(a). The NDA must also list "the patent number and the expiration date of any patent which claims the drug . . . or which claims a method of using such drug." 21 U.S.C. § 355(b)(1). After approval, information about the branded drug, including patent information, is published by the FDA in a publication entitled "Approved Drug Products with Therapeutic Equivalence Evaluations," which is generally called the "Orange Book," after the color of its cover.

The Drug Price Competition and Patent Term Restoration Act of 1984 (the "Hatch-Waxman Act"), codified at 21 U.S.C. §§ 355, 360cc and 35 U.S.C. §§ 156, 271, 282, provides a framework for the introduction of generic versions of previously approved branded drugs. Under that framework, a generic manufacturer may submit an Abbreviated New Drug Application ("ANDA") to the FDA. 21 U.S.C. § 355(j). [citation omitted] The ANDA process allows the generic manufacturer to incorporate efficacy and safety data submitted to the FDA in the NDA for a branded drug, as long as the generic drug is shown to be bioequivalent to that branded drug. 21 U.S.C. § 355(j)(2)(A). [citation omitted]

The Hatch-Waxman Act also provides a framework for the holders of pharmaceutical patents to enforce their patents against generic competitors. When filing an ANDA, a generic manufacturer must certify whether its generic drug will infringe any patents listed in the Orange Book as being associated with the branded drug. 21 U.S.C. § 355(j)(2)(A)(vii). [citation omitted] For each listed patent, the ANDA applicant must make one of four possible certifications (respectively, the Paragraph I, II, III, and IV Certifications): (I) that no patent information on the branded drug has been submitted to the FDA; (II) that the patent has expired; (III) that the patent will expire on a stated date; or (IV) that the patent is invalid or will not be infringed by the generic drug. 21 U.S.C. § 355(j)(2)(A)(vii)(I)-(IV). A Paragraph I or II Certification poses no barrier to FDA approval, and one under Paragraph III allows approval after the patent expires. 21 U.S.C. § 355(j)(5)(B)(i)-(ii). A Paragraph IV Certification, however, makes the filing of an ANDA an act of patent infringement. 35 U.S.C. § 271(e)(2)(A). Along with a Paragraph IV Certification, the applicant must provide notice to the patent holder of its invalidity or noninfringement position. 21 U.S.C. § 355(j)(2)(B)(i). The patent holder has forty-five days after receiving that notice to file a patent infringement suit. 21 U.S.C. § 355(j)(5)(B)(iii). Significantly, if an infringement suit is filed, FDA approval of the ANDA is stayed until either thirty months have passed or a court rules that the patent is invalid or not infringed. Id. [citation omitted]

Pharmacists may dispense the generic equivalent for a branded drug when the branded drug is prescribed by a physician. [citation omitted] Such substitution is allowed, however, only if the generic drug has been "AB-rated" by the FDA, which means not only that the generic drug is bioequivalent to the branded drug, but also that the generic has the same form, dosage, and strength. [citation omitted] Therefore, an approved generic drug that is not AB-rated against a currently available branded drug, because, for example, the drugs have different formulations or dosages, may not be substituted for the branded drug and may only be sold, if at all, as a separately branded, rather than generic, drug. [citation omitted]

B. Defendants' Anticompetitive Conduct

Defendants have allegedly manipulated the Hatch-Waxman framework in violation of the antitrust laws, in order to prevent generic substitution for their fenofibrate drug, TriCor. Fenofibrate is used to treat high levels of triglycerides, and also has indications for the treatment of high cholesterol. [citation omitted] Plaintiffs allege that Defendants responded to the threat of generic entry into the market by changing the formulation of TriCor, not to improve the product but simply to prevent generic formulations from becoming AB-rated for substitution with TriCor. Defendants changed the TriCor formulation twice: first, TriCor was changed from capsule form to tablet form, and second, it was changed from that initial tablet form to a second tablet form.

1. The Switch from Capsules to Tablets

Abbott has licensed from Fournier several patents covering fenofibrate formulations. [citation omitted] Abbott and Fournier are alleged to have worked together to procure patents and to market fenofibrate formulations under Abbott's TriCor brand name. In 1998, Abbott received FDA approval of its NDA for TriCor in capsule form. [citation omitted] That formulation was listed in the Orange Book, along with U.S. Patent No. 4,985,726 (the "'726 patent"), which was asserted to cover that formulation. [citation omitted] In December 1999, Novopharm filed an ANDA for 67 mg and 200 mg fenofibrate capsules, along with a Paragraph IV Certification that its formulations did not infringe any valid or enforceable claim of the '726 patent. [citation omitted] In May 2000, Impax filed a similar ANDA. [citation omitted] In response to those ANDA filings, Defendants filed lawsuits (the "Capsule Litigation") in the United States District Court for the Northern District of Illinois against Novopharm and Impax, in April and August 2000 respectively, alleging infringement of the '726 patent. [citation omitted] By that time, Novopharm had been acquired by Teva. [citation omitted] The lawsuits triggered the thirty-month Hatch-Waxman stay of FDA approval of the generic formulations. [citation omitted]

In March 2002, the Northern District of Illinois granted summary judgment for Teva, holding that Teva's fenofibrate formulations did not infringe the '726 patent because, in those formulations, fenofibrate was not comicronized with a solid surfactant, as required by the asserted claims of that patent. Abbott Labs. v. Novopharm Ltd., No. 00-C-2141, 2002 WL 433584 (N.D.Ill. Mar. 20, 2002). The United States Court of Appeals for the Federal Circuit affirmed that judgment for Teva in March 2003. Abbott Labs. v. Novopharm Ltd., 323 F.3d 1324 (Fed. Cir.2003). The District Court then granted summary judgment for Impax, also in March 2003. [citation omitted] According to the Direct Purchasers, Defendants knew that the accused formulations did not infringe and, therefore, had no probable cause to pursue the litigation against Teva and Impax. [citation omitted]

While the Capsule Litigation was pending in the Northern District of Illinois, Abbott submitted an NDA for a new fenofibrate formulation: 54 mg and 160 mg tablets. [citation omitted] That NDA was approved in September 2001, while the 30-month stay from the Capsule Litigation was still blocking approval of Teva's and Impax's ANDAs for fenofibrate capsules. [citation omitted] Defendants sought approval of a new indication for their tablet formulation, claiming that fenofibrate also could be used to increase levels of high density lipoprotein (HDL), or "good cholesterol." [citation omitted] To support the new indication, Defendants submitted data for the capsule formulation and argued that the new tablet formulation was bioequivalent to the capsule formulation. [citation omitted] According to Plaintiffs, Defendants' submission of the capsule data effectively admitted that the tablet formulation was not an improvement over the previous capsule formulation. [citation omitted]

After the NDA for the tablet formulation was approved, Defendants stopped selling TriCor capsules and also bought back the existing supplies of those capsules from pharmacies. [citation omitted] In addition, Defendants changed the code for TriCor capsules in the National Drug Data File ("NDDF") to "obsolete." [citation omitted] The NDDF is a private database that provides information about FDA-approved drugs. [citation omitted] Changing the code to "obsolete" removed the TriCor capsule drug formulation from the NDDF, which prevented pharmacies from filling TriCor prescriptions with a generic capsule formulation. [citation omitted]

Teva's ANDA for 200 mg capsules was approved on April 9, 2002, after the summary judgment in the Capsule Litigation caused the end of the Hatch-Waxman stay. [citation omitted] However, because the TriCor capsule formulation had already been removed from the market, generic substitution was no longer possible. [citation omitted] Teva has marketed fenofibrate capsules under the brand Lofibra®, but those sales have been modest. [citation omitted]

2. The Switch from Original Tablets to New Tablets

Because the only branded fenofibrate on the market was the TriCor tablet form, Teva and Impax each developed generic equivalents for that tablet formulation and submitted ANDAs for 54 mg and 160 mg tablets in June and September 2002, respectively. [citation omitted] With those ANDAs, Teva and Impax again submitted Paragraph IV Certifications stating that their formulations did not infringe any valid or enforceable patent claim listed in the Orange Book with Defendants' tablet formulation. [citation omitted] In response to those ANDA filings, Defendants filed lawsuits in this court against Teva and Impax, in October 2002 and January 2003 respectively, alleging infringement of the '726 patent, of U.S. Patent No. 6,074,670 (the "'670 patent"), and of U.S. Patent No. 6,277,405 (the "'405 patent"). [citation omitted] Again, that triggered the thirty-month Hatch-Waxman stay. The current antitrust claims brought by Teva and Impax were set forth as counterclaims in that patent litigation.

Two other related patents were subsequently listed in the Orange Book for TriCor tablets: U.S. Patent No. 6,589,552 (the "'552 patent") in July 2003, and U.S. Patent No. 6,652,881 (the "'881 patent") in December 2003. [citation omitted] Teva and Impax filed Paragraph IV Certifications as to those two patents, and, in response, Defendants filed successive patent infringement suits against Teva and Impax, first for the '552 patent and then for the '881 patent. [citation omitted]

The lawsuits against Teva and Impax for the '726, the '670, the '405, the '552, and the '881 patents will be referred to collectively as the "Tablet Litigation." The '552 suit triggered an additional thirty-month stay, but, pursuant to a change in the statute that prevented successive litigation stays,[6] the '881 suit did not. [citation omitted] Thus, the stay based on the first three patents was to expire in March 2005, and, absent an intervening court decision, the additional stay based on the '552 patent was to expire in February 2006. [citation omitted]

On May 6, 2005, I granted partial summary judgment for Teva and Impax, holding that their tablet formulations did not infringe the '552 patent. [citation omitted] Since that patent was the cause of the Hatch-Waxman stay extending beyond March 2005, Teva's ANDA was approved on May 13, 2005. Defendants then voluntarily dismissed their remaining infringement claims against Teva and Impax. [citation omitted]

According to all Plaintiffs except for Impax, Defendants pursued the Tablet Litigation without probable cause because they knew that the patents-in-suit were rendered unenforceable by inequitable conduct before the U.S. Patent and Trademark Office ("PTO") and they also knew that the accused formulations did not infringe the patents-in-suit. [citation omitted] In addition, Teva alleges that the '881 patent was obtained through fraud on the PTO. [citation omitted]

As before, while the Tablet Litigation was pending in this court, Defendants submitted an NDA for a new formulation, this time for tablets with a dosage of 145 mg and 48 mg instead of 160 mg and 54 mg. [citation omitted] For the new formulation, Defendants sought a label change stating that the new tablets no longer had to be taken with food (the "no food effect label" or "NFE label"). [citation omitted] However, according to Plaintiffs, that formulation was not an actual improvement over the previous tablets but was developed simply to prevent generic substitution. (Id.) As they had done with the TriCor capsules, Defendants stopped selling the old TriCor tablets and changed the NDDF code to implement the formulation change to the new tablets. [citation omitted]

C. Plaintiffs' Legal Claims

Based on the foregoing allegations, Teva makes ten claims [including that Defendants] have engaged in an overall scheme to monopolize the fenofibrate market, in violation of Section 2; ***

IV. Discussion ***

A. Antitrust Liability for Product Formulation Changes

Defendants argue that their conduct in changing the TriCor formulation and implementing the change cannot support an antitrust claim. [citation omitted]

---

[6] In 2003, the Hatch-Waxman Act, 21 U.S.C. § 355(j)(5)(b), was amended to limit patentees to one thirty-month stay. See Herbert Hovenkamp, Mark D. Janis & Mark A. Lemley, IP and Antitrust § 12.4c (2006) ("[L]egislative changes effective in 2004 deal effectively with the problem ... by limiting patentees to a single 30-month stay for any given drug, regardless of the number of patents listed as covering that drug.").

First, they assert that Plaintiffs have conceded in their complaints that the TriCor formulation changes were improvements, and that any product change that introduces an improvement, however minor, is per se legal under the antitrust laws. [citation omitted] Thus, according to Defendants, the antitrust claims based on those formulation changes must be dismissed. Second, Defendants argue that they have not violated the antitrust laws because Teva and Impax have not been completely foreclosed from the fenofibrate market. Third, Defendants argue that they were not required to help their competitors, and so their withdrawal of old TriCor formulations and changes to the NDDF codes do not amount to antitrust violations. Those arguments both fail to state the proper legal standards and mischaracterize Plaintiffs' factual allegations

1. The Appropriate Standard

To violate Section 2, a monopolist's conduct "must harm the competitive process and thereby harm consumers. In contrast, harm to one or more competitors will not suffice." *United States v. Microsoft Corp.*, 253 F.3d 34, 58 (D.C.Cir.2001). Thus, conduct must be examined to determine its anticompetitive effect, i.e., the effect on competition itself. Id. One of the benefits of competition is the introduction of new, improved products. *See Berkey Photo, Inc. v. Eastman Kodak Co.*, 603 F.2d 263, 286 (2d Cir.1979) ("The attempt to develop superior products is . . . an essential element of lawful competition."); IIIA Phillip E. Areeda & Herbert Hovenkamp, Antitrust Law ¶ 781a (2d ed.2002) (hereinafter "Areeda") ("[P]roduct superiority is one of the objects of competition . . . ."). Thus, while improved products may harm the sales of competitors, that harm is an aim and result of appropriate competition. *See* Herbert Hovenkamp, Mark D. Janis & Mark A. Lemley, IP and Antitrust § 12.2 (2006) (hereinafter "IP & Antitrust") ("Innovation necessarily disadvantages rivals who do not keep up."). Even a monopolist may "through technological innovation expand its market share, increase consumer brand identification, or create demand for new products," and such actions are "perfectly consistent with the competitive forces that the Sherman Act was intended to foster." *Foremost Pro Color, Inc. v. Eastman Kodak Co.*, 703 F.2d 534, 546 (9th Cir.1983).

Because, speaking generally, innovation inflicts a natural and lawful harm on competitors, a court faces a difficult task when trying to distinguish harm that results from anticompetitive conduct from harm that results from innovative competition. "[T]he error costs of punishing technological change are rather high [and] . . . [c]ourts should not condemn a product change, therefore, unless they are relatively confident that the conduct in question is anticompetitive." IP & Antitrust § 12.1. If consumers are free to choose among products, then the success of a new product in the marketplace reflects consumer choice, and "antitrust should not intervene when an invention pleases customers." Areeda ¶ 776d. If the new product is not successful, then there will be no significant injury to competitors and no need for antitrust intervention. Id. Based on those general principles, the Defendants argue that an antitrust claim premised on the introduction of new products must be supported by evidence that "the innovator knew before introducing the improvement into the market that it was absolutely no better than the prior version, and that the only purpose of the innovation was to eliminate the complementary product of a rival." (D.I. 384 at 10–11 (quoting Areeda ¶ 776d).)

That reasoning was applied in the *Berkey Photo* case, 603 F.2d 263, where the Second Circuit refused to weigh the benefits from Kodak's introduction of a new camera model and film format against the alleged harm from the product introduction, because that weighing had already occurred in the marketplace. 603 F.2d at 286–87. The fact that consumers bought Kodak's new products instead of those of its competitors accurately reflected the value of the new products, "so long as the free choice of consumers [was] preserved." *Id.* at 287. Thus, the Court concluded, the antitrust laws should not intervene. [citation omitted]

A major logical underpinning of the Second Circuit's reluctance to inquire into the alleged anticompetitive effect of Kodak's new products was the success of those products in an open market, and the related conclusion that the harm to Kodak's competitors was a matter of consumer choice. *See* Areeda ¶ 781b ("[I]f buyers want it, is an antitrust court entitled to say that buyers should not have it? We doubt that the court has any choice but to accept consumer sovereignty, especially in the absence of any criteria or calculus for deciding otherwise."). Consumers who are free to choose among various products enjoy the presence of competition rather than its absence.

By contrast, when the introduction of a new product by a monopolist prevents consumer choice, greater scrutiny is appropriate. The court in *Berkey Photo* noted that consumers in that case were "not compelled" to purchase the new film, in part because "Kodak did not remove any other films from the market when it introduced the new one." 603 F.2d at 287. Indeed, "the situation [in that case] might be completely different if, upon introduction of the [new] system, Kodak had ceased producing film in the [old] size, thereby compelling camera purchasers to buy [the new] camera." *Id.* at 287 n. 39. In the absence of free consumer choice, the basis for judicial deference is removed.

The D.C. Circuit in the *Microsoft* case, 253 F.3d 34, also recognized that "[a]s a general rule, courts are properly very skeptical about claims that competition has been harmed by a dominant firm's product design changes" because such changes are part of competition. 253 F.3d at 65. Nevertheless, that court still concluded that "[j]udicial deference to product innovation . . . does not mean that a monopolist's product design decisions are per se lawful." *Id.* In that case, Microsoft's technological integration of its web browser and Windows operating system were subject to antitrust scrutiny, *Id.* at 65–67, and the government was able to show that that integration had an anticompetitive effect, namely that it caused harm "not by making Microsoft's own [web] browser more attractive to consumers but, rather, by discouraging [the distribution of] rival products," *id.* at 65. Once the plaintiff demonstrated that anticompetitive effect, the burden shifted to Microsoft to present a procompetitive justification for its conduct. *Id.* at 59, 66–67. The D.C. Circuit said that, if such a justification were offered, the plaintiff could rebut it or, alternatively, establish antitrust liability by demonstrating that "the anticompetitive harm of the conduct outweighs the procompetitive benefit." *Id.* at 59; *see also id.* at 67.

That balancing approach embodies the familiar "rule of reason" test first articulated by the Supreme Court in Standard Oil Co. v. United States, 221 U.S. 1, 61–62, 31 S.Ct. 502, 55 L.Ed. 619 (1911). In the Microsoft case, Microsoft presented a procompetitive justification for only a portion of its technological integration, and was liable for the unjustified conduct. 253 F.3d at 66–67. As to the justified conduct, the government failed to rebut the procompetitive justification or show that it was outweighed by the anticompetitive harm, and so Microsoft was not liable under the Sherman Act. Id. at 67.

The nature of the pharmaceutical drug market, as described in Plaintiffs' allegations, persuades me that the rule of reason approach should be applied here as well. The per se standard proposed by Defendants presupposes an open market where the merits of any new product can be tested by unfettered consumer choice. But here, according to Plaintiffs, consumers were not presented with a choice between fenofibrate formulations. Instead, Defendants allegedly prevented such a choice by removing the old formulations from the market while introducing new formulations. Hence, an inquiry into the effect of Defendants' formulation changes, following the rule of reason approach, is justified. Cf. IP & Antitrust § 12.5 (inquiry as to product-switching conduct such as is alleged in this case is justified because that conduct "seems clearly to be an effort to game the rather intricate FDA rules to anticompetitive effect").

Therefore, in this case, an antitrust inquiry into the benefits provided by Defendants' product changes is appropriate. Contrary to Defendants' assertion, Plaintiffs are not required to prove that the new formulations were absolutely no better than the prior version or that the only purpose of the innovation was to eliminate the complementary product of a rival. Rather, as in Microsoft, if Plaintiffs show anticompetitive harm from the formulation changes, that harm will be weighed against any benefits presented by Defendants.[12] See 253 F.3d at 59, 66–67. ***

3. Foreclosure from the Fenofibrate Market

Defendants next argue that their introduction of new fenofibrate formulations cannot be considered anticompetitive because it has not prevented Teva or Impax from selling fenofibrate. [citation omitted] Defendants are correct that, according to Plaintiffs' allegations, Teva and Impax have not been prevented from marketing the formulations that were the subject of their ANDAs, i.e., the old TriCor formulations. If it were true that an antitrust plaintiff had to show that competition were completely foreclosed, then Defendants' argument might have merit. However, that is not the correct legal standard.

To show that conduct has an anticompetitive effect, "it is not necessary that all competition be removed from the market. The test is not total foreclosure, but

---

[12] I note the importance of the screening function that is carried out by the need for the antitrust plaintiff to show monopoly power. Only a manufacturer with monopoly power will be subject to the scrutiny under Section 2 discussed here. See United States v. Dentsply Int'l, Inc., 399 F.3d 181, 186 (3d Cir. 2005); Microsoft, 253 F.3d at 50–51. Defendants do not argue, for purposes of this Motion, that they lack the requisite monopoly power.

whether the challenged practices bar a substantial number of rivals or severely restrict the market's ambit." United States v. Dentsply Int'l, Inc., 399 F.3d 181, 191 (3d Cir. 2005). Competitors need not be barred "from all means of distribution," if they are barred "from the cost-efficient ones." Microsoft, 253 F.3d at 64. Here, while Teva and Impax may be able to market their own branded versions of the old TriCor formulations, they cannot provide generic substitutes for the current TriCor formulation, which is alleged to be their cost-efficient means of competing in the pharmaceutical drug market. That opportunity has allegedly been prevented entirely by Defendants' allegedly manipulative and unjustifiable formulation changes. Such a restriction on competition, if proven, is sufficient to support an antitrust claim in this case.

4. Actions Taken to Support the Formulation Changes

Defendants assert [citation omitted] that the actions they are alleged to have taken in support of the product changes, i.e., withdrawing the old formulations from the market and changing the NDDF codes, fail to support an antitrust claim because, according to Defendants, even a monopolist has "no general duty to aid competitors." [citation omitted] Thus, while Defendants actions may have made it more difficult for Teva and Impax to compete, because those actions blocked generic substitution for TriCor, Defendants argue that they are not required to help Teva and Impax by allowing them to "free-ride on the TriCor brand." [citation omitted]

*** [W]hile a monopolist may compete and is not required to aid its competitors, see, e.g., Microsoft, 253 F.3d at 58, "a monopolist is not free to take certain actions that a company in a competitive (or even oligopolistic) market may take, because there is no market constraint on a monopolist's behavior." LePage's Inc. v. 3M, 324 F.3d 141, 151–52 (3d Cir. 2003) (citing Aspen Skiing Co. v. Aspen Highlands Skiing Corp., 472 U.S. 585, 601–04 (1985)). Contrary to Defendants' assertion [citation omitted], Plaintiffs allege harm to competition rather than simply harm to Teva and Impax. By removing the old products from the market and changing the NDDF code, Defendants allegedly suppressed competition by blocking the introduction of generic fenofibrate. The Court in Berkey Photo noted that such conduct, which results in consumer coercion, is potentially anticompetitive. See 603 F.2d at 287 & n. 39 (finding no liability but stating that "the situation might be completely different" if the defendant stopped producing old products or removed them from the market). Thus, the allegations of product removal and NDDF code changes, like the allegations related to the product changes themselves, support Plaintiffs' antitrust claims.

Comments and Questions

1. Defendants argued "that any product change that introduces an improvement, however minor, is per se legal under the antitrust laws." Is that true?

2. The predatory innovation cases up to this point in the chapter have focused on innovators altering a particular component of a system so as to make it incompatible with a competitor's previously compatible components. The pharmaceutical

industry provides a unique predatory innovation problem. Pharmaceutical predatory innovation cases involve a sort of artificial incompatibility, which arises from the Hatch-Waxman Act. The Hatch-Waxman Act provides a means for firms to introduce generic substitutes for branded drugs, but also enables the branded drug manufacturer to receive a thirty-month stay on the introduction of generic substitutes if the product is protected by a patent. In cases involving allegedly predatory pharmaceutical product line extensions, the claim is that the branded drug manufacturer released a newer version of its drug with superficial improvements, if any, in an effort to shift the market to one without generic competition. To what extent do differences in cases of predatory product line extensions in the pharmaceutical industry and cases of predatory systems rivalry imply that courts should deal with them differently?

3. How would the Ordover-Willig approach, detailed in the notes after *Berkey Photo*, translate to cases of predatory product line extensions in the pharmaceutical industry? The second stage of the test, which focuses on product sacrifice, includes a consideration of whether the innovator stopped selling preexisting compatible components. There are no real "components" at issue in predatory product line extensions, so the analysis might shift to whether or not the innovator stopped selling previous versions of the product. Indeed, in *Abbott*, the court identified this problem with the defendants' conduct:

> [H]ere, according to Plaintiffs, consumers were not presented with a choice between fenofibrate formulations. Instead, Defendants allegedly prevented such a choice by removing the old formulations from the market while introducing new formulations.

In *Walgreen Co. et al. v. AstraZeneca Pharms.*, the United States District Court for the District of Columbia distinguished AstraZeneca's conduct from the *Abbott* defendants' decision to make a series of changes in the drug's composition, each followed by the removal of the previous version from the market. 534 F.Supp.2d 146, 151 (D.D.C. 2008). Even after AstraZeneca introduced a new version of its drug into the market (called Nexium) to the market, it continued to make the older version of the drug (called Prilosec) available. Thus, rather than constricting consumer choice through its conduct, AstraZeneca actually expanded it.

Is removing the older version from the market the only way in which pharmaceutical companies can restrict consumer choice upon release of a new version? Or are there other types of conduct with which courts should be concerned? For instance, if the *Abbott* defendants had on multiple occasions strategically altered their drug to provide a "new, improved version" each time generic substitutes were introduced, but left old versions on the market, would there still be cause for concern? What if the defendants had introduced new versions of the drug, received the thirty-month stay, and dropped the cost of the new drug below that of the still-available older versions?

4. The Delaware District Court noted that while courts should typically defer to the business judgment of decisions made in the course of product innovation,

this deference is unwarranted once it is demonstrated that "free consumer choice" has been removed. As such, the court finds that an evaluation of the benefits of the *Abbott* defendants' product is necessary. How should this evaluation of the benefits proceed? What of the *Berkey* court's contention that it is impossible to find definitively whether the qualities of one product are truly better than another?

Bibliography of Additional Resources

Guy V. Amoresano, *Branded Drug Reformulation: The Next Brand vs. Generic Antitrust Battleground*, 62 Food & Drug L.J. 249 (2007)

Kara E. Harchuck, *Microsoft IV: The Dangers of Innovation Posed by the Irresponsible Application of a Rule of Reason Analysis to Product Design Claims*, 97 Nw. U.L. Rev. 395, 493 (2002)

Janusz A. Ordover, Alan O. Sykes, & Robert D. Willig, *Predator Systems Rivalry: A Reply*, 83 Colum. L. Rev. 1150 (1983)

Ross D. Petty, *Innovation and Antitrust: Are Product Modifications Ever Predatory?*, 22 Suffolk U.L. Rev. 997 (1988)

CHAPTER 8

Deceptive Conduct before Standard-Setting Organizations

For many products, standards are necessary for safety and interoperability. Plumbing and lumber come in standard sizes so materials from different suppliers can be used together. Technical interoperability is necessary for machines to be able to interact, such as a printer with a computer. Standard-setting organizations (SSOs), comprised of members in a particular industry, may adopt and implement a common standard to help insure seamless interoperability. SSO members generally try to select the best available technical standard. But if the standard includes proprietary technology, then the IP owner may acquire market power if use of the standard would constitute infringement absent a license. The patent may not convey market power until it is included in the standard, but once it is and the standard has been widely adopted, the patentholder may be able to charge exorbitant royalties or to discriminate against its competitors in a downstream market.

The cases in this chapter discuss how antitrust law may constrain a would-be monopolist's conduct with an SSO. Because Part 2 of this casebook focuses only on unilateral conduct—primarily conduct that is potentially violative of Section Two of the Sherman Act—this chapter will focus on the conduct (and misconduct) of single firms before an SSO. However, because standard-setting organizations often involve a group of competitors agreeing to set standards—as well as royalty rates and policies—SSOs also implicate Section One of the Sherman Act, which addresses concerted action. Those issues will be addressed in Chapter 10, which discusses IP agreements that unreasonably restrain trade and thus violate the antitrust laws.

In the Matter of Dell Computer Corp.

121 F.T.C. 616 (1996)

Complaint

*** In February 1992 Dell became a member of the Video Electronics Standards Association ("VESA"), a non-profit standards-setting association composed of virtually all major U.S. computer hardware and software manufacturers. *** At or about the same time, VESA began the process of setting a design standard for a computer bus design, later to be known as the VESA Local Bus or "VL-bus." Like all computer buses, the VL-bus carries information or instructions between the computer's central processing unit and the computer's peripheral devices such as a hard disk drive, a video display terminal, or a modem. *** By June 1992 VESA's Local Bus Committee, with Dell representatives sitting as members, approved the VL-bus design standard, which improved upon then-existing technology by more quickly and efficiently meeting the transmission needs of new, video-intensive software. One year earlier, in July 1991, Dell had received United States patent number 5,036,481 (the "'481 patent"), which, according to Dell, gives it "exclusive rights to the mechanical slot configuration used on the motherboard to receive the VL-bus card." Nonetheless, at no time prior to or after June 1992 did Dell disclose to VESA's Local Bus Committee the existence of the '481 patent.

After committee approval of the VL-bus design standard, VESA sought the approval of the VL-bus design standard by all of its voting members. On July 20, 1992, Dell voted to approve the preliminary proposal for the VL-bus standard. As part of this approval, a Dell representative certified in writing that, to the best of his knowledge, "this proposal does not infringe on any trademarks, copyrights, or patents" that Dell possessed. On August 6, 1992, Dell gave final approval to the VL-bus design standard. As part of this final approval, the Dell representative again certified in writing that, to the best of his knowledge, "this proposal does not infringe on any trademarks, copyrights, or patents" that Dell possessed.

After VESA's VL-bus design standard became very successful, having been included in over 1.4 million computers sold in the eight months immediately following its adoption, Dell informed certain VESA members who were manufacturing computers using the new design standard that their "implementation of the VL-bus is a violation of Dell's exclusive rights." Dell demanded that these companies meet with its representatives to "determine ... the manner in which Dell's exclusive rights will be recognized ...." Dell followed up its initial demands by meeting with several companies, and it has never renounced the claimed infringement.

By engaging in the acts or practices described in *** this complaint, respondent Dell has unreasonably restrained competition in the following ways, among others:

(a) Industry acceptance of the VL-bus design standard was hindered because some computer manufacturers delayed their use of the design standard until the patent issue was clarified.

(b) Systems utilizing the VL-bus design standard were avoided due to concerns that patent issues would affect the VL-bus' success as an industry design standard.

(c) The uncertainty concerning the acceptance of the VL-bus design standard raised the costs of implementing the VL-bus design as well as the costs of developing competing bus designs.

Deceptive Conduct before Standard-Setting Organizations 259

(d) Willingness to participate in industry standard-setting efforts have been chilled.

The acts or practices of respondent alleged herein were and are to the prejudice and injury of the public. The acts or practices constitute unfair methods of competition in or affecting commerce in violation of Section 5 of the Federal Trade Commission Act. These acts or practices are continuing and will continue, or may recur, in the absence of the relief requested. ***

Order

It is ordered, *** That, within thirty (30) days after the date this order becomes final, and until the expiration of the '481 patent, respondent shall cease and desist all efforts it has undertaken by any means, including without limitation the threat, prosecution or defense of any suits or other actions, whether legal, equitable, or administrative, as well as any arbitrations, mediations, or any other form of private dispute resolution, through or in which respondent has asserted that any person or entity, by using or applying VL-bus in its manufacture of computer equipment, has infringed the '481 patent.

It is further ordered, That, until the expiration of the '481 patent, respondent shall not undertake any new efforts to enforce the '481 patent by threatening, prosecuting or defending any suit or other action, whether legal, equitable, or administrative, as well as any arbitration, mediation, or other form of private dispute resolution, through or in which respondent claims that any person or entity, by using or applying VL-bus in its manufacture, use or sale of computer equipment, has infringed the '481 patent.

It is further ordered, That, for a period of ten (10) years after the date this order becomes final, respondent shall cease and desist from enforcing or threatening to enforce any patent rights by asserting or alleging that any person's or entity's use or implementation of an industry design standard, or sale of any equipment using an industry design standard, infringes such patent rights, if, in response to a written inquiry from the standard-setting organization to respondent's designated representative, respondent intentionally failed to disclose such patent rights while such industry standard was under consideration. ***

Statement of the Federal Trade Commission

*** The Dell case involved an effort by the Video Electronics Standards Association ("VESA") to identify potentially conflicting patents and to avoid creating standards that would infringe those patents. In order to achieve this goal, VESA — like some other standard-setting entities — has a policy that member companies must make a certification that discloses any potentially conflicting intellectual property rights. VESA believes that its policy imposes on its members a good-faith duty to seek to identify potentially conflicting patents. This policy is designed to further VESA's strong preference for adopting standards that do not include proprietary technology.

This case involved the standard for VL-bus, a mechanism to transfer instructions between a computer's central processing unit and its peripherals. During the standard-setting process, VESA asked its members to certify whether they had any patents, trademarks, or copyrights that conflicted with the proposed VL-bus standard; Dell certified that it had no such intellectual property rights. After VESA adopted the standard—based, in part, on Dell's certification—Dell sought to enforce its patent against firms planning to follow the standard.

We believe that in the limited circumstances presented by this case, enforcement action is appropriate. In this case—where there is evidence that the association would have implemented a different non-proprietary design had it been informed of the patent conflict during the certification process, and where Dell failed to act in good faith to identify and disclose patent conflicts — enforcement action is appropriate to prevent harm to competition and consumers.[2]

The remedy in this case is carefully circumscribed. It simply prohibits Dell from enforcing its patent against those using the VL-bus standard. This relief assures that the competitive process is not harmed by the conduct addressed in the Commission's complaint. Moreover, the remedy in this case is consistent with those cases, decided under the concept of equitable estoppel, in which courts precluded patent-holders from enforcing patents when they failed properly to disclose the existence of those patents. In this case, Dell is precluded from enforcing the patent only against those implementing the relevant standard. ***

[C]ommenters asked whether the Commission intended to signal that there is a general duty to search for patents when a firm engages in a standard-setting process. The relief in this matter is carefully limited to the facts of the case. Specifically, VESA's affirmative disclosure requirement creates an expectation by its members that each will act in good faith to identify and disclose conflicting intellectual property rights. Other standard-setting organizations may have different procedures that do not create such an expectation on the part of their members. Consequently, the relief in this case should not be read to impose a general duty to search.

Others suggested that the theory supporting this enforcement action could impose liability for an unknowing (or "inadvertent") failure to disclose patent rights. Again, the Commission's enforcement action is limited to the facts of this case, in which there is reason to believe that Dell's failure to disclose the patent was not inadvertent. The order should not be read to create a general rule that inadvertence in the standard-setting process provides a basis for enforcement action.

---

[2] The Commission has reason to believe that once VESA's VL-bus standard had become widely accepted, the standard effectively conferred market power upon Dell as the patent holder. This market power was not inevitable: had VESA known of the Dell patent, it could have chosen an equally effective, non-proprietary standard. If Dell were able to impose a royalty on each VL-bus installed in 486-generation computers, prices to consumers would likely have increased. The dissent speculates that computer manufacturers could have readily shifted to a new standard. Dissenting Statement at 10. Although that alternative might be possible in some settings, it was not in this case where the market had overwhelmingly adopted the VL-bus standard.

Nor does this enforcement action contain a general suggestion that standard-setting bodies should impose a duty to disclose.

Finally, some commenters suggested that private litigation is sufficient to address this type of controversy. Although there has been private litigation for failure to disclose patent rights under equitable estoppel theories, enforcement of Section 5 of the Federal Trade Commission Act also serves an important role in this type of case, where there is a likelihood of consumer harm. Moreover, unlike other antitrust statutes, Section 5 provides only for prospective relief. In fact, the judicious use of Section 5—culminating in carefully tailored relief—is particularly appropriate in this type of case, in which the legal and economic theories are somewhat novel.

One topic considered by the Commission's hearings last fall on Global and Innovation-Based Competition was the important role of standard-setting in the technological innovation that will drive much of this nation's competitive vigor in the 21st Century. The record of those hearings is replete with discussion of the pro-competitive role of standard-setting organizations. The Commission recognizes that enforcement actions in this area should be undertaken with care, lest they chill participation in the standard-setting process. Nevertheless, a standard-setting organization may provide a vehicle for a firm to undermine the standard-setting process in a way that harms competition and consumers. We believe that the commission's enforcement action in Dell strikes the right balance between these important objectives.

[Dissenting Statement of Commissioner Mary L. Azcuenaga omitted]

Comments and Questions

1. How do network effects help a patentee (who conceals its IP rights from an SSO) acquire and maintain monopoly power? Consider the following explanation:

> Network externalities therefore may create a "positive feedback loop," which can serve to create momentum for standards. Where these positive feedback elements are strong, the market is especially prone to "tipping," which is the tendency for one standard to dominate once it has gained a sufficient advantage in popularity. If a network technology becomes dominant, its installed base of users may act as a barrier to entry for competing technologies. The combination of these effects may create a so-called first-mover advantage: network externalities may give the first introduced technology enough momentum that it can build a user base large enough that consumers will not switch to a new technology. Switching costs associated with transferring to an incompatible but superior technology will deter consumers from switching to a new technology because of lost value of network externalities. Users of an existing technology will not switch to a new superior alternative unless others switch first. This may result in stifled innovation and consumers being locked in to inferior technology.

ABA Section On Antitrust Law, Handbook on the Antitrust Aspects of Standards Setting 13–14 (2004).

2. Disclosure requirements among SSO members are common, but neither universal nor unvarying. The DOJ and FTC have noted: "Some SSOs have no disclosure requirements. The disclosure policies of those that do are diverse. Some policies state express disclosure obligations, while others impose implied obligations; the policies may cover existing patents, pending patents, or other IP rights; and they also may require an SSO member to search its own inventory for patents." U.S. Dep't of Justice & Federal Trade Commission, Antitrust Enforcement and Intellectual Property Rights: Promoting Innovation and Competition 42 (2007).

If you were developing rules for an SSO, what type of disclosure requirements would you implement and enforce?

3. Disclosure requirements are not without costs. After holding hearings on the issue, the federal antitrust agencies cautioned that

> compliance with disclosure rules may slow down standards development, which could be particularly costly in fast-paced markets with short product life cycles. Complying with differing disclosure policies in different SSOs can be costly to IP holders, especially for those with large patent portfolios who participate in many SSOs. The cost of compliance may cause some IP holders to opt out of some collaborative standard setting. As a result, "whatever they might have had to contribute to the process is going to be lost." Furthermore, IP holders that choose not to participate in an SSO are not bound by the SSO's disclosure rules. Finally, disclosure rules that are not well-crafted may not help prevent holdup. Panelists said that disclosure rules drafted by engineers and business people may reflect their authors' laudable ethos—to work collaboratively toward a standard—but sometimes fail to consider carefully the intellectual property and antitrust issues.

U.S. Dep't of Justice & Federal Trade Commission, Antitrust Enforcement and Intellectual Property Rights: Promoting Innovation and Competition 42–43 (2007).

4. Is there another area of law aside from antitrust law that could better address Dell's conduct?

Note: The Third Circuit in *Broadcom* relies in part on the FTC decision in *Rambus*, which the D.C. Circuit reversed. The D.C. Circuit opinion is presented after this excerpt from *Broadcom*.

Broadcom Corp. v. Qualcomm Inc.
501 F.3d 297 (3d Cir. 2007)

BARRY, Circuit Judge.

This appeal presents important questions regarding whether a patent holder's deceptive conduct before a private standards-determining organization may be condemned under antitrust laws and, if so, what facts must be pled to survive a motion to dismiss. Broadcom Corporation ("Broadcom") alleged that Qualcomm

Inc. ("Qualcomm"), by its intentional deception of private standards-determining organizations and its predatory acquisition of a potential rival, has monopolized certain markets for cellular telephone technology and components ***. The District Court dismissed the Complaint, and Broadcom appeals. For the reasons that follow, we conclude that Broadcom has stated claims for monopolization and attempted monopolization under § 2 of the Sherman Act-Claims 1 and 2 of the Complaint. ***

I. Background

A. Mobile Wireless Telephony and the UMTS Standard

Mobile wireless telephony is the general term for describing the technology and equipment used in the operation of cellular telephones. A cellular telephone contains one or more computer "chipsets"—the core electronics that allow it to transmit and receive information, either telephone calls or data, to and from the wireless network. Chipsets transmit information, via radio waves, to cellular base stations. Base stations, in turn, transmit information to and from telephone and computer networks. It is essential that all components involved in this transmission of information be able to communicate seamlessly with one another. Because multiple vendors manufacture these components, industry-wide standards are necessary to ensure their interoperability. In mobile wireless telephony, standards are determined privately by industry groups known as standards-determining organizations ("SDOs").

Two technology paths, or families of standards, are in widespread use today: "CDMA," which stands for "code division multiple access"; and "GSM," which stands for "global system for mobility." Cellular telephone service providers operate under one or the other path, with, for example, Verizon Wireless and Sprint Communications operating CDMA-path networks, and Cingular (now AT&T) and T-Mobile operating GSM-path networks. The CDMA and GSM technology paths are not interoperable; equipment and technologies used in one cannot be used in the other. For this reason, each technology path has its own standard or set of standards. The standard used in current generation GSM-path networks is the third generation ("3G") standard created for the GSM path, and is known as the Universal Mobile Telecommunications System ("UMTS") standard.

The UMTS standard was created by the European Telecommunications Standards Institute ("ETSI") and its SDO counterparts in the United States and elsewhere after a lengthy evaluation of available alternative equipment and technologies. Qualcomm supplies some of the essential technology that the ETSI ultimately included in the UMTS standard, and holds intellectual property rights ("IPRs"), such as patents, in this technology. Given the potential for owners of IPRs, through the exercise of their rights, to exert undue control over the implementation of industry-wide standards, the ETSI requires a commitment from vendors whose technologies are included in standards to license their technologies on fair, reasonable, and non-discriminatory ("FRAND") terms. Neither the ETSI nor the other relevant SDOs further define FRAND.

Broadcom alleged that Qualcomm was a member of the ETSI, among other SDOs, and committed to abide by its IPR policy. Specifically, Broadcom alleged, the ETSI included Qualcomm's proprietary technology in the UMTS standard only after, and in reliance on, Qualcomm's commitment to license that technology on FRAND terms. The technology in question is called Wideband CDMA ("WCDMA"), not to be confused with the CDMA technology path. Although it represents only a small component of the technologies that collectively comprise the UMTS standard, WCDMA technology is said to be essential to the practice of the standard.

B. Broadcom's Complaint

*** The Complaint alleged that Qualcomm induced the ETSI and other SDOs to include its proprietary technology in the UMTS standard by falsely agreeing to abide by the SDOs' policies on IPRs, but then breached those agreements by licensing its technology on non-FRAND terms. The intentional acquisition of monopoly power through deception of an SDO, Broadcom posits, violates antitrust law.

The Complaint also alleged that Qualcomm ignored its FRAND commitment to the ETSI and other SDOs by demanding discriminatorily higher (i.e., non-FRAND) royalties from competitors and customers using chipsets not manufactured by Qualcomm. Qualcomm, the Complaint continued, has a 90% share in the market for CDMA-path chipsets, and by withholding favorable pricing in that market, coerced cellular telephone manufacturers to purchase only Qualcomm-manufactured UMTS-path chipsets. These actions are alleged to be part of Qualcomm's effort to obtain a monopoly in the UMTS chipset market because it views competition in that market as a long-term threat to its existing monopolies in CDMA technology.

Broadcom claims to have been preparing to enter the UMTS chipset market for several years prior to its filing of the Complaint. After Broadcom purchased Zyray Wireless, Inc., a developer of UMTS chipsets, Qualcomm allegedly demanded that Broadcom license Qualcomm's UMTS technology on non-FRAND terms. Broadcom refused, and commenced this action. Qualcomm also allegedly acquired Flarion Technologies, a competitor in the development of technologies for inclusion in the forthcoming B3G and 4G standards, in an effort to extend Qualcomm's monopolies into future generations of standards. ***

C. The District Court's Opinion

Qualcomm moved to dismiss the Complaint under Federal Rule of Civil Procedure 12(b)(6) for failure to state a claim. On August 30, 2006, 2006 WL 2528545, little more than a year after the filing of the Complaint and while discovery was ongoing, the District Court granted the motion. In dismissing Broadcom's claim of monopolization in the WCDMA technology markets, the Court reasoned that Qualcomm enjoyed a legally-sanctioned monopoly in its patented technology, and that this monopoly conferred the right to exclude competition and set the terms by which that technology was distributed. Acknowledging that industry-wide standards merit "additional antitrust scrutiny", the Court nevertheless quickly concluded that the inclusion of Qualcomm's WCDMA technology in the UMTS standard did not harm competition because an absence of competition was the inevitable result of any standard-setting process. That inclusion of Qualcomm's technology may have been the product of deception was of no moment under antitrust law, the Court continued, because no matter which company's patented technology ultimately was chosen, the adoption of a standard would have eliminated competition. (Id. at A21 ("[I]t is the SDO's decision to set a standard for WCDMA technology, not Qualcomm's 'inducement,' that results in the absence of competing WCDMA technologies.").) The Court did not discuss the possibility that the FRAND commitments that SDOs required of vendors were intended as a bulwark against unlawful monopoly, nor did it consider the possibility that the SDOs might have chosen nonproprietary technologies for inclusion in the standard.

As to the claim that Qualcomm was attempting to obtain a monopoly in the UMTS chipset market by exploiting its monopolies in WCDMA technology and CDMA-path chipsets, the District Court faulted the Complaint for not providing "information on the composition or dynamics of the market for UMTS chipsets to enable the Court to infer that Qualcomm's conduct is anticompetitive." (Id. at A23.) The Court also dismissed Broadcom's claim for unlawful maintenance of monopoly, reasoning that the combination of patent rights and an industry-wide standard foreclosed the possibility of unlawful monopoly, and that the Complaint did not describe the composition of the 3G CDMA chipset market in sufficient detail. ***

III. Discussion ***

A. The District Court erred in dismissing Claim 1—the monopolization claim—on the ground that abuse of a private standard-setting process does not state a claim under antitrust law.

Claim 1 of the Complaint alleged that Qualcomm monopolized markets for WCDMA technology by inducing the relevant SDOs to include Qualcomm's patented technology as an essential element of the UMTS standard. Qualcomm did this by falsely promising to license its patents on FRAND terms, and then reneging on those promises after it succeeded in having its technology included in the standard. These actions, the Complaint alleged, violated § 2 of the Sherman Act, 15 U.S.C. § 2.

1. Unlawful Monopolization under § 2: Monopoly Power

Section 2 of the Sherman Act, in what we have called "sweeping language," makes it unlawful to monopolize, attempt to monopolize, or conspire to monopolize, interstate or international commerce. It is, we have observed, "the provision of the antitrust laws designed to curb the excesses of monopolists and near-monopolists." *LePage's Inc. v. 3M*, 324 F.3d 141, 169 (3d Cir.2003) (en banc). Liability under

§ 2 requires "(1) the possession of monopoly power in the relevant market and (2) the willful acquisition or maintenance of that power as distinguished from growth or development as a consequence of a superior product, business acumen, or historic accident." *United States v. Grinnell Corp.*, 384 U.S. 563, 570–71 (1966). Monopoly power is the ability to control prices and exclude competition in a given market. Id. at 571. If a firm can profitably raise prices without causing competing firms to expand output and drive down prices, that firm has monopoly power. *Harrison Aire, Inc. v. Aerostar Int'l, Inc.*, 423 F.3d 374, 380 (3d Cir.2005).

The existence of monopoly power may be proven through direct evidence of supracompetitive prices and restricted output. *United States v. Microsoft Corp.*, 253 F.3d 34, 51 (D.C.Cir.2001) (en banc) [citation omitted]. It may also be inferred from the structure and composition of the relevant market. *Harrison Aire*, 423 F.3d at 381; *Microsoft*, 253 F.3d at 51. To support an inference of monopoly power, a plaintiff typically must plead and prove that a firm has a dominant share in a relevant market, and that significant "entry barriers" protect that market. *Harrison Aire*, 423 F.3d at 381; *Microsoft*, 253 F.3d at 51. Barriers to entry are factors, such as regulatory requirements, high capital costs, or technological obstacles, that prevent new competition from entering a market in response to a monopolist's supracompetitive prices. *Microsoft*, 253 F.3d at 51. [citation omitted]

Proving the existence of monopoly power through indirect evidence requires a definition of the relevant market. [citation omitted] The scope of the market is a question of fact as to which the plaintiff bears the burden of proof. [citation omitted] Competing products are in the same market if they are readily substitutable for one another; a market's outer boundaries are determined by the reasonable interchangeability of use between a product and its substitute, or by their cross-elasticity of demand. [citation omitted] Failure to define the proposed relevant market in these terms may result in dismissal of the complaint. [citation omitted]

2. Unlawful Monopolization under § 2: Anticompetitive Conduct

The second element of a monopolization claim under § 2 requires the willful acquisition or maintenance of monopoly power. As this element makes clear, the acquisition or possession of monopoly power must be accompanied by some anticompetitive conduct on the part of the possessor. [citation omitted] Anticompetitive conduct may take a variety of forms, but it is generally defined as conduct to obtain or maintain monopoly power as a result of competition on some basis other than the merits. [citation omitted] Conduct that impairs the opportunities of rivals and either does not further competition on the merits or does so in an unnecessarily restrictive way may be deemed anticompetitive. [citation omitted] Conduct that merely harms competitors, however, while not harming the competitive process itself, is not anticompetitive. [citation omitted] ***

The primary goal of antitrust law is to maximize consumer welfare by promoting competition among firms. [citation omitted] Private standard setting advances this goal on several levels. In the end-consumer market, standards that ensure the interoperability of products facilitate the sharing of information among purchasers of products from competing manufacturers, thereby enhancing the utility of all products and enlarging the overall consumer market. [citation omitted] This, in turn, permits firms to spread the costs of research and development across a greater number of consumers, resulting in lower per-unit prices. [citation omitted] Industry-wide standards may also lower the cost to consumers of switching between competing products and services, thereby enhancing competition among suppliers. [citation omitted]

Standards enhance competition in upstream markets, as well. One consequence of the standard-setting process is that SDOs may more readily make an objective comparison between competing technologies, patent positions, and licensing terms before an industry becomes locked in to a standard. [citation omitted] Standard setting also reduces the risk to producers (and end consumers) of investing scarce resources in a technology that ultimately may not gain widespread acceptance. [citation omitted] The adoption of a standard does not eliminate competition among producers but, rather, moves the focus away from the development of potential standards and toward the development of means for implementing the chosen standard. [citation omitted][4]

Each of these efficiencies enhances consumer welfare and competition in the marketplace and is, therefore, consistent with the procompetitive aspirations of antitrust law. [citation omitted] Thus, private standard setting—which might otherwise be viewed as a naked agreement among competitors not to manufacture, distribute, or purchase certain types of products—need not, in fact, violate antitrust law. *See Allied Tube*, 486 U.S. at 500–01; *see also* Standards Development Organization Advancement Act of 2004, 15 U.S.C. §§ 4302, 4303 (Supp. 2004) (providing that private standard-setting conduct shall not be deemed illegal per se, and insulating such conduct from treble damages); Pub.L. 108–237, Title I, § 102, June 22, 2004, 118 Stat. 661 (noting congressional finding of "the importance of technical standards developed by voluntary consensus standards bodies to our national economy").

This is not to say, however, that acceptance, including judicial acceptance, of private standard setting is without limits. Indeed, that "private standard-setting by associations comprising firms with horizontal and vertical business relations is permitted at all under the antitrust laws [is] only on the understanding that it will be conducted in a nonpartisan manner offering procompetitive benefits," *Allied Tube*, 486 U.S. at 506–07, and in the presence of "meaningful safeguards" that "prevent the standard-setting process from being biased by members with

---

[4] In their brief, SDO Amici explain the competition that occurs between firms in the telecommunications standard-setting process. Prior to the adoption of a standard, firms compete on the basis of their respective technologies and intellectual property positions. Each SDO Amicus has policies in place to require competing firms to disclose all relevant patents and licensing commitments. Such policies facilitate an informed comparison of the firms and their technologies, and are "part of an effort to preserve the competitive benefits of ex ante technology competition." (IEEE Br. 10 (IEEE Standards Association); see also id. 12 (VITA Standards Organization); 16 (OASIS Open (Organization for the Advancement of Structured Information Standards)).) Thus, the selection of a standard is, itself, the product of a competitive process.

economic interests in stifling product competition," *id.* at 501; *Hydrolevel,* 456 U.S. at 572; *see also Clamp-All Corp. v. Cast Iron Soil Pipe Inst.,* 851 F.2d 478, 488 (1st Cir.1988) (acknowledging possibility of antitrust claim where firms both prevented SDO from adopting a beneficial standard and did so through "unfair, or improper practices or procedures"). As the Supreme Court acknowledged in *Allied Tube,* and as administrative tribunals, law enforcement authorities, and some courts have recognized, conduct that undermines the procompetitive benefits of private standard setting may, at least in some circumstances, be deemed anticompetitive under antitrust law.

a. Patent Hold-up

Inefficiency may be injected into the standard-setting process by what is known as "patent hold-up." An SDO may complete its lengthy process of evaluating technologies and adopting a new standard, only to discover that certain technologies essential to implementing the standard are patented. When this occurs, the patent holder is in a position to "hold up" industry participants ***. Industry participants who have invested significant resources developing products and technologies that conform to the standard will find it prohibitively expensive to abandon their investment and switch to another standard. They will have become "locked in" to the standard. In this unique position of bargaining power, the patent holder may be able to extract supracompetitive royalties from the industry participants. [citation omitted]

In actions brought before the Federal Trade Commission ("FTC"), patent holders have faced antitrust liability for misrepresenting to an SDO that they did not hold IPRs in essential technologies, and then, after a standard had been adopted, seeking to enforce those IPRs. In 1996, the FTC entered into a consent order with Dell Computer Corporation. The complaint issued in conjunction therewith alleged that Dell participated in an SDO's adoption of a design standard for a computer bus (i.e., an information-carrying conduit), but failed to disclose that it owned a patent for a key design feature of the standard, and even certified to the SDO that the proposed standard did not infringe any of Dell's IPRs. After the design standard proved successful, Dell attempted to assert its IPRs, prompting the FTC to commence an enforcement action under § 5 of the FTC Act, 15 U.S.C. § 45, for unfair methods of competition in or affecting commerce. Dell's actions, it was alleged, created uncertainty that hindered industry acceptance of the standard, increased the costs of implementing the standard, and chilled the willingness of industry participants to engage in the standard-setting process. In the Matter of Dell Computer Corp., 121 F.T.C. 616, 618 (May 20, 1996).

The consent order required, among other things, that Dell cease and desist from asserting that the use or implementation of the standard violated its IPRs. Significantly, the FTC's announcement that accompanied the order stated that in the "limited circumstances . . . where there is evidence that the [SDO] would have implemented a different non-proprietary design had it been informed of the patent conflict during the certification process, and where Dell failed to act in good faith to identify and disclose patent conflicts . . . enforcement action is appropriate to prevent harm to competition and consumers." *Id.* at 624. It also noted that once the standard had gained widespread acceptance, "the standard effectively conferred market power upon Dell as the patent holder. This market power was not inevitable: had [the SDO] known of the Dell patent, it could have chosen an equally effective, non-proprietary standard." *Id.* n. 2. One Commissioner, writing in dissent, conceded that "[i]f Dell had obtained market power by knowingly or intentionally misleading a standards-setting organization, it would require no stretch of established monopolization theory to condemn that conduct." *Id.* at 629. She objected, nevertheless, to imposing antitrust liability on Dell absent specific allegations in the proposed complaint that Dell misled the SDO intentionally or knowingly, and that it obtained market power as a result of its misleading statements. *Id.* at 629–30.

In 2005, the FTC entered into a consent order resolving allegations that Union Oil Company of California ("Unocal") made deceptive and bad-faith misrepresentations to a state standards-determining board concerning the status of Unocal's IPRs. The administrative complaint had alleged that the board relied on these misrepresentations in promulgating new standards governing low-emissions gasoline, and that Unocal's misrepresentations led directly to its acquisition of monopoly power and harmed competition after refiners became locked in to regulations that required the use of Unocal's proprietary technology. Unocal's anticompetitive conduct was alleged to have violated § 5 of the FTC Act. The consent order required Unocal, among other things, to cease and desist from all efforts to enforce its relevant patents. In the Matter of Union Oil Co. of Cal., No. 9305 (F.T.C. July 27, 2005), available at 2005 WL 2003365.

Most recently, a landmark, 120-page opinion in In the Matter of Rambus, Inc., was entered on the docket on August 2, 2006 by a unanimous FTC. Rambus, a developer of computer memory technologies, was found to have deceived an SDO by failing to disclose its IPRs in technology that was essential to the implementation of now-ubiquitous computer memory standards, by misleading other members of the SDO into believing that Rambus was not seeking any new patents relevant to the standard then under consideration, and by using information that it gained from its participation in the standard-setting process to amend its pending patent applications so that they would cover the ultimate standard. *Id.* at 3, 4. Noting that such conduct "has grave implications for competition," *id.* at 3, the FTC found that Rambus had distorted the standard-setting process and engaged in anticompetitive hold-up. For the first time, the FTC held that deceptive conduct of the type alleged in Dell Computer and Union Oil constituted "exclusionary conduct" under § 2 of the Sherman Act, as well as unlawful monopolization under § 5 of the FTC Act. *Id.* at 3.[5]

---

[5] In related litigation before the U.S. District Court for the Eastern District of Virginia, the Court observed of Rambus's conduct that

> even if the SSO [i.e., standard-setting organization] itself is not corrupt, the subversion of an SSO by a single industry player or by a limited subset of SSO members can result in anticompetitive outcomes. Thus, antitrust law historically has been concerned with the risk of one or a small number of participants

Rambus is particularly noteworthy for its extensive discussion of deceptive conduct in the standard-setting context and the factors that make such conduct anticompetitive under § 2 of the Sherman Act. The FTC likened the deception of an SDO to the type of deceptive conduct that the D.C. Circuit found to violate § 2 of the Sherman Act in Microsoft. There, the Court found that Microsoft had marketed software-development tools that would permit software developers to create programs that, ostensibly, did not need to run on Microsoft's ubiquitous operating system, but that, in fact, could operate properly only on Microsoft's operating system. The Court found that in an environment in which software developers reasonably expected Microsoft not to mislead them, Microsoft's deceptive conduct was anticompetitive. *Microsoft*, 253 F.3d at 76–77. Analogizing to Microsoft, the FTC found that Rambus's deception occurred in an environment-the standard-setting process-in which participants "expected each other to act cooperatively." [citation omitted]

The FTC discussed at length the unique dangers of deception in the standard-setting context. Private standard setting occurs in a consensus-oriented environment, where participants rely on structural protections, such as rules requiring the disclosure of IPRs, to facilitate competition and constrain the exercise of monopoly power. In such an environment, participants are less likely to be wary of deception and may not detect such conduct and take measures to counteract it until after lock-in has occurred. At that point, the resulting harm to competition may be very difficult to correct. [citation omitted]

These decisions reflect a growing awareness of the risks associated with deceptive conduct in the private standard-setting process. ***

b. FRAND Commitments

Against this backdrop, we must determine whether Broadcom has stated actionable anticompetitive conduct with allegations that Qualcomm deceived relevant SDOs into adopting the UMTS standard by committing to license its WCDMA technology on FRAND terms and, later, after lock-in occurred, demanding non-FRAND royalties. As Qualcomm is at pains to point out, no court nor agency has decided this precise question and, in that sense, our decision will break new ground. The authorities we have cited in our lengthy discussion that has preceded this point, however, decidedly favor a finding that Broadcom's allegations, if accepted as true, describe actionable anticompetitive conduct.

To guard against anticompetitive patent hold-up, most SDOs require firms supplying essential technologies for inclusion in a prospective standard to commit to licensing their technologies on FRAND terms. (E.g., IEEE Br. 9 & n. 13 (stating that under IEEE bylaws, the absence of irrevocable FRAND assurances will

---

capturing the economic power of an industry-wide standard and turning the SSO into a source of exclusionary power. Simply put, by hijacking or capturing an SSO, a single industry player can magnify its power and effectuate anticompetitive effects on the market in question.

Rambus, Inc. v. Infineon Techs. AG, 330 F.Supp.2d 679, 696-97 (E.D.Va.2004).

preclude approval of standards known to incorporate essential, proprietary technologies).) A firm's FRAND commitment, therefore, is a factor—and an important factor—that the SDO will consider in evaluating the suitability of a given proprietary technology vis-a-vis competing technologies. [citation omitted]

The FRAND commitment, or lack thereof, is, moreover, a key indicator of the cost of implementing a potential technology. *See Rambus*, No. 9302, at 4 (noting that FRAND commitments "may further inform [SDO] members' analysis of the costs and benefits of standardizing patented technologies"); *see also* id. at 35 (noting that predisclosure of IPRs enables SDO participants "to make their choices with more complete knowledge of the consequences"); *cf. F.T.C. v. Indiana Fed'n of Dentists*, 476 U.S. 447, 461–62 (1986) (noting that efforts to obscure "information desired by consumers for the purpose of determining whether a particular purchase is cost justified is likely enough to disrupt the proper functioning of the price-setting mechanism of the market that it may be condemned" under antitrust law). During the critical competitive period that precedes adoption of a standard [citation omitted], technologies compete in discrete areas, such as cost and performance characteristics (id. 12 n. 8). Misrepresentations concerning the cost of implementing a given technology may confer an unfair advantage and bias the competitive process in favor of that technology's inclusion in the standard. [citation omitted]

A standard, by definition, eliminates alternative technologies. *See Hydrolevel*, 456 U.S. at 559 ("Obviously, if a manufacturer's product cannot satisfy the applicable [standard], it is at a great disadvantage in the marketplace."). When a patented technology is incorporated in a standard, adoption of the standard eliminates alternatives to the patented technology. Although a patent confers a lawful monopoly over the claimed invention, [citation omitted], its value is limited when alternative technologies exist. [citation omitted] That value becomes significantly enhanced, however, after the patent is incorporated in a standard. [citation omitted] Firms may become locked in to a standard requiring the use of a competitor's patented technology. The patent holder's IPRs, if unconstrained, may permit it to demand supracompetitive royalties. It is in such circumstances that measures such as FRAND commitments become important safeguards against monopoly power. [citation omitted]

We hold that (1) in a consensus-oriented private standard-setting environment, (2) a patent holder's intentionally false promise to license essential proprietary technology on FRAND terms, (3) coupled with an SDO's reliance on that promise when including the technology in a standard, and (4) the patent holder's subsequent breach of that promise, is actionable anticompetitive conduct. This holding follows directly from established principles of antitrust law and represents the emerging view of enforcement authorities and commentators, alike. Deception in a consensus-driven private standard-setting environment harms the competitive process by obscuring the costs of including proprietary technology in a standard and increasing the likelihood that patent rights will confer monopoly power on the patent holder. *See Rambus*, No. 9302, at 68 (holding that "distorting [the SDO's] technology choices and undermining [SDO] members' ability to protect themselves against patent hold-up . . . caused harm to competition"). Deceptive FRAND commitments, no less than deceptive nondisclosure of IPRs, may result in such harm. See id. at 66 (noting that SDO's rules requiring members to disclose IPRs and commit to FRAND licensing "presented the type of consensus-oriented environment in which deception is most likely to contribute to competitive harm").[8]

3. Claim 1 States a Claim for Monopolization of WCDMA Technology Markets

The District Court's only stated reason for dismissing Broadcom's Claim 1 was that it did not plead an antitrust cause of action. Having now held that a firm's deceptive FRAND commitment to an SDO may constitute actionable anticompetitive conduct, we conclude quickly and easily that Claim 1 states a claim for monopolization under § 2 of the Sherman Act.

First, the Complaint adequately alleged that Qualcomm possessed monopoly power in the relevant market. The Complaint defined the relevant market as the market for Qualcomm's proprietary WCDMA technology, a technology essential to the implementation of the UMTS standard. [citation omitted] This technology was not interchangeable with or substitutable for other technologies [citation omitted], and adherents to the UMTS standard have become locked in [citation omitted]. With respect to monopoly power, Qualcomm had the power to extract supracompetitive prices [citation omitted], it possessed a dominant market share [citation omitted], and the market had entry barriers [citation omitted]. These allegations satisfied the first element of a § 2 monopolization claim.

Qualcomm objects to a relevant market definition that is congruent with the scope of its WCDMA patents, arguing that such a definition would result in every patent holder being condemned as a monopolist. This objection misconstrues Broadcom's theory. It is the incorporation of a patent into a standard—not the mere issuance of a patent—that makes the scope of the relevant market congruent with that of the patent.

Second, the Complaint also adequately alleged that Qualcomm obtained and maintained its market power willfully, and not as a consequence of a superior product, business acumen, or historic accident. Qualcomm excluded competition [citation omitted] and refused to compete on the merits [citation omitted]. As discussed above, the alleged anticompetitive conduct was the intentional

---

[8] We are unpersuaded by Qualcomm's argument that antitrust liability cannot turn on so vague a concept as whether licensing terms are "reasonable," although, in other contexts, we have summarily dismissed claims that turn on similarly ambiguous terms, see Lum, 361 F.3d at 226. The reasonableness of royalties is an inquiry that courts routinely undertake using the 15-factor test set forth in Georgia-Pacific Corp. v. United States Plywood Corp., 318 F.Supp. 1116, 1120 (S.D.N.Y.1970), and some courts have already applied this test in the FRAND context, see, e.g., ESS Tech., Inc. v. PC-Tel, Inc., No. C-99-20292 RMW, 2001 WL 1891713, at *3–6 (N.D.Cal. Nov.28, 2001); see also Rambus, No. 9302, at 114–15 (finding substantial evidence that Rambus's royalty rates were not reasonable). Their success persuades us that, given a fully-developed factual record, the same can be done here.

[citation omitted] false promise [citation omitted] that Qualcomm would license its WCDMA technology on FRAND terms, on which promise the relevant SDOs relied in choosing the WCDMA technology for inclusion in the UMTS standard [citation omitted], followed by Qualcomm's insistence on non-FRAND licensing terms [citation omitted]. Qualcomm's deceptive conduct induced [citation omitted] relevant SDOs to incorporate a technology into the UMTS standard that they would not have considered absent a FRAND commitment. [citation omitted] Although the Complaint did not specifically allege that Qualcomm made its false statements in a consensus-oriented environment of the type discussed in Microsoft and Rambus, this omission is not fatal in light of allegations that FRAND assurances were required [citation omitted, as well as allegations concerning the SDOs' reliance on Qualcomm's assurances (citation omitted)]. Together, these allegations satisfy the second element of a § 2 claim.

Qualcomm makes much of the Complaint's failure to allege that there were viable technologies competing with WCDMA for inclusion in the UMTS standard. [citation omitted] As Qualcomm concedes, however, the Complaint does allege that an SDO's adoption of a standard eliminates competing technologies. [citation omitted] The District Court also inferred that the relevant SDOs selected Qualcomm's WCDMA technology "to the detriment of those patent-holders competing to have their patents incorporated into the standard." [citation omitted] This inference was reasonable, particularly because even if Qualcomm's WCDMA technology was the only candidate for inclusion in the standard, it still would not have been selected by the relevant SDOs absent a FRAND commitment. [citation omitted] Thus, the allegations of the Complaint foreclose the possibility that WCDMA's inclusion in the standard was inevitable. ***

Comments and Questions

1. The Broadcom court stated: "It is the incorporation of a patent into a standard—not the mere issuance of a patent—that makes the scope of the relevant market congruent with that of the patent." Is that necessarily true?

2. Absent a FRAND promise, an IP owner could demand excessive royalties or impose onerous terms and conditions after its IP is incorporated into a widely adopted standard. This is generally referred to as patent holdup. The DOJ and FTC articulated the holdup phenomenon and its attendant risks as follows:

> The hold-up problem pertains to problems of relationship-specific investment, whereas the hold up contemplated here pertains to standards-specific investment. The hold-up problem indicates the prospect of under-investment in collaborations in which parties must sink investments that are specific to the collaboration, investments that may be costly to redeploy or have a significantly lower value if redeployed outside of the collaboration. The potential for one party to hold up another party that has sunk investments specific to the relationship may discourage that other party from investing efficiently in the collaboration in the first place. [citation omitted] In the standard-setting context, firms may make

274 Antitrust Law and Intellectual Property Rights

sunk investments in developing and implementing a standard that are specific to particular intellectual property. To the extent that these investments are not redeployable using other IP, those developing and using the standard may be held up by the IP holders. [citation omitted] Moreover, this hold up may cause firms to sink less investment in developing and implementing standards.

U.S. Dep't of Justice & Federal Trade Commission, Antitrust Enforcement and Intellectual Property Rights: Promoting Innovation and Competition 35 n.11 (2007).

SSOs require FRAND commitments in order to prevent patentees from charging excessive royalties or using its control over standard to restrict competition in the downstream market.

3. Despite the promise of FRAND commitments, there is often no accepted standard of what constitutes a FRAND royalty in most industries. It is unclear what "reasonable" is. Who decides? It is also unclear what "non-discriminatory" is. Does non-discriminatory mean that every licensee must be given the same terms, or that like licensees must be treated alike?

How does this ambiguity create an opportunity for holdup?

One way to solve the problem of ambiguous RAND commitments would be for SSO to negotiate the actual terms of licenses for IP incorporated into a standard. This raises antitrust issues under Section One since SSOs—who are generally competitors at some level—are jointly setting the price that they will pay for an important input. Some SSOs require royalty-free licenses. These issues are discussed in Chapter 9, which addresses the antitrust implications of agreements among SSO members.

4. What legal test does the Third Circuit present, for when deception before an SSO constitutes monopoly conduct?

Do you think that the legal test can be administered consistently?

Does the Broadcom opinion mean that Section Two liability is created whenever a patentee deceives an SSO by concealing its IP or breaching a FRAND commitment?

Rambus, Inc. v. FTC,
522 F.3d 456 (D.C. Cir. 2008)

Williams, Senior Circuit Judge:

Rambus Inc. develops computer memory technologies, secures intellectual property rights over them, and then licenses them to manufacturers in exchange for royalty payments. In 1990, Rambus's founders filed a patent application claiming the invention of a faster architecture for dynamic random access memory ("DRAM"). In recent years, Rambus has asserted that patents issued to protect its invention cover four technologies that a private standard-setting organization ("SSO") included in DRAM industry standards.

Before an SSO adopts a standard, there is often vigorous competition among different technologies for incorporation into that standard. After standardization, however, the dynamic typically shifts, as industry members begin adhering to the standard and the standardized features start to dominate. In this case, 90% of DRAM production is compliant with the standards at issue, and therefore the technologies adopted in those standards-including those over which Rambus claims patent rights-enjoy a similar level of dominance over their alternatives.

After lengthy proceedings, the Federal Trade Commission determined that Rambus, while participating in the standard-setting process, deceptively failed to disclose to the SSO the patent interests it held in four technologies that were standardized. Those interests ranged from issued patents, to pending patent applications, to plans to amend those patent applications to add new claims; Rambus's patent rights in all these interests are said to be sufficiently connected to the invention described in Rambus's original 1990 application that its rights would relate back to its date. [citation omitted] Finding this conduct monopolistic and in violation of § 2 of the Sherman Act, [citation omitted] the Commission went on to hold that Rambus had engaged in an unfair method of competition and unfair or deceptive acts or practices prohibited by § 5(a) of the Federal Trade Commission Act ("FTC Act") [citation omitted].

Rambus petitions for review. We grant the petition, holding that the Commission failed to sustain its allegation of monopolization. Its factual conclusion was that Rambus's alleged deception enabled it either to acquire a monopoly through the standardization of its patented technologies rather than possible alternatives, or to avoid limits on its patent licensing fees that the SSO would have imposed as part of its normal process of standardizing patented technologies. But the latter—deceit merely enabling a monopolist to charge higher prices than it otherwise could have charged—would not in itself constitute monopolization. ***

* * *

During the early 1990s, the computer hardware industry faced a "memory bottleneck": the development of faster memory lagged behind the development of faster central processing units, and this risked limiting future gains in overall computer performance. To address this problem, Michael Farmwald and Mark Horowitz began collaborating during the late 1980s and invented a higher-performance DRAM architecture. Together, they founded Rambus in March 1990 and filed Patent Application No. 07/510,898 ("the 898 application") on April 18, 1990. ***

While Rambus was developing a patent portfolio based on its founders' inventions, the computer memory industry was at work standardizing DRAM technologies. The locus of those efforts was the Joint Electron Device Engineering Council ("JEDEC") ***. Any company involved in the solid state products industry could join JEDEC by submitting an application and paying annual dues, and members could receive JEDEC mailings, participate in JEDEC committees, and vote on pending matters.

One JEDEC committee, JC 42.3, developed standards for computer memory products. Rambus attended its first JC 42.3 meeting as a guest in December 1991 and began formally participating when it joined JEDEC in February 1992. At the time,

276 *Antitrust Law and Intellectual Property Rights*

JC 42.3 was at work on what became JEDEC's synchronous DRAM ("SDRAM") standard. The committee voted to approve the completed standard in March 1993, and JEDEC's governing body gave its final approval on May 24, 1993. The SDRAM standard includes two of the four technologies over which Rambus asserts patent rights—programmable CAS latency and programmable burst length.

Despite SDRAM's standardization, its manufacture increased very slowly and asynchronous DRAM continued to dominate the computer memory market, so JC 42.3 began to consider a number of possible responses—among them specifications it could include in a next-generation SDRAM standard. As part of that process, JC 42.3 members received a survey ballot in October 1995 soliciting their opinions on features of an advanced SDRAM—which ultimately emerged as the double data rate ("DDR") SDRAM standard. Among the features voted on were the other two technologies at issue here: on-chip phase lock and delay lock loops ("on-chip PLL/DLL") and dual-edge clocking. The Committee tallied and discussed the survey results at its December 1995 meeting, which was Rambus's last as a JEDEC member. Rambus formally withdrew from JEDEC by letter dated June 17, 1996, saying (among other things) that the terms on which it proposed to license its proprietary technology "may not be consistent with the terms set by standards bodies, including JEDEC." [citation omitted]

JC 42.3's work continued after Rambus's departure. In March 1998 the committee adopted the DDR SDRAM standard, and the JEDEC Board of Directors approved it in 1999. This standard retained SDRAM features including programmable CAS latency and programmable burst length, and it added on-chip PLL/DLL and dual-edge clocking; DDR SDRAM, therefore, included all four of the technologies at issue here.

Starting in 1999, Rambus informed major DRAM and chipset manufacturers that it held patent rights over technologies included in JEDEC's SDRAM and DDR SDRAM standards, and that the continued manufacture, sale, or use of products compliant with those standards infringed its rights. It invited the manufacturers to resolve the alleged infringement through licensing negotiations. A number of manufacturers agreed to licenses, [citation omitted]; others did not, and litigation ensued [citation omitted].

On June 18, 2002, the Federal Trade Commission filed a complaint under § 5(b) of the FTC Act, 15 U.S.C. § 45(b) charging that Rambus engaged in unfair methods of competition and unfair or deceptive acts or practices in violation of the Act, *see id.* § 45(a). Specifically, the Commission alleged that Rambus breached JEDEC policies requiring it to disclose patent interests related to standardization efforts and that the disclosures it did make were misleading. By this deceptive conduct, it said, Rambus unlawfully monopolized four technology markets in which its patented technologies compete with alternative innovations to address technical issues relating to DRAM design-markets for latency, burst length, data acceleration, and clock synchronization technologies. [citation omitted]

Proceedings began before an administrative law judge, who in due course dismissed the Complaint in its entirety. [citation omitted] He concluded that Rambus did not impermissibly withhold material information about its intellectual property, [citation omitted] and that, in any event, there was insufficient evidence that, if Rambus had disclosed all the information allegedly required of it, JEDEC would have standardized an alternative technology [citation omitted].

Complaint Counsel appealed the ALJ's Initial Decision to the Commission, which reopened the record to receive additional evidence and did its own plenary review. [citation omitted] On July 31, 2006 the Commission vacated the ALJ's decision and set aside his findings of fact and conclusions of law. [citation omitted] The Commission found that while JEDEC's patent disclosure policies were "not a model of clarity," [citation omitted] members expected one another to disclose patents and patent applications that were relevant to technologies being considered for standardization, plus (though the Commission was far less clear on these latter items) planned amendments to pending applications or "anything they're working on that they potentially wanted to protect with patents down the road," [citation omitted] Based on this interpretation of JEDEC's disclosure requirements, the Commission held that Rambus willfully and intentionally engaged in misrepresentations, omissions, and other practices that misled JEDEC members about intellectual property information "highly material" to the standard-setting process. [citation omitted]

The Commission focused entirely on the allegation of monopolization. [citation omitted] In particular, the Commission held that the evidence and inferences from Rambus's purpose demonstrated that "but for Rambus's deceptive course of conduct, JEDEC either would have excluded Rambus's patented technologies from the JEDEC DRAM standards, or would have demanded RAND assurances [i.e., assurances of "reasonable and nondiscriminatory" license fees], with an opportunity for ex ante licensing negotiations." [citation omitted] Rejecting Rambus's argument that factors other than JEDEC's standards allowed Rambus's technologies to dominate their respective markets, [citation omitted] the Commission concluded that Rambus's deception of JEDEC "significantly contributed to its acquisition of monopoly power," [citation omitted].

After additional briefing by the parties, [citation omitted] the Commission rendered a separate remedial opinion and final order. [citation omitted] It held that it had the authority in principle to order compulsory licensing, but that remedies beyond injunctions against future anticompetitive conduct would require stronger proof that they were necessary to restore competitive conditions. [citation omitted] Applying that more demanding burden to Complaint Counsel's claims for relief, the Commission refused to compel Rambus to license its relevant patents royalty-free because there was insufficient evidence that "absent Rambus's deception" JEDEC would have standardized non-proprietary technologies instead of Rambus's; thus, Complaint Counsel had failed to show that such a remedy was "necessary to restore competition that would have existed in the 'but for' world." [citation omitted] Instead, the Commission decided to compel licensing at "reasonable royalty rates," which it calculated based on what it believed would have resulted from negotiations between Rambus and manufacturers before JEDEC committed to the standards. [citation omitted] The Commission's order limits Rambus's royalties for three years to 0.25% for JEDEC-compliant SDRAM and 0.5% for JEDEC-compliant DDR SDRAM (with double those royalties for certain JEDEC-compliant, non-DRAM products); after those three years, it forbids any royalty collection. [citation omitted]

*** Rambus timely petitioned ***. Rambus challenges the Commission's determination that it engaged in unlawful monopolization—and thereby violated § 5 of the FTC Act—on a variety of grounds, of which two are most prominent. First, it argues that the Commission erred in finding that it violated any JEDEC patent disclosure rules and thus that it breached any antitrust duty to provide information to its rivals. Second, it asserts that even if its nondisclosure contravened JEDEC's policies, the Commission found the consequences of such nondisclosure only in the alternative: that it prevented JEDEC either from adopting a non-proprietary standard, or from extracting a RAND commitment from Rambus when standardizing its technology. As the latter would not involve an antitrust violation, says Rambus, there is an insufficient basis for liability.

We find the second of these arguments to be persuasive, and conclude that the Commission failed to demonstrate that Rambus's conduct was exclusionary under settled principles of antitrust law. Given that conclusion, we need not dwell very long on the substantiality of the evidence, which we address only to express our serious concerns about the breadth the Commission ascribed to JEDEC's disclosure policies and their relation to what Rambus did or did not disclose.

* * *

In this case under § 5 of the FTC Act, the Commission expressly limited its theory of liability to Rambus's unlawful monopolization of four markets in violation of § 2 of the Sherman Act. [citation omitted] Therefore, we apply principles of antitrust law developed under the Sherman Act, and we review the Commission's construction and application of the antitrust laws de novo. [citation omitted]

It is settled law that the mere existence of a monopoly does not violate the Sherman Act. [citation omitted] In addition to "the possession of monopoly power in the relevant market," the offense of monopolization requires "'the willful acquisition or maintenance of that power as distinguished from growth or development as a consequence of a superior product, business acumen, or historical accident.'" [citation omitted] In this case, Rambus does not dispute the nature of the relevant markets or that its patent rights in the four relevant technologies give it monopoly power in each of those markets. [citation omitted] The critical question is whether Rambus engaged in exclusionary conduct, and thereby acquired its monopoly power in the relevant markets unlawfully.

To answer that question, we adhere to two antitrust principles that guided us in *Microsoft*. First, "to be condemned as exclusionary, a monopolist's act must have 'anticompetitive effect.' That is, it must harm the competitive process and thereby harm consumers. In contrast, harm to one or more competitors will not suffice." *Microsoft*, 253 F.3d at 58; [citation omitted] Second, it is the antitrust plaintiff—including the Government as plaintiff—that bears the burden of proving the anticompetitive effect of the monopolist's conduct. *Microsoft*, 253 F.3d at 58–59.

The Commission held that Rambus engaged in exclusionary conduct consisting of misrepresentations, omissions, and other practices that deceived JEDEC about the nature and scope of its patent interests while the organization standardized technologies covered by those interests. [citation omitted] Had Rambus fully disclosed its intellectual property, "JEDEC either would have excluded Rambus's patented technologies from the JEDEC DRAM standards, or would have demanded RAND assurances, with an opportunity for ex ante licensing negotiations." [citation omitted] But the Commission did not determine that one or the other of these two possible outcomes was the more likely. [citation omitted] The Commission's conclusion that Rambus's conduct was exclusionary depends, therefore, on a syllogism: Rambus avoided one of two outcomes by not disclosing its patent interests; the avoidance of either of those outcomes was anticompetitive; therefore Rambus's nondisclosure was anticompetitive.

We assume without deciding that avoidance of the first of these possible outcomes was indeed anticompetitive; that is, that if Rambus's more complete disclosure would have caused JEDEC to adopt a different (open, non-proprietary) standard, then its failure to disclose harmed competition and would support a monopolization claim. But while we can assume that Rambus's nondisclosure made the adoption of its technologies somewhat more likely than broad disclosure would have, the Commission made clear in its remedial opinion that there was insufficient evidence that JEDEC would have standardized other technologies had it known the full scope of Rambus's intellectual property. [citation omitted] Therefore, for the Commission's syllogism to survive—and for the Commission to have carried its burden of proving that Rambus's conduct had an anticompetitive effect—we must also be convinced that if Rambus's conduct merely enabled it to avoid the other possible outcome, namely JEDEC's obtaining assurances from Rambus of RAND licensing terms, such conduct, alone, could be said to harm competition. [citation omitted] We are not convinced.

Deceptive conduct—like any other kind—must have an anticompetitive effect in order to form the basis of a monopolization claim. "Even an act of pure malice by one business competitor against another does not, without more, state a claim under the federal antitrust laws," without proof of "a dangerous probability that [the defendant] would monopolize a particular market." *Brooke Group*, 509 U.S. at 225. Even if deception raises the price secured by a seller, but does so without harming competition, it is beyond the antitrust laws' reach. Cases that recognize deception as exclusionary hinge, therefore, on whether the conduct impaired rivals in a manner tending to bring about or protect a defendant's monopoly power. In *Microsoft*, for example, we found Microsoft engaged in anticompetitive conduct when it tricked independent software developers into believing that its software development tools could be used to design cross-platform Java applications when, in fact, they produced Windows-specific ones. The deceit had caused "developers who were opting for portability over performance . . . unwittingly [to write] Java applications that [ran] only on Windows." 253 F.3d at 76. The focus of our antitrust scrutiny, therefore, was properly placed on the resulting harms to competition rather than the deception itself.

Another case of deception with an anticompetitive dimension is *Conwood Co. v. U.S. Tobacco Co.*, 290 F.3d 768 (6th Cir.2001), where the Sixth Circuit found that U.S. Tobacco's dominance of the moist snuff market caused retailers to rely on it as a "category manager" that would provide trusted guidance on the sales strategy and in-store display for all moist snuff products [citation omitted]. Under those circumstances, the court held that its misrepresentations to retailers about the sales strength of its products versus its competitors' strength reduced competition in the monopolized market by increasing the display space devoted to U.S. Tobacco's products and decreasing that allotted to competing products. [citation omitted]

But an otherwise lawful monopolist's use of deception simply to obtain higher prices normally has no particular tendency to exclude rivals and thus to diminish competition. Consider, for example, *NYNEX Corp. v. Discon, Inc.*, 525 U.S. 128 (1998), in which the Court addressed the antitrust implications of allegations that NYNEX's subsidiary, New York Telephone Company, a lawful monopoly provider of local telephone services, charged its customers higher prices as result of fraudulent conduct in the market for the service of removing outdated telephone switching equipment (called "removal services"). Discon had alleged that New York Telephone (through its corporate affiliate, Materiel Enterprises) switched its purchases of removal services from Discon to a higher-priced independent firm (AT & T Technologies). Materiel Enterprises would pass the higher fees on to New York Telephone, which in turn passed them on to customers through higher rates approved by regulators. [citation omitted] The nub of the deception, Discon alleged, was that AT & T Technologies would provide Materiel Enterprises with a special rebate at year's end, which it would then share with NYNEX. *Id.* By thus hoodwinking the regulators, the scam raised prices for consumers; Discon, which refused to play the rebate game, was driven out of business. Discon alleged that this arrangement was anticompetitive and constituted both an agreement in restraint of trade in violation of § 1 of the Sherman Act and a conspiracy to monopolize the market for removal services in violation of § 2. [citation omitted]

As to Discon's § 1 claim, the Court held that where a single buyer favors one supplier over another for an improper reason, the plaintiff must "allege and prove harm, not just to a single competitor, but to the competitive process." [citation omitted] Nor, as Justice Breyer wrote for a unanimous Court, would harm to the consumers in the form of higher prices change the matter: "We concede Discon's claim that the [defendants'] behavior hurt consumers by raising telephone service rates. But that consumer injury naturally flowed not so much from a less competitive market for removal services, as from the exercise of market power that is lawfully in the hands of a monopolist, namely, New York Telephone, combined with a deception worked upon the regulatory agency that prevented the agency from controlling New York Telephone's exercise of its monopoly power." [citation omitted]

Because Discon based its § 2 claim on the very same allegations of fraud, the Court vacated the appellate court's decision to uphold that claim because "[u]nless those agreements harmed the competitive process, they did not amount to a conspiracy to monopolize." [citation omitted] Commission's brief doesn't mention NYNEX, much less try to distinguish it, it does cite *Broadcom Corp. v. Qualcomm Inc.*, 501 F.3d 297 (3d Cir. 2007), which in turn had cited the Commission's own "landmark" decision in the case under review here. [citation omitted] There the court held that a patent holder's intentionally false promise to a standard-setting organization that it would license its technology on RAND terms, "coupled with [the organization's] reliance on that promise when including the technology in a standard," was anticompetitive conduct, on the ground that it increased "the likelihood that patent rights will confer monopoly power on the patent holder." [citation omitted] To the extent that the ruling (which simply reversed a grant of dismissal) rested on the argument that deceit lured the SSO away from non-proprietary technology, [citation omitted] it cannot help the Commission in view of its inability to find that Rambus's behavior caused JEDEC's choice; to the extent that it may have rested on a supposition that there is a cognizable violation of the Sherman Act when a lawful monopolist's deceit has the effect of raising prices (without an effect on competitive structure), it conflicts with NYNEX.

Here, the Commission expressly left open the likelihood that JEDEC would have standardized Rambus's technologies even if Rambus had disclosed its intellectual property. Under this hypothesis, JEDEC lost only an opportunity to secure a RAND commitment from Rambus. But loss of such a commitment is not a harm to competition from alternative technologies in the relevant markets. See 2 Hovenkamp et al., IP & Antitrust § 35.5 at 35–45 (Supp.2008) [hereinafter "IP & Antitrust"] ("[A]n antitrust plaintiff must establish that the standard-setting organization would not have adopted the standard in question but for the misrepresentation or omission."). Indeed, had JEDEC limited Rambus to reasonable royalties and required it to provide licenses on a nondiscriminatory basis, we would expect less competition from alternative technologies, not more; high prices and constrained output tend to attract competitors, not to repel them.

Scholars in the field have urged that if nondisclosure to an SSO enables a participant to obtain higher royalties than would otherwise have been attainable, the "overcharge can properly constitute competitive harm attributable to the nondisclosure," as the overcharge "will distort competition in the downstream market." 2 IP & Antitrust § 35.5 at 35–47. The contention that price-raising deception has downstream effects is surely correct, but that consequence was equally surely true in NYNEX (though perhaps on a smaller scale) and equally obvious to the Court. The Commission makes the related contention that because the ability to profitably restrict output and set supracompetitive prices is the sine qua non of monopoly power, any conduct that permits a monopolist to avoid constraints on the exercise of that power must be anticompetitive. But again, as in NYNEX, an otherwise lawful monopolist's end-run around price constraints, even when deceptive or fraudulent, does not alone present a harm to competition in the monopolized market.

Thus, if JEDEC, in the world that would have existed but for Rambus's deception, would have standardized the very same technologies, Rambus's alleged deception cannot be said to have had an effect on competition in violation of the antitrust laws; JEDEC's loss of an opportunity to seek favorable licensing terms is not as such an antitrust harm. Yet the Commission did not reject this as being a possible—perhaps even the more probable—effect of Rambus's conduct. We hold, therefore, that the Commission failed to demonstrate that Rambus's conduct was exclusionary, and thus to establish its claim that Rambus unlawfully monopolized the relevant markets. ***

We set aside the Commission's orders and remand for further proceedings consistent with this opinion.

Comments and Questions

1. The D.C. Circuit noted that the FTC "refused to compel Rambus to license its relevant patents royalty-free because there was insufficient evidence that 'absent Rambus's deception' JEDEC would have standardized non-proprietary technologies instead of Rambus's." Instead, the FTC ordered Rambus to license its patents at "reasonable royalty rates." Did the FTC impose different evidentiary standards for liability and remedy? Assuming that the FTC was correct on the liability issue, do you agree with the FTC's approach to remedies?

2. The FTC assumed, without deciding, that "if Rambus's more complete disclosure would have caused JEDEC to adopt a different (open, non-proprietary) standard, then its failure to disclose harmed competition and would support a monopolization claim." Should this create liability?

How should courts address the issue of causation? In other words, how can an antitrust plaintiff prove the "but-for world" of what the SSO would have done but for the patentee concealing its IP?

What legal advice would you give an SSO that was in the process of adopting a standard?

3. The D.C. Circuit discusses and relies upon the Supreme Court decision in *NYNEX*. Are *NYNEX* and *Rambus* distinguishable? The court refers to NYNEX as "an otherwise lawful monopolist." Is Rambus "an otherwise lawful monopolist"?

4. While disclosure requirements may seem reasonable in the abstract, some people argue that SSO disclosure standards can be difficult to interpret and comply with. Should federal law standardize disclosure requirements?

Should antitrust law impose disclosure requirements separate from the disclosure requirements adopted by the particular SSO?

5. Many—if not most—SSOs have tried to address the risk of holdup by adopting policies that "fall, broadly speaking, into two nonexclusive categories: disclosure rules and licensing rules. Disclosure rules require SSO participants to disclose patents (and, sometimes, patent applications and other intellectual property or confidential information) related to a standard under consideration. Licensing rules restrict the terms that holders of such intellectual property can demand.

The most common licensing rule requires that IP holders license to users of the standard on RAND terms." U.S. Dep't of Justice & Federal Trade Commission, Antitrust Enforcement and Intellectual Property Rights: Promoting Innovation and Competition 42 (2007).

Which approach was used in Broadcom and in Rambus?

Which is the better approach to address the problem of holdups? Why?

What are the advantages and disadvantages of disclosure rules versus licensing rules?

6. The Federal Trade Commission took a different view of Rambus' conduct—both with respect to emphasizing particular actions by Rambus and the legal consequences of those actions—than did the D.C. Circuit. Federal Trade Commission, In the Matter of Rambus, Inc., 2006-2 Trade Cases P 75364, (2006). In its lengthy opinion, the Commission noted the following:

> JEDEC's policies expressly required those disclosing relevant patents or patent applications to supply full technical information and to provide RAND assurances (i.e., that royalties on patents covering any standard would be reasonable and non-discriminatory) before their patents were incorporated into JEDEC standards. *** Rambus's own documents and witnesses indicate that the company believed it should have disclosed its patent filings.
>
> Rambus, however, chose to disregard JEDEC's policy and practice, as well as the duty to act in good faith. Instead, Rambus deceived the other JEDEC members. Rambus capitalized on JEDEC's policy and practice—and also on the expectations of the JEDEC members—in several ways. Rambus refused to disclose the existence of its patents and applications, which deprived JEDEC members of critical information as they worked to evaluate potential standards. Rambus took additional actions that misled members to believe that Rambus was not seeking patents that would cover implementations of the standards under consideration by JEDEC. Rambus also went a step further: through its participation in JEDEC, Rambus gained information about the pending standard, and then amended its patent applications to ensure that subsequently-issued patents would cover the ultimate standard. Through its successful strategy, Rambus was able to conceal its patents and patent applications until after the standards were adopted and the market was locked in. Only then did Rambus reveal its patents—through patent infringement lawsuits against JEDEC members who practiced the standard.
>
> On June 17, 1996, Rambus sent a letter to JEDEC, signed by Crisp, stating that Rambus was not renewing its membership. Rambus enclosed "a list of Rambus U.S. and foreign patents" and stated that "Rambus has also applied for a number of additional patents in order to protect Rambus technology." The letter emphasized that "Rambus reserves all rights regarding its intellectual property." Rambus omitted from the list that it provided to JEDEC the only then-issued patent that Rambus believed covered technology under consideration by JEDEC - the '327 patent. Rambus's June 1996 withdrawal letter also omitted information that would have allowed JEDEC members to adopt standards that would avoid infringing Rambus's intellectual property. ***

Although Rambus terminated its JEDEC membership in 1996, Rambus continued to receive information on the activities of JEDEC after 1996. Beginning in 1997, Crisp received information from a source that he referred to as "deep throat." Crisp also received information from three other unsolicited sources known as "Mixmaster," a reporter called "Carroll Contact," and "secret squirrel." According to Crisp, these sources provided information on the features of devices being proposed for standardization. Crisp shared the information he obtained from these inside sources with Rambus's executives and engineers, and this information was used in the continuing process of filing and amending Rambus's patent applications.

Additionally, although no longer a JEDEC member, Rambus continued to conceal its relevant patent applications. Rambus CEO Tate, for example, stated in a February 1997 e-mail to Rambus executives, "do *NOT* tell customers/partners that we feel DDR may infringe—our leverage is better to wait." *** And in its October 1998 "strategy update," Rambus stated, "We should not assert patents against Direct partners until ramp reaches a point of no return." In sum, after leaving JEDEC, Rambus strategically maintained its silence, thereby prolonging the misimpression created by its prior conduct.

At the same time that Rambus was avoiding disclosure of its patent activity, Rambus was engaged in a program of amending its applications to develop a patent portfolio that would cover JEDEC's standards.

Rambus used information obtained via its participation in JEDEC to help shape and refine the very patent applications it now claims it was seeking to protect.

Do these facts, if true, affect your analysis and conclusion as to whether or not Rambus violated the antitrust laws?

7. Some commentators have suggested that reputation costs can deter misconduct by participants in SSOs. *See* U.S. DEP'T OF JUSTICE & FEDERAL TRADE COMMISSION, ANTITRUST ENFORCEMENT AND INTELLECTUAL PROPERTY RIGHTS: PROMOTING INNOVATION AND COMPETITION 40 (2007). Is this persuasive? Would you permit Rambus to participate in a SSO of which you were a member? If so, would you impose any conditions on Rambus' membership in the SSO? How would you enforce them?

8. The D.C. Circuit reasoned that "had JEDEC limited Rambus to reasonable royalties and required it to provide licenses on a nondiscriminatory basis, we would expect less competition from alternative technologies, not more; high prices and constrained output tend to attract competitors, not to repel them."

Do you agree?

How does the presence of network effects affect the antitrust analysis?

Note on Section 5 of the Federal Trade Commission Act

In 1914, Congress enacted the Federal Trade Commission Act (FTC Act) and created the Federal Trade Commission (FTC) to administer the Act. The FTC has five commissioners, appointed by the President to seven-year terms. No more than three commissioners, however, may be from the same political party. The appointment of commissioners requires Senate confirmation.

Section 5 of the FTC Act condemns "unfair methods of competition." As with the ambiguous language of the Sherman Act, Congress intended the language to be imprecise and flexible because "there were too many unfair practices to define, and after writing 20 of them into the law it would be quite possible to invent others." *FTC v. Sperry & Hutchinson Co.*, 405 U.S. 233, 239–40 (1972) (quoting Senate Report No. 597, 63d Cong., 2d Sess., 13 (1914)). In 1938, Congress amended Section 5 to also denounce "unfair or deceptive acts or practices." The additional language was, again, inexact. In 1994, however, Congress amended the FTC Act to limit the FTC's authority to declare an act or practice "unfair" only to situations where "the act or practice causes or is likely to cause substantial injury to consumers which is not reasonably avoidable by consumers themselves and not outweighed by countervailing benefits to consumers or to competition." 15 U.S.C. § 45(n).

Any conduct that violates the Sherman Act or the Clayton Act necessarily constitutes an "unfair method of competition" that also violates Section 5. But these antitrust laws do not necessarily define the limits of Section 5 liability. The Supreme Court has opined that "§5 empower[s] the Commission to define and proscribe an unfair competitive practice, even though the practice does not infringe either the letter or the spirit of the antitrust laws." *Sperry & Hutchinson Co.*, 405 U.S. at 239. A party may appeal a final decision by the FTC to the appropriate federal circuit court of appeals. Appellate courts have rejected some attempts by the FTC to condemn conduct outside the reach of other antitrust laws. See, e.g., *E.I. DuPont & Co. v. FTC*, 729 F.2d 128 (2d Cir. 1984). After initially retreating slightly in the 1980s in response to these decisions, the FTC in 1990s began to challenge conduct that it saw as anticompetitive but nonetheless falling outside of the Sherman Act, such as invitations to engage in price fixing.

The customary remedy for a proven violation of Section 5 is a cease and desist order. Noncompliance can result in civil penalties. FTC challenges are more likely to result in a consent order than litigation.

In the *Dell* case at the beginning of this chapter, the FTC brought a complaint under Section 5 of the FTC Act. In contrast, in *Rambus* the FTC pursued Rambus for allegedly violating Section Two of the Sherman Act. Both cases involved a member of a standard-setting organization charged with engaging in deceptive conduct. This raises the issue of whether the FTC should be pursuing Section Five or Section Two cases.

In *In the Matter of Negotiated Data Solutions*, 2008 WL 258308 (FTC 2008), the FTC brought a Section 5 complaint against a patent owner, Negotiated Data Solutions ("N-Data"), for violating a licensing commitment. In 1994, National Semiconductor ("National") made a commitment to a standard-setting organization—the Institute of Electrical and Electronics Engineers (IEEE)—that if the IEEE adopted an ethernet standard that included National's technology, then National would license its technology to any party for a one-time payment of $1,000. The IEEE considered several alternative technologies but ended up adopting the standard that incorporated National's technology.

National sold the relevant patents to Vertical Networks in 1998 and Vertical acknowledged that it acquired the patents subject to the representations that National had made to the IEEE. In 2002, Vertical sought to evade the earlier commitments and to charge a higher per-unit royalty to licensees, backed by the threat of infringement litigation against those companies that balked at the new terms. By this time, no viable alternative technologies existed and several firms acceded to Vertical's demands. In 2003, Vertical assigned the patents to N-Data, which was aware of National's 1994 assurance that it would license its patents for a one-time payment of $1,000 and yet continued to demand higher royalties.

The FTC issued a complaint against N-Data for violating Section 5 of the FTC Act, alleging that the conduct constituted both an unfair method of competition and an unfair act or practice. The FTC reasoned that N-Data was able to increase its price only by reneging on a prior licensing commitment and that, unchecked, this conduct would undermine standard setting more broadly. To justify its charge of an unfair method of competition, the Commission explained:

> A mere departure from a previous licensing commitment is unlikely to constitute an unfair method of competition under Section 5. The commitment here was in the context of standard-setting. The Supreme Court repeatedly has recognized the procompetitive potential of standard-setting activities. However, because a standard may displace the normal give and take of competition, the Court has not hesitated to impose antitrust liability on conduct that threatens to undermine the standard-setting process or to render it anticompetitive. The conduct of N-Data (and Vertical) at issue here clearly has that potential.

The Commission also independently challenged N-Data's attempt to evade its licensing commitments as an unfair act or practice under Section 5. Applying the language of the 1994 amendment to Section 5, the FTC reasoned that: 1) reneging on the price commitments inflicted "substantial consumer injury" because the patented technology was used in computers purchased by millions of consumers and the licensees would probably pass the higher costs on to consumers; 2) N-Data's demands for more money created no "countervailing benefit"; and 3) consumers could not avoid the injury because the standard had been adopted and relied upon, creating a "patent hold-up" situation. As with the Section 5 complaint based on unfair methods of competition, the Commission again noted that "merely breaching a prior commitment is not enough to constitute an unfair act or practice under Section 5. The standard-setting context in which National made its commitment is critical to the legal analysis."

The Commission did not treat N-Data's conduct as a species of Sherman Act violation and instead pursued the case under Section 5 as a so-called "stand-alone violation." In a footnote, the Commission noted that by bringing a "complaint alleg[ing] stand-alone violations of Section 5 rather than violations of

Section 5 that are premised on violations of the Sherman Act, this action is not likely to lead to well-founded treble damage antitrust claims in federal court." Section 5 of the FTC Act does not create a private right of action. Only the FTC may enforce the provision. A successful Section 5 action does not automatically lead to private follow-on litigation. In contrast, if the government wins a final judgment in a Sherman Act case, that victory provides prima facie evidence in subsequent private antitrust litigation. 15 U.S.C. § 16. By not characterizing its complaint against N-Data as implicating the Sherman Act, the Commission believed that it diminished the likelihood of follow-on private lawsuits.

The FTC negotiated a consent order, by which N-Data agreed to honor National's 1994 assurances on patent licensing (or to offer other terms as dictated in the consent order). Commissioner William Kovacic and Chairman Deborah Majoras dissented. Commissioner Kovacic feared that despite the absence of a Sherman Act or Clayton Act violation, "the proposed settlement could affect the application of state statutes that are modeled on the FTC Act and prohibit unfair methods of competition ('UMC') or unfair acts or practices ('UAP')." Further, he was concerned that the Commission brought separate UMC and UAP claims in a manner that broadened UAP coverage so as to make the UMC provision of Section 5 superfluous. Chairman Majoras expressed concern, among other things, that the majority was using the Commission's "consumer protection authority to protect large corporate members of a standard-setting organization."

If you were an FTC commissioner, would you challenge a monopolist's deception of a standard-setting organization as a Section Five violation or a Section Two violation? Why? What factors would you consider in deciding how to frame a complaint? What remedies would you seek?

Bibliography of Additional Resources

Daniel G. Swanson & William J. Baumol, *Reasonable and Nondiscriminatory (RAND) Royalties, Standards Selection, and Control of Market Power*, 73 ANTITRUST L.J. 1 (2005)

Joseph Kattan, *Disclosures and Commitments to Standard-Setting Organizations,* ANTITRUST 22 (Summer 2002)

Thomas F. Cotter, *Patent Holdup, Patent Remedies, and Antitrust Responses*, 34 J. CORP. L. 1151 (2009).

Michael G. Cowie & Joseph P. Lavelle, *Patents Covering Industry Standards: The Risks to Enforceability Due to Conduct Before Standard Setting Organizations*, 30 AIPLA Q.J. 95 (2002)

Herbert Hovenkamp, *Standards Ownership and Competition Policy*, 48 B.C. L. REV. 87 (2007)

Mark A. Lemley & Carl Shapiro, *Patent Holdup and Royalty Stacking*, 85 TEX. L. REV. 1991 (2007)

Mark A. Lemley, *Ten Things To Do About Patent Holdup of Standards (and One Not To)*, 48 B.C. L. REV. 149 (2007)

Janice M. Mueller, *Patenting Industry Standards*, 34 J. Marshall L. Rev. 894 (2001)

Janice M. Mueller, *Patent Misuse Through the Capture of Industry Standards*, 17 Berk. Tech. L.J. 623 (2002)

J. Gregory Sidak, *Patent Holdup and Oligopsonistic Collusion in Standard-Setting Organizations*, 5 J. Competition L. & Econ. 123 (2009)

PART THREE

THE ANTITRUST IMPLICATIONS OF HORIZONTAL AGREEMENTS INVOLVING INTELLECTUAL PROPERTY

CHAPTER 9

Price Fixing and Intellectual Property

A. Patents and Cartels

United States v. United States Gypsum Co.
333 U.S. 364 (1948)

Mr. Justice REED delivered the opinion of the Court.

The United States instituted this suit on August 15, 1940, in the District Court of the United States for the District of Columbia against United States Gypsum Company, five other corporate defendants, and seven individual defendants, as a civil proceeding under the Sherman Act. The complaint charged that the appellees had violated both §§ 1 and 2 of the Sherman Act, 15 U.S.C.A. §§ 1, 2, by conspiring to fix prices on patented gypsum board and unpatented gypsum products, to standardize gypsum board and its method of production for the purpose of eliminating competition, and to regulate the distribution of gypsum board by eliminating jobbers and fixing resale prices of manufacturing distributors. ***

I.

The appellees are engaged in the production of gypsum and the manufacture of gypsum products, including gypsum plasterboard, gypsum lath, gypsum wallboard, and gypsum plaster. At the time of the alleged conspiracy, appellees sold nearly all of the first three products which were marketed in states east of the Rocky Mountains, and a substantial portion of the plaster sold in the same area. Gypsum products are widely used in the construction industry. In 1939, the sales value of gypsum products was approximately $42,000,000, of which $23,000,000 was accounted for by gypsum board (plasterboard, lath, and wallboard), $17,000,000 by gypsum plaster and the remainder by gypsum block and tile and other products.

292   *Antitrust Law and Intellectual Property Rights*

Over 90% of all plaster used in building construction in the United States is made with gypsum.

Gypsum is found in numerous deposits throughout the country. Gypsum board is made by taking the crushed and calcined mineral, adding water, and spreading the gypsum slurry between two paper liners. When the gypsum hardens, the mineral adheres to the paper and the resulting product is used in construction. Plasterboard and lath have a rough surface and are used as a wall and ceiling base for plaster; wallboard has a finished surface and does not require the addition of plaster.

Since its organization in 1901, United States Gypsum has been the dominant concern in the gypsum industry. In 1939, it sold 55% of all gypsum board in the eastern area. By development and purchase it has acquired the most significant patents covering the manufacture of gypsum board, and beginning in 1926, United States Gypsum offered licenses under its patents to other concerns in the industry, all licenses containing a provision that United States Gypsum should fix the minimum price at which the licensee sold gypsum products embodying the patents. Since 1929, United States Gypsum has fixed prices at which the other defendants have sold gypsum board.

The other corporate appellees are National Gypsum Co., Certain-teed Products Corp., Celotex Corp., Ebsary Gypsum Co., and Newark Plaster Co. Appellee Gloyd is the owner of an unincorporated business trading under the name of Texas Cement Plaster Co. National produced 23% of all gypsum board sold in the eastern area in 1939, Certain-teed 11%, and the other four companies correspondingly smaller amounts. Seven companies which were active when the licensing plan was evolved in 1929 and before have been acquired by other companies, and defendant Celotex entered the industry in 1939 when the licensing plan was fully in effect by acquiring the assets and licenses of American Gypsum Company. The seven individual defendants are presidents of the corporate defendants. ***

Prior to 1912, gypsum board was manufactured with an open edge, leaving the gypsum core exposed on all four sides. In 1912, United States Gypsum received as assignee a patent issued to one Utzman, No. 1,034,746, covering both process and product claims on board with closed side edges, the lower paper liner being folded over the exposed gypsum core. Closed-edge board was superior in quality to open-edge board, as it was cheaper to produce, did not break so easily in shipment, and was less subject to crumbling at the edges when nailed in place. United States Gypsum also acquired a number of other patents relating to the process of making closed-edge board. In 1917, United States Gypsum sued a competitor claiming infringement of the Utzman patent and in 1921 the Circuit Court of Appeals affirmed a judgment holding that the Utzman patent was valid and infringed. United States Gypsum settled with an infringer, Beaver Products Co., in 1926, by granting Beaver a license to practice the closed-edge board patent with a provision that United States Gypsum should fix the price at which Beaver sold patented board. Shortly before the settlement with Beaver, United States Gypsum instituted suits against American Gypsum Co., Universal Gypsum and Lime Co., and gave notice of infringement to Niagara Gypsum Co. Universal did not contest the suit but accepted a license with price fixing provisions, and two other small companies followed suit in 1927. American and Niagara would not settle, and in 1928 judgment was entered against American holding that American's partially closed-edge board infringed one of United States Gypsum's patents. United States Gypsum also instituted suits for infringement against National Gypsum Co. in 1926 and 1928 which were settled by the execution of a license and payment of damages as part of the industry-wide settlement with all other defendants in 1929. In that year, two sets of license agreements were signed in which United States Gypsum licensed all but two companies manufacturing gypsum board in substantially identical terms and from that date United States Gypsum has maintained rigid control over the price and terms of sale of virtually all gypsum board. Since 1937 the control has been complete.

Up to this point there is no dispute as to the facts. The government charged that the defendants acted in concert in entering into the licensing agreements, that United States Gypsum granted licenses and the other defendants accepted licenses with the knowledge that all other concerns in the industry would accept similar licenses, and that as a result of such concert of action, competition was eliminated by fixing the price of patented board, eliminating the production of unpatented board, and regulating the distribution of patented board. To support its allegations, the government introduced in evidence the license agreements, more than 600 documentary exhibits consisting of letters and memoranda written by officers of the corporate defendants, and examined 28 witnesses, most of whom were officers of the corporate defendants. Since the appellees' motion to dismiss when the government had finished its case was sustained, the appellees introduced no evidence. They did cross-examine the government's witnesses. The documentary exhibits present a full picture of the circumstances surrounding the negotiation of the patent license agreements, and are chiefly relied on by the government to prove its case. ***

The patent licenses in force at the beginning of 1929 provided that United States Gypsum could fix prices only during the term of the principal Utzman patent, which was scheduled to expire on August 6, 1929, although the remaining features of the agreements were to remain in force until the expiration of the last patent included under the license, which was in 1937.

*** [A] meeting of representatives of all but one of the licensed manufacturers, and all unlicensed manufacturers except American and Kelley, took place in Chicago. The three unlicensed manufacturers who were present—Certain-teed, Ebsary and Niagara—signed license agreements.

At the same meeting, Avery explained to the licensees that United States Gypsum had acquired applications for a patent covering so-called 'bubble board' and suggested that the licensees take out licenses under these applications. The applications covered a process for making gypsum board by introducing a soap foam in the gypsum slurry which would result in a lighter and cheaper board. Avery subsequently mailed proposed license agreements under the 'bubble board'

294   *Antitrust Law and Intellectual Property Rights*

applications to the licensees. George M. Brown of Certain-teed on June 4th acknowledged receipt of the license proposal in a noncommittal reply, but composed a memorandum for his own files in which he commented that the savings resulting from taking a license would be doubtful ***.

On June 6th the licensees met again in Chicago to discuss the question of accepting a license under the 'bubble board' patents. Shortly thereafter Certain-teed agreed to take out a license. National also agreed to accept a license; the minutes of the meeting of the board of directors on July 23 read in part as follows:

'The President stated that the United States Gypsum Company has been working on a plan to stabilize the Gypsum Industry and has offered to license the entire Industry under the new method of manufacturing gypsum wallboard known as the 'Bubble System.' The license agreements submitted to each of the wallboard manufacturers contain price fixing clauses and under the agreements submitted the prices of wallboard would be fixed for the whole industry for the term of approximately seventeen years.'

The board passed a resolution authorizing the executive committee to negotiate a license agreement, 'provided that the United States Gypsum Company, by virtue of this agreement with this Corporation and with other manufacturers of gypsum wallboard, shall control the price of wallboard sold in the United States and its possessions.' ***

Another meeting of licensees was held in Chicago on August 6, the day on which the Utzman patent expired. In a memorandum summarizing what happened at the meeting, C. O. Brown said that it had been agreed that Universal would assign the starch patent to United States Gypsum, and the latter company would issue a single license contract covering all patents and patent applications. Brown further reported that 'All of the Independent Gypsum Companies are willing to sign on this basis' and that 'The Attorneys feel that such a contract would be exceptionally strong and price control could be maintained for the life of the Contract without difficulty.' On August 27 the board of directors of National held a meeting at which the president was authorized to sign a license with United States Gypsum covering the 'bubble board' and starch patents 'provided that all the present licensees of the United States Gypsum Company enter into a similar license and provided further that in the judgment of the President such action will result in legal stabilization of the markets.'

Soon thereafter, National, Certain-teed, Ebsary, Niagara and Atlantic executed licenses with United States Gypsum, to become effective on the date when Universal's receiver transferred the starch patents to United States Gypsum. On November 5 the starch patents were assigned to United States Gypsum, and on the same date Universal also accepted a license. On November 25 American settled its litigation with United States Gypsum and accepted a license. All manufacturers of gypsum board were now licensed by United States Gypsum, except Kelley Plasterboard Co., and that concern executed a license in April of the following year. Texas Cement Plaster, a licensee under the Utzman patent, did not accept a license under the starch and 'bubble board' patents until 1937 when the original license expired. Texas was thus free to sell board at any price from 1929 to 1937.

The contracts which became effective in November 1929 were in substantially identical terms. The license with Universal contained preferential royalty terms which were granted as consideration for the transfer of the starch patents; every other license (except that of Texas) provided that if the licensor should subsequently grant more favorable terms to any licensee (except Universal), the same more favorable terms would be granted to the first licensee. Each licensee agreed to pay as royalty a stipulated percentage on the selling price of 'all plasterboard and gypsum wallboard of every kind' whether or not made by patented processes or embodying product claims. The contract covered fifty patents and seven patent applications, including the starch patent and the 'bubble board' applications; the contract was to run until the most junior patent expired. As two 'bubble board' patents were issued in 1937, the licenses ran until 1954. The licensees agreed not to sell patented wallboard to manufacturing distributors unless United States Gypsum gave its consent as to each prospective purchaser. As in the previous contracts, United States Gypsum reserved the right to fix the minimum price at which each licensee sold wallboard embodying the licensor's patents, the licensor agreeing that such minimum price would be not greater than the price at which the licensor itself offered to sell. ***

In 1934 and 1935 United States Gypsum offered supplemental licenses to practice a patent covering metallized board, which was accepted by almost all licensees, and in 1936 United States Gypsum offered licenses under its perforated lath patent which were also accepted by most licensees. These supplemental licenses contained provisions allowing United States Gypsum to fix the minimum price on board made according to the patents which were licensed.

The government charged that the execution of the license agreements in May and November 1929 marked a turning point in the gypsum industry. The government introduced evidence tending to show that the price of first quality wallboard was raised, that United States Gypsum standardized the type of board sold by requiring its licensees to sell No. 2 wallboard and seconds at the same price as standard wallboard, and standardized the methods of sale so that no licensee could offer more favorable terms to a customer than any other licensee.

Although the license contracts gave the licensor the right only to fix the minimum price at which the licensee should sell, United States Gypsum issued a series of bulletins which defined in minute detail both the prices and terms of sale for patented gypsum board. They are printed on nearly a thousand pages of the record. The bulletins adopted a basing point system of pricing, according to which each licensee was required to quote a price determined by taking the mill price at the nearest basing point and adding the all rail freight from the basing point to the destination. The freight was to be computed on specified uniform billing weights, in order to prevent variations in freight arising from the differences in weight of board made by different manufacturers, and each licensee was directed to charge exactly the same switching, cartage, and extra delivery charges. Specified board sizes and minimum quantities were prescribed, licensees were forbidden to employ commission salesmen without the written consent of the licensor, regulations were prescribed as to the size, quantity and markings of gypsum board used for packing shipments, granting of long term credit was prohibited, sales on consignment were enjoined and licensees were forbidden to deliver board directly to a building site.

It is not practicable to quote one of the hundreds of comprehensive bulletins on prices and terms. The industry accepted directions for distribution of product as corollary to price control, so that prices would not be infringed by variations of seller contracts. ***

In order to insure compliance with the price bulletins, United States Gypsum established a wholly owned subsidiary in 1932 named Board Survey, Inc. Licensees were invited to send in complaints as to violations of pricing bulletins to Board Survey and that organization forwarded the complaints to the alleged delinquent licensees. Board Survey was authorized to make a thorough check-up of all reported violations and to take such action as it might deem necessary or proper to protect United States Gypsum's rights under the license agreements and patents. Although the record discloses no instance in which Board Survey took or even threatened to take legal action against any licensee, there are many instances in which Board Survey sent letters to licensees requesting an explanation as to alleged violations. Meetings of licensees were held at which doubtful provisions of the price bulletins were explained. The trial court found that 'in the main' licensees complied with the bulletin conditions.

The government further charged that the defendants had discontinued the production of unpatented open-edge board, eliminated jobbers by requiring jobbers to purchase board at the same price as board sold to dealers, induced manufacturing distributors to observe bulletin prices upon resale of board purchased from licensees, and stabilized the price of gypsum plaster and other unpatented products.

It is undisputed that after 1929 the defendants ceased to manufacture open-edge board; the government claims that production of the unpatented board was discontinued in order to protect the patented board from competition. Prior to 1929 open-edge board had sold at lower prices than closed-edge board, and the government's exhibits show that the officers of the corporate defendants realized that there could be no effective stabilization of prices on closed-edge board as long as open-edge board was sold without price control. The license agreements provided that royalties should be paid on the sales of all board sold, patented or unpatented, a provision which would tend to discourage and production of higher cost unpatented board. Although the government produced no evidence of any agreement between the defendants to eliminate production of open-edge board, corporate officers of the licensees testified that they anticipated that one result of industry-wide licensing would be the elimination of open-edge board. ***

To support the charge of stabilizing the price of unpatented plaster, the government cited letters written by officers of the corporate defendants showing that they anticipated that price stabilization in patented board would be accompanied with stabilization of all gypsum products. The trial court found that the price of plaster and miscellaneous gypsum products in fact did increase after 1929. The government charged that plaster prices were stabilized by requiring licensees who sold plaster together with patented board to sell plaster at prevailing prices. Board and plaster were usually sold together and the defendants claim that cutting of prices on plaster, in sales of the two together, operated in effect as a rebate on the price of board, and hence was legally subject to control. The government introduced in evidence a large number of complaints to Board Survey by licensees as to their competitors' failure to maintain prevailing prices on plaster. A bulletin provision forbidding rebates and allowances stated that a sale of board at posted prices would be in violation of the license if the licensee reduced the price of other products, and Board Survey in summarizing violations of bulletin terms revealed through audit of the licensees' books listed 'Price concessions on other material in connection with board sales.'

II.

Appellees admit that in the absence of whatever protection is afforded by valid patents the licensing arrangements described would be in violation of the Sherman Act. Accordingly, the government sought to amend its complaint to allege that the 'bubble board' patents were not valid. [*The Court held that the government could attack patent validity.*] ***

We think that the industry-wide license agreements, entered into with knowledge on the part of licensor and licensees of the adherence of others, with the control over prices and methods of distribution through the agreements and the bulletins, were sufficient to establish a prima facie case of conspiracy. Each licensee, as is shown by the uncontradicted references to the meetings and discussion that were preliminary to the execution of the licenses could not have failed to be aware of the intention of United States Gypsum and the other licensees to make the arrangements for licenses industry wide. The license agreements themselves, on their face, showed this purpose. The licensor was to fix minimum prices binding both on itself and its licensees; the royalty was to be measured by a percentage of the value of all gypsum products, patented or unpatented; the license could not be transferred without the licensor's consent; the licensee opened its books of accounts to the licensor; the licensee was protected against competition with more favorable licenses and there was a cancellation clause for failure to live up to the arrangements. Furthermore, the bulletins gave directions to the industry as to its prices and methods of operation in unmistakable terms. The District Court did not accept the foregoing facts as definite evidence of a conspiracy. To us, these facts are proof of a conspiracy. Certainly they are overwhelming evidence of a plan of the licensor and licensees to fix prices and regulate operations in the gypsum board industry.

*** Conspiracies to control prices and distribution, such as we have here, we believe to be beyond any patent privilege.

*** [T]he trial court made findings adverse to the government's claim that the defendants conspired to eliminate the production of open-edge board. The tenor of those findings is that there was no agreement among the licensees to discontinue the production of open-edge board, although the trial court conceded that it might be 'inferred' that each licensee did not expect to continue the manufacture of open-edge board. The provision in the license contracts that royalties should be paid on the production of unpatented board is strongly indicative of an agreement not to manufacture unpatented board, and the testimony of the witnesses is ample to show that there was an understanding, if not a formal agreement, that only patented board would be sold. Such an arrangement in purpose and effect increased the area of the patent monopoly and is invalid.

*** [T]he trial court dealt with the government's charge that the defendants had stabilized the price of unpatented gypsum products. Those findings hold that there was no understanding or agreement that prices would be raised or fixed upon plaster or any unpatented product, that the bulletin provision prohibiting the reduction of price on unpatented products was designed to protect the price of patented board, and was not used to stabilize the price of unpatented materials. We reject all these findings as clearly erroneous. The bulletin provision and the complaints by licensees addressed to Board Survey convince us that the defendants attempted to stabilize plaster prices, and the fact that plaster prices were stabilized only when plaster was sold in conjunction with board appears to us to be immaterial.

The foregoing discussion foreshadows our conclusion. *** These licenses and bulletins show plainly a conspiracy to violate the Sherman Act. Price fixing of this type offends. It is well settled that price fixing, without authorizing statutes is illegal, per se. *See* note 21, *United States v. Line Material Co.*, 333 U.S. 287. Patents grant no privilege to their owners of organizing the use of those patents to monopolize an industry through price control, through royalties for the patents drawn from patent-free industry products and through regulation of distribution. Here patents have been put to such uses as to collide with the Sherman Act's protection of the public from evil consequences. *United States v. National Lead Co.*, 332 U.S. 319, 327; *Hartford-Empire Co. v. United States*, 323 U.S. 386, 406; *Standard Oil Co. (Indiana) v. United States*, 283 U.S. 163, 170, 174; *Standard Sanitary Mfg. Co. v. United States*, 226 U.S. 20. The defendants did undertake to control prices and distribution in gypsum board. They did utilize an agency, Board Survey, Inc., to make this control effective. *Fashion Originators' Guild v. Federal Trade Commission*, 312 U.S. 457, 465. Such facts, together with the other indicia of intent to monopolize the gypsum board industry, hereinbefore detailed as to the agreements, bulletins and declarations, convinces us that the defendants violated the Sherman Act. ***

Reversed and remanded.

Comments and Questions

1. As discussed in Chapter 2, price-fixing cartels warrant condemnation for a number of reasons. Most cartels reduce market output in order to raise the prices of products (or services or licenses) such that some consumers are unable to afford the product, and those who are able continue to purchase the product are forced to pay higher prices. This creates both inefficiency and a transfer of wealth from consumers to suppliers.

Fortunately, price-fixing cartels are generally difficult to establish and maintain. First, coordination problems often plague cartels. Cartel members have to decide what price to charge and/or how to divide up the market. Price setting can be difficult if different members believe that the cartel will maximize profits at different price points. Also, if the cartel members have different cost structures, they may advocate different fixed prices. Thus, a low-cost member of the cartel may be comfortable with a relatively lower fixed-price then a high-cost member of the cartel. Disputes over pricing and market share can create dissension within the cartel ranks. Antitrust law complicates this process even further because the communications and debates must take place secretly because price-fixing is a crime.

Second, assuming that cartel members can agree on price, cartels are considered inherently unstable because each conspirator has an incentive to cheat on the cartel by charging a lower price or by selling more than its cartel allotment of goods. Such defection from the cartel maximizes profits in the short run more than by abiding by the cartel agreement. For example, if the only four competitors in a market agree to raise a price from $50 per unit to $60 per unit, an individual firm would be better off if it could—without getting caught—charge $55. It could take sales away from its cartel partners while still securing significant profits on each of these sales made in violation of the cartel agreement. This creates an incentive for cartel firms to cheat both as an affirmative profit-maximizing strategy and as a defensive move because abiding by a cartel agreement while others cheat—a situation that game theorists call "being the sucker"—may be less profitable than simply competing in a non-cartelized market. As cartel firms defect—either offensively or defensively because they suspect others are cheating—the cartel may unravel and devolve into competition. Consequently, if firms believe that their cartel partners will cheat, they are less likely to join a cartel in the first place. For example, the Supreme Court in *Gypsum* noted that one supplier "was afraid to sign up a license with price-fixing provisions because his competitors would grant secret rebates."

Stable cartels are those that have found a way to solve the coordination and defection problems. Cartels are more likely to be formed in concentrated markets with a relatively small number of firms. With fewer firms, cartel members can better address the coordination problems attendant with price fixing because a smaller group can more easily reach agreement on price levels and market shares. Also, with fewer members in the price-fixing conspiracy, it is easier to detect cheating on the cartel agreement, and bring defecting firms back into the fold.

How did the cartel members in *U.S. Gypsum* attempt to solve the coordination problems? In the wallboard cartel, the Supreme Court tells us that "[e]ach licensee agreed to pay as royalty a stipulated percentage on the selling price of 'all plasterboard and gypsum wallboard of every kind' whether or not made by patented processes or embodying product claims." *United States v. United States Gypsum Co.*, 333 U.S. 364 (1948). How does that constitute price fixing? Is this agreement within the legitimate scope of the defendants' patent protection? Why or why not?

In order to deter and eliminate cartel-destabilizing cheating, cartels must be able to detect defectors and punish them. Cartels employ a variety of monitoring mechanisms, including reporting of sales figures to independent auditors. What detection methods did the cartel members in Gypsum employ?

Many cartels try to deter cheating by making price more transparent, and thus cheating more evident. One policy that the cartel in the Gypsum case adopted was "a basing point system of pricing." What is base-point pricing? How does it make price more transparent and, thus, stabilize a cartel?

Even if cheating can be detected, punishing defectors can prove difficult. Perhaps the most obvious way to enforce an agreement is to sue defecting firms for breach. But antitrust law makes price-fixing arrangements illegal. A company trying to enforce a cartel agreement in court would essentially have to confess to the criminal act of price fixing, which would expose the firm to criminal fines and its executives to prison terms of up to ten years. So cartel members need to find alternative methods of disciplining cartel members who defect. Private enforcement mechanisms employed by cartels have included imposing fines on firms that sell more than their cartel allotments, inflicting a temporary price war, and employing dispute resolution systems that essentially operate as arbiters that take evidence, make findings, and impose penalties.

What enforcement and penalty mechanisms did the cartel in this case employ?

2. The first element of a price-fixing case is to prove that competitors actually agreed to set price. In the absence of direct evidence of an agreement (such as a signed contract, eyewitness testimony, or audio or video tape), antitrust plaintiffs can prove the existence of a conspiracy through circumstantial evidence. How did the government prove the existence of a price-fixing agreement in the *Gypsum* case? Do you agree that this evidence proves that an agreement exists?

3. Does the presence of patents make the licensing agreements legal?

Should it? How did the patent license agreements distort competition outside the scope of the patents?

What if the patents at issue are valid? How might this agreement have protected invalid patents?

4. What is the relevance of the fact that the licensing agreements curtailed production on unpatented product?

5. Traditionally, we think of cartels as agreements among sellers to increase price. But groups of buyers also sometimes conspire in order to reduce the price that they pay for an input or product. Such buyers' cartels can involve intellectual property. The First Circuit considered how antitrust law should deal with allegations of such a buyers' cartel in the following case:

Addamax Corp. v. Open Software Foundation, Inc.
152 F.3d 48 (1st Cir. 1998)

BOUDIN, Circuit Judge.

Addamax Corporation brought a federal antitrust suit against Open Software Foundation ("OSF"), Hewlett-Packard Company and Digital Equipment

Corporation. *** Addamax was created by Dr. Peter A. Alsberg in 1986 and, in 1987, began to focus on developing security software for Unix operating systems. Unix is a very popular operating system for larger computers, and security software is a component that can be used with the operating system to restrict outside access to sensitive information and to restrict a particular user to information consistent with that user's security classification. During this period, the National Computer Security Center, a division of the federal government's National Security Agency, rated security software, giving ratings (ranging from the most to the least secure) of A, B-3, B-2, B-1, C-2, C-1 and D. Addamax decided to produce B-1 software for Unix operating systems, a level of security demanded primarily by government users. During the years 1988–89, Addamax did develop B-1 security software for at least two different versions of Unix.

While Addamax was trying to produce its security software, a different struggle was developing between AT & T—the inventor of Unix—and a number of major computer manufacturers. Although originally Unix had been freely licensed by AT & T, it appears that in the late 1980s AT & T began restricting its licenses in the face of various software modifications being introduced by individual licensees; and at the same time, AT & T began to develop a close working relationship with Sun Microsystems, a major microprocessor manufacturer. Other hardware manufacturers professed to fear that AT & T was trying to establish a single dominant version of Unix, intending to exclude the proprietary Unix variations from the market.

Accordingly, in May 1988, a number of important computer manufacturers-including defendants Hewlett-Packard and Digital Equipment Corp.-formed the Open Software Foundation as a non-profit joint research and development venture. *** At least one of OSF's professed objectives was to develop an alternative Unix operating system, denominated OSF-1, as a competitor to the Unix system being developed jointly by AT & T and Sun Microsystems.

In 1989, while OSF-1 was still being developed, OSF decided that it should include security software at the B-1 level. At that time, only three companies—AT & T, Addamax and SecureWare, Inc.—were producing security software for the Unix system. On November 1, 1989, OSF sent a "request for technology" to Addamax and SecureWare, soliciting bids for a B-1 security component for the new OSF-1 system. Bids were submitted on November 27, 1989, and OSF selected SecureWare on December 22, 1989. There is some indication that the Addamax security software was more sophisticated—one witness agreed that the contrast was between a Cadillac and a Chevette—but the Addamax price may also have appeared more substantial. In any event, OSF-1 itself was never a very successful product.

Addamax continued to sell its own B-1 software for some period after losing the bid. Nothing prevented OSF "sponsors" (the founding members of OSF) or "members" (a great many other companies) from using Addamax security software for their own programs; and OSF sponsors and members were not the only potential buyers of Addamax's program. However, by 1991, Addamax began to phase out its B-1 security software, turning away new buyers so that it could devote its resources to the development of a new security software product, in which it appears that the company was successful.

In April 1991, Addamax filed a complaint in the district court against OSF, Hewlett-Packard and Digital, alleging various violations of federal and state antitrust law. As later amended, the complaint charged the defendants, together with other companies associated with OSF, with horizontal price fixing, boycott, and otherwise unlawful joint venture behavior in violation of the Sherman and the Clayton Acts, 15 U.S.C. §§ 1-2, 18. A central theme, although not the only one, was that the defendants had conspired to force down the price for security software below the free-market level and otherwise to limit or impair the ability of Addamax to compete as a supplier of security software. ***

1. *** [P]er se rules under section 1 of the Sherman Act have left only a couple of "serious candidates" for per se treatment: these include price or output fixing agreements (horizontal market division agreements are of essentially the same character) and "certain group boycotts or concerted refusals to deal." *U.S. Healthcare, Inc. v. Healthsource, Inc.*, 986 F.2d 589, 593 (1st Cir.1993). ***

Where a plaintiff proves conduct that falls within a per se category, nothing more is needed for liability; the defendants' power, illicit purpose and anticompetitive effect are all said to be irrelevant. *United States v. Socony-Vacuum Oil Co.*, 310 U.S. 150 (1940). But courts have been very careful to confine per se treatment to conduct of the type that is almost always actually or potentially anticompetitive and has no redeeming benefits (e.g., reduced costs, increased competition) worthy of being weighed against the negative effects. *Broadcast Music, Inc. v. Columbia Broadcasting System*, 441 U.S. 1 (1979). *** Joint venture enterprises like OFC, unless they amount to complete shams, *cf. Palmer v. BRG of Georgia*, 498 U.S. 46 (1990), are rarely susceptible to per se treatment. Where the venture is producing a new product-here, the OFC-1 software package-there is patently a potential for a productive contribution to the economy, and conduct that is strictly ancillary to this productive effort (e.g., the joint venture's decision as to the price at which it will purchase inputs) is evaluated under the rule of reason. This is so even if we accept, pursuant to the stipulation, the arguendo premise that OSF and those connected with it represented a large portion of the market for purchasing B-1 security software and represented a large portion of some kind of output market for integrated Unix software programs.

Addamax points to fragments of evidence that, assuming a full context were established, might or might not suggest that OSF was an aggressive response to the AT & T Sun venture and that Hewlett-Packard had a secret agenda to favor Secure-Ware over Addamax (for reasons that are never made quite clear), regardless of whether Addamax offered a superior product. None of the evidence pointed to by Addamax suggests that OSF-1 was other than a legitimate, if ultimately unsuccessful, product; and there is nothing to suggest that the ancillary decisions-what inputs to purchase, at what price, and from whom-were not legitimately related to this effort. In this context, flinging around terms like "cartel" and "boycott" do not convert a rule of reason claim into a per se one.

2. On the other hand, neither is a joint venture "per se" legal. Any joint venture, especially one that involves competitors, tends to be susceptible to attack under section 1's rule of reason-on the theory that the operations of the joint venture represent collaboration of the separate entities that own or control it. How far this theory can be pressed in the case of a truly integrated enterprise, whose "owners" were no more than stockholders, is a matter we need not pursue; we will assume here that the OSF joint venture, or some aspect of it, could be condemned under section 1 if the balance of harms and benefits tipped in favor of harms; questions of power and motive are primarily clues to such effects.

At this point, Addamax's most straightforward claim would be that OSF's concentration of purchasing power in the supposed "market" for acquiring B-1 security software was so great that it imposed a significant risk of forcing prices below competitive levels, and that those risks outweighed any benefit from the venture or, more plausibly, that the venture could achieve those benefits in a less restrictive fashion, i.e., without creating a substantial threat of monopsony pricing. Whether or not this theory could be proved, we are here assuming liability arguendo. The question remains whether Addamax established—either as a matter of law or based on the evidence—some causal connection between this assumed violation by defendants and Addamax's failure in the B-1 security software business. ***

Addamax's more interesting argument is its claim that the case law, and the economic theory that underlies it, require a conclusion that the conduct assumed arguendo to comprise a violation must have caused injury to Addamax. The broadest version of this proposition is Addamax's claim that under the rule of reason, conduct is condemned only because it has an anticompetitive effect. Therefore, Addamax argues, there must have been some injury to it, and the only question that remains is to calculate the amount of damages.

A more specific version of the argument, also advanced, is that in this very case the complaint's straightforward charge is that the defendants engaged in an agreement that had the effect of reducing price for B-1 security systems and since Addamax was a provider of B-1 security programs, it necessarily was injured by a reduction in price. An alternative version is Addamax's claim that the joint venturers were engaged in suppressing demand for their own output-Unix programs like OSF-1 embodying B-1 software—and this in turn reduced the demand, and presumably therefore price, volume or both, for suppliers of the input.

It is technically an overstatement to say that actual anticompetitive impact is a requirement of liability in a rule-of-reason case. True, as a practical matter, most courts would be unlikely to condemn an otherwise legitimate joint venture absent some showing of anticompetitive effect. But in principle, a sufficiently high risk of an anticompetitive effect, coupled with marginal benefits (or none at all that could not be achieved through an easily available less restrictive alternative) might justify condemnation under the rule of reason.

But all this is beside the point. Even if we assume that the OSF purchasing consortium was capable of exercising monopsony power directly or through coordination of its sponsor/members' actions, it does not follow that Addamax was a victim or that the alleged below-market price offered by the consortium materially affected Addamax. The only formal purchase by OSF involving Addamax was based on the November 1989 request for technology, in which SecureWare was the successful supplier. If below market price was paid, SecureWare, and not Addamax, was directly injured. To be sure, Addamax claims that its sales opportunities were indirectly curtailed. While the OSF sponsors and members were free to purchase B-1 security programs from anyone they wanted on an individual basis, Addamax claims that winning the OSF-1 sale would have amounted to a valuable OSF endorsement, spurring other sales. But it is hard to see this loss as a consequence of monopsony pricing. ***

3. *** We turn then to the question whether the district court erred in its factual determination that Addamax's inability to succeed in its efforts to sell its B-1 security program for Unix more widely was materially caused by the defendants' conduct. ***

Here, the district court was presented with two competing versions of reality. Addamax's witnesses took the view that Addamax developed a superior B-1 product and its failure to succeed resulted from defendants' machinations which forced down the price of the product to sub-competitive levels and suppressed output for Unix software incorporating B-1 security programs. In some places, Addamax describes itself as the target, and elsewhere as the accidental victim, of a larger conspiracy directed against AT & T.

The defense version, which the district court adopted, was derived from defense depositions, cross-examination of the plaintiffs' experts and numerous documents. In this view, Addamax engaged in risky entry into a market dominated by AT & T, an established supplier of B-1 security software for Unix; the Addamax system was oversophisticated, expensive, arrived late, and never received the important certification from NSA's National Computer Security Center. And, in a market characterized by ever-changing demands, AT & T's promised development of a follow-on B-2 system made the market for B-1 security software for Unix inherently risky and in some measure transitional. There is nothing inherently implausible about either version; everything depends on the evidence. ***

What emerges from our own review of the record is that the district court had evidence to support each of its key findings: that the business was a risky one; that Addamax entered late, with a high-priced, overbuilt and uncertified product; that AT & T and SecureWare, in different ways, posed major problems for Addamax; that many of Addamax's problems, including losses of customers, had begun before the OSF selection of SecureWare; and that changes in market conditions proved to be adverse to Addamax. Further, the evidence is largely derived from Addamax itself ***. The risky nature of Addamax's venture was stressed in its disclosures to investors, and the delays and cost overruns concerning its B-1 product emerge from its own records; it was Addamax that expressed concern with competition from AT & T and especially its ability to offer a smooth transition to its own promised B-2 offering; and the defection of existing and prospective customers to AT & T, apparently before OSF-1, can be traced through Addamax records. The district court did not commit "clear error" in finding the facts in favor of defendants. ***

Affirmed.

Comments and Questions

1. Naked price-fixing cartels run by sellers of goods or services are per se illegal.

Why should antitrust law care about buyers' cartels?

2. Should a buyers' cartel be per se illegal? Why or why not?

Would the defendants in this case be liable if such a per se rule existed? If so, would that be the correct result? Why or why not?

3. The court stated that "[i]t is technically an overstatement to say that actual anticompetitive impact is a requirement of liability in a rule-of-reason case." If there is no anticompetitive impact, can there be any antitrust damages suffered by the plaintiff?

If the plaintiff suffered no damages, why would it bring an antitrust lawsuit?

4. The court ruled against Addamax because the firm could not prove that its alleged injuries were caused by the defendants' conduct. What evidence would Addamax have needed in order to prove causation?

B. Patent Pooling and Price Fixing

DOJ-FTC Antitrust Guidelines for the Licensing of Intellectual Property, § 5.5 Cross-licensing and pooling arrangements

Cross-licensing and pooling arrangements are agreements of two or more owners of different items of intellectual property to license one another or third parties. These arrangements may provide procompetitive benefits by integrating complementary technologies, reducing transaction costs, clearing blocking positions, and avoiding costly infringement litigation. By promoting the dissemination of technology, cross-licensing and pooling arrangements are often procompetitive.

Cross-licensing and pooling arrangements can have anticompetitive effects in certain circumstances. For example, collective price or output restraints in pooling arrangements, such as the joint marketing of pooled intellectual property rights with collective price setting or coordinated output restrictions, may be deemed unlawful if they do not contribute to an efficiency-enhancing integration of economic activity among the participants. Compare NCAA 468 U.S. at 114 (output restriction on college football broadcasting held unlawful because it was not reasonably related to any purported justification) with Broadcast Music, 441 U.S. at 23 (blanket license for music copyrights found not per se illegal because the cooperative price was necessary to the creation of a new product). When cross-licensing or pooling arrangements are mechanisms to accomplish naked price fixing or market division, they are subject to challenge under the per se rule. See *United States v. New Wrinkle, Inc.*, 342 U.S. 371 (1952) (price fixing).

Settlements involving the cross-licensing of intellectual property rights can be an efficient means to avoid litigation and, in general, courts favor such settlements. When such cross-licensing involves horizontal competitors, however, the Agencies will consider whether the effect of the settlement is to diminish competition among entities that would have been actual or likely potential competitors in a relevant market in the absence of the cross-license. In the absence of offsetting efficiencies, such settlements may be challenged as unlawful restraints of trade. *Cf. United States v. Singer Manufacturing Co.*, 374 U.S. 174 (1963) (cross-license agreement was part of broader combination to exclude competitors).

Pooling arrangements generally need not be open to all who would like to join. However, exclusion from cross-licensing and pooling arrangements among parties that collectively possess market power may, under some circumstances, harm competition. *Cf. Northwest Wholesale Stationers, Inc. v. Pacific Stationery & Printing Co.*, 472 U.S. 284 (1985) (exclusion of a competitor from a purchasing cooperative not per se unlawful absent a showing of market power). In general, exclusion from a pooling or cross-licensing arrangement among competing technologies is unlikely to have anticompetitive effects unless (1) excluded firms cannot effectively compete in the relevant market for the good incorporating the licensed technologies and (2) the pool participants collectively possess market power in the relevant market. If these circumstances exist, the Agencies will evaluate whether the arrangement's limitations on participation are reasonably related to the efficient development and exploitation of the pooled technologies and will assess the net effect of those limitations in the relevant market. [citation omitted]

Another possible anticompetitive effect of pooling arrangements may occur if the arrangement deters or discourages participants from engaging in research and development, thus retarding innovation. For example, a pooling arrangement that requires members to grant licenses to each other for current and future technology at minimal cost may reduce the incentives of its members to engage in research and development because members of the pool have to share their successful research and development and each of the members can free ride on the accomplishments of other pool members. *See generally United States v. Mfrs. Aircraft Ass'n, Inc.*, 1976-1 Trade Cas. (CCH) ¶ 60,810 (S.D.N.Y. 1975); *United States v. Automobile Mfrs. Ass'n*, 307 F. Supp. 617 (C.D. Cal 1969), appeal dismissed sub nom. *City of New York v. United States*, 397 U.S. 248 (1970), modified sub nom. *United States v. Motor Vehicle Mfrs. Ass'n*, 1982-83 Trade Cas. (CCH) ¶ 65,088 (C.D. Cal. 1982). However, such an arrangement can have procompetitive benefits, for example, by exploiting economies of scale and integrating complementary capabilities of the pool members, (including the clearing of blocking positions), and is likely to cause competitive problems only when the arrangement includes a large fraction of the potential research and development in an innovation market. [citation omitted]

Standard Oil Co. v. United States,
283 U.S. 163 (1931)

Mr. Justice BRANDEIS delivered the opinion of the Court.

This suit was brought by the United States in June, 1924, in the federal court for northern Illinois, to enjoin further violation of section 1 and section 2 of the Sherman Anti-Trust Trust Act July 2, 1890. The violation charged is an illegal combination to create a monopoly and to restrain interstate commerce by controlling that part of the supply of gasoline which is produced by the process of cracking. Control is alleged to be exerted by means of seventy-nine contracts concerning patents relating to the cracking art. The parties to the several contracts are named as defendants. Four of them own patents covering their respective cracking processes, and are called the primary defendants. Three of these, the Standard Oil Company of Indiana, the Texas Company, and the Standard Oil Company of New Jersey, are themselves large producers of cracked gasoline. The fourth, Gasoline Products Company, is merely a licensing concern. The remaining forty-six defendants manufacture cracked gasoline under licenses from one or more of the primary defendants. They are called secondary defendants. ***

The violation of the Sherman Act now complained of rests substantially on the making and effect of three contracts entered into by the primary defendants. The history of these agreements may be briefly stated. For about half a century before 1910, gasoline had been manufactured from crude oil exclusively by distillation and condensation at atmospheric pressure. When the demand for gasoline grew rapidly with the widespread use of the automobile, methods for increasing the yield of gasoline from the available crude oil were sought. It had long been known that from a given quantity of crude, additional oils of high volatility could be produced by 'cracking'; that is, by applying heat and pressure to the residum after ordinary distillation. But a commercially profitable cracking method and apparatus for manufacturing additional gasoline had not yet been developed. The first such process was perfected by the Indiana Company in 1913; and for more than seven years this was the only one practiced in America. During that period the Indiana Company not only manufactured cracked gasoline on a large scale, but also had licensed fifteen independent concerns to use its process and had collected, prior to January 1, 1921, royalties aggregating $15,057, 432.46.

Meanwhile, since the phenomenon of cracking was not controlled by any fundamental patent, other concerns had been working independently to develop commercial processes of their own. Most prominent among these were the three other primary defendants, the Texas Company, the New Jersey Company, and the Gasoline Products Company. Each of these secured numerous patents covering its particular cracking process. Beginning in 1920, conflict developed among the four companies concerning the validity, scope, and ownership of issued patents. One infringement suit was begun; cross-notices of infringement, antecedent to other suits, were given; and interferences were declared on pending applications in the Patent Office. The primary defendants assert that it was these difficulties which led to their executing the three principal agreements which the United States attacks; and that their sole object was to avoid litigation and losses incident to conflicting patents.

The first contract was executed by the Indiana Company and the Texas Company on August 26, 1921; the second by the Texas Company and Gasoline Products Company on January 26, 1923; the third by the Indiana Company, the Texas Company, and the New Jersey Company, on September 28, 1923. The three agreements differ from one another only slightly in scope and terms. Each primary defendant was released thereby from liability for any past infringement of patents of the others. Each acquired the right to use these patents thereafter in its own process. Each was empowered to extend to independent concerns, licensed under its process, releases from past, and immunity from future claims of infringement of patents controlled by the other primary defendants. And each was to share in some fixed proportion the fees received under these multiple licenses. The royalties to be charged were definitely fixed in the first contract; and minimum sums per barrel, to be divided between the Texas and Indiana companies, were specified in the second and third.

*** [P]ooling arrangements may obviously result in restricting competition. [citation omitted] The limited monopolies granted to patent owners do not exempt them from the prohibitions of the Sherman Act and supplementary legislation. [citation omitted] Hence the necessary effect of patent interchange agreements, and the operations under them, must be carefully examined in order to determine whether violations of the Act result. [citation omitted] ***

The Government contends that the three agreements constitute a pooling by the primary defendants of the royalties from their several patents; that thereby competition between them in the commercial exercise of their respective rights to issue licenses is eliminated; that this tends to maintain or increase the royalty charged secondary defendants and hence to increase the manufacturing cost of cracked gasoline; that thus the primary defendants exclude from interstate commerce gasoline which would, under lower competitive royalty rates, be produced; and that interstate commerce is thereby unlawfully restrained. There is no provision in any of the agreements which restricts the freedom of the primary defendants individually to issue licenses under their own patents alone or under the patents of all the others; and no contract between any of them, and no license agreement with a secondary defendant executed pursuant thereto, now imposes any restriction upon the quantity of gasoline to be produced, or upon the price, terms, or conditions of sale, or upon the territory in which sales may be made. The only restraint thus charged is that necessarily arising out of the making and effect of the provisions for cross-licensing and for division of royalties.

The Government concedes that it is not illegal for the primary defendants to cross-license each other and the respective licensees; and that adequate consideration can legally be demanded for such grants. But it contends that the insertion of certain additional provisions in these agreements renders them illegal. It urges, first, that the mere inclusion of the provisions for the division of royalties, constitutes an unlawful combination under the Sherman Act because it evidences an intent to obtain a monopoly. This contention is unsound. Such provisions for the division of royalties are not in themselves conclusive evidence of illegality. Where there are legitimately conflicting claims or threatened interferences, a settlement by agreement, rather than litigation, is not precluded by the Act. [citation omitted] An interchange of patent rights and a division of royalties according to the value attributed by the parties to their respective patent claims is frequently necessary if technical advancement is not to be blocked by threatened litigation.[5] If the available advantages are upon on reasonable terms to all manufacturers desiring to participate, such interchange may promote rather than restrain competition. [citation omitted] ***

The Government next contends that the agreements to maintain royalties violate the Sherman Law because the fees charged are onerous. The argument is that the competitive advantage which the three primary defendants enjoy of manufacturing cracked gasoline free of royalty, while licensees must pay to them a heavy tribute in fees, enables these primary defendants to exclude from interstate commerce cracked gasoline which would, under lower competitive royalty rates, be produced by possible rivals. This argument ignores the privileges incident to ownership of patents. Unless the industry is dominated, or interstate commerce directly restrained, the Sherman Act does not require cross-licensing patentees to license at reasonable rates others engaged in interstate commerce. [citation omitted] The allegation that the royalties charged are onerous is, standing alone, without legal significance; and, as will be shown, neither the alleged domination, nor restraint of commerce, has been proved.

*** The main contention of the Government is that even if the exchange of patent rights and division of royalties are not necessarily improper and the royalties are not oppressive, the three contracts are still obnoxious to the Sherman Act because specific clauses enable the primary defendants to maintain existing royalties and thereby to restrain interstate commerce. The provisions which constitute the basis for this charge are these. The first contract specifies that the Texas Company shall get from the Indiana Company one-fourth of all royalties thereafter collected under the latter's existing license agreements; and that all royalties received under licenses thereafter issued by either company shall be equally divided. Licenses granting rights under the patents of both are to be issued at a fixed royalty-approximately that charged by the Indiana Company when its process was alone in the field. By the second contract, the Texas Company is entitled to receive one-half of the royalties thereafter collected by the Gasoline Products Company from its existing licensees, and a minimum sum per barrel for all oil cracked by its future licensees. The third contract gives to the Indiana Company one-half of all royalties thereafter paid by existing licensees of the New Jersey Company, and a

---

[5] This is often the case where patents covering improvements of a basic process, owned by one manufacturer, are granted to another. A patent may be rendered quite useless, or 'blocked,' by another unexpired patent which covers a vitally related feature of the manufacturing process. Unless some agreement can be reached, the parties are hampered and exposed to litigation. And, frequently, the cost of litigation to a patentee is greater than the value of a patent for a minor improvement. [c.o.]

similar minimum sum for each barrel treated by its future licensees,—subject in the latter case to reduction if the royalties charged by the Indiana and Texas companies for their processes should be reduced. The alleged effect of these provisions is to enable the primary defendants, because of their monopoly of patented cracking processes, to maintain royalty rates at the level established originally for the Indiana process.

The rate of royalties may, of course be a decisive factor in the cost of production. If combining patent owners effectively dominate an industry, the power to fix and maintain royalties is tantamount to the power to fix prices. [citation omitted] Where domination exists, a pooling of competing process patents, or an exchange of licenses for the purpose of curtailing the manufacture and supply of an unpatented product, is beyond the privileges conferred by the patents and constitutes a violation of the Sherman Act. The lawful individual monopolies granted by the patent statutes cannot be unitedly exercised to restrain competition. [citation omitted] But an agreement for cross-licensing and division of royalties violates the Act only when used to effect a monopoly, or to fix prices, or to impose otherwise an unreasonable restraint upon interstate commerce. [citation omitted] In the case at bar, the primary defendants own competing patented processes for manufacturing an unpatented product which is sold in interstate commerce; and agreements concerning such processes are likely to engender the evils to which the Sherman Act was directed. [citation omitted] We must, therefore, examine the evidence to ascertain the operation and effect of the challenged contracts.

*** No monopoly, or restriction of competition, in the business of licensing patented cracking processes resulted from the execution of these agreements. Up to 1920 all cracking plants in the United States were either owned by the Indiana Company alone, or were operated under licenses from it. In 1924 and 1925, after the cross-licensing arrangements were in effect, the four primary defendants owned or licensed, in the aggregate, only 55 per cent. of the total cracking capacity, and the remainder was distributed among twenty-one independently owned cracking processes. This development and commercial expansion of competing processes is clear evidence that the contracts did not concentrate in the hands of the four primary defendants the licensing of patented processes for the production of cracked gasoline. Moreover, the record does not show that after the execution of the agreements there was a decrease of competition among them in licensing other refiners to use their respective processes.

No monopoly, or restriction of competition, in the production of either ordinary or cracked gasoline has been proved. The output of cracked gasoline in the years in question was about 26 per cent. of the total gasoline production. Ordinary or straight run gasoline is indistinguishable from cracked gasoline and the two are either mixed or sold interchangeably. Under these circumstances the primary defendants could not effectively control the supply or fix the price of cracked gasoline by virtue of their alleged monopoly of the cracking processes, unless they could control, through some means, the remainder of the total gasoline production from all sources. Proof of such control is lacking. ***

No monopoly, or restriction of competition, in the sale of gasoline has been proved. On the basis of testimony relating to the marketing of both cracked and ordinary gasoline, the master found that the defendants were in active competition among themselves and with other refiners; that both kinds of gasoline were refined and sold in large quantities by other companies; and that the primary defendants and their licensees neither individually or collectively controlled the market price or supply of any gasoline moving in interstate commerce. There is ample evidence to support these findings.

Thus it appears that no monopoly of any kind, or restraint of interstate commerce, has been effected either by means of the contracts or in some other way. In the absence of proof that the primary defendants had such control of the entire industry as would make effective the alleged domination of a part, it is difficult to see how they could by agreeing upon royalty rates control either the price or the supply of gasoline, or otherwise restrain competition. By virtue of their patents they had individually the right to determine who should use their respective processes or inventions and what the royalties for such use should be. To warrant an injunction which would invalidate the contracts here in question, and require either new arrangements or settlement of the conflicting claims by litigation, there must be a definite factual showing of illegality. [citation omitted]

Comments and Questions

1. The agreement involved in *Standard Oil* is not the only way in which a "patent pool" can be structured. Consider the following attempt to offer a general definition for patent pools:

> The term "pool" has been used to describe a myriad of different arrangements in which patent owners in some manner have combined their patents. The structure of these pooling arrangements have varied dramatically, ranging from the creation of giant patent holding companies to which many pool members assign patents involving disparate technologies, to cross-licensing of related patents by two patent owners. All pools, however, have one common characteristic: two or more patent owners mutually agreeing to waive exclusive rights under their respective patents so as to grant each other rights and/or to grant jointly rights to others under their patents. The essence of a patent pool, therefore, is this mutual agreement among patent owners to waive their respective exclusive patent rights.

Roger B. Andewelt, *Practical Problems in Counseling and Litigating: Analysis of Patent Pools Under the Antitrust Laws,* 53 ANTITRUST L.J. 611, 611 (1984).

Because these definitions are not universally precise, some courts and commentators sometimes use the phrases cross-licensing and patent pooling interchangeably. But differences exist. Basic cross-licensing involves two or more firms agreeing not to sue each other for infringement of specific patents that each holds. A simple cross-license can involve one patent for each firm in the cross-licensing arrangement or hundreds. The latter situation is often called portfolio cross licensing when the parties contribute the entire sweep of patent portfolios on a particular technology to the cross license. Patent pools go one step further, in that the participants grant licenses to each other and license their patents "to third parties collectively." *Id.* at 64. Despite these differences, the language used by judges and commentators can be confusing because, as the federal antitrust agencies noted in their recent report:

> [T]he courts' terminology is inconsistent. Courts often have applied the term "patent pools" to arrangements that the Agencies would now describe as portfolio cross licenses because these "pools" did not license to third parties. *See, e.g., Hartford-Empire Co.*, 323 U.S. at 392, 413 (describing licensing agreements where defendants created a multi-firm portfolio of patents and licensed them only to each other, not to third parties, as a "patent pool"); *see also Line Material Co.*, 333 U.S. at 313 n.24 ("The words 'patent pool' are not words of art. The expression is used in this opinion to convey the idea of a linking of the right to use patents issued to more than one patentee.").

U.S. DEP'T OF JUSTICE & FEDERAL TRADE COMMISSION, ANTITRUST ENFORCEMENT AND INTELLECTUAL PROPERTY RIGHTS: PROMOTING INNOVATION AND COMPETITION 66–67 n.49 (2007).

The distinction between patent pools and cross licensing can be important from an antitrust perspective because cross-licensing agreements are often procompetitive because they make it easier for intellectual property owners to utilize each other's intellectual property efficiently. However, "[p]ooling agreements typically warrant greater antitrust scrutiny than do cross-licensing agreements due to the collective pricing of pooled patents, greater possibilities for collusion, and generally larger number of market participants." *Id.* at 58

2. Given the flexibility of such agreements, it might be fair to assume that some variations of patent pools have procompetitive benefits. Indeed, in *U.S. Philips Corp. v. Int'l Trade Comm'n*, the Federal Circuit observed that patent pools "may provide procompetitive benefits by integrating complementary technologies, reducing transaction costs, clearing blocking positions, and avoiding costly infringement litigation." 424 F.3d 1179, 1192 (Fed. Cir. 2005) (quoting U.S. Department of Justice and Federal Trade Commission, *Antitrust Guidelines for the Licensing of Intellectual Property* § 5.5 (1995)). Can you think of any other benefits?

How might "integrating complementary technologies" benefit consumers? If the complementary technologies are such that they are most useful when combined, it is likely that the licensees of the technology will want them all. In that sense, patent pools provide a "one-stop shop" for licensees. The notion that the packaging of multiple products together into a single "bundle" might reduce the transaction costs for producers and consumers has been acknowledged by courts. E.g., *United States v. Microsoft Corp.*, 253 F.3d 34, 87 (D.C. Cir. 2001) ("Bundling obviously saves distribution and consumer transaction costs."); *See United States v. Dentsply Int'l, Inc.*, 399 F.3d 181, 192 (3rd Cir. 2005) (noting that the "reduction in transaction costs and time represents a substantial benefit"). In the case of bundled discounts or rebates, a producer offers, "two or more goods or services that could be sold separately . . . [at] a lower price than the seller charges for the goods or services purchased individually." *Cascade Health Solutions v. PeaceHealth*, 515 F.3d 883, 894 (9th Cir. 2008). In terms of transaction costs savings, in what ways is the practice of bundling discounts similar to pooling patents? In what ways is it different? Is it of any importance, for instance, that transaction costs savings are concentrated on a single producer in the bundling context, whereas in the patent pool context, transaction costs savings are distributed among several different producers?

There is another reason that patent pools might benefit consumers by combining complementary technologies. The nineteenth-century French economist Augustin Cournot theorized that where there are multiple monopolists separately producing complementary products, the joint sale of those complements will actually result in a lower price than their independent sale. *See* AUGUSTIN COURNOT, RESEARCHERS INTO THE MATHEMATICAL PRINCIPLES OF THE THEORY OF WEALTH (Oxford Univ. Press 1897) (1838). This might seem counterintuitive, as the two firms might logically be expected to charge the maximum price for the bundle that would result in higher prices for consumers. However, consider a situation with two independent sellers of complementary products. If one seller increases the price of its product, the demand for both its product and the complementary product sold by the other seller will decrease. But because each individual seller does not take this externality into account when pricing its products, independent pricing will result in higher prices than joint pricing, which would force each seller to take into account the total impact on sales.

It is important to note that Cournot's theory was initially applied to the limited context of products which are useful *only* as a complement to some other product. *See* Douglas Lichtman, *Property Rights in Emerging Platform Technologies*, 29 J. Legal Stud. 615, 624 (2000). Thus, it is not immediately clear how this phenomenon applies where complementary products are functional apart from their use as complements. The applicability of the theory might depend on how "complementary" a set of products are. *See* Josh Lerner & Jean Tirole, *Efficient Patent Pools*, 94 Am. Econ. Rev. 691, 691–711 (2004) for a discussion as to how the Cournot effect applies to patent pools. If this is the case, do you think that courts are well-equipped to assess the extent to which a set of products or patents are complementary, and thus to what extent their joint pricing is welfare-enhancing?

3. In what sense might patent pools assist firms in "clearing blocking positions"? The Supreme Court in *Standard Oil* indicated that blocking patents that cover similar features in the manufacturing process could provide a legitimate basis for patent-holders to settle claims through agreement rather than litigation. But why is a patent pool necessary to resolve such disputes? Why couldn't firms contract bilaterally to resolve the issue of blocking patents? Consider the following passage:

> [E]conomists have found that, when different firms own complementary patents that are all essential to the production of a new product or the use of a new technology, individual patent holders may have both the strategic incentive and

ability to "hold up" firms that are trying to develop new products or technologies, deterring innovation. In this type of situation, patent pools are a way of clearing such blocking positions and restoring innovation incentives.

Philip B. Nelson, *Symposium: The IP Grab: The Struggle between Intellectual Property Rights and Antitrust: Patent Pools: An Economic Assessment of Current Law and Policy*, 38 RUTGERS L. J. 539, 539–40 (2007).

4. Chapter 9 dealt with the issue of patent hold up in the context of SSOs that seek to adopt a standard without putting licensees at the mercy of a patentee whose IP is incorporated into a standard. Patent pools implicate another version of the holdup problem. If patent-holders who control patents necessary to a particular endeavor sequentially engage in bilateral cross-licensing agreements, the last patent-holder will have the most leverage. Knowing this, each patent-holder will want to enter a license last, resulting in a stalemate which harms consumers by slowing or completely preventing the new innovation from coming to market. The simultaneous nature of a patent pool allows patent-holders to circumvent this problem. Seen in this light, are patent pools a legitimate mechanism to address the problem of patent holdup?

5. Of course, despite these potentially welfare-enhancing effects, it is possible for a patent pool to be anticompetitive. In large part, the concern is that a patent pool might enable collusion and serve as a cover for horizontal price-fixing. *See* Roger B. Andewelt, *Practical Problems in Counseling and Litigating: Analysis of Patent Pools Under the Antitrust Laws*, 53 ANTITRUST L.J. 611, 611 (1984). The Supreme Court in *Standard Oil* considered this possibility, observing that "the power to fix and maintain royalties is tantamount to the power to fix prices." This would make the use of patent pools to fix royalty rates per se illegal. Why then did the Supreme Court find the pooling agreement legal? However, because the Court finds that the royalty-setting could have no effect since the pool did not dominate the market, no violation is found.

The Court rejected the government's argument that the mere act of dividing royalties is in and of itself anticompetitive, or that the royalties being charged in this case were too high. The Court, noting "the privileges incident to ownership of patents," rejects this argument and holds that, unless the pool dominates the market, antitrust law does not demand that the pool make the licenses available at reasonable royalty rates. If the pool as a whole does have significant power in the market at issue, should it be required to license at a "reasonable" rate? What would that reasonable rate be?

6. Could a patent pool increase the danger of price-fixing without specific terms as to royalty rates in the pooling agreement? Courts have held that the exchange of pricing information can violate Section One of the Sherman Act. *E.g., American Column & Lumber Co. v. United States*, 257 U.S. 377, 411–12 (1921); *United States v. Container Corp. of America*, 393 U.S. 333, 336–37 (1969). But what if the information shared is not pricing information (i.e., royalty rates) as such, but information relevant to pricing? Could the sharing of information aside from royalty rates

also constitute a violation? The Supreme Court in *Maple Flooring Manufacturers Ass'n v. United States,* 268 U.S. 563, 586 (1925) suggested that it might not, in a case dealing with information that did not consist of current pricing data, but trade statistics, shipping rates, and cost data. However, the federal antitrust agencies have suggested that it could, at least in the patent pool context:

> Administering a patent pool may require the pool's licensing agent to have access to competitively sensitive proprietary information of licensors and licensees, many of which may compete against each other in downstream markets. A patent pool could serve as a mechanism that facilitates downstream price coordination among the licensors if it were used to disseminate information between them about one another's use of the pool's technologies.

U.S. DEP'T OF JUSTICE & FEDERAL TRADE COMMISSION, ANTITRUST ENFORCEMENT AND INTELLECTUAL PROPERTY RIGHTS: PROMOTING INNOVATION AND COMPETITION 81 (2007). Consider how sharing various types of non-price information might support a cartel. How might the members of a patent pool mitigate this concern in drafting the agreement? *See id.* at 82 ("Pooling agreements that limit licensors' access to each others' competitively sensitive proprietary information, such as cost data, output levels, and prices of final products, lowers the risk that licensors will be able to coordinate their activities in final product markets.").

7. Patent pools might also be anticompetitive in that they can stifle incentives to innovate among the pool members. *See* John H. Barton, *Antitrust Treatment of Oligopolies with Mutually Blocking Patent Portfolios,* 69 ANTITRUST L.J. 851, 851 (2002) for a discussion of the circumstances likely to curb innovation. The Department of Justice's Antitrust-IP Guidelines construe this as a free rider problem:

> Licensors could be discouraged from making investments in innovation if "a pooling arrangement ... requires members to grant licenses to each other at minimal cost . . . because members of the pool have to share their successful research and development and each of the members can free ride on the accomplishments of other pool members."

U.S. DEP'T OF JUSTICE & FED. TRADE COMM'N, ANTITRUST ENFORCEMENT AND INTELLECTUAL PROPERTY RIGHTS: PROMOTING INNOVATION AND COMPETITION, 67 (2007) (quoting U.S. Department of Justice and Federal Trade Commission, *Antitrust Guidelines for the Licensing of Intellectual Property* § 5.5 (1995)). Such a provision is called a grantback. The issue of grantbacks is more fully discussed in Chapter 15. Of course, these incentives are likely to vary based on how the patent pool divides profits and whether, and for what reasons, members can be forced to leave the pool. The inclusion of grantback provisions in a pool agreement can also modify the incentives of innovators, "by rewarding first innovators for enabling follow-on innovation by others." *Id.* at 81.

However, patent pools might also stifle the incentives to innovate of non-members. If non-members cannot easily enter the pool upon developing an improved version of one of the patented technologies, there will be little incentive to engage in R&D in that area. Can you think of how a patent pool might be designed so as to avoid stifling the innovation incentives of non-members? Could the pooling agreement contain a provision allowing for the replacement of members under certain circumstances? How could such a provision be designed in order to adequately compensate the original pool members on the occasion of replacement such that the incentives to join the pool in the first place would be sufficient?

8. The duration of a patent pool can vary—for the life of the patents, for the life cycle of the licensed technology or standard, or for a fixed period of time. Should antitrust law care about how the duration of the patent pool is determined? Why or why not?

Matsushita Electrical Industrial Co. v. Cinram,
299 F.Supp.2d 370 (D. Del. 2004)

SUE L. ROBINSON, Chief Judge.

I. Introduction

Matsushita Electric Industrial Co., Ltd. ("MEI") filed an action against Cinram International, Inc. ("Cinram") on December 20, 2001 for patent infringement of five patents related to optical discs, including digital versatile discs ("DVDs"). ***

Cinram filed four antitrust counterclaims against MEI on March 13, 2002. [citation omitted] Cinram specifically charges that MEI has conspired to restrain trade by participating in the non-exclusive DVD 6C Licensing Agency (the "6C Pool") in violation of Section 1 of the Sherman Act, 15 U.S.C. § 1. *** Cinram alleges that it has experienced harm to its business and properties and been forced to pay excessive patent royalties as a result of MEI's illegal actions. It also alleges that it is unable to license and exercise patents related to DVD technology on competitive terms. To redress these injuries, "Cinram seeks to have MEI license 6C Pool members and independent licensees, through the 6C Pool and individually, on non-discriminatory terms, so that pool members and independent licensees pay the same royalties (while each pool member receives a share of pool royalties collected based on its patent contribution). In short, Cinram ... [seeks] to level the unlevel playing field." ***

II. Background

1. The Technology

DVDs are high-capacity media that permit the storage and readout of information in a digital format. DVDs are used for the storage and reproduction of video images in a format called DVD-Video. DVDs are also used for the storage and reading of digital information for use with computers in a format called DVD-ROM.

2. The 6C Pool

The DVD Forum is an international association of companies that are engaged in the research, development, manufacture, and/or sales related to DVD technology.

The DVD Forum was founded in 1995 by MEI under the name "DVD Consortium." Around 1995, the DVD Forum agreed on specifications for the recording, production, replication, and use of both DVDs and DVD equipment (the "DVD Standard Specification").

After establishing the DVD Standard Specification, six members of the DVD Forum, namely MEI, Hitachi, Mitsubishi, Toshiba, JVC, and AOL-Time Warner, organized the "6C Pool" and entered an agreement to manage the intellectual property rights around their DVD patented technology (the "6C Pool Formation Agreement"). [citation omitted] Under the terms of the 6C Pool Formation Agreement, each member of the 6C Pool contributed one or more of its patents related to DVD technology to the pool to form a collection of patents "essential" to DVD production.[3]

Each pool member acquired a cross-license to the other members' "essential" patents in exchange for its contribution. The members agreed as part of formation to offer a non-exclusive, non-transferable license to these pooled patents to non-member companies interested in replicating DVDs in compliance with the DVD Standard Specification ("independent replicator"). To this end, the members drafted a standard license agreement to facilitate licensing the pooled patents (the "6C Pool License"). Section 2.1 of the 6C Pool License specifically recites:

> Licensor hereby grants to Licensee and its Affiliates a non-exclusive, non-transferrable license to make, have made, use, sell, and otherwise dispose of DVD Products under the DVD Patents or any of their claims pursuant to the Conditions of Exhibit 3.

Also as part of formation, each member consented to offer individual licenses to its "essential" DVD patents on a non-exclusive basis to interested third party licensees as an alternative to the 6C Pool License. [citation omitted] The members incorporated this option into the 6C Pool License to notify potential licensees of a separate means of acquiring licenses for "essential" patents.

*** [A]n independent replicator who wishes to make DVDs without infringing any DVD patent, therefore, has the option of approaching either the 6C Pool for a 6C Pool License or each member of the 6C Pool for individual licenses.

The 6C Pool initially charged independent replicators $0.075 per disc under the 6C Pool License. The members later lowered the price to $0.065 or $0.05 per disc, depending upon when the independent replicator negotiated its 6C Pool License. MEI serves as the licensing agent to the Americas on behalf of the 6C Pool.

In addition to owning patents relating to DVD technology, MEI, JVC, AOL-Time Warner, and Mitsubishi commercially replicate DVDs. These four pool members, consequently, are in competition with independent replicators who

---

[3] "Essential" patents are defined in the 6C Pool License to mean "[1] necessarily infringed when implementing the DVD Standard Specifications or [2] claiming technologies for which there is no realistic alternative in implementing the DVD Standard Specifications." In other words, these patents are understood to have no substitutes, to be complementary to each other, and to be necessary to comply with the DVD Standard Specifications.

must take either a 6C Pool License or individual licenses to avoid patent infringement. Indeed, MEI is a direct competitor of Cinram in the market for wholesale production of DVDs in the DVD-Video and DVD-ROM formats. Moreover, MEI may practice DVD technology in compliance with the DVD Standard Specification without owing the same per disc license fees that Cinram must pay as a 6C Pool licensee; MEI only pays a $0.0015 per disc royalty whereas Cinram must pay a $0.05 per disc royalty.

3. Business Review Letter from the United States Department of Justice

In October 1998, the 6C Pool requested a Business Review Letter from the United States Department of Justice ("DOJ") pursuant to the DOJ's Business Review Procedure, 28 C.F.R. § 50.6. The 6C Pool specifically asked for a statement of the DOJ's antitrust enforcement intentions with respect to the 6C Pool's plan to assemble and offer a package license to "essential" patents, to manufacture products in compliance with the DVD-ROM and DVD-Video formation, and to distribute royalty income to members of the 6C Pool. The 6C Pool represented that "the pool will make the essential DVD patents available to licensees on fair, reasonable and non-discriminatory terms for the manufacture of products conforming to the [DVD Standard] Specifications." It also represented that the terms would entitle "any licensee to the benefit of favorable royalty terms offered to any other licensee." Furthermore, the 6C Pool represented that they would "make their DVD patents available individually, outside the [6C] [P]ool, on fair, reasonable, and non-discriminatory terms." Finally, the 6C Pool represented that "royalties will be a sufficiently small element of the final cost of DVD products so as to preclude them from serving as a device to coordinate downstream product prices."

Based on these assurances, the DOJ issued a Business Review Letter on June 10, 1999 indicating that it would not initiate an enforcement action. The DOJ found that the 6C Pool was "likely to combine complementary patent rights, thereby lowering the costs of manufacturers that need access to them in order to produce discs, players and decoders in conformity with the DVD-Video and DVD-ROM formats." The DOJ concluded that the 6C Pool was not likely to violate antitrust laws. ***

IV. Discussion

Under Section 1 of the Sherman Act, "[e]very contract, combination ... conspiracy, in restraint of trade or commerce ... is hereby declared to be illegal." *** The Supreme Court has advised that "[t]he Sherman Act has always been discriminatingly applied in the light of economic realities." *Broadcast Music, Inc. v. Columbia Broad. Sys. Inc.*, 441 U.S. 1, 14 (1979). In addition, the Supreme Court has stated that "[t]here are situations in which competitors have been permitted to form joint selling agencies or other pooled activities, subject to strict limitations under the antitrust laws to guarantee against abuse of the collective power thus created." *Id.*

rule of reason OR per se?

Price Fixing and Intellectual Property

In determining whether a pooled activity violates antitrust laws, courts must consider whether to employ a per se or a rule of reason analysis. The per se approach treats certain practices as being so plainly anti-competitive and without redeeming virtue as to be per se unreasonable. [citation omitted] The rule of reason approach, in contrast, broadly examines the business practices and related market factors to determine whether the questioned practice imposes an unreasonable restraint on competition. [citation omitted] The Supreme Court has recognized that patent pools should be addressed under the rule of reason analysis, except for arrangements where the only apparent purpose is naked price fixing. *United States v. Line Material,* 333 U.S. 287 (1948). In this context, the rule of reason analysis predominantly focuses on identifying pro-competitive benefits and balancing them against potential anti-competitive effects. [citation omitted]

Patent pooling arrangements may serve valid competitive objectives, especially in situations involving "blocking" and "complementary" patents. "For example, where patents 'block' one another in the sense that neither can be used without infringing the other, pooling becomes necessary to remove the stalemate and facilitate exploitation of the patents." [citation omitted] Similarly, if multiple patents complement each other to protect related but separate parts of a larger product or process, then pooling may be needed to produce a complete item. *Id.* Pooling likewise may be justified as the best way of solving a patent interference or infringement dispute. [citation omitted]

pooling can be pro-competitive

On the other hand, courts have recognized that certain types of pooling arrangements may significantly hurt competition. This is especially true when patents protect substitute goods that compete against each other in the marketplace. [citation omitted] In these situations, patent pools should be scrutinized for naked price-fixing, output restraints, exclusionary practices, and foreclosure of competition in downstream or related markets. [citation omitted]

"Trade is restrained, sometimes unreasonably, when the rights to use individual copyrights or patents may be obtained only by payment for a pool of such rights, but that the opportunity to acquire a pool of rights does not restrain trade if an alternative opportunity to acquire individual rights is realistically available." [citation omitted] However, "[a]n antitrust plaintiff is not obliged to pursue any imaginable alternative, regardless of cost or efficiency, before it can complain that a practice has restrained competition." [citation omitted] The true issue in situations involving a pool of rights is whether the antitrust plaintiff lacked a "realistic opportunity" as a "practical matter" to obtain individual licenses from individual owners as opposed to a single license from the pool. [citation omitted] If the antitrust plaintiff has the opportunity to license independently, then the pool of rights does not restrain trade in violation of Section 1 of the Sherman Act. ***

MEI argues that the 6C Pool members each contractually agreed when they formed the 6C Pool to offer individual licenses for their "essential" patents to interested parties on fair, reasonable, and non-discriminatory terms as an alternative to the 6C Pool License. MEI points out that both the 6C Pool Formation Agreement and the actual 6C Pool License contain provisions reciting this obligation. In light of its contractual duties, MEI asserts that it is willing to grant an individual license to any company interested in its individual "essential" patents.

MEI maintains that it repeatedly notified prospective licensees of the availability of individual licenses. *** MEI argues that Cinram did not respond to any of these notifications, nor did it seek to negotiate an individual license or ask for individual licensing rates, even though it met with 6C Pool representatives on seven occasions from August 2000 to February 2002. Moreover, MEI points out that Cinram did not approach other 6C Pool members to inquire about individual licenses. On this basis, MEI asserts that Cinram cannot meet its burden to establish that individual licenses are not a realistic alternative.

To counter MEI's argument, Cinram asserts that MEI's contractual obligation to offer individual licenses is illusory because, in reality, it does not offer such licenses on fair, reasonable, and non-discriminatory terms. To this end, Cinram maintains that the structure of the 6C Pool discourages individual licenses because such licenses would undercut the pool price. As well, Cinram charges that as its direct competitor in the DVD manufacturing area, MEI is less inclined to offer low individual licensing fees because it does not want to help the competition.

Cinram also argues that the terms for individual licenses are cost-prohibitive. Cinram explains that the cost for individual licenses from four of the six 6C Pool members totaled $0.11. Cinram points out that this total substantially exceeds the $0.05 per disc royalty that it currently pays for a 6C Pool License, thereby making individual licenses entirely impractical. Cinram substantiates its argument by noting that DOCdata Quanta, Metatec, Asustek Computer Inc., Wistron Corp., CMC Magnetics Corp., Cyberlink, Richoh, and Nippon Columbia all explored the possibility of individual licenses with 6C Pool members, but abandoned efforts in favor of a 6C Pool License. Cinram further validates its position by noting that MEI told Mr. Ritchie [Chief Financial Officer, Executive Vice President of Finance and Administration, and Corporate Secretary of Cinram] on two separate occasions that individual licenses would be "more costly" than a 6C Pool License and not a realistic alternative.

Finally, Cinram maintains that MEI and other 6C Pool members purposefully delayed in responding to inquiries regarding individual licenses. Cinram points out that Metatac contacted MEI and the other 6C Pool members for individual licensing terms in August 1999, but only received feedback from JVC and Hitachi after several months of delay. Particularly, JVC waited until June 2000 to respond, but did not quote any terms. JVC then took an additional ten months until April 2001 to provide a rate quote. Hitachi delayed fourteen months to provide its quotation to Metatec. With regard to MEI, Metatec renewed its request several times in 2001 and finally received a term sheet from MEI two and one-half years after its initial request. ***

Viewing the evidence of record and all reasonable inferences to be drawn therefrom in a light most favorable to Cinram as the non-moving party, the court finds that there are no genuine issues of material fact regarding whether individual licenses are a realistic alternative to the 6C Pool License. While this court previously recognized in *Broadcast Music, Inc., v. Moor Law, Inc.*, 484 F.Supp. 357, 367 (D.Del.1980) [citations omitted] that a plaintiff is not required to attempt individual licensing negotiations before suing under antitrust law when it is clear that such gesture would be futile, the court concludes that Cinram realistically could avail itself of individual licenses to "essential" DVD patents. Cinram was presented with a plethora of information regarding individual licensing terms from MEI through letters, brochures, and a direct presentation; it simply chose to pursue a 6C Pool License instead. Additionally, the court concludes that MEI did not seek to entirely avoid discussions with independent replicators about individual licensing terms. Rather, the court finds that MEI showed a willingness to discuss such terms based upon its two conversations with Mr. Ritchie. While MEI's slowness could be construed as purposeful delay as suggested by Cinram, the court understands that communications often proceed very slowly and deliberately in the business world, particularly when such communications occur on a global scale as in the instant case.

Moreover, despite the fact that numerous independent replicators approached MEI for individual licenses but eventually settled on a 6C Pool License, the court is not persuaded that MEI merely gave lip service to the option of individual licenses. The 6C Pool License is the simplest way to acquire a license to all the "essential" DVD patents. It likewise is the most economical approach, given that (1) the cost of a 6C Pool License is less than the cost of obtaining multiple individual licenses and (2) the per disc royalty under the 6C Pool License is $0.05 whereas the per disc royalty under individual licenses exceeds $0.11. The Second Circuit has stated that the only valid test to prove that an alternative is too costly to be a realistic alternative is whether the price for such a license, in an objective sense, is higher than the value of the intellectual property rights being conveyed. [citation omitted] In accord with this reasoning, the court concludes that the per disc royalty differential only causes the individual licensing option to be an unrealistic alternative if it is higher than the value of the DVD rights conveyed. The court finds that the facts at bar do not show this to be the case.

Furthermore, the court does not overlook the fact that the DOJ issued a Business Review Letter concluding that the 6C Pool was not likely to violate antitrust laws. The court appreciates the DOJ's familiarity and experience analyzing complex pooling arrangements and is strongly persuaded by the DOJ's conclusions. In light of these considerations, the court finds that there is enough evidence of record to enable a jury to reasonably decide that individual licenses present a realistic alternative to the 6C Pool License and that the 6C Pool, in turn, does not violate antitrust laws. Accordingly, the court concludes that summary judgment is appropriate and grants MEI's motion as to Cinram's antitrust claims. ***

Comments and Questions

1. The Department of Justice's Antitrust Division is not authorized to give advisory opinions to firms. However, the Division has developed a procedure for issuing so-called Business Review Letters in response to written submissions from

businesses seeking review of their proposed conduct. "The requesting parties are under an affirmative obligation to make full and true disclosure with respect to the business conduct for which review is requested." 28 C.F.R. § 50.6. In response to the request, and accompanying data and documents, the Division may do one of three things: "state its present enforcement intention with respect to the proposed business conduct; decline to pass on the request; or take such other position or action as it considers appropriate." *Id.* Letters that state an intention not to bring an enforcement action do not bind the Division and it "remains completely free to bring whatever action or proceeding it subsequently comes to believe is required by the public interest." *Id.* Nevertheless, the Division's issuance of a Business Review Letter provides some modicum of assurance to firms considering a venture that they fear could arguably be seen as anticompetitive. Furthermore, although a Business Review Letter does not bind courts in subsequent antitrust litigation, see *United States v. Western Elec. Co.*, 154 F.R.D. 1, 4 (D.D.C.1994), aff'd, 46 F.3d 1198 (D.C.Cir.1995), courts sometimes give weight to them, as seen in the *Cinram* opinion.

The Business Review Letter did not consider the price differentials and the delays in responding. Should the Business Review Letter protect the defendant's conduct in this case?

The applicants made several assurances in their request for a Business Review Letter. What should happen if those assurances were violated? Were the assurances violated in this case?

2. Courts draw a distinction between complementary and substitute patents. Why?

Patent pools may involve as few as two and as many as hundreds of patents. When hundreds of patents are involved, it can be exceedingly difficult to determine whether the component patents are essential and complementary. Is it always clear whether patents in a pool are substitutes or complementary? See U.S. Dep't of Justice & Federal Trade Commission, Antitrust Enforcement and Intellectual Property Rights: Promoting Innovation and Competition 74 (2007) ("categorizing patents as complements or substitutes is not a simple task. In many cases, patents in a pool are not pure complements or pure substitutes, but display characteristics of both.").

3. The court reasoned that "[t]he true issue in situations involving a pool of rights is whether the antitrust plaintiff lacked a 'realistic opportunity' as a 'practical matter' to obtain individual licenses from individual owners as opposed to a single license from the pool." Did the plaintiff have a reasonable opportunity as a practical matter, given the facts alleged by the plaintiff?

Cinram claimed that the cost of obtaining individual licenses from each pool member was greater than the cost of obtaining a single pool license. The District Court was not persuaded that this was enough to show that an alternative opportunity was not "realistically available." Should it have been? When should a claim of excessive cost of the alternative opportunity be enough to show that it was not realistically available?

Cinram claimed that the pool members purposefully delayed responding to requests for individual licenses. JVC waited ten months to respond to an individual license request and then another ten months to provide any terms for the license. Other members were similarly sluggish in responding to individual license requests. At what point is a delay tantamount to the refusal to make the license available? Does the court provide any guidance as to this question? What kinds of factors could courts consider in determining whether a delay is excessive?

Was the delay in this case tantamount to the members of the patent pool saying "no individual licenses"? Why or why not?

4. The plaintiff objected to the fact that "MEI may practice DVD technology in compliance with the DVD Standard Specification without owing the same per disc license fees that Cinram must pay as a 6C Pool licensee; MEI only pays a $0.0015 per disc royalty whereas Cinram must pay a $0.05 per disc royalty."

Consequently, the royalty that Cinram paid was more than 33 times more expensive than the royalty paid by Matsushita. Why doesn't the FRAND requirement solve this? Should MEI pay a lower disk royalty fee?

5. The court granted summary judgment to the defendant, reasoning that "the court finds that there is enough evidence of record to enable a jury to reasonably decide that individual licenses present a realistic alternative to the 6C Pool License and that the 6C Pool, in turn, does not violate antitrust laws." *Matsushita Electrical Industrial Co. v. Cinram*, 299 F.Supp.2d 370 (D. Del. 2004). Is that the correct issue? Given the posture of the case, shouldn't the issue be whether there is enough for a jury to find that an individual license is *not* a realistic alternative? Why does the distinction matter?

The court claimed that it was "[v]iewing the evidence of record and all reasonable inferences to be drawn therefrom in a light most favorable to Cinram" when it held "that Cinram realistically could avail itself of individual licenses to "essential" DVD patents." Did it view the evidence in the light most favorable to Cinram?

6. Assuming that the plaintiff had prevailed on the issue of liability, what would be the appropriate remedy in a case like this? Why?

Cinram had requested damages and the following injunctive relief: "(1) that MEI withdraw from any licensing or cross-licensing agreements with 6C Pool members for DVD technology, particularly involving 'essential' technology, that offer terms to members more favorable than those given to Cinram; (2) that MEI discontinue entering into licensing or cross-licensing agreements for DVD technology, particularly involving the "essential" technology, that offer terms more favorable than those given to Cinram; and (3) that MEI offer a license to its DVD technology on fair, reasonable, and non-discriminatory terms." Is that appropriate?

Federal Trade Commission In the Matter of Summit Technology

127 F.T.C. 208 (February 23, 1999)

This consent order, among other things, prohibits the Massachusetts-based marketer of laser equipment for eye surgery from entering into, enforcing or maintaining any contract, agreement, joint venture or other combination with VISX, Inc., to fix, maintain or control any price or the terms or conditions associated with the purchase, license or use of any product, device or technology that uses a laser to perform any medical procedure, including ophthalmic surgery.

Complaint

Pursuant to the provisions of the Federal Trade Commission Act, and by virtue of the authority vested in it by said Act, the Federal Trade Commission, having reason to believe that Summit Technology Inc. ("Summit"), a corporation, and VISX, Inc. ("VISX"), a corporation, hereinafter sometimes referred to as respondents, have violated the provisions of said Act, and it appearing to the Commission that a proceeding by it in respect thereof would be in the public interest, hereby issues its complaint, stating its charges as follows:

Background ***

4. Photorefractive keratectomy ("PRK") is a form of eye surgery use to correct vision disorders. PRK uses specialized, computer-guided laser equipment to reshape the cornea.

5. Before VISX and Summit pooled their patents, each firm owned or controlled numerous patents related to PRK.

6. VISX and Summit are the only firms whose laser equipment has received marketing approval from the United States Food and Drug Administration ("FDA") for performing PRK. As a result, VISX and Summit are the only two firms legally able to market laser equipment to be used for PRK in the United States.

7. Except to the extent that VISX and Summit have restrained competition as alleged herein, they have been, and are now, in competition with each other in connection with the sale or lease of PRK equipment and the licensing of technology related to PRK.

The Patent Pool

8. On or about June 3, 1992, pursuant to a series of agreements hereinafter collectively referred to as the "PPP Agreement," VISX and Summit pooled most of their existing, as well as certain future, patents related to PRK in a newly created partnership, called Pillar Point Partners ("PPP"). VISX and Summit have pooled at least 25 patents, containing more than 500 method and apparatus claims, in PPP ("PPP Patents"). Notwithstanding these patents, in the absence of the PPP Agreement, VISX and Summit could have and would have competed with one another in the sale or lease of PRK equipment by using their respective patents, licensing them, or both. In addition, VISX and Summit would have engaged in competition with each other in connection with the licensing of technology related to PRK.

9. Under the PPP Agreement, PPP has the right to license the PPP Patents to persons engaged in the business of manufacturing PRK equipment, and VISX and

Price Fixing and Intellectual Property

Summit each have relinquished the right to unilaterally license to any such person any patent that either firm contributed to PPP.

10. Under the PPP Agreement, VISX and Summit each have the unilateral right and power to prevent PPP from licensing any of the PPP Patents to other persons engaged in the business of manufacturing PRK equipment.

11. Under the PPP Agreement, PPP has licensed back to VISX and Summit all of the PPP Patents. Also under the PPP Agreement VISX and Summit each may sell, lease or otherwise make available PRK equipment covered by the PPP Patents to laser users and may sublicense those users to perform PRK and related procedures.

12. With certain exceptions, under the PPP Agreement, VISX and Summit each must pay a fee to PPP each time any laser user performs a PRK procedure under any PPP Patents sublicensed by Summit or VISX. Under the PPP Agreement, the level of this Per-Procedure Fee can range from $30 to $250, and is set at the higher of the amounts separately proposed by VISX and Summit. Since receiving FDA approval to market their lasers, VISX and Summit have set this Per-Procedure Fee at $250. Since receiving FDA approval to market their lasers, VISX and Summit each has charged its sublicensees a $250 per-procedure fee, with certain minor exceptions. Under the PPP Agreement, all third party manufacturers that might be licensed by PPP would be required to pay this Per-Procedure Fee to PPP.

13. As a result of their agreement with respect to Per-Procedure Fee under the PPP Agreement, VISX and Summit charged consumers significantly more than they would have been charged in the absence of the agreement. Based on the number of procedures performed in 1996, it is likely that this overcharge exceeded $10.5 million. Based on estimates for procedures performed in 1997, it is likely that this overcharge exceeded $30 million. ***

The Relevant Markets

22. The sale or lease of PRK equipment, including the licensing of patents for use in performing PRK, is a relevant line of commerce in which to analyze the effects of respondents' conduct.

23. The licensing of technology related to PRK is a relevant line of commerce in which to analyze the effects of respondents' conduct.

24. A relevant geographic area in which to analyze the effects of respondents' conduct is the United States.

Violations of Section Five of the FTC Act

Count I

25. The acts and practices of respondents as alleged herein constitute a contract, combination or conspiracy in restraint of commerce, and have had, and continue to have, the purpose, effect, tendency and capacity to, among other things:

   a. Raise, fix, stabilize and maintain the price that physicians must pay to perform PRK procedures;

b. Raise the cost of, prevent entry into and deter the sale or leasing of PRK equipment and the licensing of technology related to PRK;

c. Deprive consumers of the benefits of competition in the sale and leasing of PRK equipment and the licensing of technology related to PRK.

26. The acts and practices of respondents as alleged herein were and are to the prejudice and injury of the public, will continue in the absence of the relief herein requested, and constitute unfair methods of competition in or affecting commerce in violation of Section 5 of the Federal Trade Commission Act.

Count II

27. The acts and practices of respondents as alleged herein constitute the willful acquisition and maintenance of a monopoly, or a conspiracy or attempt to monopolize, and had the purpose, effect, tendency and capacity to, among other things:

a. Create, maintain or have a dangerous probability of creating, a monopoly in the sale or leasing of PRK equipment and the licensing of technology related to PRK;

b. Raise, fix, stabilize and maintain the price that physicians must pay to perform PRK procedures;

c. Raise the cost of, prevent entry into and deter the sale or leasing of PRK equipment and the licensing of technology related to PRK; and

d. Deprive consumers of the benefits of competition in the sale and leasing of PRK equipment and the licensing of technology related to PRK.

28. The acts and practices of respondents as alleged herein were and are to the prejudice and injury of the public, will continue in the absence of the relief herein requested, and constitute unfair methods of competition in or affecting commerce in violation of Section 5 of the Federal Trade Commission Act. ***

Order

*** It is *** ordered, That respondent, directly or indirectly, or through any person or other device, in or in connection with activities in or affecting commerce, *** cease and desist, except as provided in paragraph III of this order or in the Settlement and Dissolution Agreement, from entering into, adhering to, participating in, enforcing or maintaining any contract, agreement, understanding, joint venture, pool, partnership, cross-license or other combination with VISX:

A. (1) To fix, construct, stabilize, standardize, raise, maintain, or otherwise affect or control any price, royalty or fee for, any aspect of any price, royalty or fee for, or the terms or conditions associated with the purchase, license or use of any product, device, method, patent, intellectual property, or technology that uses or is used in conjunction with, or claims, covers, embodies or incorporates in whole or in part the use of, a laser to perform any medical procedure, including but not limited to ophthalmic surgery; or

(2) To establish, require, charge, collect or pay any Per-Procedure Fee;

B. (1) To restrict the right or ability of respondent or VISX to sell or license any product, device, method, patent, intellectual property, or technology that uses or is used in conjunction with, or claims, covers, embodies or incorporates in whole or in part the use of, a laser to perform any medical procedure, including but not limited to ophthalmic surgery; or

(2) To grant respondent or VISX the right or ability to prevent the sale or license by respondent or VISX of any product, device, method, patent, intellectual property, or technology that uses or is used in conjunction with, or claims, covers, embodies or incorporates in whole or in part the use of, a laser to perform any medical procedure, including but not limited to ophthalmic surgery. ***

It is further ordered, That respondent shall, no later than twenty (20) days from the date this order becomes final, license to VISX the patents that respondent contributed to, or agreed to contribute to, PPP *** and any divisions, reissues, reexaminations, continuations, continuations in part, renewals, extensions and additions thereof. Such license(s) shall be royalty-free and non-exclusive as set forth in the Settlement and Dissolution Agreement. ***

Comments and Questions

1. What is the difference between the agreement in *Standard Oil* and the agreement between Summit and VISX?

2. Were the patents in the Summit-VISX pool complementary or substitutes? How does your answer affect the antitrust analysis?

C. Blanket Licensing of Copyrighted Works

Broadcast Music, Inc. v. CBS,
441 U.S. 1 (1979)

Mr. Justice WHITE delivered the opinion of the Court.

This case involves an action under the antitrust and copyright laws brought by respondent Columbia Broadcasting System, Inc. (CBS), against petitioners, American Society of Composers, Authors and Publishers (ASCAP) and Broadcast Music, Inc. (BMI), and their members and affiliates. The basic question presented is whether the issuance by ASCAP and BMI to CBS of blanket licenses to copyrighted musical compositions at fees negotiated by them is price fixing per se unlawful under the antitrust laws.

I

CBS operates one of three national commercial television networks, supplying programs to approximately 200 affiliated stations and telecasting approximately 7,500 network programs per year. Many, but not all, of these programs make use of copyrighted music recorded on the soundtrack. CBS also owns television and radio stations in various cities. It is "the giant of the world in the use of music rights," the "No. 1 outlet in the history of entertainment."

328 *Antitrust Law and Intellectual Property Rights*

Since 1897, the copyright laws have vested in the owner of a copyrighted musical composition the exclusive right to perform the work publicly for profit, but the legal right is not self-enforcing. In 1914, Victor Herbert and a handful of other composers organized ASCAP because those who performed copyrighted music for profit were so numerous and widespread, and most performances so fleeting, that as a practical matter it was impossible for the many individual copyright owners to negotiate with and license the users and to detect unauthorized uses. "ASCAP was organized as a 'clearing-house' for copyright owners and users to solve these problems" associated with the licensing of music. [citation omitted] As ASCAP operates today, its 22,000 members grant it nonexclusive rights to license nondramatic performances of their works, and ASCAP issues licenses and distributes royalties to copyright owners in accordance with a schedule reflecting the nature and amount of the use of their music and other factors.

BMI, a nonprofit corporation owned by members of the broadcasting industry, was organized in 1939, is affiliated with or represents some 10,000 publishing companies and 20,000 authors and composers, and operates in much the same manner as ASCAP. Almost every domestic copyrighted composition is in the repertory either of ASCAP, with a total of three million compositions, or of BMI, with one million.

Both organizations operate primarily through blanket licenses, which give the licensees the right to perform any and all of the compositions owned by the members or affiliates as often as the licensees desire for a stated term. Fees for blanket licenses are ordinarily a percentage of total revenues or a flat dollar amount, and do not directly depend on the amount or type of music used. Radio and television broadcasters are the largest users of music, and almost all of them hold blanket licenses from both ASCAP and BMI. Until this litigation, CBS held blanket licenses from both organizations for its television network on a continuous basis since the late 1940's and had never attempted to secure any other form of license from either ASCAP or any of its members. [citation omitted]

The complaint filed by CBS charged various violations of the Sherman Act and the copyright laws. CBS argued that ASCAP and BMI are unlawful monopolies and that the blanket license is illegal price fixing, an unlawful tying arrangement, a concerted refusal to deal, and a misuse of copyrights. The District Court, though denying summary judgment to certain defendants, ruled that the practice did not fall within the per se rule. [citation omitted] After an 8-week trial, limited to the issue of liability, the court dismissed the complaint, rejecting again the claim that the blanket license was price fixing and a per se violation of § 1 of the Sherman Act, and holding that since direct negotiation with individual copyright owners is available and feasible there is no undue restraint of trade, illegal tying, misuse of copyrights, or monopolization. [citation omitted]

Though agreeing with the District Court's factfinding and not disturbing its legal conclusions on the other antitrust theories of liability, the Court of Appeals held that the blanket license issued to television networks was a form of price fixing illegal per se under the Sherman Act. [citation omitted] This conclusion, without more, settled the issue of liability under the Sherman Act, established copyright misuse, and required reversal of the District Court's judgment, as well as a remand to consider the appropriate remedy.

ASCAP and BMI petitioned for certiorari ***. Because we disagree with the Court of Appeals' conclusions with respect to the per se illegality of the blanket license, we reverse its judgment and remand the cause for further appropriate proceedings.

II

In construing and applying the Sherman Act's ban against contracts, conspiracies, and combinations in restraint of trade, the Court has held that certain agreements or practices are so "plainly anticompetitive," [citation omitted] and so often "lack . . . any redeeming virtue," [citation omitted], that they are conclusively presumed illegal without further examination under the rule of reason generally applied in Sherman Act cases. This pro se [sic] rule is a valid and useful tool of antitrust policy and enforcement.[11] And agreements among competitors to fix prices on their individual goods or services are among those concerted activities that the Court has held to be within the per se category. But easy labels do not always supply ready answers.

A

To the Court of Appeals and CBS, the blanket license involves "price fixing" in the literal sense: the composers and publishing houses have joined together into an organization that sets its price for the blanket license it sells. But this is not a question simply of determining whether two or more potential competitors have literally "fixed" a "price." As generally used in the antitrust field, "price fixing" is a shorthand way of describing certain categories of business behavior to which the per se rule has been held applicable. The Court of Appeals' literal approach does not alone establish that this particular practice is one of those types or that it is "plainly anticompetitive" and very likely without "redeeming virtue." Literalness is overly simplistic and often overbroad. When two partners set the price of their goods or services they are literally "price fixing," but they are not per se in violation of the Sherman Act. [citation omitted] Thus, it is necessary to characterize the challenged conduct as falling within or without that category of behavior to which we apply the label "per se price fixing." That will often, but not always, be a simple matter.

---

[11] "This principle of per se unreasonableness not only makes the type of restraints which are proscribed by the Sherman Act more certain to the benefit of everyone concerned, but it also avoids the necessity for an incredibly complicated and prolonged economic investigation into the entire history of the industry involved, as well as related industries, in an effort to determine at large whether a particular restraint has been unreasonable–an inquiry so often wholly fruitless when undertaken." Northern Pac. R. Co. v. United States, 356 U.S. 1, 5 (1958). [c.o.]

Consequently, as we recognized in *United States v. Topco Associates, Inc.*, 405 U.S. 596, 607–608 (1972), "[i]t is only after considerable experience with certain business relationships that courts classify them as per se violations . . . ." [citation omitted] We have never examined a practice like this one before; indeed, the Court of Appeals recognized that "[i]n dealing with performing rights in the music industry we confront conditions both in copyright law and in antitrust law which are sui generis." [citation omitted] And though there has been rather intensive antitrust scrutiny of ASCAP and its blanket licenses, that experience hardly counsels that we should outlaw the blanket license as a per se restraint of trade.

B

This litigation and other cases involving ASCAP and its licensing practices have arisen out of the efforts of the creators of copyrighted musical compositions to collect for the public performance of their works, as they are entitled to do under the Copyright Act. As already indicated, ASCAP and BMI originated to make possible and to facilitate dealings between copyright owners and those who desire to use their music. Both organizations plainly involve concerted action in a large and active line of commerce, and it is not surprising that, as the District Court found, "[n]either ASCAP nor BMI is a stranger to antitrust litigation." 400 F.Supp., at 743.

The Department of Justice first investigated allegations of anticompetitive conduct by ASCAP over 50 years ago. A criminal complaint was filed in 1934, but the Government was granted a midtrial continuance and never returned to the courtroom. In separate complaints in 1941, the United States charged that the blanket license, which was then the only license offered by ASCAP and BMI, was an illegal restraint of trade and that arbitrary prices were being charged as the result of an illegal copyright pool. The Government sought to enjoin ASCAP's exclusive licensing powers and to require a different form of licensing by that organization. The case was settled by a consent decree that imposed tight restrictions on ASCAP's operations. Following complaints relating to the television industry, successful private litigation against ASCAP by movie theaters, and a Government challenge to ASCAP's arrangements with similar foreign organizations, the 1941 decree was reopened and extensively amended in 1950.

Under the amended decree, which still substantially controls the activities of ASCAP, members may grant ASCAP only nonexclusive rights to license their works for public performance. Members, therefore, retain the rights individually to license public performances, along with the rights to license the use of their compositions for other purposes. ASCAP itself is forbidden to grant any license to perform one or more specified compositions in the ASCAP repertory unless both the user and the owner have requested it in writing to do so. ASCAP is required to grant to any user making written application a nonexclusive license to perform all ASCAP compositions either for a period of time or on a per-program basis. ASCAP may not insist on the blanket license, and the fee for the per-program license, which is to be based on the revenues for the program on which ASCAP music is played, must offer the applicant a genuine economic choice between the per-program license and the more common blanket license. If ASCAP and a putative licensee are unable to agree on a fee within 60 days, the applicant may apply to the District Court for a determination of a reasonable fee, with ASCAP having the burden of proving reasonableness.[20]

The 1950 decree, as amended from time to time, continues in effect, and the blanket license continues to be the primary instrument through which ASCAP conducts its business under the decree. The courts have twice construed the decree not to require ASCAP to issue licenses for selected portions of its repertory. It also remains true that the decree guarantees the legal availability of direct licensing of performance rights by ASCAP members; and the District Court found, and in this respect the Court of Appeals agreed, that there are no practical impediments preventing direct dealing by the television networks if they so desire. Historically, they have not done so. Since 1946, CBS and other television networks have taken blanket licenses from ASCAP and BMI. It was not until this suit arose that the CBS network demanded any other kind of license.

Of course, a consent judgment, even one entered at the behest of the Antitrust Division, does not immunize the defendant from liability for actions, including those contemplated by the decree, that violate the rights of nonparties. [citation omitted] But it cannot be ignored that the Federal Executive and Judiciary have carefully scrutinized ASCAP and the challenged conduct, have imposed restrictions on various of ASCAP's practices, and, by the terms of the decree, stand ready to provide further consideration, supervision, and perhaps invalidation of asserted anticompetitive practices. In these circumstances, we have a unique indicator that the challenged practice may have redeeming competitive virtues and that the search for those values is not almost sure to be in vain. Thus, although CBS is not bound by the Antitrust Division's actions, the decree is a fact of economic and legal life in this industry, and the Court of Appeals should not have ignored it completely in analyzing the practice. [citation omitted] That fact alone might not remove a naked price-fixing scheme from the ambit of the per se rule, but, as discussed infra, Part III, here we are uncertain whether the practice on its face has the effect, or could have been spurred by the purpose, of restraining competition among the individual composers.

After the consent decrees, the legality of the blanket license was challenged in suits brought by certain ASCAP members against individual radio stations for copyright infringement. The stations raised as a defense that the blanket license was a form of price fixing illegal under the Sherman Act. The parties stipulated that it would be nearly impossible for each radio station to negotiate with each copyright holder separate licenses for the performance of his works on radio. Against this background, and relying heavily on the 1950 consent judgment, the Court of Appeals for the Ninth Circuit rejected claims that ASCAP was a combination

---

[20] BMI is in a similar situation. ***

in restraint of trade and that the blanket license constituted illegal price fixing. [citation omitted]

The Department of Justice, with the principal responsibility for enforcing the Sherman Act and administering the consent decrees relevant to this case, agreed with the result reached by the Ninth Circuit. In a submission amicus curiae opposing one station's petition for certiorari in this Court, the Department stated that there must be "some kind of central licensing agency by which copyright holders may offer their works in a common pool to all who wish to use them." [citation omitted] And the Department elaborated on what it thought that fact meant for the proper application of the antitrust laws in this area:

> "The Sherman Act has always been discriminatingly applied in the light of economic realities. There are situations in which competitors have been permitted to form joint selling agencies or other pooled activities, subject to strict limitations under the antitrust laws to guarantee against abuse of the collective power thus created. *** This case appears to us to involve such a situation. The extraordinary number of users spread across the land, the ease with which a performance may be broadcast, the sheer volume of copyrighted compositions, the enormous quantity of separate performances each year, the impracticability of negotiating individual licenses for each composition, and the ephemeral nature of each performance all combine to create unique market conditions for performance rights to recorded music." Id., at 10 (footnote omitted).

The Department concluded that, in the circumstances of that case, the blanket licenses issued by ASCAP to individual radio stations were neither a per se violation of the Sherman Act nor an unreasonable restraint of trade.

As evidenced by its amicus brief in the present case, the Department remains of that view. Furthermore, the United States disagrees with the Court of Appeals in this case and urges that the blanket licenses, which the consent decree authorizes ASCAP to issue to television networks, are not per se violations of the Sherman Act. It takes no position, however, on whether the practice is an unreasonable restraint of trade in the context of the network television industry.

Finally, we note that Congress itself, in the new Copyright Act, has chosen to employ the blanket license and similar practices. Congress created a compulsory blanket license for secondary transmissions by cable television systems and provided that "[n]otwithstanding any provisions of the antitrust laws, . . . any claimants may agree among themselves as to the proportionate division of compulsory licensing fees among them, may lump their claims together and file them jointly or as a single claim, or may designate a common agent to receive payment on their behalf." 17 U.S.C. App. § 111(d)(5)(A). And the newly created compulsory license for the use of copyrighted compositions in jukeboxes is also a blanket license, which is payable to the performing-rights societies such as ASCAP unless an individual copyright holder can prove his entitlement to a share. § 116(c)(4). Moreover, in requiring noncommercial broadcasters to pay for their use of copyrighted music, Congress again provided that "[n]otwithstanding any provision of the antitrust laws" copyright owners "may designate common agents to negotiate, agree to, pay, or receive payments." § 118(b). Though these provisions are not directly controlling, they do reflect an opinion that the blanket license, and ASCAP, are economically beneficial in at least some circumstances.

There have been District Court cases holding various ASCAP practices, including its licensing practices, to be violative of the Sherman Act, but even so, there is no nearly universal view that either the blanket or the per-program licenses issued by ASCAP at prices negotiated by it are a form of price fixing subject to automatic condemnation under the Sherman Act, rather than to a careful assessment under the rule of reason.

III

Of course, we are no more bound than is CBS by the views of the Department of Justice, the results in the prior lower court cases, or the opinions of various experts about the merits of the blanket license. But while we must independently examine this practice, all those factors should caution us against too easily finding blanket licensing subject to per se invalidation. ***

B

In the first place, the line of commerce allegedly being restrained, the performing rights to copyrighted music, exists at all only because of the copyright laws. Those who would use copyrighted music in public performances must secure consent from the copyright owner or be liable at least for the statutory damages for each infringement and, if the conduct is willful and for the purpose of financial gain, to criminal penalties. Furthermore, nothing in the Copyright Act of 1976 indicates in the slightest that Congress intended to weaken the rights of copyright owners to control the public performance of musical compositions. Quite the contrary is true. Although the copyright laws confer no rights on copyright owners to fix prices among themselves or otherwise to violate the antitrust laws, we would not expect that any market arrangements reasonably necessary to effectuate the rights that are granted would be deemed a per se violation of the Sherman Act. Otherwise, the commerce anticipated by the Copyright Act and protected against restraint by the Sherman Act would not exist at all or would exist only as a pale reminder of what Congress envisioned. ***

C

More generally, in characterizing this conduct under the per se rule, our inquiry must focus on whether the effect and, here because it tends to show effect, *see United States v. United States Gypsum Co.*, 438 U.S. 422, 436 n. 13 (1978), the purpose of the practice are to threaten the proper operation of our predominantly free-market economy–that is, whether the practice facially appears to be one that would always or almost always tend to restrict competition and decrease output, and in what portion of the market, or instead one designed to "increase economic efficiency and render markets more, rather than less, competitive." Id. at 441 n. 16 [citation omitted].

The blanket license, as we see it, is not a "naked restrain[t] of trade with no purpose except stifling of competition," *White Motor Co. v. United States,* 372 U.S. 253, 263 (1963), but rather accompanies the integration of sales, monitoring, and enforcement against unauthorized copyright use. See L. Sullivan, Handbook of the Law of Antitrust § 59, p. 154 (1977). *** ASCAP and the blanket license developed together out of the practical situation in the marketplace: thousands of users, thousands of copyright owners, and millions of compositions. Most users want unplanned, rapid, and indemnified access to any and all of the repertory of compositions, and the owners want a reliable method of collecting for the use of their copyrights. Individual sales transactions in this industry are quite expensive, as would be individual monitoring and enforcement, especially in light of the resources of single composers. Indeed, as both the Court of Appeals and CBS recognize, the costs are prohibitive for licenses with individual radio stations, nightclubs, and restaurants, [citation omitted] and it was in that milieu that the blanket license arose.

A middleman with a blanket license was an obvious necessity if the thousands of individual negotiations, a virtual impossibility, were to be avoided. Also, individual fees for the use of individual compositions would presuppose an intricate schedule of fees and uses, as well as a difficult and expensive reporting problem for the user and policing task for the copyright owner. Historically, the market for public-performance rights organized itself largely around the single-fee blanket license, which gave unlimited access to the repertory and reliable protection against infringement. When ASCAP's major and user-created competitor, BMI, came on the scene, it also turned to the blanket license.

With the advent of radio and television networks, market conditions changed, and the necessity for and advantages of a blanket license for those users may be far less obvious than is the case when the potential users are individual television or radio stations, or the thousands of other individuals and organizations performing copyrighted compositions in public.[34] But even for television network licenses, ASCAP reduces costs absolutely by creating a blanket license that is sold only a few, instead of thousands,[35] of times, and that obviates the need for closely monitoring the networks to see that they do not use more than they pay for. ASCAP also provides the necessary resources for blanket sales and enforcement, resources unavailable to the vast majority of composers and publishing houses. Moreover, a bulk license of some type is a necessary consequence of the integration necessary to achieve these efficiencies, and a necessary consequence of an aggregate license is that its price must be established.

---

[34] And of course changes brought about by new technology or new marketing techniques might also undercut the justification for the practice.

[35] The District Court found that CBS would require between 4,000 and 8,000 individual license transactions per year. [c.o.]

D

This substantial lowering of costs, which is of course potentially beneficial to both sellers and buyers, differentiates the blanket license from individual use licenses. The blanket license is composed of the individual compositions plus the aggregating service. Here, the whole is truly greater than the sum of its parts; it is, to some extent, a different product. The blanket license has certain unique characteristics: It allows the licensee immediate use of covered compositions, without the delay of prior individual negotiations and great flexibility in the choice of musical material. Many consumers clearly prefer the characteristics and cost advantages of this marketable package, and even small performing rights societies that have occasionally arisen to compete with ASCAP and BMI have offered blanket licenses. Thus, to the extent the blanket license is a different product, ASCAP is not really a joint sales agency offering the individual goods of many sellers, but is a separate seller offering its blanket license, of which the individual compositions are raw material.[40] ASCAP, in short, made a market in which individual composers are inherently unable to compete fully effectively.

E

Finally, we have some doubt—enough to counsel against application of the per se rule—about the extent to which this practice threatens the "central nervous system of the economy," [citation omitted] that is, competitive pricing as the free market's means of allocating resources. Not all arrangements among actual or potential competitors that have an impact on price are per se violations of the Sherman Act or even unreasonable restraints. Mergers among competitors eliminate competition, including price competition, but they are not per se illegal, and many of them withstand attack under any existing antitrust standard. Joint ventures and other cooperative arrangements are also not usually unlawful, at least not as price-fixing schemes, where the agreement on price is necessary to market the product at all.

Here, the blanket-license fee is not set by competition among individual copyright owners, and it is a fee for the use of any of the compositions covered by the license. But the blanket license cannot be wholly equated with a simple horizontal arrangement among competitors. ASCAP does set the price for its blanket license, but that license is quite different from anything any individual owner could issue. The individual composers and authors have neither agreed not to sell individually in any other market nor use the blanket license to mask price fixing in such other markets. Moreover, the substantial restraints placed on ASCAP and its members by the consent decree must not be ignored. The District Court found that there

---

[40] Moreover, because of the nature of the product—a composition can be simultaneously "consumed" by many users—composers have numerous markets and numerous incentives to produce, so the blanket license is unlikely to cause decreased output, one of the normal undesirable effects of a cartel. And since popular songs get an increased share of ASCAP's revenue distributions, composers compete even within the blanket license in terms of productivity and consumer satisfaction.

was no legal, practical, or conspiratorial impediment to CBS's obtaining individual licenses; CBS, in short, had a real choice.

With this background in mind, which plainly enough indicates that over the years, and in the face of available alternatives, the blanket license has provided an acceptable mechanism for at least a large part of the market for the performing rights to copyrighted musical compositions, we cannot agree that it should automatically be declared illegal in all of its many manifestations. Rather, when attacked, it should be subjected to a more discriminating examination under the rule of reason. It may not ultimately survive that attack, but that is not the issue before us today. ***

The judgment of the Court of Appeals is reversed, and the cases are remanded to that court for further proceedings consistent with this opinion.

It is so ordered.

Comments and Questions

1. In determining whether to apply the per se rule or the rule of reason to blanket licenses, the Supreme Court notes that "the blanket license involves 'price fixing' in the literal sense" but that "this is not a question simply of determining whether two or more potential competitors have literally 'fixed' a 'price.'" What does this mean? Is it no longer the case that price fixing is per se illegal?

After analyzing sections of the Copyright Act, the Court noted: "Though these provisions are not directly controlling, they do reflect an opinion that the blanket license, and ASCAP, are economically beneficial in at least some circumstances." What is the legal significance of this finding?

The Court notes that "[i]t is only after considerable experience with certain business relationships that courts classify them as *per se* violations." Upon claiming that it has "never examined a practice like this one before," the Court goes on to assess the previous forty years of treatment of blanket licenses. The Court examines a consent decree imposing restrictions on ASCAP, but allowing the blanket license to continue, a few judicial decisions, and the incorporation of blanket licenses into the Copyright Act. In footnote 11, the Court emphasizes the virtues of the per se rule: that it provides certainty to market participants so that they can abide by the law, and that it spares judicial resources by avoiding the "incredibly complicated and prolonged economic investigation into the entire history of the industry involved."

By declaring that literal price-fixing is not the same as per se illegal price fixing and engaging in a thorough analysis of forty years of exposure to the practice by several different institutions, has the Court entirely stripped the per se rule of these virtues?

2. Recall that in the case of patent pools, courts are generally more lenient when the patents are complementary. Are the performance rights at issue in this case substitutes or complements? It is certainly the case that the artists generating the performances are competitors, and in that sense, their performances are substitutes. But isn't it also the case that the licensee radio or television broadcasters

value each performance more as the number of performances to which they have access increases? Does the substitute-complement distinction offer any guidance to the Court as to how this particular blanket license should be treated?

3. The crux of the Court's decision here seems to be that the blanket license is not just a combination of the efforts of individual competitors, but the creation of an entirely different product that would not exist otherwise:

> Here, the whole is truly greater than the sum of its parts; it is, to some extent, a different product. *** [T]o the extent the blanket license is a different product, ASCAP is not really a joint sales agency offering the individual goods of many sellers, but is a separate seller offering its blanket license, of which the individual compositions are raw material.

There are a few important details to take note of here. First, the idea of a "different product" put forth by the Court is not simply the consolidation of several parts into a packaged whole, but the creation of something "unique." Second, as the Court later observes, the "license is quite different from anything any individual owner could issue." In other words, were it not for the aggregation of copyrighted works into the blanket license, this product *could not exist*. The blanket license was thus necessary to the creation of this product. Third, the Court emphasizes the efficiencies provided by the new product: it reduces the transaction costs of individual negotiations and completely eliminates the time required to locate performers.

Should the creation of a new, efficient product that could not exist but for the license provide a bar to antitrust liability? How should courts consider this argument in the future?

4. On remand, the Second Circuit found that because the licensees were able to secure individual licenses from the copyright owners, there was no violation of Section One of the Sherman Act. *Columbia Broadcasting System, Inc. v. American Soc. of Composers, Authors and Publishers,* 620 F.2d 930, 936 (2nd 1980).

5. The rights granted are nonexclusive so CBS could license directly from the copyright owners. The Court notes that CBS "never attempted to secure any other form of license from either ASCAP or any of its members." Does that make the case moot? What is CBS' antitrust injury?

The Supreme Court noted that "[t]he District Court found that there was no legal, practical, or conspiratorial impediment to CBS's obtaining individual licenses; CBS, in short, had a real choice." How does that compare to the situation that the district court found in Matsushita v. Cinram? Does it affect the antitrust analysis?

6. Why is a blanket license necessary to effectuate the copyright owners' rights?

The Court notes that "of course changes brought about by new technology or new marketing techniques might also undercut the justification for the practice." Does the Internet reduce search costs and transactions costs in a manner that makes blanket licensing less necessary? If so, should that affect the antitrust analysis?

7. How is blanket licensing different than a price-fixing cartel, such as the one discussed in *U.S. v. Gypsum*?

Note on Agreements to Fix a Maximum Price

Most price-fixing conspiracies challenged in antitrust litigation are agreements to fix a minimum price. Plaintiffs generally allege that defendants are members of a cartel that have combined to hike prices above the competitive level in an effort to increase the cartelists' profits. Consumers who are injured by the higher prices have standing to bring antitrust claims. Price-fixing cases have also been brought by producers who claim that their competitors have conspired to set an artificially low price in order to prevent the plaintiff-seller from entering the market. When the fixed price is below the defendants' cost, the alleged agreement may be characterized as a predatory pricing conspiracy. Courts are generally wary of such claims. See *Matsushita Elec. Indus. Co., Ltd. v. Zenith Radio Corp.*, 475 U.S. 574 (1986). Such claims are particularly difficult to prove in the context of intellectual property, which has high fixed costs and low marginal costs.

In *Wallace v. International Business Machines Corp.*, 467 F.3d 1104 (7th Cir. 2006), the plaintiff challenged the provision of copyrighted software under the General Public License ("GPL"). The Free Software Foundation, Inc. designed the license, under which authors permit free copying and the creation of derivative works, so long as the people who may make and distribute the derivative works do not charge for them and offer the derivative work on the same license terms as those governing the original work. As a result, the Seventh Circuit explained, "the GPL propagates from user to user and revision to revision: neither the original author, nor any creator of a revised or improved version, may charge for the software or allow any successor to charge. Copyright law, usually the basis of limiting reproduction in order to collect a fee, ensures that open-source software remains free: any attempt to sell a derivative work will violate the copyright laws, even if the improver has not accepted the GPL." The Linux operating system is an example of free, open-source software. Because the GPL covers only the software, firms can still charge for physical media, paper manuals, and technical assistance. Thus, firms like Red Hat and IBM can profitably operate businesses based on open-source software even though the software itself is free.

The plaintiff claimed that he wanted to compete against Linux—by creating a derivative work or an entirely new operating system—but he could not because the Linux software and its derivatives were available for free. The plaintiff characterized the GPL as the focal point of a price-fixing conspiracy among the Free Software Foundation, IBM, Red Hat, and others to set the price of operating system software at zero in order to deter competition. The Seventh Circuit rejected the plaintiff's effort

> to characterize people who accept the GPL as "conspirators." Although the antitrust laws forbid conspiracies "in restraint of trade," [citation omitted] the GPL does not restrain trade. It is a cooperative agreement that facilitates production of new derivative works, and agreements that yield new products that would not arise

through unilateral action are lawful. See, e.g., *Broadcast Music, Inc. v. Columbia Broadcasting System, Inc.,* 441 U.S. 1 (1979) [citation omitted]

Nor does it help to call the GPL "price fixing." Although it sets a price of zero, agreements to set maximum prices usually assist consumers and therefore are evaluated under the Rule of Reason. *See State Oil Co. v. Khan,* 522 U.S. 3 (1997). Intellectual property can be used without being used up; the marginal cost of an additional user is zero (costs of media and paper to one side), so once a piece of intellectual property exists the efficient price of an extra copy is zero, for that is where price equals marginal cost. Copyright and patent laws give authors a right to charge more, so that they can recover their fixed costs (and thus promote innovation), but they do not require authors to charge more. No more does antitrust law require higher prices. Linux and other open-source projects have been able to cover their fixed costs through donations of time; as long as that remains true, it would reduce efficiency and consumers' welfare to force the authors to levy a charge on each new user. ***

The GPL and open-source software have nothing to fear from the antitrust laws.

The Seventh Circuit affirmed the district court's grant of summary judgment to the defendants.

The court cited the Supreme Court opinion in *Broadcast Music* for support. How is the GPL like the blanket license in *Broadcast Music*? How is it different? Do you think that *Broadcast Music* dictates the result in this case? Why or why not?

The Seventh Circuit cited *State Oil* for the proposition that agreements to set maximum prices benefit consumers and, consequently, should be evaluated under the Rule of Reason. *State Oil* involved vertical price fixing. Was the conspiracy alleged in *Wallace* vertical or horizontal? On what facts do you base your characterization?

Should antitrust law condemn horizontal agreements to set a maximum price? Why or why not?

Do the *Microsoft* decision, and the facts underlying that case, help inform your opinion about whether the plaintiff's claims in *Wallace* are persuasive?

D. Standard-setting Organizations

Standard setting can raise issues under both Section 1 and Section 2 of the Sherman Act. Section 2 is implicated when a single firm manipulates the standard-setting process so that it secures monopoly power (or attempts to) through illegitimate means. Chapter 9 dealt with these issues. Because standard-setting organizations (SSOs) often involve agreements among competitors, SSOs may violate Section 1 when competitors adopt a standard in order to exclude rival products or to use the SSO in order to facilitate price-fixing and other cartel behavior. Drawing the line between legitimate and illegal agreements can be difficult because standard setting is sometimes inherently anticompetitive; the selection of one standard necessarily excludes other standards. But that exclusionary effect alone cannot create antitrust liability. Otherwise, efficient standards would not be adopted.

340 *Antitrust Law and Intellectual Property Rights*

U.S. Dep't of Justice & Federal Trade Commission,
Antitrust Enforcement and Intellectual Property Rights:
Promoting Innovation and Competition (2007)

Industry standards are widely acknowledged to be one of the engines driving the modern economy. Standards can make products less costly for firms to produce and more valuable to consumers. They can increase innovation, efficiency, and consumer choice; foster public health and safety; and serve as a "fundamental building block for international trade." Standards make networks, such as the Internet and wireless telecommunications, more valuable by allowing products to interoperate. The most successful standards are often those that provide timely, widely adopted, and effective solutions to technical problems.

The process by which industry standards are set varies. Commonly, businesses collaborate to establish standards by working through standard-setting organizations ("SSOs") to develop a standard that all firms, regardless of whether they participate in the process, then can use in making products. However, standards also may be set in the marketplace where firms vigorously compete in a winner-take-all standards war to establish their own technology as the *de facto* standard.

Firms that choose to work through an SSO to develop and adopt standards may be competitors within their particular industry. Thus, agreement among competitors about which standard is best suited for them replaces consumer choice and the competition that otherwise would have occurred in the market to make their product the consumer-chosen standard. In many contexts, this process can produce substantial benefits. By agreeing on an industry standard, firms may be able to avoid many of the costs and delays of a standards war, thus substantially reducing transaction costs to both consumers and firms.

Sony Electronics, Inc. v. Soundview Technologies, Inc.

157 F.Supp.2d 180 (D.Conn. 2001)

ARTERTON, District Judge.

Declaratory judgment defendant and counterclaim plaintiff Soundview Technologies, Inc. (Soundview) is the holder of a patent for technology related to the so-called "V-chip," a device mandated by the FCC to be included in all television sets manufactured after January 1, 2000, to allow parents to block the display of violent or sexually explicit programming, with the standards for the technology to be set by industry. [citation omitted] Defendants are a trade association and numerous television manufacturers who are alleged to have infringed Soundview's patent and engaged in a conspiracy to fix prices for licenses to the V-chip technology, or to refuse to deal with Soundview altogether. Counterclaim defendant Sony Corporation of America (Sony) now moves to dismiss Soundview's antitrust claim, arguing that Soundview has not sufficiently alleged antitrust injury. ***

Factual Background

Soundview's antitrust allegations can be summarized as follows. The industry association, known as EIA or CEMA, formed a subcommittee to discuss V-chip implementation, the "R4.3 Television Data Systems Subcommittee." [citation omitted] The R4.3 Subcommittee undertook to investigate "U.S. patents which might be infringed by those manufacturers who build equipment for receiving and decoding content advisories information" using the methods contained in the EIA-formulated standard, and retained an outside patent attorney to determine "which patents exist that impact" use of this technology. [citation omitted] The subcommittee reported the results of its search that "[s]ome patents were found to be essential to the standard" to the R-4 Video Systems Committee, the parent committee of the R4.3 subcommittee. [citation omitted] A then-Soundview consultant attending the meeting at which the results were reported stated that the subcommittee acknowledged that "six patents that had been previously identified could pose a problem." [citation omitted]

EIA's investigation revealed, in total, 43 patents belonging to 40 separate entities, and communicated this information to its members, including the statement that the six patents it categorized as "most relevant" "have, generally speaking, broader claims, which are more easily infringed." [citation omitted] Soundview's patent, '584, was first on the list of the six "most relevant" patents identified by EIA. Id. EIA's vice-president of Engineering, George Hanover, also sent a memorandum to EIA's members outlining the possibility of enlisting the FCC to help television manufacturers "avoid unreasonable royalty demands" by, for instance, extending the effective dates of the regulations until the "intellectual property situation is resolved" or exploring the FCC's "legal ability to preempt the intellectual property rights of holders unwilling to license the use of their patents on fair and reasonable terms." [citation omitted] Hanover also conceded, however, that these strategies would likely "encounter serious legal and jurisdictional problems" due to the FCC's lack of authority to take such actions. Id. EIA continued to circulate the list of "potentially applicable content advisory patents" to its members on several occasions ***.

On November 10, 1998 Soundview formally informed EIA, and its constituent members, of its plans to license its patent to television manufacturers on reasonable terms "on a non-exclusive, non-discriminatory basis." [citation omitted] EIA allegedly never responded to this letter, id., but instead circulated a memorandum to its members in February of 1999 explaining:

> [EIA] is aware that the owners of several patents claim that use of their patented technology is necessary for television set manufacturers to comply with the [FCC's] regulations mandating the incorporation of the V-chip in certain television sets .... EIA, at the request of some of its members, is in the process of evaluating these patents and assessing all of the options available to television manufacturers .... [I]f any members have non-confidential information relating to the patent issues that they would like the EIA to be aware of in connection with EIA's study of the situation (such as patents called to their attention, offered license terms, relevant prior art, etc.) please provide that information to George Hanover.

[citation omitted] The decision to circulate the above memorandum was made during a February 17, 1999 meeting, and was allegedly accompanied by a discussion of Soundview Technologies, although the substance of this discussion is not yet known by Soundview. [citation omitted] Soundview finds it sufficiently ominous that its consultant attending the meeting reported that he understood the discussion would not have taken place if the participants had known that he had been retained by Soundview; shortly thereafter this consultant terminated his relationship with Soundview, citing an unidentified "conflict of interest." Id. Soundview also cites its failure to receive copies of the minutes for two EIA meetings (of which it is a member) discussing the V-chip, despite repeated requests, as further support for its allegation that something untoward was discussed at those meetings. [citation omitted]

During a telephone conversation between EIA's Hanover and Soundview's president and vice president, Hanover allegedly revealed that EIA and the industry manufacturing members actually had agreed upon a uniform price for a license under the Soundview patent: 5 cents per television set. [citation omitted] Soundview maintains that the above facts sufficiently allege the outlines of a conspiracy to fix prices for patent licenses relating to the V-chip and to boycott sellers of licenses.

Discussion

Sony characterizes Soundview's antitrust claims as a strained attempt "to force the square peg of a patent dispute into the round hole of an antitrust action," and urges the Court to dismiss all antitrust claims to allow this case to proceed "to the real dispute-whether Soundview has a valid patent claim." [citation omitted] According to Sony, Soundview's counterclaim fails to allege sufficient antitrust injury, that is, injury to the competitive process itself, and that concerted action to seek to take down a patent is not the sort of injury the antitrust statutes were meant to address. ***

B. Antitrust Injury

As a prerequisite to recovery for an antitrust violation, a claimant must allege an antitrust injury, which is to say:

> injury of the type the antitrust laws were intended to prevent and that flows from that which makes defendants' acts unlawful. The injury should reflect the anticompetitive effect either of the violation or of anticompetitive acts made possible by the violation.

Brunswick Corp. v. Pueblo Bowl-O-Mat, 429 U.S. 477, 489 (1977). To meet this initial burden, an individual claiming violations of the Sherman Act must "show more than just that he was harmed by defendants' conduct." *K.M.B. Warehouse Distribs., Inc. v. Walker Mfg. Co.*, 61 F.3d 123, 127 (2d Cir.1995). This requirement stems from the fundamental principle that "[t]he antitrust laws ... were enacted for the protection of competition, not competitors." *Brunswick,* 429 U.S. at 489. In *Brunswick,* the Supreme Court found no antitrust injury where the defendant had preserved, rather than dampened, competition by acquiring a number of the plaintiff's bowling alley competitors that would otherwise have gone out of business. 429 U.S. at 488. In responding to plaintiff's claim that the defendant's actions deprived it of profits that it would have received had its competition been allowed to fail, the Court stated "[i]t is inimical to the purposes of [the antitrust] laws to award damages for the type of injury claimed here." *Id.* ***

1. The Economic Theory of Monopsony

Although Sony's argument takes many forms, it boils down to the position that Soundview has not alleged any injury of the nature the antitrust laws were intended to prevent, but instead seeks to enhance the remedies available for its patent claim beyond those allowed by law. According to Sony, the conduct alleged in the counterclaim does not amount to an antitrust violation, because it is not destructive of competition, but is rather pro-competitive, since the law and public policy encourage the challenge of disputed patents in order to prevent the continued existence of an unwarranted monopoly resulting from an invalid patent. The antitrust laws were designed for the benefit of consumers, Sony's argument continues, and consumers would only benefit from lower production costs (here, lower costs resulting from the alleged conspiracy to pay only 5 cents per television as a licensing fee), because they would lead to lower consumer prices. In response, Soundview counters that is has adequately pleaded what is called a monopsony, or an arrangement where a buyer uses its market share power to reduce the purchase price of goods that it will use to produce its own products.[1]

Sony challenges the economic validity of Soundview's theory, as the monopsony model upon which Soundview relies is predicated upon production reductions, resulting in higher consumer prices. See Areeda & Turner, Antitrust Law, § 574 at ¶ 299 (1999). Sony and the counterclaim defendants, however, are not alleged to have reduced input prices simply by buying fewer licenses; to the contrary, they seek a lower per unit price for those licenses, presumably to allow them to continue manufacturing a large number of television sets with the required technology. Nothing in the counterclaims alleged here indicate that Sony and the counterclaim defendants are producing fewer television sets, or that their conspiracy was to do so.

Soundview also relies on the purported harm done to the "market for innovation" by monopsonistic pricing policies, with the sole basis for this contention being the affidavit of Allyn Strickland, *** an Industrial Organization economist who opines that "monopsonistic price fixing is, analytically, similar to monopolistic

---

[1] While both parties refer to a monopsony, the correct term would actually be oligopsony, which refers to a group of buyers with market power that collude to depress the price of one or more key inputs used in their production processes. See Roger D. Blair, Antitrust Policy and Monopsony, 76 Cornell L.Rev. 297 (1991). As Soundview utilizes the term monopsony, as do a number of the relevant cases, however, this Court will follow suit.

price fixing and poses significant harm to competition and consumer welfare" and that "[t]he economic harm inflicted by this alleged price-fixing conspiracy can affect both the technology and innovation markets in which Soundview and other firms participate by reducing their incentives to innovate and develop new technologies for television sets." [citation omitted] Strickland's affidavit does not provide an economic rationale for this opinion, other than that it is proffered by an expert, and Sony attacks Strickland's conclusion as being logically untenable. According to Sony, it would be in the interest of the television manufacturers here to foment increased competition amongst providers of the V-chip technology: the more companies there are competing to develop and license the technology, the better chance that prices will be driven down to the 5 cents per set threshold. Fewer companies providing the technology would mean increased leverage on the part of the sellers, as the V-chip technology is crucial to the manufacture of television sets as long as the current regulations are extant.

While Sony's argument does point out some flaws in the economic underpinnings of Soundview's claims, the Court does not accept entirely Sony's argument that the scheme alleged in the counterclaims could have no anticompetitive effects. As outlined by Professor Blair, monopsonistic pricing conspiracies can have distributional injuries, such as where a group of buyers gets together and agrees on an all-or-nothing pricing scheme (as is alleged here), as contrasted with the Areeda & Turner theory about reducing the quantity of raw materials purchased in order to lower production costs. The all-or-nothing price set by these colluding purchasers can depress the price below the optimal price that would obtain if usual market forces of supply and demand were at work. The price to consumers does not decrease, but there may be social welfare consequences in the long run, because suppliers will leave the industry (or, as Soundview has it, will cease to innovate and invent). Blair, 76 Cornell L.Rev. at 367.

While this may seem counterintuitive because, for the reasons discussed above, the monopsonist purchaser's interests are not served by reducing the numbers of suppliers, business conduct is not always rational, and economic actors do not always have access to perfect information, the utopian ideal of economics. See id., (discussing possible long-term consequences of all-or-nothing monopsony scenarios). Further, in the context of licenses for technology required by the government, different interests may be at work, as the manufacturers need only overturn the regulation or "invent around the patent" in order to obviate the need for Soundview's technology in the first place. ***

The allegations in the instant counterclaims do involve claims of anticompetitive behavior, and allege that the rejection of Soundview's license offer was not the result of marketplace economics. Soundview has alleged that the television manufacturers agreed on a license price, and that they engaged in a joint boycott and concerted refusal to deal. [citation omitted] Under what Soundview terms the "key monopsonization decisions," such agreements may violate the antitrust laws. *Jones Knitting Corp. v. Morgan*, 244 F.Supp. 235, 237 (E.D.Pa.1965) ("[c]oncerted refusals to buy are no less a violation of the antitrust law than concerted refusals to sell"), aff'd, 361 F.2d 451 (3d Cir.1966); [citation omitted].

The Court is also not persuaded by Sony's argument that Jones Knitting and its progeny have been undermined by more recent Supreme Court guidance on antitrust injury, such as *Atlantic Richfield Co. v. USA Petroleum Co.*, 495 U.S. 328 (1990). All of the cases cited by plaintiff save the Jones Knitting opinion itself post-date the Supreme Court's seminal pronouncement on antitrust injury in the *Pueblo Bowl-O-Mat* case. Sony is correct that these cases do not discuss the requirement of antitrust injury, but they do discuss the restraints on individual liberty that these "group boycotts" involve. In the Court's view, the nature of this restraint is conceptually similar-if the individual television manufacturers are constrained by the alleged agreement from negotiating with Soundview for a license or from accepting more than five cents a set, then competition is impeded, because the individual manufacturers thus cannot make their own economic decisions. While Sony charges that the allegations of a group boycott and a concerted refusal to buy are contrived conclusions that blatantly cadge the language of Jones Knitting, the Counterclaims do include some factual support, such as the two EIA meetings for which minutes have not been provided, the failure of EIA members to respond to Soundview's November memo offering to license its patent, the discussion of various strategies to "avoid unreasonable royalty demands," [citation omitted] and the Soundview consultant's description of the discussion at an EIA meeting and his subsequent decision to terminate his relationship with Soundview. [citation omitted] The Court is thus not persuaded that Jones Knitting and analytically similar decisions are no longer good law, and declines to dismiss the counterclaims on this ground.

*** The Court concludes that the monopsony conspiracy outlined in Soundview's counterclaim adequately alleges the elements of an antitrust claim, including antitrust injury to competition. Whether the counterclaim defendants in this case were acting as rational economic decision-makers or participants in an illegal price-fixing conspiracy cannot be determined on the pleadings alone. ***

Comments and Questions

1. When the process of standard setting involves joint *ex ante* licensing activity, this creates the risk of a buyers' cartel, in which the licensees (who are voting members of the SSO) coerce patentholders to accept lower royalties in exchange for having their patents incorporated into the standard. SSOs create countervailing potential antitrust concerns (if not violations). On the one hand, if the IP owner has its patent included in the standard without any restrictions, after the standard is adopted and implemented, the IP owner can act like a monopolist by charging excessive royalties and can disrupt competition in downstream markets. This implicates Section 2 of the Sherman Act.

On the other hand, if the SSO members attempt to prevent excessive royalties by setting low royalties before the standard is adopted, their actions might be considered illegal price fixing. Courts have suggested such a buyers' cartel could violate

Section One of the Sherman Act. *See Addamax Corp. v. Open Software Found.*, 152 F.3d 48, 51–52 (1st Cir. 1998).

Given the complexity and nuance involved in joint ex ante licensing activity, in their report on innovation and competition, the Department of Justice and the Federal Trade Commission explained their approach to the issue in detail:

> Because of the strong potential for procompetitive benefits, the Agencies will evaluate joint *ex ante* activity to establish licensing terms under the rule of reason. The Agencies' general approach to these issues is outlined below.
>
> First, an IP holder's voluntary and unilateral disclosure of its licensing terms, including its royalty rate, is not a collective act subject to review under section 1 of the Sherman Act. Further, a unilateral announcement of a price before "selling" the technology to the standard-setting body (without more) cannot be exclusionary conduct and therefore cannot violate section 2.
>
> Second, bilateral *ex ante* negotiations about licensing terms that take place between an individual SSO member and an individual intellectual property holder (without more) outside the auspices of the SSO also are unlikely to require any special antitrust scrutiny because IP rights holders are merely negotiating terms with individual buyers.
>
> Third, *per se* condemnation is not warranted for joint SSO activities that mitigate hold up and that take place before deciding which technology to include in a standard. Rather, the Agencies will apply the rule of reason when evaluating joint activities that mitigate hold up by allowing the "buyers" (members of the SSO who are potential licensees of the standard) to negotiate licensing terms with the "sellers" (the rival IP holders) before competition among the technologies ends and potentially confers market power (or additional market power) on the holder of the chosen technology. Such joint activities could take various forms, including joint *ex ante* licensing negotiations or an SSO rule that requires intellectual property holders to announce their intended (or maximum) licensing terms for technologies being considered for adoption in a standard. The Department recently analyzed an SSO's proposal to require member firms to disclose their intended most restrictive licensing terms for patents essential to a standard. Pursuant to the rule of reason, the Department concluded that it would not take enforcement action if the policy were adopted because the policy preserved competition between technologies during the standard-setting process.
>
> If intellectual property holders turn joint *ex ante* licensing discussions into a sham to cover up naked agreements on the licensing terms each IP holder will offer the SSO, *per se* condemnation of such agreements among "sellers" of IP rights may be warranted. Similarly, *ex ante* discussion of licensing terms within the standard-setting process may provide an opportunity for SSO members to reach side price-fixing agreements that are *per se* illegal. The Agencies will almost certainly treat as *per se* illegal any effort by manufacturing rivals to fix the price of the standardized products they "sell" instead of discussing the price of the terms on which they will "buy" a technology input that is needed to comply with the standard. However, such risks are not sufficient to condemn *all* multilateral

> *ex ante* licensing negotiations, particularly given the fact that "[t]hose developing standards already have extensive experience managing this risk."
>
> The Agencies do not suggest that SSOs are required to sponsor such discussions during the standard-setting process. Concerns about legitimate licensing discussions spilling over into dangerous antitrust territory may dissuade some groups from conducting them in the first place. Moreover, it is fully within the legitimate purview of each SSO and its members to conclude that *ex ante* licensing discussions are unproductive or too time consuming or costly. An SSO may also fear that requiring *ex ante* commitments to licensing terms would deter some IP holders from participating in the standard-setting process, depriving the standard-setting process of the expertise of those IP holders.
>
> The Agencies take no position as to whether SSOs should engage in joint *ex ante* discussion of licensing terms but recognize that joint *ex ante* activity to establish licensing terms as part of the standard-setting process will not warrant *per se* condemnation. Such activity might mitigate the potential for IP holders to hold up those seeking to use a standard by demanding licensing terms greater than they would have received before their proprietary technology was included in the standard. Given the strong potential for procompetitive benefits, the Agencies will evaluate joint *ex ante* negotiation of licensing terms pursuant to the rule of reason.

U.S. Dep't of Justice & Federal Trade Commission, Antitrust Enforcement and Intellectual Property Rights: Promoting Innovation and Competition 54–56 (2007).

2. Should SSOs perform auctions in which patent owners bid against each other (i.e., lower royalties) for the SSO to adopt the standard that includes their IP? At the FTC-DOJ hearings on antitrust and intellectual property,

> the economist [Stanley Besen] described a stylized setting in which an SSO needed to select one of multiple alternative protected technologies. He suggested that the SSO could hold an auction and require the holders of the IP to submit "bids" describing the licensing terms to which they would agree if their technology were incorporated into the standard. He explained that, under his simplifying assumptions, one would expect such an auction to result in the SSO selecting the efficient technology, and that the terms of the licensing agreement would reflect the relative benefit of the selected technology. Several panelists expressed concern that such auctions or negotiations could slow down the standard-setting process, raise the costs of participation, and potentially result in antitrust liability. For these reasons, many SSOs and companies strictly prohibit discussions of licensing terms within SSOs.

U.S. Dep't of Justice & Federal Trade Commission, Antitrust Enforcement and Intellectual Property Rights: Promoting Innovation and Competition 49 (2007).

3. Some SSOs require royalty-free licenses. *See, e.g.*, Press Release, World Wide Web Consortium, World Wide Web Consortium Approves Patent Policy (May 21, 2003) (announcing finalized royalty-free patent policy).

http://www.w3.org/2003/05/patentpolicy-pressrelease.html.en.

Why would a firm give a royalty-free license?

Consider this: "Some asserted that giving a royalty-free license might be of little competitive consequence to an intellectual property holder that is a market player. Such might be the case because the intellectual property holder could retain a first-mover advantage and be in the best position to implement the standard, or the IP holder could license its other protected technologies that are complements to those incorporated in the standard." U.S. DEP'T OF JUSTICE & FEDERAL TRADE COMMISSION, ANTITRUST ENFORCEMENT AND INTELLECTUAL PROPERTY RIGHTS: PROMOTING INNOVATION AND COMPETITION 48 (2007). *See also* Edward F. Sherry, *Standards Setting and Antitrust*, 87 MINN. L. REV. 1913, 1954 (2003) ("[A] patent holder may be willing to license its patents royalty-free to all interested parties . . . . [T]his is most likely to occur . . . when the patent holder will benefit from others' adoption of its patented technology as a standard because the patent holder has other complementary capabilities that will enable it to profit from its innovation in a manner other than collecting royalties.").

Is there a risk that if SSOs can require royalty-free licensing, firms will have insufficient incentives to engage in important research and development?

4. In addition to the possibility that SSO members could conspire against patent owners in order to artificially reduce royalty payments, SSOs also create a corresponding risk that members may fix the price of products that they manufacture pursuant to the agreed upon standard. The federal antitrust agencies have warned that "if manufacturers use the cover of multilateral licensing negotiations to reach naked agreements on the prices of the products they sell downstream, summary condemnation is warranted. Meeting to discuss royalty rates within an SSO may give manufacturers an opportunity to discuss downstream prices with less risk of detection, making collusion less expensive." U.S. DEP'T OF JUSTICE & FEDERAL TRADE COMMISSION, ANTITRUST ENFORCEMENT AND INTELLECTUAL PROPERTY RIGHTS: PROMOTING INNOVATION AND COMPETITION 51 (2007). The agencies have noted that they would treat such activity as per se illegal. *Id.* at 37.

5. Even absent naked price fixing, competitors who are members of an SSO may innocently or intentionally share sensitive pricing information. SSOs may attempt to reduce that risk by screening out executives with pricing authority from participating in SSO activities, and thus having contact with competitors. See ABA SECTION ON ANTITRUST LAW, HANDBOOK ON THE ANTITRUST ASPECTS OF STANDARDS SETTING 68–69 (2004)

6. In order to encourage efficient standard setting—and to reduce the potential chilling effect of antitrust liability—Congress enacted the Standards Development Organization Advancement Act of 2004 ("SDOAA"). The provides that courts will provide rule of reason analysis in an antitrust case against a standard-setting "organization that plans, develops, establishes, or coordinates voluntary consensus standards using procedures that incorporate the attributes of openness, balance of interests, due process, an appeals process, and consensus. . ." Qualifying SSOs will also only be liable for single damages, not treble damages, in the event

of antitrust liability. Notably, the SDOAA excludes from the definition of "standards development organization" the individual "parties participating in the standards development organization." 15 U.S.C. § 4301(a)(8). *See also* Philip J. Weiser, *Making the World Safe for Standard Setting*, UNIV. OF COLORADO LAW SCHOOL LEGAL STUDIES RESEARCH PAPER SERIES, WORKING PAPER NO. 08-06 (Mar. 13, 2008), at 32 (noting that the "statute only applies to formal standard setting bodies (and not other standard setting bodies or individual members of formal standard setting bodies)"), *available at* http://ssrn.com/abstract=1003432. The SDOAA can be found in Appendix A of this casebook.

7. The SDOAA is concerned about procedural safeguards to prevent anticompetitive abuses by SSOs members. The case law presents examples of procedural deficiencies. For example, in *Allied Tube & Conduit Corp. v. Indian Head, Inc.*, 486 U.S. 492 (1988), the producers and sellers of steel conduit manipulated an SSO meeting by purchasing memberships for people whose sole function was to vote against expanding the standard to allow plastic conduit, which would pose a competitive threat to the steel conduit industry. The Supreme Court affirmed antitrust liability.

8. Both the individual members and the SSO itself can be held liable for violating the Sherman Act. The Supreme Court has explained that "a rule that imposes liability on the standard-setting organization—which is best situated to prevent antitrust violations ***—is most faithful to the congressional intent that the private right of action deter antitrust violations." American Society of Mechanical Engineers v. Hydrolevel Corp., 456 U.S. 556, 572–73 (1982). By making SSOs legally responsible for the anticompetitive activities of their agents, "organizations can react to potential antitrust liability by making their associations less subject to fraudulent manipulation." *Id.* at 574 n.13.

9. SSOs are not the only source of product standards. Most standards are a result of government regulation. In 1995, federal agencies imposed approximately 52,000, compared to 41,500 from private entities. ABA SECTION ON ANTITRUST LAW, HANDBOOK ON THE ANTITRUST ASPECTS OF STANDARDS SETTING 5 (2004). These figures do include the standards enacted by various state, county, and local governments. However, there is an important interplay between government and SSOs, because the government often adopts the standards proposed by SSOs. This can give a private SSOs considerable power.

10. The written standards of a standards setting organization should, in general, be protected by copyright law. After all, the standard shows originality and is fixed in a tangible medium. However, some standards are structured as model codes with the hope that they will be adopted by local, state, or federal decision-makers. When a private standard is enacted into law, it may lose its copyright protection. Veeck v. Southern Building Code Congress Int'l Inc., 293 F.3d 791 (5th Cir. 2002).

Bibliography of Additional Resources

Roger B. Andewelt, *Analysis of Patent Pools under the Antitrust Laws*, 53 ANTITRUST L.J. 611 (1985)

John H. Barton, *Antitrust Treatment of Oligopolies with Mutually Blocking Patent Portfolios*, 69 ANTITRUST L.J. 851 (2002)

Steven C. Carlson, *Patent Pools and the Antitrust Dilemma*, 16 YALE J. ON REG. 359 (1999)

Michael A. Carrier, *Why Antitrust Should Defer to the Intellectual Property Rules of Standard-Setting Organizations: A Commentary on Teece & Sherry*, 87 MINN. L. REV. 2019 (2003)

Michael A. Einhorn, *Intellectual Property and Antitrust: Music Performing Rights in Broadcasting*, 24 COLUM.-VLA J.L. & ARTS 349 (2001)

Daniel J. Gifford, *Developing Models for a Coherent Treatment of Standard-Setting Issues under the Patent, Copyright, and Antitrust Laws*, 43 IDEA 331 (2003)

Richard J. Gilbert, *Antitrust for Patent Pools: A Century of Policy Evolution*, 2004 STAN. TECH. L. REV. 3 (2004)

Peter Grindley, et al., *Standards Wars: The Use of Standard Setting as a Means of Facilitating Cartels*, 3 INT'L J. COMM. . L. & POL'Y 1, 32 (Summer 1999)

John E. Haapala, Jr., *Patent Pools and Antitrust Concerns in Plant Biotechnology*, 19 J. ENVTL. L. & LITIG. 475 (2004)

Carole E. Handler & Julian Brew, *The Application of Antitrust Rules to Standards in the Information Industries—Anomaly or Necessity?*, 14 COMPUTER LAW 1 (Nov. 1997)

Mary Katherine Kennedy, *Blanket Licensing of Music Performing Rights: Possible Solutions to the Copyright-Antitrust Conflict*, 37 VAND. L. REV. 183 (1984)

Ramon A. Klitzke, *Patent Licensing: Concerted Action by Licensees*, 13 DEL. J. CORP. L. 459 (1988)

Michael A. Lavine, *Ripples in the Patent Pool: The Impact and Implications of the Evolving Essentiality Analysis*, 4 N.Y.U. J. L. & BUS. 605 (2008)

Mark A. Lemley, *Intellectual Property Rights and Standard-Setting Organizations*, 90 CAL. L. REV. 1889 (2002)

Bradley J. Levang, *Evaluating the Use of Patent Pools For Biotechnology: A Refutation to the USPTO White Paper Concerning Biotechnology Patent Pools*, 19 SANTA CLARA COMPUTER & HIGH TECH. L.J. 229 (2002)

Janice M. Mueller, *Patent Misuse through the Capture of Industry Standards*, 17 BERKELEY TECH. L.J. 623 (2002)

David J. Teece & Edward F. Sherry, *Standards Setting and Antitrust*, 87 MINN. L. REV. 1913 (2003)

CHAPTER 10

Market Allocation and Intellectual Property Rights

A. Patents and Market Allocation

Hartford-Empire Co. v. United States,
323 U.S. 386 (1945)

Mr. Justice ROBERTS delivered the opinion of the Court.

These are appeals from a decree awarding an injunction against violations of §§1 and 2 of the Sherman Act, as amended, and s 3 of the Clayton Act. Two questions are presented. Were violations proved? If so, are the provisions of the decree right?

The complaint named as defendants 12 corporations and 101 individuals associated with them as officers or directors. It was dismissed as to 3 corporations and 40 individuals. The corporations are the leaders in automatic glass-making machinery and in the glassware industry. The charge is that all the defendants agreed, conspired, and combined to monopolize, and did monopolize and restrain interstate and foreign commerce by acquiring patents covering the manufacture of glass-making machinery, and by excluding others from a fair opportunity freely to engage in commerce in such machinery and in the manufacture and distribution of glass products. The gravamen of the case is that the defendants have cooperated in obtaining and licensing patents covering glass-making machinery, have limited and restricted the use of the patented machinery by a network of agreements, and have maintained prices for unpatented glassware. ***

In 1912 Hartford-Fairmont Company was organized to combine the activities of two existing companies interested in glass manufacture with those of a group of engineers who desired to obtain and exploit patents for automatic glass-making machinery. The defendant Corning Glass Works was, at that time, engaged primarily in the production and distribution of incandescent bulbs, sign and optical

352 *Antitrust Law and Intellectual Property Rights*

ware, heat-resisting ware and other specialty glassware. Its field may be defined roughly as the pressed and blown field, or the noncontainer field. It has not made, and does not now make, containers save a limited amount of tumblers. In 1909 persons interested in Corning organized Empire Machine Company as a patent holding and developing company.

The defendant Owens-Illinois Glass Company (hereafter called Owens) is a large manufacturer of glass. Mr. Owens of that company produced the first fully automatic machine for blowing bottles, which is known as a suction type machine. He was interested in companies engaged in developing and manufacturing this type of machine and exercising the rights represented by the Owens and related patents. From about 1904 the Owens group followed the policy of granting exclusive licenses, in limited fields, for the manufacture of glass-ware by the suction process. Owens itself was, and is, mainly interested in what is known as narrow neck container ware. Prior to the Owens inventions glass making had been largely a hand process. Thereafter, due to Owens' restrictive licensing policy, many glass manufacturers were threatened with extinction unless some other competing machine could be devised. Ultimately a process, called suspended gob feeding, was invented, which was more economical for certain ware than the suction process, and could be applied in the manufacture of diversified glassware. The introduction of the gob feeder machine threatened Owens' domination of the glass machinery field and Owens, in self-protection, obtained patents and patent rights on gob feeders and licensed some companies for their use.

Hartford-Fairmont was interested in the development of the gob feeder. It applied for some patents and acquired others. In the meantime, it licensed gob feeder machinery, as Owens had done with the suction machine, by restricting its use to the manufacture of specified ware. Empire owned certain patent applications which were in interference with Hartford-Fairmont gob feeder applications.

June 30, 1916, Hartford-Fairmont and Empire made an agreement whereby Empire was given an exclusive license to use Hartford-Fairmont's patents for pressed and blown glassware and Hartford-Fairmont was given an exclusive license to use Empire's patents for production of containers. Thus Corning obtained exclusive rights, under the patents, for Corning's line of ware,-pressed and blown glass,- and Hartford obtained the patent rights of both companies in respect of other glassware. Negotiations led to agreements, October 6, 1922, whereby Hartford-Empire (hereinafter called Hartford) was formed and took over all assets of Hartford-Fairmont and of Empire relating to glass machinery. Empire received 43% of the stock of the company and Corning retained approximately the same exclusive interest that Empire had enjoyed under the 1916 agreement. *** Empire was dissolved in 1941.

After 1916 Hartford-Fairmont (and its successor Hartford) and Owens were competitors in the gob feeding field; their applications were in interference in the Patent Office with each other and with those of other applicants; and they were in litigation. As a result of negotiations for a settlement of their disputes, they entered into an agreement April 9, 1924, whereby Owens granted Hartford an exclusive license under Owens' patents for gob feeder and forming machines and Hartford granted Owens a nonexclusive, nonassignable, and nondivisible license to make and use machines and methods embodying patents then or thereafter owned or acquired by Hartford for the manufacture of glassware, but Owens was not to sell or license gob feeding machinery and was excluded from the pressed and blown field previously reserved to Corning. Owens was to receive one-half of Hartford's divisible income from licenses over and above $600,000 per annum. Owens retained a veto power on Hartford's granting new licenses on machines embodying Owens' inventions. This provision was eliminated in 1931. The agreement left Owens in full control of its patented suction process.

As soon as the agreement had been made, Hartford and Owens combined to get control of all other feeder patents. In this endeavor they pooled the efforts of their legal staffs and contributed equally to the purchase of patents and the expenses of litigation.

While patent claims upon applications controlled by Hartford and Owens were pending in the Patent Office, Hartford purchased, under the joint arrangement, certain feeder patents and applications belonging to outsiders, and persons to whom feeders had been sold or licensed by such outsiders were persuaded to take licenses from Hartford. As a result of Hartford's and Owens' joint efforts in connection with patent applications and purchases of applications and patents of others, Hartford obtained what it considered controlling patents on gob feeders in 1926.

Hazel-Atlas Glass Company (hereinafter called Hazel) was second to Owens in the manufacture and sale of glass containers. It had been using feeders of its own design and manufacture. To build up further patent control, to discourage use of machinery not covered by their patents, and to influence glass makers to take licenses under Hartford's inventions, Hartford and Owens desired that Hazel should become a partner-licensee.***

As of June 1, 1932, Hartford, Owens, and Hazel executed a series of agreements Hartford licensed Hazel under Hartford's patents, excluding from the license the pressed and blown field reserved to Corning and with restrictions against sale or license by Hazel to anyone else.

[The Thatcher Manufacturing Company and Ball Brothers also took licenses from Hartford for making milk bottles and fruit jars, respectively.]

In granting licenses under the pooled patents Hartford always reserved the rights within Corning's field. Further, it not only limited its licensees to certain portions of the container field but, in many instances, limited the amount of glassware which might be produced by the licensee and, in numerous instances, as a result of conferences with Owens, Hazel, Thatcher and Ball, refused licenses to prevent overstocking of the glassware market and to 'stabilize' the prices at which such ware was sold.

In the automatic manufacture of glassware, other machines are used in connection with the feeders. These are known as forming machines, stackers, and lehrs. The purpose of Hartford and Owens, participated in by the other three large manufacturers mentioned, was that there should be gathered into the pool patents covering and monopolizing these adjunct machines so that automatic glass manufacture, without consent of the parties to the pool, would become difficult if not impossible.

In 1919 the Glass Container Association of America was formed. Prior to 1933 its members produced 82% of the glass containers made in the United States and since have produced 92%. Since 1931 (except while the National Industrial Recovery Act, 48 Stat. 195, was in force) the Association has had a statistical committee of seven, on which Owens, Hazel, Thatcher, and, since 1933, Ball were represented. These appellants also were represented in the Board of Directors. Hartford, though not a member, has closely cooperated with the officers of the association in efforts to discourage outsiders from increasing production of glassware and newcomers from entering the field. The court below, on sufficient evidence, has found that the association, through its statistical committee, assigned production quotas to its members and that they and Hartford were zealous in seeing that these were observed.

In summary, the situation brought about in the glass industry, and existing in 1938, was this: Hartford, with the technical and financial aid of others in the conspiracy, had acquired, by issue to it or assignment from the owners, more than 600 patents. These, with over 100 Corning controlled patents, over 60 Owens patents, over 70 Hazel patents, and some 12 Lynch patents, had been, by cross-licensing agreements, merged into a pool which effectually controlled the industry. This control was exercised to allot production in Corning's field to Corning, and that in restricted classes within the general container field to Owens, Hazel, Thatcher, Ball, and such other smaller manufacturers as the group agreed should be licensed. The result was that 94% of the glass containers manufactured in this country on feeders and formers were made on machinery licensed under the pooled patents.

The district court found that invention of glass making machinery had been discouraged, that competition in the manufacture and sale or licensing of such machinery had been suppressed, and that the system of restricted licensing had been employed to suppress competition in the manufacture of unpatented glassware and to maintain prices of the manufactured product. The findings are full and adequate and are supported by evidence, much of it contemporary writings of corporate defendants or their officers and agents. ***

We affirm the District Court's findings and conclusions that the corporate appellants combined in violation of the Sherman Act, that Hartford and Lynch contracted in violation of the Clayton Act, and that the individual appellants with exceptions to be noted participated in the violations in their capacities as officers and directors of the corporations.

Little need be said concerning the legal principles which vindicate the District Court's findings and conclusions as to the corporate appellants and the individual appellants who as officers or directors participated in the corporate acts which forwarded the objects of the conspiracy. As was said in Standard Sanitary Mfg. Co. v. United States, 226 U.S. 20, 49: 'Rights conferred by patents are indeed very definite and extensive, but they do not give any more than other rights a universal license against positive prohibitions. The Sherman law is a limitation of rights,-rights which may be pushed to evil consequences and therefore restrained.'

The difference between legitimate use and prohibited abuse of the restrictions incident to the ownership of patents by the pooling of them is discussed in Standard Oil Co. v. United States, 283 U.S. 163. Application of the tests there announced sustains the District Court's decision. It is clear that, by cooperative arrangements and binding agreements, the appellant corporations, over a period of years, regulated and suppressed competition in the use of glass making machinery and employed their joint patent position to allocate fields of manufacture and to maintain prices of unpatented glassware.

The explanations offered by the appellants are unconvincing. It is said, on behalf of Hartford, that its business, in its inception, was lawful and within the patent laws; and that, in order to protect its legitimate interests as holder of patents for automatic glass machinery, it was justified in buying up and fencing off improvement patents, the grant of which, while leaving the fundamental inventions untouched, would hamper their use unless tribute were paid to the owners of the so-called improvements which, of themselves, had only a nuisance value.

The explanation fails to account for the offensive and defensive alliance of patent owners with its concomitant stifling of initiative, invention, and competition. ***

Comments and Questions

1. On what basis did the parties allocate the market?
2. How are the licensing agreements anticompetitive?
3. Should the presence of patent immunize the agreements? Why or why not?

B. Trademarks and Market Allocation

Timken Roller Bearing Co. v. United States,
341 U.S. 593 (1951)

Mr. Justice BLACK delivered the opinion of the Court.

The United States brought this civil action to prevent and restrain violations of the Sherman Act by appellant, Timken Roller Bearing Co., an Ohio corporation. The complaint charged that appellant, in violation of §§ 1 and 3 of the Act, combined, conspired and acted with British Timken, Ltd. (British Timken), and Societe Anonyme Francaise Timken (French Timken) to restrain interstate and foreign commerce by eliminating competition in the manufacture and sale of antifriction bearings in the markets of the world. After a trial of more than a month the District Court made detailed findings of fact which may be summarized as follows:

As early as 1909 appellant and British Timken's predecessor had made comprehensive agreements providing for a territorial division of the world markets for antifriction bearings. Beginning in [1928], appellant, British Timken and French

Timken have continuously kept operative 'business agreements' regulating the manufacture and sale of antifriction bearings by the three companies and providing for the use by the British and French corporations of the trademark 'Timken.'

Under these agreements the contracting parties have (1) allocated trade territories among themselves; (2) fixed prices on products of one sold in the territory of the others; (3) cooperated to protect each other's markets and to eliminate outside competition; and (4) participated in cartels to restrict imports to, and exports from, the United States.

On these findings, the District Court concluded that appellant had violated the Sherman Act as charged, and entered a comprehensive decree designed to bar future violations. 83 F.Supp. 284. The case is before us on appellant's direct appeal under 15 U.S.C. s 29, 15 U.S.C.A. s 29. ***

Appellant *** contends that the restraints of trade so clearly revealed by the District Court's findings can be justified as 'reasonable,' and therefore not in violation of the Sherman Act, because they are 'ancillary' to allegedly 'legal main transactions,' namely, *** an exercise of appellant's right to license the trademark 'Timken.' ***

Nor can the restraints of trade be justified as reasonable steps taken to implement a valid trademark licensing system, even if we assume with appellant that it is the owner of the trademark 'Timken' in the trade areas allocated to the British and French corporations. Appellant's premise that the trade restraints are only incidental to the trademark contracts is refuted by the District Court's finding that the 'trademark provisions (in the agreements) were subsidiary and secondary to the central purpose of allocating trade territories.' Furthermore, while a trademark merely affords protection to a name, the agreements in the present case went far beyond protection of the name 'Timken' and provided for control of the manufacture and sale of antifriction bearings whether carrying the mark or not. A trademark cannot be legally used as a device for Sherman Act violation. ***

Comments and Questions

1. The *Timken* Court implied that if "the trade restraints were merely incidental to an otherwise legitimate 'joint venture,'" then the restraint might survive antitrust scrutiny. How should courts determine whether a trade restraint is "merely incidental"?

2. The *Timken* Court held that the various members of the Timken family of corporations were capable of agreeing with each other for Section 1 purposes: "The fact that there is common ownership or control of the contracting corporations does not liberate them from the impact of the antitrust laws." That statement does not represent the current state of antitrust law. In *Copperweld Corp. v. Independence Tube Corp.*, 467 U.S. 752 (1984), the Supreme Court held that parent corporation is legally incapable of agreeing with a wholly owned subsidiary because "in reality a parent and a wholly owned subsidiary always have a 'unity of purpose or a common design.' They share a common purpose whether or not the parent keeps a tight rein over the subsidiary; the parent may assert full control at any moment if the subsidiary fails to act in the parent's best interests."

The Supreme Court recently applied *Copperweld* to trademark licensing in *American Needle, Inc. v. National Football League*, __ U.S. __ (2010). The 32 teams in the National Football League (NFL) formed a corporate entity that granted an exclusive license to Reebok to manufacture and sell trademarked headwear with the various teams' insignias. Another vendor sued, claiming that the NFL teams violated Section 1 of the Sherman Act. The Seventh Circuit held that the teams were incapable of agreeing with each other under *Copperweld* because in the context of IP licensing, the teams acted as a single entity collectively promoting NFL football. The Supreme Court reversed, holding that "NFL teams do not possess either the unitary decisionmaking quality or the single aggregation of economic power characteristic of independent action. Each of the teams is a substantial, independently owned, and independently managed business. … [T]he teams compete in the market for intellectual property. To a firm making hats, the Saints and the Colts are two potentially competing suppliers of valuable trademarks." This does not mean that the agreement to collectively license their trademarks necessarily violates antitrust laws; rather, the agreement is not immune from antitrust scrutiny. The Supreme Court remanded the case for determination of whether the collective licensing arrangement unreasonably restrained trade.

United States v. Sealy,
388 U.S. 350 (1967)

Mr. Justice FORTAS delivered the opinion of the Court.

Appellee and its predecessors have, for more than 40 years, been engaged in the business of licensing manufacturers of mattresses and bedding products to make and sell such products under the Sealy name and trademarks. In this civil action the United States charged that appellee had violated § 1 of the Sherman Act [] by conspiring with its licensees to fix the prices at which the retail customers of the licensees might resell bedding products bearing the Sealy name, and to allocate mutually exclusive territories among such manufacturer-licensees.

After trial, the District Court found that the appellee was engaged in a continuing conspiracy with its manufacturer-licensees to agree upon and fix minimum retail prices on Sealy products and to police the prices so fixed. It enjoined the appellee from such conduct, 'Provided, however, that nothing herein contained shall be construed to prohibit the defendant from disseminating and using suggested retail prices for the purpose of national advertising of Sealy products.' Appellee did not appeal the finding or order relating to price-fixing.

With respect to the charge that appellee conspired to allocate mutually exclusive territory among its manufacturers, the District Court held that the United States had not proved conduct 'in unreasonable restraint of trade in violation of Section 1 of the Sherman Act.' The United States appealed ***

There is no dispute that exclusive territories were allotted to the manufacturer-licensees. Sealy agreed with each licensee not to license any other person to manufacture or sell in the designated area; and the licensee agreed not to manufacture or sell 'Sealy products' outside the designated area. A manufacturer could make and sell his private label products anywhere he might choose.

Because this Court has distinguished between horizontal and vertical territorial limitations for purposes of the impact of the Sherman Act, it is first necessary to determine whether the territorial arrangements here are to be treated as the creature of the licensor, Sealy, or as the product of a horizontal arrangement among the licensees. *White Motor Co. v. United States*, 372 U.S. 253 (1963).

If we look at substance rather than form, there is little room for debate. These must be classified as horizontal restraints. [citation omitted]

There are about 30 Sealy 'licensees.' They own substantially all of its stock. Sealy's bylaws provide that each director must be a stockholder or a stockholder-licensee's nominee. Sealy's business is managed and controlled by its board of directors. Between board meetings, the executive committee acts. It is composed of Sealy's president and five board members, all licensee-stockholders. Control does not reside in the licensees only as a matter of form. It is exercised by them in the day-to-day business of the company including the grant, assignment, reassignment, and termination of exclusive territorial licenses. Action of this sort is taken either by the board of directors or the executive committee of Sealy, both of which, as we have said, are manned, wholly or almost entirely, by licensee-stockholders.

Appellee argues that 'there is no evidence that Sealy is a mere creature or instrumentality of its stockholders.' In support of this proposition, it stoutly asserts that 'the stockholders and directors wore a 'Sealy hat' when they were acting on behalf of Sealy.' But the obvious and inescapable facts are that Sealy was a joint venture of, by, and for its stockholder-licensees; and the stockholder-licensees are themselves directly, without even the semblance of insulation, in charge of Sealy's operations.

For example, some of the crucial findings of the District Court describe actions as having been taken by 'stockholder representatives' acting as the board or a committee.

It is true that the licensees had an interest in Sealy's effectiveness and efficiency, and, as stockholders, they welcomed its profitability-at any rate within the limits set by their willingness as licensees to pay royalties to the joint venture. But that does not determine whether they as licensees are chargeable with action in the name of Sealy. We seek the central substance of the situation, not its periphery; and in this pursuit, we are moved by the identity of the persons who act, rather than the label of their hats. The arrangements for exclusive territories are necessarily chargeable to the licensees of appellee whose interests such arrangements were supposed to promote and who, through select members, guaranteed or withheld and had the power to terminate licenses for inadequate performance. The territorial arrangements must be regarded as the creature of horizontal action by the licensees. It would violate reality to treat them as equivalent to territorial limitations imposed by a manufacturer upon independent dealers as incident to the sale of a trademarked product. Sealy, Inc., is an instrumentality of the licensees for purposes of the horizontal territorial allocation. It is not the principal. ***

In the present case, we are [] faced with an 'aggregation of trade restraints.' Since the early days of the company in 1925 and continuously thereafter, the prices to be charged by retailers to whom the licensee-stockholders of Sealy sold their products have been fixed and policed by the licensee-stockholders directly, by Sealy itself, and by collaboration between them. As the District Court found:

> 'the stockholder-licensee representatives * * * as the board of directors, the Executive Committee, or other committees of Sealy, Inc. * * * discuss, agree upon and set
>
> '(a) The retail prices at which Sealy products could be sold;
> '(b) The retail prices at which Sealy products could be advertised;
> '(c) The comparative retail prices at which the stockholder-licensees and the Sealy retailers could advertise Sealy products;
> '(d) The minimum retail prices below which Sealy products could not be advertised;
> '(e) The minimum retail prices below which Sealy products could not be sold; and
> '(f) The means of inducing and enforcing retailers to adhere to these agreed upon and set prices.'

These activities, as the District Court held, constitute a violation of the Sherman Act. Their anticompetitive nature and effect are so apparent and so serious that the courts will not pause to assess them in light of the rule of reason. [citation omitted]

Appellee has not appealed the order of the District Court enjoining continuation of this price-fixing, but the existence and impact of the practice cannot be ignored in our appraisal of the territorial limitations. In the first place, this flagrant and pervasive price-fixing, in obvious violation of the law, was, as the trial court found, the activity of the 'stockholder representatives' acting through and in collaboration with Sealy mechanisms. This underlines the horizontal nature of the enterprise, and the use of Sealy, not as a separate entity, but as an instrumentality of the individual manufacturers. In the second place, this unlawful resale price-fixing activity refutes appellee's claim that the territorial restraints were mere incidents of a lawful program of trademark licensing. Cf. Timken Roller Bearing Co. v. United States.[3] The territorial restraints were a part of the unlawful price-fixing and policing. As specific findings of the District Court show, they gave to each licensee an enclave in which it could and did zealously and effectively maintain resale

---

[3] In Timken, as in the present case, it was argued that the restraints were reasonable steps incident to a valid trademark licensing system. But the Court summarily rejected the argument, as we do here. It pointed out that the restraints went far beyond the protection of the trademark and included nontrademarked items, and it concluded that: 'A trademark cannot be legally used as a device for Sherman Act violation.' 341 U.S., at 599, 71 S.Ct., at 975. Cf. § 33 of the Lanham Act, 60 Stat. 438, as amended, 15 U.S.C. § 1115(b) (7). In Timken, the restraints covered nonbranded merchandise as well as the 'Timken' line. In the present case the restraints were in terms of 'Sealy products' only. As to their private label products, the licensees were free to sell outside of the given territory, and, so far as appears, without resale price collaboration or enforcement. But this difference in fact is not consequential in this case. A restraint such as is here involved of the resale price of a trademarked article, not otherwise permitted by law, cannot be defended as ancillary to a trademark licensing scheme. [c.o.]

prices, free from the danger of outside incursions. It may be true, as appellee vigorously argues, that territorial exclusivity served many other purposes. But its connection with the unlawful price-fixing is enough to require that it be condemned as an unlawful restraint and that appellee be effectively prevented from its continued or further use.

It is urged upon us that we should condone this territorial limitation among manufacturers of Sealy products because of the absence of any showing that it is unreasonable. It is argued, for example, that a number of small grocers might allocate territory among themselves on an exclusive basis as incident to the use of a common name and common advertisements, and that this sort of venture should be welcomed in the interests of competition, and should not be condemned as per se unlawful. But condemnation of appellee's territorial arrangements certainly does not require us to go so far as to condemn that quite different situation, whatever might be the result if it were presented to us for decision. For here, the arrangements for territorial limitations are part of 'an aggregation of trade restraints' including unlawful price-fixing and policing. Within settled doctrine, they are unlawful under § 1 of the Sherman Act without the necessity for an inquiry in each particular case as to their business or economic justification, their impact in the marketplace, or their reasonableness.

Accordingly, the judgment of the District Court is reversed and the case remanded for the entry of an appropriate decree.

Reversed and remanded.

Mr. Justice HARLAN, dissenting.

I cannot agree that on this record the restrictive territorial arrangements here challenged are properly to be classified as 'horizontal,' and hence illegal per se under established antitrust doctrine. I believe that they should be regarded as 'vertical' and thus, as the Court recognizes, subject to different antitrust evaluation.

Sealy, Inc., is the owner of trademarks for Sealy branded bedding. Sealy licenses manufacturers in various parts of the country to produce and sell its products. In addition, Sealy provides technical and managerial services for them, conducts advertising and other promotional programs, and engages in technical research and quality control activities. The Government's theory of this case in the District Court was essentially that the allocation of territories by Sealy to its various licensees was unlawful per se because in spite of these other legitimate activities Sealy was actually a 'front' created and used by the various manufacturers of Sealy products 'to camouflage their own collusive activities. * * *' Plaintiff's Brief in Opposition to Defendants' Briefs [citation omitted].

If such a characterization of Sealy had been proved at trial I would agree that the division of territories is illegal per se. Horizontal agreements among manufacturers to divide territories have long been held to violate the antitrust laws without regard to any asserted justification for them. [citation omitted] The reason is that territorial divisions prevent open competition, and where they are effected horizontally by manufacturers or by sellers who in the normal course of things would be competing among themselves, such restraints are immediately suspect. As the Court noted in *White Motor Co. v. United States,* 372 U.S. 253, 263, they are 'naked restraints of trade with no purpose except stifling of competition.' On the other hand, vertical restraints-that is, limitations imposed by a manufacturer on its own dealers, as in White Motor Co., or by a licensor on his licensees-may have independent and valid business justifications. The person imposing the restraint cannot necessarily be said to be acting for anticompetitive purposes. Quite to the contrary, he can be expected to be acting to enhance the competitive position of his product vis-a-vis other brands.

With respect to vertical restrictions, it has long been recognized that in order to engage in effective interbrand competition, some limitations on ~~interbrand~~ [intrabrand] competition may be necessary. Restraints of this type 'may be allowable protections against aggressive competitors or the only practicable means a small company has for breaking into or staying in business. [citation omitted] For these reasons territorial limitations imposed vertically should be tested by the rule of reason, namely, whether in the context of the particular industry, 'the restraint imposed is such as merely regulates and perhaps thereby promotes competition or whether it is such as may suppress or even destroy competition.' [citation omitted] ***

The question in this case is whether Sealy is properly to be regarded as an independent licensor which, as a prima facie matter, can be deemed to have imposed these restraints on its licensees for its own business purposes, or as equivalent to a horizontal combination of licensees, that is as simply a vehicle for effectuating horizontal arrangements between its licensees. On the basis of the findings made by the District Court, I am unable to accept the Court's classification of these restraints as horizontally contrived. The District Court made the following findings:

> '84. The proceding (detailed factual) findings indicate the type of evidence in this record that demonstrates that there has never been a central conspiratorial purpose on the part of Sealy and its licensees to divide the United States into territories in which competitors would not compete. Their main purpose has been the proper exploitation of the Sealy name and trademarks by licensing bedding manufacturers to manufacture and sell Sealy products in exchange for royalties to Sealy. The fact remains that each licensee was restricted in the territory in which he could manufacture and sell Sealy products. However, the record shows that this restriction was imposed by Sealy and was also secondary, or ancillary, to the main purpose of Sealy's license contracts.

> '119. Plaintiff's evidence, read as a whole, conclusively proves that the Sealy licensing arrangements were developed in the early 1920's for entirely legitimate business purposes, including royalty income to Sugar Land Industries, which owned the Sealy name, trademarks and patents, and the benefits to licensees of joint purchasing, research, engineering, advertising and merchandising. These objectives were carried out by successor companies, including defendant, whose activities have been directed not toward market division among licensees but toward obtaining additional licensees and more intensive sales coverage.'

The Solicitor General in presenting the appeal to this Court stated explicitly that he did not contend 'that Sealy, Inc. was no more than a facade for a conspiracy to suppress competition,' Brief, p. 12, since it admittedly did have genuine and lawful purposes. For me these District Court findings, which the Government accepts for purposes of this appeal, take this case out of the category of horizontal agreements, and thus out of the per se category as well. Sealy has wholly legitimate interests and purposes of its own: it is engaged in vigorous interbrand competition with large integrated bedding manufacturers and with retail chains selling their own products. Sealy's goal is to maximize sales of its products nationwide, and thus to maximize its royalties. The test under such circumstances should be the same as that governing other vertical relationships, namely, whether in the context of the market structure of this industry, these territorial restraints are reasonable business practices, given the true purposes of the antitrust laws. [citation omitted] It is true that in this case the shareholders of Sealy are the licensees. Such a relationship no doubt requires special scrutiny. But I cannot agree that this fact by itself automatically requires striking down Sealy's policy of territorialization. The correct approach, in my view, is to consider Sealy's corporate structure and decision-making process as one (but only one) relevant factor in determining whether the restraint is an unreasonable one. [citation omitted]

I find nothing in the Court's opinion that persuades me to abandon the traditional 'rule of reason' approach to this type of business practice in the context of the facts found by the trial court. ***

I would affirm the dismissal of this aspect of the case by the District Court.

Comments and Questions

1. The key issue in *Sealy* is whether the restraint is better characterized as vertical or horizontal. Do you think that the agreement among Sealy licensees is vertical or horizontal? Do you think that this line of inquiry is worthwhile? Why or why not?

2. Did the Court apply the per se rule or the rule of reason? How do you know?

3. In his dissent, Justice Harlan states: "With respect to vertical restrictions, it has long been recognized that in order to engage in effective interbrand competition, some limitations on interbrand competition may be necessary." That sentence appears to be a mistake (perhaps a typo). How should the sentence read and why does it matter?

United States v. Topco Associates, Inc.

405 U.S. 596 (1972)

Mr. Justice MARSHALL delivered the opinion of the Court.

The United States brought this action for injunctive relief against alleged violation by Topco Associates, Inc. (Topco), of § 1 of the Sherman Act.*** Following a trial on the merits, the United States District Court for the Northern District of Illinois entered *** and we now reverse the judgment of the District Court.

Market Allocation and Intellectual Property Rights

I

Topco is a cooperative association of approximately 25 small and medium-sized regional supermarket chains that operate stores in some 33 States. Each of the member chains operates independently; there is no pooling of earnings, profits, capital, management, or advertising resources. No grocery business is conducted under the Topco name. Its basic function is to serve as a purchasing agent for its members.[2] In this capacity, it procures and distributes to the members more than 1,000 different food and related nonfood items, most of which are distributed under brand names owned by Topco. The association does not itself own any manufacturing, processing, or warehousing facilities, and the items that it procures for members are usually shipped directly from the packer or manufacturer to the members. Payment is made either to Topco or directly to the manufacturer at a cost that is virtually the same for the members as for Topco itself.

All of the stock in Topco is owned by the members, with the common stock, the only stock having voting rights, being equally distributed. The board of directors, which controls the operation of the association, in drawn from the members and is normally composed of high-ranking executive officers of member chains. It is the board that elects the association's officers and appoints committee members, and it is from the board that the principal executive officers of Topco must be drawn. Restrictions on the alienation of stock and the procedure for selecting all important officials of the association from within the ranks of its members give the members complete and unfettered control over the operations of the association.

Topco was founded in the 1940's by a group of small, local grocery chains, independently owned and operated, that desired to cooperate to obtain high quality merchandise under private labels in order to compete more effectively with larger national and regional chains.[3] With a line of canned, dairy, and other

---

[2] In addition to purchasing various items for its members, Topco performs other related functions: e.g., it insures that there is adequate quality control on the products that it purchases; it assists members in developing specifications on certain types of products (e.g., equipment and supplies); and it also aids the members in purchasing goods through other sources.

[3] The founding members of Topco were having difficulty competing with larger chains. This difficulty was attributable in some degree to the fact that the larger chains were capable of developing their own private-label programs.

Private-label products differ from other brand-name products in that they are sold at a limited number of easily ascertainable stores. A&P, for example, was a pioneer in developing a series of products that were sold under an A&P label and that were only available in A&P stores. It is obvious that by using private-label products, a chain can achieve significant cost economies in purchasing, transportation, warehousing, promotion, and advertising. These economies may afford the chain opportunities for offering private-label products at lower prices than other band-name products. This, in turn, provides many advantages of which some of the more important are: a store can offer national-brand products at the same price as other stores, while simultaneously offering a desirable, lower priced alternative; or, if the profit margin is sufficiently high on private-brand goods, national-brand products may be sold at reduced price. Other advantages include: enabling a chain to bargain more favorably with national-brand manufacturers by creating a broader supply base of manufacturers, thereby decreasing dependence on a few, large national-brand manufacturers; enabling a chain to create a 'price-mix' whereby prices on special items can be lowered to attract customers while profits are maintained on other items; and creation of general goodwill by offering lower priced, higher quality goods

products, the association began. It added frozen foods in 1950, fresh produce in 1958, more general merchandise equipment and supplies in 1960, and a branded bacon and carcass beef selection program in 1966. By 1964, Topco's members had combined retail sales of more than $2 billion; by 1967, their sales totaled more than $2.3 billion, a figure exceeded by only three national grocery chains.

Members of the association vary in the degree of market share that they possess in their respective areas. The range is from 1.5% to 16%, with the average being approximately 6%. While it is difficult to compare these figures with the market shares of larger regional and national chains because of the absence in the record of accurate statistics for these chains, there is much evidence in the record that Topco members are frequently in as strong a competitive position in their respective areas as any other chain. The strength of this competitive position is due, in some measure, to the success of Topco-brand products. Although only 10% of the total goods sold by Topco members bear the association's brand names, the profit on these goods is substantial and their very existence has improved the competitive potential of Topco members with respect to other large and powerful chains.

It is apparent that from meager beginnings approximately a quarter of a century ago, Topco has developed into a purchasing association wholly owned and operated by member chains, which possess much economic muscle, individually as well as cooperatively.

II

Section 1 of the Sherman Act provides, in relevant part: "Every contract, combination in the form of trust or otherwise, or conspiracy, in restraint of trade or commerce among the several States, or with foreign nations, is declared to be illegal...."

The United States charged that, beginning at least as early as 1960 and continuing up to the time that the complaint was filed, Topco had combined and conspired with its members to violate § 1 in two respects. First, the Government alleged that there existed: 'a continuing agreement, understanding and concert of action among the co-conspirator member firms acting through Topco, the substantial terms of which have been and are that each co-conspirator or member firm will sell Topco-controlled brands only within the marketing territory allocated to it, and will refrain from selling Topco-controlled brands outside such marketing territory.' The division of marketing territories to which the complaint refers consists of a number of practices by the association. Article IX, § 2, of the Topco bylaws establishes three categories of territorial licenses that members may secure from the association:

> '(a) Exclusive-An exclusive territory is one in which the member is licensed to sell all products bearing specified trademarks of the Association, to the exclusion of all other persons.
>
> '(b) Non-exclusive-A non-exclusive territory is one in which a member is licensed to sell all products bearing specified trademarks of the Association, but not to the

exclusion of others who may also be licensed to sell products bearing the same trademarks of the Association in the same territory.

'(c) Coextensive-A coextensive territory is one in which two (2) or more members are licensed to sell all products bearing specified trademarks of the Association to the exclusion of all other persons. . . .'

When applying for membership, a chain must designate the type of license that it desires. Membership must first be approved by the board of directors, and thereafter by an affirmative vote of 75% of the association's members. If, however, the member whose operations are closest to those of the applicant, or any member whose operations are located within 100 miles of the applicant, votes against approval, an affirmative vote of 85% of the members is required for approval. Bylaws, Art. I, § 5. Because, as indicated by the record, members cooperate in accommodating each other's wishes, the procedure for approval provides, in essence, that members have a veto of sorts over actual or potential competition in the territorial areas in which they are concerned.

Following approval, each new member signs an agreement with Topco designating the territory in which that member may sell Topco-brand products. No member may sell these products outside the territory in which it is licensed. Most licenses are exclusive, and even those denominated 'coextensive' or 'nonexclusive' prove to be de facto exclusive. Exclusive territorial areas are often allocated to members who do no actual business in those areas on the theory that they may wish to expand at some indefinite future time and that expansion would likely be in the direction of the allocated territory. When combined with each member's veto power over new members, provisions for exclusivity work effectively to insulate members from competition in Topco-brand goods. Should a member violate its license agreement and sell in areas other than those in which it is licensed, its membership can be terminated under Art. IV, §§ 2 (a) and 2(b) of the bylaws. Once a territory is classified as exclusive, either formally or de facto, it is extremely unlikely that the classification will ever be changed. See Bylaws, Art. IX.

The Government maintains that this scheme of dividing markets violates the Sherman Act because it operates to prohibit competition in Topco-brand products among grocery chains engaged in retail operations. The Government also makes a subsidiary challenge to Topco's practices regarding licensing members to sell at wholesale. Under the bylaws, members are not permitted to sell any products supplied by the association at wholesale, whether trademarked or not, without first applying for and receiving special permission from the association to do so. Before permission is granted, other licensees (usually retailers), whose interests may potentially be affected by wholesale operations, are consulted as to their wishes in the matter. If permission is obtained, the member must agree to restrict the sale of Topco products to a specific geographic area and to sell under any conditions imposed by the association. Permission to wholesale has often been sought by members, only to be denied by the association. The Government contends that this amounts not only to a territorial restriction violative of the Sherman Act, but also to a restriction on customers that in itself is violative of the Act.

366 *Antitrust Law and Intellectual Property Rights*

From the inception of this lawsuit, Topco accepted as true most of the Government's allegations regarding territorial divisions and restrictions on wholesaling, although it differed greatly with the Government on the conclusions, both factual and legal, to be drawn from these facts.

Topco's answer to the complaint is illustrative of its posture in the District Court and before this Court:

> 'Private label merchandising is a way of economic life in the food retailing industry, and exclusivity is the essence of a private label program; without exclusivity, a private label would not be private. Each national and large regional chain has its own exclusive private label products in addition to the nationally advertised brands which all chains sell. Each such chain relies upon the exclusivity of its own private label line to differentiate its private label products from those of its competitors and to attract and retain the repeat business and loyalty of consumers. Smaller retail grocery stores and chains are unable to compete effectively with the national and large regional chains without also offering their own exclusive private label products.
>
> 'The only feasible method by which Topco can procure private label products and assure the exclusivity thereof is through trademark licenses specifying the territory in which each member may sell such trademarked products.' Answer, App. 11.

Topco essentially maintains that it needs territorial divisions to compete with larger chains; that the association could not exist if the territorial divisions were anything but exclusive; and that by restricting competition in the sale of Topco brand goods, the association actually increases competition by enabling its members to compete successfully with larger regional and national chains. ***

III

On its face, § 1 of the Sherman Act appears to bar any combination of entrepreneurs so long as it is 'in restraint of trade.' Theoretically, all manufacturers, distributors, merchants, sellers, and buyers could be considered as potential competitors of each other. Were § 1 to be read in the narrowest possible way, any commercial contract could be deemed to violate it. [citation omitted] The history underlying the formulation of the antitrust laws led this Court to conclude, however, that Congress did not intend to prohibit all contracts, nor even all contracts that might in some insignificant degree or attenuated sense restrain trade or competition. In lieu of the narrowest possible reading of § 1, the Court adopted a 'rule of reason' analysis for determining whether most business combinations or contracts violate the prohibitions of the Sherman Act. [citation omitted] An analysis of the reasonableness of particular restraints includes consideration of the facts peculiar to the business in which the restraint is applied, the nature of the restraint and its effects, and the history of the restraint and the reasons for its adoption. [citation omitted]

While the Court has utilized the 'rule of reason' in evaluating the legality of most restraints alleged to be violative of the Sherman Act, it has also developed the doctrine that certain business relationships are per se violations of the Act without regard to a consideration of their reasonableness. In *Northern Pacific R. Co. v.*

United States, 356 U.S. 1, 5 (1958), Mr. Justice Black explained the appropriateness of, and the need for, per se rules:

> '(T)here are certain agreements or practices which because of their pernicious effect on competition and lack of any redeeming virtue are conclusively presumed to be unreasonable and therefore illegal without elaborate inquiry as to the precise harm they have caused or the business excuse for their use. This principle of per se unreasonableness not only makes the type of restraints which are proscribed by the Sherman Act more certain to the benefit of everyone concerned, but it also avoids the necessity for an incredibly complicated and prolonged economic investigation into the entire history of the industry involved, as well as related industries, in an effort to determine at large whether a particular restraint has been unreasonable-an inquiry so often wholly fruitless when undertaken.'

It is only after considerable experience with certain business relationships that courts classify them as per se violations of the Sherman Act. [citation omitted] One of the classic examples of a per se violation of § 1 is an agreement between competitors at the same level of the market structure to allocate territories in order to minimize competition. Such concerted action is usually termed a 'horizontal' restraint, in contradistinction to combinations of persons at different levels of the market structure, e.g., manufacturers and distributors, which are termed 'vertical' restraints. This Court has reiterated time and time again that '(h)orizontal territorial limitations . . . are naked restraints of trade with no purpose except stifling of competition.' White Motor Co. v. United States, 372 U.S. 253, 263 (1963). Such limitations are per se violations of the Sherman Act. [citation omitted]

We think that it is clear that the restraint in this case is a horizontal one, and, therefore, a per se violation of § 1. The District Court failed to make any determination as to whether there were per se horizontal territorial restraints in this case and simply applied a rule of reason in reaching its conclusions that the restraints were not illegal. [citation omitted] In so doing, the District Court erred.

United States v. Sealy, Inc., is, in fact, on all fours with this case. Sealy licensed manufacturers of mattresses and bedding to make and sell products using the Sealy trademark. Like Topco, Sealy was a corporation owned almost entirely by its licensees, who elected the Board of Directors and controlled the business. Just as in this case, Sealy agreed with the licensees not to license other manufacturers or sellers to sell Sealy-brand products in a designated territory in exchange for the promise of the licensee who sold in that territory not to expand its sales beyond the area demarcated by Sealy. The Court held that this was a horizontal territorial restraint, which was per se violative of the Sherman Act.

Whether or not we would decide this case the same way under the rule of reason used by the District Court is irrelevant to the issue before us. The fact is that courts are of limited utility in examining difficult economic problems. Our inability to weigh, in any meaningful sense, destruction of competition in one sector of the economy against promotion of competition in another sector is one important reason we have formulated per se rules.

In applying these rigid rules, the Court has consistently rejected the notion that naked restraints of trade are to be tolerated because they are well intended or because they are allegedly developed to increase competition. [citation omitted]

Antitrust laws in general, and the Sherman Act in particular, are the Magna Carta of free enterprise. They are as important to the preservation of economic freedom and our free-enterprise system as the Bill of Rights is to the protection of our fundamental personal freedoms. And the freedom guaranteed each and every business, no matter how small, is the freedom to compete-to assert with vigor, imagination, devotion, and ingenuity whatever economic muscle it can muster. Implicit in such freedom is the notion that it cannot be foreclosed with respect to one sector of the economy because certain private citizens or groups believe that such foreclosure might promote greater competition in a more important sector of the economy. [citation omitted]

The District Court determined that by limiting the freedom of its individual members to compete with each other, Topco was doing a greater good by fostering competition between members and other large supermarket chains. But, the fallacy in this is that Topco has no authority under the Sherman Act to determine the respective values of competition in various sectors of the economy. On the contrary, the Sherman Act gives to each Topco members and to each prospective member the right to ascertain for itself whether or not competition with other supermarket chains is more desirable than competition in the sale of Topco-brand products. Without territorial restrictions, Topco members may indeed '(cut) each other's throats.' *Cf. White Motor Co., supra,* 372 U.S., at 278, 83 S.Ct., at 710 (Clark, J. dissenting). But we have never found this possibility sufficient to warrant condoning horizontal restraints of trade.

The Court has previously noted with respect to price fixing, another per se violation of the Sherman Act, that:

> 'The reasonable price fixed today may through economic and business changes become the unreasonable price of tomorrow. Once established, it may be maintained unchanged because of the absence of competition secured by the agreement for a price reasonable when fixed.' United States v. Trenton Potteries Co., 273 U.S. 392, 397, 47 S.Ct. 377, 379, 71 L.Ed. 700 (1927).

A similar observation can be made with regard to territorial limitations. [citation omitted]

There have been tremendous departures from the notion of a free-enterprise system as it was originally conceived in this country. These departures have been the product of congressional action and the will of the people. If a decision is to be made to sacrifice competition in one portion of the economy for greater competition in another portion this too is a decision that must be made by Congress and not by private forces or by the courts. Private forces are too keenly aware of their own interests in making such decisions and courts are ill-equipped and ill-situated for such decisionmaking. To analyze, interpret, and evaluate the myriad of competing interests and the endless data that would surely be brought to bear on such decisions, and to make the delicate judgment on the relative values to society of competitive areas of the economy, the judgment of the elected representatives of the people is required.

Just as the territorial restrictions on retailing Topco-brand products must fall, so must the territorial restrictions on wholesaling. The considerations are the same, and the Sherman Act requires identical results.

We reverse the judgment of the District Court and remand the case for entry of an appropriate decree.

It is so ordered.

Reversed and remanded.

Mr. Justice POWELL and Mr. Justice REHNQUIST took no part in the consideration or decision of this case. [Blackman concurrence and Burger dissent omitted]

Comments and Questions

1. The *Topco* majority states that "the Court has consistently rejected the notion that naked restraints of trade are to be tolerated because they are well intended or because they are allegedly developed to increase competition." Should good intent save a potentially anticompetitive restraint from antitrust liability? Why or why not?

2. The *Topco* Court states that it cannot trade off reduced intrabrand competition for increased interbrand competition because that is "a decision that must be made by Congress and not by private forces or by the courts." But five years later in *Continental TV v. Sylvania*, 433 U.S. 36 (1977), the Court reached an opposing result in a case challenging a non-price vertical restraint, noting that "[t]he market impact of vertical restrictions is complex because of their potential for a simultaneous reduction of intrabrand competition and stimulation of interbrand competition." The Court reversed its prior application of the per se rule to non-price vertical restrictions such as a manufacturer assigning exclusive territories to its distributors. But the Court maintained that *Topco* was still good law, as it applied to horizontal non-price restraints. Nevertheless, the reasoning of *Topco* was undermined.

3. Regarding the per se rule and experience, the Court asserted: "It is only after considerable experience with certain business relationships that courts classify them as per se violations of the Sherman Act." Do you think that the Court had considerable experience with this particular type of business arrangement before declaring it per se illegal?

4. On remand, the district court allowed Topco to create areas or territories of primary responsibility for member firms (so long as they did not create de facto exclusive territories) and to terminate members that did not adequately promote Topco brands. The Supreme Court summarily affirmed the district court's holding. *United States v. Topco Associates, Inc.*, 414 U.S. 801 (1973).

Palmer v. BRG of Georgia, Inc.
498 U.S. 46 (1990)

PER CURIAM.

In preparation for the 1985 Georgia Bar Examination, petitioners contracted to take a bar review course offered by respondent BRG of Georgia, Inc. (BRG). In this litigation they contend that the price of BRG's course was enhanced by reason of an unlawful agreement between BRG and respondent Harcourt Brace Jovanovich Legal and Professional Publications (HBJ), the Nation's largest provider of bar review materials and lecture services. The central issue is whether the 1980 agreement between respondents violated § 1 of the Sherman Act.

HBJ began offering a Georgia bar review course on a limited basis in 1976, and was in direct, and often intense, competition with BRG during the period from 1977 to 1979. BRG and HBJ were the two main providers of bar review courses in Georgia during this time period. In early 1980, they entered into an agreement that gave BRG an exclusive license to market HBJ's material in Georgia and to use its trade name "Bar/Bri." The parties agreed that HBJ would not compete with BRG in Georgia and that BRG would not compete with HBJ outside of Georgia.[2] Under the agreement, HBJ received $100 per student enrolled by BRG and 40% of all revenues over $350. Immediately after the 1980 agreement, the price of BRG's course was increased from $150 to over $400. ***

In *United States v. Socony-Vacuum Oil Co.*, 310 U.S. 150 (1940), we held that an agreement among competitors to engage in a program of buying surplus gasoline on the spot market in order to prevent prices from falling sharply was unlawful, even though there was no direct agreement on the actual prices to be maintained. We explained that "[u]nder the Sherman Act a combination formed for the purpose and with the effect of raising, depressing, fixing, pegging, or stabilizing the price of a commodity in interstate or foreign commerce is illegal per se." *Id.*, at 223. [citation omitted]

The revenue-sharing formula in the 1980 agreement between BRG and HBJ, coupled with the price increase that took place immediately after the parties agreed to cease competing with each other in 1980, indicates that this agreement was "formed for the purpose and with the effect of raising" the price of the bar review course. *** [T]he District Court and the Court of Appeals erred when they assumed that an allocation of markets or submarkets by competitors is not unlawful unless the market in which the two previously competed is divided between them.

In *United States v. Topco Associates, Inc.*, 405 U.S. 596 (1972), we held that agreements between competitors to allocate territories to minimize competition are illegal:

> "One of the classic examples of a per se violation of § 1 is an agreement between competitors at the same level of the market structure to allocate territories in order to minimize competition. . . . This Court has reiterated time and time again that '[h]orizontal territorial limitations . . . are naked restraints of trade with no

---

[2] The 1980 agreement contained two provisions, one called a "Covenant Not to Compete" and the other called "Other Ventures." The former required HBJ not to "directly or indirectly own, manage, operate, join, invest, control, or participate in or be connected as an officer, employee, partner, director, independent contractor or otherwise with any business which is operating or participating in the preparation of candidates for the Georgia State Bar Examination." Plaintiffs' Motion for Partial Summary Judgment, Attachment E, p. 10. The latter required BRG not to compete against HBJ in States in which HBJ currently operated outside the State of Georgia. *Id.*, at 15.

Market Allocation and Intellectual Property Rights 371

purpose except stifling of competition.' Such limitations are per se violations of the Sherman Act." [citation omitted]

The defendants in *Topco* had never competed in the same market, but had simply agreed to allocate markets. Here, HBJ and BRG had previously competed in the Georgia market; under their allocation agreement, BRG received that market, while HBJ received the remainder of the United States. Each agreed not to compete in the other's territories. Such agreements are anticompetitive regardless of whether the parties split a market within which both do business or whether they merely reserve one market for one and another for the other. Thus, the 1980 agreement between HBJ and BRG was unlawful on its face. ***

It is so ordered.

[Justice Marshall dissent omitted]

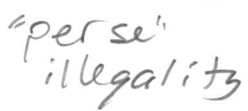

Comments and Questions

1. The Court condemned the challenged agreement under the per se rule. What would have happened if the Court had applied the rule of reason?

2. How much weight did the Court give to the fact that the market allocation provision took place in the context of a trademark agreement? Would you have taken a different approach? Why?

In addition to their trademarks, the businesses in *Palmer* also depended on their copyrighted works of authorship, which would have been affected by the agreement. Should the combination of trademarks and copyrights affect the antitrust analysis of their agreement?

3. Although many observers thought that the *Sylvania* opinion had substantially undermined the *Topco* decision, "by finding market allocation, the [*Palmer*] Court breathed life into the *Topco* decision, which a number of commentators prematurely had declared dead." ABA ANTITRUST SECTION, MONOGRAM NO. 23, THE RULE OF REASON MONOGRAPH 86 (1999).

Clorox Co. v. Sterling Winthrop, Inc.

117 F.3d 50 (2nd Cir. 1997)

PARKER, Circuit Judge:

I. Background

A. The Parties and Their Products

*** Clorox makes and sells household cleaner-disinfectant products, including Pine-Sol-brand products acquired from Cyanamid in 1990. Pine-Sol is the oldest and best-selling pine-oil cleaner. The trademark has been used since 1945, and possibly as early as 1929. It has been federally registered since 1957. *** Clorox is one of the largest producers of cleaning products in the world. In addition to the Pine-Sol brand, it manufactures bleaches and cleaners under many famous trademarks *** Overall, as of June 1996, Clorox enjoyed a thirty-seven percent share of the all-purpose household cleaning market. Sterling acquired the Lysol mark in 1966. Reckitt purchased Sterling's assets in 1994, including the Lysol line. As of June 1996, Reckitt enjoyed close to fifteen percent of the all-purpose household cleaning market, in contrast to Clorox's market share of thirty-seven percent.

The Lysol brand name arrived on the market a few decades before Pine-Sol. Lysol has been a federally registered trademark for disinfectants since 1906, and for cleaning products in general since the 1920s. Lysol is famous as an aerosol spray disinfectant. *** The Lysol name has become virtually synonymous with household disinfectants. The Lysol aerosol spray disinfectant is in a class of its own, as only small brand-name products compete against it.

B. The History of the Dispute

The Lysol and Pine-Sol marks have not coexisted amicably. The owners of these marks have been battling ever since the owners of Pine-Sol sought to register the trademark with the U.S. Patent office in the 1940s. When the maker of Pine-Sol products initially attempted to register the Pine-Sol mark, the owner of the Lysol mark opposed the registration. The Examiner in Chief of the U.S. Patent Office denied registration of Pine-Sol on account of what the Examiner determined to be a confusing similarity between the Pine-Sol and Lysol marks. At the time, Pine-Sol was written as one word, similar to the way Lysol appears. The Examiner reasoned that "Pine" can be slurred as "Pi" and "Pi-Sol" can thereby be confused with "Lysol." [citation omitted]

Despite the Examiner's decision, the owners of the Pine-Sol mark continued to use it. [The owner of the Lysol mark brought a trademark infringement suit, which settled.] The 1967 Agreement prohibited the use of the Pine-Sol mark on any "disinfectant product," including "any product which is offered for sale, sold or promoted solely or in part" as a disinfectant or "as possessing or containing any disinfectant." In return, the 1967 Agreement granted Cyanamid the right to introduce various cleaning products under the Pine-Sol name, including "soaps or detergents, laundry preparations, finishing products for hard or soft surfaces, or deodorants." It also allowed Cyanamid to introduce agricultural fungicides, and insecticides and rodenticides, under the Pine-Sol mark. The 1967 Agreement provided that Cyanamid could continue to promote Pine-Sol as primarily a liquid cleaner with disinfecting properties, subject to the same limitations provided in the 1956 Agreement. Cyanamid agreed to discontinue manufacturing the Pine-Sol spray disinfectant, the subject of the 1965 lawsuit.

Nearly two decades later, in 1983, the battle resumed. Cyanamid sued Sterling for marketing a product called Lysol PINE ACTION in a bottle similar to the one used by Pine-Sol. Cyanamid argued that the 1967 Agreement contained a negative covenant prohibiting Sterling from introducing Lysol in the pine-oil product category. Cyanamid also claimed that Sterling's actions constituted unfair competition and trade dress infringement.

A few years later, with the 1983 action still pending, Cyanamid attempted to market a non-aerosol pump spray disinfectant under the Pine-Sol name.

As a result, Sterling sued Cyanamid in 1987. Sterling and Cyanamid resolved both lawsuits in the 1987 Agreement. The 1987 Agreement modified the terms of the 1967 Agreement in important ways. Cyanamid obtained the ability to market a "multi-purpose pump spray household cleaner with disinfecting properties." Cyanamid obtained this limited consent from Sterling subject to many conditions, however. These include the following, which Clorox now characterizes as the 1987 Agreement's "most anticompetitive provisions":

- ¶ 3(c)-(d) and ¶ 4(e)-restricts the sale of "disinfectant products" under the Pine-Sol mark: only the basic liquid cleaner and a pump spray may be sold "in part" as disinfectants under the mark. The product restrictions allow only one "form, scent or formula" of these two Pine-Sol products to be sold "in a single geographic area at the same time." The provisions permit Clorox to market other disinfectant products with the Pine-Sol mark used as an endorsement mark for products sold under other trademarks, subject to limitations on the size and placement of the mark.
- ¶ 4(a)-requires that the original Pine-Sol product be "sold, advertised, and promoted primarily as a cleaner rather than primarily as a disinfectant product." This includes the requirement that the words "cleans" or "cleaner" be set forth before the words "disinfectant" or "disinfects" and that the words "cleans" or "cleaner" be more prominent.
- ¶ 4(c)-prevents Pine-Sol products from being sold as anything other than generic cleaners, as opposed to special purpose cleaners like bathroom cleaners.

In return for allowing Cyanamid to market the disinfectant spray, Sterling obtained Cyanamid's permission to market Lysol Pine Action Cleaner.

Clorox purchased the Pine-Sol assets in 1990, subject to the 1987 Agreement.

C. Proceedings Below

Clorox brought this action alleging that the 1987 Agreement serves no legitimate trademark purpose because there is no longer the likelihood of consumers confusing the Lysol and Pine-Sol marks. Clorox claims that in restricting the way Clorox can use the Pine-Sol mark to compete, it violates the prohibition in Section One of the Sherman Act of unlawful agreements in restraint of trade. See 15 U.S.C. § 1. *** The high barrier to introducing new household cleaning products, in the form of advertising costs and high risk, according to Clorox, requires that Clorox be allowed to use the already famous Pine-Sol mark to compete effectively against Reckitt in the alleged markets Lysol products dominate. *** [The district court granted summary judgment to the defendant and Clorox appealed.]

II. Discussion

On appeal, Clorox pursues its claim that the 1987 Agreement between Cyanamid and Sterling serves no valid trademark purpose and is therefore an illegal agreement in restraint of trade. ***

B. Agreement in Restraint of Trade: Sherman Act Section One

Section One of the Sherman Antitrust Act makes illegal "[e]very contract, combination in the form of trust or otherwise, or conspiracy, in restraint of trade or commerce among the several States, or with foreign nations. . . ." 15 U.S.C. § 1. Clorox argues that the 1987 Agreement is unlawful because it serves no legitimate trademark purpose in preventing Clorox from advertising Pine-Sol products primarily as disinfectants and prohibiting Clorox from producing certain disinfectant products under the Pine-Sol name.

We must first determine the proper framework for analyzing Clorox's Section One claim. We begin with the fact that Clorox challenges a trademark agreement. Such agreements are common, and favored, under the law. [citation omitted] Unlike trademark agreements that in reality serve to divide markets, *see, e.g., Timken Roller Bearing Co. v. United States,* 341 U.S. 593 (1951), and thus have been condemned as illegal per se under the antitrust laws, the agreement at issue here merely regulates the way a competitor *56 can use a competing mark. Contrary to Clorox's argument, the agreement does not effect any of the types of restraints that have historically been condemned as illegal per se, such as price fixing, market divisions, tying arrangements, or boycotts. Accordingly, we must examine the summary judgment evidence in accordance with "rule of reason" analysis. [citation omitted]

Applying rule of reason analysis, we must determine whether the restraints in the agreement are reasonable in light of their actual effects on the market and their pro-competitive justifications. [citation omitted] As we outlined in *K.M.B.,* "[e]stablishing a violation of the rule of reason involves three steps." 61 F.3d at 127. First, the "'[p]laintiff bears the initial burden of showing that the challenged action has had an actual adverse effect on competition as a whole in the relevant market. . . .'" *Id.* [citation omitted] Then, "[i]f the plaintiff succeeds, the burden shifts to the defendant to establish the 'pro-competitive "redeeming virtues"' of the action. Should the defendant carry this burden, the plaintiff must then show that the same pro-competitive effect could be achieved through an alternative means that is less restrictive of competition." *Id.* [citation omitted] Ultimately, the goal is to determine whether restrictions in an agreement among competitors potentially harm consumers. *See SCFC ILC, Inc. v. Visa USA, Inc.,* 36 F.3d 958, 965 (10th Cir.1994). The focus of the inquiry on consumers "cannot be overemphasized and is especially essential when a successful competitor," as here, "alleges antitrust injury at the hands of a rival." *Id.* We examine Clorox's Section One claim according to this analytical framework.

1. Adverse Effects

We begin by noting that Clorox faces a difficult task of proving that the 1987 Agreement harms competition in general. As other courts and commentators have observed, trademarks are by their nature non-exclusionary. A trademark, unlike other intellectual property rights, does not confer a legal monopoly on any good or idea; it confers rights to a name only. Because a trademark "merely enables the owner to bar others from use of the mark, as distinguished from competitive manufacture and sale of identical goods bearing another mark, ... the opportunity for effective antitrust misuse of a trademark, as distinguished from collateral anti-competitive activities on the part of the manufacturer or seller of the goods bearing the mark, is so limited that it poses a far less serious threat to the economic health of the nation." *Carl Zeiss Stiftung v. V.E.B. Carl Zeiss, Jena*, 298 F.Supp. 1309, 1314 (S.D.N.Y.1969), aff'd in relevant part, 433 F.2d 686 (2d Cir.1970); see also 4 McCarthy § 31:96, at 31–145 ("[B]ecause the economic exclusivity of a trademark is far less than that of a patent, there is far less opportunity for a trademark to play and integral role in violations of the antitrust laws."). As Judge Mansfield noted in *Carl Zeiss*, "in almost every reported instance where the antitrust misuse of a trademark has been raised as a defense [in a trademark infringement suit], it has been rejected. In the great majority of such cases the evidence revealed the antitrust activities to be collateral" to trademark protection. *See* 298 F.Supp. at 1314.

The trademark agreement at issue here does no more than regulate how the name Pine-Sol may be used; it does not in any way restrict Clorox from producing and selling products that compete directly with the Lysol brand, so long as they are marketed under a brand name other than Pine-Sol. Accordingly, at first blush it would not appear to restrict Clorox's, much less any other competitor's, ability to compete in the markets Lysol products allegedly dominate.

*** [I]t is difficult to show that an unfavorable trademark agreement raises antitrust concerns. Even if such an agreement only marginally advances trademark policies, the antitrust laws do not exist to protect competitors from agreements that in retrospect turn out to be unfavorable to the complaining party. The antitrust laws protect consumers by prohibiting agreements that unreasonably restrain overall competition; thus, in order to fulfill the requirement of showing an actual adverse effect in the relevant market, "the plaintiff must show more than just that he was harmed by the defendant's conduct." *See K.M.B.*, 61 F.3d at 127. Accordingly, Clorox cannot make a case under the antitrust laws unless it demonstrates that the 1987 Agreement may significantly harm competition as a whole, regardless of whether the agreement is entirely necessary to protect Reckitt's trademark rights. ***

Clorox is free to market a cleaner-disinfectant that competes head-to-head against Lysol liquid disinfectant cleaner. Clorox is only hampered by the restriction that Pine-Sol be advertised primarily as a cleaner rather than primarily as a disinfectant. There is no prohibition on Clorox promoting the original Pine-Sol product-a product that has enjoyed enormous success despite the limitations imposed by the 1987 Agreement-in part as a disinfectant. It did so until recently. Although the agreement prohibits Clorox from producing an aerosol disinfectant spray under the Pine-Sol name, it does not prevent Clorox from producing such a spray using an endorsement mark indicating that the product is from the makers of Pine-Sol, although Clorox's ability to do so is subject to limitations on the size and placement of the mark.

It may well be that the restrictions in the agreement prevent Clorox from competing as effectively as it otherwise might. Endorsement marks may not be as effective as using a name brand as a primary mark, advertising a product primarily as a disinfectant may be more lucrative, and using the Clorox name may be less effective than using the popular Pine-Sol name to market disinfectant products. The antitrust laws do not guarantee competitors the right to compete free of encumbrances, however, so long as competition as a whole is not significantly affected. [citation omitted] ***

In light of the fact that the agreement leaves many other companies who produce cleaning products capable of competing against Reckitt's Lysol products, including Clorox, we find unavailing Clorox's attempt to bolster its Section One claim with evidence of Reckitt's market power in various alleged cleaner-disinfectant categories. *** [E]ven if true, Clorox's claim that Reckitt maintains a seventy-percent share of the alleged pure liquid disinfectant cleaner market, and over a ninety-percent share of the alleged aerosol spray disinfectant market, and that Lysol products now earn super-competitive profits, does not establish that the restrictions in the 1987 Agreement violate Section One. The agreement simply does not significantly restrict Clorox's, or other competitors', ability to enter these alleged markets.

2. Pro-Competitive Justifications

Only if a plaintiff succeeds in establishing the actual adverse effects of an alleged restraint does the burden shift to the defendant to establish its pro-competitive redeeming virtues. [citation omitted] Accordingly, as Clorox has not shown that the 1987 Agreement can significantly affect competition as a whole, it is immaterial whether the Agreement is entirely necessary to protect the senior Lysol mark. [citation omitted]

We note, however, that the pro-competitive justifications of the agreement bolster our conclusion that the agreement does not violate the antitrust laws. As we stated previously, trademark agreements are favored in the law as a means by which parties agree to market products in a way that reduces the likelihood of consumer confusion and avoids time-consuming litigation. Parties such as Clorox, Sterling, and their predecessors, are in a position to structure such agreements in the way that the parties believe best accommodates their interests in light of trademark law. Accordingly, in the absence of any evidence that the provisions relating to trademark protection are auxiliary to an underlying illegal agreement between competitors-such as the territorial market division condemned in Timken-and absent exceptional circumstances, we believe the parties' determination of the scope of needed trademark protections is entitled to substantial weight. At the time of the execution of such an agreement, the parties are in the best position to determine what protections are needed and how to resolve disputes concerning earlier trademark agreements between themselves. While the intent of the parties may not always be determinative, it is usually unwise for courts to second-guess such decisions. In the absence of evidence to the contrary it is reasonable to presume that such arms-length agreements are pro-competitive.

The fact is, Clorox now complains about the antitrust consequences of the very agreement its predecessor freely entered, and which it voluntarily assumed, an agreement Clorox now claims harms its ability to compete. There is no evidence that Cyanamid entered the agreement under duress. Although Clorox raises some ambiguous evidence to suggest Sterling's anticompetitive intent, there is not a scintilla of evidence that Cyanamid intended to conspire with Sterling to violate the antitrust laws in any way. Rather, each competitor bargained freely over the potential use of the Pine-Sol name, in light of prior trademark agreements and the history of the trademark dispute between the owners of the competing Lysol and Pine-Sol marks.

While it is settled that a good intention will not relieve a party from civil antitrust liability, intent is nonetheless important in judging the pro-competitive purposes, and thus the likely overall competitive effects, of an alleged restraint. [citation omitted] Efforts to protect trademarks, even aggressive ones, serve the competitive purpose of furthering trademark policies. Where large competitors each represent their respective trademark interests, unless one party is irrational, the result should accord with how the parties view their respective rights. ***

Comments and Questions

1. Clorox brought this case because Sterling had convinced a New Jersey state court to issue obtained a preliminary injunction against a television commercial for one of Clorox's Pine-Sol products. Sterling had argued that the commercial violated the 1987 Agreement because the commercial emphasized Pine-Sol's disinfectant properties.

2. Are pine-scented cleaners a relevant product market? Why or why not? How does the answer affect the antitrust analysis?

3. "Cyanamid argued that the 1967 Agreement contained a negative covenant prohibiting Sterling from introducing Lysol in the pine-oil product category." Is that a form of market allocation? If so, why isn't the restraint per se illegal?

4. The Second Circuit discusses intent. What should intent play in a case like this? Does it matter whether the court is using a per se or rule-of-reason approach?

5. The Second Circuit cited earlier case law for the proposition that a trademark agreement, such as the one before it, "did not restrict a competitor's ability to market products under names other than the one precluded by the agreement" and thus "did not state an antitrust claim." (The court cited *California Packing Corp. v. Sun-Maid Raisin Growers*, 165 F.Supp. 245 (S.D.Cal.1958), aff'd, 273 F.2d 282 (9th Cir.1959), and *The Seven-Up Co. v. No-Cal Corp.*, 183 U.S.P.Q. 165, 1974 WL 886 (E.D.N.Y.1974). At one point, the Second Circuit asserted that "trademarks are non-exclusionary." Is that necessarily true?

6. Clorox also brought a Section 2 claim, asserting that the defendant had used the previous settlement agreement to illegally monopolize "various disinfectant cleaning markets." The Second Circuit affirmed summary judgment for the defendant by referring to its Section 1 analysis and concluding that the challenged

378 *Antitrust Law and Intellectual Property Rights*

agreement left "Clorox, as well as other viable competitors in the household-cleaning industry, free to compete against Reckitt's Lysol brand in the markets these products allegedly dominate."

After losing its Section 1 claim, does Clorox's Section 2 have to fail as a matter of law?

7. How is the agreement in Clorox, which the Second Circuit found lawful, distinguishable for the agreements in Timken, Sealy, Topco, and Palmer, all of which the Supreme Court condemned as violating Section 1 of the Sherman Act?

C. Copyrights and Market Allocation

Auwood v. Harry Brandt Booking Office, Inc.
850 F.2d 884 (2nd Cir. 1988)

KEARSE, Circuit Judge:

Plaintiffs William Auwood and Neal S. Ossen, as Trustees in bankruptcy for Liberty Theatre Corporation ("Liberty"), appeal from a final judgment entered in the United States District Court for the District of Connecticut following a jury trial before Peter C. Dorsey, Judge, awarding them $3.00 as treble damages for injury suffered by Liberty as a result of an agreement or conspiracy among the defendants to allocate "first-run" films among theatres other than Liberty, in violation of § 1 of the Sherman Antitrust Act, 15 U.S.C. § 1 (1982), 647 F.Supp. 1551. On appeal, plaintiffs contend that the district court erred (1) in denying their motion for a new trial on the issue of damages, and (2) in reducing the jury's damage award of $75,000, labeled by the jury as "nominal," to $1. Defendants Harry Brandt Booking Office, Inc. ("Brandt"), Groton Cinema, Inc. ("Groton Cinema"), and United Artists Communications, Inc. ("UA Communications"), cross-appeal, contending (1) that the court should have granted judgment in their favor notwithstanding the verdict ("n.o.v.") because plaintiffs failed to prove a conspiracy of which defendants were members and failed to prove injury, ***

I. Background

From 1976 to 1981, Liberty operated a movie theatre in Uncasville, Connecticut, midway between the cities of Norwich and New London. In the operation of its business, Liberty sought to license motion pictures for exhibition on a "first-run" basis, i.e., to give the first exhibition of a film released by a major film distributor in a given geographical market. It secured few first-run films, and in 1981 it declared bankruptcy.

In 1979, Liberty and Auwood, its principal, commenced the present action against several theatre chains and film distributors, alleging that the defendants had entered into an agreement among themselves to allocate the rights to license first-run films among the exhibitor parties to the agreement, to the exclusion of Liberty, thereby causing injury to Liberty in its business and property in violation of § 1 of the Sherman Act, 15 U.S.C. § 1. ***

After some years of discovery, several of the defendants entered into settlement agreements with plaintiffs. They paid plaintiffs a total of at least $97,000 and were dismissed from the case. The case proceeded to trial against the present defendants: Groton Cinema, which operated a movie theatre in New London; UA Communications, which is Groton Cinema's parent (also referred to as "UATC"); and Brandt, which was a booking agent for Groton Cinema and a theatre in Norwich (the "Norwich Cinema"). ***

A 13-day jury trial was held, with the jury considering separately the issues of liability and damages. ***

On the liability issues, the jury found that Brandt, Groton Cinema, and UA Communications had formed, joined, or participated in a conspiracy, combination, or agreement which was intended to and did constitute an unreasonable restraint of trade. It found that these actions adversely affected Liberty's opportunities to obtain a fair allocation of first-run films and proximately caused injury to Liberty's business. ***

II. Discussion

On the present appeals, defendants contend principally that the district court should have granted their motions for judgment n.o.v. because plaintiffs failed to prove (a) the existence of a conspiracy to allocate first-run films, (b) the participation by the defendants in such a conspiracy, or (c) any quantifiable injury resulting from unlawful conduct on the part of the defendants. ***

A. The Denial of Judgment N.O.V. as to Liability

Defendants' contentions that they were entitled to judgment in their favor notwithstanding the jury's findings against them on the issues of liability need not detain us long. ***

As the district court noted, there was ample evidence that the first-run exhibition of acclaimed films was more profitable than the subsequent exhibition of such films or the first exhibition of so-called "dogs." Despite the evidence that Liberty's gross income potential for first-run films was comparable to that of Norwich Cinema, Liberty received less than half as many first-run films as Norwich Cinema; it received only some 60% as many first-run films as other theatres whose gross income potential was less than that of Liberty. The evidence as to the cause of Liberty's receipt of so few first-run films included the testimony of a witness experienced in the film distribution business who testified that an agreement among distributors and theatres to allocate, or "split," first-run films among participating theatres caused certain first-run films bid on by Liberty to be licensed to Groton Cinema or other participating theatres and not to Liberty. From about 1967 to 1980, James Engle had been employed at various times in New England as a branch manager for Warner Brothers Pictures, or as an assistant branch manager and branch manager for Paramount Pictures; he had been a partner in Jed Parker Films, an independent film distribution company in Boston, and had owned his own film distribution company. As Boston branch manager for Warner Brothers

Pictures in 1976–1978, Engle's territory included the New London-Norwich area. He testified that

> [t]he splitting had been going on for some time in that area, long before I ever reached Warner Brothers. I found that out working at Jed Parker Films and also at Paramount Pictures.
>
> Q. When you were at Warner Brothers, would exhibitors call up from time to time and say anything that would indicate that there might be a split?
>
> A. Yes. I would get calls from RKO and Warner, "It's my picture, put it in on a particular availability date."
>
> I would get calls from UATC, from Nat Harris [UATC's booker], telling me the same thing.

As an example of the denial of films to Liberty because of the allocation agreement, Engle testified that when he had been at Warner Brothers some two and one-half months, Liberty made a bid on "All the President's Men," and Engle recommended that Liberty be allowed to show that film at the same time as Groton Cinema. His recommendation was met by "a very irate" telephone call from his division manager, asking "who the hell the Liberty Theater was."

> Q. Did he say anything?
>
> A. He said, "Don't be stupid." He said, "The picture belongs to UATC and that's where it's going to play."
>
> Q. Did you have any understanding with respect to how that picture was sold?
>
> A. That picture was awarded on a split basis.

Engle testified that even when the ostensible reason for licensing a film to another theatre instead of to Liberty was a higher bid or guarantee from the other theatre, the latter often in fact paid less than the amount of Liberty's bid. The motive for distributors to adhere to the allocation agreement was that the participating theatres were required to show "dogs" as well as acclaimed films, thereby assuring distributors of outlets for all of their films, not just the most popular. We conclude that the evidence in the record as a whole was sufficient to permit the jury to infer that there existed a conspiracy to allocate first-run films, that the defendants were parties to that conspiracy, and that the operation of the conspiracy caused injury to Liberty. Although there was also evidence that there might have been other reasons for Liberty's failure to receive more first-run films, the district court properly noted that the resolution of the conflicting evidence was a matter for the jury. The jury was not required to accept defendants' explanations, and we are not entitled to overturn the jury's credibility evaluations or the inferences it chose to draw. The motions for judgment n.o.v. were properly denied. ***

Comments and Questions

1. The 2nd Circuit reinstated the jury award of $75,000, which was trebled to $225,000, and then deducted the previous settlements from it.

2. How is the split arrangement similar to and different from block-booking?

3. Where is the anticompetitive effect? Should antitrust care about movie splits?

D. International Intellectual Property Regimes and Market Allocation

Metro Industries, Inc. v. Sammi Corp.
82 F.3d 839 (9th Cir. 1996)

WIGGINS, Circuit Judge:

Metro Industries, Inc. ("Metro"), an importer and wholesaler of kitchenware, sued Sammi Corp. ("Sammi"), a South Korean exporting company, and two of its American subsidiaries alleging, inter alia, that a Korean design registration system, which gives Korean holloware producers the exclusive right to export a particular holloware design for three years, constituted a market division that is a per se violation of section 1 of the Sherman Antitrust Act, 15 U.S.C. § 1. Metro alleges that Sammi used this registration system in 1983 to prevent Metro and other kitchenware importers from acquiring Korean-made stainless steal steamers from any of Sammi's competitors in Korea.

Metro appeals the district court's grant of Sammi's motion for summary judgment on Metro's Sherman Act § 1 claim, which was based on the district court record from *Vollrath Co. v. Sammi Corp.,* 9 F.3d 1455 (9th Cir.1993), cert. denied, 511 U.S. 1142, 114 S.Ct. 2163, 128 L.Ed.2d 886 (1994), a case in which another importer of Korean kitchenware sued Sammi for alleged violations of §§ 1 and 2 of the Sherman Act. We have jurisdiction pursuant to 28 U.S.C. § 1291 and AFFIRM.

Facts and Procedural History

Metro is an importer and distributor of kitchenware products. Metro started a stainless steel kitchenware business in about 1977, importing mixing bowls from a Korean supplier called Haidong. In 1978 it began to purchase bowls from Sammi, and over the next few years, expanded its business to include other kitchenware. By 1981, importing and selling stainless steel kitchenware constituted Metro's principal business activity.

Sammi is a large Korean trading company that purchases a wide variety of finished products, including stainless steel steamers, for export to the United States and other countries. Sammi is a member of the Korea Holloware Association. See *Vollrath,* 9 F.3d at 1462. This association, through a thirteen-member design registration committee, grants pattern and design registration rights for particular products based on the shape, appearance, and color of the products. Id. The registration committee consists of members from manufacturing companies, trading companies, the Korea Association of patent attorneys, and three members of

Korean government organizations. A trading company, such as Sammi, can only hold a pattern design right jointly with a manufacturer. *Id.* Registration gives the design holder the exclusive right to export a particular design for three years, and the rights can be extended for three additional years.

According to Metro, in late 1981, it raised the idea of a line of stainless steel steamers with Sammi, provided Sammi with models, and asked Sammi to develop samples and to prepare to supply the steamers. Sammi registered the steamer design and began to supply Metro with steamers. Metro experienced a disruption of steamer deliveries from Sammi at some time during 1983. Metro alleges that its attempts to order the steamers from another company were blocked by Sammi. Eventually, in late 1983, Metro was able to secure a source of steamers from a Korean company called Sambo and apparently had no further disruptions in its steamer shipments.

In December 1983, Metro filed a complaint in the United States District Court for the Central District of California against Sammi and two of its American subsidiaries alleging violations of §§ 1 and 2 of the Sherman Act (15 U.S.C. §§ 1 and 2) and §§ 2, 3, and 7 of the Clayton Act (15 U.S.C. §§ 13, 14, and 18), and various violations of California law. In June 1984, the claims against Sammi were dismissed for lack of personal jurisdiction. ***

[After a related case was decided] Metro began arguing a new theory-that the Korean design registration system under which Sammi had the exclusive rights to manufacture a particular steamer design constituted a market division that was illegal per se under § 1 of the Sherman Act. In May 1994, Sammi filed a motion to dismiss all claims against Sammi and its subsidiaries pursuant to Rules 52(c) and 56(b) of the Federal Rules of Civil Procedure. Metro filed an opposition and cross-motion for partial summary judgment on the liability portion of the market division claim, relying entirely on the Vollrath record. The district court granted Sammi's motion for summary judgment and denied Metro's cross-motion, finding that Metro had failed to present sufficient evidence to carry its burden on any of its claims.

Discussion

Metro appeals only the district court's grant of summary judgment in favor of Sammi on Metro's Sherman Act § 1 market division claim and the court's denial of Metro's cross-motion for summary judgment. We review a district court's grant of summary judgment de novo. [citation omitted]

Section 1 of the Sherman Antitrust Act, as amended in 1990, reads, in relevant part:

> Every contract, combination in the form of trust or otherwise, or conspiracy, in restraint of trade or commerce among the several States, or with foreign nations, is hereby declared to be illegal.

15 U.S.C. § 1 (1994). Metro alleges that the Korean Holloware Association registration system constitutes a "naked" market division agreement, which is per se illegal

under the Sherman Act. Thus, Metro argues, an examination of the impact of the registration system on competition in the United States is not necessary to find a violation of § 1.

Because conduct occurring outside the United States is only a violation of the Sherman Act if it has a sufficient negative impact on commerce in the United States, per se analysis is not appropriate. ***

I. Per Se Treatment is Inappropriate in This Case

"Ordinarily, whether particular concerted activity violates § 1 of the Sherman Act is determined through case-by-case application of the so-called rule of reason-that is, 'the factfinder weighs all of the circumstances of a case in deciding whether a restrictive practice should be prohibited as imposing an unreasonable restraint on competition.' "*Business Elecs. Corp. v. Sharp Elecs. Corp.*, 485 U.S. 717, 723 (1988) (quoting *Continental T.V., Inc. v. GTE Sylvania Inc.*, 433 U.S. 36, 49 (1977)). "Certain categories of agreements, however, have been held to be per se illegal, dispensing with the need for case-by-case evaluation." *Id.* "Such agreements are those that always or almost always tend to restrict competition and decrease output." *United States v. Brown*, 936 F.2d 1042, 1045 (9th Cir.1991) (internal citations omitted). In general, "[a] market allocation agreement between competitors at the same market level is a classic per se antitrust violation." *Id.*

A. The Korean Registration System is Not Illegal Per Se

Where the conduct at issue is not a garden-variety horizontal division of a market, we have eschewed a per se rule and instead have utilized rule of reason analysis. *Northrop Corp. v. McDonnell Douglas Corp.*, 705 F.2d 1030, 1050 (9th Cir.) [citation omitted] In deciding whether to extend the per se rule to a previously unexamined business practice, we are to examine whether "the practice facially appears to be one that would always or almost always tend to restrict competition and decrease output, ... or instead one designed to 'increase economic efficiency and render markets more, rather than less, competitive.' "*Broadcast Music, Inc. v. Columbia Broadcasting Sys.*, 441 U.S. 1, 19-20 (1979) (quotation omitted).

The Korean registration system is not a classic horizontal market division agreement in which competitors at the same level agree to divide up the market for a given product. Metro does not point to, and we have not found, a single instance in which an arrangement similar to the Korean manufacturer-exporter design registration system has undergone judicial scrutiny in the Sherman Act context. The novelty of this arrangement, "strongly supports application of rule-of-reason analysis." *Northrop*, 705 F.2d at 1051; *see also United States v. Topco Assoc., Inc.*, 405 U.S. 596, 607–08 (1972) ("It is only after considerable experience with certain business relationships that courts classify them as per se violations of the Sherman Act.").

Further, as discussed below, there is no evidence of a negative effect on competition, which also militates against extension of the per se rule. *Northrop*, 705 F.2d at 1052; *Cascade Cabinet Co. v. Western Cabinet & Millwork Inc.*, 710 F.2d 1366,

1372 (9th Cir.1983). The record reveals that the registration protection was limited to particular designs of a product "based on shape, appearance, and color of the products." *Vollrath*, 9 F.3d at 1462. The protection extends for only three years, renewable for three additional years. Contrary to Metro's assertions, the record does reveal the output increasing potential of the registration system. Sammi's general manager of housewares indicated that tooling and production of a new product takes several years. Thus, the limited protection could encourage manufacturers to develop and produce new products, knowing that they would have the exclusive right to export a particular design for a limited period of time.

Finally, there is no evidence that the purpose of the design registration system was to restrain trade, which also counsels in favor of rule of reason analysis. *Northrop*, 705 F.2d at 1053. The Korean association was apparently a quasi-governmental group (in that it was sanctioned by the Korean government and three of its thirteen members were representatives of the Korean government) that was formed to ensure product and design quality and to protect from copying. Sammi's general manager of housewares indicated that the system was designed "to promote the manufacturer to develop better quality product, a better quality design, and protect them from copy[ing] by other manufacturers."

Accordingly, rule of reason analysis is appropriate in this case.

B. Foreign Conduct Cannot Be Examined Under the Per Se Rule

Even if Metro could prove that the registration system constituted a "market division" that would require application of the per se rule if the division occurred in a domestic context, application of the per se rule is not appropriate where the conduct in question occurred in another country. Determining whether the registration system was a violation of the antitrust laws would still require an examination of the impact of the system on commerce in the United States. "The Sherman Act does reach conduct outside our borders, but only when the conduct has an effect on American commerce." *Matsushita Elec. Indus. Co. v. Zenith Radio Corp.*, 475 U.S. 574, 582 n. 6 (1986). *See also Hartford Fire Ins. Co. v. California*, 509 U.S. 764, 796 (1993) ("[I]t is well established by now that the Sherman Act applies to foreign conduct that was meant to produce and did in fact produce some substantial effect in the United States."). According to a leading treatise:

> [T]he conventional assumptions that courts make in appraising restraints in domestic markets are not necessarily applicable in foreign markets. A foreign joint venture among competitors, for example, might be more "reasonable" than a comparable domestic transaction in several respects: the actual or potential harms touching American commerce may be more remote; the parties' necessities may be greater in view of foreign market circumstances; and the alternatives may be fewer, more burdensome, or less helpful.
>
> The fact that foreign conduct would be a per se offense-one that is condemned without proof of particular effects and with little regard for possible justifications in the particular case-when entirely domestic does not call for a fundamentally different analysis. Domestic antitrust policy uses per se rules for conduct that, in most of

its manifestations, is potentially very dangerous with little or no redeeming virtue. That rationale would be inapplicable to foreign restraints that, in many instances, either pose very little danger to American commerce or have more persuasive justifications than are likely in similar restraints at home. For example, price fixing in a foreign country might have some but very little impact on United States commerce.

1 Phillip Areeda & Donald F. Turner, Antitrust Law ¶ 237 (1978). Thus, the potential illegality of actions occurring outside the United States requires an inquiry into the impact on commerce in the United States, regardless of the inherently suspect appearance of the foreign activities. Consequently, where a Sherman Act claim is based on conduct outside the United States, we apply rule of reason analysis to determine whether there is a Sherman Act violation. *** [The court went on to conclude that, despite the foreign origin of the restraint, federal courts have jurisdiction to review that challenged arrangement under the rule of reason, but that Metro's claim nevertheless failed because it produced no evidence of injury to competition in the United States.]

Comments and Questions

1. Can you define the relevant market in a way that the defendants have market power? What type of evidence would you need to develop?

2. Should the Sherman Act reach foreign-based conduct? If so, under what circumstances?

3. The court noted that "Sammi's general manager of housewares indicated that tooling and production of a new product takes several years." If that is true, why do they need three years of protection?

E. DOJ-FTC Antitrust Guidelines for the Licensing of Intellectual Property, Sec. 5.1

5.1 Horizontal restraints

The existence of a restraint in a licensing arrangement that affects parties in a horizontal relationship (a "horizontal restraint") does not necessarily cause the arrangement to be anticompetitive. As in the case of joint ventures among horizontal competitors, licensing arrangements among such competitors may promote rather than hinder competition if they result in integrative efficiencies. Such efficiencies may arise, for example, from the realization of economies of scale and the integration of complementary research and development, production, and marketing capabilities.

Following the general principles outlined in section 3.4, horizontal restraints often will be evaluated under the rule of reason. In some circumstances, however, that analysis may be truncated; additionally, some restraints may merit per se treatment, including price fixing, allocation of markets or customers, agreements to reduce output, and certain group boycotts.

EXAMPLE 9

Situation:

Two of the leading manufacturers of a consumer electronic product hold patents that cover alternative circuit designs for the product. The manufacturers assign their patents to a separate corporation wholly owned by the two firms. That corporation licenses the right to use the circuit designs to other consumer product manufacturers and establishes the license royalties. None of the patents is blocking; that is, each of the patents can be used without infringing a patent owned by the other firm. The different circuit designs are substitutable in that each permits the manufacture at comparable cost to consumers of products that consumers consider to be interchangeable. One of the Agencies is analyzing the licensing arrangement.

Discussion:

In this example, the manufacturers are horizontal competitors in the goods market for the consumer product and in the related technology markets. The competitive issue with regard to a joint assignment of patent rights is whether the assignment has an adverse impact on competition in technology and goods markets that is not outweighed by procompetitive efficiencies, such as benefits in the use or dissemination of the technology. Each of the patent owners has a right to exclude others from using its patent. That right does not extend, however, to the agreement to assign rights jointly. To the extent that the patent rights cover technologies that are close substitutes, the joint determination of royalties likely would result in higher royalties and higher goods prices than would result if the owners licensed or used their technologies independently. In the absence of evidence establishing efficiency-enhancing integration from the joint assignment of patent rights, the Agency may conclude that the joint marketing of competing patent rights constitutes horizontal price fixing and could be challenged as a per se unlawful horizontal restraint of trade. If the joint marketing arrangement results in an efficiency-enhancing integration, the Agency would evaluate the arrangement under the rule of reason. However, the Agency may conclude that the anticompetitive effects are sufficiently apparent, and the claimed integrative efficiencies are sufficiently weak or not reasonably related to the restraints, to warrant challenge of the arrangement without an elaborate analysis of particular industry circumstances (see section 3.4).

CHAPTER 11

Pharmaceutical Settlements and Reverse Payments

In re Cardizem CD Antitrust Litigation,
332 F.3d 896 (6th Cir. 2003)

OBERDORFER, District Judge.

This antitrust case arises out of an agreement entered into by the defendants, Hoescht Marion Roussel, Inc. ("HMR"), the manufacturer of the prescription drug Cardizem CD, and Andrx Pharmaceuticals, Inc. ("Andrx"), then a potential manufacturer of a generic version of that drug. The agreement provided, in essence, that Andrx, in exchange for quarterly payments of $10 million, would refrain from marketing its generic version of Cardizem CD even after it had received FDA approval (the "Agreement"). The plaintiffs are direct and indirect purchasers of Cardizem CD who filed complaints challenging the Agreement as a violation of federal and state antitrust laws. After denying the defendants' motions to dismiss, see *In re Cardizem CD Antitrust Litigation,* 105 F.Supp.2d 618 (E.D.Mich.2000) ("Dist.Ct.Op. I") and granting the plaintiffs' motions for partial summary judgment, *id.,* 105 F.Supp.2d 682 (E.D.Mich.2000) ("Dist.Ct.Op. II"), the district court certified two questions for interlocutory appeal: ***

> (2) . . . In determining whether Plaintiffs' motions for partial judgment were properly granted, whether the Defendants' September 24, 1997 Agreement constitutes a restraint of trade that is illegal per se under section 1 of the Sherman Antitrust Act, 15 U.S.C. § 1, and under the corresponding state antitrust laws at issue in this litigation. ***
>
> *Answer to Second Certified Question*: Yes. The Agreement whereby HMR paid Andrx $40 million per year not to enter the United States market for Cardizem CD and its generic equivalents is a horizontal market allocation agreement and,

388 *Antitrust Law and Intellectual Property Rights*

as such, is per se illegal under the Sherman Act and under the corresponding state antitrust laws. Accordingly, the district court properly granted summary judgment for the plaintiffs on the issue of whether the Agreement was per se illegal.

I. Background ***

A. Statutory Framework

In 1984, Congress enacted the Hatch-Waxman Amendments, see Drug Price Competition & Patent Term Restoration Act of 1984, Pub. L. No. 98-417, 98 Stat. 1585 (1984), to the Federal Food, Drug, and Cosmetic Act, 21 U.S.C. §§ 301-399. Those amendments permit a potential generic[1] manufacturer of a patented pioneer drug to file an abbreviated application for approval with the Food and Drug Administration ("FDA") (known as an Abbreviated New Drug Application ("ANDA")). See 21 U.S.C. § 355(j)(1). Instead of submitting new safety and efficacy studies, an ANDA may rely on the FDA's prior determination, made in the course of approving an earlier "pioneer" drug, that the active ingredients of the proposed new drug are safe and effective. Id. § 355(j)(2)(A). Every ANDA must include a "certification that, in the opinion of the applicant and to the best of his knowledge, the proposed generic drug does not infringe any patent listed with the FDA as covering the pioneer drug." Id. § 355(j)(2)(A)(vii). That certification can take several forms. Relevant here is the so-called "paragraph IV certification" whereby the applicant certifies that any such patent "is invalid or will not be infringed by the manufacture, use, or sale of the new drug for which the application is submitted." Id. § 355(j)(2)(A)(vii)(IV). An applicant filing a paragraph IV certification must give notice to the patent-holder, id. § 355(j)(2)(B); the patent-holder then has forty-five days to file a patent infringement action against the applicant. Id. § 355(j)(5)(B)(iii). If the patent-holder files suit, a thirty-month stay goes into effect, meaning that unless before that time the court hearing the patent infringement case finds that the patent is invalid or not infringed, the FDA cannot approve the generic drug before the expiration of that thirty-month period. Id. § 355(j)(5)(B)(iii)(I). In order to encourage generic entry, and to compensate for the thirty-month protective period accorded the patent holder, the first generic manufacturer to submit an ANDA with a paragraph IV certification receives a 180-day period of exclusive marketing rights, during which time the FDA will not approve subsequent ANDA applications. Id. § 355(j)(5)(B)(iv). The 180-day period of exclusivity begins either (1) when the first ANDA applicant begins commercial marketing of its generic drug (the marketing trigger) or (2) when there is a court decision ruling that the patent is invalid or not infringed (the court decision trigger), whichever is earlier. Id.

---

[1] A "generic" drug contains the same active ingredients but not necessarily the same inactive ingredients as a "pioneer" drug sold under a brand name.

B. Facts

Unless otherwise noted, the following facts are undisputed. HMR manufactures and markets Cardizem CD, a brand-name prescription drug which is used for the treatment of angina and hypertension and for the prevention of heart attacks and strokes. The active ingredient in Cardizem CD is diltiazem hydrochloride, which is delivered to the user through a controlled-release system that requires only one dose per day. HMR's patent for diltiazem hydrochloride expired in November 1992.

On September 22, 1995, Andrx filed an ANDA with the FDA seeking approval to manufacture and sell a generic form of Cardizem CD. On December 30, 1995, Andrx filed a paragraph IV certification stating that its generic product did not infringe any of the patents listed with the FDA as covering Cardizem CD. Andrx was the first potential generic manufacturer of Cardizem CD to file an ANDA with a paragraph IV certification, entitling it to the 180-day exclusivity period once it received FDA approval.

In November 1995, the United States patent office issued Carderm Capital, L.P. ("Carderm") U.S. Patent No. 5, 470, 584 ("'584 patent"), for Cardizem CD's "dissolution profile," which Carderm licensed to HMR. [citation omitted] The dissolution profile claimed by the '584 patent was for 0–45% of the total diltiazem to be released within 18 hours ("45%–18 patent").

In January 1996, HMR and Carderm filed a patent infringement suit against Andrx in the United States District Court for the Southern District of Florida, asserting that the generic version of Cardizem CD that Andrx proposed would infringe the '584 patent. [citation omitted] The complaint sought neither damages nor a preliminary injunction. Id. However, filing that complaint automatically triggered the thirty-month waiting period during which the FDA could not approve Andrx's ANDA and Andrx could not market its generic product. In February 1996, Andrx brought antitrust and unfair competition counterclaims against HMR [citation omitted] In April 1996, Andrx amended its ANDA to specify that the dissolution profile for its generic product was not less than 55% of total diltiazem released within 18 hours ("55%–18 generic"). HMR nonetheless continued to pursue its patent infringement litigation against Andrx in defense of its 45%–18 patent. On June 2, 1997, Andrx represented to the patent court that it intended to market its generic product as soon as it received FDA approval. [citation omitted]

On September 15, 1997, the FDA tentatively approved Andrx's ANDA, indicating that it would be finally approved as soon as it was eligible, either upon expiration of the thirty-month waiting period in early July 1998, or earlier if the court in the patent infringement action ruled that the '584 patent was not infringed.

Nine days later, on September 24, 1997, HMR and Andrx entered into the Agreement. [citation omitted] It provided that Andrx would not market a bioequivalent or generic version of Cardizem CD in the United States until the earliest of: (1) Andrx obtaining a favorable, final and unappealable determination in the patent infringement case; (2) HMR and Andrx entering into a license agreement; or (3) HMR entering into a license agreement with a third party. Andrx also agreed to dismiss its antitrust and unfair competition counterclaims, to diligently prosecute its ANDA, and to not "relinquish or otherwise compromise any right accruing thereunder or pertaining thereto," including its 180-day period of exclusivity. In exchange, HMR agreed to make interim payments to Andrx in the amount of $40 million per year, payable quarterly, beginning on the date Andrx received final FDA approval.[3] HMR further agreed to pay Andrx $100 million per year,[4] less whatever interim payments had been made, once: (1) there was a final and unappealable determination that the patent was not infringed; (2) HMR dismissed the patent infringement case; or (3) there was a final and unappealable determination that did not determine the issues of the patent's validity, enforcement, or infringement, and HMR failed to refile its patent infringement action.[5] HMR also agreed that it would not seek preliminary injunctive relief in the ongoing patent infringement litigation.[6]

On July 8, 1998, the statutory thirty-month waiting period expired. On July 9, 1998, the FDA issued its final approval of Andrx's ANDA. Pursuant to the Agreement, HMR began making quarterly payments of $10 million to Andrx, and Andrx did not bring its generic product to market.

On September 11, 1998, Andrx, in a supplement to its previously filed ANDA, sought approval for a reformulated generic version of Cardizem CD. Andrx informed HMR that it had reformulated its product; it also urged HMR to reconsider its infringement claims. On February 3, 1999, Andrx certified to HMR that its reformulated product did not infringe the '584 patent.

On June 9, 1999, the FDA approved Andrx's reformulated product. That same day, HMR and Andrx entered into a stipulation settling the patent infringement case and terminating the Agreement. At the time of settlement, HMR paid Andrx a final sum of $50.7 million, bringing its total payments to $89.83 million. On June 23, 1999, Andrx began to market its product under the trademark Cartia XT, and its 180-day period of marketing exclusivity began to run. Since its release, Cartia XT has sold for a much lower price than Cardizem CD and has captured a substantial portion of the market.

---

[3] The payments were scheduled to end on the earliest of: (1) a final and unappealable order or judgment in the patent infringement case; (2) if HMR notified Andrx that it intended to enter into a license agreement with a third party, the earlier of: (a) the expiration date of the required notice period or (b) the date Andrx effected its first commercial sale of the Andrx product; or (3) if Andrx exercised its option to acquire a license from HMR, the date the license agreement became effective.

[4] HMR and Andrx stipulated that, for the purposes of the Agreement, Andrx would have realized $100 million per year in profits from the sale of its generic product after receiving FDA approval.

[5] HMR had to notify Andrx within thirty days of such a determination that it continued to believe that Andrx's generic version of the drug infringed its patent and that it intended to refile its patent infringement action.

[6] HMR also agreed that it would give Andrx copies of changes it proposed to the FDA regarding Cardizem CD's package insert and immediate container label, that it would notify Andrx of any labeling changes pending before or approved by the FDA, and that it would grant Andrx an irrevocable option to acquire a nonexclusive license to all intellectual property HMR owned or controlled that Andrx might need to market its product in the United States.

C. Procedural History

*** [T]he district court denied the defendants' motions to dismiss for failure to allege antitrust injury.

The plaintiffs then moved for partial summary judgment on the issue of whether the Agreement was a per se illegal restraint of trade. The district court concluded that the Agreement, specifically the fact that HMR paid Andrx $10 million per quarter not to enter the market with its generic version of Cardizem CD, was a naked, horizontal restraint of trade and, as such, per se illegal. [citation omitted]

II. Discussion

*** [W]e address first whether the Agreement was a per se illegal restraint of trade before considering whether the plaintiffs adequately alleged antitrust injury.

A. Per Se Illegal Restraint of Trade ***

1. Relevant Antitrust Law

Section 1 of the Sherman Act provides that "Every contract, combination in the form of trust or otherwise, or conspiracy, in restraint of trade or commerce among the several States, or with foreign nations, is declared to be illegal. . . ." 15 U.S.C. § 1. Read "literally," section 1 "prohibits every agreement in restraint of trade." *Arizona v. Maricopa Cty. Medical Soc.*, 457 U.S. 332, 342 (1982). However, the Supreme Court has long recognized that Congress intended to outlaw only "unreasonable" restraints. *State Oil Co. v. Khan*, 522 U.S. 3, 10 (1997) [citation omitted]. Most restraints are evaluated using a "rule of reason." *State Oil*, 522 U.S. at 10. Under this approach, the "finder of fact must decide whether the questioned practice imposes an unreasonable restraint on competition, taking into account a variety of factors, including specific information about the relevant business, its condition before and after the restraint was imposed, and the restraint's history, nature, and effect." *Id.* [citation omitted]

Other restraints, however, "are deemed unlawful per se" because they "have such predictable and pernicious anticompetitive effect, and such limited potential for procompetitive benefit." *Id.* [citation omitted] "Per se treatment is appropriate '[o]nce experience with a particular kind of restraint enables the Court to predict with confidence that the rule of reason will condemn it.'" *Id.* [citation omitted] The per se approach thus applies a "conclusive presumption" of illegality to certain types of agreements, *Maricopa Cty.*, 457 U.S. at 344; where it applies, no consideration is given to the intent behind the restraint, to any claimed pro-competitive justifications, or to the restraint's actual effect on competition.[11]

---

[11] The risk that the application of a per se rule will lead to the condemnation of an agreement that a rule of reason analysis would permit has been recognized and tolerated as a necessary cost of this approach. *See, e.g., Maricopa Cty.*, 457 U.S. at 344 ("As in every rule of general application, the match between the presumed and the actual is imperfect. For the sake of business certainty and litigation efficiency, we have tolerated the invalidation of some agreements that a full-blown inquiry might have proved to be reasonable."); *United States v. Topco Associates, Inc.*, 405 U.S. 596, 609 (1972)

National College Athletic Ass'n ("NCAA") v. Board of Regents, 468 U.S. 85, 100 (1984). As explained by the Supreme Court, "[t]he probability that anticompetitive consequences will result from a practice and the severity of those consequences must be balanced against its procompetitive consequences. Cases that do not fit the generalization may arise, but a per se rule reflects the judgment that such cases are not sufficiently common or important to justify the time and expense necessary to identify them." *Continental T.V., Inc. v. GTE Sylvania Inc.*, 433 U.S. 36, 50 n. 6 (1977).

The Supreme Court has identified certain types of restraints as subject to the per se rule. The classic examples are naked, horizontal restraints pertaining to prices or territories. [citation omitted]

2. Application

In answering the question whether the Agreement here was per se illegal, the following facts are undisputed and dispositive. The Agreement guaranteed to HMR that its only potential competitor at that time, Andrx, would, for the price of $10 million per quarter, refrain from marketing its generic version of Cardizem CD even after it had obtained FDA approval, protecting HMR's exclusive access to the market for Cardizem CD throughout the United States until the occurrence of one of the end dates contemplated by the Agreement. (In fact, Andrx and HMR terminated the Agreement and the payments in June 1999, before any of the specified end dates occurred.) In the interim, however, from July 1998 through June 1999, Andrx kept its generic product off the market and HMR paid Andrx $89.83 million. By delaying Andrx's entry into the market, the Agreement also delayed the entry of other generic competitors, who could not enter until the expiration of Andrx's 180-day period of marketing exclusivity, which Andrx had agreed not to relinquish or transfer. There is simply no escaping the conclusion that the Agreement, all of its other conditions and provisions notwithstanding, was, at its core, a horizontal agreement to eliminate competition in the market for Cardizem CD throughout the entire United States, a classic example of a per se illegal restraint of trade.

None of the defendants' attempts to avoid per se treatment is persuasive. As explained in greater detail in the district court's opinion, [citation omitted] the Agreement cannot be fairly characterized as merely an attempt to enforce patent rights or an interim settlement of the patent litigation. As the plaintiffs point out, it is one thing to take advantage of a monopoly that naturally arises from a patent, but another thing altogether to bolster the patent's effectiveness in inhibiting competitors by paying the only potential competitor $40 million per year to stay out of the market. Nor does the fact that this is a "novel" area of law preclude per se treatment, *see Maricopa Cty.*, 457 U.S. at 349. To the contrary, the Supreme Court has held that "'[w]hatever may be its peculiar problems and characteristics, the Sherman Act, so far as price-fixing agreements are concerned, establishes

("Whether or not we would decide this case the same way under the rule of reason used by the District Court is irrelevant to the issue before us.").

one uniform rule applicable to all industries alike.'" *Id.* at 349 [citation omitted]. We see no reason not to apply that rule here, especially when the record does not support the defendants' claim that the district court made "errors" in its analysis. Finally, the defendants' claims that the Agreement lacked anticompetitive effects and had pro-competitive benefits are simply irrelevant. *See, e.g., Maricopa Cty.*, 457 U.S. at 351. To reiterate, the virtue/vice of the per se rule is that it allows courts to presume that certain behaviors as a class are anticompetitive without expending judicial resources to evaluate the actual anticompetitive effects or procompetitive justifications in a particular case. As the Supreme Court explained in Maricopa County:

> The respondents' principal argument is that the per se rule is inapplicable because their agreements are alleged to have procompetitive justifications. The argument indicates a misunderstanding of the per se concept. The anticompetitive potential inherent in all price-fixing agreements justifies their facial invalidation even if procompetitive justifications are offered for some. Those claims of enhanced competition are so unlikely to prove significant in any particular case that we adhere to the rule of law that is justified in its general application.

457 U.S. at 351. Thus, the law is clear that once it is decided that a restraint is subject to per se analysis, the claimed lack of any actual anticompetitive effects or presence of procompetitive effects is irrelevant. Of course, our holding here does not resolve the issues of causation and damages, both of which will have to be proved before the plaintiffs can succeed on their claim for treble damages under the Clayton Act.

III. Conclusion

For the foregoing reasons, we answer [] the district court's certified question[] as follows: it properly grant[ed] the plaintiffs' motions for summary judgment that the defendants had committed a per se violation of the antitrust laws.

Comments and Questions

1. Does the court hold that all reverse payment settlements are per se illegal? If not all reverse payment settlements warrant per se condemnation, which features of this settlement tipped the balance in favor of per se treatment?

2. Would making reverse payment settlements per se illegal be good policy? If reverse payments were per se illegal, how might parties try to craft settlements in order to circumvent the per se rule? Could those settlements be more anticompetitive than reverse payments?

3. Sitting by designation as a district court judge, Judge Richard Posner asserted: "A ban on reverse-payment settlements would reduce the incentive to challenge patents by reducing the challenger's settlement options should he be sued for infringement, and so might well be thought anticompetitive." *Asahi Glass Co. v. Pentech Pharm., Inc.*, 289 F.Supp.2d 986, 992 (N.D. Ill. 2003) (Posner., J.). What do you think of Judge Posner's argument? Would a per se rule against reverse-payment settlements reduce competition and innovation?

4. It appears unusual that a plaintiff would pay a defendant to settle a lawsuit. After all, if the plaintiff wants the litigation to end, it can seek to voluntarily dismiss its lawsuit. See Fed. R. Civ. Proc. 41(a). Are there legitimate—not anticompetitive—reasons why a patentholder would pay an accused infringer to settle?

5. Some have advanced the argument that reverse-payment settlements are a legitimate mechanism for patentholders to any uncertainty associated with infringement litigation, including the risk that their patents could be invalidated. See ABA SECTION OF ANTITRUST LAW, INTELLECTUAL PROPERTY AND ANTITRUST HANDBOOK 10 (2007). Does this justify removing such settlements from the per se illegal category? If so, does it mean that such agreements should be per se legal? Why or why not?

Schering-Plough Corp. v. F.T.C.

402 F.3d 1056 (11th Cir. 2005)

FAY, Circuit Judge:

Pharmaceutical companies Schering-Plough Corp. and Upsher-Smith Laboratories, Inc. petition for review of an order of the Federal Trade Commission ("FTC") that they cease and desist from being parties to any agreement settling a patent infringement lawsuit, in which a generic manufacturer either (1) receives anything of value; and (2) agrees to suspend research, development, manufacture, marketing, or sales of its product for any period of time. The issue is whether substantial evidence supports the conclusion that the Schering-Plough settlements unreasonably restrain trade in violation of Section 1 of the Sherman Antitrust Act, 15 U.S.C. § 1, and Section 5 of the Federal Trade Commission Act ("FTC Act"), 15 U.S.C. § 45(a). We have jurisdiction pursuant to 15 U.S.C. § 45(c), and, for the reasons discussed below, we grant the petition for review and set aside and vacate the FTC's order.

I. Factual Background

A. The Upsher Settlement

Schering-Plough ("Schering") is a pharmaceutical corporation that develops, markets, and sells a variety of science-based medicines, including antihistamines, corticosteroids, antibiotics, anti-infectives and antiviral products. Schering manufactures and markets an extended-release microencapsulated potassium chloride product, K-Dur 20, which is a supplement generally taken in conjunction with prescription medicines for the treatment of high blood pressure or congestive heart disease. The active ingredient in K-Dur 20, potassium chloride, is commonly used and unpatentable. Schering, however, owns a formulation patent on the extended-release coating, which surrounds the potassium chloride in K-Dur 20, patent number 4,863,743 (the "'743 patent"). The '743 patent expires on September 5, 2006.

The '743 patent claims a pharmaceutical dosage unit in tablet form for oral administration of potassium chloride. The tablet contains potassium chloride crystals coated with a cellulose-type material. The novel feature in the '743 patent is the viscous coating, which is applied to potassium chloride crystals. The coating provides a sustained-release delivery of the potassium chloride.

In late 1995, Upsher-Smith Laboratories ("Upsher"), one of Schering's competitors, sought Food and Drug Administration ("FDA") approval to market Klor Con M20 ("Klor Con"), a generic version of K-Dur 20. Asserting that Upsher's product was an infringing generic substitute, Schering sued for patent infringement. K-Dur 20 itself was the most frequently prescribed potassium supplement, and generic manufacturers such as Upsher could develop their own potassium-chloride supplement as long as the supplement's coating did not infringe on Schering's patent.

In 1997, prior to trial, Schering and Upsher entered settlement discussions. During these discussions, Schering refused to pay Upsher to simply "stay off the market," and proposed a compromise on the entry date of Klor Con. Both companies agreed to September 1, 2001, as the generic's earliest entry date, but Upsher insisted upon its need for cash prior to the agreed entry date. Although still opposed to paying Upsher for holding Klor Con's release date, Schering agreed to a separate deal to license other Upsher products. Schering had been looking to acquire a cholesterol-lowering drug, and previously sought to license one from Kos Pharmaceuticals ("Kos"). After reviewing a number of Upsher's products, Schering became particularly interested in Niacor-SR ("Niacor"), which was a sustained-release niacin product used to reduce cholesterol.

Upsher offered to sell Schering an exclusive license to market Niacor worldwide, except for North America. The parties executed a confidentiality agreement in June 1997, and Schering received licenses to market five Upsher products, including Niacor. In relation to Niacor, Schering received a data package, containing the results of Niacor's clinical studies. The cardiovascular products unit of Schering's Global Marketing division, headed by James Audibert ("Audibert") evaluated Niacor's profitability and effectiveness.

According to the National Institute of Health, niacin was the only product known to have a positive effect on the four lipids related to cholesterol management. Immediate-release niacin, however, created an annoying-but innocuous-side effect of "flushing," which reduced patient compliance. On the other hand, previous versions of sustained-release niacin supplements, like Niacor, had been associated with substantial elevations in liver enzyme levels.

Schering knew of the effects associated with niacin supplements, but continued with its studies of Niacor because it had passed the FDA's medical review and determined that it would likely be approved. More important, the clinical trials studied by Audibert demonstrated that Niacor reduced the flushing effect to one-fourth of the immediate-release niacin levels and only increased liver enzymes by four percent, which was generally consistent with other cholesterol inhibitors. Based on this data, Audibert constructed a sales and profitability forecast, and concluded that Niacor's net present value at that time would be between $245–265 million.

On June 17, 1997, the day before the patent trial was scheduled to begin, Schering and Upsher concluded the settlement. The companies negotiated a three-part license deal, which called for Schering to pay (1) $60 million in initial royalty fees;

396 *Antitrust Law and Intellectual Property Rights*

(2) $10 million in milestone royalty payments; and (3) 10% or 15% royalties on sales. Schering's board approved of the licensing transaction after determining the deal was valuable to Schering. This estimation corresponds to the independent valuation that Schering completed in relation to Kos' Niaspan, a substantially similar product to Niacor. That evaluation fixed Niaspan's net present value between $225–265 million. The sales projections for both the Kos and Upsher products are substantially similar. Raymond Russo ("Russo") estimated Niaspan (Kos' supplement) sales to reach $174 million by 2005 for the U.S. market. Comparably, and more conservatively, Audibert predicted Niacor (Upsher's supplement) to reach $136 million for the global market outside the United States, Canada, and Mexico, which is either equal to or larger than U.S. market alone.

After acquiring the licensing rights to Niacor, Schering began to ready its documents for overseas filings. In late 1997, however, Kos released its first-quarter sales results for Niaspan, which indicated a poor performance and lagging sales. Following this announcement, Kos' stock price dramatically dropped from $30.94 to $16.56, and eventually bottomed out at less than $6.00. In 1998, with Niaspan's disappointing decline as a precursor, Upsher and Schering decided further investment in Niacor would be unwise.

B. The ESI Settlement

In 1995, ESI Lederle, Inc. ("ESI"), another pharmaceutical manufacturer, sought FDA approval to market its own generic version of K-Dur 20 called "Micro-K 20." Schering sued ESI in United States District Court ***. The trial court appointed U.S. Magistrate Judge Thomas Rueter ("Judge Rueter") to mediate the fifteen-month process, which resulted in nothing more than an impasse.

Finally, in December 1997, Schering offered to divide the remaining patent life with ESI and allow Micro-K 20 to enter the market on January 1, 2004-almost three years ahead of the patent's September 2006 expiration date.[6] ESI accepted this offer, but demanded on receiving some form of payment to settle the case. At Judge Rueter's suggestion, Schering offered to pay ESI $5 million, which was attributed to legal fees, however, ESI insisted upon another $10 million. Judge Rueter and Schering then devised an amicable settlement whereby Schering would pay ESI up to $10 million if ESI received FDA approval by a certain date. Schering doubted the likelihood of this contingency happening, and Judge Rueter intimated that if Schering's prediction proved true, it would not have to pay the $10 million. The settlement was signed in Judge Rueter's presence on January 23, 1998.

C. The FTC Complaint

On March 30, 2001, more than three years after the ESI settlement, and nearly four years after the Schering settlement, the FTC filed an administrative complaint

---

[6] There was also a side agreement in this settlement that provided for a payment of $15 million in return for the right to license generic enalpril and buspirone from ESI.

against Schering, Upsher, and ESI's parent, American Home Products Corporation ("AHP"). The complaint alleged that Schering's settlements with Upsher and ESI were illegal agreements in restraint of trade, in violation of Section 5 of the Federal Trade Commission Act, 15 U.S.C. § 45, and in violation of Section 1 of the Sherman Act, 15 U.S.C. § 1. The complaint also charged that Schering monopolized and conspired to monopolize the potassium supplement market.

II. Procedural History

The Complaint was tried before an Administrative Law Judge (ALJ) from January 23, 2002 to March 28, 2002. Numerous exhibits were admitted in evidence, and the ALJ heard testimony from an array of expert witnesses presented by both sides. In his initial decision, the ALJ found that both agreements were lawful settlements of legitimate patent lawsuits, and dismissed the complaint. Specifically, the ALJ ruled that the theories advanced by the FTC, namely, that the agreements were anticompetitive, required either a presumption of (1) that Schering's '743 patent was invalid; or (2) that Upsher's or ESI's generic products did not infringe the '743 patent. The ALJ concluded that such presumptions had no basis in law or fact. Moreover, the ALJ noted that Schering's witnesses went unrebutted by FTC complaint counsel, and credibly established that the licensing agreement with Upsher was a "bona-fide arm's length transaction."

The ALJ further found that the presence of payments did not make the settlement anticompetitive, per se. Rather, the strength of the patent itself and its exclusionary power needed to be assessed. The initial decision highlighted the FTC's failure to prove that, absent a payment, either better settlement agreements or litigation results would have effected an earlier entry date for the generics. Finally, the ALJ found no proof that Schering maintained an illegal monopoly within the relevant potassium chloride supplement market.

The FTC's complaint counsel appealed this decision to the full Commission. On December 8, 2003, the Commission issued its opinion, reversing the ALJ's initial decision, and agreeing with complaint counsel that Schering's settlements with ESI and Upsher had violated the FTC Act and the Sherman Act. Although it refrained from ruling that Schering's payments to Upsher and ESI made the settlements per se illegal, the Commission concluded that the quid pro quo for the payment was an agreement to defer the entry dates, and that such delay would injure competition and consumers.

In contrast to the ALJ's inquiry into the merits of the '743 patent litigation, the Commission turned instead to the entry dates that "might have been" agreed upon in the absence of payments as the determinative factor. Despite the Commission's assumption that the parties could have achieved earlier entry dates via litigation or non-monetary compromises, it also acknowledged that the settled entry dates were non-negotiable. Upon review of the settlement payments, the Commission determined that neither the $60 million to Upsher nor the $30 million to ESI represented legitimate consideration for the licenses granted by Upsher or ESI's ability to secure FDA approval of its generic.[10] Consequently, the Commission prohibited settlements under which the generic receives anything of value and agrees to defer its own research, development, production or sales activities. Nevertheless, the Commission carved out one arbitrary exception for payments to the generic: beyond a "simple compromise" to the entry date, if payments can be linked to litigation costs (not to exceed $2 million), and the Commission is notified of the settlement, then the parties need not worry about a later antitrust attack. Neither of the Schering agreements fit this caveat, and Schering and Upsher timely petition for review. ***

IV. Discussion

The question remains whether the Commission's conclusions are legally sufficient to establish a violation of the Sherman Act and the FTC Act-that is, whether Schering's agreements with Upsher and ESI amount to an "unreasonable" restraint of trade. In *Valley Drug*, this Court stated that the "ultimate purpose of the antitrust inquiry is to form a judgment with respect to the competitive significance of the restraint at issue." *Valley Drug Co. v. Geneva Pharm., Inc.*, 344 F.3d 1294, 1303-04 (11th Cir.2003) [citation omitted]. We wrote that the focus of antitrust analysis should be on "what conclusions regarding the competitive impact of a challenged restraint can confidently be drawn from the facts demonstrated by the parties." *Valley Drug*, 344 F.3d at 1304.

Valley Drug involved an interim settlement agreement between a patent-holding pharmaceutical company and its potential generic competitor. Under the agreement, the patent holder paid the generic manufacturer $4.5 million per month to keep its product off the market until resolution of the underlying patent infringement suit. The lower court determined that the payments amounted to a per se violation of antitrust laws. *See In re Terazosin Hydrochloride Antitrust Litig.*, 164 F.Supp.2d 1340 (S.D.Fla.2000). We reversed that decision, and concluded that monetary payments made to an alleged infringer as part of a patent litigation settlement did not constitute a per se violation of antitrust law. *Valley Drug*, 344 F.3d at 1309.

Although we acknowledged in *Valley Drug* that an agreement to allocate markets is "clearly anticompetitive," resulting in reduced competition, increased prices, and a diminished output, we nonetheless reversed for a rather simple reason: one of the parties owned a patent. *Id.* at 1304. We recognized the effect of agreements that employ extortion-type tactics to keep competitors from entering the market. In the context of patent litigation, however, the anticompetitive effect may be no more broad than the patent's own exclusionary power. To expose those agreements to antitrust liability would "obviously chill such settlements." *Id.* at 1309.

---

[10] The contradictory nature of the Commission's opinion is exemplified by its assessment of the ESI settlement. Although the Commission found the payment to be unjustified and in violation of the law, it simultaneously explained that "[a]s a matter of prosecutorial discretion, we might not have brought a stand-alone case based on such relatively limited evidence."

Both the ALJ and the Commission analyzed the Schering agreements according to the rule of reason analysis, albeit under two different methodologies. To the contrary, the district court in *Valley Drug* approached the agreements in that case from the perspective of whether they were a per se violation of antitrust laws. Under the Supreme Court's guidance, an alleged restraint may be found unreasonable either because it fits within a category of restraints that has been held to be "per se" unreasonable, or because it violates the so-called "Rule of Reason." The rule of reason tests "'whether the restraint imposed is such as merely regulates and perhaps thereby promotes competition or whether it is such as may suppress or even destroy competition.' "*FTC v. Indiana Federation of Dentists,* 476 U.S. 447, 457, 106 S.Ct. 2009, 2017, 90 L.Ed.2d 445 (1986) (quoting *Board of Trade of City of Chicago v. United States,* 246 U.S. 231, 238, 38 S.Ct. 242, 244, 62 L.Ed. 683, (1918)).

Both the ALJ's initial decision and the Commission's opinion rejected the per se approach, and instead employed the rule of reason. The traditional rule of reason analysis requires the factfinder to "weigh all of the circumstances of a case in deciding whether a restrictive practice should be prohibited as imposing an unreasonable restraint on competition." *Continental T.V., Inc. v. GTE Sylvania Inc.,* 433 U.S. 36, 49 (1977). The plaintiff bears an initial burden of demonstrating that the alleged agreement produced adverse, anti-competitive effects within the relevant product and geographic markets, i.e., market power. [citation omitted]

Once the plaintiff meets the burden of producing sufficient evidence of market power, the burden then shifts to the defendant to show that the challenged conduct promotes a sufficiently pro-competitive objective. A restraint on competition cannot be justified solely on the basis of social welfare concerns. [citation omitted] In rebuttal then, the plaintiff must demonstrate that the restraint is not reasonably necessary to achieve the stated objective. [citation omitted]

In the present case, the Commission emphasized that its rule of reason standard required a methodology different from that set out by the ALJ's initial decision. The Commission chided the ALJ's approach-which evaluated the strength of the patent, defined the relevant geographic and product markets, calculated market shares, and then drew inferences from the shares and other industry characteristics-as an inappropriate manner of analyzing the competitive effects of the parties' activities. Instead, the Commission's rule of reason dictated application of the Indiana Federation exception, in that complaint counsel need not prove the relevant market. See 476 U.S. at 460-61, 106 S.Ct. 2009. Rather, the FTC was only required to show a detrimental market effect. Thus, under the Commission's standard, once the FTC met the low threshold of demonstrating the anticompetitive nature of the agreements, it found that Schering and Upsher did not sufficiently establish that the challenged activities were justified by procompetitive benefits. Despite the appearance that it openly considered Schering and Upsher's procompetitive affirmative defense, the Commission immediately condemned the settlements because of their absolute anti-competitive nature, and discounted the merits of the patent litigation. It would seem as though the Commission clearly made its decision before it considered any contrary conclusion.

We think that neither the rule of reason nor the per se analysis is appropriate in this context. We are bound by our decision in *Valley Drug* where we held both approaches to be ill-suited for an antitrust analysis of patent cases because they seek to determine whether the challenged conduct had an anticompetitive effect on the market. 344 F.3d 1294, 1311 n. 27.[14] By their nature, patents create an environment of exclusion, and consequently, cripple competition. The anticompetitive effect is already present. "What is required here is an analysis of the extent to which antitrust liability might undermine the encouragement of innovation and disclosure, or the extent to which the patent laws prevent antitrust liability for such exclusionary effects." *Id.* Therefore, in line with *Valley Drug*, we think the proper analysis of antitrust liability requires an examination of: (1) the scope of the exclusionary potential of the patent; (2) the extent to which the agreements exceed that scope; and (3) the resulting anticompetitive effects. *Valley Drug*, 344 F.3d at 1312.[15]

A. The '743 Patent

"A patent shall be presumed valid." 35 U.S.C. § 282. [citation omitted] Engrafted into patent law is the notion that a patent grant bestows "the right to exclude others from profiting by the patented invention." *Dawson Chem. Co. v. Rohm & Haas Co.*, 448 U.S. 176, 215, 100 S.Ct. 2601, 65 L.Ed.2d 696 (1980); see *Valley Drug*, 344 F.3d at 1304 ("A patent grants its owner the lawful right to exclude others."). Thus, the Patent Act essentially provides the patent owner "with what amounts to a permissible monopoly over the patented work." *Telecom Technical Services Inc. v. Rolm Co.*, 388 F.3d 820, 828 (11th Cir.2004) [citation omitted] The Patent Act also explicitly allows for the assignability of a patent; providing the owner with a right to "grant or convey an exclusive right under his application for patent . . . to the whole or any specified part of the United States." 35 U.S.C. § 261.

---

[14] On remand, the district court in *Valley Drug* still applied a per se analysis, and found those agreements to be illegal. See *In re Terazosin Hydrochloride Antitrust Litigation*, 352 F.Supp.2d 1279 (S.D.Fla.2005). We note that the case at bar is wholly different from *Valley Drug*. The critical difference is that the agreements at issue in Valley Drug did not involve final settlements of patent litigation, and, moreover, the *Valley Drug* agreements did not permit the generic company to market its product before patent expiration. On remand, the district court emphasized that the "[a]greement did not resolve or even simplify Abbott's patent infringement action . . . to the contrary, the Agreement tended to prolong that dispute to Abbott's advantage, delaying generic entry for a longer period of time than the patent or any reasonable interpretation of the patent's protections would have provided." *In re Terazosin Hydrochloride Antitrust Litigation*, 352 F.Supp.2d 1279 (S.D.Fla.2005). Given these material distinctions, the same analysis cannot apply.

[15] The Commission wrote that it would neither address the exclusionary power of Schering's patent nor compare the patent's scope to the exclusionary effect of the settlements. Rather, the Commission grounds its decision in the untenable supposition that without a payment there would have been different settlements with both ESI and Schering, resulting in earlier entry dates: "we cannot assume that Schering had a right to exclude Upsher's generic competition for the life of the patent any more than we can assume that Upsher had the right to enter earlier. In fact we make neither assumption, but focus on the effect that Schering's payment to Upsher was likely to have on the generic entry date which the parties would otherwise have agreed to in a settlement."

By virtue of its '743 patent, Schering obtained the legal right to exclude Upsher and ESI from the market until they proved either that the '743 patent was invalid or that their products, Klor-Con and Micro-K 20, respectively, did not infringe Schering's patent. Although the exclusionary power of a patent may seem incongruous with the goals of antitrust law, a delicate balance must be drawn between the two regulatory schemes. Indeed, application of antitrust law to markets affected by the exclusionary statutes set forth in patent law cannot discount the rights of the patent holder. [citation omitted] Therefore, a patent holder does not incur antitrust liability when it chooses to exclude others from producing its patented work. [citation omitted]

A patent gives its owner the right to grant licenses, if it so chooses, or it may ride its wave alone until the patent expires. [citation omitted] What patent law does not do, however, is extend the patentee's monopoly beyond its statutory right to exclude. *Mallinckrodt, Inc. v. Medipart, Inc.*, 976 F.2d 700, 708 (Fed.Cir.1992); *see also, United States v. Singer Mfg. Co.*, 374 U.S. 174, 196–197 (1963) ("[B]eyond the limited monopoly which is granted, the arrangements by which the patent is utilized are subject to the general law. . . . [T]he possession of a valid patent or patents does not give the patentee any exemption from the provisions of the Sherman Act beyond the limits of the patent monopoly."). If the challenged activity simply serves as a device to circumvent antitrust law, then that activity is susceptible to an antitrust suit. *Asahi Glass Co., Ltd. v. Pentech Pharmaceuticals, Inc.*, 289 F.Supp.2d 986, 991 (N.D.Ill.2003), In *Asahi*, Judge Posner gave an illustrative example of when certain conduct transcends the confines of the patent:

> Suppose a seller obtains a patent that it knows is almost certainly invalid (that is, almost certain not to survive a judicial challenge), sues its competitors, and settles the suit by licensing them to use its patent in exchange for their agreeing not to sell the patented product for less than the price specified in the license. In such a case, the patent, the suit, and the settlement would be devices-masks-for fixing prices, in violation of antitrust law.

Id.

It is uncontested that potassium chloride is the unpatentable active ingredient in Schering's brand-name drug K-Dur 20. Schering won FDA approval in 1986 to sell its K-Dur 20 tablets. Under the Hatch-Waxman scheme, in order for Upsher and ESI to obtain FDA approval to market their generic versions of an approved drug product like K-Dur 20, they simply needed to demonstrate that the drugs were bioequivalent [sic], i.e., that the "active ingredient of the new drug is the same as that of the listed drug." 21 U.S.C. § 355(j)(2)(A)(ii)(I). K-Dur 20's uniqueness, and hence the reason for a patent, is the time-release capsule that surrounds the potassium chloride. Because the patent only covers the individualized delivery method (the sustained-release formula), and not the active ingredient itself, it is termed a "formulation" patent.

No one disputes that the '743 patent gave Schering the lawful right to exclude infringing products from the market until September 5, 2006. Nor is there any dispute that Schering's agreement with Upsher gave it a license under the '743 patent to sell a microencapsulated form of potassium chloride more than five years before the expiration of the '743 patent.[17] Likewise, ESI gained a license under the '743 patent to sell its microencapsulated version more than two years before the '743 patent expired. Perhaps most important, and which the ALJ duly noted, is that FTC complaint counsel acknowledged that it could not prove that Upsher and ESI could have entered the market on their own prior to the '743 patent's expiration on September 5, 2006. This reinforces the validity and strength of the patent.

Although the FTC alleges that Schering's settlement agreements are veiled attempts to disguise a quid pro quo arrangement aimed at preserving Schering's monopoly in the potassium chloride supplement market, there has been no allegation that the '743 patent itself is invalid or that the resulting infringement suits against Upsher and ESI were "shams." Additionally, without any evidence to the contrary, there is a presumption that the '743 patent is a valid one, which gives Schering the ability to exclude those who infringe on its product. Therefore, the proper analysis now turns to whether there is substantial evidence to support the Commission's conclusion that the challenged agreements restrict competition beyond the exclusionary effects of the '743 patent. *Valley Drug*, 344 F.3d at 1306; see also *In re Ciprofloxacin Hydrochloride Antitrust Litig.*, 261 F.Supp.2d 188, 196 (E.D.N.Y.2003).[18]

B. The Scope of Schering's Agreements

1. The Upsher Settlement

The FTC's complaint characterized the agreements at the center of this contest as "horizontal market allocation agreements," whereby Schering reserved its sales of K-Dur 20 for several years, while Upsher and ESI refrained from selling their generic versions of K-Dur 20 during that same time period. Adding to the FTC's ire is the presence of "reverse payments," represented by settlement payments from the patent owner to the alleged infringer. The Commission ruled that the coupling of reverse payments with an agreement by the generics not to enter the market before a particular date, "raise[d] a red flag that distinguishes this particular litigation settlement from most other patent settlements, and mandates a further inquiry." [citation omitted]

In the context of Schering's settlement with Upsher, the FTC argues that the $60 million payment from Schering to Upsher was not a bona fide royalty payment under the licenses Schering obtained for Niacor and five other Upsher products. Instead, according to the FTC, the royalty payments constituted payoffs to delay

---

[17] Upsher began selling Klor Con M20 on September 1, 2001.
[18] It is patently obvious that the Commission's opinion did not employ this analysis; preferring, instead, to proceed through its laborious rule of reason framework, eventually branding the challenged restraints to be illegal horizontal market allocation agreements. The Commission was ostensibly silent with regard to the '743 patent, yet it cavalierly dismissed our holding in Valley Drug, stating that a determination on the merits of the underlying patent disputes was "not supported by law or logic."

the introduction of Upsher's generic. The FTC concedes that its position fails if it cannot prove a direct causal link between the payments and the delay.

The trial before the ALJ covered 8,629 pages of transcript, involved forty-one witnesses, and included thousands of exhibits. The trial revealed that Schering personnel evaluated Niacor, and forecast its profit stream with a net present value of $225–265 million. Upsher itself had invested significant time and financial resources in Niacor. Moreover, Schering had a long-documented and ongoing interest in licensing an extended-release niacin product, as evidenced by its efforts to acquire Niaspan from Kos Pharmaceuticals.

Evidence at trial also demonstrated that the personnel who evaluated Niaspan's potential were unaware of the ongoing litigation between Upsher and Schering, and had little, if any, incentive to inflate Niacor's value. Indeed, many of the estimates in conjunction with the Niacor evaluation traced the independent conclusions of the team that evaluated Niaspan. Schering's witnesses corroborated the documentary evidence, and the ALJ found the $60 million payment to Upsher to be a bona fide fair-value payment.

The Commission chose to align its opinion with the two witnesses presented by the FTC. One witness, Dr. Nelson Levy ("Levy") was proffered as an expert in pharmaceutical licensing and valuation. He concluded that the $60 million payment was "grossly excessive," and that Schering's due diligence in evaluating Niacor fell astonishingly short of industry standards. Levy cited Upsher and Schering's post-settlement behavior, as proof of the agreement's artificial nature. We are troubled by Levy's testimony. Interestingly, Levy arrived at his conclusions without performing a quantitative analysis of Niacor or any of the other Upsher products licensed by Schering. Additionally, Levy lacked expertise in the area of cholesterol-lowering drugs and niacin supplements. Finally, Levy's unpersuasive appraisal of the post-settlement behavior blatantly ignored the parties' ongoing communications and the fact that the niacin market essentially bottomed out. Although the Commission's opinion does not state that it in relying on Levy's testimony, it curiously mirrors each of Levy's conclusions.

The FTC also offered Professor Timothy Bresnahan ("Bresnahan") to prove that Schering's payment was not for the Niacor license. While Bresnahan neither challenged Niacor's sales projections nor discounted its economic value, Bresnahan nonetheless opined that the payment was for Upsher's delayed entry, and not Niacor. Bresnahan based his conclusions on his interpretation of the parties' subjective incentives to trade a payment for delay. Bresnahan specifically pointed to Schering's failed transactions with Kos and the lack of other competitors vying for Niacor as evidence that the payment was not connected to the license.

Like the Levy testimony, the Commission did not expressly adopt Bresnahan's theories, but his rationale and the Commission's conclusions became one and the same. The Commission is quite comfortable with assenting to Bresnahan's rather amorphous "incentive" theory despite its lack of empirical foundation. Unfortunately, Bresnahan's so-called incentives do not rise to the level of legal conclusions. We understand that certain incentives may rank high in these transactions, but it also true that the possibility of an outside impetus often lays dormant. The simple presence of economic motive weighs little on the scale of probative value. [citation omitted]

The ALJ rejected the FTC's experts, concluding that testimony from Schering's witnesses "provides direct evidence that the parties did not exchange money for delay." The Commission disagreed, and determined that Niacor was not worth $60 million. To prove its point, the Commission relied on somewhat forced evidence: (1) the unconvincing fact that doctors gave Kos' niacin product mixed reviews, causing Schering to value those profits at an apparently contemptible $254 million; (2) the meretricious argument that Schering's personnel did not adequately assess Niacor's safety; (3) the Commission's questionable non-expert opinion that Schering should have done more due diligence; (4) the Commission's belief that the European market-where Schering held the Niacor license-for a niacin product was less desirable than the U.S. market; and (5) Schering's post-settlement decision to discontinue its Niacor efforts in light of the poor sales effected by Kos' Niaspan.[23]

To borrow from the Commission's own words, we think its conclusion that Niacor was not worth $60 million, and that settlement payment was to keep Upsher off the market is "not supported by law or logic." Substantial evidence requires a review of the entire record at trial, and that most certainly includes the ALJ's credibility determinations and the overwhelming evidence that contradicts the Commission's conclusion. [citation omitted]

The ALJ made credibility findings based upon his observations of the witnesses' demeanor and the testimony given at trial. The Commission rejected these findings, and instead relied on information that was not even in the record. The Supreme Court has noted the importance of an examiner's determination of credibility, and explained that evidence which supports an administrative agency's fact-finding "may be less substantial when an impartial, experienced examiner who has observed the witnesses and lived with the case has drawn conclusions different from the [agency's] . . ." *Id.* Additionally, the Court instructs that "[t]he findings of the examiner are to be considered along with the consistency and inherent probability of testimony." *Id.*

We think that this record consistently demonstrates the factors that Schering considered, and there is nothing to undermine the clear findings of the ALJ that this evidence was reliable. The Commission's finding that the "Upsher licenses were worth nothing to Schering" overlooks the very nature of the pharmaceutical industry where licenses are very often granted on drugs that never see the market.[25] Likewise, the essence of research and development is the need to encourage

---

[23] Niaspan's sales were in fact disappointing. Market analysts predicted its 1999 sales to reach $169.3 million, and Schering's more conservative estimate calculated $101 million for the same year. In actuality, the sales were only $37.9 million.

[25] At trial, the FTC selected eight products that Schering had licensed from companies other than Upsher for comparative analysis. Five of those eight products were never marketed.

and foster new innovations, which necessarily involves exploring licensing options and selecting which products to pursue.

Finally, we note that the terms of the Schering-Upsher agreement expressly describes three payments totaling $60 million as "up-front royalty payments." The surrounding negotiations, trial testimony, and the record all evidence that both parties intended "royalty" to denote its traditional meaning: that Schering would pay Upsher for the licenses and production rights of Upsher's products. [citation omitted] There is nothing to refute that these payments are a fair price for Niacor and the other Upsher products. Schering-Plough made a stand-alone determination that it was getting as much in return from these products as it was paying, and just because the agreement also includes Upsher's entry date into the potassium chloride supplement market, one cannot infer that the payments were solely for the delay rather than the licenses. [citation omitted] Thus, the substantial and overwhelming evidence undercuts the Commission's conclusion that Schering's agreement with Upsher was illegal.

2. The ESI Settlement

The Commission separately addressed Schering's settlement with ESI. Although it purported to analyze this agreement under the same scheme as it did the Upsher settlement, there is far less development of the factual record to support the Commission's conclusion that the settlement was unreasonable. At trial, the FTC called no fact witnesses to testify about the ESI settlement, and its economic expert offered only brief testimony. The Commission's opinion itself spends little time on the ESI settlement, and begins with the recognition that the case is based on "relatively limited evidence." On the other hand, Schering produced experts who posited that Schering would have won the patent case, and that the ESI's January 1, 2004, entry date reasonably reflected the strength of Schering's case. The FTC did not rebut this testimony, but rather ignored it.

It seems the sole indiscretion committed in the context of the ESI settlement is the inclusion of monetary payments. The Commission ignored the lengthy mediation process, and insisted that the parties could have reached an alternative settlement with an earlier entry date. We do not pretend to understand the Commission's profound concern with this settlement, but it takes particular exception to the $10 million payment, which was contingent on FDA approval of the generic product. The Commission also subtly questions the validity of the $5 million for legal costs. We might only guess that if the legal fee tallied $2 million-the arbitrary cap the Commission would allow for such settlements-it would not garner the same scrutiny.

The Commission, however, refused to consider the underlying patent litigation, and its certainty to be a bitter and prolonged process. All of the evidence of record supports the conclusion of the ALJ that this is not the case of a "naked payment" aimed to delay the entry of product that is "legally ready and able to compete with Schering." The litigation that unfolded between Schering and ESI was fierce and impassioned. Fifteen months of mediation demonstrates the doubt of a peaceful conclusion (or a simple compromise, as the Commission would characterize it).

That the parties to a patent dispute may exchange consideration to settle their litigation has been endorsed by the Supreme Court. *See Standard Oil Co. v. United States*, 283 U.S. 163, 170-71 n. 5 (1931) (noting that the interchange of rights and royalties in a settlement agreement "may promote rather than restrain competition"). Veritably, the Commission's opinion would leave settlements, including those endorsed and facilitated by a federal court, with little confidence. The general policy of the law is to favor the settlement of litigation, and the policy extends to the settlement of patent infringement suits. [citation omitted] Patent owners should not be in a worse position, by virtue of the patent right, to negotiate and settle surrounding lawsuits. We find the terms of the settlement to be within the patent's exclusionary power, and "reflect a reasonable implementation" of the protections afforded by patent law. *Valley Drug*, 344 F.3d at 1312.

C. The Anticompetitive Effects

Our final line of inquiry turns to whether these agreements were indeed an "unfair method of competition." The FTC Act's prohibition on such agreements encompasses violations of other antitrust laws, including the Sherman Act, which prohibits agreements in restraint of trade. 15 U.S.C. § 45(a); *California Dental Ass'n.*, 526 U.S. at 763 n. 3. In California Dental, the Supreme Court required that the anticompetitive effect cannot be hypothetical or presumed. Rather, the probe must turn to "whether the effects actually are anticompetitive." *Id.* at 775 n. 12.

The restraints at issue here covered any "sustained release microencapsulated potassium chloride tablet." Such a specific clause-an "ancillary restraint"-is routine to define the parameters of the agreement and to prevent future litigation over what may or may not infringe upon the patent. *See Rothery Storage & Van Co. v. Atlas Van Lines, Inc.*, 792 F.2d 210, 224 (D.C.Cir.1986) ("The ancillary restraint is subordinate and collateral in the sense that it serves to make the main transaction more effective in accomplishing its purpose."). Ancillary restraints are generally permitted if they are "reasonably necessary" toward the contract's objective of utility and efficiency. [citation omitted]

The efficiency-enhancing objectives of a patent settlement are clear, and "[p]ublic policy strongly favors settlement of disputes without litigation." *Aro Corp. v. Allied Witan Co.*, 531 F.2d 1368, 1372 (6th Cir.1976). *See also Schlegal Mfg. Co. v. U.S.M. Corp.*, 525 F.2d 775, 783 (6th Cir.1975) ("The importance of encouraging settlement of patent-infringement litigation . . . cannot be overstated."). In order for a condition to be ancillary, an agreement limiting competition must be secondary and collateral to an independent and legitimate transaction. *Rothery Storage*, 792 F.2d at 224. Naturally, the restraint imposed must relate to the ultimate objective, and cannot be so broad that some of the restraint extinguishes competition without creating efficiency. Even restraints ancillary in form can in substance be illegal if they are part of a general plan to gain monopoly control of a market. *United States v. Addyston Pipe & Steel Co.*, 85 F. 271, 282–83 (6th Cir.1898). Such a restraint, then, is not ancillary.

Under the Schering-Upsher agreement, the scope of the products subject to the September 1, 2001 entry date demonstrate an efficient narrowness. No other products were delayed by the ancillary restraints contained in the agreements. The '743 patent claims a "controlled release [microencapsulated] potassium chloride tablet." The language in the Schering-Upsher agreement covers the identical reach of the '743 patent. There is no broad provision that detracts from the efficiency of settling the underlying patent litigation. Nevertheless, the Commission rejected the notion that the narrow restraints were legitimate and reasonable means of accomplishing the settlement, and refused to consider that this settlement preserved public and private resources, and that the resultant certainty ultimately led to more intense competition.

The Commission's opinion requires the conclusion that but for the payments, the parties would have fashioned different settlements with different entry dates. Although it claimed to apply a rule of reason analysis, which we disagree with on its own, the Commission pointedly states that it logically concluded that "quid pro quo for the payment was an agreement by the generic to defer entry date beyond the date that represents an otherwise reasonable litigation compromise." We are not sure where this "logic" derives from, particularly given our holding in *Valley Drug*. "It is not obvious that competition was limited more than that lawful degree by paying potential competitors for their exit . . . litigation is a much more costly mechanism to achieve exclusion, both to the parties and to the public, than is settlement." *Id.* at 1309.

The Commission rationalizes its decision not to consider the exclusionary power of the patent by asserting that the parties could have attained an earlier entry without the role of payments. There is simply no evidence in the record, however, that supports this conclusion. The Commission even recognized that the January 1, 2004 entry date in the ESI settlement was "non-negotiable." For its part, Schering presented experts who testified to the litigation truism that settlements are not always possible. Indeed, Schering's experts agreed that ancillary agreements may be the only avenue to settlement.

The proposition that the parties could have "simply compromised" on earlier entry dates is somewhat myopic, given the nature of patent litigation and the role that reverse payments play in settlements. It is uncontested that parties settle cases based on their perceived risk of prevailing in and losing the litigation. Pre-Hatch-Waxman, Upsher and ESI normally would have had to enter the market with their products, incurring the costs of clinical trials, manufacturing and marketing. This market entry would have driven down Schering's profits, as it took sales away. As a result, Schering would have sued ESI and Upsher, seeking damages for lost profits and willful infringement. Assuming the patent is reasonably strong, and the parties then settled under this scenario, the money most probably would flow from the infringers to Schering because the generics would have put their companies at risk by making infringing sales.

By contrast, the Hatch-Waxman Amendments grant generic manufacturers standing to mount a validity challenge without incurring the cost of entry or risking enormous damages flowing from any possible infringement. *See In re Ciprofloxacin Hydrochloride Antitrust Litigation,* 261 F.Supp.2d 188, 251 (E.D.N.Y.2003). Hatch-Waxman essentially redistributes the relative risk assessments and explains the flow of settlement funds and their magnitude. *Id.* Because of the Hatch-Waxman scheme, ESI and Upsher gained considerable leverage in patent litigation: the exposure to liability amounted to litigation costs, but paled in comparison to the immense volume of generic sales and profits. This statutory scheme could then cost Schering its patent.

By entering into the settlement agreements, Schering realized the full potential of its infringement suit-a determination that the '743 patent was valid and that ESI and Upsher would not infringe the patent in the future. Furthermore, although ESI and Upsher obtained less than what they would have received from successfully defending the lawsuits (the ability to immediately market their generics), they gained more than if they had lost. A conceivable compromise, then, directs the consideration from the patent owner to the challengers. *Id.* Ultimately, the consideration paid to Upsher and ESI was arguably less than if Schering's patent had been invalidated, which would have resulted in the generic entry of potassium chloride supplements.

In fact, even in the pre-Hatch-Waxman context, "implicit consideration flows from the patent holder to the alleged infringer." *Id.* If Schering had been able to prove damages from infringing sales, and settled before trial for a sum less than the damages, the result is a windfall to the generic manufacturers who essentially keep a portion of the profits. If this were true, then under the Commission's analysis, such a settlement would be a violation of antitrust law because the infringer reaped the benefit of the patent holder's partial surrender of damages. Like the reverse payments at issue here, "such a rule would discourage any rational party from settling a patent case because it would be an invitation to antitrust litigation." *Id.*

The Commission's inflexible compromise-without-payment theory neglects to understand that "[r]everse payments are a natural by-product of the Hatch-Waxman process." *Id.* Pure compromise ignores that patents, payments, and settlement are, in a sense, all symbiotic components that must work together in order for the larger abstract to succeed. As Judge Posner emphasized in Asahi, "[i]f any settlement agreement can be characterized as involving 'compensation' to the defendant, who would not settle unless he had something to show for the settlement. If any settlement agreement is thus classified as involving a forbidden 'reverse payment,' we shall have no more patent settlements." *Asahi Glass Co.,* 289 F.Supp.2d at 994. We agree. If settlement negotiations fail and the patentee prevails in its suit, competition would be prevented to the same or an even greater extent because the generic could not enter the market prior to the expiration of the patent. *See In re Ciprofloxacin Hydrochloride Antitrust Litigation,* 261 F.Supp.2d 188, 250–52 (E.D.N.Y.2003). A prohibition on reverse-payment settlements would "reduce the incentive to challenge patents by reducing the challenger's settlement options should he be sued for infringement, and so might well be thought anticompetitive." *Asahi Glass Co.,* 289 F.Supp.2d at 994.

There is no question that settlements provide a number of private and social benefits as opposed to the inveterate and costly effects of litigation. See generally D. Crane, "Exit Payments in Settlement of Patent Infringement Lawsuits: Antitrust Rules and Economic Implications," 54 Fla. L.Rev. 747, 760 (2002). Patent litigation breeds a litany of direct and indirect costs, ranging from attorney and expert fees to the expenses associated with discovery compliance. Other costs accrue for a variety of reasons, be it the result of uncompromising legal positions, differing strategic objectives, heightened emotions, lawyer incompetence, or sheer moxie. Id.; see also, S. Carlson, Patent Pools and the Antitrust Dilemma, 16 Yale. J. Reg. 359, 380 (1999) (U.S. patent litigation costs $1 billion annually).

Finally, the caustic environment of patent litigation may actually decrease product innovation by amplifying the period of uncertainty around the drug manufacturer's ability to research, develop, and market the patented product or allegedly infringing product. The intensified guesswork involved with lengthy litigation cuts against the benefits proposed by a rule that forecloses a patentee's ability to settle its infringement claim. See In re Tamoxifen Citrate Antitrust Litig., 277 F.Supp.2d 121, 133 (E.D.N.Y.2003) (noting that the settlement resolved the parties' complex patent litigation, and in so doing, "cleared the field" for other ANDA filers). Similarly, Hatch-Waxman settlements, likes the ones at issue here, which result in the patentee's purchase of a license for some of the alleged infringer's other products may benefit the public by introducing a new rival into the market, facilitating competitive production, and encouraging further innovation. See H. Hovenkamp, et al., Anticompetitive Settlement of Intellectual Property Disputes 87 Minn. L.Rev. at 1719, 1750–51 (2003); see also H. Hovenkamp Antitrust Law: An Analysis of Antitrust Principles and Their Application, ¶ 1780a (1999).

Despite the associated benefits of settlements-which include the avoidance of the burdensome costs and the resolution of uncertainty regarding the respective rights and obligations of party litigants-the Commission manufactured a rule that would make almost any settlement involving a payment illegal. Furthermore, the Commission's minimal allowance for $ 2 million in litigation costs is rather naive. While we agree that a settlement cannot be more anticompetitive than litigation, see Valley Drug, 344 F.3d at 1312, we must recognize "[a] suitable accommodation between antitrust law's free competition requirement and the patent regime's incentive system." 344 F.3d at 1307.

We have said before, and we say it again, that the size of the payment, or the mere presence of a payment, should not dictate the availability of a settlement remedy. Due to the "asymmetries of risk and large profits at stake, even a patentee confident in the validity of its patent might pay a potential infringer a substantial sum in settlement." Id. at 1310. An exception cannot lie, as the Commission might think, when the issue turns on validity (Valley Drug) as opposed to infringement (the Schering agreements).[27] The effect is the same: a generic's entry into the

---

[27] The Schering agreements would necessarily be stronger than those in Valley Drug, where the facts demonstrated the likelihood of an invalid patent, because a valid patent could operate to exclude all infringing products for the life of the patent.

market is delayed. What we must focus on is the extent to which the exclusionary effects of the agreement fall within the scope of the patent's protection. Id. Here, we find that the agreements fell well within the protections of the '743 patent, and were therefore not illegal.

V. Conclusion

*** Given the costs of lawsuits to the parties, the public problems associated with overcrowded court dockets, and the correlative public and private benefits of settlements, we fear and reject a rule of law that would automatically invalidate any agreement where a patent-holding pharmaceutical manufacturer settles an infringement case by negotiating the generic's entry date, and, in an ancillary transaction, pays for other products licensed by the generic. Such a result does not represent the confluence of patent and antitrust law. Therefore, this Court grants the petition for review. Accordingly, we SET ASIDE the decision of the Federal Trade Commission and VACATE its cease and desist order.

Comments and Questions

1. Why does the court examine the $60 million dollar royalty for the Niacor license? What is the legal significance if the royalty significantly exceeds the true value of the license? How can the court determine whether the payment is excessive? What factors should the court consider in making this determination? Should the court grant any deference to the FTC's finding that the payment was excessive? If so, why?

2. What test does the court employ to evaluate the settlement in *Schering*? Rule of Reason? Per se? Quick look? Traditional rule of reason analysis asks courts to balance pro and anti-competitive aspects of an agreement—is this test appropriate for this case? Professors Hovenkamp, Janis, and Lemley's oft-cited article argued, in part, against a traditional rule of reason analysis:

> This middle set of cases—where the agreement itself looks like an antitrust violation but the presence of IP rights might absolve it—is much more problematic and requires special treatment. The traditional "rule of reason" analysis is not a good fit for practices that would be unlawful per se but for the presence of an IP claim. The rule of reason is designed to assess whether a practice tends to diminish market-wide output. By contrast, the disputed issue in these middle cases concerns the likely validity and scope of the claimed IP rights, and the reasonableness of the settlement as one among many outcomes of the IP dispute. That is, these cases should be decided on IP grounds because the agreements in this middle category are pro-competitive if, but only if, the patent in question is valid and infringed. Antitrust's rule of reason cannot help with that IP inquiry. All antitrust can do is narrow the class of cases for which inquiry into the IP merits is required.

Herbert Hovenkamp, Mark Janis, and Mark A. Lemley, *Anticompetitive Settlement of Intellectual Property Disputes,* 87 MINN. L. REV. 1719, 1724–25 (2003) (internal citations omitted).

3. Does Schering-Plough hold that it is per se legal for parties to settle non-sham litigation as long as the settlement does not go beyond the scope of the patent? See Ronald W. Davis, *Reverse Payment Patent Settlements: A View into the Abyss, And a Modest Proposal,* 21-Fall ANTITRUST 26, 28 (2006) (suggesting such an interpretation).

4. The FTC appealed the *Schering* decision to the Supreme Court, but cert. was denied. Professor Holman summarized the FTC's argument:

> The FTC's position relies heavily on a body of scholarly literature that stresses the uncertainty of patent litigation and the "probabilistic" nature of patent rights. These theories characterize the patent right as inherently "probabilistic" because of the general uncertainty with respect to validity and scope of a patent prior to court decision. As expressed by Hovenkamp et al., a patent is best viewed not as a right to exclude competition, but more correctly as "a right to try to exclude competition."
>
> The FTC has essentially taken the position that in every Paragraph IV litigation, consumers have an expectation interest in the finite probability that the patent challenge will succeed. In effect, the FTC would treat this consumer expectation as a probabilistic property right. The FTC argues that any settlement between the parties that deprives consumers of the value of this expectation interest is a presumptive violation of the antitrust laws.
>
> The FTC would allow parties to settle by compromising on an entry date prior to the patent's expiration, without cash payments, because "the resulting settlement presumably would reflect the parties' own assessment of the strength of the patent." The FTC views these agreements as neutral, or even pro-competitive, since they resolve the uncertainty of the litigation early and provide some guaranteed benefit to consumers in proportion to the probability that the patent challenge would succeed. The FTC would generally find any reverse payment settlement anticompetitive, because it fails to provide as much consumer benefit as what it considers to be the "benchmark" agreement with a negotiated early entry date and no payments to the patent challenger. The FTC would infer that any payment is a quid pro quo for delayed generic entry, and that were it not for the payment the parties would have either settled on an earlier entry date, or not settled and litigated the case to completion—either scenario benefiting consumers relative to the reverse payment settlement. Note that under the FTC's approach, essentially any reverse payment settlement will be found illegal, regardless of the strength or weakness of the patent case. This is consistent with the FTC's position that an inquiry into the merits of the underlying patent case is inappropriate, except in cases of an objectively baseless or sham patent suit.

Christopher M. Holman, *Do Reverse Payment Settlements Violate Antitrust Laws?,* 23 SANTA CLARA COMPUTER & HIGH TECH. L.J. 489, 533–34 (2007). Should the government protect consumers' "probabilistic" property rights? More specifically, should it be an antitrust violation for settlements to bargain away consumers' probabilistic property rights?

5. After the FTC petitioned the Supreme Court to take the case, the Antitrust Division of the Department of Justice filed an amicus brief, advising the Court

to deny the FTC's petition for certiorari. It is relatively rare for the two federal antitrust agencies to disagree so publicly. In its brief, the DOJ argued that the *Schering-Plough* case was not an appropriate vehicle for the Court to consider the appropriate antitrust treatment for patent settlements involving reverse payments and, also, that there was no split between the circuits. The Court did, in fact, deny the FTC's cert. petition. Do you agree with the DOJ that no circuit split existed?

C. Scott Hemphill, An Aggregate Approach to Antitrust: Using New Data and Rulemaking to Preserve Drug Competition, 109 COLUMBIA LAW REVIEW 629 (2009)

The intensity of antitrust enforcement affects not only the fact, but also the form, of monetary settlements. The first monetary settlements *** blocked entry until patent expiration, and the brand-name firm paid cash. Starting in 1997, and with increasing frequency after 2000, settling firms changed the standard form of settlements in two ways, both likely responses to increased pressure from antitrust enforcers. First, settlements began to include some pre-expiration entry. That shift provides drug makers with the rhetorical opportunity to argue that the settlement guarantees some competition. Some entry looks better than no entry. From this perspective, the law has shifted in the drug makers' favor even further than they may have anticipated, given the prevailing view of appellate courts that it is fine to pay for settlements with no pre-expiration entry.

Second, starting in 1997, settlements frequently included not only payment and delay, but also additional contractual terms that tend to obscure whether payment has occurred. ***

In the wake of increased antitrust scrutiny, naked payments have given way to more complex arrangements. Today, side deals take two complementary forms: overpayment by the brand-name firm for value contributed by the generic firm, and underpayment by the generic firm for value provided by the brand-name firm.

1. Overpayment by the Brand-Name Firm.—In the most common type of side deal, the generic firm contributes—in addition to delayed entry—some further value, such as an unrelated product license. The additional term provides an opportunity to overstate the value contributed by the generic firm and claim that the cash is consideration for the contributed value, rather than for delayed entry. In reviewing K-Dur, the earliest settlement with this type of side deal, the Eleventh Circuit accepted such a factual assertion, which provided a basis for rejecting antitrust liability.

Side deals are now a regular feature of entry-delaying settlements. The contributed value can include a wide range of product development, manufacturing, and promotional services. In some deals, the generic firm offers a product or patent license, or agrees to develop a new product. In one variant, the generic firm develops a new formulation of the brand-name drug. In other deals, it agrees to furnish manufacturing services to the brand-name producer, or to provide inventory, or even to provide "backup" manufacturing services. In some cases, the generic firm provides promotional services as to the product at issue, related drugs, or unrelated products. For some drugs, the brand-name firm reaches entry-delaying settlements with multiple generic firms, each with side deals.

Some of these arrangements are suspect on their face. It may seem clear that the brand-name firm does not need a patent license that does not clearly cover its product, new drug development that is unrelated to its current core business, a new source of raw material supply, backup manufacturing, or additional promotion. However, not all such settlements are facially absurd. In some cases, the generic firm has plausible expertise in the subject of the side deal. It is very difficult to be certain that a deal is collusive without a deep and complex inquiry into the business judgment of the two drug makers.

2. Underpayment by the Generic Firm.—The brand-name firm, rather than paying too much, can charge too little. One mechanism involves "authorized generic" sales. These are sales made by a generic firm under the brand-name firm's FDA approval. The brand-name firm supplies the product to the generic firm at a discount, which the generic firm then resells under its own label at a profitable price. The compensation is buried in the discounted price offered by the brand-name firm.

In several early settlements, the authorized generic product was launched at the time of settlement. This practice fell out of favor after a court concluded that the authorized generic sales triggered the 180-day period. Some modern settlements avoid the trigger problem by providing for authorized generic sales only after another generic firm enters, or of a drug other than the subject of the generic firm's ANDA filing, or in another country.

In a related form of discounted sale, which avoids the trigger issue, the brand-name firm sells an entire product line to the generic firm. One settlement involving an extended-release version of a drug, for example, transferred (for a possibly discounted price) the immediate-release version to the generic firm. In a more complicated set of deals, a brand-name firm may have sold a generic firm rights to one product, and the generic firm delayed entry in two other products. *** Once again, it is very difficult as a practical matter for a decisionmaker to know whether the transfer price provides compensation from the brand-name firm to the generic firm, and if so, how much. ***

Outside of settlement, brand-name firms seldom contract with generic firms for help with the activities that form the basis of side deals. Indeed, as a general matter, brand-name and generic firms seldom execute major deals outside the settlement context, with the exception of authorized generic arrangements, which necessarily are reached between a brand-name firm and a generic firm.

In re Tamoxifen Citrate Antitrust Litigation
466 F.3d 187 (2nd Cir. 2006)

SACK, Circuit Judge.

This appeal, arising out of circumstances surrounding a lawsuit in which a drug manufacturer alleged that its patent for the drug tamoxifen citrate ("tamoxifen")

414 *Antitrust Law and Intellectual Property Rights*

was about to be infringed, and the suit's subsequent settlement, requires us to address issues at the intersection of intellectual property law and antitrust law. Although the particular factual circumstances of this case are unlikely to recur, the issues presented have been much litigated and appear to retain their vitality.

The plaintiffs appeal from a judgment of the United States District Court for the Eastern District of New York (I. Leo Glasser, Judge) dismissing their complaint pursuant to Federal Rule of Civil Procedure 12(b)(6). The plaintiffs claim that the defendants conspired, under an agreement settling a patent infringement lawsuit among the defendants in 1993 while an appeal in that lawsuit was pending, to monopolize the market for tamoxifen—the most widely prescribed drug for the treatment of breast cancer—by suppressing competition from generic versions of the drug. The settlement agreement included, among other things, a so-called "reverse payment" of $21 million from the defendant patent-holders Zeneca, Inc., AstraZeneca Pharmaceuticals LP, and AstraZeneca PLC (collectively "Zeneca") to the defendant generic manufacturer Barr Laboratories, Inc. ("Barr"), and a license from Zeneca to Barr allowing Barr to sell an unbranded version of Zeneca-manufactured tamoxifen. The settlement agreement was contingent on obtaining a vacatur of the judgment of the district court that had heard the infringement action holding the patent to be invalid.

The district court in the instant case concluded that the settlement did not restrain trade in violation of the antitrust laws, and that the plaintiffs suffered no antitrust injury from that settlement. Because we conclude that we have jurisdiction to hear the appeal and that the behavior of the defendants alleged in the complaint would not violate antitrust law, we affirm the judgment of the district court.

Regulatory Background

[*This has been removed because it was covered in the previous cases. Editor*] ***

Factual and Procedural Background

Tamoxifen, the patent for which was obtained by Imperial Chemical Industries, PLC, ("ICI") on August 20, 1985, is sold by Zeneca (a former subsidiary of ICI which succeeded to the ownership rights of the tamoxifen patent) under the trade name Nolvadex®.[6] Tamoxifen is the most widely prescribed drug for the treatment of breast cancer. Indeed, it is the most prescribed cancer drug in the world. In December 1985, four months after ICI was awarded the patent, Barr filed an ANDA with the FDA requesting the agency's approval for Barr to market a generic version of tamoxifen that it had developed. Barr amended its ANDA in September 1987 to include a paragraph IV certification.

In response, on November 2, 1987-within the required forty-five days of Barr's amendment of its ANDA to include a paragraph IV certification—ICI filed a patent

---

[6] In 2001, Zeneca's domestic sales of tamoxifen amounted to $442 million.

infringement lawsuit against Barr and Barr's raw material supplier, Heumann Pharma GmbH & Co. ("Heumann"), in the United States District Court for the Southern District of New York. See *Imperial Chem. Indus., PLC v. Barr Labs., Inc.,* 126 F.R.D. 467, 469 (S.D.N.Y.1989). On April 20, 1992, the district court (Vincent L. Broderick, Judge) declared ICI's tamoxifen patent invalid based on the court's conclusion that ICI had deliberately withheld "crucial information" from the Patent and Trademark Office regarding tests that it had conducted on laboratory animals with respect to the safety and effectiveness of the drug. See *Imperial Chem. Indus., PLC v. Barr Labs., Inc.,* 795 F.Supp. 619, 626–27 (S.D.N.Y.1992) ("Tamoxifen I"). Those tests had revealed hormonal effects "opposite to those sought in humans," which, the court found, could have "unpredictable and at times disastrous consequences." *Id.* at 622.

ICI appealed the district court's judgment to the United States Court of Appeals for the Federal Circuit. In 1993, while the appeal was pending, the parties entered into a confidential settlement agreement (the "Settlement Agreement") which is the principal subject of this appeal. In the Settlement Agreement, Zeneca (which had succeeded to the ownership rights of the patent) and Barr agreed that in return for $21 million and a non-exclusive license to sell Zeneca-manufactured tamoxifen in the United States under Barr's label, rather than Zeneca's trademark Nolvadex®, Barr would change its ANDA paragraph IV certification to a paragraph III certification, thereby agreeing that it would not market its own generic version of tamoxifen until Zeneca's patent expired in 2002. See *In re Tamoxifen Citrate Antitrust Litig.,* 277 F.Supp.2d 121, 125–26 (E.D.N.Y.2003) ("Tamoxifen II"). Zeneca also agreed to pay Heumann $9.5 million immediately, and an additional $35.9 million over the following ten years. The parties further agreed that if the tamoxifen patent were to be subsequently declared invalid or unenforceable in a final and (in contrast to the district court judgment in Tamoxifen I) unappealable judgment by a court of competent jurisdiction, Barr would be allowed to revert to a paragraph IV ANDA certification. Thus if, in another lawsuit, a generic marketer prevailed as Barr had prevailed in Tamoxifen I, and that judgment was either not appealed or was affirmed on appeal, Barr would have been allowed to place itself in the same position (but for the 180-day head start, if it was available) that it would have been in had it prevailed on appeal in *Tamoxifen I,* rather than settling while its appeal was pending in the Federal Circuit.

The plaintiffs allege that as a part of the Settlement Agreement, Barr "understood" that if another generic manufacturer attempted to market a version of tamoxifen, Barr would seek to prevent the manufacturer from doing so by attempting to invoke the 180-day exclusivity right possessed by the first "paragraph IV" filer. Compl. ¶ 58. According to the plaintiffs, this understanding among the defendants effectively forestalled the introduction of any generic version of tamoxifen, because, five years later—only a few weeks before other generic manufacturers were to be able to begin marketing their own versions of tamoxifen—Barr did in fact successfully claim entitlement to the exclusivity period. It thereby prevented those manufacturers from entering the tamoxifen market until 180 days after Barr triggered the period by commercially marketing its own generic version of the drug. In fact, Barr had not yet begun marketing its own generic version and had little incentive to do so because, pursuant to the Settlement Agreement, it was already able to market Zeneca's version of tamoxifen.

Meanwhile, pursuant to the Settlement Agreement which was contingent on the vacatur of the district court judgment in Tamoxifen I, Barr and Zeneca filed a "Joint Motion to Dismiss the Appeal as Moot and to Vacate the Judgment Below." See Tamoxifen II, 277 F.Supp.2d at 125. The Federal Circuit granted the motion, thereby vacating the district court's judgment that the patent was invalid. [citation omitted] Such a vacatur, while generally considered valid as a matter of appellate procedure by courts at the time of the Settlement Agreement, see U.S. Philips Corp. v. Windmere Corp., 971 F.2d 728, 731 (Fed.Cir.1992), was shortly thereafter held to be invalid in nearly all circumstances by the Supreme Court, see U.S. Bancorp Mortgage Co. v. Bonner Mall P'ship, 513 U.S. 18, 27–29 (1994).[8]

In the years after the parties entered into the Settlement Agreement and the Federal Circuit vacated the district court's judgment,[9] three other generic manufacturers filed ANDAs with paragraph IV certifications to secure approval of their respective generic versions of tamoxifen: Novopharm Ltd., in June 1994, Mylan Pharmaceuticals, Inc., in January 1996, and Pharmachemie, B.V., in February 1996. See Tamoxifen II, 277 F.Supp.2d at 126–27. Zeneca responded to each of these certifications in the same manner that it had responded to Barr's: by filing a patent infringement lawsuit within the forty-five day time limit provided by 21 U.S.C. § 355(j)(5)(B)(iii). See id. In each case, the court rejected the generic manufacturer's attempt to rely on the vacated Tamoxifen I decision, and-contrary to the Tamoxifen I judgment-upheld the validity of Zeneca's tamoxifen patent. [citation omitted] ***

Proceedings in the District Court

While these generic manufacturers were litigating the validity of Zeneca's patent on tamoxifen, consumers and consumer groups in various parts of the United States filed some thirty lawsuits challenging the legality of the 1993 Settlement Agreement between Zeneca and Barr. See Tamoxifen II, 277 F.Supp.2d at 127. Those lawsuits were subsequently transferred by the Judicial Panel on Multidistrict Litigation to the United States District Court for the Eastern District of New York. Subsequently, a consolidated class action complaint embodying the claims was filed. In re Tamoxifen Citrate Antitrust Litig., 196 F.Supp.2d 1371 (2001); Tamoxifen II, 277 F.Supp.2d at 127. In the consolidated lawsuit, the plaintiffs alleged that the Settlement Agreement unlawfully (1) enabled Zeneca and Barr to resuscitate a patent that the district court had already held to be invalid and unenforceable;

---

[8] The rule in U.S. Bancorp does not apply retroactively. [c.o.]
[9] After the Settlement Agreement was entered into and the vacatur ordered, Barr began to market its licensed version of Zeneca's tamoxifen, selling its product to distributors and wholesalers at a 15 percent discount to the brand-name price, which translated into a price to consumers about five percent below Zeneca's otherwise identical Nolvadex® brand-name version. Barr soon captured about 80 percent of the tamoxifen market.

(2) facilitated Zeneca's continuing monopolization of the market for tamoxifen; (3) provided for the sharing of unlawful monopoly profits between Zeneca and Barr; (4) maintained an artificially high price for tamoxifen; and (5) prevented competition from other generic manufacturers of tamoxifen. See *Tamoxifen II*, 277 F.Supp.2d at 127-28. At the heart of the lawsuit was the contention that the Settlement Agreement enabled Zeneca and Barr effectively to circumvent the district court's invalidation of Zeneca's tamoxifen patent in *Tamoxifen I*, which, the plaintiffs asserted, would have been affirmed by the Federal Circuit. The result of such an affirmance, according to the plaintiffs, would have been that Barr would have received approval to market a generic version of tamoxifen; Barr would have begun marketing tamoxifen, thereby triggering the 180-day exclusivity period; other generic manufacturers would have introduced their own versions of tamoxifen upon the expiration of the exclusivity period, with Zeneca collaterally estopped from invoking its invalidated patent as a defense; and, as a result, the price for tamoxifen would have declined substantially below the levels at which the Zeneca-manufactured drug in fact sold in the market shared by Zeneca and Barr through the Settlement Agreement. *Id.* at 128. The defendants moved to dismiss the class action complaint pursuant to Federal Rule of Civil Procedure 12(b)(6) for failure to state a claim upon which relief can be granted.

On May 15, 2003, in a thorough and thoughtful opinion, the district court granted the defendants' motion to dismiss. [citation omitted] The court noted that although market-division agreements between a monopolist and a potential competitor ordinarily violate the Sherman Act, they are not necessarily unlawful when the monopolist is a patent holder. [citation omitted] Pursuant to a patent grant, the court reasoned, a patent holder may settle patent litigation by entering into a licensing agreement with the alleged infringer without running afoul of the Sherman Act. [citation omitted] Yet, the court continued, a patent holder is prohibited from acting in bad faith "beyond the limits of the patent monopoly" to restrain or monopolize trade. [citation omitted]

Analyzing the terms and impact of the Settlement Agreement, the district court concluded that the agreement permissibly terminated the litigation between the defendants, which "cleared the field for other generic manufacturers to challenge the patent." *Id.* at 133. "Instead of leaving in place an additional barrier to subsequent ANDA filers, the Settlement Agreement in fact removed one possible barrier to final FDA approval-namely, the existence of ongoing litigation between an existing ANDA filer and a subsequent filer." *Id.* To the court, this factor distinguished the case from similar cases in which other circuits had held settlement agreements to be unlawful, where the agreement in question did not conclude the underlying litigation and instead prolonged the period during which other generic manufacturers could not enter the market. [citation omitted]

The district court was also of the view that the defendants could not be held liable for Barr's FDA petition to preserve its 180-day exclusivity period even if this was a term of the defendants' negotiated Settlement Agreement. [citation omitted] It reasoned that at the time of settlement, Barr could not have successfully pursued its FDA application because the FDA continued to apply the "successful defense" rule until 1997. [citation omitted] It was only after 1997 that Barr petitioned the FDA to preserve its exclusivity period. The court concluded that Barr's petition was

> an attempt to petition a governmental body in order to protect an arguable interest in a statutory right based on recent developments in the court and at the FDA. As such, the FDA Petition was protected activity under the First Amendment, and long-settled law established that the Sherman Act, with limited exceptions, does not apply to petitioning administrative agencies.

Id. at 135. The court concluded that the plaintiffs' complaint therefore did not sufficiently allege a bad-faith settlement in violation of the Sherman Act. [citation omitted]

The district court also concluded that even if the plaintiffs had stated an antitrust violation, they did not suffer antitrust injury from either Barr's exclusivity period or the Settlement Agreement and the resulting vacatur of the district court's judgment in *Tamoxifen I* invalidating the tamoxifen patent. [citation omitted] The court noted that "[a]ntitrust injury . . . must be caused by something other than the regulatory action limiting entry to the market." *Id.* at 137. The court attributed "the lack of competition in the market" not to "the deployment of Barr's exclusivity period, but rather [to] the inability of the generic companies to invalidate or design around" the tamoxifen patent, and their consequent loss of the patent litigation against Zeneca. *Id.* This was so, the district court concluded, even if Barr's petition to the FDA had delayed the approval of Mylan's ANDA. *Id.* at 137. Any "injury" suffered by the plaintiffs, said the court, "is thus not antitrust injury, but rather the result of the legal monopoly that a patent holder possesses." *Id.* at 138.

The district court also rejected the plaintiffs' contention that "the settlement and vacatur deprived other generic manufacturers of the ability to make the legal argument that the [*Tamoxifen I*] judgment (if affirmed) would collaterally estop Zeneca from claiming the [tamoxifen] patent was valid in future patent litigation with other ANDA filers." *Id.* It reasoned that there is no basis for the assertion that "forcing other generic manufacturers to litigate the validity of the [tamoxifen] patent[] is an injury to competition." *Id.* The court also referred to the other generic manufacturers' subsequent litigation against Zeneca over the validity of the tamoxifen patent, in which Zeneca prevailed, as additional reason to reject the plaintiffs' assertion that the Federal Circuit would have affirmed Judge Broderick's judgment invalidating the tamoxifen patent. *Id.*

The district court therefore dismissed the plaintiffs' Sherman Act claims. *** The plaintiffs appeal the dismissal of their claims. ***

Discussion ***

III. The Plaintiffs' Antitrust Claims

A. The Tension between Antitrust Law and Patent Law

With the ultimate goal of stimulating competition and innovation, the Sherman Act prohibits "[e]very contract, combination in the form of trust or otherwise, or conspiracy, in restraint of trade or commerce among the several States," 15 U.S.C. § 1, and "monopoliz[ation], or attempt[s] to monopolize, or combin[ations] or conspir[acies] . . . to monopolize any part of the trade or commerce among the several States," id. § 2. By contrast, also with the ultimate goal of stimulating competition and innovation, patent law grants an innovator "the right to exclude others from making, using, offering for sale, or selling the invention throughout the United States or importing the invention into the United States" for a limited term of years. 35 U.S.C. § 154(a)(1)-(2); *see also Dawson Chem. Co. v. Rohm & Haas Co.*, 448 U.S. 176, 215 (1980) ("[T]he essence of a patent grant is the right to exclude others from profiting by the patented invention."). It is the tension between restraints on anti-competitive behavior imposed by the Sherman Act and grants of patent monopolies under the patent laws, as complicated by the Hatch-Waxman Act, that underlies this appeal. [citation omitted]

In most cases, however, conduct will be evaluated under a "rule of reason" analysis, "according to which the finder of fact must decide whether the questioned practice imposes an unreasonable restraint on competition, taking into account a variety of factors, including specific information about the relevant business, its condition before and after the restraint was imposed, and the restraint's history, nature, and effect." [citation omitted]

The rule-of-reason analysis has been divided into three steps. First, a plaintiff must demonstrate "that the challenged action has had an actual adverse effect on competition as a whole in the relevant market." [citation omitted] If the plaintiff succeeds in doing so, "the burden shifts to the defendant to establish the 'pro-competitive "redeeming virtues" ' of the action." [citation omitted] If the defendant succeeds in meeting its burden, the plaintiff then has the burden of "show[ing] that the same pro-competitive effect could be achieved through an alternative means that is less restrictive of competition." [citation omitted]

B. The Plaintiffs' Allegations

1. Settlement of a Patent Validity Lawsuit. The plaintiffs contend that several factors—including that *Tamoxifen I* was settled after the tamoxifen patent had been held invalid by the district court, making the patent unenforceable at the time of settlement–indicate that if their allegations are proved, the defendants violated the antitrust laws. They argue that the district court in the case before us erred by treating the tamoxifen patent as valid and enforceable. Instead, they say, in accordance with the never-reviewed judgment in Tamoxifen I, the district court in this case should have treated the patent as presumptively invalid for purposes of assaying the sufficiency of the plaintiffs' complaint.

We begin our analysis against the backdrop of our longstanding adherence to the principle that "courts are bound to encourage" the settlement of litigation. [citation omitted] It is well settled that "[w]here there are legitimately conflicting [patent] claims . . ., a settlement by agreement, rather than litigation, is not precluded by the [Sherman] Act," although such a settlement may ultimately have an adverse effect on competition. Standard Oil Co. v. United States, 283 U.S. 163, 171 (1931) [citation omitted]

Rules severely restricting patent settlements might also be contrary to the goals of the patent laws because the increased number of continuing lawsuits that would result would heighten the uncertainty surrounding patents and might delay innovation. *See Valley Drug,* 344 F.3d at 1308; Daniel A. Crane, *Exit Payments in Settlement of Patent Infringement Lawsuits: Antitrust Rules and Economic Implications,* 54 Fla. L.Rev. 747, 749 (2002). Although forcing patent litigation to continue might benefit consumers in some instances, "patent settlements can . . . promote efficiencies, resolving disputes that might otherwise block or delay the market entry of valuable inventions." Joseph F. Brodley & Maureen A. O'Rourke, *Preliminary Views: Patent Settlement Agreements,* Antitrust, Summer 2002, at 53. As the Fourth Circuit has observed, "It is only when settlement agreements are entered into in bad faith and are utilized as part of a scheme to restrain or monopolize trade that antitrust violations may occur." *Duplan Corp.,* 540 F.2d at 1220.

We cannot judge this post-trial, pre-appeal settlement on the basis of the likelihood vel non of Zeneca's success had it not settled but rather pursued its appeal. ***

As the plaintiffs correctly point out, the Federal Circuit would have reviewed Judge Broderick's factual findings underlying his conclusion of invalidity with considerable deference, rather than engaging in a presumption of validity. [citation omitted] But it takes no citation to authority to conclude that appellants prevail with some frequency in federal courts of appeals even when a high degree of deference is accorded the district courts from which the appeals are taken. Accordingly, it does not follow from the deference that was due by the Federal Circuit to the district court in *Tamoxifen I* that Zeneca would have been unsuccessful on appeal. [citation omitted] ***

The fact that the settlement here occurred after the district court ruled against Zeneca seems to us to be of little moment. There is a risk of loss in all appeals that may give rise to a desire on the part of both the appellant and the appellee to settle before the appeal is decided. Settlements of legitimate disputes, even antitrust and patent disputes of which an appeal is pending, in order to eliminate that risk, are not prohibited. That Zeneca had sufficient confidence in its patent to proceed to trial rather than find some means to settle the case first should hardly weigh against it.

We conclude, then, that without alleging something more than the fact that Zeneca settled after it lost to Barr in the district court that would tend to establish that the Settlement Agreement was unlawful, the assertion that there was a bar-antitrust or otherwise-to the defendants' settling the litigation at the time that they did is unpersuasive.

2. *Reverse Payments.* Payments pursuant to the settlement of a patent suit such as those required under the Settlement Agreement are referred to as "reverse" payments because, by contrast, "[t]ypically, in patent infringement cases the payment flows from the alleged infringer to the patent holder." David A. Balto, *Pharmaceutical Patent Settlements: The Antitrust Risks,* 55 Food & Drug L.J. 321, 335 (2000). Here, the patent holder, which, if its patent is valid, has the right to prevent the

alleged infringer from making commercial use of it, nonetheless pays that party not to do so. Seeking to supply the "something more" than the fact of settlement that would render the Settlement Agreement unlawful, the plaintiffs allege that the value of the reverse payments from Zeneca to Barr thereunder "greatly exceeded the value of Barr's 'best case scenario' in winning the appeal . . . and entering the market with its own generic product." Appellants' Br. at 27.

It is the size, not the mere existence, of Zeneca's reverse payment that the plaintiffs point to in asserting that they have successfully pleaded a Sherman Act cause of action. In explaining our analysis, though, it is worth exploring the notion advanced by others that the very existence of reverse payments establishes unlawfulness. See Balto, supra, at 335 ("A payment flowing from the innovator to the challenging generic firm may suggest strongly the anticompetitive intent of the parties in entering the agreement and the rent-preserving effect of that agreement."); Herbert Hovenkamp et al., Anticompetitive Settlement of Intellectual Property Disputes, 87 Minn. L.Rev. 1719, 1751 (2003) ("[T]he problem of exclusion payments can arise whenever the patentee has an incentive to postpone determination of the validity of its patent.").

Heeding the advice of several courts and commentators, we decline to conclude (and repeat that the plaintiffs do not ask us to conclude) that reverse payments are per se violations of the Sherman Act such that an allegation of an agreement to make reverse payments suffices to assert an antitrust violation. We do not think that the fact that the patent holder is paying to protect its patent monopoly, without more, establishes a Sherman Act violation. *See Valley Drug,* 344 F.3d at 1309 (concluding that the presence of a reverse payment, by itself, does not transform an otherwise lawful settlement into an unlawful one); Asahi Glass, 289 F.Supp.2d at 994 (asserting that "[a] ban on reverse-payment settlements would reduce the incentive to challenge patents by reducing the challenger's settlement options should he be sued for infringement, and so might well be thought anticompetitive," and observing that if the parties decided not to settle, and the patent holder ultimately prevailed in the infringement lawsuit, there would be the same level of competition as in the reverse payment case); Thomas F. Cotter, Refining the "Presumptive Illegality" Approach to Settlements of Patent Disputes Involving Reverse Payments: A Commentary on Hovenkamp, Janis & Lemley, 87 Minn. L.Rev. 1789, 1807 (2003) (noting that "the plaintiff often will have an incentive to pay the defendant not to enter the market, regardless of whether the former expects to win at trial," which "suggests that reverse payments should not be per se illegal, since they are just as consistent with a high probability of validity and infringement as they are with a low probability. It also suggests that reverse payments should not be per se legal for the same reason."). *But see Cardizem,* 332 F.3d at 911 (calling a forty-million-dollar reverse payment to a generic manufacturer "a naked, horizontal restraint of trade that is per se illegal because it is presumed to have the effect of reducing competition in the market for Cardizem CD and its generic equivalents to the detriment of consumers").

*** [M]oreover, reverse payments are particularly to be expected in the drug-patent context because the Hatch-Waxman Act created an environment that encourages them. [citation omitted]

In the typical patent infringement case, the alleged infringer enters the market with its drug after the investment of substantial sums of money for manufacturing, marketing, legal fees, and the like. The patent holder then brings suit against the alleged infringer seeking damages for, inter alia, its lost profits. If the patent holder wins, it receives protection for the patent and money damages for the infringement. And in that event, the infringer loses not only the opportunity to continue in the business of making and selling the infringing product, but also the investment it made to enter the market for that product in the first place. And it must pay damages to boot. It makes sense in such a circumstance for the alleged infringer to enter into a settlement in which it pays a significant amount to the patent holder to rid itself of the risk of losing the litigation.

By contrast, under the Hatch-Waxman Act, the patent holder ordinarily brings suit shortly after the paragraph IV ANDA has been filed—before the filer has spent substantial sums on the manufacturing, marketing, or distribution of the potentially infringing generic drug. The prospective generic manufacturer therefore has relatively little to lose in litigation precipitated by a paragraph IV certification beyond litigation costs and the opportunity for future profits from selling the generic drug. Conversely, there are no infringement damages for the patent holder to recover, and there is therefore little reason for it to pursue the litigation beyond the point at which it can assure itself that no infringement will occur in the first place.

Accordingly, a generic marketer has few disincentives to file an ANDA with a paragraph IV certification. The incentive, by contrast, may be immense: the profits it will likely garner in competing with the patent holder without having invested substantially in the development of the drug, and, in addition, possible entitlement to a 180-day period (to be triggered at its inclination) during which it would be the exclusive seller of the generic drug in the market.

The patent holder's risk if it loses the resulting patent suit is correspondingly large: It will be stripped of its patent monopoly. At the same time, it stands to gain little from winning other than the continued protection of its lawful monopoly over the manufacture and sale of the drug in question.

"Hatch-Waxman essentially redistributes the relative risk assessments and explains the flow of settlement funds and their magnitude. Because of the Hatch-Waxman scheme, [the generic challengers] gain[] considerable leverage in patent litigation: the exposure to liability amount[s] to litigation costs, but pale[s] in comparison to the immense volume of generic sales and profits." *Schering-Plough*, 402 F.3d at 1074 (citation omitted).

Under these circumstances, we see no sound basis for categorically condemning reverse payments employed to lift the uncertainty surrounding the validity and scope of the holder's patent.

3. "Excessive" Reverse Payments. As we have noted, although there are those who contend that reverse payments are in and of themselves necessarily unlawful, the plaintiffs are not among them. They allege instead that "[t]he value of the consideration provided to keep Barr's product off the market . . . greatly exceeded the value Barr could have realized by successfully defending its trial victory on appeal and entering the market with its own competitive generic product." Appellants' Br. at 15. The plaintiffs assert that it is that excessiveness that renders the Settlement Agreement unlawful. We agree that even if "reverse payments are a natural by-product of the Hatch-Waxman process," *Cipro II*, 261 F.Supp.2d at 252, it does not follow that they are necessarily lawful. [citation omitted] But

> [o]nly if a patent settlement is a device for circumventing antitrust law is it vulnerable to an antitrust suit. Suppose a seller obtains a patent that it knows is almost certainly invalid (that is, almost certain not to survive a judicial challenge), sues its competitors, and settles the suit by licensing them to use its patent in exchange for their agreeing not to sell the patented product for less than the price specified in the license. In such a case, the patent, the suit, and the settlement would be devices—masks—for fixing prices, in violation of antitrust law.

Asahi Glass, 289 F.Supp.2d at 991. "If, however, there is nothing suspicious about the circumstances of a patent settlement, then to prevent a cloud from being cast over the settlement process a third party should not be permitted to haul the parties to the settlement over the hot coals of antitrust litigation." *Id.* at 992.

There is something on the face of it that does seem "suspicious" about a patent holder settling patent litigation against a potential generic manufacturer by paying that manufacturer more than either party anticipates the manufacturer would earn by winning the lawsuit and entering the newly competitive market in competition with the patent holder. Why, after all-viewing the settlement through an antitrust lens-should the potential competitor be permitted to receive such a windfall at the ultimate expense of drug purchasers? We think, however, that the suspicion abates upon reflection. In such a case, so long as the patent litigation is neither a sham nor otherwise baseless, the patent holder is seeking to arrive at a settlement in order to protect that to which it is presumably entitled: a lawful monopoly over the manufacture and distribution of the patented product.

If the patent holder loses its patent monopoly as a result of defeat in patent litigation against the generic manufacturer, it will likely lose some substantial portion of the market for the drug to that generic manufacturer and perhaps others. The patent holder might also (but will not necessarily) lower its price in response to the competition. The result will be, unsurprisingly, that (assuming that lower prices do not attract significant new purchasers for the drug) the total profits of the patent holder and the generic manufacturer on the drug in the competitive market will be lower than the total profits of the patent holder alone under a patent-conferred monopoly. In the words of the Federal Trade Commission: "The anticipated profits of the patent holder in the absence of generic competition are greater than the sum of its profits and the profits of the generic entrant when the two compete." *In re Schering-Plough Corp.*, slip op. at 27, 2003 WL 22989651 (Fed. Trade Comm'n Dec. 8, 2003), 2003 FTC LEXIS 187, vacated, 402 F.3d 1056 (11th Cir.2005). It might therefore make economic sense for the patent holder to pay some portion of that difference to the generic manufacturer to maintain the patent-monopoly market for itself. And, if that amount exceeds what the generic manufacturer sees as its likely profit from victory, it seems to make obvious economic sense for the generic manufacturer to accept such a payment if it is offered. We think we can safely assume that the patent holder will seek to pay less if it can, but under the circumstances of a paragraph IV Hatch-Waxman filing, as we have discussed, the ANDA filer might well have the whip hand. [citation omitted]

Of course, the law could provide that the willingness of the patent holder to settle at a price above the generic manufacturer's projected profit betrays a fatal disbelief in the validity of the patent or the likelihood of infringement, and that the patent holder therefore ought not to be allowed to maintain its monopoly position. Perhaps it is unwise to protect patent monopolies that rest on such dubious patents. But even if large reverse payments indicate a patent holder's lack of confidence in its patent's strength or breadth, we doubt the wisdom of deeming a patent effectively invalid on the basis of a patent holder's fear of losing it.

> [T]he private thoughts of a patentee, or of the alleged infringer who settles with him, about whether the patent is valid or whether it has been infringed is not the issue in an antitrust case. A firm that has received a patent from the patent office (and not by fraud . . .), and thus enjoys the presumption of validity that attaches to an issued patent, 35 U.S.C. § 282, is entitled to defend the patent's validity in court, to sue alleged infringers, and to settle with them, whatever its private doubts, unless a neutral observer would reasonably think either that the patent was almost certain to be declared invalid, or the defendants were almost certain to be found not to have infringed it, if the suit went to judgment. It is not "bad faith" to assert patent rights that one is not certain will be upheld in a suit for infringement pressed to judgment and to settle the suit to avoid risking the loss of the rights. No one can be certain that he will prevail in a patent suit.

Asahi Glass, 289 F.Supp.2d at 992-93 (citation omitted) (emphasis in original).

Such a rule would also fail to give sufficient consideration to the patent holder's incentive to settle the lawsuit without reference to the amount the generic manufacturer might earn in a competitive market, even when it is relatively confident of the validity of its patent-to insure against the possibility that its confidence is misplaced, or, put another way, that a reviewing court might (in its view) render an erroneous decision. *Cf. Schering-Plough*, 402 F.3d at 1075–76. Whatever the degree of the patent holder's certainty, there is always some risk of loss that the patent holder might wish to insure against by settling.

This case is illustrative. It is understandable that however sure Zeneca was at the outset that its patent was valid, settlement might have seemed attractive once it lost in the district court, especially in light of the deferential standard the Federal

Circuit was expected to apply on review. But its desire to settle does not necessarily belie Zeneca's confidence in the patent's validity. Indeed, Zeneca's pursuit of subsequent litigation seeking to establish the tamoxifen patent's validity, and the success of that litigation, strongly suggest that such confidence persisted and was not misplaced. Neither do we think that the settlement's entry after the district court rendered a judgment against Zeneca should counsel against the settlement's propriety. It would be odd to handicap the ability of Zeneca to settle after it had displayed sufficient confidence in its patent to risk a finding of invalidity by taking the case to trial.

We are unsure, too, what would be accomplished by a rule that would effectively outlaw payments by patent holders to generic manufacturers greater than what the latter would be able to earn in the market were they to defend successfully against an infringement claim. A patent holder might well prefer such a settlement limitation-it would make such a settlement cheaper—while a generic manufacturer might nonetheless agree to settle because it is less risky to accept in settlement all the profits it expects to make in a competitive market rather than first to defend and win a lawsuit, and then to enter the marketplace and earn the profits. If such a limitation had been in place here, Zeneca might have saved money by paying Barr the maximum such a rule might allow-what Barr was likely to earn if it entered the market—and Barr would have received less than it could have if it were free to negotiate the best deal available-as it did here. But the resulting level of competition, and its benefit to consumers, would have been the same. The monopoly would have nonetheless endured—but, to no apparent purpose, at less expense to Zeneca and less reward for Barr.

It strikes us, in other words, as pointless to permit parties to enter into an agreement settling the litigation between them, thereby protecting the patent holder's monopoly even though it may be based on a relatively weak patent, but to limit the amount of the settlement to the amount of the generic manufacturer's projected profits had it won the litigation.

We are not unaware of a troubling dynamic that is at work in these cases. The less sound the patent or the less clear the infringement, and therefore the less justified the monopoly enjoyed by the patent holder, the more a rule permitting settlement is likely to benefit the patent holder by allowing it to retain the patent. But the law allows the settlement even of suits involving weak patents with the presumption that the patent is valid and that settlement is merely an extension of the valid patent monopoly. So long as the law encourages settlement, weak patent cases will likely be settled even though such settlements will inevitably protect patent monopolies that are, perhaps, undeserved.

*** An alternative rule is, of course, possible. As suggested above, the antitrust laws could be read to outlaw all, or nearly all, settlements of Hatch-Waxman infringement actions. Patent holders would be required to litigate each threatened patent to final, unappealable judgment. Only patents that the courts held were valid would be entitled to confer monopoly power on their proprietors. But such a requirement would be contrary to well-established principles of law. As we have rehearsed at some length above, settlement of patent litigation is not only suffered, it is encouraged for a variety of reasons even if it leads in some cases to the survival of monopolies created by what would otherwise be fatally weak patents. It is too late in the journey for us to alter course.

We generally agree, then, with the Eleventh Circuit insofar as it held in *Valley Drug* that "'simply because a brand-name pharmaceutical company holding a patent paid its generic competitor money cannot be the sole basis for a violation of antitrust law,' unless the 'exclusionary effects of the agreement' exceed the 'scope of the patent's protection.'" *Cipro III*, 363 F.Supp.2d at 538 (*quoting Schering-Plough*, 402 F.3d at 1076 (alteration omitted)). Whatever damage is done to competition by settlement is done pursuant to the monopoly extended to the patent holder by patent law unless the terms of the settlement enlarge the scope of that monopoly. "Unless and until the patent is shown to have been procured by fraud, or a suit for its enforcement is shown to be objectively baseless, there is no injury to the market cognizable under existing antitrust law, as long as competition is restrained only within the scope of the patent." *Cipro III*, 363 F.Supp.2d at 535.

We further agree with the *Cipro III* court that absent an extension of the monopoly beyond the patent's scope, an issue that we address in the next section of this opinion, and absent fraud, which is not alleged here, the question is whether the underlying infringement lawsuit was "objectively baseless in the sense that no reasonable litigant could realistically expect success on the merits." *Prof'l Real Estate Investors, Inc. v. Columbia Pictures Indus., Inc.*, 508 U.S. 49, 60 (1993). In this case, the plaintiffs do not contend that they can—and we conclude that in all likelihood they cannot—establish that Zeneca's patent litigation was baseless, particularly in light of the subsequent series of decisions upholding the validity of the same patent. *Cf. id.* at 60 n. 5 ("A winning lawsuit is by definition a reasonable effort at petitioning for redress and therefore not a sham."). Payments, even "excessive" payments, to settle the dispute were therefore not necessarily unlawful.

4. The Terms of the Settlement Agreement. Inasmuch as we conclude that neither the fact of settlement nor the amount of payments made pursuant thereto as alleged by the plaintiffs would render the Settlement Agreement unlawful, we must assess its other terms to determine whether they do. As we have explained in the previous section of this opinion, we think that the question is whether the "exclusionary effects of the agreement" exceed the "scope of the patent's protection." *Schering-Plough*, 402 F.3d at 1076. Looking to other courts that have addressed similar cases for guidance, and accepting the plaintiffs' allegations as true, we conclude that the Settlement Agreement did not unlawfully extend the reach of Zeneca's tamoxifen patent.

First, the Settlement Agreement did not extend the patent monopoly by restraining the introduction or marketing of unrelated or non-infringing products. It is thus unlike the agreement the Sixth Circuit held per se illegal in *Cardizem*, 332 F.3d at 908, which included not only a substantial reverse payment but also an agreement that the generic manufacturer would not market non-infringing products. [citation omitted] ***

Second, the Settlement Agreement ended all litigation between Zeneca and Barr and thereby opened the tamoxifen patent to immediate challenge by other potential generic manufacturers ***.

Finally, the Settlement Agreement did not entirely foreclose competition in the market for tamoxifen. It included a license from Zeneca to Barr that allowed Barr to begin marketing Zeneca's version of tamoxifen eight months after the Settlement Agreement became effective. The license ensured that money also flowed from Barr to Zeneca, decreasing the value of the reverse payment. By licensing tamoxifen to Barr, Zeneca added a competitor to the market, however limited the competition may have been. Unlike reverse payment settlements that leave the competitive situation as it was prior to the litigation, the reverse payment in this case was pursuant to an agreement that increased competition in the market for Tamoxifen—even if only a little-almost nine years before the tamoxifen patent was to expire. [citation omitted]

The Settlement Agreement almost certainly resulted in less price competition than if Barr had introduced its own generic version, of course. The plaintiffs allege that the Barr-distributed, Zeneca-manufactured tamoxifen sold at retail for just five percent less than the Zeneca-branded version, compared with what the plaintiffs allege is a typical initial drop of sixteen percent or more, and an eventual drop in a truly competitive market of thirty to eighty percent. [citation omitted] This was competition nonetheless. It was certainly more competition than would have occurred had there been no settlement and had Zeneca prevailed on appeal. [citation omitted]

We conclude that the facts as alleged in the plaintiffs' complaint, if proved, would not establish that the terms of the Settlement Agreement violated the antitrust laws. In the absence of any plausible allegation that the reverse payment provided benefits to Zeneca outside the scope of the tamoxifen patent, the plaintiffs have not stated a claim for relief with respect to the Settlement Agreement. [citation omitted]***

Conclusion

For the foregoing reasons, the judgment of the district court is affirmed.

[Dissent omitted]

Comments and Questions

1. Some observers consider the Second Circuit's opinion in *In re Tamoxifen Citrate Antitrust Litigation*, 466 F.3d 187 (2nd Cir. 2006), to be a particularly controversial case involving reverse payments by a patentee. Quoting Eleventh Circuit opinions, as well as others, the Second Circuit held: "simply because a brand-name pharmaceutical company holding a patent paid its generic competitor money cannot be the sole basis for a violation of antitrust law, unless the 'exclusionary effects of the agreement' exceed the 'scope of the patent's protection.' Whatever damage is done to competition by settlement is done pursuant to the monopoly

extended to the patent holder by patent law unless the terms of the settlement enlarge the scope of that monopoly." *Id.* at 212 (internal citations and quotations omitted).

Do you agree that antitrust plaintiffs fail to state a claim sufficient to survive a Rule 12(b)(6) motion when they allege that a patentee has paid a generic competitor not to challenge its patent?

What if the patent at issue were invalid?

The district court had held ICI's tamoxifen patent invalid. How should that initial determination affect the antitrust analysis of the subsequent agreement between the parties?

2. Prior to the Second Circuit's decision in *Tamoxifen*, a district court wrestled with a similar motion to dismiss in In re Ciprofloxacin Hydrochloride Antitrust Litig., 261 F. Supp. 2d 188 (E.D.N.Y. 2003) (*see also* 363 F. Supp. 2d 513 (E.D.N.Y. 2005)). In this case, consumers sued Bayer Corporation and several generic manufacturers who reached individual settlements covering Bayer's patent on the market's leading antibiotic. Though the terms of the settlements varied, the settlements roughly stated that the generic manufacturers acknowledged the validity of Bayer's patent and agreed not to enter the market until the patent expired, and in return Bayer would pay the generics hundreds of millions of dollars. *Id.* at 195–96. The defendants moved to dismiss the case pursuant to Fed. R. Civ. P. 12(b)(6). The Court rejected the plaintiff's argument that per se analysis should be used, noting:

> [E]ven in the traditional context, implicit consideration flows from the patent holder to the alleged infringer. For instance, suppose a case is ready for trial and the patent holder can prove damages (infringing sales) of $100 million. The parties settle before trial with the alleged infringer paying the patent holder $40 million and agreeing to cease sales of its product. In addition to the $40 million payment to the patent holder, there is an implicit $60 million payment to the alleged infringer to cease its sales. In reality, what has occurred is the alleged infringer is permitted to keep a portion of the profits from its sales. Under plaintiffs' analysis, a settlement such as this, where the patent holder forgoes collecting all damages due, would be a *per* se violation. Such a rule would discourage any rational party from settling a patent case because it would be an invitation to antitrust litigation.

Id. at 252.

Ultimately, the Court decided that the settlements should not be evaluated under the per se rule, but denied the defendants' motion to dismiss anyway in order to permit further discovery. *Id.* at 257–58.

Does the *Tamoxifen* decision effectively prevent discovery in reverse payments cases? Should it?

3. In a footnote, the Second Circuit cited "authority for the proposition that when its patent monopoly is ended, the patent holder might actually raise the price on its branded product, rather than lower it in response to generic competition." How likely do you think that is? Why or why not?

4. Over the last century, Congress has regularly amended laws covering food and drug safety in response to court decisions and changing market conditions.

   a. In the 19th century, states attempted to promote safe food and drugs with a patchwork of different regulations, yet the states were largely ineffective at protecting their citizens from drugs imported from other states. "State regulators encouraged, indeed implored, the national government to create a federal agency to aid in regulation . . . ." Mary J. Davis, *The Battle Over Implied Preemption: Products Liability and the FDA*, 48 B.C. L. Rev. 1089, 1100 (2007). The federal government responded with the Pure Food and Drug Act of 1906, 34 Stat. 768, creating the Food and Drug Administration (FDA), a federal agency authorized to condemn and seize misbranded or "adulterated" (containing harmful ingredients) drugs. *See* United States v. Lexington Mill & Elevator Co., 232 U.S. 399, 409 (1914).

   b. In 1938 Congress passed the Food, Drug, and Cosmetic Act (FDCA), 21 U.S.C. § 301 *et seq.*, a brief statute that increased penalties for regulatory violations, mandated that drugs include labels instructing the user in the safe use of the drug, and authorized the FDA to screen new drugs for safety. Jodie M. Gross and Judi Abbott Curry, *The Federal Debate in Pharmaceutical Labeling Product Liability Actions*, 43 Tort Trial & Ins. Prac. L.J. 35, 43 (2007).

   c. In 1962, Congress passed several amendments to the FDCA, including the Kefauver-Harris amendment, which drastically increased the FDA's role in clinical trials, which had to demonstrate both the safety of new drugs and that drugs would have their intended effects. *Pub. L. No. 87-781; 76 Stat. 780 (1962); David A. Kessler and David C. Vladeck, A Critical Examination of the FDA's Efforts to Preempt Failure-to-Warn Claims*, 96 Geo. L.J. 461, 469 (2008). The 1962 amendments did not distinguish between genuinely new drugs and generic versions of drugs; thus, under the 1962 regime, generic drugs had to undergo virtually all of the same expensive clinical trials as the older patented versions. "Even though the active ingredients used in the generic drugs had already been successfully tested and approved by the [FDA] for the brand-name drug companies, the generic drug manufacturers were compelled to run their own separate clinical trials to establish safety and efficacy before FDA review could even begin. Relying on the clinical trials already approved by the FDA for the brand-name drugs . . . could have saved the generic manufacturers time, effort, and money." Marcy L. Lobanoff, *Anti-Competitive Agreements Cloaked as "Settlements" Thwart the Purposes of the Hatch-Waxman Act*, 50 Emory L.J. 1331, 1333 (2001).

   d. The generic pharmaceuticals industry became increasingly vocal after Roche Prods., Inc. v. Bolar Pharm. Co., 733 F.2d 858 (D.C. Cir. 1984). The Court held that generic manufacturer Bolar infringed Roche's patent on a drug because Bolar began clinical testing of the drug's active ingredient to prepare for the time when Roche's patent would expire and Bolar could apply to the FDA for approval to make a generic. Id. at 861. The case did not "break[] new legal ground," but it did highlight the fact that drug patent holders could effectively extend the life of their patent by forcing manufacturers to refrain from beginning the lengthy FDA testing period until after the patent expired. Joseph P. Reid, Note, A Generic Drug Price Scandal: Too Bitter a Pill for the Drug Price Competition and Patent Term Restoration Act to Swallow?, 75 NOTRE DAME L. REV. 309, 313 (1999); Lobanoff, *supra*, at 1333 n.9.

e. Due to public outcry over increasing drug costs and the generic pharmaceutical manufacturing industry's lobbying, Congress passed the Drug Price Competition and Patent Term Restoration Act of 1984 ("Hatch-Waxman Act"). PL 98-417; 98 Stat 1585; Reid, *supra*, at 316–317. Title I of the Hatch-Waxman Act created the Abbreviated New Drug Approval (ANDA) system, which shortened and streamlined clinical testing for generic drugs that were virtually certain to acquire FDA approval because they did not depart significantly from the name-brand drug. Title I contains the thirty-month stay and the 180-day exclusivity provisions at issue in these cases. Title II overturned *Roche,* amending the patent code to allow generic manufacturers to use patented processes or products in order to prepare for generics for FDA approval.

f. In response to Federal Trade Commission (FTC) requests, Congress modified the Hatch-Waxman scheme with Title XI of the Medicare Modernization Act of 2003, which, among other changes, required that if parties settle litigation arising out of an ANDA application, they must file the settlement with the FTC.

g. The FTC and some members of Congress reacted negatively to *Schering*. Senators Kohl, Leahy, Grassley, and Schumer introduced the "Preserve Access to Affordable Generics Act." S. 3582. The relevant portion of that bill read as follows:

> (1) It shall be considered an unfair method of competition affecting commerce under subsection (a)(1) for a person, in connection with the sale of a drug product, to directly or indirectly be a party to any agreement resolving or settling a patent infringement claim in which—
> (A) an ANDA filer receives anything of value; and
> (B) the ANDA filer agrees not to research, develop, manufacture, market, or sell the ANDA product for any period of time.
>
> (2) Construction-Nothing in this subsection shall prohibit a resolution or settlement of patent infringement claim in which the value paid by the NDA holder to the ANDA filer as a part of the resolution or settlement of the patent infringement claim includes no more than the right to market the ANDA product prior to the expiration of the patent that is the basis for the patent infringement claim.

What would be the effect of this legislation? Per se illegality? Can you find any loopholes that would allow reverse payments? Furthermore, is it wise to ban all reverse payments? Does Schering convince you that courts should have a policy to encourage settlement?

FTC Commissioner Jon Leibowitz testified in favor of the legislation, noting that in the fiscal year following the decision in Schering:

> We have seen significantly more settlements with payments and a restriction on entry—seven of ten agreements between brand-name and generic companies included a payment from the brand-name to the generic company and an agreement to defer generic entry.

Prepared Statement of the Federal Trade Commission on Barriers to Generic Entry, Special Committee on Aging, U. S. Senate, Delivered by FTC Commissioner Jon Leibowitz, (July 20, 2006) (Leibowitz Testimony), *available at* http://www.ftc.gov/os/2006/07/P052103BarrierstoGenericEntryTestimonySenate07202006.pdf.

Commissioner Leibowitz also argued that *Schering* was wrongly decided:

> The court purported to assess whether the agreement exceeded the exclusionary potential of Schering's patent, but in doing so, the court relied on the incorrect supposition that the patent provided Schering with "the legal right to exclude Upsher and ESI from the market until they proved either that the . . . patent was invalid or that their products . . . did not infringe Schering's patent," and noted that there was no allegation that the patent claim was a "sham." In particular, the court ruled that a payment by the patentee, accompanied by an agreement by the challenger to defer entry, could not support an inference that the challenge must have agreed to a later date in return for such payment, even if there was no other plausible explanation for the payment.

Id.

Is Commissioner Leibowitz correct that it is an "incorrect supposition" that a patent holder may exclude generics until the generics manufacturers prove patent invalidity or that the generics did not infringe? What would the *Schering* court say in response?

Despite the FTC's urging, Congress did not act on the Preserve Access to Affordable Generics Act. Should it have? Is there a less extreme legislative solution that might motivate Congress to act?

Bibliography of Additional Resources

David A. Balko, *Pharmaceutical Patent Settlements: The Antitrust Risks*, 55 FOOD & DRUG L.J. 321, 335 (2000)

Kent S. Bernard, *Antitrust Treatment Of Pharmaceutical Patent Settlements: The Need For Context And Fidelity To First Principles*, 15 FED. CIRCUIT B.J. 617 (2006)

Thomas F. Cotter, *Antitrust Implications of Patent Settlements Involving Reverse Payments: Defending a Rebuttable Presumption of Illegality in Light of Some Recent Scholarship*, 71 ANTITRUST L.J. 1069 (2004)

Thomas F. Cotter, *Refining The "Presumptive Illegality" Approach To Settlements Of Patent Disputes Involving Reverse Payments: A Commentary On Hovenkamp, Janis And Lemley*, 87 MINN. L. REV. 1789 (2003)

Daniel A. Crane, *Exit Payments in Settlement of Patent Infringement Lawsuits: Antitrust Rules and Economic Implications*, 54 FLA. L. REV. 747 (2002)

Joshua P. Davis & Steig Olson, *Efforts to Delay Competition from Generic Drugs: Litigation along a Seismic Fault between Antitrust and Intellectual Property Law*, 39 U.S.F. L. REV. 1 (2004)

Alan Devlin, *Exclusionary Strategies In The Hatch-Waxman Context*, 2007 MICH. ST. L. REV. 631 (2007)

Stacey L. Dogan & Mark A. Lemley, *Antitrust Law and Regulatory Gaming*, 87 TEX. L. REV. 685 (2009)

Bruce R. Genderson, *Settlements in Hatch-Waxman Act Patent Litigation: Resolving Conflicting Intellectual Property and Antitrust Concerns*, 3 SEDONA CONF. J. 43 (2002)

Stephanie Greene, *A Prescription For Change: How The Medicare Act Revises Hatch-Waxman To Speed Market Entry Of Generic Drugs*, 30 J. CORP. L. 309 (2005)

C. Scott Hemphill, *Paying for Delay: Pharmaceutical Patent Settlement as a Regulatory Design Problem*, 81 N.Y.U. L. REV. 1553 (2006)

Robert J. Hoerner, *Antitrust Pitfalls in Patent Litigation Settlement Agreements*, 8 FED. CIRCUIT B.J. 113 (1998)

Christopher M. Holman, *Review Do Reverse Payment Settlements Violate The Antitrust Laws?*, 23 SANTA CLARA COMPUTER & HIGH TECH. L.J. 489 (2007)

Herbert Hovenkamp, Mark D. Janis & Mark A. Lemley, *Anticompetitive Settlement of Intellectual Property*, 87 MINN. L. REV. 1719 (2003)

Mark L. Kovner, Colin R. Kass, and Avery W. Gardiner, *Applying the Noerr Doctrine in Pharmaceutical Patent Litigation Settlements*, 71 ANTITRUST L.J. 609 (2003)

John E. Lopatka, *A Comment on the Antitrust Analysis of Reverse Payment Patent Settlements: Through the Lens of the Hand Formula*, 79 TUL. L. REV. 235 (2004)

M. Howard Morse, *Settlement of Intellectual Property Disputes in the Pharmaceutical and Medical Device Industries: Antitrust Rules*, 10 GEO. MASON L. REV. 359 (2002)

Christine S. Paine, *Brand-Name Drug Manufacturers Risk Antitrust Violations by Slowing Generic Production through Patent Layering*, 33 SETON HALL L. REV. 479 (2003)

James F. Ponsoldt, *The Antitrust Legality Of Pharmaceutical Patent Litigation Settlements*, 2006 U. ILL. J.L. TECH. & POL'Y 37 (2006)

Laura J. Robinson, *Analysis Of Recent Proposals To Reconfigure Hatch-Waxman*, 11 J. INTELL. PROP. L. 47 (2003)

Julia Rosenthal, *Collusive Settlements: Hatch-Waxman Use or Abuse? Collusive Settlements Between Brand-Name and Generic Drug Manufacturers*. 17 BERKELEY TECH. L.J. 317, 325 (2002)

Jeff Thomas, *Schering-Plough and In re Tamoxifen: Lawful Reverse Payments in the Hatch-Waxman Context?*, 23 BERKELEY TECH. L.J. 12 (2007).

CHAPTER 12

Agreements to Buy and Sell Intellectual Property as an Antitrust Violation

The Supreme Court famously opined in 1950 that "[t]he mere accumulation of patents, no matter how many, is not in and of itself illegal." *Automatic Radio Mfg. Co. v. Hazeltine Research, Inc.*, 339 U.S. 827 (1950). While at first glance the Court's language may suggest that acquisition of intellectual property rights is exempt from antitrust scrutiny, the acquisition of IP can implicate Section One of the Sherman Act when the acquisition is made pursuant to an antitrust conspiracy, Section Two of the Sherman Act if the acquisition results in an illegal monopoly, or Section Seven of the Clayton Act if the acquisition violates merger law. The three sections in Chapter 4 discuss each of these potential antitrust violations.

A. Acquisition of IP as a Conspiracy to Restrain Trade

United States v. Singer Manufacturing, Co.
374 U.S. 174 (1963)

Mr. Justice CLARK delivered the opinion of the Court.

This is a direct appeal from the judgment of the United States District Court for the Southern District of New York, 205 F.Supp. 394, dismissing a civil antitrust action brought by the United States against the Singer Manufacturing Company to prevent and restrain alleged violations of §§ 1 and 2 of the Sherman Act. The complaint alleged that Singer combined and conspired with two competitors, Gegauf of Switzerland and Vigorelli of Italy, to restrain and monopolize and that Singer unilaterally attempted to monopolize interstate and foreign trade in the importation, sale and distribution of household zigzag sewing machines. The District Court dismissed after an extended trial, concluding that the charges were without merit. The United States appealed under § 2 of the Expediting Act, 15 U.S.C. § 29, but has abandoned its claim as to attempted monopolization. *** We have examined the record (1,723 pages) in detail, as is necessary in these direct appeals, and upon consideration of it, as well as the briefs and argument of counsel, have concluded that there was a conspiracy to exclude Japanese competitors in household zigzag sewing machines and that the judgment must be reversed.

I.

The details of the facts are long and complicated. ***

A. As the District Court stated, this action 'concerns only the United States trade and commerce arising from the importation into the United States of a particular type of household sewing machine known as the 'machine-carried multicam zigzag machine." [citation omitted] The zigzag stitch machine produces various ornamental and functional zigzag stitches as well as straight ones. The automatic multicam zigzag machine, unlike the manually operated zigzag and the replaceable cam machine, each of which requires hand manipulation or insertion, operates in response to the turning of a knob or dial on the exterior of the machine. While the multicam machines involved here function in slightly different ways, all are a variant of the same basic principle.

B. Singer is the sole United States manufacturer of household zigzag sewing machines. *** Singer's sales comprised approximately 61.4% of all domestic sales in multicam zigzag machines in the United States in 1959. During the same year some 22.6% were imported from Japan and about 16% from Europe. In 1958 Singer's percentage was 69.6%, Japanese imports 20.7% and European imports 9.7%. Further, Singer's 1959 and 1960 domestic sales of multicam machines amounted to approximately $46 million per year, in each of which years such sales accounted for about 45% of all its domestic sewing machine sales.

C. It appears that Singer by April 29, 1953, through its experimental department, had completed a design of a multiple cam zigzag mechanism in what it calls the Singer '401' machine. It is disclosed in Singer's Johnson Patent. In 1953 Singer was also developing its Perla Patent as used in its '306' replaceable cam machine and in 1954 its '319' machine-carried multiple cam machine. In September of 1953 Vigorelli, an Italian corporation, introduced in the United States a sewing machine incorporating a stack of cams with a single follower. Singer concluded that Vigorelli had on file applications covering its machine in the various patent offices in the world and that the Singer design would infringe. On June 10, 1955, Singer bought for $8,000 a patent disclosing a plurality of cams with a single cam follower from Carl Harris, a Canadian. It was believed that this patent, filed June 9, 1952, might be reissued with claims covering the Singer 401 as well as its 319 machine, and that the reissued patent would dominate the Vigorelli machine as well as a Japanese one introduced into the United States in September 1954 by Brother International Corporation. Thereafter Singer concluded that litigation would result between it and Vigorelli unless a cross-licensing agreement could be made, and this was effected on November 17, 1955. The license was nonexclusive, world-wide and royalty free. The trial court found that Singer's only purpose was to effect a cross-licensing, but certain correspondence does cast some shadow upon these negotiations. The agreement also contained provisions by which each of the parties agreed not to bring any infringement action against the other 'in any country' or institute against the other any opposition, nullity or invalidation proceedings in any country. In accordance with this agreement Singer withdrew its opposition to Vigorelli's patent application in Brazil and Vigorelli later (1958) abandoned a United States interference to the Johnson application which cleared the way for the Johnson Patent to issue on December 2 of that year.

D. While Singer was negotiating the cross-license agreement with Vigorelli it learned that Gegauf, a Swiss corporation, had a patent covering a multiple cam mechanism. This placed an additional cloud over Singer's Harris reissue plan because the Gegauf patent enjoyed an effective priority date in Italy of May 31, 1952. This was nine days earlier than Singer's Harris patent filing date in the United States. In December 1955 Singer learned that Gegauf and Vigorelli had entered a cross-licensing agreement covering their multiple cam patents similar to the Vigorelli-Singer agreement. In January 1956 Singer found that Gegauf had pending an application in the United States Patent Office and assumed that it was based on the same priority date, i.e., May 31, 1952. If this was true Singer could use its Harris reissue patent only to oppose through interference the allowance of broad claims to Gegauf. It therefore made preparation to negotiate with Gegauf, first approaching Vigorelli in order to ascertain how the latter had induced Gegauf to grant him a royalty-free license and drop any claim of infringement. Singer made direct arrangements for a conference with Gegauf for April 12, 1956, and the license agreement was made April 14, 1956.

The setting for this meeting was that Gegauf had a dominant Swiss patent with applications in Germany, Italy, and the United States all prior to Singer. In addition, Singer's counsel had examined Gegauf's Swiss patent and advised that it was valid. Singer opened conversation with indications of coming litigation on the Harris patent, concealing the Johnson and Perla applications. Gegauf felt secure in his patent claims but insecure with reference to the inroads the Japanese machines were making on the United States market. It was this 'lever' which Singer used to secure the license, pointing out that without an agreement Gegauf and Singer might litigate for a protracted period; that they should not be fighting each other as that would only delay the issue of their respective patents; and, finally, that they should license each other and get their respective patents 'so they could be enforced by whoever would own the particular patent.' Singer in the discussions worked upon these Gegauf fears of Japanese competition 'because one of the strong points' of its argument was that an agreement should be made 'in order to fight against this Japanese competition in their building a machine that in any way reads on the patents of ourselves and of Bernina (Gegauf) which are in conflict.' ***

The parties agreed in the first paragraph of the agreement 'not to do anything, either directly or indirectly and in any country, the result of which might restrict the scope of the claims of the other party relating to the subject matter of the above mentioned patents and patent applications.' In addition 'each undertakes, in accordance with the laws and regulations of the Patent Office concerned, to facilitate the allowance in any country of claims as broad as possible, as regards the subject matter of the patents and patent applications referred to above.' The parties also agreed not to sue one another on the basis of any of the patents or applications. Singer agreed not to make a 'slavish' copy of Gegauf's machine and to give Gegauf 'the amical assistance of its patent attorneys for the defense of any of the above mentioned Gegauf patents or patent applications against an action in cancellation.' The agreement made no mention of Singer's Perla or Johnson applications, the existence of which Singer did not wish Gegauf to know.

E. Approximately one week after the Gegauf cross-license agreement Singer met with Vigorelli at Milan, Italy, at the latter's request. *** [In] a May 7, 1956, letter from Mr. Stanford [Singer's patent attorney] to Patent Department employees of Singer *** he said, 'When in Italy we laid careful plans for Gegauf to be advised by a third party that Singer could best handle the patent situation if we owned the Gegauf U.S. Patent.' *** Mr. Majnoni [Vigorelli's patent attorney] reported in June 1956 that he had the 'opportunity of talking to the Patent Attorneys of Mr. F. Gegauf on a number of occasions' concerning 'the question of the advantage of the American Singer Company being in possession of the different patents which might be useful in defence of sewing machines with multiple cams * * *.' He stated that 'the particular character of the question,' i.e., 'the possibility and advantage that the Gegauf patent application in the States be assigned to Singer,' required that the approach be in 'such a way as to prompt an initiative to this end by Gegauf.' He was hopeful that this had been accomplished. Thereafter on September 19 Dr. S. Lando, Singer representative in Milan, reported that Majnoni advised that Gegauf 'is today effectively willing to transfer his patent application in the U.S. to the Singer, without regard or with little regard to the financial side of the matter.' ***

In the summer of 1956 Mr. F. Gegauf, Jr., and his sister attended a sewing machine convention at Kansas City. On returning home they met with Singer (Messrs. Waterman & Stanford) in Singer's office in New York City. Gegauf expressed concern over the number of Japanese machines that he had seen at the convention. Singer again found opportunity to employ the Japanese problem and stressed to Gegauf, Jr., the difficulties of enforcing a patent in the United States—namely, large number of importers, size of the country, number of judicial circuits, etc. Singer emphasized that these all presented problems to the owner of a United States patent. Singer being in the United States could, they said, enforce the patent better than Gegauf could. They asked Gegauf, Jr., whether he thought his father would be interested in selling the patent to Singer. Thereafter, on September 3, Gegauf, Jr. wrote Mr. Waterman that Singer's suggestion had been taken up with Gegauf, Sr., and 'we might be interested in such an agreement.' The closing paragraph says: 'We agree that something should be done against Japanese competition in your country and maybe South America and are therefore looking forward to your early reply.'

Agreements to Buy and Sell Intellectual Property as an Antitrust Violation

*** And on October 24 Singer wrote Mr. Gegauf advising that the United States Patent Office had declared an interference between their patent applications; that their cross-license agreement provided that this interference be settled in accordance with the patent laws of the United States; that 'since * * * interference proceedings are usually time consuming and costly to the parties involved, it would appear that it would be advantageous for us to settle the interference between ourselves rather than to continue the proceeding and rely on the United States Patent Office finally to award a priority'; and finally Singer suggested that the attorneys for the parties in the United States get together with a view to settling the interference. Singer abandoned its interference on March 15, 1957, and the Gegauf claim was taken verbatim from the Singer Harris reissue claim.

Nothing more was done by Singer toward securing the Gegauf application until September 12, 1957, when Singer wrote Gegauf that its Harris application was about to be issued as a patent. It also anticipated that several other patents relating to ornamental stitch machines would soon be issued to it and presumed Gegauf's application would soon be granted. Then followed this paragraph:

> '*** A proper enforcement of these patents may make it necessary to instigate patent suits against each of the importers in the United States, of whom there will perhaps be many. I think you will agree with me that neither one of us alone can protect himself most effectively.'

This letter brought on a meeting of the parties in Zurich on October 16, 1957. Gegauf's position was that, as the trial court found, 'while it had no objection 'to making an agreement with Singer, in order to stop as far as possible Japanese competitors in the United States market,' it was willing to do so only under certain conditions.' [citation omitted] Finally, as the trial court found, Gegauf demanded $125,000 plus certain conditions declaring that it 'was cheap and that it could not go lower since it could get more money if it licensed the invention. Kirker (of Singer) replied that there was no comparison since a sale to Singer was insurance against common competitors and that was why Singer was willing to pay.' ***

Finally Gegauf assigned to Singer its application and all rights in the invention claimed and to all United States patents which might be granted under it for $90,000. The accompanying agreement provided that (1) Singer would grant Gegauf a nonexclusive royalty-free license to sell in the United States sewing machines made in Gegauf's factory in Switzerland; (2) Singer would not institute, without the consent of Gegauf, legal proceedings asserting the patents when issued against Pfaff in Germany or Vigorelli in Italy with respect to machines manufactured in their home factories; and (3) Singer would not make a 'slavish' copy of Gegauf's Bernina machine.

F. The Gegauf patent issued on April 29, 1958, and Singer filed two infringement suits against Brother, the largest domestic importer of Japanese machines. It also sued two other distributors of multicam machines, those actions terminating in consent decrees. Finally, in January 1959, eight months after the patent was issued, Singer brought a proceeding before the United States Tariff Commission under § 337 of the Tariff Act of 1930, 19 U.S.C. § 1337. It sought an order of the President of the United States excluding all imported machines coming within the claims of the Gegauf patent for the term of the patent, naming European as well as Japanese infringers. *** Upon commencement of this action by the United States, the Commission stayed the proceedings, and they are now in abeyance pending our disposition of this case.

II.

First it may be helpful to set out what is not involved in this case. There is no claim by the Government that it is illegal for one merely to acquire a patent in order to exclude his competitors; or that the owner of a lawfully acquired patent cannot use the patent laws to exclude all infringers of the patent; or that a licensee cannot lawfully acquire the covering patent in order better to enforce it on his own account, even when the patent dominates an industry in which the licensee is the dominant firm. Therefore, we put all these matters aside without discussion.

What is claimed here is that Singer engaged in a series of transactions with Gegauf and Vigorelli for an illegal purpose, i.e., to rid itself and Gegauf, together, perhaps, with Vigorelli, of infringements by their common competitors, the Japanese manufacturers. The Government claims that in this respect there were an identity of purpose among the parties and actions pursuant thereto that in law amount to a combination or conspiracy violative of the Sherman Act. ***

[T]he fact that the cross-license agreement provided that Singer and Gegauf would facilitate the allowance to each other of claims 'as broad as possible' indicates a desire to secure as broad coverage for the patent as possible, the more effectively to stifle competition, the overwhelming percentage of which was Japanese. This effect was accomplished, for when the Patent Office placed the Harris (Singer) and Gegauf patents in interference, Singer abandoned the proceeding, thus facilitating the issuance of broad claims to Gegauf.

We now come to the assignment of the Gegauf patent to Singer. The trial court found: (1) that six days after the license agreement was made with Gegauf, Singer proceeded to Italy where a conference was held with Vigorelli. At this meeting two events took place that led to the later acquisition of the patent by Singer. The first was Vigorelli's proposal that Singer, Gegauf and himself act 'in concert against others' in enforcing the patent. This was rejected by Singer's representatives, who said it was best for each 'to prosecute his own patents.' At the same meeting, however, Singer proposed to Vigorelli that it could prosecute the Gegauf patent in the United States better than Gegauf and, after Vigorelli agreed, solicited his help in getting Gegauf to agree to assign the patent. (2) Vigorelli went to Gegauf 'acting as Singer's agent,' 205 F.Supp., at 414, and convinced the latter sufficiently for him to write Singer that he favored the idea of doing something 'against Japanese competition.' (3) Singer replied to Gegauf by letter that an arrangement could be reached 'equally advantageous to both.' (4) Singer went to Europe but was not able to agree on Gegauf's terms and thereafter, in September 1957, wrote the latter that 'their mutual interests required that something be done to protect themselves from the Japanese infringing machines.' (5) Gegauf replied that he would be happy to meet Singer to discuss 'mutual enforcement' of its United States application and the Harris reissue. Then, (6) in the final conferences in Europe Gegauf told Singer that he had no objection 'to making an agreement with Singer, in order to stop as far as possible Japanese competitors in the United States market.' Further, the trial court found that Singer assured Gegauf that 'Singer was insurance against common competitors' and Gegauf's fears that if Singer stopped the Japanese infringements in the United States they (the Japanese) would go to Europe, where Gegauf was not in as good a position to stop them, were unfounded because a greater risk was run in Europe if Singer were not permitted to first stop infringements in the United States. Finally, the court found that (7) Singer was determined 'to drive home the point' that Gegauf stood to benefit more by enforcement of the patents in the United States because the 'Brother Pacesetter' machine, a big selling and patent infringing Japanese-made machine, was in direct competition with the Gegauf machine in the United States. As the trial court put it, '(t)he point apparently reached home'—Gegauf ultimately assigned the patent for only $90,000, much less than its original asking price and much less than Gegauf believed it would realize annually from a license grant. Gegauf's beliefs as to the inadequacy of the monetary consideration were well founded, since Singer received more than twice that amount in a two-year period from the one license it granted under the Gegauf patent. That license, incidentally, was to Sears, Roebuck & Company, which imported machines from Europe.

III.

*** The trial court held that the fact that Singer had a purpose, which 'Gegauf well knew,' of enforcing the patent upon its acquisition, that the enforcement 'would most certainly include Japanese manufacturers who were the principal infringers,' and 'that Gegauf shared with Singer a common concern over Japanese competition' did not establish a conspiracy. [citation omitted] Given the court's own findings and the clear import of the record, it is apparent that its conclusions were predicated upon 'an erroneous interpretation of the standard to be applied. * * *' *** Whether the conspiracy was achieved by agreement, by tacit understanding, or by 'acquiescence * * * coupled with assistance in effectuating its purpose is immaterial.' [citation omitted] Here the patent was put in Singer's hands to achieve the common purpose of enforcement 'equally advantageous to both' Singer and Gegauf and to Vigorelli as well.[8] What Singer had refused Vigorelli, i.e., acting 'in concert against others,' was thus achieved by the simple expedient of transferring the patent to Singer.

Thus by entwining itself with Gegauf and Vigorelli in such a program Singer went far beyond its claimed purpose of merely protecting its own 401 machine—it was protecting Gegauf and Vigorelli, the sole licensees under the patent at the time, under the same umbrella. This the Sherman Act will not permit. As the Court held in *Frey & Son, Inc. v. Cudahy Packing Co.*, 256 U.S. 208, 210 (1921), the conspiracy arises implicitly from the course of dealing of the parties, here resulting in Singer's obligation to enforce the patent to the benefit of all three parties.

440 *Antitrust Law and Intellectual Property Rights*

While there was no contract so stipulating, the facts as found by the trial court indicate a common purpose to suppress the Japanese machine competition in the United States through the use of the patent, which was secured by Singer on the assurances to Gegauf and its colicensee, Vigorelli, that such would certainly be the result. [citation omitted]. Singer cannot, of course, contend that it sought the assignment of the patent merely to assure that it could produce and sell its machines, since the preceding cross-license agreement had assured that right. The fact that the enforcement plan likewise served Singer is of no consequence, the controlling factor being the overall common design, i.e., to destroy the Japanese sale of infringing machines in the United States by placing the patent in Singer's hands the better to achieve this result. It is this concerted action to restrain trade, clearly established by the course of dealings, that condemns the transactions under the Sherman Act. As we said in United States v. Parke, Davis & Co., 362 U.S. at 44, 'whether an unlawful combination or conspiracy is proved is to be judged by what the parties actually did rather than by the words they used.'

Moreover this overriding common design to exclude the Japanese machines in the United States is clearly illustrated by Singer's action before the United States Tariff Commission. Less than eight months after the patent was issued it started this effort to bar infringers in one sweep. As an American corporation, it was the sole company of the three that was able to bring such an action. *** While the tariff application was leveled against nine European as well as the Japanese competitors, the allegations were clearly beamed at the infringing Japanese machines to which Singer attributed the destruction of all American domestic household sewing machine companies save itself. As the parties to the agreements and assignment well knew, and as the trial court itself stated, '(b)y far the largest number of infringers of the Gegauf patent and invention were the Japanese. [citation omitted]

It is strongly urged upon us that application of the antitrust laws in this case will have a significantly deleterious effect on Singer's position as the sole remaining domestic producer of zigzag sewing machines for household use, the market for which has been increasingly preempted by foreign manufacturers. Whether economic consequences of this character warrant relaxation of the scope of enforcement of the antitrust laws, however, is a policy matter committed to congressional or executive resolution. It is not within the province of the courts, whose function is to apply the existing law. It is well settled that '(b)eyond the limited monopoly which is granted, the arrangements by which the patent is utilized are subject to the general law,' [citation omitted] and it 'is equally well settled that the possession of a valid patent or patents does not give the patentee any exemption from the provisions of the Sherman Act beyond the limits of the patent monopoly. By aggregating patents in one control, the holder of the patents cannot escape the prohibitions of the Sherman Act.' [citation omitted] That Act imposes strict limitations on the concerted activities in which patent owners may lawfully engage. [citation omitted]

The judgment of the District Court is reversed and the case is remanded for the entry of an appropriate decree in accordance with this opinion. It is so ordered.

Reversed and remanded.

Agreements to Buy and Sell Intellectual Property as an Antitrust Violation 441

Mr. Justice WHITE, concurring.

There are two phases to the Government's case here: one, the conspiracy to exclude the Japanese from the market, and the other, the collusive termination of a Patent Office interference proceeding pursuant to an agreement between Singer and Gegauf to help one another to secure as broad a patent monopoly as possible, invalidity considerations notwithstanding. The Court finds a violation of § 1 of the Sherman Act in the totality of Singer's conduct, and intimates no views as to either phase of the Government's case standing alone. Since, in my view, either branch of the case is sufficient to warrant relief, I join the Court's opinion***

As to the conspiracy to exclude the Japanese, there is involved, as the Court points out, more than the transfer of the patent from one competitor to another; implicit in the arrangement is Singer's undertaking to enforce the patent on behalf of both itself and Gegauf. Moreover, Singer was the dominant manufacturer in the American sewing machine industry and was acquiring a patent which dominated the multicam field, an aspect of this case which in itself raises serious questions, in my view, and which is saved by the Court for future consideration. [citation omitted]

More must be said about the interference settlement. In 1956, Singer's 'Harris' multicam zigzag reissue-patent application was pending in the United States Patent Office; Gegauf had an application pending at the same time covering substantially the same subject matter, but enjoying a nine-day earlier priority date. [citation omitted] In the circumstances, it appeared to Singer that, between Singer and Gegauf, Gegauf would have a better claim to a patent on the multicam zigzag, at least on the broad and thus more valuable claims. But it was by no means certain that either of them would get the patent. In cases where several applicants claim the same subject matter, the Patent Office declares an 'interference.' This is an adversary proceeding between the rival applicants, primarily for the purpose of determining relative priority. But a party to an interference also can, by drawing additional prior art to the attention of the Patent Office which will require the Office to issue no patent at all to anyone, [citation omitted] prevent his rival from securing a patent which if granted might exclude him from the manufacture of the subject matter. [citation omitted] Gegauf, after Singer approached it to negotiate an agreement before the Office declared an interference, feared that Singer might in self-defense draw to the attention of the Patent Office certain earlier patents the Office was unaware of, and which might cause the Gegauf claims to be limited or invalidated; Singer 'let them know that we thought we could knock out their claims but that in so doing we were probably going to hurt both of us.'

The result was that in April 1956 Singer and Gegauf entered a general cross-licensing agreement providing that the parties were not to attack one another's patent applications 'directly or indirectly,' not to do anything to restrict one another's claims in patents or applications, and to facilitate the allowance to one another of 'claims as broad as possible.' In August 1956 the Patent Office declared the anticipated interference. Singer and Gegauf settled the interference pursuant to their prior agreement: Singer withdrew its interfering claims and in April 1957 the Patent Office dissolved the interference proceeding before it had ever reached the litigation stage. [citation omitted] Eventually the Gegauf patent issued and was sold to Singer as part of the concerted action to exclude the Japanese which is involved in the first branch of the case.

In itself the desire to secure broad claims in a patent may well be unexceptionable—when purely unilateral action is involved. And the settlement of an interference in which the only interests at stake are those of the adversaries, as in the case of a dispute over relative priority only and where possible invalidity, because of known prior art, is not involved, may well be consistent with the general policy favoring settlement of litigation. But the present case involves a less innocuous setting. Singer and Gegauf agreed to settle an interference, at least in part, to prevent an open fight over validity. There is a public interest here, [citation omitted] which the parties have subordinated to their private ends—the public interest in granting patent monopolies only when the progress of the useful arts and of science will be furthered because as the consideration for its grant the public is given a novel and useful invention. [citation omitted] When there is no novelty and the public parts with the monopoly grant for no return, the public has been imposed upon and the patent clause subverted. [citation omitted] Whatever may be the duty of a single party to draw the prior art to the Office's attention, [citation omitted] clearly collusion among applicants to prevent prior art from coming to or being drawn to the Office's attention is an inequitable imposition on the Office and on the public. [citation omitted] In my view, such collusion to secure a monopoly grant runs afoul of the Sherman Act's prohibitions against conspiracies in restraint of trade—if not bad per se, then such agreements are at least presumptively bad. [citation omitted] The patent laws do not authorize, and the Sherman Act does not permit, such agreements between business rivals to encroach upon the public domain and usurp it to themselves.

It should be noted that the present agreement involved a specific promise not to attack one another's patents directly or indirectly in addition to a promise to cooperate in interference proceedings. ***

Comments and Questions

1. Despite the fact that *Singer* is a Section One case, the majority does not employ traditional Section One analysis. Section One cases generally ask whether or not a challenged agreement unreasonably restrains trade. Because the *Singer* case predates quick-look analysis, courts at the time either condemned a challenged restraint as per se illegal or evaluated the agreement under the rule of reason. The majority neither denounces the concerted action among the defendants as per se illegal nor utilizes the traditional Rule of Reason framework in which the factfinder defines the relevant market and determines whether any anticompetitive effect occurred in that market. In short, it is odd that the court found a Section One violation while neither invoking the per se rule nor finding an anticompetitive

effect under the Rule of Reason approach. (Only in Justice White's concurrence is the concept of per se illegality mentioned, and then only in passing.)

Does the market power associated with the patent affect the Section One analysis? If the patent does not confer market power, then would this agreement violate antitrust laws?

2. The Court's opinion never reaches the core patent issues of whether the defendant's patents were valid and infringed. The Court assumes infringement—and perhaps patent validity—without any real inquiry. How might the issue of patent validity affect the antitrust analysis in this case? Should antitrust liability turn on whether the Japanese firms were actually infringing valid patents held by the defendants?

Assume the Japanese firms were infringing the patents. If so, shouldn't they be sued and kept out of the American market? In order to stop the infringement, the patent holders had to consolidate their patents because it was harder for the Europeans to enforce their patents in the United States.

3. In its opinion, the Court devoted much discussion to the fact that Singer preyed on Gegauf's fear of Japanese competition to get Gegauf to sell Singer its patent. From an antitrust perspective, is there anything inherently wrong with either Singer's tactics or its acquisition of the Gegauf patent? The majority suggests that Singer was in a better position to enforce the patent, but is it unreasonably anticompetitive for one company to sell its patent to another company because the latter can more efficiently enforce the patent?

4. Even after their agreement, Singer, Gegauf, and Vigorelli could still compete against each other in the American market. The firms did not divide up the world market or fix prices. To the extent that all three sewing machine manufacturers had nonexclusive licenses and remained viable sellers, why wasn't their agreement procompetitive?

5. The *Singer* Court emphasized the fact that "[t]he agreement also contained provisions by which each of the parties agreed not to bring any infringement action against the other 'in any country' or institute against the other any opposition, nullity or invalidation proceedings in any country." How is that anticompetitive? Did the agreement illegitimately expand the scope of the co-conspirators' patents? If the defendant had refrained from agreeing not to challenge each other's patents, should their arrangements violate antitrust law?

6. The context in which the cross licensing agreement between Singer and Vigorelli is made is critical. The PTO had called for an interference, which is "an adversary proceeding in the Patent Office in which the Office establishes who among competing applicants for a patent is the first inventor under United States law." *United States v. FMC Corp.*, 717 F.2d 775, 776 n. 1 (3d Cir. 1983). During the interference proceeding, the PTO may discover new evidence (e.g., prior art) that may lead to neither party receiving the patent, or the resulting patent being significantly limited in scope. In order to eliminate this risk, Singer and Vigorelli settled their dispute, thus insuring that a broad patent remained.

Largely in response to Singer's agreement with Vigorelli, Congress amended the patent laws to require the parties to any settlement of an interference to file their agreement with the PTO. 35 U.S.C.A. § 135(c). The law provides, in part:

> Any agreement or understanding between parties to an interference, including any collateral agreements referred to therein, made in connection with or in contemplation of the termination of the interference, shall be in writing and a true copy thereof be filed in the Patent and Trademark Office before the termination of the interference as between the said parties to the agreement or understanding.... Failure to file the copy of such agreement or understanding shall render permanently unenforceable such agreement or understanding and any patent of such parties involved in the interference or any patent subsequently issued on any application of such parties so involved....

The law was designed to expose and deter anticompetitive settlements between parties in a patent interference because the parties' failure to file their settlement agreement renders the underlying patents involved in the interference permanently unenforceable. See *CTS Corp. v. Piher Int'l Corp.*, 727 F.2d 1550, 1555–56 (Fed. Cir. 1984). However, the statute does not apply if the parties in dispute settle their disagreement before the PTO actually initiates the interference proceeding. See *CCPI, Inc. v. American Premier, Inc.*, 967 F.Supp. 813, 819–20 (D. Del. 1997). Nevertheless, such settlements could still violate Section One of the Sherman Act. Settlements of patent litigation, including interference proceedings, are often seen as a positive outcome. Settlements generally lead to a quicker resolution of a patent conflict and they save judicial and business resources. How can courts distinguish between efficient settlements and those that unreasonably restrain trade?

B. Agreements to Acquire Intellectual Property and Merger Law

DOJ-FTC Antitrust Guidelines for the Licensing of Intellectual Property § 5.7

5.7 Acquisition of intellectual property rights

Certain transfers of intellectual property rights are most appropriately analyzed by applying the principles and standards used to analyze mergers, particularly those in the 1992 Horizontal Merger Guidelines. The Agencies will apply a merger analysis to an outright sale by an intellectual property owner of all of its rights to that intellectual property and to a transaction in which a person obtains through grant, sale, or other transfer an exclusive license for intellectual property (i.e., a license that precludes all other persons, including the licensor, from using the licensed intellectual property). Such transactions may be assessed under section 7 of the Clayton Act, sections 1 and 2 of the Sherman Act, and section 5 of the Federal Trade Commission Act.

Antitrust Modernization Commission: Report and Recommendations (2007)

Section 7 of the Clayton Act, enacted in 1914 and amended in 1950, prohibits mergers or acquisitions where "the effect of such acquisition may be substantially

Agreements to Buy and Sell Intellectual Property as an Antitrust Violation 445

to lessen competition, or to tend to create a monopoly" in a relevant market.1 Both the substance and the procedures of antitrust merger enforcement have changed significantly in recent decades. These changes are to some extent interrelated.

Before 1976, antitrust challenges typically occurred after a merger already had been consummated; such challenges sometimes took years to litigate. In cases where a court ultimately ruled the merger illegal and ordered the merged firm to divest the acquired assets, it was sometimes difficult to recreate a competitively viable firm—that is, to "unscramble the eggs"—and effectively restore lost competition.

Passage of the Hart-Scott-Rodino Antitrust Improvements Act in 1976 (HSR Act) changed this dynamic. The HSR Act requires firms that propose mergers or acquisitions of a certain size to notify the antitrust agencies and to adhere to certain waiting periods before consummating the proposed transaction. The HSR Act enables the agencies to obtain documents and other information to assess whether to challenge the proposed transaction. Either the agencies can sue to block the entire transaction, or they can seek the divestiture of assets in order to resolve competitive concerns while allowing the overall transaction to proceed. In practice, merging companies most often consent to relief sought by the agencies in order to avoid time-consuming litigation that would delay closing the transaction and the realization of related efficiencies.

As a result, there have been fewer litigated merger cases interpreting application of the antitrust laws to mergers and acquisitions and greater reliance on agency enforcement guidelines and other guidance explaining how the agencies assess mergers and exercise their prosecutorial discretion. This development has made merger enforcement more predictable, due to the issuance of agency guidelines and other guidance and the fact that the enforcement agencies systematically review a greater number of transactions than was the case prior to enactment of the HSR Act. Such expanded review has led to the development of substantial expertise within the agencies. Agency guidelines have served as both a source of guidance to business and a mechanism through which advances in economic learning have been integrated into substantive merger analysis. At the same time, the paucity of litigated court cases has made the merger review process much more administrative in nature.

Over time, the antitrust agencies and courts have moved away from the stringent enforcement standards that prevailed during the 1950s and 1960s, when mergers resulting in a merged firm's market share as small as 5 percent had sometimes been found unlawful. ***

Federal antitrust merger enforcement has evolved significantly since enactment of the Clayton Act in 1914. It has shifted in emphasis from a litigation-based system focused on judicial review of consummated deals to an administrative regime in which two federal agencies, the Antitrust Division of the Department of Justice (DOJ) and the Federal Trade Commission (FTC), review mergers above a certain size prior to consummation. In recent years, the DOJ/FTC Horizontal Merger Guidelines (Merger Guidelines or Guidelines) have described the analytical framework used by the agencies for merger enforcement and guided the agencies' enforcement approach.

The Antitrust Division (under Assistant Attorney General Donald Turner) issued its first set of merger enforcement guidelines in 1968.10 The DOJ explained that its purpose in publishing the 1968 Merger Guidelines was to inform business, counsel, and others of "the standards currently being applied by the Department of Justice in determining whether to challenge corporate acquisitions and mergers." The 1968 Merger Guidelines used concentration within the relevant market as a guidepost for whether enforcement action should be taken, setting thresholds by which merger challenges became more likely as market concentration and the market shares of the merging firms increased.

In 1982 the DOJ issued a revised set of merger guidelines, under the leadership of Assistant Attorney General William Baxter. To measure market concentration, the 1982 Merger Guidelines introduced use of the Herfindahl-Hirschman Index (HHI)$^\Phi$ and established revised concentration thresholds, which are still in

---

$^\Phi$ [Editor:] The current Merger Guidelines explain the process of calculating an HHI—and its significance in merger analysis as follows:

1.5 Concentration and Market Shares

Market concentration is a function of the number of firms in a market and their respective market shares. As an aid to the interpretation of market data, the Agency will use the Herfindahl-Hirschman Index ("HHI") of market concentration. The HHI is calculated by summing the squares of the individual market shares of all the participants. [Footnote 17: For example, a market consisting of four firms with market shares of 30 percent, 30 percent, 20 percent, and 20 percent has an HHI of 2600 ($30^2 + 30^2 + 20^2 + 20^2 = 2600$). The HHI ranges from 10,000 (in the case of a pure monopoly) to a number approaching zero (in the case of an atomistic market). Although it is desirable to include all firms in the calculation, lack of information about small firms is not critical because such firms do not affect the HHI significantly.] ***

The Agency divides the spectrum of market concentration as measured by the HHI into three regions that can be broadly characterized as unconcentrated (HHI below 1000), moderately concentrated (HHI between 1000 and 1800), and highly concentrated (HHI above 1800). Although the resulting regions provide a useful framework for merger analysis, the numerical divisions suggest greater precision than is possible with the available economic tools and information. Other things being equal, cases falling just above and just below a threshold present comparable competitive issues.

1.51 General Standards

In evaluating horizontal mergers, the Agency will consider both the post-merger market concentration and the increase in concentration resulting from the merger. Market concentration is a useful indicator of the likely potential competitive effect of a merger. The general standards for horizontal mergers are as follows:

a) Post-Merger HHI Below 1000. The Agency regards markets in this region to be unconcentrated. Mergers resulting in unconcentrated markets are unlikely to have adverse competitive effects and ordinarily require no further analysis.

b) Post-Merger HHI Between 1000 and 1800. The Agency regards markets in this region to be moderately concentrated. Mergers producing an increase in the HHI of less than 100 points in moderately concentrated markets post-merger are unlikely to have adverse competitive consequences and ordinarily require no further analysis. Mergers producing an increase in the HHI of more than 100 points in moderately concentrated markets post-merger potentially raise significant competitive concerns depending on [other relevant] factors ***.

c) Post-Merger HHI Above 1800. The Agency regards markets in this region to be highly concentrated. Mergers producing an increase in the HHI of less than 50 points, even in highly concentrated markets post-merger, are unlikely to have adverse competitive consequences and ordinarily require no further analysis. Mergers producing an increase in the HHI of more than 50 points in highly concentrated markets post-merger potentially raise significant competitive concerns, depending on [other relevant] factors. Where the post-merger HHI exceeds 1800, it will be presumed that mergers producing an increase in the HHI of use today. More important, the 1982 Merger Guidelines expanded merger analysis beyond concentration thresholds to explain how mergers may raise competitive concerns and to include an assessment of additional factors in the markets of relevance to the merger.

The 1982 Merger Guidelines explained that antitrust law seeks to prevent mergers that could increase the likelihood of collusion, either tacit or explicit, in a post-merger market. Thus, merger enforcement is one of the ways in which antitrust enforcers attempt to prevent tacit coordination in oligopolistic markets. Antitrust law also seeks to prevent mergers that would enhance market power by creating or strengthening a dominant firm, the 1982 Merger Guidelines explained.

To ground the analytical framework of merger analysis more firmly, the 1982 Merger Guidelines set forth a methodology for assessing market definition based on the behavior that would be profitable post-merger for a hypothetical profit-maximizing monopolist. Market definition requires an assessment of substitutes to which customers could turn if the merged firm attempted to raise price. The 1982 Merger Guidelines also introduced the concept that entry by other firms into the relevant market might deter or counteract attempts by a merged firm to raise prices post-merger, thus negating a merger's potential anticompetitive effects.

Several factors, including ongoing economic research that questioned the extent to which market concentration was correlated with reduced competition, prompted these revisions to merger analysis. In 1984 the DOJ made modest revisions to update the 1982 Merger Guidelines with recent thinking and "to correct any misperception that the Merger Guidelines are a set of rigid mathematical formulas that ignore market realities, and rely solely on a static view of the marketplace."

In 1992 the DOJ and the FTC jointly issued merger guidelines, the first time both agencies set forth a unified approach to merger analysis. For market definition, the 1992 Merger Guidelines continued to ask whether a hypothetical monopolist could successfully impose a small but significant non-transitory increase in price. The 1992 Merger Guidelines further deemphasized the HHI thresholds. Although mergers that would increase concentration by a certain amount in a highly concentrated market remained subject to a presumption of anticompetitive effects, the 1992 Merger Guidelines explained that "market share and concentration data provide only the starting point for analyzing the competitive impact of a merger."

Once past this starting point, the 1992 Merger Guidelines emphasized a need to explain how the proposed transaction could harm competition and which factors suggest the likelihood of such harm. The 1992 Merger Guidelines articulated more fully two mechanisms of anticompetitive effects: (1) coordinated effects, that is explicit or tacit collusion, and (2) unilateral effects resulting from the relaxation

---

more than 100 points are likely to create or enhance market power or facilitate its exercise. The presumption may be overcome by a showing that [other relevant] factors *** make it unlikely that the merger will create or enhance market power or facilitate its exercise, in light of market concentration and market shares.

U.S. DEPARTMENT OF JUSTICE AND FEDERAL TRADE COMMISSION, HORIZONTAL MERGER GUIDELINES (1992, as amended 1997).

of competitive constraints on the combined firm due to the acquisition of a close competitor. For each mechanism, the Guidelines outlined how particular factors might be more or less conducive to a particular theory of anticompetitive effects. In addition, the Guidelines refined the analysis of entry to focus on the potential entrants' need to sink costs in a relevant market as a key determinant of whether entry would be "timely, likely, and sufficient" to deter or counteract anticompetitive effects.

In 1997 the FTC and the DOJ revised the 1992 Merger Guidelines to elaborate on the treatment of merger-related efficiencies. The revisions recognized that the main benefit of mergers to the economy is their potential to achieve efficiencies. The Guidelines explained that merging parties must show that the efficiencies resulting from the merger "would be sufficient to reverse the merger's potential to harm consumers in the relevant market, e.g., by preventing price increases in the market."

Although the Merger Guidelines have not been altered since 1997, the FTC and the DOJ issued a Commentary on the Horizontal Merger Guidelines in 2006. The Commentary provides further explication of the Merger Guidelines, including examples of how the agencies have applied them in particular matters. The Commentary does not change the standards of the Merger Guidelines, however. Rather, the antitrust agencies issued the Commentary "to provide greater transparency and foster deeper understanding regarding antitrust law enforcement." ***

U.S. Merger Policy is Sufficiently Flexible to Address Industries in Which Innovation, Intellectual Property, and Technological Change are Central Features

... [T]he common-law development of antitrust doctrine has permitted the courts and the agencies to adapt the contours of the antitrust laws to new economic learning, changes in markets, shifting consumer and business behavior, and numerous other factors. Innovation has driven the U.S. economy since before the passage of the Sherman Act. In some respects, the challenges for antitrust analysis presented by dynamic, innovation-driven industries today are analogous to those presented in past years. Current merger policy has met this challenge. It is well grounded in economics and is sufficiently flexible to provide a sound competitive assessment in matters involving industries in which innovation, intellectual property, and technological change are central features.

As described above, merger analysis has moved away from structural presumptions, which presume increased concentration will likely lead to anticompetitive outcomes, toward a more complex analysis that predicts competitive effects using modern economic tools. Furthermore *** current merger analysis requires an evaluation of procompetitive efficiencies that may result from transactions and an assessment of whether these efficiencies offset the potential anticompetitive effects of a merger. These changes have positioned U.S. merger policy so that it does not currently need substantial change to account for innovation, intellectual property, and technological change.

Merger law and policy—as it has developed through both agency guidelines and case law—has incorporated new or improved economic learning.

'Industries characterized by innovation, intellectual property, and technological change will continue to evolve, and economic learning will progress. Guidelines and case law provide flexible vehicles through which antitrust analysis can continue to develop. In contrast, efforts to adjust antitrust analysis though statutory change would likely prove difficult, and would require continual amendment or pose the risk of codifying economic learning at only one point in time.

A Note on Technology and Innovation Markets

Traditional merger analysis deals with product markets where the firms in a properly defined market each has a quantifiable market share that can be used to measure market concentration (such as by calculating the Herfindahl-Hirschman Index or "HHI"). In established product markets, the conventional analysis is relatively static. However, in dynamic markets, a proposed merger may affect competition for products that do not yet exist. In their *Antitrust Guidelines for the Licensing of Intellectual Property,* the federal antitrust agencies' recognize this and delineate three types of markets that may exist in industries that rely heavily on intellectual property.

DOJ-FTC Antitrust Guidelines for the Licensing of Intellectual Property §3.2

3.2.1 Goods markets

A number of different goods markets may be relevant to evaluating the effects of a licensing arrangement. A restraint in a licensing arrangement may have competitive effects in markets for final or intermediate goods made using the intellectual property, or it may have effects upstream, in markets for goods that are used as inputs, along with the intellectual property, to the production of other goods. In general, for goods markets affected by a licensing arrangement, the Agencies will approach the delineation of relevant market and the measurement of market share in the intellectual property area as in section 1 of the U.S. Department of Justice and Federal Trade Commission Horizontal Merger Guidelines.

3.2.2 Technology markets

Technology markets consist of the intellectual property that is licensed (the "licensed technology") and its close substitutes—that is, the technologies or goods that are close enough substitutes significantly to constrain the exercise of market power with respect to the intellectual property that is licensed. When rights to intellectual property are marketed separately from the products in which they are used, the Agencies may rely on technology markets to analyze the competitive effects of a licensing arrangement. ***

3.2.3 Research and development: innovation markets

If a licensing arrangement may adversely affect competition to develop new or improved goods or processes, the Agencies will analyze such an impact either as a separate competitive effect in relevant goods or technology markets, or as a competitive effect in a separate innovation market. A licensing arrangement may have competitive effects on innovation that cannot be adequately addressed through the analysis of goods or technology markets. For example, the arrangement may affect the development of goods that do not yet exist. Alternatively, the arrangement may affect the development of new or improved goods or processes in geographic markets where there is no actual or likely potential competition in the relevant goods.

An innovation market consists of the research and development directed to particular new or improved goods or processes, and the close substitutes for that research and development. The close substitutes are research and development efforts, technologies, and goods that significantly constrain the exercise of market power with respect to the relevant research and development, for example by limiting the ability and incentive of a hypothetical monopolist to retard the pace of research and development. The Agencies will delineate an innovation market only when the capabilities to engage in the relevant research and development can be associated with specialized assets or characteristics of specific firms.

In assessing the competitive significance of current and likely potential participants in an innovation market, the Agencies will take into account all relevant evidence. When market share data are available and accurately reflect the competitive significance of market participants, the Agencies will include market share data in this assessment. The Agencies also will seek evidence of buyers' and market participants' assessments of the competitive significance of innovation market participants. Such evidence is particularly important when market share data are unavailable or do not accurately represent the competitive significance of market participants. The Agencies may base the market shares of participants in an innovation market on their shares of identifiable assets or characteristics upon which innovation depends, on shares of research and development expenditures, or on shares of a related product. When entities have comparable capabilities and incentives to pursue research and development that is a close substitute for the research and development activities of the parties to a licensing arrangement, the Agencies may assign equal market shares to such entities.

The precise contours of innovation markets—and their use in antitrust analysis—remain controversial. The concept of technology markets has, to date, received greater acceptance by courts. But the theory underlying these alternative markets informs agency decision-making, including mergers between firms with extensive intellectual property portfolios.

Federal Trade Commission In the Matter of Ciba-Geigy Ltd., et al.
123 F.T.C. 842 (1997)

This consent order requires, among other things, the licensing of specified gene therapy technology and patent rights to Rhone-Poulenc Rorer, Inc., to put

Rhone-Poulene in a position to compete against the combined firm. The consent order also requires divestiture of the Sandoz U.S. and Canadian corn herbicide assets to BASF *** or another Commission-approved buyer:

*** Complaint

Pursuant to the provisions of the Federal Trade Commission Act and of the Clayton Act, and by virtue of the authority vested in it by said Acts, the Federal Trade Commission ***, having reason to believe that respondents Ciba-Geigy Ltd. *** and Sandoz Ltd. *** have agreed to merge into Novartis Ltd. ("Novartis"), a corporation, in violation of Section 7 of the Clayton Act [citation omitted], and Section 5 of the Federal Trade Commission Act [citation omitted], and it appearing to the Commission that a proceeding in respect thereof would be in the public interest, hereby issues, its complaint, stating its charges as follows:

I. Respondents

1. Respondent Ciba-Geigy Limited is a corporation *** engaged in the discovery, development, manufacture and sale of agricultural crop protection chemicals, proprietary and generic pharmaceutical products, and animal health products. Ciba participates in the field of gene therapy in the United States through the Chiron Corporation. ***

3. Respondent Sandoz Ltd. is a corporation *** engaged in the discovery, development, manufacture and sale of agricultural crop protection chemicals, proprietary and generic pharmaceutical products, and animal health products. Sandoz participates in the field of gene therapy ***

5. Respondent Chiron Corporation ("Chiron") is a corporation organized, existing, and doing business under and by virtue of the laws of Delaware ***. Ciba-Geigy Limited, together with its subsidiaries, is the largest shareholder of Chiron, holding, not solely for investment, approximately 46.5% of the Chiron capital stock as of September 30, 1996. Chiron is engaged in the discovery, development, manufacture and sale of proprietary and generic pharmaceutical products, including gene therapy products. Ciba has agreed to fund research at Chiron and guarantee its debt, and has the right to appoint members of its board of directors and to veto specified actions of the company. ***

III. The Proposed Merger

8. On or about March 6, 1996, Ciba and Sandoz signed a merger agreement providing that both companies will merge with Novartis Ltd., a Swiss company jointly formed by Ciba and Sandoz to effectuate the merger of their businesses. The total value of the stock involved in the transaction is in excess of $63 billion. The merged entity, Novartis, will control worldwide assets valued at approximately $80 billion.

IV. The Relevant Markets

9. One relevant line of commerce in which to analyze the effects of the proposed merger is gene therapy technology and research and development of gene therapies ***. Specific gene therapy product markets, in which the effects of the proposed merger may be analyzed include the research, development, manufacture and sale of:

   (a) Herpes simplex virus-thymidine kinase ("HSV-tk") gene therapy for the treatment of cancer;
   (b) HSV-tk gene therapy for the treatment of graft versus host disease;
   (c) Gene therapy for the treatment of hemophilia; and
   (d) Chemoresistance gene therapy.

Gene therapy is a therapeutic intervention in humans based on modification of the genetic material of living cells. ***

10. While no gene therapy product has yet been approved by the FDA, gene therapy treatments now in clinical trials offer patients the prospect of significant medical improvements or cures for diseases, particularly in oncology, transplantation and central nervous system diseases. The first regulatory approvals for commercial sales of gene therapy products, expected by the year 2000, will most likely be in the area of oncology. These oncology gene therapy products are anticipated to have sales exceeding $600 million by 2002 and will likely use the HSV-tk gene with viral vectors, the means of delivering the gene. Sales of all gene therapy products are projected to reach $45 billion by 2010, resulting from approvals for additional gene therapies using the HSV-tk gene and other gene therapies. *** There are no economic substitutes for gene therapy products. ***

13. The United States is a relevant geographic area in which to analyze the effects of the merger. U.S. Environmental Protection Agency ("EPA") and Food and Drug Administration ("FDA") regulations impose substantial barriers on the introduction of products which do not meet those agencies' regulations.

V. Structure of the Markets

Gene Therapy

14. The market for the research and development of gene therapy is highly concentrated. Ciba and Chiron together, and Sandoz, are two of only a few entities capable of commercially developing gene therapy products. Only Ciba together with Chiron, and Sandoz control the substantial proprietary rights necessary to commercialize gene therapy products and possess the technological, manufacturing, clinical, regulatory expertise and manufacturing capability to commercially develop gene therapy products. Each is either in clinical development or near clinical development for the treatment of human diseases for which there are large unmet medical needs.

15. Ciba and Chiron together, and Sandoz are the two leading commercial developers of gene therapy technologies and control critical gene therapy proprietary portfolios, including patents, patent applications, and know-how.

16. The market for the research and development of HSV-tk gene therapy for the treatment of cancer is highly concentrated. Only two companies are capable of commercially developing HSV-tk gene therapy products with viral vectors and are either in clinical development or near clinical development to treat cancer. Sandoz and Chiron are the leading commercial developers of these gene therapy technologies and control critical proprietary intellectual property portfolios, including patents, patent applications, and know-how. [The FTC made similar findings for other gene therapies] ***

VI. Entry Conditions

25. Entry into the relevant markets would not be timely, likely, or sufficient in its magnitude, character, and scope to deter or counteract anticompetitive effects of the merger. Regulations by the Food and Drug Administration ("FDA") covering gene therapy products *** create long lead times for the introduction of new products. Additionally, patents and other intellectual property create large and potentially insurmountable barriers to entry.

Gene Therapy

26. Entry into the gene therapy markets requires lengthy clinical trials, data collection and analysis, and expenditures of significant resources over many years to qualify manufacturing facilities with the FDA. Entry into each gene therapy market can extend up to and beyond 10 to 12 years. The most significant barriers to entry include technical, regulatory, patent, clinical and production barriers. The FDA must approve all phases of gene therapy development, including extensive preclinical and clinical work. No company may reach advanced stages of development in the relevant gene therapy markets without: (1) clinical gene therapy expertise; (2) scientific research that requires years to complete; (3) patent rights to all the necessary proprietary inputs into the gene therapy product sufficient to provide the company with reasonable assurances of freedom to operate; and (4) clinical grade product manufacturing expertise, regulatory approvals and capacity to complete clinical development. The necessary proprietary inputs include genes, vectors and vector manufacturing technology, and cytokines, proteins necessary for many gene therapy applications. ***

VII. Effects of the Proposed Merger

31. The effects of the merger, if consummated, may be substantially to lessen competition or tend to create a monopoly in the relevant markets in violation of Section 7 of the Clayton Act [citation omitted], and Section 5 of the FTC Act [citation omitted]. Specifically the merger will:

   a. Eliminate Ciba and Sandoz as substantial, independent competitors; eliminate actual, direct, and substantial competition between Ciba and Sandoz, including the reduction in, delay of or redirection of research and development projects; and increase the level of concentration in the relevant markets;

454 *Antitrust Law and Intellectual Property Rights*

    b. Eliminate actual potential and perceived potential competition in the relevant markets;
    c. Increase barriers to entry into the relevant markets;

Gene Therapy

    d. Combine alternative technologies, and reduce innovation competition among researchers and developers of gene therapy products, including reduction in, delay of or redirection of research and development tracks;
    e. Increase the merged firm's ability to exercise market power, either unilaterally or through coordinated interaction with Chiron, in the gene therapy markets, because the merged firm will have both complete ownership of the Sandoz gene therapy research and development and a 46.5% stock ownership interest in Chiron, the only other firm in a position to commercialize work in gene therapy;
    f. Heighten barriers to entry by combining portfolios of patents and patent applications of uncertain breadth and validity, requiring potential entrants to invent around or declare invalid a greater array of patents;
    g. Create a disincentive in the merged firm to license intellectual property rights to or collaborate with other companies as compared to premerger incentives ***

VIII. Violations Charged

*** 33. The merger, if consummated, would constitute a violation of Section 5 of the FTC Act, 15 U.S.C. 45, and Section 7 of the Clayton Act, 15 U.S.C. 18.

Decision and Order

*** The respondents, their attorneys, and counsel for the Commission *** thereafter executed an agreement containing a consent order ***

Order ***

IX.

It is further ordered, That:

    A.1. On or before September 1, 1997, each respondent shall (i) grant a nonexclusive license to RPR [Rhone-Poulene Rorer] to make, use and sell HSV-tk Licensed Products under such respondent's HSV-tk Patent Rights, in a manner that has received prior Commission approval ***; or (ii) grant a nonexclusive license to make, use and sell HSV-tk Licensed Products under such respondent's HSV-tk Patent Rights to an HSV-tk Licensee that receives the prior approval of the Commission and in a manner that receives the prior approval of the Commission, in perpetuity and in good faith, at no minimum price. In consideration for the HSV-tk License, each respondent may request from the HSV-tk Licensee compensation in the form of royalties and/or an equivalent cross-license.

2. At the option of RPR or the HSV-tk Licensee, Novartis shall, in good faith, within one (1) year of execution of said HSV-tk License, or within one (1) year of the execution of any sublicense to the HSV-tk Patent Rights by RPR or the HSV-tk Licensee, provide to RPR or the HSV-tk Licensee, or the HSV-tk Sublicensee(s), technical information, know-how or material owned or controlled by Novartis as of the date on which this order become final, as is necessary to develop the HSV-tk Licensed Products. Such technical assistance may include reasonable consultation with knowledgeable employees of Novartis and training at RPR or the HSV-tk Licensee's facilities, or the HSV-tk Sublicensee's facilities, or at such other place as is mutually satisfactory to Novartis and RPR or the HSV-tk Licensee or the HSV-tk Sublicensee(s), such consultation to be for a period of time within the one-year period reasonably sufficient to satisfy RPR or the HSV-tk Licensee or the HSV-tk Sublicensee(s).

3. RPR or the HSV-tk Licensee may sublicense, to any HSV-tk Sublicensee, fields that are not being developed by RPR or said HSV-tk Licensee.

4. The purpose for the HSV-tk License is to ensure the continuation of HSV-tk gene therapy research and development for an HSV-tk Gene Therapy product to be approved by the FDA for sale in the United States and to remedy the lessening of competition resulting from the Merger as alleged in the Commission's complaint.

5. Pending licensing of the HSV-tk Patent Rights, each respondent shall take such action as is necessary to maintain the viability and marketability of the HSV-tk Patent Rights and the HSV-tk Licensed Products, including, but not limited to, maintaining in the ordinary course the research and development of HSV-tk products. ***

Any violation of the Consent Order *** may subject Ciba, Sandoz and Novartis to civil penalties and other relief as provided by law.

Statement of Commissioner Mary L. Azcuenaga, Concurring in Part and Dissenting in Part

The order in this matter seeks to remedy the alleged anticompetitive effects of the merger of Ciba-Geigy Limited and Sandoz Ltd. in several product markets ***. I do not concur with the order in the gene therapy markets, in which the Commission has bypassed the obvious, simple and effective remedy of divestiture in favor of a complex regulatory concoction that promises to be less effective and more costly.

Given the allegations of the complaint, the obvious remedy in the gene therapy markets is to require the divestiture of the gene therapy business of either Ciba-Geigy or Sandoz. A divestiture of GTI or of Ciba-Geigy's interest in Chiron would eliminate the alleged anticompetitive overlaps in the gene therapy markets and preserve the competition that existed before the merger. It is a remedy that would be simple, complete, and easily reviewable. Normally, divestiture would be the remedy of choice, and no persuasive reason for a different remedy has been presented in this case.

The order of the Commission instead imposes licensing requirements that do not necessarily preserve the competition that existed before the merger. ***

The order permits Ciba-Geigy and Sandoz to combine their research and development projects in the HSV-tk gene therapy markets and requires them to license their combined intellectual property to an entity approved by the Commission. Instead of preserving the premerger competition between Ciba-Geigy and Sandoz, the order allows the allegedly anticompetitive combination to stand, as long as it clones its intellectual property. Novartis remains free to "combine alternative technologies," as alleged in the complaint. The diversity of research projects is an element of the premerger competition between Sandoz and Ciba-Geigy that is worth preserving, but the order does not ensure that it is preserved. ***

The complaint also alleges a market for "the research and development of gene therapy," in which Ciba-Geigy and Sandoz are "two of only a few entities capable of commercially developing gene therapy products" and in which they control "critical gene therapy proprietary portfolios." In this overall market for the research and development of gene therapy, the merger allegedly would "heighten barriers to entry by combining portfolios of patents and patent applications of uncertain breadth and validity" and "create a disincentive in the merged firm to license intellectual property rights" to others. The remedy for the alleged violation is to require the licensing of intellectual property rights at a "low" royalty rate stipulated in the order.

Remedies that require the Commission to police prices generally are disfavored as highly regulatory, difficult to enforce and likely to distort the normal functioning of the market. They should be particularly disfavored in cases such as this in which a clean, simple divestiture of a gene therapy business is readily available and would not impede consummation of the remainder of the transaction, which is neutral or procompetitive. ***

A divestiture of the gene therapy business of either Ciba-Geigy or Sandoz would resolve the alleged anticompetitive overlap in all the gene therapy markets. It would preserve the competition in research and development that existed before the merger, without compulsory licensing under order, without the mandating by the Commission of "reasonable" fees, and without creating possible disincentives for innovative research.

I dissent from the order in the gene therapy markets.

Separate Statement of Chairman Robert Pitofsky and Commissioners Janet D. Steiger, Roscoe B. Starek, III and Christine A. Varney[*]

We write to respond to Commissioner Azcuenaga's suggestion that the Commission erred by requiring licensing rather than divestiture in order to remedy competitive problems in the gene therapy markets.

---

[*] Editor's note: In the original FTC opinion, this statement preceded Commissioner Azcuenaga's. The order of the statements has been reversed here because the majority is responding to Commissioner Azcuenaga's concerns.

The Commission's complaint in this matter alleges that the merger of Ciba-Geigy Ltd. ("Ciba") and Sandoz Ltd. ("Sandoz") may substantially lessen competition or tend to create a monopoly in several gene therapy markets, including "gene therapy technologies" and "research and development of gene therapies" as well as specific gene therapy product markets. No gene therapy product is currently marketed or even approved by the Food and Drug Administration, and none is expected to obtain regulatory approval until the year 2000. The complaint notes, however, that sales of gene therapy products are projected to reach $45 billion by 2010. The complaint emphasizes that patent rights to proprietary inputs sufficient to provide a firm in this industry with reasonable assurances of freedom to operate are necessary for the firm to reach advanced stages of development. Moreover, the complaint alleges not only that Ciba and Sandoz "are two of only a few" entities capable of commercially developing gene therapy products, but also that they "control the substantial proprietary rights necessary to commercialize gene therapy products" and "control critical gene therapy proprietary portfolios, including patents, patent applications, and know-how." We are left with a post-merger picture of potentially life-saving therapies whose competitive development could be hindered by the merged firm's control of substantially all of the proprietary rights necessary to commercialize gene therapy products. Preserving long-run innovation in these circumstances is critical.

Commissioner Azcuenaga argues that the Commission should have required the divestiture of Ciba's or Sandoz's gene therapy businesses, rather than licensing, in order to "preserve the competition that existed before the merger." Of course, an injunction or divestiture is often the remedy chosen to resolve competition problems arising from mergers and acquisitions. In this case, however, patent licensing not only alleviated the competitive problems but also avoided divestiture's potentially disruptive effects on the parties' ongoing research. ***

Commissioner Azcuenaga asks why the Commission could not have ordered a divestiture of Sandoz's wholly-owned Gene Therapy, Inc. ("GTI") subsidiary or Ciba's partially-owned Chiron Corporation subsidiary. It may be appealing to call for divestiture of businesses acquired only two or three years ago—as both GTI and Chiron were—particularly when one such business is only partially owned. Ciba and Chiron, however, have numerous joint efforts that would have to be unraveled to separate the two companies. And GTI's U.S. clinical development is being closely coordinated with trials that Sandoz is conducting in Europe. Divestiture in this case would not be simple. To divest a business that would have such extensive continuing entanglements with the merged firm—its principal competitor—not only could hamper efficiency but also could be less effective in restoring competition if it led to coordinated interaction or left the divested business at the mercy of the merged firm.

Instead of divestiture, the order requires the merged firm to license gene therapy technology and patent rights to Rhône-Poulenc Rorer Inc. ("RPR"), so as to put RPR in a position to compete against the combined firm. In this way, RPR will be able to continue its research to develop HSV-tk gene therapy products for cancer and graft versus host disease. ***

In short, requiring Novartis to license the key gene therapy patent rights is the best way to maintain competition and preserve the efficiencies gained in this transaction.

Comments and Questions

1. In addition to performing research in gene therapy, both of the merging companies also competed in similar product markets, including those for corn herbicides and flea control products. Because these were product markets, the FTC could measure market concentration using the Herfindahl-Hirschmann Index (HHI). For example, with respect to corn herbicides, the commissioners calculated that the "proposed merger would increase concentration, as measured by the HHI, by approximately 700 points for dollar sales, and by approximately 1000 points for treated acres, to approximately 3000 for sales and approximately 3300 for treated acres." After concluding that the merger created a risk that the merged entity (Novartis) would be able to unilaterally raise price—as well as engage in coordinated action with its remaining competitors—the FTC conditioned its approval of the merger on the parties' divesting the Sandoz Corn Herbicide Business, i.e., selling it to another firm that would compete against Novartis in the market for corn herbicides. Is this the type of divestiture remedy that Commissioner Azcuenaga is advocating for gene therapy research?

2. Commissioner Azcuenaga argued that divestiture "is a remedy that would be simple, complete, and easily reviewable." Do you agree in this case?

3. The majority of commissioners noted "No gene therapy product is currently marketed or even approved by the Food and Drug Administration." Thus, the commissioners treated the relevant antitrust market to be a field of research and development before a marketable product exists. How does that complicate the antitrust analysis?

4. The order required Novartis to provide "technical assistance" to its competitor RPR, "including reasonable consultation with knowledgeable employees of Novartis and training at RPR or the HSV-tk Licensee's facilities." Is it possible for the FTC to insure that this provision is fairly and efficiently implemented? Does this "technical assistance" raise anticompetitive concerns of its own?

5. The order also limited the parties' ability to acquire certain stocks and required the parties to notify the FTC of certain stock acquisitions and to file compliance reports with the FTC. Furthermore, in case the parties did not comply with the divestiture requirements in a timely manner, the order also provided for the appointment of a trustee who would undertake the necessary divestitures on the affected product markets.

CHAPTER 13

Group Boycotts and Concerted Refusals to Deal or License

A. Antitrust Treatment of Concerted Refusals to Deal

Fashion Originators Guild of America v. Federal Trade Commission,
312 U.S. 457 (1941)

Mr. Justice BLACK delivered the opinion of the Court.

The Circuit Court of Appeals *** affirmed a Federal Trade Commission decree ordering petitioners to cease and desist from certain practices found to have been done in combination and to constitute 'unfair methods of competition' tending to monopoly. Determination of the correctness of the decision below requires consideration of the Sherman, Clayton, and Federal Trade Commission Acts.

Some of the members of the combination design, manufacture, sell and distribute women's garments-chiefly dresses. Others are manufacturers, converters or dyers of textiles from which these garments are made. Fashion Originators' Guild of America (FOGA), an organization controlled by these groups, is the instrument through which petitioners work to accomplish the purposes condemned by the Commission. The garment manufacturers claim to be creators of original and distinctive designs of fashionable clothes for women, and the textile manufacturers claim to be creators of similar original fabric designs. After these designs enter the channels of trade, other manufacturers systematically make and sell copies of them, the copies usually selling at prices lower than the garments copied. Petitioners call this practice of copying unethical and immoral, and give it the name of 'style piracy.' And although they admit that their 'original creations' are neither copyrighted nor patented, and indeed assert that existing legislation affords them no protection against copyists, they nevertheless urge that sale of copied designs constitutes an unfair trade practice and a tortious invasion of their rights. Because of these alleged wrongs, petitioners, while continuing to compete with one another in many respects, combined among themselves to combat and, if possible, destroy all competition from the sale of garments which are copies of their 'original creations.' They admit that to destroy such competition they have in combination purposely boycotted and declined to sell their products to retailers who follow a policy of selling garments copied by other manufacturers from designs put out by Guild members. As a result of their efforts, approximately 12,000 retailers throughout the country have signed agreements to 'cooperate' with the Guild's boycott program, but more than half of these signed the agreements only because constrained by threats that Guild members would not sell to retailers who failed to yield to their demands—threats that have been carried out by the Guild practice of placing on red cards the names of noncooperators (to whom no sales are to be made), placing on white cards the names of cooperators (to whom sales are to be made), and then distributing both sets of cards to the manufacturers.

The one hundred and seventy-six manufacturers of women's garments who are members of the Guild occupy a commanding position in their line of business. In 1936, they sold in the United States more than 38% of all women's garments wholesaling at $6.75 and up, and more than 60% of those at $10.75 and above. The power of the combination is great; competition and the demand of the consuming public make it necessary for most retail dealers to stock some of the products of these manufacturers. And the power of the combination is made even greater by reason of the affiliation of some members of the National Federation of Textiles, Inc.—that being an organization composed of about one hundred textile manufacturers, converters, dyers, and printers of silk and rayon used in making women's garments. Those members of the Federation who are affiliated with the Guild have agreed to sell their products only to those garment manufacturers who have in turn agreed to sell only to cooperating retailers.

The Guild maintains a Design Registration Bureau for garments, and the Textile Federation maintains a similar Bureau for textiles. The Guild employs 'shoppers' to visit the stores of both cooperating and non-cooperating retailers, 'for the purpose of examining their stocks, to determine and report as to whether they contain *** copies of registered designs ***.' An elaborate system of trial and appellate tribunals exists, for the determination of whether a given garment is in fact a copy of *463 a Guild member's design. In order to assure the success of its plan of registration and restraint, and to ascertain whether Guild regulations are being violated, the Guild audits its members books. And if violations of Guild requirements are discovered, as, for example, sales to red-carded retailers, the violators are subject to heavy fines. ***

If the purpose and practice of the combination of garment manufacturers and their affiliates runs counter to the public policy declared in the Sherman and Clayton Acts, the Federal Trade Commission has the power to suppress it as an unfair method of competition. ***

Section 1 of that Act makes illegal every contract, combination or conspiracy in restraint of trade or commerce among the several states ***. Under the Sherman Act 'competition, not combination, should be the law of trade.' [citation omitted] And among the many respects in which the Guild's plan runs contrary to the policy of the Sherman Act are these: it narrows the outlets to which garment and textile manufacturers can sell and the sources from which retailers can buy [citation omitted]; subjects all retailers and manufacturers who decline to comply with the Guild's program to an organized boycott [citation omitted]; takes away the freedom of action of members by requiring each to reveal to the Guild the intimate details of their individual affairs [citation omitted]; and has both as its necessary tendency and as its purpose and effect the direct suppression of competition from the sale of unregistered textiles and copied designs [citation omitted]. In addition to all this, the combination is in reality an extra-governmental agency, which prescribes rules for the regulation and restraint of interstate commerce, and provides extra-judicial tribunals for determination and punishment of violations, and thus 'trenches upon the power of the national legislature and violates the statute.' [citation omitted]. ***

Petitioners, however, argue that the combination cannot be contrary to the policy of the Sherman and Clayton Acts, since the Federal Trade Commission did not find that the combination fixed or regulated prices, parcelled out or limited production, or brought about a deterioration in quality. But action falling into these three categories does not exhaust the types of conduct banned by the Sherman and Clayton Acts. And *** it was the object of the Federal Trade Commission Act to reach not merely in their fruition but also in their incipiency combinations which could lead to these and other trade restraints and practices deemed undesirable. ***

But petitioners further argue that their boycott and restraint of interstate trade is not within the ban of the policies of the Sherman and Clayton Acts because 'the practices of FOGA were reasonable and necessary to protect the manufacturer, laborer, retailer and consumer against the devastating evils growing from the pirating of original designs and had in fact benefited all four.' The Commission declined to hear much of the evidence that petitioners desired to offer on this subject. As we have pointed out, however, the aim of petitioners' combination was the intentional destruction of one type of manufacture and sale which competed with Guild members. The purpose and object of this combination, its potential power, its tendency to monopoly, the coercion it could and did practice upon a rival method of competition, all brought it within the policy of the prohibition declared by the Sherman and Clayton Acts. *** Under these circumstances it was not error to refuse to hear the evidence offered, for the reasonableness of the methods pursued by the combination to accomplish its unlawful object is no more material than would be the reasonableness of the prices fixed by unlawful combination. [citation omitted] Nor can the unlawful combination be justified upon the argument that systematic copying of dress designs is itself tortious, or should now be declared so by us. In the first place, whether or not given conduct is tortious is a question of state law ***. In the second place, even if copying were an acknowledged tort under the law of every state, that situation would not justify petitioners in combining together to regulate and restrain interstate commerce in violation of federal law. ***

Affirmed.

Comments and Questions

1. Chapter 7 discussed unilateral refusals to deal, which includes unilateral refusals to license. The cases in this chapter deal with concerted refusals to deal or license. Unlike unilateral refusals, concerted ones implicate Section One of the Sherman Action, which addresses agreements in restraint of trade. As noted in Chapter 2 of this casebook, Section One has a lower threshold for liability than Section Two of the Sherman Act. This means that conduct—such as refusing to deal with another firm or to license—that is perfectly legal when done unilaterally may violate antitrust laws when done pursuant to an agreement with another firm.

2. Did the Supreme Court take a per se approach? What language in the opinion provides the answer to that question?

3. The *Fashion Originators'* Court noted that the "'original creations' are neither copyrighted nor patented." Should it change the result if they had been? Why or why not?

4. The case is decided before the creation and evolution of the Noerr-Pennington Doctrine. See discussion in Chapter 5. That doctrine protects collective action to enforce rights—including intellectual property rights—in some circumstances. Would the defendants' conduct in this case fall within the ambit of Noerr protection?

5. What conduct by the Guild members looks less like policing "copyists" and more like classic cartel behavior?

B. Concerted Refusals to Deal with a Patentee

Jones Knitting Corp. v. Morgan,
244 F.Supp. 235 (E.D.Pa. 1965)

CALEB M. WRIGHT, District Judge.

*** On June 24, 1958 United States Patent No. 2,838.909 was issued to John E. Morgan. The patent application covered a 'knitted fabric'. Morgan claimed that this patent gave him proprietary rights to 'knitted circular thermal fabric and garments' made by using his patent. ***

Morgan's announcement caused consternation among manufacturers of circular knit thermal underwear which imitated the newly patented fabric. ***

Representatives of twelve companies attended [a] meeting. It was decided that an attorney should be retained by the twelve (the plaintiff group) to make a search of the new patent and render an opinion as to its validity. Each company pledged $2,000 to pay counsel fees and to be used to defend any one of the group which might be sued for infringement.

Group Boycotts and Concerted Refusals to Deal or License   463

At this July 16 meeting the plaintiff group also made an agreement which defendants claim produced an illegal boycott. Since it is this boycott which concerns the court here, the offending agreement will be carefully focused upon in the succeeding pages. For the moment, however, it can be stated as defendant, Morgan, sees it:

> (1) No member was to approach Morgan individually regarding a license until after completion of the search, without first consulting with the others, and
>
> (2) in the event Morgan approached any member of the group, that member would do nothing until after he had notified the others in the group.

A second meeting of the plaintiff group was held in New York on September 16, 1958. At that meeting, the attorney who had been retained by the group, Roberts B. Larson, reported that, in his opinion, the Morgan patent was invalid. He posed several courses of action to be considered by those present. The group could take licenses under the patent; continue to make and sell the fabric and wait to be sued for infringement; or bring a declaratory judgment action to have the patent declared invalid.

After hearing their attorney's procedural alternatives, the members of the plaintiff group determined to institute a declaratory judgment action in the name of those knitting mills which had already received cease and desist notices from Morgan. It was further agreed that each company would contribute $5,000 to bring the action and to defend any infringement suit which might be brought against a member of the group. The portentous agreement of the July meeting that no member would negotiate with Morgan without notifying the others was to continue in effect until a judicial decision was obtained.

On September 23, 1958 the declaratory judgment action to declare the patent invalid was brought in this court. At that time the defendants counterclaimed for patent infringement. Subsequently, defendants requested permission to add a second counterclaim charging violation of the antitrust laws and unfair competition. The court granted leave to file an amended answer and counterclaim. On April 10, 1964, the court held the Morgan patent invalid on the basis of indefiniteness of claims, anticipation in the prior art, and lack of invention. [citation omitted] This opinion deals with defendants' second counterclaim.

In the counterclaim defendants charge:

> '* * * the plaintiffs have agreed, combined and conspired among themselves to seek to induce, and have in fact induced, others not parties to this action to join with them in forming a group to boycott and to refuse to deal with defendants, and have agreed, combined and conspired with and among themselves and with and among such others to refuse to accept any license under said Morgan patent and, if approached by said defendants John E. Morgan or John E. Morgan Patents, Inc., to refuse to deal with defendants or to discuss with defendants the terms under which such patent licenses might be granted.'

*** They do not claim that formation of a group to take action against a patent and prorate the expense of litigation is unlawful. However, defendants assert that the agreement went beyond this. They charge that when a group and its members agree to refuse to deal with a patent owner, and act collectively to relinquish or inhibit their individual freedom in doing so, they overstep the lawful boundary of combination.

Group boycotts are per se violations of the Sherman Act. [citation omitted] A group boycott is group action to coerce third parties to conform to the pattern of conduct desired by the group or to secure their removal from competition. Concerted refusals to buy are no less a violation of the antitrust law than concerted refusals to sell. Thus, group action to refuse to take a license runs afoul of the Sherman Act as a group boycott and transgresses § 1 of the Sherman Act. ***

It seems plain that the participants at the July 16 meeting did not contemplate an across the board refusal to deal with Morgan with regard to licenses but only an undertaking to notify the other members of the group should they decide individually to negotiate with Morgan.

Taking this characterization of the agreement, defendants argue that the intent of the parties was inimical to the purpose of the antitrust laws. By requiring such communication, defendants argue, the group hoped to ensure that its members would refrain from dealing individually with Morgan. 'Subjecting each members' individual freedom to negotiate to prior review by the others effectively snuffed out that freedom.'

Plaintiffs argue that the July 16 agreement did not constitute a group boycott. They maintain that it is only reasonable that joint plaintiffs should keep one another advised of individual settlement negotiations. But plaintiffs agreement went farther than that. They agreed not to negotiate with Morgan without first communicating with the others. Their individual freedom was impeded, however slightly, by the promise to communicate before acting. It does not matter that each plaintiff considered himself to be free to negotiate with Morgan. Each had, in fact, circumscribed his freedom by promising not to take a license until he had informed the others, should he contact Morgan or be contacted by Morgan.

Thus a group was formed not only for purposes of bringing suit, but also for purposes of refusing to negotiate with Morgan for licenses. Whether or not the plan was designed to allow the group to force a dissenter back into line- by peaceful persuasion or overt coercion—and whether or not any individual considered his freedom of action impeded, that freedom was in fact impeded. The freedom of each plaintiff to deal freely with Morgan was restrained by the requirement of giving notice.

The Court is aware that the mechanics of giving notice could in fact be an insignificant factor. A given plaintiff's freedom to act might be diminished only by the time and effort necessary to make a phone call or dictate a telegram. Usually when § 1 of the Sherman Act is concerned, restraint of trade by persons acting in concert means undue restraint of trade. *House of Materials, Inc. v. Simplicity Pattern Co. Inc.*, 298 F.2d 867 (2 Cir. 1962). But where the per se rules are in effect, a given activity is condemned out of hand and a court may not sift the reasonableness of the restraint, however minor, or look to justification for it. ***

Here this Court has found a group boycott. Since the Supreme Court has declared such group boycotts illegal per se, this Court must find that plaintiffs have restrained trade in violation of § 1 of the Sherman Act.

[cease & desist remedy since no damages]

However, since this Court has found the Morgan patent invalid, Morgan suffered no damage because of the group boycott. If by some conceptual machination damage could be shown, it would be de minimus. If, absent the group boycott, it is reasonable to assume some one of the twelve would have taken a license and thus paid royalties to Morgan, Morgan would have been unjustly enriched since he did not have a valid patent from which a valid license could stem. ***

Comments and Questions

1. The Third Circuit reversed on the issue of patent invalidity, and held that the patent was, in fact, valid. The district court had disposed of the antitrust claim by holding the patent invalid and concluding that the patentee, therefore, could not have suffered antitrust injury. The Third Circuit revisited the antitrust issue briefly as follows:

> Upon examination of the record, we agree with the fact-finding of the district court [citation omitted] that the twelve member plaintiff group did more than merely enter into an agreement to challenge the validity of the Morgan Patent; that the "group was formed not only for purposes of bringing suit, but also for purposes of refusing to negotiate with Morgan for licenses," and that under the terms of the agreement "the freedom of each plaintiff to deal freely with Morgan was restrained by the requirement of giving notice" of any dealing with Morgan to all the members of the group. We further agree with the district court's ultimate finding of fact that the plaintiffs engaged in a "group boycott," and its conclusion of law "that plaintiffs have restrained trade in violation of § 1 of the Sherman Act." [citation omitted] Since the district court based its denial of damages on its ruling that the patent is invalid, our holding that the patent is valid will require it, on remand, to reach the issue of damages with respect to this phase of the litigation.

Jones Knitting Corp. v. Morgan, 361 F.2d 451 (3d Cir. 1966).

2. Generally speaking, patent pools can be open or closed. In an open pool, third parties can relatively easily purchase a license from the pool. In contrast, in a closed pool, the pool members may agree not to license third parties (or may require unanimous consent of pool members before any such licenses are granted). Should a closed patent pool be condemned as a concerted refusal to license? Why or why not?

3. In what ways was the patent pool agreement between Summit and VISX a concerted refusal to deal?

C. Group Boycotts and Copyrights

Primetime 24 Joint Venture v. National Broadcasting Co.
219 F.3d 92 (2nd Cir. 2000)

WINTER, Chief Judge:

This appeal arises out of an antitrust action brought by PrimeTime 24 Joint Venture ("PrimeTime") against the major television networks, their affiliates' trade associations, independent television stations, and the National Association of Broadcasters. The complaint alleged that appellees violated Section 1 of the Sherman Act, 15 U.S.C. § 1, through concerted, baseless, signal-strength challenges brought under the Satellite Home Viewer Act, 17 U.S.C. § 119 (1995), and through a concerted refusal to license copyrighted television programming to PrimeTime. Judge McKenna granted appellees' motion to dismiss under Fed.R.Civ.P. 12(b)(6) on the ground that their conduct was protected under the *Noerr-Pennington* doctrine. We reverse.

[Editor: The facts of the case were excerpted in Chapter 5, which addressed the *Noerr-Pennington* issues. This excerpt assumes familiarity with the facts presented in Chapter 5.]

The complaint *** alleged a concerted refusal to deal in that appellees agreed among themselves not to license content to PrimeTime, notwithstanding the fact that it would be in their interests, acting individually, to do so. Specifically, the complaint alleged that the NAB, bargaining on behalf of appellees, offered a per-viewer license at a price that it believed to be prohibitive. When PrimeTime immediately agreed to negotiate that price, the offer was withdrawn. Subsequently, according to the complaint, appellees engaged in a concerted effort not to deal with PrimeTime, and the NAB copied a letter to its members telling them not to deal with PrimeTime. The complaint further alleged that the networks discouraged their affiliates from dealing with PrimeTime and that none of the networks have dealt with PrimeTime. ***

Concerted Refusal to Deal Claim

PrimeTime's concerted refusal to deal claim alleged that it attempted to deal individually with each of the affiliated stations, [citation omitted] but that "[t]he NAB and other [appellees] organized a campaign to ensure that no affiliate would break ranks and enter into discussions with PrimeTime," [citation omitted] PrimeTime further alleged that none of the network-affiliated stations has "engaged in any real negotiation" with PrimeTime, that many have sent identical rejection letters, and that NBC and ABC have specifically discouraged their affiliated stations from dealing with PrimeTime. [citation omitted] PrimeTime alleged "a horizontal agreement among direct competitors," a classic per se violation of the Sherman Act. *NYNEX Corp. v. Discon, Inc.*, 525 U.S. 128, 135-36 (1998); *see also Klor's, Inc. v. Broadway-Hale Stores, Inc.*, 359 U.S. 207, 212 (1959) ("Group boycotts, or concerted refusals . . . to deal . . ., have long been held to be [per se antitrust violations].").

Appellees assert, and the district court held, that their conduct "amounted to the rejection of settlement offer, which constitutes protected petitioning activity" under *Noerr-Pennington* [citation omitted]. In so holding, the court relied largely on the Ninth Circuit's opinion in *Columbia Pictures*, 944 F.2d 1525. In that case, plaintiff had alleged that defendants, after they had instituted a copyright infringement action, conspired to frustrate plaintiff's attempts to obtain licenses. [citation omitted] The court granted summary judgment in favor of the defendants on plaintiffs' concerted refusal to deal claim. See *id.* at 1528–33. Significantly, the Ninth Circuit ruled that "[o]n the facts of this case, [plaintiff]'s request for licensing amounted to an offer to settle the lawsuit." *Id.*

However, it is hardly clear from the complaint here, including supporting letters and documentation, that PrimeTime's attempts to deal individually with the networks and stations were only "an offer to settle the lawsuit[s]." Although appellees had made the disputed SHVA signal-strength challenges when PrimeTime sought to deal with the networks and stations individually, PrimeTime's initial offer predated the copyright infringement lawsuits. [citation omitted] Moreover, by proposing to offer each station a fee for each local subscriber, PrimeTime may have been seeking to obtain licenses prospectively, allowing ongoing legal actions to survive. Although coordinated efforts to enforce copyrights against a common infringer may be permissible, copyright holders may not agree to limit their individual freedom of action in licensing future rights to such an infringer before, during, or after the lawsuit. See *Broadcast Music*, 441 U.S. at 19. Such an agreement would, absent litigation, violate the Sherman Act, *see id.*; *NYNEX*, 525 U.S. at 136 (noting that horizontal agreements among competitors are per se antitrust violations (citing *Klor's*, 359 U.S. at 212–13)), and cannot be immunized by the existence of a common lawsuit.

Nothing in the SHVA itself, or its legislative history, suggests a congressional intent to limit the Sherman Act's applicability to such conduct. As noted, although the House Judiciary Committee Report did contemplate cooperation among copyright holders to monitor satellite carriers' compliance with the SHVA, see H.R.Rep. No. 100-887(I), at 19 (1988), reprinted in 1988 U.S.C.C.A.N. 5611, 5622, it specifically stated that the SHVA did not countenance "anti-competitive ancillary restraints," id. at 20, reprinted in 1988 U.S.C.C.A.N. at 5623 ("Although the Committee expects and approves of . . . cooperation in achieving compliance with the [SHVA], any restraints ancillary to such activities would be governed by existing law.").

Although the networks and their affiliates compete with each other through common technology, PrimeTime offers similar services through a different technology that is a common competitive threat to the networks and affiliates. A concerted refusal to license copyrighted programming to PrimeTime in order to prevent competition from it is a boycott that, if proven, violates the Sherman Act. See *Klor's*, 359 U.S. at 212; see also *Broadcast Music*, 441 U.S. at 19.

Comments and Questions

1. If individual copyright (or patent) owners have a right to refuse to license their intellectual property, why should antitrust law care if they collectively decide to exercise their statutory rights?

2. *Jones Knitting* involved non-IP owners—who were potential licensees—allegedly engaging in a group boycott of a patentholder, whereas *PrimeTime 24* involved IP owners allegedly engaging in a group boycott of a potential licensee.

Should the antitrust analysis change based on whether the IP owner is a perpetrator or a target of a group boycott? Why or why not?

The Movie 1 & 2 v. United Artists Communications, Inc.

909 F.2d 1245 (1990)

BREWSTER, District Judge:

The Movie 1 & 2 ("The Movie") appeals a district court judgment dismissing its case against numerous antitrust defendants. This case involves allegations that two motion picture exhibitors in Santa Cruz, California, entered into an illegal film licensing agreement in which 19 national film distributors participated ***. The United States District Court for the Northern District of California, excluding from evidence certain statements offered by The Movie that the court deemed inadmissible, granted the defendants' multiple motions for summary judgment as to all of the antitrust claims. ***

I. Background

Appellant The Movie is a general partnership consisting of Harold Snyder and his two sons, David and Larry Snyder. In February of 1984, the Snyders opened a motion picture theatre in Santa Cruz, California. The two-screen theatre, which has 225 seats in each auditorium, is located in downtown Santa Cruz in a converted storefront which it shares with a moped shop. The Snyders' intent was to exhibit both "commercial" and "art" films on a first-run basis.

The exhibitor defendants in this case were two of The Movie's competitors, UA, which operates five theatres in Santa Cruz with a total of twelve screens, and the Nickelodeon, which operates two theatres with a total of four screens. The distributor defendants included ten major motion picture distributors ("Group I") and nine smaller independent distribution companies ("Group II").

The relevant geographic market in this case is the greater Santa Cruz area ***. The relevant product market is first-run motion pictures. Although theatres can either show "first-run" films or subsequently run "sub-run" films, first-run films provide the greatest grossing potential. The Santa Cruz area has only ten theatres at present. UA's five theatres exhibit primarily first-run "commercial" films. The Nickelodeon's two theatres exhibit primarily first-run and vintage "art" films. The only other competitors in Santa Cruz are two non-defendant independent exhibitors who apparently show primarily sub-run films.

The appellant alleges that The Movie was unable to obtain licenses to first-run commercial or art films from the defendant distributors, who concertedly refused to deal with it. Appellant alleges that the distributors cooperated in an illegal "split agreement" between UA and the Nickelodeon, whereby nearly all first-run commercial films were licensed to UA and nearly all first-run art films were licensed to the Nickelodeon. A split agreement is an exhibitor agreement which divides a normally competitive market by allocating films to particular members with the understanding that there will be no bidding among members for licensing rights to the films assigned. [citation omitted]

Appellant alleges that the split agreement in this case was part of a boycott against The Movie, which had the purpose of eliminating it as a competitor, a restraint of trade in violation of section 1 of the Sherman Act, 15 U.S.C. § 1 (1982).

***

On December 22, 1987, the district court, after excluding several items of evidence which it deemed inadmissible, granted the defendants' multiple motions for summary judgment as to *** the section 1 claim[] ***.

III. Discussion

B. Section 1 Claims: Agreement in Restraint of Trade

Section 1 of the Sherman Act prohibits "[e]very contract, combination ... or conspiracy, in restraint of trade." 15 U.S.C. § 1 (1982). Appellant's section 1 claims allege an illegal agreement between the exhibitors and the distributors in the form of a "group boycott" aimed at excluding The Movie from the Santa Cruz theatre market.

The Supreme Court has emphasized, however, that the Sherman Act does not restrict "the long recognized right of a trader ... engaged in an entirely private business, freely to exercise his own independent discretion as to the parties with whom he will deal." *United States v. Colgate & Co.*, 250 U.S. 300, 307 (1919). Because of a supplier's right to choose his customers and set his own terms, "antitrust plaintiffs are required to do more than merely allege conspiracy and unequal treatment in order to take a case to trial." *Harkins Amusement Enterprises v. General Cinema Corp.*, 850 F.2d 477, 483 (9th Cir.1988). According to the law of this circuit, once a defendant rebuts the allegations of conspiracy with "probative evidence supporting an alternative interpretation of a defendant's conduct," the plaintiff must come forward with specific factual support of its conspiracy allegations to avoid summary judgment. *Barnes v. Arden Mayfair, Inc.*, 759 F.2d 676, 680 (9th Cir.1985).

The defendants in this case did offer some evidence from which a trier of fact could reasonably have found that their refusal to deal with The Movie was based on legitimate and sound business judgment. Following such a showing of a plausible and justifiable reason for a defendant's conduct, a plaintiff must provide specific factual support for its allegations of conspiracy which tends to show that the defendant was not acting independently. Accordingly, we examine appellant's evidence in support of its conspiracy allegations.

1. The Distributor Defendants

The distributors possessed an absolute right to refuse to license films to The Movie as long as their decisions were based upon independent business judgment. *Colgate*, 250 U.S. at 307. The distributors presented evidence to the trial court from which a trier of fact could find that the decision to license films to UA and the

Nickelodeon rather than to The Movie was based on such factors as the perceived inferiority and consequently lower grossing potential of The Movie's theatre house and the allegedly inferior terms offered in The Movie's bids. Thus, under Barnes, the defendants rebutted the allegations of conspiracy, and it was incumbent upon the plaintiff to come forward with specific factual support of its conspiracy claim. We believe the plaintiff did present ample evidence to rebut defendants' evidence of independent business decisions and to support plaintiff's allegations of an illegal boycott. We, therefore, reverse the trial court's summary adjudication of the section 1 claims against all of the Group I distributor defendants.

Appellees contend that the lower court's record contained no admissible evidence or assertion of any defendant distributors' having received superior bids from The Movies and having rejected them in favor of defendant exhibitors. ***While it could be argued, as appellees also urge here, that none of the appellant's bids were superior, that determination is an issue of fact which should be decided by summary judgment only if the trial court can find that no reasonable jury could find on that question in favor of the non-moving party. [citation omitted] Some of the bids were arguably superior.

There was evidence before the trial court indicating that these distributors had refused to even receive bids from The Movie until they received threatening correspondence from The Movie's attorney. The distributors have cited no legitimate business justification for a refusal to even receive an exhibitor's bid, nor can this court conceive of how such conduct could reflect sound business judgment. To the contrary, such behavior raises the inference that the distributors would not have licensed films to The Movie even if presented with consistent lucrative bids superior to those of the other exhibitors. This circuit has recognized that a distributor's repeated rejection of lucrative bids in an anticompetitive market environment raises an inference of conspiratorial antitrust conduct. See *Harkins*, 850 F.2d at 484. The evidence that UA reaped roughly 96.9% of all revenues from first-run commercial films shown in Santa Cruz reflects an anticompetitive market situation. In such an environment, the distributors' refusal to even receive a new exhibitor's bids "tends to exclude the possibility of independent action," and at least raises an issue of fact as to their participation in the alleged boycott.

This circuit has recognized that it is not necessary for a plaintiff to show an explicit agreement among defendants in support of a Sherman Act conspiracy, and that "concerted action may be inferred from circumstantial evidence of the defendant's conduct and course of dealings." *Harkins*, 850 F.2d at 477 (quoting *Dimidowich v. Bell & Howell*, 803 F.2d 1473, 1479 (9th Cir.1986). We conclude, therefore, that appellant did present sufficient evidence to present a triable issue on the section 1 claim of conspiracy to restrain trade in the form of a group boycott of appellant through split agreements. Our conclusion is reached in the context of evidence before the trial court of awards of films without any bids at all, bid negotiations excluding appellant, bid-tipping, adjustments to licensing agreements made to UA regularly, but to appellant rarely, if ever, and the statistics of film licenses awarded. The appellant should, therefore, have been allowed to proceed to trial on the section 1 claims against the Group I distributors. We accordingly reverse the trial court's grant of summary judgment as to these defendants.

2. Defendant Exhibitor United Artists

The appellant also presented evidence to the trial court which raises a material issue of fact as to UA's participation in an agreement in restraint of trade. [Some] statements, which the court erroneously excluded, provided some evidence in support of the allegations of UA's participation in an illegal split agreement. The absence of any evidence that UA and the Nickelodeon ever bid against each other for a film during the relevant period, as well as the pattern evidence indicating that UA had 96.9% of the revenue from first-run commercial films which played in Santa Cruz during the relevant period while Nickelodeon had 69.9% of the revenue from first-run art films shown during that period, provided further evidence in support of the allegations of participation in an illegal split agreement.

Appellees first argue that it is impossible to classify types of films. They admit, however, that the exhibitors in this lawsuit did differ in the types of films they preferred to play: the Nickelodeon specializing in foreign and more sophisticated subject films, UATC and Scotts Valley playing mostly general audience films. Appellees' contention, however, that no "pattern" existed besides the independent, legitimate business, and artistic decisions of the exhibitors misses the point. The question is not whether an individual exhibitor has the "right" to specialize; it cannot be disputed that every exhibitor has the right, and perhaps even laudable business acumen to "specialize" in one type of film, such as "art" or "commercial." The relevant inquiry, rather, is whether the defendant exhibitors conspired to exclude any and all other entrants into the movie exhibition market. For this, the statistical pattern evidence, along with other evidence, contributes to the raising of a material issue of fact.

Appellant further offered evidence of specific instances where UA advertised films prior to the completion of bidding, allegedly indicating confidence and ultimate knowledge that it would obtain the films. Although UA argues that it is a common practice in the film industry to obtain and display promotional posters for films that have not yet been licensed, UA offered no explanation for the evidence that, in addition to displaying posters, on at least one occasion it had placed an advertisement in a local newspaper advertising a film it had not yet been awarded.

Appellant also presented to the trial court a letter sent to Hal Snyder from The Movie's film buyer, documenting an instance where a non-defendant distributor had agreed to license a particular film to The Movie, assuring the film buyer that The Movie could have it because UA had shown no interest in the film in northern California. The distributor later informed The Movie that it was canceling its agreement in order to license the film to UA. This evidence suggests that UA wielded such power in the Santa Cruz market that a distributor would rather breach an agreement with The Movie than deny UA a film.

Viewing the above evidence and the inferences that may be drawn therefrom collectively and in the light most favorable to the appellant, we cannot say that there was an absence of any genuine issue of material fact. Therefore, UA was not entitled to prevail as a matter of law. The summary adjudication of the section 1 claims in favor of UA must be reversed.

3. Evaluation of the Unreasonable Restraint of Trade Allegations Under the "Per Se" Rule or the "Rule of Reason"

To the extent that the district court held that a split agreement should be evaluated under the rule of reason because it constituted a non-price restraint of trade, the court erred. It should have applied the illegal per se rule.

This circuit has recently ruled on this issue. In *Harkins*, 850 F.2d at 486, we noted that per se treatment is appropriate "where joint efforts by firms disadvantage competitors by inducing suppliers or customers to deny relationships the competitors need in order to compete." We concluded that an alleged split agreement, if proven, would be illegal per se. Appellees dispute the appellant's reliance on *Harkins* on several grounds. First, they claim that the "per se rule" in that case was only dicta. Second, they claim that all cases finding per se treatment appropriate for a split agreement have demonstrated that the agreement was to depress film rentals to the distributors, eliminate guarantees to those distributors, or otherwise affect the terms of licensing for films, i.e., antitrust injury. Appellees contend that appellants have failed to even allege these factors. One of the cases relied on in *Harkins*, appellees point out, *Northwest Wholesale Stationers, Inc. v. Pacific Stationery & Printing Co.*, 472 U.S. 284 (1985), supports the proposition that a per se analysis is not appropriate where no antitrust injury has been alleged. The United States Supreme Court in that case found that plaintiff failed to prove an antitrust violation when it demonstrated injury to itself but not to competition. *Northwest Wholesale Stationers*, 472 U.S. at 297 n. 9.

In the instant case, however, the split agreement is allegedly employed to restrict entry of other exhibitors into the Santa Cruz market for any film. If so, such conduct would cause antitrust injury in the form of a boycott, a conspiracy in restraint of trade in violation of 15 U.S.C. § 1. In fact, in *Northwest Wholesale Stationers*, 472 U.S. at 294, the court opined that in cases of group boycotts that directly or indirectly cut off necessary access to customers or suppliers, the per se rule applies because the likelihood of antitrust injury is clear.

On remand, the trial court should instruct the jury accordingly. ***

Comments and Questions

1. In *Auwood* in Chapter 11, the court treated a movie split as a form of market allocation. Here, the court evaluated a movie split as a form of group boycott. Is one court correct and the other wrong? Does the characterization matter? How does the characterization affect the antitrust analysis?

If you were representing the plaintiff, would you characterize the claim as a market allocation scheme or as a group boycott? Why?

2. Why are the distributors participating in this alleged conspiracy?

PART FOUR

THE ANTITRUST IMPLICATIONS OF VERTICAL AGREEMENTS INVOLVING INTELLECTUAL PROPERTY

CHAPTER 14

Vertical Price Restraints and Intellectual Property

The cases in this chapter illustrate the evolution of thinking on vertical price restraints generally, as well as in the context of intellectual property owners, who may have more latitude to impose vertical price restraints. In the context of real products, vertical price fixing is often called resale price maintenance. However, this nomenclature may not accurately describe licensor-licensee relationships in which there is not technically a sale, but instead a license.

Until recently, the first excerpted case, *Dr. Miles*, represented the state of the law. However, in its 2007 *Leegin* decision, the Supreme Court reversed the 96-year-old precedent. Still, *Dr. Miles* informed vertical price restraint jurisprudence for almost a century and it remains an important historical decision. It may continue to influence judicial thinking post-*Leegin*.

A. The Foundation of Antitrust's Treatment of Vertical Price Restraints

Dr. Miles Medical Co. v. John D. Park & Sons Co.
220 U.S. 373 (1911)

Statement by Mr. Justice Hughes:

*** The complainant, Dr. Miles Medical Company, an Indiana corporation, is engaged in the manufacture and sale of proprietary medicines, prepared by means of secret methods and formulas, and identified by distinctive packages, labels, and trademarks. It has established an extensive trade throughout the United States and in certain foreign countries. It has been its practice to sell its medicines to jobbers and wholesale druggists, who in turn sell to retail druggists for sale to the consumer. In the case of each remedy, it has fixed not only the price of its own sales to jobbers

476 Antitrust Law and Intellectual Property Rights

and wholesale dealers, but also the wholesale and retail prices. The bill alleged that most of its sales were made through retail druggists, and that the demand for its remedies largely depended upon their good will and commendation, and their ability to realize a fair profit; that certain retail establishments, particularly those known as department stores, had inaugurated a 'cutrate' or 'cut-price' system which had caused 'much confusion, trouble, and damage' to the complainant's business, and 'injuriously affected the reputation' and 'depleted the sales' of its remedies; that this injury resulted 'from the fact that the majority of retail druggists as a rule cannot, or believe that they cannot, realize sufficient profits' by the sale of the medicines 'at the cut-prices announced by the cut-rate and department stores,' and therefore are 'unwilling to, and do not keep' the medicines 'in stock,' or, 'if kept in stock, do not urge or favor sales thereof, but endeavor to foist off some similar remedy or substitute, and from the fact that in the public mind an article advertised or announced at 'cut' or 'reduced' price from the established price suffers loss of reputation and becomes of inferior value and demand.'

***The defendant is a Kentucky corporation conducting a wholesale drug business. The bill alleged that the defendant had formerly dealt with the complainant, and had full knowledge of all the facts relating to the trade in its medicines; that it had been requested, and refused, to enter into the wholesale contract required by the complainant; that in the city of Cincinnati, Ohio, where the defendant conducted a wholesale drug store, there were a large number of wholesale and retail druggists who had made contracts of the sort described, with the complainant, and kept its medicines on sale pursuant to the agreed terms and conditions. It was charged that the defendant, 'in combination and conspiracy with a number of wholesale and retail dealers in drugs and proprietary medicines, who have not entered into said wholesale and retail contracts' required by the complainant's system, and solely for the purpose of selling the remedies to dealers 'to be advertised, sold, and marketed at cut rates,' and 'to thus attract and secure custom and patronage for other merchandise, and not for the purpose of making or receiving a direct money profit' from the sales of the remedies, had unlawfully and fraudulently procured them from the complainant's 'wholesale and retail agents' by means 'of false and fraudulent representations and statements, and by surreptitious and dishonest methods, and by persuading and inducing, directly and indirectly,' a violation of their contracts. ***

Mr. Justice Hughes, after making the above statement, delivered the opinion of the court:

The complainant, a manufacturer of proprietary medicines which are prepared in accordance with secret formulas, presents by its bill a system, carefully devised, by which it seeks to maintain certain prices fixed by it for all the sales of its products, both at wholesale and retail. Its purpose is to establish minimum prices at which sales shall be made by its vendees and by all subsequent purchasers who traffic in its remedies. Its plan is thus to govern directly the entire trade in the medicines it manufactures, embracing interstate commerce as well as commerce within the state respectively. To accomplish this result it has adopted two forms of restrictive agreements limiting trade in the articles to those who become parties to one or the other. The one sort of contract, known as 'Consignment Contract—Wholesale,' has been made with over four hundred jobbers and wholesale dealers, and the other described as 'Retail Agency Contract,' with twenty-five thousand retail dealers in the United States.

The defendant is a wholesale drug concern which has refused to enter into the required contract, and is charged with procuring medicines for sale at 'cut prices' by inducing those who have made the contracts to violate the restrictions. The complainant invokes the established doctrine that an actionable wrong is committed by one who maliciously interferes with a contract between two parties, and induces one of them to break that contract, to the injury of the other, and that, in the absence of an adequate remedy at law, equitable relief will be granted. [citation omitted]

The principal question is as to the validity of the restrictive agreements. *** That these agreements restrain trade is obvious. That, having been made, as the bill alleges, with 'most of the jobbers and wholesale druggists and a majority of the retail druggists of the country,' and having for their purpose the control of the entire trade, they relate directly to interstate as well as intrastate trade, and operate to restrain trade or commerce among the several states, is also clear. [citation omitted]

But it is insisted that the restrictions are not invalid either at common law or under the act of Congress of July 2, 1890, [the Sherman Act], upon the following grounds, which may be taken to embrace the fundamental contentions for the complainant: (1) That the restrictions are valid because they relate to proprietary medicines manufactured under a secret process; and (2) that, apart from this, a manufacturer is entitled to control the prices on all sales of his own products.

First. The first inquiry is whether there is any distinction, with respect to such restrictions as are here presented, between the case of an article manufactured by the owner of a secret process and that of one produced under ordinary conditions. The complainant urges an analogy to right secured by letters patent. *E. Bement & Sons v. National Harrow Co.* 186 U. S. 70. In the case cited, there were licenses for the manufacture and sale of articles covered by letters patent, with stipulations as to the prices at which the licensee should sell. The court said, referring to the act of July 2, 1890: 'But that statute clearly does not refer to that kind of a restraint of interstate commerce which may arise from reasonable and legal conditions imposed upon the assignee or licensee of a patent by the owner thereof, restricting the terms upon which the article may be used and the price to be demanded therefor. Such a construction of the act we have no doubt was never contemplated by its framers.'

But whatever rights the patentee may enjoy are derived from statutory grant under the authority conferred by the Constitution. This grant is based upon public considerations. The purpose of the patent law is to stimulate invention by protecting inventors for a fixed time in the advantages that may be derived from exclusive manufacture, use, and sale. ***

The complainant has no statutory grant. So far as appears, there are no letters patent relating to the remedies in question. The complainant has not seen fit to make the disclosure required by the statute, and thus to secure the privileges it confers. Its case lies outside the policies of the patent law, and the extent of the right which that law secures is not here involved or determined. ***

Second. We come, then, to the second question,—whether the complainant, irrespective of the secrecy of its process, is entitled to maintain the restrictions by virtue of the fact that they relate to products of its own manufacture.

The basis of the argument appears to be that, as the manufacturer may make and sell, or not, as he chooses, he may affix conditions as to the use of the article or as to the prices at which purchasers may dispose of it. The propriety of the restraint is sought to be derived from the liberty of the producer.

But because a manufacturer is not bound to make or sell, it does not follow in case of sales actually made he may impose upon purchasers every sort of restriction. Thus, a general restraint upon alienation is ordinarily invalid. ***

With respect to contracts in restraint of trade, the earlier doctrine of the common law has been substantially modified in adaptation to modern conditions. But the public interest is still the first consideration. To sustain the restraint, it must be found to be reasonable both with respect to the public and to the parties, and that it is limited to what is fairly necessary, in the circumstances of the particular case, for the protection of the covenantee. Otherwise restraints of trade are void as against public policy. *** The question is whether, under the particular circumstances of the case and the nature of the particular contract involved in it, the contract is, or is not, unreasonable. *** But agreements or combinations between dealers, having for their sole purpose the destruction of competition and the fixing of prices, are injurious to the public interest and void. They are not saved by the advantages which the participants expect to derive from the enhanced price to the consumer. [citation omitted]

The complainant's plan falls within the principle which condemns contracts of this class. It, in effect, creates a combination for the prohibited purposes. No distinction can properly be made by reason of the particular character of the commodity in question. It is not entitled to special privilege or immunity. It is an article of commerce, and the rules concerning the freedom of trade must be held to apply to it. Nor does the fact that the margin of freedom is reduced by the control of production make the protection of what remains, in such a case, a negligible matter. And where commodities have passed into the channels of trade and are owned by dealers, the validity of agreements to prevent competition and to maintain prices is not to be determined by the circumstance whether they were produced by several manufacturers or by one, or whether they were previously owned by one or by many. The complainant having sold its product at prices satisfactory to itself, the public is entitled to whatever advantage may be derived from competition in the subsequent traffic. ***

[Dissent by Mr. Justice Holmes omitted]

Comments and Questions

1. What rationale did Dr. Miles provide for why it needed to impose resale price maintenance? Is it persuasive?

2. The Court never uses the phrase "per se," but subsequent courts, including the Supreme Court itself, interpreted *Dr. Miles* as holding that resale price maintenance is illegal per se. Why? What language in the case suggests a per se rule against vertical price fixing?

3. Although *Dr. Miles* created the per se rule against resale price maintenance, the case is actually not an antitrust case. Rather, Dr. Miles was suing John D. Park & Sons for tortious interference with contract because Park was inducing Dr. Miles' customers into breaching their contracts by selling products to Park, who then resold them outside of the control of Dr. Miles' resale price maintenance scheme. Park defended itself by arguing that it could not be liable for tortious interference because the contracts interfered with were illegal due to their resale price maintenance provisions.

4. The Court states "a general restraint upon alienation is ordinarily invalid." What is a restraint upon alienation?

The concern about restraints on alienation exists independent of antitrust law. In general, restraints on alienation do not necessarily affect the competitiveness of markets. For example, in a market with twenty sellers of equal market share, if one seller attempted to restrict its customers from reselling, competition would not be injured despite the restraint on alienation. Of course, a horizontal agreement to impose restraints on alienation would probably violate Section One of the Sherman Act.

5. Dr. Miles claimed that its medicines were protected by trade secret. Under trade secret law, an innovator's secrets are protected against misappropriation (so long as the innovator implements reasonable safeguards). What does resale price maintenance have to do with trade secrets? Does fixing the resale price of a product made pursuant to a secret process help protect that secrecy?

6. Dr. Miles' products were not protected by patents, but the Court notes that they were protected by trademarks. Do you think that the *Dr. Miles'* per se rule against resale price maintenance should apply to trademarked goods? Why or why not?

The issue of fixing the resale price of trademarked goods is discussed later in this chapter.

7. *Dr. Miles* seems to suggest that resell price maintenance is not okay with copyrighted works that may be okay with patented products. Even if there is a statutory basis for the distinction, is there any policy reason to treat resale price maintenance differently between copyrighted works and patented products?

8. Chapter 3 noted that in the early Supreme Court case of *E. Bement & Sons v. National Harrow*, 186 U.S. 70 (1902), the Court interpreted antitrust law in a manner that was highly deferential to patent owners. This was certainly true with respect to a patentee's effort to fix the resale price charged by its licensees. Writing for a

unanimous Court in *Bement*, Justice Peckham opined: "The owner of a patented article can, of course, charge such price as he may choose, and the owner of a patent may assign it, or sell the right to manufacture and sell the article patented, upon the condition that the assignee shall charge a certain amount for such article."

Can you reconcile *Bement* and *Dr. Miles*?

Both the *Bement* and *Dr. Miles* opinions have been controversial in their own ways. Respected scholars have challenged the Court's reasoning in *Bement*. For example, Professor Herbert Hovenkamp observed: "The Court's logic was bizarre. If Ford owns three automobile production plants, it has the legal right both to produce cars in the plants and to set their price. But it does not follow that Ford could sell one of the plants to Chrysler while "retaining" the right to set the price on the cars that Chrysler made in that plant. Once the plant had passed into Chrysler's hands, any attempt by Ford to set the price of Chrysler cars would be naked price-fixing." HERBERT HOVENKAMP, 256 ANTITRUST ENTERPRISE (2005).

Criticism of the *Dr. Miles* opinion is presented in the *Leegin* case, excerpted later in this chapter, in which the Supreme Court reversed *Dr. Miles*.

B. *General Electric* and the Ability of Patent Owners to Set Resale Prices

United States v. Line Materials Co.
333 U.S. 287 (1948)

Mr. Justice REED delivered the opinion of the Court.

The United States sought an injunction under §§ 1 and 4 of the Sherman Act in the District Court against continuance of violations of that Act by an allegedly unlawful combination or conspiracy between appellees, through contracts, to restrain interstate trade in certain patented electrical devices. The restraint alleged arose from a cross-license arrangement between the patent owners, Line Material Company and Southern States Equipment Corporation, to fix the sale price of the devices to which arrangement the other appellees, licensees to make and vend, adhered by supplemental contracts. ***

I. The Facts.

The challenged arrangements center around three product patents, which are useful in protecting an electric circuit from the dangers incident to a short circuit or other overload. Two of them are dropout fuse cutouts and the third is a housing suitable for use with any cutout. Dropout fuse cutouts may be used without any housing. The District Court found that 40.77% of all cutouts manufactured and sold by these defendants were produced under these patents. This was substantially all the dropout fuse cutouts made in the United States. There are competitive devices that perform the same functions manufactured by appellees and others under different patents than those here involved.

The dominant patent *** in the field of dropout fuse cutouts with double jointed hinge construction was issued March 7, 1939, to the Southern States Equipment Corporation, assignee, on an application of George N. Lemmon. This patent reads upon a patent *** issued October 17, 1939 to Line Material Company, assignee, on an application by Schultz and Steinmayer. The housing *** was issued November 18, 1930 to Line, assignee, on an application by W. D. Kyle. The Kyle patent covers a wet-process porcelain box with great dielectric strength, which may be economically constructed and has been commercially successful. We give no weight to the presence of the Kyle patent in the licenses.

The applications for the Lemmon and Schultz patents were pending simultaneously. They were declared in interference and a contest resulted. The decision of the Patent Office, awarding dominant claims to Southern and subservient claims to Line on the Lemmon and the Schultz applications made it impossible for any manufacturer to use both patents when later issued without some cross-licensing arrangement. [citation omitted] Only when both patents could be lawfully used by a single maker could the public or the patentees obtain the full benefit of the efficiency and economy of the inventions. Negotiations were started by Line which eventuated in the challenged arrangements.

The first definitive document was a bilateral, royalty-free, cross-license agreement of May 23, 1938, between Southern and Line after the patent office award but before the patents issued. *** Sublicense royalties and expenses were to be divided between Line and Southern. Although a memorandum of agreement of January 12, 1938, between the parties had no such requirement, Line agreed to sell equipment covered by the Southern patent at prices not less than those fixed by Southern. Southern made the same agreement for equipment covered solely by the Line patent. No requirement for price limitation upon sales by other manufacturers under license was included.

Six of the other manufacturers here involved were advised by Line by letter, dated June 13, 1938, that Southern had authority to grant licenses under the Schultz prospective patent. On October 3, 1938, Kearney took from Southern a license to practice the Lemmon and Schultz patents. The license had a price, term and condition of sale clause, governed by Southern's prices, which bound Kearney to maintain the prices on its sales of devices covered by the patents. On October 7, 1938, the five other manufacturers *** were offered by Southern the same contract as the standard licensor's agreement. ***

The price maintenance feature was reflected in all the licenses to make and vend granted by Line, under the Line-Southern contract, to the other appellees. There were variations in the price provisions that are not significant for the issues of this case. *** There can be no doubt, however, that each licensee knew of the proposed price provisions in the licenses of other licensees from the circulation of proposed from of license on October 6, 1939, subsequent consultations among the licensees and an escrow agreement, fulfilled July 11, 1940. That agreement was entered into after General Electric took its license and required for fulfillment the acceptance of identical licenses by Matthews, Kearney and Railway. The licenses that were the subject of the escrow contained the price provisions of General Electric's license. This awareness by each signer of the price provisions in prior contracts is conceded by appellees' brief. A price schedule became effective January 18, 1941. Thereafter, all the appellees tried to maintain prices. Where there was accidental variation, Line wrote the licensee calling attention to the failure.

The licenses were the result of arm's length bargaining in each instance. Price limitation was actively opposed in toto or restriction of its scope sought by several of the licensees, including General Electric, the largest producer of the patented appliances. A number tried energetically to find substitutes for the devices. All the licensees, however, were forced to accept the terms or cease manufacture. By accepting they secured release from claims for past infringement through a provision to that effect in the license. The patentees through the licenses sought system in their royalty collections and pecuniary reward for their patent monopoly. Undoubtedly one purpose of the arrangements was to make possible the use by each manufacturer of the Lemmon and Schultz patents. These patents in separate hands produced a deadlock. Lemmon by his basic patent 'blocked' Schultz' improvement. Cross-licenses furnished appellees a solution.

On consideration of the agreements and the circumstances surrounding their negotiation and execution, the District Court found that the arrangements, as a whole, were made in good faith, to make possible the manufacture by all appellees of the patented devices, to gain a legitimate return to the patentees on the inventions and apart from the written agreements there was no undertaking between the appellees or any of them to fix prices. Being convinced *** that the General Electric case controlled and permitted such price arrangements as are disclosed in the contracts the District Court dismissed the complaint. The Government attacks the rationale of the General Electric case and urges that it be overruled, limited and explained or differentiated.

II. The General Electric Case

That case was decided in 1926 by a unanimous court, Chief Justice Taft writing. It involved a bill in equity to enjoin further violations of the Sherman Act. While violations of the Act by agreements fixing the resale price of patented articles (incandescent light bulbs) sold to dealers also were alleged in the bill, so far as here material the pertinent alleged violation was an agreement between General Electric and Westinghouse Company through which Westinghouse was licensed to manufacture lamps under a number of General Electric's patents, including a patent on the use of tungsten filament in the bulb, on condition that it should sell them at prices fixed by the licensor. On considering an objection to the fixing of prices on bulbs with a tungsten filament, the price agreement was upheld as a valid exercise of patent rights by the licensor.

Speaking of the arrangement, this Court said: 'If the patentee *** licenses the selling of the articles (by a licensee to make), may he limit the selling by limiting the method of sale and the price? We think he may do so provided the conditions of sale are normally and reasonably adapted to secure pecuniary reward for the patentee's monopoly.' [citation omitted] This proviso must be read as directed at agreements between a patentee and a licensee to make and vend. The original context of the words just quoted makes clear that they carry no implication of approval of all a patentee's contracts which tend to increase earnings on patents. The opinion recognizes the fixed rule that a sale of the patented article puts control of the purchaser's resale price beyond the power of the patentee. [citation omitted] Nor can anything be found in the *General Electric* case which will serve as a basis to argue otherwise than that the precise terms of the grant define the limits of a patentee's monopoly and the area in which the patentee is freed from competition of price, service, quality or otherwise. [citation omitted]

General Electric is a case that has provoked criticism and approval. It had only bare recognition in *Ethyl Gasoline Corporation v. United States*, 309 U.S. 436, 456. That case emphasized the rule against the extension of the patent monopoly [citation omitted] to resale prices or to avoid competition among buyers. [citation omitted] We found it unnecessary to reconsider the rule in *United States v. Masonite Corporation*, 316 U.S. 265, 277, although the arrangement there was for sale of patented articles at fixed prices by dealers whom the patentee claimed were del credere agents. As we concluded the patent privilege was exhausted by a transfer of the articles to certain agents who were part of the sales organization of competitors, discussion of the price fixing limitation was not required. *** Other courts have explained or distinguished the *General Electric* rule. *** Furthermore, the point is made that there is such a 'host of difficult and unsettled questions' arising from the *General Electric* holding that the simplest solution is to overrule the precedent on the power of a patentee to establish sale prices of a licensee to make and vend a patented article.

Such a liquidation of the doctrine of a patentee's power to determine a licensee's sale price of a patented article would solve problems arising from its adoption. Since 1902, however, when *E. Bement & Sons v. National Harrow Co.*, 186 U.S. 70, was decided, a patentee has been able to control his licensee's sale price within the limits of the patent monopoly. Litigation that the rule has engendered proves that business arrangements have been repeatedly, even though hesitatingly, made in reliance upon the contractors' interpretation of its meaning. Appellees urge that Congress has taken no steps to modify the rule. Such legislative attitude is to be weighed with the counter balancing fact that the rule of the *General Electric* case grew out of a judicial determination. The writer accepts the rule of the *General Electric* case as interpreted by the third subdivision of this opinion. As a majority of the Court does not agree with that position, the case cannot be reaffirmed on that basis. Neither is there a majority to overrule *General Electric*. In these circumstances, we must proceed to determine the issues on the assumption that *General Electric* continues as a precedent. *** On that assumption where a conspiracy to restrain trade or an effort to monopolize is not involved, a patentee may license another to make and vend the patented device with a provision that the licensee's sale price shall be fixed by the patentee. The assumption is stated in this was so as to leave aside the many variables of the *General Electric* rule that may arise. For example, there may be an aggregation of patents to obtain dominance in a patent field, broad or narrow, or a patent may be used as a peg upon which to attach contracts with former or prospective competitors, touching business relations other than the making and vending of patented devices. Compare *United States v. United States Gypsum Co.*, decided today; *United States v. Masonite Corporation*, 316 U.S. 265. ***

III. The Determination of the Issue

Under the above-mentioned assumption as to *General Electric*, the ultimate question for our decision on this appeal may be stated, succinctly and abstractly, to be as to whether in the light of the prohibition of § 1 of the Sherman Act, [citation omitted] two or more patentees in the same patent field may legally combine their valid patent monopolies to secure mutual benefits for themselves through contractual agreements between themselves and other licensees, for control of the sale price of the patented devices. ***

If the patent rights do not empower the patentees to fix sale prices for others, the agreements do violate the Act. *** As the Schultz patent could not be practiced without the Lemmon, the result of the agreement between Southern and Line for Line's sublicensing of the Lemmon patent was to combine in Line's hands the authority to fix the prices of the commercially successful devices embodying both the Schultz and Lemmon patents. Thus though the sublicenses in terms followed the pattern of *General Electric* in fixing prices only on Line's own patents, the additional right given to Line by the license agreement of January 12, 1940, between Southern and Line, to be the exclusive licensor of the dominant Lemmon patent, made its price fixing of its own Schultz devices effective over devices embodying also the necessary Lemmon patent. By the patentees' agreement the dominant Lemmon and the subservient Schultz patents were combined to fix prices. In the absence of patent or other statutory authorization, a contract to fix or maintain prices in interstate commerce has long been recognized as illegal per se under the Sherman Act. This is true whether the fixed price is reasonable or unreasonable. It is also true whether it is a price agreement between producers for sale or between producer and distributor for resale.

It is equally well settled that the possession of a valid patent or patents does not give the patentee any exemption from the provisions of the Sherman Act beyond the limits of the patent monopoly. By aggregating patents in one control, the holder of the patents cannot escape the prohibitions of the Sherman Act. [citation omitted] ***

We are thus called to make an adjustment between the lawful restraint on trade of the patent monopoly and the illegal restraint prohibited broadly by the Sherman Act. That adjustment has already reached the point, as the precedents now stand, that a patentee may validly license a competitor to make and vend with a price limitation under the *General Electric* case and that the grant of patent rights is the limit of freedom from competition ***.

With the postulates in mind that price limitations on patented devices beyond the limits of patent monopoly violate the Sherman Act and that patent grants are to be construed strictly, the question of the legal effect of the price limitations in these agreements may be readily answered. Nothing in the patent statute specifically gives a right to fix the price at which a licensee may vend the patented article. [citation omitted] While the *General Electric* case holds that a patentee may, under certain conditions, lawfully control the price the licensee of his several patents may charge for the patented device, no case of this Court has construed the patent and anti-monopoly statutes to permit separate owners of separate patents by cross-licenses or other arrangements to fix the prices to be charged by them and their licensees for their respective products. Where two or more patentees with competitive, non-infringing patents combine them and fix prices on all devices produced under any of the patents, competition is impeded to a greater degree than where a single patentee fixes prices for his licensees. The struggle for profit is less acute. Even when, as here, the devices are not commercially competitive because the subservient patent cannot be practiced without consent of the dominant, the statement holds good. The stimulus to seek competitive inventions is reduced by the mutually advantageous price fixing arrangement. Compare, as to acts by a single entity and those done in combination with others. [citation omitted] The merging of the benefits of price fixing under the patents restrains trade in violation of the Sherman Act in the same way as would the fixing of prices between producers of nonpatentable goods.

If the objection is made that a price agreement between a patentee and a licensee equally restrains trade, the answer is not that there is no restraint in such an arrangement but, when the validity of the *General Electric* case is assumed, that reasonable restraint accords with the patent monopoly granted by the patent law. Where a patentee undertakes to exploit his patent by price fixing through agreements with anyone, he must give consideration to the limitations of the Sherman Act on such action. The patent statutes give an exclusive right to the patentee to make, use, and vend and to assign any interest in this monopoly to others. The *General Electric* case construes that as giving a right to a patentee to license another to make and vend at a fixed price. There is no suggestion in the patent statutes of authority to combine with other patent owners to fix prices on articles covered by the respective patents. As the Sherman Act prohibits agreements to fix prices, any arrangement between patentees runs afoul of that prohibition and is outside the patent monopoly.

We turn now to the situation here presented of an agreement where one of the patentees is authorized to fix prices under the patents. The argument of respondents is that if a patentee may contract with his licensee to fix prices, it is logical to permit any number of patentees to combine their patents and authorize one patentee to fix prices for any number of licensees. In this present agreement Southern and Line have entered into an arrangement by which Line is authorized to and has fixed prices for devices produced under the Lemmon and Schultz patents. It seems to us, however, that such argument fails to take into account the cumulative effect of such multiple agreements in establishing an intention to restrain. The obvious purpose and effect of the agreement was to enable Line to fix prices for the patented devices. Even where the agreements to fix prices are limited to a small number of patentees, we are of the opinion that it crosses the barrier erected by the Sherman Act against restraint of trade though the restraint is by patentees and their licensees. ***

Even if a patentee has a right in the absence of a purpose to restrain or monopolize trade, to fix prices on a licensee's sale of the patented product in order to exploit properly his invention or inventions, when patentees join in an agreement as here to maintain prices on their several products, that agreement, however advantageous it may be to stimulate the broader use of patents, is unlawful per se under the Sherman Act. It is more than an exploitation of patents. There is the vice that patentees have combined to fix prices on patented products. It is not the cross-licensing to promote efficient production which is unlawful. There is nothing unlawful in the requirement that a licensee should pay a royalty to compensate the patentee for the invention and the use of the patent. The unlawful element is the use of the control that such cross-licensing gives to fix prices. The mere fact that a patentee uses his patent as whole or part consideration in a contract by which he and another or other patentees in the same patent field arrange for the practice of any patent involved in such a way that royalties or other earnings or benefits from the patent or patents are shared among the patentees, parties to the agreement, subjects that contract to the prohibitions of the Sherman Act whenever the selling price, for things produced under a patent involved, is fixed by the contract or a license, authorized by the contract. Licensees under the contract who as here enter into license arrangements, with price fixing provisions, with knowledge of the contract, are equally subject to the prohibitions. ***

Comments and Questions

1. Although the 1926 *General Electric* case concerns a vertical agreement in that General Electric and Westinghouse had a licensor-licensee relationship, the arrangement also had horizontal elements because GE and Westinghouse were competitors in the market for light bulbs. Because the case was interpreted as allowing a patentee to set the resale price charged by licensees, this vertical aspect is what this chapter—and the excerpted cases—focuses on.

2. Judge Posner summarized the facts of *General Electric* as follows:

General Electric licensed its principal competitor, Westinghouse, to manufacture light bulbs using the GE patents. GE had 69 percent of the market, Westinghouse 16 percent, and other licensees of GE 8 percent, for a total of 93 percent. The effect of the licensing agreement was to solidify the monopoly conferred by the GE patents. The license fixed a minimum price at which Westinghouse could sell the light bulbs. The royalty rate was only 2 percent but was to rise to 10 percent if Westinghouse's share of the light-bulb market exceeded 15 percent, which, as the figures above reveal, it did by the time the case was tried. The very low starting royalty rate suggests that the right to use the GE patents was not worth a lot to Westinghouse, and the rate escalation keyed to Westinghouse's market share suggests that the parties were trying to minimize competition, which was anyway the effect of the minimum-price term in the licensing agreement. The Court upheld the arrangement but I doubt that it would do so today, at least without a further inquiry into the strength of the patents and the rationale for the licensing arrangement.

Asahi Glass Co. v. Pentech Pharm., Inc., 289 F.Supp.2d 986, 992 (N.D. Ill. 2003) (Posner., J.). Judge Posner described the Supreme Court's opinion as "an elderly and much-criticized decision." *Id.*

3. How does the Court in *Line Materials* distinguish the facts of *General Electric*?

4. In *Newburgh Moire Co. v. Superior Moire Co.*, 237 F.2d 283, (3rd Cir. 1956), the Third Circuit explained how the Supreme Court dealt with the issue of cabining *General Electric* opinion, without reversing it:

BIGGS, Chief Judge.

The principle enunciated in *Bement & Sons v. National Harrow Co.*, 1902, 186 U.S. 70, and followed in *United States v. General Electric Co.*, 1926, 272 U.S. 476, permitted a patentee to fix the price the licensee of the patent may charge for the device. It is difficult to say how much of this principle remains in the law. This question came to a head but was not resolved in *United States v. Line Material Co.*, 1948, 333 U.S. 287, 312. The Line decision dealt with arrangements made between two patentees for the cross-licensing of their interdependent product patents and for the licensing by one of them of other manufacturers under both patents. The Court held that price maintenance by the various types of agreements constituted a violation of Section 1 of the Sherman Act. Four Justices thought that the *General Electric* decision should be overruled. Three thought otherwise and dissented. One Justice did not participate. Mr. Justice Reed, voicing an opinion for a divided Court, distinguished the *General Electric* decision and construed the patent statutes as giving a patentee a right to license 'another to make and vend at a fixed price.' [citation omitted] ***

On the same day as the Line decision a unanimous Supreme Court, albeit with two Justices not participating, decided *United States v. United States Gypsum Co.*, 1948, 333 U.S. 364. In *Gypsum* there was no cross-licensing, but rather industry-wide licensing under several patents held by Gypsum Company. Mr. Justice Reed stated for the Court: 'We think that the industry-wide license agreements, entered into with knowledge on the part of licensor and licensees of the adherence of others, with the control over prices and methods of distribution through the agreements and the bulletins, were sufficient to establish a prima facie case of conspiracy.' [citation omitted] The licensing agreements extended to unpatented as well as to Patented Gypsum products but the Supreme Court did not seem to rely on this fact. Mr. Justice Reed went on to say: 'Even in the absence of the specific abuses in this case, which fall within the traditional prohibitions of the Sherman Act, it would be sufficient to show that the defendants, constituting all former competitors in an entire industry, had acted in concern to restrain commerce in an entire industry under patent licenses in order to organize the industry and stabilize prices. That conclusion follows despite the assumed legality of each separate patent license, for it is familiar doctrine that lawful acts may become unlawful when taken in concert. Such concerted action is an effective deterrent to competition; * * *.' [citation omitted]

In the second *Gypsum* case, 1950, 340 U.S. 76, the Supreme Court explained that conspiracy to restrain commerce was the basis of the first *Gypsum* decision. Mr. Justice Reed stated: 'There was no holding in our first opinion in *Gypsum* that mere multiple licensing violated the Sherman Act.' [citation omitted] Footnote 4 cited to the text, to the sentence just quoted, seems to indicate that the dissenters in Line Material would not have concurred in the first *Gypsum* opinion were it not for the conspiracy element in that case. The footnote should be repeated here. 'The dissenters in Line * * * joined in the *United States Gypsum* opinion, since the concerted action in the *United States Gypsum* case was thought to violate the Sherman Act, despite their view that the mere multiplication of licenses, as in *Line*, 'produces a repetition of the same issue (as in General Electric) rather than a different issue.' [citation omitted]

Other/subsequent opinions narrowed the holding of *General Electric* further, suggesting that if the patentee's patent covered a small part of a larger good, then the patentee could not set the resale price of the larger good even though it incorporated the patentee's intellectual property. See U.S. v. General Elec. Co., 82 F. Supp. 753 (D.N.J. 1949).

Explaining this limitation on the *General Electric* rule, Roscoe Steffen explained: "if the Chief Justice meant precisely what he said, price fixing, where permissible at all, must be tailored carefully to fit the particular patent. In a crowded field, where many prior patents have contributed to the development of the article sought to be controlled, it is difficult, as a practical matter, to see how any price fixing whatever could be sanctioned. It would scarcely be possible to permit price control of the whole article, as that would be giving the latest inventor not only a 'pecuniary reward for the patentee's monopoly,' but would be permitting him and his licensees to collect a tribute from the public on the work of many other inventors as well." Roscoe Steffen, *Invalid Patents and Price Control*, 56 YALE L.J. 1, 4 (1946).

5. Aside from the specific restrictions at issue, is there any inherent problem with the parties in Line Materials engaging in cross-licensing?

6. One reason that antitrust law condemned vertical price fixing is because it could be used to maintain a buyers' cartel. What evidence suggests that the vertical price fixing is not serving that function in this case?

7. While the *General Electric* holding is arguably inconsistent with *Dr. Miles*, the holding in *General Electric* can be seen as upholding the Court's 1902 decision in *Bement*, discussed above. If the medicines in *Dr. Miles* had been patented, should the result have been different?

The medicines had been protected by trade secret and their packaging— with which Park & Sons had allegedly tampered— had been protected by trademark. Should these forms of intellectual property protection have been sufficient to apply the reasoning of *General Electric* to the facts of *Dr. Miles*?

8. Even if the *General Electric* rule is sound on its terms, should the rule protect patentees whose patents are invalid?

If not, how should courts deal with issues of patent validity in antitrust litigation?

9. Some courts have held that a vertical price-fixing provision in a patent license may make the patent unenforceable, but the patentee can purge the misuse by waiving the vertical price-fixing provision, which makes the patent enforcement. See Westinghouse Electric Corp. v. Bulldog, 179 F.2d 139, 145 (4th Cir. 1950).

C. Vertical Price Fixing and Copyrighted Works

United States v. Paramount Pictures, Inc.
334 U.S. 131 (1948)

Mr. Justice DOUGLAS delivered the opinion of the Court.

These cases are here on appeal from a judgment of a three-judge District Court holding that the defendants had violated § 1 and § 2 of the Sherman Act, [citation omitted] and granting an injunction and other relief. [citation omitted]

The suit was instituted by the United States under § 4 of the Sherman Act, 15 U.S.C.A. § 4, to prevent and restrain violations of it. The defendants fall into three groups: (1) Paramount Pictures, Inc., Loew's, Incorporated, Radio-Keith-Orpheum Corporation, Warner Bros. Pictures, Inc., Twentieth Century-Fox Film Corporation, which produce motion pictures, and their respective subsidiaries or affiliates which distribute and exhibit films. These are known as the five major defendants or exhibitor-defendants. (2) Columbia Pictures Corporation and Universal Corporation, which produce motion pictures, and their subsidiaries which distribute films. (3) United Artists Corporation, which is engaged only in the distribution of motion pictures. The five majors, through their subsidiaries or affiliates, own or control theatres; the other defendants do not.

*** The complaint charged that all the defendants, as distributors, had conspired to restrain and monopolize and had restrained and monopolized interstate trade in the distribution and exhibition of films by specific practices which we will shortly relate. It also charged that the five major defendants had engaged in a conspiracy to restrain and monopolize, and had restrained and monopolized, interstate trade in the exhibition of motion pictures in most of the larger cities of the country. It charged that the vertical combination of producing, distributing, and exhibiting motion pictures by each of the five major defendants violated § 1 and § 2 of the Act. It charged that each distributor-defendant had entered into various contracts with exhibitors which unreasonably restrained trade. ***

No film is sold to an exhibitor in the distribution of motion pictures. The right to exhibit under copyright is licensed. The District Court found that the defendants in the licenses they issued fixed minimum admission prices which the exhibitors agreed to charge, whether the rental of the film was a flat amount or a percentage of the receipts. It found that substantially uniform minimum prices had been established in the licenses of all defendants. Minimum prices were established in master agreements or franchises which were made between various defendants as distributors and various defendants as exhibitors and in joint operating agreements made by the five majors with each other and with independent theatre owners covering the operation of certain theatres. By these later contracts minimum admission prices were often fixed for dozens of theatres owned by a particular defendant in a given area of the United States. Minimum prices were fixed in licenses of each of the five major defendants. The other three defendants made the same requirement in licenses granted to the exhibitor-defendants. ***

The District Court found that two price-fixing conspiracies existed—a horizontal one between all the defendants, a vertical one between each distributor-defendant and its licensees. The latter was based on express agreements and was plainly established. The former was inferred from the pattern of price-fixing disclosed in the record. We think there was adequate foundation for it too. It is not necessary to find an express agreement in order to find a conspiracy. It is enough that a concert of action is contemplated and that the defendants conformed to the arrangement. [citation omitted] That was shown here.

On this phase of the case the main attack is on the decree which enjoins the defendants and their affiliates from granting any license, except to their own theatres, in which minimum prices for admission to a theatre are fixed in any manner or by any means. The argument runs as follows: *United States v. General Electric Co.*, 272 U.S. 476, held that an owner of a patent could, without violating the Sherman Act, grant a license to manufacture and vend and could fix the price at which the licensee could sell the patented article. It is pointed out that defendants do not sell the films to exhibitors, but only license them and that the Copyright Act, [citation omitted] like the patent statutes, grants the owner exclusive rights. And it is argued that if the patentee can fix the price at which his licensee may sell the patented article, the owner of the copyright should be allowed the same privilege. It is maintained that such a privilege is essential to protect the value of the copyrighted films.

We start, of course, from the premise that so far as the Sherman Act is concerned, a price-fixing combination is illegal per se. [citation omitted] We recently held in *United States v. United States Gypsum Co.*, 333 U.S. 364, that even patentees could not regiment an entire industry by licenses containing price-fixing agreements. What was said there is adequate to bar defendants, through their horizontal conspiracy, from fixing prices for the exhibition of films in the movie industry. Certainly the rights of the copyright owner are no greater than those of the patentee.

Nor can the result be different when we come to the vertical conspiracy between each distributor-defendant and his licensees. The District Court stated in its findings [citation omitted]: 'In agreeing to maintain a stipulated minimum admission price, each exhibitor thereby consents to the minimum price level at which it will compete against other licensees of the same distributor whether they exhibit on the same run or not. The total effect is that through the separate contracts between the distributor and its licensees a price structure is erected which regulates the licensees' ability to compete against one another in admission prices.'

That consequence seems to us to be incontestable. We stated in *United States v. United States Gypsum Co.*, that 'The rewards which flow to the patentee and his licensees from the suppression of competition through the regulation of an industry are not reasonably and normally adapted to secure pecuniary reward for the patentee's monopoly.' The same is true of the rewards of the copyright owners and their licensees in the present case. For here too the licenses are but a part of the general plan to suppress competition. The case where a distributor fixes admission prices to be charged by a single independent exhibitor, no other licensees or exhibitors being in contemplation, seems to be wholly academic, as the District Court pointed out. It is, therefore, plain that *United States v. General Electric Co.*, as applied in the patent cases, affords no haven to the defendants in this case. For a copyright may no more be used than a patent to deter competition between rivals in the exploitation of their licenses. [citation omitted] ***

Comments and Questions

1. Should movie studios or distributors be able to set the price that theaters charge moviegoers? Why or why not?

One antitrust concern is that higher-priced theaters in a particular city might attempt to convince their distributors to impose price restrictions (i.e., to set the ticket prices) in order to prevent discount theaters from charging a lower price. The Supreme Court addressed this issue in *Interstate Circuit v. U.S.*, 306 U.S. 208 (1939), in which a group of exhibitors convinced distributors to refuse to license their movies to theaters that either charged lower prices or showed high-quality movies as part of a double feature.

The *Interstate Circuit* Court inferred an agreement among the movie distributors because the exhibitors had openly invited all of the distributors to participate in the scheme to discipline discount theaters and the distributors each imposed the same price restrictions on discount theaters, despite the fact that it would have been economically irrational absent an agreement among distributors. The Court further indicated that an agreement among distributors to license their movies only to theaters that charged a certain price—and did not show double features— violated the Sherman Act.

The case indicates how vertical price fixing can be part of a larger price-fixing scheme that is horizontal in nature.

2. The *Interstate Circuit* case shows why a movie distributor might set a minimum resale price. Why might movie distributors—or other manufacturers—set a maximum resale price?

If the movie distributors had tried to set a maximum ticket price, how might the exhibitors attempt to circumvent the restriction?

3. Despite an antitrust decree in the *Paramount* case that precludes movie distributors from setting ticket prices, uniform pricing remains the norm in American movie theaters, which charge the same price for all movies shown regardless of the variations in quality, demand, and lengths of movies. Professor Barak Orbach explains how this may be a result of the *Paramount* decree in *Antitrust and Pricing in the Motion Picture Industry*, 21 YALE J. ON REG. 317 (2004).

For more on the antitrust history of the motion picture industry, see Alexandra Gil, *Breaking the Studios: Antitrust and the Motion Picture Industry*, 3 N.Y.U. J. L. & LIBERTY 83 (2008).

4. The *Paramount* Court states: "Certainly the rights of the copyright owner are no greater than those of the patentee." United States v. Paramount Pictures, Inc., 334 U.S. 131, 143 (1948). Should they be?

LucasArts Entertainment Co. v. Humongous Entertainment Co.

870 F.Supp. 285 (N.D. Cal. 1993)

WALKER, District Judge.

This suit arises as a result of an agreement between Electronic Arts, Inc. ("Electronic Arts") and defendant Humongous Entertainment Company ("Humongous"), granting Electronic Arts the right to distribute Humongous' products, including a computer video game entitled Putt Putt Joins the Parade. Humongous' principals are former employees of plaintiff LucasArts Entertainment Company ("LucasArts"), who created a software tool called the Script Creation Utility for Maniac Mansion ("SCUMM") System. The SCUMM System is a tool used in the development of computer video games. LucasArts subsequently licensed the SCUMM System to Humongous under limited terms and conditions. Among other things, the license agreement states that Humongous may not sell its games which utilize the SCUMM program to any third party distributor other than LucasArts for less than a certain price and that Humongous must verify its compliance with the licensing agreement at LucasArts' request. The precise language as outlined in section A.1.1.1(b) of the license agreement is as follows:

> For a period of three (3) years commencing on the Effective Date, [Humongous] may not sell any product it develops using the SCUMM System to any third party distributors in North America other than [LucasArts] for less than seventy-five percent (75%) of the six month rolling average wholesale price, net of any promotional allowances, at which such products are re-sold to North American retailers (current examples of which include Software, Etc.; Babbages; and Electronic Boutique). [LucasArts] reserves the right to verify such wholesale price upon [LucasArts'] request in writing to Licensee. After such three year period, the foregoing price restriction will be inapplicable.

LucasArts brings this suit alleging, among other things, that Humongous violated the terms of the licensing agreement by (1) failing to follow the terms of the price restriction provision ***. Humongous and Electronic Arts deny such allegations and bring counterclaims for violation of federal and state antitrust laws ***.

*** Electronic Arts moves for partial summary judgment on its antitrust claims on the grounds that: (1) the price restriction in section A.1.1.1(b) of the Licensing Agreement between LucasArts and Humongous is per se illegal and unenforceable; (2) the restriction constitutes a per se illegal and unenforceable boycott; ***

Electronic Arts moves for partial summary judgment on its antitrust counterclaims, which allege that section A.1.1.1(b) constitutes an illegal price fixing agreement and an illegal boycott in violation of the Sherman and Cartwright Acts.* Further, Electronic Arts contends that LucasArts' enforcement of section A.1.1.1(b) constitutes copyright misuse, thereby preventing enforcement of LucasArts' copyright.

In support of its argument that section A.1.1.1(b) constitutes a per se illegal price fixing agreement, Electronic Arts cites some of the antitrust laws' greatest hits: *United States v. Socony-Vacuum Oil Company*, 310 U.S. 150, 223 (1940); *United States v. New Wrinkle, Inc.*, 342 U.S. 371, 377 (1952) ("[P]rice fixing in commerce, reasonable or unreasonable, has been considered a per se violation of the Sherman Act."); *Northern Pacific Railway Co. v. United States*, 356 U.S. 1, 5 (1958) (certain practices, including price fixing, "are conclusively presumed to be unreasonable and therefore illegal without elaborate inquiry as to the precise harm they have caused or the business excuse for their use"); *Arizona v. Maricopa County Medical Society*, 457 U.S. 332, 351 (1982) (the anticompetitive potential inherent in all price-fixing agreements justifies their facial invalidation even if procompetitive justifications are offered for some).

LucasArts correctly notes that none of these cases involve intellectual property rights of the type here and citation to these cases merely begs the principle question in this case; namely, whether section A.1.1.1(b) falls outside the safe harbor accorded to intellectual property owners by the Supreme Court in *United States v. General Electric*, 272 U.S. 476 (1926).

In *General Electric*, the Supreme Court held that the statutory right of intellectual property owners to forbid entirely sales by licensees necessarily includes the power to restrict the prices at which such licensees may sell licensed material:

> The patentee may make and grant a license to another to make and use the patented articles but withhold his right to sell them * * *. [If the licensee] sells [the patented articles,] he infringes the right of the patentee, and may be held for damages and enjoined. If the patentee goes further, and licenses the selling of the articles, may he limit the selling by limiting the method of sale and the price? We think he may do so provided the conditions of sale are normally and reasonably adapted to secure pecuniary reward for the patentee's monopoly * * *. It would seem entirely reasonable that he should say to the licensee, "Yes, you may make and sell articles under my patent but not so as to destroy the profit that I wish to obtain by making them and selling them myself."

Id. at 490.

Applying the foregoing principle to the case at bar, the court finds that the price restriction found in section A.1.1.1(b) of the Licensing Agreement does not

---

* Editor: The Cartwright Act is California's state antitrust statute.

violate the Sherman or Cartwright Acts because it is "reasonably adapted to secure pecuniary reward for the [LucasArts' lawful] monopoly."

In any event, the per se rule is reserved only where experience has demonstrated that anticompetitive effects predictably and regularly flow from a particular practice, [citation omitted] or where the potential harm to competition is "so clear and so great," [citation omitted] or where the challenged activity would almost always tend to have a predominantly anticompetitive effect, [citation omitted]. The present case involves a licensing provision which is plainly procompetitive, namely the licensing of SCUMM code to Humongous so that Humongous can create more computer video games. There can be no serious question that such licensing activities foster consumer welfare.

Limitations imposed by the antitrust laws are thought to improve consumer welfare because they force firms to increase output from monopolistic to competitive levels. This is based upon the notion that firms face increasing marginal costs (i.e., the laws of diminishing returns). If returns to scale are increasing, however (i.e., falling marginal costs), the competitive model upon which the antitrust laws are premised is stood on its head and "the role of imperfect competition plays." [citation omitted] Where "imperfect competition" provides the economic standard, the antitrust laws' restrictions against extension of monopoly should not apply. Here, the high initial costs of programming code compared to the relatively low cost of producing copies of the code, make application of traditional antitrust concepts inappropriate. In such a setting, marginal costs decline with increases in production rather than the other way around, the situation to which the antitrust laws apply. As such, the application of the per se rule in judging the legality of the license agreement does not comport with the principles underlying the establishment of the per se rule.

Even if the foregoing were not true, section A.1.1.1(b) runs afoul of the antitrust laws only if it forecloses Electronic Arts from competition. It does not.

Electronic Arts relies on *Northwest Wholesale Stationers, Inc. v. Pacific Stationery and Printing Co.*, 472 U.S. 284 (1985), correctly reading that decision as barring unreasonable concerted refusals to deal or group boycotts. In this case, however, the court finds nothing unreasonable in LucasArts, a holder of a valid copyright in the SCUMM System Code, imposing on its licensee resale price restrictions on the copyrighted material or material derived therefrom. Such conduct in no way forecloses Electronic Arts from offering competing copyrighted material if it produces such material or licenses it from others. In short, competition can suffer no injury from section A.1.1.1(b).

Finally, the court notes that the essence of a copyright interest is the power to exclude use of the copyrighted work by those who did not originate it or who are not authorized to use it. The right to license a patent or copyright (and to dictate the terms of such a license) is the "untrammeled right" of the intellectual property owner. [citation omitted] In *Simpson v. Union Oil Co.*, 377 U.S. 13, 24 (1964), the Supreme Court noted that the laws of intellectual property "are in pari materia with the antitrust laws and modify them pro tanto." Accordingly, a court must tread gingerly before permitting an antitrust plaintiff to modify the scope of the statutory copyright grant that Congress has seen fit to impose. Applying the foregoing considerations to the present case, the court declines to find anything unreasonable or illegal in the resale price restriction found in section A.1.1.1(b).

Comments and Questions

1. Does the pricing restriction in this case reduce output?

Should antitrust only be concerned about reduced output? Or do higher prices alone create antitrust injury?

The court suggests that the per se rule should not apply when marginal costs are declining. Would that essentially allow cartelization in such industries? If so, is the court's reasoning too broad?

2. The *LucasArts* Court held that "the Licensing Agreement does not violate the Sherman or Cartwright Acts because it is 'reasonably adapted to secure pecuniary reward for the [LucasArts' lawful] monopoly.'"

Do you agree?

Why couldn't the licensor simply charge a higher royalty "to secure pecuniary reward"?

3. If the price restriction in this case is permissible, why shouldn't LucasArts be able to impose a tying requirement?

A Note on the First Sale Doctrine

Independent of antitrust law, copyright law also condemns resale price maintenance. However, copyright law employs different terminology: the first sale doctrine. In *Quality King Distributors, Inc. v. L'anza Research Int'l, Inc.*, 523 U.S. 135 (1998), the Supreme Court explained:

> we first endorsed the first sale doctrine in a case involving a claim by a publisher that the resale of its books at discounted prices infringed its copyright on the books. Bobbs-Merrill Co. v. Straus, 210 U.S. 339 (1908).
>
> In that case, the publisher, Bobbs-Merrill, had inserted a notice in its books that any retail sale at a price under $1 would constitute an infringement of its copyright. The defendants, who owned Macy's department store, disregarded the notice and sold the books at a lower price without Bobbs-Merrill's consent. We held that the exclusive statutory right to "vend" applied only to the first sale of the copyrighted work:
>
>> "What does the statute mean in granting 'the sole right of vending the same'? Was it intended to create a right which would permit the holder of the copyright to fasten, by notice in a book or upon one of the articles mentioned within the statute, a restriction upon the subsequent alienation of the subject-matter of copyright after the owner had parted with the title to one who had acquired full dominion over it and had given a satisfactory price for it? It is not denied that one who has sold a copyrighted article, without restriction, has parted with all right to control the sale of it. The purchaser of a book, once sold by authority of the owner of the copyright, may sell it again, although he could not publish a new edition of it.

"In this case the stipulated facts show that the books sold by the appellant were sold at wholesale, and purchased by those who made no agreement as to the control of future sales of the book, and took upon themselves no obligation to enforce the notice printed in the book, undertaking to restrict retail sales to a price of one dollar per copy."

Id., at 349–350.

The statute in force when *Bobbs-Merrill* was decided provided that the copyright owner had the exclusive right to "vend" the copyrighted work. Congress subsequently codified our holding in *Bobbs-Merrill* that the exclusive right to "vend" was limited to first sales of the work. Under the 1976 Act, the comparable exclusive right granted in 17 U.S.C. § 106(3) is the right "to distribute copies . . . by sale or other transfer of ownership." The comparable limitation on that right is provided not by judicial interpretation, but by an express statutory provision.

Id. at 1128–29 (citing 17 U.S.C. § 109(a)).

The first sale doctrine allows used book stores to sell—and libraries to lend out—physical copies of the books that they own without either infringing a copyright or being subjected to resale price restrictions imposed by the copyright owner.

A copyright owner may attempt to characterize its sales as licenses in order to evade the first sale doctrine. (Notice that both *Paramount* and *LucasArts* involved licenses.) For example, a software company may sell a disk with its program on it but claim that it is not selling a copy of its product but merely selling a license to use the copyrighted product subject to the licensing restrictions. The software may then impose a licensing restriction prevents licensees from disposing of their copy of the program by selling it to another person.

Why would a software company impose such a restriction?

What are the potential anticompetitive effects of such a restriction?

If you believe that there are potential anticompetitive effects, does that mean that such policies necessarily violate antitrust laws?

D. Resale Price Maintenance and Trademarked Goods

U.S. v. Frankfort Distilleries,
324 U.S. 293 (1945)

The facts alleged in the indictment ***indicate a pattern which bears all the earmarks of a traditional restraint of trade. The participants are producers, middlemen, and retailers. They have agreed among themselves to adopt a single course in making contracts of sale and to boycott all others who would not adopt the same course.

The effect, and if it were material, the purpose of the combination charged was to fix prices at an artificial level. Such combinations, affecting commerce among the states, tend to eliminate competition, and violate the Sherman Act per se. [citation omitted] Price maintenance contracts fall under the same ban, *Ethyl Gasoline Corp. v. United States*, 309 U.S. 436, 458, except as provided by the

1937 Miller-Tydings Amendment to the Sherman Act. [citation omitted] The combination charged against respondents does not fall within this exception. It permits the seller of an article which bears his trade mark, brand, or name, to prescribe a minimum resale price by contract, if such contracts are lawful in the state where the resale is to be made and if the trademarked article is in free and open competition with other articles of the same commodity. This type of 'Fair Trade' price maintenance contract is lawful in Colorado. [citation omitted] But the Miller-Tydings Amendment to the Sherman Act does not permit combinations of business men to coerce others into making such contracts, and Colorado has not attempted to grant such permission. Both the federal and state 'Fair Trade' Acts expressly provide that they shall not apply to price maintenance contracts among producers, wholesalers and competitors. It follows that whatever may be the rights of an individual producer under the Miller-Tydings Amendment to make price maintenance contracts or to refuse to sell his goods to those who will not make such contracts, a combination to compel price maintenance in commerce among the states violates the Sherman Act. [citation omitted]

Hudson Distributors, Inc. v. Eli Lilly & Co.
377 U.S. 386 (1964)

Mr. Justice GOLDBERG delivered the opinion of the Court.

These appeals raise the question of whether the McGuire Act, 66 Stat. 631, 15 U.S.C. §§ 45(a)(1)-(5), permits the application and enforcement of the Ohio Fair Trade Act against appellant in support of appellees' systems of retail price maintenance.

*** Appellant, Hudson Distributors, Inc., owns and operates a retail drug chain in Cleveland, Ohio. Appellee, Eli Lilly & Co., manufactures pharmaceutical products bearing its trademarks and trade names. Lilly sells its products directly to wholesalers and makes no sales to retailers. Hudson purchases Lilly brand products from Regal D.S., Inc., a Michigan wholesaler.

In June 1959, the Ohio Legislature enacted a new Fair Trade Act [cit]. Subsequently Lilly sent letters to all Ohio retailers of Lilly products, including Hudson, to notify them of Lilly's intention to establish minimum retail resale prices for its trademarked products pursuant to the new Ohio Act and to invite the retailers to enter into written fair-trade contracts. More than 1,400 Ohio retailers of Lilly products (about 65% of all the retail pharmacists in Ohio) signed fair-trade contracts with Lilly. Hudson, however, refused to enter into a written contract with Lilly and ignored the specified minimum resale prices. Lilly formally notified Hudson that the Ohio Act required Hudson to observe the minimum retail resale prices for Lilly commodities. Hudson, nevertheless, continued to purchase and then to resell Lilly products at less than the stipulated minimum retail resale prices.

Hudson thereupon filed a petition in the Court of Common Pleas for Cuyahoga County, Ohio, for a judgment declaring the Ohio Act invalid under the State

Constitution and federal law. Lilly answered and cross-petitioned for enforcement of the Ohio Act against Hudson. ***

Hudson contends that the provisions of the Ohio Act under which Lilly established minimum resale prices are not authorized by the McGuire Act, 66 Stat. 631, 15 U.S.C. §§ 45(a)(1)–(5). Section 2 of the McGuire Act provides in pertinent part as follows:

> 'Nothing contained in this section or in any of the Antitrust Acts shall render unlawful any contracts or agreements prescribing minimum or stipulated prices, * * * when contracts or agreements of that description are lawful as applied to intrastate transactions under any statute, law, or public policy now or hereafter in effect in any State * * *.'

Section 3 of the McGuire Act reads as follows:

> 'Nothing contained in this section or in any of the Antitrust Acts shall render unlawful the exercise or the enforcement of any right or right of action created by any statute, law, or public policy now or hereafter in effect in any State, Territory, or the District of Columbia, which in substance provides that willfully and knowingly advertising, offering for sale, or selling any commodity at less than the price or prices prescribed in such contracts or agreements whether the person so advertising, offering for sale, or selling is or is not a party to such a contract or agreement, is unfair competition and is actionable at the suit of any person damaged thereby.'

Before the enactment of the McGuire Act, this Court in 1951 in *Schwegmann Bros. v. Calvert Distillers Corp.*, 341 U.S. 384, considered whether the Miller-Tydings Act [citation omitted] removed from the prohibition of the Sherman Act [citation omitted] a state statute which authorized a trademark owner, by notice, to require a retailer who had not executed a written contract to observe resale price maintenance. Respondents in that case argued that since the Sherman Act outlawed 'contracts' in restraint of trade and since the Miller-Tydings amendment to the Sherman Act excepted 'contracts or agreements prescribing minimum prices for the resale' of a commodity where such contracts or agreements were lawful under state law, the Miller-Tydings Act therefore immunized all arrangements involving resale price maintenance authorized by state law. [citation omitted] After examining the history of the Miller-Tydings Act, the Court concluded that Congress had intended the words 'contracts or agreements' as contained in that Act to be used 'in their normal and customary meaning,' [citation omitted] and to cover only arrangements whereby the retailer voluntarily agreed to be bound by the resale price restrictions. The Court held therefore that the state resale price maintenance law could not be applied to nonsigners–'recalcitrants * * * dragged in by the heels and compelled to submit to price fixing.' [citation omitted] The Court stated that:

> 'It should be remembered that it was the state laws that the federal law was designed to accommodate. Federal regulation was to give way to state regulation. When state regulation provided for resale price maintenance by both those who

contracted and those who did not, and the federal regulation was relaxed only as respects 'contracts or agreements,' the inference is strong that Congress left the noncontracting group to be governed by preexisting law.' Id., 341 U.S. at 395.

Shortly after the Schwegmann decision, Congress passed the McGuire Act [citation omitted]. The Report of the House Committee on Interstate and Foreign Commerce, which accompanied the McGuire Act, declared that:

> 'The primary purpose of the (McGuire) bill is to reaffirm the very same proposition which, in the committee's opinion, the Congress intended to enact into law when it passed the Miller-Tydings Act * * *, to the effect that the application and enforcement of State fair-trade laws-including the nonsigner provisions of such laws-with regard to interstate transactions shall not constitute a violation of the Federal Trade Commission Act or the Sherman Antitrust Act. This reaffirmation is made necessary because of the decision of a divided Supreme Court in Schwegmann v. Calvert Distillers Corporation (341 U.S. 384, May 21, 1951). In that case, six members of the Court held that the Miller-Tydings Act did not exempt from these Federal laws enforcement of State fair trade laws with respect to nonsigners. Three members of the Court held that the Miller-Tydings Act did so apply.
>
> 'The end result of the Supreme Court decision has been seriously to undermine the effectiveness of the Miller-Tydings Act and, in turn, of the fair-trade laws enacted by 45 States. H.R. 5767, as amended, is designed to restore the effectiveness of these acts by making it abundantly clear that Congress means to let State fair-trade laws apply in their totality; that is, with respect to nonsigners as well as signers.' (Emphasis added.) H.R. Rep.No.1437, 82d Cong., 2d Sess., at 1–2.

This authoritative report evinces the clear intention of Congress that, where sanctioned by a state fair-trade act, a trademark owner such as Lilly could be permitted to enforce, even against a nonsigning retailer such as Hudson, the stipulated minimum prices established by written contracts with other retailers.[7]

*** The price fixing authorized by the Ohio Fair Trade Act and involving goods moving in interstate commerce would be, absent approval by Congress, clearly illegal under the Sherman Act, *Dr. Miles Medical Co. v. John D. Park & Sons Co.*, 220 U.S. 373. 'Fixing minimum prices, like other types of price fixing, is illegal per se.' *Schwegmann Bros. v. Calvert Distillers Corp.*, 341 U.S. at 386. Congress, however, in the McGuire Act has approved state statutes sanctioning resale price maintenance schemes such as those involved here. Whether it is good policy to permit such laws is a matter for Congress to decide. Where the statutory language and the legislative history clearly indicate the purpose of Congress that purpose must be upheld. ***

Affirmed.

---

[7] See United States v. McKesson & Robbins, Inc., 351 U.S. 305, 311, n. 14, 76 S.Ct. 937, 941, 100 L.Ed. 1209: 'The McGuire Act * * * specifically exempts from the antitrust laws price fixing under 'fair trade' agreements which bind not only retailers who are parties to the agreement but also retailers who refuse to sign the agreement.'

Comments and Questions

1. Should the manufacturers of trademarked products be able to set the resale price of their goods?

If so, why should the ability to fix resale price be limited to manufacturers of trademarked products?

2. In 1975, Congress repealed Miller-Tydings Act because it was dissatisfied with the competitive effects of state fair trade laws. This restored *Dr. Miles* as the state of the law and resale price maintenance— including of trademarked goods— became per se illegal again.

The effect of the Miller-Tydings Act on consumer prices is discussed by the competing opinions in *Leegin* in the following excerpt.

E. The Demise of *Dr. Miles*

Leegin Creative Leather Products, Inc. v. PSKS, Inc.
127 S.Ct. 2705 (2007)

Justice KENNEDY delivered the opinion of the Court.

In *Dr. Miles Medical Co. v. John D. Park & Sons Co.*, 220 U.S. 373 (1911), the Court established the rule that it is per se illegal under § 1 of the Sherman Act, 15 U.S.C. § 1, for a manufacturer to agree with its distributor to set the minimum price the distributor can charge for the manufacturer's goods. The question presented by the instant case is whether the Court should overrule the per se rule and allow resale price maintenance agreements to be judged by the rule of reason, the usual standard applied to determine if there is a violation of § 1. The Court has abandoned the rule of per se illegality for other vertical restraints a manufacturer imposes on its distributors. Respected economic analysts, furthermore, conclude that vertical price restraints can have procompetitive effects. We now hold that *Dr. Miles* should be overruled and that vertical price restraints are to be judged by the rule of reason. ***

The Court has interpreted *Dr. Miles Medical Co. v. John D. Park & Sons Co.*, 220 U.S. 373 (1911), as establishing a per se rule against a vertical agreement between a manufacturer and its distributor to set minimum resale prices. [citation omitted] In *Dr. Miles* the plaintiff, a manufacturer of medicines, sold its products only to distributors who agreed to resell them at set prices. The Court found the manufacturer's control of resale prices to be unlawful. It relied on the common-law rule that "a general restraint upon alienation is ordinarily invalid." [citation omitted] The Court then explained that the agreements would advantage the distributors, not the manufacturer, and were analogous to a combination among competing distributors, which the law treated as void. [citation omitted]

The reasoning of the Court's more recent jurisprudence has rejected the rationales on which *Dr. Miles* was based. By relying on the common-law rule against restraints on alienation, [citation omitted] the Court justified its decision based on "formalistic" legal doctrine rather than "demonstrable economic effect," [citation omitted] The Court in *Dr. Miles* relied on a treatise published in 1628, but failed to discuss in detail the business reasons that would motivate a manufacturer situated in 1911 to make use of vertical price restraints. Yet the Sherman Act's use of "restraint of trade" "invokes the common law itself, . . . not merely the static content that the common law had assigned to the term in 1890." [citation omitted] The general restraint on alienation, especially in the age when then-Justice Hughes used the term, tended to evoke policy concerns extraneous to the question that controls here. Usually associated with land, not chattels, the rule arose from restrictions removing real property from the stream of commerce for generations. The Court should be cautious about putting dispositive weight on doctrines from antiquity but of slight relevance. We reaffirm that "the state of the common law 400 or even 100 years ago is irrelevant to the issue before us: the effect of the antitrust laws upon vertical distributional restraints in the American economy today." [citation omitted]

Dr. Miles, furthermore, treated vertical agreements a manufacturer makes with its distributors as analogous to a horizontal combination among competing distributors. [citation omitted] Our recent cases formulate antitrust principles in accordance with the appreciated differences in economic effect between vertical and horizontal agreements, differences the *Dr. Miles* Court failed to consider.

The reasons upon which *Dr. Miles* relied do not justify a per se rule. As a consequence, it is necessary to examine, in the first instance, the economic effects of vertical agreements to fix minimum resale prices, and to determine whether the per se rule is nonetheless appropriate. [citation omitted]

A

Though each side of the debate can find sources to support its position, it suffices to say here that economics literature is replete with procompetitive justifications for a manufacturer's use of resale price maintenance. [c.o] The few recent studies documenting the competitive effects of resale price maintenance also cast doubt on the conclusion that the practice meets the criteria for a per se rule. [citation omitted]

The justifications for vertical price restraints are similar to those for other vertical restraints. [citation omitted] Minimum resale price maintenance can stimulate interbrand competition—the competition among manufacturers selling different brands of the same type of product—by reducing intrabrand competition-the competition among retailers selling the same brand. [citation omitted] The promotion of interbrand competition is important because "the primary purpose of the antitrust laws is to protect [this type of] competition." [citation omitted] A single manufacturer's use of vertical price restraints tends to eliminate intrabrand price competition; this in turn encourages retailers to invest in tangible or intangible services or promotional efforts that aid the manufacturer's position as against rival manufacturers. Resale price maintenance also has the potential to give consumers more options so that they can choose among low-price, low-service brands; high-price, high-service brands; and brands that fall in between.

Absent vertical price restraints, the retail services that enhance interbrand competition might be underprovided. This is because discounting retailers can free ride on retailers who furnish services and then capture some of the increased demand those services generate. [citation omitted] Consumers might learn, for example, about the benefits of a manufacturer's product from a retailer that invests in fine showrooms, offers product demonstrations, or hires and trains knowledgeable employees. [citation omitted] Or consumers might decide to buy the product because they see it in a retail establishment that has a reputation for selling high-quality merchandise. [citation omitted] If the consumer can then buy the product from a retailer that discounts because it has not spent capital providing services or developing a quality reputation, the high-service retailer will lose sales to the discounter, forcing it to cut back its services to a level lower than consumers would otherwise prefer. Minimum resale price maintenance alleviates the problem because it prevents the discounter from undercutting the service provider. With price competition decreased, the manufacturer's retailers compete among themselves over services.

Resale price maintenance, in addition, can increase interbrand competition by facilitating market entry for new firms and brands. "[N]ew manufacturers and manufacturers entering new markets can use the restrictions in order to induce competent and aggressive retailers to make the kind of investment of capital and labor that is often required in the distribution of products unknown to the consumer." [citation omitted] New products and new brands are essential to a dynamic economy, and if markets can be penetrated by using resale price maintenance there is a procompetitive effect.

Resale price maintenance can also increase interbrand competition by encouraging retailer services that would not be provided even absent free riding. It may be difficult and inefficient for a manufacturer to make and enforce a contract with a retailer specifying the different services the retailer must perform. Offering the retailer a guaranteed margin and threatening termination if it does not live up to expectations may be the most efficient way to expand the manufacturer's market share by inducing the retailer's performance and allowing it to use its own initiative and experience in providing valuable services. [citation omitted]

B

While vertical agreements setting minimum resale prices can have procompetitive justifications, they may have anticompetitive effects in other cases; and unlawful price fixing, designed solely to obtain monopoly profits, is an ever present temptation. Resale price maintenance may, for example, facilitate a manufacturer cartel. [citation omitted] An unlawful cartel will seek to discover if some manufacturers are undercutting the cartel's fixed prices. Resale price maintenance could assist the cartel in identifying price-cutting manufacturers who benefit from the lower prices they offer. Resale price maintenance, furthermore, could discourage a manufacturer from cutting prices to retailers with the concomitant benefit of cheaper prices to consumers. [citation omitted]

Vertical price restraints also "might be used to organize cartels at the retailer level." [citation omitted] A group of retailers might collude to fix prices to consumers and then compel a manufacturer to aid the unlawful arrangement with resale price maintenance. In that instance the manufacturer does not establish the practice to stimulate services or to promote its brand but to give inefficient retailers higher profits. Retailers with better distribution systems and lower cost structures would be prevented from charging lower prices by the agreement. [citation omitted]

A horizontal cartel among competing manufacturers or competing retailers that decreases output or reduces competition in order to increase price is, and ought to be, per se unlawful. See *Texaco*, 547 U.S., at 5; *GTE Sylvania*, 433 U.S., at 58, n. 28. To the extent a vertical agreement setting minimum resale prices is entered upon to facilitate either type of cartel, it, too, would need to be held unlawful under the rule of reason. This type of agreement may also be useful evidence for a plaintiff attempting to prove the existence of a horizontal cartel.

Resale price maintenance, furthermore, can be abused by a powerful manufacturer or retailer. A dominant retailer, for example, might request resale price maintenance to forestall innovation in distribution that decreases costs. A manufacturer might consider it has little choice but to accommodate the retailer's demands for vertical price restraints if the manufacturer believes it needs access to the retailer's distribution network. [citation omitted] A manufacturer with market power, by comparison, might use resale price maintenance to give retailers an incentive not to sell the products of smaller rivals or new entrants. [citation omitted] As should be evident, the potential anticompetitive consequences of vertical price restraints must not be ignored or underestimated.

C

*** Respondent contends, nonetheless, that vertical price restraints should be per se unlawful because of the administrative convenience of per se rules. [citation omitted] That argument suggests per se illegality is the rule rather than the exception. This misinterprets our antitrust law. Per se rules may decrease administrative costs, but that is only part of the equation. Those rules can be counterproductive. They can increase the total cost of the antitrust system by prohibiting procompetitive conduct the antitrust laws should encourage. [citation omitted] They also may increase litigation costs by promoting frivolous suits against legitimate practices. The Court has thus explained that administrative "advantages are not sufficient in themselves to justify the creation of per se rules," [citation omitted] and has relegated their use to restraints that are "manifestly anticompetitive," [citation omitted] Were the Court now to conclude that vertical price restraints should be per se illegal based on administrative costs, we would undermine, if not overrule, the traditional "demanding standards" for adopting per se rules. [citation omitted] Any possible reduction in administrative costs cannot alone justify the *Dr. Miles* rule.

Respondent also argues the per se rule is justified because a vertical price restraint can lead to higher prices for the manufacturer's goods. [citation omitted]

Respondent is mistaken in relying on pricing effects absent a further showing of anticompetitive conduct. [citation omitted] For, as has been indicated already, the antitrust laws are designed primarily to protect interbrand competition, from which lower prices can later result. [citation omitted] The Court, moreover, has evaluated other vertical restraints under the rule of reason even though prices can be increased in the course of promoting procompetitive effects. [citation omitted] And resale price maintenance may reduce prices if manufacturers have resorted to costlier alternatives of controlling resale prices that are not per se unlawful. [citation omitted]

Respondent's argument, furthermore, overlooks that, in general, the interests of manufacturers and consumers are aligned with respect to retailer profit margins. The difference between the price a manufacturer charges retailers and the price retailers charge consumers represents part of the manufacturer's cost of distribution, which, like any other cost, the manufacturer usually desires to minimize. [citation omitted] A manufacturer has no incentive to overcompensate retailers with unjustified margins. The retailers, not the manufacturer, gain from higher retail prices. The manufacturer often loses; interbrand competition reduces its competitiveness and market share because consumers will "substitute a different brand of the same product." [citation omitted] As a general matter, therefore, a single manufacturer will desire to set minimum resale prices only if the "increase in demand resulting from enhanced service . . . will more than offset a negative impact on demand of a higher retail price." [citation omitted]

The implications of respondent's position are far reaching. Many decisions a manufacturer makes and carries out through concerted action can lead to higher prices. A manufacturer might, for example, contract with different suppliers to obtain better inputs that improve product quality. Or it might hire an advertising agency to promote awareness of its goods. Yet no one would think these actions violate the Sherman Act because they lead to higher prices. The antitrust laws do not require manufacturers to produce generic goods that consumers do not know about or want. The manufacturer strives to improve its product quality or to promote its brand because it believes this conduct will lead to increased demand despite higher prices. The same can hold true for resale price maintenance.

Resale price maintenance, it is true, does have economic dangers. If the rule of reason were to apply to vertical price restraints, courts would have to be diligent in eliminating their anticompetitive uses from the market. This is a realistic objective, and certain factors are relevant to the inquiry. For example, the number of manufacturers that make use of the practice in a given industry can provide important instruction. When only a few manufacturers lacking market power adopt the practice, there is little likelihood it is facilitating a manufacturer cartel, for a cartel then can be undercut by rival manufacturers. [citation omitted] Likewise, a retailer cartel is unlikely when only a single manufacturer in a competitive market uses resale price maintenance. Interbrand competition would divert consumers to lower priced substitutes and eliminate any gains to retailers from their price-fixing agreement over a single brand. [citation omitted] Resale price maintenance should be subject to more careful scrutiny, by contrast, if many competing manufacturers adopt the practice. [citation omitted]

The source of the restraint may also be an important consideration. If there is evidence retailers were the impetus for a vertical price restraint, there is a greater likelihood that the restraint facilitates a retailer cartel or supports a dominant, inefficient retailer. [citation omitted] If, by contrast, a manufacturer adopted the policy independent of retailer pressure, the restraint is less likely to promote anticompetitive conduct. [citation omitted] A manufacturer also has an incentive to protest inefficient retailer-induced price restraints because they can harm its competitive position.

As a final matter, that a dominant manufacturer or retailer can abuse resale price maintenance for anticompetitive purposes may not be a serious concern unless the relevant entity has market power. If a retailer lacks market power, manufacturers likely can sell their goods through rival retailers. [citation omitted] And if a manufacturer lacks market power, there is less likelihood it can use the practice to keep competitors away from distribution outlets.

The rule of reason is designed and used to eliminate anticompetitive transactions from the market. This standard principle applies to vertical price restraints. A party alleging injury from a vertical agreement setting minimum resale prices will have, as a general matter, the information and resources available to show the existence of the agreement and its scope of operation. As courts gain experience considering the effects of these restraints by applying the rule of reason over the course of decisions, they can establish the litigation structure to ensure the rule operates to eliminate anticompetitive restraints from the market and to provide more guidance to businesses. Courts can, for example, devise rules over time for offering proof, or even presumptions where justified, to make the rule of reason a fair and efficient way to prohibit anticompetitive restraints and to promote procompetitive ones.

For all of the foregoing reasons, we think that were the Court considering the issue as an original matter, the rule of reason, not a per se rule of unlawfulness, would be the appropriate standard to judge vertical price restraints.

IV

We do not write on a clean slate, for the decision in *Dr. Miles* is almost a century old. So there is an argument for its retention on the basis of stare decisis alone. Even if *Dr. Miles* established an erroneous rule, "[s]tare decisis reflects a policy judgment that in most matters it is more important that the applicable rule of law be settled than that it be settled right." [citation omitted] And concerns about maintaining settled law are strong when the question is one of statutory interpretation. [citation omitted]

Stare decisis is not as significant in this case, however, because the issue before us is the scope of the Sherman Act. [citation omitted] From the beginning the Court has treated the Sherman Act as a common-law statute. [citation omitted] Just as the common law adapts to modern understanding and greater experience, so too does the Sherman Act's prohibition on "restraint[s] of trade" evolve to meet the dynamics of present economic conditions. The case-by-case adjudication contemplated by the rule of reason has implemented this common-law approach. [citation omitted] Likewise, the boundaries of the doctrine of per se illegality should not be immovable. For "[i]t would make no sense to create out of the single term 'restraint of trade' a chronologically schizoid statute, in which a 'rule of reason' evolves with new circumstance and new wisdom, but a line of per se illegality remains forever fixed where it was." [citation omitted]

A

Stare decisis, we conclude, does not compel our continued adherence to the per se rule against vertical price restraints. As discussed earlier, respected authorities in the economics literature suggest the per se rule is inappropriate, and there is now widespread agreement that resale price maintenance can have procompetitive effects. [citation omitted] It is also significant that both the Department of Justice and the Federal Trade Commission-the antitrust enforcement agencies with the ability to assess the long-term impacts of resale price maintenance-have recommended that this Court replace the per se rule with the traditional rule of reason. [citation omitted] In the antitrust context the fact that a decision has been "called into serious question" justifies our reevaluation of it. [citation omitted] ***

B

Respondent's arguments for reaffirming *Dr. Miles* on the basis of stare decisis do not require a different result. Respondent looks to congressional action concerning vertical price restraints. In 1937, Congress passed the Miller-Tydings Fair Trade Act, [citation omitted] which made vertical price restraints legal if authorized by a fair trade law enacted by a State. Fifteen years later, Congress expanded the exemption to permit vertical price-setting agreements between a manufacturer and a distributor to be enforced against other distributors not involved in the agreement. [citation omitted] In 1975, however, Congress repealed both Acts. Consumer Goods Pricing Act, 89 Stat. 801. That the *Dr. Miles* rule applied to vertical price restraints in 1975, according to respondent, shows Congress ratified the rule.

This is not so. The text of the Consumer Goods Pricing Act did not codify the rule of per se illegality for vertical price restraints. It rescinded statutory provisions that made them per se legal. Congress once again placed these restraints within the ambit of § 1 of the Sherman Act. And, as has been discussed, Congress intended § 1 to give courts the ability "to develop governing principles of law" in the common-law tradition. [citation omitted] Congress could have set the *Dr. Miles* rule in stone, but it chose a more flexible option. We respect its decision by analyzing vertical price restraints, like all restraints, in conformance with traditional § 1 principles, including the principle that our antitrust doctrines "evolv[e] with new circumstances and new wisdom." [citation omitted]

The rule of reason, furthermore, is not inconsistent with the Consumer Goods Pricing Act. Unlike the earlier congressional exemption, it does not treat vertical price restraints as per se legal. In this respect, the justifications for the prior exemption are illuminating. Its goal "was to allow the States to protect small retail establishments that Congress thought might otherwise be driven from the marketplace by large-volume discounters." [citation omitted] The state fair trade laws also appear to have been justified on similar grounds. [citation omitted] The rationales for these provisions are foreign to the Sherman Act. Divorced from competition and consumer welfare, they were designed to save inefficient small retailers from their inability to compete. The purpose of the antitrust laws, by contrast, is "the protection of competition, not competitors." [citation omitted] To the extent Congress repealed the exemption for some vertical price restraints to end its prior practice of encouraging anticompetitive conduct, the rule of reason promotes the same objective.

Respondent also relies on several congressional appropriations in the mid-1980's in which Congress did not permit the Department of Justice or the Federal Trade Commission to use funds to advocate overturning *Dr. Miles*. [citation omitted] We need not pause long in addressing this argument. The conditions on funding are no longer in place [citation omitted] and they were ambiguous at best. As much as they might show congressional approval for *Dr. Miles*, they might demonstrate a different proposition: that Congress could not pass legislation codifying the rule and reached a short-term compromise instead.***

For these reasons the Court's decision in *Dr. Miles Medical Co. v. John D. Park & Sons Co.*, 220 U.S. 373 (1911), is now overruled. Vertical price restraints are to be judged according to the rule of reason. ***

Justice BREYER, with whom Justice STEVENS, Justice SOUTER, and Justice GINSBURG join, dissenting.

In *Dr. Miles Medical Co. v. John D. Park & Sons Co.*, 220 U.S. 373, 394, 408–409 (1911), this Court held that an agreement between a manufacturer of proprietary medicines and its dealers to fix the minimum price at which its medicines could be sold was "invalid . . . under the [Sherman Act, 15 U.S.C. § 1]." This Court has consistently read *Dr. Miles* as establishing a bright-line rule that agreements fixing minimum resale prices are per se illegal. [citation omitted] That per se rule is one upon which the legal profession, business, and the public have relied for close to a century. Today the Court holds that courts must determine the lawfulness of minimum resale price maintenance by applying, not a bright-line per se rule, but a circumstance-specific "rule of reason." [citation omitted] And in doing so it overturns *Dr. Miles*. ***

Those who express concern about the potential anticompetitive effects find empirical support in the behavior of prices before, and then after, Congress in 1975 repealed the Miller-Tydings Fair Trade Act [citation omitted] and the McGuire Act [citation omitted]. Those Acts had permitted (but not required) individual States to enact "fair trade" laws authorizing minimum resale price maintenance. At the time of repeal minimum resale price maintenance was lawful in 36 States; it was unlawful in 14 States. [citation omitted] Comparing prices in the former States with prices in the latter States, the Department of Justice argued that minimum resale price maintenance had raised prices by 19% to 27%. [citation omitted]

After repeal, minimum resale price maintenance agreements were unlawful per se in every State. The Federal Trade Commission (FTC) staff, after studying numerous price surveys, wrote that collectively the surveys "indicate[d] that [resale price maintenance] in most cases increased the prices of products sold with [resale price maintenance]." [citation omitted] Most economists today agree that, in the words of a prominent antitrust treatise, "resale price maintenance tends to produce higher consumer prices than would otherwise be the case." 8 Areeda & Hovenkamp ¶ 1604b, at 40 (finding "[t]he evidence . . . persuasive on this point"). See also Brief for William S. Comanor and Frederic M. Scherer as Amici Curiae 4 ("It is uniformly acknowledged that [resale price maintenance] and other vertical restraints lead to higher consumer prices"). ***

We write, not on a blank slate, but on a slate that begins with Dr. Miles and goes on to list a century's worth of similar cases, massive amounts of advice that lawyers have provided their clients, and untold numbers of business decisions those clients have taken in reliance upon that advice. [citation omitted] ***

I can find no change in circumstances in the past several decades that helps the majority's position. In fact, there has been one important change that argues strongly to the contrary. In 1975, Congress repealed the McGuire and Miller-Tydings Acts. [citation omitted] And it thereby consciously extended Dr. Miles' per se rule. Indeed, at that time the Department of Justice and the FTC, then urging application of the per se rule, discussed virtually every argument presented now to this Court as well as others not here presented. And they explained to Congress why Congress should reject them. [citation omitted] Congress fully understood, and consequently intended, that the result of its repeal of McGuire and Miller-Tydings would be to make minimum resale price maintenance per se unlawful. See, e.g., S.Rep. No. 94–466, pp. 1–3 (1975), U.S.Code Cong. & Admin.News 1975, pp. 1569, 1570–71 ("Without [the exemptions authorized by the Miller-Tydings and McGuire Acts,] the agreements they authorize would violate the antitrust laws. . . . [R]epeal of the fair trade laws generally will prohibit manufacturers from enforcing resale prices"). See also Sylvania, supra, at 51, n. 18 ("Congress recently has expressed its approval of a per se analysis of vertical price restrictions by repealing those provisions of the Miller-Tydings and McGuire Acts allowing fair-trade pricing at the option of the individual States").

Congress did not prohibit this Court from reconsidering the per se rule. But enacting major legislation premised upon the existence of that rule constitutes important public reliance upon that rule. ***

The only safe predictions to make about today's decision are that it will likely raise the price of goods at retail and that it will create considerable legal turbulence as lower courts seek to develop workable principles. I do not believe that the majority has shown new or changed conditions sufficient to warrant overruling a decision of such long standing. All ordinary stare decisis considerations indicate the contrary. For these reasons, with respect, I dissent.

Comments and Questions

1. Shifting from per se illegality to rule of reason analysis in vertical price-fixing cases should make the antitrust analysis more complicated. What factors does the *Leegin* Court indicate are relevant in a rule of reason analysis of resale price maintenance? What other factors do you think should be considered?

2. Professor Barak Orbach has argued that resale price maintenance can be a mechanism to protect the value of certain status goods (such as trademarked luxury items) because higher prices may create value in the minds of status-conscious consumers. Barak Orbach, *Antitrust Vertical Myopia: The Allure of High Prices*, 50 Ariz. L. Rev. 50 (2008). Do you agree?

If so, how would you incorporate this into a rule of reason analysis?

Is it possible to distinguish between higher prices that create value by conferring luxury status and higher prices that simply reduce consumer surplus?

3. The *Leegin* dissent argued that stare decisis considerations counseled in favor of not reversing the *Dr. Miles* opinion. In *Line Materials*, the Supreme Court opined: "Litigation that the rule has engendered proves that business arrangements have been repeatedly, even though hesitatingly, made in reliance upon the contractors' interpretation of its meaning."

Does this same reasoning counsel against reversing *Dr. Miles*, or are the two situations distinguishable?

4. Following the announcement of the *Leegin* decision, some members of Congress have sought to reverse the decision legislatively. The sponsors of the Discount Pricing Consumer Protection Act of 2009 hope to restore the Dr. Miles rule of per se illegality for vertical price fixing. In April of 2009, FTC Commissioner Pamela Jones Harbour testified in favor of congressional repeal of *Leegin*. To date, Congress has not passed legislation in response to *Leegin*.

5. State legislatures have proven more successful in their efforts to reverse the effects of the *Leegin* decision as applied to state antitrust claims. For example, Maryland amended its state antitrust law to provide that "a contract, combination, or conspiracy that establishes a minimum price below which a retailer, wholesaler, or distributor may not sell a commodity or service is an unreasonable restraint of trade or commerce." Md. Code, Commercial Law, § 11-204(B).

How does this provision reestablish the pre-*Leegin* per se rule against resale price maintenance?

CHAPTER 15

Non-price Licensing Restrictions

DOJ-FTC Antitrust Guidelines for the Licensing of Intellectual Property, § 2.3

Procompetitive benefits of licensing:

"Intellectual property typically is one component among many in a production process and derives value from its combination with complementary factors. Complementary factors of production include manufacturing and distribution facilities, workforces, and other items of intellectual property. The owner of intellectual property has to arrange for its combination with other necessary factors to realize its commercial value. Often, the owner finds it most efficient to contract with others for these factors, to sell rights to the intellectual property, or to enter into a joint venture arrangement for its development, rather than supplying these complementary factors itself.

Licensing, cross-licensing, or otherwise transferring intellectual property (hereinafter "licensing") can facilitate integration of the licensed property with complementary factors of production. This integration can lead to more efficient exploitation of the intellectual property, benefiting consumers through the reduction of costs and the introduction of new products. Such arrangements increase the value of intellectual property to consumers and to the developers of the technology. By potentially increasing the expected returns from intellectual property, licensing also can increase the incentive for its creation and thus promote greater investment in research and development.

Sometimes the use of one item of intellectual property requires access to another. An item of intellectual property "blocks" another when the second cannot be practiced without using the first. For example, an improvement on a patented machine can be blocked by the patent on the machine. Licensing may promote the coordinated development of technologies that are in a blocking relationship.

512 *Antitrust Law and Intellectual Property Rights*

Field-of-use, territorial, and other limitations on intellectual property licenses may serve procompetitive ends by allowing the licensor to exploit its property as efficiently and effectively as possible. These various forms of exclusivity can be used to give a licensee an incentive to invest in the commercialization and distribution of products embodying the licensed intellectual property and to develop additional applications for the licensed property. The restrictions may do so, for example, by protecting the licensee against free-riding on the licensee's investments by other licensees or by the licensor. They may also increase the licensor's incentive to license, for example, by protecting the licensor from competition in the licensor's own technology in a market niche that it prefers to keep to itself. These benefits of licensing restrictions apply to patent, copyright, and trade secret licenses, and to know-how agreements."

B. Braun Med., Inc. v. Abbott Labs,
124 F.3d 1419 (Fed Cir. 1997)

CLEVENGER, Circuit Judge.

B. Braun Medical, Inc. (Braun) appeals from the district court's judgment, following a jury trial, that Braun misused its patent, was equitably estopped from asserting its patent, and that, in any event, the accused devices did not infringe the asserted claims of Braun's patent. ***

I

The patent in suit, U.S. Patent No. 4,683,916 (the '916 patent), is generally directed to a reflux valve that attaches to an intravenous (IV) line and permits injection or aspiration of fluids by means of a needleless syringe. This type of valve provides safety benefits to health care professionals by reducing the risk of needlestick injuries, which might transmit blood-borne pathogens. Since 1987, Braun has sold an embodiment of the patented reflux valve under the commercial name SafSite (R). ***

Beginning in early 1991, Braun and Abbott representatives discussed the purchase by Abbott of the patented SafSite (R) valves. Braun informed Abbott that although it was willing to sell SafSite (R) valves to Abbott for use on Abbott's primary line and piggyback sets, it would not sell those valves for use on an extension set.[1] In a letter dated October 23, 1991, Randy Prozeller, Abbott's General Manager of Fluid Systems, agreed that his company would abide by these restrictions: "We will honor your company's demand that we not use the valve in question for list

---

[1] The primary line and piggyback sets allow a needleless syringe to be attached directly to an IV. An extension set incorporating the SafSite (R) valve consists of a tube with a SafSite (R) valve on one end, and one or more connectors on the other end. These extension sets permit the delivery of additional fluids and drugs.

Non-price Licensing Restrictions 513

numbers other than our primary and primary piggyback sets." Pursuant to this arrangement, Abbott purchased approximately 536,000 SafSite (R) valves.

Meanwhile, negotiations continued between Abbott and Braun for purchase of the SafSite (R) valves for use with Abbott's extension sets. Because the parties could not reach agreement on these terms, Abbott requested that NP Medical, Inc. (NP Medical) develop a substitute valve. After extensive development, NP Medical developed the accused product: the NP Medical Luer Activated Valve (LAV). The novel aspects of this new valve were claimed in U.S. Patent No. 5,190,067 to Paradis and Kotsifas.

On July 20, 1993, Braun sued Abbott and NP Medical, alleging that the NP Medical LAV infringed claims 1 and 2 of the '916 patent. ***

The defendants denied infringement, challenged validity and asserted the equitable defenses of patent misuse, estoppel and implied license. Over Braun's objections, the district court submitted all issues, including interpretation of the claims in suit, to the jury. In November 1994, the jury determined that the '916 patent was not invalid and not infringed by the accused NP Medical LAV. *** The jury also determined that Braun was estopped from charging the defendants with infringement, and that Braun had misused the '916 patent. ***

On the basis of the patent misuse finding, Abbott sought damages pursuant to its declaratory judgment counterclaim. Following an additional eight-day trial on this issue, the jury decided that Braun's alleged patent misuse had not caused any damages to Abbott. After the district court entered judgment on all issues, Abbott filed a motion for attorney fees, contending that the case was exceptional. The district court denied this motion and explained that Braun had presented "sufficient evidence and legal support to more than negate the possibility of bad faith or gross negligence on its part in bringing the infringement claim." Both parties appeal those portions of the district court's judgment that are adverse to them. ***

V.

The jury also found Braun guilty of patent misuse based on the following instruction from the district court (emphasis added):

> [A] patent holder is not allowed to place restrictions on customers which prohibit resale of the patented product, or allow the customer to resell the patented product only in connection with certain products. ... If you find, by a preponderance of the evidence, that Braun placed such restrictions on its customers, including Abbott, you *must* find that Braun is guilty of patent misuse.

Braun contends that this jury instruction is legally erroneous because it essentially creates per se liability for any conditions that Braun placed on its sales. We agree.

The resolution of this issue is governed by our precedent in *Mallinckrodt, Inc. v. Medipart, Inc.*, 976 F.2d 700 (Fed. Cir. 1992). In that case, we canvassed precedent concerning the legality of restrictions placed upon the post-sale use of patented goods. As a general matter, we explained that an unconditional sale of a patented device exhausts the patentee's right to control the purchaser's use of the device thereafter. 976 F.2d at 706. The theory behind this rule is that in such a transaction, the patentee has bargained for, and received, an amount equal to the full value of the goods. [citation omitted] This exhaustion doctrine, however, does not apply to an expressly conditional sale or license. In such a transaction, it is more reasonable to infer that the parties negotiated a price that reflects only the value of the "use" rights conferred by the patentee. As a result, express conditions accompanying the sale or license of a patented product are generally upheld. See Mallinckrodt, 976 F.2d at 708; cf. *General Talking Pictures Corp. v. Western Elec. Co.*, 305 U.S. 124, 127 (1938) ("That a restrictive license is legal seems clear."). Such express conditions, however, are contractual in nature and are subject to antitrust, patent, contract, and any other applicable law, as well as equitable considerations such as patent misuse. Mallinckrodt, 976 F.2d at 703. Accordingly, conditions that violate some law or equitable consideration are unenforceable. On the other hand, violation of valid conditions entitles the patentee to a remedy for either patent infringement or breach of contract. See Mallinckrodt, 976 F.2d at 707 n. 6. This, then, is the general framework.

In *Mallinckrodt*, we also outlined the framework for evaluating whether an express condition on the post-sale use of a patented product constitutes patent misuse. The patent misuse doctrine, born from the equitable doctrine of unclean hands, is a method of limiting abuse of patent rights separate from the antitrust laws. The key inquiry under this fact-intensive doctrine is whether, by imposing the condition, the patentee has "impermissibly broadened the 'physical or temporal scope' of the patent grant with anticompetitive effect." *Windsurfing Int'l, Inc. v. AMF, Inc.*, 782 F.2d 995, 1001–02 (Fed.Cir.1986); see also *Mallinckrodt*, 976 F.2d at 704. Two common examples of such impermissible broadening are using a patent which enjoys market power in the relevant market, see 35 U.S.C. § 271(d)(5) (1994), to restrain competition in an unpatented product or employing the patent beyond its 17-year term. In contrast, field of use restrictions (such as those at issue in the present case) are generally upheld, see *General Talking Pictures*, 305 U.S. at 127, and any anticompetitive effects they may cause are reviewed in accordance with the rule of reason. See *Mallinckrodt*, 976 F.2d at 708.

Because the district court improperly instructed the jury that it must find Braun guilty of patent misuse if Braun placed any use restrictions on its sales of the SafSite (R) valves, rather than instructing the jury pursuant to the *Mallinckrodt* framework, we remand the case for further proceedings. On remand, the district court must first determine whether Braun's restriction exceeds the scope of the patent grant. If it does not, then Braun cannot be guilty of patent misuse.

If it does, the restriction must be evaluated under the rule of reason.[4] ***

---

[4] In its appeal briefs, Abbott contends that Braun's restrictions constitute a horizontal restraint that violates the antitrust laws per se. We briefly address this issue in the event that it is reached on remand. Simply put, the restriction imposed by Braun is not a per se illegal horizontal restraint because Braun and Abbott are not horizontal competitors in the relevant markets. The two markets

VIII

In conclusion, *** the district court erred by instructing the jury that it must find patent misuse if Braun placed any post-sale restrictions on use of the SafSite (R) valves it sold to Abbott. [R]emanded.

Comments and Questions

1. The Federal Circuit states that "patent misuse doctrine . . . is . . . separate from the antitrust laws." But then the court states that patent misuse occurs when "the patentee has "impermissibly broadened the 'physical or temporal scope' of the patent grant with anticompetitive effect." Can you discern the relationship between patent misuse and antitrust law? Does the court imply that patent misuse is essentially a type of antitrust violation? How?

If not, what forms of patent misuse are not also antitrust violations?

What should be the relationship between patent misuse and antitrust law? Why?

2. *Braun* is not an antitrust case. If you were representing Abbott, what antitrust claims would you consider bringing against Braun?

What would you need to prove in order for such an antitrust claim to succeed? What is your likelihood of success?

A Note on Exhaustion Doctrine

Chapter 14 discussed the copyright law's first sale doctrine, which limits a copyright owner's ability to set the resale price or other terms of resale. The analog in patent law is the exhaustion doctrine (sometimes also called the first sale doctrine). The Supreme Court recently explained exhaustion doctrine in *Quanta Computer, Inc. v. LG Electronics, Inc.*, 128 S.Ct. 2109 (2008):

> The longstanding doctrine of patent exhaustion provides that the initial authorized sale of a patented item terminates all patent rights to that item. This Court first applied the doctrine in 19th-century cases addressing patent extensions on the Woodworth planing machine. Purchasers of licenses to sell and use the machine

---

at issue are those for (i) a SafSite (R) valve, alone, and (ii) an extension set incorporating a SafSite (R) valve. By virtue of its patent rights to the SafSite (R) valve, Braun has the right to exclude competition altogether in each of these markets. Therefore, the restricted sale does not constitute a per se illegal horizontal restraint. If anything, Braun's sale to Abbott—for further sale to Abbott's customers—is akin to a vertical restraint, which *Mallinckrodt* specifically stated should be analyzed under the rule of reason. See *Mallinckrodt*, 976 F.2d at 706, 708. Abbott relies upon an earlier district court decision in *Baldwin-Lima-Hamilton Corp. v. Tatnall Measuring Systems Co.*, 169 F.Supp. 1 (E.D.Pa.1958), for the proposition that Braun's actions constitute a per se antitrust violation. That case does not control here. The result in Baldwin was driven by the court's belief that any condition placed on a sale constituted patent misuse. 169 F.Supp. at 29–30. As we have explained, however, that reasoning was rejected in *Mallinckrodt*. See *Mallinckrodt*, 976 F.2d at 708. In addition, the court in Baldwin viewed the conduct of the patentee in that case as being akin to a tie-in, which is not alleged in the present case. 169 F.Supp. at 30–31.

for the duration of the original patent term sought to continue using the licenses through the extended term. The Court held that the extension of the patent term did not affect the rights already secured by purchasers who bought the item for use "in the ordinary pursuits of life." *Bloomer v. McQuewan*, 14 How. 539, 549 (1853); *see also ibid.* ("[W]hen the machine passes to the hands of the purchaser, it is no longer within the limits of the monopoly"); *Bloomer v. Millinger*, 1 Wall. 340, 351 (1864). In *Adams v. Burke*, 17 Wall. 453 (1873), the Court affirmed the dismissal of a patent holder's suit alleging that a licensee had violated postsale restrictions on where patented coffin-lids could be used. "[W]here a person ha[s] purchased a patented machine of the patentee or his assignee," the Court held, "this purchase carrie[s] with it the right to the use of that machine so long as it [is] capable of use." *Id.*, at 455.

Although the Court permitted postsale restrictions on the use of a patented article in *Henry v. A.B. Dick Co.*, 224 U.S. 1 (1912),[2] that decision was short lived. In 1913, the Court refused to apply *A.B. Dick* to uphold price-fixing provisions in a patent license. See *Bauer & Cie v. O'Donnell*, 229 U.S. 1, 14–17 (1913). Shortly thereafter, in *Motion Picture Patents Co. v. Universal Film Mfg. Co.*, 243 U.S. 502, 518 (1917), the Court explicitly overruled *A.B. Dick*. In that case, a patent holder attempted to limit purchasers' use of its film projectors to show only film made under a patent held by the same company. The Court noted the "increasing frequency" with which patent holders were using *A.B. Dick*-style licenses to limit the use of their products and thereby using the patents to secure market control of related, unpatented items. 243 U.S., at 509, 516–517. Observing that "the primary purpose of our patent laws is not the creation of private fortunes for the owners of patents but is 'to promote the progress of science and useful arts,'" *id.*, at 511 (quoting U.S. Const., Art. I, § 8, cl. 8), the Court held that "the scope of the grant which may be made to an inventor in a patent, pursuant to the [patent] statute, must be limited to the invention described in the claims of his patent." 243 U.S., at 511. Accordingly, it reiterated the rule that "the right to vend is exhausted by a single, unconditional sale, the article sold being thereby carried outside the monopoly of the patent law and rendered free of every restriction which the vendor may attempt to put upon it." *Id.*, at 516.

This Court most recently discussed patent exhaustion in *Univis*, 316 U.S. 241, on which the District Court relied. Univis Lens Company, the holder of patents on eyeglass lenses, licensed a purchaser to manufacture lens blanks by fusing together different lens segments to create bi- and tri-focal lenses and to sell them to other

---

[2] The A.B. Dick Company sold mimeograph machines with an attached license stipulating that the machine could be used only with ink, paper, and other supplies made by the A.B. Dick Company. The Court rejected the notion that a patent holder "can only keep the article within the control of the patent by retaining the title," *A.B. Dick*, 224 U.S., at 18, and held that "any . . . reasonable stipulation, not inherently violative of some substantive law" was "valid and enforceable," *id.*, at 31. The only requirement, the Court held, was that "the purchaser must have notice that he buys with only a qualified right of use," so that a sale made without conditions resulted in "an unconditional title to the machine, with no limitations upon the use." *Id.*, at 26.

Univis licensees at agreed-upon rates. Wholesalers were licensed to grind the blanks into the patented finished lenses, which they would then sell to Univis-licensed prescription retailers for resale at a fixed rate. Finishing retailers, after grinding the blanks into patented lenses, would sell the finished lenses to consumers at the same fixed rate. The United States sued Univis under the Sherman Act, 15 U.S.C. §§ 1, 3, 15, alleging unlawful restraints on trade. Univis asserted its patent monopoly rights as a defense to the antitrust suit. The Court granted certiorari to determine whether Univis' patent monopoly survived the sale of the lens blanks by the licensed manufacturer and therefore shielded Univis' pricing scheme from the Sherman Act.

The Court assumed that the Univis patents containing claims for finished lenses were practiced in part by the wholesalers and finishing retailers who ground the blanks into lenses, and held that the sale of the lens blanks exhausted the patents on the finished lenses. *Univis*, 316 U.S., at 248-249. The Court explained that the lens blanks "embodi[ed] essential features of the patented device and [were] without utility until ... ground and polished as the finished lens of the patent." *Id.*, at 249. The Court noted that:

> "where one has sold an uncompleted article which, because it embodies essential features of his patented invention, is within the protection of his patent, and has destined the article to be finished by the purchaser in conformity to the patent, he has sold his invention so far as it is or may be embodied in that particular article." *Id.*, at 250–251.

In sum, the Court concluded that the traditional bar on patent restrictions following the sale of an item applies when the item sufficiently embodies the patent-even if it does not completely practice the patent-such that its only and intended use is to be finished under the terms of the patent.

Id. at 2115–16.

How might exhaustion doctrine affect antitrust analysis?

Would it be potentially relevant if you were representing Abbott in an antitrust suit against Braun? If so, how?

United States v. Studiengesellschaft Kohle,
670 F.2d 1122 (D.C. Cir. 1981)

OBERDORFER, District Judge [sitting by designation]:

This is a civil antitrust enforcement action brought by the United States against Studiengesellschaft Kohle m.b.H. (S.K.) and its licensees. Essentially, the complaint challenged certain arrangements which granted an exclusive license to sell the product of a patented process as an unreasonable restraint of trade and an attempt to monopolize a part of trade or commerce in violation of Sections 1 and 2 of the Sherman Act, 15 U.S.C. §§ 1, 2. Before trial, the district court denied defendants' motion for summary judgment, holding that the patents did not immunize the challenged arrangements from antitrust scrutiny. *United States v. Studiengesellschaft*

Kohle, m.b.H., 426 F.Supp. 143 (D.D.C.1976). After a trial without a jury, the district court found that the license provisions in question, stripped of any patent law protection, violated Sections 1 and 2 of the Sherman Act. The court entered a decree enjoining defendant S.K. from enforcing any agreement limiting sales of the product of its process patent, and requiring defendant to license the patented process to all applicants at a reasonable royalty. This appeal followed. For reasons stated below, we reverse the judgment of the district court and remand with instructions that it enter judgment for the defendant.

I. Facts

Between 1953 and 1954, Dr. Karl Ziegler, the Director of the Max Planck Institute in Mulheim, West Germany, developed a new process for the production of aluminum trialklys (ATAs), a catalytic agent and chemical reactant. For this and other related discoveries of organic-metallic catalysts and processes, Dr. Ziegler was awarded the 1963 Nobel Prize in Chemistry. He was also awarded with a number of U.S. patents on his process for producing ATAs.

Prior to Ziegler's invention, ATAs were known but had no commercial uses. [citation omitted] Experience with the invention shows that ATAs produced by the Ziegler process cost an estimated 5% of what it cost to produce ATAs using the prior art. As the district court found, Ziegler's process "is so economical that no other process can be commercially competitive with it." Primarily as a result of these economies, the number of uses for ATAs increased dramatically. ATAs are now consumed in large quantities as a reactant in the manufacture of biodegradable household detergents and as a catalyst in the manufacture of synthetic rubber for tires. [citation omitted] But since Ziegler did not discover the product ATAs, he was not awarded a patent on ATAs, but only on the process which he invented for their more economical manufacture.

In 1954 Dr. Ziegler concluded an agreement with Hercules Incorporated (formerly Hercules Powder Company) to exploit his process patents. Hercules had followed his research for a number of years and had previously expressed interest in obtaining licenses for the exploitation of his inventions. This Ziegler/Hercules agreement, designated by the parties as the "Technical Field Contract," granted Hercules a nonexclusive license to manufacture ATAs by the Ziegler process for use in Hercules' own manufacturing operations. It also granted to Hercules "an exclusive license to sell in the United States the aluminum trialkyl produced within the scope of the Technical Field." [citation omitted] Ziegler's agreement with Hercules permitted him to grant nonexclusive licenses to a number of other manufacturers as long as they used, but did not sell, the ATAs manufactured pursuant to the license. Accordingly, Ziegler granted licenses to Ethyl Corporation (Ethyl), Continental Oil Co. (Conoco) and others to use his process to manufacture ATAs for internal use.

In 1959 Hercules entered into a joint venture with Stauffer Chemical Co. in an effort to exploit the exclusive license to manufacture ATAs for sale. Together they formed Texas Alkyls, Inc. (Texas); Stauffer contributed capital while Hercules contributed its exclusive license. This transaction purported to give Texas the exclusive right to sell ATAs in the United States, diluted only by licenses authorizing ATA users such as Conoco and Ethyl to manufacture ATAs for internal consumption. Several nonexclusive licensees sought licenses from Ziegler to use his patented process to produce ATAs for sale in competition with Texas, but he consistently denied these applications.

Ethyl was one such disappointed licensee. In 1959 it reacted to Ziegler's denial of its application for a license to sell by filing a declaratory judgment action in the United States District Court for Delaware challenging Ziegler's right to enforce the license provisions banning ATA sales by Ethyl. Before that case came to issue, the parties agreed that, whatever the outcome, Ethyl would be permitted to sell ATAs-by right if the result was in favor of Ethyl, and if otherwise, according to the terms of a special license that would require Ethyl to pay Hercules an additional 2% royalty on sales of ATAs.[2] The Delaware Court ultimately found that the license restrictions were a valid exercise of the monopoly power inherent in Ziegler's process patent. *Ethyl Corp. v. Hercules Powder Co.*, 232 F.Supp. 453 (D.Del.1964). Ethyl took no appeal, but began selling ATAs, subject only to an obligation to pay the 2% royalty agreed upon in partial settlement of the Delaware litigation. Only Hercules and Ethyl have sold industrial quantities of ATAs since that time.

II. This Litigation

On April 24, 1970, the United States filed the complaint in this case against Dr. Ziegler, Hercules, Stauffer, and Texas. After extensive discovery, defendants moved for summary judgment on the ground that the exclusive license to market ATAs manufactured by the Ziegler process was protected by the patent laws and thus immune from attack under the antitrust laws. The district court denied this motion, finding, contrary to the Delaware decision, that the patent laws did not protect the Ziegler licensing agreement. [citation omitted] The court emphasized that S.K. (which was substituted as a defendant upon the death of Dr. Ziegler) held a process patent and not a product patent. The court concluded that a restriction on sales of the product by the nonexclusive process licensees exceeded the scope of a process patent. According to the district court, Ziegler's

> "... patent claim gave him the right to exclude others from marketing, using, or selling his process. He therefore never had protection under the patent laws when he sought by whatever means to extend his process claim to restrict use or distribution of the unpatented product, the ATAs. . . . The holder of a process patent could not . . . license several companies to use the process and attempt to limit the manner in which some of those companies decided to use the ultimate product."

---

[2] There was no restriction on the price or other terms under which Ethyl could sell ATAs, nor any restriction on Ethyl's use and sale of ATAs manufactured by some other process.

426 F.Supp. at 148, 149 and n.3. Having denied defendants' motion for summary judgment, the court set the case for trial on the issue of whether the agreements limiting sales violated the Sherman Act.

With trial pending, defendants Hercules, Stauffer and Texas agreed to consent judgments and decrees. After a trial in which S.K. was the sole remaining defendant, the district court entered findings of fact and conclusions of law. The court found essentially four anticompetitive effects from the restrictions at issue: (1) the nonexclusive licensees, prospective sellers of ATAs, were excluded from the market, (2) the price of ATAs exceeded competitive levels, (3) the development of new uses for ATAs was retarded because of their supracompetitive price, and (4) trade in certain aluminum alkyls other than ATAs was restrained as a result of the restrictions on the Ziegler process. [citation omitted] Without discussion of relevant authorities, the district court concluded that the agreements constituted an attempt to monopolize the sale of the ATAs in the United States in violation of Section 2 of the Sherman Act, 15 U.S.C. § 2, and were illegal restraints of trade under Section 1 of the Sherman Act, 15 U.S.C. § 1, both under a per se rule and as measured by the rule of reason. On March 15, 1979, the court entered an amended final decree that, inter alia, prohibited defendants from enforcing or granting limited licenses and mandated compulsory licensing at reasonable and nondiscriminatory rates of the Ziegler process, including the right to sell any ATAs so produced.

On appeal, the parties make a number of contentions, not all of which need be addressed in view of the conclusion we reach. Appellant renews its argument below in support of its motion for summary judgment that its conduct is protected by the patent laws because (1) it effected no greater restraint than the patent granted, and (2) it could have legally imposed a much greater restraint by granting Hercules an absolutely exclusive license to use the Ziegler process, thereby automatically vesting Hercules with the exclusive right to sell ATA's manufactured by that process. In addition, appellant argues that the restraints challenged here should be upheld as permissible quantity restrictions on the use of the process. [citation omitted] Finally, appellant argues that the government's failure to prove a relevant market is fatal to its claim under both Section 1 and Section 2.

The government grounds its position to the contrary on the summary judgment ruling by the district court below, that the agreements were designed to expand a legal monopoly of the process into an impermissible monopoly of the unpatented product. Arguing that a process patentee has no authority to control the sales of the unpatented product of the process, the government maintains that such an attempt is per se illegal as well as effecting an unreasonable restraint of trade. It also disagrees with the analogy to quantity limitations which defendant asserts, arguing that the license here restrains the use of the products and not the amount of the product which the licensee may produce. Finally, the government argues that it is not required to prove a relevant market, and that in any event the district court made adequate findings that ATAs constitute a relevant market. We conclude that, even assuming arguendo that ATAs constitute a relevant market and that the agreements are not defensible as quantity restrictions, the judgment must be reversed because defendant did not expand its monopoly or impose restraints beyond the scope of the monopoly which its patent gave it.

III. Analysis

A. The patent laws, authorized by the Constitution, were enacted by Congress to stimulate invention and reward innovation by granting the patentee a 17-year monopoly of the making, using, and selling of the patented invention. U.S.Const., art. I, sec. 8; 35 U.S.C. § 154. Such a grant is in inevitable tension with the general hostility against monopoly expressed in the antitrust laws, 15 U.S.C. § 1 et seq. Therefore, courts normally construe patent rights narrowly in deference to the public interest in competition. [citation omitted] As a result, there has been a stream of litigation down through the years flowing from the conflict between the monopoly rights created by the patent laws on one hand and the national policy favoring competition expressed in the antitrust laws on the other.

The essential rights of a patentee may be briefly summarized. A patentee has the right to exclude others from profiting from the patented invention. [citation omitted] This includes the right to suppress the invention while continuing to prevent all others from using it [citation omitted], to license others, or to refuse to license, and to charge such royalty as the leverage of the patent monopoly permits. [citation omitted] A patentee may grant one exclusive license or may grant many licenses. [citation omitted]

A license is an agreement by the patentee, usually for a consideration, not to sue the licensee of the patent for infringement of the patent. A patentee has the right to an injunction barring use of the patented process or product without his permission and the additional right to recover damages caused by such an infringement. The license waives this right to judicial relief against what, but for the license, would be an infringement. Frequently, a patentee grants licenses on certain conditions, in addition to the requirement that the licensee pay royalties. The validity of various restrictions in licensing agreements has been the focus of much patent-antitrust litigation. [citation omitted]

A patent may be awarded for either a product or a process. A product patent creates a monopoly over the manufacture, use, and sale of a product; a process patent creates a monopoly over the manufacture, use, and sale of a process. The essential difference between the two relates to scope. A product patent gives the patentee the right to restrict the use and sale of the product regardless of how and by whom it was manufactured. A process patentee's power extends only to those products made by the patented process. [citation omitted] A process patent thus "leaves the field open to ingenious men to invent and to employ other processes." [citation omitted]

A sale of a product made by a patented process does not itself infringe the patent; it is the unauthorized use of the process that infringes the patent. [citation omitted] Here the several licenses contained conditions restricting sales by the nonexclusive licensees of the product of the patented process. Such sales would violate the license agreement and therefore expose the seller to infringement claims by Hercules and S.K., unless the antitrust laws rendered those conditions unenforceable. [citation omitted] The validity of these restrictions in the nonexclusive licenses under the antitrust laws is the issue which we must resolve.

B. The district court treated the question of the interaction between the patent laws and the antitrust laws here in two stages: it first determined that the restriction imposed was outside the scope of the patent protection, then examined the unprotected restriction to determine if it constituted an attempt to monopolize or an unlawful restraint of trade. [citation omitted] Although in the second step of its analysis the court purported to assess the reasonableness of the competitive effects of the restriction, in fact, its method of analysis had the effect of applying a per se rule. This is so because once the protection of the patent was removed, the license conditions, like the patent itself, inevitably had the effect of restricting competition.

Such a formalistic, two-step analysis forecloses adequate consideration of the fundamental fact that a patent by definition restrains trade, and in effect makes most exclusive patent licenses per se violations of the antitrust laws. But as the Supreme Court noted in *E. Bement & Sons v. National Harrow Co.*, 186 U.S. 70, 91 (1902); "(t)he very object of (the patent laws) is monopoly. . . . The fact that the conditions in the contract keep up the monopoly does not render them illegal." Thus, as appears more fully below, we conclude that a rule of reason rather than a per se rule applies here. Under our analysis, the protection of the patent laws and the coverage of the antitrust laws are not separate issues. Rather, the conduct at issue is illegal if it threatens competition in areas other than those protected by the patent, and is otherwise legal. The patentee is entitled to exact the full value of his invention but is not entitled to endanger competition in other areas by manipulating his patent monopoly. It was thus error to consider the scope of the patent protection irrespective of any competitive effects in the first phase of the case, and then rule separately on the anticompetitive effects of the arrangement without consideration of the protection of the patent.

If the four anticompetitive effects found by the district court are examined, it is clear that all of them were restraints on what the patent lawfully protects: ATAs manufactured by the Ziegler process. The effects as stated were (1) the exclusion from the market of potential sellers of ATAs manufactured by that process, (2) supracompetitive prices, (3) retarded development of new uses for ATAs because of supracompetitive prices, and (4) restraint on certain other aluminum alkyls which resulted from restrictions on the Ziegler process. None of these restraints go beyond what the patent itself authorizes. Such an exclusion of competitors and charging of supracompetitive prices are at the core of the patentee's rights, and are legitimate rewards of the patent monopoly. [citation omitted] Similarly, the restraint on aluminum alkyls other than ATAs produced by the Ziegler process was a legitimate reward of the patent. All of these "anticompetitive effects" of the restriction on sales by licensees would have resulted from a conventional grant of an exclusive license to Hercules to practice the patented process. In fact, the anticompetitive effects of such an exclusive license would be even greater.

The government contends and the district court concluded that defendant's conduct in this case was an attempt to extend its monopoly of the process for making ATAs into a monopoly of the product, ATAs, which are themselves unpatented. As already noted previously, the defendant was not given a product patent on the ATAs because he did not invent them. S.K. thus has no right to prevent others from selling ATAs which are manufactured by another process. An attempt by defendant to expand its monopoly to cover such an unpatented product manufactured by another process would be an attempt to enlarge its monopoly beyond what the patent law gives it and would thus be subject to antitrust attack. For example, if S.K. had required its licensees to refrain from selling any ATAs, even if they were made by other processes, it might well be in violation of the antitrust laws. [citation omitted] A requirement by defendant that any licensee who discovered an alternative process grant back to S.K. a license under that process might similarly be illegal, since such a license might dampen the incentive to invent around the patent. But S.K. did neither of these things. It merely restricted the sale of ATAs which were manufactured by its process. Such a restriction does not in any way operate to limit competition between ATAs manufactured pursuant to the Ziegler process and ATAs manufactured by other processes, now or hereafter available. Nor does this restriction make it less likely that such process will be discovered.

Defendant has thus sought nothing beyond what the patent itself gave it. The patent gives it the unlimited right to exclude others from utilizing its process. This process is, in fact, so superior to other processes that a monopoly over the process gives its holder a de facto monopoly over the product. But there is no danger that defendant can, by manipulating its process patent, "convert a process patent into a product patent." [citation omitted] S.K. has no monopoly over ATAs not produced by the Ziegler patent. Its monopoly of the product can continue only so long as its process remains "so superior to other processes that ATAs made by those other processes could not compete commercially..." [citation omitted] The district court's ruling that Ziegler could not restrict sales of products made by the patented process, without a showing that trade in some article other than ATAs made by that process was restrained, amounted to a rule that restraints on sales by a process patentee, though not by a product patentee, are per se unlawful.

Even were we otherwise attracted to this purely formalistic distinction between a process patent and a product patent, however, it is clear that such a per se approach is no longer acceptable in the wake of the Supreme Court's decision in *Continental TV, Inc. v. GTE Sylvania, Inc.*, 433 U.S. 36 (1977). Prior to *Continental TV*, restrictions by a seller upon the territories in which dealers could sell were per se illegal when title to the relevant goods had passed from the seller to the dealer, but were governed by the rule of reason when the seller retained title. *United States v. Arnold Schwinn & Co.*, 388 U.S. 365 (1967). This distinction, based as it was essentially upon a "restraints on alienation" theory, was criticized by the *Continental TV* Court as overly formalistic and insufficiently attentive to the real economic effects of the particular challenged restraint. *Continental TV* is a message to lower courts that antitrust violations should be based upon economic effects rather than upon formal distinctions. ***

What the district court did below and the government urges here is subject to similar criticism. The government would have us declare that any restraint on products produced by a process patent is outside the protection of the patent laws and illegal per se regardless of the effects of the restraint, on the theory that licensing of the process exhausts the patentee's rights in that process. In the absence of "demonstrable economic effects," however, such a conclusion would be wholly unrelated to any realistic distinction between a process patent and a product patent, and would be just the sort of "formalistic line-drawing" which the Supreme Court condemned.

This conclusion is further supported by the Supreme Court's decision in *Broadcast Music, Inc. v. Columbia Broadcasting System, Inc.*, 441 U.S. 1 (1979). There the Court again cautioned against a willingness to invoke per se rules lightly, stating that it is only after considerable experience with a restraint that courts should classify it as per se illegal. This is particularly true where, as here, the restraint is not a "naked restraint of trade with no purpose except stifling of competition." 441 U.S. at 10 [citation omitted]. In addition, the Court noted in the related context of copyrights that "we would not expect that any market arrangements reasonably necessary to effectuate the rights that are granted would be deemed a per se violation of the Sherman Act." 441 U.S. at 19.

While it is possible that some restraints in a patent license, such as tying restrictions, may be illegal per se after *Continental TV* and *Broadcasting Music, Inc.*, it would be necessary at least to show that the restraints involved had no purpose except restraining trade, and had unequivocally anticompetitive effects in the vast majority of cases. *** In our view these authorities, along with numerous patent licensing cases discussed below, require that the result turn on a careful analysis of whether the restriction imposed here constituted an unreasonable restraint of trade. We proceed to consideration of that question.

C. Defendant's reasonableness claim rests primarily on its assertion that it effected no more control over ATAs than it could have exercised if it had given Hercules an absolutely exclusive license. The law is settled that S.K. could legally have licensed Hercules alone to use the patented process. [citation omitted] The actual licensing arrangement here is less restrictive than an exclusive license. Because other nonexclusive licensees are free to manufacture for their own use, demand for ATAs produced by Texas, and therefore the benefit of its exclusive license, is lessened. This lesser restraint, which has fewer anti-competitive effects than a lawful exclusive license, gives the Ziegler arrangement an important badge of reasonableness.

The government attempts to respond by pointing out that antitrust scrutiny of a patent arrangement is not foreclosed simply because the patentee had the power to license less widely than it did. Of course, it is not the case that merely because the patentee has the right to refuse to license anyone, he has the right to license upon any condition he chooses; that position was rejected as early as *Motion Picture Patents Co. v. Universal Film Mfg. Co.*, 243 U.S. 502 (1917). But in all of the cases which the government cites, and which are discussed below, the restriction imposed itself had competitive dangers which were not present in purely legal arrangements. The government has cited no case, and we are not aware of any, which found antitrust infirmities in a restriction that posed only the restraint on competition imposed by the patent itself or by exercise of legal rights corollary to those created by the patent. ***

The so-called "field-of-use" cases, which are perhaps most closely related to the case at bar, illustrate well the distinction between lawful use of the patent monopoly and uses which operate to extend the patent monopoly. *General Talking Pictures v. Western Elec. Co.*, 304 U.S. 175, aff'd on rehearing, 305 U.S. 124 (1938), involved a typical "field-of-use" restriction. The patentee there licensed patents relating to amplifiers which could be used both in motion picture exhibition equipment and in private radio reception equipment. The defendant was licensed only to practice the patent in equipment for noncommercial use, while others were licensed to use the patent in equipment used commercially. The Supreme Court upheld this restriction, concluding that it was well within the scope of the patentee's monopoly ***. Courts have generally followed *General Talking Pictures* in holding legal such field-of-use restraints as a restriction on classes of customers to which licensees could sell and a restriction on the kinds of objects on which the process could be used. But courts have occasionally distinguished General Talking Pictures and held the restraint illegal where they perceived that the field-of-use restriction was being used to extend the patent into areas not protected by the patent monopoly, such as a requirement that a patented strain gauge only be sold with the licensee's machines.

Viewed in perspective, these authorities, underscored by *Continental TV*, expose the vice of the government's position and the decision below. The government urges and the district court essentially adopted a formalistic approach. Under the government's theory, a process patentee has only the right to restrict the use of his process. By analogy to Univis and similar cases, it suggests that the process patent's protection is exhausted once the process is used, and the patentee may not restrict disposition of the product once the process is completed. The government accepts the proposition that if Ziegler held a product patent, the license arrangement permitting nonexclusive licensees to use but not to sell ATAs would be legal. Thus, according to the government, the arrangement should be held illegal here solely because the defendant holds only a process patent instead of a product patent.

No functional difference between a process patent and a product patent supports the purely formal distinction the government urges. *** Ziegler did not invent ATAs, and thus he was not awarded any right to prevent others from making, using, or selling ATAs manufactured by a process other than his own. Any discoverer of an equally (or more) efficient process was and is free to compete in the market for ATAs despite S.K.'s patent. Ziegler's nonexclusive licensees are completely free to manufacture, use and sell any ATAs manufactured by a process not patented by Ziegler. ***

The situation here is thus quite different from those obtaining where the patentee threatened to extend its monopoly beyond those rights accruing under the patent. None of the anticompetitive effects found by the district court involve this danger. Moreover, these same anticompetitive effects would be created if

Ziegler had given Hercules an exclusive license. Thus, none of the effects found will support a finding that the license restraints at issue violated Section 1 of the Sherman Act under the rule of reason. Since we have rejected both a per se rule and the district court's rule-of-reason approach which, in effect, applied a per se rule, the district court's conclusion that defendant violated Section 1 must be reversed. The conclusion that the restraints violated Section 2 because they constitute an attempt to monopolize must similarly be reversed: defendant cannot be guilty of attempting to monopolize the market for ATAs manufactured by the Ziegler process. That is the very market which the patent authorizes its grantee to monopolize. [citation omitted]

D. *** None of the anticompetitive effects of the challenged restriction found by the district court exceed the anticompetitive effects which the patent authorized. There is no basis in the record for a finding of other anticompetitive effects, and with one exception, which is discussed below, the government is unable to point to any other possible effect on competition. Finally, analysis of the arrangement itself demonstrates that it is no more restrictive than a legal exclusive license, and in fact has certain procompetitive effects not created by such a license.

As stated earlier, Dr. Ziegler lawfully could have licensed Hercules alone to practice the patented process. Such an exclusive license would, by definition, have given Hercules a monopoly over ATAs manufactured by his process, and would have effectively granted Hercules a monopoly over the sale of ATAs, since no other process is now commercially competitive with the Ziegler process. Exclusive licenses are tolerated because they normally threaten competition to no greater extent than is threatened by the patent itself. [citation omitted] Equally important from the perspective of the rule of reason, many potential licensees might be unwilling to undertake the expense necessary to develop and promote a product but for assurances against attempts by later licensees to exploit the early licensee's development and promotion. [citation omitted] An exclusive license protects licensees against such "free rider" problems, and thereby serves the interests of both the patentee and the public by facilitating more rapid and widespread use of new inventions.

The license restriction at issue here has similar virtues with somewhat fewer vices. It prevents other licensees from taking advantage of any promotional or developmental efforts by Hercules, but leaves them free to utilize the patented technology in their own operations. The prohibition on sales is thus a more narrowly tailored version of the exclusive license, having most of its benefits but fewer of its liabilities. The same considerations that lead courts to validate exclusive licenses lead us to approve the restriction at issue here. ***

A number of scholars have also noted that some patent arrangements, such as field-of-use restrictions, have a potential for facilitating market division by giving each participant a stake in the patent in the form of an exclusive territory, or by parceling out to each competitor exclusive access to particular customers. Thus, such agreements give potential competitors incentives to remain in cartels rather than turning to another product, inventing around the patent, or challenging its validity. [citation omitted] In this case by contrast, only Hercules enjoys any advantage from the limitation on sales, and the advantage it enjoys is far less than the advantage which a conventional exclusive license would give it. All other competitors, bound as they are by the prohibition on sales, have every incentive to compete or challenge the defendant's patent and thereby become entitled to sell ATAs.

In addition, market division is a much more serious problem where the product restricted is also produced by other means. Each of the cases cited involved a product which was generic: other processes existed and competed with the patented process. If one of twenty competitors makes a slight improvement in existing technology and proceeds to divide the country into exclusive territories for the purpose of exploiting the patent, the danger that his competitors might abandon the existing technology in favor of the patented technology in order to divide markets is manifest. If the patentee invents a clearly superior technology, whether a product or process, and divides the country into exclusive territories, the case is completely different; there would be a de facto monopoly irrespective of whether the territories were divided. *** The commercial superiority of the Ziegler process is clear. The strength of the Ziegler patent and the inherent value of the process itself give the patentee a monopoly of all ATAs. The licensing arrangement adds nothing. ***

Indeed, it may well be that striking down the restraint at issue here would itself injure competition. There is a reasonable likelihood that had the defendant been unable to issue licenses for internal use only, it would have issued only an exclusive license to Hercules. *** We should hesitate before we impose a legal rule that would force a patentee to follow the more anticompetitive route of a single exclusive license. ***

IV. Summary

*** [W]e reverse the decision of the district court and remand with directions to enter judgment for defendant.

Comments and Questions

1. What are the anticompetitive risks posed by field-of-use restrictions imposed by a patentee?

Why does the presence of a patent make these anticompetitive risks tolerable, or at least not illegal, according to the D.C. Circuit?

2. The D.C. Circuit in *Studiengesellschaft Kohle* suggests that field-of-use restrictions are generally permissible. When, if ever, might a patentee's imposition of field-of-use restrictions violate antitrust laws? Could a field-of-use restriction help strengthen an illegal cartel?

DOJ-FTC Antitrust Guidelines for the Licensing of Intellectual Property, Examples of Licensing

EXAMPLE 1

Situation:

ComputerCo develops a new, copyrighted software program for inventory management. The program has wide application in the health field. ComputerCo licenses the program in an arrangement that imposes both field of use and territorial limitations. Some of ComputerCo's licenses permit use only in hospitals; others permit use only in group medical practices. ComputerCo charges different royalties for the different uses. All of ComputerCo's licenses permit use only in specified portions of the United States and in specified foreign countries. The licenses contain no provisions that would prevent or discourage licensees from developing, using, or selling any other program, or from competing in any other good or service other than in the use of the licensed program. None of the licensees are actual or likely potential competitors of ComputerCo in the sale of inventory management programs.

Discussion:

The key competitive issue raised by the licensing arrangement is whether it harms competition among entities that would have been actual or likely potential competitors in the absence of the arrangement. Such harm could occur if, for example, the licenses anticompetitively foreclose access to competing technologies (in this case, most likely competing computer programs), prevent licensees from developing their own competing technologies (again, in this case, most likely computer programs), or facilitate market allocation or price-fixing for any product or service supplied by the licensees. If the license agreements contained such provisions, the Agency evaluating the arrangement would analyze its likely competitive effects as described in parts 3–5 of these Guidelines. In this hypothetical, there are no such provisions and thus the arrangement is merely a subdivision of the licensor's intellectual property among different fields of use and territories. The licensing arrangement does not appear likely to harm competition among entities that would have been actual or likely potential competitors if ComputerCo had chosen not to license the software program. The Agency therefore would be unlikely to object to this arrangement. Based on these facts, the result of the antitrust analysis would be the same whether the technology was protected by patent, copyright, or trade secret. The Agency's conclusion as to likely competitive effects could differ if, for example, the license barred licensees from using any other inventory management program.

Transparent-Wrap Machine Corp. v. Stokes & Smith Co.
329 U.S. 637 (1947)

Mr. Justice DOUGLAS delivered the opinion of the Court.

This is a suit for a declaratory judgment [citation omitted] and an injunction, instituted by respondent for the determination of the legality and enforceability of a provision of a patent license agreement. The District Court *** entered judgment for petitioner, holding the provision valid. The Circuit Court of Appeals reversed by a divided vote [citation omitted] being of the opinion that the provision in question was illegal ***.

Petitioner, organized in 1934, has patents on a machine which bears the trademark 'Transwrap'. This machine makes transparent packages, simultaneously fills them with such articles as candy, and seals them. In 1937 petitioner sold and respondent acquired the Transwrap business in the United States, Canada, and Mexico, the right to use the trade-mark 'Transwrap', and an exclusive license to manufacture and sell the Transwrap machine under the patents petitioner then owned or might acquire. The agreement contained a formula by which royalties were to be computed and paid. The term of the agreement was ten years with an option in respondent to renew it thereafter for five year periods during the life of the patents covered by the agreement. The agreement could be terminated by petitioner on notice for specified defaults on respondent's part. The provision of the agreement around which the present controversy turns is a covenant by respondent to assign to petitioner improvement patents applicable to the machine and suitable for use in connection with it.

The parties had operated under the agreement for several years when petitioner ascertained that respondent had taken out certain patents on improvements in the machine. Petitioner notified respondent that its failure to disclose and assign these improvements constituted a breach of the agreement and called on respondent to remedy the default. When that did not occur petitioner notified respondent that the agreement would be terminated on a day certain. Thereupon respondent instituted this action asking that the provisions respecting the improvement patents be declared illegal and unenforceable and that petitioner be enjoined from terminating the agreement. In a long and consistent line of cases the Court has held that an owner of a patent may not condition a license so as to tie to the use of the patent the use of other materials, processes or devices which lie outside of the monopoly of the patent. ***

An improvement patent may, like a patent on a step in a process, have great strategic value. For it may, on expiration of the basic patent, be the key to a whole technology. One who holds it may therefore have a considerable competitive advantage. And one who assigns it and thereby loses negative command of the art may by reason of his assignment have suffered a real competitive handicap. For thereafter he will have to pay toll to the assignee, if he practices the invention. But the competitive handicap or disadvantage which he suffers is no greater and no less whether the consideration for the assignment be the right to use the basic patent or something else of value. That is to say, the freedom of one who assigns a patent is restricted to the same degree whether the assignment is made pursuant to a license agreement or otherwise.

If Congress, by whose authority patent rights are created, had allowed patents to be assigned only for a specified consideration, it would be our duty to permit no exceptions. But here Congress has made no such limitation. *** The fact that a patentee has the power to refuse a license does not mean that he has the power to grant a license on such conditions as he may choose. *United States v. Masonite Corporation*, 316 U.S. 265, 277.

As we have noted, such a power, if conceded, would enable the patentee not only to exploit the invention but to use it to acquire a monopoly not embraced in the patent. Thus, if he could require all licensees to use his unpatented materials with the patent, he would have, or stand in a strategic position to acquire, a monopoly in the unpatented materials themselves. Beyond the 'limited monopoly' granted by the patent, the methods by which a patent is exploited are 'subject to the general law'. *United States v. Masonite Corporation, supra*, 316 U.S. at page 277. Protection from competition in the sale of unpatented materials is not granted by either the patent law or the general law. He who uses his patent to obtain protection from competition in the sale of unpatented materials extends by contract his patent monopoly to articles as respects which the law sanctions neither monopolies nor restraints of trade.

*** An improvement patent, like the basic patent to which it relates, is a legalized monopoly for a limited period. The law permits both to be bought and sold. One who uses one patent to acquire another is not extending his patent monopoly to articles governed by the general law and as respects which neither monopolies nor restraints of trade are sanctioned. He is indeed using one legalized monopoly to acquire another legalized monopoly. ***

It is true that for some purposes the owner of a patent is under disabilities with which owners of other property are not burdened. Thus where the use of unpatented materials is tied to the use of a patent, a court will not lend its aid to enforce the agreement though control of the unpatented article falls short of a prohibited restraint of trade or monopoly. *Morton Salt Co. v. S. S. Suppiger Co., supra*. There is a suggestion that the same course should be followed in this case since the tendency of the practice we have here would be in the direction of concentration of economic power that might run counter to the policy of the anti-trust laws. The difficulty is that Congress has not made illegal the acquisition of improvement patents by the owner of a basic patent. The assignment of patents is indeed sanctioned. And as we have said, there is no difference in the policy of the assignment statute whatever consideration may be used to purchase the improvement patents. And apart from violations of the anti-trust laws to which we will shortly advert, the end result is the same whether the owner of a basic patent uses a license to obtain improvement patents or uses the wealth which he accumulates by exploiting his basic patent for that purpose. In sum, a patent license may not be used coercively to exact a condition contrary to public policy. But what falls within the terms of the assignment statute is plainly not per se against the public interest.

It is, of course, true that the monopoly which the licensor obtains when he acquires the improvement patents extends beyond the term of his basic patent. But as we have said, that is not creating by agreement a monopoly which the law otherwise would not sanction. The grant of the improvement patent itself creates the monopoly. On the facts of the present case the effect on the public interest would seem to be the same whether the licensee or the licensor owners the improvement patents.

There is a suggestion that the enforcement of the condition gives the licensee less incentive to make inventions when he is bound to turn over to the licensor the products of his inventive genius. Since the primary aim of the patent laws is to promote the progress of science and the useful arts [citation omitted], an arrangement which diminishes the incentive is said to be against the public interest. Whatever force that argument might have in other situations, it is not persuasive here. Respondent pays no additional royalty on any improvement patents which are used. By reason of the agreement any improvement patent can be put to immediate use and exploited for the account of the licensee. And that benefit continues so long as the agreement is renewed. The agreement thus serves a function of supplying a market for the improvement patents. Whether that opportunity to exploit the improvement patents would be increased but for the agreement depends on vicissitudes of business too conjectural on this record to appraise.

***We are quite aware of the possibilities of abuse in the practice of licensing a patent on condition that the licensee assign all improvement patents to the licensor. Conceivably the device could be employed with the purpose or effect of violating the anti-trust laws. He who acquires two patents acquires a double monopoly. As patents are added to patents a whole industry may be regimented. The owner of a basic patent might thus perpetuate his control over an industry long after the basic patent expired. Competitors might be eliminated and an industrial monopoly perfected and maintained. Through the use of patents pools or multiple licensing agreements the fruits of invention of an entire industry might be systematically funneled into the hands of the original patentee. [citation omitted]

A patent may be so used as to violate the anti-trust laws. [citation omitted] Such violations may arise through conditions in the license whereby the licensor seeks to control the conduct of the licensee by the fixing of prices [citation omitted] or by other restrictive practices. [citation omitted] Moreover, in the Clayton Act [citation omitted] Congress made it unlawful to condition the sale or lease of one article on an agreement not to use or buy a competitor's article (whether either or both are patented), where the effect is 'to substantially lessen competition or tend to create a monopoly'. [citation omitted] Congress, however, has made no specific prohibition against conditioning a patent license on the assignment by the licensee of improvement patents. But that does not mean that the practice we have here has immunity under the anti-trust laws. ***

We only hold that the inclusion in the license of the condition requiring the licensee to assign improvement patents is not per se illegal and unenforceable.

Reversed.

Comments and Questions

1. Grantbacks represent another type of non-price licensing restrictions with antitrust implications. A grantback is a provision in a license that requires the licensee to give a license to the original licensor on any improvement patents that the licensee were to obtain on the original licensor's patented invention.

Depending on their structure, grantbacks can have either anti- or pro-competitive effects. On the one hand, grantbacks raise antitrust concerns because they could reduce innovation if the provision requires the innovator-licensee to grantback an exclusive license to the original licensor. Such a provision could eliminate a licensee's incentive to engage in research and improve the patented product that it has licensed because it would not reap any of the rewards from its improvement patent. *See* U.S. Dep't of Justice & Federal Trade Commission, Antitrust Enforcement and Intellectual Property Rights: Promoting Innovation and Competition 92–93 (2007) ("Panelists stated that the primary anticompetitive concern presented by grantbacks is their potential for adverse effects on innovation. Some have expressed concern that an exclusive grantback that allows only the original licensor to reap the rewards of any follow-on invention can deter innovation because the licensee will receive none of the benefits from any future improvements it might make."). Additionally, "[s]ome have argued that grantbacks also have the potential to extend improperly a patentee's market power because 'numerous improvements made by different licensees all come back to the original patentee. The patentee can then use all the improvements, not merely to obtain control of the affected technology during the life of the original patent, but often for a subsequent time as well.'" *Id.* at 93 (quoting 1 Hovenkamp, et al., IP and Antitrust § 25.3, at 25–7).

On the other hand, grantbacks can facilitate innovation because absent "the security of a grantback provision, a licensor may be hesitant to share its intellectual property with others, fearing that it might be prevented from accessing and benefitting from follow-on improvements to its own technology." *Id.* at 93. If the alternative to grantbacks is a reduction in licensing, then some innovations may not make it to market, *id.* at 80–81; if so, consumers and overall efficiency suffer. A nonexclusive grantback may allow a licensor to charge a lower royalty rate, knowing that it can share in any patented advancements on its technology made by its licensees. *Id.* at 92.

2. Although the Court in *Transparent Wrap* took a deferential approach to grantbacks, such provisions may nonetheless violate antitrust laws. Consider the district court's treatment of grantback provisions in *General Electric*:

> *Licensing on condition that the licensee or agent should assign or cross-license future patent rights.* The Carboloy Company ensured for itself access to any patent rights which any of its manufacturing licensees or agents might subsequently acquire. In the case of the manufacturing licensees, Carboloy was either automatically licensed, or was required to be licensed on request, to any such patent rights. In the majority of cases, these licenses, in effect, were exclusive. The agency contracts required the agents 'upon request of the Company at any time,' to 'assign to the Company, without further charge, all such inventions and applications for United States patents which relate to cemented hard metal carbide or similar material or to the manufacture thereof, and the Agent shall receive back without further charge, full, free, non-exclusive, non-divisible, non-transferable licenses * * * .' Both licenses and agents were obligated to do everything possible to secure the rights to any inventions made by any of their employees. In fact, though some patents were offered by agents, Carboloy never accepted any. In Transparent-Wrap Machine Corp. v. Stokes & Smith Co., 1947, 329 U.S. 637, a clause requiring the licensee to assign over to the patentee any patentable improvements that might be made by

the licensee was held not to be illegal, per se, but the Supreme Court remanded the case for an anti-trust finding. On remand, the arrangement was upheld[citation omitted]. In that case, however, the contracting parties were two relatively small concerns and were without an extensive control of market conditions. *** [I]n *United States v. National Lead Co.,* D.C., 63 F.Supp. 513, *** affirmed by the Supreme Court in 1947, after the *Transparent-Wrap* case was decided. [citation omitted] [O]ne of the factors relied upon [in the lower court opinion] in condemning the arrangements between the leading producers in the field, was that they 'applied to patents not yet issued and to inventions not yet imagined. * * * They embraced acknowledgment of patent validity with respect to patents not yet issued, nor applied for, and concerning inventions not yet conceived. * * * '(63 F.Supp. 524.) The trade position of the present defendants closely approximates that of the defendants in the *National Lead* case, and not that which is found in the Transparent-Wrap case. The employment of basic patents, or patents which may be basic, to compel the transfer of future patent rights, is condemned per se, when practiced on a scale such as is found in this suit. With regard to this question, there would seem to be no difference between licensing a patent with such a condition, and granting an agency conditional on such a clause.

United States v. General Electric Co. et al, 80 F.Supp. 989, 1005–06 (S.D.N.Y. 1948).

The district court claimed to condemn the restriction "per se." Is there a per se rule against grantbacks? Did the district court actually apply a per se rule in this case?

3. In their Antitrust Guidelines for the Licensing of Intellectual Property, the Department of Justice Antitrust Division and Federal Trade Commission addressed the issue of grantbacks:

> A grantback is an arrangement under which a licensee agrees to extend to the licensor of intellectual property the right to use the licensee's improvements to the licensed technology. Grantbacks can have procompetitive effects, especially if they are nonexclusive. Such arrangements provide a means for the licensee and the licensor to share risks and reward the licensor for making possible further innovation based on or informed by the licensed technology, and both promote innovation in the first place and promote the subsequent licensing of the results of the innovation. Grantbacks may adversely affect competition, however, if they substantially reduce the licensee's incentives to engage in research and development and thereby limit rivalry in innovation markets.
>
>   A non-exclusive grantback allows the licensee to practice its technology and license it to others. Such a grantback provision may be necessary to ensure that the licensor is not prevented from effectively competing because it is denied access to improvements developed with the aid of its own technology. Compared with an exclusive grantback, a non-exclusive grantback, which leaves the licensee free to license improvements technology to others, is less likely to have anticompetitive effects.
>
>   The Agencies will evaluate a grantback provision under the rule of reason, see generally Transparent-Wrap Machine Corp. v. Stokes & Smith Co., 329 U.S. 637,

645–48 (1947) (grantback provision in technology license is not per se unlawful), considering its likely effects in light of the overall structure of the licensing arrangement and conditions in the relevant markets. An important factor in the Agencies' analysis of a grantback will be whether the licensor has market power in a relevant technology or innovation market. If the Agencies determine that a particular grantback provision is likely to reduce significantly licensees' incentives to invest in improving the licensed technology, the Agencies will consider the extent to which the grantback provision has offsetting procompetitive effects, such as (1) promoting dissemination of licensees' improvements to the licensed technology, (2) increasing the licensors' incentives to disseminate the licensed technology, or (3) otherwise increasing competition and output in a relevant technology or innovation market. *See* section 4.2. In addition, the Agencies will consider the extent to which grantback provisions in the relevant markets generally increase licensors' incentives to innovate in the first place.

DOJ-FTC Antitrust Guidelines for the Licensing of Intellectual Property, § 5.6

4. Standard-setting organizations sometimes require licensees to agree to grantback improvement patents such that the standard can progress and still be made available. ABA SECTION ON ANTITRUST LAW, HANDBOOK ON THE ANTITRUST ASPECTS OF STANDARDS SETTING 74 (2004). The grantback may prevent future opportunities for patent holdups. Discussing the role of grantbacks in the standard-setting context, the ABA Section on Antitrust Law has noted:

> In applying the rule of reason to grant-backs, courts have considered a number of factors, most of which relate to effects on the licensee's incentives to innovate, including (1) whether the grant-back is exclusive or non-exclusive; (2) whether the licensee retains the right to use the improvements; (3) the extent to which the licensor may grant sublicenses of the improvements; (4) whether the grant-back covers patents that would not infringe the licensed patent; (5) the duration of the grant-back; (6) whether the grant-back is royalty free; and (7) the market power of the parties and whether the parties are competitors. Broadly speaking, the greater the burden imposed by the grant-back on the licensee, the greater the potential anticompetitive effect on innovation.

Id. at 75.

Why are these factors relevant under a rule of reason analysis?

Bibliography of Additional Resources

John H. Barton, *Patents and Antitrust: A Rethinking in Light of Patent Breadth and Sequential Innovation*, 65 ANTITRUST L.J. 449, 461–62 (1997)

Douglas H. Ginsburg, *Vertical Restraints: De Facto Legality under the Rule of Reason*, 60 ANTITRUST L. J. 67 (1991)

Michael J. Meurer, *Vertical Restraints and Intellectual Property Law: Beyond Antitrust*, 87 MINN. L. REV. 1871 (2003)

CHAPTER 16

The Antitrust Implications of Structuring Royalties

Collecting Royalties based on a percentage of the licensee's sales regardless of whether the apparatus sold used the patents in question

Automatic Radio Manufacturing v. Hazeltine Research,
339 U.S. 827 (1950)

Mr. Justice MINTON delivered the opinion of the Court

This is a suit by respondent Hazeltine Research, Inc., as assignee of the licensor's interest in a nonexclusive patent license agreement covering a group of 570 patents and 200 applications, against petitioner Automatic Radio Manufacturing Company, Inc., the licensee, to recover royalties. The patents and applications are related to the manufacture of radio broadcasting apparatus. Respondent and its corporate affiliate and predecessor have for some twenty years been engaged in research, development, engineering design and testing and consulting services in the radio field. Respondent derives income from the licensing of its patents, its policy being to license any and all responsible manufacturers of radio apparatus at a royalty rate which for many years has been approximately one percent. Petitioner manufactures radio apparatus, particularly radio broadcasting receivers.

The license agreement in issue, which appears to be a standard Hazeltine license, was entered into by the parties in September 1942, for a term of ten years. By its terms petitioner acquired permission to use, in the manufacture of its 'home' products, any or all of the patents which respondent held or to which it might acquire rights. Petitioner was not, however, obligated to use respondent's patents in the manufacture of its products. For this license, petitioner agreed to pay respondent's

535

536 *Antitrust Law and Intellectual Property Rights*

assignor royalties based upon a small percentage of petitioner's selling price of complete radio broadcasting receivers, and in any event a minimum of $10,000 per year. It further agreed to keep a record of its sales and to make monthly reports thereof.

This suit was brought to recover the minimum royalty due for the year ending August 31, 1946, for an accounting of other sums due, and for other relief. Petitioner answered and both parties filed motions for summary judgment and affidavits in support of the motions. The District Court . . . sustained the motion of respondent for judgment. The validity of the license agreement was upheld against various charges of misuse of the patents, and judgment was entered for the recovery of royalties and an accounting, and for a permanent injunction restraining petitioner from failing to pay royalties, to keep records, and to render reports during the life of the agreement. [citation omitted] The Court of Appeals affirmed, one judge dissenting, [citation omitted] and we granted certiorari [citation omitted] in order to consider important questions concerning patent misuse and estoppel to challenge the validity of licensed patents.

The questions for determination are whether a misuse of patents has been shown, and whether petitioner may contest the validity of the licensed patents, in order to avoid its obligation to pay royalties under the agreement.

First. It is insisted that the license agreement cannot be enforced because it is a misuse of patents to require the licensee to pay royalties based on its sales, even though none of the patents are used. Petitioner directs our attention to the 'Tie-in' cases. These cases have condemned schemes requiring the purchase of unpatented goods for use with patented apparatus or processes, prohibiting production or sale of competing goods, and conditioning the granting of a license under one patent upon the acceptance of another and different license. Petitioner apparently concedes that these cases do not, on their facts, control the instant situation. It is obvious that they do not. There is present here no requirement for the purchase of any goods. Hazeltine does not even manufacture or sell goods; it is engaged solely in research activities. Nor is there any prohibition as to the licensee's manufacture or sale of any type of apparatus. The fact that the license agreement covers only 'home' apparatus does not mean that the licensee is prohibited from manufacturing or selling other apparatus. And finally, there is no conditioning of the license grant upon the acceptance of another and different license. . . .

But petitioner urges that this case 'is identical in principle' with the 'Tie-in' cases. It is contended that the licensing provision requiring royalty payments of a percentage of the sales of the licensee's products constitutes a misuse of patents because it ties in a payment on unpatented goods. Particular reliance is placed on language from *United States v. U.S. Gypsum*, 333 U.S. 364, 389, 400.[5] That case was a prosecution under the Sherman Act [citation omitted] for an alleged conspiracy

---

[5] '* * * the royalty was to be measured by a percentage of the value of all gypsum products, patented or unpatented * * *.' 333 U.S. at page 389. 'Patents grant no privilege to their owners of organizing the use of those patents to monopolize an industry through price control, through royalties for the patents drawn from patent-free industry products and through regulation of distribution.' 333 U.S. at page 400.

of Gypsum and its licensees to extend the monopoly of certain patents and to eliminate competition by fixing prices on patented and unpatented gypsum board. The license provisions based royalties on all sales of gypsum board, both patented and unpatented. It was held that the license provisions, together with evidence of an understanding that only patented board would be sold, showed a conspiracy to restrict the production of unpatented products which was an invalid extension of the area of the patent monopoly. There is no indication here of conspiracy to restrict production of unpatented or any goods to effectuate a monopoly, and thus the Gypsum case does not aid petitioner. That which is condemned as against public policy by the 'Tie-in' cases is the extension of the monopoly of the patent to create another monopoly or restraint of competition—a restraint not countenanced by the patent grant. See, e.g., *Mercoid Corp. v. Mid-Continent Investment Co.*, 320 U.S. 661, 665-666; *Morton Salt Co. v. Suppiger Co.*, 314 U.S. 488; *Ethyl Gasoline Corp. v. United States*, 309 U.S. 436, 456. The principle of those cases cannot be contorted to circumscribe the instant situation. This royalty provision does not create another monopoly; it creates no restraint of competition beyond the legitimate grant of the patent. The right to a patent includes the right to market the use of the patent at a reasonable return. See 46 Stat. 376, 35 U.S.C. § 40, 35 U.S.C.A. § 40; *Hartford-Empire Co. v. United States*, 323 U.S. 386, 417; Id., 324 U.S. 570, 574.

The licensing agreement in issue was characterized by the District Court as essentially a grant by Hazeltine to petitioner of a privilege to use any patent or future development of Hazeltine in consideration of the payment of royalties. Payment for the privilege is required regardless of use of the patents. The royalty provision of the licensing agreement was sustained by the District Court and the Court of Appeals on the theory that it was a convenient mode of operation designed by the parties to avoid the necessity of determining whether each type of petitioner's product embodies any of the numerous Hazeltine patents. [citation omitted] The Court of Appeals reasoned that since it would not be unlawful to agree to pay a fixed sum for the privilege to use patents, it was not unlawful to provide a variable consideration measured by a percentage of the licensee's sales for the same privilege. [citation omitted] Numerous District Courts which have had occasion to pass on the question have reached the same result on similar grounds, [citation omitted] and we are of like opinion.

The mere accumulation of patents, no matter how many, is not in and of itself illegal. [citation omitted] And this record simply does not support incendiary, yet vague, charges that respondent uses its accumulation of patents 'for the exaction of tribute' and collects royalties 'by means of the overpowering threat of disastrous litigation.' We cannot say that payment of royalties according to an agreed percentage of the licensee's sales is unreasonable. Sound business judgment could indicate that such payment represents the most convenient method of fixing the business value of the privileges granted by the licensing agreement. We are not unmindful that convenience cannot justify an extension of the monopoly of the patent. See, e.g., *Mercoid Corp. v. Mid-Continent Investment Co.*, 320 U.S. 661, 666; *B.B. Chemical Co. v. Ellis*, 314 U.S. 495, 498. But as we have already indicated, there is in this royalty provision no inherent extension of the monopoly of the patent. Petitioner cannot complain because it must pay royalties whether it uses Hazeltine patents or not. What it acquired by the agreement into which it entered was the privilege to use any or all of the patents and developments as it desired to use them. If it chooses to use none of them, it has nevertheless contracted to pay for the privilege of using existing patents plus any developments resulting from respondent's continuous research. We hold that in licensing the use of patents to one engaged in a related enterprise, it is not per se a misuse of patents to measure the consideration by a percentage of the licensee's sales. . . .

The judgment of the Court of Appeals is affirmed.

Mr. Justice DOUGLAS, with whom Mr. Justice BLACK concurs, dissenting.

. . . One who holds a patent on article A may not license the use of the patent on condition that B, an unpatented article, be bought. Such a contract or agreement would be an extension of the grant of the patent contrary to a long line of decisions. [citation omitted] For it would sweep under the patent an article that is unpatented or unpatentable. Each patent owner would become his own patent office and, by reason of the leverage of the patent, obtain a larger monopoly of the market than the Constitution or statutes permit.

That is what is done here. Hazeltine licensed Automatic Radio to use 570 patents and 200 patent applications. Of these Automatic used at most 10. Automatic Radio was obligated, however, to pay as royalty a percentage of its total sales in certain lines without regard to whether or not the products sold were patented or unpatented. The inevitable result is that the patentee received royalties on unpatented products as part of the price for the use of the patents.

The patent owner has therefore used the patents to bludgeon his way into a partnership with this licensee, collecting royalties on unpatented as well as patented articles.

A plainer extension of a patent by unlawful means would be hard to imagine. . . .

Comments and Questions

1. The Court in *Gypsum*, excerpted in Chapter 9, condemned a licensing agreement that extended to unpatented products. In *Automatic Radio*, the Court upheld a licensing agreement whereby the licensee had to pay royalties on total output whether or not each unit actually incorporated the licensor's patent. Are the cases inconsistent or can you distinguish the two cases?

Although this case involves patent misuse, not antitrust law, that is not the distinction upon which the Court relied, probably because the doctrines overlap. *See* Chapter 9. Rather, the issue is whether the agreements have different competitive consequences. Do they?

2. The *Automatic Radio* Court concluded that "there is in this royalty provision no inherent extension of the monopoly of the patent." Do you agree?

3. The dissent notes that "Hazeltine licensed Automatic Radio to use 570 patents and 200 patent applications. Of these Automatic used at most 10. Automatic Radio

was obligated, however, to pay as royalty a percentage of its total sales in certain lines without regard to whether or not the products sold were patented or unpatented."

Does the relatively low number of patents used compared to patents licensed affect the anticompetitive potential of the licensing agreement?

Brulotte v. Thys Co.
379 U.S. 29 (1964)

Mr. Justice DOUGLAS delivered the opinion of the Court.

Respondent, owner of various patents for hop-picking, sold a machine to each of the petitioners for a flat sum and issued a license for its use. Under that license there is payable a minimum royalty of $500 for each hop-picking season or $3.33 1/3 per 200 pounds of dried hops harvested by the machine, whichever is greater. The licenses by their terms may not be assigned nor may the machines be removed from Yakima County. The licenses issued to petitioners listed 12 patents relating to hop-picking machines;[2] but only seven were incorporated into the machines sold to and licensed for use by petitioners. Of those seven all expired on or before 1957. But the licenses issued by respondent to them continued for terms beyond that date.

Petitioners refused to make royalty payments accruing both before and after the expiration of the patents. This suit followed. One defense was misuse of the patents through extension of the license agreements beyond the expiration date of the patents. The trial court rendered judgment for respondent and the Supreme Court of Washington affirmed.

We conclude that the judgment below must be reversed insofar as it allows royalties to be collected which accrued after the last of the patents incorporated into the machines had expired.

The Constitution by Art. I, § 8 authorizes Congress to secure 'for limited times' to inventors 'the exclusive right' to their discoveries. *** The right to make, the right to sell, and the right to use 'may be granted or conferred separately by the patentee.' [citation omitted] But these rights become public property once the 17-year period* expires. [citation omitted] As stated by Chief Justice Stone, speaking for the Court in *Scott Paper Co. v. Marcalus Mfg. Co.*, 326 U.S. 249, 256:

> "* * * any attempted reservation or continuation in the patentee or those claiming under him of the patent monopoly, after the patent expires, whatever the legal device employed, runs counter to the policy and purpose of the patent laws.'

The Supreme Court of Washington held that in the present case the period during which royalties were required was only 'a reasonable amount of time over which to spread the payments for the use of the patent.' [citation omitted]

---

[2] All but one of the 12 expired prior to the expiration of the license agreements. The exception was a patent whose mechanism was not incorporated in these machines.

* Ed: Patents now last 20 years.

But there is intrinsic evidence that the agreements were not designed with that limited view. As we have seen, the purchase price in each case was a flat sum, the annual payments not being part of the purchase price but royalties for use of the machine during that year. The royalty payments due for the post-expiration period are by their terms for use during that period, and are not deferred payments for use during the pre-expiration period. Nor is the case like the hypothetical ones put to us where non-patented articles are marketed at prices based on use. The machines in issue here were patented articles and the royalties exacted were the same for the post-expiration period as they were for the period of the patent. That is peculiarly significant in this case in view of other provisions of the license agreements. The license agreements prevent assignment of the machines or their removal from Yakima County after, as well as before, the expiration of the patents.

Those restrictions are apt and pertinent to protection of the patent monopoly; and their applicability to the post-expiration period is a telltale sign that the licensor was using the licenses to project its monopoly beyond the patent period. They forcefully negate the suggestion that we have here a bare arrangement for a sale or a lease at an undetermined price based on use. The sale or lease of unpatented machines on long-term payments based on a deferred purchase price or on use would present wholly different considerations. Those arrangements seldom rise to the level of a federal question. But patents are in the federal domain; and 'whatever the legal device employed' [citation omitted] a projection of the patent monopoly after the patent expires is not enforceable. The present licenses draw no line between the term of the patent and the post-expiration period. The same provisions as respects both use and royalties are applicable to each. The contracts are, therefore, on their face a bald attempt to exact the same terms and conditions for the period after the patents have expired as they do for the monopoly period. We are, therefore, unable to conjecture what the bargaining position of the parties might have been and what resultant arrangement might have emerged had the provision for post-expiration royalties been divorced from the patent and nowise subject to its leverage.

In light of those considerations, we conclude that a patentee's use of a royalty agreement that projects beyond the expiration date of the patent is unlawful per se. If that device were available to patentees, the free market visualized for the post-expiration period would be subject to monopoly influences that have no proper place there.

Automatic Radio Co. v. Hazeltine, 339 U.S. 827, is not in point. While some of the patents under that license apparently had expired, the royalties claimed were not for a period when all of them had expired. That license covered several hundred patents and the royalty was based on the licensee's sales, even when no patents were used. The Court held that the computation of royalty payments by that formula was a convenient and reasonable device. We decline the invitation to extend it so as to project the patent monopoly beyond the 17-year period.

A patent empowers the owner to exact royalties as high as he can negotiate with the leverage of that monopoly. But to use that leverage to project those royalty payments beyond the life of the patent is analogous to an effort to enlarge the monopoly of the patent by tieing the sale or use of the patented article to the purchase or use of unpatented ones. See *Ethyl Gasoline Corp. v. United States*, 309 U.S. 436; *Mercoid Corp. v. Mid-Continent Inv. Co.*, 320 U.S. 661, 664–665, and cases cited. The exaction of royalties for use of a machine after the patent has expired is an assertion of monopoly power in the post-expiration period when, as we have seen, the patent has entered the public domain. We share the views of the Court of Appeals in *Ar-Tik Systems, Inc. v. Dairy Queen, Inc.*, 3 Cir., 302 F.2d 496, 510, that after expiration of the last of the patents incorporated in the machines 'the grant of patent monopoly was spent' and that an attempt to project it into another term by continuation of the licensing agreement is unenforceable.

Reversed.

Dissent by Justice Harlan omitted.

Comments and Questions

1. Is a royalty payment after expiration *necessarily* a royalty payment for an expired patent? See *Pitney Bowes, Inc. v. Mestre*, 701 F.2d 1365, 1373 (11th Cir. 1983) (holding that licensing rights and obligations applying in both the pre- and post-expiration period signaled that "at least some part of the post-expiration payment" compensated "for patent rights beyond the patent period").

The *Brulotte* Court suggests that deferred payments would be permissible. ("The royalty payments due for the post-expiration period are by their terms for use during that period, and are not deferred payments for use during the pre-expiration period."; "The sale or lease of unpatented machines on long-term payments based on a deferred purchase price or on use would present wholly different considerations.")

What is the difference with respect to anticompetitive effects?

Why is the arrangement in Brulotte not merely a "deferred payment"?

2. "The license agreements prevent assignment of the machines or their removal from Yakima County after, as well as before, the expiration of the patents."

How is this provision potentially anti-competitive?

Does it exceed the scope of the patent?

3. The Court "conclude[s] that a patentee's use of a royalty agreement that projects beyond the expiration date of the patent is unlawful per se."

Does that mean that it is a per se violation of the Sherman Act?

4. The Court analogizes the challenged conduct to tying: "A patent empowers the owner to exact royalties as high as he can negotiate with the leverage of that monopoly. But to use that leverage to project those royalty payments beyond the life of the patent is analogous to an effort to enlarge the monopoly of the patent by tieing the sale or use of the patented article to the purchase or use of unpatented ones."

How is it like tying, and how is it different?

Should tying law inform how antitrust law addresses royalty provisions that require payments after the patent has expired?

5. An interesting question arises when a royalty agreement is entered into before a patent application successfully results in a patent issuing. In *Aronson v. Quick Point Pencil Co.*, 440 U.S. 257 (1979), the Supreme Court addressed this issue when a patent applicant entered into a royalty agreement before a patent had issued. The contract provided that the manufacturer-licensee would pay a 5 percent royalty rate, however, if a patent did not issue, then the manufacturer would pay a 2.5 percent royalty indefinitely. The patent never issued and the manufacturer sued to avoid paying the 2.5 percent royalty, claiming that that part of the contract was inconsistent with federal patent law. The Court rejected the claim:

> Enforcement of the royalty agreement here is also consistent with the principles treated in Brulotte v. Thys Co., 379 U.S. 29 (1964). There, we held that the obligation to pay royalties in return for the use of a patented device may not extend beyond the life of the patent. The principle underlying that holding was simply that the monopoly granted under a patent cannot lawfully be used to "negotiate with the leverage of that monopoly." The Court emphasized that to "use that leverage to project those royalty payments beyond the life of the patent is analogous to an effort to enlarge the monopoly of the patent . . . ." Id., at 33. Here the reduced royalty which is challenged, far from being negotiated "with the leverage" of a patent, rested on the contingency that no patent would issue within five years. No doubt a pending patent application gives the applicant some additional bargaining power for purposes of negotiating a royalty agreement. The pending application allows the inventor to hold out the hope of an exclusive right to exploit the idea, as well as the threat that the other party will be prevented from using the idea for 17 years. However, the amount of leverage arising from a patent application depends on how likely the parties consider it to be that a valid patent will issue. Here, where no patent ever issued, the record is entirely clear that the parties assigned a substantial likelihood to that contingency, since they specifically provided for a reduced royalty in the event no patent issued within five years. This case does not require us to draw the line between what constitutes abuse of a pending application and what does not. It is clear that whatever role the pending application played in the negotiation of the 5% royalty, it played no part in the contract to pay the 2 1/2% royalty indefinitely.

Aronson v. Quick Point Pencil Co., 440 U.S. 257, 264–65 (1979).

Why would a firm agree to pay a royalty to manufacture an unpatented product? Part of the answer may lie in the possibility that the invention may have been protected by state trade secret law. How would that affect the negotiations?

The *Aronson* opinion might seem to suggest that agreements made before a patent issues may avoid the *Brulotte* rule. However, in *Boggild v. Kenner Products, Div. of CPG Products Corp.*, 776 F.2d 1315 (6th Cir. 1985), the Sixth Circuit did not so hold.

> In *Boggild*, the plaintiffs invented a toy extruder to be used with Play-Doh. These plaintiffs sold an exclusive license to make, use, and sell the extruder to Kuto/ Products, which subsequently assigned its rights to Kenner Products. No patents

for the extruder had been applied for when the agreement was executed. However, the agreement required the plaintiffs to apply promptly for mechanical and design patents on the extruder. Patents were subsequently issued. The agreement required Kenner Products to make royalty payments for 25 years, regardless of whether the patents issued. The Sixth Circuit held that the *Brulotte* rule of per se invalidity precluded enforcement of license terms that were entered into in anticipation of patent protection and that required royalty payments beyond the life of the patent. *Id.* at 1319. Because the agreement did not contain provisions for reduction of post-expiration royalties and because the use restrictions on the extruder were the same in the post-expiration and pre-expiration periods, it was held unlawful. *Id.* at 1321.

Meehan v. PPG0 Industries, Inc., 802 F.2d 881, 884-85 (7th Cir. 1986) (explaining *Boggild*). The Seventh Circuit in *Meehan* followed a similar approach, noting that the "*Aronson* Court held that absent an issued patent, federal patent law will not preempt state contract law. *Id.* at 265. The Court explicitly noted, however, that had the patent issued, enforcement of the royalty for exclusive rights beyond the life of the patent would have been precluded." That suggests that in some cases, licensors may make more money in the long run if their patent applications are rejected. Does that make sense? Should either antitrust or patent law care?

Zenith Radio Corp. v. Hazeltine Research, Inc.
395 U.S. 100 (1969)

Mr. Justice WHITE delivered the opinion of the Court.

Petitioner Zenith Radio Corporation (Zenith) is a Delaware Corporation which for many years has been successfully engaged in the business of manufacturing radio and television sets for sale in the United States and foreign countries. A necessary incident of Zenith's operations has been the acquisition of licenses to use patented devices in the radios and televisions it manufactures, and its transactions have included licensing agreements with respondent Hazeltine Research, Inc. (HRI), an Illinois corporation which owns and licenses domestic patents, principally in the radio and television fields. ***

Until 1959, Zenith had obtained the right to use all HRI domestic patents under HRI's so-called standard package license. In that year, however, with the expiration of Zenith's license imminent, Zenith declined to accept HRI's offer to renew, asserting that it no longer required a license from HRI. Negotiations proceeded to a stalemate, and in November 1959, HRI brought suit in the Northern District of Illinois, claiming that Zenith television sets infringed HRI's patents on a particular automatic control system. Zenith's answer alleged invalidity of the patent asserted and noninfringement, and further alleged that HRI's claim was unenforceable because of patent misuse as well as unclean hands through conspiracy with foreign patent pools. On May 22, 1963, more than three years after its answer had been filed, Zenith filed a counterclaim against HRI for treble damages and injunctive relief, alleging violations of the Sherman Act by misuse of HRI patents, including the one in suit, as well as by conspiracy among HRI, Hazeltine, and patent pools in Canada, England, and Australia. ***

The District Court, sitting without a jury, ruled for Zenith in the infringement action, [citation omitted] and its judgment in that respect, which was affirmed by the Court of Appeals, [citation omitted] is not in issue here. On the counterclaim, the District Court ruled, first that HRI had misused its domestic patents by attempting to coerce Zenith's acceptance of a five-year package license, and by insisting on extracting royalties from unpatented products. [citation omitted] Judgment was entered in Zenith's favor for treble the amount of its actual damages of approximately $50,000, and injunctive relief against further patent misuse was awarded. ***

On appeal by HRI and Hazeltine, the Court of Appeals set aside entirely the judgments for damages and injunctive relief entered against Hazeltine ***. [citation omitted] With respect to Zenith's patent misuse claim, the Court of Appeals affirmed the treble-damage award against HRI, but modified in certain respects the District Court's injunction against further misuse. [citation omitted] ***

III. The Patent-Misuse Issue

Since the District Court's treble damage award for patent misuse was affirmed by the Court of Appeals, and HRI has not challenged that award in this Court, the only misuse issue we need consider at length is whether the Court of Appeals was correct in striking the last clause from Paragraph A of the injunction, which enjoined HRI from

'A. Conditioning directly or indirectly the grant of a license to defendant-counterclaimant, Zenith Radio Corporation, or any of its subsidiaries, under any domestic patent upon the taking of a license under any other patent *or upon the paying of royalties on the manufacture, use or sale of apparatus not covered by such patent.*' (Emphasis added.)

This paragraph of the injunction was directed at HRI's policy of insisting upon acceptance of its standard five-year package license agreement, covering the 500-odd patents within its domestic licensing portfolio and reserving royalties of the licensee's total radio and television sales, irrespective of whether the licensed patents were actually used in the products manufactured.[28]

In striking the last clause of Paragraph A the Court of Appeals, in effect, made two determinations. First, under its view of *Automatic Radio Mfg. Co. v. Hazeltine Research, Inc.*, 339 U.S. 827 (1950), conditioning the grant of a patent license upon payment of royalties on unpatented products was not misuse of the patent.

---

[28] The District Court concluded: "Plaintiff's demands that royalties be paid on admittedly unpatented apparatus constitute misuse of its patent rights and plaintiff cannot justify such use of the monopolies of its patents, by arguing the necessities and convenience to it of such a policy. While parties in an arms-length transaction are free to select any royalty base that may suit their mutual convenience, a patentee has no right to demand or force the payment of royalties on unpatented products." 239 F.Supp., at 77.

Second, since such conduct did not constitute patent misuse, neither could it be violative of the antitrust laws within the meaning of § 16 of the Clayton Act, under which Zenith had sought and the District Court had granted the injunction. With respect to the first determination, we reverse the Court of Appeals. We hold that conditioning the grant of a patent license upon payment of royalties on products which do not use the teaching of the patent does amount to patent misuse.

The trial court's injunction does not purport to prevent the parties from serving their mutual convenience by basing royalties on the sale of all radios and television sets, irrespective of the use of HRI's inventions. The injunction reaches only situations where the patentee directly or indirectly 'conditions' his license upon the payment of royalties on unpatented products—that is, where the patentee refuses to license on any other basis and leaves the licensee with the choice between a license so providing and no license at all. Also, the injunction takes effect only if the license is conditioned upon the payment of royalties 'on' merchandise not covered by the patent—where the express provisions of the license or their necessary effect is to employ the patent monopoly to collect royalties, not for the use of the licensed invention, but for using, making, or selling an article not within the reach of the patent.

A patentee has the exclusive right to manufacture, use, and sell his invention. [citation omitted] The heart of his legal monopoly is the right to invoke the State's power to prevent others from utilizing his discovery without his consent. [citation omitted] The law also recognizes that he may assign to another his patent, in whole or in part, and may license others to practice his invention. [citation omitted] But there are established limits which the patentee must not exceed in employing the leverage of his patent to control or limit the operations of the licensee. Among other restrictions upon him, he may not condition the right to use his patent on the licensee's agreement to purchase, use, or sell, or not to purchase, use, or sell, another article of commerce not within the scope of his patent monopoly. [citation omitted] His right to set the price for a license does not extend so far, whatever privilege he has 'to exact royalties as high as he can negotiate.' Brulotte v. Thys Co., 379 U.S. 29, 33 (1964). And just as the patent's leverage may not be used to extract from the licensee a commitment to purchase, use, or sell other products according to the desires of the patentee, neither can that leverage be used to garner as royalties a percentage share of the licensee's receipts from sales of other products; in either case, the patentee seeks to extend the monopoly of his patent to derive a benefit not attributable to use of the patent's teachings.

In Brulotte v. Thys Co., supra, the patentee licensed the use of a patented machine, the license providing for the payment of a royalty for using the invention after, as well as before, the expiration date of the patent. Recognizing that the patentee could lawfully charge a royalty for practicing a patented invention prior to its expiration date and that the payment of this royalty could be postponed beyond that time, we noted that the post-expiration royalties were not for prior use but for current use, and were nothing less than an effort by the patentee to extend the term of his monopoly beyond that granted by law. Brulotte thus articulated in a particularized context the principle that a patentee may not use the power of his patent to levy a charge for making, using, or selling products not within the reach of the monopoly granted by the Government.

Automatic Radio is not to the contrary; it is not authority for the proposition that patentees have carte blanche authority to condition the grant of patent licenses upon the payment of royalties on unpatented articles. In that case, Automatic Radio acquired the privilege of using all present and future HRI patents by promising to pay a percentage royalty based on the selling price of its radio receivers, with a minimum royalty of $10,000 per year. HRI sued for the minimum royalty and other sums. Automatic Radio asserted patent misuse in that the agreement extracted royalties whether or not any of the patents were in any way used in Automatic Radio receivers. The District Court and the Court of Appeals approved the agreement as a convenient method designed by the parties to avoid determining whether each radio receiver embodied an HRI patent. The percentage royalty was deemed an acceptable alternative to a lump-sum payment for the privilege to use the patents. This Court affirmed.

Finding the tie-in cases such as *International Salt Co. v. United States*, 332 U.S. 392 (1947), inapposite, and distinguishing *United States v. United States Gypsum Co.*, 333 U.S. 364 (1948), as involving a conspiracy between patentee and licensees to eliminate competition, the Court considered reasonable the 'payment of royalties according to an agreed percentage of the licensee's sales,' since '(s)ound business judgment could indicate that such payment represents the most convenient method of fixing the business value of the privileges granted by the licensing agreement.' 339 U.S., at 834. It found nothing 'inherent' in such a royalty provision which would extend the patent monopoly. Finally, the holding by the Court was stated to be that in licensing the use of patents 'it is not per se a misuse of patents to measure the consideration by a percentage of the licensee's sales.' Ibid.

Nothing in the foregoing is inconsistent with the District Court's injunction against conditioning a license upon the payment of royalties on unpatented products or with the principle that patent leverage may not be employed to collect royalties for producing merchandise not employing the patented invention. The Court's opinion in *Automatic Radio* did not deal with the license negotiations which spawned the royalty formula at issue and did not indicate that HRI used its patent leverage to coerce a promise to pay royalties on radios not practicing the learning of the patent. No such inference follows from a mere license provision measuring royalties by the licensee's total sales even if, as things work out, only some or none of the merchandise employs the patented idea or process, or even if it was foreseeable that some undetermined portion would not contain the invention. It could easily be, as the Court indicated in *Automatic Radio*, that the licensee as well as the patentee would find it more convenient and efficient from several standpoints to base royalties on total sales than to face the burden of figuring royalties based on actual use.[29] If convenience of the parties rather than patent power

---

[29] The record and oral argument in Automatic Radio disclose no basis for the conclusion that Automatic Radio was forced into accepting the total-sales royalty rate by HRI's use of its patent leverage.

dictates the total-sales royalty provision, there are no misuse of the patents and no forbidden conditions attached to the license.

The Court also said in *Automatic Radio* that if the licensee bargains for the privilege of using the patent in all of his products and agrees to a lump sum or a percentage-of-total-sales royalty, he cannot escape payment on this basis by demonstrating that he is no longer using the invention disclosed by the patent. We neither disagree nor think such transactions are barred by the trial court's injunction. If the licensee negotiates for 'the privilege to use any or all of the patents and developments as (he) desire(s) to use them,' 339 U.S., at 834, he cannot complain that he must pay royalties if he chooses to use none of them. He could not then charge that the patentee had refused to license except on the basis of a total-sales royalty.

But we do not read *Automatic Radio* to authorize the patentee to use the power of his patent to insist on a total-sales royalty and to override protestations of the licensee that some of his products are unsuited to the patent or that for some lines of his merchandise he has no need or desire to purchase the privileges of the patent. In such event, not only would royalties be collected on unpatented merchandise, but the obligation to pay for nonuse would clearly have its source in the leverage of the patent.

We also think patent misuse inheres in a patentee's insistence on a percentage-of-sales royalty, regardless of use, and his rejection of licensee proposals to pay only for actual use. Unquestionably, a licensee must pay if he uses the patent. Equally, however, he may insist upon paying only for use, and not on the basis of total sales, including products in which he may use a competing patent or in which no patented ideas are used at all. There is nothing in the right granted the patentee to keep others from using, selling, or manufacturing his invention which empowers him to insist on payment not only for use but also for producing products which do not employ his discoveries at all.

Of course, a licensee cannot expect to obtain a license, giving him the privilege of use and insurance against infringement suits, without at least footing the patentee's expenses in dealing with him. He cannot insist upon paying on use alone and perhaps, as things turn out, pay absolutely nothing because he finds he can produce without using the patent. If the risks of infringement are real and he would avoid them, he must anticipate some minimum charge for the license-enough to insure the patentee against loss in negotiating and administering his monopoly, even if in fact the patent is not used at all. But we discern no basis in the statutory monopoly granted the patentee for his using that monopoly to coerce an agreement to pay a percentage royalty on merchandise not employing the discovery which the claims of the patent define.

Although we have concluded that *Automatic Radio* does not foreclose the injunction entered by the District Court, it does not follow that the injunction was otherwise proper. Whether the trial court correctly determined that HRI was conditioning the grant of patent licenses upon the payment of royalties on unpatented products has not yet been determined by the Court of Appeals. And if there was such patent misuse, it does not necessarily follow that the misuse embodies the ingredients of a violation of either § 1 or § 2 of the Sherman Act, or that Zenith was threatened by a violation so as to entitle it to an injunction under § 16 of the Clayton Act. [citation omitted] Whether the findings and the evidence are sufficient to make out an actual or threatened violation of the antitrust laws so as to justify the injunction issued by the District Court has not been considered by the Court of Appeals, and we leave the matter to be dealt with by that court in the first instance. ***

Mr. Justice HARLAN, concurring in part and dissenting in part.

*** I do not join Part III, in which the Court holds that a patent license provision which measures royalties by a percentage of the licensee's total sales is lawful if included for the 'convenience' of both parties but unlawful if 'insisted upon' by the patentee.

My first difficulty with this part of the opinion is that its test for validity of such royalty provisions is likely to prove exceedingly difficult to apply and consequently is apt to engender uncertainty in this area of business dealing, where certainty in the law is particularly desirable. In practice, it often will be very hard to tell whether a license provision was included at the instance of both parties or only at the will of the licensor. District courts will have the unenviable task of deciding whether the course of negotiations establishes 'insistence' upon the suspect provision. Because of the uncertainty inherent in such determinations, parties to existing and future licenses will have little assurance that their agreements will be enforced. And it may be predicted that after today's decision the licensor will be careful to embellish the negotiations with an alternative proposal, making the court's unravelling of the situation that much more difficult.

Such considerations lead me to the view that any rule which causes the validity of percentage-of-sales royalty provisions to depend upon subsequent judicial examination of the parties' negotiations will disserve rather than further the interests of all concerned. Hence, I think that the Court has fallen short in failing to address itself to the question whether employment of such royalty provisions should invariably amount to patent misuse.[1]

My second difficulty with this part of the Court's opinion is that in reality it overrules an aspect of a prior decision of this Court, *Automatic Radio Mfg. Co. v. Hazeltine Research, Inc.*, 339 U.S. 827 (1950), without offering more than a shadow of a reason in law or economics for departing from that earlier ruling. ***

Comments and Questions

1. The Court apparently conflates patent misuse and antitrust when it states: "With respect to Zenith's patent misuse claim, the Court of Appeals affirmed the treble-damage award against HRI. . ." It is important to remember that patent misuse is a defense, not a cause of action. So, when the Court affirms the treble-damage

---

[1] I find it unnecessary to consider the further question whether inclusion of such a provision should be held to violate the antitrust laws.

award, it must be affirming antitrust liability, not a patent misuse claim as the opinion suggests.

2. The *Zenith* Court states: "A patentee has the exclusive right to manufacture, use, and sell his invention." That is incorrect. A patent does not confer any rights to make or sell an invention. Patent rights are exclusionary rights, these are rights to stop others from manufacturing or using in a manner that infringes the patent, not affirmative rights to produce or sell.

3. The Court makes a critical distinction between voluntary and coerced agreements. How should one determine whether a total-sales royalty rate is the result of mutual agreement or coercion?

Strategically, shouldn't a licensee protest before agreeing to a total-sales royalty rate in order preserve legal arguments in later litigation?

4. In his dissent, Justice Harlan argued that the *Zenith* majority overruled the Court's prior decision in *Automatic Radio*. Do you agree?

If not, how would you reconcile the two cases?

5. Total-output royalties can also raise antitrust concerns in the copyright context. In the 1990s, Microsoft licensed its copyrighted operating systems to makers of personal computers on the basis of total sales, such that a PC maker would have to pay a royalty on each of its computers regardless of whether it contained a copy of Microsoft's operating system. The government argued that Microsoft's royalty provisions were exclusionary conduct under Section Two of the Sherman Act because PC makers would be less likely to license competing operating systems since they would have to pay for two licenses even if the machine only contained the non-Microsoft operating system. The government settled the case with Microsoft with a consent decree that constrained Microsoft's ability to use anti-competitive royalty provisions. *U.S. v. Microsoft Corp.*, 1995-2 Trade Cas. (CCH) P 71096, 1995 WL 505998 (D.D.C. 1995).

Scheiber v. Dolby Laboratories, Inc.

293 F.3d 1014 (7th Cir. 2002)

Posner, Circuit Judge.

The plaintiff in a suit to enforce a patent licensing agreement appeals to us from the grant of summary judgment to the defendants, Dolby for short. Scheiber, the plaintiff, a musician turned inventor who held U.S. and Canadian patents on the audio system known as "surround sound," sued Dolby in 1983 for infringement of his patents. The parties settled the suit by agreeing that Scheiber would license his patents to Dolby in exchange for royalties. The last U.S. patent covered by the agreement was scheduled to expire in May 1993, while the last Canadian patent was not scheduled to expire until September 1995. During the settlement negotiations Dolby suggested to Scheiber that in exchange for a lower royalty rate the license agreement provide that royalties on all the patents would continue until the Canadian patent expired, including, therefore, patents that had already expired.

That way Dolby could, it hoped, pass on the entire royalty expense to its sublicensees without their balking at the rate. Scheiber acceded to the suggestion and the agreement was drafted accordingly, but Dolby later refused to pay royalties on any patent after it expired, precipitating this suit. ***

Dolby argues that the duty to pay royalties on any patent covered by the agreement expired by the terms of the agreement itself as soon as the patent expired, because the royalties were to be based on Dolby's sales of equipment within the scope of the patents and once a patent expires, Dolby argues, there is no equipment within its scope. The argument would make meaningless the provision that Dolby itself proposed for continuing the payment of royalties until the last patent expired. Anyway the reference to equipment within the scope of the patent was clearly meant to identify the equipment on which royalties would be based (Dolby makes equipment that does not utilize Scheiber's patents as well as equipment that does) rather than to limit the duration of the obligation to pay royalties.

Dolby's principal argument is that the Supreme Court held in a decision that has never been overruled that a patent owner may not enforce a contract for the payment of patent royalties beyond the expiration date of the patent. The decision was *Brulotte v. Thys Co.*, 379 U.S. 29 (1964), dutifully followed by lower courts *** [citation omitted]. *Brulotte* involved an agreement licensing patents that expired at different dates, just like this case; the two cases are indistinguishable. The decision has, it is true, been severely, and as it seems to us, with all due respect, justly, criticized ***. The Supreme Court's majority opinion reasoned that by extracting a promise to continue paying royalties after expiration of the patent, the patentee extends the patent beyond the term fixed in the patent statute and therefore in violation of the law. That is not true. After the patent expires, anyone can make the patented process or product without being guilty of patent infringement. The patent can no longer be used to exclude anybody from such production. Expiration thus accomplishes what it is supposed to accomplish. For a licensee in accordance with a provision in the license agreement to go on paying royalties after the patent expires does not extend the duration of the patent either technically or practically, because, as this case demonstrates, if the licensee agrees to continue paying royalties after the patent expires the royalty rate will be lower. The duration of the patent fixes the limit of the patentee's power to extract royalties; it is a detail whether he extracts them at a higher rate over a shorter period of time or a lower rate over a longer period of time.

This insight is not original with us. "The *Brulotte* rule incorrectly assumes that a patent license has significance after the patent terminates. When the patent term ends, the exclusive right to make, use or sell the licensed invention also ends. Because the invention is available to the world, the license in fact ceases to have value. Presumably, licensees know this when they enter into a licensing agreement. If the licensing agreement calls for royalty payments beyond the patent term, the parties base those payments on the licensees' assessment of the value of the license during the patent period. These payments, therefore, do not represent an extension in time of the patent monopoly.... Courts do not remove the obligation of the consignee to pay because payment after receipt is an extension of market power—it is simply a division of the payment-for-delivery transaction. Royalties beyond the patent term are no different. If royalties are calculated on post-patent term sales, the calculation is simply a risk-shifting credit arrangement between patentee and licensee. The arrangement can be no more than that, because the patentee at that time has nothing else to sell." Harold See & Frank M. Caprio, "The Trouble with Brulotte: the Patent Royalty Term and Patent Monopoly Extension," 1990 Utah L.Rev. 813, 814, 851; to similar effect see Rochelle Cooper Dreyfuss, "Dethroning Lear: Licensee Estoppel and the Incentive to Innovate," 72 Va. L.Rev. 677, 709–12 (1986). "[T]he Supreme Court refused to see that typically such post-expiration royalties merely amortize the price of using patented technology." 10 Phillip E. Areeda et al., Antitrust Law §§ 1782c2-c3, pp. 505-11 (1996) [citation omitted].

These criticisms might be wide of the mark if *Brulotte* had been based on an interpretation of the patent clause of the Constitution, or of the patent statute or any other statute; but it seems rather to have been a free-floating product of a misplaced fear of monopoly ("a patentee's use of a royalty agreement that projects beyond the expiration date of the patent is unlawful per se. If that device were available to patentees, the free market visualized for the post-expiration period would be subject to monopoly influences that have no proper place there," 379 U.S. at 32–33, that was not even tied to one of the antitrust statutes. 10 Areeda et al., supra, at §§ 1782c2, 1782c3, pp. 505, 511. The doctrinal basis of the decision was the doctrine of patent misuse, of which more later.

A patent confers a monopoly, and the longer the term of the patent the greater the monopoly. The limitation of the term of a patent, besides being commanded by the Constitution, see U.S. Const. art. I, § 8, cl. 8 [citation omitted], and necessary to avoid impossible tracing problems (imagine if some caveman had gotten a perpetual patent on the wheel), serves to limit the monopoly power conferred on the patentee. But as we have pointed out, charging royalties beyond the term of the patent does not lengthen the patentee's monopoly; it merely alters the timing of royalty payments. This would be obvious if the license agreement between Scheiber and Dolby had become effective a month before the last patent expired. The parties could have agreed that Dolby would pay royalties for the next 100 years, but obviously the royalty rate would be minuscule because of the imminence of the patent's expiration.

However, we have no authority to overrule a Supreme Court decision no matter how dubious its reasoning strikes us, or even how out of touch with the Supreme Court's current thinking the decision seems. ***

Brulotte called extending the royalty obligation beyond the term of the patent analogous to tying, [citation omitted] because the traditional objection to tying as we noted is that by telling the buyer that he can't buy the tying product unless he agrees to buy a separate product from the seller as well, the seller is trying to "lever" or "extend" his monopoly to the market for that separate product: only extending it in product space rather than in time. Yet if the seller tries to charge a monopoly price for that separate product, the buyer will not be willing to pay as much for the tying product as he would if the separate product, which he has to buy also, were priced at a lower rate. Acquiring monopoly power in the tied-product market comes at the expense of losing it in the tying-product market. [citation omitted] Thus, as these cases and a tidal wave of legal and economic scholarship point out, the idea that you can use tying to lever your way to a second (or, in the post-expiration patent royalty setting, a longer and therefore greater) monopoly is economic nonsense, imputing systematic irrationality to businessmen. ***

AFFIRMED.

Comments and Questions

1. Judge Posner argued that "charging royalties beyond the term of the patent does not lengthen the patentee's monopoly; it merely alters the timing of royalty payments."

Do you agree? Why or why not?

2. Judge Posner asserted that "After the patent expires, anyone can make the patented process or product without being guilty of patent infringement. The patent can no longer be used to exclude anybody from such production."

Is that true?

If the licensee must continue to pay a royalty— lest he be held liable for breach of contract for producing the now-unpatented product without paying— is the patent still exclusionary?

In other words, if the patent is leveraged to extract a contract term that "excludes" competitors by driving up their production costs after the patent has expired— in the same manner that owners of valid patents can do during the life of the patent— why isn't that exclusionary?

3. Judge Posner assumes that "if the licensee agrees to continue paying royalties after the patent expires the royalty rate will be lower."

Is that necessarily true?

If it isn't, how does that affect the antitrust analysis?

In their 2007 Report, the federal antitrust agencies agree with Judge Posner's analysis: "Collecting royalties beyond a patent's statutory term can be efficient. Although there are limitations on a patent owner's ability to collect royalties beyond a patent's statutory term, that practice may permit licensees to pay lower royalty rates over a longer period of time, which reduces the deadweight loss associated with a patent monopoly and allows the patent holder to recover the full value of the patent, thereby preserving innovation incentives." U.S. DEP'T OF JUSTICE & FEDERAL TRADE COMMISSION, ANTITRUST ENFORCEMENT AND INTELLECTUAL PROPERTY RIGHTS: PROMOTING INNOVATION AND COMPETITION 12 (2007); see *id.* at 118 ("Economists agree [with Judge Posner in Scheiber], contending that agreements that extend royalty payments beyond the patent term actually can 'reduce the deadweight loss from a patent monopoly' because per-period royalties are low, and yet the licensor recoups the same present value rent from licensing the patent.').")

4. Judge Posner concluded that "Scheiber would be entitled to such relief only if the amount of royalties that Dolby did pay was less than the fair market value of Dolby's use of the patents, which of course it may not have been."

Is this concession inconsistent with Judge Posner's defense of post-expiration royalties more generally?

5. Ultimately, the federal antitrust agencies have opined that "the antitrust laws are not concerned with agreements that allow a licensee to amortize royalty payments beyond the life of the licensed patent if the patent itself does not confer market power." U.S. DEP'T OF JUSTICE & FEDERAL TRADE COMMISSION, ANTITRUST ENFORCEMENT AND INTELLECTUAL PROPERTY RIGHTS: PROMOTING INNOVATION AND COMPETITION 118 n.20 (2007).

6. If a patentee bundles her about-to-expire patent with a recently issued patent, does that expand the life of the first patent in a way that antitrust law should care about? Why or why not?

7. Another antitrust issue involving royalty arrangement is whether differential royalty rates violate antitrust laws. When a patentee charges different royalty rates to different licensees, it can affect competition in the marketplace. After all, the licensee charged a higher royalty is at a competitive disadvantage to those charged a lower rate. While some litigants have argued that charging different royalties to different licensees constitutes patent misuse, Judge Posner in *USM Corp. v. SPS Technologies, Inc.*, 694 F.2d 505 (7th Cir. 1982) reasoned that such patent misuse claims should be evaluated pursuant to "conventional antitrust principles" and thus royalty differentials are not illegal unless the challenger presents "evidence of actual or probable anticompetitive effect in a relevant market." *Id.* at 512. Other courts have held that an alleged conspiracy to charge discriminatory royalties is not per se illegal. *See, e.g., Hennessy Industries Inc. v. FMC Corp.*, 779 F.2d 402 (7th Cir. 1985). At least one court has found discriminatory royalties to violate Section 5 of the FTC Act. *See LaPeyre v. F.T.C.*, 366 F.2d 117 (5th Cir. 1966).

Bibliography of Additional Resources

Michael Koenig, *Patent Royalties Extending Beyond Expiration: An Illogical Ban from Brulotte to Scheiber*, 2003 DUKE L. & TECH. REV. 5 (March 4, 2003).

Robin C. Feldman, *The Insufficiency of Antitrust Analysis for Patent Misuse*, 55 HASTINGS L.J. 399, 448 (2003).

PART FIVE

INJURY, REMEDIES, JURISDICTION AND PROCEDURAL ISSUES

CHAPTER 17

Standing and Antitrust Injury

A. Competitor Standing

Handgards, Inc. v. Ethicon, Inc.
743 F.2d 1282 (9th Cir. 1984)

*** The Antitrust Standing of Handgards

In order to receive treble damages under 15 U.S.C. § 15 (1982), Handgards must prove that it has been injured by reason of a violation of the antitrust laws. The Supreme Court recently observed that the question of antitrust standing "requires us to evaluate the plaintiff's harm, the alleged wrongdoing by the defendants, and the relationship between them." *Associated General Contractors of California, Inc. v. California State Council of Carpenters*, 459 U.S. 519 (1983). The Supreme Court articulated six factors that should be considered in determining whether a plaintiff has antitrust standing:

> (1) The causal connection between the alleged antitrust violation and the harm to the plaintiff; (2) Improper motive; (3) Whether the injury was of a type that Congress sought to redress with the antitrust laws; (4) The directness between the injury and the market restraint; (5) The speculative nature of the damages; (6) The risk of duplicate recoveries or complex damage apportionment.

McDonald v. Johnson & Johnson, 722 F.2d 1370, 1374 (8th Cir. 1983) [citation omitted]. Because these factors focus upon the relationship between the type of injury for which damages are sought and the harmful conduct, we shall examine the relationship between each of Handgards' damage elements and the harmful conduct.

A. Handgards' Lost Profits as a Result of the Pendency of the Bad Faith Litigation

The jury awarded Handgards lost profits as a result of the pendency of the bad faith litigation from 1964 to 1973. To justify such an award, Handgards had presented evidence to support all six factors of "antitrust standing" required by Associated General Contractors.[19] Ethicon directly attacks the jury's finding that the lost profits injury was of a type that Congress sought to redress with the antitrust laws. It presents three arguments to support its contention that no antitrust injury exists.

First, Ethicon argues that its license offers to Handgards on both the Gerard and Orsini patents preclude a finding of antitrust injury. [citation omitted] *** Ethicon brought a bad faith infringement suit. Any offer to license a patent that it knew was invalid cannot preclude a finding of antitrust injury as a matter of law.

Second, Ethicon argues that Handgards' alleged lost profits are attributable to the entry of additional competition, not an antitrust injury. *See Brunswick Corp. v. Pueblo Bowl-O-Mat, Inc.*, 429 U.S. 477 (1977). To have earned the alleged profits, it contends that Handgards would have had to exclude two subsequent competitors, Poly-Version and Clairol, from the relevant market. We disagree. The district judge explicitly instructed the jury that Handgards could not recover for losses resulting from an increase in competition. Also, as Handgards points out, Poly-Version did not become a viable competitor until 1971 when it entered into a joint venture with Clairol. Handgards does not seek Poly-Version's profits from the joint venture. It only looks to these profits as a rational method of calculating profits Handgards would have received had Ethicon not stopped its efforts to form a joint venture in 1965 and 1968. Aside from the lost joint venture business, Handgards presented evidence that the Gerard patent suit impaired significantly its ability to raise capital to remain "technologically competitive" and Ethicon's letter to Handgards' potential customers frightened many of them away.

Ethicon's conduct not only damaged Handgards but it also had an anticompetitive effect. *See California Computer Products, Inc. v. International Business Machines Corp.*, 613 F.2d 727, 732 (9th Cir. 1979). The bad faith suit not only excluded Ethicon's only significant competitor, Handgards, it also checked possible future competitors until the Gerard patent had been declared invalid. Although subsequent to that date several competitors entered the market, that did not alleviate the harm to competition that resulted from the prosecution of a suit for a patent that was known to be invalid. We conclude, therefore, that Handgards' lost profits injury meets the *Brunswick* test: "Plaintiffs must prove *antitrust* injury, which is to say injury of the type the antitrust laws were intended to prevent and that flows from that which makes the defendants' acts unlawful." 429 U.S. at 489 (emphasis in original).

---

[19] Handgards introduced evidence of (1) Ethicon's prosecution of the Gerard patent suit and its effect of excluding Handgards from the relevant market; (2) Ethicon's bad faith; (3) the anticompetitive effect of Ethicon's conduct and its "antitrust injury"; (4) the direct impact of the bad faith patent infringement suit; (5) damages supported by schedules and expert testimony; and (6) an appropriate damages apportionment to exclude the effect of the valid Orsini patent when necessary.

B. The Legal Expenses, Attorneys' Fees, and Costs Incurred in Defending the Gerard Patent Infringement Litigation

Ethicon does not challenge the jury's award of damages for the costs incurred to defend its Gerard patent suit. This is because in *Handgards I*, 601 F.2d at 997, we found that "[i]n a suit alleging antitrust injury based upon a bad faith prosecution theory it is obvious that the costs incurred in defense of the prior patent infringement suit are an injury which 'flows' from the antitrust wrong." We do not believe this conclusion is affected by the antitrust standing principles enunciated in Associated General Contractors [citation omitted].

VI. Damage Award Properly Supported by Evidence

Ethicon argues that Handgards' damage schedules are insufficient as a matter of law. We disagree. Once the fact of antitrust injury is proven, we have traditionally required a lesser quantum of proof to support the amount of damages. [citation omitted] An antitrust plaintiff must simply provide evidence to support a "'just and reasonable estimate of the damage.'" [citation omitted] A jury's finding of the amount of damages must be upheld unless the amount is "grossly excessive or monstrous," clearly not supported by the evidence, or "only based on speculation or guesswork." [citation omitted] In this case Ethicon has failed to demonstrate such error in the jury's damage verdict.

Comments and Questions

1. Antitrust injury differs from the traditional injury required to get standing in federal court, in that an antitrust plaintiff's injury must be caused by the anticompetitive effects of the defendant's conduct. Why, and when, are litigation costs an antitrust injury?

2. In addition to proving antitrust injury, an antitrust plaintiff must be able to calculate its damages and prove that these damages were *caused* by the defendant's antitrust violation. The issues of injury, causation, and damages are, of course, interconnected:

> To establish fact of injury, [an antitrust plaintiff] must demonstrate "a causal connection between the defendant's actions violative of the Sherman Act and the actual injury to the plaintiff's business." [citation omitted] Damage issues in antitrust cases, however, do not lend themselves to the sort of detailed proof of injury which surfaces in other types of claims. A plaintiff's burden to show a fact of injury, therefore, "'is satisfied by its proof of some damage flowing from the unlawful conspiracy' which may be established by reasonable inference drawn from circumstantial evidence." World of Sleep at 1478 (quoting Zenith Radio Corp. v. Hazeltine Research, Inc., 395 U.S. 100, 114 n. 9 (1969)).

Beal Corp. Liquidating Trust v. Valleylab, Inc., 927 F.Supp. 1350 (D.Colo. 1996).

When an antitrust plaintiff loses business, how might it prove that the losses were caused by the defendant's antitrust violation?

560 *Antitrust Law and Intellectual Property Rights*

3. Antitrust damages are automatically trebled, pursuant to section 4 of the Clayton Act, 15 U.S.C. § 15(a), which provides, in part:

> [A]ny person who shall be injured in his business or property by reason of anything forbidden in the antitrust laws may sue therefor in any district court of the United States in the district in which the defendant resides or is found or has an agent, without respect to the amount in controversy, and shall recover threefold the damages by him sustained, and the cost of suit, including a reasonable attorney's fee.

15 U.S.C. § 15(a) (1988). Some statutory exceptions exist, for example, for certain joint ventures and standard-setting organizations, which must pay only single damages in the event of antitrust liability. 15 U.S.C. §§ 4301, 4303 (2006).

4. In cases of price-fixing and illegal monopolization, antitrust damages are measured by the overcharge, i.e., the difference between the market price that would have prevailed but for the antitrust violation and the price actually charged by the antitrust defendant.

In cases of illegal tying, damages may be hard to estimate because two separate markets are involved and the tying seller may give a discount in the tying product market in order to induce customers to accept the tying requirement. The Fifth Circuit held that *Siegel v. Chicken Delight*, excerpted in Chapter 5,

> stands for the proposition that injury resulting from a tie-in must be shown by establishing that payments for both the tied and tying products exceeded their combined fair market value. The rationale behind this requirement is apparent: A determination of the value of the tied products alone would not indicate whether the plaintiff indeed suffered any net economic harm, since a lower price might conceivably have been exacted by the franchisor for the tying product. Unless the fair market value of both the tied and tying products are determined and an overcharge in the complete price found, no injury can be claimed; suit, then, would be foreclosed.

Kypta v. McDonald's Corp., 671 F.2d 1282, 1285 (5th Cir. 1982).

Do you think that that is the correct measure of damages? Why or why not?

Bourns, Inc. v. Raychem Corp.

331 F.3d 704 (9th Cir. 2003)

NOONAN, Circuit Judge.

*** Facts

PPTCs are used in a variety of products, including automobiles, batteries, computers, consumer electronics, industrial controls, and instruments of telecommunications. PPTCs are not the only devices available to control excess current but, depending on price and supply, may be preferable in many contexts to competing methods such as fuses or ceramic positive temperature coefficients or bimetallics breakers. Raychem used its patents to achieve a dominant position where PPTCs were highly preferred.

Beginning in 1988 with its role as a PPTC distributor for Raychem in Europe, Bourns contemplated the possibility of itself becoming a maker of PPTCs. Indeed, as Bourns puts it in its brief, as early as 1987 Bourns had "proposed the obvious—a marriage in which Raychem contributed its technology with Bourns to provide the manufacturing and marketing expertise." The proposal was not accepted. Bourns took no steps to prepare to manufacture PPTCs until sometime in 1994. On December 2, 1994, its board approved a proposal to produce PPTC ***.

Proceedings

In 1995, *** Bourns brought this suit against Raychem in the district court. Bourns' first amended complaint charged Raychem with a variety of acts violative of Sections 1 and 2 of the Sherman Act and Section 7 of the Clayton Act. In the course of the proceedings, a number of these charges were eliminated by rulings of the district court that have not been appealed. The heart of Bourns' case remained: Raychem had prevented Bourns from competing in the PPTC business by threatened enforcement of its invalid patents.

The jury that heard the case returned a special verdict, stating that Bourns had proved by clear and convincing evidence that Raychem had acquired four specified patents by intentional fraud on the Patent Office and had threatened to enforce these patents against Bourns and that Raychem "acquired or maintained monopoly power in a relevant market" by these threats. To the question, "identify the relevant market or relevant markets in which Raychem willfully acquired or maintained monopoly power," the jury replied: "PPTC/Primary Lithium Batteries." To the question, "On what date after May, 1994, did Bourns first have the intent and preparedness to enter the business of making and selling PPTC devices?" The jury answered: "December 1, 1994." The jury stated that the damages Bourns suffered amounted to $64 million.

Raychem moved for judgment notwithstanding the verdict on the ground that Bourns had established no antitrust injury after December 1, 1994, the date the jury had determined that it had antitrust standing as a potential competitor. The district court denied the motion, stating, "Here the jury could have reasonably concluded that Raychem's threatened enforcement of the challenged patents in both May and September 1994 had continuing effects on Bourns so as to cause antitrust injury." ***

Analysis

Antitrust Injury. Bourns' case rested on what is referred to as its "Walker Process claim," shorthand for reference to *Walker Process Equip., Inc. v. Food Mach. & Chem. Corp.*, 382 U.S. 172 (1965). In that case the Supreme Court held that possession and use of a fraudulently-acquired patent was not a per se violation of the Sherman Act but could be treated as an offense under the antitrust laws if the patent was employed to produce monopoly power in a specified market. Bourns' successful attack on the Raychem patents and its establishment of the lithium batteries market as affected by the patents was not the end of Bourns' case. Bourns had to show that, at the time Raychem threatened it with patent litigation, it was more than a hopeful bystander. Bourns had to show that Raychem's fraudulent bluffing had inflicted antitrust injury on it.

Only an actual competitor or one ready to be a competitor can suffer antitrust injury. The district court ruled that as a matter of law Bourns did not have the intent and preparedness to be a competitor in the PPTC business prior to May, 1994. The jury found that the necessary intent and preparedness were not present until the day before the Bourns' board action of December 2, 1994. Bourns challenges this determination, but we cannot say that either the district court's ruling or the jury's finding was against the weight of the evidence.

Bourns points to evidence of its desire to get into the PPTC business: its "marriage proposal" to Raychem in 1987; its acceptance of the private licensing agreement from Raychem; its repeated efforts to get a manufacturing license from Raychem. Each of these examples of Bourns' desire to enter the business might count as evidence of intent to enter the business. At the same time each example shows Bourns unprepared to enter the business. Bourns was wishing; it was not assembling the personnel, the equipment, the facilities, nor acquiring the knowledge, nor allocating the capital to put it into the production of PPTCs. It was unprepared to compete. [citation omitted]

As the district court observed in its ruling that Bourns was unprepared, that Bourns was an electronics firm did not establish that it "had the experience and background necessary to manufacture PPTCs." Bourns had no experience working with carbon black or with the processes of extrusion and lamination. Bourns did not have a place or equipment to produce the PPTCs. When on December 2, 1994, Bourns voted to embark on the business, it opened a new facility in Hong Kong to do the manufacturing and purchased new equipment for the facility. Before it acquired Hogge, Chan, and Zhang, Bourns did not have the people for the PPTC business. Until the Bourns board acted on December 2, 1994, Bourns had not decided to allocate funds. Bourns failed every test of preparedness to be a PPTC competitor prior to December 1, 1994. [citation omitted] *** Bourns had no product and no contracts or arrangements to produce the product. [citation omitted] Up to the date determined by the jury, Bourns was a bystander.

The threats that Bourns showed were made by Raychem to enforce its patents were made in May 1994 and September 1994. They were threats to a bystander who was pawing the ground: don't get into our turf. They were not threats to a competitor or to a business prepared to be a competitor. They did constitute an abuse of Raychem's invalid patents. They did not constitute antitrust injury for the threats were not addressed to a business in the market or to a business that was prepared to enter the market.

The district court, denying Raychem's motion for judgment notwithstanding the verdict, speculated that the threats could have "continuing effects on Bourns so as to constitute antitrust injury." What were these continuing effects? Bourns does not name them. Bourns does argue that but for the threats it would have been ready to sell "its own PPTC product by December 1, 1994." It is very difficult to see how this claim can be made. Working as hard as it could after December 1, 1994, with the help of the ex-Raychem employees, Bourns had no product to sell for another 20 months. Not the slightest evidence was offered that any threat of Raychem prevented Bourns from selling PPTCs prior to September 1996 when Bourns actually entered the market.

Standing to bring an antitrust action is a requirement because antitrust injury is a necessary element of an antitrust suit. See P. Areeda and H. Hovenkamp, Antitrust Law (2d ed.2001) ¶ 337. A "nascent" business—one that is merely a gleam in the eye and a hope in the heart of its promoters—does not possess the property to which antitrust injury can be done. Id. ¶ 349. Bourns, up until December 1994, was such a firm so far as the PPTC business was concerned. Suffering no antitrust injury before the December date because it was unprepared, and suffering no antitrust injury after the December date because no patent threats were thereafter made, Bourns has no antitrust case. Raychem is entitled to judgment as a matter of law. ***

PREGERSON, Circuit Judge, concurring in part and dissenting in part:

*** The majority does not question the jury's special verdict that Bourns had proved by clear and convincing evidence that Raychem unlawfully procured four of its PPTC patents by intentional fraud on the United States Trademark and Patent Office, or that Bourns had anti-trust standing to bring suit against Raychem on December 1, 1994. The majority also does not dispute that Raychem made several threats to Bourns to enforce its fraudulently obtained patents against Bourns if Bourns entered the PPTC market. Instead, the majority reversed the jury's verdict in favor of Bourns because (1) Bourns did not present adequate evidence that it suffered antitrust injury since it had no product to sell for twenty months after it acquired standing to bring a *Walker Process* claim, and (2) Raychem threatened to enforce its fraudulent patents against Bourns before the date that Bourns acquired its anti-trust standing.

The majority's reliance on whether Bourns had a PPTC product in the market as an indicator that Bourns suffered anti-trust injury misses the point of the *Walker Process* inquiry: a *Walker Process* claim is designed to prohibit a dominant party from willfully and fraudulently monopolizing a market by deterring another company's attempt to enter that market. As the Supreme Court described in *Walker Process*:

> A patent by its very nature is affected with a public interest. * * * (It) is an exception to the general rule against monopolies and to the right to access to a free and open market. The far-reaching social and economic consequences of a patent, therefore, give the public a paramount interest in seeing that patent monopolies spring from backgrounds free from fraud or other inequitable conduct and that such monopolies are kept within their legitimate scope.

Walker Process, 382 U.S. at 177 [citation omitted]. Because a party who wishes to enter a market often is deterred from doing so as a direct result of a monopolizing party's threats to enforce its fraudulent patents, *Walker Process* only requires that to have standing to sue, a company which wishes to enter the market demonstrate that it was a potential competitor, not an actual competitor. Thus, "our circuit, along with most circuits, has held that a potential competitor has standing if he can show a genuine intent to enter the market and a preparedness to do so." [citation omitted] The majority errs by holding that Raychem's threats to enforce its patents against Bourns could not have caused Bourns anti-trust injury because it took Bourns twenty months to enter the PPTC market after it acquired standing to bring a *Walker Process* claim. ***

Comments and Questions

1. The majority holds that antitrust standing is limited to "an actual competitor or one ready to be a competitor." How can you determine whether an antitrust plaintiff is sufficiently "ready to be a competitor" that it has antitrust standing to sue a monopolist-patentee that has acquired its patents through fraud?

2. What are the risks of defining antitrust standing too broadly? What are the risks of defining antitrust standing too narrowly? How should courts balance those risks to ensure that they are defining antitrust standing properly?

3. In his dissent, Judge Pregerson argues that Bourns had suffered antitrust injury and therefore did have standing to pursue its claim. Do you think that the majority or the dissent offers a more persuasive argument? Why?

B. Consumer Standing

In re Ciprofloxacin Hydrochloride Antitrust Litigation,
363 F.Supp.2d 514 (E.D.N.Y. 2005)

Trager, District Judge

*** Consumer Antitrust Standing

As the law now stands, the validity of a patent may be challenged only by an alleged infringer as an affirmative defense or counterclaim to an infringement action brought by the patentee, or by a declaratory judgment plaintiff ***. Therefore, at present, non-infringing consumers of patented products who may feel that they are being charged supracompetitive prices by the patentee have no cause of action to invalidate the patent. ***

Given that consumers are often subjected to monopoly prices for invalid patents, it is tempting to suggest that, as a policy matter, a rule should be fashioned giving consumers of drugs—and perhaps patented goods generally—the right to challenge the validity of patents. In other words, plaintiffs should be afforded the opportunity to challenge the exclusion-payment scheme at issue here—and licensing arrangements as well—by folding in a predicate challenge to the underlying patent itself. Under the proposed rule, the consumers would have to show by clear and convincing evidence—as accused infringers must—that the subject patent was invalid. This proposal would have the effect of allowing non-infringing consumers of a patented product to seek to invalidate the patent in order to allow price-reducing competitors to enter the market. The desirability of such a change is a complex issue which is not within the competence of judges. A thorough examination of the consequences of such a change would have to be made. For example, would such a change negatively impact the willingness of drug manufacturers to invest in research and development? Should consumers be permitted to recover punitive damages for the overcharges they have suffered? As Justice Harlan noted, patents are often set aside for any number of technical reasons. *Walker Process*, 382 U.S. at 179–80. Perhaps permitting only declaratory relief, together with attorneys' fees, would solve the problem of unduly punishing those who in good faith sought patents that ultimately were shown to be invalid. Another possible alternative is to limit the consumer recovery to the amount of the monopolistic overcharges. These questions lead to the inevitable conclusion that such a change in public policy should be made by Congress, and not by the courts. ***

Molecular Diagnostics Laboratories v. Hoffmann-La Roche Inc.
402 F.Supp.2d 276 (D.D.C. 2005)

Kennedy, District Judge

*** In *Walker Process*, the Supreme Court permitted plaintiffs to seek treble damages under the antitrust laws when the fraudulent procurement of a patent is coupled with a violation of section 2 of the Sherman Act. [citation omitted] Here, MDL maintains that Applera and Roche used the '818 patent, procured by fraud, to monopolize the market for Taq.* Because MDL is a direct consumer of Taq, MDL asserts that it has standing to prosecute a *Walker Process* claim as an injured party under the antitrust laws. In response, both Applera and Roche argue that the *Walker Process* decision did not contemplate direct consumers as suitable plaintiffs in this type of action. Rather, they contend, the only entity with standing to bring a *Walker Process* claim is a competitor or, more specifically, an entity against whom a fraudulently obtained patent is, or could be, enforced.[4]

Applera and Roche rely on *In re Remeron Antitrust Litig.*, 335 F.Supp.2d 522 (D.N.J.2004) *** in support of the proposition that *Walker Process* claims are

---

* Editor's note: The court defined Taq earlier: "Taq is a thermostable enzyme derived from Thermus aquaticus bacteria and an important component of a process known as "polymerase chain reaction" ("PCR"). PCR is a technique used to replicate DNA, allowing small DNA samples to yield larger quantities that can then be studied or manipulated. During the PCR process, a sample of DNA is subjected to rapid fluctuations between extreme temperatures–Taq is able to withstand these volatile temperature changes and still remain an effective catalyst for the replication of DNA."

[4] Defendants are indeed correct that the vast majority of Walker Process claims are brought by parties against whom a patent is enforced. See *Nobelpharma AB v. Implant Innovations, Inc.*, 141 F.3d 1059, 1067 (Fed.Cir.1998) ("[A]n antitrust claim premised on stripping a patentee of its immunity from the antitrust laws is typically raised as a counterclaim by a defendant in a patent infringement suit.") (citing *Argus Chem. Corp. v. Fibre Glass-Evercoat Co.*, 812 F.2d 1381, 1383 (Fed.Cir.1987)). Indeed, with the exception of the two cases discussed infra, neither the parties nor the court have been able to identify an instance in which a customer litigated a Walker Process claim.

available exclusively to those against whom a patent is enforced. *** The court in *In re Remeron*, by comparison, did find that a direct purchaser lacked standing to bring a *Walker Process* claim. However, the court offered little justification for its holding, stating:

> Plaintiffs, as direct purchasers, neither produced mirtzapine nor would have done so; moreover, Plaintiffs were not party to the initial patent infringement suits. Plaintiffs may not now claim standing to bring a Walker Process claim by donning the cloak of a Clayton Act monopolization claim.

335 F.Supp.2d at 529. The holding cites no controlling precedent, nor offers any compelling justification for its conclusion.

The inclusion of the fact that the plaintiffs were not parties in the initial patent infringement suits suggests that the court confused the harm addressed through a *Walker Process* claim. The court appears to believe that, standing alone, the enforcement of the fraudulently procured patent is the relevant injury in a *Walker Process* claim, hence the court's assertion that a plaintiff must be an actual or potential competitor. This, however, is not the case. *Walker Process* claims are intended to address antitrust injury, thus the requirement that a plaintiff be able to allege a violation of Section 2 of the Sherman Act. [citation omitted] A *Walker Process* claim is not a fraud claim, as the court intonates, but an antitrust violation. The harm is not the invalid patent, but the use of the invalid patent to establish a monopoly.

Viewed properly as an antitrust claim, there is little reason to think that standing requirements for *Walker Process* claims differ from standing requirements in more conventional antitrust actions. [citation omitted] As plaintiff notes, direct purchasers are generally recognized as having standing to prosecute antitrust claims. [citation omitted] In the absence of a compelling reason to the contrary, the court is hesitant to restrict a direct purchaser's ability to sue for treble damages under § 4 of the Clayton Act. [citation omitted]

The court appreciates that a number of factors should be considered before adopting a broad rule with respect to standing. Conferring standing upon every individual tangentially affected by an alleged antitrust violation presents the risk of duplicative recovery, and may subject defendants to an onslaught of litigation. [citation omitted] Recognizing these dangers, courts are counseled to "examine other factors in addition to antitrust injury, such as the potential for duplicative recovery, the complexity of apportioning damages, and the existence of other parties that have been more directly harmed, to determine whether a party is a proper plaintiff under § 4." [citation omitted]

Examining these factors, the court sees no reason to limit standing to competitors. While entities facing enforcement actions are more likely to rely on *Walker Process*, this reflects more that they are in a stronger position to detect wrongdoing than a Congressional preference. If one believes that one of the primary purposes of a treble damages action is deterrence, then increasing the number of parties scrutinizing the actions of potential monopolists will further that goal. Moreover, because direct purchasers have frequent interactions with the defendants, they have a strong incentive to discover and litigate the offense. *See* William H. Page, The Scope of Liability For Antitrust Violations, 37 Stan. L. Rev. 1445, 1488 (1985). Those against whom a patent is enforced, by comparison, will generally have limited contact with a defendant unless there is the suspicion of infringement.

Nor is there any particular difficulty in determining damages for direct purchasers. As the Supreme Court stated in *Illinois Brick*, direct purchasers are a preferred plaintiff, in part, for the ease of apportioning damages: "We conclude that the legislative purpose in creating a group of 'private attorneys general' to enforce the antitrust laws under § 4 is better served by holding direct purchasers to be injured to the full extent of the overcharge paid by them than by attempting to apportion the overcharge among all that may have absorbed a part of it." 431 U.S. at 746 (citations omitted).

Based on the foregoing analysis, the court finds that direct purchasers have standing to pursue *Walker Process* claims.

Comments and Questions

1. Which court do you think took the correct approach? Should consumers have standing to pursue *Walker Process* claims? Why or why not?

How could expanding standing doctrine to include consumers potentially interfere with the patent system?

2. The *Molecular Diagnostics Laboratories* court talks about "direct purchasers" because indirect purchasers do not have standing to bring antitrust claims for overcharges in federal court. *See* Illinois Brick Co. v. Illinois, 431 U.S. 720 (1977).

Bibliography of Additional Resources

Joseph P. Bauer, *The Stealth Assault on Antitrust Enforcement: Raising the Barriers for Antitrust Injury and Standing*, U. Pitt. L. Rev. 437 (2001)

Roger D. Blair, *Rethinking Antitrust Injury*, 42 Vand. L. Rev. 1539 (1989)

Teague I. Donahey, *Antitrust Counterclaims in Patent Infringement Litigation: Clarifying the Supreme Court's Enigmatic* Mercoid *Decision*, 39 IDEA 225 (1999)

C. Douglas Floyd, *Antitrust Victims Without Antitrust Remedies: The Narrowing of Standing in Private Antitrust Actions*, 82 Minn. L. Rev. 1 (1997)

Michael S. Jacobs, *Lessons from Pharmaceutical Antitrust Litigation: Indirect Purchasers, Antitrust Standing, and Antitrust Federalism*, 42 St. Louis U. L.J. 59 (1998)

Christopher R. Leslie, *The Role of Consumers in* Walker Process *Litigation*, 13 Sw. J. of L. and Trade in the Am. 281 (2007)

John E. Lopatka & William H. Page, *Brunswick at 25: Antitrust Injury and the Evolution of Antitrust Law*, 17 Antitrust 20 (Fall 2002)

William H. Page, *Optimal Antitrust Penalties and Competitors' Injury*, 88 Mich. L. Rev. 2151 (1990)

Catherine Parrish, *Unilateral Refusals to License Software: Limitations on the Right to Exclude and the Need for Compulsory Licensing*, 68 Brook. L. Rev. 557 (2002)

William H. Rooney, *Consumer Injury in Antitrust Litigation: Necessary, But By What Standard?* 75 St. John's L. Rev. 561 (2001)

Joseph A. Yosick, *Compulsory Patent Licensing for Efficient Use of Inventions*, 2001 U. Ill. L. Rev. 1275 (2001)

CHAPTER 18

Remedies

[Handwritten annotations:]
Civil:
Most common: 1) Treble damages
2) Injunction
3) IP owner required to license its IP

Criminal:
1) double gains received by violator
2) double losses by damaged party
3) Imprisonment
4) Injunction

The most notable remedy for antitrust violations is treble damages to the successful private plaintiff. In criminal cases, the federal government can ask for double the gains received by the antitrust violator or double the losses inflicted by the violation. Given the overcharges associated with some international cartels, this could amount to over $1 billion of damages. Also, guilty individuals can be imprisoned for a maximum of ten years. However, the government only brings criminal cases against naked restraints like hard-core cartel activity, and agreements involving IP owners are only rarely brought as criminal antitrust actions.

In civil cases, both the government and private plaintiffs can also request injunctive relief. This usually takes the form of conduct restrictions that forbid the antitrust violator from undertaking specified actions in the future, such as acquiring competitors. But antitrust cases against owners of intellectual property present the opportunity for an additional form of conduct remedy: the IP owner can be compelled to license its IP, either for a reasonable royalty or no royalty at all. The following case and accompanying notes discuss whether compulsory licensing is an appropriate antitrust remedy. *[Issue]*

U. S. v. Glaxo Group Ltd.
410 U.S. 52 (1973)

Mr. Justice WHITE delivered the opinion of the Court.

*** We are asked to decide whether the Government may challenge the validity of patents involved in illegal restraints of trade, when the defendants do not rely upon the patents in defense of their conduct, and whether the District Court erred in refusing certain relief requested by the Government. *[Issue]*

I

Appellees, Imperial Chemical Industries Ltd. (ICI) and Glaxo Group Ltd. (Glaxo), are British drug companies engaged in the manufacture and sale of griseofulvin. Griseofulvin is an antibiotic compound that may be cut with inert ingredients and administered orally in the form of capsules or tablets to humans or animals for the treatment of external fungus infections. There is no substitute for dosage-form griseofulvin in combating certain infections. Griseofulvin itself is unpatented and unpatentable. ICI owns various patents on the dosage form of the drug. Glaxo owns various patents on a method for manufacturing the drug in bulk form, as well as a patent on the finely ground, 'microsize' dosage form of the drug.

On April 26, 1960, ICI and Glaxo entered into a formal agreement pooling their griseofulvin patents. At the time of the execution of the agreement, ICI held patents on the dosage form of the drug, and Glaxo held bulk-form manufacturing patents. Pursuant to the agreement, ICI acquired the right to manufacture bulk-form griseofulvin under Glaxo's patents, to sell bulk-form griseofulvin, and to sublicense under Glaxo's patents. Glaxo was authorized to manufacture dosage-form griseofulvin and to sublicense under ICI's patents. As part of the agreement, ICI undertook 'not to sell and to use its best endeavors to prevent its subsidiaries and associates from selling any griseofulvin in bulk to any independent third party without Glaxo's express consent in writing.' ***

On March 4, 1968, the United States filed a civil antitrust suit against ICI and Glaxo, pursuant to § 4 of the Sherman Act, 15 U.S.C. § 4, to restrain alleged violations of § 1 of the Act, 26 Stat. 209, as amended, 15 U.S.C. § 1. The Government charged that the restrictions on the sale and resale of bulk-form griseofulvin, contained in the 1960 ICI-Glaxo agreement and the various sublicensing agreements, were unreasonable restraints of trade. The Government also challenged the validity of ICI's dosage-form patent.

The District Court, citing this Court's decision in *United States v. Arnold, Schwinn & Co.*, 388 U.S., 365 (1967),* held that the bulk-sales restrictions contained in the ICI-AMHO agreement were per se violations of § 1 of the Sherman Act. [citation omitted] Because ICI had filed an affidavit disclaiming any desire to rely on its patent in defense of the antitrust claims, the District Court struck the claims of patent invalidity from the Government's complaint, ruling that the Government could not challenge ICI's patent when it was not relied upon as a defense to the antitrust claims. The District Court also denied the Government's motion to amend its complaint to allege the invalidity of Glaxo's patent on 'microsize' griseofulvin.

Subsequently, in separate, unreported orders, the bulk-sales restrictions in the Glaxo-J & J, the Glaxo-Schering, and the Glaxo-ICI agreements were found to be per se violations of § 1. The court enjoined future use of the bulk-sales restrictions, but refused the Government's request to order mandatory, nondiscriminatory

---

* Editor's note: The reversed the *Schwinn* decision in *Continental T. V., Inc. v. GTE Sylvania Inc.*, 433 U.S. 36 (1977). That reversal does not affect the discussion in Glaxo about compulsory licensing.

sales of the bulk form of the drug and reasonable-royalty licensing of the ICI and Glaxo patents as part of the relief. [citation omitted] ***

The District Court was then faced with the Government's attack on the pertinent patents as well as its demand for mandatory sales and reasonable-royalty licensing, the latter being well-established forms of relief when necessary to an effective remedy, particularly where patents have provided the leverage for or have contributed to the antitrust violation adjudicated. [citation omitted] Appellees opposed mandatory sales and compulsory licensing, asserting that the Government would 'deny defendants an essential ingredient of their rights under the patent system,' and that there was no warrant for 'such a drastic forfeiture of their rights.' In this context, where the court would necessarily be dealing with the future enforceability of the patents, we think it would have been appropriate, if it appeared that the Government's claims for further relief were substantial, for the court to have also entertained the Government's challenge to the validity of those patents.

In arriving at this conclusion, we do not recognize unlimited authority in the Government to attack a patent by basing an antitrust claim on the simple assertion that the patent is invalid. Cf. *Walker Process Equipment v. Food Machinery & Chemical Corp.*, 382 U.S. 172 (1965). Nor do we invest the Attorney General with a roving commission to question the validity of any patent lurking in the background of an antitrust case. But the district courts have jurisdiction to entertain and decide antitrust suits brought by the Government and, where a violation is found, to fashion effective relief. This often involves a substantial question as to whether it is necessary to limit the rights normally vested in the owners of patents, which in itself can be a complex and difficult issue. The litigation would usually proceed on the assumption that valid patents are involved, but if this basic assumption is itself challenged, we perceive no good reason, either in terms of the patent system or of judicial administration, for refusing to hear and decide it.

The District Court, therefore, erred in striking the allegations of the Government's complaint dealing with the patent validity issue and in refusing to permit the Government to amend its complaint with respect to this issue. On remand, the District Court should consider the validity of the ICI dosage-form patent and the Glaxo microsize patent.

III

The question remains whether the Government's case for additional relief was sufficient to provide the appropriate predicate for a consideration of its challenge to the validity of these patents. For this purpose, as we have said, its case need not be conclusive, but only substantial enough to warrant the court's undertaking what could be a large inquiry, one which could easily obviate other questions of remedy if the patent is found invalid and which, if the patent is not invalidated, would lend substance to a defendant's claim that a valid patent should not be limited, absent the necessity to provide effective relief for an antitrust violation to which the patent has contributed. Here, we think not only that the United States presented a substantial case for additional relief, but that it was sufficiently convincing that the

District Court, wholly aside from the question of patent validity, should have ruled favorably on the demand for mandatory sales and compulsory licensing.

In the first place, it is clear from the evidence that the ICI dosage-form patent, along with other ICI and Glaxo patents, gave the appellees the economic leverage with which to insist upon and enforce the bulk-sales restrictions imposed on the licensees. Glaxo apparently considered the bulk-sales restriction to be a prerequisite to the granting of a sublicense, for it rejected a draft of the ICI-AMHO agreement because, among other things, it would have permitted AMHO to sell griseofulvin in bulk form. There are indications, also, that Glaxo refused a sublicense to others than Schering and J & J because of fears that the companies would sell in bulk form or pressure Glaxo to allow such sales. The source of the patent-pooling agreement pursuant to which such licenses were permitted and which contained the bulk-sales restriction was simple: Glaxo needed the ICI dosage-form patent to assure its licensees the right to use the patent and sell in dosage form. Pooling permitted ICI to engage in bulk manufacture, and, in exchange, ICI imposed the bulk-sales restrictions upon its licensees. There can be little question that the patents involved here were intimately associated with and contributed to effectuating the conduct that the District Court held to be a per se restraint of trade in griseofulvin.

Secondly, we think that ICI and Glaxo should have been required to sell bulk-form griseofulvin on reasonable and nondiscriminatory terms and to grant patent licenses at reasonable-royalty rates to all bona fide applicants in order to 'pry open to competition' the griseofulvin market that 'has been closed by defendants' illegal restraints.' International Salt Co., 332 U.S., at 401.

The United States griseofulvin market consists of three wholesalers, all licensees of appellees, that account for nearly 100% of United States sales totaling approximately eight million dollars. Glaxo and ICI have never sold in bulk to others than the licensees and have prohibited bulk sales and resales by the licensees. In practice, the licensees have not manufactured griseofulvin under the bulk-form patents, preferring instead to purchase in bulk form from ICI and Glaxo. The licensees sell the drug in dosage and microsize form to retail outlets at virtually identical prices. The effect of appellees' refusal to sell in bulk and prohibition of such sales by the licensees has been that bulk griseofulvin has not been available to any but appellees' three licensees and that these three are the only sources of dosage-form griseofulvin in the United States.

There is little reason to think that the appellees or their licensees, now that the bulk-sales restrictions have been declared illegal, will begin selling in bulk. It is in their economic self-interest to maintain control of the bulk form of the drug in order to keep the dosage-form, wholesale market competition-free. Bulk sales would create new competition among wholesalers, by enabling other companies to convert the bulk drug into dosage and microsize forms and sell to retail outlets, and would presumably lead to price reductions as the result of normal competitive forces. There is, in fact, substantial evidence in the record to the effect that other drug companies would not only have entered the market, had they been able to make bulk purchases, but also would have charged substantially lower wholesale prices for the dosage and microsize forms of the drug. Only by requiring the appellees to sell bulk-form griseofulvin on nondiscriminatory terms to all bona fide applicants will the dosage-form, whole-sale market become competitive.

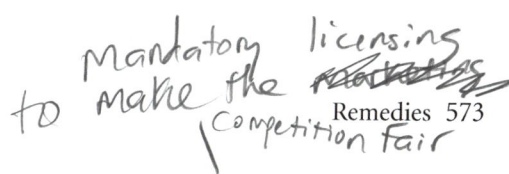

Relief in the form of compulsory sales may not, however, alone insure a competitive market. Glaxo and ICI could choose to discontinue bulk-form manufacturing or the sale of griseofulvin in bulk form. The patent licensees might then begin to practice the bulk-form manufacturing patents pursuant to the patent licenses to fill their needs for the bulk drug. The licensees, of course, are not parties to this action, and a mandatory-sales order would not affect them. They would not be required to make the economically less advantageous bulk sales. The bulk form of the drug would be controlled by the licensees, and the appellees, because they would be required under the Government's proposed relief to sell to all applicants only so long as they sell to any United States purchasers, could easily avoid the mandatory-sales requirement. Unless other American firms are licensed to manufacture griseofulvin, competition in the United States market will depend entirely upon appellees' willingness to continue to supply their present licensees with the bulk form of the drug.

This Court has repeatedly recognized that '(t)he framing of decrees should take place in the District rather than in Appellate Courts' and has generally followed the principle that district courts 'are invested with large discretion to model their judgments to fit the exigencies of the particular case.' *International Salt Co. v. United States, supra*, 332 U.S., at 400–401 [citation omitted]. The Court has not, however, treated that power as one of discretion, subject only to reversal for gross abuse, but has recognized 'an obligation to intervene in this most significant phase of the case' when necessary to assure that the relief will be effective. *United States v. United States Gypsum Co.*, 340 U.S., at 89. Accordingly, we have ordered the affirmative relief that the District Court refused to implement. *See e.g., United States v. United States Gypsum Co.* The purpose of relief in an antitrust case is 'so far as practicable, (to) cure the ill effects of the illegal conduct, and assure the public freedom from its continuance.' Id., at 88. Mandatory selling on specified terms and compulsory patent licensing at reasonable charges are recognized antitrust remedies. *See, e.g., Besser Mfg. Co. v. United States*, 343 U.S. 444 (1952); *International Salt Co. v. United States*, 332 U.S. 392 (1947); *Hartford-Empire Co. v. United States*, 323 U.S. 386 (1945). The District Court should have ordered those remedies in this case.

To the extent indicated in this opinion, the judgment of the District Court is reversed.

So ordered.

Judgment reversed.

[Dissent by Justice Rehnquist omitted]

Comments and Questions

1. In his dissent, Justice Rehnquist argued that the "total lack of proof of any relationship also defeats for me the granting of compulsory licensing of the United States patents. Compulsory licensing is a recognized remedy in patent misuse cases,

see, e.g., International Salt Co. v. United States, 332 U.S. 392 (1947), Hartford-Empire Co. v. United States, 323 U.S. 386 (1945), but here the District Court specifically found there was no patent misuse or other abuse of patent rights."

Do you agree? If an antitrust violator has not abused its patents, should compulsory licensing be off the table as a possible antitrust remedy?

2. Even if patentholders have a general right to refuse to license their intellectual property—without being held liable for violating antitrust laws, *see* Chapter 7—does that mean that firms found to have actually violated the antitrust laws should not be subject to compulsory licensing?

Under what circumstances, if any, is compulsory licensing an appropriate antitrust remedy? Why?

3. The Supreme Court has observed that "[c]ompulsory licensing is a rarity in our patent system." Dawson Chemical Co. v. Rohm and Haas Co., 448 U.S. 176, 214–15 (1980).

Although compulsory licensing is generally disfavored in the American legal system, several statutory regimes provide for it. For example, the Clean Air Act, 42 U.S.C. § 7608, and the Atomic Energy Act, 42 U.S.C. § 2183(c), provide for compulsory licensing of patents. *See* Jeffry C. Gerber & Peter W. Kitson, *Compulsory Licensing of Patents Under the Clean Air Act of 1970*, 54 J. PAT. OFF. SOC'Y 650 (1972); Warren F. Schwartz, *Mandatory Patent Licensing of Air Pollution Control Technology*, 57 VA. L. REV. 719, 742 (1971); Stefan A. Riesenfeld, *Patent Protection and Atomic Energy Legislation*, 46 CAL. L. REV. 40 (1958); Dean C. Dunlavey, *Government Regulation of Atomic Industry*, 105 U. PA. L. REV. 295 (1957).

Copyright law has several provisions for compulsory licensing, including for certain musical works (17 U.S.C. § 115), songs in jukeboxes (17 U.S.C. § 116), and secondary transmissions of television programming by satellite carriers (17 U.S.C. §§ 119, 122), as discussed in *PrimeTime 24*, excerpted in Chapter 5.

Does that mean that courts should be more willing to impose a compulsory licensing remedy in antitrust cases involving copyright owners instead of patent owners?

4. The Supreme Court has upheld compulsory licensing as a remedy in antitrust cases. *See, e.g., United States v. National Lead Co.*, 332 U.S. 319, 355–56 (1947); *Hartford-Empire Co. v. U.S.*, 323 U.S. 386 (1945). The Court required that the licenses by made at reasonable royalties, not royalty-free.

5. Federal antitrust officials have negotiated consent decrees that include royalty-free compulsory licensing provisions.

Should that affect the willingness of courts to impose that as an antitrust remedy?

6. If courts were to require compulsory licensing that was not royalty-free, it would raise the issue of how to determine the reasonable royalty that the antitrust defendant could charge. Some commentators have "argued that the courts and Agencies are not well-equipped to determine appropriate licensing terms and conditions and, as a result, compulsory licensing would be problematic." U.S. DEP'T

of Justice & Federal Trade Commission, Antitrust Enforcement and Intellectual Property Rights: Promoting Innovation and Competition 22 (2007).

Professor Janice Mueller has argued that panels of industry could construct licensing fee schedules that set the reasonable royalties for compulsory licensing remedies. Janice M. Mueller, *Patenting Industry Standards*, 34 J. Marshall L. Rev. 897, 933–34 (2001).

7. In some cases, compulsory licensing alone may be insufficient to restore competition to the relevant market. For example, the "transfer of some technologies requires not only a patent license, but also the transfer of related know-how, and it may be difficult for courts to enforce a requirement that this know-how be transferred." U.S. Dep't of Justice & Federal Trade Commission, Antitrust Enforcement and Intellectual Property Rights: Promoting Innovation and Competition 23 (2007).

In an important historic case involving the tin can industry, the court required the antitrust defendant to license its patents for reasonable royalties and to provide all necessary technical information for five years following the judgment. See Simon N. Whitney, 2 Antitrust policies 218 (1958) (discussing the remedy in *American Can*).

8. Another concern associated with compulsory licensing as an antitrust remedy is that firms may shift to using trade secret protection to keep their innovations from competitors, instead of relying on patent protection. To the extent that patent protection increases societal efficiency by requiring public disclosure of inventions (in exchange for short-term exclusionary rights), a shift from patent to trade secret protection could reduce innovation and efficiency.

Do you think that the fear for compulsory licensing would cause firms to reduce patenting activity?

Why or why not?

9. Other countries are generally more accepting of compulsory licensing, in general as well as to remedy prior anticompetitive conduct. For example, the Doha Round allows countries to provide for compulsory licensing for certain pharmaceuticals.

Should that influence the willingness of American courts to employ compulsory licensing as an antitrust remedy?

10. Courts are less likely to impose compulsory licensing of trademarks than patents because trademarks provide consumers with important information about the source of the goods. If the owner of an established trademark were forced to license it to the owner's competitors as a remedy in an antitrust case, consumers could be confused about from whom they were actually purchasing their products.[1]

---

[1] *See* Herbert Hovenkamp, The Antitrust Enterprise: Principle and Execution 269 (2005) ("Trademark law is generally hostile toward compulsory licensing because of its concern that the owners of trademarks be responsible for the quality of the goods that they represent. We don't want,

But that doesn't mean compulsory licensing of trademarks has never been attempted. *See* Richard Schmalensee, *On the Use of Economic Models in Antitrust: The ReaLemon Case*, 127 U. PA. L. REV. 994, 1028–31 (1979) (discussing the *ReaLemon* case).

Bibliography of Additional Resources

Richard P. Beem, *Recovering Attorney Fees & Damages When Defending Against Bad Faith Patent Litigation*, 80 J. PAT. & TRADEMARK OFF. SOC'Y 81 (1998)

William E. Kovacic, *Designing Antitrust Remedies for Dominant Firm Misconduct*, 31 CONN. L. REV. 1285 (1999).

Lawrence Schlam, *Compulsory Royalty-Free Licensing as an Antitrust Remedy for Patent Fraud: Law, Policy and the Patent-Antitrust Interface Revisited*, 7 CORNELL J.L. & PUB. POL'Y 467 (1998)

John M. Taladay & James N. Carlin, Jr., *Compulsory Licensing of Intellectual Property Under the Competition Laws of the United States and European Community*, 10 GEO. MASON L. REV. 443 (2002)

---

say, Del Monte to license its trademark to any canner it wishes without being involved to at least some extent in that firm's food production.").

CHAPTER 19

Jurisdiction and Procedural Issues

Congress created the Court of Appeals for the Federal Circuit with the Federal Courts Improvement Act of 1982. The Federal Circuit exercises exclusive jurisdiction over appeals in cases arising under the patent law. Congress intended the new court to bring uniformity to patent law by fashioning a single, cohesive body of patent law, instead of different circuits announcing varying, and sometimes conflicting, interpretations of patent principles. In adjudicating non-patent issues in patent cases, the Federal Circuit was supposed to apply the law of the regional circuit where the district court whose decision the Federal Circuit was reviewing. However, in *Nobelpharma AB v. Implant Innovations, Inc.*, the Federal Circuit reversed its prior precedent, noting:

> an antitrust claim premised on stripping a patentee of its immunity from the antitrust laws is typically raised as a counterclaim by a defendant in a patent infringement suit. [citation omitted] Because most cases involving these issues will therefore be appealed to this court, we conclude that we should decide these issues as a matter of Federal Circuit law, rather than rely on various regional precedents. *** Accordingly, we hereby change our precedent and hold that whether conduct in procuring or enforcing a patent is sufficient to strip a patentee of its immunity from the antitrust laws is to be decided as a question of Federal Circuit law. This conclusion applies equally to all antitrust claims premised on the bringing of a patent infringement suit.

Nobelpharma AB v. Implant Innovations, Inc., 141 F.3d 1059 (Fed. Cir. 1998).

As the Federal Circuit began developing its body of antitrust law—where antitrust law intersects with patent law—it created the possibility for divergent antitrust doctrine in the Federal Circuit versus the various regional circuit. For litigants in district court, this meant that the ultimate outcome of their cases could be a function over

Christianson v. Colt Industries Operating Corp.
486 U.S. 800 (1988)

Justice BRENNAN delivered the opinion of the Court.

This case requires that we decide a peculiar jurisdictional battle between the Court of Appeals for the Federal Circuit and the Court of Appeals for the Seventh Circuit. Each court has adamantly disavowed jurisdiction over this case. Each has transferred the case to the other. And each insists that the other's jurisdictional decision is "clearly wrong." ***

I

Respondent Colt Industries Operating Corp. is the leading manufacturer, seller, and marketer of M16 rifles and their parts and accessories. Colt's dominant market position dates back to 1959, when it acquired a license for 16 patents to manufacture the M16's precursor. Colt continued to develop the rifle, which the United States Army adopted as its standard assault rifle, and patented additional improvements. Through various devices, Colt has also maintained a shroud of secrecy around certain specifications essential to the mass production of interchangeable M16 parts. For example, Colt's patents conceal many of the manufacturing specifications that might otherwise be revealed by its engineering drawings, and when Colt licenses others to manufacture M16 parts or hires employees with access to proprietary information, it contractually obligates them not to disclose specifications.

Petitioner Christianson is a former Colt employee who acceded to such a nondisclosure agreement. Upon leaving respondent's employ in 1975, Christianson established petitioner International Trade Services, Inc. (ITS), and began selling M16 parts to various customers domestically and abroad. Petitioners' business depended on information that Colt considers proprietary. Colt expressly waived its proprietary rights at least as to some of petitioners' early transactions. The precise scope of Colt's waiver is a matter of considerable dispute. In 1983, however, Colt joined petitioners as defendants in a patent-infringement lawsuit against two companies that had arranged a sale of M16's to El Salvador. Evidence suggested that petitioners supplied the companies with certain M16 specifications, and Colt sought a court order enjoining petitioners from any further disclosures. When the District Court declined the motion, Colt voluntarily dismissed its claims against petitioners. In the meantime, Colt notified several of petitioners' current and potential customers that petitioners were illegally misappropriating Colt's trade secrets, and urged them to refrain from doing business with petitioners.

Three days after their dismissal from the lawsuit, petitioners brought this lawsuit in the District Court against Colt "pursuant to Section 4 ... (15 U.S.C. § 15) and Section 16 of the Clayton Act (15 U.S.C. § 26) for damages, injunctive and equitable relief by reason of its violations of Sections 1 and 2 of the Sherman Act (15 U.S.C. §§ 1 & 2). . . ." [citation omitted]. The complaint alleged that Colt's letters, litigation tactics, and "[o]the[r] . . . conduct" drove petitioners out of business. ***

Petitioners' motion for summary judgment raised only a patent-law issue ***—that Colt's patents were invalid from their inception for failure to disclose sufficient information to "enable any person skilled in the art . . . to make and use the same" as well as a description of "the best mode contemplated by the inventor of carrying out his invention." 35 U.S.C. § 112. Since Colt benefited from the protection of the invalid patents, the argument continues, the "trade secrets" that the patents should have disclosed lost any state-law protection. Petitioners therefore argued that the District Court should hold that "Colt's trade secrets are invalid and that [their] claim of invalidity shall be taken as established with respect to all claims and counterclaims to which said issue is material." [citation omitted]

The District Court awarded petitioners summary judgment as to liability on both the antitrust and the tortious-interference claims, essentially relying on the § 112 theory articulated above. In the process, the District Court invalidated nine of Colt's patents, declared all trade secrets relating to the M16 unenforceable, enjoined Colt from enforcing "any form of trade secret right in any technical information relating to the M16," and ordered Colt to disgorge to petitioners all such information. [citation omitted]

Respondent appealed to the Court of Appeals for the Federal Circuit, which, after full briefing and argument, concluded that it lacked jurisdiction and issued an unpublished order transferring the appeal to the Court of Appeals for the Seventh Circuit. [citation omitted] The Seventh Circuit, however, raising the jurisdictional issue sua sponte, concluded that the Federal Circuit was "clearly wrong" and transferred the case back. [citation omitted] The Federal Circuit, for its part, adhered to its prior jurisdictional ruling, concluding that the Seventh Circuit exhibited "a monumental misunderstanding of the patent jurisdiction granted this court," [citation omitted] and was "clearly wrong," [citation omitted]. Nevertheless, the Federal Circuit proceeded to address the merits in the "interest of justice," [citation omitted] and reversed the District Court. We granted certiorari [citation omitted] and now vacate the judgment of the Federal Circuit.

II

As relevant here, 28 U.S.C. § 1295(a)(1) grants the Court of Appeals for the Federal Circuit exclusive jurisdiction over "an appeal from a final decision of a district court of the United States . . . if the jurisdiction of that court was based, in whole or in part, on [28 U.S.C.] section 1338. . . ." Section 1338(a), in turn, provides in relevant part that "[t]he district courts shall have original jurisdiction of any civil action arising under any Act of Congress relating to patents. . . ." Thus, the jurisdictional issue before us turns on whether this is a case "arising under" a federal patent statute, for if it is then the jurisdiction of the District Court was based at least "in part" on § 1338.

A

In interpreting § 1338's precursor, we held long ago that in order to demonstrate that a case is one "arising under" federal patent law "the plaintiff must set up some right, title or interest under the patent laws, or at least make it appear that some right or privilege will be defeated by one construction, or sustained by the opposite construction of these laws." [citation omitted] *** § 1338(a) jurisdiction *** extend[s] only to those cases in which a well-pleaded complaint establishes either that federal patent law creates the cause of action or that the plaintiff's right to relief necessarily depends on resolution of a substantial question of federal patent law, in that patent law is a necessary element of one of the well-pleaded claims. [citation omitted]

The most superficial perusal of petitioners' complaint establishes, and no one disputes, that patent law did not in any sense create petitioners' antitrust or intentional-interference claims. Since no one asserts that federal jurisdiction rests on petitioners' state-law claims, the dispute centers around whether patent law "is a necessary element of one of the well-pleaded [antitrust] claims." *See Merrell Dow Pharmaceuticals Inc. v. Thompson*, 478 U.S. 804, 813 (1986). *** Under the well-pleaded complaint rule, as appropriately adapted to § 1338(a), whether a claim "arises under" patent law "'must be determined from what necessarily appears in the plaintiff's statement of his own claim in the bill or declaration, unaided by anything alleged in anticipation or avoidance of defenses which it is thought the defendant may interpose.'" [citation omitted] Thus, a case raising a federal patent-law defense does not, for that reason alone, "arise under" patent law, "even if the defense is anticipated in the plaintiff's complaint, and even if both parties admit that the defense is the only question truly at issue in the case."

Nor is it necessarily sufficient that a well-pleaded claim alleges a single theory under which resolution of a patent-law question is essential. If "on the face of a well-pleaded complaint there are . . . reasons completely unrelated to the provisions and purposes of [the patent laws] why the [plaintiff] may or may not be entitled to the relief it seeks," [citation omitted] then the claim does not "arise under" those laws. [citation omitted] Thus, a claim supported by alternative theories in the complaint may not form the basis for § 1338(a) jurisdiction unless patent law is essential to each of those theories.

B

Framed in these terms, our resolution of the jurisdictional issue in this case is straightforward. Petitioners' antitrust count can readily be understood to encompass both a monopolization claim under § 2 of the Sherman Act and a group-boycott claim under § 1. The patent-law issue, while arguably necessary to at least one theory under each claim, is not necessary to the overall success of either claim.

Section 2 of the Sherman Act condemns "[e]very person who shall monopolize, or attempt to monopolize...." 15 U.S.C. § 2. The thrust of petitioners' monopolization claim is that Colt has "embarked on a course of conduct to illegally extend its monopoly position with respect to the described patents and to prevent ITS from engaging in any business with respect to parts and accessories of the M-16." [citation omitted] The complaint specifies several acts, most of which relate either to Colt's prosecution of the lawsuit against petitioners or to letters Colt sent to petitioners' potential and existing customers. To make out a § 2 claim, petitioners would have to present a theory under which the identified conduct amounted to a "willful acquisition or maintenance of [monopoly] power as distinguished from growth or development as a consequence of a superior product, business acumen, or historic accident." *United States v. Grinnell Corp.*, 384 U.S. 563, 570–571 (1966). Both the Seventh Circuit and Colt focus entirely on what they perceive to be "the only basis Christianson asserted in the complaint for the alleged antitrust violation," [citation omitted] that Colt made false assertions in its letters and pleadings that petitioners were violating its trade secrets, when those trade secrets were not protected under state law because Colt's patents were invalid under § 112. Thus, Colt concludes, the validity of the patents is an essential element of petitioners' prima facie monopolization theory and the case "arises under" patent law.

We can assume without deciding that the invalidity of Colt's patents is an essential element of the foregoing monopolization theory rather than merely an argument in anticipation of a defense. [citation omitted] The well-pleaded complaint rule, however, focuses on claims, not theories, [citation omitted] and just because an element that is essential to a particular theory might be governed by federal patent law does not mean that the entire monopolization claim "arises under" patent law.

Examination of the complaint reveals that the monopolization theory that Colt singles out (and on which petitioners ultimately prevailed in the District Court) is only one of several, and the only one for which the patent-law issue is even arguably essential. So far as appears from the complaint, for example, petitioners might have attempted to prove that Colt's accusations of trade-secret infringement were false not because Colt had no trade secrets, but because Colt authorized petitioners to use them. [citation omitted] In fact, most of the conduct alleged in the complaint could be deemed wrongful quite apart from the truth or falsity of Colt's accusations. According to the complaint, Colt's letters also (1) contained "copies of inapplicable court orders" and "suggest[ed] that these court orders prohibited [the recipients] from doing business with" petitioners; and (2) "falsely stat[ed] that 'Colt's right' to proprietary data had been 'consistently upheld in various courts.'" [citation omitted] Similarly, the complaint alleges that Colt's lawsuit against petitioners (1) was designed "to contravene the permission previously given";

(2) was "[p]ursued . . . in bad faith by subjecting [petitioners] to substantial expense in extended discovery procedures"; and (3) was brought only to enable Colt "to urge customers and potential customers of [petitioners] to refrain from doing business with them." [citation omitted] Since there are "reasons completely unrelated to the provisions and purposes" of federal patent law why petitioners "may or may not be entitled to the relief [they] see[k]" under their monopolization claim, [citation omitted] the claim does not "arise under" federal patent law.

The same analysis obtains as to petitioners' group-boycott claim under § 1 of the Sherman Act, which provides that "[e]very contract, combination . . ., or conspiracy, in restraint of trade or commerce . . . is declared to be illegal," 15 U.S.C. § 1. This claim is set forth in the allegation that "virtually all suppliers of ITS and customers of ITS have agreed with Colt to refrain from supplying and purchasing M-16 parts and accessories to or from ITS, which has had the effect of requiring ITS to close its doors and no longer transact business." [citation omitted] As this case unfolded, petitioners attempted to prove that the alleged agreement was unreasonable because its purpose was to protect Colt's trade secrets from petitioners' infringement and, given the patents' invalidity under § 112, Colt had no trade secrets to infringe. Whether or not the patent-law issue was an "essential" element of that group-boycott *theory*, however, petitioners could have supported their group-boycott *claim* with any of several theories having nothing to do with the validity of Colt's patents. Equally prominent in the complaint, for example, is a theory that the alleged agreement was unreasonable not because Colt had no trade secrets to protect, but because Colt authorized petitioners to use them. Once again, the appearance on the complaint's face of an alternative, non-patent theory compels the conclusion that the group-boycott claim does not "arise under" patent law.

III

*** Colt correctly observes that one of Congress' objectives in creating a Federal Circuit with exclusive jurisdiction over certain patent cases was "to reduce the widespread lack of uniformity and uncertainty of legal doctrine that exist[ed] in the administration of patent law." H.R.Rep. No. 97-312, p. 23 (1981). Colt might be correct (although not clearly so) that Congress' goals would be better served if the Federal Circuit's jurisdiction were to be fixed "by reference to the case actually litigated," rather than by an ex ante hypothetical assessment of the elements of the complaint that might have been dispositive. [citation omitted] Congress determined the relevant focus, however, when it granted jurisdiction to the Federal Circuit over "an appeal from . . . a district court . . . if the jurisdiction of *that court* was based . . . on section 1338." 28 U.S.C. § 1295(a)(1) (emphasis added). Since the district court's jurisdiction is determined by reference to the well-pleaded complaint, not the well-tried case, the referent for the Federal Circuit's jurisdiction must be the same. The legislative history of the Federal Circuit's jurisdictional provisions confirms that focus. See, e.g., H.R.Rep. No. 97-312, supra, at 41 (cases fall within the Federal Circuit's patent jurisdiction "in the same sense that cases are said to 'arise under' federal law for purposes of federal question jurisdiction"). In view of that clear congressional intent, we have no more authority to read § 1295(a)(1) as granting the Federal Circuit jurisdiction over an appeal where the well-pleaded complaint does not depend on patent law, than to read § 1338(a) as granting a district court jurisdiction over such a complaint. See Pratt, 168 U.S., at 259. ***

We vacate the judgment of the Court of Appeals for the Federal Circuit and remand with instructions to transfer the case to the Court of Appeals for the Seventh Circuit. See 28 U.S.C. § 1631.

It is so ordered.

[Concurrence by Justice Stevens omitted]

Holmes Group, Inc. v. Vornado Air Circulation Systems, Inc.

535 U.S. 826 (2002)

Justice SCALIA delivered the opinion of the Court.

In this case, we address whether the Court of Appeals for the Federal Circuit has appellate jurisdiction over a case in which the complaint does not allege a claim arising under federal patent law, but the answer contains a patent-law counterclaim.

I

Respondent, Vornado Air Circulation Systems, Inc., is a manufacturer of patented fans and heaters. In late 1992, respondent sued a competitor, Duracraft Corp., claiming that Duracraft's use of a "spiral grill design" in its fans infringed respondent's trade dress. The Court of Appeals for the Tenth Circuit found for Duracraft, holding that Vornado had no protectable trade-dress rights in the grill design. [citation omitted] (*Vornado I*).

Nevertheless, on November 26, 1999, respondent lodged a complaint with the United States International Trade Commission against petitioner, The Holmes Group, Inc., claiming that petitioner's sale of fans and heaters with a spiral grill design infringed respondent's patent and the same trade dress held unprotectable in *Vornado I*. Several weeks later, petitioner filed this action against respondent in the United States District Court for the District of Kansas, seeking, inter alia, a declaratory judgment that its products did not infringe respondent's trade dress and an injunction restraining respondent from accusing it of trade-dress infringement in promotional materials. Respondent's answer asserted a compulsory counterclaim alleging patent infringement.

The District Court granted petitioner the declaratory judgment and injunction it sought. *** Respondent appealed to the Court of Appeals for the Federal Circuit. Notwithstanding petitioner's challenge to its jurisdiction, the Federal Circuit vacated the District Court's judgment *** We granted certiorari to consider whether the Federal Circuit properly asserted jurisdiction over the appeal. [citation omitted]

II

Congress vested the Federal Circuit with exclusive jurisdiction over "an appeal from a final decision of a district court of the United States . . . if the jurisdiction *of that court* was based, in whole or in part, on [28 U.S.C. §] 1338 . . . ." 28 U.S.C. § 1295(a)(1) (emphasis added). Section 1338(a), in turn, provides in relevant part that "[t]he district courts shall have original jurisdiction of any civil action arising under any Act of Congress relating to patents . . . ." Thus, the Federal Circuit's jurisdiction is fixed with reference to that of the district court, and turns on whether the action arises under federal patent law.

Section 1338(a) uses the same operative language as 28 U.S.C. § 1331, the statute conferring general federal-question jurisdiction, which gives the district courts "original jurisdiction of all civil actions *arising under* the Constitution, laws, or treaties of the United States." (Emphasis added.) We said in *Christianson v. Colt Industries Operating Corp.*, 486 U.S. 800, 808 (1988), that "[l]inguistic consistency" requires us to apply the same test to determine whether a case arises under § 1338(a) as under § 1331.

The well-pleaded-complaint rule has long governed whether a case "arises under" federal law for purposes of § 1331. [citation omitted] As "appropriately adapted to § 1338(a)," the well-pleaded-complaint rule provides that whether a case "arises under" patent law "must be determined from what necessarily appears in the plaintiff's statement of his own claim in the bill or declaration . . . ." *Christianson*, 486 U.S., at 809. The plaintiff's well-pleaded complaint must "establis[h] either that federal patent law creates the cause of action or that the plaintiff's right to relief necessarily depends on resolution of a substantial question of federal patent law . . . ." Ibid. Here, it is undisputed that petitioner's well-pleaded complaint did not assert any claim arising under federal patent law. The Federal Circuit therefore erred in asserting jurisdiction over this appeal.

A

Respondent argues that the well-pleaded-complaint rule, properly understood, allows a counterclaim to serve as the basis for a district court's "arising under" jurisdiction. We disagree.

Admittedly, our prior cases have only required us to address whether a federal defense, rather than a federal counterclaim, can establish "arising under" jurisdiction. Nevertheless, those cases were decided on the principle that federal jurisdiction generally exists "only when a federal question is presented on the face of the *plaintiff's* properly pleaded complaint." *Caterpillar Inc. v. Williams*, 482 U.S. 386, 392 (1987) (emphasis added). As we said in *The Fair v. Kohler Die & Specialty Co.*, 228 U.S. 22, 25 (1913), whether a case arises under federal patent law "cannot depend upon the answer." Moreover, we have declined to adopt proposals that "the answer as well as the complaint . . . be consulted before a determination [is] made whether the case 'ar[ises]' under' federal law . . . ." [citation omitted] It follows that a counterclaim—which appears as part of the defendant's answer, not as part of the plaintiff's complaint—cannot serve as the basis for "arising under" jurisdiction. [citation omitted]

*** [W]e decline to transform the longstanding well-pleaded-complaint rule into the "well-pleaded-complaint-or-counterclaim rule" urged by respondent.

B

Respondent argues, in the alternative, that even if a counterclaim generally cannot establish the original "arising under" jurisdiction of a district court, we should interpret the phrase "arising under" differently in ascertaining the Federal Circuit's jurisdiction. In respondent's view, effectuating Congress's goal of "promoting the uniformity of patent law," [citation omitted] requires us to interpret §§ 1295(a)(1) and 1338(a) to confer exclusive appellate jurisdiction on the Federal Circuit whenever a patent-law counterclaim is raised.

We do not think this option is available. Our task here is not to determine what would further Congress's goal of ensuring patent-law uniformity, but to determine what the words of the statute must fairly be understood to mean. It would be difficult enough to give "arising under" the meaning urged by respondent if that phrase appeared in § 1295(a)(1)—the jurisdiction-conferring statute—itself. [citation omitted] Even then the phrase would not be some neologism that might justify our adverting to the general purpose of the legislation, but rather a term familiar to all law students as invoking the well-pleaded-complaint rule. [citation omitted] But the present case is even weaker than that, since § 1295(a)(1) does not itself use the term, but rather refers to jurisdiction under § 1338, where it is well established that "arising under any Act of Congress relating to patents" invokes, specifically, the well-pleaded-complaint rule. It would be an unprecedented feat of interpretive necromancy to say that § 1338(a)'s "arising under" language means one thing (the well-pleaded-complaint rule) in its own right, but something quite different (respondent's complaint-or-counterclaim rule) when referred to by § 1295(a)(1).

Not all cases involving a patent-law claim fall within the Federal Circuit's jurisdiction. By limiting the Federal Circuit's jurisdiction to cases in which district courts would have jurisdiction under § 1338, Congress referred to a well-established body of law that requires courts to consider whether a patent-law claim appears on the face of the plaintiff's well-pleaded complaint. Because petitioner's complaint did not include any claim based on patent law, we vacate the judgment of the Federal Circuit and remand the case with instructions to transfer the case to the Court of Appeals for the Tenth Circuit. *See* 28 U.S.C. § 1631.

It is so ordered.

[Concurrences by Justices Stevens and Ginsburg are omitted.]

Comments and Questions

1. Does Vornado risk undermining the purpose of the Federal Circuit? Why or why not?

2. Should Congress give the Federal Circuit exclusive jurisdiction over all appeals that involve the intersection of antitrust law and intellectual property law? Why or why not? What would be the risks and benefits of such an approach?

3. In light of *Vornado*, the order in which litigants file their claims may determine which court will hear any appeals. If the patentee files an infringement action and the alleged infringer files an antitrust counterclaim, the Federal Circuit will hear the appeal. Conversely, if an antitrust plaintiff brings a claim and the defendant brings a patent infringement counterclaim, the regional circuit in which the district court sits will hear the appeal. This matters because some litigants perceive the Federal Circuit to be relatively hostile to antitrust claims. This means that an antitrust plaintiff who wants to avoid having the Federal Circuit decide its case could either file its antitrust claim *before* the patentee files an infringement action or, at least, decline to file its antitrust claim as a counterclaim in an infringement suit (and instead file it as a separate case). The first strategy is not possible when the antitrust claim is based on the patentee's infringement suit. Patentees have tried to eliminate the second strategy by arguing that antitrust claims are compulsory counterclaims. Consequently, they assert that if the infringement defendant does not file their antitrust lawsuit as a counterclaim (whose appeal would be heard by the Federal Circuit), then the antitrust claim is barred. This leads to the legal question of whether antitrust counterclaims are compulsory, an issue addressed in the following case:

Hydranautics v. FilmTec Corp.
70 F.3d 533 (9th Cir. 1995)

[Editor's Note: The background facts of this case are excerpted in a note in Chapter 4.]

A. Compulsory Counterclaim

It was permissible for Hydranautics to delay suing FilmTec for predatory patent litigation until it had succeeded in defeating the infringement case. The Supreme Court in Mercoid Corp. v. Mid-Continent Investment Co., 320 U.S. 661 (1944), said that "the fact that [an antitrust counterclaim for damages] might have been asserted . . . in the prior suit . . . does not mean that the failure to do so renders the prior judgment res judicata as respects it." Mercoid, 320 U.S. at 671. A claim that patent infringement litigation violated an antitrust statute is a permissive, not a mandatory, counterclaim in a patent infringement case, and is not barred in a subsequent suit by failure to raise it in the infringement suit. See Id. at 669–71.

An answer must state as a counterclaim a claim which "arises out of the same transaction or occurrence" as the plaintiff's claim:

> (a) Compulsory counterclaims. A pleading shall state as a counterclaim any claim which at the time of serving the pleading the pleader has against any opposing party, if it arises out of the same transaction or occurrence that is the subject matter of the opposing party's claim. . . .

(b) Permissive counterclaims. A pleading may state as a counterclaim any claim against an opposing party not arising out of the transaction or occurrence that is the subject matter of the opposing party's claim.

Fed.R.Civ.P. 13. If a party has a counterclaim which is compulsory and fails to plead it, it is lost, and cannot be asserted in a second, separate action after conclusion of the first. [citation omitted]

We determine whether a claim arises out of the same transaction or occurrence by analyzing "whether the essential facts of the various claims are so logically connected that considerations of judicial economy and fairness dictate that all the issues be resolved in one lawsuit."

While there may be cases where resolving both issues at once is preferable, *Mercoid* leaves open the possibility of raising antitrust claims as permissive counterclaims in an infringement action, or in a separate and subsequent action.

In many cases even if the antitrust counterclaim were asserted by counterclaim, the court would sever the issues and resolve the infringement case first. The evidence for patent infringement and antitrust damages may differ considerably, depending on the particulars of the case. If the plaintiff wins the patent infringement suit, then the antitrust counterclaim may ordinarily be disposed of expeditiously on motion, instead of by a time consuming and expensive trial. ***

Appeals from patent infringement decisions now go to the Federal Circuit, but appeals from antitrust decisions go to the regional circuit in which the district court sits. [citation omitted] If the antitrust counterclaim were treated as compulsory, then any appeal of the antitrust decision would go to the Federal Circuit, not the regional circuit. This may generate a difference between the antitrust law generally applicable within each regional circuit, and antitrust law in predatory patent infringement cases. That Congress has provided for regional courts of appeals to decide antitrust appeals, and for the federal circuit to decide patent appeals, suggests that Congress perceived a distinction between the kinds of facts giving rise to one or the other.

The antitrust claim attacks the patent infringement lawsuit itself as the wrong which furnishes the basis for antitrust damages. ***

Comments and Questions

1. When, if ever, should antitrust claims be considered compulsory counterclaims to a patent infringement lawsuit? Does the Federal Circuit's decision in *Nobelpharma* to decide certain antitrust-patent issues as a matter of Federal Circuit, and not regional circuit, law affect your answer?

2. Long before the creation of the Federal Circuit, antitrust scholars and enforcement officials debated how to handle patent infringement lawsuits in which the defendant asserts an antitrust violation as either a defense or a counterclaim. The influential 1955 Attorney General's National Committee to Study the Anti-trust Laws recommended that courts "should order separate trials of the antitrust issues

and the patent issues. Separation may be essential not only 'in furtherance of convenience and to avoid prejudice' but also 'to serve the ends of justice.'" *Components, Inc. v. Western Elec. Co.*, 318 F.Supp. 959, 966 (Me. 1970) (quoting Report at 249).

Do you agree? Why or why not?

Bibliography of Additional Resources

David T. DeZern, *Federal Circuit Antitrust Law and the Legislative History of the Federal Court's Improvement Act of 1982*, 26 Rev. Litig. 457 (2007)

John Donofrio & Edward C. Donovan, *Christianson v. Colt Industries Operating Corp.: The Application of Federal Question Precedent to Federal Circuit Jurisdiction Decisions*, 45 Am. U. L. Rev. 1835 (1996)

Rochelle Cooper Dreyfuss, *The Federal Circuit: A Case Study in Specialized Courts*, 64 N.Y.U. L. Rev. 1 (1989)

Claudette Espanol, *The Federal Circuit: Jurisdictional Expansion into Antitrust Issues Relating to Patent Enforcement*, 2 Seton Hall Circuit Rev. 307 (2005)

James B. Gambrell, *The Evolving Interplay of Patent Rights and Antitrust Restraints in the Federal Circuit*, 9 Tex. Intell. Prop. L.J. 137 (2001)

Karen C. Hermann, *Are Antitrust Counterclaims in Patent Infringement Suits Permissive or Compulsory?*, 26 AIPLA Q.J. 437 (1998)

Paul M. Janicke, *Two Unsettled Aspects of the Federal Circuit's Patent Jurisdiction*, 11 Va. J.L. & Tech 3 (Spring 2006)

Ronald S. Katz & Adam J. Safer, *Should One Patent Court Be Making Antitrust Law for the Whole Country?*, 69 Antitrust L. J. 687 (2002)

Gentry Crook McLean, *Vornado Hits the Midwest: Federal Circuit Jurisdiction in Patent and Antitrust Cases after* Holmes v. Vornado, 82 Tex. L. Rev. 1091 (2004)

Ravi V. Sitwala, *In Defense of Holmes v. Vornado: Addressing the Unwarranted Criticism*, 79 N.Y.U. L. Rev. 452 (2004)

APPENDICES

Appendix A: Statutory Supplement
    Antitrust Statutes
        Excerpts from The Sherman Act
        Excerpts from The Clayton Act
        The National Cooperative Research Act of 1984, as amended by the National Cooperative Research and Production Act of 1993 and the Standards Development Organization Advancement Act of 2004
    Patent Statutes
    Copyright Statutes
    Trademark Statutes
Appendix B: Antitrust Guidelines for the Licensing of Intellectual Property
Appendix C: Microeconomic Analysis and Graphs

APPENDIX A

Statutory Supplement

Antitrust Statutes

Excerpts from The Sherman Act

15 U.S.C.A. § 1

§ 1. Trusts, etc., in restraint of trade illegal; penalty

Every contract, combination in the form of trust or otherwise, or conspiracy, in restraint of trade or commerce among the several States, or with foreign nations, is declared to be illegal. Every person who shall make any contract or engage in any combination or conspiracy hereby declared to be illegal shall be deemed guilty of a felony, and, on conviction thereof, shall be punished by fine not exceeding $100,000,000 if a corporation, or, if any other person, $1,000,000, or by imprisonment not exceeding 10 years, or by both said punishments, in the discretion of the court.

15 U.S.C.A. § 2

§ 2. Monopolizing trade a felony; penalty

Every person who shall monopolize, or attempt to monopolize, or combine or conspire with any other person or persons, to monopolize any part of the trade or commerce among the several States, or with foreign nations, shall be deemed guilty of a felony, and, on conviction thereof, shall be punished by fine not exceeding $100,000,000 if a corporation, or, if any other person, $1,000,000, or by imprisonment not exceeding 10 years, or by both said punishments, in the discretion of the court.

Excerpts from The Clayton Act

15 U.S.C.A. § 14. Sale, etc., on agreement not to use goods of competitor

It shall be unlawful for any person engaged in commerce, in the course of such commerce, to lease or make a sale or contract for sale of goods, wares, merchandise, machinery, supplies, or other commodities, whether patented or unpatented, for use, consumption, or resale within the United States or any Territory thereof or the District of Columbia or any insular possession or other place under the jurisdiction of the United States, or fix a price charged therefor, or discount from, or rebate upon, such price, on the condition, agreement, or understanding that the lessee or purchaser thereof shall not use or deal in the goods, wares, merchandise, machinery, supplies, or other commodities of a competitor or competitors of the lessor or seller, where the effect of such lease, sale, or contract for sale or such condition, agreement, or understanding may be to substantially lessen competition or tend to create a monopoly in any line of commerce.

15 U.S.C.A. § 15. Suits by persons injured

(a) Amount of recovery; prejudgment interest

Except as provided in subsection (b) of this section, any person who shall be injured in his business or property by reason of anything forbidden in the antitrust laws may sue therefor in any district court of the United States in the district in which the defendant resides or is found or has an agent, without respect to the amount in controversy, and shall recover threefold the damages by him sustained, and the cost of suit, including a reasonable attorney's fee. The court may award under this section, pursuant to a motion by such person promptly made, simple interest on actual damages for the period beginning on the date of service of such person's pleading setting forth a claim under the antitrust laws and ending on the date of judgment, or for any shorter period therein, if the court finds that the award of such interest for such period is just in the circumstances. In determining whether an award of interest under this section for any period is just in the circumstances, the court shall consider only—

> (1) whether such person or the opposing party, or either party's representative, made motions or asserted claims or defenses so lacking in merit as to show that such party or representative acted intentionally for delay, or otherwise acted in bad faith;
>
> (2) whether, in the course of the action involved, such person or the opposing party, or either party's representative, violated any applicable rule, statute, or court order providing for sanctions for dilatory behavior or otherwise providing for expeditious proceedings; and
>
> (3) whether such person or the opposing party, or either party's representative, engaged in conduct primarily for the purpose of delaying the litigation or increasing the cost thereof.

(b) Amount of damages payable to foreign states and instrumentalities of foreign states

(1) Except as provided in paragraph (2), any person who is a foreign state may not recover under subsection (a) of this section an amount in excess of the actual damages sustained by it and the cost of suit, including a reasonable attorney's fee.

(2) Paragraph (1) shall not apply to a foreign state if—

(A) such foreign state would be denied, under section 1605(a)(2) of Title 28, immunity in a case in which the action is based upon a commercial activity, or an act, that is the subject matter of its claim under this section;

(B) such foreign state waives all defenses based upon or arising out of its status as a foreign state, to any claims brought against it in the same action;

(C) such foreign state engages primarily in commercial activities; and

(D) such foreign state does not function, with respect to the commercial activity, or the act, that is the subject matter of its claim under this section as a procurement entity for itself or for another foreign state.

(c) Definitions

For purposes of this section—

(1) the term "commercial activity" shall have the meaning given it in section 1603(d) of Title 28, and

(2) the term "foreign state" shall have the meaning given it in section 1603(a) of Title 28.

15 U.S.C.A. § 15a. Suits by United States; amount of recovery; prejudgment interest

Whenever the United States is hereafter injured in its business or property by reason of anything forbidden in the antitrust laws it may sue therefor in the United States district court for the district in which the defendant resides or is found or has an agent, without respect to the amount in controversy, and shall recover threefold the damages by it sustained and the cost of suit. The court may award under this section, pursuant to a motion by the United States promptly made, simple interest on actual damages for the period beginning on the date of service of the pleading of the United States setting forth a claim under the antitrust laws and ending on the date of judgment, or for any shorter period therein, if the court finds that the award of such interest for such period is just in the circumstances. In determining whether an award of interest under this section for any period is just in the circumstances, the court shall consider only—

(1) whether the United States or the opposing party, or either party's representative, made motions or asserted claims or defenses so lacking in merit as to show that such party or representative acted intentionally for delay or otherwise acted in bad faith;

(2) whether, in the course of the action involved, the United States or the opposing party, or either party's representative, violated any applicable rule, statute, or court order providing for sanctions for dilatory behavior or otherwise providing for expeditious proceedings;

(3) whether the United States or the opposing party, or either party's representative, engaged in conduct primarily for the purpose of delaying the litigation or increasing the cost thereof; and

(4) whether the award of such interest is necessary to compensate the United States adequately for the injury sustained by the United States.

15 U.S.C.A. § 15b. Limitation of actions

Any action to enforce any cause of action under section 15, 15a, or 15c of this title shall be forever barred unless commenced within four years after the cause of action accrued. No cause of action barred under existing law on the effective date of this Act shall be revived by this Act.

The National Cooperative Research Act of 1984, as amended by the National Cooperative Research and Production Act of 1993 and the Standards Development Organization Advancement Act of 2004 15 U.S.C. §§ 4301–4305

15 U.S.C. § 4301. Definitions

(a) For purposes of this chapter:

(1) The term "antitrust laws" has the meaning given it in subsection (a) of section 12 of this title, except that such term includes section 45 of this title to the extent that such section 45 applies to unfair methods of competition.

(2) The term "Attorney General" means the Attorney General of the United States.

(3) The term "Commission" means the Federal Trade Commission.

(4) The term "person" has the meaning given it in subsection (a) of section 12 of this title.

(5) The term "State" has the meaning given it in section 15g(2) of this title.

(6) The term "joint venture" means any group of activities, including attempting to make, making, or performing a contract, by two or more persons for the purpose of—

(A) theoretical analysis, experimentation, or systematic study of phenomena or observable facts,

(B) the development or testing of basic engineering techniques,

(C) the extension of investigative findings or theory of a scientific or technical nature into practical application for experimental and demonstration purposes, including the experimental production and testing of models, prototypes, equipment, materials, and processes,

(D) the production of a product, process, or service,

(E) the testing in connection with the production of a product, process, or service by such venture,

(F) the collection, exchange, and analysis of research or production information, or

(G) any combination of the purposes specified in subparagraphs (A), (B), (C), (D), (E), and (F), and may include the establishment and operation of facilities for the conducting of such venture, the conducting of such venture on a protected and proprietary basis, and the prosecuting of applications for patents and the granting of licenses for the results of such venture, but does not include any activity specified in subsection (b) of this section.

(7) The term "standards development activity" means any action taken by a standards development organization for the purpose of developing, promulgating, revising, amending, reissuing, interpreting, or otherwise maintaining a voluntary consensus standard, or using such standard in conformity assessment activities, including actions relating to the intellectual property policies of the standards development organization.

(8) The term "standards development organization" means a domestic or international organization that plans, develops, establishes, or coordinates voluntary consensus standards using procedures that incorporate the attributes of openness, balance of interests, due process, an appeals process, and consensus in a manner consistent with the Office of Management and Budget Circular Number A-119, as revised February 10, 1998. The term "standards development organization" shall not, for purposes of this chapter, include the parties participating in the standards development organization.

(9) The term "technical standard" has the meaning given such term in section 12(d)(4) of the National Technology Transfer and Advancement Act of 1995.

(10) The term "voluntary consensus standard" has the meaning given such term in Office of Management and Budget Circular Number A-119, as revised February 10, 1998.

(b) The term "joint venture" excludes the following activities involving two or more persons:

(1) exchanging information among competitors relating to costs, sales, profitability, prices, marketing, or distribution of any product, process, or service if such information is not reasonably required to carry out the purpose of such venture,

(2) entering into any agreement or engaging in any other conduct restricting, requiring, or otherwise involving the marketing, distribution, or provision by any person who is a party to such venture of any product, process, or service, other than—

(A) the distribution among the parties to such venture, in accordance with such venture, of a product, process, or service produced by such venture,

(B) the marketing of proprietary information, such as patents and trade secrets, developed through such venture formed under a written agreement entered into before June 10, 1993, or

(C) the licensing, conveying, or transferring of intellectual property, such as patents and trade secrets, developed through such venture formed under a written agreement entered into on or after June 10, 1993,

(3) entering into any agreement or engaging in any other conduct—

(A) to restrict or require the sale, licensing, or sharing of inventions, developments, products, processes, or services not developed through, or produced by, such venture, or

(B) to restrict or require participation by any person who is a party to such venture in other research and development activities, that is not reasonably required to prevent misappropriation of proprietary information contributed by any person who is a party to such venture or of the results of such venture,

(4) entering into any agreement or engaging in any other conduct allocating a market with a competitor,

(5) exchanging information among competitors relating to production (other than production by such venture) of a product, process, or service if such information is not reasonably required to carry out the purpose of such venture,

(6) entering into any agreement or engaging in any other conduct restricting, requiring, or otherwise involving the production (other than the production by such venture) of a product, process, or service,

(7) using existing facilities for the production of a product, process, or service by such venture unless such use involves the production of a new product or technology, and

(8) except as provided in paragraphs (2), (3), and (6), entering into any agreement or engaging in any other conduct to restrict or require participation by any person who is a party to such venture, in any unilateral or joint activity that is not reasonably required to carry out the purpose of such venture.

(c) The term "standards development activity" excludes the following activities:

(1) Exchanging information among competitors relating to cost, sales, profitability, prices, marketing, or distribution of any product, process, or service that is not reasonably required for the purpose of developing or promulgating a voluntary consensus standard, or using such standard in conformity assessment activities.

(2) Entering into any agreement or engaging in any other conduct that would allocate a market with a competitor.

(3) Entering into any agreement or conspiracy that would set or restrain prices of any good or service.

15 U.S.C. § 4302. Rule of reason standard

In any action under the antitrust laws, or under any State law similar to the antitrust laws, the conduct of—

(1) any person in making or performing a contract to carry out a joint venture, or

(2) a standards development organization while engaged in a standards development activity, shall not be deemed illegal per se; such conduct shall be judged on the basis of its reasonableness, taking into account all relevant factors affecting competition, including, but not limited to, effects on competition in properly defined, relevant research, development, product, process, and service markets. For the purpose of determining a properly defined, relevant market, worldwide capacity shall be considered to the extent that it may be appropriate in the circumstances.

§ 4303. Limitation on recovery

(a) Amount recoverable

Notwithstanding section 15 of this title and in lieu of the relief specified in such section, any person who is entitled to recovery on a claim under such section shall recover the actual damages sustained by such person, interest calculated at the rate specified in section 1961 of Title 28 on such actual damages as specified in subsection (d) of this section, and the cost of suit attributable to such claim, including a reasonable attorney's fee pursuant to section 4304 of this title if such claim—

(1) results from conduct that is within the scope of a notification that has been filed under section 4305(a) of this title for a joint venture, or for a standards development activity engaged in by a standards development organization against which such claim is made, and

(2) is filed after such notification becomes effective pursuant to section 4305(c) of this title.

(b) Recovery by States

Notwithstanding section 15c of this title, and in lieu of the relief specified in such section, any State that is entitled to monetary relief on a claim under such section shall recover the total damage sustained as described in subsection (a)(1) of such section, interest calculated at the rate specified in section 1961 of Title 28 on such total damage as specified in subsection (d) of this section, and the cost of suit attributable to such claim, including a reasonable attorney's fee pursuant to section 15c of this title if such claim—

(1) results from conduct that is within the scope of a notification that has been filed under section 4305(a) of this title for a joint venture, or for a standards development activity engaged in by a standards development organization against which such claim is made, and

(2) is filed after such notification becomes effective pursuant to section 4305(c) of this title.

(c) Conduct similar under State law

Notwithstanding any provision of any State law providing damages for conduct similar to that forbidden by the antitrust laws, any person who is entitled to recovery on a claim under such provision shall not recover in excess of the actual damages sustained by such person, interest calculated at the rate specified in section 1961 of Title 28 on such actual damages as specified in subsection (d) of this section, and the cost of suit attributable to such claim, including a reasonable attorney's fee pursuant to section 4304 of this title if such claim—

(1) results from conduct that is within the scope of a notification that has been filed under section 4305(a) of this title for a joint venture, or for a standards development activity engaged in by a standards development organization against which such claim is made, and

(2) is filed after notification has become effective pursuant to section 4305(c) of this title.

(d) Interest

Interest shall be awarded on the damages involved for the period beginning on the earliest date for which injury can be established and ending on the date of judgment, unless the court finds that the award of all or part of such interest is unjust in the circumstances.

(e) Subsections (a), (b), and (c) of this section shall not be construed to modify the liability under the antitrust laws of any person (other than a standards development organization) who—

(1) directly (or through an employee or agent) participates in a standards development activity with respect to which a violation of any of the antitrust laws is found,

(2) is not a fulltime employee of the standards development organization that engaged in such activity, and

(3) is, or is an employee or agent of a person who is, engaged in a line of commerce that is likely to benefit directly from the operation of the standards development activity with respect to which such violation is found.

(f) Applicability

This section shall be applicable only if the challenged conduct of a person defending against a claim is not in violation of any decree or order, entered or issued after October 11, 1984, in any case or proceeding under the antitrust laws or any State law similar to the antitrust laws challenging such conduct as part of a joint venture, or of a standards development activity engaged in by a standards development organization.

15 U.S.C. § 4304. Award of costs, including attorney's fees, to substantially prevailing party; offset

(a) Notwithstanding sections 15 and 26 of this title, in any claim under the antitrust laws, or any State law similar to the antitrust laws, based on the conducting of a joint venture, or of a standards development activity engaged in by a standards development organization, the court shall, at the conclusion of the action—

(1) award to a substantially prevailing claimant the cost of suit attributable to such claim, including a reasonable attorney's fee, or

(2) award to a substantially prevailing party defending against any such claim the cost of suit attributable to such claim, including a reasonable attorney's fee,

if the claim, or the claimant's conduct during the litigation of the claim, was frivolous, unreasonable, without foundation, or in bad faith.

(b) The award made under subsection (a) of this section may be offset in whole or in part by an award in favor of any other party for any part of the cost of suit, including a reasonable attorney's fee, attributable to conduct during the litigation by any prevailing party that the court finds to be frivolous, unreasonable, without foundation, or in bad faith.

(c) Subsections (a) and (b) of this section shall not apply with respect to any person who—

> (1) directly participates in a standards development activity with respect to which a violation of any of the antitrust laws is found,
>
> (2) is not a fulltime employee of a standards development organization that engaged in such activity, and
>
> (3) is, or is an employee or agent of a person who is, engaged in a line of commerce that is likely to benefit directly from the operation of the standards development activity with respect to which such violation is found.

15 U.S.C. § 4305. Disclosure of joint venture

(a)(1) Written notifications; filing

> Any party to a joint venture, acting on such venture's behalf, may, not later than 90 days after entering into a written agreement to form such venture or not later than 90 days after October 11, 1984, whichever is later, file simultaneously with the Attorney General and the Commission a written notification disclosing—
>
>> (A) the identities of the parties to such venture,
>>
>> (B) the nature and objectives of such venture, and
>>
>> (C) if a purpose of such venture is the production of a product, process, or service, as referred to in section 4301(a)(6)(D) of this title, the identity and nationality of any person who is a party to such venture, or who controls any party to such venture whether separately or with one or more other persons acting as a group for the purpose of controlling such party.

Any party to such venture, acting on such venture's behalf, may file additional disclosure notifications pursuant to this section as are appropriate to extend the protections of section 4303 of this title. In order to maintain the protections of section 4303 of this title, such venture shall, not later than 90 days after a change in its membership, file simultaneously with the Attorney General and the Commission a written notification disclosing such change.

(2) A standards development organization may, not later than 90 days after commencing a standards development activity engaged in for the purpose of developing or promulgating a voluntary consensus standards or not later than 90 days after June 22, 2004, whichever is later, file simultaneously

with the Attorney General and the Commission, a written notification disclosing—

(A) the name and principal place of business of the standards development organization, and

(B) documents showing the nature and scope of such activity.

Any standards development organization may file additional disclosure notifications pursuant to this section as are appropriate to extend the protections of section 4303 of this title to standards development activities that are not covered by the initial filing or that have changed significantly since the initial filing.

(b) Publication; Federal Register; notice

Except as provided in subsection (e) of this section, not later than 30 days after receiving a notification filed under subsection (a) of this section, the Attorney General or the Commission shall publish in the Federal Register a notice with respect to such venture that identifies the parties to such venture and that describes in general terms the area of planned activity of such venture, or a notice with respect to such standards development activity that identifies the standards development organization engaged in such activity and that describes such activity in general terms. Prior to its publication, the contents of such notice shall be made available to the parties to such venture or available to such organization, as the case may be.

(c) Effect of notice

If with respect to a notification filed under subsection (a) of this section, notice is published in the Federal Register, then such notification shall operate to convey the protections of section 4303 of this title as of the earlier of—

(1) the date of publication of notice under subsection (b) of this section, or

(2) if such notice is not so published within the time required by subsection (b) of this section, after the expiration of the 30-day period beginning on the date the Attorney General or the Commission receives the applicable information described in subsection (a) of this section.

(d) Exemption; disclosure; information

Except with respect to the information published pursuant to subsection (b) of this section—

(1) all information and documentary material submitted as part of a notification filed pursuant to this section, and

(2) all other information obtained by the Attorney General or the Commission in the course of any investigation, administrative proceeding, or case, with respect to a potential violation of the antitrust laws by the joint venture, or the standards development activity, with respect to which such notification was filed, shall be exempt from disclosure under section 552 of Title 5, and shall not be made publicly available by any agency of the United States to which such section applies except in a judicial or administrative proceeding in which such information and material is subject to any protective order.

(e) Withdrawal of notification

Any person or standards development organization that files a notification pursuant to this section may withdraw such notification before notice of the joint venture involved is published under subsection (b) of this section. Any notification so withdrawn shall not be subject to subsection (b) of this section and shall not confer the protections of section 4303 of this title on any person or any standards development organization with respect to whom such notification was filed.

(f) Judicial review; inapplicable with respect to notifications

Any action taken or not taken by the Attorney General or the Commission with respect to notifications filed pursuant to this section shall not be subject to judicial review.

(g) Admissibility into evidence; disclosure of conduct; publication of notice; supporting or answering claims under antitrust laws

(1) Except as provided in paragraph (2), for the sole purpose of establishing that a person or standards development organization is entitled to the protections of section 4303 of this title, the fact of disclosure of conduct under subsection (a) of this section and the fact of publication of a notice under subsection (b) of this section shall be admissible into evidence in any judicial or administrative proceeding.

(2) No action by the Attorney General or the Commission taken pursuant to this section shall be admissible into evidence in any such proceeding for the purpose of supporting or answering any claim under the antitrust laws or under any State law similar to the antitrust laws.

Patent Statutes

35 U.S.C. § 101. Inventions patentable

Whoever invents or discovers any new and useful process, machine, manufacture, or composition of matter, or any new and useful improvement thereof, may obtain a patent therefor, subject to the conditions and requirements of this title.

35 U.S.C. § 102. Conditions for patentability; novelty and loss of right to patent

A person shall be entitled to a patent unless—

(a) the invention was known or used by others in this country, or patented or described in a printed publication in this or a foreign country, before the invention thereof by the applicant for patent, or

(b) the invention was patented or described in a printed publication in this or a foreign country or in public use or on sale in this country, more than one year prior to the date of the application for patent in the United States, or

(c) he has abandoned the invention, or

(d) the invention was first patented or caused to be patented, or was the subject of an inventor's certificate, by the applicant or his legal representatives or assigns in a foreign country prior to the date of the application for patent in this country on an application for patent or inventor's certificate filed more than twelve months before the filing of the application in the United States, or

(e) the invention was described in (1) an application for patent, published under section 122(b), by another filed in the United States before the invention by the applicant for patent or (2) a patent granted on an application for patent by another filed in the United States before the invention by the applicant for patent, except that an international application filed under the treaty defined in section 351(a) shall have the effects for the purposes of this subsection of an application filed in the United States only if the international application designated the United States and was published under Article 21(2) of such treaty in the English language; or

(f) he did not himself invent the subject matter sought to be patented, or

(g)(1) during the course of an interference conducted under section 135 or section 291, another inventor involved therein establishes, to the extent permitted in section 104, that before such person's invention thereof the invention was made by such other inventor and not abandoned, suppressed, or concealed, or (2) before such person's invention thereof, the invention was made in this country by another inventor who had not abandoned, suppressed, or concealed it. In determining priority of invention under this subsection, there shall be considered not only the respective dates of conception and reduction to practice of the invention, but also the reasonable diligence of one who was first to conceive and last to reduce to practice, from a time prior to conception by the other.

35 U.S.C. § 103. Conditions for patentability; non-obvious subject matter

(a) A patent may not be obtained though the invention is not identically disclosed or described as set forth in section 102 of this title, if the differences between the subject matter sought to be patented and the prior art are such that the subject matter as a whole would have been obvious at the time the invention was made to a person having ordinary skill in the art to which said subject matter pertains. Patentability shall not be negatived by the manner in which the invention was made. ***

35 U.S.C. § 154. Contents and term of patent; provisional rights

(a) In general.—

(1) Contents.—Every patent shall contain a short title of the invention and a grant to the patentee, his heirs or assigns, of the right to exclude others from making, using, offering for sale, or selling the invention throughout the United States or importing the invention into the United States, and, if the invention is a process, of the right to exclude others from using, offering for sale or selling throughout the United States, or importing into the United States, products made by that process, referring to the specification for the particulars thereof.

(2) Term.—Subject to the payment of fees under this title, such grant shall be for a term beginning on the date on which the patent issues and ending 20 years from the date on which the application for the patent was filed in the United States or, if the application contains a specific reference to an earlier filed application or applications under section 120, 121, or 365(c) of this title, from the date on which the earliest such application was filed.

35 U.S.C.A. § 271. Infringement of patent

(a) Except as otherwise provided in this title, whoever without authority makes, uses, offers to sell, or sells any patented invention, within the United States or imports into the United States any patented invention during the term of the patent therefor, infringes the patent.

(b) Whoever actively induces infringement of a patent shall be liable as an infringer.

(c) Whoever offers to sell or sells within the United States or imports into the United States a component of a patented machine, manufacture, combination or composition, or a material or apparatus for use in practicing a patented process, constituting a material part of the invention, knowing the same to be especially made or especially adapted for use in an infringement of such patent, and not a staple article or commodity of commerce suitable for substantial noninfringing use, shall be liable as a contributory infringer.

(d) No patent owner otherwise entitled to relief for infringement or contributory infringement of a patent shall be denied relief or deemed guilty of misuse or illegal extension of the patent right by reason of his having done one or more of the following:

(1) derived revenue from acts which if performed by another without his consent would constitute contributory infringement of the patent;

(2) licensed or authorized another to perform acts which if performed without his consent would constitute contributory infringement of the patent;

(3) sought to enforce his patent rights against infringement or contributory infringement;

(4) refused to license or use any rights to the patent; or

(5) conditioned the license of any rights to the patent or the sale of the patented product on the acquisition of a license to rights in another patent or purchase of a separate product, unless, in view of the circumstances, the patent owner has market power in the relevant market for the patent or patented product on which the license or sale is conditioned.

***

35 U.S.C. § 283. Injunction

The several courts having jurisdiction of cases under this title may grant injunctions in accordance with the principles of equity to prevent the violation of any right secured by patent, on such terms as the court deems reasonable.

35 U.S.C. § 284. Damages

Upon finding for the claimant the court shall award the claimant damages adequate to compensate for the infringement, but in no event less than a reasonable royalty for the use made of the invention by the infringer, together with interest and costs as fixed by the court.

When the damages are not found by a jury, the court shall assess them. In either event the court may increase the damages up to three times the amount found or assessed. Increased damages under this paragraph shall not apply to provisional rights under section 154(d) of this title.

The court may receive expert testimony as an aid to the determination of damages or of what royalty would be reasonable under the circumstances.

Copyright Statutes

17 U.S.C. § 102

Subject matter of copyright: In general

(a) Copyright protection subsists, in accordance with this title, in original works of authorship fixed in any tangible medium of expression, now known or later developed, from which they can be perceived, reproduced, or otherwise communicated, either directly or with the aid of a machine or device. Works of authorship include the following categories:

(1) literary works;

(2) musical works, including any accompanying words;

(3) dramatic works, including any accompanying music;

(4) pantomimes and choreographic works;

(5) pictorial, graphic, and sculptural works;

(6) motion pictures and other audiovisual works;

(7) sound recordings; and

(8) architectural works.

(b) In no case does copyright protection for an original work of authorship extend to any idea, procedure, process, system, method of operation, concept, principle, or discovery, regardless of the form in which it is described, explained, illustrated, or embodied in such work.

17 U.S.C. § 106. Exclusive rights in copyrighted works

Subject to sections 107 through 122, the owner of copyright under this title has the exclusive rights to do and to authorize any of the following:

(1) to reproduce the copyrighted work in copies or phonorecords;

(2) to prepare derivative works based upon the copyrighted work;

(3) to distribute copies or phonorecords of the copyrighted work to the public by sale or other transfer of ownership, or by rental, lease, or lending;

(4) in the case of literary, musical, dramatic, and choreographic works, pantomimes, and motion pictures and other audiovisual works, to perform the copyrighted work publicly;

(5) in the case of literary, musical, dramatic, and choreographic works, pantomimes, and pictorial, graphic, or sculptural works, including the individual images of a motion picture or other audiovisual work, to display the copyrighted work publicly; and

(6) in the case of sound recordings, to perform the copyrighted work publicly by means of a digital audio transmission.

17 U.S.C. § 107. Limitations on exclusive rights: Fair use

Notwithstanding the provisions of sections 106 and 106A, the fair use of a copyrighted work, including such use by reproduction in copies or phonorecords or by any other means specified by that section, for purposes such as criticism, comment, news reporting, teaching (including multiple copies for classroom use), scholarship, or research, is not an infringement of copyright. In determining whether the use made of a work in any particular case is a fair use the factors to be considered shall include—

(1) the purpose and character of the use, including whether such use is of a commercial nature or is for nonprofit educational purposes;

(2) the nature of the copyrighted work;

(3) the amount and substantiality of the portion used in relation to the copyrighted work as a whole; and

(4) the effect of the use upon the potential market for or value of the copyrighted work.

The fact that a work is unpublished shall not itself bar a finding of fair use if such finding is made upon consideration of all the above factors.

17 U.S.C. § 109. Limitations on exclusive rights: Effect of transfer of particular copy or phonorecord

(a) Notwithstanding the provisions of section 106(3), the owner of a particular copy or phonorecord lawfully made under this title, or any person authorized by such owner, is entitled, without the authority of the copyright owner, to sell or otherwise dispose of the possession of that copy or phonorecord. Notwithstanding the preceding sentence, copies or phonorecords of works subject to restored copyright under section 104A that are manufactured before the date of restoration of copyright or, with respect to reliance parties, before publication or service of notice under section 104A(e), may be sold or otherwise disposed of without the authorization of the owner of the restored copyright for purposes of direct or indirect commercial advantage only during the 12-month period beginning on—

(1) the date of the publication in the Federal Register of the notice of intent filed with the Copyright Office under section 104A(d)(2)(A), or

(2) the date of the receipt of actual notice served under section 104A(d)(2)(B),
whichever occurs first.

***

17 U.S.C. § 115. Scope of exclusive rights in nondramatic musical works: Compulsory license for making and distributing phonorecords

In the case of nondramatic musical works, the exclusive rights provided by clauses (1) and (3) of section 106, to make and to distribute phonorecords of such works, are subject to compulsory licensing under the conditions specified by this section.

(a) Availability and Scope of Compulsory License.—

(1) When phonorecords of a nondramatic musical work have been distributed to the public in the United States under the authority of the copyright owner, any other person, including those who make phonorecords or digital phonorecord deliveries, may, by complying with the provisions of this section, obtain a compulsory license to make and distribute phonorecords of the work. A person may obtain a compulsory license only if his or her primary purpose in making phonorecords is to distribute them to the public for private use, including by means of a digital phonorecord delivery. A person may not obtain a compulsory license for use of the work in the making of phonorecords duplicating a sound recording fixed by another, unless: (i) such sound recording was fixed lawfully; and (ii) the making of the phonorecords was authorized by the owner of copyright in the sound recording or, if the sound recording was fixed before February 15, 1972, by any person who fixed the sound recording pursuant to an express license from the owner of the copyright in the musical work or pursuant to a valid compulsory license for use of such work in a sound recording.

(2) A compulsory license includes the privilege of making a musical arrangement of the work to the extent necessary to conform it to the style or manner of interpretation of the performance involved, but the arrangement shall not change the basic melody or fundamental character of the work, and shall not be subject to protection as a derivative work under this title, except with the express consent of the copyright owner.

(b) Notice of Intention to Obtain Compulsory License.—

(1) Any person who wishes to obtain a compulsory license under this section shall, before or within thirty days after making, and before distributing any phonorecords of the work, serve notice of intention to do so on the copyright owner. If the registration or other public records of the Copyright Office do not identify the copyright owner and include an address at which notice can be served, it shall be sufficient to file the notice of intention in the Copyright Office. The notice shall comply, in form, content, and manner of service, with requirements that the Register of Copyrights shall prescribe by regulation.

(2) Failure to serve or file the notice required by clause (1) forecloses the possibility of a compulsory license and, in the absence of a negotiated license, renders the making and distribution of phonorecords actionable as acts of

infringement under section 501 and fully subject to the remedies provided by sections 502 through 506 and 509.

(c) Royalty Payable under Compulsory License.—

(1) To be entitled to receive royalties under a compulsory license, the copyright owner must be identified in the registration or other public records of the Copyright Office. The owner is entitled to royalties for phonorecords made and distributed after being so identified, but is not entitled to recover for any phonorecords previously made and distributed.

(2) Except as provided by clause (1), the royalty under a compulsory license shall be payable for every phonorecord made and distributed in accordance with the license. For this purpose, and other than as provided in paragraph (3), a phonorecord is considered "distributed" if the person exercising the compulsory license has voluntarily and permanently parted with its possession. With respect to each work embodied in the phonorecord, the royalty shall be either two and three-fourths cents, or one-half of one cent per minute of playing time or fraction thereof, whichever amount is larger.

(3)(A) A compulsory license under this section includes the right of the compulsory licensee to distribute or authorize the distribution of a phonorecord of a nondramatic musical work by means of a digital transmission which constitutes a digital phonorecord delivery, regardless of whether the digital transmission is also a public performance of the sound recording under section 106(6) of this title or of any nondramatic musical work embodied therein under section 106(4) of this title. For every digital phonorecord delivery by or under the authority of the compulsory licensee—

> (i) on or before December 31, 1997, the royalty payable by the compulsory licensee shall be the royalty prescribed under paragraph (2) and chapter 8 of this title; and
>
> (ii) on or after January 1, 1998, the royalty payable by the compulsory licensee shall be the royalty prescribed under subparagraphs (B) through (E) and chapter 8 of this title.

(B) Notwithstanding any provision of the antitrust laws, any copyright owners of nondramatic musical works and any persons entitled to obtain a compulsory license under subsection (a)(1) may negotiate and agree upon the terms and rates of royalty payments under this section and the proportionate division of fees paid among copyright owners, and may designate common agents on a nonexclusive basis to negotiate, agree to, pay or receive such royalty payments. Such authority to negotiate the terms and rates of royalty payments includes, but is not limited to, the authority to negotiate the year during which the royalty rates prescribed under this subparagraph and subparagraphs (C) through (E) and chapter 8 of this title shall next be determined.

(C) Proceedings under chapter 8 shall determine reasonable rates and terms of royalty payments for the activities specified by this section during the period beginning with the effective date of such rates and terms, but not earlier than January 1 of the second year following the year in which the petition requesting the proceeding is filed, and ending on the effective date of successor rates and terms, or such other period as the parties may agree. Such terms and rates shall distinguish between (i) digital phonorecord deliveries where the reproduction or distribution of a phonorecord is incidental to the transmission which constitutes the digital phonorecord delivery, and (ii) digital phonorecord deliveries in general. Any copyright owners of nondramatic musical works and any persons entitled to obtain a compulsory license under subsection (a)(1) may submit to the Copyright Royalty Judges licenses covering such activities. The parties to each proceeding shall bear their own costs.

(D) The schedule of reasonable rates and terms determined by the Copyright Royalty Judges shall, subject to subparagraph (E), be binding on all copyright owners of nondramatic musical works and persons entitled to obtain a compulsory license under subsection (a)(1) during the period specified in subparagraph (C), such other period as may be determined pursuant to subparagraphs (B) and (C), or such other period as the parties may agree. Such terms and rates shall distinguish between (i) digital phonorecord deliveries where the reproduction or distribution of a phonorecord is incidental to the transmission which constitutes the digital phonorecord delivery, and (ii) digital phonorecord deliveries in general. In addition to the objectives set forth in section 801(b)(1), in establishing such rates and terms, the Copyright Royalty Judges may consider rates and terms under voluntary license agreements described in subparagraphs (B) and (C). The royalty rates payable for a compulsory license for a digital phonorecord delivery under this section shall be established de novo and no precedential effect shall be given to the amount of the royalty payable by a compulsory licensee for digital phonorecord deliveries on or before December 31, 1997. The Copyright Royalty Judges shall also establish requirements by which copyright owners may receive reasonable notice of the use of their works under this section, and under which records of such use shall be kept and made available by persons making digital phonorecord deliveries.

(E)(i) License agreements voluntarily negotiated at any time between one or more copyright owners of nondramatic musical works and one or more persons entitled to obtain a compulsory license under subsection (a)(1) shall be given effect in lieu of any determination by the Librarian of Congress and Copyright Royalty Judges. Subject to clause (ii), the royalty rates determined pursuant to subparagraph (C) and (D) shall be given effect as to digital phonorecord deliveries in lieu of any contrary royalty rates specified in a contract pursuant to which a recording artist who is the author of a nondramatic musical work grants a license under that person's exclusive rights in the musical work under paragraphs (1) and (3) of section 106 or commits another person to grant a license in that musical work under paragraphs (1) and (3) of section 106, to a person desiring to fix in a tangible medium of expression a sound recording embodying the musical work.

(ii) The second sentence of clause (i) shall not apply to—

(I) a contract entered into on or before June 22, 1995, and not modified thereafter for the purpose of reducing the royalty rates determined pursuant to subparagraph (C) and (D) or of increasing the number of musical works within the scope of the contract covered by the reduced rates, except if a contract entered into on or before June 22, 1995, is modified thereafter for the purpose of increasing the number of musical works within the scope of the contract, any contrary royalty rates specified in the contract shall be given effect in lieu of royalty rates determined pursuant to subparagraph (C) and (D) for the number of musical works within the scope of the contract as of June 22, 1995; and

(II) a contract entered into after the date that the sound recording is fixed in a tangible medium of expression substantially in a form intended for commercial release, if at the time the contract is entered into, the recording artist retains the right to grant licenses as to the musical work under paragraphs (1) and (3) of section 106.

(F) Except as provided in section 1002(e) of this title, a digital phonorecord delivery licensed under this paragraph shall be accompanied by the information encoded in the sound recording, if any, by or under the authority of the copyright owner of that sound recording, that identifies the title of the sound recording, the featured recording artist who performs on the sound recording, and related information, including information concerning the underlying musical work and its writer.

(G)(i) A digital phonorecord delivery of a sound recording is actionable as an act of infringement under section 501, and is fully subject to the remedies provided by sections 502 through 506 and section 509, unless—

(I) the digital phonorecord delivery has been authorized by the copyright owner of the sound recording; and

(II) the owner of the copyright in the sound recording or the entity making the digital phonorecord delivery has obtained a compulsory license under this section or has otherwise been authorized by the copyright owner of the musical work to distribute or authorize the distribution, by means of a digital phonorecord delivery, of each musical work embodied in the sound recording.

(ii) Any cause of action under this subparagraph shall be in addition to those available to the owner of the copyright in the nondramatic musical work under subsection (c)(6) and section 106(4) and the owner of the copyright in the sound recording under section 106(6).

(H) The liability of the copyright owner of a sound recording for infringement of the copyright in a nondramatic musical work embodied in the sound recording shall be determined in accordance with applicable law, except that the owner of a copyright in a sound recording shall not be liable for a digital phonorecord delivery by a third party if the owner of the copyright in the sound recording does not license the distribution of a phonorecord of the nondramatic musical work.

(I) Nothing in section 1008 shall be construed to prevent the exercise of the rights and remedies allowed by this paragraph, paragraph (6), and chapter 5 in the event of a digital phonorecord delivery, except that no action alleging infringement of copyright may be brought under this title against a manufacturer, importer or distributor of a digital audio recording device, a digital audio recording medium, an analog recording device, or an analog recording medium, or against a consumer, based on the actions described in such section.

(J) Nothing in this section annuls or limits (i) the exclusive right to publicly perform a sound recording or the musical work embodied therein, including by means of a digital transmission, under sections 106(4) and 106(6), (ii) except for compulsory licensing under the conditions specified by this section, the exclusive rights to reproduce and distribute the sound recording and the musical work embodied therein under sections 106(1) and 106(3), including by means of a digital phonorecord delivery, or (iii) any other rights under any other provision of section 106, or remedies available under this title, as such rights or remedies exist either before or after the date of enactment of the Digital Performance Right in Sound Recordings Act of 1995.

(K) The provisions of this section concerning digital phonorecord deliveries shall not apply to any exempt transmissions or retransmissions under section 114(d)(1). The exemptions created in section 114(d)(1) do not expand or reduce the rights of copyright owners under section 106(1) through (5) with respect to such transmissions and retransmissions.

(4) A compulsory license under this section includes the right of the maker of a phonorecord of a nondramatic musical work under subsection (a)(1) to distribute or authorize distribution of such phonorecord by rental, lease, or lending (or by acts or practices in the nature of rental, lease, or lending). In addition to any royalty payable under clause (2) and chapter 8 of this title, a royalty shall be payable by the compulsory licensee for every act of distribution of a phonorecord by or in the nature of rental, lease, or lending, by or under the authority of the compulsory licensee. With respect to each nondramatic musical work embodied in the phonorecord, the royalty shall be a proportion of the revenue received by the compulsory licensee from every such act of distribution of the phonorecord under this clause equal to the proportion of the revenue received by the compulsory licensee from distribution of the phonorecord under clause (2) that is payable by a compulsory licensee under that clause and under chapter 8. The Register of Copyrights shall issue regulations to carry out the purpose of this clause.

(5) Royalty payments shall be made on or before the twentieth day of each month and shall include all royalties for the month next preceding. Each monthly payment shall be made under oath and shall comply with requirements that the Register of Copyrights shall prescribe by regulation. The Register shall also prescribe regulations under which detailed cumulative annual statements of account, certified by a certified public accountant, shall be filed for every compulsory license under this section. The regulations covering both the monthly and the annual statements of account shall prescribe the form, content, and manner of certification with respect to the number of records made and the number of records distributed.

(6) If the copyright owner does not receive the monthly payment and the monthly and annual statements of account when due, the owner may give written notice to the licensee that, unless the default is remedied within thirty days from the date of the notice, the compulsory license will be automatically terminated. Such termination renders either the making or the distribution, or both, of all phonorecords for which the royalty has not been paid, actionable as acts of infringement under section 501 and fully subject to the remedies provided by sections 502 through 506 and 509.

(d) Definition.—As used in this section, the following term has the following meaning: A "digital phonorecord delivery" is each individual delivery of a phonorecord by digital transmission of a sound recording which results in a specifically identifiable reproduction by or for any transmission recipient of a phonorecord of that sound recording, regardless of whether the digital transmission is also a public performance of the sound recording or any nondramatic musical work embodied therein. A digital phonorecord delivery does not result from a real-time, non-interactive subscription transmission of a sound recording where no reproduction of the sound recording or the musical work embodied therein is made from the inception of the transmission through to its receipt by the transmission recipient in order to make the sound recording audible.

17 U.S.C. § 116. Negotiated licenses for public performances by means of coin-operated phonorecord players

(a) Applicability of section.—This section applies to any nondramatic musical work embodied in a phonorecord.

(b) Negotiated Licenses.—

(1) Authority for negotiations.—Any owners of copyright in works to which this section applies and any operators of coin-operated phonorecord players may negotiate and agree upon the terms and rates of royalty payments for the performance of such works and the proportionate division of fees paid among copyright owners, and may designate common agents to negotiate, agree to, pay, or receive such royalty payments.

(2) Chapter 8 proceeding.—Parties not subject to such a negotiation may have the terms and rates and the division of fees described in paragraph (1) determined in a proceeding in accordance with the provisions of chapter 8.

(c) License agreements superior to determinations by Copyright Royalty Judges.—License agreements between one or more copyright owners and one or more operators of coin-operated phonorecord players, which are negotiated in accordance with subsection (b), shall be given effect in lieu of any otherwise applicable determination by the Copyright Royalty Judges.

(d) Definitions.—As used in this section, the following terms mean the following:

(1) A "coin-operated phonorecord player" is a machine or device that—

(A) is employed solely for the performance of nondramatic musical works by means of phonorecords upon being activated by the insertion of coins, currency, tokens, or other monetary units or their equivalent;

(B) is located in an establishment making no direct or indirect charge for admission;

(C) is accompanied by a list which is comprised of the titles of all the musical works available for performance on it, and is affixed to the phonorecord player or posted in the establishment in a prominent position where it can be readily examined by the public; and

(D) affords a choice of works available for performance and permits the choice to be made by the patrons of the establishment in which it is located.

(2) An "operator" is any person who, alone or jointly with others—

(A) owns a coin-operated phonorecord player;

(B) has the power to make a coin-operated phonorecord player available for placement in an establishment for purposes of public performance; or

(C) has the power to exercise primary control over the selection of the musical works made available for public performance on a coin-operated phonorecord player.

17 U.S.C. § 504. Remedies for infringement: Damages and profits

(a) In General.—Except as otherwise provided by this title, an infringer of copyright is liable for either—

(1) the copyright owner's actual damages and any additional profits of the infringer, as provided by subsection (b); or

(2) statutory damages, as provided by subsection (c).

(b) Actual Damages and Profits.—The copyright owner is entitled to recover the actual damages suffered by him or her as a result of the infringement, and any profits of the infringer that are attributable to the infringement and are not taken into account in computing the actual damages. In establishing the infringer's profits, the copyright owner is required to present proof only of the infringer's gross revenue, and the infringer is required to prove his or her deductible expenses and the elements of profit attributable to factors other than the copyrighted work.

(c) Statutory Damages.—

(1) Except as provided by clause (2) of this subsection, the copyright owner may elect, at any time before final judgment is rendered, to recover, instead

of actual damages and profits, an award of statutory damages for all infringements involved in the action, with respect to any one work, for which any one infringer is liable individually, or for which any two or more infringers are liable jointly and severally, in a sum of not less than $750 or more than $30,000 as the court considers just. For the purposes of this subsection, all the parts of a compilation or derivative work constitute one work.

(2) In a case where the copyright owner sustains the burden of proving, and the court finds, that infringement was committed willfully, the court in its discretion may increase the award of statutory damages to a sum of not more than $150,000. In a case where the infringer sustains the burden of proving, and the court finds, that such infringer was not aware and had no reason to believe that his or her acts constituted an infringement of copyright, the court in its discretion may reduce the award of statutory damages to a sum of not less than $200. The court shall remit statutory damages in any case where an infringer believed and had reasonable grounds for believing that his or her use of the copyrighted work was a fair use under section 107, if the infringer was: (i) an employee or agent of a nonprofit educational institution, library, or archives acting within the scope of his or her employment who, or such institution, library, or archives itself, which infringed by reproducing the work in copies or phonorecords; or (ii) a public broadcasting entity which or a person who, as a regular part of the nonprofit activities of a public broadcasting entity (as defined in subsection (g) of section 118) infringed by performing a published nondramatic literary work or by reproducing a transmission program embodying a performance of such a work.

(3) (A) In a case of infringement, it shall be a rebuttable presumption that the infringement was committed willfully for purposes of determining relief if the violator, or a person acting in concert with the violator, knowingly provided or knowingly caused to be provided materially false contact information to a domain name registrar, domain name registry, or other domain name registration authority in registering, maintaining, or renewing a domain name used in connection with the infringement.

(B) Nothing in this paragraph limits what may be considered willful infringement under this subsection.

(C) For purposes of this paragraph, the term "domain name" has the meaning given that term in section 45 of the Act entitled "An Act to provide for the registration and protection of trademarks used in commerce, to carry out the provisions of certain international conventions, and for other purposes" approved July 5, 1946 (commonly referred to as the "Trademark Act of 1946"; 15 U.S.C. 1127).

(d) Additional damages in certain cases.—In any case in which the court finds that a defendant proprietor of an establishment who claims as a defense that its activities were exempt under section 110(5) did not have reasonable grounds to believe that its use of a copyrighted work was exempt under such section, the plaintiff shall be entitled to, in addition to any award of damages under this section, an additional award of two times the amount of the license fee that the proprietor of the establishment concerned should have paid the plaintiff for such use during the preceding period of up to 3 years.

Trademark Statutes

15 U.S.C. § 1117. Recovery for violation of rights

(a) Profits; damages and costs; attorney fees
When a violation of any right of the registrant of a mark registered in the Patent and Trademark Office, a violation under section 1125(a) or (d) of this title, or a willful violation under section 1125(c) of this title, shall have been established in any civil action arising under this chapter, the plaintiff shall be entitled, subject to the provisions of sections 1111 and 1114 of this title, and subject to the principles of equity, to recover (1) defendant's profits, (2) any damages sustained by the plaintiff, and (3) the costs of the action. The court shall assess such profits and damages or cause the same to be assessed under its direction. In assessing profits the plaintiff shall be required to prove defendant's sales only; defendant must prove all elements of cost or deduction claimed. In assessing damages the court may enter judgment, according to the circumstances of the case, for any sum above the amount found as actual damages, not exceeding three times such amount. If the court shall find that the amount of the recovery based on profits is either inadequate or excessive the court may in its discretion enter judgment for such sum as the court shall find to be just, according to the circumstances of the case. Such sum in either of the above circumstances shall constitute compensation and not a penalty. The court in exceptional cases may award reasonable attorney fees to the prevailing party.

(b) Treble damages for use of counterfeit mark
In assessing damages under subsection (a) of this section, the court shall, unless the court finds extenuating circumstances, enter judgment for three times such profits or damages, whichever is greater, together with a reasonable attorney's fee, in the case of any violation of section 1114(1)(a) of this title or section 220506 of Title 36 that consists of intentionally using a mark or designation, knowing such mark or designation is a counterfeit mark (as defined in section 1116(d) of this title), in connection with the sale, offering for sale, or distribution of goods or services. In such cases, the court may in its discretion award prejudgment interest on such amount at an annual interest rate established under section 6621(a)(2) of Title 26, commencing on the date of the service of the claimant's pleadings setting forth the claim for such entry and ending on the date such entry is made, or for such shorter time as the court deems appropriate.

(c) Statutory damages for use of counterfeit marks
In a case involving the use of a counterfeit mark (as defined in section 1116(d) of this title) in connection with the sale, offering for sale, or distribution of goods or services, the plaintiff may elect, at any time before final judgment is rendered by the trial court, to recover, instead of actual damages and profits under subsection

(a) of this section, an award of statutory damages for any such use in connection with the sale, offering for sale, or distribution of goods or services in the amount of—

(1) not less than $500 or more than $100,000 per counterfeit mark per type of goods or services sold, offered for sale, or distributed, as the court considers just; or

(2) if the court finds that the use of the counterfeit mark was willful, not more than $1,000,000 per counterfeit mark per type of goods or services sold, offered for sale, or distributed, as the court considers just.

(d) Statutory damages for violation of section 1125(d)(1)

In a case involving a violation of section 1125(d)(1) of this title, the plaintiff may elect, at any time before final judgment is rendered by the trial court, to recover, instead of actual damages and profits, an award of statutory damages in the amount of not less than $1,000 and not more than $100,000 per domain name, as the court considers just.

(e) Rebuttable presumption of willful violation

In the case of a violation referred to in this section, it shall be a rebuttable presumption that the violation is willful for purposes of determining relief if the violator, or a person acting in concert with the violator, knowingly provided or knowingly caused to be provided materially false contact information to a domain name registrar, domain name registry, or other domain name registration authority in registering, maintaining, or renewing a domain name used in connection with the violation. Nothing in this subsection limits what may be considered a willful violation under this section.

APPENDIX B

Antitrust Guidelines for the Licensing of Intellectual Property

Issued by the U.S. Department of Justice[1] and the Federal Trade Commission
April 6, 1995

Table of Contents

1. Intellectual Property Protection and the Antitrust Laws
2. General Principles
    2.1 Standard Antitrust Analysis Applies to Intellectual Property
    2.2 Intellectual Property and Market Power
    2.3 Procompetitive Benefits of Licensing
3. Antitrust Concerns and Modes of Analysis
    3.1 Nature of the Concerns
    3.2 Markets Affected by Licensing Arrangements
        3.2.1 Goods Markets
        3.2.2 Technology Markets
        3.2.3 Research and Development: Innovation Markets
    3.3 Horizontal and Vertical Relationships
    3.4 Framework for Evaluating Licensing Restraints

---

[1] These Guidelines supersede section 3.6 in Part I, "Intellectual Property Licensing Arrangements," and cases 6, 10, 11, and 12 in Part II of the U.S. Department of Justice 1988 Antitrust Enforcement Guidelines for International Operations.

4. General Principles Concerning the Agencies' Evaluation of Licensing Arrangements
    4.1 Analysis of Anticompetitive Effects
        4.1.1 Market Structure, Coordination, and Foreclosure
        4.1.2 Licensing Arrangements Involving Exclusivity
    4.2 Efficiencies and Justifications
    4.3 Antitrust "Safety Zone"
5. Application of General Principles
    5.1 Horizontal Restraints
    5.2 Resale Price Maintenance
    5.3 Tying Arrangements
    5.4 Exclusive Dealing
    5.5 Cross-Licensing and Pooling Arrangements
    5.6 Grantbacks
    5.7 Acquisition of Intellectual Property Rights
6. Enforcement of Invalid Intellectual Property Rights

1. Intellectual Property Protection and the Antitrust Laws

1.0 These Guidelines state the antitrust enforcement policy of the U.S. Department of Justice and the Federal Trade Commission (individually, "the Agency," and collectively, "the Agencies") with respect to the licensing of intellectual property protected by patent, copyright, and trade secret law, and of know-how.[2] By stating their general policy, the Agencies hope to assist those who need to predict whether the Agencies will challenge a practice as anticompetitive. However, these Guidelines cannot remove judgment and discretion in antitrust law enforcement. Moreover, the standards set forth in these Guidelines must be applied in unforeseeable circumstances. Each case will be evaluated in light of its own facts, and these Guidelines will be applied reasonably and flexibly.[3]

    In the United States, patents confer rights to exclude others from making, using, or selling in the United States the invention claimed by the patent for a period of

---

[2] These Guidelines do not cover the antitrust treatment of trademarks. Although the same general antitrust principles that apply to other forms of intellectual property apply to trademarks as well, these Guidelines deal with technology transfer and innovation-related issues that typically arise with respect to patents, copyrights, trade secrets, and know-how agreements, rather than with product-differentiation issues that typically arise with respect to trademarks.

[3] As is the case with all guidelines, users should rely on qualified counsel to assist them in evaluating the antitrust risk associated with any contemplated transaction or activity. No set of guidelines can possibly indicate how the Agencies will assess the particular facts of every case. Parties who wish to know the Agencies' specific enforcement intentions with respect to any particular transaction should consider seeking a Department of Justice business review letter pursuant to 28 C.F.R. § 50.6 or a Federal Trade Commission Advisory Opinion pursuant to 16 C.F.R. §§ 1.1–1.4.

seventeen years from the date of issue.[4] To gain patent protection, an invention (which may be a product, process, machine, or composition of matter) must be novel, nonobvious, and useful. Copyright protection applies to original works of authorship embodied in a tangible medium of expression.[5] A copyright protects only the expression, not the underlying ideas.[6] Unlike a patent, which protects an invention not only from copying but also from independent creation, a copyright does not preclude others from independently creating similar expression. Trade secret protection applies to information whose economic value depends on its not being generally known.[7] Trade secret protection is conditioned upon efforts to maintain secrecy and has no fixed term. As with copyright protection, trade secret protection does not preclude independent creation by others.

The intellectual property laws and the antitrust laws share the common purpose of promoting innovation and enhancing consumer welfare.[8] The intellectual property laws provide incentives for innovation and its dissemination and commercialization by establishing enforceable property rights for the creators of new and useful products, more efficient processes, and original works of expression. In the absence of intellectual property rights, imitators could more rapidly exploit the efforts of innovators and investors without compensation. Rapid imitation would reduce the commercial value of innovation and erode incentives to invest, ultimately to the detriment of consumers. The antitrust laws promote innovation and consumer welfare by prohibiting certain actions that may harm competition with respect to either existing or new ways of serving consumers.

2. General Principles

2.0 These Guidelines embody three general principles:
  a. for the purpose of antitrust analysis, the Agencies regard intellectual property as being essentially comparable to any other form of property;

---

[4] *See* 35 U.S.C. § 154 (1988). Section 532(a) of the Uruguay Round Agreements Act, Pub. L. No. 103–465, 108 Stat. 4809, 4983 (1994) would change the length of patent protection to a term beginning on the date at which the patent issues and ending twenty years from the date on which the application for the patent was filed.

[5] *See* 17 U.S.C. § 102 (1988 & Supp. V 1993). Copyright protection lasts for the author's life plus 50 years, or 75 years from first publication (or 100 years from creation, whichever expires first) for works made for hire. *See* 17 U.S.C. § 302 (1988). The principles stated in these Guidelines also apply to protection of mask works fixed in a semiconductor chip product (*see* 17 U.S.C. § 901 *et seq.* (1988)), which is analogous to copyright protection for works of authorship.

[6] *See* 17 U.S.C. § 102(b) (1988).

[7] Trade secret protection derives from state law. *See generally Kewanee Oil Co. v. Bicron Corp.*, 416 U.S. 470 (1974).

[8] "[T]he aims and objectives of patent and antitrust laws may seem, at first glance, wholly at odds. However, the two bodies of law are actually complementary, as both are aimed at encouraging innovation, industry and competition." *Atari Games Corp. v. Nintendo of America, Inc.*, 897 F.2d 1572, 1576 (Fed. Cir. 1990).

b. the Agencies do not presume that intellectual property creates market power in the antitrust context; and
c. the Agencies recognize that intellectual property licensing allows firms to combine complementary factors of production and is generally procompetitive.

2.1 Standard Antitrust Analysis Applies to Intellectual Property

The Agencies apply the same general antitrust principles to conduct involving intellectual property that they apply to conduct involving any other form of tangible or intangible property. That is not to say that intellectual property is in all respects the same as any other form of property. Intellectual property has important characteristics, such as ease of misappropriation, that distinguish it from many other forms of property. These characteristics can be taken into account by standard antitrust analysis, however, and do not require the application of fundamentally different principles.[9]

Although there are clear and important differences in the purpose, extent, and duration of protection provided under the intellectual property regimes of patent, copyright, and trade secret, the governing antitrust principles are the same. Antitrust analysis takes differences among these forms of intellectual property into account in evaluating the specific market circumstances in which transactions occur, just as it does with other particular market circumstances.

Intellectual property law bestows on the owners of intellectual property certain rights to exclude others. These rights help the owners to profit from the use of their property. An intellectual property owner's rights to exclude are similar to the rights enjoyed by owners of other forms of private property. As with other forms of private property, certain types of conduct with respect to intellectual property may have anticompetitive effects against which the antitrust laws can and do protect. Intellectual property is thus neither particularly free from scrutiny under the antitrust laws, nor particularly suspect under them.

The Agencies recognize that the licensing of intellectual property is often international. The principles of antitrust analysis described in these Guidelines apply equally to domestic and international licensing arrangements. However, as described in the 1995 Department of Justice and Federal Trade Commission Antitrust Enforcement Guidelines for International Operations, considerations particular to international operations, such as jurisdiction and comity, may affect enforcement decisions when the arrangement is in an international context.

---

[9] As with other forms of property, the power to exclude others from the use of intellectual property may vary substantially, depending on the nature of the property and its status under federal or state law. The greater or lesser legal power of an owner to exclude others is also taken into account by standard antitrust analysis.

2.2 Intellectual Property and Market Power

Market power is the ability profitably to maintain prices above, or output below, competitive levels for a significant period of time.[10] The Agencies will not presume that a patent, copyright, or trade secret necessarily confers market power upon its owner. Although the intellectual property right confers the power to exclude with respect to the *specific* product, process, or work in question, there will often be sufficient actual or potential close substitutes for such product, process, or work to prevent the exercise of market power.[11] If a patent or other form of intellectual property does confer market power, that market power does not by itself offend the antitrust laws. As with any other tangible or intangible asset that enables its owner to obtain significant supracompetitive profits, market power (or even a monopoly) that is solely "a consequence of a superior product, business acumen, or historic accident" does not violate the antitrust laws.[12] Nor does such market power impose on the intellectual property owner an obligation to license the use of that property to others. As in other antitrust contexts, however, market power could be illegally acquired or maintained, or, even if lawfully acquired and maintained, would be relevant to the ability of an intellectual property owner to harm competition through unreasonable conduct in connection with such property.

2.3 Procompetitive Benefits of Licensing

Intellectual property typically is one component among many in a production process and derives value from its combination with complementary factors. Complementary factors of production include manufacturing and distribution facilities, workforces, and other items of intellectual property. The owner of intellectual property has to arrange for its combination with other necessary factors to realize its commercial value. Often, the owner finds it most efficient to contract with others for these factors, to sell rights to the intellectual property, or to enter into a

---

[10] Market power can be exercised in other economic dimensions, such as quality, service, and the development of new or improved goods and processes. It is assumed in this definition that all competitive dimensions are held constant except the ones in which market power is being exercised; that a seller is able to charge higher prices for a higher-quality product does not alone indicate market power. The definition in the text is stated in terms of a seller with market power. A buyer could also exercise market power (e.g., by maintaining the price below the competitive level, thereby depressing output).

[11] The Agencies note that the law is unclear on this issue. *Compare Jefferson Parish Hospital District No. 2 v. Hyde*, 466 U.S. 2, 16 (1984) (expressing the view in dictum that if a product is protected by a patent, "it is fair to presume that the inability to buy the product elsewhere gives the seller market power") *with id.* at 37 n.7 (O'Connor, J., concurring) ("[A] patent holder has no market power in any relevant sense if there are close substitutes for the patented product."). *Compare also Abbott Laboratories v. Brennan*, 952 F.2d 1346, 1354–55 (Fed. Cir. 1991) (no presumption of market power from intellectual property right), *cert. denied*, 112 S. Ct. 2993 (1992) *with Digidyne Corp. v. Data General Corp.*, 734 F.2d 1336, 1341–42 (9th Cir. 1984) (requisite economic power is presumed from copyright), *cert. denied*, 473 U.S. 908 (1985).

[12] *United States v. Grinnell Corp.*, 384 U.S. 563, 571 (1966); *see also United States v. Aluminum Co. of America*, 148 F.2d 416, 430 (2d Cir. 1945) (Sherman Act is not violated by the attainment of market power solely through "superior skill, foresight and industry").

joint venture arrangement for its development, rather than supplying these complementary factors itself.

Licensing, cross-licensing, or otherwise transferring intellectual property (hereinafter "licensing") can facilitate integration of the licensed property with complementary factors of production. This integration can lead to more efficient exploitation of the intellectual property, benefiting consumers through the reduction of costs and the introduction of new products. Such arrangements increase the value of intellectual property to consumers and to the developers of the technology. By potentially increasing the expected returns from intellectual property, licensing also can increase the incentive for its creation and thus promote greater investment in research and development.

Sometimes the use of one item of intellectual property requires access to another. An item of intellectual property "blocks" another when the second cannot be practiced without using the first. For example, an improvement on a patented machine can be blocked by the patent on the machine. Licensing may promote the coordinated development of technologies that are in a blocking relationship.

Field-of-use, territorial, and other limitations on intellectual property licenses may serve procompetitive ends by allowing the licensor to exploit its property as efficiently and effectively as possible. These various forms of exclusivity can be used to give a licensee an incentive to invest in the commercialization and distribution of products embodying the licensed intellectual property and to develop additional applications for the licensed property. The restrictions may do so, for example, by protecting the licensee against free-riding on the licensee's investments by other licensees or by the licensor. They may also increase the licensor's incentive to license, for example, by protecting the licensor from competition in the licensor's own technology in a market niche that it prefers to keep to itself. These benefits of licensing restrictions apply to patent, copyright, and trade secret licenses, and to know-how agreements.

EXAMPLE 1[13]

Situation:

ComputerCo develops a new, copyrighted software program for inventory management. The program has wide application in the health field. ComputerCo licenses the program in an arrangement that imposes both field of use and territorial limitations. Some of ComputerCo's licenses permit use only in hospitals; others permit use only in group medical practices. ComputerCo charges different royalties for the different uses. All of ComputerCo's licenses permit use only in specified portions of the United States and in specified foreign countries.[14] The licenses contain no provisions that would prevent or discourage licensees from

---

[13] The examples in these Guidelines are hypothetical and do not represent judgments about, or analysis of, any actual market circumstances of the named industries.
[14] These Guidelines do not address the possible application of the antitrust laws of other countries to restraints such as territorial restrictions in international licensing arrangements.

developing, using, or selling any other program, or from competing in any other good or service other than in the use of the licensed program. None of the licensees are actual or likely potential competitors of ComputerCo in the sale of inventory management programs.

Discussion:

The key competitive issue raised by the licensing arrangement is whether it harms competition among entities that would have been actual or likely potential competitors in the absence of the arrangement. Such harm could occur if, for example, the licenses anticompetitively foreclose access to competing technologies (in this case, most likely competing computer programs), prevent licensees from developing their own competing technologies (again, in this case, most likely computer programs), or facilitate market allocation or price-fixing for any product or service supplied by the licensees. (*See* section 3.1.) If the license agreements contained such provisions, the Agency evaluating the arrangement would analyze its likely competitive effects as described in parts 3–5 of these Guidelines. In this hypothetical, there are no such provisions and thus the arrangement is merely a subdivision of the licensor's intellectual property among different fields of use and territories. The licensing arrangement does not appear likely to harm competition among entities that would have been actual or likely potential competitors if ComputerCo had chosen not to license the software program. The Agency therefore would be unlikely to object to this arrangement. Based on these facts, the result of the antitrust analysis would be the same whether the technology was protected by patent, copyright, or trade secret. The Agency's conclusion as to likely competitive effects could differ if, for example, the license barred licensees from using any other inventory management program.

3. Antitrust Concerns and Modes of Analysis

3.1 Nature of the Concerns

While intellectual property licensing arrangements are typically welfare-enhancing and procompetitive, antitrust concerns may nonetheless arise. For example, a licensing arrangement could include restraints that adversely affect competition in goods markets by dividing the markets among firms that would have competed using different technologies. *See, e.g.*, Example 7. An arrangement that effectively merges the research and development activities of two of only a few entities that could plausibly engage in research and development in the relevant field might harm competition for development of new goods and services. *See* section 3.2.3. An acquisition of intellectual property may lessen competition in a relevant antitrust market. *See* section 5.7. The Agencies will focus on the actual effects of an arrangement, not on its formal terms.

The Agencies will not require the owner of intellectual property to create competition in its own technology. However, antitrust concerns may arise when a licensing arrangement harms competition among entities that would have been actual or likely potential competitors[15] in a relevant market in the absence of the license (entities in a "horizontal relationship"). A restraint in a licensing arrangement may harm such competition, for example, if it facilitates market division or price-fixing. In addition, license restrictions with respect to one market may harm such competition in another market by anticompetitively foreclosing access to, or significantly raising the price of, an important input,[16] or by facilitating coordination to increase price or reduce output. When it appears that such competition may be adversely affected, the Agencies will follow the analysis set forth below. *See generally* sections 3.4 and 4.2.

3.2 Markets Affected by Licensing Arrangements

Licensing arrangements raise concerns under the antitrust laws if they are likely to affect adversely the prices, quantities, qualities, or varieties of goods and services[17] either currently or potentially available. The competitive effects of licensing arrangements often can be adequately assessed within the relevant markets for the goods affected by the arrangements. In such instances, the Agencies will delineate and analyze only goods markets. In other cases, however, the analysis may require the delineation of markets for technology or markets for research and development (innovation markets).

3.2.1 Goods Markets

A number of different goods markets may be relevant to evaluating the effects of a licensing arrangement. A restraint in a licensing arrangement may have competitive effects in markets for final or intermediate goods made using the intellectual property, or it may have effects upstream, in markets for goods that are used as inputs, along with the intellectual property, to the production of other goods. In general, for goods markets affected by a licensing arrangement, the Agencies will approach the delineation of relevant market and the measurement of market share in the intellectual property area as in section 1 of the U.S. Department of Justice and Federal Trade Commission Horizontal Merger Guidelines.[18]

---

[15] A firm will be treated as a likely potential competitor if there is evidence that entry by that firm is reasonably probable in the absence of the licensing arrangement.

[16] As used herein, "input" includes outlets for distribution and sales, as well as factors of production. *See, e.g.*, sections 4.1.1 and 5.3–5.5 for further discussion of conditions under which foreclosing access to, or raising the price of, an input may harm competition in a relevant market.

[17] Hereinafter, the term "goods" also includes services.

[18] U.S. Department of Justice and Federal Trade Commission, Horizontal Merger Guidelines (April 2, 1992) (hereinafter "1992 Horizontal Merger Guidelines"). As stated in section 1.41 of the 1992 Horizontal Merger Guidelines, market shares for goods markets "can be expressed either in dollar terms through measurement of sales, shipments, or production, or in physical terms through measurement of sales, shipments, production, capacity or reserves."

3.2.2 Technology markets

Technology markets consist of the intellectual property that is licensed (the "licensed technology") and its close substitutes—that is, the technologies or goods that are close enough substitutes significantly to constrain the exercise of market power with respect to the intellectual property that is licensed.[19] When rights to intellectual property are marketed separately from the products in which they are used,[20] the Agencies may rely on technology markets to analyze the competitive effects of a licensing arrangement.

EXAMPLE 2

Situation:

Firms Alpha and Beta independently develop different patented process technologies to manufacture the same off-patent drug for the treatment of a particular disease. Before the firms use their technologies internally or license them to third parties, they announce plans jointly to manufacture the drug, and to assign their manufacturing processes to the new manufacturing venture. Many firms are capable of using and have the incentive to use the licensed technologies to manufacture and distribute the drug; thus, the market for drug manufacturing and distribution is competitive. One of the Agencies is evaluating the likely competitive effects of the planned venture.

Discussion:

The Agency would analyze the competitive effects of the proposed joint venture by first defining the relevant markets in which competition may be affected and then evaluating the likely competitive effects of the joint venture in the identified markets. (*See* Example 4 for a discussion of the Agencies' approach to joint venture analysis.) In this example, the structural effect of the joint venture in the relevant goods market for the manufacture and distribution of the drug is unlikely to be significant, because many firms in addition to the joint venture compete in that market. The joint venture might, however, increase the prices of the drug produced using Alpha's or Beta's technology by reducing competition in the relevant market for technology to manufacture the drug.

The Agency would delineate a technology market in which to evaluate likely competitive effects of the proposed joint venture. The Agency would identify other technologies that can be used to make the drug with levels of effectiveness and cost per dose comparable to that of the technologies owned by Alpha and Beta.

---

[19] For example, the owner of a process for producing a particular good may be constrained in its conduct with respect to that process not only by other processes for making that good, but also by other goods that compete with the downstream good and by the processes used to produce those other goods.

[20] Intellectual property is often licensed, sold, or transferred as an integral part of a marketed good. An example is a patented product marketed with an implied license permitting its use. In such circumstances, there is no need for a separate analysis of technology markets to capture relevant competitive effects.

In addition, the Agency would consider the extent to which competition from other drugs that are substitutes for the drug produced using Alpha's or Beta's technology would limit the ability of a hypothetical monopolist that owned both Alpha's and Beta's technology to raise its price.

To identify a technology's close substitutes and thus to delineate the relevant technology market, the Agencies will, if the data permit, identify the smallest group of technologies and goods over which a hypothetical monopolist of those technologies and goods likely would exercise market power—for example, by imposing a small but significant and nontransitory price increase.[21] The Agencies recognize that technology often is licensed in ways that are not readily quantifiable in monetary terms.[22] In such circumstances, the Agencies will delineate the relevant market by identifying other technologies and goods which buyers would substitute at a cost comparable to that of using the licensed technology.

In assessing the competitive significance of current and likely potential participants in a technology market, the Agencies will take into account all relevant evidence. When market share data are available and accurately reflect the competitive significance of market participants, the Agencies will include market share data in this assessment. The Agencies also will seek evidence of buyers' and market participants' assessments of the competitive significance of technology market participants. Such evidence is particularly important when market share data are unavailable, or do not accurately represent the competitive significance of market participants. When market share data or other indicia of market power are not available, and it appears that competing technologies are comparably efficient,[23] the Agencies will assign each technology the same market share. For new technologies, the Agencies generally will use the best available information to estimate market acceptance over a two-year period, beginning with commercial introduction.

3.2.3 Research and Development: Innovation Markets

If a licensing arrangement may adversely affect competition to develop new or improved goods or processes, the Agencies will analyze such an impact either as a separate competitive effect in relevant goods or technology markets, or as a competitive effect in a separate innovation market. A licensing arrangement may have competitive effects on innovation that cannot be adequately addressed through the analysis of goods or technology markets. For example, the arrangement may affect

---

[21] This is conceptually analogous to the analytical approach to goods markets under the 1992 Horizontal Merger Guidelines. Cf. § 1.11. Of course, market power also can be exercised in other dimensions, such as quality, and these dimensions also may be relevant to the definition and analysis of technology markets.

[22] For example, technology may be licensed royalty-free in exchange for the right to use other technology, or it may be licensed as part of a package license.

[23] The Agencies will regard two technologies as "comparably efficient" if they can be used to produce close substitutes at comparable costs.

the development of goods that do not yet exist.[24] Alternatively, the arrangement may affect the development of new or improved goods or processes in geographic markets where there is no actual or likely potential competition in the relevant goods.[25]

An innovation market consists of the research and development directed to particular new or improved goods or processes, and the close substitutes for that research and development. The close substitutes are research and development efforts, technologies, and goods[26] that significantly constrain the exercise of market power with respect to the relevant research and development, for example by limiting the ability and incentive of a hypothetical monopolist to retard the pace of research and development. The Agencies will delineate an innovation market only when the capabilities to engage in the relevant research and development can be associated with specialized assets or characteristics of specific firms.

In assessing the competitive significance of current and likely potential participants in an innovation market, the Agencies will take into account all relevant evidence. When market share data are available and accurately reflect the competitive significance of market participants, the Agencies will include market share data in this assessment. The Agencies also will seek evidence of buyers' and market participants' assessments of the competitive significance of innovation market participants. Such evidence is particularly important when market share data are unavailable or do not accurately represent the competitive significance of market participants. The Agencies may base the market shares of participants in an innovation market on their shares of identifiable assets or characteristics upon which innovation depends, on shares of research and development expenditures, or on shares of a related product. When entities have comparable capabilities and incentives to pursue research and development that is a close substitute for the research and development activities of the parties to a licensing arrangement, the Agencies may assign equal market shares to such entities.

EXAMPLE 3

Situation:

Two companies that specialize in advanced metallurgy agree to cross-license future patents relating to the development of a new component for aircraft

---

[24] *E.g., Sensormatic*, FTC Inv. No. 941-0126, 60 Fed. Reg. 5428 (accepted for comment Dec. 28, 1994); *Wright Medical Technology, Inc.*, FTC Inv. No. 951-0015, 60 Fed. Reg. 460 (accepted for comment Dec. 8, 1994); *American Home Products*, FTC Inv. No. 941-0116, 59 Fed. Reg. 60,807 (accepted for comment Nov. 28, 1994); *Roche Holdings Ltd.*, 113 F.T.C. 1086 (1990); *United States v. Automobile Mfrs. Ass'n*, 307 F. Supp. 617 (C.D. Cal. 1969), *appeal dismissed sub nom. City of New York v. United States*, 397 U.S. 248 (1970), *modified sub nom. United States v. Motor Vehicles Mfrs. Ass'n*, 1982–83 Trade Cas. (CCH) ¶ 65,088 (C.D. Cal. 1982).

[25] *See* Complaint, *United States v. General Motors Corp.*, Civ. No. 93-530 (D. Del., filed Nov. 16, 1993).

[26] For example, the licensor of research and development may be constrained in its conduct not only by competing research and development efforts but also by other existing goods that would compete with the goods under development.

jet turbines. Innovation in the development of the component requires the capability to work with very high tensile strength materials for jet turbines. Aspects of the licensing arrangement raise the possibility that competition in research and development of this and related components will be lessened. One of the Agencies is considering whether to define an innovation market in which to evaluate the competitive effects of the arrangement.

Discussion:

If the firms that have the capability and incentive to work with very high tensile strength materials for jet turbines can be reasonably identified, the Agency will consider defining a relevant innovation market for development of the new component. If the number of firms with the required capability and incentive to engage in research and development of very high tensile strength materials for aircraft jet turbines is small, the Agency may employ the concept of an innovation market to analyze the likely competitive effects of the arrangement in that market, or as an aid in analyzing competitive effects in technology or goods markets. The Agency would perform its analysis as described in parts 3–5.

If the number of firms with the required capability and incentive is large (either because there are a large number of such firms in the jet turbine industry, or because there are many firms in other industries with the required capability and incentive), then the Agency will conclude that the innovation market is competitive. Under these circumstances, it is unlikely that any single firm or plausible aggregation of firms could acquire a large enough share of the assets necessary for innovation to have an adverse impact on competition.

If the Agency cannot reasonably identify the firms with the required capability and incentive, it will not attempt to define an innovation market.

EXAMPLE 4

Situation:

Three of the largest producers of a plastic used in disposable bottles plan to engage in joint research and development to produce a new type of plastic that is rapidly biodegradable. The joint venture will grant to its partners (but to no one else) licenses to all patent rights and use of know-how. One of the Agencies is evaluating the likely competitive effects of the proposed joint venture.

Discussion:

The Agency would analyze the proposed research and development joint venture using an analysis similar to that applied to other joint ventures.[27] The Agency would begin by defining the relevant markets in which to analyze the joint venture's likely competitive effects. In this case, a relevant market is an innovation

---

[27] *See, e.g.,* U.S. Department of Justice and Federal Trade Commission, Statements of Enforcement Policy and Analytical Principles Relating to Health Care and Antitrust 20–23, 37–40, 72–74 (September 27, 1994). This type of transaction may qualify for treatment under the National Cooperative Research and Production Act of 1993, 15 U.S.C.A §§ 4301–05.

market—research and development for biodegradable (and other environmentally friendly) containers. The Agency would seek to identify any other entities that would be actual or likely potential competitors with the joint venture in that relevant market. This would include those firms that have the capability and incentive to undertake research and development closely substitutable for the research and development proposed to be undertaken by the joint venture, taking into account such firms' existing technologies and technologies under development, R&D facilities, and other relevant assets and business circumstances. Firms possessing such capabilities and incentives would be included in the research and development market even if they are not competitors in relevant markets for related goods, such as the plastics currently produced by the joint venturers, although competitors in existing goods markets may often also compete in related innovation markets.

Having defined a relevant innovation market, the Agency would assess whether the joint venture is likely to have anticompetitive effects in that market. A starting point in this analysis is the degree of concentration in the relevant market and the market shares of the parties to the joint venture. If, in addition to the parties to the joint venture (taken collectively), there are at least four other independently controlled entities that possess comparable capabilities and incentives to undertake research and development of biodegradable plastics, or other products that would be close substitutes for such new plastics, the joint venture ordinarily would be unlikely to adversely affect competition in the relevant innovation market (*cf.* section 4.3). If there are fewer than four other independently controlled entities with similar capabilities and incentives, the Agency would consider whether the joint venture would give the parties to the joint venture an incentive and ability collectively to reduce investment in, or otherwise to retard the pace or scope of, research and development efforts. If the joint venture creates a significant risk of anticompetitive effects in the innovation market, the Agency would proceed to consider efficiency justifications for the venture, such as the potential for combining complementary R&D assets in such a way as to make successful innovation more likely, or to bring it about sooner, or to achieve cost reductions in research and development.

The Agency would also assess the likelihood that the joint venture would adversely affect competition in other relevant markets, including markets for products produced by the parties to the joint venture. The risk of such adverse competitive effects would be increased to the extent that, for example, the joint venture facilitates the exchange among the parties of competitively sensitive information relating to goods markets in which the parties currently compete or facilitates the coordination of competitive activities in such markets. The Agency would examine whether the joint venture imposes collateral restraints that might significantly restrict competition among the joint venturers in goods markets, and would examine whether such collateral restraints were reasonably necessary to achieve any efficiencies that are likely to be attained by the venture.

3.3 Horizontal and Vertical Relationships

As with other property transfers, antitrust analysis of intellectual property licensing arrangements examines whether the relationship among the parties to the arrangement is primarily horizontal or vertical in nature, or whether it has substantial aspects of both. A licensing arrangement has a vertical component when it affects activities that are in a complementary relationship, as is typically the case in a licensing arrangement. For example, the licensor's primary line of business may be in research and development, and the licensees, as manufacturers, may be buying the rights to use technology developed by the licensor. Alternatively, the licensor may be a component manufacturer owning intellectual property rights in a product that the licensee manufactures by combining the component with other inputs, or the licensor may manufacture the product, and the licensees may operate primarily in distribution and marketing.

In addition to this vertical component, the licensor and its licensees may also have a horizontal relationship. For analytical purposes, the Agencies ordinarily will treat a relationship between a licensor and its licensees, or between licensees, as horizontal when they would have been actual or likely potential competitors in a relevant market in the absence of the license.

The existence of a horizontal relationship between a licensor and its licensees does not, in itself, indicate that the arrangement is anticompetitive. Identification of such relationships is merely an aid in determining whether there may be anticompetitive effects arising from a licensing arrangement. Such a relationship need not give rise to an anticompetitive effect, nor does a purely vertical relationship assure that there are no anticompetitive effects.

The following examples illustrate different competitive relationships among a licensor and its licensees.

EXAMPLE 5

Situation:
AgCo, a manufacturer of farm equipment, develops a new, patented emission control technology for its tractor engines and licenses it to FarmCo, another farm equipment manufacturer. AgCo's emission control technology is far superior to the technology currently owned and used by FarmCo, so much so that FarmCo's technology does not significantly constrain the prices that AgCo could charge for its technology. AgCo's emission control patent has a broad scope. It is likely that any improved emissions control technology that FarmCo could develop in the foreseeable future would infringe AgCo's patent.

Discussion:
Because FarmCo's emission control technology does not significantly constrain AgCo's competitive conduct with respect to its emission control technology, AgCo's and FarmCo's emission control technologies are not close substitutes for each other. FarmCo is a consumer of AgCo's technology and is not an actual competitor of AgCo in the relevant market for superior emission control technology of the kind licensed by AgCo. Furthermore, FarmCo is not a likely potential competitor of AgCo in the

relevant market because, even if FarmCo could develop an improved emission control technology, it is likely that it would infringe AgCo's patent. This means that the relationship between AgCo and FarmCo with regard to the supply and use of emissions control technology is vertical. Assuming that AgCo and FarmCo are actual or likely potential competitors in sales of farm equipment products, their relationship is horizontal in the relevant markets for farm equipment.

EXAMPLE 6

Situation:

FarmCo develops a new valve technology for its engines and enters into a cross-licensing arrangement with AgCo, whereby AgCo licenses its emission control technology to FarmCo and FarmCo licenses its valve technology to AgCo. AgCo already owns an alternative valve technology that can be used to achieve engine performance similar to that using FarmCo's valve technology and at a comparable cost to consumers. Before adopting FarmCo's technology, AgCo was using its own valve technology in its production of engines and was licensing (and continues to license) that technology for use by others. As in Example 5, FarmCo does not own or control an emission control technology that is a close substitute for the technology licensed from AgCo. Furthermore, as in Example 5, FarmCo is not likely to develop an improved emission control technology that would be a close substitute for AgCo's technology, because of AgCo's blocking patent.

Discussion:

FarmCo is a consumer and not a competitor of AgCo's emission control technology. As in Example 5, their relationship is vertical with regard to this technology. The relationship between AgCo and FarmCo in the relevant market that includes engine valve technology is vertical in part and horizontal in part. It is vertical in part because AgCo and FarmCo stand in a complementary relationship, in which AgCo is a consumer of a technology supplied by FarmCo. However, the relationship between AgCo and FarmCo in the relevant market that includes engine valve technology is also horizontal in part, because FarmCo and AgCo are actual competitors in the licensing of valve technology that can be used to achieve similar engine performance at a comparable cost. Whether the firms license their valve technologies to others is not important for the conclusion that the firms have a horizontal relationship in this relevant market. Even if AgCo's use of its valve technology were solely captive to its own production, the fact that the two valve technologies are substitutable at comparable cost means that the two firms have a horizontal relationship.

As in Example 5, the relationship between AgCo and FarmCo is horizontal in the relevant markets for farm equipment.

3.4 Framework for Evaluating Licensing Restraints

In the vast majority of cases, restraints in intellectual property licensing arrangements are evaluated under the rule of reason. The Agencies' general approach in analyzing a licensing restraint under the rule of reason is to inquire whether the restraint is likely to have anticompetitive effects and, if so, whether the restraint is reasonably necessary to achieve procompetitive benefits that outweigh those anticompetitive effects. *See Federal Trade Commission v. Indiana Federation of Dentists,* 476 U.S. 447 (1986); *NCAA v. Board of Regents of the University of Oklahoma,* 468 U.S. 85 (1984); *Broadcast Music, Inc. v. Columbia Broadcasting System, Inc.,* 441 U.S. 1 (1979); 7 Phillip E. Areeda, *Antitrust Law* § 1502 (1986). *See also* part 4.

In some cases, however, the courts conclude that a restraint's "nature and necessary effect are so plainly anticompetitive" that it should be treated as unlawful per se, without an elaborate inquiry into the restraint's likely competitive effect. *Federal Trade Commission v. Superior Court Trial Lawyers Association,* 493 U.S. 411, 433 (1990); *National Society of Professional Engineers v. United States,* 435 U.S. 679, 692 (1978). Among the restraints that have been held per se unlawful are naked price-fixing, output restraints, and market division among horizontal competitors, as well as certain group boycotts and resale price maintenance.

To determine whether a particular restraint in a licensing arrangement is given per se or rule of reason treatment, the Agencies will assess whether the restraint in question can be expected to contribute to an efficiency-enhancing integration of economic activity. *See Broadcast Music,* 441 U.S. at 16–24. In general, licensing arrangements promote such integration because they facilitate the combination of the licensor's intellectual property with complementary factors of production owned by the licensee. A restraint in a licensing arrangement may further such integration by, for example, aligning the incentives of the licensor and the licensees to promote the development and marketing of the licensed technology, or by substantially reducing transactions costs. If there is no efficiency-enhancing integration of economic activity and if the type of restraint is one that has been accorded per se treatment, the Agencies will challenge the restraint under the per se rule. Otherwise, the Agencies will apply a rule of reason analysis.

Application of the rule of reason generally requires a comprehensive inquiry into market conditions. (*See* sections 4.1–4.3.) However, that inquiry may be truncated in certain circumstances. If the Agencies conclude that a restraint has no likely anticompetitive effects, they will treat it as reasonable, without an elaborate analysis of market power or the justifications for the restraint. Similarly, if a restraint facially appears to be of a kind that would always or almost always tend to reduce output or increase prices,[28] and the restraint is not reasonably related to efficiencies, the Agencies will likely challenge the restraint without an elaborate analysis of particular industry circumstances.[29] *See Indiana Federation of Dentists,* 476 U.S. at 459–60; *NCAA,* 468 U.S. at 109.

---

[28] Details about the Federal Trade Commission's approach are set forth in *Massachusetts Board of Registration in Optometry,* 110 F.T.C. 549, 604 (1988). In applying its truncated rule of reason inquiry, the FTC uses the analytical category of "inherently suspect" restraints to denote facially anticompetitive restraints that would always or almost always tend to decrease output or increase prices, but that may be relatively unfamiliar or may not fit neatly into traditional per se categories.

[29] Under the FTC's *Mass. Board* approach, asserted efficiency justifications for inherently suspect restraints are examined to determine whether they are plausible and, if so, whether they are valid in the context of the market at issue. *Mass. Board,* 110 F.T.C. at 604.

EXAMPLE 7

Situation:

Gamma, which manufactures Product X using its patented process, offers a license for its process technology to every other manufacturer of Product X, each of which competes world-wide with Gamma in the manufacture and sale of X. The process technology does not represent an economic improvement over the available existing technologies. Indeed, although most manufacturers accept licenses from Gamma, none of the licensees actually uses the licensed technology. The licenses provide that each manufacturer has an exclusive right to sell Product X manufactured using the licensed technology in a designated geographic area and that no manufacturer may sell Product X, however manufactured, outside the designated territory.

Discussion:

The manufacturers of Product X are in a horizontal relationship in the goods market for Product X. Any manufacturers of Product X that control technologies that are substitutable at comparable cost for Gamma's process are also horizontal competitors of Gamma in the relevant technology market. The licensees of Gamma's process technology are technically in a vertical relationship, although that is not significant in this example because they do not actually use Gamma's technology.

The licensing arrangement restricts competition in the relevant goods market among manufacturers of Product X by requiring each manufacturer to limit its sales to an exclusive territory. Thus, competition among entities that would be actual competitors in the absence of the licensing arrangement is restricted. Based on the facts set forth above, the licensing arrangement does not involve a useful transfer of technology, and thus it is unlikely that the restraint on sales outside the designated territories contributes to an efficiency-enhancing integration of economic activity. Consequently, the evaluating Agency would be likely to challenge the arrangement under the per se rule as a horizontal territorial market allocation scheme and to view the intellectual property aspects of the arrangement as a sham intended to cloak its true nature.

If the licensing arrangement could be expected to contribute to an efficiency-enhancing integration of economic activity, as might be the case if the licensed technology were an advance over existing processes and used by the licensees, the Agency would analyze the arrangement under the rule of reason applying the analytical framework described in this section.

In this example, the competitive implications do not generally depend on whether the licensed technology is protected by patent, is a trade secret or other know-how, or is a computer program protected by copyright; nor do the competitive implications generally depend on whether the allocation of markets is territorial, as in this example, or functional, based on fields of use.

4. General Principles Concerning the Agencies' Evaluation of Licensing Arrangements Under the Rule of Reason

4.1 Analysis of Anticompetitive Effects

The existence of anticompetitive effects resulting from a restraint in a licensing arrangement will be evaluated on the basis of the analysis described in this section.

4.1.1 Market Structure, Coordination, and Foreclosure

When a licensing arrangement affects parties in a horizontal relationship, a restraint in that arrangement may increase the risk of coordinated pricing, output restrictions, or the acquisition or maintenance of market power. Harm to competition also may occur if the arrangement poses a significant risk of retarding or restricting the development of new or improved goods or processes. The potential for competitive harm depends in part on the degree of concentration in, the difficulty of entry into, and the responsiveness of supply and demand to changes in price in the relevant markets. *Cf.* 1992 Horizontal Merger Guidelines §§ 1.5, 3.

When the licensor and licensees are in a vertical relationship, the Agencies will analyze whether the licensing arrangement may harm competition among entities in a horizontal relationship at either the level of the licensor or the licensees, or possibly in another relevant market. Harm to competition from a restraint may occur if it anticompetitively forecloses access to, or increases competitors' costs of obtaining, important inputs, or facilitates coordination to raise price or restrict output. The risk of anticompetitively foreclosing access or increasing competitors' costs is related to the proportion of the markets affected by the licensing restraint; other characteristics of the relevant markets, such as concentration, difficulty of entry, and the responsiveness of supply and demand to changes in price in the relevant markets; and the duration of the restraint. A licensing arrangement does not foreclose competition merely because some or all of the potential licensees in an industry choose to use the licensed technology to the exclusion of other technologies. Exclusive use may be an efficient consequence of the licensed technology having the lowest cost or highest value.

Harm to competition from a restraint in a vertical licensing arrangement also may occur if a licensing restraint facilitates coordination among entities in a horizontal relationship to raise prices or reduce output in a relevant market. For example, if owners of competing technologies impose similar restraints on their licensees, the licensors may find it easier to coordinate their pricing. Similarly, licensees that are competitors may find it easier to coordinate their pricing if they are subject to common restraints in licenses with a common licensor or competing licensors. The risk of anticompetitive coordination is increased when the relevant markets are concentrated and difficult to enter. The use of similar restraints may be common and procompetitive in an industry, however, because they contribute to efficient exploitation of the licensed property.

4.1.2 Licensing Arrangements Involving Exclusivity

A licensing arrangement may involve exclusivity in two distinct respects. First, the licensor may grant one or more *exclusive licenses,* which restrict the right of the licensor to license others and possibly also to use the technology itself. Generally, an exclusive license may raise antitrust concerns only if the licensees themselves, or the licensor and its licensees, are in a horizontal relationship. Examples of arrangements involving exclusive licensing that may give rise to antitrust concerns include cross-licensing by parties collectively possessing market power (*see* section 5.5), grantbacks (*see* section 5.6), and acquisitions of intellectual property rights (*see* section 5.7).

A non-exclusive license of intellectual property that does not contain any restraints on the competitive conduct of the licensor or the licensee generally does not present antitrust concerns even if the parties to the license are in a horizontal relationship, because the non-exclusive license normally does not diminish competition that would occur in its absence.

A second form of exclusivity, *exclusive dealing,* arises when a license prevents or restrains the licensee from licensing, selling, distributing, or using competing technologies. *See* section 5.4. Exclusivity may be achieved by an explicit exclusive dealing term in the license or by other provisions such as compensation terms or other economic incentives. Such restraints may anticompetitively foreclose access to, or increase competitors' costs of obtaining, important inputs, or facilitate coordination to raise price or reduce output, but they also may have procompetitive effects. For example, a licensing arrangement that prevents the licensee from dealing in other technologies may encourage the licensee to develop and market the licensed technology or specialized applications of that technology. *See, e.g.,* Example 8. The Agencies will take into account such procompetitive effects in evaluating the reasonableness of the arrangement. *See* section 4.2.

The antitrust principles that apply to a licensor's grant of various forms of exclusivity to and among its licensees are similar to those that apply to comparable vertical restraints outside the licensing context, such as exclusive territories and exclusive dealing. However, the fact that intellectual property may in some cases be misappropriated more easily than other forms of property may justify the use of some restrictions that might be anticompetitive in other contexts.

As noted earlier, the Agencies will focus on the actual practice and its effects, not on the formal terms of the arrangement. A license denominated as non-exclusive (either in the sense of exclusive licensing or in the sense of exclusive dealing) may nonetheless give rise to the same concerns posed by formal exclusivity. A non-exclusive license may have the effect of exclusive licensing if it is structured so that the licensor is unlikely to license others or to practice the technology itself. A license that does not explicitly require exclusive dealing may have the effect of exclusive dealing if it is structured to increase significantly a licensee's cost when it uses competing technologies. However, a licensing arrangement will not automatically raise these concerns merely because a party chooses to deal with a single licensee or licensor, or confines his activity to a single field of use or location, or because only a single licensee has chosen to take a license.

EXAMPLE 8

Situation:

NewCo, the inventor and manufacturer of a new flat panel display technology, lacking the capability to bring a flat panel display product to market, grants BigCo an exclusive license to sell a product embodying NewCo's technology. BigCo does not currently sell, and is not developing (or likely to develop), a product that would compete with the product embodying the new technology and does not control rights to another display technology. Several firms offer competing displays, BigCo accounts for only a small proportion of the outlets for distribution of display products, and entry into the manufacture and distribution of display products is relatively easy. Demand for the new technology is uncertain and successful market penetration will require considerable promotional effort. The license contains an exclusive dealing restriction preventing BigCo from selling products that compete with the product embodying the licensed technology.

Discussion:

This example illustrates both types of exclusivity in a licensing arrangement. The license is exclusive in that it restricts the right of the licensor to grant other licenses. In addition, the license has an exclusive dealing component in that it restricts the licensee from selling competing products.

The inventor of the display technology and its licensee are in a vertical relationship and are not actual or likely potential competitors in the manufacture or sale of display products or in the sale or development of technology. Hence, the grant of an exclusive license does not affect competition between the licensor and the licensee. The exclusive license may promote competition in the manufacturing and sale of display products by encouraging BigCo to develop and promote the new product in the face of uncertain demand by rewarding BigCo for its efforts if they lead to large sales. Although the license bars the licensee from selling competing products, this exclusive dealing aspect is unlikely in this example to harm competition by anticompetitively foreclosing access, raising competitors' costs of inputs, or facilitating anticompetitive pricing because the relevant product market is unconcentrated, the exclusive dealing restraint affects only a small proportion of the outlets for distribution of display products, and entry is easy. On these facts, the evaluating Agency would be unlikely to challenge the arrangement.

4.2 Efficiencies and Justifications

If the Agencies conclude, upon an evaluation of the market factors described in section 4.1, that a restraint in a licensing arrangement is unlikely to have an anticompetitive effect, they will not challenge the restraint. If the Agencies conclude that the restraint has, or is likely to have, an anticompetitive effect, they will consider whether the restraint is reasonably necessary to achieve procompetitive efficiencies.

If the restraint is reasonably necessary, the Agencies will balance the procompetitive efficiencies and the anticompetitive effects to determine the probable net effect on competition in each relevant market.

The Agencies' comparison of anticompetitive harms and procompetitive efficiencies is necessarily a qualitative one. The risk of anticompetitive effects in a particular case may be insignificant compared to the expected efficiencies, or vice versa. As the expected anticompetitive effects in a particular licensing arrangement increase, the Agencies will require evidence establishing a greater level of expected efficiencies.

The existence of practical and significantly less restrictive alternatives is relevant to a determination of whether a restraint is reasonably necessary. If it is clear that the parties could have achieved similar efficiencies by means that are significantly less restrictive, then the Agencies will not give weight to the parties' efficiency claim. In making this assessment, however, the Agencies will not engage in a search for a theoretically least restrictive alternative that is not realistic in the practical prospective business situation faced by the parties.

When a restraint has, or is likely to have, an anticompetitive effect, the duration of that restraint can be an important factor in determining whether it is reasonably necessary to achieve the putative procompetitive efficiency. The effective duration of a restraint may depend on a number of factors, including the option of the affected party to terminate the arrangement unilaterally and the presence of contract terms (e.g., unpaid balances on minimum purchase commitments) that encourage the licensee to renew a license arrangement. Consistent with their approach to less restrictive alternative analysis generally, the Agencies will not attempt to draw fine distinctions regarding duration; rather, their focus will be on situations in which the duration clearly exceeds the period needed to achieve the procompetitive efficiency.

The evaluation of procompetitive efficiencies, of the reasonable necessity of a restraint to achieve them, and of the duration of the restraint, may depend on the market context. A restraint that may be justified by the needs of a new entrant, for example, may not have a procompetitive efficiency justification in different market circumstances. *Cf. United States v. Jerrold Electronics Corp.*, 187 F. Supp. 545 (E.D. Pa. 1960), *aff'd per curiam*, 365 U.S. 567 (1961).

4.3 Antitrust "Safety Zone"

Because licensing arrangements often promote innovation and enhance competition, the Agencies believe that an antitrust "safety zone" is useful in order to provide some degree of certainty and thus to encourage such activity.[30] Absent extraordinary circumstances, the Agencies will not challenge a restraint in an intellectual

---

[30] The antitrust "safety zone" does not apply to restraints that are not in a licensing arrangement, or to restraints that are in a licensing arrangement but are unrelated to the use of the licensed intellectual property.

property licensing arrangement if (1) the restraint is not facially anticompetitive[31] and (2) the licensor and its licensees collectively account for no more than twenty percent of each relevant market significantly affected by the restraint. This "safety zone" does not apply to those transfers of intellectual property rights to which a merger analysis is applied. See section 5.7.

Whether a restraint falls within the safety zone will be determined by reference only to goods markets unless the analysis of goods markets alone would inadequately address the effects of the licensing arrangement on competition among technologies or in research and development.

If an examination of the effects on competition among technologies or in research development is required, and if market share data are unavailable or do not accurately represent competitive significance, the following safety zone criteria will apply. Absent extraordinary circumstances, the Agencies will not challenge a restraint in an intellectual property licensing arrangement that may affect competition in a technology market if (1) the restraint is not facially anticompetitive and (2) there are four or more independently controlled technologies in addition to the technologies controlled by the parties to the licensing arrangement that may be substitutable for the licensed technology at a comparable cost to the user. Absent extraordinary circumstances, the Agencies will not challenge a restraint in an intellectual property licensing arrangement that may affect competition in an innovation market if (1) the restraint is not facially anticompetitive and (2) four or more independently controlled entities in addition to the parties to the licensing arrangement possess the required specialized assets or characteristics and the incentive to engage in research and development that is a close substitute of the research and development activities of the parties to the licensing agreement.[32]

The Agencies emphasize that licensing arrangements are not anticompetitive merely because they do not fall within the scope of the safety zone. Indeed, it is likely that the great majority of licenses falling outside the safety zone are lawful and procompetitive. The safety zone is designed to provide owners of intellectual property with a degree of certainty in those situations in which anticompetitive effects are so unlikely that the arrangements may be presumed not to be anticompetitive without an inquiry into particular industry circumstances. It is not intended to suggest that parties should conform to the safety zone or to discourage parties falling outside the safety zone from adopting restrictions in their license arrangements that are reasonably necessary to achieve an efficiency-enhancing integration of economic activity. The Agencies will analyze arrangements falling outside the safety zone based on the considerations outlined in parts 3–5.

The status of a licensing arrangement with respect to the safety zone may change over time. A determination by the Agencies that a restraint in a licensing

---

[31] "Facially anticompetitive" refers to restraints that normally warrant per se treatment, as well as other restraints of a kind that would always or almost always tend to reduce output or increase prices. See section 3.4.

[32] This is consistent with congressional intent in enacting the National Cooperative Research Act. See H.R. Conf. Rpt. No. 1044, 98th Cong., 2d Sess., 10, reprinted in 1984 U.S.C.C.A.N. 3105, 3134–35.

arrangement qualifies for inclusion in the safety zone is based on the factual circumstances prevailing at the time of the conduct at issue.[33]

5. Application of General Principles

5.0 This section illustrates the application of the general principles discussed above to particular licensing restraints and to arrangements that involve the cross-licensing, pooling, or acquisition of intellectual property. The restraints and arrangements identified are typical of those that are likely to receive antitrust scrutiny; however, they are not intended as an exhaustive list of practices that could raise competitive concerns.

5.1 Horizontal Restraints

The existence of a restraint in a licensing arrangement that affects parties in a horizontal relationship (a "horizontal restraint") does not necessarily cause the arrangement to be anticompetitive. As in the case of joint ventures among horizontal competitors, licensing arrangements among such competitors may promote rather than hinder competition if they result in integrative efficiencies. Such efficiencies may arise, for example, from the realization of economies of scale and the integration of complementary research and development, production, and marketing capabilities.

Following the general principles outlined in section 3.4, horizontal restraints often will be evaluated under the rule of reason. In some circumstances, however, that analysis may be truncated; additionally, some restraints may merit per se treatment, including price fixing, allocation of markets or customers, agreements to reduce output, and certain group boycotts.

EXAMPLE 9

Situation:
Two of the leading manufacturers of a consumer electronic product hold patents that cover alternative circuit designs for the product. The manufacturers assign their patents to a separate corporation wholly owned by the two firms. That corporation licenses the right to use the circuit designs to other consumer product manufacturers and establishes the license royalties. None of the patents is blocking; that is, each of the patents can be used without infringing a patent owned by the other firm. The different circuit designs are substitutable in that each permits the manufacture at comparable cost to consumers of products that consumers consider to be interchangeable. One of the Agencies is analyzing the licensing arrangement.

---

[33] The conduct at issue may be the transaction giving rise to the restraint or the subsequent implementation of the restraint.

Discussion:

In this example, the manufacturers are horizontal competitors in the goods market for the consumer product and in the related technology markets. The competitive issue with regard to a joint assignment of patent rights is whether the assignment has an adverse impact on competition in technology and goods markets that is not outweighed by procompetitive efficiencies, such as benefits in the use or dissemination of the technology. Each of the patent owners has a right to exclude others from using its patent. That right does not extend, however, to the agreement to assign rights jointly. To the extent that the patent rights cover technologies that are close substitutes, the joint determination of royalties likely would result in higher royalties and higher goods prices than would result if the owners licensed or used their technologies independently. In the absence of evidence establishing efficiency-enhancing integration from the joint assignment of patent rights, the Agency may conclude that the joint marketing of competing patent rights constitutes horizontal price fixing and could be challenged as a per se unlawful horizontal restraint of trade. If the joint marketing arrangement results in an efficiency-enhancing integration, the Agency would evaluate the arrangement under the rule of reason. However, the Agency may conclude that the anticompetitive effects are sufficiently apparent, and the claimed integrative efficiencies are sufficiently weak or not reasonably related to the restraints, to warrant challenge of the arrangement without an elaborate analysis of particular industry circumstances (*see* section 3.4).

5.2 Resale Price Maintenance

Resale price maintenance is illegal when "commodities have passed into the channels of trade and are owned by dealers." *Dr. Miles Medical Co. v. John D. Park & Sons Co.*, 220 U.S. 373, 408 (1911). It has been held per se illegal for a licensor of an intellectual property right in a product to fix a licensee's *resale* price of that product. *United States v. Univis Lens Co.*, 316 U.S. 241 (1942); *Ethyl Gasoline Corp. v. United States*, 309 U.S. 436 (1940).[34] Consistent with the principles set forth in section 3.4, the Agencies will enforce the per se rule against resale price maintenance in the intellectual property context.

---

[34] *But cf. United States v. General Electric Co.*, 272 U.S. 476 (1926) (holding that an owner of a product patent may condition a license to manufacture the product on the fixing of the *first* sale price of the patented product). Subsequent lower court decisions have distinguished the *GE* decision in various contexts. *See, e.g., Royal Indus. v. St. Regis Paper Co.*, 420 F.2d 449, 452 (9th Cir. 1969) (observing that *GE* involved a restriction by a patentee who also manufactured the patented product and leaving open the question whether a nonmanufacturing patentee may fix the price of the patented product); *Newburgh Moire Co. v. Superior Moire Co.*, 237 F.2d 283, 293–94 (3rd Cir. 1956) (grant of multiple licenses each containing price restrictions does not come within the *GE* doctrine); *Cummer-Graham Co. v. Straight Side Basket Corp.*, 142 F.2d 646, 647 (5th Cir.) (owner of an intellectual property right in a process to manufacture an unpatented product may not fix the sale price of that product), *cert. denied*, 323 U.S. 726 (1944); *Barber-Colman Co. v. National Tool Co.*, 136 F.2d 339, 343–44 (6th Cir. 1943) (same).

5.3 Tying Arrangements

A "tying" or "tie-in" or "tied sale" arrangement has been defined as "an agreement by a party to sell one product . . . on the condition that the buyer also purchases a different (or tied) product, or at least agrees that he will not purchase that [tied] product from any other supplier." *Eastman Kodak Co. v. Image Technical Services, Inc.*, 112 S. Ct. 2072, 2079 (1992). Conditioning the ability of a licensee to license one or more items of intellectual property on the licensee's purchase of another item of intellectual property or a good or a service has been held in some cases to constitute illegal tying.[35] Although tying arrangements may result in anticompetitive effects, such arrangements can also result in significant efficiencies and pro-competitive benefits. In the exercise of their prosecutorial discretion, the Agencies will consider both the anticompetitive effects and the efficiencies attributable to a tie-in. The Agencies would be likely to challenge a tying arrangement if: (1) the seller has market power in the tying product,[36] (2) the arrangement has an adverse effect on competition in the relevant market for the tied product, and (3) efficiency justifications for the arrangement do not outweigh the anticompetitive effects.[37] The Agencies will not presume that a patent, copyright, or trade secret necessarily confers market power upon its owner.

Package licensing—the licensing of multiple items of intellectual property in a single license or in a group of related licenses—may be a form of tying arrangement if the licensing of one product is conditioned upon the acceptance of a license of another, separate product. Package licensing can be efficiency enhancing under some circumstances. When multiple licenses are needed to use any single item of intellectual property, for example, a package license may promote such efficiencies. If a package license constitutes a tying arrangement, the Agencies will evaluate its competitive effects under the same principles they apply to other tying arrangements.

5.4 Exclusive Dealing

In the intellectual property context, exclusive dealing occurs when a license prevents the licensee from licensing, selling, distributing, or using competing technologies. Exclusive dealing arrangements are evaluated under the rule of reason. *See Tampa Electric Co. v. Nashville Coal Co.*, 365 U.S. 320 (1961) (evaluating legality of exclusive dealing under section 1 of the Sherman Act and section 3 of the Clayton Act); *Beltone Electronics Corp.*, 100 F.T.C. 68 (1982) (evaluating legality of exclusive dealing under section 5 of the Federal Trade Commission Act).

---

[35] *See, e.g., United States v. Paramount Pictures, Inc.*, 334 U.S. 131, 156–58 (1948) (copyrights); *International Salt Co. v. United States*, 332 U.S. 392 (1947) (patent and related product).

[36] *Cf.* 35 U.S.C. § 271(d) (1988 & Supp. V 1993) (requirement of market power in patent misuse cases involving tying).

[37] As is true throughout these Guidelines, the factors listed are those that guide the Agencies' internal analysis in exercising their prosecutorial discretion. They are not intended to circumscribe how the Agencies will conduct the litigation of cases that they decide to bring.

In determining whether an exclusive dealing arrangement is likely to reduce competition in a relevant market, the Agencies will take into account the extent to which the arrangement (1) promotes the exploitation and development of the licensor's technology and (2) anticompetitively forecloses the exploitation and development of, or otherwise constrains competition among, competing technologies.

The likelihood that exclusive dealing may have anticompetitive effects is related, inter alia, to the degree of foreclosure in the relevant market, the duration of the exclusive dealing arrangement, and other characteristics of the input and output markets, such as concentration, difficulty of entry, and the responsiveness of supply and demand to changes in price in the relevant markets. (*See* sections 4.1.1 and 4.1.2.) If the Agencies determine that a particular exclusive dealing arrangement may have an anticompetitive effect, they will evaluate the extent to which the restraint encourages licensees to develop and market the licensed technology (or specialized applications of that technology), increases licensors' incentives to develop or refine the licensed technology, or otherwise increases competition and enhances output in a relevant market. (*See* section 4.2 and Example 8.)

5.5 Cross-licensing and Pooling Arrangements

Cross-licensing and pooling arrangements are agreements of two or more owners of different items of intellectual property to license one another or third parties. These arrangements may provide procompetitive benefits by integrating complementary technologies, reducing transaction costs, clearing blocking positions, and avoiding costly infringement litigation. By promoting the dissemination of technology, cross-licensing and pooling arrangements are often procompetitive.

Cross-licensing and pooling arrangements can have anticompetitive effects in certain circumstances. For example, collective price or output restraints in pooling arrangements, such as the joint marketing of pooled intellectual property rights with collective price setting or coordinated output restrictions, may be deemed unlawful if they do not contribute to an efficiency-enhancing integration of economic activity among the participants. *Compare NCAA* 468 U.S. at 114 (output restriction on college football broadcasting held unlawful because it was not reasonably related to any purported justification) *with Broadcast Music*, 441 U.S. at 23 (blanket license for music copyrights found not per se illegal because the cooperative price was necessary to the creation of a new product). When cross-licensing or pooling arrangements are mechanisms to accomplish naked price fixing or market division, they are subject to challenge under the per se rule. *See United States v. New Wrinkle, Inc.*, 342 U.S. 371 (1952) (price fixing).

Settlements involving the cross-licensing of intellectual property rights can be an efficient means to avoid litigation and, in general, courts favor such settlements. When such cross-licensing involves horizontal competitors, however, the Agencies will consider whether the effect of the settlement is to diminish competition among entities that would have been actual or likely potential competitors in a relevant market in the absence of the cross-license. In the absence of offsetting efficiencies, such settlements may be challenged as unlawful restraints of trade.

Cf. United States v. Singer Manufacturing Co., 374 U.S. 174 (1963) (cross-license agreement was part of broader combination to exclude competitors).

Pooling arrangements generally need not be open to all who would like to join. However, exclusion from cross-licensing and pooling arrangements among parties that collectively possess market power may, under some circumstances, harm competition. *Cf. Northwest Wholesale Stationers, Inc. v. Pacific Stationery & Printing Co.*, 472 U.S. 284 (1985) (exclusion of a competitor from a purchasing cooperative not per se unlawful absent a showing of market power). In general, exclusion from a pooling or cross-licensing arrangement among competing technologies is unlikely to have anticompetitive effects unless (1) excluded firms cannot effectively compete in the relevant market for the good incorporating the licensed technologies and (2) the pool participants collectively possess market power in the relevant market. If these circumstances exist, the Agencies will evaluate whether the arrangement's limitations on participation are reasonably related to the efficient development and exploitation of the pooled technologies and will assess the net effect of those limitations in the relevant market. *See* section 4.2.

Another possible anticompetitive effect of pooling arrangements may occur if the arrangement deters or discourages participants from engaging in research and development, thus retarding innovation. For example, a pooling arrangement that requires members to grant licenses to each other for current and future technology at minimal cost may reduce the incentives of its members to engage in research and development because members of the pool have to share their successful research and development and each of the members can free ride on the accomplishments of other pool members. *See generally United States v. Mfrs. Aircraft Ass'n, Inc.*, 1976-1 Trade Cas. (CCH) ¶ 60,810 (S.D.N.Y. 1975); *United States v. Automobile Mfrs. Ass'n*, 307 F. Supp. 617 (C.D. Cal 1969), *appeal dismissed sub nom. City of New York v. United States*, 397 U.S. 248 (1970), *modified sub nom. United States v. Motor Vehicle Mfrs. Ass'n*, 1982–83 Trade Cas. (CCH) ¶ 65,088 (C.D. Cal. 1982). However, such an arrangement can have procompetitive benefits, for example, by exploiting economies of scale and integrating complementary capabilities of the pool members, (including the clearing of blocking positions), and is likely to cause competitive problems only when the arrangement includes a large fraction of the potential research and development in an innovation market. *See* section 3.2.3 and Example 4.

EXAMPLE 10

Situation:

As in Example 9, two of the leading manufacturers of a consumer electronic product hold patents that cover alternative circuit designs for the product. The manufacturers assign several of their patents to a separate corporation wholly owned by the two firms. That corporation licenses the right to use the circuit designs to other consumer product manufacturers and establishes the license royalties. In this example, however, the manufacturers assign to the separate corporation only patents that are blocking. None of the patents assigned to the corporation can be used without infringing a patent owned by the other firm.

Discussion:

Unlike the previous example, the joint assignment of patent rights to the wholly owned corporation in this example does not adversely affect competition in the licensed technology among entities that would have been actual or likely potential competitors in the absence of the licensing arrangement. Moreover, the licensing arrangement is likely to have procompetitive benefits in the use of the technology. Because the manufacturers' patents are blocking, the manufacturers are not in a horizontal relationship with respect to those patents. None of the patents can be used without the right to a patent owned by the other firm, so the patents are not substitutable. As in Example 9, the firms are horizontal competitors in the relevant goods market. In the absence of collateral restraints that would likely raise price or reduce output in the relevant goods market or in any other relevant antitrust market and that are not reasonably related to an efficiency-enhancing integration of economic activity, the evaluating Agency would be unlikely to challenge this arrangement.

5.6 Grantbacks

A grantback is an arrangement under which a licensee agrees to extend to the licensor of intellectual property the right to use the licensee's improvements to the licensed technology. Grantbacks can have procompetitive effects, especially if they are nonexclusive. Such arrangements provide a means for the licensee and the licensor to share risks and reward the licensor for making possible further innovation based on or informed by the licensed technology, and both promote innovation in the first place and promote the subsequent licensing of the results of the innovation. Grantbacks may adversely affect competition, however, if they substantially reduce the licensee's incentives to engage in research and development and thereby limit rivalry in innovation markets.

A non-exclusive grantback allows the licensee to practice its technology and license it to others. Such a grantback provision may be necessary to ensure that the licensor is not prevented from effectively competing because it is denied access to improvements developed with the aid of its own technology. Compared with an exclusive grantback, a non-exclusive grantback, which leaves the licensee free to license improvements technology to others, is less likely to have anticompetitive effects.

The Agencies will evaluate a grantback provision under the rule of reason, *see generally Transparent-Wrap Machine Corp. v. Stokes & Smith Co.*, 329 U.S. 637, 645–48 (1947) (grantback provision in technology license is not per se unlawful), considering its likely effects in light of the overall structure of the licensing arrangement and conditions in the relevant markets. An important factor in the Agencies' analysis of a grantback will be whether the licensor has market power in a relevant technology or innovation market. If the Agencies determine that a particular grantback provision is likely to reduce significantly licensees' incentives to invest in improving the licensed technology, the Agencies will consider the extent to which the grantback provision has offsetting procompetitive effects, such as (1) promoting dissemination of licensees' improvements to the licensed technology, (2) increasing the licensors' incentives to disseminate the licensed technology, or (3) otherwise increasing competition and output in a relevant technology or innovation market. *See* section 4.2. In addition, the Agencies will consider the extent to which grantback provisions in the relevant markets generally increase licensors' incentives to innovate in the first place.

5.7 Acquisition of Intellectual Property Rights

Certain transfers of intellectual property rights are most appropriately analyzed by applying the principles and standards used to analyze mergers, particularly those in the 1992 Horizontal Merger Guidelines. The Agencies will apply a merger analysis to an outright sale by an intellectual property owner of all of its rights to that intellectual property and to a transaction in which a person obtains through grant, sale, or other transfer an exclusive license for intellectual property (i.e., a license that precludes all other persons, including the licensor, from using the licensed intellectual property).[38] Such transactions may be assessed under section 7 of the Clayton Act, sections 1 and 2 of the Sherman Act, and section 5 of the Federal Trade Commission Act.

EXAMPLE 11

Situation:

Omega develops a new, patented pharmaceutical for the treatment of a particular disease. The only drug on the market approved for the treatment of this disease is sold by Delta. Omega's patented drug has almost completed regulatory approval by the Food and Drug Administration. Omega has invested considerable sums in product development and market testing, and initial results show that Omega's drug would be a significant competitor to Delta's. However, rather than enter the market as a direct competitor of Delta, Omega licenses to Delta the right to manufacture and sell Omega's patented drug. The license agreement with Delta is nominally nonexclusive. However, Omega has rejected all requests by other firms to obtain a license to manufacture and sell Omega's patented drug, despite offers by those firms of terms that are reasonable in relation to those in Delta's license.

Discussion:

Although Omega's license to Delta is nominally nonexclusive, the circumstances indicate that it is exclusive in fact because Omega has rejected all reasonable offers by other firms for licenses to manufacture and sell Omega's patented drug. The facts of this example indicate that Omega would be a likely potential competitor of Delta in the absence of the licensing arrangement, and thus they are

---

[38] The safety zone of section 4.3 does not apply to transfers of intellectual property such as those described in this section.

in a horizontal relationship in the relevant goods market that includes drugs for the treatment of this particular disease. The evaluating Agency would apply a merger analysis to this transaction, since it involves an acquisition of a likely potential competitor.

6. Enforcement of Invalid Intellectual Property Rights

The Agencies may challenge the enforcement of invalid intellectual property rights as antitrust violations. Enforcement or attempted enforcement of a patent obtained by fraud on the Patent and Trademark Office or the Copyright Office may violate section 2 of the Sherman Act, if all the elements otherwise necessary to establish a section 2 charge are proved, or section 5 of the Federal Trade Commission Act. *Walker Process Equipment, Inc. v. Food Machinery & Chemical Corp.*, 382 U.S. 172 (1965) (patents); *American Cyanamid Co.*, 72 F.T.C. 623, 684–85 (1967), *aff'd sub. nom. Charles Pfizer & Co.*, 401 F.2d 574 (6th Cir. 1968), *cert. denied*, 394 U.S. 920 (1969) (patents); *Michael Anthony Jewelers, Inc. v. Peacock Jewelry, Inc.*, 795 F. Supp. 639, 647 (S.D.N.Y. 1992) (copyrights). Inequitable conduct before the Patent and Trademark Office will not be the basis of a section 2 claim unless the conduct also involves knowing and willful fraud and the other elements of a section 2 claim are present. *Argus Chemical Corp. v. Fibre Glass-Evercoat, Inc.*, 812 F.2d 1381, 1384–85 (Fed. Cir. 1987). Actual or attempted enforcement of patents obtained by inequitable conduct that falls short of fraud under some circumstances may violate section 5 of the Federal Trade Commission Act, *American Cyanamid Co., supra*. Objectively baseless litigation to enforce invalid intellectual property rights may also constitute an element of a violation of the Sherman Act. See *Professional Real Estate Investors, Inc. v. Columbia Pictures Industries, Inc.*, 113 S. Ct. 1920, 1928 (1993) (copyrights); *Handgards, Inc. v. Ethicon, Inc.*, 743 F.2d 1282, 1289 (9th Cir. 1984), *cert. denied*, 469 U.S. 1190 (1985) (patents); *Handgards, Inc. v. Ethicon, Inc.*, 601 F.2d 986, 992–96 (9th Cir. 1979), *cert. denied*, 444 U.S. 1025 (1980) (patents); *CVD, Inc. v. Raytheon Co.*, 769 F.2d 842 (1st Cir. 1985) (trade secrets), *cert. denied*, 475 U.S. 1016 (1986).

APPENDIX C

Microeconomic Analysis and Graphs

Microeconomics explores the efficient use of scarce resources, including the relationships between cost and output, between supply and demand, and between consumers and producers. Basic microeconomic texts run hundreds of pages. In contrast, this overview is significantly circumscribed. Many important microeconomic concepts are omitted, not because they are irrelevant to the economics of intellectual property protection, but because antitrust courts generally do not discuss these more advanced concepts. For those students who wish greater immersion in microeconomics, some excellent texts are listed at the end of this appendix.

A. The Demand Curve

The demand curve reflects how many units of a product consumers will purchase in the aggregate at a given price. Economists communicate the relationship between price and quantity graphically, as represented in Figure 1. Price is represented on the y-axis, which shows vertical movement in the area of the graph. Price increases as one moves up the y-axis. The quantity demanded is represented on the x-axis, which illustrates horizontal movement. Quantity increases as one moves right along the x-axis.

The demand curve slopes downward to reflect the fact that for most goods, as price increases, the number of units purchased decreases.[1] If the market price is *P1*, then consumers will demand the quantity represented as *Q1*. If the market price goes down to *P2*, then consumers will demand more of the product. Their new demand is determined by moving down along the demand curve to the point where a horizontal line originating at *P2* intersects the demand curve. At this point, a vertical line is drawn down to the x-axis and we denote this point as *Q2*, which

---

[1] This may not be true for all goods. There may be some luxury goods where a higher price increases demand because consumers perceive the goods as having more cachet due to the higher price.

647

648 Microeconomic Analysis and Graphs

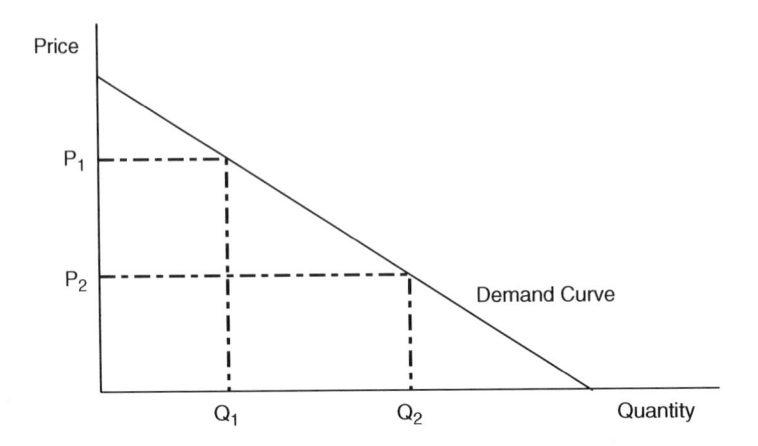

Figure 1

represents how many units of the product consumers demand at the *P2* price. As the price goes down from *P1* to *P2*, the quantity demanded increases from *Q1* to *Q2*.

The downward-sloping demand curve applies to individual consumers and to market demand as a whole for a particular product. Every consumer has his or her own demand curve for every product (although for some products the demand curve is vertical at zero because an individual desires none of the product no matter what the price). In general, these individual demand curves are downward-sloping for most products. For example, as the price of gasoline increases, an individual consumer will normally purchase less. Similarly, for the market as a whole, we see that as the price of gasoline goes up, national consumption declines.

The downward-sloping demand curve applies to consumer goods and to inputs used by businesses. Firms have a demand curve for each input that they use to produce their wares. For example, as wages increase, businesses may consume less labor and shift to greater consumption of technology, for example, by using robotics in auto-manufacturing plants. Thus, as the price of labor increases, demand for labor decreases. This means that businesses have a downward-sloping demand for labor.

In reality, the linear demand curve in Figure 1 is a Platonic ideal, an archetype that rarely reflects reality. In the real world, demand curves are not linear. Demand curves bend and become concave or convex; they can be discontinuous when demand drops off precipitously at a particular price point. Basic economics texts generally draw the oversimplified linear demand curve because it makes it easier to illustrate and explain the broad concepts that economics students need to understand.

Demand curves also have varying degrees of steepness. If a demand curve is very steep, as in Figure 2, demand is said to be inelastic, which means that a large percentage increase in price causes a relatively small percentage decrease in consumption. Conversely, if a demand curve is relatively flat, as in Figure 3, then demand is considered very elastic, which means that a small percentage increase in price causes a relatively large percentage decrease in consumption. Thus, in Figure 2, when the price increases significantly from *P1* to *P2*, demand decreases relatively little. Contrast this with Figure 3, in which the price increases slightly from *P1* to *P2*, but demand decreases substantially.

Demand elasticity is affected by several factors, including the nature of the product and the availability of substitutes. For example, if the product is a patented drug to treat a particular form of cancer and there are no non-infringing alternative

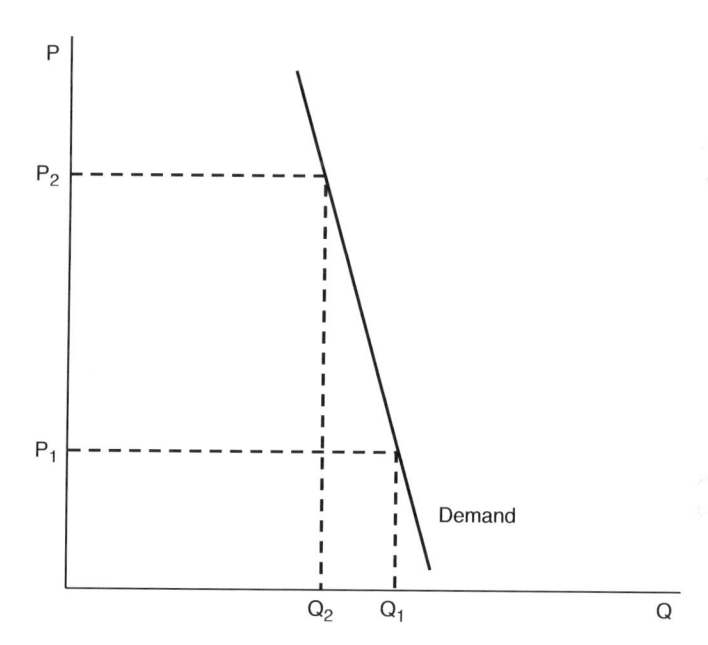

Figure 2

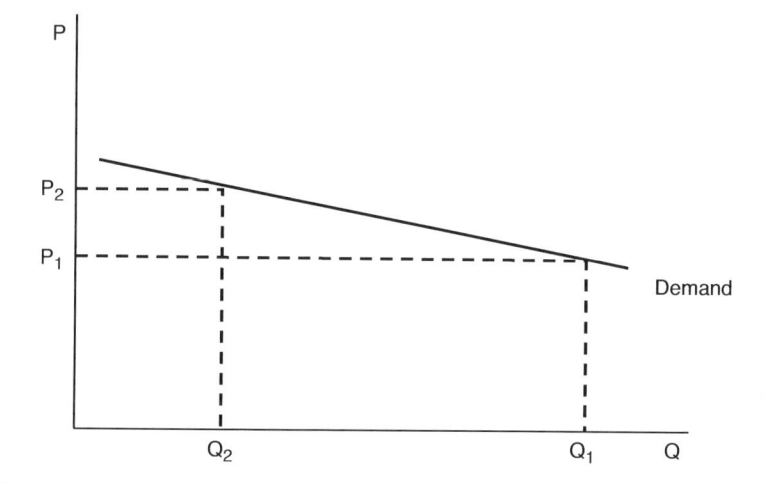

Figure 3

drugs, we expect demand to be relatively inelastic. Even if the price increases significantly, patients will pay the higher price. If, however, low-priced, equally effective, non-infringing drugs were widely available to treat the same disease, demand for the patented drug would be elastic because if the patentee raised the price of its drug, consumers would shift to the alternatives.

B. Cost Curves

Production of goods and services entails costs. Costs are often categorized as either fixed or variable. Fixed costs are those costs that a firm incurs regardless of its level of output. For example, if a new business needs to buy or build a factory in order to produce its product, that cost is generally considered fixed because it is the same whether the firm makes 1 unit of product or 1,000. Fixed costs are represented by the line in Figure 4 in which the cost of producing a unit of the product is represented on the y-axis and the quantity of product produced is measured on the x-axis. The line remains horizontal over the entire range of output.

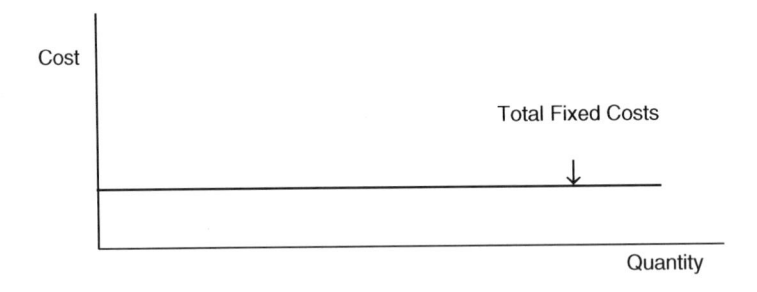

Figure 4

In contrast to fixed costs, variable costs fluctuate over the range of output. Each additional unit of output incurs an additional cost. Types of variable costs include labor and physical inputs that are consumed during production. For example, if a manufacturer of tires has to purchase rubber to make tires, then the more tires that it produces, the more rubber that it will need to purchase. So, the cost of rubber is a variable cost—it increases as output increases. (Economists sometimes argue that in the long run all costs are variable because fixed costs will eventually become recurring, such as when the tire factory needs to be replaced.)

An example of a variable cost curve can be found in the graph in Figure 5. The precise shape of a variable cost curve differs from product to product. Often, variable cost curves are depicted so that the variable costs rise steeply in early production and less steeply in the middle range where the firm is achieving economies of scale. As reflected in Figure 5, the total variable costs are drawn to eventually increase at a higher rate; this reflects a diseconomy of scale.

Intellectual property is a necessary input for many products. As reflected in the cases in this casebook, many manufacturers cannot build products without a patent or copyright license, theaters cannot show movies without a copyright license, and franchisees cannot operate their stores without a trademark license. Costs associated with intellectual property may represent either fixed or variable

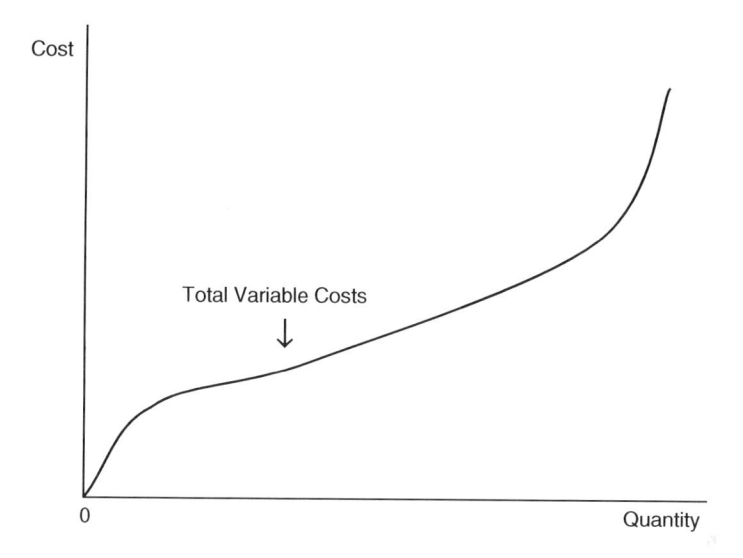

[Figure 5: Graph showing Total Variable Costs curve, with Cost on y-axis and Quantity on x-axis.]

Figure 5

costs, depending on the terms of the license. For example, you cannot legally write a novel based on a copyrighted play unless you acquire a license from the copyright owner. If she grants you a license for a lump sum, then this is a fixed cost because you pay her the same amount of money regardless of how many copies of the book you actually publish and sell. Conversely, you could acquire a license that requires you to pay a royalty for every copy of the book that you sell. In this case, the costs of acquiring the IP would be a variable cost, one that increases with output.

The total cost of making any product or providing a service is reflected in the total cost curve. This is constructed by vertically summing the fixed cost curve and variable cost curve. In other words, for each quantity of output, we add the fixed costs and the variable costs associated with that particular quantity. An example of a total cost curve that sums the fixed and variable costs represented in Figure 4 and 5 is represented in Figure 6.

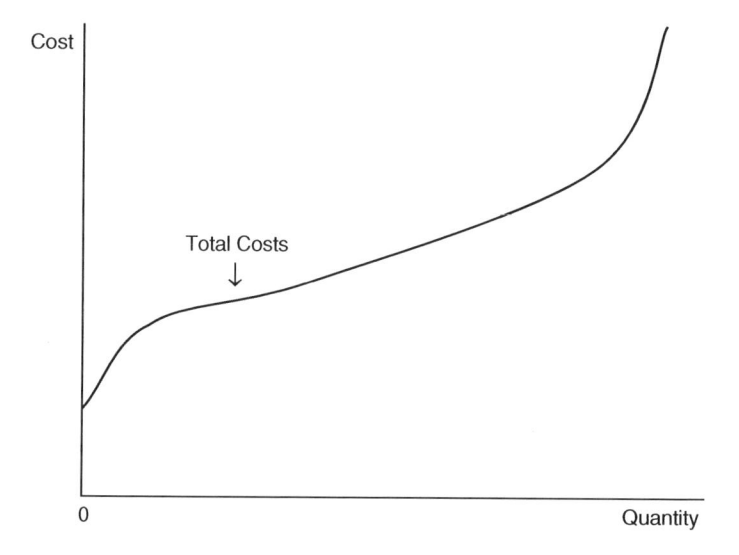

[Figure 6: Graph showing Total Costs curve, with Cost on y-axis and Quantity on x-axis.]

Figure 6

Once a firm knows its total cost curve, it can calculate its average total cost curve (ATC). It does so by dividing total cost by the number of units produced. This generally yields a U-shaped curve, such as the curve labeled ATC in Figure 7.

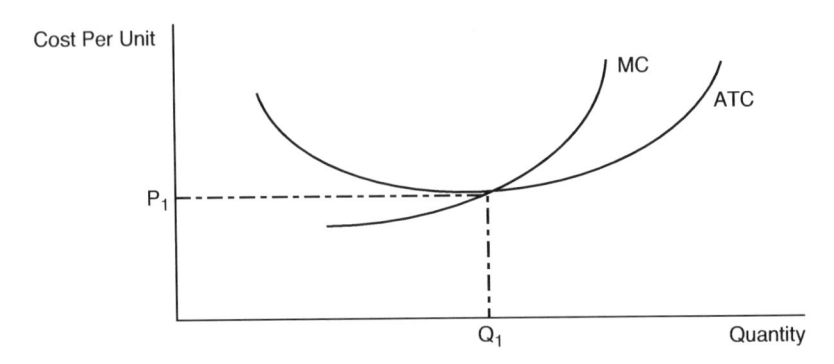

Figure 7

Another measure of cost is marginal cost (MC). Marginal cost refers to the cost of making the next unit of product. For example, if it costs a total of $10 to make one unit, $14 to make two units, and $15 to make three units, then the marginal cost of the second unit is $4 and the marginal cost of the third unit is $1. Note that as marginal cost is declining, so is the average total cost; using the above numbers, the average total cost for one, two, and three units is $10, $7, and $5, respectively. The quantity produced during the downward sloping section of the average total cost curve until the marginal cost curve intersects the ATC curve can be thought of as the production that takes place when the firm was enjoying economies of scales. The upward sloping section of the ATC curve to the right of the intersection reflects a diseconomy of scale in which the firm is not producing as efficiently as it was during the earlier production.

Marginal cost also generally starts off declining as the firm is achieving economies of scale. Eventually, at higher levels of production, marginal cost increases. This can be explained by diseconomies of scale or the increasing costs of inputs because, in theory, firms use the cheapest and most efficient inputs first.

As shown in Figure 7, the MC curve intersects the ATC curve from below at the lowest point in the ATC curve. As long as marginal cost is below average total cost, then average total cost is declining. Once marginal cost exceeds average total cost, then average total cost must increase.

C. The Supply Curve

At any given price, suppliers are willing to sell a particular amount of a good or service. Like the demand curve, the supply curve shows the relationship between price and quantity. Whereas the demand curve illustrates this relationship from the consumers' perspective, the supply curve does it from the sellers' perspective.

In contrast to the downward-sloping demand curve, the supply curve slopes upward. This reflects the observation that as market price increases, the quantity available for sale will increase as well, as illustrated in Figure 8. The supply curve is created by horizontally aggregating the cost curves of all the firms in the industry (i.e., at each price along the x-axis we determine how many units each individual firm would supply and we add these numbers up). Thus, the supply curve is also a measure of the cost of bringing a particular quantity of product to market. To the extent that the least expensive inputs are used first, a higher price is necessary to induce sellers to supply larger quantities that will be more costly to produce. As consumers are willing to pay more, sellers should be willing to supply more.

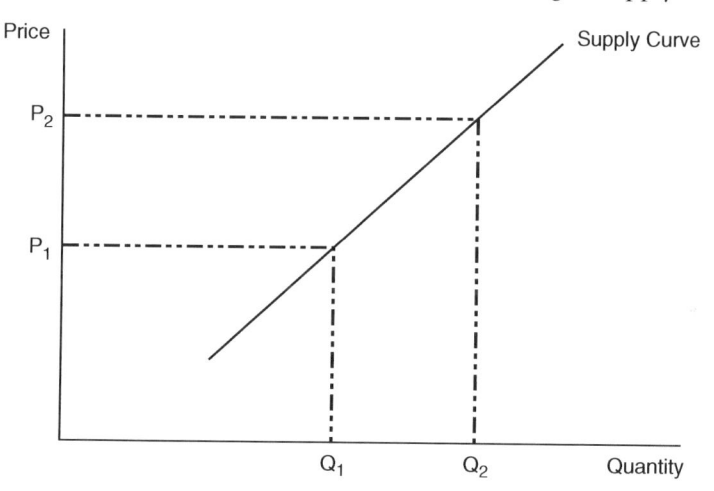

Figure 8

As with the stylized demand curves discussed above, the supply curve in Figure 8 does not reflect reality. For example, when the price is very low—approaching zero—no quantity will be supplied because manufacturers cannot cover their fixed costs. In the real world, businesses do not spend much time considering the extreme ends of the supply curve where the quantity is either too insignificant to warrant participating in the market or too large to reflect the reality of how much product will be manufactured and sold. The demand and supply curves are drawn this way, in part, because it makes it easier to illustrate relevant economic concepts such as consumer surplus and producer surplus, discussed next.

D. The Efficient Equilibrium

In a perfectly competitive market, the market output for a product will be where the demand and supply curves intersect, represented as Q_c in Figure 9. All consumers will be charged the same price, P_c, which is the market-clearing price. At this price, many consumers enjoy a surplus because they were willing to pay a higher amount. The demand curve represents how much consumers valued each unit of output, with the first units being valued more. The difference between the amount that consumers were willing to pay (represented by the demand curve) and the amount that they actually paid (represented by the horizontal line at P_c) constitutes consumer surplus. The area of consumer surplus is represented by the area labeled *CS* in Figure 9.

Figure 9

Figure 9

Producers, too, enjoy a surplus in a perfectly competitive market, though their surplus is measured differently. The supply curve shows the price at which a supplier would be willing to sell each unit of product and the horizontal line at P_c denotes how much the producer actually received on each unit. This difference between these constitutes producer surplus, represented by the area labeled *PS* in Figure 9.

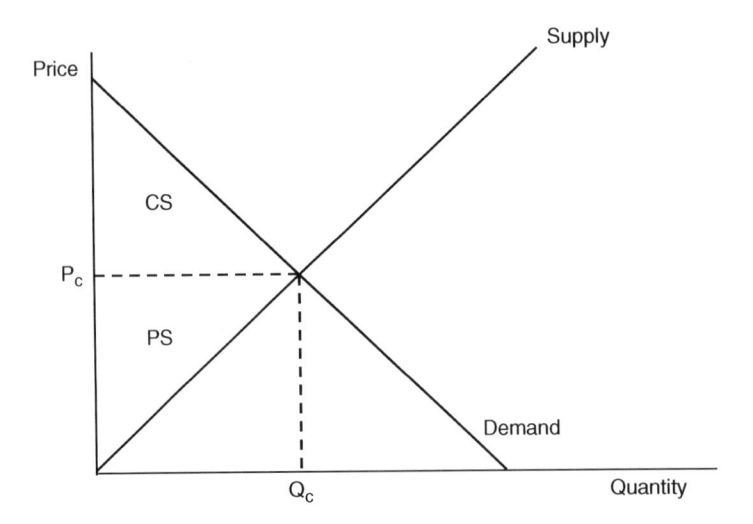

The level of output associated with the intersection of the demand and supply curves, Q_c, represents the efficient equilibrium for the market. If more than quantity Q_c were sold, this would be inefficient. To the extent that the demand curve represents how much consumers value each additional unit of output and the supply curve represents the marginal cost of each additional unit of output, sales to the right of Q_c are inefficient because these units cost more to make than society values them. Conversely, if the quantity supplied is less than Q_c, then sales that should be occurring—because society values these sales more than the cost of making these additional units of product—are not taking place. This form of inefficiency is called deadweight loss, which is discussed below.

The efficient equilibrium is not unvarying. It can change based on shifts in the demand or supply curve. The demand curve for a product, such as a trademarked brand of clothing, can shift out if the product suddenly becomes desirable due to a change in fashion. At the new equilibrium, a larger quantity is sold and the price is higher. Similarly, the supply curve can shift in or out based on exogenous shocks to the market or other factors. For example, if an oil embargo reduces the availability of oil, then any market whose products require oil as an input should see its supply curve shift in, so that a new equilibrium is created at a higher price and a lower quantity. Alternatively, if a copyrighted novel enters the public domain, we should expect the supply curve to shift out because whereas previously only the copyright owner could publish new copies of the book, now any publisher can publish the book (without paying for a license or risking an infringement lawsuit). This dynamic is illustrated in Figure 10. As the supply curve shifts from *T1* to *T2*,

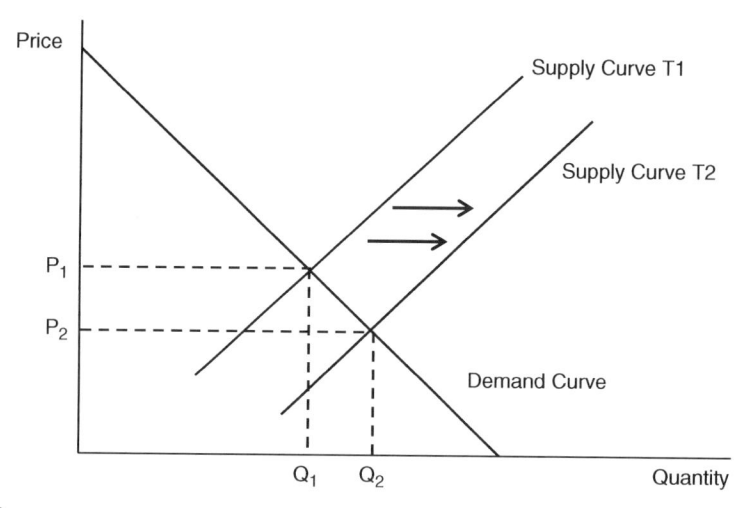

Figure 10

the market price decreases and the quantity supplied increases. A new efficient equilibrium is created.

As the price of inputs decreases, the supply curve will shift out because at a given price, suppliers are willing to sell more. In theory this means that when a patent expires or a copyrighted work enters the public domain, the supply curve for products that use that intellectual property as an input should shift out because the cost of making such goods will decrease since manufacturers will no longer have to pay for an IP license. Conversely, when licensing fees for IP inputs unexpectedly increase, the supply curve should shift in and a new equilibrium results at a lower quantity and higher price.

E. Deviations from the Efficient Equilibrium

A profit-maximizing firm will produce output at the level where its marginal cost (MC) of production equals its marginal revenue (MR). Because marginal cost is increasing (i.e., upward sloping) at this point, if the firm were to produce more than this quantity, it would lose money on the additional sales because these extra units cost more to make than the revenue that they generate. For a firm in a competitive market, marginal revenue is the market price represented by Pc in Figure 9. So a firm will produce output up to the point where its marginal cost is equal to the market price. It would lose money on sales beyond that point, i.e., where MC > MR. As a price taker, the firm cannot affect market price. Whether it produces a lot or a little, the market price remains unchanged.

For a firm with monopoly power, marginal revenue is downward sloping. This reflects the fact that the monopolist is a price maker and its output decisions determine the market price for the product. In contrast to firms in a competitive market—which are price takers—a firm with market power is a price maker. It has the ability to set market price by manipulating the quantity available for purchase. If the monopolist produces very little output, then the market price will be high. If the monopolist expands output, then the market price will decrease. Assuming that all consumers pay the same price (i.e., that there is no price discrimination), this means that as the monopolist expands output, it will forego some of the money that high-value consumers were willing to pay. In other words, by lowering the price in order to secure sales to lower-value consumers, the monopolist will lose some money from high-end consumers. As a result, expanding output reduces the amount of marginal revenue associated with each additional sale and this is reflected in a downward-sloping marginal revenue curve. Like firms in a competitive market, the monopolist will produce output at the point where its marginal revenue and marginal cost curves intersect. It will then determine the price by drawing a vertical line up to the demand curve (at Qm in Figure 11) and then charging the price associated with that point on the demand curve by drawing a horizontal line to the y-axis (at Pm in Figure 11).

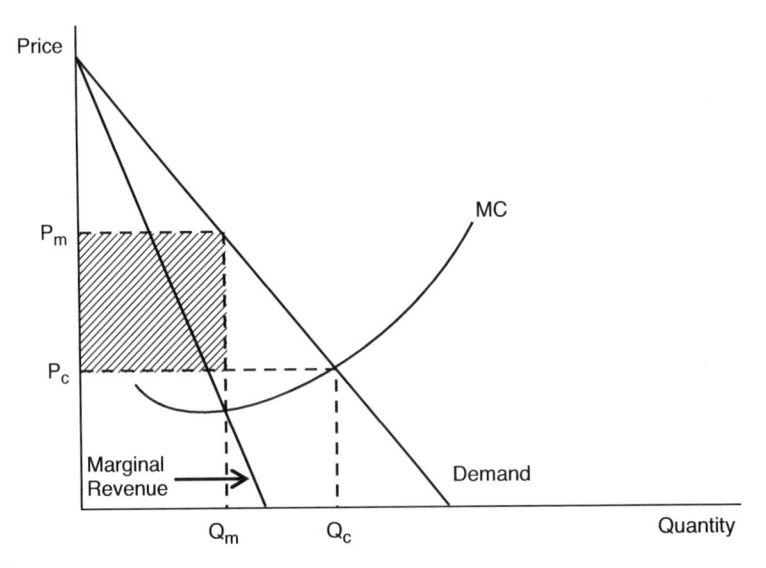

Figure 11

If a firm were an archetypal monopolist, it could restrict quantity without the unmet demand being satisfied by other suppliers. That means that the monopolist can restrict supply in order to increase price. Pursuing this strategy, the monopolist can convert some consumer surplus into producer surplus. As Figure 12 shows, if a monopolist can increase the price from *P1* to *P2*, then the quantity sold will decrease from *Q1* to *Q2*. As a result, consumer surplus shrinks from the large triangle represented by *ABC* to the smaller triangle represented by *AEF*. The eliminated consumer surplus is represented by the trapezoid *EBCF*. Some of this lost consumer surplus is converted into producer surplus. This transfer of wealth from consumers to producers is represented by the rectangle *EBGF*. This is the equivalent of the shaded area in Figure 11.

The remaining triangle of lost consumer surplus, represented by triangle GCF, is deadweight loss. Deadweight loss is a form of inefficiency associated with

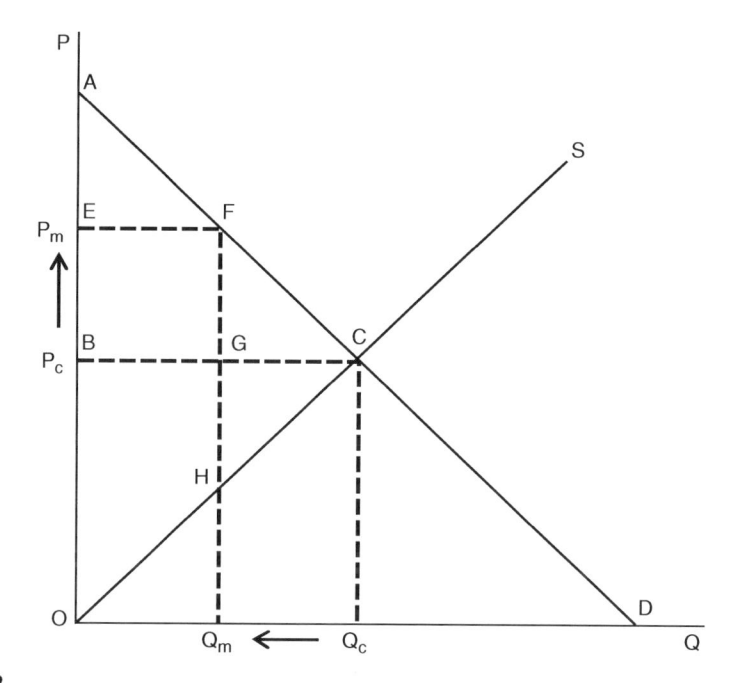

Figure 12

reduced output. When a monopolist reduces sales in order to increase price, socially beneficial transactions do not occur, and this harm is called deadweight loss.

With the reduction of output, some producer surplus is also lost. This is represented by the triangle *GHC*. Thus, the total deadweight loss associated with a monopolist's decision to reduce quantity is represented by the triangle *FHC*. The monopolist is willing to create this deadweight loss so long as her gain (measured by *EBGF*) is greater than her personal loss (measured by *GHC*). The monopolist is indifferent to the deadweight loss associated with the reduction in consumer surplus (measured by *GCF*). The net result is that monopoly pricing maximizes the monopolist's profit but imposes inefficiency on society.

Cartels can have the same economic effect as monopolies. In a cartel, competitors in the market agree to reduce their output in order to increase the market price. As with a monopoly, this reduction in quantity leads to an increase in price and converts consumer surplus into producer surplus, which the cartel members allocate among one another. The result is higher profits for the price-fixing firms and the creation of deadweight loss.

Antitrust law attempts to address the inefficiency associated with monopoly pricing and cartel behavior by limiting what firms can do in their quest for monopoly power and by limiting what agreements firms can enter into. The cases excerpted in this casebook demonstrate how courts apply antitrust law to these situations when the defendants possess intellectual property rights. Some courts discuss inefficiency explicitly, while others do not. As you read and discuss the cases in this book, you should ask yourself whether the challenged conduct inhibits or facilitates efficient market behavior.

Bibliography of Additional Reading

Roger D. Blair & David L. Kaserman, Antitrust Economics (2nd ed. 2008)

Jack Hirshleifer, Amihai Glazer, & David Hirshleifer, Price Theory and Applications: Decisions, Markets, and Information (2005)

William M. Landes & Richard A. Posner, The Economic Structure of Intellectual Property Law (2003)

Robert Pindyck & Daniel Rubinfeld, Microeconomics (7th ed. 2008)

Paul Samuelson & William Nordhaus, Economics (2009)

Frederic M. Scherer & David Ross, Industrial Market Structure and Economic Performance (3rd ed. 1990)

W. Kip Viscusi, Joseph E. Harrington, & John M. Vernon, Economics of Regulation and Antitrust (4th ed. 2005)

TABLE OF CASES

Principal cases are indicated by italic page numbers.

A

Abbott Labs. v. Brennan 621*n*11
Abbott Labs. v. Teva Pharms. USA, Inc. *245*
ABC, Inc. v. Prime Time 24 128
Addamax Corp. v. Open Software Found., Inc. *300*, 346
Alabama Power Co. v. FCC 84
Alaska Airlines, Inc. v. United Airlines, Inc. 227
Alcatel USA, Inc. v. DGI Techs., Inc. 65
Aldridge v. Microsoft Corp. 213
Allied Tube & Conduit Corp. v. Indian Head, Inc. 349
Aluminum Co. of Am.; United States v. 621*n*12
American Broad. Co. v. Prime Time 24 Joint Venture 128
American Column & Lumber Co. v. United States 314
American Cyanamid Co. 646
American Needle, Inc. v. National Football League 357
American Soc'y of Mech. Eng'rs v. Hydrolevel Corp. 349
Appalachian Coals v. United States 41*n*11
Argus Chem. Corp. v. Fibre Glass-Evercoat, Inc. 646
Arnold, Schwinn & Co.; United States v. 41*n*16
Aronson v. Quick Point Pencil Co. 542
Asahi Glass Co. v. Pentech Pharm., Inc. 54, 393, 487
Aspen Skiing Co. v. Aspen Highlands Skiing Corp. 31*n*17, 242
Assessment Techs. of WI, LLC v. WIREdata, Inc. 65, 202

Atari Games Corp. v. Nintendo of Am., Inc. 44–45, 197–98, 619n8
Atlantic Richfield Co. v. USA Petroleum Co. 36n33
Automatic Radio Mfg. Co. v. Ford Motor Co. 243
Automatic Radio Mfg. Co. v. Hazeltine Research, Inc. 433, 535, 538–39
Automobile Mfrs. Ass'n; United States v. 306, 643
Auwood v. Harry Brandt Booking Office, Inc. 378
Aveda Corp. v. Evita Mktg. 17n23

B

Barber-Colman Co. v. Nat'l Tool Co. 640n34
B. Braun Med.,Inc. v. Abbott Labs 512
Beal Corp. Liquidating Trust v. Valleylab, Inc. 559
Beltone Elecs. Corp. 641
Berkey Photo, Inc. v. Eastman Kodak Co. 215
Boggild v. Kenner Prods.,Div. of CPG Prods. Corp. 542
Boulware v. Nevada Dep't of Human Res. 121
Bourns, Inc. v. Raychem Corp. 560
Broadcast Music, Inc. v. CBS 26n4, 327, 339, 632, 642
Broadcom Corp. v. Qualcomm Inc. 262
Brooke Group Ltd. v. Brown & Williamson
Tobacco Corp. 23
Brown Shoe Co. v. United States 23, 41n18
Brulotte v. Thys Co. 539, 541, 542
Brunswick Corp. v. Riegel Textile Corp. 100

C

California Dental Ass'n v. FTC 27n7
California E. Lab., Inc. v. Gould 93
California Motor Transp. Co. v. Trucking Unlimited 112–13
California Packing Corp. v. Sun-Maid Raisin Growers 377
Cardizem CD Antitrust Litig., In re 387
Cardtoons, LC v. Major League Baseball Players Ass'n 119
Carl Zeiss Stiftung v. V.E.B. Carl Zeiss, Jena 66
Cascade Health Solutions v. PeaceHealth 313
CBS v. American Soc. of Composers, Authors and Publishers 337
CBS v. Prime Time 24 Joint Venture 128
CCPI, Inc. v. American Premier, Inc., ... 444
Cement Inst.; FTC v., ... 35n32
Chamberlain Group, Inc. v. Skylink Tech., Inc. 202
Charles Pfizer & Co. 646
Christianson v. Colt Indus. Operating Corp. 578
Ciba-Geigy, Ltd., FTC in the Matter of 450

Ciprofloxacin Hydrochloride Antitrust Litig., In re, 261
F.Supp. 2d 188 (E.D.N.Y., 2003) 428
Ciprofloxacin Hydrochloride Antitrust Litig., In re, 363
F.Supp. 2d 514 (E.D.N.Y., 2005) 564
City of. *See name of city*
Clark, In re 15n16
Clorox Co. v. Sterling Winthrop, Inc. 371, 377
Columbia Broad. Sys., Inc. v. American Soc'y of Composers,
Authors and Publishers 337
Columbia Broad. Sys., Inc. v. Prime Time 24 Joint Venture 128
Components, Inc. v. Western Elec. Co. 588
Container Corp. of Am.; United States v. 314
Continental T.V., Inc. v. GTE Sylvania Inc. 27n10, 42, 369
Copperweld Corp. v. Independence Tube Corp. 356, 357
County Materials Corp. v. Allan Block Corp. 57
Crane & Shovel Sales Corp. v. Bucyrus-Erie Co. 230
C.R. Bard, Inc. v. M3 Sys., Inc. 236, 242–43
CSU, LLC v. Xerox Corp. 202
CTS Corp. v. Piher Int'l Corp. 444
Cummer-Graham Co. v. Straight Side Basket Corp. 640n34
CVD, Inc. v. Raytheon Co. 104, 110–11, 646

D

Data Gen. Corp. v. Grumman Sys. Support Corp. 167, 202
Dawson Chem. Co. v. Rohm & Haas Co. 574
Dell Computer Corp., In the Matter of 257
Dentsply Int'l, Inc.; United States v. 312
Digidyne Corp. v. Data Gen. Corp. 149, 621n11
Digital Equip. Corp. v. Uniq Digital Techs., Inc. 200
Dippin' Dots, Inc. v. Mosey 94
Dr. Miles Med. Co. v. John D. Park & Sons Co. 41n15, 475, 479, 640
DSC Commc'ns Corp. v. Pulse Commc'ns, Inc. 64–65
DuPont v. Berkley & Co. 94

E

Eastern R.R. Presidents Conference v. Noerr Motor
Freight, Inc. 111, 112
Eastman Kodak Co. v. Image Tech.
Servs., Inc. 33n25, 33n27, 131, 199–200, 202, 641
E. Bement & Sons v. National Harrow Co. 39–40, 42n23, 479
E.I. du Pont de Nemours & Co. v. FTC 285
E.I. du Pont de Nemours & Co.; United States v. 29n15, 30n16

662 Table of Cases

Estée Lauder, Inc. v. Fragrance Counter, Inc. 66–67
Ethyl Gasoline Corp. v. United States 640
Expert Masonry, Inc. v. Boone County, Ky. 230

F

Fashion Originators' Guild of Am. v. FTC *459*
Federal Trade Comm'n v. *See name of opposing party*
Filmtec Corp. v. Hydranautics, 67 F.3d 931 (Fed. Cir. 1995) 120–21, 122n1
Fineman v. Armstrong World Indus., Inc. 227
Firemen's Ins. Servs. v. CIGNA Prop. & Cas. Ins. Agency 19n24
FMC Corp. v. Manitowoc Co. 93
FMC Corp.; United States v. 443
Foremost Pro Color, Inc. v. Eastman Kodak Co. *231*
Frankfort Distilleries; United States v. *496*
FTC v. *See name of opposing party*

G

Gershwin Pub. Corp. v. Columbia Artists Mgmt., Inc. 13n13
Glaxo Group Ltd.; United States v. *569*
Globetrotter Software, Inc. v. Elan Computer Group, Inc. 119
Grinnell Corp.; United States v. 28n12, 31–32, 621n12

H

Hack v. Yale College 34n29
Handgards, Inc. v. Ethicon, Inc., 601 F.2d 986 (9th Cir. 1979) 92–93, 646
Handgards, Inc. v. Ethicon, Inc., 743 F.2d 1282 (9th Cir. 1984), ... *557*, 646
Hartford-Empire Co. v. United States 312, *351*, 574
Haynes v. Monson 61
Heaton-Peninsular Button-Fastener Co. v. Eureka Specialty Co. 39
Hennessy Indus., Inc. v. FMC Corp. 553
Henry v. A.B. Dick 33n24, 40
Holmes Group, Inc. v. Vornado Air Circulation Sys., Inc. 583, 586
Hornsby Oil Co. v. Champion Spark Plug Co. 29n13
Hudson Distrib., Inc. v. Eli Lilly & Co. *497*
Hydranautics v. FilmTec Corp. 121–22, 586
Hydril Co. v. Grant Prideco LP 93

I

IBM Peripheral EDP Devices Antitrust Litig., In re 230, 240, 241
IBM v. United States 40n8

ILC Peripherals v. International Bus. Machs. 231
Illinois Brick Co. v. Illinois 567
Illinois Tool Works v. Independent Ink, Inc. 47, 55
Image Tech. Serv. v. Eastman Kodak *178*, 196–97
Independent Serv. Orgs. Antitrust Litig. (Xerox), In re *190*, 195, 196–97
Indiana Fed'n of Dentists; FTC v. 632
In re. *See name of party*
Intergraph Corp. v. Intel Corp. *203*, 213
International Salt Co. v. United States 41*n*21, *132*, 136–37, 574, 641*n*35
Interstate Circuit v. United States 491
Inwood Labs v. Ives Labs 16*n*20

J

Jayco Sys., Inc. v. Savin Bus. Mach. Corp. 29*n*14
Jefferson Parish Hosp. Dist. No. 2 v. Hyde 33*n*25, 34*n*30, 138, 158, 621*n*11
Jerrold Elecs. Corp.; United States v. 637
Jones Knitting Corp. v. Morgan *462*, 465, 467

K

Kentucky Fried Chicken Corp. v. Diversified Packaging Corp. 165
KP Permanent Make-Up, Inc. v. Lasting Impression I, Inc. 17*n*22
Krehl v. Baskin-Robbins Ice Cream Co. *158*
Kypta v. McDonald's Corp. 560

L

LaPeyre v. FTC 553
Lasercomb Am., Inc. v. Reynolds 61, 65
Leegin Creative Leather Prods., Inc. v. PSKS, Inc. 27*n*10, *500*, 509
Lexington Mill & Elevator Co.; United States v. 429
Line Materials Co.; United States v. *480*
Loew's, Inc.; United States v. *141*
LucasArts Entm't Co. v. Humongous Entm't Co. 492

M

Mallinckrodt, Inc. v. Medipart, Inc. 60
Manufacturers Aircraft Ass'n, Inc.; United States v. 306, 643
Maple Flooring Mfrs. Ass'n v. United States 315
Massachusetts Bd. of Registration in Optometry,
FTC In the Matter of 632*n*28
Matsushita Elec. Indus. Co. v. Cinram *316*, 323

Matsushita Elec. Indus. Co. v. Zenith Radio Corp. 338
Meehan v. PPG0 Indus., Inc. 543
Metro Indus., Inc. v. Sammi Corp. *381*
Michael Anthony Jewelers, Inc. v. Peacock Jewelry, Inc. 646
Microsoft Corp.; United States v., 253 F.3d 34 (D.C. Cir. 2001) 73, 230, 312
Microsoft Corp; United States v., 1995-2 Trade Cas.
(CCH) ¶ 71096 549
Miller Insituform, Inc. v. Insituform of North Am., Inc. 197
Molecular Diagnostics Labs. v. Hoffmann-La Roche, Inc. 565, 567
Morton Salt Co. v. G. S. Suppiger Co. 66
Motion Picture Patents Co. v. Universal Film Mfg. Co. 56–57, 198
Motor Vehicle Mfrs. Ass'n; United States v. 306, 643
Movie 1 & 2 v. United Artists Commc'ns, Inc. *468*
Mozart Co. v. Mercedes Benz of N. Am., Inc. 137
Multistate Legal Studies, Inc. v. Harcourt Brace
Jovanovich Legal and Prof'l Publ'g, Inc. 32n23

N

National Collegiate Athletic Ass'n v. Board of Regents of Univ. of Okla. 27n8
National Lead Co.; United States v. 574
National Soc'y of Prof'l Eng'rs v. United States 26n5
Negotiated Data Solutions, In the Matter of 285
Newburgh Moire Co. v. Superior Moire Co. 487, 640n34
New Wrinkle, Inc.; United States v. 306, 642
New York, City of v. United States 306
Nobelpharma AB v. Implant Innovations, Inc. 577
Northern Pac. Ry. Co. v. United States 33n25, 41n14, 55
North Miss. Commc'ns, Inc. v. Jones 32n23
Northwestern Corp. v. Gabriel Mfg. Co., Inc. 66
Northwest Wholesale Stationers, Inc. v. Pacific Stationery &
Printing Co. 26n4, 306, 643

O

Oahu Gas Serv., Inc. v. Pac. Res., Inc. 228
Olympia Equip. Leasing Co. v. Western Union Tel. Co. 241
Outlet Commc'ns, Inc. v. King World Prods., Inc. *147*

P

Palmer v. BRG of Ga., Inc. *369*
Paramount Pictures, Inc.; United States v. *139, 489, 492,* 641n35
Pfizer, Inc. v. Gov't of India 36n34

Pitney Bowes, Inc. v. Mestre 541
Practice Mgmt. Info. Corp. v. American Med. Ass'n 65
Precision Instrument Mfg. Co. v. Automobile Maint. Mach. Co. 41n20
Primetime 24 Joint Venture v. National Broad. Co. 123, 465, 467, 574
Professional Real Estate Invs. v. Columbia Pictures *113*, 118, 119, 121, 122, 646

Q

Quality King Distribs., Inc. v. L'anza Research Int'l, Inc. 495
Quanta Computer, Inc. v. LG Elecs., Inc. 515

R

Rambus, Inc., Matter of 283–84
Rambus, Inc. v. FTC *274*
Rental Car of N.H. v. Westinghouse Elec. Corp. 158
Ringling Bros. Barnum & Bailey Combined Shows v.
Utah Div. of Travel Dev. 17n21
Roche Prods., Inc. v. Bolar Pharm. Co. 429
Royal Indus. v. St. Regis Paper Co. 640n34
Rural Tel. Servs. Co., Inc. v. Feist Publ'ns, Inc. 241

S

Saturday Evening Post Co. v. Rumbleseat Press, Inc. 65
Scheiber v. Dolby Labs., Inc. 549
Schering-Plough Corp. v. FTC *394*
SCM Corp. v. Xerox Corp. 197
Sealy; United States v. 357
Sega Enter. Ltd. v. Accolade, Inc. 14n14
Seven-Up Co. v. No-Cal Corp. 377
Siegel v. Chicken Delight, Inc. 154, 158, 560
Singer Mfg, Co.; United States v. 306, 433, 643
Six W. Retail Acquisition, Inc. v. Sony Theatre Mgmt. Corp. 140
Socony-Vacuum Oil Co.; United States v. 41n13
Sony Elec., Inc. v. Soundview Techs., Inc. 340
Spectrum Sports, Inc. v. McQuillan 31–32, 31n18, 32n19, 32n21, 227
Sperry & Hutchinson Co.; FCC v. 285
Standard Oil Co. v. United States 25n3, 307
State Oil Co. v. Khan 25n2, 27n6, 339
Studiengesellschaft Kohle; United States v. 517
Summit Tech., FTC In the Matter of 323
Superior Court Trial Lawyers Ass'n; FTC v. 27n11, 632
Systemcare, Inc. v. Wang Labs. Corp. 146

T

Tamoxifen Citrate Antitrust Litig., In re 413, 427
Tampa Elec. Co. v. Nashville Coal Co. 641
Technical Res. Serv. v. Dornier Med. Sys. 33n27
Terminal R.R. Ass'n; United States v. 212
Terminal R.R. & Otter Tail Power Co. v. United States 212
Texaco, Inc. v. Dagher 26n5
Thompson Med. Co. v. Pfizer, Inc. 16n19
Tic-X-Press, Inc. v. Omni Promotions Co. 33n27
Times Picayune Publ'g Co. v. United States 32n22, 135
Timken Roller Bearing Co. v. United States 355, 356
Tominaga v. Shepherd 162, 165
Topco Assocs., Inc.; United States v. 23, 27n9, 41n17, 362, 369
Total Ben. Serv., Inc. v. Group Ins. Admin., Inc. 46n31
Townshend v. Rockwell Int'l Corp. 198
Town Sound & Custom Tops, Inc. v. Chrysler Motors Corp. 33n28
Transparent-Wrap Mach. Corp. v. Stokes & Smith Co. 528, 532, 644
Two Pesos, Inc. v. Taco Cabana, Inc. 16n19

U

United Farmers Agents Ass'n v. Farmers Ins. Exch. 34n29, 138
United Mine Workers v. Pennington 112
United States v. *See name of opposing party*
United States Anchor Mfg., Inc. v. Rule Indus., Inc. 32n23
United States Gypsum Co.; United States v. 291, 299
Universal City Studios v. Corley 201
Univis Lens Co.; United States v. 640
USM Corp. v. SPS Techs., Inc. 65, 553
U.S. Philips Corp. v. International Trade Comm'n 312
USS-POSCO Indus. v. Contra Costa County Bldg. &
Const. Trades Council 113

V

Veeck v. Southern Bldg. Code Cong. Int'l Inc. 349
Verizon Commc'ns Inc. v. FCC 84
Verizon Commc'ns Inc. v. Law Offices of Curtis V. Trinko, LLP 213
Virginia Panel Corp. v. MAC Panel Co. 61
Von's Grocery Co.; United States v. 41nn18–19

W

Walgreen Co. v. AstraZeneca Pharms. 254
Walker Process Equip. v. Food Mach. & Chem. Corp. 89, 92–93, 99, 122, 646
Wallace v. International Bus. Machs. Corp. 338
Warriner Hermetics, Inc. v. Copeland Refrigeration Corp. 158
Western Elec. Co.; United States v. 322
Westinghouse Elec. Corp. v. Bulldog 489
Westinghouse Elec. Corp.; United States v. 42n23

Z

Zenith Radio Corp. v. Hazeltine Research, Inc. 543, 549, 559

INDEX

A

ABA Section on Antitrust Law. *See* American Bar Association (ABA), Section on Antitrust Law
Abandonment of trademarks, 16, 20
Abbreviated New Drug Approval (ANDA) system, 430
Acquisition of intellectual property rights
  Clayton Act, 433
  conspiracy to restrain trade, 433–44
    competition, impact on, 443
    cross-licensing arrangements, 443
    FTC interference proceedings, anticompetitive settlements in, 443–44
    market power, 443
    patent infringement, relevance of, 443
    per se rules re, 442–43
    rule of reason analysis, 442–43
    validity of patent, relevance of, 443
  DOJ/FTC *Antitrust Guidelines*, 645–46
  mergers, 444–58
    divestiture requirements, 458
    goods markets, 449
    innovation markets, 449–50
    technology markets, 449
  patents generally, 5–7
  Sherman Act, 433, 444
Advisory opinions, 321
Aftermarkets
  circumvention in, 201–2
  DMCA, 200–202
  market power in, 199–200

Alienation, restraints on, 479
American Bar Association (ABA), Section on Antitrust Law
  on grantbacks, 534
  on market allocation and trademarks, 371
  on reverse payment settlements, 394
  on SSOs, 261
ANDA (Abbreviated New Drug Approval) system, 387–430
Andewelt, Roger B., 43–44, 311
Antitrust Division. *See* Justice Department
Antitrust Guidelines for the Licensing of Intellectual Property (DOJ/FTC)
  For reprint of text, see pages 617–646
  acquisition of intellectual property rights, 645–46
  cross-licensing arrangements, 305–6, 642–44
  efficiency, 636–37
  enforcement of invalid rights, 646
  exclusive dealing arrangements, 635–36, 641–42
  general principles, 619–23
  goods markets, 624
  grantbacks, 533–34, 644–45
  horizontal restraints, 639–40
  innovation markets, 626–29
  issuance, 45
  licensing of intellectual property, 511–12, 527–28
  market power, 46–47, 621
  mergers, 444

669

Antitrust Guidelines for the Licensing of Intellectual Property (DOJ/FTC) (*cont.*)
  modes of analysis, 623–33
  patent pooling, 315
  pooling arrangements, 642–44
  price fixing, 305–6
  rule of reason analysis, 634–39
  "safety zone," 637–39
  technology markets, 625–26
  tying arrangements, 131–32, 641
  unilateral refusals to license or deal, 167
  vertical price restraints, 640
Antitrust law generally
  competitor standing in, 557–64
  concerted refusals to license or deal in, 459–62
  consumer standing in, 564–67
  copyright misuse, relationship with, 65
  efficiency, maximizing of, 72–73
  fraudulently procured patents in, 103
  generally, 23–35
  historical background, 25
  jurisdiction of Federal Circuit, 577–88
  market allocation. *See* Market allocation
  patent misuse, relationship with, 60–61
  predatory innovation. *See* Predatory innovation
  price discrimination. *See* Price discrimination
  price fixing. *See* Price fixing
  remedies. *See* Remedies in antitrust law
  reverse payment settlements. *See* Pharmaceuticals
  royalty structuring. *See* Royalty structuring
  tension with intellectual property, 39–46
  trademark misuse, relationship with, 67
  tying arrangements. *See* Tying arrangements
  vertical price restraints. *See* Vertical price restraints
Antitrust Modernization Commission
  on mergers, 444–49
  on price discrimination, 70–71
Arbitrage, 68–70
Atomic Energy Act, 574
Attempted monopolization, 31–32, 36
Attorney General's National Committee to Study the Anti-trust Laws, 587–88
Atwood, James R., 119
Auctions by SSOs, 347

B
Barnett, Thomas O., 72–73
Barriers to entry, 30
Baxter, William F., 43
Bifurcation of trials, 587–88
Black markets, 55–56
Blanket licensing of copyrighted works. *See* Price fixing
Block-booking, 139–48
  Clayton Act, 146
  coercion in, 140
  competition, impact on, 140
  motion pictures, 139–46
  per se rules re, 146
  price discrimination, 140–41
  rule of reason analysis, 141
  Sherman Act, 146
  split arrangements compared, 378–81
  television, 141–49
  tying arrangements, 140
Blocking patents, 7, 313–14
Bork, Robert, 135
Business Review Letters, 321–22
Buyers' cartels, 488

C
Cartels
  buyers' cartels, 488
  competition, impact on, 24
  price fixing. *See* Price fixing
Causation
  antitrust law, 559
  price fixing, 305
Cease and desist orders under FTCA §5, 285
"Cellophane Fallacy," 30
Chicago School, 135–37
Circumvention, 201–2
Civil penalties. *See* Penalties
Clayton Act
  acquisition of intellectual property rights, 433
  block-booking, 146
  excerpts, 592–94
  exclusive dealing arrangements, 34
  FTCA compared, 35, 287
  mergers, 34–35, 444–45
  overview, 33–35
  treble damages, 560
  tying arrangements, 33–34, 40, 146
Clean Air Act, 574
Clinical trials of drugs, 449
Closed patent pools, 465
Compensatory pricing, 228
Competition
  acquisition of intellectual property rights, impact of, 443
  block-booking, impact of, 140
  cartels, impact of, 24
  dynamic competition, 23–24
  grantbacks, impact of, 531–32
  patent misuse, 61
  patent pooling, impact of, 312–14

predatory innovation, impact of, 241
reverse payment settlements, impact of, 393
static competition, 23
tying arrangements, impact of, 135
unfair competition, 119, 284–87
Competitor standing in antitrust law, 557–64
Complementary copyrights, 336–37
Complementary patents, 322, 327
Compulsory counterclaims in patent
   infringement cases, 586–87
Compulsory licensing as remedy, 569–76
Computer hardware
   SSOs for, 257–61
   unilateral refusals to license or deal in, 203–13
Concerted refusals to license or deal, 459–72
   antitrust law, 459–62
   copyrights, 465–72
   Noerr-Pennington doctrine, 462
   patent pooling, 462–65
   patents, 462–65
   Sherman Act, 462
Conditional refusals to license or deal, 198
Conspiracy
   acquisition of intellectual property rights
      as conspiracy to restrain trade.
      See Acquisition of intellectual property rights
   monopolization, 32–33
   price fixing. *See* Price fixing
Constitution
   intellectual property in, 56
   patents in, 5
Consumer protection, 36–37
Consumer standing in antitrust law, 564–67
Consumer welfare standard, 229
Contract law, relationship with patents, 543
Copyright Act
   excerpts, 604–14
   price fixing, 336
   unilateral refusals to license or deal, 173–77,
      193–95
Copyright infringement, 13–14
   circumvention as, 201–2
   defenses to, 14, 61–65
   encryption as, 201–2
   remedies, 13
   sham litigation re, 128
Copyright Office, 11
Copyrights
   acquisition of protection, 11–12
   blanket licensing. *See* Price fixing
   block-booking. *See* Block-booking
   complementary rights, 336–37
   concerted refusals to license or deal, 465–72
   duration of protection, 12–13
   first sale doctrine, 495–96

fraudulent procurement, patents contrasted,
   92–93
group boycotts, 465–72
infringement. *See* Copyright infringement
market allocation, 371, 378–81
misuse, 61–65
overview, 11–14
price discrimination, 69
price fixing through blanket licensing.
   See Price fixing
scope of protection, 12
split arrangements, 378–81
SSO standards, protection of, 349
substitute rights, 336–37
tying arrangements
   block-booking. *See* Block-booking
   software, 149–53
vertical price restraints, 489–96
Cost curve, 650–52
Cotter, Thomas F., 61
Counterclaims in patent
   infringement cases, 583–88
Cournot, Augustin, 313
Court of Appeals for the Federal Circuit, 577–88
Covenants not to compete, 61
Creighton, Susan A., 128–29
Criminal violations, 36, 569
Cross-licensing arrangements
   acquisition of intellectual property rights as
      conspiracy to restrain trade, 443
   DOJ/FTC *Antitrust Guidelines,* 305–6, 642–44
   DOJ/FTC *Promoting Innovation and
      Competition,* 311–12
   patent pooling distinguished, 311–12

D
Damages
   antitrust law, 559
   monopolization, for, 560
   predatory innovation, for, 240
   price fixing, for, 560
   treble damages, 35–36, 560, 569
   tying arrangements, for, 560
Davis, Mary J., 429
Deadweight loss, 24, 552
Deceptive conduct before SSOs. *See* Standard-
      setting organizations (SSOs)
Defenses
   copyright infringement, to, 14, 61–65
   copyright misuse as, 61–65
   patent infringement, to. *See* Patent
      infringement
   patent misuse as, 10–11, 55–61, 63
   trademark misuse as, 66–67
Delacourt, John T., 118, 128

672 Index

Demand curve, 647–50
Design changes. *See* Predatory innovation
Digital Millennium Copyright Act (DMCA), 200–202
Digital rights management (DRM), 20
Dilution of trademarks, 17
Disclosure
   predatory innovation, duty of disclosure, 227–28
   SSO requirements, 262, 282
Discount Pricing Consumer Protection Act of 2009, 509
Discovery in reverse payment settlement cases, 428
Distributors, vertical price restraints by. *See* Vertical price restraints
Divestiture, 458
DMCA (Digital Millennium Copyright Act), 200–202
DOJ. *See* Justice Department
Downstream markets
   circumvention in, 201–2
   DMCA, 200–202
   market power in, 199–200
DRM (Digital rights management), 20
Drug Price Competition and Patent Term Restoration Act of 1984, 254, 430
Drug safety laws, 429–31
Drugs. *See* Pharmaceuticals
Dynamic competition, 23–24
Dynamic efficiency, 24, 72

E
Efficiency
   DOJ/FTC *Antitrust Guidelines*, 636–37
   dynamic efficiency, 24, 72
   overview, 72–73
   price fixing, effect of, 298
   static efficiency, 24, 72
Efficient equilibrium, 653–57
Encryption, 201–2
Enforcement of intellectual property rights, 89–129
   fraudulently procured patents. *See* Fraudulently procured patents
   inequitable conduct, effect of, 99
   patent infringement, 93
   sham litigation. *See* Sham litigation
Essential facilities doctrine, 207–13
Exclusionary rights, 4–5, 54–55
Exclusive dealing arrangements
   Clayton Act, 34
   DOJ/FTC *Antitrust Guidelines*, 635–36, 641–42
   Sherman Act, 34
   tying arrangements contrasted, 158
Exhaustion doctrine, 515—517

F
Fair, reasonable, and non-discriminatory (FRAND) terms, 262–74, 323
FDCA (Food, Drug, and Cosmetic Act), 429
Federal Circuit Court of Appeals, 577–88
Federal Courts Improvement Act of 1982, 577
Federal Trade Commission (FTC)
   Antitrust Guidelines for the Licensing of Intellectual Property. *See* Antitrust Guidelines for the Licensing of Intellectual Property (DOJ/FTC)
   enforcement powers, 36
   interference proceedings, anticompetitive settlements in, 443–44
   Merger Guidelines, 445–48
   mergers and acquisitions, authority to challenge, 34
   Promoting Innovation and Competition. *See* Promoting Innovation and Competition (DOJ/FTC)
   on reverse payment settlements, 411–12
   on SSOs, 283–84
Federal Trade Commission Act (FTCA)
   cease and desist orders, 285
   civil penalties, 285
   Clayton Act compared, 35, 287
   §5 actions, 284–87
   injunctive relief, 35–36
   overview, 35–36
   Sherman Act compared, 35, 287
   unfair competition, 284–87
Field-of-use restrictions, 517–27
First sale doctrine, 495–96
Food, Drug, and Cosmetic Act (FDCA), 429
Food safety laws, 429–31
Franchises and tying arrangements, 154–65
   exclusive dealing arrangements compared, 158
   lists of approved suppliers, 165
   quality assurance, 158
   separate product requirement, 157–58, 162
FRAND. *See* Fair, reasonable, and non-discriminatory (FRAND) terms
Fraudulently procured patents, 89–104
   antitrust law, 103
   copyrights contrasted, 92–93
   Handgards claims, 92–93
   inequitable conduct distinguished, 99, 119
   invalidity distinguished, 94
   monopolization, 93, 99
   Noerr-Pennington doctrine, 119
   sham litigation, relationship with, 119
   Sherman Act, 93
   theft of patents, 103

trade secrets contrasted, 92–93
trademarks contrasted, 92–93
"Free riding," 242, 315
FTC. *See* Federal Trade Commission
FTCA. *See* Federal Trade Commission Act

G
Gene therapy, 450–58
General public licenses (GPL), 339–39
Generic drugs
    overpayment by brand-name firms, 412–13
    reverse payment settlements.
        See Pharmaceuticals
    safety laws, 429–31
    underpayment by generic firms, 413
Gilbert, Richard, 229
Goods markets, 449, 624
GPL (General public licenses), 339–39
Grantbacks
    ABA Section on Antitrust Law, 534
    antitrust law, 532–33
    competition, impact on, 531–32
    deference to, 532
    DOJ/FTC *Antitrust Guidelines*, 533–34, 644–45
    patent pooling, 315
    patents, 528–34
    per se rules re, 533
    SSOs, 534
Grinnell test, 31–32
Group boycotts
    copyrights, 465–72
    movie splits as, 472

H
Handgards claims, 92–93
Hart–Scott–Rodino Antitrust Improvements Act, 34, 445
Hatch–Waxman Act, 254, 430
Hemphill, C. Scott, 412–13
Herfindahl–Hirschman Index (HHI), 446, 449, 458
Hoffman, D. Bruce, 128–29
Holman, Christopher M., 411
Horizontal restraints
    DOJ/FTC *Antitrust Guidelines*, 639–40
    market allocation, 362, 385–86
    Sherman Act, 27
Hovenkamp, Herbert, 140, 158, 189, 196–97, 213, 410

I
Inequitable conduct
    fraudulent procurement of patents distinguished, 99, 119
    patent infringement, as defense to, 10, 99

Infringement
    copyrights. *See* Copyright infringement
    patents. *See* Patent infringement
    trademarks, 17
Injunctive relief
    FTCA, 35–36
    predatory innovation, against, 245
    requests for, 569
    unilateral refusals to license or deal, against, 203–13
Innovation
    efficiency and, 73
    patent pooling, effect of, 315–16
    predatory innovation. *See* Predatory innovation
    Promoting Innovation and Competition.
        See Promoting Innovation and Competition (DOJ/FTC)
Innovation markets, 449–50, 626–29
Intellectual property generally
    acquisition of rights. *See* Acquisition of intellectual property rights
    Constitutional authority, 56
    copyrights. *See* Copyrights
    defined, 3
    enforcement of rights. *See* Enforcement of intellectual property rights
    exclusionary rights, 4–5, 54–55
    generally, 3–5
    licensing. *See* Licensing of intellectual property
    market power, relationship with, 46–56
    nonrivalrous consumption, 3–4, 20–21
    other property rights compared, 56
    patents. *See* Patents
    tension with antitrust law, 39–46
    trade secrets. *See* Trade secrets
    trademarks. *See* Trademarks
Intent
    market allocation and trademarks, relevance to, 369, 377
    predatory innovation, relevance to, 240–41
    sham litigation, relevance to, 118–19, 195
    unilateral refusals to license or deal, relevance to, 195
Interference proceedings, 443–44
International intellectual property regimes, market allocation in, 381–85
Invalidity of patents
    acquisition of intellectual property rights as conspiracy to restrain trade, relevance to, 443
    extent of, 93–94
    fraud distinguished, 94
    patent infringement, as defense to, 9–10

Invalidity of patents (*cont.*)
  reverse payment settlements, relevance to, 428
  sham litigation, effect on, 119

J
Janis, Mark, 196–97, 213, 410
Jurisdiction of Federal Circuit, 577–88
Justice Department (DOJ)
  advisory opinions, 321
  Antitrust Guidelines for the Licensing of Intellectual Property. See Antitrust Guidelines for the Licensing of Intellectual Property (DOJ/FTC)
  Business Review Letters, 321–22
  enforcement powers, 36
  Merger Guidelines, 445–48
  mergers and acquisitions, authority to challenge, 34
  "Nine No-No's," 42–46
  Promoting Innovation and Competition. See Promoting Innovation and Competition (DOJ/FTC)
  reverse payment settlements, 411–12

K
Kefauver–Harris Amendment, 429
Krattenmaker, Thomas G., 128–29

L
Lanham Act
  excerpts, 614–15
  trademarks, 15, 17
Legal expenses as antitrust injury, 110–11
Legitimate business justification, 176—177
Leibowitz, Jon, 431
Lemley, Mark A., 196–97, 213, 410
Leslie, Christopher R., 69–70
Leverage School, 135–37
Licensing of intellectual property
  blanket licensing of copyrighted works. *See* Price fixing
  compulsory licensing as remedy, 569–76
  concerted refusals. *See* Concerted refusals to license or deal
  conditional refusals, 198
  DOJ/FTC *Antitrust Guidelines*, 511–12, 527–28, 617–46
  general public licenses (GPL), 339–39
  non-price restrictions. *See* Non-price licensing restrictions
  royalty-free licenses and SSOs, 274, 282, 347–48
  unconditional refusals, 198
  unilateral refusals. *See* Unilateral refusals to license or deal
Lobanoff, Marcy L., 429
Lobbying as basis of antitrust injury, 111–13

M
Manufacturers, vertical price restraints by. *See* Vertical price restraints
Market allocation, 351–86
  copyrights, 371, 378–81
  historical background, 41
  horizontal restraints, 362, 385–86
  international intellectual property regimes, 381–85
  movie splits as, 472
  patents, 351–55
  trademarks, 355–78
    ABA Section on Antitrust Law on, 371
    copyrights compared, 371
    intent, relevance of, 369, 377
    intrabrand competition *versus* interbrand competition, 369
    "merely incidental" restraints, 356
    monopolization, 377–78
    parent/subsidiary relationship, 356
    per se rules re, 362, 369, 371
    rule of reason analysis, 362, 371
    Sherman Act, 357, 369
    sports leagues, 357
    vertical *versus* horizontal restraint, 362
Market power
  acquisition of intellectual property rights as conspiracy to restrain trade, 443
  aftermarkets, 199–200
  black markets, 55–56
  DOJ/FTC *Antitrust Guidelines*, 46–47, 621
  downstream markets, 199–200
  intellectual property, relationship with, 46–56
  patents, 55
  pharmaceuticals, 55
  price discrimination, 68, 71
  royalty structuring, 553
  software, 55
  tying arrangements, 46–56, 153
  unilateral refusals to license or deal, 197–200
Market share, 29
Medical technology, predatory innovation in, 236–43
Medicare Modernization Act of 2003, 430
Mergers
  acquisition of intellectual property rights in, 444–58
  divestiture requirements, 458

goods markets, 449
innovation markets, 449–50
technology markets, 449
Antitrust Modernization Commission on, 444–49
Clayton Act, 34–35, 444–45
DOJ/FTC *Antitrust Guidelines,* 444
DOJ/FTC *Merger Guidelines,* 445–48
Meurer, Michael, 69
Microeconomic analysis, 647–58
Miller-Tydings Act, 497–500
Misappropriation of trade secrets, 18–19
Misuse of intellectual property
copyrights, 61–65
patents. *See* Patent misuse
trademarks, 66–67
MNF (Most favored nations) clauses, 137
Monopolization
attempted monopolization, 31–32, 36
barriers to entry, 30
"Cellophane Fallacy," 30
conspiracy to monopolize, 32–33
damages, 560
fraudulently procured patents, 93, 99
Grinnell test, 31–32
market allocation and trademarks, 377–78
market share, 29
monopoly conduct, 30–31
monopoly leveraging doctrine, 227
network effects, 83–84, 261
non-price licensing restrictions as, 517–27
overview, 28–33
patents, exclusionary rights contrasted, 54–55
possession of monopoly power in relevant market, 28–30
price discrimination, 68, 70–71
royalty structuring as, 538
Spectrum Sports test, 31–32
SSOs, 345–46
trade secrets, 110
tying arrangements, 135–36
unilateral refusals to license or deal as, 176–178, 196–97
Monopoly leveraging doctrine, 227
Monopoly pricing, 24
Most favored nations (MNF) clauses, 137
Motion pictures
black markets in, 55–56
block-booking, 139–46
movie splits, 378–81, 472
sham litigation re, 113–19
vertical price restraints in, 489–92
Mueller, Janice, 575
Music industry, black markets in, 55–56

N
Nagata, Ernest A., 128–29
National Cooperative Research Act of 1984
enactment of, 44
excerpts, 594–601
National Cooperative Research and Production Act of 1993, 594–601
National Recovery Administration, 41
Nelson, Philip B., 313–14
Network effects, 73–84
monopolization, 83–84, 261
non-price licensing restrictions, 84
"Nine No-No's," 42–46
"No economic sense" test, 230
Noerr-Pennington doctrine
concerted refusals to license or deal, 462
sham litigation, 111–13, 119, 121–23
Non-price licensing restrictions, 511–34
exhaustion doctrine, 515–517
field-of-use restrictions, 517–27
grantbacks, 528–34
monopolization, 517–27
network effects, 84
patent misuse, 512–15
Noncompetition covenants, 61
Nonobviousness of patents, 6
Nonrivalrous consumption, 3–4, 20–21
Novelty of patents, 6

O
Oil industry, price fixing in, 307–16
Open patent pools, 465
Ordover, Janusz A., 228–29, 254

P
Parent/subsidiary relationship and market allocation, 356
Patent Act of 1790, 5
Patent Act of 1952
enactment of, 5
excerpts, 601–4
Patent and Trademark Office (PTO)
fraudulently procured patents. *See* Fraudulently procured patents
interference proceedings, 443–44
patents, 5–6
trademarks, 15
"Patent holdup," 273–74, 282, 314
Patent infringement
conspiracy to restrain trade, relevance to, 443
counterclaims, 586–588
defenses to, 9–11
inequitable conduct, 10, 99
invalidity, 9–10

Patent infringement (*cont.*)
   non-infringement, 9
   patent misuse, 10–11, 55–61, 63
   enforcement of intellectual property
     rights, 93
   overview, 8–11
   predatory innovation, relevance to, 242
   remedies, 9
   sham litigation re, 120–23
Patent misuse
   antitrust law, relationship with, 60–61
   competition, 61
   copyright misuse compared, 63
   defense to patent
     infringement, 10–11, 55–61, 63
   historical background, 41–42
   non-price licensing restrictions, 512–15
   per se misuse, 61
   royalty structuring, 538, 548–49
   trademark misuse compared, 66
   tying arrangements as, 44
   unilateral refusals to license or deal, 197
Patent Misuse Reform Act of 1988, 44, 197
Patent pooling
   blocking patents, 313–14
   closed patent pools, 465
   collusion, 314
   competition, impact on, 312–14
   concerted refusals to license or deal, 462–65
   cross-licensing arrangements distinguished,
     311–12
   defined, 311
   DOJ/FTC *Antitrust Guidelines,* 315, 642–44
   DOJ/FTC *Promoting Innovation and
     Competition,* 311–12, 315
   "free riding," 315
   grantbacks, 315
   innovation, impact on, 315–16
   integrating complementary
     technologies, 312–13
   open patent pools, 465
   overview, 39–40
   "patent holdup," 314
   price fixing. *See* Price fixing
   royalties, 314–15, 323
   Sherman Act, 314–15
Patents
   acquisition of rights, 5–7
   blocking patents, 7, 313–14
   complementary patents, 322, 327
   concerted refusals to license or deal, 462–65
   Constitutional authority, 5
   contract law, relationship with, 543
   deference to patent holders, 39–41, 43
   disclosure, 7
   duration of protection, 8
   exhaustion doctrine, 515—517
   field-of-use restrictions, 517–27
   fraudulent procurement. *See* Fraudulently
     procured patents
   grantbacks, 528–34
   historical background, 5
   infringement. *See* Patent infringement
   invalidity
     acquisition of intellectual property rights
       as conspiracy to restrain trade,
       relevance to, 443
     extent of, 93–94
     fraud distinguished, 94
     patent infringement, as defense to, 9–10
     reverse payment settlements,
       relevance to, 428
     sham litigation, effect on, 119
   jurisdiction of Federal Circuit, 577–88
   market allocation, 351–55
   market power, 55
   misuse. *See* Patent misuse
   monopolization, exclusionary rights
     contrasted, 54–55
   "Nine No-No's," 42–46
   nonobviousness, 6
   novelty, 6
   overview, 5–11
   "patent holdup," 273–74, 282, 314
   pooling arrangements. *See* Patent pooling
   price fixing. *See* Price fixing
   priority of, 7
   PTO authority, 5–6
   royalty structuring. *See* Royalty structuring
   scope of protection, 7–8
   statutory bars, 7
   substitute patents, 322, 327
   theft of, 103
   tying arrangements. *See* Tying arrangements
   unilateral refusals to license or deal, 167–213
   utility, 6
   vertical price restraints, 479–89
Penalties
   cartels imposing, 300
   FTCA §5, 285
Per se rules
   block-booking, 146
   grantbacks, 533
   market allocation and
     trademarks, 362, 369, 371
   patent misuse, 61
   predatory innovation, 253
   price fixing

blanket licensing of copyrighted works, 336
cartels, 305
SSOs, 348
reverse payment
  settlements, 393, 410–11, 428
royalty structuring, 541
Sherman Act, 26
tying arrangements, 138, 146
unilateral refusals to license or deal, 197
vertical price restraints, 42–43, 475–80
Permissive counterclaims in patent infringement cases, 586–87
Pharmaceuticals, 387–432
  Abbreviated New Drug Approval (ANDA) system, 387–430
  black markets in, 55–56
  clinical trials, 449
  generic drugs
    overpayment by brand-name firms, 412–13
    safety laws, 429–31
    underpayment by generic firms, 413
  market power in, 55
  predatory innovation, 245–55
  reverse payment settlements
    ABA Section on Antitrust Law on, 394
    after expiration of patent, 428
    competition, impact on, 393
    discovery in, 428
    DOJ on, 411–12
    exclusionary effects, 427–28
    FTC on, 411–12
    invalidity of patent, relevance of, 428
    per se rules re, 393, 410–11, 428
    plaintiffs' reasons for, 394
    probabilistic property rights, 411
    quick look analysis, 410
    royalties, 410
    rule of reason analysis, 410
  safety laws, 429–31
  vertical price restraints, 475–80
Photocopiers, unilateral refusals to license or deal in, 178–90
Photography industry, predatory innovation in, 215–36
Pooling arrangements. *See* Patent pooling
Predatory innovation, 215–55
  business judgment, deference to, 254–55
  chilling effect on innovation, 241–42
  coercion requirement, 235
  compensatory pricing, 228
  competition, impact on, 241
  consumer welfare standard, 229
  damages, 240

disclosure, duty of, 227–28
free consumer choice, 254–55
"free riding," 242
injunctive relief against, 245
intent, relevance of, 240–41
judicial quality assessment, necessity of, 230–31
medical technology, 236–43
monopoly leveraging doctrine, 227
"no economic sense" test, 230
patent infringement, relevance of, 242
per se rules re, 253
pharmaceuticals, 245–55
photography industry, 215–36
price discrimination, 236
profit sacrifice test, 229–30, 254
simultaneous product releases, 228
technological incompatibility, 235
total economic welfare standard, 229
tying arrangements, 235–36
Preserve Access to Affordable Generics Act, 430–31
Price discrimination
  block-booking as, 140–41
  consumer demand, 68–69
  copyrights, 69
  market power, 68, 71
  monopolization, 68, 70–71
  predatory innovation, 236
  Robinson–Patman Act, 70–71
  tying arrangements, 69–70, 136
Price fixing, 291–350
  blanket licensing of copyrighted works, 327–38
    cartels compared, 338
    complementary rights, 336–37
    justification of, 337
    new product concept, 337
    nonexclusive rights, 337
    per se rules re, 336
    rule of reason analysis, 336
    Sherman Act, 337
    substitute rights, 336–37
  Business Review Letters, 321–22
  cartels, 291–305
    agreement requirement, 300
    blanket licensing of copyrighted works compared, 338
    causation, 305
    competition, impact on, 305
    coordination problems, 299
    defection problems, 299–300
    difficulty in establishing, 299
    efficiency, effect on, 298

Price fixing (*cont.*)
   instability, 299–300
   per se rules re, 305
   SSOs compared, 345–46
   unpatented products, 300
  damages, 560
  general public licenses (GPL), 339–39
  historical background, 41
  maximum price, 338–39
  oil industry, 307–16
  patent pooling, 305–27
   blocking patents, 313–14
   collusion, 314
   competition, impact on, 312–14
   complementary patents, 322, 327
   cross-licensing arrangements distinguished, 311–12
   DOJ/FTC *Antitrust Guidelines,* 305–6, 315
   DOJ/FTC *Promoting Innovation and Competition,* 311–12, 315
   "free riding," 315
   grantbacks, 315
   innovation, impact on, 315–16
   integrating complementary technologies, 312–13
   "patent holdup," 314
   realistic opportunity to obtain licenses, 322–23
   remedies, 323
   royalties, 314–15, 323
   Sherman Act, 314–15
   substitute patents, 322, 327
  software, 300–305
  SSOs, 339–49
   auctions by, 347
   cartels compared, 345–46
   DOJ/FTC *Promoting Innovation and Competition,* 340, 345–48
   joint *ex ante* licensing, 345–47
   monopolization, 345–46
   per se rules re, 348
   procedural deficiencies, 349
   royalties, 345–46
   royalty-free licenses, 347–48
   screening, 348
   Sherman Act, 339, 345–46, 349
  tying arrangements, 137–38
  V-chip, 340–49
  vertical price restraints. *See* Vertical price restraints
Price-protection clauses, 136–38
Probabilistic property rights, 411
Profit sacrifice test, 229–30, 254

Promoting Innovation and Competition (DOJ/FTC)
  cross-licensing arrangements, 311–12
  patent pooling, 311–12, 315
  SSOs, 262, 274, 283–84, 340, 345–48
  tying arrangements, 131
  unilateral refusals to license or deal, 195–98
PTO. *See* Patent and Trademark Office
Publicity rights, 19
Punitive damages, 35

Q
Quick look analysis
  reverse payment settlements, 410
  Sherman Act, 27

R
Refusals to license or deal
  concerted refusals. *See* Concerted refusals to license or deal
  conditional refusals, 198
  unconditional refusals, 198
  unilateral refusals. *See* Unilateral refusals to license or deal
Relevant market, 176–77, 189–90
Remedies in antitrust law, 569–76
  compulsory licensing as, 569–76
  copyright infringement, for, 13
  criminal violations, 36, 569
  damages. *See* Damages
  injunctive relief
   FTCA, 35–36
   predatory innovation, against, 245
   requests for, 569
   unilateral refusals to license or deal, against, 203–13
  patent infringement, for, 9
  price fixing, for, 323
  punitive damages, 35
  treble damages, 35–36, 560, 569
  unilateral refusals to license or deal, for, 199, 212
Repetitive petitioning, 128–29
Resale price maintenance. *See* Vertical price restraints
Restatement of the Law of Unfair Competition, 18
Restraint of trade. *See* Monopolization
Restraints on alienation, 479
Reverse payment settlements. *See* Pharmaceuticals
Robinson–Patman Act, 70–71
Royalties
  patent pooling, 314–15, 323
  SSOs, 345–46

Royalty-free licenses and SSOs, 274, 282, 347–48
Royalty structuring, 535–53
  after expiration of patent, 541, 552–53
  bundling of patents, 553
  deferred payments, 541
  differential rates, 553
  before issuance of patent, 542–43
  market power, 553
  monopolization, 538
  patent misuse, 538, 548–49
  per se rules re, 541
  protesting, 549
  Sherman Act, 541
  total output, based on, 538–39, 549
  trade secrets, 542
  tying arrangements compared, 541
  unpatented products, incorporating, 538, 542
  voluntary *versus* coerced agreements, 549
Rule of reason analysis
  acquisition of intellectual property rights as conspiracy to restrain trade, 442–43
  block-booking, 141
  DOJ/FTC *Antitrust Guidelines,* 634–39
  market allocation, 362, 371
  price fixing, 336
  reverse payment settlements, 410
  Sherman Act, 26–27
  tying arrangements, 141
  vertical price restraints, 500–509

S
"Safety zone," 637–39
Schumpeter, Joseph, 72
Settlements
  FTC interference proceedings, anticompetitive settlements in, 443–44
  reverse payment settlements. *See* Pharmaceuticals
Sham litigation, 104–29
  copyright infringement, re, 128
  fraudulently procured patents, relationship with, 119
  intent, relevance of, 118–19, 195
  invalidity of patent, effect of, 119
  legal expenses as antitrust injury, 110–11
  lobbying compared, 111–13
  motion pictures, re, 113–19
  Noerr-Pennington doctrine, 111–13, 119, 121–23
  objective baselessness, 118
  patent infringement, re, 120–23
  prevailing in litigation, effect of, 118
  repetitive petitioning, 128–29

Sherman Act, 120
  subjective motivation, 118–19, 195
  television, re, 123–129
  trade secrets, re, 110–11
Sherman Act
  acquisition of intellectual property rights, 433, 444
  agreement requirement, 26
  block-booking, 146
  concerted refusals to license or deal, 462
  criminal violations, 36
  essential facilities doctrine, 212–13
  excerpts, 591
  exclusive dealing arrangements, 34
  foreign-based conduct, 385
  fraudulently procured patents, 93
  FTCA compared, 35, 287
  horizontal restraints, 27
  market allocation and trademarks, 357, 369
  monopolization. *See* Monopolization
  overview, 25–33
  per se rules, 26
  price fixing
    blanket licensing of copyrighted works, 337
    patent pooling, 314–15
    SSOs, 339, 345–46, 349
  quick look analysis, 27
  royalty structuring, 541
  rule of reason analysis, 26–27
  SSOs, deceptive conduct before, 257
  tying arrangements, 33–34, 40, 146
  unreasonable restraints of trade, 26–27
  vertical price restraints, 27, 491
Sidak, Joseph Gregory, 236
Software
  market power in, 55
  price fixing in, 300–305
  SSOs for, 274–84
  tying arrangements in, 149–53
  unilateral refusals to license or deal in, 167–78, 190–99
Spectrum Sports test, 31–32
Split arrangements, 378–81
Sports leagues, market allocation in, 357
Standard-setting organizations (SSOs), 257–88
  ABA Section on Antitrust Law on, 261
  auctions by, 347
  computer hardware, for, 257–61
  copyright protection of standards, 349
  disclosure requirements, 262, 282
  DOJ/FTC *Promoting Innovation and Competition,* 262, 274, 283–84, 340, 345–48
  fair, reasonable, and non-discriminatory (FRAND) terms, 273–74

Standard-setting organizations (SSOs) (cont.)
   FTC on, 283–84
   FTCA §5 actions, 284–87
   government agencies, relationship with, 349
   grantbacks, 534
   licensing requirements, 282–83
   monopolization, 345–46
   monopoly conduct before, 274
   "patent holdup," 273–74, 282
   price fixing. *See* Price fixing
   royalty-free licenses, 274, 282, 347–48
   Sherman Act, 257
   software, for, 274–84
   wireless communications, for, 262–73
Standards Development Organization Advancement Act of 2004
   enactment of, 44
   excerpts, 594–601
   overview, 348–49
Standing in antitrust law, 557–67
   competitor standing, 557–64
   consumer standing, 564–67
Static competition, 23
Static efficiency, 24, 72
Stigler, George J., 140–41
Structuring royalties. *See* Royalty structuring
Subsidiaries and market allocation, 356
Substitute copyrights, 336–37
Substitute patents, 322, 327
Supply curve, 652–53

T
Technology markets, 449, 625–26
Television
   block-booking, 141–49
   sham litigation re, 123–29
Tension between antitrust law and intellectual property, 39–46
Theft of patents, 103
Tortious interference with contract, 479
Total economic welfare standard, 229
Trade secrets
   acquisition of protection, 18
   duration of protection, 19
   fraudulent procurement, patents contrasted, 92–93
   misappropriation, 18–19
   monopolization, 110
   overview, 18–19
   royalty structuring, 542
   scope of protection, 18
   sham litigation re, 110–11
   vertical price restraints, 479, 489

Trademarks
   abandonment of, 20
   acquisition of protection, 15
   dilution of, 17
   distinctiveness, 15–16
   duration of protection, 16–17
   fraudulent procurement, patents contrasted, 92–93
   infringement, 17
   Lanham Act, 15, 17
   market allocation. *See* Market allocation
   misuse, 66–67
   non-functionality, 16
   overview, 14–17
   PTO authority, 15
   requirements, 15
   scope of protection, 17
   tying arrangements, 154–65
      exclusive dealing arrangements compared, 158
      lists of approved suppliers, 165
      quality assurance, 158
      separate product requirement, 157–58, 162
   use in commerce, 16
   vertical price restraints, 479, 489, 496–500
Treble damages, 35–36, 560, 569
Tying arrangements, 131–65
   block-booking. *See* Block-booking
   Clayton Act, 33–34, 40, 146
   copyrights
      block-booking. *See* Block-booking
      software, 149–53
   damages, 560
   defined, 131–32
   DOJ/FTC *Antitrust Guidelines*, 131–32, 641
   DOJ/FTC *Promoting Innovation and Competition,* 131
   exclusive dealing arrangements contrasted, 158
   franchises, 154–65
      exclusive dealing arrangements compared, 158
      lists of approved suppliers, 165
      quality assurance, 158
      separate product requirement, 157–58, 162
   historical background, 39–41
   market power, 46–56, 153
   patent misuse, 44
   patents, 132–38
      Chicago School on, 135–37
      competition, impact on, 135
      goodwill arrangements, 137
      Leverage School on, 135–37
      market share, 136
      monopolization, 135–36

most favored nations (MNF) clauses, 137
per se rules re, 138
price discrimination, 136
price fixing, 137–38
price-protection clauses, 136–38
price regulation, evading, 137
Volume Tying Theory, 138
per se rules re, 138, 146
predatory innovation, 235–36
price discrimination, 69–70
royalty structuring compared, 541
rule of reason analysis, 141
separate product
    requirement, 153, 157–58, 162
Sherman Act, 33–34, 40, 146
software, 149–53
trademarks, 154–65
    exclusive dealing arrangements
        compared, 158
    lists of approved suppliers, 165
    quality assurance, 158
    separate product
        requirement, 157–58, 162
unilateral refusals to license or
    deal as, 196–97

U

Unconditional refusals to license or deal, 198
Unfair competition, 119, 284–87
Uniform Trade Secrets Act, 18
Unilateral refusals to license or deal, 167–214
    aftermarkets, market power in, 199–200
    computer hardware, 203–13
    conditional refusals, 198
    Copyright Act, 177
    DOJ/FTC *Antitrust Guidelines,* 167
    DOJ/FTC *Promoting Innovation and Competition,* 195–98
    downstream markets, market
        power in, 199–200
    essential facilities doctrine, 212–13
    injunctive relief against, 203–13
    intellectual property justification, 196
    intent, relevance of, 195
    legitimate business justification, 176–77

market power, 197–200
monopolization, 176–78, 196–97
patent misuse, 197
per se rules re, 197
photocopiers, 178–90
presumptive validity, 176–77
relevant market, defining, 176–77, 189–90
remedies for, 199, 212
scope of patent, relevance of, 196
software, 167–78, 190–99
subjective motivation, 195
tying arrangements, 196–97
unconditional refusals, 198
unpatented products, 190

V

V-chip, 340–49
Vertical price restraints, 475–509
    antitrust law, 475–80
    buyers' cartels, 488
    copyrights, 479, 489–96
    DOJ/FTC *Antitrust Guidelines,* 640
    Dr. Miles case, 475–80
    first sale doctrine, 495–96
    General Electric rule, 480–89
    historical background, 41
    Leegin case, 475, 500–509
    motion pictures, 489–92
    patents, 479–89
    per se rules re, 42–43, 475–80
    pharmaceuticals, 475–80
    rule of reason analysis, 500–509
    Sherman Act, 27, 491
    trade secrets, 479, 489
    trademarks, 479, 489, 496–500
    video games, 492–95
    waivers, 489
Video games, vertical price restraints in, 492–95
Volume Tying Theory, 138

W

Willig, Robert D., 228–29, 254
Wireless communications, SSOs for, 262–73